Human Resource Management

Eighth Edition

HUMAN RESOURCE MANAGEMENT

EIGHTH EDITION

ROBERT L. MATHIS
University of Nebraska at Omaha

JOHN H. JACKSON
University of Wyoming

West Publishing Company
Minneapolis/St. Paul ❖ New York ❖ Los Angeles ❖ San Francisco

Copy Editor: Beverly Peavler, Naples Editorial Services
Indexer: Maggie Jarpey
Proofreader: Angela-Zobel-Rodriguez
Composition: Parkwood Composition Services

WEST'S COMMITMENT TO THE ENVIRONMENT
In 1906, West Publishing Company began recycling materials left over from the production of books. This began a tradition of efficient and responsible use of resources. Today, 100% of our legal bound volumes are printed on acid-free, recycled paper consisting of 50% new fibers. West recycles nearly 27,700,000 pounds of scrap paper annually—the equivalent of 229,300 trees. Since the 1960s, West has devised ways to capture and recycle waste inks, solvents, oils, and vapors created in the printing process. We also recycle plastics of all kinds, wood, glass, corrugated cardboard, and batteries, and have eliminated the use of polystyrene book packaging. We at West are proud of the longevity and the scope of our commitment to the environment.

West pocket parts and advance sheets are printed on recyclable paper and can be collected and recycled with newspapers. Staples do not have to be removed. Bound volumes can be recycled after removing the cover.

Production, Prepress, Printing and Binding by West Publishing Company.

Printed with Printwise
Environmentally Advanced Water Washable Ink

British Library Cataloguing-in-Publication Data. A catalogue record for this book is available from the British Library.

Printed in the United States of America

04 03 02 01 00 99 98 97 8 7 6 5 4 3 2 1 0

Library of Congress Cataloging-in-Publication Data

Mathis, Robert L., 1944–
Human resource management / Robert L. Mathis, John H. Jackson.
8th ed.
p. cm.
Includes bibliographical references and index.
ISBN 0-314-08248-7 (hardcover: alk. paper)
1. Personnel management. I. Jackson, John Harold. II. Title.
HF5549.M3349 1997
658.3—dc20 96-26108
CIP

TO
Jo Ann Mathis
who manages me

❖

R. D. and M. M. Jackson
who have been successful managers of people for many years

❖ Contents in Brief ❖

❖ CONTENTS ❖

❖ Preface ❖

> *"The future has suddenly and dramatically become the present."*
> —*R. Babson*

Organizations today face many challenges in the management of their human resources. Every week brings news media reports on organizational downsizings, workforce diversity, shortages of skilled workers in many areas and industries, and many other concerns. The thrust of this book is to identify and explain developments in the field of human resource (HR) management that managers will face to the year 2000.

The eighth edition of this book continues the successful tradition established in the past, but the authors have made many changes in this edition in order to address newly emerging issues, and to reflect changes in the way HR management activities are being addressed. The goal is to build on past excellence and to continue as one of the leading HR management texts. Every line and word of content from the previous edition has been reviewed and major revisions have been made in most areas. We believe that the eighth edition continues the standards of currentness, readability, and excellence associated with the previous editions.

There are a number of reasons for someone to read this book. Certainly not everyone who reads it will become an HR manager. In fact, many students who take HR courses will not even become HR generalists or specialists. But everyone who works in any organization will come in contact with HR management–both effective and ineffective. Those who become operating managers must be able to manage HR activities because every manager's HR actions can have major consequences for every organization. One continuing feature of the book is specifying the areas of contact between operating managers and the HR unit. Throughout the book these "interfaces" describe typical divisions of HR responsibilities, even though some variations occur depending on the size of the organization, its technology, history, and other factors.

Another important audience for the book is composed of practicing HR professionals. Previous editions of the book have aided hundreds of HR professionals to enhance their knowledge and prepare for one of the professional exams so that they can become PHR or SPHR certified by the Human Resource Certification Institute (HRCI). This edition will continue to be valuable to HR professionals, and conscious efforts have been made by the authors to provide content coverage of the topics on the HRCI approved outline, which is reproduced in Appendix E.

❖ Features of the Eighth Edition

Each chapter begins with an example of an HR problem, situation, or practice in an actual organization that illustrates a facet of the content that follows in the chapter. Within each chapter, there are vignettes called *HR Perspective* that highlight specific practices by employers, research studies on HR management topics, and/or ethical issues in HR management. New to this edition is the *Logging On* feature which identifies some useful sources of HR information on the Internet. Specific World Wide Web addresses are given in every chapter. All of the cases at the end of chapters are "real-life" problems and situations using actual organizations as examples. As a result of suggestions from students and instructors who have used the previous edition, key terms and concepts are listed at the end of each chapter along with the Review and Discussion Questions.

Possibly the most exciting addition to the eighth edition has been the inclusion of Learning Media for each of the six sections of the book. There are two features of the Learning Media: one is a sample HRIS system and the second contains video cases. Regarding the sample HRIS system, at the beginning of the book a brief profile of a fictitious company, SME-TEK, is presented. Then using the data on employees at SME-TEK located on the CD that is available with the text, readers can access computer-based training applications of an actual human resource information system (HRIS) in use in many organizations. Produced by Ceridian Employer Services, one of the best known suppliers of human resource information and payroll services, students may see how the Ceridian© CII HR information system is used to perform specific HR activities. On the CD in the *Features and Processes* component of the Ceridian-produced CD, students may see typical HRIS screens. In the *Concepts* section, background material on the various content areas may be reviewed to augment the appropriate text coverage.

The video cases cover management issues in smaller firms, with the HR management aspect being highlighted by the questions in the text. Instructors wishing to use these video cases may order them either from West Publishing or their area West sales representative, and they are available at no cost to adopters.

❖ Organization of the Eighth Edition

Section 1 of the eighth edition opens with an overview of HR as a field of study, with Chapter 1 stressing both the strategic and administrative roles of HR management. The second chapter examines strategic HR planning and why strategic HR planning is growing in importance. A virtually new Chapter 3 focuses on human resources as they affect organizational competitiveness. The chapter specifically addresses the impact that human resources have on productivity, quality, and service in organizations. Reengineering, self-directed work teams, production cells, and Total Quality Management (TQM) are all topics covered as they relate to the management of human resources. The increasing global nature of organizations has led to a new Chapter 4 on Global Human Resource management. Extensive coverage is given to the cultural effects HR management has on operating globally.

Major revisions have been made in Chapters 5 and 6 that comprise Section 2 on Equal Employment Opportunity. The authors believe that the issues of diversity and equal employment are closely linked, and Chapter 5 begins with a discussion of diversity and HR management's role with managing diversity. The legal framework for EEO is covered, along with both sides of the contentious debate on affirmative action. Chapter 6 contains a detailed look at various aspects of implementing equal employment, such as sexual harassment, age discrimination, the glass ceiling, and many others.

Section 3 on Analyzing and Staffing Jobs begins with Chapter 7, which covers job analysis. That chapter provides details on preparation and use of job descriptions and job specifications, as well as content on identifying essential job functions as required by the ADA. In Chapter 8 on recruiting new content highlights the use of the Internet for recruiting and flexible staffing approaches. Chapter 9 continues its solid coverage of the employment process and selection activities.

Chapter 10 on training contains comprehensive coverage on employee orientation and major issues associated with training. Specific content addresses the effects of educational and skill deficiencies of U.S. workers and how employers are addressing those deficiencies. Chapter 11 discusses employee development and career planning and the importance of HR activities in these areas. The final chapter of Section 4 has new content on performance management and the role of performance appraisal as a part of enhancing the performance of human resources in organizations.

Section 5 on Compensating Human Resources covers pay administration, incentives, and benefits. Information has been included on new approaches such as broadbanding and skill-based pay to augment the detailed coverage of pay-for-performance, gainsharing, and other incentive programs that are presented in Chapters 13 and 14. Changes in content have been made in Chapter 15 on benefits in order to highlight the growing cost concerns facing managers and organizations. Special coverage of mandated benefits, health-care cost management, and family-related benefits highlight current challenges, while discussion of flexible benefits systems identifies one response of employers to those challenges.

Employees and labor relations activities are covered in Section 6. Chapter 16 on health, safety, and security has been reorganized and additional coverage has been included on hazard communications, personal protective equipment, blood-born pathogens, and other OSHA compliance issues. Content on workplace violence and security issues also has been added. Chapter 17 discusses the various issues associated with employee rights and discipline, such as employment-at-will, privacy rights, and substance abuse. The coverage of union-management relations in Chapters 18 and 19 highlights the legal framework for unionism, emerging trends in unionism, collective bargaining, and effective grievance management. The text concludes with a chapter on assessing HR effectiveness. Significant revisions have been made in this chapter as well.

The instructor's manual, prepared by Jack A. Hill (University of Nebraska at Omaha) represents one of the most exciting, professionally-useful instructor's aids available. The test bank contains approximately 2000 test questions prepared by Roger Dean (Washington and Lee University). That test bank is available in computerized form also from West Publishing, as are over 60 color transparencies. An excellent student resource guide prepared by Sally A. Coltrin (University of North Florida) and Roger Dean contains sample test questions, cases, and exercises to supplement the learning potential of this text.

❖ Acknowledgments

Producing any book requires assistance from many others. The authors are especially grateful to those individuals who provided reviews and numerous helpful comments for this edition, including the following who did comprehensive reviews:

Larry B. Brandt	Nova Southeastern University
Wendy Eager	Eastern Washington University
Gundars Kaupins	Boise State University
Jonathan S. Monat	Cal State University at Long Beach
Robert A. Reber	Western Kentucky University
Gene Szwajkowski	University of Illinois
Ann C. Wendt	Wright State University
George L. Whaley	San Jose State University
Carolyn Wiley	University of Tennessee at Chattanooga

In addition, specific suggestions from Carl Thornton (General Motors Institute) were appreciated.

Finally, some leading HR professionals provided ideas and assistance and appreciation is expressed to: Nicholas Dayan, SPHR; William L. Kelly, SPHR; Michael R. Losey, SPHR; Jerry L. Sellentin, SPHR; S. Gary Snodgrass; and Raymond B. Weinberg, SPHR.

Those involved in changing messy scrawls into printed ideas deserve special recognition. At the top of that list is JoAnn Mathis whose guidance and prodding made this book better. Another who assisted with many critical details included Carolyn Foster. Special thanks for their support and encouragement throughout the production process go to Carole Balach and Denise Simon of West Publishing.

The authors are confident that this edition will continue to be the standard for the HR field. We believe that it is a relevant and interesting text for those learning more about HR management and we are optimistic that those who use the book will agree.

Robert L. Mathis, SPHR
Omaha, Nebraska

John H. Jackson
Laramie, Wyoming

SME-TEK, INC.

COMPANY PROFILE

SME-TEK, INC. is a fictional company developed specifically for the exercises on the CD-ROM accompanying this text. Its workforce has been structured by Ceridian to depict HR activities in a company its size.

SME-TEK INC. headquarters is located in Boulder, Colorado and the manufacturing facility is in New York, New York. SME-TEK Inc. was started in 1975 by Samuel Jacobs, Joe Bailey, and Howard Robinson.

SME-TEK Industrial was formed and started manufacturing small pins and rollers for use in automated assembly lines. Over the next five years, the company expanded its foothold in this industry and started manufacturing almost all components used in the mechanical or automated portions of assembly lines.

During the 1980s, the focus on quality and technology improvements led many customers to start asking SME-TEK, for help in designing and implementing manufacturing operations. The company decided to capitalize on its internal knowledge and expertise to meet this developing market.

Thus, in 1983, SME-TEK Inc. started a consulting company based out of San Francisco, California called ST&D Consulting Group. This company's primary role was to provide implementation, training and documentation services to meet the customized solutions requested by customers for improving manufacturing systems.

Today there are 109 employees working for SME-TEK Inc. in ten different states across the U.S.

During the progression of the CD-ROM exercises in this text, SME-TEK will acquire a small accounting firm, CEB & Associates, which will be operated as a separate company. Also, a small communications firm will be acquired and become part of SME-TEK as its Advertising Department. Otherwise, all of the operating entities of SME-TEK are shown on the corporate organization chart below.

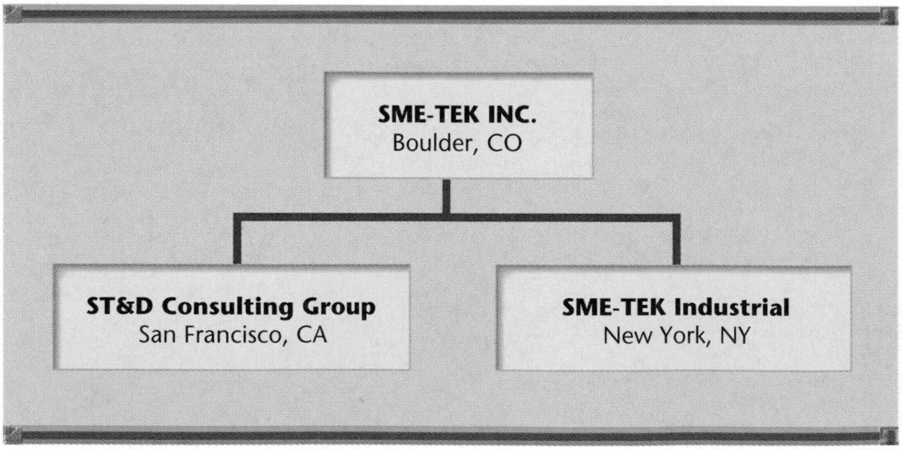

FIGURE P–1
SME-TEK, INC.
CORPORATE ORGANIZATION

NOTE: CD-ROM exercises appear at the end of each section of the text. These exercises are produced exclusively for *Human Resource Management, Eighth Edition* by Ceridian Employer Services, a leading supplier of human resource information systems (HRIS) to the business community. The exercises are adapted from and will introduce the student to using the Ceridian© CII HR information system. Technical information, system requirements, and installation instructions are contained on the endsheet of the text opposite the CD which is provided free with the textbook.

SECTION 1

PERSPECTIVES ON HUMAN RESOURCE MANAGEMENT

CHAPTER 1

THE STRATEGIC NATURE OF HUMAN RESOURCE MANAGEMENT

After you have read this chapter, you should be able to . . .

- Discuss the goals of HR management and tell how they link with the two roles of HR management.
- Define organizational culture and discuss its link to HR strategy.
- Identify four major HR challenges currently facing organizations and managers.
- List and define each of the six major categories of HR activities.
- Explain why HR professionals and operating managers must view HR management as an interface.
- Discuss why ethical issues and professionalism affect HR management.

HR in Transition

Rebuilding an Organization from the Ground Up!

Change is sweeping work organizations throughout the United States. It is brought about by competition, changes in society, and economics. The shifts have huge effects on people and the way they do their work. Human resource (HR) management is in a state of flux as well. But what comes from the changes *can be* much better than what came before them.

St. Francis Regional Medical Center in Wichita, Kansas, offers an example of a successful transformation. Examining the two-year journey of this large hospital to adapt to changes illustrates many of the issues facing HR management today. The many changes were guided by the CEO of the medical center, Sister M. Sylvia Egan.

Like many U.S. organizations, St. Francis tried downsizing in the 1980s. In fact, it laid off 400 people. It was a horrible experience for both those who went and those who stayed. Then the institution began to face changes in the health-care industry in the 1990s. In the past, the strategy had been to fill as many of the 630 beds as possible because health insurance paid for filled beds. But the future of health care appears to be in keeping people *out* of hospitals. The environment of the medical care business was changing, and a strategy shift emphasizing outpatient care and cost efficiency was necessary.

Decisions are made at lower levels, faster, without the loss of good ideas to red tape. The new corporate culture involves much more management by contact.

The old structure of 11 vice-presidents and traditional departments had become cumbersome. Over time, more and more levels of management had been added until decisions were made too slowly, costs had become too high, and patient care was inefficient.

To deal with these problems, Sister Egan dissolved the existing structure by doing away with *all positions*. Then, with the help of a task force of employees at St. Francis, job descriptions were rewritten for the jobs that really needed to be done. People who had worked for the medical center, as well as people from outside, were invited to apply for the jobs that best fit them. A consulting firm was called in to help with the transition, interview job candidates, provide career and self-assessment counseling, and assist with outplacement for those individuals who were not selected.

The result was terror, confusion, upheaval, and finally understanding, cooperation, and success. Management ultimately was cut by 200 positions. The CEO calls the process "rightsizing" rather than downsizing and feels the result is a much closer, stronger management team. Instead of spending all their time in the office, upper management practices more "management by walking around," and most employees say they themselves are both thinking and acting differently.

A major concern was that there would be a massive exodus of individuals from the organization when the changes began. That did not happen, apparently because the task force had presented good feedback and the consultants provided assistance in bringing a sensible vision to completion.[1]

Changes like the ones at St. Francis are a big part of the environment in which human resource management is operating today. They will be covered in the following chapters.

> *"The changes are so deep and far reaching that there are no simple descriptions or answers as to the real nature of work and employment in the 21st century."*
>
> *—Jeffrey J. Hallett*

Human resource (HR) management is a key ingredient affecting organizational competitiveness and its ability to fulfill its mission. The effectiveness of an organization in providing a product or service that fits customers' needs is critical if it is to survive. That product or service is provided in part (or entirely) by people. Employees are not only among the most important resources a firm has, they also are among the most expensive and sometimes the most problematic. Organizational human resources have grown as a strategic interest to upper management recently because effective use of people in the organization can provide a *competitive advantage* both domestically and abroad. Human resource (HR) systems that focus on high-performance HR work practices have been shown to improve the financial performance of organizations.[2] **Human resource (HR) management** deals with the design of formal systems in an organization to ensure the effective and efficient use of human talent to accomplish the organizational goals.

***Human resource (HR) management**
The design of formal systems in an organization to ensure the effective and efficient use of human talent to accomplish organizational goals.

❖ HR Management and Competitive Advantage

The activities that focus on HR management can provide a direct contribution to organizational performance. Such a contribution can be positive or negative, depending on the effectiveness of the design and implementation of the HR policies and systems. Human resources are frequently "underutilized" because employees often perform below their potential. The design of HR activities can affect the effectiveness and efforts of employees by influencing their jobs, skills, and motivation.

❖ Human Capital

***Human capital**
The total value of organizational human resources.

The way HR management is practiced also influences "**human capital**," which is the total *value* of human resources to the organization. Further, the choices made about HR systems and practices can be used to guide changes in the performance of organizations.[3] The combination of HR practices chosen can be highly effective or highly ineffective. Research suggests that effectiveness is most likely to result when HR practices fit the overall strategy of organizations. Both market performance and productivity are stronger when there is consistency among HR practices, philosophy, and business strategy.[4]

Human resources include all of the experience, skills, judgment, abilities, knowledge, contacts, risk taking, and wisdom of the individuals associated with an organization.[5] A complete understanding of strategic sources of competitive advantages must include an analysis of the internal strengths and weaknesses of an organization. Sustained competitive advantage depends on the unique characteristics of all the resources—including human resources—that an organization uses as it competes in its environment.[6]

Various experts on human capital have predicted a skills shortage for U.S. organizations that would hurt their competitive edge unless more investment is made in human capital. Serious skills shortages have developed in a number of fields and geographic areas. If that trend spreads as predicted, the role of HR management as the organizational link to labor markets will become even more important. Evidence that some organizations are using more productive HR strategies now can be seen in the fact that the Fortune 500 companies seem to be increasing profits without having to hire additional workers.[7] This result may indicate more productivity per existing worker.

❖ Goals of HR Management

While a CEO's goals for HR management are usually to have productive employees that contribute to a competitive advantage for the organization, HR executives concern themselves with the more specific objectives necessary to reach those goals. A recent national survey identified the top concerns of HR executives. The most important concerns identified were productivity, quality and service.[8]

Productivity Improving productivity has become even more important as global competition has increased, particularly when technology keeps changing. Organizations are discovering that the traditional approach of cutting costs, specifically labor costs, may be counterproductive in some cases because some human resources may hold the keys to productivity improvement. Productivity can be generally identified as the amount of output per employee.

Quality and Service Because human resources are the ones producing the products or services offered by an organization, they must be included in identifying any quality and service blockages and redesigning operational processes. Involving all employees, not just managers, in problem solving often requires a change in corporate culture, leadership styles, and HR policies and practices. But as more and more managers have discovered, the quantity and composition of human resources available to organizations today are dramatically different from those in previous decades. Some of those changes are highlighted later in this chapter.

The push for quality that followed Japan's successful competitive moves into the United States has become a way of life in some firms. Total quality management (TQM), an approach championed by W. Edwards Deming, focuses on employee communication, continuous improvement, training, and worker involvement, among other HR-oriented issues.

A true TQM approach requires continuous changes aimed at improving work processes. That need opens the door for reengineering the work. Some argue that "business process reengineering" (discussed later in this chapter) may replace TQM, but regardless of changes in the labels of programs, the quality issue appears to be one that will remain primary in business. Customer value received and satisfaction become the bases for judging success, along with more traditional HR measures of performance and efficiency. The emphasis on quality is forcing some HR departments toward making difficult changes in their operations.[9]

❖ Strategic and Operational Roles of HR Management

At the heart of the evolution of HR management is the fact that there are two major roles associated with the management of human resources in organizations. As Figure 1–1 shows, those roles are the strategic role and the operational role. HR management began as an operational function, but its strategic role is growing.

Strategic Role of HR Management The strategic role of HR management emphasizes that the people in an organization are valuable resources representing a significant investment of organizational efforts. These human resources can be a source of competitive strength if they are managed effectively.

Strategically, then, human resources must be viewed in the same context as the financial, technological, and other resources that are managed in organiza-

❖ FIGURE 1–1 ❖
HR MANAGEMENT ROLES

Role	Focus	HR Often Reports to	Typical Activities
Strategic	Global, long-run, innovative	CEO/ President	• Human resource planning • Tracking evolving legal issues • Assessing workforce trends and issues • Engaging in community economic development • Assisting in organizational restructuring and downsizing • Advising on mergers or acquisitions • Managing compensation planning and strategies
Operational	Administrative, short-term, maintenance-oriented	Corporate Vice-President of Administration	• Recruiting and selecting for current openings • Conducting employee orientation • Reviewing safety and accident reports • Resolving employee complaints and grievances • Administering employee benefits programs

tions. HR supply and demand must be viewed from a strategic standpoint. For example, consider the following situations:

- ❖ At a computer software firm, growth is being limited by shortages of programmers and systems analysts. The company plans to open a new facility in another state so that a different labor market can be tapped, and the HR Director heads up the site-selection team.
- ❖ In a firm with 100 employees, the HR Director is developing career plans and succession charts to determine if the firm has sufficient human resources to operate and manage the 70% growth it expects over the upcoming four years.
- ❖ In a firm with 1,000 employees, the Vice-President of Human Resources spends one week in any firm that is proposed for merger or acquisition to determine if the "corporate cultures" of the two entities are compatible. Two potential acquisitions that were viable financially were not made because he determined that the organizations would not mesh well and that some talented employees in both organizations probably would quit.

Note that the strategic focus of HR must be long term for planning to be effective. The strategic role of HR is discussed further in Chapter 2.

OPERATIONAL ROLE OF HR MANAGEMENT Operational activities are both tactical and administrative in nature. Compliance with equal employment opportunity and other laws must be ensured, applicants must be interviewed, new employees must be oriented to the organization, supervisors must be trained, safety problems must be resolved, and wages and salaries must be administered. In short, a wide variety of activities typically associated with the day-to-day management of people in organizations must be performed efficiently and appropriately. It is this collection of activities that often has been referred to as "the personnel function," and the newer strategic focus of HR management has not eliminated it. However, instead of performing both roles, many HR practitioners are, unfortunately, continuing to perform only the operational role. This emphasis still exists in some organizations partly because of individual limitations and partly because of top management's resistance to an expanded HR role.

❖ Organizational Life Cycles, Organizational Culture, and HR Strategy

Human resource management as a field is changing, and organizations go through evolutionary life cycles as well. In addition, organizations have cultures, just as nations and regions do. Both the life-cycle stage and culture of an organization guide appropriate HR strategies.

❖ Life-Cycle Stages and HR Strategy

As noted, organizations go through evolutionary life cycles, and the stage in which an organization finds itself affects what human resource strategies it should use. For example, the HR needs of a small, three-year-old high-tech software firm will be different from those of a large computer company. Apple Computer is a good illustration. At one time, Apple, founded by Steven Jobs and Stephen Wozniak, was a laid-back, entrepreneurial organization. But as the company grew, the need for more structure and formalization of plans and policies became evident. A new president, John Scully, was hired from PepsiCo, and within two years, the founders left Apple. Scully reduced staff to eliminate duplicate jobs and instituted more formalized policies throughout the company. Apple had passed from the growth to the maturity stage of its life cycle. When Scully left Apple, evolution in the company continued, and today, Apple faces major changes to avoid decline.

The relationships between the life cycle of an organization and HR activities are profiled in Figure 1–2. A discussion of each follows.

Introduction At the introduction stage, a high-risk and entrepreneurial spirit pervades the organization. The founders often operate with limited financial resources; consequently, HR activities are handled reactively, and training seems less important. When skills are needed, the organization recruits and hires individuals who are already trained. A simple strategy is associated with good performance.[10]

Growth During the growth stage, the organization continues to take risks and invest in marketing and operations. The organization needs investments to expand facilities, marketing, and human resources to take advantage of the demand for its products and services. Often, backlogs and scheduling problems indicate that the organization has grown faster than its ability to handle the demand. The decisions made during the growth stage have a critical impact on the organization as it moves into maturity. Consequently, just as in the Apple Computer situation, some formalization of policies and rules must occur. Inadequate staffing becomes a major concern, so the organization begins to focus on recruitment and selection of workers. It recognizes the need to make HR plans rather than just react to immediate pressures, and it institutes some simple HR planning procedures.

❖ FIGURE 1–2 ❖
ORGANIZATIONAL LIFE-CYCLE STAGES AND HR ACTIVITIES

LIFE-CYCLE STAGE	HR MANAGEMENT ISSUES			
	Staffing	Compensation	Training and Development	Labor/Employee Relations
Introduction	Attract best technical and professional talent.	Meet or exceed labor market rates to attract needed talent.	Define future skill requirements and begin establishing career ladders.	Set basic employee relations philosophy of organization.
Growth	Recruit adequate numbers and mix of qualified workers. Plan management succession. Manage rapid internal labor market movements.	Meet external market but consider internal equity effects. Establish formal compensation structures.	Mold effective management team through management development and organizational development.	Maintain labor peace, employee motivation, and morale.
Maturity	Encourage sufficient turnover to minimize layoffs and provide new openings. Encourage mobility as reorganizations shift jobs around.	Control compensation costs.	Maintain flexibility and skills of an aging workforce.	Control labor costs and maintain labor peace. Improve productivity.
Decline	Plan and implement workforce reductions and reallocations. Downsizing and outplacement may occur during this stage.	Implement tighter cost control.	Implement retraining and career consulting services.	Improve productivity and achieve flexibility in work rules. Negotiate job security and employment adjustment policies.

SOURCE: Thomas A. Kochan and Thomas A. Barocci, *Human Resource Management and Industrial Relations: Text, Readings, and Cases,* 105. Copyright © 1985 by Thomas A. Kochan and Thomas A. Barocci. Adapted by permission of Scott, Foresman and Company.

MATURITY In the maturity stage, the organization and its culture are stabilized. Size and success enable the organization to develop even more formalized plans, policies, and procedures. It now reaps the fruits of its past risky labors. Often, organizational politics flourish, and HR activities expand. At the same time, managers are concerned about keeping costs under control. Compensation programs become a major focus for HR efforts. HR planning becomes vital, especially for workforce shifts that occur as demand for some products and services slows.

DECLINE The organization in the decline stage faces resistance to change. Numerous examples can be cited in the manufacturing sectors of the U.S. economy. Manufacturing firms have had to reduce their workforces, close plants, and use their accumulated profits from the past to diversify into other industries. During the decline stage, employers try certain HR practices such as productivity-enhancement, and cost-reduction programs. Unionized workers resist the decline by demanding no pay cuts and greater job-security provisions in their contracts. Nevertheless, employers are compelled to reduce their workforces through attrition, early retirement incentives, and major facility closings.

❖ Effects of Organizational Culture on HR Strategy

Not only the life cycle stage but also the culture of an organization affects HR strategy. **Organizational culture** is a pattern of shared values and beliefs giving members of an organization meaning and providing them with rules for behavior. These values are inherent in the ways organizations and their members view themselves, define opportunities, and plan strategies. Much as personality shapes an individual, organizational culture shapes its members' responses and defines what an organization can or is willing to do.

❖Organizational culture
A pattern of shared values and beliefs giving members of an organization meaning and providing them with rules for behavior.

The culture of an organization is seen in the norms of expected behaviors, values, philosophies, rituals, and symbols used by its employees. Culture evolves over a period of time. Only if an organization has a history in which people have shared experiences for years does a culture stabilize. A relatively new firm, such as a business existing for less than two years, probably has not developed a stabilized culture.

Culture is important because it tells people how to behave (or not to behave). It is relatively constant and enduring over time. Newcomers learn the culture from the senior employees, and so the rules of behavior are perpetuated. These rules may or may not be beneficial. In other words, the culture can either facilitate or limit performance.

Managers must consider the culture of the organization because otherwise excellent strategies can be negated by a culture that is incompatible. For example, both AT&T and IBM have had to shift from a process-oriented culture to a results-oriented culture in the aftermath of company restructuring in an attempt to address such incompatibilities.

For another example, consider the case of an insurance firm whose culture was highly stable, resistant to innovation, and low on customer service and marketing. The firm wanted to start a financial services unit and modified its strategic plan accordingly. To be successful in this venture, the firm knew it would have to make an extensive number of service contracts and rapid financial marketing adjustments. Unfortunately, because of a mismatch between culture and strategy, the firm decided it could not implement this strategy, even though it was a viable possibility from a business standpoint. In contrast, the accompanying HR Perspective shows how corporate culture issues were overcome in a successful strategic alliance.

The culture of an organization also affects the way external forces are viewed. In one culture, external events are seen as threatening, whereas another culture views risks and changes as challenges requiring immediate responses. The latter type of culture can be a source of competitive advantage, especially if it is unique and hard to duplicate.

❖ The Challenging Environment for HR Management Today

The environment in which HR management takes place is very much in a state of flux. Changes are occurring rapidly across a wide range of issues. Some of the more visable changes present challenges to HR Management and are discussed next:

- ❖ Economic and employment shifts
- ❖ Education and training
- ❖ Organizational restructuring
- ❖ Demographic diversity
- ❖ Balancing work and family

HR PERSPECTIVE

Corporate Culture's Role in Strategic Alliances

A strategic alliance is a way in which two firms can join together to carry out a specific project, to quickly add capacities, or to enter new markets. Strategic alliances are *not* mergers or acquisitions—just partnerships. General Electric has entered into more than 100 such cooperative ventures and Ford Motor Company more than 40. Strategic alliances have been formed between the following companies: trucking company J. B. Hunt and IBM, to produce a software program to manage the process of matching loads to truckers; Microsoft Corporation and Dream Works, to produce entertainment; and AT&T and Universal Card Services, to market the AT&T Universal credit card. The long list goes on. Indeed, in a recent five-year period, it is estimated that 20,000 alliances were formed in the United States. But in spite of the popularity of strategic alliances, about 40% are considered failures, because they do not achieve their objectives. There are many potential reasons for this problem, including difficulties in reconciling two different operating cultures.

An example of how cultures can differ is provided by Dresser Industries and Ingersoll-Rand. Together, the two companies were forming a new entity, IDP, in Corning, New York, to manufacture compressors and gas turbines. The new company was to stand on its own, draw employees from both firms, and use the parents as consultants. Both firms had cultures in which the average employee tenure was about 14 years, and both were engineering firms; but their work styles were very different. One had an "East Coast" style; the other, a "Texas" style. As a result, some employees were used to working in a more formal way and others in a more casual manner. HR management took on the problem of differing cultures by arranging special events and van pools to try and break down differences and shift employees' focus to the new organization. It followed up with team building and total quality management (TQM) initiatives. The alliance became so successful that the companies also combined their pump businesses; and today, IDP is a huge global enterprise with $900 million in sales and 7,000 employees. The differences in corporate cultures were a strategic consideration but were successfully overcome.[11]

❖ Economic and Employment Shifts

Several economic changes have occurred that have altered employment and occupational patterns in the United States. A major one is the shift of jobs from manufacturing and agriculture to service industries and telecommunications. Additionally, pressures from global competitors have forced many U.S. firms to close facilities, adapt their management practices, and increase productivity and decrease labor costs in order to become more competitive. For instance, in a recent two-year period, over 3.7 million jobs were eliminated by major U.S. firms. Over half of the jobs cut were in manufacturing, indicating that significant shifts in industries and occupations continue to occur.

The U.S. economy increasingly has become a service economy, and that shift is expected to continue. Over 80% of U.S. jobs are in service industries, and most new jobs created by the year 2005 also will be in services. It is estimated that manufacturing jobs will represent only 12% to 15% of all U.S. jobs by that date. From 1990 to 2005, the number of service jobs will increase 35%, while the number of manufacturing jobs will decrease 3%.

Occupational Projections to 2005 Service-sector jobs generally include jobs in industries such as financial services, health care, transportation, retailing, fast food and restaurants, legal and social services, education, and computer systems. The fastest-growing occupations in terms of percentage are predominately in the computer and health-care fields. Figure 1–3 indicates the occupations with the largest growth in the numbers of jobs. Another facet of change is the pattern of

OCCUPATIONS	PERCENT GROWTH	NUMERICAL GROWTH
Computer scientists, systems analysts	91%	755,000
Homeworker-home health aides	107	640,000
School teachers	22	634,000
Retail sales people	14	584,000
Janitors, cleaners	18	582,000
Cashiers	19	562,000
Food/beverage service workers	12	537,000
Chefs, cooks, kitchen help	16	502,000
Registered nurses	25	473,000
Handlers, equipment cleaners, laborers	10	471,000
General managers, top executives	15	466,000
Services sales representatives	72	441,000
Guards	48	415,000
Nursing and psychiatric aides	29	400,000
Secretaries	12	390,000
Teacher aides	39	364,000
Preschool teachers, child-care workers	33	358,000
Information clerks	24	355,000
Receptionists	31	318,000
Truckdrivers	10	299,000

❖ **FIGURE 1–3** ❖
OCCUPATIONS WITH LARGEST PROJECTED NUMERICAL JOB GROWTH, 1994–2005

SOURCE: U.S. Department of Labor, Bureau of Labor Statistics, *Occupational Outlook Handbook, 1996–97.* Available for $32 in softcover or $38 in hardcover from BLS Publications Sales Center, P.O. Box 2145, Chicago, IL 60690-2145; (312) 353-1880.

job growth or shrinkage in firms of varying sizes. Whereas many large firms have cut jobs by reducing their workforces, many smaller firms have continued to create jobs.

EDUCATION AND "KNOWLEDGE JOBS" Many occupational groups and industries will require more educated workers in the coming years. The number of jobs requiring advanced knowledge is expected to grow at a much more rapid rate than the number of other jobs. This growth means that people without high school diplomas or appropriate college degrees increasingly will be at a disadvantage, as their employment opportunities are confined to the lowest-paying service jobs. In short, there is a growing gap between the knowledge and skills required by many jobs and those possessed by employees and applicants. Several different studies and projections all point to the likelihood that employers in many industries will have difficulties obtaining sufficiently educated and trained workers.

❖ EDUCATION AND TRAINING

Quite simply, there is an education and training crisis in the United States that increasingly will affect the quality of the human resources available to employers. One estimate by the American Society for Training and Development (ASTD) is that close to half of the U.S. workforce (about 50 million workers) need or will need new or enhanced workplace training to adapt to the myriad of job and technological changes that are occurring.

A special task force set up through the U.S. Department of Labor, the Secretary's Commission on Achieving Necessary Skills (SCANS), found that effective job performance is defined by workplace know-how, which is built on a foundation of skills and competencies, as well as certain personal characteristics. In a harsh commentary, the SCANS report stated that many persons entering the U.S. workforce or those already in it are deficient in some of the foundation skills. Unless major efforts are made to improve educational systems, especially those serving minorities, employers will be unable to find enough qualified workers for the growing number of "knowledge jobs."[12] The HR Perspective highlights ways in which employers are addressing the deficiencies many employees have in basic literacy and mathematics skills.

Increased emphasis on remedial education and job training for employees will be a continuing HR management concern. Implications are as follows:

- New training methods, such as interactive videos and individualized computerized training, will grow in usage.
- Training for future jobs and skills must be available for employees at all levels, not just managers and professionals.
- More accurate skill assessment for existing employees and jobs will be critical. Screening applicants for specific skills will be necessary.
- Remedial and literacy training programs will be offered by more employers.
- Employers increasingly will become active partners with public school systems to aid in the upgrading of the skills of high school graduates.

❖ ORGANIZATIONAL RESTRUCTURING

Many organizations have "rightsized" either by: (1) eliminating layers of managers, (2) closing facilities, (3) merging with other organizations, or (4) outplacing workers. A common transformation has been to make organizations flatter by removing several layers of management. Three ideas related to such organizational restructuring are reengineering, downsizing, and outsourcing.

❖Business process reengineering The fundamental rethinking and redesign of work to improve cost, service, and speed.

REENGINEERING **Business process reengineering** (BPR) is the fundamental rethinking and redesign of work processes to improve cost, service, and speed. Reengineering work involves an attempt to rethink and redesign the way work gets done. The idea is to make improvements in cost, quality, service, and speed. The process is somewhat like that followed by St. Francis Medical Center in the chapter-opening discussion. Reengineering is widespread and not always comfortable for either employees or the organization.

Reengineering is seen as part of a "clarification" of lines of business; the clarification involves deciding on the *core business* and diverting investment away from marginal activities. One study found that such clarification pays, as the stocks of firms that clarified operations outperformed the market as a whole.[13]

HR PERSPECTIVE

Employers' Responses to Basic Skills Deficiencies in Employees

Approximately 23 million Americans cannot read well enough to comprehend the daily newspaper. A study of 360 companies by the National Association of Manufacturers found that a third of the employers consistently reject job applicants for not having sufficient reading and/or writing skills. Also, over half of the firms said that there were major deficiencies in basic skills within their existing workforces. For example, a paper company in Georgia installed automated equipment that required operators to use 10th grade math and reading skills. But when the firm surveyed its workers, most of whom had high school diplomas, one-third did not have the necessary skills. Consequently, the company established a math and reading center on site, spending $200,000. After three years, virtually all of the employees had obtained the necessary skills.

Many companies have had similar experiences:

- Motorola has spent over $50 million teaching seventh-grade math and English to its thousands of workers.
- Adolph Coors established a learning center for employees and families to aid them in obtaining general equivalency diplomas.
- Loxcreen, in West Columbia, South Carolina, participates in a state-sponsored program to teach employees basic skills after work hours. Loxcreen pays workers 50% of their wage rates for the time spent in class.
- Valmont Corporation, a manufacturer of steel and aluminum lighting and irrigation systems, based in Valley, Nebraska, conducted a year-long program to train 350 employees in math, English, and science skills. Employees participating in the program work as machine operators, welders, and material handlers, as well as in other plant jobs.
- IBM taught basic high school algebra to thousands of workers so they could run its computers in Burlington, Vermont, factories.

Given the demographic trends and the declining educational skills in the United States, it is likely that basic skills training will grow in importance.[14]

Reengineering begins with asking, "Why do we do what we do?" It requires wiping the existing slate of procedures clean and analyzing every functional activity to see if there is a better way to perform them. As a result, jobs are redesigned, and people are affected. For example, reengineering the HR function at Texas Instruments resulted in a complete rethinking of the benefits information function; the result was automation of that function along with several other changes to make it more flexible and less expensive.[15] Not every "reengineering" attempt is really that. In some cases, organizations focus only on the cost side (often labor cost) and are really downsizing rather than reengineering.[16]

Downsizing A strategy to reduce costs, most often through a reduction in payroll.

DOWNSIZING **Downsizing** is an intentional strategy to reduce costs—most often through a reduction in payroll. Unit labor costs in the United States have fallen an average of 6.4% a year since 1985.[17] One of the reasons for downsizing has been the past practice of American businesses to accumulate employees. Figure 1–4 shows the layoffs associated with downsizing in the last several years. The rate has slowed some, but there is much to suggest that the trend will continue for awhile.[18] The human cost associated with downsizing has been much discussed in the popular press: a survivor's mentality for those who remain, unfulfilled cost saving estimates, loss of loyalty, and many people looking for new jobs.[19]

Outsourcing Contracting with another organization to provide operations that were previously handled internally.

OUTSOURCING Related to clarification of the core business through downsizing and reengineering is a practice that is growing rapidly—outsourcing. **Outsourcing** is contracting with another organization to provide operations that previously were handled internally. An example is hiring a janitorial firm to keep the

❖ FIGURE 1–4 ❖
DOWNSIZING AND LAYOFFS, 1989–1995

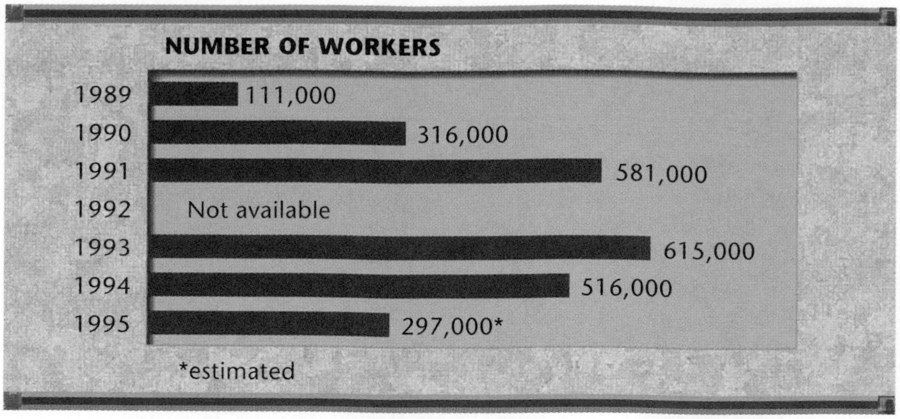

SOURCE: U.S. Department of Labor, Bureau of Labor Statistics, 1995.

building clean instead of hiring janitors. The process both eliminates and creates jobs as tasks are shifted from one organization to another.

Many organizations have decided to outsource because they do not want to hire their own employees to meet future needs. This partially may be a reaction to increased numbers of federal employment regulations, which are viewed by some employers as impediments to attempts to increase productivity. There have been an average of 200 new federal employment laws each year since 1985.[20]

Successful outsourcing requires a different mindset for management. Control may be viewed as critical for success, and outsourcing requires giving up some of that control to a third party. Meshing the outsider's goals and priorities with the company's is not easy, and written contracts have some very real limits.

Outsourcing is not new. Organizations have hired outside providers for many years to help with accounting, foodservice, and other functions. What is different now is the range of services being provided by sources outside the company. For instance, a growing number of organizations are outsourcing human resource functions, real estate management, and tax services. It is estimated that outsourcing computer services will grow to a $65 billion industry by 1998.[21] Phillips Petroleum has contracted out its employee benefits administration, engineering design, computer programming, and some research and development. Freeport McMoRan, Inc., contracted with former employees to run its entire industrial film department and set up a profit-sharing plan with them. In contrast, Atlantic Richfield does little outsourcing, arguing that their managers still have to manage the functions that are contracted out.[22]

Managers note several advantages of outsourcing: the company is not as likely to end up with an out-of-date system that it cannot afford to upgrade, there is less up-front financial commitment, and there is no long-term commitment.[23] But outsourcing has definite downsides as well.[24]

First, unions *do not* like outsourcing, and unionized firms face a fight over the practice. For example, General Motors and the United Auto Workers have had major disagreements on outsourcing. Further, the payoffs from outsourcing may be less than expected. For example, typically consultants promise savings averaging 20% to 40%, but one firm found that average savings for outsourcing were around 9%. There are other problems as well. Southern Pacific Railroad suffered through many computer breakdowns after outsourcing its computers to IBM. General Electric was late introducing a new washing machine because production was delayed by a key contractor to which GE had contracted work. Critics note, too, that increasingly fragmented work cultures result from the presence of lower-paid individuals working for contractors who simply get the work done with little enthusiasm or attention to quality.

❖ Demographics and Diversity

The U.S. workforce has been changing dramatically. It is more diverse racially; by 2000, nearly a third of the workforce will be members of racial minority groups. Further, women are in the labor force in much greater numbers than ever before, now comprising close to 50% of the workforce. The age distribution has changed as well, and the average age of the workforce is now considerably older than before. In addition, today's employees have different expectations about their roles in the workplace and different work values.[25] These diversity topics will be covered in later chapters.

❖ Balancing Work and Family

For many workers in the United States, balancing the demands of family and work is a significant challenge. While this was always a concern in the past, the 1980s saw major growth in the number of working women and dual-career couples. Family composition also is changing in the 1990s.

Family Composition Just as the workforce and population have become more diverse, so too have the living patterns and household composition of families. According to data from the U.S. Census Bureau, families and households today can be described as follows:

- The number of married couples who are childless or without children living at home exceeds the number of couples with children at home by 3 million.
- 60% of all U.S. households will have no children at home by 2010.
- Dual-career couples comprise 58% of all married couples, representing 30.3 million couples.
- Households headed by a single parent make up 27% of all families, with women heading most of these households.
- Single-parent households are less prevalent among whites than among other racial/ethnic groups.
- About two-thirds of all women with children under age six are in the workforce, and 55% of all women with children under age three are working.
- Both men and women are marrying at later ages, with the median age of first marriage for men about 27 and for women about 24.
- A majority of both men and women aged 18 to 24 still live with their parents or are considered dependents.

These statistics reveal that the traditional pattern (in which the father works, the mother stays home, and there are several children) exists only in some families and in the misperceptions of some managers who think that it is widely prevalent. Actually, the "traditional family" represents only about 10% of modern American households.

Care of Dependents To respond to changes in the composition of families, employers are facing growing pressures to provide "family-friendly" policies and benefits. The assistance given by employers ranges from maintaining references on child-care providers to establishing on-site child-care and elder-care facilities. Elder-care benefits are offered by some employers because about one-third of all

LOGGING ON

ElderCare Web
Contains reference materials and resources on elder care issues.

http://www.ice.net/~kstevens/ELDERWEB.HTM

workers have significant responsibilities for caring for elderly relatives, and these responsibilities can detract from job performance and increase absenteeism. Finally, legislation requiring employers with at least 50 workers to provide up to 12 weeks of unpaid parental/family leave is required by the Family and Medical Leave Act.

CHANGES IN FAMILY AND WORK ROLES The decline of the traditional family and the increasing numbers of dual-career couples and working single parents place more stress on employees to balance family and work. For instance, many employees are less willing than in the past to accept relocations and transfers if it means sacrificing family or leisure time. Organizations that do get employees to relocate often must offer employment assistance for spouses. Such assistance can include contacting other employers, providing counseling and assistance in resume development, and hiring employment search firms to assist the relocated spouse.

Balancing work and family concerns has particular career implications for women, because they more than men tend to interrupt careers for child rearing. According to Felice Schwartz, employers should recognize that there are two groups of women managers and professionals:

- *Career-primary women*—those who forgo or de-emphasize family responsibilities to be executives
- *Career-and-family women*—those who stay in middle management and professional jobs and accept less pay in exchange for more family time and flexibility

It is this second group that gave rise to the "mommy track," a name given by critics to a subtle classification in the business world of women who were paid less and offered fewer opportunities because they had chosen to have families.[26] As would be expected, this dual-track view continues to be controversial. The balancing of work and family issues is sure to affect the management of human resources throughout the late 1990s and beyond.

❖ HR MANAGEMENT ACTIVITIES

As Figure 1–5 depicts, HR management is composed of several groups of interrelated activities. All managers with HR responsibilities must consider legal, political, economic, social, cultural, and technological forces when addressing these activities. The activities are as follows:

- HR Planning and Analysis
- Equal Employment Opportunity Compliance
- Staffing
- HR Development
- Compensation and Benefits
- Employee and Labor/Management Relations

❖ HR PLANNING AND ANALYSIS

HR planning and analysis activities have several facets. Through *HR planning,* managers attempt to anticipate forces that will influence the future supply of and demand for employees. *HR analysis* comprises information, communications, and assessment systems that are vital to the coordination of HR activities. These topics are examined in Chapters 2 and 20.

❖ Figure 1–5 ❖
HR Management Activities

❖ Equal Employment Opportunity Compliance

Compliance with equal employment opportunity (EEO) laws and regulations affects all other HR activities. For instance, strategic HR plans must ensure sufficient availability of a diversity of individuals to meet *affirmative action* requirements. In addition, when recruiting, selecting, and training individuals, all managers must be aware of EEO requirements. The nature of EEO compliance is discussed in Chapters 5 and 6.

❖ Staffing

The aim of staffing is to provide an adequate supply of appropriately qualified individuals to fill the jobs in an organization. *Job analysis* is the foundation for the staffing function. From job analysis information, *job descriptions* and *job specifications* can be prepared to *recruit* applicants for job openings. The *selection* process is concerned with choosing the most qualified individuals to fill jobs in the organization. Staffing activities are discussed in Chapters 7, 8, and 9.

❖ HR Development

Beginning with the *orientation* of new employees, HR training and development also includes *job-skill training*. As jobs evolve and change, *retraining* is necessary to accommodate technological changes. Encouraging *development* of all employees, including supervisors and managers, is necessary to prepare organizations for future challenges. *Career planning* identifies paths and activities for individual employees as they develop within the organization. Assessing how well employees are doing their jobs is the focus of *performance appraisal*. Activities associated with training and development are examined in Chapters 10, 11, and 12.

❖ Compensation and Benefits

Compensation rewards people for performing organizational work through *pay, incentives,* and *benefits*. Employers must develop and refine their basic *wage and salary* systems. Also, *incentive programs* such as gainsharing and productivity rewards are growing in usage. The rapid increase in the costs of *benefits*, especially health-care benefits, will continue to be a major issue. Compensation and benefits activities are discussed in Chapters 13, 14, and 15.

❖ Employee and Labor/Management Relations

The relationship between managers and their employees must be handled effectively if both the employees and the organization are to prosper together. Whether or not some of the employees are represented by a union, activities associated with employee *health, safety,* and *security* must be addressed in all organizations. To facilitate good employee relations, *employee rights* must be addressed. It is important to develop, communicate, and update HR *policies and rules* so that managers and employees alike know what is expected. In some organizations, *union/management relations* must be addressed as well. Activities associated with employee and labor/management relations are discussed in Chapters 16, 17, 18, and 19.

❖ Managing HR Activities

Managers and supervisors throughout organizations are responsible for the effective use of all of the resources available to them. Therefore, effective management of the human resources is integral to any manager's job, whether as a hospital head nurse, assistant manager in a retail store, director of engineering, or president of a nonprofit agency.

Moreover, cooperation among people who specialize in HR and other managers is critical to organizational success. This cooperation requires contact, or **interface**, between the HR unit and managers within the organization. These points of contact represent the "boundaries" that determine who does what in the various HR activities. In organizations, decisions must be made to manage "people-related" activities; they cannot be left to chance.

***Interfaces**
Areas of contact between the HR unit and managers within the organization.

Figure 1–6 illustrates how some of the responsibilities in the process of selection interviewing might be divided between the HR unit and other managers. A possible division of HR responsibilities is outlined throughout the book, illustrating HR responsibilities in a particular area and who typically performs what portion of them. These are not attempts to indicate "the one way" all organizations should perform HR activities but are simply illustrations of how these activities can be divided. For example, in one medium-sized bank, all new non-management employees are hired by the HR department. In another equally successful company, applicants are screened by the HR department, but the new employees actually are selected by the supervisors for whom they will work.

❖ FIGURE 1–6 ❖
TYPICAL SELECTION INTERVIEWING INTERFACE BETWEEN HR UNIT AND OTHER MANAGERS

HR UNIT	MANAGERS
• Develops legal, effective interviewing techniques • Trains managers in selection interviewing • Conducts interviews and testing • Sends top three applicants to managers for final interview • Checks references • Does final interviewing and hiring for certain job classifications	• Advise HR of job openings • Decide whether to do own final interviewing • Receive interview training from HR unit • Do final interviewing and hiring where appropriate • Review reference information • Provide feedback to HR unit on hiring/rejection decisions

In smaller organizations without separate HR departments, cooperation among managers at different levels and in different departments also is essential if HR activities are to be performed well. For instance, in a small distribution firm hiring a new sales representative, the sales manager coordinates with the office supervisor, who may place a recruiting ad in a local newspaper, respond to telephone inquiries about the job from interested applicants, and conduct a telephone screening interview.

❖ EVOLUTION OF HR MANAGEMENT

What traditionally were called "personnel departments" now are usually termed "human resource departments." But more than the name has changed. The focus of such departments has shifted, and their responsibilities have expanded. Figure 1–7 highlights the major shifts that have occurred in the field.

Before 1900, improving the working life of individuals was a major concern of reformers. Some employees attempted to start unions or strike for improved conditions. As far back as 1786, the Philadelphia Cordwainers (shoemakers) went on strike to obtain a $6 per week minimum wage.

THE INCEPTION OF HR MANAGEMENT HR management as a specialized function in organizations began its formal emergence shortly before 1900. Before that time, most hiring, firing, training, and pay-adjustment decisions were made by individual supervisors. Some organizations adopted programs to benefit some employees, such as American Express which established a pension plan in 1875. Also, the scientific management studies conducted by Frederick W. Taylor and others, beginning in 1885, helped management identify ways to make work more efficient and less fatiguing, thus increasing worker productivity.

As organizations grew larger, many managerial functions such as purchasing and personnel began to be performed by specialists. The growth of organizations also led to the establishment of the first personnel departments about 1910. Work by individuals such as Frank and Lillian Gilbreth dealt with task design and efficiency. The Hawthorne Studies, conducted by Elton Mayo in the mid-1920s, revealed the impact of work groups on individual workers. Ultimately, these studies led to the development and use of employee counseling and testing in industry.[27]

1930S TO 1950S In the 1930s, the passage of several major labor laws, such as the National Labor Relations Act of 1935, led to the growth of unions. The

❖ FIGURE 1–7 ❖
CHANGING CONCERNS OF HR MANAGEMENT

TIME PERIOD	SUBJECT OF PRIMARY CONCERN TO MANAGEMENT	MANAGERIAL PERCEPTIONS OF EMPLOYEES	HR ACTIVITIES
Before 1890	Production technologies	Indifference to needs	Discipline systems
1890 to 1910	Employee welfare	Employees need safe conditions and economic opportunity	Safety programs, English-language classes, inspirational programs
1910 to 1920	Task efficiency	Employees need high earnings made possible with higher productivity	Motion and time studies
1920 to 1930	Individual differences	Employees' individual differences considered	Psychological testing, employee counseling
1930 to 1940	Unionization	Employees as management adversaries	Employee communication programs, anti-unionization techniques
1940 to 1950	Economic security	Employees need economic protection	Employee pension plans, health plans, benefits
1950 to 1960	Human relations	Employees need considerate supervision	Supervisor training (role playing, sensitivity training)
1960 to 1970	Participation	Employees need involvement in task decisions	Participative management techniques (MBO, etc.)
1970 to 1980	Task challenge	Employees need work that is challenging and congruent with abilities	Job enrichment, integrated task teams, etc.
1980 to 1990	Employee displacement	Employees need jobs to replace those lost through economic downturns, international competition, and technology changes	Outplacement, retraining, restructuring
1990 to 2000	Workforce changes and shortages	Employees need more flexibility in work schedules, benefits, policies	Strategic HR planning, employee rights, training, flexible benefits, computerization, etc.

SOURCE: Adapted from Stephen J. Carroll and Randall S. Schuler, "Professional HRM: Changing Functions and Problems," in *Human Resources Management in the 1980s,* edited by Stephen J. Carroll and Randall S. Schuler (Washington D.C.: Bureau of National Affairs, 1983), 8–10. Used with permission.

importance of collective bargaining and union/management relations following the labor unions' rise to power in the 1940s and 1950s expanded the responsibilities of the personnel area in many organizations, especially those in manufacturing, utilities, and transportation. Such work as keeping payroll and retirement records, arranging stockholder visits, managing school relations, and organizing company picnics were often the major tasks of personnel departments. The role of the HR department in the organization as a staff function to support operational (line) departments expanded during this period, and line/staff issues grew to influence HR departments in the following decades.

1960s to 1980s Increased legal requirements and constraints arising from the social legislation of the 1960s and 1970s forced dramatic changes in the HR departments of most organizations.[28] HR departments had to become much more professional and more concerned about the legal ramifications of policies and practices.[29] Also, organizations took a new look at employee involvement and quality of work as a result of concerns about the impact of automation and job design on worker productivity.

During the 1980s, the strategic role of HR management became essential as organizations reduced staff, closed plants, or "restructured." The ability of foreign firms from Japan, Korea, and other countries to outperform U.S.–based manufacturing companies forced U.S. organizations to become more productive. Outplacement of employees and retraining of those kept became prime concerns of HR departments. Containment of the costs of health-care benefits also grew in importance.

1990s to the Present For the 1990s, organizational restructuring has continued. Another major area of emphasis in HR management is workforce diversity. Computerization of HR activities, even in small firms, has received attention as well. Finally, growth in issues involving employee rights, such as drug testing and smoking restrictions, are affecting how HR activities are managed. The movement toward direct participation of HR executives in the strategic planning for the organization continues, with three-quarters of HR executives in large companies reporting to the CEO. Further, many of those executives report major changes in their influence on strategic issues and organizational direction.[30]

❖ Organizing the HR Unit

HR management as an organizational function traditionally was viewed as a *staff* function. Staff functions provide advisory, control, or support services to the *line*

❖ Figure 1–8 ❖
Common Organizational Arrangements for HR

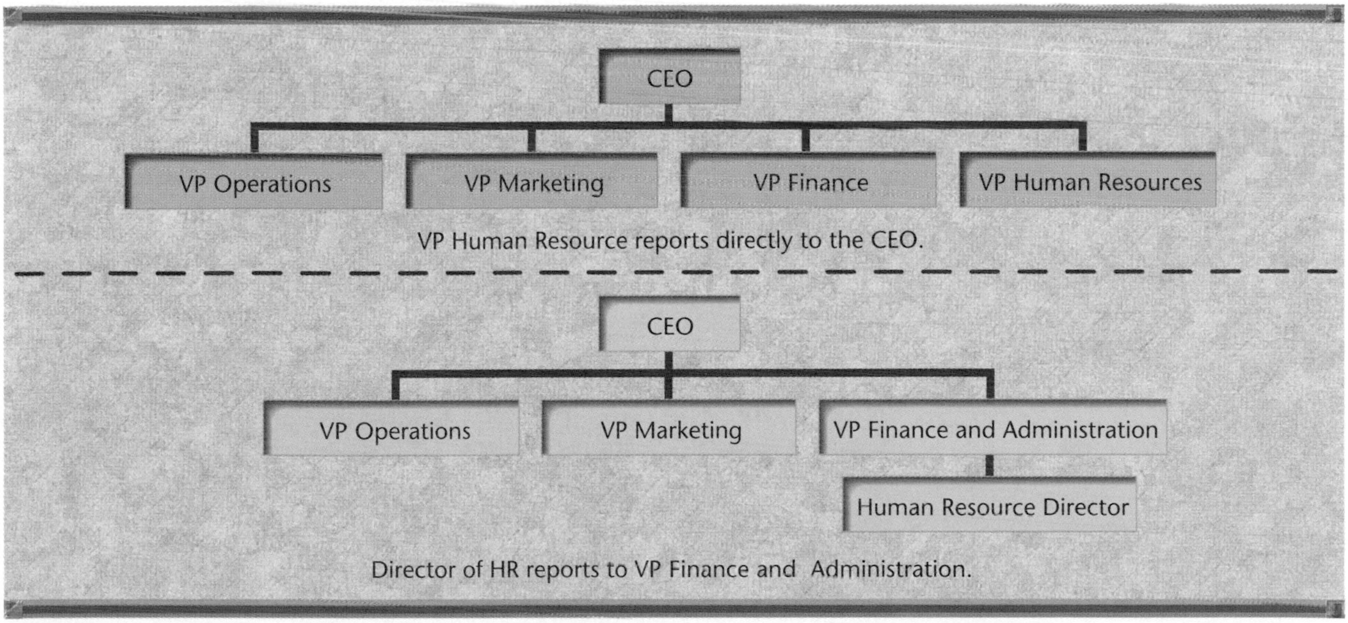

functions. Line functions are those portions of the organization directly concerned with operations resulting in products or services. Line authority gives people the right to make decisions regarding their part of the work flow; however, traditional staff authority only gives people the right to advise the line managers who will make the decisions.

Figure 1–8 on the previous page shows two different organizational arrangements that include an HR department. The upper arrangement shown in the figure is becoming more common, yet the lower structure is still frequently found. The HR function reporting directly to the CEO is likely to result in greater status and access to the strategy-making process in organizations.

HR Management Costs As an organization grows, so does the need for a separate HR department, especially in today's climate of increasing emphasis on human resources. As might be expected, the number of HR-unit employees needed to serve 800 employees is not significantly different from the number needed to serve 2800 employees. The same activities simply must be provided for more people. Consequently, the cost per employee of having an HR department is greater in organizations with fewer than 250 employees, as Figure 1–9 shows.

Outsourcing HR Activities In a growing number of organizations, some specialty HR activities are being outsourced to outside providers and consultants. For example, one firm with 1,500 employees has many processing activities related to employee benefits performed by a service bureau instead of hiring two full-time benefits technicians. A study of larger employers found that 85% have outsourced or are planning to outsource some HR activities. Portions of HR activities that are most frequently outsourced are in order:[31]

- 401(K) savings plan administration
- Employee assistance plans
- Relocation services
- Employee benefits administration
- Management development programs
- Skills training for employees
- Payroll administration

Outsourcing some HR activities can be beneficial for organizations for several reasons. First, the contractor is likely to maintain more current systems and processes, so that the employer does not have to keep buying new items, such as computer software, programs, and hardware. Also, many contractors have special expertise that is unavailable with HR managers in smaller organizations, whose time and experience both may be limited. A major benefit is to reduce HR payroll costs and shift them to the outsourcing contractor. This shift means that the HR department has fewer people and more flexibility in changing its structure and operations as organizational changes require.

But outsourcing HR activities has some disadvantages also. First, the success of outsourcing rests in the competence of the outside vendor. Having a contract that identifies what will be done and what continuing support will be provided is crucial. Obviously, selecting an outsider that does not produce services or results reflects negatively on the HR staff in the organization. Second, some concerns exist about "losing control" by utilizing outsourcing. When data are available from and services are provided by an outsider, the HR staff may feel less important and more anxious because they do not have as much access and control. Partially this concern can be addressed by clearly identifying the outsourc-

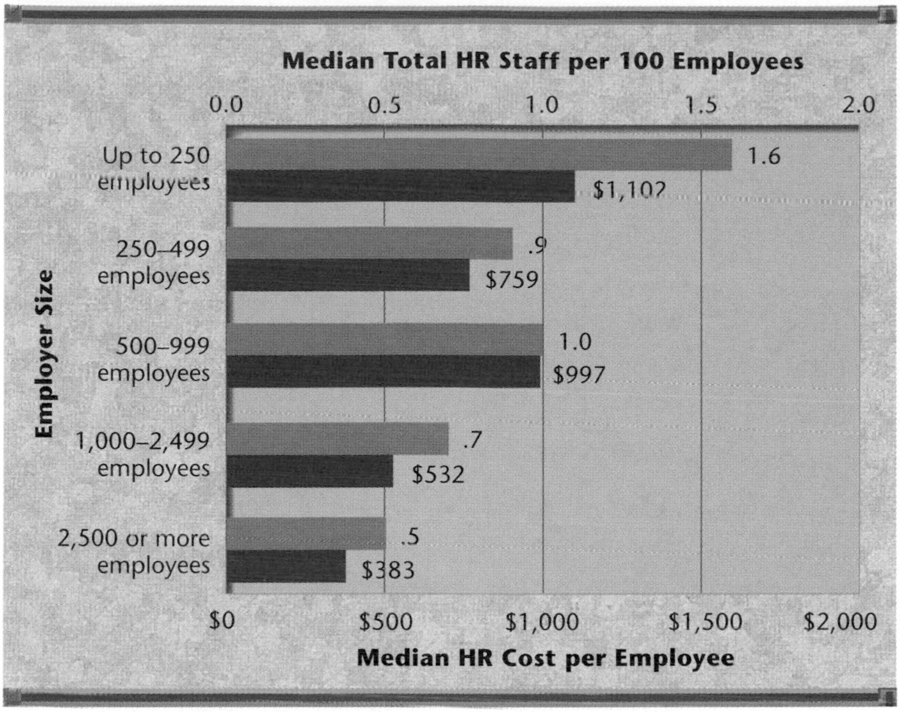

❖ FIGURE 1–9 ❖
COSTS OF THE HR FUNCTION

SOURCE: Adapted from SHRM-BNA Survey #61, "Human Resources Activities, Budgets, and Staffs: 1995–1996," *Bulletin to Management,* June 27, 1996.

ing relationship.[32] In addition, sometimes outsourcing may cost more than providing some HR activities in-house, particularly if the contract is not clear on a variety of factors. In summary, there definitely are risks associated with outsourcing, but there are distinct advantages as well. Detailed analyses should be done by the HR manager before outsourcing is done.

❖ ETHICS AND HR MANAGEMENT

As the issues faced by HR managers have increased in number and complexity, so have the pressures and challenges of acting ethically. Ethical issues in HR management pose fundamental questions about fairness, justice, truthfulness, and social responsibility. Concerns have been raised about the ethical standards used by managers, particularly those in business organizations.

❖ ETHICAL ISSUES IN HR MANAGEMENT

Specific ethical issues that create difficulty in the HR area include the following:

- ❖ How much information on a problem employee should be given to or withheld from another potential employer?
- ❖ Should an employment manager check credit agency or law enforcement records on applicants without informing them?
- ❖ What obligations are owed a long-term employee who has become an ineffective performer because of changes in the job skills required?
- ❖ What impact should an employee's off-the-job lifestyle have on promotion decisions if on-the-job work performance has been satisfactory?
- ❖ Should employees who smoke be forced to stop smoking on the job when new no-smoking restrictions are implemented by the employer?

HR PERSPECTIVE

SHRM Code of Ethics

As a member of the Society for Human Resource Management (SHRM), I pledge myself to:

- ❖ Maintain the highest standards of professional and personal conduct.
- ❖ Strive for personal growth in the field of human resource management.
- ❖ Support the Society's goals and objectives for developing the human resource management profession.
- ❖ Encourage my employer to make the fair and equitable treatment of all employees a primary concern.
- ❖ Strive to make my employer profitable both in monetary terms and through the support and encouragement of effective employment practices.
- ❖ Instill in the employees and the public a sense of confidence about the conduct and intentions of my employer.
- ❖ Maintain loyalty to my employer and pursue its objectives in ways that are consistent with the public interest.
- ❖ Uphold all laws and regulations relating to my employer's activities.
- ❖ Refrain from using my official positions, either regular or volunteer, to secure special privilege, gain or benefit for myself.
- ❖ Maintain the confidentiality of privileged information.
- ❖ Improve public understanding of the role of human resource management.

This Code of Ethics for members of the Society for Human Resource Management has been adopted to promote and maintain the highest standards of personal conduct and professional standards among its members. Adherence to this code is required for membership in the Society and serves to assure public confidence in the integrity and service of human resource management professionals.

SOURCE: Society for Human Resource Management, used with permission.

Should an employer be allowed to reject a job applicant on the basis of off-the-job smoking?

- ❖ Should an otherwise qualified applicant be refused employment because the applicant's dependent child has major health problems that would raise the employer's insurance costs?
- ❖ How should coworkers' "right to know" be balanced with individual privacy rights when a worker discloses he or she has AIDS?

These and many other situations pose both ethical and legal questions, which may involve a variety of conflicting facts, concerns, and options.[33] With HR management in an international environment, other ethical pressures arise. Such practices as gift giving and hiring vary in other countries, and some of those practices would not be accepted as ethical in the United States. Consequently, all managers, including HR managers, must deal with ethical issues and be sensitive to how they interplay with HR activities.[34]

Firms as diverse in size as Levi Strauss, Johnson and Johnson, and Cannondale, a bicycle maker, have found it profitable to behave ethically. A recent survey found that 60% of American companies have formal codes of ethics.[35] The accompanying HR Perspective features the code of ethics adopted by the Society for Human Resource Management (SHRM).

What Is Ethical Behavior? Ethics deals with what "ought" to be done. For the HR manager, there are ethical ways in which the manager *ought* to act relative to a given human resource issue. However, determining specific actions is not always easy. Ethical issues in management, including HR issues, often have five dimensions:[36]

1. **Extended consequences.** Ethical decisions have consequences beyond the decisions themselves. Closing a plant and moving it to another location to avoid unionization of a workforce has an impact on the affected workers, their families, the community, and other businesses.
2. **Multiple alternatives.** Various alternatives exist in most decision-making situations, so the issue may involve how far to "bend" rules. For example, deciding how much flexibility to offer employees with family problems, while denying other employees similar flexibility, may require considering various alternatives.
3. **Mixed outcomes.** Decisions with ethical dimensions often involve weighing some beneficial outcomes against some negative ones. For example, preserving the jobs of some workers in a plant might require eliminating the jobs of others. The result would be a mix of negative and positive outcomes for the organization and the affected employees.
4. **Uncertain consequences.** The consequences of decisions with ethical dimensions often are not known. Should employees' personal lifestyles or family situations eliminate them from promotion even though they clearly are the most qualified candidates?
5. **Personal effects.** Ethical decisions often affect the personal lives of employees, their families, and others. Allowing foreign customers to dictate that they will not have a female or minority sales representative call on them may help with the business relationship short term, but what are the impacts on the employees denied career opportunities?

RESPONDING TO ETHICAL SITUATIONS To respond to situations with ethical elements, the following guides are suggested for thought:[37]

1. Does the behavior or result achieved comply with all *applicable laws, regulations,* and *government codes?*
2. Does the behavior or result achieved comply with all *organizational standards* of ethical behavior?
3. Does the behavior or result achieved comply with *professional standards* of ethical behavior?

The complete study of ethics is philosophical, complex, and beyond the scope of this book. The intent here is to highlight ethical aspects of HR management. Various ethical issues are highlighted throughout the text.

❖ HR MANAGEMENT AS A CAREER FIELD

As HR activities become more and more complex, the demands placed on individuals who make the HR field their career specialty are increasing. Although many of the readers of this book will not become HR managers, it is important that they know about HR as a career field so that they can appreciate the professional preparation required.

A wide variety of jobs can be performed in HR departments. As a firm grows large enough to need someone to focus primarily on HR activities, the role of the **HR generalist** emerges—that is, a person who has responsibility for performing a variety of HR activities. Further growth leads to adding **HR specialists** who are individuals who have in-depth knowledge and expertise in a limited area. Intensive knowledge of an activity such as benefits, testing, training, or affirmative action compliance typifies the work of HR specialists.

❖HR generalist
A person with responsibility for performing a variety of HR activities.

❖HR specialist
A person with in-depth knowledge and expertise in a limited area of HR.

LOGGING ON

This site contains HR News On-Line and information on all of the services and products available through the Society for Human Resource Management (SHRM).

http://www.shrm.org

SPECIFIC HR KNOWLEDGE The idea that "liking to work with people" is the major qualification necessary for success in HR is one of the greatest myths about the field. It ignores the technical knowledge and education needed. Depending on the job, HR professionals may need considerable knowledge about tax laws, finance, statistics, or computers. In all cases, they need extensive knowledge about equal employment opportunity regulations and wage/hour regulations. The body of knowledge of the HR field, as used by the Human Resource Certification Institute (HRCI), is contained in Appendix E. This outline reveals the breadth and depth of knowledge necessary for HR professionals. Additionally, those who want to succeed in the field must update their knowledge continually. Reading HR publications, such as those listed in Appendix A, is one way to do this.

The broad range of issues faced by HR professionals has made professional involvement important. For HR generalists, the largest organization is the Society for Human Resource Management (SHRM). Public-sector HR professionals tend to be concentrated in the International Personal Management Association (IPMA). Other major functional specialty HR organizations exist, such as the International Association for Human Resource Information Management (IHRIM), the American Compensation Association (ACA), and the American Society for Training and Development (ASTD). A listing of major HR-related associations and organizations is contained in Appendix B.

CERTIFICATION One of the characteristics of a professional field is having a means to certify the knowledge and competence of members of the profession. The C.P.A. for accountants and the C.L.U. for life insurance underwriters are well-known examples. The most well-known certification program for HR generalists is administered by the Human Resource Certification Institute (HRCI), which is affiliated with SHRM. The program has seen significant growth in those certified in the 1990s. Increasingly, employers hiring or promoting HR professionals are requesting certification as a "plus." Certification by HRCI is available at two levels; and both levels have education and experience requirements, as noted in the HR Perspective.

Additional certification programs exist for both specialists and generalists sponsored by other organizations. For specialists, the most well-known programs include the following:

- Certified Compensation Professional (CCP), sponsored by the American Compensation Association.
- Certified Employee Benefits Specialist (CEBS), sponsored by the International Foundation of Employee Benefits Plans.
- Certified Benefits Professional, sponsored by the American Compensation Association.
- Certified Safety Professional, sponsored by the Board of Certified Safety Professionals.
- Occupational Health and Safety Technologist, given by the American Board of Industrial Hygiene and the Board of Certified Safety Professionals.

Regardless of the certification attained, those individuals who are certified demonstrate their professional commitment and competence. Also, certification may enhance job and career prospects.

HR PERSPECTIVE

HR Certification

Professional in Human Resources (PHR) Requirements[a]

- ❖ A minimum of four years of HR professional experience,
- ❖ *or* an HR-related bachelor's degree and two years of HR professional experience,
- ❖ *or* an HR-related master's degree and one year of HR professional experience.
- ❖ **Students**: Special provisions for the PHR allow students to take the PHR exam within one year of graduation, even though they do not have the required experience. If they pass the examination, they receive a letter certifying examination results. Then they have four years in which to complete the specific experience requirements to earn certification. Full certification is granted as soon as they submit evidence of meeting the work experience requirements.

Senior Professional in Human Resources (SPHR) Requirements[a]

- ❖ Eight years of professional HR experience,
- ❖ *or* an HR-related bachelor's degree and six years of HR professional experience,
- ❖ *or* an HR-related master's degree and five years of HR professional experience.

[a]For information regarding the above HR certification, contact the Human Resource Certification Institute, 606 North Washington St., Alexandria, VA 22314 (703-548-3440).

SUMMARY

❖ The management of human resources (HR) is important because it affects the human capital in organizations.

❖ The primary goals of HR management are aimed at affecting organizational productivity, quality, and service.

❖ HR management is involved in both strategic and operational management of activities to enhance the performance of the human resources in an organization.

❖ The dominant strategic HR concerns vary with the stages of the organizational life cycle.

❖ HR challenges faced by managers and organizations include those involving economic and employment shifts, education and training, organizational restructuring, demographics and diversity, and balancing of family and work.

❖ HR management activities can be grouped as follows: HR planning and analysis, equal employment opportunity compliance, staffing, HR development, compensation and benefits, and employee and labor/management relations.

❖ A sharing of HR responsibilities between the HR unit and operating managers creates an interface on HR activities.

❖ Transitions in HR management over the past 100 years have paralleled general social changes, and the field has become increasingly complex and multi-faceted.

❖ Costs for providing HR activities vary by organizational size.

❖ HR as a career field requires maintaining current knowledge in HR management.

❖ Professional certification has grown in importance for HR generalists and specialists.

Review and Discussion Questions

1. Why are both the strategic and operational roles of HR management necessary in organizations today?
2. Discuss how HR management is affected by organizational culture and organizational life cycle stages.
3. How have some of the HR challenges listed in the book affected organizations at which you have worked?
4. What are the six major sets of HR activities, and what activities fall within each set?
5. Discuss the following statement: "In many ways, all managers are and must be HR managers."
6. What are three specifically HR-oriented ethical issues?

Terms to Know

business process reengineering 12
downsizing 13
HR generalist 25
HR specialist 25
human capital 4
Human resource (HR) management 4
interfaces 18
organizational culture 9
outsourcing 13

Case

HR Management at Hewlett-Packard

The role of the HR function at Hewlett-Packard (HP) is changing. No longer the solvers of "people" problems, HR professionals have become "management enhancers"—that is, they help the managers themselves solve people problems. Rather than being a catch-all for everything management wishes to delegate in this regard, the HR unit now facilitates, measures, and improves the quality of the management process. It has meant a complete change in functional perspective.

The firm was founded in 1939 by Bill Hewlett and David Packard—two Stanford electrical engineers from Palo Alto whose efforts in technology gave birth to California's Silicon Valley. Early on, the growing company became known for innovation in people-oriented practices and values, embodied later in a set of organizational values called *The HP Way*.

It was not until 1956, 17 years after the company was founded, that Hewlett and Packard agreed to have an HR function. Their earlier reluctance had been founded in their strong belief that managers should be responsible for the people-related aspects of the business. The creation of a separate department, they feared, might lead to diminished managerial effectiveness in these areas. "The pendulum within our company swung in the direction that Dave and Bill feared," says Pete Peterson, Vice-President of Personnel. "Now we're moving it back a little bit in the other direction." Hewlett-Packard's HR department is becoming a complement to management, not a substitute for it.

Overall, the revised strategic intent of the HR function is to *create an environment* conducive to increasing human value, providing higher quality, and utilizing resources more efficiently. Along with the senior managers of the HR function at Hewlett-Packard, Peterson formulated a revised vision for the department:

- Facilitate, measure, and improve the quality of management and teamwork.
- Contribute to business decision making and facilitate changes consistent with the basic values of Hewlett-Packard.
- Manage people-related processes, which are defined as those processes for which the HR department is directly responsible.

One HR goal that Peterson has set to help meet company goals is to achieve a ratio of one HR professional to every 75 employees. When the department embarked on the goal, the ratio was 1 to 56. About two years later, it was 1 to 68, which represented a 26% improvement in two years—and departmental savings of more than $25 million.

Goals already achieved include the following impressive list:

- An accelerated 12-month development program aimed at advancing high-potential women and minorities, each of whom has a senior management mentor.
- A technical women's conference that showcased the achievements of female engineers and scientists.
- Benefits for part-time employees working at least 20 hours a week.
- A video on the company's management-development efforts.
- Procedures for measuring the connection between general managers' performance appraisals and the results of their management, such as employee morale surveys, marketing plans, profitability, growth, and new-product success.
- An action plan to increase the hiring and promotion of women, people with disabilities, and older workers in Japan, Taiwan, Germany, and other countries in which Hewlett-Packard operates.
- An on-line database called the *Practices Hotline,* which links HR professionals in the organization worldwide.
- A workforce balancing plan that helps the company avoid layoffs and achieve its no-layoff goal.
- A flex-force program, which gives the company more flexibility in redistributing personnel to various areas of the organization as needed.

These changes have reinforced the importance of HR management to the organizational success of HP. The revitalizing of HR management is a continuing challenge for all organizations, including Hewlett-Packard.[28]

Questions

1. Explain the changes in HR management at HP in light of organizational life cycles.
2. If you had to predict what changes HP will face in the future in light of organizational life cycles, what would those changes be?

Notes

1. Adapted from Sister M. Sylvia Egan, "Reorganization as Rebirth," *HR Magazine,* January 1995, 84–88.

2. Mark Huselid, "The Impact of Human Resource Management Practices on Turnover, Productivity, and Corporate Financial Performance," *Academy of Management Journal,* 38 (1995) 635–672.

3. J. B. Arthur, "Effects of Human Resources Systems on Manufacturing Performance and Turnover," *Academy of Management Journal,* 37 (1994) 670–687.

4. "Bottom-Line Reasons Support HR's Place at CEO's Table," *1995 SHRM/CCH Survey,* June 21, 1995, 1–12.

5. J. B. Barney, "Looking Inside for Competitive Advantage," *Academy of Management Executive,* November 1995, 50.

6. E. Burack and D. M. Miller, "New Paradigm Approaches in Strategic Human Resources Management," *Group and Organization Management,* June 1994, 141–159.

7. J. M. Rosenberg, "Fortune 500 Earns More with Little Worker Growth," *Denver Post,* April 9, 1996, 3D.

8. "HR Pros Less Worried About Benefits Costs," *Benefits & Compensation Solutions,* September 1995, 47.

9. Robert L. Cardy and Gregory H. Dobbins, "HRM in a Total Quality Organizational Environment: Shifting from a Traditional to a TQHRM Approach," *Journal of Quality Management* 1 (1996), 5–18.

10. G. T. Lumpkin and G. G. Dess, "Simplicity As a Strategy-Making Process: The Effects of Stage of Organizational Development and Environment on Performance," *Academy of Management Journal,* 38 (1995), 1386–1407.

11. B. P. Sunoo, "Wedding HR to Strategic Alliances," *Personnel Journal,* May 1995, 28–36, and C. S. Sankar, *et al.,* "Building a World-Class Alliance: The Universal Card—TSYS Case," *Academy of Management Executive,* May 1995, 20–29.

12. K. G. Salwen and P. Thomas, "Job Programs Flunk at Training," *The Wall Street Journal,* December 16, 1993, A1.

13. S. Rothwell, "Restructuring and Re-

(Notes continued on following page)

▼Notes, continued

Engineering Organizations," *Manager Update,* Summer 1995, 23–41, and "In a Clear Light," *The Economist,* November 11, 1995, 74.

14. N. Ramsey, "What Companies Are Doing," *Fortune,* November 29, 1993, 142–162.

15. "TI Re-Engineers Human Resources," *Teleprofessional,* March 1996, 44–45.

16. Laura Hills, "BPR Meets HR," *Benefits & Compensation Solutions,* June 1995, 30.

17. "Upsizing," *The Economist,* February 10, 1996, 61.

18. B. Wysocki, "Big Corporate Layoffs Are Slowing Down," *The Wall Street Journal,* June 12, 1995.

19. "Workers See Pain, No Gain in Downsizing," *Omaha World Herald,* December 24, 1995, G1, and Del Jones, "Managers Study Up for Downsizing," *USA Today,* January 19, 1996, 1B.

20. R. Rolf, "HR's Future Points to Strategic Outsourcing," *The Right Report,* 1995; B. Gow, "Analyze Your Options," *Paytech,* July/August 1994, 30; B. Zimmerman and K. Ramnath, "Outsourcing Benefits," *Benefits & Compensation Solutions,* April 1995, 28; and Steve Tessler, "Employee-Free Forever," *Benefits & Compensation Solutions,* January 1995, 40.

21. "Performance Management and Outsourcing," *Issues in HR,* September/October 1995, 3.

22. "Labor Letter," *The Wall Street Journal,* September 20, 1994, 1.

23. S. E. O'Connell, "Outsourcing: A Technology Based Decision," *HR Magazine,* February 1995, 35, and J. C. Spree, "Addition by Subtraction," *HR Magazine,* March 1995, 38.

24. Adapted from John Byrne, "Has Outsourcing Gone Too Far?" *Business Week,* April 1, 1996, 26–28.

25. G. Spreitzer, "Psychological Empowerment in the Workplace," *Academy of Management Journal,* 38 (1995) 1442–1465.

26. Felice Schwartz, "The Mommy Track," *Harvard Business Review,* January–February 1989.

27. For more details on the Hawthorne Studies, see Alfred A. Bolton, "Hawthorne a Half Century Later," *International Journal of Public Administration* 17 (1994), 255–430.

28. M. M. Markowich, "Who Is Running HR?—Attorneys?" *Personnel Journal,* May 1994, 150.

29. "Special Survey Report: Legal Oversight of the HR Department," *Bulletin to Management,* BNA Policy and Practice Series (Washington, DC: BNA, Inc.), February 2, 1995, 1–12.

30. Frank B. Manley and Company Consultants, "Survey Report: Changing Perspectives in HR Management," Society for Human Resource Management, 1994, 8.

31. Bill Leonard, "The New Age of Manageable Flexibility," *HR Magazine,* July 1994, 53–54.

32. J. C. Spee, "Addition By Subtraction: Outsourcing Strengthens Business Focus," *HR Magazine,* March 1995, 38–43.

33. D. Greising, "A Company That Knows How to Put Out a Fire," *Business Week,* February 27, 1995, 50, and "How to Make Lots of Money and Save the Planet Too," *The Economist,* June 3, 1995, 57–59.

34. Kate Walter, "Ethics Hot Lines Tap Into More Than Wrongdoing," *HR Magazine,* September 1995, 79–85.

35. "Good Grief," *The Economist,* April 8, 1995, 57.

36. Based on information in Larue T. Hosmer, *The Ethics of Management,* (Homewood, IL: Richard D. Irwin, 1987), 12–14.

37. Robert D. Gatewood and Archie B. Carrell, "Assessment of Ethical Performance of Organization Members: A Conceptual Framework," *Academy of Management Review* 16 (1991), 667–690.

38. W. Woods, "Taking On the Last Bureaucracy," *Fortune,* January 15, 1996, and Jennifer J. Laabs, "HR at Hewlett-Packard Marries the Best of Old and New Approaches," *Personnel Journal,* January 1993, 52–53.

CHAPTER 2

STRATEGIC HUMAN RESOURCE PLANNING

After you have read this chapter, you should be able to . . .

- Identify HR practices associated with two strategic business approaches.
- Define HR planning and discuss management and HR-unit responsibilities for it.
- Outline the HR planning process.
- Discuss why external environmental scanning is an important part of HR planning.
- Explain how auditing current jobs and skills relates to HR planning.
- Identify factors to be considered in forecasting the supply and demand for human resources in an organization.
- Discuss several ways to manage a surplus of human resources.

HR in Transition

Strategy and HR Planning at the "Go-Go Goliaths"

The "people department" at Southwest Airlines was having a busy Saturday. But unlike the "people" units at a lot of companies, which seem often to be busy writing out pink slips, those at Southwest were interviewing 200 internal candidates for 100 management jobs in reservations. The company was simply growing very fast.

As other corporate giants downsize, rightsize, and lay off their way to a "lean and mean" organization, a group of big companies are following a different approach. They are following the paths taken by the smaller firms headed by entrepreneurs: Grabbing new markets and building new and better products while still controlling creeping costs and bureaucracy.

Companies like Wal-Mart, Hewlett-Packard, Motorola, Intel, Home Depot, Microsoft, Southwest Airlines, and others have called into question the conventional wisdom that big is bad and that large organizations cannot compete. These "Go-Go Goliaths" far outperform their large corporate brothers. Many of them are adding human resources at a rapid pace. These companies have cultures that deal well with change and adapt to new market realities as they occur. They have managed to stay forward-looking, flexible, and customer focused.

The challenge is to make sure bigness does not mean bureaucracy and inefficiency.

The payoff for thinking big but acting small is experiencing growth in sales when competitors are only holding their own. For example, at Home Depot, revenues climbed an average 36% a year over a five year period (the rate was around 50% at Microsoft), while the *average* sales increases for companies in the $2 billion–plus range have been only 7% annually. A recent study found that in the stock market, investors will pay 50% more for an added dollar of profit generated by growth than for that same dollar produced by cost savings.

Shrinking company size has been absolutely necessary in many cases, but it has been correctly noted that "lean and mean is not a business strategy." For most of the industrial history of America, bigger has been better. Economies of scale, market clout, and resources of capital, technology, and talent have allowed big companies to expand at home and abroad.

Microsoft follows the *n*-minus-one theory of HR planning. If five people are needed for a job, Microsoft will allocate four. The work gets done anyway.

Despite organizational downsizing efforts currently popular, at some future point organizations may require more employees. Indeed, these companies *have* been hiring. At Microsoft, staff counts have grown 32% a year for several years, while the average payroll of all big companies has grown by less than 1% per year.

Decentralizing responsibility and decision making has improved response to the marketplace in big firms. Of course, if people lower in the organization are to have more responsibility, they must have the right skills. At Motorola, which recently added 13,000 employees in one year, *every* job candidate goes through three days of interviews and takes four and a half hours of tests in math, problem solving, composition, and teamwork. One candidate in 10 gets a job. Motorola wants to make sure its employees have the right skills. Also, training is critical and a Motorola employee gets 40 hours of training annually to improve skills.

This decade could offer some of the best opportunities for an organizational strategy of growth for big companies. Many promising markets are opening up abroad. Motorola is already pushing forward along the Pacific Rim, especially in China, where it expects sales to equal its U.S. sales by 2000. The Latin American expansion timetable was somewhat slowed by problems in Mexico, but the potential is there, too. Whether at home or abroad, the most successful organizations will follow the strategy of growth and the lessons that have brought them this far:

- *Accept change.* The market is in a constant state of flux.
- *Listen to customers.* Listening helps guard against isolation and arrogance.
- *Decentralize authority.* The lower the level decisions are made, the closer the solutions are to customers.
- *Hire carefully.* Employ skilled people who are versatile and flexible.
- *Control costs.* Pursue a frugal corporate culture, not lavish perks.
- *Teach continuously.* Identify and improve needed skills.[1]

> "Plan ahead: It wasn't raining when Noah built the ark."
> —Richard Cushing

Strategic Planning The process of identifying organizational objectives and the actions needed to achieve those objectives.

This chapter deals with planning for the human resources the organization will need in the future. But any description of HR planning must begin on a level one step higher—with the overall strategic plan of the organization. **Strategic planning** can be defined as the process of identifying organizational objectives and the actions needed to achieve those objectives. It involves analyzing such areas as finance, marketing, and human resources to determine the capacities of the organization to meet its objectives.

Strategic planning must include planning for human resources to carry out the rest of the plan. Figure 2–1 shows the relationship among the variables that ultimately determine the HR plans an organization will develop. Business strategy affects strategies and activities in the HR area. For example, several years ago, a large bank began planning to become one of the top financial institutions in the country. Two parts of its strategic plan were: (1) to adopt a global focus and (2) to improve service. HR plans to support global goals included integrating compensation and benefits systems and hiring policies for international operations and domestic operations. Service improvement plans hinged on well-trained, capable first-level employees. But an HR diagnosis turned up basic skills deficiencies in employees. As a result of HR planning, a series of programs designed to remedy basic skills problems in the workforce was developed. The coordination of companywide strategic planning and strategic HR planning was successful in this case because HR plans supported corporate strategic plans.

The amount of strategic planning an organization conducts affects its financial performance; more strategic planning produces better financial performance. This is true at least in part because strategic planning promotes "adaptive thinking" about keeping an organization aligned with its environment.[2] Further, the inherently logical idea is that organizational performance will be improved if the various component parts (such as human resources) are integrated into a coordinated whole.[3]

❖ Organizational Strategy and HR Planning

Proper staffing and training are at the heart of how organizations must plan for human resources to maintain a competitive advantage. Having the correct num-

❖ Figure 2–1 ❖
Factors That Determine HR Plans

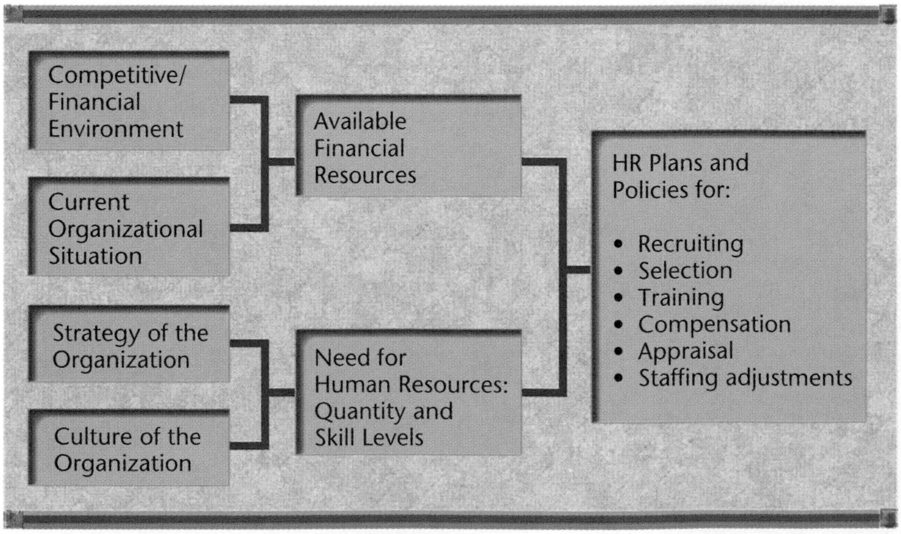

❖ **FIGURE 2–2** ❖
BUSINESS STRATEGY AND HR STRATEGY LINKS

	DEFENDER (Lower Price, High Quality)	**PROSPECTOR** (New Products, New Markets)
The Orgainization Needs:	• Efficiency • Stability • Division of Labor • Control of Expenses	• Growth • Innovation • Decentralization • Informal Control
HR Strategy:	• Long HR Planning Horizon • Build Skill in Existing Employees • Skill Specializations: Production and Control • The Correct Specialization Is Critical	• Shorter HR Planning Horizon • Hire the Skills You Need • Skills Needed: Marketing, Sales/R + D • Flexibility Is Critical
HR Practices:	• Promote from Within • Extensive Training • Hire and Train for Narrow Skills	• External Staffing • Less Training • Hire and Train Broad Skills

SOURCE: Adapted from S. Ragburam and R. Arvey, "Business Strategy Links with Staffing and Training Practices," *Human Resource Planning* 17, (1994), 58.

ber of people with the correct mix of skills at the correct time is an important part of meeting organizational strategic objectives. An appropriate pool of talented people in an organization may help the organization create and maintain competitive advantage.

There are many possible approaches to understanding the strategies an organization may choose. To illustrate the relationship between strategy and HR, two basic business strategies have been defined: *defender* and *prospector.* The defender strategy may be appropriate in a relatively stable business environment. It approaches competition on the basis of low price and high quality of product or service. The prospector strategy is more appropriate in an unstable environment with rapid change (such as the computer software industry). It requires finding new products and new markets. The categories of defender and prospector may not be mutually exclusive, as it is possible for an organization to pursue one strategy with one product line and a different one with another. Figure 2–2 compares HR needs under each strategy and the HR approaches that may be most appropriate.

Defender strategies require an organization to "build" its own employees to fit its specialized needs. This approach requires a longer HR planning horizon. In contrast, prospector organizations tend to "buy" their human resources rather than "grow" them internally. When specific skills are found to be needed for a new market or product, it is difficult to develop them quickly internally under "crash" conditions.[4] The HR Perspective "Shifting Strategic Gears" shows the difficulty Bell and Howell Holdings had in changing from one strategy to another and the impact on HR activities.

Whatever strategy an organization chooses, it must deal with changes in basic relationships within the economy. One such change in today's business environment involves staffing levels during economic downturns and upturns—an area obviously important in HR planning.

HR PERSPECTIVE

Shifting Strategic Gears

Bell and Howell Holdings Co., a Skokie, Illinois, imaging and information services firm, has seen both sides of the prospector and defender strategies.

Several years ago, Bell and Howell was a cash-flow-driven firm with a short-term orientation. Management bonuses were geared to cash flow and profit. Then, in a change of philosophy, Bell and Howell adopted a defender strategy. Inventories were slashed, and an entire level of management disappeared. Spending on research and development continued, but the company no longer took as many risks on new products or markets. Operating profits grew about 15% a year, but revenue increased 3% a year.

Five years later, top management realized that Bell and Howell could not save its way into the future. It needed revenue growth, but the cost-cutting mentality was very tough to break. The Executive VP noted that "The culture had to change; we almost had to encourage people . . . to invest in products and personnel that speed growth."

One change was an infusion of growth-oriented management that was hired from outside the company. Of the five divisions, four added new managers. In addition, Bell and Howell changed executive bonus formulas by tying 30% of bonuses to sales growth. As a result of the changes, revenue rose 7% and operating income went up 23%. The painful restructuring helped reported results—but worker productivity did not go up, and earnings did not go up.

Like many companies, Bell and Howell had chosen to "defend" its territory by downsizing parts of the workforce, such as the sales force. When the need to grow comes again for such companies, the decimated sales forces have difficulty responding. Salespeople may be doubling as customer service representatives and have less time in the field to sell. For example, at Westwood-Squibb Pharmaceuticals in Buffalo, New York, sales districts were cut from 15 to 11 and the sales force from 145 to 122. When whole levels of management were removed, the survivors had to take up the slack, and the work was not getting done.

One prescription is to "invest in people and buy companies that can expand the range of expertise," a decidedly prospector-like idea. Notes one management consultant, "The biggest driver of shareholder value is profitable growth; rising stock prices follow a growing business."[5]

Traditionally, when the economy turns down, many organizations lay off workers as the demand for the products and services decreases. When the economy picks up again, organizations increase overtime work until it is clear that the corner has indeed been turned, and then more regular employees are hired. But as the recession of the early 1990s ended, it was clear the old relationships were no longer holding.

Overtime increased—but such increases were not always followed by the hiring of full-time employees. Instead of replacing the regular full-time employees they had laid off, many employers hired contingent workers—part-time and temporary workers, consultants, and independent contractors—when overtime became insufficient to meet workloads. Employers can save money by hiring contingents because it usually is not necessary to provide them with health insurance, retirement benefits, or even the assurance of a job tomorrow.

Meanwhile, regular, full-time workers had been working significant amounts of overtime before any additional workers were hired. Ironically, while the underemployed would like more hours of work, those who are employed and are working overtime regularly would like more free time—even at the expense of a smaller paycheck.

As employers struggle to control costs to be competitive in world markets, they must deal with costs of capital, raw materials, and technology that are relatively *fixed* to the business. The cost of the workforce—total payroll—is often the only major opportunity for making costs more flexible. For many organizations, change and adaptive restructuring have been the only ways to survive.

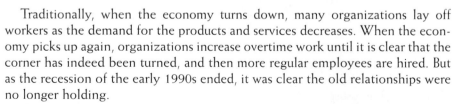

This phenomenon is not confined to the United States. Many businesses in Germany, which has the highest wage costs in the world, are making investments abroad in more cost-effective countries. Companies that cannot move abroad are trimming staff to reduce production costs. Other European countries are moving to reduce production costs as well.

All of these changes in the basic relationships within an economy make HR planning both difficult and critical. Without strategic planning, employers are sure to experience more problems with surpluses or shortages of employees.

❖ THE STRATEGIC PLANNING PROCESS

The strategic planning process can be thought of as circular in nature. As Figure 2–3 shows, the process begins with identification and recognition of the philosophy and mission of the organization. This first step addresses the most fundamental questions about the organization:

- ❖ Why does the organization exist?
- ❖ What is the unique contribution it makes?
- ❖ What are the underlying values and motivations of key managers and owners?

Once the philosophy and mission of the organization are identified, the next requirement is to scan the environment. **Environmental scanning** is the process of studying the environment to pinpoint opportunities and threats. Scanning is especially important when rapid changes are occurring, such as in the last several years. HR managers also need the results of environmental scanning. For example, some questions might be: What recruiting approaches are competitors currently using to attract scarce specialties? How are competitors using greater access to inexpensive Mexican labor made possible by the North American Free

❖Environmental Scanning The process of studying the environment of the organization to pinpoint opportunities and threats.

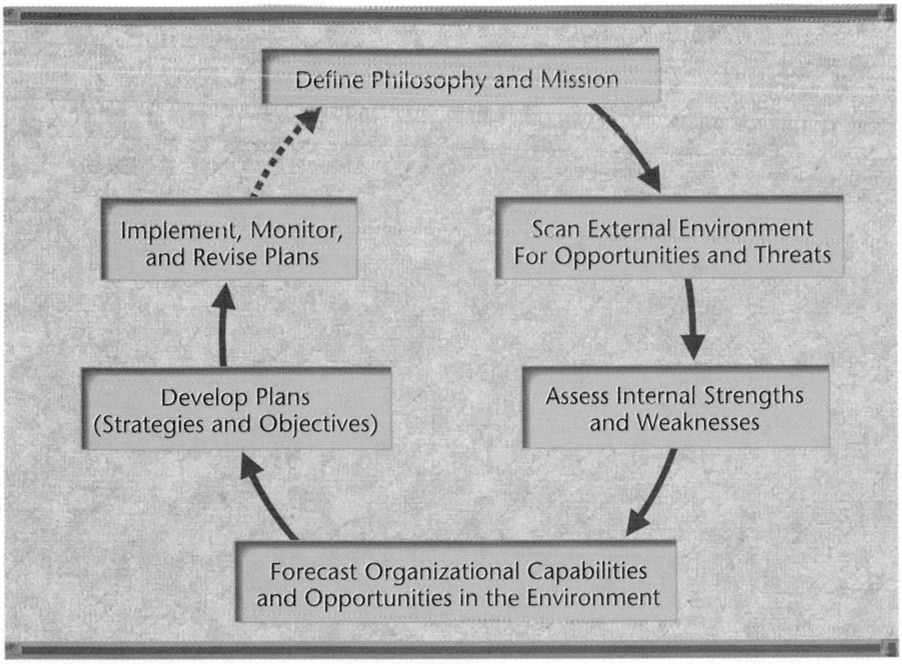

❖ FIGURE 2–3 ❖
STRATEGIC PLANNING PROCESS

Trade Agreement (NAFTA)? Will a new product under development require a labor-intensive production process? HR managers must be able to predict what type of future employees will be needed to implement the business strategy. Workforce patterns and conditions, social values and lifestyles, and technological developments are some external factors to consider.

After external forces are examined, an internal assessment is made of what the organization *can* do before a decision is reached on what it *should* do. Internal strengths and weaknesses must be identified in light of the philosophy and culture of the organization. Factors such as current workforce skills, retirement patterns, and demographic profiles of current employees are items that relate to human resource capabilities.

Next comes forecasting organizational capabilities and future opportunities in the environment to match organizational objectives and strategies. Finally, specific plans are developed to identify how strategies will be implemented. Details of the plans become the basis for implementation and later adjustments. Like all plans, they must be monitored, adjusted, and updated continually. The strategic planning process is circular, since the environment is always changing and a specific step in the process must be repeated over and over again.

❖ HR Planning

Human Resource (HR) Planning The process of analyzing and identifying the need for and availability of human resources so that the organization can meet its objectives.

The competitive organizational strategy of the firm as a whole becomes the basis for **human resource (HR) planning,** which is the process of analyzing and identifying the need for and availability of human resources so that the organization can meet its objectives. This section discusses HR planning responsibilities, the importance of HR planning in small and entrepreneurial organizations, and the HR planning process.

❖ HR Planning Responsibilities

In most organizations that do HR planning, the top HR executive and subordinate staff specialists have most of the responsibilities for this planning. However, as Figure 2–4 indicates, other managers must provide data for the HR specialists to analyze. In turn, those managers need to receive data from the HR unit. Because top managers are responsible for overall strategic planning, they usually ask the HR unit to project the human resources needed to implement overall organizational goals.

❖ HR Planning in Evolving Small and Entrepreneurial Organizations

HR management and ultimately HR planning are critical in small and entrepreneurial organizations. "People problems" are among the most frustrating ones faced by small-business owners and entrepreneurs.

Evolution of HR Activities At the beginning of a small business's existence, only very basic HR activities must be performed. Compensation and government-mandated benefits must be paid. As the organization evolves, more employees must be recruited and selected. Also, some orientation and on-the-job training are necessary, though they are usually haphazardly done.

The evolution of the business proceeds through several stages. The focus of each stage reflects the needs of the organization at the time. In the initial stage, the organization first hires an HR clerk, then possibly an HR administrator. As

HR Unit	Managers
❖ Prepares objectives for HR planning ❖ Participates in strategic planning process for overall organization ❖ Designs HR planning data systems ❖ Compiles and analyzes data from managers on staffing needs ❖ Identifies HR strategies ❖ Implements HR plan as approved by top management	❖ Identify supply-and-demand needs for each division/department ❖ Review/discuss HR planning information with HR specialists ❖ Integrate HR plan with departmental plans ❖ Monitor HR plan to identify changes needed ❖ Review employee succession plans and career paths in line with HR plan

❖ FIGURE 2–4 ❖
TYPICAL HR PLANNING RESPONSIBILITIES

the organization grows, it may add more HR professionals, often including an employment or benefits specialist. With further growth, other specialists, such as trainers, may be needed. From this point, additional clerical and specialist employees can be added, and separate functional departments (employment, compensation, benefits, and training) can evolve.

FAMILY RELATIONSHIPS AND HR MANAGEMENT One factor often affecting the planning of HR activities in small firms is family relationships. Particular difficulties arise when a growing business is passed on from one generation to another, resulting in a mix of family and nonfamily employees. Some family members may use employees as "pawns" in disagreements with other family members in the firm. Also, nonfamily employees may see different HR policies and rules being used for family members than for them. Key to the successful transition of a business from one generation to another is having a clearly identified succession plan, along with an estate financial plan.[6] Small businesses, depending on how small they are, may use the HR planning process that follows, but the process is much more intuitive and often done entirely by the top executive.

❖ THE HR PLANNING PROCESS

Figure 2–5 shows the steps in the HR planning process. These steps are considered in depth in later sections.

Effective HR planning cannot take place in a void. As suggested earlier, it must be guided by and coordinated with top management plans. For example, in planning for human resources, an organization must consider the allocation of people to jobs over long periods of time—not just for the next month or even the next year. This allocation requires knowledge of any foreseen expansions or reductions in operations and any technological changes that may affect the organization. On the basis of such analyses, plans can be made for shifting employees within the organization, laying off or otherwise cutting back the number of employees, or retraining present employees. Factors to consider include the current level of employee knowledge, skills, and abilities in an organization and the expected vacancies resulting from retirement, promotion, transfer, sick leave, or discharge.

Further, the pay system has to fit with the performance appraisal system, which must fit with selection decisions, and so on. The different activities in the

❖ FIGURE 2–5 ❖
STEPS IN HR PLANNING

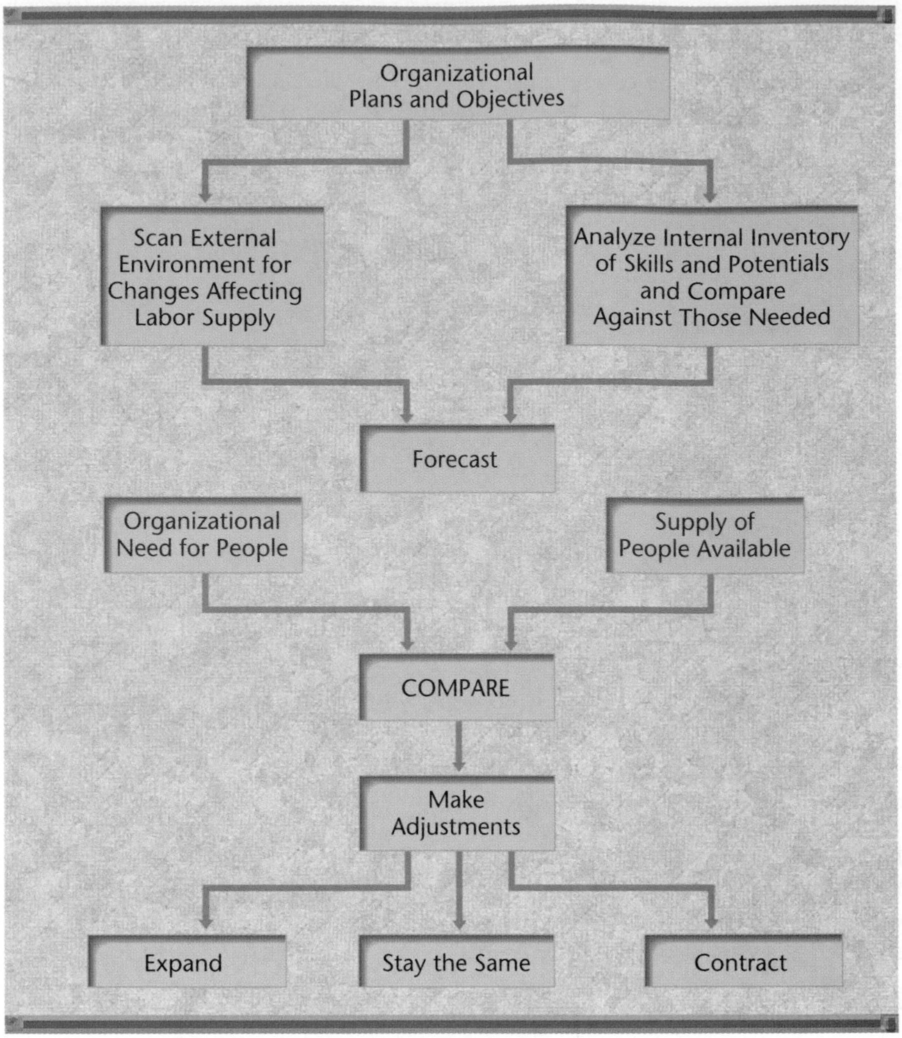

HR area must be in tune with the general business strategy, as well as the overall HR strategy, in order to provide support for business goals.

❖ SCANNING THE EXTERNAL ENVIRONMENT

At the heart of strategic planning is the knowledge gained from scanning the external environment for changes. Scanning especially affects HR planning because each organization must draw from the same labor market that supplies all other employers. Indeed, one measure of organizational effectiveness is the ability of an organization to compete for critical human resources. Many factors can influence the supply of labor available to an employer. The reputation of the organization is one factor, but labor market conditions and the HR plan also must be considered. Some of the more significant environmental factors are identified in Figure 2–6. They include workforce composition, work patterns, government influences, and economic, geographic, and competitive conditions.

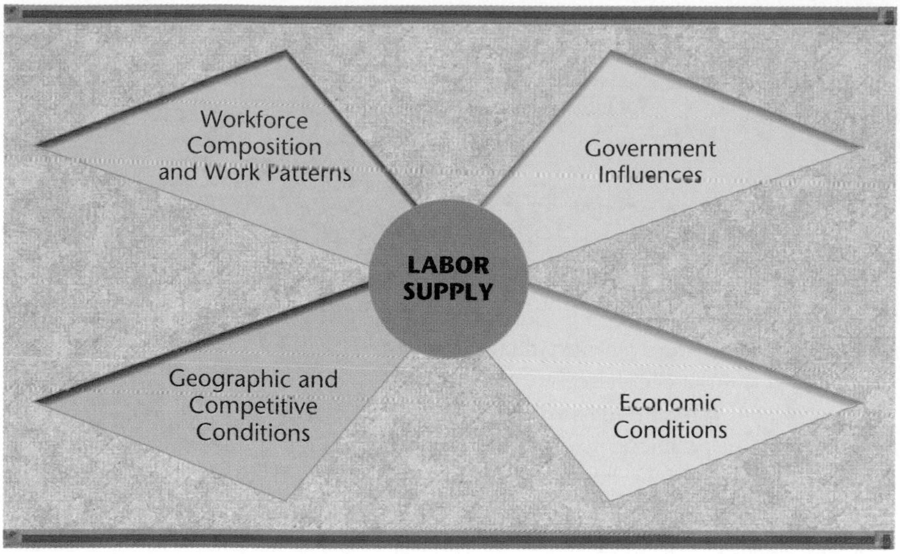

❖ FIGURE 2–6 ❖
EXTERNAL ENVIRONMENTAL FACTORS AFFECTING LABOR SUPPLY FOR AN ORGANIZATION

❖ WORKFORCE COMPOSITION AND WORK PATTERNS

Changes in the composition of the U.S. workforce combine with the use of contingent workers and alternative work schedules to create a workplace very different from that of a generation ago. HR planners need up-to-date information on these changes. Such information is available in libraries through sources such as *Monthly Labor Review,* a publication of the U.S. Bureau of Labor Statistics.[7]

WORKFORCE DIVERSITY The shifting makeup of the U.S. population accounts for today's increased workforce diversity. A major study by the Hudson Institute entitled *Workforce 2000* brought management's attention to these multifaceted shifts.[8] On its release, the report received extensive media attention.

CONTINGENT WORKFORCE TRENDS In the past, temporary workers were used for vacation relief, maternity leave, or peaks of workload. Today "contingent workers" (temporary workers, independent contractors, leased employees, and part-timers) represent 20% of the workforce. Many employers operate with a core group of regular employees with critical skills and then expand and contract the workforce through the use of contingent workers.

This practice requires determining staffing needs and deciding in advance which employees or positions should form the "core" and which should be more fluid. At one large firm, about 5% of the workforce is contingent now. The company sees contingent employees as a way to stabilize the workforce. Instead of hiring regular workers when work piles up and then firing them when the work is finished, the company relies more on temporary workers and independent contractors. Productivity is measured in the output per hour. Thus, if employees are paid only when they are working (as contingents are), overall productivity increases.

The nature of the work to be done (volume, timing, whether the work is cyclical) is a big part of the decision to use contingents. Further, the cost is an issue. Many companies think using contingent workers saves money because the companies may not be paying benefits, Social Security, or workers compensation for the contingent workers. However, those costs may increase if the contingents are hired through a third party agency, such as Manpower International.

LOGGING ON

Data on workforce composition and trends are available from the U.S. Department of Labor, Bureau of Labor Statistics.

http://stats.bls.gov/sahome.html

Another concern is the potential for developing a "two-tiered workforce." Both contingent and regular employees often are resented by the others. In one study, nearly a third of regular employees said they see contingent workers as a threat, and 25% of each group reported tension or conflict between regular and contingent workers.[9]

❖ Government Influences

Another major element that affects labor supply is the government. Today, managers are confronted with an expanding and often bewildering array of government rules as regulation of HR activities has steadily increased. As a result, HR planning must be done by individuals who understand the legal requirements of various government regulations.

Government trade policies and restrictions can affect HR planning. For example, government policies on importing Japanese cars affect the plans of automakers like General Motors, Ford, and Chrysler. Under a *closed-import policy,* foreign firms may establish more American-based manufacturing operations using American labor. An *open-import policy,* on the other hand, creates an entirely different economic labor environment.

Tax legislation at local, state, and federal levels also affects HR planning. Pension provisions and Social Security legislation may change retirement patterns and funding options. Elimination or expansion of tax benefits for job-training expenses might alter some job-training activities associated with workforce expansions. Employee benefits may be affected significantly by tax law changes. Tax credits for employee day care and financial aid for education may affect employer practices in recruiting and retaining workers. In summary, an organization must consider a wide variety of government policies, regulations, and laws when doing HR planning.[10]

❖ Economic Conditions

The general business cycle of recessions and booms also affects HR planning.[11] Such factors as interest rates, inflation, and economic growth help determine the availability of workers and figure into organizational plans and objectives. Decisions on wages, overtime, and hiring or laying off workers all hinge on economic conditions. For example, suppose economic conditions lead to a decrease in the unemployment rate. There is a considerable difference between finding qualified applicants in a 5% unemployment market and in a 9% unemployment market. In the 5% unemployment market, significantly fewer qualified applicants are likely to be available for any kind of position. Those who are available may be less employable because they are less educated, less skilled, or unwilling to work. As the unemployment rate rises, the number of qualified people looking for work increases, making it easier to fill jobs.[12]

❖ Geographic and Competitive Concerns

Employers must consider the following geographic and competitive concerns in making HR plans:

- Net migration into the area
- Other employers in the area
- Employee resistance to geographic relocation
- Direct competitors in the area
- Impact of international competition on the area

HR PERSPECTIVE

Global Workforce Composition

In Europe, the labor market now contains people from *at least* 12 nations, each with its own language, culture, and traditions. The goal for many European companies and American multinationals has been to create organizations where the full cultural diversity present in Europe is reflected in the professionals employed.

However, HR planners might need to consider some additional issues that suggest possible problems. Not only is the population in Europe aging but it also will begin to decrease in numbers.

To keep pace with the need for skilled people, a company planning for human resources in Europe will need to assure not only that a Greek and a Danish engineer can work together effectively, but that a young Turkish employee will be able to fit into the company without prejudice. Such multicultural hiring raises issues of comparable credentials and training and of cultural differences in the styles of interviewing, communication, and management. Yet competition for the best people will require that such problems be solved.

During the 1990s, workers who have the skills and education most in demand will be valuable in world labor markets. If opportunities are poor in their native countries, better jobs will be available elsewhere. This will put yet more pressure on immigration, already a sore spot in most European countries. Patterns of immigration will vary depending on what skills the local markets demand.[13]

	PERCENTAGE OF WORKERS UNDER 34 YRS		PERCENTAGE OF POPULATION OVER 65 YRS	
	1985	2000	1985	2000
United States	50.4%	39.5%	12.3%	12.9%
Germany	45.7	37.4	14.2	16.0
United Kingdom	43.6	38.8	15.5	15.4
France	47	41.5	13.6	15.6
Italy	48	44.6	14.0	16.7
Spain	49.9	49.0	9.1	11.5
Sweden	38.7	36.3	16.9	17.2
WORLD	57.1	51.7	5.9	6.8

The *net migration* into a particular region is important. For example, after World War II, the population of northern U.S. cities grew rapidly and provided a ready source of labor. Recently there has been a shift to the Sunbelt.

Other employers in a geographic region can greatly expand or diminish the labor supply. If, for example, a large military facility is closing or moving to another geographic location, a large supply of good civilian labor, previously employed by the military, may be available for a while. In contrast, the opening of a new plant may decrease the supply of potential employees in a labor market for some time.

Within the last decade, there has been growing reluctance on the part of many workers, especially those with working spouses, to accept *geographic relocation* as a precondition of moving up in the organization. This trend has forced organizations to change their employee development policies and practices and their HR plans.

Direct competitors are another important external force in staffing. Failure to consider the competitive labor market and to offer pay scales and benefits competitive with those of organizations in the same general industry and geographic location may cost a company dearly in the long run. Underpaying or "under-competing" may result in a much lower-quality workforce.

Finally, the impact of *international competition*, as well as numerous other external factors, must be considered as part of environmental scanning. A global competition for labor appears to be developing. For an example, see the HR Perspective on the composition of the European workforce and how it influences HR planning.

❖ Internal Analysis of Jobs and People

Analyzing the jobs that will need to be done and the skills of people currently available to do them is the next part of HR planning. The needs of the organization must be compared against the labor supply available.

❖ Auditing Jobs

The starting point for evaluating internal strengths and weaknesses is an audit of jobs currently being done in the organization. A comprehensive analysis of all current jobs provides a basis for forecasting what jobs will need to be done in the future. A planner should examine the following questions:

- ❖ What jobs now exist?
- ❖ How many individuals are performing each job?
- ❖ What are the reporting relationships of jobs?
- ❖ How essential is each job?
- ❖ What jobs will be needed to implement the organizational strategy?
- ❖ What are the characteristics of anticipated jobs?

Much of the data to answer these questions should be available from existing organization charts. However, determining how essential each job is may require some judgment on the part of planners.[14]

❖ Auditing Skills

As planners gain an understanding of current jobs and the new jobs that will be necessary to carry out organizational plans, they can make a detailed audit of current employees and their skills. The basic source of data on employees and their skills is the HR records of the organization. Increasingly, employers are making use of a computerized human resource information system (HRIS) to compile such records.

HRIS and Organizational Skills Inventories Human resource information systems (HRIS) have numerous applications which are discussed in more detail in Chapter 20. They are most frequently used for routine and time-consuming tasks such as payroll, record keeping, and benefits administration.[15] By integrating different data bases, HR has been able to add such valuable applications as **skills inventories**, which can be used to identify existing skills throughout the organization. That information can be the basis for determining which additional skills will be needed in the future workforce. Planners can use skills inventories to determine long-range needs for recruiting, selection, and training, as well as the feasibility of making bids for new work. The HR Perspective on page 46 describes how two firms have used skills inventories.

❖**Skills Inventories**
Listings of the skills of all employees in an organization.

In general terms, a skills inventory should consist of:

- Individual employee demographics (age, length of service in the organization, time in present job)
- Individual career progression (jobs held, time in each job, promotions or other job changes, pay rates)
- Individual performance data (work accomplishment, growth in skills)

These three types of information can be expanded to include:

- Education and training
- Mobility and geographic preference
- Specific aptitudes, abilities, and interests
- Areas of interest and internal promotion ladders
- Promotability ratings
- Anticipated retirement

All the information that goes into an employee's skills inventory affects the employee's career. Therefore, the data and their use must meet the same standards of job-relatedness and nondiscrimination as those used when the employee was initially hired. Furthermore, security of such information is important to ensure that sensitive information is available only to those who have specific use for it.

AGGREGATE WORKFORCE PROFILES Data on individual employees can be aggregated into a profile of the organization's current workforce. This profile will reveal many of the organization's strengths and weaknesses. The absence of some skills, such as computer skills, may affect the ability of an organization to take advantage of new technological developments. If a large group of skilled employees are all in the same age bracket, their retirement could lead to high turnover and leave a major void in the organization. For example, in one case, eight skilled line workers in a small rural electric utility were due to retire within a three-year period. Yet it takes seven years of apprenticeship and on-the-job training for a person to be qualified for a senior skilled job within the utility.

Other areas often profiled include turnover, mobility restrictions of current workers, and specialized job qualifications. A number of these factors are ones over which the organization has little control. Some employees will die, leave the firm, retire, or otherwise contribute to a reduction in the current employee force. It can be helpful to plot charts giving an overview of the employee situation for each department in an organization, suggesting where external candidates might be needed to fill future positions. Similarly, the chart may indicate where there is a reservoir of trained people that the employer can tap to meet future conditions.[16]

❖ FORECASTING

The information gathered from external environmental scanning and assessment of internal strengths and weaknesses is used to predict or *forecast* HR supply and demand in light of organizational objectives and strategies. **Forecasting** uses information from the past and present to identify expected future conditions. Projections for the future are, of course, subject to error. Changes in the conditions on which the projections are based might even completely invalidate them, which is the chance forecasters take. Usually, though, experienced people are able to forecast with enough accuracy to benefit organizational long-range planning.

Forecasting Identifying expected future conditions based on information from the past and present.

Approaches to forecasting human resources range from a manager's best guess to a rigorous and complex computer simulation. Simple assumptions may be suf-

HR PERSPECTIVE

HRIS Skills Inventory Aids HR Planning

As part of the HR planning efforts, it is important to know the skills available in the existing employees in an organization. Numerous firms have found value in establishing computerized skills inventories and continually maintaining them. Two such companies are Farmer's Insurance Company and National Semiconductor.

Farmer's Insurance Company, a Los Angeles–based firm with 18,000 employees at 20 sites across the country, has modernized its skills inventory. The company tracks job histories, skills, languages, licenses, and performance appraisals. Through the use of optical mark readers and scannable forms, employees can update records of their skills, training, and the like. Supervisors fill in performance appraisal ratings, thoughts about advancement potential, and career interests that employees have. This approach has decreased human error because fewer people handle the data. In summary, the HRIS skills inventory is used for HR planning and to make sure the right people are considered for the right jobs.[17]

National Semiconductor used a similar HRIS approach when it was restructuring and needed a skills inventory to help some employees find new positions in the company. An automated resume scanning and processing system that had been used to match outside candidates to jobs was used to scan the resumes of current employees and match them to existing positions. Thousands of resumes were quickly scanned and matched.[18]

ficient in certain instances, but complex models may be necessary for others. It is beyond the scope of this text to discuss in detail the numerous methods of forecasting available, but a few of the more prominent ones will be highlighted.

Despite the availability of sophisticated mathematical models and techniques, forecasting is still a combination of quantitative method and subjective judgment. The facts must be evaluated and weighed by knowledgeable individuals, such as managers and HR experts, who use the mathematical models as a tool rather than relying on them blindly.

❖ Forecasting Periods

HR forecasting should be done over three planning periods: short range, intermediate, and long range. The most commonly used planning period is *short-range,* usually a period of six months to one year. This level of planning is routine in many organizations because very few assumptions about the future are necessary for such short-range plans. These short-range forecasts offer the best estimates of the immediate HR needs of an organization. Intermediate and long-range forecasting are much more difficult processes. *Intermediate* plans usually project one to five years into the future, and *long-range* plans extend beyond five years.

❖ Forecasting the Need for Human Resources (Demand)

The main emphasis in HR forecasting to date has been on forecasting organizational need for human resources, or HR demand. Forecasts of demand may be either judgmental or mathematical. As mentioned before, mathematical methods still require considerable judgmental human input. Figure 2–7 summarizes judgmental and mathematical approaches to forecasting HR demand.

The demand for employees can be calculated on an organization-wide basis and/or calculated based on the needs of individual units in the organization. For example, to forecast that the firm needs 125 new employees next year might mean less than to forecast that it needs 25 new people in sales, 45 in production,

❖ FIGURE 2–7 ❖
METHODS FOR FORECASTING HR DEMAND

JUDGMENTAL METHODS

Estimates can be either top-down or bottom-up, but essentially people who are in a position to know are asked, "How many people will you need next year?"

Rules of thumb rely on general guidelines applied to a specific situation within the organization. For example, a guideline of "one operations manager per five reporting supervisors" aids in forecasting the number of supervisors needed in a division. However, it is important to adapt the guidelines to recognize widely varying departmental needs.

The Delphi technique uses input from a group of experts. The exprts anonymously is sought by separate questionnaires on what forecasted situations will be. These expert opinions are then aggregated and returned to the experts for a second anonymous opinion. The process continues through several rounds until the experts essentially agree on a judgment.

The nominal group technique, unlike the Delphi method, requires people to meet face to face. Their ideas are usually generated independently at first and then discussed as a group.

MATHEMATICAL METHODS

Statistical regression analysis makes a statistical comparison of past relationships among various factors. For example, a statistical relationship between gross sales and number of employees in a retail chain may be useful in forecasting the number of employees that will be needed if the retailer's sales increase 30%.

Simulation models are representations of real situations in abstract form. They may include available economic models. Numerous simulation methods and techniques are available, but surveys reveal that the more complex simulation techniques are used by relatively few firms.

Productivity ratios—calculate the average number of units produced per employee. These averages can be applied to sales forecasts to determine the number of employees needed.

Staffing ratios—can by used to estimate indirect labor. For example, if the company usually uses one clerical person for every 25 production employees, that ratio can be used to help estimate the need for clerical people.

20 in accounting, 5 in HR, and 30 in the warehouse. This unit breakdown obviously allows for more consideration of the specific skills needed than the aggregate method does.

A *demand-pull approach* to forecasting (as contrasted with a *supply-push approach,* covered later) considers specific openings that are likely to occur and uses that as the basis for planning. The openings (or demands) are created when employees leave a position because of promotions, transfers, and terminations. The analysis always begins with the top positions in the organization, because from those there can be no promotions to a higher level. Consider the example of loaders and drivers on the loading dock.[19] The loading dock has two basic job classifications, loaders and drivers, and there are two levels of each. Currently the staffing situation is as follows:

	LOADERS	DRIVERS	
Level II	50	30	
Level I	90	60	
			Total 230

Decision rules (or "fill rates") are developed for each position or level. For example, a rule might state that 50% of loader Level II openings will be filled through promotions from loader Level I, 25% through promotions from driver Level I, and 25% from new hires. Suppose anticipated openings are estimated to be:

+8 Openings due to predicted turnover
+6 Added loaders due to expansion
14 openings

Since 50% of loader Level II jobs are to be filled through promotions from loader Level I, it is forecast that 7 will come from that source, and so on. Forecasters must be aware of chain effects throughout, because as people are promoted, their previous positions become available.

❖ Forecasting Availability of Human Resources (Supply)

Not only the need for human resources but also their availability must be identified. Forecasting the availability of human resources considers both *external* and *internal* supplies. Although the internal supply is easier to calculate, it is important to calculate the external supply as well.

External Supply The external supply of potential employees available to the organization can be estimated based on the following factors:

- Net migration into and out of the area
- Individuals entering and leaving the workforce
- Individuals graduating from schools and colleges
- Changing workforce composition and patterns
- Economic forecasts for the next few years
- Technological developments and shifts
- Actions of competing employers
- Government regulations and pressures
- Factors affecting persons entering and leaving the workforce

Internal Supply Figure 2–8 shows in general terms how the internal supply can be calculated. This supply is influenced by training and development programs, transfer and promotion policies, and retirement policies, among other factors.

A *supply-push approach* to estimating internal supply considers that employees move from their current jobs into others through promotions, lateral moves, and terminations. Again consider the example of the loading dock with two basic job

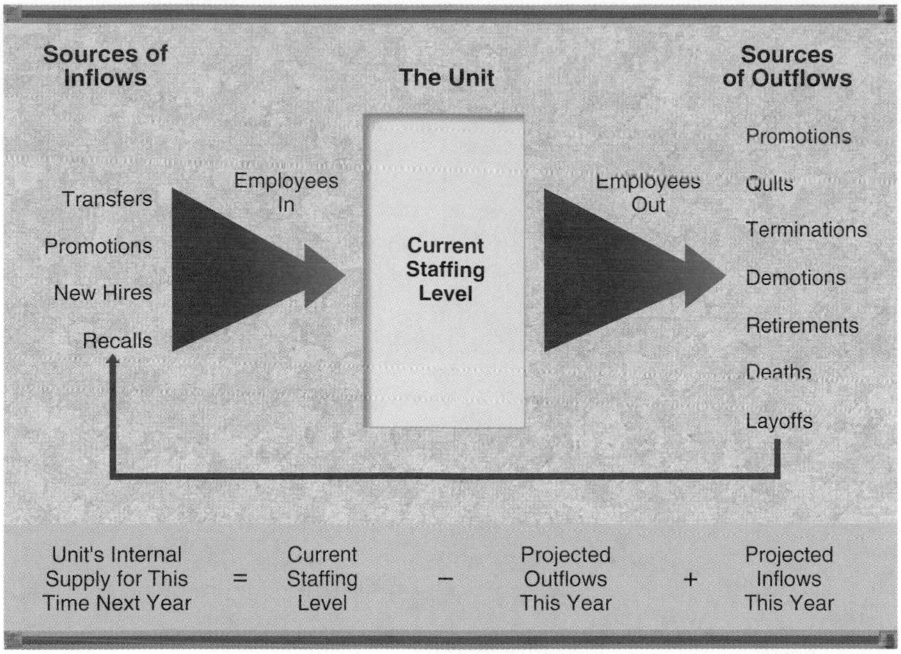

❖ FIGURE 2–8 ❖
ESTIMATING INTERNAL LABOR SUPPLY FOR A GIVEN UNIT

classifications—loaders and drivers—and two levels of each. Suppose the following situation exists:

Level II	15 Loaders + 6 Drivers	21
Level I	25 Loaders + 10 Drivers	35
TOTAL	Loaders and Drivers	56

Now suppose that the following happens:

25	(Beginning number of loaders at Level I)
−8	(Promoted to loader Level II)
−1	(Promoted to driver Level II)
−1	(Fired)
+1	(Transferred in from driver Level I)
+5	(New hires)
21	(Loaders remaining at Level I)

These historical data on the proportions of Level I loaders that were promoted, fired, or transferred can form the basis for estimates for next year.

Internally, *succession analysis* is a widely used method to forecast the supply of people for certain positions. It relies on *replacement charts,* which are succession plans developed to identify potential personnel changes, select backup candidates, promote individuals, and keep track of attribution (resignations, retirements) for each department in an organization. Replacement charts are the most widely used forecasting technique in HR planning.

A *transition matrix,* or *Markov matrix,* can be used to model the internal flow of human resources. These matrices simply show as probabilities the average rate of historical movement from one job to another. Figure 2–9 presents a very simple transition matrix. For a line worker, for example, there is a 20% probability

❖ FIGURE 2–9 ❖
TRANSITION MATRIX FOR 12-MONTH PERIOD

	EXIT	MANAGER	SUPERVISOR	LINE WORKER
Manager	.15	.85	.00	.00
Supervisor	.10	.15	.70	.05
Line Worker	.20	.00	.15	.65

of being gone in 12 months, a 0% probability of promotion to manager, a 15% probability of promotion to supervisor, and a 65% probability of being a line worker this time next year. Such transition matrices form the bases for computer simulations of the internal flow of people through a large organization over time.

❖ MANAGING A HUMAN RESOURCE SURPLUS

With all the data collected and forecasts done, an organization has the information it needs to develop an HR plan. Such a plan can be extremely sophisticated or rather rudimentary. Regardless of its degree of complexity, the ultimate purpose of the plan is to enable managers in the organization to match the available supply of labor with the forecasted demands in light of the strategies of the firm. If the necessary skill level does not exist in the present workforce, employees may need to be trained in the new skill, or outside recruiting may need to be undertaken. Likewise, if the plan reveals that the firm employs too many people for its needs, workforce reductions may be necessary.

The HR plan provides a "road map" for the future, identifying where employees are likely to be obtained, when employees will be needed, and what training and development employees must have. Through career and succession planning, employee *career paths* can be tailored to individual needs that are consistent with organizational requirements.

All efforts involved in HR planning will be futile unless management takes action to implement the plans. Managerial actions vary depending on whether a surplus or a shortage of workers has been forecast. Consideration will be given here to managing a surplus of employees, since dealing with a shortage is considered later, in the recruiting and training chapters (Chapters 8 and 10). A surplus of workers can be managed within an HR plan in a variety of ways. But regardless of the means, the actions are difficult because they require that some employees be removed from the organization.

❖ DOWNSIZING

❖Downsizing
Reducing the size of an organizational workforce.

The 1980s saw the introduction of a trend toward downsizing, which has continued through the 1990s. **Downsizing** is reducing the size of an organizational workforce. A wave of merger and acquisition activity in the United States has often left the new, combined companies with redundant departments, plants, and people. Another cause for downsizing is the need to meet foreign competition and cut costs.

Downsizing has inspired a variety of innovative ways of removing people from the payroll, sometimes on a massive scale. For example, at one major company, more than 40,000 employees were given the option of leaving the company voluntarily or taking a chance that their jobs would be among the ones retained. To encourage volunteers, an early retirement buyout plan was offered to anyone over 50 years of age who had at least 15 years' service. Improved pensions were offered to people who took retirement. For those not eligible for the early retirement buyout, a lump-sum settlement of approximately two weeks' pay for each year of service was offered. Further, those entitled to regular pensions could still get them when they became eligible later in life. For both the volunteers who chose to leave and the employees laid off, employee relations specialists developed retirement counseling seminars, outplacement assistance to aid former employees in finding other jobs, and stress counseling. Ultimately, over 6,000 employees elected to leave under the program.

This first major *reduction in force (RIF)* of workers ever undertaken in that firm gave a major jolt to the way in which employees viewed the company. Bitterness, anger, disbelief, and shock were common reactions. For those who survived the cuts, the paternalistic culture and image of the firm as a "lifetime" employer were gone forever. This situation is typical when downsizing occurs.

Overall, studies of the effects of downsizing show mixed results. Cost control is most often the reason given for downsizing, but whether downsizing increases profitability in all cases is questionable. Some studies show a negative or at best indifferent effects on quality, productivity, and morale.[20] But corporate leaders point out that layoffs *do* cut costs, and that the competition is getting leaner and quicker.[21] Arguments are made for continuous, selective cutting of the workforce to offset growth in areas that are not adding value. In fact, nearly one in four companies recently reporting job cuts had no net change in head count.[22]

A decade of experience with downsizing has led to some wisdom on how to deal with it if necessary:

- *Investigate alternatives to downsizing.* Given the potential problems of downsizing, alternatives should be seriously considered first.
- *Involve those people necessary for success in the planning for downsizing.* This involvement frequently is not done; those who have to make the downsizing operation work often are not involved in its planning.
- *Develop a comprehensive communications plan.* Employees are entitled to advance notice so they can make plans.
- *Nurture the survivors.* Remaining employees may be confused about their future careers. These and other concerns obviously can have negative effects.
- *Outplacement pays off.* Helping separated employees find new work is good both for the people and for the reputation of the firm.

There are several alternatives to immediate downsizing. Attrition, early retirement buyouts, and layoffs are the ones most frequently used.

ATTRITION AND HIRING FREEZES *Attrition* occurs when individuals who quit, die, or retire are not replaced. With this approach, no one is cut out of a job, but those who remain must handle the same workload with fewer people. Unless turnover is high, attrition will eliminate only a relatively small number of employees. Therefore, employers may use a method that combines attrition with a freeze on hiring. This method is usually received with better employee understanding than many of the other methods. It is usually the first method used to downsize.[23]

EARLY RETIREMENT BUYOUTS Early retirement is a means of encouraging more senior workers to leave the organization early. To provide an incentive, employers make additional payments to employees so that they will not be penalized too much economically until their pensions and Social Security benefits take effect. Such voluntary termination programs, or buyouts, entice employees to quit with financial incentives. They are widely viewed as ways to accomplish workforce reduction without resorting to layoffs and individual firings.

Buyouts appeal to employers because they can reduce payroll costs significantly over time. Although there are some up-front costs, the organization does not incur the continuing payroll costs. One hospital saved $2 for every $1 spent on early retirees. As noted, early retirement buyouts are viewed as a more humane way to reduce staff than terminating long-service, loyal employees. In addition, as long as buyouts are truly voluntary, the organization is less exposed to age discrimination suits.

Most early retirement buyout programs offer a one-time "window." Employees must decide during that window, typically 60 to 90 days, whether to take early retirement or take their chances that their jobs will not be eliminated in future restructuring efforts. Both employees whom the company wishes would stay and those it wishes would leave can take advantage of the buyout. Consequently, some individuals whom the employer would rather retain often are among those who take a buyout.[24]

LAYOFFS Layoffs occur when employees are put on unpaid leaves of absence. If business improves for the employer, then employees can be called back to work. Layoffs may be an appropriate downsizing strategy if there is a temporary downturn in an industry. Nevertheless, careful planning of layoffs is essential. Managers must consider the following questions:

- How are decisions made about whom to lay off (seniority, performance records)?
- How will call-backs be made if all workers cannot be recalled at the same time?
- Will any benefits coverage be given workers who are laid off?
- If workers take other jobs, do they forfeit their call-back rights?

Companies have no legal obligation to provide a financial cushion to laid-off employees; however, many do. When a provision exists for severance pay, the most common formula is one week's pay for every year of employment. Larger companies tend to be more generous. Loss of medical benefits is a major problem for laid-off employees. But under a federal law (COBRA) displaced workers can retain their medical group coverage for up to 18 months, and up to 36 months for dependents if they pay the premiums themselves.

There may be no kind way to lay off employees. The HR Perspective "Ethics—Watch What We Did, Not What We Said" shows the irony and public relations difficulties associated with layoffs.

❖ MANAGING SURPLUS HUMAN RESOURCES CREATED BY MERGERS AND ACQUISITIONS

During the 1980s in the United States, a large number of firms acquired or merged with other firms. Some of these mergers were large. Others were smaller, such as the merger of two local hospitals. But a common result of most mergers and acquisitions is that there is an excess of employees once the firms have been combined. Because much of the rationale for combinations is financial, elimination of employees with overlapping responsibilities is a primary concern. The natural response of employees is anxiety about their futures: Who will be eliminated? What operations will be closed? Who will be required to relocate or lose employment? Stress follows anxiety because the climate and culture of the organization are strained.

HR PERSPECTIVE

Ethics—Watch What We Did, Not What We Said

Organizations in a recent year combined record profits with record layoffs. Here are some leaders' comments at the *beginning* of the year in the chairman's letter accompanying the annual report. In parentheses are the *number laid off* during the year that followed.[25]

From 1994 annual reports:

"It would not have been possible without the tremendous effort put forth by . . . more than 5,000 dedicated employees. They made it happen." *William Roemer,* **Integra Financial Corp. (1,200 cuts)**

"I want to thank our employees, who are applying more creative energy than ever before." *Robert Williams,* **James River Corp. (4,400 cuts)**

"Our skilled, dedicated, and hard-working employees remain our most important asset. . . . I thank all of our employees for their outstanding efforts in 1994." *John Stafford,* **American Home Products (6,500 cuts)**

"To . . . our associates . . . thanks for your confidence and support, and your belief in the exciting future that awaits Woolworth." *Roger Farah,* **Woolworth (2,000 cuts)**

"Satisfied employees are a necessary precondition for satisfied customers. . . . We deeply appreciate the accomplishments of thousands of dedicated employees." *Iran Stepanian and Charles Gifford,* **Bank of Boston (2,000 cuts)**

"Much of the credit goes to our employees. Their dedication and commitment . . . prove we're capable of reaching our goal." *Thomas O'Brien,* **PNC Bank Corp. (2,000 cuts)**

"Relationships . . . expertise . . . innovation . . . these qualities have served Bankers Trust well in the past, and with the continued dedication of our talented professionals around the world, they will serve us well in the future." *Charles Sanford,* **Bankers Trust (1,400 cuts)**

"I am confident because I am so proud of the job being done by AT&T people (more than 300,000 of them)." *Robert Allen,* **AT&T (8,500 cuts, plus 72,000 buyout offers)**

"There are a number of reasons for this improvement, but none is more important than the hard work of Digital's employees. The company's success is the direct result of their dedication and determination." *Robert Palmer,* **Digital Equipment Corp. (4,500 cuts)**

"I have enormous confidence in the ability of the men and women of Boeing to meet the challenges ahead." *Frank Shomtz and Philip Condit,* **Boeing (17,500 cuts)**

HR experts can help employees with these adjustments. At the same time, HR specialists must be involved in identifying and planning how the combined firms will operate. They must evaluate options for reducing the surplus and implement the selected options. Different HR policies, benefit programs, compensation plans, and human resource information systems must be integrated. In sum, many of top factors to be considered after a merger are related directly to human resources.[26]

❖ Managing Survivors of Downsizing

A common myth is that those who are still around after downsizing in any of its many forms are so glad to have a job that they pose no problems to the organization. However, some observers draw an analogy between those who survive downsizing and those who survive wartime but experience guilt because they were spared while their friends were not. The result is that the performance of the survivors may be affected.[27]

Survivors need information as to why the actions had to be taken and what the future holds for them personally. The more that employees are involved in the regrouping, the more likely the transition will be smooth.[28] One employer set aside some of the money saved from downsizing to reward employee suggestions for getting more work done with fewer employees, thereby involving and rewarding the survivors.

❖ Outplacement

Outplacement
A group of services provided to displaced employees to give them support and assistance.

Outplacement is a group of services provided to displaced employees to give them support and assistance. It most often is used with those involuntarily removed because of plant closings or elimination of departments. A variety of services may be available to displaced employees. Outplacement services typically include personal career counseling, resume preparation and typing services, interviewing workshops, and referral assistance. Such services are generally provided by outside firms that specialize in outplacement assistance. Additionally, special severance pay arrangements may be used. Firms commonly continue medical benefit coverage for a period of time at the same company-paid level as before. Other aids include retraining for different jobs, establishing on-site career centers, and contacting other employers for job placement possibilities.

There are several reasons why a company should consider such a seemingly costly and time-consuming program even though employees are terminated because of financial burdens:[29]

1. *Cost.* It may not be as great as it seems. For example, helping workers find jobs more quickly can cut down on unemployment benefits.
2. *Company image.* Outplacement efforts typically project an image of the company as a caring employer.
3. *Legal issues.* The longer employees are out of work, the more likely they are to consider suing for damages.
4. *Social responsibility.* Some believe that employers have a moral or ethical obligation to former employees.

❖ Evaluating HR Planning

HR planning is a critical part of managing human resources in an organization. If it is poorly done, there may be too few people to staff the company or, conversely, massive layoffs may be necessary—with all the attendant problems. If HR planning is done well, the following benefits should result:

- Upper management has a better view of the human resource dimensions of business decisions.
- HR costs may be less because management can anticipate imbalances before they become unmanageable and expensive.
- More time is available to locate talent because needs are anticipated and identified before the actual staffing is required.
- Better opportunities exist to include women and minority groups in future growth plans.
- Development of managers can be better planned.

To the extent that these results can be measured, they can form the basis for evaluating the success of HR planning. Another approach is to measure projected levels of demand against actual levels at some point in the future. But the most telling evidence of successful HR planning is an organization in which the human resources are consistently aligned with the needs of the business over a period of time.[30]

SUMMARY

❖ HR planning involves analyzing and identifying the future needs for and availability of human resources for the organization.

❖ HR planning is tied to the broader process of strategic planning, beginning with identification of the philosophy and mission of the organization. The HR unit has major responsibilities in HR planning, but managers must provide supportive information and input.

❖ Different organizational strategies require different approaches to selection and development of human resources.

❖ HR planning in small entrepreneurial firms is concerned with different issues from those in larger firms.

❖ Assessment of internal strengths and weaknesses as a part of HR planning requires that current jobs and employee skills be audited and aggregate workforce profiles developed.

❖ Information on past and present conditions is used to identify expected future conditions and forecast the supply and demand for human resources. This process can be carried out with a variety of methods and for differing periods of time.

❖ Changes in organization patterns, government influences, competitive factors, and economic conditions affect the supply of human resources.

❖ Supply-push and demand-pull approaches to forecasting help identify specific needs.

❖ Management of HR surpluses may require downsizing and outplacement. Attrition and early retirement are common means.

❖ "Survivors" of downsizing often are changed and may require different management after downsizing.

REVIEW AND DISCUSSION QUESTIONS

1. What is HR planning, and how do the HR planning responsibilities of HR specialists differ from those of managers?
2. Discuss how business strategy and HR practices are related.
3. Why must HR planning be seen as a process flowing from the organizational strategic plan?
4. Assume you have to develop an HR plan for a local bank. What specific external factors would be important for you to consider? Why?
5. At a computer software firm, how would you audit the current jobs and skills of employees?
6. Why are the time frame and methods used to forecast supply and demand for human resources so important?
7. Assume that as a result of HR planning, a hospital identifies a shortage of physical therapists but a surplus of administrative workers. Discuss what actions might be taken to address these problems and why they must be approached carefully.

Terms to Know

downsizing **50**
environmental scanning **37**
forecasting **45**
human resource (HR) planning **38**
outplacement **54**
skills inventories **44**
strategic planning **34**

CASE

Tailoring HR Management to Fit at Levi Strauss & Co.

Just as Levi Strauss & Co. tailors its products to fit a variety of markets, it also has tailored its HR management activities to fit a variety of employee and corporate needs. Several years ago the company redefined the role of HR management, as well as the company as a whole. The senior management of the firm met to identify the basic values and mission for the company.

Following the development of a mission statement, the senior management specified the principles of leadership necessary to fulfill these aspirations:

- New leadership behavior
- Greater valuing of the diversity of people in Levi's workforce
- Greater recognition for individual and team contributions
- Ethical management practices
- Timely communications with employees
- Empowerment of employees to act

Fulfilling these lofty aspirations in a company of 31,000, of whom 8,000 are located outside the United States (in 78 facilities worldwide), has been the challenge of the HR professionals at Levi's, headed by the Senior Vice-President of Human Resources.

One critical focus of Levi's HR management is to become a truly global company. Accordingly, HR programs are adapted or revised to fit local cultural differences in the European, Asian, and Latin American countries where Levi's operates. Cross-country movement of managers and professionals has aided the career development of employees while also expanding the company's global perspectives. International jobs are posted throughout Levi's. The firm does not have specifically targeted career tracks for individuals but expects them and their managers to develop their abilities in the directions they desire.

Extensive investment in training has been required. A core curriculum of classes was started in which every employee participates. Topics in the core focus on the key dimensions of the aspiration statement. Extensive time is spent on values, diversity, and ethics. Understanding people with different backgrounds and lifestyles is explored through a variety of exercises.

Another area of concern at Levi's is aiding employees in balancing their personal/family and professional/work responsibilities. A Work/Family Taskforce identified major individual issues and developed a survey for employees throughout the United States. Over 17,000 employees (representing 73% of Levi's workforce) completed the 27-page survey. As a result of the survey, the following programs were implemented:

- Training to make managers and supervisors aware of work and family issues
- A "time-off with pay" program that replaces vacation, sick leave, and floating holidays.
- Expanded child-care and elder-care leaves for individuals with family problems
- Financial support to improve existing child-care programs in communities where Levi's operates

One result of this expanded view of HR is that the corporate personnel policy manual decreased from 300 to 24 pages. The idea is to allow managers, HR professionals, and employees to adapt policies to fit individual and local needs.[31]

Questions

1. Levi Strauss has an image as a caring employer. If the company had to downsize by 10%, how could it best be done in a way to keep that image with its employees?
2. Describe why HR planning is especially important to Levi Strauss.

Notes

1. Based on B. P. Sunoo, "How Fun Flies at Southwest Airlines," *Personnel Journal*, June 1995, 62–73; and Wendy Zelner et al., "Go-Go Goliaths," *Business Week*, February 13, 1995, 64–70.
2. C. Miller and L. Cardinal, "Strategic Planning and Firm Performance: A Synthesis of More Than Two Decades of Research," *Academy of Management Journal*, December 1994, 1649–1665.
3. Paul Swiercz, "Research Update," *Human Resource Planning* 18 (1995), 5–7.
4. S. Ragburam and R. Arvey, "Business Strategy Links with Staffing and Training Practices," *Human Resource Planning* 17 (1994), 57.
5. Adapted from B. Wysocki, "Lean and Frail," *The Wall Street Journal*, July 15, 1995, 1.
6. Sharon Nelton, "What It Takes to Be a Winner," *Nation's Business*, June 1995, 49.
7. Throughout the following section, various statistics on workforce composition and trends are taken from U.S. Department of Labor, Bureau of Labor Statistics, and Census Bureau data widely available in various reference and news media reports. For additional details, pertinent issues of the *Monthly Labor Review* can be consulted.
8. W. B. Johnston and A. E. Parker, *Workforce 2000: Work and Workers for the 21st Century* (Indianapolis: The Hudson Institute, 1987).
9. Shari Caudron, "Contingent Workforce Spurs HR Planning," *Personnel Journal*, July 1994, 58.
10. A. Bernstein, "Wage Squeeze," *Business Week*, July 17, 1995, 54–62; H. Gleckman, *et al.*, "Downsizing Government," *Business Week*, January 23, 1995, 34.
11. L. S. Richman, "The Economy," *Fortune*, August 7, 1995, 157–160.
12. Lee Smith and E. M. Davies, "Riskiest Industries," *Fortune*, April 1, 1996, 76.
13. "Misplaced Panics," *The Economist*, February 11, 1995, 23; Barry Rubin, "Europeans Value Diversity," *HR Magazine*, January 1991, 38; Jim Kennedy and Anna Everest, "Put Diversity in Context," *Personnel Journal*, September 1991, 50–54. Statistics from International Labour Office, *Economically Active Population 1950–2025*.
14. See Donald Jarrell, *Human Resource Planning* (Englewood Cliffs, NJ: Prentice Hall, 1993).
15. A. Yeung and W. Brockbank, "Lower Cost, Higher Value: HR Function in Transition," *Human Resource Planning* 17, no. 3 (1994), 7.
16. A. Yeung, "Reengineering HR through Information Technology," *Human Resource Planning* 18–2 (1995), 24–37.
17. J. Konkling, "A New Way to Monitor Talent," *Solutions*, November 1995, 22–23.
18. William Matlack, "Automated Job Placement," *Benefits & Compensation Solutions*, June 1995.
19. The examples of supply push and demand-pull analysis were adapted from T. Bechet and W. Maki, "Modeling and Forecasting Focusing on People As a Strategic Resource," *Human Resource Planning* 10 (1987), 214–217.
20. L. Baggerman, "The Futility of Downsizing," *Industry Week*, January 18, 1993, 27–29; J. Gutknecht and J. Keys, "Mergers, Acquisitions and Takeovers: Maintaining Morale of Survivors," *Academy of Management Executive*, August 1993, 26.
21. Matt Murphy, "Thanks, Goodbye," *The Wall Street Journal*, May 4, 1995, A1; and Alex Markels and Matt Murphy, "Call It Dumbsizing," *The Wall Street Journal*, May 14, 1996, A1.
22. Joann S. Lublin, "Don't Stop Cutting Staff, Study Suggests," *The Wall Street Journal*, September 27, 1994, B1; John Byrne, "Why Downsizing Looks Different These Days," *Business Week*, October 10, 1994, 43.
23. AMA Survey on Downsizing, 1994 (New York: American Management Association, 1994), 3.
24. "Fire and Forget?," *The Economist*, April 20, 1996, 51–52.
25. Adapted from Ani Hadjiian, "Watch What We Did, Not What We Said," *Fortune*, April 15, 1996, 140.
26. R. Gandossy and J. Jeffary, "HR Issues in Mergers and Acquisitions: A Strategic Overview," *ACA Journal*, Winter 1995, 26–31; T. Dadone and J. Radford, "Lessons Learned along the Road of Mergers and Acquisition," *ACA Journal*, Winter 1995, 48.
27. M. Armstrong Stassen, "Coping with Transition: A Study of Layoff Survivors," *Journal of Organizational Behavior* 15 (1994), 597–621.
28. J. Robert J. Grossman, "Damaged, Downsized Souls . . . ", *HR Magazine*, May 1996, 54–64.
29. R. Bigus, "Outplacement Services Work," *Kansas City Star*, October 29, 1995, E1.
30. "Misplaced Panics," *The Economist*, February 11, 1995, 13.
31. Adapted from Jennifer J. Laabs, "HR's Vital Role at Levi Strauss," *Personnel Journal*, December 1992, 34–36. Reprinted with the permission of *Personnel Journal*, ACC Communications, Inc., Costa Mesa, CA; all rights reserved.

Chapter 3

Human Resources and Organizational Competitiveness

After you have read this chapter, you should be able to . . .

- Discuss why and how the psychological contract between employees and employers is being transformed.
- Explain the expectancy theory of motivation.
- Define *job design* and identify the five components of the job-characteristics model.
- Describe three types of teams used for jobs.
- Define *job satisfaction* and *organizational commitment* and discuss how they relate to absenteeism and turnover.
- Identify several ways to control absenteeism and turnover.
- Describe the importance of national, organizational, and individual productivity.
- Define *Total Quality Management (TQM)* and explain HR's role in it.
- Identify the five dimensions of service.

HR in Transition

Quality Cup Rewards Teamwork, Quality, and Service

Efforts to improve quality and service while also raising productivity have been made in hundreds of organizations. Some of the efforts are successful, but others have been short-term programs dropped in favor of the next management fad. Some managers have recognized that attempting to change organizations to emphasize quality and service may not work as well as focusing on departments and units in organizations. Often, such efforts have relied on extensive employee involvement and use of work teams.

To recognize teams of employees that have been successful in using teamwork and enhancing quality and service, the Quality Cup was created in 1992, and awards have been given each year thereafter. The sponsors of the Quality Cup are *USA Today* and the Rochester Institute of Technology of Rochester, New York. Each year, a team of judges selected by the sponsors reviews information from numerous organizations and teams. Each year the number of applicants has grown, and now 200 or more entries are received annually. Teams that enter represent a wide variety of organizations, from health care to construction. A brief look at one of the cup winners in a recent year illustrates the value of teamwork and quality.

In other contexts, this approach has been called reengineering, but the Medical Director called it "dropping a bomb" on the existing system.

Most people who have been to a hospital emergency room (ER) likely have experienced delays, inefficiencies, and confusion. Too often, the staff in a typical emergency room is extremely busy, overworked, and somewhat frustrated as they attempt to help injured and ill patients. At Harris Methodist Hospital in Ft. Worth, Texas, the staff had been expanded so more people could provide help, but many problems seemed to remain. The ER group even had offered free coffee and hot chocolate to try to improve the way that patients and their families viewed ER "customer service." But all efforts had been less successful than hoped.

Finally, the Medical Director for ER identified a radical approach to improve ER for staff, patients, and others: wipe out the old system, start from scratch, and redesign the ER system from the beginning. In other contexts, this approach has been called *reengineering*, but the Medical Director called it "dropping a bomb" on the existing system.

A team of employees was formed representing all areas affecting the services delivered by ER. To emphasize the need for change early in the redesign process, the team watched a video in which patients described their ER experiences. Such issues as having to repeat information several times to different people, experiencing long delays for test results, and waiting for treatment of minor problems as well as major problems were voiced repeatedly.

When the team began addressing the process redesign, another significant discovery was made: The various departments did not work well together, and did not even like working with other departments. Each department blamed other departments for problems. Ultimately, by getting people from all departments together and discussing their concerns and problems, the team recognized that when ER processes were improved, many of the conflicts and difficulties would disappear. In essence, the ER process and systems were the cause of the conflicts, not the people in the various departments. Some of the changes decided upon by the team and implemented have included the following:

- The ER admission process was reorganized. Instead of completing admission forms in the ER lobby and then sitting and waiting to be sent to a treatment room, a patient first is sent to a treatment room. Then ER admissions staff members get all administrative and medical forms completed while the patient is waiting for medical staff members to begin treatment. This change has given the admissions staff a greater feeling of inclusion in providing patient service.
- A separate subunit for ER patients with minor problems was established so that they could be treated more quickly. The average amount of time spent in ER by those with minor injuries and illnesses has declined to less than an hour, a decrease of 40 minutes.
- The time needed to have prescriptions filled by the pharmacy and to receive lab test results has been reduced significantly through changing the flow of requests and transferring information using pneumatic tubes and other means.

By getting greater employee involvement and allowing teams of employees to address the redesign of jobs and work, organizations such as Harris Methodist Hospital are tapping their employees' knowledge and capabilities to improve organizational operations. These improvements likely will have long-term payoffs with customers as well as employees.[1]

> *"Job security is an oxymoron. I have no security because tomorrow I may have no job."*
>
> *—Anonymous employee at AT&T following 1996 downsizing*

The opening quote illustrates an interesting paradox in many organizations in the United States today. Despite economic statistics and statements from politicians, many employees do not feel that the economy is sound or that they are important to their employers. As organizational mergers, restructuring, and "rightsizing" have spread throughout many industries, more and more employees believe that the loyalty and effort they have shown is not being returned by their employers. Consequently, there is a need to transform the relationships between organizations and individuals.

❖ The Changing Nature of Organization-Individual Relationships

A recent poll by *Business Week* found that over 75% of the respondents rated large corporations *poor* or *fair* at providing job security and showing loyalty to their employees.[2] Another study by a major consulting firm found far too many "demoralized, underutilized workers poorly led by out-of-touch managers."[3] Although unemployment in the United States has stayed low, the primary reason is that many "rightsized" employees have taken jobs having lower pay and/or are working in multiple part-time jobs.

Similar problems have been noted in a number of other developed countries, such as Great Britain, France, and Germany. But those countries have many more governmental restrictions on employers eliminating jobs and workers. Therefore, a growing number of European employers have moved jobs to countries where wages and benefits costs are lower and productivity is higher. As a result, in Europe, economic growth has slowed, unemployment has climbed, and many younger workers cannot find jobs. The decline in the competitiveness of large, state-owned firms in Europe, particularly Eastern Europe, has spread employee anxieties through that part of the world. Even Japan has seen growing unemployment and the inability of younger workers to obtain jobs appropriate to their skills. In summary, in many parts of the world, many individuals are anxious and concerned about their longer-term security and whether they will be able to maintain their standards of living.

❖ Economic Anxiety and Job Insecurity

Downsizing, reengineering, and "delayering" have done recognizable damage to loyalty. The older hierarchical approach offered career progression in a single firm. Job security allowed large firms to demand sacrifices such as moving families regularly. It also allowed the companies to invest in training and development of their employees, confident they would not immediately go to another firm. But it is clear that the "one-company-for-life" attitude that existed during the period from 1950 to 1990 definitely has changed.

Employee disenchantment is being seen in a number of ways. Opinion surveys of employees have shown that even employees with jobs are experiencing economic anxiety because "they could be the next" affected by organizational restructuring and downsizing.[4] Workers who once wanted higher wages and benefits now simply want to keep current jobs and wages. One sign has been a shift in U.S. labor-management negotiations. In many manufacturing industries, bargaining emphasizes maintaining current wages and benefits and providing job security guarantees for existing workers.

❖ Declining Living Standards

A recent survey in the United States found that only 26% of those surveyed saw the economy as being good and only 24% believed that their children would have living standards as good as or better than theirs.[5] These anxieties have a basis in the reality of economic statistics. Even though over three million jobs were added to the U.S. labor force in a recent year, many individuals have focused on the one million jobs eliminated. One cause for this pessimism is that the average pay for many of the new jobs is significantly lower than the pay levels for the jobs eliminated. Figure 3–1 shows this decline clearly in U.S. wages and compensation for both blue-collar and white-collar workers. In fact, the median household income declined on average about 2.7% per year in the first half of the 1990s.

❖ Downsizing and Executive Pay Increases

Another cause of rising anger and disenchantment among employees is that top executives have continued to receive large salaries and bonuses, even though they make decisions to eliminate thousands of jobs to cut operating costs.[6] In fact, from 1990 to 1995, compensation for CEOs in large companies increased 92%, but worker pay rose only 16%, and worker layoffs increased 39%.[7] For instance, AT&T announced that approximately 40,000 jobs would be eliminated so the company would be more cost-competitive as telecommunications deregulation progressed. But the CEO from AT&T, Robert Allen, received total compensation of $2.67 million, which included an "annual performance bonus" of $1.52 million for one year. He also received $1.86 million in long term compensation incentives, making the total compensation he received in one year

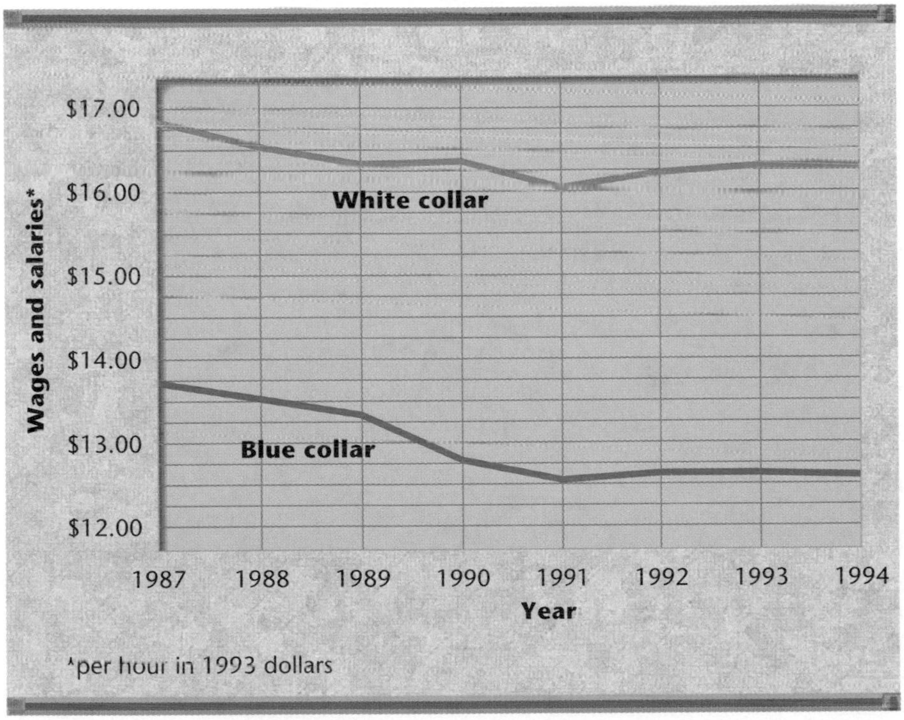

❖ Figure 3–1 ❖
Changes in U.S. Wages and Salaries 1987–1994

SOURCE: U.S. Department of Labor, Bureau of Labor Statistics, 1995.

$5.16 million.[8] Similar examples have been seen in other firms in which large numbers of jobs have been eliminated.

❖ The Psychological Contract

Psychological Contract The unwritten expectations that employees and employers have about the nature of their work relationships.

The long-term economic health of most organizations depends on the efforts of employees with the appropriate knowledge, skills, and abilities. One concept that has been useful in discussing employees' relationship with the organization is that of a **psychological contract**, which refers to the unwritten expectations that employees and employers have about the nature of their work relationships. Because the psychological contract is individual and subjective in nature, it focuses on expectations about "fairness" that may not be defined clearly by employees.[9] Both tangible items (such as wages, benefits, employee productivity, and attendance) and intangible items (such as loyalty, fair treatment, and job security) are encompassed by psychological contracts between employers and employees. Many employers may attempt to detail their expectations through employee handbooks and policy manuals, but those materials are only part of the total "contractual" relationship.

❖ Traditional Psychological Contract

In the "good old days," employees exchanged their efforts and capabilities for a secure job that offered rising wages, comprehensive benefits, and career progression withn the organization. But as organizations have downsized and cut workers who have given long and loyal service, a growing number of employees question whether they should be loyal to their employers.

There are two general forces pushing for changes in organizations and hence in the psychological contract in the developed countries, such as the United States, France, Germany, Australia, and Japan. One force is the pressures caused by *globalization* and maintaining international competitiveness, which is discussed in more detail in Chapter 4. The other force is *technology*, which is driving changes in many industries. Using a variety of statistics, the CEO of a major U.S. company concluded that one of every six U.S. workers has a job that is vulnerable because of technological developments and automation.[10]

❖ Transforming the Psychological Contract

The transformation in the psychological contract mirrors an evolution in which organizations have moved from employing individuals just to perform tasks, to employing individuals expected to produce results. Rather than just paying them to follow orders and put in time, increasingly employers are expecting employees to utilize their skills and capabilities to accomplish organizational results. According to one expert, the new psychological contract rewards employees for contributing to organizational success in the competitive marketplace for goods and services.[11]

This focus on organizational results also means that individuals are seen as contributing jointly with other employees. Consequently, a growing number of employers will expect their employees to be able to work with others in teams and on projects. If employees are to do their jobs and be full members of an organizational team, management will have to provide open communication about organizational results and activities. Gainsharing and other team reward programs will grow in importance as ways to link employee rewards more closely to organizational success and results.

❖ Linking Individuals and Jobs for Organizational Success

In a competitive environment, many organizations do not succeed over the long term. Those that do need ongoing contributions from the human resources in the organization to become successful and continue their success over time. The remainder of this chapter will utilize the conceptual model shown in Figure 3–2. This model depicts the linkages, beginning with individual and job characteristics, that lead to job satisfaction and organizational commitment. Also organizational outcomes are affected. The outcomes—productivity, quality, and service—are reflections of the broader goals by which organizational success is measured.

❖ Individual Characteristics and Motivation

The behaviors that employers look for in individuals rest on motivation. **Motivation** is the desire within a person causing that person to act. People usually act for one reason: to reach a goal. Thus, motivation is a goal-directed drive, and as such, it seldom occurs in a void. The words *need, want, desire,* and *drive* are all similar to *motive,* from which the word *motivation* is derived.

Motivation
The desire within a person causing that person to act.

Approaches to understanding motivation differ because many individual theorists have developed their own views and theories. They approach motivation from different starting points, with different ideas in mind, and from different backgrounds. No one approach is considered to be the "correct" one. Each has contributed to the understanding of human behavior.

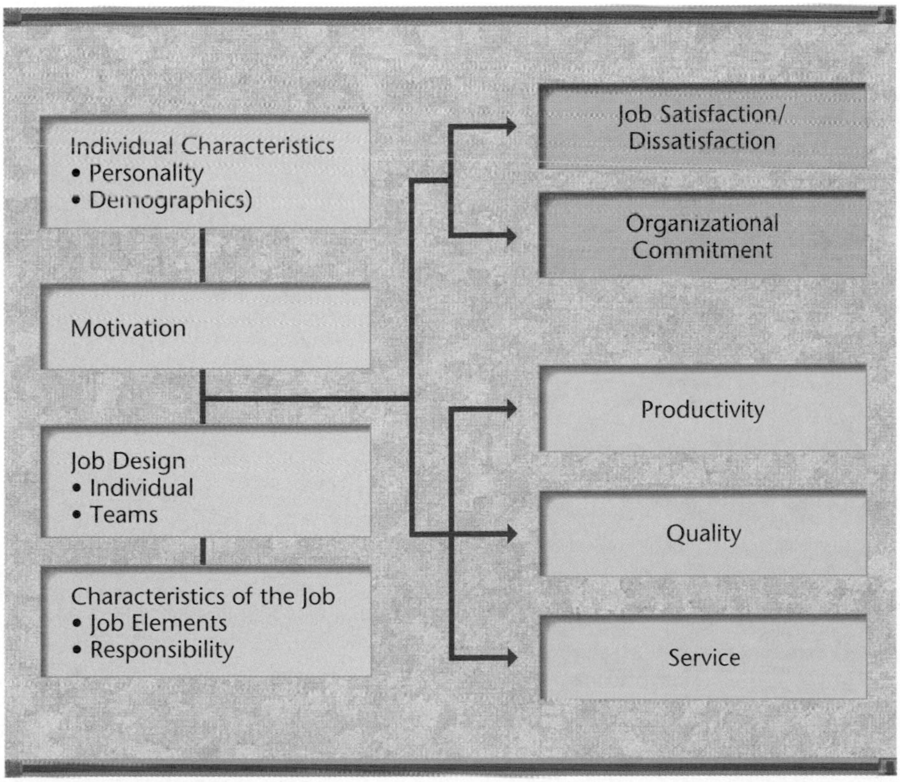

❖ Figure 3–2 ❖
Model of Individual/Organizational Performance

❖ Content Theories of Motivation

Content theories of motivation are concerned with the needs that people are attempting to satisfy. The most well-known theories are highlighted briefly next.

Maslow's Hierarchy of Needs One theory of human motivation that has received a great deal of exposure in the past was developed by Abraham Maslow. In this theory, Maslow classified human needs into five categories that ascend in a definite order. Until the more basic needs are adequately fulfilled, a person will not strive to meet higher needs. Maslow's well-known hierarchy is composed of: (1) physiological needs, (2) safety and security needs, (3) belonging and love needs, (4) esteem needs, and (5) self-actualization needs.[12]

An assumption often made by those using Maslow's hierarchy is that workers in modern, technologically advanced societies basically have satisfied their physiological, safety, and belonging needs. Therefore, they will be motivated by the needs for self-esteem, esteem of others, and then self-actualization. Consequently, conditions to satisfy these needs should be present at work; the job itself should be meaningful and motivating.

Herzberg's Motivation/Hygiene Theory Frederick Herzberg's motivation/hygiene theory assumes that one group of factors, *motivators,* accounts for high levels of motivation. Another group of factors, *hygiene,* or maintenance, factors, can cause discontent with work. Figure 3–3 compares Herzberg's motivators and hygiene factors with Maslow's needs hierarchy.

The implication of Herberg's research for management and HR practices is that although managers must carefully consider hygiene factors in order to avoid employee dissatisfaction, even if all these maintenance needs are addressed, people may not be motivated to work harder. Only motivators cause employees to exert more effort and thereby attain more productivity, and this theory suggests that managers should use the motivators as tools to enhance employee performance.

❖ Figure 3–3 ❖
Maslow's and Herzberg's Ideas Compared

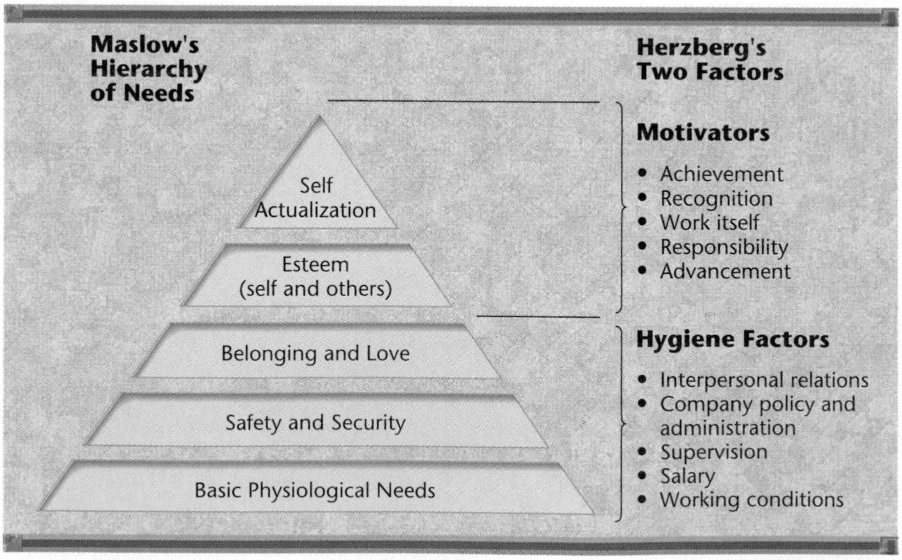

❖ Process Theories of Motivation

The various process theories of motivation focus on employee motivation through the satisfaction of needs to enhance individual performance. The most prominent process theory is *expectancy theory.* At the heart of expectancy theory are the *perceptions* that individuals have of effort, performance, and rewards.[13] Figure 3–4 depicts a simplified model of expectancy theory.

Theorists such as Victor Vroom, Lyman Porter, and E. E. Lawler III have noted that people act in order to reach goals.[14] But whether they will act at all depends on whether they believe their behavior will help them achieve their goals. In charting a path to goals, people choose among various actions based on their prediction of the outcome of each action. For example, does hard work lead to more money in the pay envelope? Some people think that it does, and others think that it does not, depending on past experiences with hard work and earning more money.

The relationship between the behavior of individuals and the outcomes of their actions is affected by individual factors and organizational factors. Individual factors include a person's needs, skills, abilities, and others. Organizational factors include reward systems, performance appraisals, training, and supervisory support. For motivated behavior to occur, three elements are important: effort-performance expectancy, performance-reward instrumentality, and valence of rewards.

- ❖ *Effort-Performance Expectancy* In this context, **expectancy** is the probability that if the employee puts forth more effort, it will lead to performance. For example, if individual employees believe that they lack the skills to do their jobs and that even if they work harder their performance will not improve, their motivation to perform will be affected.
- ❖ *Performance-Reward Instrumentality* The relationship between performance and rewards is described by **instrumentality**, which is the probability that performance will lead to the desired rewards. If employees believe that high performance will not be rewarded sufficiently, then they may not be

❖Expectancy
The probability that if the employee puts forth more effort, it will lead to performance.

❖Instrumentality
The probability that performance will lead to the desired rewards.

❖ Figure 3–4 ❖
Simplified Model of Expectancy Theory of Motivation

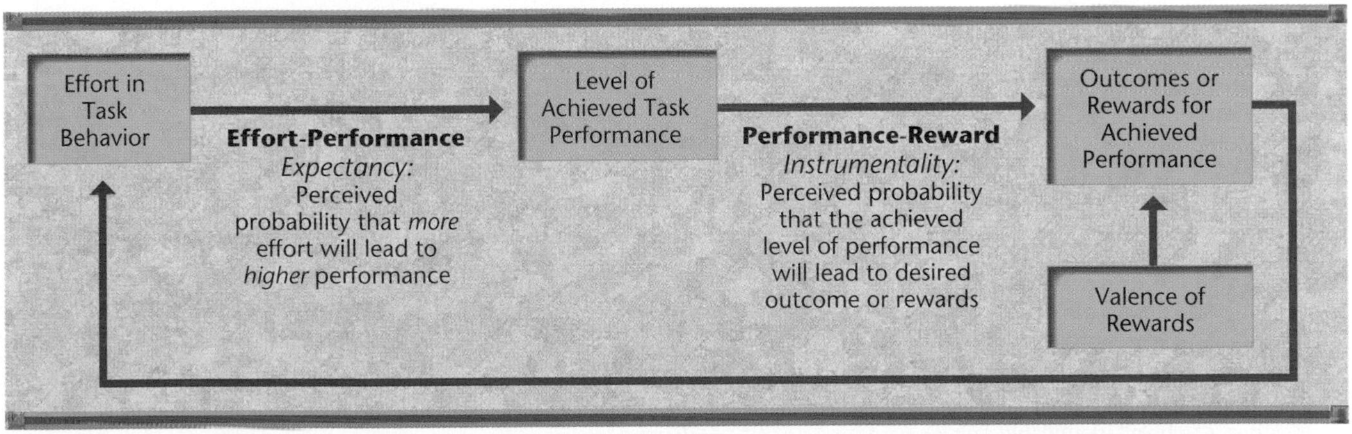

SOURCE: Michael A. Hitt, R. Dennis Middlemist, and Robert L. Mathis, *Management: Concepts and Effective Practice,* 3rd ed. (St. Paul: West Publishing Co., 1989), 324.

motivated to perform at a high level. That is the problem with automatic pay raises in which all employees get the same percentage increases, regardless of level of performance.

Valence
The strength of the individual's valuation of the reward.

- *Valence* **Valence** is the strength of the individual's valuation of the reward. The valence of an outcome or reward is not the reward itself; rather, it describes the individual's internal desire or need for the reward and the individual's perception of the reward as more desirable or less desirable.

The expectancy model of motivation says that a person's motivation depends first on expectancy, the person's expectation that a particular behavior will result in reaching a desired goal, and second on instrumentality, the probability that the performance will be rewarded.

Job Characteristics and Job Design

Individual responses to jobs vary. A job may be fascinating to one person but not to someone else. Also, depending on how jobs are designed, they may provide more or less opportunity for employees to satisfy their job-related needs. For example, a sales job may furnish a good opportunity to satisfy social needs, whereas a training assignment may satisfy a person's need to be an expert in a certain area. A job that gives little latitude may not satisfy an individual's need to be creative or innovative. Therefore, managers and employees alike are finding that understanding the characteristics of jobs requires broader perspectives than it did in the past.[15]

Nature of Jobs

Job Design
Organizing tasks, duties, and responsibilities into a productive unit of work.

Designing or redesigning jobs encompasses many factors. **Job design** refers to organizing tasks, duties, and responsibilities into a productive unit of work. It involves the content of jobs and the effect of jobs on employees. Identifying the components of a given job is an integral part of job design.

Job Characteristics

The job-characteristics model developed by Hackman and Oldham identifies five important design characteristics of jobs.[16] Figure 3–5 shows that *skill variety, task identity,* and *task significance* affect meaningfulness of work. *Autonomy* stimulates responsibility, and *feedback* provides knowledge of results. Following is a description of each characteristic.

Skill Variety
The extent to which the work requires several different activities for successful completion.

Job Rotation
The process of shifting a person from job to job.

Job Enlargement
Broadening the scope of a job by expanding the number of different tasks to be performed.

Skill Variety The extent to which the work requires several different activities for successful completion indicates its **skill variety.** For example, low skill variety exists when an assembly-line worker performs the same two tasks repetitively. The more skills involved, the more meaningful the work.

Skill variety can be enhanced in several ways. The technique known as **job rotation** can break the monotony of an otherwise routine job with little scope by shifting a person from job to job. **Job enlargement** involves broadening the scope of a job by expanding the number of different tasks to be performed.

Task Identity
The extent to which the job includes a "whole" identifiable unit of work that is carried out from start to finish and that results in a visible outcome.

Task Identity The extent to which the job includes a "whole" identifiable unit of work that is carried out from start to finish and that results in a visible outcome is its **task identity.** For example, GTE Corporation changed its customer service processes so that when a customer calls with a problem, one employee, called a Customer Care Advocate, handles most or all facets of the problem from

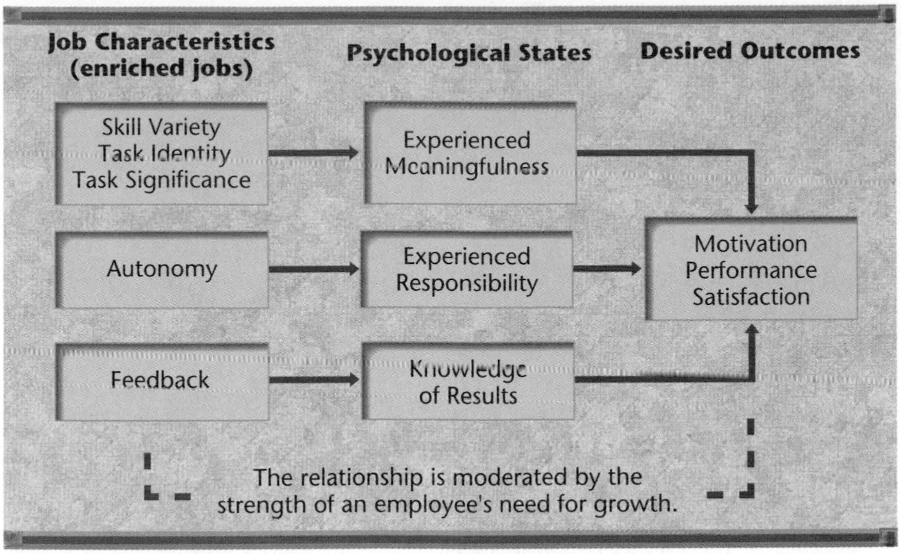

❖ FIGURE 3–5 ❖
JOB-CHARACTERISTICS MODEL

maintenance to repair. As a result, more than 40% of customer problems are resolved by one person while the customer is still on the line. Previously, less than 1% of the customer problems were resolved immediately because the customer service representative had to complete paperwork and forward it to operations, which then followed a number of separate steps using different people to resolve problems. In the current system, the Customer Care Advocate can identify more closely with solving a customer's problem.[17]

TASK SIGNIFICANCE The amount of impact the job has on other people indicates its **task significance.** A job is more meaningful if it is importanat to other people for some reason. For instance, a soldier may experience more fulfillment when defending his or her country from a real threat than when merely training to stay ready in case such a threat arises. In the GTE example, the Customer Care Advocate's task has significance because it affects customers considerably.

❖Task Significance
The amount of impact the job has on other people.

AUTONOMY The extent of individual freedom and discretion in the work and its scheduling indicates **autonomy.** More autonomy leads to a greater feeling of personal responsibility for the work. Efforts to increase autonomy may lead to what was characterized as job enrichment by Frederick Herzberg. **Job enrichment** is increasing the depth of a job by adding responsibility for planning, organizing, controlling, and evaluating the job. Examples of actions that increase autonomy include giving more freedom and authority so the employee can perform the job as he or she sees fit and increasing an employee's accountability for work by reducing external control.

❖Autonomy
The extent of individual freedom and discretion in the work and its scheduling.

❖Job Enrichment
Increasing the depth of a job by adding employee responsibility for planning, organizing, controlling, and evaluating the job.

FEEDBACK The amount of information employees receive about how well or how poorly they have performed is **feedback.** The advantage of feedback is that it helps employees to understand the effectiveness of their performance and contributes to their overall knowledge about the work. At one firm, feedback reports from customers who contact the company with problems are given directly to the employees who handle the customers' complaints, instead of being given only to the department manager.

❖Feedback
The amount of information received about how well or how poorly one has performed.

❖ Consequences of Job Design

Jobs designed to take advantage of these important job characteristics are more likely to be positively received by employees. Such characteristics help distinguish between "good" and "bad" jobs.[18] Many of the approaches to enhancing productivity and quality to be discussed later in this chapter reflect efforts to expand some of the job characteritics. Today, more attention is being paid to job design for three major reasons, all of which can reduce turnover and absenteeism and thus costs:

- ❖ Job design can influence *performance* in certain jobs, especially those where employee motivation can make a substantial difference.
- ❖ Job design can affect *job satisfaction*. Because people are more satisfied with certain job configurations than with others, it is important to be able to identify what makes a "good" job.
- ❖ Job design can affect both *physical and mental health*. Problems such as hearing loss, backache, and leg pain sometimes can be traced directly to job design, as can stress and related high blood pressure and heart disease.[19]

Because of the effects of job design on performance, employee satisfaction, health, and many other factors, many organizations are changing or have already changed the design of some jobs. A broader approach is reengineering work and jobs.

❖ Reengineering Work and Jobs

❖**Reengineering**
Rethinking and redesigning work to improve cost, service, and speed.

One movement that has affected the design and characteristics of jobs and work is reengineering. As defined in the first chapter, **reengineering** is rethinking and redesigning work to improve cost, service, and speed. The reengineering process may include such techniques as creating work teams, training employees in multiple skills so they can do multiple jobs, pushing decision making as far down the organizational hierarchy as possible, and reorganizing operations and offices to simplify and speed work.

The thrust of reengineering is not downsizing or restructuring the organization but focusing on the flow of work and how jobs themselves need to change to improve the processes associated with work.[20] Reengineering assumes that the ultimate focus of all organizational work should be the customer, and it attempts to generate dramatic improvement in organizational productivity, quality, and service. As a result, many jobs are changed, and greater use of technology is made, particularly of information systems and computers.

One of the more dramatic examples of reengineering occurred in the federal Social Security Administration (SSA). To handle a doubling in the number of calls to a toll-free line to 74.6 million calls per year, the agency had to rethink its handling of customer calls. Detailed analyses of the customer response process revealed numerous problems. As a result, the telephone systems were upgraded, employees were retrained, temporary staff were added to handle the large number of calls in January every year, and numerous other changes were made. A team of SSA employees visited private companies such as Land's End and Federal Express to observe their customer service procedures. The reengineering process worked so well that the SSA received national recognition for its efforts.[21]

Organizations that have reengineered their HR departments have found that a variety of goals were met. According to a study of reengineering efforts at 34 major companies, improved customer service and reduced costs were cited by

HR PERSPECTIVE

The Virtual Office

Traditionally, office workers have left home and commuted to an office to do their work. Many professional, administrative, and clerical employees still follow this pattern daily. Others telecommute from their homes using electronic technology. Still others utilize *hoteling, virtual offices,* and other arrangements some of the time.

A growing number of employers allow workers to work at home some, come in to an office some, and share office space with other "office nomads." In *hoteling,* workers check in with an office concierge, carry their own name plates with them, and are assigned to work cubicles or small offices. A worker uses the assigned office for a day or more, but other workers may use the same office in later days and weeks. At Ernst & Young, the large accounting and consulting company, the concierge assigns each individual an office, then forwards the individual's phone number to that office and may even send a personalized screen saver, such as a child's photograph, to the computer in the office.

Other employees have *virtual offices,* which means that their offices are wherever they are whenever they are there. An office could be a customer's project room, an airport conference room, a work suite in a hotel resort, a business-class seat on an international airline flight, or even a rental car.

The shift to such arrangements means that work is done anywhere, anytime, and that people are judged more on results than on "putting in time." Greater trust, less direct supervision, and more self-scheduling are all job characteristics of those with virtual offices and other less traditional arrangements.[22]

over 75% of the responding executives. However, much of the cost reduction came through reducing HR staff and outsourcing HR activities.[23]

❖ Alternative Work Schedules and Arrangements

The traditional work schedule, in which employees work full time, 8 hours a day, 5 days a week at the employer's place of operations, is in transition. Organizations have been experimenting with many different possibilities for change: the 4-day, 40-hour week; the 4-day, 32-hour week; the 3-day week; and flexible scheduling. According to the Bureau of Labor Statistics, about 60% of all employers have adopted some flexibility in work schedules and in the location of work. Changes of this nature require some major adjustments for organizations: but in some cases, they have been very useful. They allow organizations to make better use of workers by matching work demands to work hours. Workers are helped to balance their work and family responsibilities; and ultimately, everyone benefits—the employer, the employee, and society at large. The accompanying HR Perspective discusses the virtual office to illustrate the flexibility of working arrangements and schedules.[24]

Flextime In a type of schedule redesign called **flextime,** employees work a set number of hours per day but vary starting and ending times. The traditional starting and ending times of the eight-hour work shift can vary up to one or more hours at the beginning and end of the normal workday. Flextime allows management to relax some of the traditional "time clock" control of employees.

❖Flextime
A scheduling arrangement in which employees work a set number of hours per day but vary starting and ending times.

Compressed Workweeks Another way to change work patterns is with the **compressed workweek,** in which a full week's work is accomplished in fewer than five days. Compression simply alters the number of hours per day per employee, usually resulting in longer working times each day and a decreased number of days worked per week.

❖Compressed Workweek
Workweek in which a full week's work is accomplished in fewer than five days.

Dilbert® reprinted by permission of United Feature Syndicate, Inc.

Working at Home and Telecommuting A growing number of people in the United States do not leave home to go to work. One estimate is that about 40 million U.S. workers work at home on job-related tasks at least part time, including corporate employees working at home after hours. According to some estimates, over 8 million workers earn all of their income at home. Other estimates are lower, as low as 2 million.[25]

Telecommuting
The process of going to work via electronic computing and telecommunications equipment.

Telecommuting is the process of going to work via electronic computing and telecommunications equipment. Many U.S. employers have telecommuting employees or are experimenting with them, including such firms as American Express, Travelers Insurance, and J.C. Penney Co. Other types of nontraditional work arrangements have been labeled in various ways.

❖ Jobs and Teams

Typically, a job is thought of as something done by one person. However, where it is appropriate, jobs may be designed for teams. In an attempt to make jobs more meaningful and to take advantage of the increased productivity and commitment that can follow, more organizations are using teams of employees instead of individuals for jobs. One study of 1,800 employers found that about two-thirds of them use teams in their workplaces.[26] Some firms have gone as far as dropping the terms *workers* and *employees,* replacing them with *teammates, crew members, cast members,* and others that emphasize teamwork.[27]

Special-purpose Team
An organizational team that is formed to address specific problems and may continue to work together to improve work processes or the quality of products and services.

Quality Circle
A small group of employees who monitor productivity and quality and suggest solutions to problems.

Special-Purpose Teams and Quality Circles Several types of teams are used in organizations today that function outside the scope of members' normal jobs and meet from time to time. One is the **special-purpose team,** which is formed to address specific problems and may continue to work together to improve work processes or the quality of products and services. Often, these teams are a mixture of employees, supervisors, and managers. Another kind of team is the **quality circle,** a small group of employees who monitor productivity and quality and suggest solutions to problems. In many organizations, these problem-solving teams are part of Total Quality Management (TQM) efforts (discussed later). Care must be taken that such teams do not violate federal labor laws. As is discussed in Chapter 19, in a number of court cases, teams selected by and dominated by managers have been ruled to violate provisions of the National Labor Relations Act.[28]

PRODUCTION CELLS Another way work is restructured is through the use of production cells. As used in a number of manufacturing operations, **production cells** are groupings of workers who produce entire products or components of products. As many as fifty employees and as few as two can be grouped into a production cell and each cell has all necessary machines and equipment. The cells ultimately replace the assembly line as the primary means of production. The HR Perspective describes how several well-known firms have used production cells successfully.

Production Cells
Groupings of workers who produce entire products or components of products.

SELF-DIRECTED WORK TEAMS The **self-directed work team** is composed of individuals who are assigned a cluster of tasks, duties, and responsibilities to be accomplished. Unlike special-purpose teams, these teams become the regular entities in which team members work.

Self-directed Work Team
An organizational team composed of individuals who are assigned a cluster of tasks, duties, and responsibilities to be accomplished.

One of the interesting challenges for self-directed work teams involves the emergence or development of team leaders. This role is different from the traditional role played by supervisors or managers. Rather than directing and giving orders, the team leader becomes a facilitator to assist the team, mediate and resolve conflicts among team members, and interact with other teams and managers in other parts of the organization.[29] Shared leadership may be necessary; here, team members rotate leadership for different phases of projects in which special expertise may be beneficial.[30]

HR PERSPECTIVE

PRODUCTION CELLS CHANGE MANUFACTURING

Cell manufacturing techniques are being adopted widely in manufacturing firms in the United States and other countries. The extent of the popularity of manufacturing cells is seen in a survey of about 1,000 U.S. factories. The survey found that about 75% of the manufacturing firms with over 100 employees are using production cell techniques, whereas only 40% of the smaller manufacturers have adopted such an approach.

In cell manufacturing, workers are grouped into production teams of up to 50 employees. All of the equipment necessary to manufacture a complete component or product is placed in one area. Workers in the cell are trained or retrained so that they can perform several different tasks. The cell is responsible for quality, including checking and inspecting the products it produces. Often, the products are packaged, labeled, and shipped by the cell. Any customer complaints about the products must be addressed by cell members and resolved at the cell site.

At Compaq, the production of computers in plants in Texas and Scotland makes use of production cells instead of the traditional assembly lines. Each production cell is composed of four people: one worker who lays out components, two who assemble the computers, and one who checks the completed machines. The computers are assembled according to specific customer orders, which allows each machine to be configured according to customer specifications. Compaq can ship a computer within two days of when an order is placed. Other firms also have found production cells to be beneficial. Among them are Harley-Davidson (motorcycles), Lexmark (computer printers), and W. L. Gore (Gore-Tex fabric).

Conversion to production cells should be considered carefully. A great deal of planning must be done so that each cell has the tools, equipment, processes, and people needed. Also, a change from the traditional production line often creates significant resistance among production employees—and their unions, if they are covered by a collective bargaining agreement. Extensive training and discussions with those affected by the changes are essential. Despite these concerns, the use of production cells is growing in manufacturing.[31]

❖ FIGURE 3–6 ❖
SHAMROCK TEAM

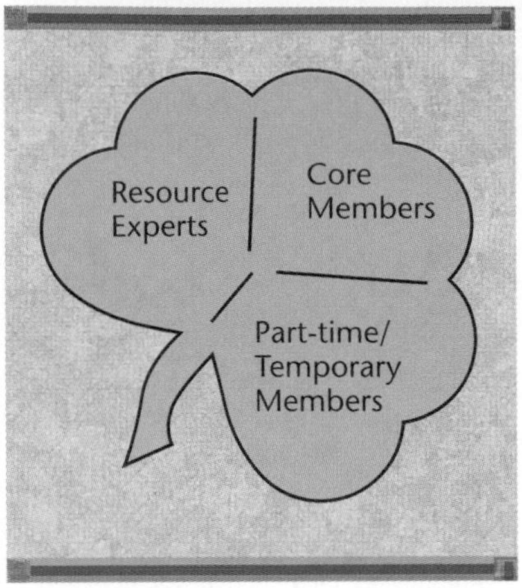

Shamrock Team
An organizational team composed of a core of members, resource experts who join the team as appropriate, and part-time/temporary members as needed.

Three characteristics have been identified for the successful use of self-directed work teams in the United States:[32]

1. *Teams value and endorse dissent.* The effective use of self-directed work teams requires that conflict and dissent be recognized and addressed. Contrary to what some might believe, suppressing dissent and conflict to preserve "harmony" ultimately becomes destructive to the effective operations of the team.
2. *Teams use "shamrock" structures and have some variation in membership.* As Figure 3–6 shows, a **shamrock team** is composed of a core of members, resource experts who join the team as appropriate, and part-time/temporary members as needed. As identified by Charles Handy, the presence of core members provides stability, but the infusion of the resource experts and part-time/temporary members provides renewal and change to the team.[33]
3. *Teams have authority to make decisions.* For self-directed work teams to be effective, they must be allowed to function with sufficient authority to make decisions about team activities and operations. As transition to self-directed work teams occurs, significant efforts are necessary to define the areas and scope of the authority of the teams as well as their goals.

HR ACTIVITIES AND TEAMS Self-directed work teams are not created easily, nor do they always operate effectively. The greatest problem is that teams may be created for incorrect reasons, such as to follow the latest management fad or because they work well at a competing company. Set up improperly, the teams may not function effectively. Some team members may withdraw or become reluctant to voice dissent, and legitimate concerns may be ignored in the rush to create teams.[34] The following guidelines may be useful for the establishment of teams in an organization.

- Match teams with the organizational culture
- Train individuals to be on teams
- Make compensation team-based

The growing use of teams and other changes in working arrangements are designed to foster greater employee job satisfaction and organizational commitment, which hopefully will lead to enhanced productivity, quality, and service. Job satisfaction and organizational commitment are examined next.

❖ JOB SATISFACTION AND ORGANIZATIONAL COMMITMENT

The characteristics of individuals and jobs interact through the perceptions, expectations, and experiences that people have in organizations. Ultimately, all of those factors affect the job satisfaction and commitment that individuals make to work organizations.

❖ JOB SATISFACTION

Job Satisfaction
A positive emotional state resulting from evaluating one's job experiences.

In its most basic sense, **job satisfaction** is a positive emotional state resulting from evaluating one's job experiences. Job *dis*satisfaction occurs when these expectations are not met. For example, if an employee expects clean and safe working conditions on the job, then the employee is likely to be dissatisfied if the workplace is dirty and dangerous.

Job satisfaction has many dimensions. Some include satisfaction with the work itself, wages, recognition, rapport with supervisors and coworkers, and organizational culture and philosophy. Each dimension contributes to an overall feeling of satisfaction with the job itself, but the "job" is defined differently by different people.

There is no simple formula for predicting a worker's satisfaction. Furthermore, the relationship between productivity and job satisfaction is not entirely clear. The critical factor is what employees expect from their jobs and what they are receiving as rewards from their jobs. Although job satisfaction itself is interesting and important, perhaps the "bottom line" is the impact that job satisfaction has on organization commitment, which affects the ultimate goals of productivity, quality, and service.

❖ Organizational Commitment

If employees are committed to an organization, they are more likely to be more productive. **Organizational commitment** is the degree to which employees believe in and accept organizational goals and desire to remain with the organization. Several types of organizational commitment have been identified.[35]

Organizational Commitment The degree to which employees believe in and accept organizational goals and desire to remain with the organization.

- *Affective commitment:* how strongly the individual identifies with and is involved in the organization
- *Continuance commitment:* the perceived consequences of leaving the organization
- *Normative commitment:* the responsibility that individuals feel toward the organization and its goals.

Research has revealed that job satisfaction and organizational commitment tend to influence each other. What this finding suggests is that people who are relatively satisfied with their jobs will be somewhat more committed to the organization and also that people who are relatively committed to the organization are more likely to have greater job satisfaction.[36]

A logical extension of organizational commitment focuses specifically on continuance commitment factors, which suggest that decisions to remain with or leave an organization ultimately are reflected in employee absenteeism and turnover statistics. Individuals who are not as satisfied with their jobs or who are not as committed to the organization are more likely to withdraw from the organization, either occasionally through absenteeism or permanently through turnover.

❖ Absenteeism

Absenteeism is expensive, as seen in estimates that absenteeism nationally costs $505 per year per employee.[37] Being absent from work may seem like a small matter to an employee. But if a manager needs 12 people in a unit to get the work done, and 4 of the 12 are absent most of the time, the unit's work will probably not get done, or additional workers will have to be hired.

Types of Absenteeism Employees can be absent from work for several reasons. Figure 3–7 depicts the reasons for unscheduled absences. Clearly, some absenteeism is unavoidable. People do get sick and have family issues such as sick children that make it impossible for them to attend work. This is usually referred to as *involuntary* absenteeism. However, much absenteeism is avoidable; it is called *voluntary* absenteeism. Often, a relatively small number of individuals in the workplace are responsible for a disproportionate share of the total absenteeism in an organization.

Because illness, death in the family, and other personal reasons for absences are unavoidable and understandable, many employers have sick-leave policies

❖ FIGURE 3–7 ❖
REASONS FOR UNSCHEDULED ABSENCES

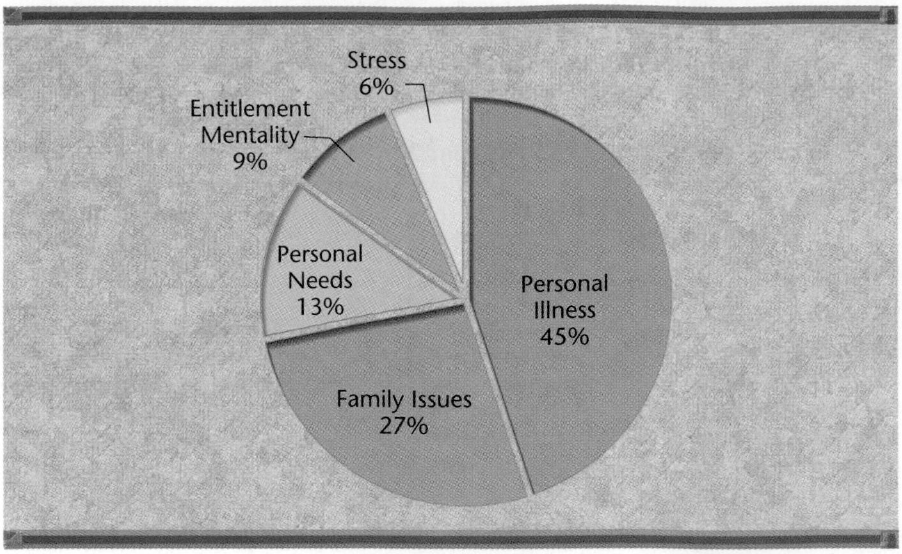

SOURCE: Reproduced with permission from *CCH Human Resource Management Ideas & Trends,* May 24, 1995, 86, published and copyrighted by CCH INCORPORATED.

that allow employees a certain number of paid absent days per year. Sick-leave programs are discussed in more detail in Chapter 15, as part of employee benefits programs.

Absenteeism tends to be highest in governmental agencies, utilities, and manufacturing firms. Absenteeism is lowest in retail/wholesale firms, possibly because those industries use a large percentage of part-time workers.[38]

MEASUREMENT OF ABSENTEEISM Controlling or reducing absenteeism must begin with continuous monitoring of the absenteeism statistics in work units. Such monitoring helps managers pinpoint employees who are frequently absent and departments that have excessive absenteeism.

Various methods of measuring or computing absenteeism exist.[39] One formula for computing absenteeism rates, suggested by the U.S. Department of Labor, is as follows:

$$\frac{\text{Number of person-days lost through job absence during period}}{\text{(Average number of employees)} \times \text{(Number of work days)}} \times 100$$

(This rate can be based on number of hours instead of number of days.)

CONTROL OF ABSENTEEISM Controlling voluntary absenteeism is easier if managers understand its causes more clearly. Nevertheless, there are a variety of thoughts about reducing voluntary absenteeism. Organizational policies on absenteeism should be stated clearly in an employee handbook and stressed by supervisors and managers. The policies and rules an organization uses to govern absenteeism may provide a clue to the effectiveness of its control. Studies indicate that absence rates are highly related to the policies used to control absenteeism.[40]

Absenteeism control options fall into three categories: (1) discipline, (2) positive reinforcement, and (3) a combination of both. A brief look at each follows.

- *Disciplinary approach.* Many employers use a disciplinary approach. People who are absent the first time receive an oral warning, but subsequent absences bring written warnings, suspension, and finally dismissal.
- *Positive reinforcement.* Positive reinforcement includes such methods as giving employees cash, recognition, time off, or other rewards for meeting

attendance standards. Offering rewards for good attendance, giving bonuses for missing fewer than a certain number of days, and "buying back" unused sick leave are all positive methods of reducing absenteeism.

- *Combination approach.* Combination approaches ideally reward desired behaviors and punish undesired behaviors. One of the most effective absenteeism control methods is to provide paid sick-leave banks for employees to use up to some level. Once that level is exhausted, then the employees may face the loss of some pay if they miss additional work unless they have major illnesses in which long-term disability insurance coverage would begin.

  Another method is known as a *"no-fault" absenteeism* policy. Here, the reasons for absences do not matter, but the employees must manage their time rather than having managers make decisions about excused and unexcused absences. Once absenteeism exceeds normal limits, then disciplinary action up to and including termination of employment can occur.

  Some firms have extended their policies to provide a *paid time-off (PTO)* program in which vacation time, holidays, and sick leave for each employee are combined into a PTO account. Employees use days from their accounts at their discretion for illness, personal time, or vacation. If employees run out of days in their accounts, then they are not paid for any additional days missed. The PTO programs generally have reduced absenteeism, particularly one-day absences, but overall, time away from work often increases because employees use all of "their" time off by taking unused days as vacation days.

TURNOVER

Turnover occurs when employees leave an organization and have to be replaced. Excessive turnover can be a very costly problem, one with a major impact on productivity. One firm had a turnover rate of more than 120% per year! It cost the company $1.5 million a year in lost productivity, increased training time, increased employee selection time, lost work efficiency, and other indirect costs. But cost is not the only reason turnover is important.[41] Lengthy training times, interrupted schedules, overtime for others, mistakes, and not having knowledgeable employees in place are some of the frustrations associated with excessive turnover.

Turnover
Process in which employees leave the organization and have to be replaced.

TYPES OF TURNOVER Turnover often is classified as *voluntary* or *involuntary* in nature. *Involuntary turnover* occurs when an employee is fired. *Voluntary turnover* occurs when an employee leaves by his or her own choice and can be caused by many factors. Causes include lack of challenge, better opportunity elsewhere, pay, supervision, geography, and pressure. Certainly, not all turnover is negative. Some workforce losses are quite desirable, especially if those workers who leave are lower-performing, less reliable individuals.

MEASUREMENT OF TURNOVER The turnover rate for an organization can be computed in a number of different ways. The following formula from the U.S. Department of Labor is widely used. (*Separations* are people who left the organization.)

$$\frac{\text{Number of employee separations during the month}}{\text{(Total number of employees at midmonth)}} \times 100$$

Common turnover figures range from almost zero to over 100% per year, and normal turnover rates vary among industries. Organizations that require entry-level employees to have few skills are likely to have higher turnover rates among those employees than among managerial personnel. As a result, it is important that turnover rates be computed by work units. For instance, one organization had a companywide turnover rate that was not severe—but 80% of the turnover occurred within one department. This imbalance indicated that some action was needed to resolve problems in that unit.

Control of Turnover Turnover can be controlled in a number of ways. During the *recruiting* process, the job should be outlined and a realistic preview of the job presented, so that the reality of the job matches the expectations of the new employee. A good way to eliminate voluntary turnover is to *improve selection* and to better match applicants to jobs. By fine-tuning the selection process and hiring people who will not have disciplinary problems and low performance, employers can reduce involuntary turnover.

Good *employee orientation* also will help reduce turnover, because new employees are more likely to leave than employees who have been on the job longer. Also, employees who are properly inducted into the company and are well trained tend to be less likely to leave. If people receive some basic information about the company and the job to be performed, they can determine early whether they want to stay.

Compensation also is important. A fair and equitable pay system can help prevent turnover. An employee who is underpaid relative to employees in other jobs with similar skills may leave if there is an inviting alternative job available. An awareness of employee problems and dissatisfaction may provide a manager with opportunities to resolve them before they become so severe that employees leave. The HR Perspective discusses findings that inadequate rewards may lead to voluntary turnover, especially with employees such as salespeople, whose compensation is tied directly to their performance.

Career planning and *internal promotion* can help an organization keep employees, because if individuals believe they have no opportunities for career advancement, they may leave the organization. One study identified career "shocks" that may lead to turnover.[42] Shocks include being turned down for a promotion, being transferred to a new location without adequate training, and believing that the imediate supervisor will not be fair as a result of a negative performance review. Some voluntary turnover may involve people who "voluntarily quit" because they recognize that their performance deficiencies could result in their employment's being terminated in the near future.

Finally, voluntary turnover may be linked to personal factors that are not controllable by the organization. This is particularly true with part-time workers. Among the many reasons employees quit that cannot be controlled by the organization are the following: (1) the employee moves out of the geographic area, (2) the employee decides to stay home for family reasons, (3) the employee's spouse is transferred, or (4) a student employee graduates from college.

Even though some turnover is inevitable, organizations must take steps to control turnover, particularly that which is caused by organizational factors such as poor supervising, inadequate training, and inconsistent policies. HR activities should be examined as part of turnover control efforts.

❖ Organizational Productivity, Quality, and Service

The performance of organizations significantly affects their survival and their growth or decline. In the competitive environment that exists in many industries

HR PERSPECTIVE

Research on Performance and Voluntary Turnover

An employee's performance is a determining factor in whether turnover of that employee is considered "good" or "bad." Certainly, employees who are performing poorly or below standards are not missed as much when they leave the organization as good performers are. However, no manager wants to lose the best performers; when they leave the organization, it is considered "bad" turnover. Williams and Livingstone compared the relationship between performance and turnover and reported their results in the *Academy of Management Journal*.

The study was a "meta-analysis," in which the researchers review previous studies, reanalyze data from a number of those studies, and then attempt to identify broader patterns of findings and more general conclusions from all the previous work done in an area. In this study, Williams and Livingstone analyzed 55 previous studies on the turnover/performance relationship.

They found a strong relationship between voluntary turnover and poor performance. As would be expected, individuals who performed poorly tended to have more frequent turnover. Further, when organizations gave rewards such as pay raises or promotions that were contingent on performance, the relationship was even stronger—that is, poor performers showed an even greater tendency to leave.

The authors noted that this pattern suggests that employers who choose to reward good performance can encourage better performers to stay and poorer performers to leave. As they observed, retention of better-performing workers is important to continuing organizational performance, while voluntary separation of poorer performers is also beneficial for the organization. Apparently, poorer performers tend to be less satisfied than better performers when rewards are tied to meeting performance standards; therefore, the poor performers are more likely to quit. The results suggest that pay-for-performance systems and other HR programs that emphasize performance will "encourage" poor performers to leave and better performers to stay. However, HR practices that treat all employees alike and are not performance-based, such as those emphasizing seniority and giving across-the-board pay raises, are not as likely to cause the poor performers leave and may result in more turnover of better-performing employees.[43]

today, the performance of the organization often is linked to the performance of the human resources in that organization. At the organizational level and even at the national level, productivity is one means of determining competitiveness.

❖ Productivity

Productivity is a measure of the quantity and quality of work done, considering the cost of the resources it took to do the work. It is also useful to view productivity as a ratio between inputs and outputs. This ratio indicates the *value added* by an organization or in an economy.

❖Productivity
A measure of the quantity and quality of work done, considering the cost of the resources it took to do the work.

Global Competitiveness and Productivity At the national level, productivity is of concern for several reasons. First, high productivity leads to high standards of living, as symbolized by the greater ability of a country to pay for what its citizens want. Next, increases in national wage levels without increases in national productivity lead to inflation. This means an increase in costs and a decrease in purchasing power. Finally, lower rates of productivity make for higher labor costs and a less competitive position for a nation's products in the world marketplace.

Figure 3–8 shows that the United States now leads the other major developed industrial nations in productivity, as measured by growth in manufacturing output per hour worked. In service industries, the United States has an even larger lead. Even more impressive is an international ranking of nations on economic

❖ FIGURE 3–8 ❖
GLOBAL PRODUCTIVITY COMPARISONS

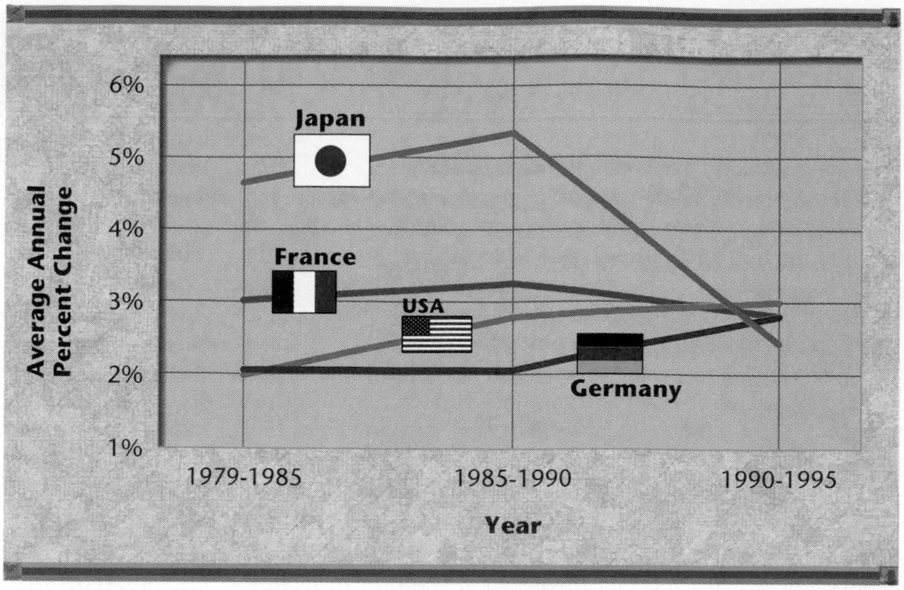

SOURCE: U.S. Department of Labor, Bureau of Labor Statistics, 1995.

competitiveness. Based on 120 criteria, out of 48 countries evaluated, the top 5 nations were, in order: (1) the United States, (2) Singapore, (3) Hong Kong, (4) Japan, and (5) Switzerland. The bottom five countries were, from the bottom up: Russia, Venezuela, Hungary, Poland, and Mexico.[44] Much of the productivity growth in the United States has been due to a high level of investment in technology, especially computers. For instance, in U.S. industries, there are 53 personal computers per 100 workers, compared with only 17 per 100 workers in Japan.[45]

The problems caused by becoming less competitive internationally can be seen by examining Germany. Among the nations of the world, it has had the highest labor costs for several years. These costs result from very short workweeks, long vacations, short careers, students staying in school for many years, and rampant holidays. High wage costs and restrictive union work rules keep German machines running 20% fewer hours than those in the United States and many Asian countries.[46] Consequently, German companies are refusing to create jobs at home; instead, they are opening up new plants and operations throughout the world. The Mercedes-Benz plant in Alabama and the BMW automobile plant in South Carolina are only two examples of hundreds of operations established by German firms globally, with productivity concerns being a major contributing factor.

ORGANIZATIONS AND PRODUCTIVITY Productivity at the level of the organization ultimately affects profitability and competitiveness in a for-profit organization and total costs in a not-for-profit organization. Decisions to close (or open) plants often are the result of productivity concerns.

Perhaps none of the resources for productivity are so closely scrutinized as human resources. Many of the activities undertaken in an HR system deal with individual or organizational productivity. Pay, appraisal systems, training, selection, job design, and incentives are HR issues concerned with productivity very directly.

Unit Labor Cost
The total labor cost per unit of output, which is the average wages of workers divided by their levels of productivity.

A useful way to measure organizational HR productivity is by **unit labor cost**, or the total labor cost per unit of output, which is computed by dividing the average wages of workers by their levels of productivity. Using the unit labor cost, it can be seen that a company paying relatively high wages still can be economically competitive if it can also achieve an offsetting high productivity level.

INDIVIDUAL PRODUCTIVITY The productivity of an individual depends on: (1) the person's innate *ability* (*A*) to do the job, (2) the level of *effort* (*E*) that he or she is willing to exert, and (3) the *support* (*S*) given that person. The relationship of these factors, widely acknowledged in management literature, is that *performance* (*P*) is a result of effort times ability times support ($P = E \times A \times S$). Performance is diminished if *any* of these factors is reduced or absent. Earlier in the chapter, the importance of effort and ability were discussed as they affect the motivation of an individual in an organization. HR management has a role in each factor.

Recruiting and selection are directly connected with the first factor, which involves choosing the person with the right talents and interests for a given job. The second factor, the effort expended by an individual, is influenced by many HR issues, such as compensation, incentives, and job design. Organizational support, the third factor, includes training, equipment provided, and knowledge of expectations. HR activities involved here include training and development and performance appraisal.

In summary, productivity is an important means of measuring the performance of national economies, organizations, and individuals. Another important factor affecting organizational competitiveness is quality.

❖ QUALITY

Quality must be closely tied to productivity. The alternative may be to trade off quality of production for quantity of production. Currently, goods and services produced by some organizations in various nations suffer from an image of poor quality as a result of this very trade-off. As it relates to U.S. organizations, some observers blame the problem on the failure of U.S. manufacturers to make quality a first priority. W. Edwards Deming, an American quality expert, argued that, "Fifteen to forty percent of the cost of almost any American product you buy is for the waste embedded in it."[47] He advocated "getting the job done right the first time" through individual pride in craftsmanship, vigorous training, and an unwillingness to tolerate delays, defects, and mistakes.

Organizations throughout the world are proceeding on the quality front in many different ways, ranging from general training of workers on improving and maintaining quality to better engineering of products prior to manufacturing. One way in which organizations have focused on quality is by using international quality standards.

ISO 9000 A set of quality standards called the ISO 9000 standards have been derived by the International Standards Organization in Geneva, Switzerland. These standards cover everything from training to purchasing and are being implemented widely in European countries. Companies that meet the standards are awarded a certificate. The purpose of the ISO 9000 certification is to show that an organization has documented its management processes and procedures and has a trained staff so that customers can be confident that organizational goods and services will be consistent in quality.

Organizations seeking ISO approval must document how employees perform every function that affects quality.[48] There are standards for 20 different functions, including design, process control, purchasing, service, inspection and testing, and training practices.

LOGGING ON

An ISO 9000 bibliography lists many English-language books on the ISO 9000 group of standards.

http://www.exit109.com/~leebee/bibiog.htm

Baldrige Awards The U.S. Department of Commerce gives the Malcolm Baldrige Awards annually for quality improvement in American companies. These awards require that companies examine their operations to identify ways to improve quality. Then they must make necessary changes and describe them in the Baldrige applications. The link between human resources and quality is very strong in the judging of the Baldrige Awards.[49]

Although many of the Baldrige Award winners have benefitted from their efforts to improve quality, not all of the news is positive. The detailed documentation processes and compilation of supporting data is extremely time-consuming and costly, especially when all employees' time is factored in. Also, some firms have made winning the award the goal, rather than improving quality, so that the award-winning status could be hyped in marketing and public relations efforts.[50]

❖ Total Quality Management (TQM)

Total Quality Management (TQM) A comprehensive management process focusing on the continuous improvement of organizational activities to enhance the quality of the goods and services supplied.

Many organizations that have made major improvements in the quality of their operations have recognized that a broad-based quality effort has been needed. **Total Quality Management (TQM)** is a comprehensive management process focusing on the continuous improvement of organizational activities to enhance the quality of the goods and services supplied. TQM programs have become quite popular as organizations strive to improve their productivity and quality.

At the heart of TQM is the concept that it is *customer focused,* which means that every organizational activity should be evaluated and analyzed to determine if it contributes to meeting customers' needs and expectations.[51] Another characteristic of TQM is the importance of *employee involvement.* Often, quality improvement teams or other group efforts are used to ensure that all employees understand the importance of quality and how their efforts affect quality. *Benchmarking* is another facet of TQM, in which quality efforts are measured and compared with measures both for the industry and for other organizations. It is hoped that providing measurement information to quality teams will help to make continuous improvements in quality a part of the organizational culture. Benchmarking is discussed in more detail in Chapter 20.

HR's Role in TQM Integral to TQM is the involvement and utilization of the capabilities and skills of the human resources in the organization. Therefore, HR professionals have key roles to play in TQM efforts. As both experts on and advocates for the human resources in an organization, HR professionals become internal consultants on the development and implementation of TQM initiatives.[52] The HR staff work with senior executives, operational managers and supervisors, and employees to help them address changes from traditional authority structures to structures utilizing significant amounts of employee involvement.

The role of HR in TQM efforts was the focus of a survey of over 300 HR professionals and 300 non-HR respondents. *Training* was identified as the most important HR activity in terms of TQM and other quality initiatives. Training activities were necessary to explain the quality process, to create awareness of the changes in organizational culture needed to support quality initiatives, and to develop strategies to improve cooperation between employees and managers.[53]

Other HR activities also may be affected by TQM efforts in organizations. If teams are to be used extensively, then skill-based and team-based *pay and incentive* programs may replace or augment traditional compensation plans. Measurement of individual and team performance may require alternative means of *appraising performance* and using appraisal information for employee development. *Selection processes* may have to be changed to reflect the need for employees to be able to work well with others. The means to identify and screen individuals for such abilities may require development of different assessment methods. In summary, the HR activities in an organization must be aligned with TQM efforts.

LOGGING ON

Describes in both English and French the TQM experience of Hydro-Quebec, a large Canadian utility.

http://gig-tqm.envir.hydro.qc.ca/

SUCCESSES AND FAILURES OF TQM When TQM first became popular in the early 1990s, many glowing statements were made about how it would revolutionize organizations worldwide. Virtually all organizations were advised to consider adopting TQM. For some organizations, the promises of TQM have been realized, but for others, TQM became a short-term program that later was dropped. A nationwide study of over 1,000 executives and managers found that only 45% of the organizations that had implemented TQM thought their programs had been successful. Middle managers are even more negative toward TQM efforts, probably because their roles are affected the most when employee involvement becomes more widespread. Furthermore, even if quality is improved, the improvement does not guarantee success, particularly if the goods or services fall behind those offered by competitors.

Finally, far too many organizations implemented TQM as a short-term "fix" rather than viewing it as a longer-term approach requiring significant changes in organizational cultures, management styles, production and service, delivery processes, and employee participation in decision making. In conclusion, TQM may be easier to discuss than to implement.[54]

❖ SERVICE

Delivering high-quality customer service is another important outome that affects organizational competitiveness. Service begins with the design of the product or service and ultimately is reflected in customers' satisfaction with the product or service. For instance, a U.S. automobile manufacturer discovered that a major negative for customers considering the purchase of the firm's cars was the design of the pull-out cup holders.

Overall, customer satisfaction has declined in the United States and other countries. The American Customer Satisfaction Index revealed that in many U.S. industries, customers are growing more dissatisfied with the customer service that they receive.[55] If their expectations are met, however, customers are likely to be more satisfied, make favorable comments to others, and/or become repeat customers. Consequently, organizations working to enhance their competitiveness must work to enhance service.

DIMENSIONS OF SERVICE Service is much like beauty: It is difficult to define, but people know it when they see it. The dimensions of service and the relative importance of each dimension are depicted in Figure 3–9.[56] Each factor is described briefly next in order of importance.

- *Reliability.* The product/service performs dependably and accurately, as promised.
- *Responsiveness.* The organization provides assistance to customers in a timely manner.
- *Assurance.* Knowledgeable employees create trust and confidence in customers.

❖ FIGURE 3–9 ❖
DIMENSIONS OF CUSTOMER SERVICE AND RELATIVE IMPORTANCE OF EACH DIMENSION

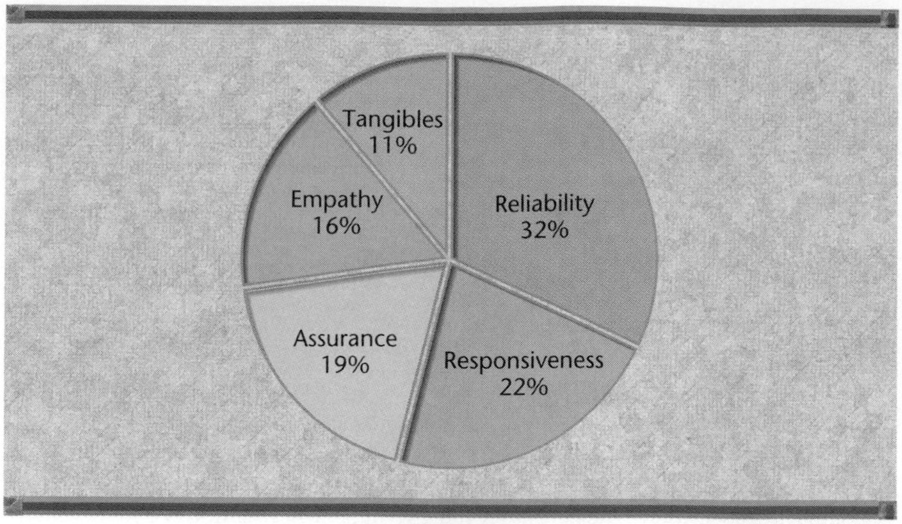

SOURCE: Based on information in L. L. Berry, A. Parasuraman, and V. A. Zeithami, "Improving Service Quality in America: Lessons Learned," *Academy of Management Executive,* May 1994, 32–45.

- *Empathy.* Individualized attention is given to customers, which reflects the organizational care and concern about meeting customer expectations.
- *Tangibles.* Telecommunications and other equipment is easily used, and the appearance of physical facilities and employees creates positive images.

HR'S ROLE IN SERVICE In many organizations, service quality is affected significantly by the employees who interact with customers. But as the cup-holder example above indicates, the design of products and services can put well-meaning employees at a disadvantage.

To have human resources who can provide high-quality service, *employee selection* is critical. The individuals who deliver service to customers must have the requisite knowledge, skills, and abilities. Also, a key HR activity is *training.* Once individuals have been selected, they must receive training both in the technical facets of products or services and in providing customer service. Ongoing training in customer service must be provided also.

Recognition and reward programs must focus on recognizing and rewarding employees who demonstrate exceptional customer service. Often, incentive programs are used. In addition, *teams* are used externally to focus on improving customer service. Often, the teams return to the design of the product or service and then follow the customer service process all the way through. Such thoroughness is essential if service quality is to be enhanced through reengineering. What all of the discussions in this chapter have emphasized is that the human resources in organizations significantly affect productivity, quality, and customer service.

SUMMARY

❖ The relationships between individuals and organizations have changed as a result of economic insecurity throughout the world, which is reflected in declining living standards for some workers.

❖ A psychological contract contains the unwritten expectations that employees and employers have about the nature of their work relationships. Those contracts are being transformed in some organizations.

❖ Motivation deals with the "whys" of human behavior, and employers want motivated employees.

❖ Various theories of motivation have been developed. Maslow's hierarchy of needs and Herzberg's motivation/hygiene theory are widely known content theories.

❖ The expectancy theory of motivation is the most prominent process theory of motivation. It focuses on the linkages among effort-performance expectancies, performance-reward instrumentalities, and the valence of rewards.

❖ Job design is organizing tasks, duties, and responsibilities into a productive unit of work.

❖ The job-characteristics model suggests that five characteristics of jobs (skill variety, task identity, task significance, autonomy, and feedback from the organization) affect motivation, performance, and satisfaction.

❖ Work has been redesigned through reengineering and through use of alternative work schedules and arrangements.

❖ Teams increasingly are being used in organizations. Special-purpose teams, production cells, and self-directed work teams have all been used successfully.

❖ Self-directed work teams are more successful when dissent is valued, membershp is flexible, and teams have decision-making authority.

❖ Job satisfaction affects commitment to the organization, which, in turn, affects the rates of absenteeism and turnover.

❖ Absenteeism is expensive, but it can be controlled by discipline, positive reinforcement, or some combination of the two.

❖ Turnover has been studied extensively and appears to be strongly related to certain external, work-related, and personal factors.

❖ Productivity at national, organizational, and individual levels is critical for organizational success.

❖ The ISO 9000 standards are international standards for quality, and the Baldrige Awards reward quality improvements in U.S.–based firms.

❖ Total Quality Management (TQM) is a comprehensive management process focusing on the continuous improvement of organizational activities to enhance the quality of the goods and services supplied. But TQM's success has been mixed.

❖ Service is critical to meeting customer expectations, and HR must support service through selection, training, and other activities.

Review and Discussion Questions

1. Why are many workers worried about their jobs, even though traditional macroeconomic measures indicate that the U.S. economy is relatively strong?
2. Apply the expectancy model of motivation to your motivation in your current job.
3. Describe your current job using the job-characteristics model (Figure 3–5).
4. Discuss the advantages and disadvantages of self-directed work teams.
5. Apply the various types of organizational commitment to jobs you have had.
6. Contrast the use of discipline with the use of positive reinforcement and rewards to reduce absenteeism and turnover.
7. Discuss why productivity in an organization depends to a large extent on individual productivity.
8. Discuss the following statement: "For too many organizations, total quality management (TQM) was a passing fad rather than reflecting a commitment to quality."
9. Give two examples that apply the dimensions of service, one example of good service and one of poor service.

Terms to Know

autonomy 67
compressed workweek 69
expectancy 65
feedback 67
flextime 69
instrumentality 65
job design 66
job enlargement 66
job enrichment 67
job rotation 66
job satisfaction 72
motivation 63
organizational commitment 73
production cells 71
productivity 77
psychological contract 62
quality circle 70
reengineering 68
self-directed work team 71
shamrock team 72
skill variety 66
special-purpose team 70
task identity 66
task significance 67
telecommuting 69
Total Quality Management (TQM) 80
turnover 75
unit labor cost 78
valence 66

CASE

PRODUCTIVITY IN THE AUTO INDUSTRY

In the 1980s, productivity became a major concern of U.S. automakers. Japanese automobile imports were priced well below American products. The U.S. auto companies, feeling the crunch of foreign competition, looked closely at output per employee. The companies tried a wide variety of techniques to improve productivity, ranging from automation and work redesign to "motivation programs" and attempts at psychological "involvement," but the results were mixed.

One often-mentioned illustration of the contrast between U.S. and Japanese automakers' productivity involves the General Motors assembly plant in Fremont, California. In the early 1980s, the absenteeism rate was about 20%. There were 5,000 outstanding grievances, frequent wildcat strikes, and constant feuds between management and labor. Finally, General Motors shut the plant down and turned it over to Toyota Motor Corporation as part of a joint venture called New Unit Motor Manufacturing, Inc. (NUMMI). Adding little new technology, Toyota implemented a typical Toyota production system with just-in-time delivery of parts and components and flexible assembly lines run by teams of workers in charge of their own jobs. The firm hired back the United Auto Workers (UAW) members who wanted to work, including their militant leaders. Several years later, 2,500 employees were assembling what it formerly took 5,000 people to produce with GM. Significantly, absenteeism decreased to about 2%, and outstanding grievances averaged only about two at a time.

The melding of Japanese technology and U.S. workers generally has made extensive use of work teams. The employees in the Toyota plant in Georgetown, Kentucky, participate in compensation programs to reward teamwork and continuity of production. Gift certificates are given for suggestions that result in improved efficiency and productivity. However, there have been cultural adjustment problems between some Japanese managers and American workers. Also, some have charged that the role of women in plants has not been accepted well, as evidenced by sexual harassment claims at Mitsubishi Motors Plant in Illinois.

Productivity (including quality) in U.S.–owned plants in the United States still is below that in Japanese plants (both in Japan and in the United States); and the chairman of Toyota recently created some controversy when he said that U.S. Toyota factories had too many quality problems and were below Toyota's standards in Japan. U.S.–owned plants do better than some plants in Europe, however.

One U.S. success story involves GM's Saturn division, which has utilized employee-involvement and quality-improvement techniques to make a success of its Saturn autos. Saturn has not been able to produce enough cars to meet demand, so customers have long waits for cars. GM could "lean on" Saturn for an improvement in productivity. But when employees and equipment are pushed too far, quality suffers. Saturn employees' pay is tied to quality targets, and Saturn management and employees have demonstrated they will not compromise quality. When GM's management pushed through a production increase that raised the number of defects, employees staged a work slowdown until those production goals were eased. Saturn is another illustration of how productivity, quality, and employee involvement are interrelated.[57]

Questions

1. In what ways does this case illustrate the importance of teamwork in improving quality and productivity, even when strong unions are present?
2. How would jobs have to be redesigned to shift from the traditional production line to that used at the Toyota plants described in the case?

Notes

1. Based on Paul Wiseman, "ER Workers Help Patients Lose the Wait," *USA Today,* May 3, 1996, 6B.
2. Michael J. Mandel, "Economic Anxiety," *Business Week,* March 11, 1996, 50–56.
3. "Study Claims Poor Management Is Alienating American Workers," November 19, 1995, G1.
4. L. S. Richman, "Getting Past Economic Insecurity," *Fortune,* April 17, 1995, 161–168; and J. Harwood, "Economic Insecurity Is Widespread," *The Wall Street Journal,* May 16, 1996, A20.
5. R. C. Longworth and S. Stein, "Troubled Middle Class," *The Denver Post,* September 15, 1995, 25A.
6. R. F. Yates, "Shining Surface of U.S. Business Hides Rising Fury," *The Chicago Tribune,* October 1, 1995, Section 5, 1, 4.
7. J. A. Byrne, "How High Can CEO Pay Go?" *Business Week,* April 22, 1996, 100–106.
8. "Executive Pay Survey," *The Wall Street Journal,* April 11, 1996, R17.
9. R. A. Guzzo, K. A. Noonan, and E. Elron, "Expatriate Managers and the Psychological Contract," *Journal of Applied Psychology* 79 (1994), 617–626; and E. H. Schein, *Organizational Psychology,* 3rd ed. (Englewood Cliffs, NJ: Prentice-Hall, 1980).
10. G. P. Zachary, "High Tech Explains Widening Wage Gaps," *The Wall Street Journal,* April 22, 1996, A1.
11. Judith Bardwick, "From Entitlement to Earning," *Benefits & Compensation Solutions,* September 1994, 27.
12. Abraham H. Maslow, *Motivation and Personality* (New York: Harper & Row, 1954).
13. Adapted from a discussion in Michael A. Hitt, R. Dennis Middlemist, and Robert L. Mathis, *Management: Concepts and Effective Practice,* 3rd ed. (St. Paul: West Publishing Co., 1989), 324–326.
14. Victor H. Vroom, *Work and Motivation* (New York: Wiley, 1964); and Lyman W. Porter and E. E. Lawler III, *Managerial Attitudes and Performance* (Homewood, IL: Richard D. Irwin, 1968).
15. D. G. Langdon and K. S. Whiteside, "Redefining Jobs and Work in Changing Organizations," *HR Magazine,* May 1996, 97–101.
16. J. R. Hackman and G. R. Oldham, *Work Design* (Reading, MA: Addison-Wesley, 1980), 72–73.
17. Michael Hammer and Steven A. Stanton, *The Reengineering Revolution* (New York: Harper Collins, 1995), 7–9.
18. P. Spector and S. Jex, "Relations of Job Characteristics from Multiple Data Sources with Employee Affect," *Journal of Applied Psychology* 76 (1991), 46–53; and J. Kelley, "Does Job Redesign Theory Explain Job Redesign Outcomes?" *Human Relations* 45 (1992), 753.
19. John Schaubroeck, Daniel C. Ganster, and Barbara E. Kemmerer, "Job Complexity: 'Type A Behavior and Cardiovascular Disorder," *Academy of Management Journal* 37 (1994), 426–439.
20. Michael Hammer and Steven A. Stanton, *The Reengineering Revolution* (New York: Harper Collins, 1995).
21. M. T. Moore, "Agency Puts Focus on Its Customers," *USA Today,* August 30, 1995, B1.
22. Based on "The New Workplace," *Business Week,* April 29, 1996, 106–117; and L. S. Vines, "Managing the Virtual Office," *Benefits & Compensation Solutions,* January 1995, 29–33.
23. "Reengineering Goals Are Generally Met," *HR Series Policies and Practices,"* August 25, 1995, 17.
24. Elizabeth Sheley, "Flexible Work Options: Beyond 9 to 5," *HR Magazine,* February 1996, 52–58.
25. W. P. Barrett, "8 Million, 22 Million . . . But Who's Counting?" *Worth,* July/August 1995, 80.
26. "Teams Become Commonplace," *The Wall Street Journal,* November 28, 1995, A1.
27. "Wanted: Teammates, Crew Members, Cast Members," *The Wall Street Journal,* April 30, 1996, A1.
28. Janice Stanger *et al.,* "Alternatives to Employee Task Forces," *Employee Benefits Journal,* June, 1994, 18–22.
29. K. A. Guinn, "Performance Management for Evolving Self-Directed Work Teams," *ACA Journal,* Winter 1995, 74–81.
30. Val Arnold, "Organizational Development: Making Teams Work," *HR Focus,* February 1996, 12–14.
31. Based on "The Celling Out of America," *The Economist,* December 17, 1994, 63–64; and M. Loeb, "Leadership Lost and Regained," *Fortune,* April 17, 1995, 217–218.
32. Based on ideas suggested by A. Nahavandi and E. Aranda, "Restructuring Teams for the Re-engineered Organization," *Academy of Management Executive,* November 1994, 58–68.
33. Charles Handy, *Age of Unreason* (Cambridge, MA: Harvard Business School Press, 1990).
34. P. M. Mulvey, J. F. Veiga, and P. M. Elsass, "When Teammates Raise a White Flag," *Academy of Management Executive,* February 1996, 40–49.
35. N. Allen and J. P. Meyer, "Organizational Commitment: Evidence of Career Stage Effects?" *Journal of Business Research* 26 (1993), 49–61.
36. Peter W. Hom and Rodger W. Griffeth, *Employee Turnover* (Cincinnati: South-Western Publishing Co. 1995), 94–100.
37. "Worker Absenteeism Still on the Rise," *Benefits & Compensation Solutions,* December 1995, 8.
38. *CCH Ideas & Trends,* May 24, 1995, 85–96.
39. R. P. Steel and J. R. Rentsch, "Influence of Cumulation Strategies on the Long-Range Prediction of Absenteeism," *Academy of Management Journal* 38 (1995), 1616–1634.

(Notes continued on following page)

Notes, continued

40. I. A. Miners *et al.*, "Time-Serial Substitution Effects of Absence Control on Employee Time-Off," *Human Relations* 48 (1995), 307–326.

41. Jeffrey B. Archer, "Efforts of Human Resource Systems on Manufacturing Performance and Turnover," *Academy of Management Journal* 37 (1994), 670–687.

42. T. W. Lee, T. R. Mitchell, L. Wise, and S. Fireman, "An Unfolding Model of Voluntary Employee Turnover," *Academy of Management Journal* 39 (1996), 5–36.

43. Charles R. Williams and Linda P. Livingstone, "Another Look at the Relationship between Performance and Voluntary Turnover," *Academy of Management Journal* 37 (1994), 269–398.

44. "U.S. Leader of the Pack in Global Competitiveness," *Omaha World-Herald*, September 6, 1995, 18.

45. C. Farrell and Michael J. Mandel, "Riding High," *Business Week*, October 9, 1995, 134–146.

46. "Is the Model Broken?" *The Economist*, May, 4, 1996, 17–19.

47. K. R. Sheets, "Showdown on the Dollar," *U.S. News and World Report*, February 2, 1989, 20.

48. For more details on ISO 9000, see John T. Rabbit and Peter A. Bergh, *The ISO 9000 Book: A Global Competitor's Guide to Compliance and Certification* (New York: Amacom Books, 1993).

49. L. Dobyns and C. Crawford-Mason, *Quality or Use* (Boston: Houghton-Mifflin, 1991), 181.

50. R. C. Hill, "When the Going Gets Rough: A Baldrige Award Winner on the Line," *Academy of Management Executive*, August 1993, 75–79.

51. C. C. Pegels, *Total Quality Management* (Danvers, MA: boyd & fraser, 1995), 29–38.

52. Robert L. Cardy and Gregory H. Dobbins, "Human Resource Management in a Total Quality Organizational Environment," *Journal of Quality Management* 1 (1996), 5–20.

53. "Quality Challenge for HR: Linking Training to Quality Program Goals," *1994 SHRM/CCH Survey*, June 22, 1994, 1–12.

54. R. Reger *et al.*, "Reframing the Organization: Why Implementing Total Quality Is Easier Said Than Done," *Academy of Management Review* 19 (1994), 565–584.

55. T. A. Stewart, "After All You've Done for Your Customers . . .," *Fortune*, December 11, 1995, 178–182.

56. L. L. Berry, A. Parasuraman, and V. A. Zeithami, "Improving Service Quality in America: Lessons Learned," *Academy of Management Executive*, May 1994, 32–45.

57. D. Woodruff, "Saturn," *Business Week*, August 17, 1992, 87–88; and Terry L. Beeser, "Rewards and Organizational Goal Achievement: A Case Study of Toyota Motor Manufacturing in Kentucky," *Journal of Management Studies* 32 (1995), 383–399.

CHAPTER 4

GLOBAL HUMAN RESOURCE MANAGEMENT

After you have read this chapter, you should be able to . . .

- Discuss the major factors influencing global HR management.
- Define *culture* and explain how national cultures can be classified.
- Differentiate among importing and exporting companies, multinational enterprises, and global organizations.
- List and define several types of international employees.
- Explain why staffing activities are more complex for international jobs than for domestic ones.
- Discuss three areas of international training and development.
- Identify several international compensation practices.
- Describe several international health, safety, and security concerns.

HR in Transition

Global HR at McDonald's

One of the best-known companies worldwide is McDonald's Corporation. The fast-food chain, with its symbol of the golden arches, has spread from the United States into 91 countries. With over 18,000 restaurants worldwide, McDonald's serves 33 million people each day. International sales are an important part of McDonald's business, and over 50% of the company's operating income results from sales outside the United States. To generate these sales, McDonald's employs over one million people, and by 2000, McDonald's anticipates having two million employees.

Operating in so many different countries means that McDonald's has had to adapt its products, services, and HR practices to legal, political, economic, and cultural factors in each one of those countries. A few examples illustrate how adaptations have been made. In some countries, such as India, beef is not acceptable as a food to a major part of the population, so McDonald's uses lamb or mutton. To appeal to Japanese customers, McDonald's has developed teriyaki burgers. Separate dining rooms for men and women have been constructed in McDonald's restaurants in some Middle Eastern countries.

Before beginning operations in a different country, HR professionals at McDonald's research the country and determine how HR activities must be adjusted.

HR practices also have had to be adapted. Before beginning operations in a different country, HR professionals at McDonald's research the country and determine how HR activities must be adjusted. One method of obtaining information is to contact HR professionals from other U.S. firms operating in the country and ask them questions about laws, political factors, and cultural issues. In addition, the firm conducts an analysis using a detailed outline to ensure that all relevant information has been gathered. Data gathered might include what employment restrictions exist on ages of employees and hours of work, what benefits must be offered to full-time and part-time employees (if part-time work is allowed), and other operational requirements. For instance, in some of the former communist countries in Eastern Europe, employers provide locker rooms and showers for employees. These facilities are necessary because shower facilities, and even consistent water supplies, are unavailable in many homes, particularly in more rural areas around major cities. Also, public transportation must be evaluated to ensure that employees have adequate means to travel to work.

Once a decision has been made to begin operations in a new country, the employment process must begin. Often, McDonald's is seen as a desirable employer, particularly when its first restaurant is being opened in a country. For instance, in Russia, 27,000 people initially applied to work at the first Moscow McDonald's, which currently has over 1,500 employees. Because customer service is so important to McDonald's, recruiting and selection activities focus on obtaining employees with customer service skills. For worker positions such as counter representative and cashier, the focus is to identify individuals who will be friendly, customer-service-oriented employees. A "trial" process whereby some applicants work for a few days on a conditional basis may be used to ensure that these individuals will represent McDonald's appropriately and will work well with other employees.

For store managers, the company uses a selection profile emphasizing leadership skills, high work expectations, and management abilities appropriate to a fast-paced restaurant environment. Once applicant screening and interviews have been completed, individuals are asked to work for up to a week in a restaurant. During that time, both the applicants and the company representatives evaluate one another to see if the job "fit" is appropriate. After the first group of store managers and assistant managers are selected, future managers and assistant managers are chosen using internal promotions based on job performance.

Once the restaurants are staffed, training becomes crucial to acquaint new employees with their jobs and the McDonald's philosophy of customer service and quality. McDonald's has taken its Hamburger University curriculum from the United States and translated it into 22 different languages to use in training centers throughout the world. Once training has been done for trainers and managers, they then conduct training for all employees selected to work at McDonald's locations in the foreign countries. Every facet from customer service to the appropriate way to prepare hamburgers and french fries is covered. When actual equipment had not arrived in one country, the trainers made replicas of grills and fryers out of cardboard. The trainees practiced "cooking" on the cardboard models. Thus, the training was completed and the restaurant opened as scheduled. This is just one example of how McDonald's ensures that it maintains quality and service in its global operations.[1]

> "The world hates change but it is the only thing that has brought progress."
>
> —C. F. Kettering

❖ Global Competition and HR Management

Unprecedented political realignments and a changing world economic order have guaranteed a new era for international business. The reunification of Germany, the transformation of the Soviet bloc, the redevelopment of the Eastern European countries, the growing economic might of Asian countries, and new opportunities in Latin America and Africa have begun shaping the world and the organizations that operate in it.

Truly the world has become a global economy. Many U.S. firms receive a substantial portion of their profits and sales from outside the United States. Estimates are that the largest 100 U.S. multinational firms have foreign sales of more than $500 billion in one year. For firms such as Colgate and Coca-Cola, foreign sales and profits account for over 60% of total sales and profits. Other U.S. firms have substantial operations in other countries as well.

Global competition is driving changes in organizations throughout the world. As a result, the number and types of jobs in firms have changed. The impact of global competition can be seen in many U.S. industries. The automobile, steel, and electronics industries have closed unproductive facilities or reduced employment because of competition from firms in Japan, Taiwan, Korea, Germany, and other countries. At the same time, foreign-owned firms have been investing in plants and creating jobs in the United States. The growth in employment resulting from foreign investments has helped to replace some of the jobs lost at U.S. firms.

At the end of 1994, the General Agreement on Tariffs and Trade (GATT) was signed by many nations. Although the purpose of GATT was to provide general guidelines on trade practices among nations, there were a number of provisions in GATT that are likely to affect HR practices in the various countries, including the United States.[2] The brief look at the various areas of the world that follows illustrates the changing nature of international economic linkages.

❖ North America

The United States, Canada, and Mexico have recognized the importance of world trade by eliminating barriers and working more closely together, starting in North America. One aspect of this cooperation is that U.S. firms, as well as firms from other nations such as Japan, South Korea, and Taiwan, have taken advantage of the lower Mexican wage rates to establish operations in Mexico. The HR Perspective describes one type of operation in Mexico, *maquiladoras*. The signing of the North American Free Trade Agreement (NAFTA) in 1992 expanded trade opportunities among Canada, the United States, and Mexico. But NAFTA also placed restrictions on employers to ensure that their HR practices in Mexico met certain standards. The Commission on Labor Cooperation (CLC) was established as part of NAFTA to review complaints filed in the United States, Canada, or Mexico regarding occupational safety and health, child labor, benefits, and labor-management relations.[3]

❖ Latin America

One highlight of recent years in Latin America is the resurgence of the economies of the largest countries, specifically Brazil, Argentina, and Chile. Economic austerity programs in those countries have reduced their inflation rates to more normal levels. Expanding populations created by relatively high birthrates

HR PERSPECTIVE

MAQUILADORAS

Many firms based in highly developed nations such as the United States have attempted to maintain competitive prices for their products by establishing manufacturing plants in less-developed countries having lower labor costs. One illustration is the establishment of *maquiladora* plants, called so from the Spanish word meaning "someone who makes goods for market." In many of the *maquiladoras*, parts are shipped to Mexico, and then the goods are assembled in the plants for shipment to the United States. Depending on the currency exchange rate, wage rates for Mexican workers at *maquiladoras* average about 12 to 15% of U.S. wages for comparable work.

Such diverse corporations as Outboard Marine, RCA, General Motors, Zenith, Sunbeam, and R. G. Barry have *maquiladoras*. One estimate is that over 2,400 plants employing approximately 475,000 Mexican workers have been established. Although many of the *maquiladoras* are located near the U.S. border, they can be located anywhere in Mexico except Mexico City.

Firms that establish *maquiladoras* are required by Mexican government regulations to offer such benefits as health insurance, vacation time, holiday pay, and a 15-day cash bonus at holiday time. Other benefits that are not government-mandated include subsidized or free lunches, free transportation to and from work, and others.

But the *maquiladoras* have some negative factors. First, the wage rates are even lower than the typical wage rates in assembly plants in the interior of Mexico. Thus, U.S. labor union officials and others criticize *maquiladoras* as being "sweatshops." Second, the growth in the number of plants has resulted in border-town housing shortages, transportation problems, and even labor shortages.

More and more U.S. firms will be tapping Mexico's labor supply as a result of the North America Free Trade Agreement. Whether the *maquiladoras* will continue to proliferate, and where, are questions with significant human resource implications.[1]

have led to those countries being seen as attractive for foreign investment, and many multinational organizations based in the United States, Asian countries, and European nations have expanded operations through joint ventures with host-country firms.

❖ ASIA

In Asia, Japan's economy has been maturing, and Japanese society has been changing because of a rapidly aging population. Also, younger Japanese are becoming more "westernized" and are buying more imported goods. Gradually, the Japanese government has had to open up its markets and make changes in its economy in response to pressure from the United States and other countries.

Economic relations between foreign firms and firms in such Asian countries as Taiwan, South Korea, Singapore, and Malaysia have become more complex, and their exports have increased dramatically. The rapid growth of the economies in those Asian countries, as well as in Indonesia, Thailand, and Vietnam, has led more foreign firms to establish manufacturing facilities there and to increase trade opportunities.

Two other Asian countries, India and China, have huge populations. Consequently, a growing number of foreign firms are establishing operations in those nations. But the difficulty of attracting foreign managers and professionals to these countries and the costs of providing for them have created a shortage of qualified human resources in both India and China.

❖ EUROPE

Changes in Europe include the disintegration of the USSR into 14 independent states. The opening of Eastern European countries such as Poland and Romania gives U.S.–based and other firms dramatically expanded opportunities to sell products and services. Also, the ample supply of workers available in those countries, whose wage rates are relatively low, means that labor-intensive manufacturing facilities can be established to tap the available labor pools.

In Western Europe, efforts to create a unified European economic market have led to cross-country mergers of firms and greater cooperation by European governments. At the same time, those efforts may have the effect of limiting the import of U.S. and Japanese-made goods to participating European countries. Therefore, U.S. and Asian firms have added offices and production facilities in Europe to avoid potential trade restrictions.

The stagnation of the economies and high costs imposed on employers in Western European countries such as Germany and France have led to double-digit unemployment rates. As a result, many European-headquartered organizations have shifted production to new plants in the United States and other countries.

❖ Africa

In many parts of Africa, opportunities for international operations are inhibited by civil strife and corrupt governments. Also, the infrastructure in many countries is inadequate. A more positive outlook has existed for South Africa since its discredited apartheid policy was repealed. As a result, foreign firms are entering South Africa and establishing operations and joint ventures. But race relations still must be considered by HR professionals in global organizations operating in South Africa.

❖ Global Factors Influencing HR Management

Doing business globally requires that adaptations be made to reflect cultural and other factors that differ from country to country and continent to continent. It is crucial that the various factors be seen as interrelated by managers and professionals as they do business and establish operations globally. Figure 4–1 depicts some of the more important factors to be considered by HR managers with global responsibilities. Each of those factors will be examined briefly.

❖ Legal and Political Factors

The nature and stability of political systems vary from country to country. U.S. firms are accustomed to a relatively stable political system. The same is true in many of the other developed countries in Europe. Although presidents, prime ministers, premiers, governors, senators, and representatives may change, the legal systems are well-established, and global firms can depend on continuity and consistency.

In many other nations, the legal and political systems are much more turbulent. Some governments can be overthrown by military coups. Others are ruled by dictators and despots who use their power to require international firms to buy goods and services from host-country firms owned or controlled by the rulers or the rulers' families. In some parts of the world, one-party rule has led to pervasive corruption, while in others there are so many parties that governments change regularly. Also, legal systems vary in character and stability, with contracts suddenly becoming unenforceable because of internal political factors. International firms may have to decide strategically when to comply with certain

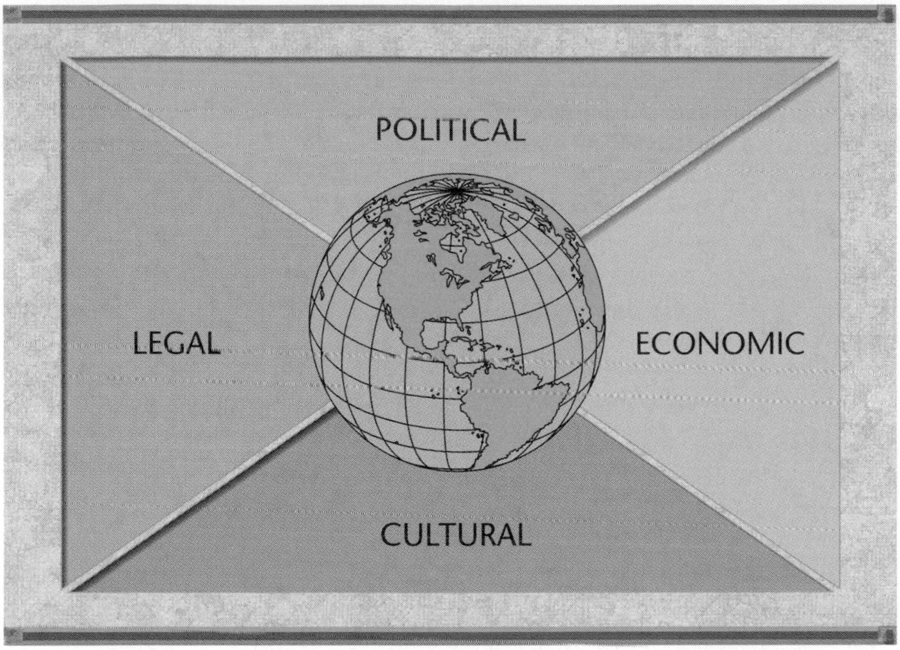

❖ FIGURE 4–1 ❖
SOME FACTORS AFFECTING GLOBAL HR MANAGEMENT

laws and regulations and when to ignore them because of operational or political reasons.[5] Another issue involves ethics. Because of restrictions imposed on U.S.–based firms through the Foreign Corrupt Practices Act, a fine line exists between paying agent fees, which is legal, and bribery, which is illegal. The HR Perspective on the next page highlights how ethical issues vary globally.

HR regulations and laws vary among countries in character and detail. In many countries in Western Europe, laws on labor unions and employment make it difficult to reduce the number of workers because required payments to ex-employees can be very high. Equal employment legislation exists to varying degrees. In some countries, laws address issues such as employment discrimination and sexual harassment. In others, because of religious or ethical differences, employment discrimination may be an accepted practice.

It is crucial for HR professionals to conduct a comprehensive review of the political environment and employment-related laws before beginning operations in a country. The role and nature of labor unions also should be investigated.

❖ ECONOMIC FACTORS

Economic conditions vary from country to country. Many lesser-developed nations are receptive to foreign investment in order to create jobs for their growing populations. Global firms often obtain significantly cheaper labor rates in these countries than they do in Europe and the United States. However, whether firms can realize significant profits may be determined by currency fluctuations and restrictions on transfer of earnings. Also, political instability can lead to situations in which the assets of foreign firms are seized. In addition, nations with weak economies may not be able to invest in maintaining and upgrading the elements of their infrastructures, such as roads, electric power, and telecommunica-

HR PERSPECTIVE

ETHICAL ISSUES IN GLOBAL HR

Cultural differences among countries have led to different ethical values. What is deemed acceptable or normal in one country may be deemed unethical in another. Both major and minor ethical issues must be confronted by those with international HR responsibilities. Several examples illustrate:

- In one Eastern European country, obtaining a new telephone line in less than three months requires making a cash payment, referred to as an "expediting charge," to the local manager of the telephone office. All parties to the deal know that the manager will retain the cash, but a telephone is essential for doing business internationally.
- Foreign firms wishing to do business in one Asian Pacific country must hire a "business representative" in order to obtain appropriate licenses and operating permits. In this country, it is well known that the two best representatives are relatives of the head of the country. It also is common to give the representative 10–20% ownership in the business as a "gift" for completing the licensing process in a timely manner.

A U.S.–based firm engaged in such practices could be violating the Foreign Corrupt Practices Act (FCPA), which prohibits U.S. firms from engaging in bribery and other practices in foreign countries that would be illegal in the United States. However, competing firms from other countries are not bound by similar restrictions.

Specifically relating to HR management, a major concern is the use of child labor and prison labor. According to one estimate, over 80 million children under age 18 are working in factories and fields for international companies.[6] In some places, children as young as six years old work eight hours per day. In some countries, people convicted of "political crimes" are forced to work in factories that manufacture goods to be sold to U.S. and European firms.

When stories of these types of situations have been publicized, customer boycotts and news media coverage have focused unfavorable attention on the companies involved. To counter such concerns, firms such as Levi's and Starbuck's Coffee, among others, have established minimum standards that must be met by all operations of their subcontractors and suppliers. But other firms have not been as aggressive.

Consequently, an effort was made by the U.S. government to establish a voluntary code of ethics to be followed by U.S. firms with foreign operations. The code includes five basic principles. U.S. firms and their suppliers and subcontractors are expected to:

- Provide a safe and healthy workplace
- Practice fair employment, including not using child or forced labor
- Respect the right of association, including the right of workers and unions to bargain collectively, and the right of freedom of expression
- Provide environmental protection for natural resources such as water, air, and rain forests
- Comply with U.S. laws restricting bribery and illicit payments

Although laudable in intent, the code has been criticized as being too vague and idealistic, rather than requiring that specific practices be discontinued. Another concern is that few other countries have adopted even such vague and general codes of conduct. Therefore, a U.S. firm trying to comply with the code may decrease its operations but then see a European- or Asian-based firm take over the operations and continue the undesirable practices. In summary, appropriate ethics for HR management in other countries may not be easy to identify or practice, given differences in what is regarded as ethical.[7]

tions. The absence of good infrastructures may make it more difficult to convince managers from the United States or Europe to take assignments overseas.

In many developed countries, especially in Europe, unemployment has grown, but employment restrictions and wage levels remain high. Consequently, many European firms are transferring jobs to lower-wage countries. In addition, both personal and corporate tax rates are quite high. These factors all must be evaluated by HR professionals as part of the process of deciding whether to begin or purchase operations in foreign countries.

❖ Cultural Factors

Cultural forces represent another important concern affecting international HR management. The culture of organizations was discussed earlier in the text, and of course, national cultures exist also. **Culture** is composed of the societal forces affecting the values, beliefs, and actions of a distinct group of people. Cultural differences certainly exist between nations, but significant cultural differences exist within countries also. One only has to look at the conflicts caused by religion or ethnicity in Central Europe and other parts of the world to see the importance of culture on international organizations. Even getting individuals from different ethnic or tribal backgrounds to work together may be difficult in some parts of the world.

❖Culture
The societal forces affecting the values, beliefs, and actions of a distinct group of people.

One widely used way to classify and compare cultures has been developed by Geert Hofstede, a Dutch scholar and researcher. Hofstede conducted research on over 100,000 IBM employees in 53 countries, and he identified five dimensions useful in identifying and comparing culture. A review of each of those dimensions follows.[8]

Power Distance The dimension of **power distance** refers to the inequality among the people of a nation. In countries such as Germany, the Netherlands, and the United States, there is a smaller power distance—which means there is less inequality—than in such countries as France, Indonesia, Russia, and China. As power distance increases, there are greater status and authority differences between superiors and subordinates.

❖Power Distance
Dimension of culture referring to the inequality among the people of a nation.

One way in which differences on this dimension affect HR activities is that reactions to management authority differ among cultures. In addition, one study found that styles of management differed among U.S. managers, European managers, and Japanese managers.[9] Another study compared participatory management systems in a firm's plants in Italy, Mexico, Spain, Great Britain, and the United States. The study found that plants in the United States were more participatory, while the management style used in plants in the other countries was relatively autocratic in nature.[10]

Individualism Another dimension of culture identified by Hofstede is **individualism**, which is the extent to which people in a country prefer to act as individuals instead of members of groups. On this dimension, people in Asian countries tend to be less individualistic and more group-oriented, whereas those in the United States score the highest in individualism.

❖Individualism
Dimension of culture referring to the extent to which people in a country prefer to act as individuals instead of members of groups.

An implication of these differences is that more collective action and less individual competition is likely in those countries that deemphasize individualism. For instance, one study that compared the reactions of Canadian executives and Chinese executives to conflict found that Chinese executives were more likely to avoid conflicts and discontinue negotiations when conflicts arose, particularly those that were individually based.[11]

Masculinity/Femininity The cultural dimension of **masculinity/femininity** refers to the degree to which "masculine" values prevail over "feminine" values. Masculine values identified by Hofstede were assertiveness, performance orientation, success, and competitiveness, whereas feminine values included quality of life, close personal relationships, and caring. Respondents from Japan had the highest masculinity scores, while those from the Netherlands had more femininity-oriented values. Differences on this dimension may be tied to the role of women in the culture. Considering the different roles of women and what is "acceptable"

❖Masculinity/Femininity
Dimension of culture referring to the degree to which "masculine" values prevail over "feminine" values.

for women in the United States, Saudi Arabia, Japan, and Mexico suggests how this dimension might affect the assignment of women expatriates to managerial jobs in the various countries.

Uncertainty Avoidance Dimension of culture referring to the preference of people in a country for structured situations instead of unstructured situations.

UNCERTAINTY AVOIDANCE The dimension of **uncertainty avoidance** refers to the preference of people in a country for structured situations instead of unstructured situations. A structured situation is one in which rules can be established and there are clear guides on how people are expected to act. Nations high on this factor, such as Japan, France, and Russia, tend to be more resistant to change and more rigid. In contrast, people in places such as Hong Kong, the United States, and Indonesia tend to have more "business energy" and to be more flexible.

A logical use of differences on this factor is to anticipate how people in different countries will react to changes instituted in organizations. In more flexible cultures, what is less certain may be more intriguing and challenging, which may lead to greater entrepreneurship and risk taking than in the more "rigid" countries.

Long-Term Orientation Dimension of culture referring to values people hold that emphasize the future, as opposed to short-term values, which focus on the present and the past.

LONG-TERM ORIENTATION The dimension of **long-term orientation** refers to values people hold that emphasize the future, as opposed to short-term values, which focus on the present and the past. Long-term values include thrift and persistence, while short-term values include respecting tradition and fulfilling social obligations. People scoring the highest on long-term orientation were China and Hong Kong, while people in Russia, the United States, and France tended to have a more shot-term orientation.

It is interesting to note that one of the criticisms of U.S. firms is that they have too great a focus on short-term earnings, compared with Japanese firms, which tend to have longer-term views. Hofstede notes that the countries with the highest rates of economic growth in the past two decades have been the countries with the greatest long-term orientation, which are Asian countries.

Differences in many other facets of culture could be discussed. An obvious one is language differences, while another is differences in time pressures. The purpose of this overview of culture is to stress that international HR managers and professionals must recognize that cultural dimensions differ from country to country and even within countries. Therefore, the HR activities appropriate in one culture or country may have to be altered to fit appropriately into another culture or country.

❖ TYPES OF GLOBAL ORGANIZATIONS

A growing number of organizations that operate only within one country are recognizing that they must change and develop a more international perspective. Organizations may pass through three stages as they broaden out into the world, as shown in Figure 4–2. A discussion of each stage follows.[12]

Importing and Exporting The phase of international interaction in which an organization begins selling and buying goods and services with organizations in other countries.

IMPORTING AND EXPORTING The first phase of international interaction consists of **importing and exporting.** Here, an organization begins selling and buying goods and services with organizations in other countries. Most of the international contacts are made by the sales and marketing staff and a limited number of other executives who negotiate contracts. Generally, HR activities are not affected except for travel policies for those going abroad.

Multinational Enterprise (MNE) An organization with units located in foreign countries.

MULTINATIONAL ENTERPRISES As firms develop and expand, they identify opportunities to begin operating in other countries. A **multinational enterprise** (MNE)

❖ FIGURE 4–2 ❖
TRANSITION TO GLOBAL ORGANIZATION

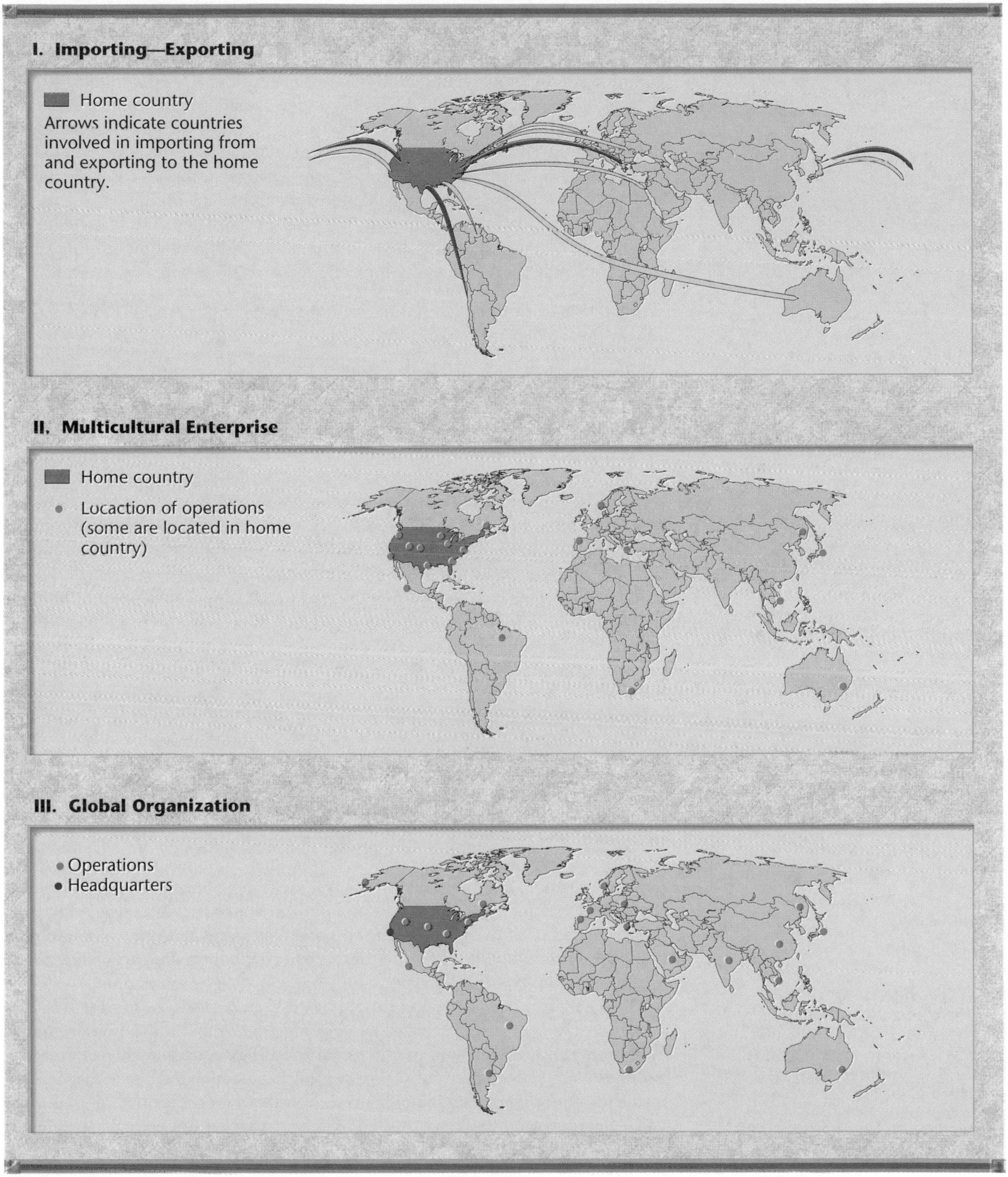

is one in which organizational units are located in foreign countries. Typically these units provide goods and services for the geographic areas surrounding the countries where operations exist. Key management positions in the foreign operations are filled with employees from the home country of the corporation. As the MNE expands, it hires workers from the countries in which it has operations. HR practices for employees sent from corporate headquarters must be developed so that these employees and their dependents may continue their economic lifestyles while stationed outside the home country. Ways to link these individuals to the parent company are also critical, especially if the international job assignment is two to three years long. There are likely to be laws and regulations that differ from those in the home country that must be considered. As a result, the HR professionals in the parent organization must become knowledgeable about each country in which the MNE operates and know how staffing, training, compensation, health and safety, and labor relations must be adapted.

Global Organization The MNE can be thought of as an *international* firm, in that it operates in various countries but each foreign business unit is operated separately. In contrast, a **global organization** has corporate units in a number of countries that are integrated to operate as one organization worldwide. An MNE may evolve into a global organization as operations in various countries become more integrated. That certainly describes what has occurred with McDonald's.

Global Organization
An organization that has corporate units in a number of countries that are integrated to operate as one organization worldwide.

Another example of making the transition from MNE to global organization involves Ford Motor Co. in the early 1990s. Ford started shifting from having a separate, relatively autonomous unit on each continent to operating as a global firm. One facet of Ford's approach illustrates the shift. Previously, Ford had its major design centers in the United States, and centers elsewhere adapt U.S.–designed vehicles to market needs in various countries. If separate Ford vehicles were developed, they often differed in model name and style. Under the global approach, Ford is merging design facilities and people from all over the world. In centers located in several countries, designers, engineers, and production specialists will work in teams to develop cars. Ford plans to develop a common "platform" and model for what it hopes will become a "world car" that can be produced and sold throughout the world. It will differ in different countries only in having the steering wheel and instrumentation on the right for such countries as Great Britain and Australia.

HR management in truly global organizations moves people, especially key managers and professionals, throughout the world. Individuals who speak several languages fluently are highly valued, and they will move among divisions and countries as they assume more responsibilities and experience career growth. As much as possible, international HR management must be viewed strategically in these organizations.[13] Global HR policies and activities are developed, but decentralization of decision making to subsidiary units and operations in other countries is necessary in order for country-specific adjustments to be made.

International Staffing and Selection

When organizations expand to other countries, they often must develop operations and staff the operations in those countries. Large MNEs and global organizations typically employ individuals from throughout the world. Thus, staffing and selection activities must be tailored to obtaining individuals specifically suited for international responsibilities.

❖ Staffing Philosophies for International Assignments

The corporate philosophy and managerial attitudes in a firm affect the assignment of managers and professionals to international operations. Four distinct attitudinal sets can be identified.[14]

- ❖ *Ethnocentric.* Assignment of managers and professionals from the home-country office
- ❖ *Polycentric.* Assignment of host-country nationals to professional and managerial jobs
- ❖ *Regiocentric.* Assignment of managers and professionals to a broad area, such as the Caribbean basin or European Community countries
- ❖ *Geocentric.* Assignment of managers and professionals from anywhere to any world location

Finding a sufficient number of qualified managers for global assignments is an increasing problem for MNEs and global organizations. The results of two different surveys illustrate the difficulties. In one study of 1,000 CEOs in firms throughout the world, fewer than half of them indicated that they had staffed international management jobs successfully. Another study of 440 European executives found that a third of them currently were experiencing difficulties in locating managers with sufficient international experience, and over 70% said they expected that problem to continue in the future.[15]

The shortage of global talent represents one problem. Another is the high cost of establishing a manager or professional in another country; costs can run as high as $1 million for a three-year job assignment.[16] The actual costs for placing a key manager outside the United States often are twice the manager's annual salary.[17] For instance, if the manager is going to Japan, the costs may be even higher when housing costs, schooling subsidies, and tax equalization payments are calculated. Further, if a manager or professional executive quits an international assignment prematurely or insists on a transfer home, associated costs can equal or exceed the annual salary. One survey found that "failure" rates for managers sent to other countries ran as high as 45%.[18] Consequently, international HR management practices focus heavily on staffing and selection.

❖ Types of International Employees

International employees can be placed in three different classifications:

- ❖ An **expatriate** is an employee working in a unit or plant who is not a citizen of the country in which the unit or plant is located but is a citizen of the country in which the organization is headquartered.
- ❖ A **host-country national** is an employee working in a unit or plant who is a citizen of the country in which the unit or plant is located, but where the unit or plant is operated by an organization headquartered in another country.
- ❖ A **third-country national** is a citizen of one country, working in a second country, and employed by an organization headquartered in a third country.

Each of these individuals presents some unique HR management challenges. Because in a given situation each is a citizen of a different country, different tax laws and other factors apply. HR professionals have to be knowledgeable about the laws and customs of each country. They must establish appropriate payroll and record-keeping procedures, among other activities, to ensure compliance with varying regulations and requirements.

❖Expatriate
An employee working in a unit or plant who is not a citizen of the country in which the unit or plant is located but is a citizen of the country in which the organization is headquartered.

❖Host-Country National
An employee working in a unit or plant who is a citizen of the country in which the unit or plant is located, but where the unit or plant is operated by an organization headquartered in another country.

❖Third-Country National
An employee who is a citizen of one country, working in a second country, and employed by an organization headquartered in a third country.

USE OF EXPATRIATES Many MNEs use expatriates to ensure that foreign operations are linked effectively with the parent corporations. Generally, expatriates also are used to develop international capabilities within an organization. Experienced expatriates can provide a pool of talent that can be tapped as the organization expands its operations more broadly into even more countries. Japanese-owned firms with operations in the United States have rotated Japanese managers through U.S. operations in order to expand the knowledge of U.S. business practices in the Japanese firms.

Several types of expatriates may be differentiated by job assignment, because not all individuals who decide to work as expatriates are similar in the assignments undertaken.[19]

- *Volunteer expatriates.* These are persons who want to work abroad for a period of time because of career or self-development interests. Often, these expatriates volunteer for shorter-term assignments of less than a year so that they can experience other cultures and travel to desired parts of the world.
- *Traditional expatriates.* These are professionals and managers assigned to work in foreign operations for one to three years. They then rotate back to the parent corporation in the home country.
- *Career development expatriates.* These individuals are placed in foreign jobs to develop the international management capabilities of the firm. They may serve one to three "tours" in different countries, so that they can develop a broader understanding of international operations.
- *Global expatriates.* The broadest category comprises those individuals who move from one country to another. Often, they prefer to work internationally rather than in the home country.

USE OF HOST-COUNTRY NATIONALS Using host-country nationals is important for several reasons. It is important if the organization wants to establish clearly that it is making a commitment to the host country and not just setting up a foreign operation. Host-country nationals often know the culture, the politics, the laws, and how business is done better than an outsider would.[20] Also, tapping into the informal "power" network may be important. In one Southeast Asian country, foreign companies have learned that a firm's problems are resolved more quickly if a member of the family of the president of the country is a consultant to the firm or a member of its management. But U.S. firms must take care that the individuals used perform work for the company; the "salary" must not be a disguised bribe paid in order to obtain contracts. Otherwise, the firms could be in violation of U.S. foreign corrupt practices legislation. Another reason to use host-country nationals is to provide employment in the country. In many lesser-developed countries, pay rates are significantly lower than in the United States, so U.S. firms can gain cost advantages by using host-country nationals to staff many jobs.

USE OF THIRD-COUNTRY NATIONALS The use of third-country nationals is a way to emphasize that a global approach is being taken. Often, these individuals are used to handle responsibilities throughout a continent or region. For instance, a major U.S.–based electronics company has its European headquarters in Brussels, Belgium. While most employees on the clerical staff are Belgians, only about 20% of the professionals and managers are from Belgium. Most of the rest, except for five U.S. expatriates, are from other Western European countries. This approach reflects a regiocentric or geocentric philosophy for staffing jobs. More and more organizations are following this strategy in order to broaden their perspectives on global operations.

❖ Selection for International Assignments

The selection process for an international assignment should provide a realistic picture of the life, work, and culture to which the employee may be sent. HR managers should prepare a comprehensive description of the job to be done. The description especially should note responsibilities that would be unusual in the home nation. Those responsibilities might include negotiating with public officials; interpreting local work codes; and responding to ethical, moral, and personal issues such as religious prohibitions and personal freedoms. Figure 4–3 shows the most frequently cited selection criteria for expatriates.

Cultural Adaptability Most staffing "failures" for those selected for foreign assignments occur because of cultural adjustment problems, not because of difficulties with the jobs or inadequate technical skills. Organizational support for the employees is particularly important in this area. Once employees have been selected for international assignments, continuing organizational support for the employees is crucial. One study found that the intention of expatriates to quit and their commitment to their organizations are affected significantly by how they view the support given to them by their employers.[21]

Throughout the selection process, especially in the selection interviews, it is crucial to assess the potential employee's ability to accept and adapt to different customs, management practices, laws, religious values, and infrastructure conditions. For example, in Nigeria, the local telephone system is so inefficient that overseas calls can be made more easily than crosstown calls, especially in Lagos, the capital city. A U.S. citizen who is accustomed to the convenience and reliability of the U.S. telephone system may become impatient and angry when confronted with such delays.

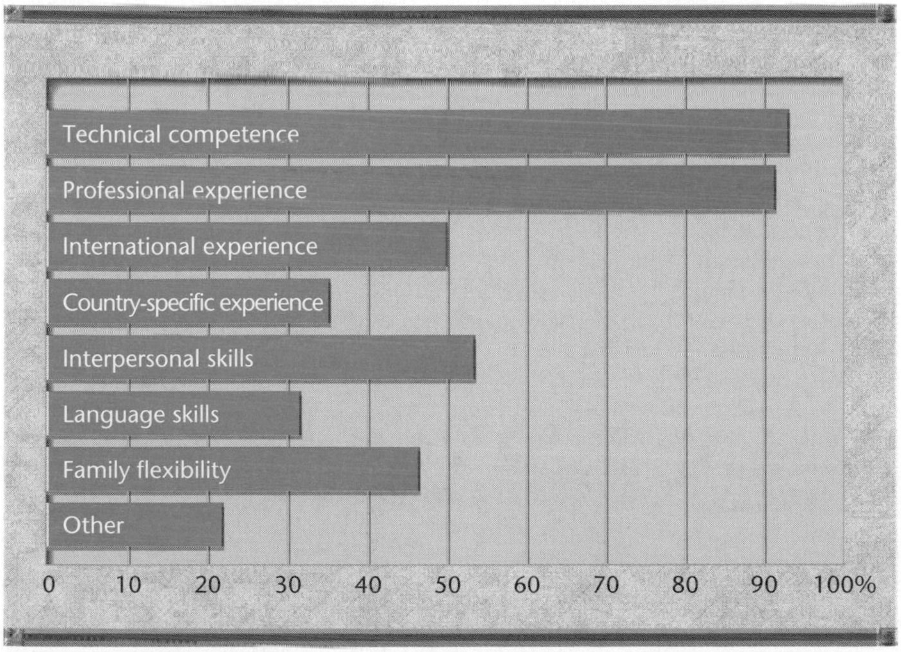

❖ Figure 4–3 ❖
Expatriate Selection Criteria

SOURCE: Windham International, as presented in Charlene M. Solomon, "Success Abroad Depends on More Than Job Skills," *Personnel Journal,* April 1994, 51–60. Used with permission.

Communication Skills One of the most basic skills needed by expatriate employees is the ability to communicate orally and in writing in the host-country language. Inability to communicate adequately in the language may significantly inhibit the success of an expatriate. Numerous firms with international operations select individuals based on their technical and managerial capabilities and then have the selected individuals take foreign language training. Intensive 10-day courses offered by Berlitz and other schools teach basic foreign language skills.

Family Factors The preferences and attitudes of spouses and other family members also are major staffing considerations. One study found that the most common reasons for turning down international assignments were family considerations (81%) and spouses' careers (53%).[22] With the growth in dual-career couples, the difficulty of transferring international employees is likely to increase, particularly given work-permit restrictions common in many countries. Some international firms have begun career services to assist spouses in getting jobs with other international firms.[23]

The availability of good schooling opportunities, the roles of men and women in the foreign country, and the availability of employment opportunities for the spouse must be considered. The international employee may adjust more easily than the spouse or other family members because of involvement in work activities. The HR Perspective highlights a study on ways to improve the adjustment of spouses to international assignments.

Women Employees Overseas For years in many U.S. firms, women were not considered for overseas jobs. Because of cultural values and historical traditions in some foreign countries, women who worked as professionals were a rarity, if such employment was allowed at all. Unaccompanied women still have difficulty obtaining visas to enter some countries, particularly those in the Middle East and Far East. Also, the male-dominated cultures of some countries have continued to pose significant problems for women who attempt to represent U.S. firms to top-

HR PERSPECTIVE

Global Assignments and Spousal Adjustment

The importance of spouses' acceptance of and adjustment to international assignments has been well documented. Black and Gregersen conducted a research study to identify the effectiveness of various HR actions in aiding such adjustment. Questionnaires were mailed to expatriates located in France, Great Britain, Hong Kong, Japan, Korea, the Netherlands, and Taiwan. A total of 321 were returned. The questionnaire asked the expatriates and spouses to evaluate international adjustment, pre-departure training, pre-move visits, desire to move prior to departure, social support in the host country, family support, living conditions, and culture. Data also were obtained on previous international experience and length of stay in the host countries.

The study found that spousal adjustment was positively related to pre-move visits, an attempt by the firm to seek spousal input about the assignment, and pre-departure cross-cultural training. Favorable living conditions, host-country social support, and family support also related positively to the adjustment of spouses. However, there was not a significant relationship between previous international experience and spouses' adjustment.

One interesting result was that the more a spouse, on his or her own initiative, sought cross-cultural training, the greater the eventual adjustment. Therefore, the authors recommend providing self-study materials and cross-cultural materials to augment formal training. The study generally suggests that if the employer ignores the spouse in the pre-departure planning, the probability of expatriate failure increases. Black and Gregersen said, "U.S. firms would likely have more adjusted and committed spouses and expatriates by providing rigorous pre-departure training, especially when individuals are being sent to novel cultures."[24]

level host-country executives. However, when given the opportunity, women function effectively in foreign countries. Those women who do obtain overseas assignments are expected to be more qualified professionally and personally than men in similar positions, according to many observers. Nevertheless, a growing number of women are interested in international assignments. It is estimated that women will be 20% of all expatriates by 2000, up from 13% in 1995.[25]

EQUAL EMPLOYMENT OPPORTUNITY (EEO) CONCERNS The assignment of women and members of racial/ethnic minorities to international posts can involve legal issues, as these individuals may be protected by Equal Employment Opportunity (EEO) regulations. Many U.S. firms operating internationally have limited assignments of women and other protected-class individuals in deference to cultural concerns. In a case brought by a Lebanese American working in Saudi Arabia who was fired by Aramco Oil Company, [26] the U.S. Supreme Court ruled that the EEO regulations of Title VII did not cover U.S. employees working for U.S. firms internationally.

The Civil Rights Act of 1991 overturned this decision and extended coverage of EEO laws and regulations to U.S. citizens working internationally for U.S.–controlled companies. However, the act states that if laws in a foreign country require actions that conflict with U.S. EEO laws, the foreign laws will apply. If no laws exist, only customs or cultural considerations, then the U.S. EEO laws will apply.

In a related area, some foreign firms in the United States, particularly Japanese-owned ones, have "reserved" top-level positions for those from the home country. Consequently, EEO charges have been brought against these firms. A circuit court decision ruled that because of a treaty between Japan and the United States, Japanese subsidiaries can give preference to Japanese over U.S. citizens.[27] However, it should be noted that most other EEO regulations and laws apply to foreign-owned firms.

Women have brought sexual harassment charges against foreign managers, and other protected-class individuals have brought EEO charges for refusal to hire or promote them.[28] In those cases, courts have treated the foreign-owned firms just as they would U.S.–owned employers.

❖ International Training and Development

Employees working internationally face special situations and pressures, and training and development activities must be tailored to address them. As illustrated in Figure 4–4, these activities are of three types:

1. Orientation and training of the expatriate employee and the employee's family before the international assignment begins
2. Continuing employee development in which the employee's broadened skills can be fitted into career planning and corporate development programs
3. Readjustment training and development to prepare the employee for a return to the home-country culture and to prepare the expatriate's new subordinates and supervisor for the return

❖ Pre-Departure Orientation and Training

The orientation and training that expatriates and their families receive before departure have a major impact on the success of the overseas assignment. Three

❖ FIGURE 4–4 ❖
INTERNATIONAL TRAINING AND DEVELOPMENT

areas affect the cross-cultural adjustment process: (a) work adjustment, (b) interaction adjustment, and (c) general adjustment.[29] Permeating all of those areas is the need for training in foreign language and culture familiarization. Many firms have formal training programs for expatriates and their families, and this training has been found to have a positive effect on cross-cultural adjustment.

Individuals selected to work outside the United States for MNEs need answers to many specific questions about their host countries. Such areas as language, political and historical forces, geographic and climatic conditions, and general living conditions are topics frequently covered in the orientation and training sessions on the culture of the host country. Expatriates and their families also must receive detailed, country-specific training on customs in the host country. Such knowledge will greatly ease their way in dealing with host-country counterparts. Training in such customs and practices also should be part of the training programs for individuals who will not live outside the home country but will travel to other countries for business purposes.

A related issue is the promotion and transfer of foreign citizens to positions in the United States. As more global organizations start or expand U.S. operations, more cross-cultural training will be necessary for international employees relocated to the United States.[30] For example, many Japanese firms operating in the United States have training programs to prepare Japanese for the food, customs, and other practices of U.S. life. The acceptance of a foreign boss by U.S. workers is another concern.[31] All these issues point to the importance of training and development for international adjustment.

Once global employees arrive in the host country, they will need assistance in "settling in." Arrangements should be made for someone to meet them and assist them. Obtaining housing, establishing bank accounts, obtaining driver's licenses, arranging for admissions to schools for dependent children, and establishing a medical provider relationship are all basics when relocating to a new city, internationally or not. But differences in culture, language, and laws may complicate these activities in a foreign country. The sooner the expatriates and their families can establish a "normal" life, the better the adjustment will be, and the less likely that expatriate failure will occur.

❖ Continuing Employee Development

Career planning and continued involvement of expatriates in corporate employee development activities are essential. One of the greatest deterrents to accepting foreign assignments is employees' concern that they will be "out of sight, out of mind." If they do not have direct and regular contact with others at the corporate headquarters, many expatriates experience anxiety about their continued career progression.[32] Therefore, the international experiences of expatriates must be seen as beneficial to the employer and to the expatriate's career.

One way to overcome problems in this area is for firms to invite the expatriates back for regular interaction and development programs with other company managers and professionals. Another useful approach is to establish a mentoring system. In this system, an expatriate is matched with a corporate executive in the headquarters. This executive talks with the expatriate frequently, ensures that the expatriate's name is submitted during promotion and development discussions at the headquarters, and resolves any headquarters-based problems experienced by the expatriate.[33]

Opportunities for continuing education represent another way for international employees to continue their development. In some of the more developed European countries, foreign executives and professionals may enroll in Master of Business Administration (MBA) programs at well-respected universities. By obtaining an MBA while on the international assignment, the expatriate keeps up with those with similar jobs in the home country who pursue advanced degrees while working full time.

❖ Readjustment Training and Development

The process of bringing expatriates home is called **repatriation.** Some major difficulties can arise when it is time to bring expatriates home. For example, the special compensation packages often available to expatriates are dropped, which means that the expatriates experience a net decrease in total income, even if they receive promotions and pay increases. In addition to concerns about personal finances, repatriated employees must readjust to a closer working and reporting relationship with other corporate employees. Often, expatriates have a greater degree of flexibility, autonomy, and independent decision making than do their counterparts in the United States.[34]

❖Repatriation
The process of bringing expatriates home.

Expatriates often must also be reacclimatized to U.S. lifestyles, transportation services, and other cultural practices, especially if they have been living in less-developed countries. For example, the wife of a U.S. expatriate was accustomed to bargaining for lower prices when she shopped in the foreign country. During the first week after her return to the United States, she tried to bargain with the checkout cashier at a supermarket before she realized that she was back in a place where this practice was not normal.

❖ International Compensation

Organizations with employees in many different countries face some special compensation pressures. Variations in laws, living costs, tax policies, and other factors all must be considered in establishing the compensation for expatriate managers and professionals. Even fluctuations in the value of the U.S. dollar must be tracked and adjustments made as the dollar rises or falls in relation to currency rates in other countries. Add to all of these concerns the need to com-

❖ FIGURE 4–5 ❖
TYPICAL EXPATRIATE COMPENSATION COMPONENTS

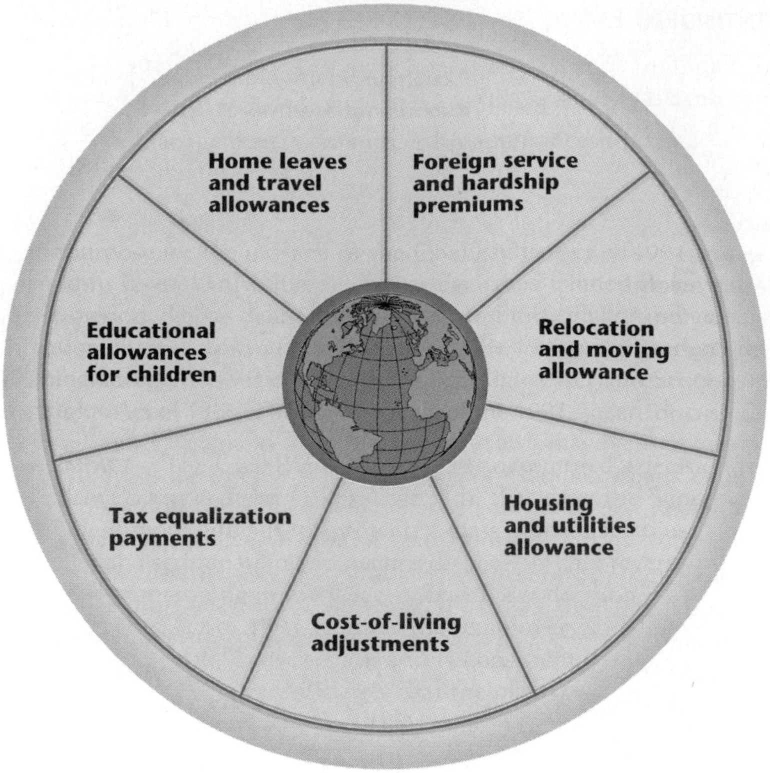

pensate employees for the costs of housing, schooling of children, and yearly transportation home for themselves and their family members. When all these different issues are considered, it is evident that international compensation is extremely complex. Typical components of an international compensation package for expatriates are shown in Figure 4–5. Several approaches to international compensation are discussed next.

❖ BALANCE-SHEET APPROACH

***Balance-Sheet Approach**
An approach to international compensation that provides international employees with a compensation package that equalizes cost differences between the international assignment and the same assignment in the home country of the individual or the corporation.

Many multinational firms have compensation programs that use the balance-sheet approach. The **balance-sheet approach** provides international employees with a compensation package that equalizes cost differences between the international assignment and the same assignment in the home country of the individual or the corporation. The balance-sheet approach is based on some key assumptions, which are discussed next.[35]

HOME-COUNTRY REFERENCE POINT The compensation package is developed to keep global employees at a level appropriate to their jobs in relation to similar jobs in the home country. Special benefits or allowances are provided to allow the global employees to maintain a standard of living at least equivalent to what they would have in the home country. Figure 4–6 shows a compensation package for a U.S. expatriate employee located in Japan.

LIMITED DURATION OF GLOBAL ASSIGNMENT Another basic premise of the balance-sheet approach is that expatriate employees generally have international assignments lasting two to three years. The international compensation package is designed to keep the expatriates "whole" for a few years until they can be rein-

❖ FIGURE 4–6 ❖
COMPARATIVE COSTS FOR U.S. EXPATRIATE IN JAPAN

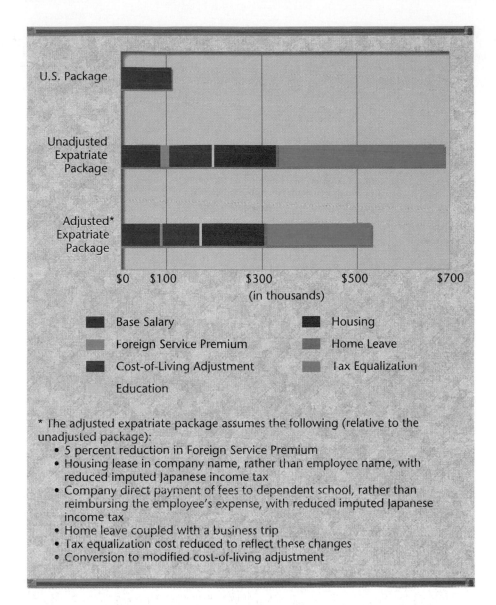

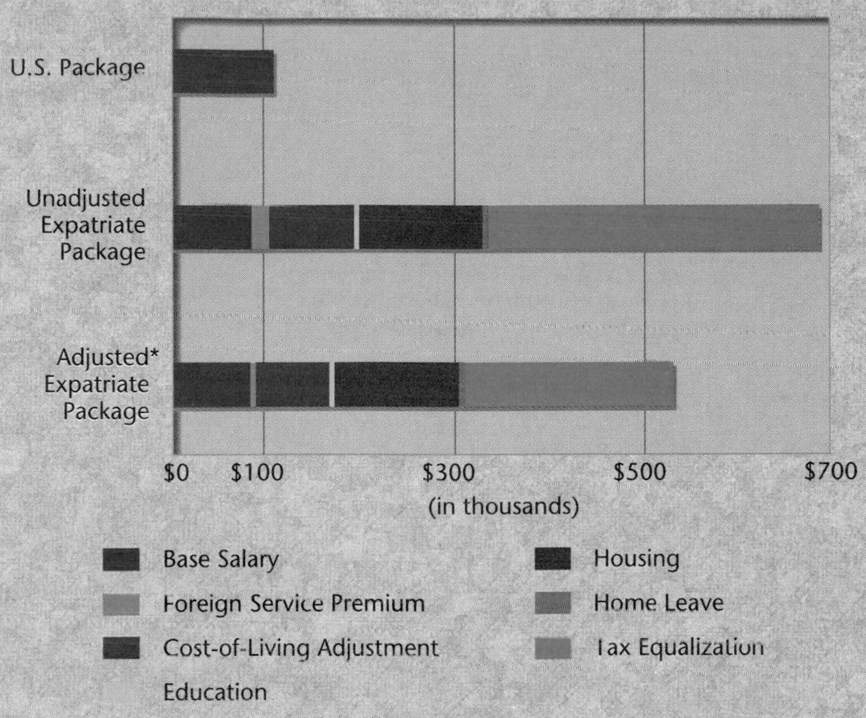

* The adjusted expatriate package assumes the following (relative to the unadjusted package):

- 5 percent reduction in Foreign Service Premium
- Housing lease in company name, rather than employee name, with reduced imputed Japanese income tax
- Company direct payment of fees to dependent school, rather than reimbursing the employee's expense, with reduced imputed Japanese income tax
- Home leave coupled with a business trip
- Tax equalization cost reduced to reflect these changes
- Conversion to modified cost-of-living adjustment

SOURCE: Jack W. Eads and Douglas J. Carey, "Expatriate Compensation: Managing the Bottom Line," *Journal of International Compensation & Benefits*, May/June 1994, 32. Used with permission.

tegrated into the home-country compensation program. Thus, the "temporary" compensation package for the international assignment must be structured to make it easy for the repatriated employee to reenter the domestic compensation and benefits programs. Also, it is assumed that the international employee will retire in the home country, so pension and other retirement benefits will be home-country-based.

❖ GLOBAL MARKET APPROACH

Increasingly, global organizations have recognized that attracting, retaining, and motivating managers with global capabilities requires taking a broader perspective than just sending expatriates overseas. As mentioned earlier, in many large multinational enterprises, key executives have worked in several countries and may be of many different nationalities. These executives are moved from one part of the world to another and to corporate headquarters wherever the firms are based. It appears that there is a high demand for these global managers, and they almost form their own "global market" for compensation purposes.

Unlike the balance-sheet approach, a global market approach to compensation requires that the international assignment be viewed as continual, not just temporary, though the assignment may take the employee to different countries for differing lengths of time. This approach is much more comprehensive in that the core components, such as insurance benefits and relocation expenses, are present regardless of the country to which the employee is assigned. But pegging the appropriate pay level, considering rates in the host country, home country, and/or headquarters country, becomes more complex.[36] Further, the acceptability of distributing compensation unequally based on performance varies from country to country.[37] Therefore, global compensation requires greater flexibility, more detailed analyses, and greater administrative effort. One study of 100 foreign subsidiaries of MNEs found that some of the factors affecting executive compensation included the "cultural distance" from headquarters and how much responsibility and autonomy the subsidiary had for products and services.[38]

❖ Tax Concerns

❖**Tax Equalization Plan**
Compensation plan used to protect expatriates from negative tax consequences.

Many international compensation plans attempt to protect expatriates from negative tax consequences by using a **tax equalization plan.** Under this plan, the company adjusts an employee's base income downward by the amount of estimated U.S. tax to be paid for the year. Thus, the employee pays only the foreign-country tax. The intent of the tax equalization plan is to ensure that expatriates will not pay any more or less in taxes than if they had stayed in the United States if they are U.S. citizens. One survey of U.S. MNEs found that 92% of them have tax equalization plans for use with expatriates.[39]

Currently, under U.S. Internal Revenue Service rules, U.S. citizens living overseas can exclude up to $70,000 of income earned abroad from taxes. Also, credits against U.S. income taxes are given for a portion of the foreign income taxes paid by U.S. expatriates beyond the $70,000 level.[40]

❖ Global Employee and Labor Relations

The nature of employee and labor relations varies from country to country. When international operations are considered, concerns related to health, safety, and security must be evaluated. Also, it is important to understand the applicable labor-management laws, regulations, and practices before commencing operations in foreign countries. A look at several facets of employee and labor relations follows.

❖ Global Health, Safety, and Security

Health, safety, and security are important for international operations and personnel, just as they are vital in the home country. Some aspects of global health, safety, and security are discussed next.

International Health and Safety Safety and health laws and regulations vary from country to country, ranging from virtually nonexistent to more stringent than in the United States. For instance, one study found that the importance placed on workplace safety varies among different countries.[41]

With more and more expatriates working internationally, especially in some of the less-developed countries, significant health and safety issues are arising, and addressing these issues is part of the HR role. For instance, in many parts of the former Soviet Union, medical facilities are more primitive, treatment is not as available, and pharmaceuticals are less easily obtained. U.S. expatriates traveling to such countries as Turkmenistan and Tajikistan commonly take antibiotics, other medications, and syringes and needles with them in case they need them. Similar practices are recommended for those traveling or working in some African and lesser-developed Asian countries, including China.[42]

Another consideration is provision of emergency evacuation services. For instance, how to evacuate and care for an expatriate employee who sustains internal injuries in a car accident in the Ukraine or Sierra Leone may be a major issue. Many global firms purchase coverage for their international employees from an organization that provides emergency services, such as International SOS, Global Assistance Network, or U.S. Assist. To use such a service, an employer pays a membership fee per employee, and all employee travelers are given emergency contact numbers. If an emergency arises, the emergency services company will dispatch physicians or even transport employees by chartered aircraft. If adequate medical assistance can be obtained locally, the emergency services company maintains a referral list and will make arrangements for the expatriate to receive treatment. Legal counsel in foreign countries, emergency cash for medical expenses, and assistance in retrieving lost documents or having them reissued also are provided by emergency services firms.

International Security and Terrorism As more U.S. firms operate internationally, the threat of terrorist actions against those firms and the employees working for them increases. U.S. citizens are especially vulnerable to extortions, kidnapping, bombing, physical harassment, and other terrorist activities. In a three-month period in a recent year, several hundred terrorist acts were aimed at businesses and businesspeople. Many of these acts targeted company facilities and offices. Nevertheless, individual employees and their families living abroad must constantly be aware of security issues.[43]

Many firms provide bodyguards who escort executives everywhere. Different routes of travel are used, so that "normal" patterns of movement are difficult for terrorists to identify. Family members of employees also receive training in security. Children are told to avoid wearing sweatshirts with U.S. logos and to be discreet when meeting friends. Schools for American children have instituted tight security measures, including sign-in procedures for visitors, guards for the grounds, and improved security fences and surveillance equipment.

Firms themselves are taking other actions. For example, one U.S. firm removed its large signs from facilities in a Latin American country. Removal of signs identifying offices and facilities reduces the visibility of the firm and thus reduces its potential as a target for terrorist acts. Many international firms screen all employees, and many use metal detectors to scan all packages, briefcases, and other items. Physical barriers, such as iron security fences, concrete barricades, bulletproof glass, and electronic surveillance devices, are common in offices. In some countries, such items are used at the homes of executives. Some global organizations have developed policies regarding payment of ransom for kidnaped employees and executives should such situations arise, even though they may be considered unlikely. Others have "disaster plans" to deal with evacuating expatriates if natural disasters, civil conflicts, or wars occur.

LOGGING ON

U.S. State Department Warnings and Consider Advisory Sheets are distributed by St. Olaf College (Minnesota) on all countries at

http://www.stolaf.edu/network/travelisories.html

❖ GLOBAL LABOR-MANAGEMENT RELATIONS

The strength and nature of unions differ from country to country. In some countries, unions either do not exist at all or are relatively weak. Such is the case in China and a number of African countries. In other countries, unions are extremely strong and are closely tied to political parties. This is the case in some European countries. In still other countries, such as the United States and Great Britain, unions have declined in influence and membership during the last decade.

***Co-Determination**
A practice whereby union or worker representatives are given positions on a company's board of directors.

Some countries require that firms have union or worker representatives on their boards of directors. This practice is very common in European countries, where it is called **co-determination.** Economic stagnation has hit many European countries, and unemployment has risen dramatically in France, Sweden, Germany, and Italy. One major cause for economic problems in those countries has been the high costs for wages and benefits forced on employers. As a result, many European firms have moved operations to the United States and other countries with less restrictive employment practices, higher productivity rates, and lower wage and benefit costs. But unions in several European countries have resisted changing the laws and removing government benefits. For instance, in France, a 21-day strike was called by French unions—not because of 12% unemployment but because of proposals to reduce state-provided pension and welfare benefits.[44] Union militancy is increasing in some lesser-developed countries such as Brazil, Mexico, Poland, and Romania.

Differences from country to country in how collective bargaining occurs are quite noticeable.[45] In the United States, local unions bargain with individual employers to set wages and working conditions. In Australia, unions argue their cases before arbitration tribunals. In Scandinavia, national agreements with associations of employers are the norms. In France and Germany, industrywide or regionwide agreements are common. In Japan, local unions do the bargaining but combine at some point to determine national wage patterns. In spite of these differences, unions appear to have somewhat similar effects internationally in most situations regarding employment and provision of benefits.

SUMMARY

❖ International HR activities must be adapted to reflect what is appropriate in different countries.

❖ The factors that most influence global HR management are legal, political, economic, and cultural factors.

❖ Culture is composed of the societal forces affecting the values, beliefs, and actions of a distinct group of people.

❖ One scheme for classifying national cultures considers power distance, individualism, masculinity/femininity, uncertainty avoidance, and long-term orientation.

❖ Organizations doing business internationally may evolve from organizations engaged in importing and exporting activities, to multinational enterprises, to global organizations.

❖ Staffing international jobs can be costly, and selection criteria must include a wide range of skills, abilities, and family factors in addition to the required business knowledge and experience.

❖ Training and development activities for international employees focus on pre-departure orientation and training, continued employee development, and readjustment training for repatriates.

❖ Compensation practices for international employees are much more complex than those for domestic employees because many more factors must be considered.

❖ Global organizations must be concerned about the health, safety, and security of their employees.

❖ Labor-management relations vary from country to country.

Review and Discussion Questions

1. Discuss the following statement: "Shifts in the types of jobs and the industries in which jobs are gained or lost reflect global competition and other economic shifts that are occurring in the United States."
2. Select a country and identify how you believe it would stand on Hofstede's five dimensions of culture.
3. Describe how a medium-sized firm with no international presence could evolve into a global organization.
4. What are some advantages and disadvantages associated with using expatriate managers instead of host-country nationals?
5. Assume you have been asked to consider a job in a foreign country with a U.S.–based corporation. Develop a list of questions and issues that the corporation should address with you before you make your decision.
6. Assuming you accepted a foreign job, what should the content of the pre-departure training be for you and your family?
7. Discuss the following statement: "Global compensation packages should keep expatriates even with what they would receive at home but not allow them to get rich."
8. Suppose an expatriate employee is to work in Bulgaria for two years. What health, safety, and security issues should be addressed?

Terms to Know

balance-sheet approach **106**
co-determination **110**
culture **95**
expatriate **99**
global organization **98**
host-country national **99**
importing and exporting **96**
individualism **95**
long-term orientation **96**
masculinity/femininity **95**
multinational enterprise (MNE) **96**
power distance **95**
repatriation **105**
tax equalization plan **108**
third-country national **99**
uncertainty avoidance **96**

Case

Utell International and Global HR Management

Founded during the Depression by Henry Utell, an Austrian travel journalist, by 1975 Utell International was doing business in 27 locations around the world. Utell International's core business is receiving and processing worldwide hotel reservations for over 6,500 hotels, including major international chains and smaller single-location properties. Hotels served by Utell operate in over 144 countries, and Utell processes several million reservations per year. The growth of international travel is expected to provide Utell with the opportunity to be generating 40 million reservations per year by the year 2000. Currently, Utell has 48 offices located in numerous countries, including locations in Asia-Pacific, Western and Eastern Europe, Africa, Latin America, and North America. Today, Utell's global headquarters is in London, England, and Utell International is now part of the Reed Travel Group, a division of Reed Elsevier, an Anglo-Dutch conglomerate with annual revenues exceeding $7 billion.

In addition to processing hotel reservations, Utell provides a financial service that enables customers to pay in local currency when reserving hotel accommodations in the far reaches of the globe. For example, a Utell customer in the United States can pay in U.S. dollars for a hotel reservation in Bombay, India, rather than having to pay in Indian rupees. Also, customized advertising and marketing services are offered to Utell's hotel clients.

It is evident that Utell has established itself as a significant international business, and its ability to provide its services depends on its human resources located throughout the world. The HR division was established formally when Utell opened a major U.S. operations center in Omaha, Nebraska, in January 1986. Humble beginnings describe the HR development effort over the past 10 years,

Utell International and Global HR Management, continued

starting with the development of the nuts and bolts of Utell's Omaha HR department. The HR department juggled multiple projects, including employment applications, job descriptions, wage and salary administration, a performance review process, employee benefits programs, training, affirmative action reporting procedures, and employee relations. Over several years, the HR director in Omaha added key support managers and specialists in the HR division to support Utell's U.S. operations.

The Omaha office soon became Utell's regional hub for North America and Latin America and still provides some HR support to 15 offices in the region, in addition to other affiliated companies located the United States. But Utell recognized that as global human resource issues emerged, a global human resource plan and accompanying strategies were needed. The need for a more strategic approach to HR throughout Utell became evident as the firm expanded into more locations. Consequently, several years ago, an experienced senior-level HR executive, Rachid "Ben" Bengougam, was hired to be Executive Corporate Director of Human Resources at headquarters in London, England.

Thanks in part to Bengougam's efforts, the Utell executive team has given its full support to the adoption of a formal HR strategy, which currently is being implemented in each region by regional HR professionals. At the heart of that strategy is that HR will be a significant force influencing Utell globally. Because payroll costs worldwide exceed $35 million and consume 40% of gross revenues, HR must produce results, not just be a cost-center. To ensure that HR receives appropriate direction and attention, additional HR professionals have been added in major global centers throughout the world. Two key HR directors were added in Europe and Asia-Pacific, and both speak two or more languages fluently, as does the HR director in Omaha who works with Utell operations in Central and South America. Language barriers can impair HR communications, and the need to recruit multilingual professionals has grown in recent years.

Currently, Utell is shifting its business emphasis from being a processor of reservations to being seen as a contributing partner to increasing the business of the hotels it represents. As a result, a part of the HR strategic efforts is to manage change and shift the culture to emphasize the sales, marketing and customer service skills of its employees. One part of this shift is the development of compensation programs in both Omaha and corporate headquarters that aid in positioning Utell as an employer of choice in the labor markets in which operations exist. Once those programs have been completed and implemented, they will be adapted and implemented in other regions. Bengougam has said, "The job evaluation process will be a cornerstone to ensure that Utell has the right people, in the right jobs, with equitable compensation and incentive programs worldwide." Also, aggressive efforts are being made to implement management development and leadership training programs throughout all regions. But care has had to be taken to reflect cultural differences in the various countries in which Utell operates.

In the future, efforts are planned in the HR areas of staffing, strategic planning, and HRIS support in order to provide an HR base to propel Utell International into the next century. In summary, it appears that Bengougam and the HR professionals at Utell International have developed a map complete with markers and clear directions on how to achieve Utell's business objectives and are well on their worldwide journey to effective HR management.[46]

Questions

1. Discuss how Utell has evolved into a global organization in its HR activities and why that has been important.
2. Describe, using specific examples, how the compensation and management development programs and processes might have to be altered for different parts of the world.

Notes

1. Based on Charlene M. Solomon, "Big Mac's McGlobal HR Secrets," *Personnel Journal,* April 1996, 47–54.
2. For technical details of GATT, see O. Morrissey and Y. Rai, "The GATT Agreement on Trade-Related Investment Measures," *Journal of Development Studies* 31 (1995), 702–725.
3. *International HR News,* January 1994, B10.
4. Mariah E. de Forest, "Thinking of a Plant in Mexico?" *Academy of Management Executive,* February 1994, 33–40.
5. J. J. Boddewyn and T. L. Brewer, "International-Business Political Behavior: New Theoretical Directions," *Academy of Management Review* 19 (1994), 119–143.
6. M. I. Finney, "Global Success Rides on Keeping Top Talent," *HR Magazine,* April 1996, 69–72.
7. Based on "Ethical Guidelines for Multinationals Take the Forefront," *WorldLink,* September–October 1995, 1; and "U.S. Develops Voluntary Code of Conduct for Business Overseas," *International HR Update,* July 1995, 5.
8. Based on information in Geert Hofstede, "Business Cultures," *UNESCO Courier,* April 1994, 12–17; and Geert Hofstede, "Cultural Constraints in Management Theories," *Academy of Management Executive,* February 1993, 81–94.
9. R. Calori and B. Dufour, "Management European Style," *Academy of Management Executive,* August 1995, 61–73.
10. Cynthia Pavett and Tom Morris, "Management Styles within a Multinational Corporation: A Five Country Comparative Study," *Human Relations* 48 (1995), 1171–1192.
11. D. K. Tse, J. Francis, and Jan Walls, "Cultural Differences in Conducting Intra- and Inter-Cultural Negotiations: A Sino-Canadian Comparison," *Journal of International Business Studies* 25 (1994), 537–554.
12. Based on information in David J. Cherrington and Laura Z. Middleton, "An Introduction to Global Business Issues," *HR Magazine,* June 1995, 124–130.
13. Randall S. Schuler, Peter J. Dowling, and Helen DeCieri, "An Integrative Framework of Strategic International Human Resource Management," *Journal of Management* 19 (1993), 419–459.
14. H. V. Perlmutter and D. A. Heenan, "How Multinational Should Your Top Managers Be?" *Harvard Business Review,* November 1974, 121–132.
15. "The Shortage of Global Managers," *Issues in HR,* March/April 1995, 2.
16. Bill Leonard, "Guardian Angels Help Overseas Employees," *HR Magazine,* April 1994, 59–60.
17. Based on data from Runzheimer International, 1996.
18. "Study of Global Sourcing and Selection Finds Troubling Rate of Assignment 'Failure,'" *International HR Update,* March 1996, 6.
19. Adapted from S. Barciela, "Expatriate Employees Sometimes Get Short End of Deal," *Omaha World-Herald,* April 14, 1996, G1.
20. Charlene M. Soloman, "Learning to Manage Host-Country Nationals," *Personnel Journal,* March 1995, 60–67.
21. R. A. Guzzo, K. A. Noonan, and E. Elron, "Expatriate Managers and the Psychological Contract," *Journal of Applied Psychology* 79 (1994), 617–626.
22. "Saying No to Work Abroad," *USA Today,* June 1, 1995, B1.
23. Reyer A. Swaak, "Today's Expatriate Family: Dual Careers and Other Obstacles," *Compensation & Benefits Review,* January–February 1995, 21–26.
24. Adapted from J. Stewart Black and Hal B. Gregersen, "The Other Half of the Picture: Antecedents of Spouse Cultural Adjustment," *Journal of International Business Studies* 22 (1991), 461–477.
25. *Global Relocation Trends: 1995 Survey Report* (New York: Windham International, 1995), 5.
26. *EEOC and Boureslan v. Aramco,* 111 SCt 1227 (1991).
27. *Fortino v. Quasar Co.* 950 F.2d 289 (7th Cir. 1991).
28. W. Hardman and J. Heidelberg, "When Sexual Harassment Is a Foreign Affair," *Personnel Journal,* April 1996, 91–97.
29. Mark E. Mendelhall and Carolyn Wiley, "Strangers in a Strange Land: The Relationship between Expatriate Adjustment and Impression Management," *American Behavioral Scientist,* March–April 1994, 605–621.
30. K. S. Dhir and A. Tagawa, "Cross-Cultural Training for International Employees and Families Relocated to the U.S.," *International HR Update,* July 1995, 1–2.
31. D. C. Thomas and E. C. Ravlin, "Responses of Employees to Cultural Adaptation by a Foreign Manager," *Journal of Applied Psychology* 80 (1995), 133–147.
32. L. Genasci, "Expatriate Workers Find Uncertainty at Home," *The San Juan Star,* August 7, 1995, B39.
33. Deborah Conlan, "Mentors Are Key to Expatriate Success," *Journal of International Compensation & Benefits,* May/June 1994, 62–64.
34. F. F. Mueller-Maerki, "Expatriates Need Not Apply," *The Wall Street Journal,* October 16, 1995, A16.
35. T. S. Tilghman, "Developing Alternative Approaches to Compensation," *ACA Journal,* Summer 1994, 36–49.
36. Brent M. Longnecker and Wendy Powell, "Executive Compensation in a Global Market," *Benefits & Compensation Solutions,* April 1996, 40–43.

(Notes continued on following page)

Notes, continued

37. Chao C. Chen, "New Trends in Rewards Allocation Preferences: A Sino–U.S. Comparison," *Academy of Management Journal* 38 (1995), 408–428.

38. S. Wetlaufer, "Determining Executive Compensation: Companies with Foreign Subsidiaries," *Harvard Business Review,* March 1996, 11–12.

39. Charlene M. Soloman, "Global Compensation: Learn the ABCs," *Personnel Journal,* July 1995, 70–76.

40. Jane Howard, "Earned-Income Tax Exclusion Levels Global Playing Field," *International HR News,* February 1996, B1.

41. M. Janssens, J. M. Brett, and F. J. Smith, "Confirmatory Cross-Cultural Research Testing the Viability of a Corporation-Wide Safety Policy," *Academy of Management Journal* 38 (1995), 364–382.

42. R. B. Palchak and R. T. Schmidt, "Protecting the Health of Employees Abroad," *Occupational Health & Safety,* February 1996, 53–56.

43. Patricia Digh Howard, "Circle of Impact: HR Professionals Respond to War Riot, Terrorism," *Employment Relations Today,* Spring 1991, 29–38.

44. M. Hunter, "Vive le Welfare State! Say French Strikers," *Fortune,* January 15, 1996, 15–17; and J. Warner, "Clinging to the Safety Net," *Business Week,* March 11, 1996, 62.

45. Harry C. Katz, "The Decentralization of Collective Bargaining," *Industrial and Labor Relations Review* 47 (1993), 3–22.

46. Used with permission. Utell International, 1996, Nicholas E. Dayan, Director of Human Resources and Training, The Americas.

EXERCISE 1 - Analysis

The issues of melding Human Resources after mergers and acquisitions were covered in several places in the first section. Among the observations made were the necessity for integrating the acquired firm with the existing company. Integrating cultures is an important issue. On a very operational level integrating the compensation, vacation plans, retirement plans and other benefits is a major issue as well.

SME-TEK has just acquired CEB and Associates, a small accounting firm that will be maintained as a separate company. However, the new acquisition will need to mesh with the SME-TEK culture and organization.

1. What difficulties would you anticipate in getting records and databases incorporated between the two companies?
2. Enter CEB and Associates organizational levels (region, office, and unit) into the existing database. Use cross validation for the new company as has been done for the rest of SME-TEK. This will provide you with an overview of a portion of the HRIS.

SME-TEK

MEMO

TO: *HUMAN RESOURCES MANAGEMENT USER*

Great news! We just acquired CEB & Associates, a small accounting firm that we are going to maintain as a separate company. I need you to enter their organizational levels (Region, Office, and Unit) into the database. We will use cross validation for the new company as we have for the rest of SME-TEK INC.

Thanks,

Pat

EXERCISE 1 - Procedure

Before completing the memo's request, you need to access the Human Resources module and review the topic "Company Organizational Structure Overview" in the "Introduction to Tables" lesson of the Concepts section.

To fulfill the memo's request, access the "Organizational Structure" lesson of the Human Resources Features & Processes section. Then, review the topics "Defining the Organizational Levels" and "Data Entry." The Practice and Checkpoint topics are optional.

EXERCISE 2 - Analysis

Material in the first section discussed outsourcing, its advantages and disadvantages. The opposite of outsourcing, having an in-house operation to handle various necessary functions, is a strategy that SME-TEK has just begun for its advertising, promotion, and media research.

The company has just acquired a small communications firm to handle those functions. The firm will be treated as a new department in the company. SME-TEK will also need to hire a creative copy director to coordinate the production of creative advertising for the new department.

1. What are the advantages of having an in-house operation to do these functions and what requirements would you have for a "creative copy director"?
2. Set up the data record for the new advertising department in the HRIS. In addition, add the job of creative copy director to the job tables in the HRIS.

SME-TEK

MEMO

TO: *HUMAN RESOURCES MANAGEMENT USER*

We have just acquired a small communications firm to handle our advertising, promotions, and media research needs. We need to set up a new record for the new Advertising department in the Department table.

We'll also be looking for a Creative Copy Director to coordinate the production of creative advertising copy for the new department. I need you to add this job to the Job table ASAP so we can begin our search.

Thanks!

Elizabeth

EXERCISE 2 - Procedure

Before completing the memo's request, you need to access the Human Resources module and review the topic "Purpose of the Job and Department Tables" in the "Introduction to Tables" lesson of the Concepts section.

To fulfill the memo's request, access the "Department Table" lesson of the Human Resources Features & Processes section. Then, review the topic "Setting Up the Department Table." When done, access the "Job Table" lesson of the Human Resources Features & Processes section and review the topic "Setting Up the Job Table." The Practice and Checkpoint topics in both lessons are optional.

SECTION VIDEO CASES

❖ CASE 1
BEALL'S ROSES
Making a Business Bloom Again

Johna Beall faced thorny problems when she took over the family business in 1991. A single mom with three small kids, she was heading a company whose production facility was 5,000 miles away, in a country scarred by drug-cartel violence. Beall's Roses had lost key executives—her gravely ill father and a burned-out older sister—and sales. It suffered from increased competition, lower product quality, and higher costs.

In business since 1889, Beall's had grown roses near Palo Alto, Calif., until 1973, when it bought a farm outside Bogota, Colombia, on an Andean plateau rich in soil and sunlight. Company headquarters were and are in Seattle, Wash.

Beall's had done well for years on the Miami wholesale market with its roses, but they now seemed no longer to be consistently of high quality. Meanwhile, Johna Beall says, consumers, because of excess rose production in many countries, were accepting mediocre roses at medium prices, and her company's costs were rising because Colombia's government requires annual payroll increases in line with inflation—generally between 22 and 25 percent.

Her challenges were to develop cost-efficient quality management in rural Colombia and to find new markets.

Beall says the farm was blessed with long-term employees who had integrity and skill. She put some in charge of teams to solve greenhouse, grading, and shipping problems. She began giving bonuses for increases in rose quantity and in quality—i.e., longer stem length and lower disease rates. She also offered bonuses for continued education, and she improved a day-care center, a lunchroom, and workers' transportation and health-care coverage.

"I made my commitment to the workers' quality of life very clear and asked them in return to apply themselves to resurrecting and maintaining the quality of our product," Beall says. To reflect consumer demand, she invested $80,000 in new varieties of roses from Europe.

At headquarters in Seattle, Beall improved cost-efficiency, launched customer satisfaction surveys, and—to generate new wholesale accounts—formed a marketing alliance with another producer of premium Colombian roses.

Moving into retailing, she opened a small store in downtown Seattle and a larger one in a suburb, telling the public it could buy magnificent roses, at a fair price, that would last.

"We have proven that high-end rose stores can be made profitable relatively quickly," Beall says. The downtown store was in the black in 14 months but it took the suburban store 16 to reach break-even—a learning experience, Beall says, that indicates the direction of retail expansion she is planning.

Today productivity and production at the farm have increased, and so has quality. In the wholesale market, sales turned up after two tough years, and Beall expects a 20 percent increase this year. Customers say they can't rely on anyone else for comparable roses, she reports.

Beall plans a stock ownership plan for the company's 24 U.S. employees (up from five) and continued solicitude for its 165 Colombian employees (up from 145). Since a rose symbolizes love, she says, if the company doesn't care for its workers, it will have missed the point.

1. Explain the HR challenges associated with the global nature of this business.

2. How has the need for competitiveness driven some of the HR policies of Beall's Flowers?

(Excerpts reprinted by permission of The Blue Chip Enterprise Initiative©, *Real-World Lessons for America's Small Businesses* pp. 1,2; copyright 1994 by Connecticut Mutual Life Insurance Company.) ❖

❖ CASE 2
STONES RIVER UTILITIES
A New Tack in Electrical Contracting

The daughter of an electrical contractor, Jami Wilson knew the darker side of the business.

Her father had to close up shop after several general contractors, forced out of business themselves in a construction recession, couldn't pay what they owed him. An electrical contracting enterprise that she and her brother later started was also unprofitable because of difficult economic times.

Wilson accepted a managerial job at another company, but she really wanted her own business. She tried again, taking a new approach in order to avoid the obstacles she was familiar with.

Instead of working in new construction, her Stones River Utilities, Inc., of Nashville, Tenn., looks for clients that want to outsource electrical maintenance. Businesses and government agencies often can save money by having someone else handle lighting and other electrical servicing, rather than keep people on their payroll to do the job.

Stones River has one contract with the local power company, Nashville Electric Service, to read 1.4 million meters annually and a second to relamp 70,000 street lights. It also has contracts with the Metro Government Water Services (treatment plants and pumping stations), the Nashville Department of Parks and Recreation, the State of Tennessee (over 40 state buildings), and private enterprises including McDonald's restaurants.

Wilson, unable to get a loan initially, started her company with one electrician. Sales volume was $70,000 the first year and rising. With the company shown to be viable, Wilson was able to get capital from an outside investor.

In three years her volume has risen to $800,000 and her staff—ranging from people who do simple tasks like meter reading to skilled employees like journeyman electricians and crane operators—has increased to 25.

Wilson emphasizes sharing ideas with employees, opportunity for advancement, and good benefits. She has developed a bonus-for-attendance program that supplants sick pay. An employee gets four hours' extra pay for a month without an absence. "When our men are not working, our trucks are not working," Wilson explains. She also emphasizes quality in service. For example, a Nashville Electric Service customer with a complaint about meter reading is called personally by Wilson, who corrects the problem and reports to the power company in writing.

Success has made borrowing possible, and Wilson has now bought another firm, Light Incorporated, which owned a fleet of trucks and equipment for light and electrical-sign installation and maintenance. She projects that the two companies, with 45 employees between them, will have a $2 million volume this year.

A "major consideration" in the purchase of Light Incorporated was continuing maintenance contracts it has that will provide revenue during economic downturns, Wilson says. She hopes to win more such contracts. Wilson had a basic philosophy in launching her business that reflected her earlier experiences with electrical contracting. It was, she says, that her company "would not be as affected by adverse conditions in the economy as in the past."

1. What difficulties had to be addressed when Stones River merged with Light Incorporated?

2. Why is the Concept of Outsourcing by customers important for Stones Rivers?

(Excerpts reprinted by permission of The Blue Chip Enterprise Initiative©, *Real-World Lessons for America's Small Businesses* pp. 15, 16; copyright 1994 by Connecticut Mutual Life Insurance Company.) ❖

❖ CASE 3 FLETCHER-TERRY
On the Cutting Edge

TV hostess Oprah Winfrey, notes a report from the Fletcher-Terry Co., once defined luck as "when opportunity meets preparation." Fletcher-Terry, a Farmington, Conn., manufacturer of glass-cutting equipment, was about to get lucky.

Sales rose 16.4 percent that year, 15.4 percent the next year, and 8.6 percent the next. They have continued upward. A preliminary figure for 1993 indicates sales growth for the six-year period totaled 82.5 percent.

It wasn't ever thus.

Fletcher-Terry, which has a plant in Bristol, Conn., as well as one in Farmington, traces its roots to 1868. That was when Samuel Monce, an employee in a Bristol machine shop, improved on a new device that substituted hardened steel for costly diamonds in cutting glass. He invented a steel-wheel cutter and went into partnership with his boss to make it.

In 1894 Monce's nephew, Fred S. Fletcher, who worked for him, got a patent on a replaceable-wheel cutter, and in 1903 manufacturing of Fletcher's device began on the property of Fletcher's father-in-law and partner, Franklin Terry. The Fletcher-Terry Co. bought the Monce Co. in 1935.

The family-owned firm's president and chairman today is Terry B. Fletcher, a grandson of Fred S. Fletcher. In the 1970s the company enjoyed greater growth than ever before, making its traditional product lines of hand-held glass cutters and cutting wheels for the glass, glazing, and hardware markets. Then two distributors, its largest customers, introduced their own private-label cutters, made offshore. Fletcher Terry's sales of hand-held glass cutters were down a staggering 45 percent by the end of 1982. Profits plunged.

Fletcher-Terry invested substantially in technology to cut costs by automating, but the technology never worked. Then the company expanded its products with an imported, private-label line that brought it into competition with its two big customers. But the dollar weakened, and what price advantage the line had was lost. The line was abandoned, with a substantial write-off.

"We realized we would have to change to survive," the company says.

It began a strategic business-planning process, drafting a mission statement and setting objectives that included (1) increasing market share where it was already strong and penetrating other markets with new products; (2) providing technological expertise for its product development; (3) promoting employee involvement and personal growth; and (4) achieving a company growth rate twice the real growth of gross domestic product.

The company invested in plant and process improvements, to cut costs and increase quality. It researched markets in behalf of products old and new and launched marketing and advertising efforts that re-established a traditional claim of being "the first choice of professionals" in its product areas. It established a participatory management environment that fosters creativity and calculated risk-taking.

Today Fletcher-Terry is no longer just "a manufacturer of relatively simple hand tools and equipment for the glass, glazing, and hardware markets," the company says. It is "a manufacturer of mechanically complex equipment and tools for the professional picture framing, photography, sign, hobby, craft, and art markets as well." It can boast of winning awards for quality and of increasing sales abroad as well as at home.

This 126-year-old business still looks proudly at the past. It also looks confidently at the future.

1. Discuss how the implementation of the Strategic Business Plan required a change in the management of Human Resources in the organization.

2. Explain how the training and involvement of employees were critical to Fletcher-Terry's Total Quality Plan.

(Excerpts reprinted by permission of The Blue Chip Enterprise Initiative©, *Real-World Lessons for America's Small Businesses* pp. 54, 55; copyright 1994 by Connecticut Mutual Life Insurance Company.) ❖

SECTION 2

EQUAL EMPLOYMENT OPPORTUNITY

❖

CHAPTER 5
DIVERSITY AND EQUAL EMPLOYMENT OPPORTUNITY

❖

CHAPTER 6
IMPLEMENTING EQUAL EMPLOYMENT

Chapter 5

Diversity and Equal Employment Opportunity

After you have read this chapter, you should be able to . . .

- Define *diversity management,* and discuss what it encompasses.
- Differentiate among diversity management, equal employment opportunity (EEO), and affirmative action.
- Discuss several reasons supporting and opposing affirmative action.
- Explain how to identify when illegal discrimination occurs, and define five basic EEO concepts.
- Discuss the key provisions of the Civil Rights Act of 1964, Title VII, and the Civil Rights Act of 1991.
- Discuss the two general approaches that can be used to comply with the 1978 Uniform Guidelines on Employee Selection Procedures.
- Define *validity* and *reliability,* and explain three approaches to validating employment requirements.

HR IN TRANSITION

THE EEOC AND HOOTERS GUYS

For more than three decades, the focus of most equal employment opportunity (EEO) laws and regulations has been to increase employment opportunities for women and minorities. But one group of individuals increasingly has become embittered about all the efforts to advance women and minorities: white males, particularly those 40 years of age or younger. Their anger and disgust with what they view as *reverse discrimination* has led to current attacks on affirmative action efforts.

Recently, some men have been finding ways to use EEO laws and regulations to raise claims of discriminatory treatment on the basis of their gender. The best-known example involves Hooters, a company that has staffed its restaurants with attractive women, known as *Hooters Girls.* The uniforms of the Hooters Girls consist of short shorts, tank tops or half shirts, and suntan-colored hose. By 1994, in approximately 150 Hooters restaurants, the food staff was virtually all female, and males tended to be hired into kitchen, cook, or "back-room" jobs. Many women's groups criticized the "blatant sexist" appeal used at Hooters restaurants to attract and entertain customers. Meanwhile, employment practices at Hooters caused enough concern that the federal Equal Employment Opportunity Commission (EEOC) began an intensive investigation of Hooters starting in 1991. By 1995, the EEOC had concluded that Hooters was violating EEO laws and regulations by refusing to hire men as wait staff, bartenders, and hosts. The EEOC concluded that the major purpose of Hooters was to be a restaurant and that the use of Hooters Girls was not relevant. Hooters and the EEOC held initial discussions in which the EEOC demanded the following:

Recently, some men have been finding ways to use EEO laws and regulations to raise claims of discriminatory treatment on the basis of their gender.

- ❖ Hooters would establish a fund estimated at over $22 million for men who had been denied employment. Any male who claimed to have applied for one of the "female-designated" jobs would be entitled to up to $10,000.
- ❖ Hooters would run newspaper ads inviting males to file claims and encouraging them to apply at Hooters.
- ❖ Hooters henceforth would be guilty of violating EEO laws anytime the number of men hired fell below 40% of the total hiring rate.
- ❖ Hooters would discontinue using the Hooters Girls in advertising discouraging males from applying for jobs.
- ❖ Hooters would provide sensitivity training to teach Hooters employees how to be more sensitive to men's needs.

Hooters rejected the EEOC demands and ran full-page ads in many newspapers showing a burly man with a mustache wearing a blond wig, tank top, short shorts, and tennis shoes and holding a plate of chicken wings and a sign saying "Washington–Get a Grip." Specifically in response to the EEOC, Hooters' legal counsel stated that "The business of Hooters is predominantly the provision of entertainment, diversion, and amusement based on the sex appeal of the Hooters Girls." That reasoning may seem unusual, but there are legal precedents for using it. In the 1970s and 1980s, Playboy Clubs used similar arguments and won a number of court victories by claiming its policy of hiring attractive women was based on Bona Fide Occupational Qualifications, which are allowed under the 1964 Civil Rights Act.

Hooters also claimed that the EEOC drastically overstated the number of men who had applied for the jobs in question, so that if a male applicant put "any job" on an employment application, he was deemed to have been discriminated against. Consequently, Hooters felt that the EEOC was being so unreasonable that it decided to take the offensive.

As a result of the furor caused by all of the publicity, the EEOC announced that it was dropping its investigation of Hooters. The EEOC Chairman said, "It is wiser for the EEOC to devote its scarce litigation resources to other cases."

The purpose in highlighting this dispute here is not to defend either Hooters or the EEOC but to illustrate how EEO issues have shifted since the passage of the 1964 Civil Rights Act. Readers are encouraged to discuss the issues involved and monitor the legal progress of other cases in which men claim that discrimination against them has occurred.[1]

> "Injustice anywhere is a threat to justice everywhere."
> —Martin Luther King

Organizations are microcosms of the society in which they exist. Therefore, changes and problems in society ultimately will be faced internally by managers. The opening discussion on the EEOC and Hooters illustrates how societal changes can create legal issues for organizations. Until the mid-1980s, employers rarely were confronted with such issues as AIDS policies, smoke-free workplaces, employee drug testing, employer-sponsored child-care assistance, workplace violence, and workforce diversity training. Yet today all of these issues and many others must be addressed in organizations of all sizes and industries by all managers, including HR managers. The purpose of this chapter is to identify why the management of diversity is important and how it is linked to legal requirements related to providing equal employment opportunity for individuals working in organizations.

❖ Nature of Diversity

Diversity Differences among people.

The workforce today is composed of individuals of differing races, ages, cultural and geographic origins, abilities and disabilities, and genders. In addition, varied lifestyles, personalities, family arrangements, and other factors affect individual performance. In summary, people do differ from each other; **diversity** recognizes that people have different characteristics.

The existence of diversity is apparent in most organizations, and it has both positive and negative consequences. On the positive side, it provides organizations opportunities to tap a broader, more diverse set of ideas and experiences of people. Diversity is particularly valuable in an organization because it often reflects the diversity of customers and the marketplace. By capitalizing on the diversity internally, organizations may be able to adapt better to the subtle differences in various customer markets.

On the down side, diversity may initially lead to increased tensions and conflicts in the workplace. People who are part of well-established groups in organizations who have relatively similar backgrounds and racial or ethnic heritages have demonstrated reluctance to accept people who are "different." Fortunately, outright hostility and physical resistance have been seen in relatively few work situations. But certainly the tensions have increased in many other circumstances as diversity efforts have been reflected in work settings. Communication difficulties and conflicts between workers may occur with greater frequency when greater diversity of people is introduced into organizations. Consequently, organizations must be *proactive* in addressing diversity concerns by existing employees, as well as providing support for the individuals with differing backgrounds and heritages.[2] Probably the worst response to diversity is to ignore it. Therefore, the concept of diversity should be viewed broadly, as Figure 5–1 indicates. Any of these factors can create conflict between people at work, which is why organizations have addressed diversity as a strategic human resource issue.

❖ Demographics and Diversity

Diversity is seen in demographic differences in the workforce. The shifting makeup of the U.S. population accounts for today's increased workforce diversity as many organizations follow projections by the U.S. Labor Department:[3]

Organizations today have been seeing the effects of these trends for several years. A more detailed look at some of the key changes follows.

❖ FIGURE 5–1 ❖
DIMENSIONS OF DIVERSITY

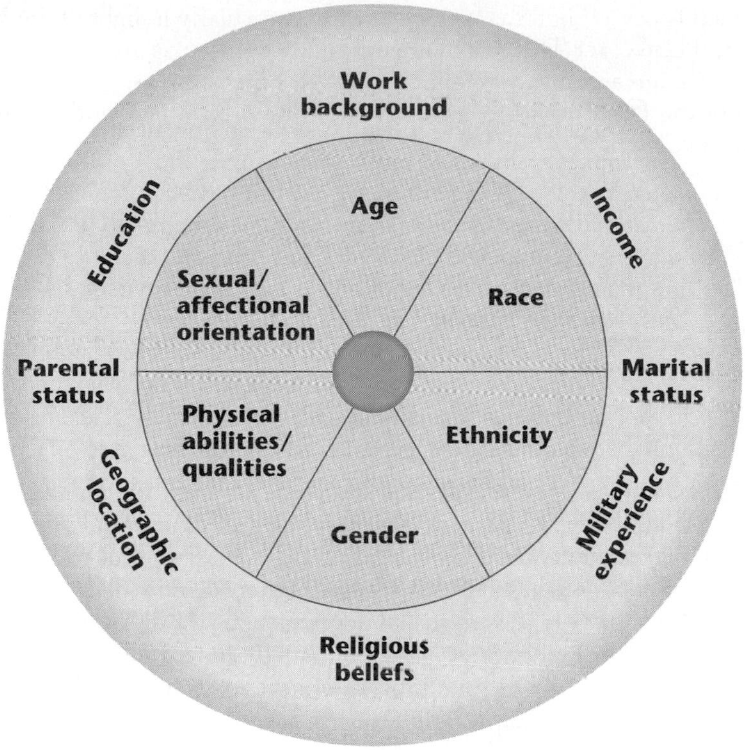

SOURCE: Marilyn Loden and Judy Rosener. *Workforce America! Managing Employee Diversity as a Vital Resource.* Copyright © 1991 by Irwin: Business One. Reprinted with permission from Richard D. Irwin, Inc.

- ❖ Total workforce growth will be slower between 1996 and 2006 than in previous decades.
- ❖ Only one-third of the entrants to the workforce between 1990 and 2005 will be white males.
- ❖ Women will constitute a greater proportion of the labor force than in the past, and 63% of all U.S. women will be in the workforce by 2005.
- ❖ Minority racial and ethnic groups will account for a growing percentage of the overall labor force. Immigrants will expand this growth.
- ❖ The average age of the U.S. population will increase, and more workers who retire from full-time jobs will work part time. The total number of individuals aged 16 to 24 available to enter the workforce will decrease.
- ❖ As a result of these shifts, employers in a variety of industries will face shortages of qualified workers.

WOMEN IN THE WORKFORCE The influx of women into the workforce has major social and economic consequences. From 1970 to 1990, the percentage of women of working age in the workforce rose from 43% to 57%. It is projected that 63% of all women of working age, and over 80% of women from 25 to 40 years old, will be working or looking for work by 2000. This increase will mean that women will make up 47% of the total workforce by 2005. Further, about half of all working women are single, separated, divorced, widowed, or otherwise single heads of households. Consequently, they are "primary" income earners, not co–income providers.

One major consequence of having an increased percentage of women in the workforce is that balancing work and family issues will continue to grow in importance. As mentioned in Chapter 2, employers increasingly are having to address such issues as child care and elder care, particularly in light of the Family and Medical Leave Act (FMLA) requirements. In summary, as more women enter the workforce, greater diversity will be found in organizations.

Some of the implications for HR activities of more women working include the following:

- Greater flexibility in work patterns and schedules to accommodate women with family responsibilities, part-time work interests, or other pressures.
- More variety in benefits programs and HR policies, including child-care assistance and parental-leave programs.
- Job placement assistance for working spouses whose mates are offered relocation transfers.
- Greater employer awareness of gender-related legal issues such as sexual harassment and sex discrimination.

Racial/Ethnic Diversity in the Workforce The fastest-growing segments of the U.S. population are minority racial and ethnic groups, especially Hispanics, African Americans, and Asian Americans. By 2000, about 30% of the U.S. population will be from such groups. Already, "minority" individuals make up a majority in many cities of at least 100,000 population in California, Texas, and Florida. Some of the changes in racial/ethnic groups are as follows:

- The population of Asian Americans increased 108% from 1980 to 1990 and is expected to jump fivefold from 1990 to 2050, with half of these people being foreign born.
- The number of African Americans in the labor force is expected to grow twice as fast as the number of whites from 1990 to 2000.
- Hispanics will be the largest minority group by 2010. Projections are that about 20% of the U.S. population will be Hispanic by 2020, with the number of Hispanics having tripled by then. Also, the percentage of Hispanics in the workforce will double by 2010.

Much of the growth in the various racial and ethnic groups is due to immigration from other countries. Approximately 700,000 immigrants are arriving annually in the United States. As Figure 5–2 shows, immigration patterns have changed over the past four decades. During the 1950s, most immigrants were Europeans, whereas in the 1990s, Hispanics and Asians predominated. Today, about one-third of immigrants have less than a high school education, while about one-fourth are college graduates. Increasingly, people with advanced degrees in science and engineering being hiring by U.S. firms are foreign born.[4]

Implications of the increase in racial and ethnic cultural diversity are as follows:

- The potential for work-related conflicts among various racial and ethnic groups will increase.
- Extensive employer-sponsored cultural awareness and diversity training will be required to defuse conflicts and promote multicultural understanding.
- Training in communication skills for those with English as a second language will increase, and job training will have to accommodate the different language abilities of a multicultural workforce.
- Employees skilled in more than one language will be vital, particularly in service industries in certain geographic locales.
- Greater cultural diversity in dress, customs, and lifestyles will be permitted by employers.

Figure 5–2
Origins of Immigrants to the United States
SOURCE: Based on data from the U.S. Immigration and Naturalization Service, 1995.

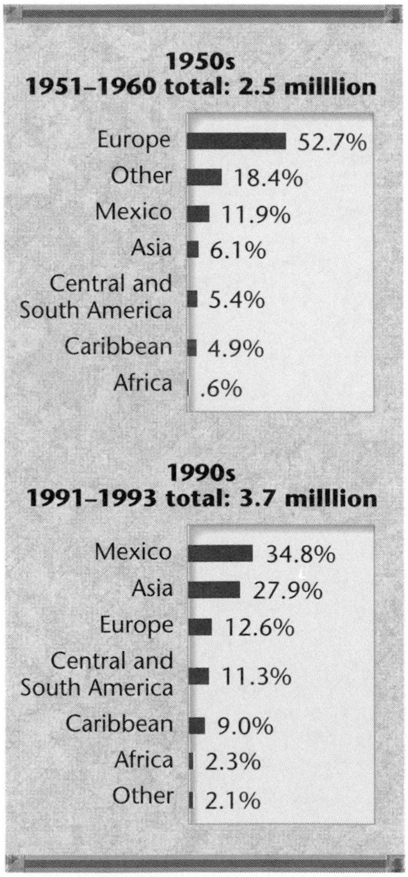

Aging of the Workforce Most of the developed countries are experiencing an aging of their populations—including Australia, Japan, most European countries, and the United States. In the United States, the median age will increase from 31.5 in 1986 to 39 by 2000. This increase is due in part to people living longer and in part to a decrease in the number of children, particularly in the 16–24 age bracket. Little growth in this "teen" age group is projected until at least 2000.

One of the major implications of the age shift is that employers such as hotels, fast-food chains, and retailers will continue to face significant staffing difficulties. Employers are attracting more older persons to return to the workforce through the use of part-time and other scheduling options. According to the U.S. Bureau of Labor Statistics, the number of workers aged 55 to 64 holding part-time jobs has been increasing. Many of these older workers are people who lost their jobs in organizational restructurings or who took early retirement buyout packages.

A 1996 change in Social Security regulations allows individuals over age 65 to earn more per year without affecting their Social Security payments. As a result, it is likely that the number of older workers interested in working part time will increase and that they will work more hours than previously. By 2002, the earnings limit will be $30,000 per year, up from $11,520 in 1996.[5]

Implications of the shifting age of the U.S. workforce include the following:

- Retirement will change in character as organizations and older workers choose phased retirements, early retirement buyouts, and part-time work.
- Service industries will actively recruit senior workers for many jobs.
- Retirement benefits will increase in importance, particularly pension and health-care coverage for retirees.
- Fewer promotion opportunities will exist for midcareer baby boomers and the baby busters below them in experience.
- Baby boomers will have more "multiple" careers as they leave organizations (voluntarily or through organizational restructurings) and/or as they start their own businesses.

Individuals with Disabilities in the Workforce Another group adding diversity to the workforce is composed of individuals with disabilities. With the passage of the Americans with Disabilities Act (ADA) in 1990, employers were reminded of their responsibilities for employing individuals with disabilities. At least 43 million Americans with disabilities are covered by the ADA. The disabilities of this group are shown in Figure 5–3 on page 126. Estimates are that up to 10 million of these individuals could be added to the workforce if appropriate accommodations were made. The number of individuals with disabilities is expected to continue growing as the workforce ages. Also, people with AIDS or other life-threatening illnesses are considered disabled, and their numbers are expected to increase. The ADA is discussed further in Chapter 6.

Implications of greater employment of individuals with disabilities include the following:

- Employers must define more precisely what are the essential tasks in jobs and what knowledge, skills, and abilities are needed to perform each job.
- Accommodating individuals with disabilities will become more common by providing more flexible work schedules, altering facilities, and purchasing special equipment.
- Nondisabled workers will be trained in ways to work with coworkers with disabilities.

❖ FIGURE 5–3 ❖
DISABLED POPULATION IN THE UNITED STATES

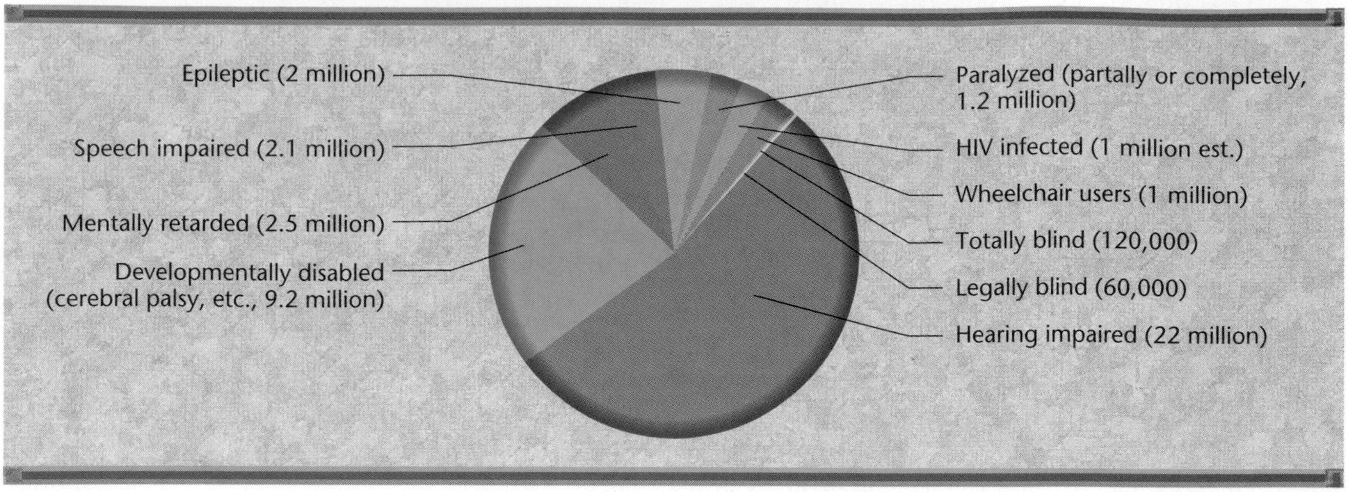

SOURCE: Office of Special Education and Rehabilitative Services, Centers for Disease Control.

- ❖ Employment-related health and medical examination requirements will be revised to avoid discriminating against individuals with disabilities.

INDIVIDUALS WITH DIFFERING SEXUAL ORIENTATIONS IN THE WORKFORCE As if demographic diversity did not place pressure enough on managers and organizations, individuals in the workforce today have widely varying lifestyles that can have work-related consequences. A growing number of employers are facing legislative efforts to protect individuals with differing sexual orientations from employment discrimination, though at present, only a few cities and states have passed such laws. In addition, there are growing concerns about balancing employee privacy rights with legitimate employer requirements.

Some of the implications of these issues include the following:

- ❖ The potential for workplace conflicts is heightened as people with different lifestyles and sexual orientations work together. Training to reduce such conflicts will be necessary.
- ❖ Access to employee records will be limited, and the types of information kept must be reviewed.
- ❖ Generally, managers must recognize that they should not attempt to "control" off-the-job behavior of employees unless it has a direct, negative effect on the organization. Even then, difficulties may exist.

❖ MANAGEMENT OF DIVERSITY

Diversity Management
Efforts concerned with developing organizational initiatives that value all people equally, regardless of their differences.

All of these changes have led organizations and HR professionals to make management of diversity part of their change processes. **Diversity management** is concerned with developing organizational initiatives that value all people equally, regardless of their differences. With the management of diversity at the forefront of HR, organizations have taken various approaches to diversity.

APPROACHES TO DIVERSITY According to Roosevelt Thomas of the American Institute for Managing Diversity, there are three approaches to diversity.[6]

- *Traditional.* The traditional approach requires that diverse individuals be assimilated into the workforce by use of affirmative action programs, so that an employee "melting pot" is achieved.
- *Understanding.* The objective of understanding diversity is to expand the abilities of employees to understand, accept, and value differences among coworkers.
- *Managing.* Management of diversity is a continuing process requiring a variety of proactive efforts by employers, managers, and employees.

Employers' Efforts to Address Diversity A growing number of employers have taken steps to address diversity issues and incorporate management of diversity throughout their organizations. One study of the 50 largest corporations in the United States found that 72% of them have formal programs for managing diversity. Except in some manufacturing areas, these programs go beyond traditional approaches and focus on diversity training.[7] Figure 5–4 shows the wide range of areas that can be addressed in managing diversity.

Figure 5–4
Spheres of Activity in Management of Cultural Diversity

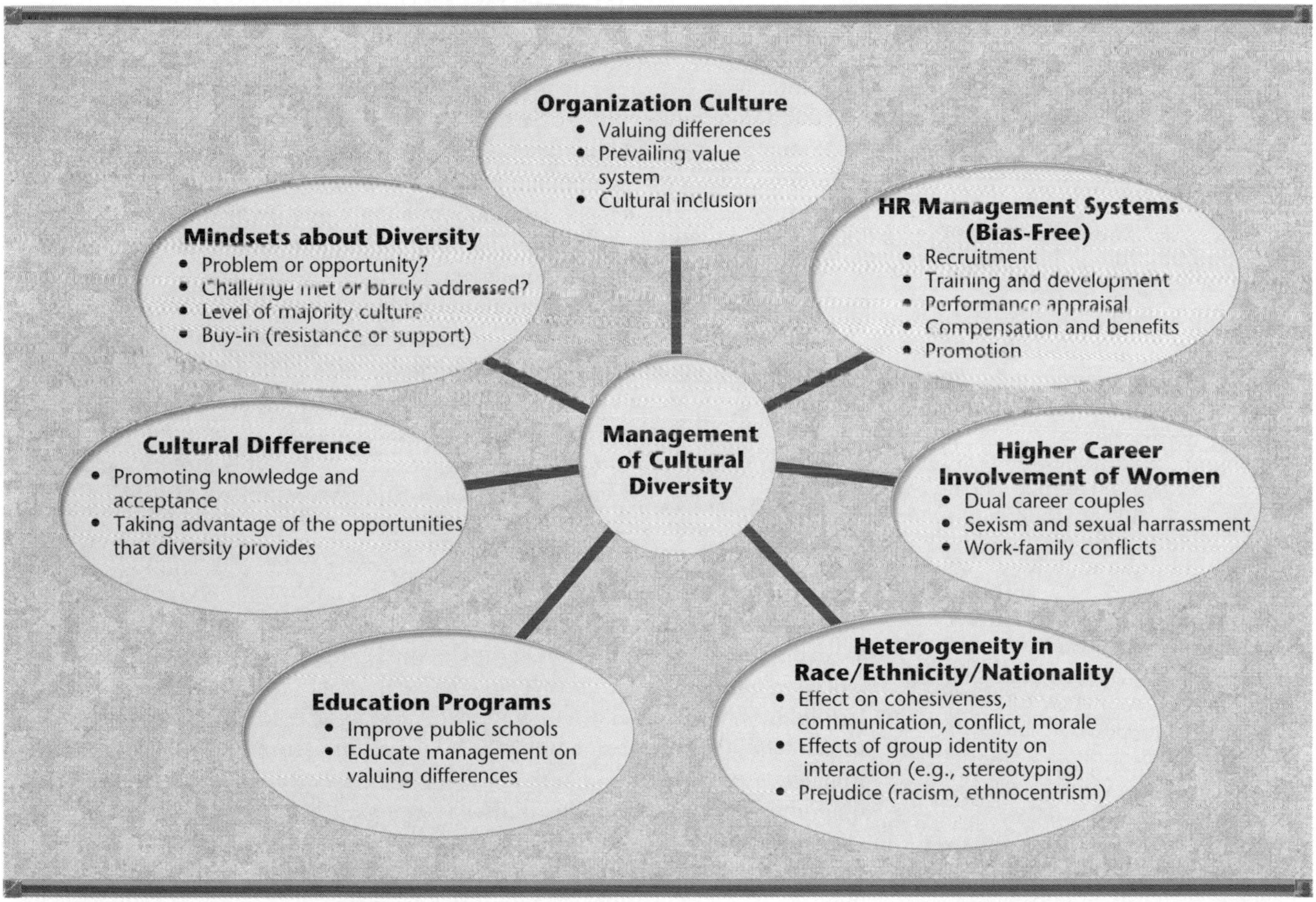

SOURCE: Taylor H. Cox and Stacey Blake, "Managing Cultural Diversity: Implications for Organizational Competitiveness," *The Academy of Management EXECUTIVE,* August 1991, 46.

In contrast, a study of 785 employers of all sizes found that diversity was rated by a majority of responding HR professionals as lower in priority than profitability, market share, capital investments, health-care costs, total quality management, and restructuring and downsizing. The study indicated that legal concerns still dominate diversity efforts among respondents, with sexual harassment policies, access for individuals with disabilities, and EEO/affirmative action policies and programs cited frequently as diversity efforts.[8] One conclusion based on this study was that many of the firms had not gone beyond the traditional approach to diversity, which stresses compliance with various laws and regulations.

But there are numerous examples of employers that have found that cultural diversity efforts benefit their organizations.[9] For instance, at Harvard's Pilgrim Health Care, which employs 8,000 people in four states, managers and executives have diversity management as a component of their performance goals, and their compensation can be affected positively or negatively by their diversity management efforts.[10]

By addressing diversity issues and managing them effectively, organizations benefit in various ways. Conflicts within the organization can be ameliorated, better productivity can result, and the organization can be more attractive to potential applicants and current employees.[11]

❖ Diversity, Equal Employment, and Affirmative Action

It is very easy to state that diversity exists, and most people recognize that there are differences between themselves and others. However, acceptance of diversity is another matter when the rights of an individual are affected by someone else because of such differences. The debate about differences and how they should be handled in employment situations has led to various effects. To assist in identifying the issues involved in workplace diversity, it is critical that terminology often used generally and incorrectly be clarified.

Figure 5–5 shows that diversity management is the highest level at which organizations have addressed diversity issues. To review, diversity management is concerned with developing organizational initiatives that value all people equally, regardless of their differences. In the management of diversity, organizational efforts are made by both the organization and the individuals in it to adapt to and accept the importance of diversity.

As the figure shows, organizations can also address diversity issues in more restricted ways: equal employment opportunity and affirmative action. These levels are discussed next.

❖ Equal Employment Opportunity

Equal Employment Opportunity (EEO)
The concept that individuals should have equal treatment in all employment-related actions.

Protected Class
Those individuals who fall within a group identified for protection under equal employment laws and regulations.

Equal employment opportunity (EEO) is a broad concept holding that individuals should have equal treatment in all employment-related actions. Individuals who are covered under equal employment laws are protected from illegal discrimination, which occurs when individuals having a common characteristic are discriminated against based on that characteristic. Various laws have been passed to protect individuals who share certain characteristics, such as race, age, or gender. Those having the designated characteristics are referred to as a protected class or as members of a protected group. A **protected class** is composed of individuals who fall within a group identified for protection under equal employment laws and regulations. Many of the protected classes historically have been subjected to illegal discrimination. The following bases for protection have been identified by various federal laws:

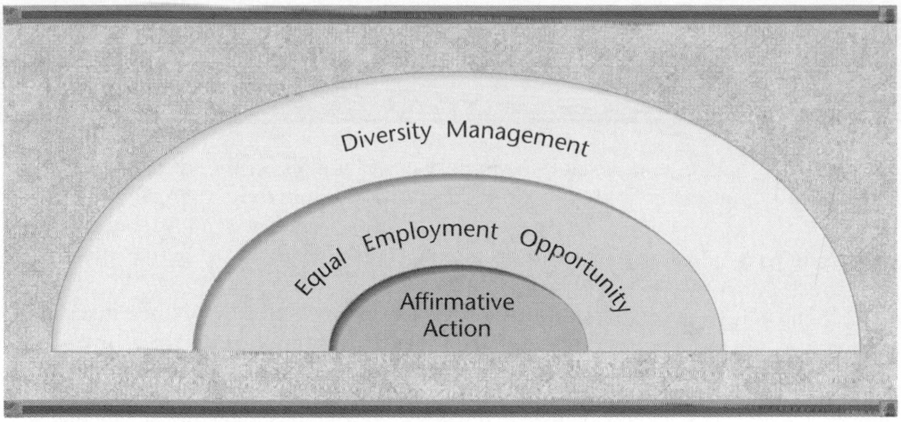

❖ FIGURE 5–5 ❖
DIVERSITY MANAGEMENT, EQUAL EMPLOYMENT OPPORTUNITY, AND AFFIRMATIVE ACTION

- *Race, ethnic origin, color* (African Americans, Hispanics, Native Americans, Asian Americans)
- *Gender* (women, including those who are pregnant)
- *Age* (individuals over 40)
- *Individuals with disabilities* (physical or mental)
- *Military experience* (Vietnam-era veterans)
- *Religion* (special beliefs and practices)

For instance, suppose a firm that is attempting to comply with EEO regulations has relatively few Hispanic managers. To increase the number of Hispanics, the firm will take steps to recruit and interview Hispanics who meet the minimum qualifications for the management jobs. Notice that what the firm is providing is equal employment opportunity for *qualified* individuals to be considered for employment. To remedy areas in which it appears that individuals in protected classes have not had equal employment opportunities, some employers have developed affirmative action policies.

❖ AFFIRMATIVE ACTION

Affirmative action occurs when employers identify problem areas, set goals, and take positive steps to guarantee equal employment opportunities for people in a protected class. Affirmative action focuses on hiring, training, and promoting of protected-class members where they are *underrepresented* in an organization in relation to their availability in the labor markets from which recruiting occurs. Sometimes employers have instituted affirmative action voluntarily, but many times employers have been required to do so because they are government contractors having over 50 employees and over $50,000 in government contracts annually.

***Affirmative Action**
A process in which employers identify problem areas, set goals, and take positive steps to guarantee equal employment opportunities for people in a protected class.

AFFIRMATIVE ACTION VERSUS REVERSE DISCRIMINATION When equal employment opportunity regulations are discussed, probably the most volatile issues concern the view that affirmative action leads to *quotas, preferential selection,* and *reverse discrimination.* At the heart of the conflict is the employers' role in selecting, training, and promoting protected-class members when they are underrepresented in various jobs in an organization. Those who are not members of any protected class have claimed that they are being discriminated against in reverse.[12] **Reverse discrimination** is said to exist when a person is denied an opportunity because of preferences given to a member of a protected class who may be less qualified. Specifically, some critics charge that white males are at a disadvantage

***Reverse Discrimination**
A condition that may exist when a person is denied an opportunity because of preferences given to protected-class individuals who may be less qualified.

HR PERSPECTIVE

Debate: Why Affirmative Action Is Needed

Supporters have offered many reasons why affirmative action is necessary and important. Some of the common reasons are given here.

1. **Affirmative action is needed to overcome past injustices or eliminate the effects of those injustices.** Proponents of affirmative action believe it is necessary because of the historical inequities that have existed in the United States. In particular, women and racial minorities have long been subjected to unfair employment treatment by being relegated to lower positions (such as clerical and low-paying jobs), not being considered qualified, and being discriminated against for promotions. Without affirmative action, the inequities will continue to exist for individuals who are not white males.
2. **Women and minorities have taken the brunt of the inequality in the past; but now more equality can be created, even if temporary injustice to some may result.** White males in particular may be disadvantaged temporarily in order for affirmative action to create broader opportunities for all—the greatest good. Proponents argue that there must be programs to ensure that women and minorities be considered for employment opportunities so that they can be competitive with males and nonminorities. An often-cited example is that in a running contest, someone running against a well-trained athlete starts at a disadvantage. Women and minorities have had such a disadvantage. Consequently, for a period of time, they should be given a head start in order to ensure that a truly competitive contest occurs.
3. **Raising the employment level of women and minorities will benefit U.S. society in the long run.** Statistics consistently indicate that the greatest percentage of those in lower socioeconomic groups belong to minority groups. If affirmative action assists these minorities, then it is a means to address socioeconomic disparities. Without affirmative action, proponents believe that a large percentage of the U.S. population will be consigned to being permanently economically disadvantaged. When economic levels are low, other social ills proliferate, such as single-parent families, crime, drug use, and educational disparities. Ultimately, then, a vicious circle of desperation will continue unless special efforts are made to provide access to better jobs for all individuals.
4. **Properly used, affirmative action does not discriminate against males or nonminorities.** An affirmative action plan should remedy a situation in which disproportionately few women and minorities are employed compared with their numbers in the labor markets from which they are drawn. The plan should have a deadline for accomplishing its long-term goals. All individuals must meet the qualifications for jobs. Once all of these job criteria are established, qualified women or minorities should be chosen. In this way, those not selected are discriminated against only in the sense that they did not get the jobs.

   Proponents of affirmative action also stress that affirmative action involves not *quotas* but *goals*. The difference is that quotas are specific, required numbers, whereas goals are targets for "good faith" efforts to ensure that protected-class individuals truly are given consideration when employment-related decisions are made.
5. **Affirmative action promotes long-term civility and tolerance through forced interaction.** The United States is a diverse country facing social integration issues, and change is occurring rapidly. In order to staff their jobs, employers will have to tap the talents of the diverse members of the U.S. labor force and to find ways for all inhabitants to work together effectively. When women and minorities are placed in widely varying work environments and males and nonminorities interact and work with them, there will be greater understanding among the diverse peoples in the United States. Additionally, women and minorities who are given opportunities can become role models that will make preferences in the future unnecessary. Thus, if successful, affirmative action ultimately may no longer be necessary.

today, even though they traditionally have held many of the better jobs. These critics say that white males are having to "pay for the sins of their fathers."[13] The accompanying HR Perspectives provide both views.[14]

It has been stated by some that the use of affirmative action to remedy under-representation of protected-class members is really a form of *quotas,* or "hiring by the numbers." However, the Civil Rights Act of 1991 specifically prohibits the

HR PERSPECTIVE

Debate: Why Affirmative Action Should Be Eliminated

While proponents argue in favor of affirmative action, opponents argue against it. They offer the following reasons why affirmative action should be eliminated.

1. **Creating preferences for women and minorities results in reverse discrimination.** Those opposed to affirmative action believe that discriminating *for* someone means discriminating *against* someone else. If equality is the ultimate aim, then discriminating for or against anyone on any basis other than the knowledge, skills, and abilities needed to perform jobs is wrong. Equal employment opportunity means that people should compete for jobs according to their qualifications. If any factor such as gender or race is considered in addition to qualifications, then there is discrimination in reverse, which is counter to creating a truly equal society.
2. **Affirmative action results in greater polarization and separatism along gender and racial lines.** The opponents of affirmative action believe that affirmative action establishes two groups: women and minorities who are in protected classes and everyone else. For any job, a person will clearly fall into one group or the other. In reality, according to affirmative action classification efforts, women may or may not fall into the "special" category, depending on whether there has been disparate impact on them. Thus, affirmative action may be applicable to some groups but not to others in various employment situations. Regardless of the basis for classification, affirmative action results in males and nonminorities being affected negatively because of their gender or race. Consequently, they become bitter against the protected groups, leading to greater racism or prejudice.
3. **Affirmative action stigmatizes those it is designed to help.** The opponents of affirmative action cite examples wherein less qualified women and minorities were given jobs or promotions over more qualified males and nonminorities. When protected-class individuals perform poorly in jobs because they do not have the knowledge, skills, and abilities needed, the result is to reinforce gender or racial stereotypes.

   Because affirmative action has come to be viewed by some people as placing unqualified women and minorities in jobs, it reinforces the beliefs held by some that women and minorities could not succeed on their own efforts. Thus, any women or minority members who have responsible positions are only there because of who they are, not because of what they can do and have done.
4. **Affirmative action penalizes individuals (males and nonminorities) even though they have not been guilty of practicing discrimination.** Opponents argue that affirmative action is unfair to "innocent victims"—males and nonminorities. These "innocent victims" had nothing to do with past discrimination or disparate impact and were not even present at the time. Thus, the opponents of affirmative action wonder why these individuals should have to pay for the remediation of these discriminatory actions.
5. **Preferences through affirmative action lead to conflicts between protected groups.** In this argument, opponents cite examples that illustrate how using preferences for one underrepresented racial minority group has led to discrimination against women or members of another racial minority group when these groups were adequately represented. Conflicts between African American organizations and Asian American organizations are one example. Another is the situation in which Hispanics have sued employers because African Americans were overrepresented.

   Closely related is the difficulty of "classifying" people at all. While gender is a bit clearer, melding of races and backgrounds has made racial/ethnic classification difficult. If someone has parents and grandparents from three different ethnic groups, it is difficult to determine how the person should be classified. Thus, focusing on someone's racial/ethnic background may lead to multiple or inaccurate classifications. This process points out the difficulties of classifying people in any way other than by their qualifications and abilities according to those opposed to affirmative action.

use of quotas. It also sets limits on when affirmative action plans can be challenged by individuals who are not members of a protected class. Some of the phrases that are used to convey that affirmative action goals are not quotas include "relative numbers," "appropriately represented," "representative sample," and "balanced workforce."

Along with the economic restructuring of many organizations has come a growing backlash against affirmative action. As noted, some see it as an unfair quota system rather than sound HR management. Proponents of affirmative action maintain that it is a proactive way for employers to ensure that protected-class members have equal opportunity in all aspects of employment and that it is indeed sound management. The accompanying HR Perspective provides both viewpoints.[14]

Court Decisions and Legislation on Affirmative Action Increasingly, court decisions and legislative efforts have focused on restricting the use of affirmative action. One example is the California Civil Rights Initiative (CCRI) which stated that the State of California and its subdivisions

> shall not discriminate against or grant preferential treatment to any individual or group on the basis of race, sex, color, ethnicity or national origin in the operation of public employment, public education, or public contracting.[15]

The philosophy behind the CCRI has been seen in U.S. federal court decisions also. For instance, in the *Adarand Constructors v. Peña* case, involving the "setting aside" of a percentage of government contracts for firms owned by women or minorities, the U.S. Supreme Court by a 5- to 4-vote ruled that federal affirmative action efforts designed to benefit racial minorities and remedy past discrimination must meet "strict scrutiny" standards. This means that, as stated by Justice O'Connor in the majority decision,

> strict scrutiny of all government racial classifications is essential to distinguish between legitimate programs that redress past discrimination and programs that are in fact motivated by illegitimate notions of racial inferiority or single racial politics.[16]

The decision did not say that affirmative action plans were unconstitutional, however.

As a result of this decision, President Bill Clinton directed that all federal agencies eliminate programs that create quotas, use preferences for unqualified individuals, or create reverse discrimination. However, in later speeches, Clinton strongly backed continued use of affirmative action efforts that do not violate the Supreme Court standards.

Further legal clarification of affirmative action came from a 1996 federal court decision regarding admission standards at the University of Texas Law School. The university used separate admissions committees to evaluate minority and nonminority applicants. The suit was brought by Cheryl Hopwood and three other students who were denied admission to the law school, even though they had test scores and grade point averages significantly higher than those of a majority of African Americans and Hispanics who were admitted.

Clarifying an earlier case, *Bakke v. University of California,*[17] the Fifth Circuit Court of Appeals in *Hopwood v. State of Texas* ruled:

> The use of race in admissions for diversity in higher education contradicts, rather than furthers, the aims of equal protection. Diversity fosters, rather than minimizes, the use of race. It treats minorities as a group, rather than as individuals. It may further remedial purposes, but just as likely, may promote improper racial stereotypes, thus fueling racial hostility.[18]

That clear statement illustrates the idea that affirmative action as a concept is under major attack by courts, employers, and males and nonminorities. Upon appeal, the U.S. Supreme Court allowed the previous decision to stand. Whether that trend continues will depend on future changes in the makeup of the U.S. Supreme Court and the results of presidential and Congressional elections.

The authors of this text believe that whether one supports or opposes affirmative action, it is important to understand why its supporters believe that it is needed and why its opponents believe it should be discontinued. Because the "final" status of affirmative action has not been determined, we have presented the arguments on both sides of the debate without advocating one position or the other.

❖ IMPORTANCE OF EEO AND DIVERSITY MANAGEMENT

Regardless of the ultimate outcome of the debate on affirmative action, it is critical that employers recognize the diversity of their workforces and that diversity issues be addressed. Many employers have stated that their employees truly are assets and represent human capital that has accumulated value for the organization. As a result, managing diversity effectively and providing equal employment opportunities are elements of good business, resulting in the full use of the talents present in the widely diverse workforce of today. The accompanying HR Perspective describes a research study on how the effectiveness of EEO efforts are affected by HR management.

First and most important, effective management of human resources requires understanding that all people have knowledge, skills, and abilities that can be used by organizations today. For instance, the necessary level of manual dexterity or creative reasoning required by a job is not limited to certain race, gender, or age groups. Nor are mathematical aptitudes or computer skills factors that are genetically exclusive to some and not to others. In summary, tapping the potential of all individuals in order to achieve organizational goals and objectives is basic to HR management.

HR PERSPECTIVE

RESEARCH ON EEO EFFECTIVENESS AND HR MANAGEMENT

The link between EEO policies and practices and the effectiveness of HR management has been discussed extensively. To gather data on this link and address it specifically, Konrad and Linnehan conducted a study the results of which were published in the *Academy of Management Journal.* The authors studied several facets of the issue by developing a survey based on interviews with some HR executives and consultants. The survey contained 119 questions asking how formalized HR structures and practices were. Of the 350 survey questionnaires mailed to HR executives in the Philadelphia area, 138 surveys were returned.

One major topic examined was the effect of governmental EEO efforts on HR practices. As would be expected, the study revealed that the EEO requirements had caused more firms to develop policies and practices to reduce their EEO risks. In particular, the researchers found that EEO enforcement efforts had been applied to firms with poorer EEO records. Also, the attitudes of top managers were found to be significant in predicting the effectiveness of EEO efforts.

The importance of the efforts of the HR department in ensuring equal employment was highlighted. The study found that because EEO efforts often are decentralized and then administered by HR professionals for the entire organization, the actions of the HR department play a major role in determining the effectiveness of organizational efforts for EEO.

In summary, the study found that two major factors contribute to the effectiveness of EEO efforts in organizations. If those efforts are 1) supported by top management and 2) implemented and administered well by the HR department, then EEO is more likely to be integrated throughout the organization.[19]

Even if an organization has no regard for the principles of EEO, it must follow federal, state, and local EEO laws and regulations to avoid costly penalties. Whether violations of such laws occur intentionally, accidently, or through ignorance, many employers have learned the hard way that they may be required to pay back wages, reinstate individuals to their jobs, reimburse attorneys' fees, and possibly pay punitive damages. Even if not guilty, the employer still will have considerable costs in HR staff and managerial time involved and legal fees. Therefore, it is financially prudent to establish an organizational culture in which compliance with EEO laws and regulations is expected.

❖ Interpretations of EEO Laws and Regulations

Laws establishing the legal basis for equal employment opportunity generally have been written broadly. Consequently, only through application to specific organizational situations can one see how the laws affect employers.

❖ Interpretation Difficulties

The broad nature of the laws has led enforcement agencies to develop guidelines and to enforce the acts as they deem appropriate. However, agency rulings and the language of those rulings have caused confusion and have been interpreted differently by employers. Interpretation of ambiguous provisions in the laws also shifts as the membership of the agencies changes.

The court system is left to resolve the disputes and issue interpretations of the laws. The courts, especially the lower courts, have issued conflicting rulings and interpretations. The ultimate interpretation often has rested on decisions by the U.S. Supreme Court, although Supreme Court rulings, too, have been interpreted differently. Thus, equal employment opportunity is an evolving concept that often is confusing.

❖ When Does Illegal Discrimination Occur?

Equal employment laws and regulations address concerns about discrimination in employment practices. The word *discrimination* simply means that differences among items or people are recognized. Thus, discrimination involves choosing among alternatives. For example, employers must discriminate (choose) among applicants for a job on the basis of job requirements and candidates' qualifications. However, discrimination can be illegal in employment-related situations in which either: (1) different standards are used to judge different individuals, or (2) the same standard is used, but it is not related to the individuals' jobs.

When deciding if and when illegal discrimination has occurred, courts and regulatory agencies have had to consider the following issues:

- ❖ Employer intentions
- ❖ Disparate treatment
- ❖ Disparate impact
- ❖ Business necessity and job-relatedness
- ❖ Bona fide occupational qualifications
- ❖ Burden of proof
- ❖ Retaliation

Disparate Treatment and Disparate Impact It would seem that the motives or intentions of the employer might enter into the determination of whether discrimination has occurred—but they do not. It is the outcome of the employer's actions, not the intent, that will be considered by the regulatory agencies or courts when deciding if illegal discrimination has occurred. Two concepts used to activate this principle are *disparate treatment* and *disparate impact.*

Disparate treatment occurs when protected-class members are treated differently from others. For example, if female applicants must take a special skills test not given to male applicants, then disparate treatment may be occurring. If disparate treatment has occurred, the courts generally have said that intentional discrimination exists.

Disparate Treatment Situation that exists when protected-class members are treated differently from others.

Disparate impact occurs when there is a substantial underrepresentation of protected-class members as a result of employment decisions that work to their disadvantage. The landmark case that established the importance of disparate impact as a legal foundation of EEO law is *Griggs v. Duke Power* (1971).[20] The decision of the U.S. Supreme Court established two major points:

Disparate Impact Situation that exists when there is a substantial underrepresentation of protected-class members as a result of employment decisions that work to their disadvantage.

1. It is not enough to show a lack of discriminatory intent if the employment tool results in a disparate impact that discriminates against one group more than another or continues a past pattern of discrimination.
2. The employer has the burden of proving that an employment requirement is directly job related as a "business necessity." Consequently, the intelligence test and high school diploma requirements of Duke Power were ruled not to be related to the job.

Business Necessity and Job-Relatedness A **business necessity** is a practice necessary for safe and efficient organizational operations. Business necessity has been the subject of numerous court decisions. Educational requirements often are based on business necessity. However, an employer who requires a minimum level of education, such as a high school diploma, must be able to defend the requirement as essential to the performance of the job. For instance, equating a degree or diploma with the possession of math or reading abilities is considered questionable. Having a general requirement for a degree cannot always be justified on the basis of the need for a certain level of ability. All requirements must be *job related,* or proven necessary for job performance. Determining and defending the job-relatedness of employment requirements through validation procedures is discussed later in this chapter.

Business Necessity A practice necessary for safe and efficient organizational operations.

Bona Fide Occupational Qualification (BFOQ) Title VII of the 1964 Civil Rights Act specifically states that employers may discriminate on the basis of sex, religion, or national origin if the characteristic can be justified as a "bona fide occupational qualification reasonably necessary to the normal operation of the particular business or enterprise."[21] Thus, a **bona fide occupational qualification (BFOQ)** is a legitimate reason why an employer can exclude persons on otherwise illegal bases of consideration. What constitutes a BFOQ has been subject to different interpretations in various courts across the country.

Bona Fide Occupational Qualification (BFOQ) A characteristic providing a legitimate reason why an employer can exclude persons on otherwise illegal bases of consideration.

Burden of Proof Another legal issue that arises when discrimination is alleged is the determination of which party has the *burden of proof.* At issue is what individuals who are filing suit against employers must prove in order to establish that illegal discrimination has occurred.

Based on the evolution of court decisions, current laws and regulations state that the plaintiff charging discrimination (1) must be a protected-class member and (2) must prove that disparate impact or disparate treatment existed. For instance, in *McDonnell Douglas v. Green* (1973), the U.S. Supreme Court ruled that a preliminary *(prima facie)* case of discrimination existed by showing that: (1) the person (Green) was a member of a protected class, (2) the person applied for and was qualified for a job but was rejected, and (3) the employer (McDonnell Douglas) continued to seek other applicants after the rejection occurred.[22]

This case indicates that once a court rules that a *prima facie* case has been made, the burden of proof shifts to the employer. The employer then must show that the bases for making employment-related decisions were specifically job related and consistent with considerations of business necessity.

In *Texas Department of Community Affairs v. Burdine* in 1981, the Supreme Court, in ruling against Burdine, decided that an employer need only establish a business-related nondiscriminatory reason for not hiring or promoting a member of a protected group. The employer does not have to prove that the hired individual was *more qualified* than the protected-class person. Thus, the individual charging illegal discrimination has the burden of establishing that illegal discrimination occurred.[23]

***Retaliation**
Punitive actions taken by employers against individuals who exercise their legal rights.

RETALIATION Employers are prohibited by EEO laws from retaliating against individuals who file discrimination charges. **Retaliation** occurs when employers take punitive actions against individuals who exercise their legal rights. For example, an employer was ruled to have engaged in retaliation when an employee who filed a discrimination charge was assigned undesirable hours and his work schedule was changed frequently.[24] Various laws, including Title VII of the Civil Rights Act of 1964, protect individuals who have: (1) "made a charge, testified, assisted, or participated in any investigation, proceeding, or hearing" or (2) "opposed any practice made unlawful."[25]

❖ CIVIL RIGHTS ACTS OF 1964 AND 1991

Numerous federal, state, and local laws address equal employment opportunity concerns. As the chart in Figure 5–6 indicates, some laws have a general civil rights emphasis, while others address specific EEO issues and concerns. At this point, it is important to discuss two major broad-based civil rights acts that encompass many areas. In the next chapter, specific acts and priorities will be discussed.

❖ CIVIL RIGHTS ACT OF 1964, TITLE VII

Although the first Civil Rights Act was passed in 1866, it was not until the passage of the Civil Rights Act of 1964 that the keystone of antidiscrimination legislation was put into place. The Civil Rights Act of 1964 was passed in part to bring about equality in all employment-related decisions. As is often the case, the law contains ambiguous provisions giving considerable leeway to agencies that enforce the law. The Equal Employment Opportunity Commission (EEOC) was established to enforce the provisions of Title VII, the portion of the act that deals with employment.

PROVISIONS OF TITLE VII In Title VII, Section 703(a) of the act it states:

> It shall be unlawful employment practice for an employer: (1) to fail or refuse to hire or to discharge any individual, or otherwise to discriminate against any individual with respect to his compensation, terms, conditions, or privileges of employment, because of such individual's race, color, religion, sex, or national origin; or (2) to limit, segregate, or classify his employees in any way which would deprive or tend to deprive any individual of employment opportunities or otherwise adversely affect his status as an employee because of such individual's race, color, religion, sex, or national origin.[26]

❖ FIGURE 5–6 ❖

MAJOR FEDERAL EQUAL EMPLOYMENT OPPORTUNITY LAWS AND REGULATIONS

ACT	YEAR	PROVISIONS
Equal Pay Act	1963	Requires equal pay for men and women performing substantially the same work
Title VII, Civil Rights Act of 1964	1964	Prohibits discrimination in employment on basis of race, color, religion, sex, or national origin
Executive Orders 11246 and 11375	1965 1967	Require federal contractors and subcontractors to eliminate employment discrimination and prior discrimination through affirmative action
Age Discrimination in Employment Act (as amended in 1978 and 1986)	1967	Prohibits discrimination against persons over age 40 and restricts mandatory retirement requirements, except where age is a bona fide occupational qualification
Executive Order 11478	1969	Prohibits discrimination in the U.S. Postal Service and in the various government agencies on the basis of race, color, religion, sex, national origin, handicap, or age
Vocational Rehabilitation Act Rehabilitation Act of 1974	1973 1974	Prohibit employers with federal contracts over $2,500 from discriminating against individuals with disabilities
Vietnam-Era Veterans Readjustment Act	1974	Prohibits discrimination against Vietnam-era veterans by federal contractors and the U.S. government and requires affirmative action
Pregnancy Discrimination Act	1978	Prohibits discrimination against women affected by pregnancy, childbirth, or related medical conditions; requires that they be treated as all other employees for employment-related purposes, including benefits
Immigration Reform and Control Act	1986 1990 1996	Establishes penalties for employers who knowingly hire illegal aliens; prohibits employment discrimination on the basis of national origin or citizenship
Americans with Disabilities Act	1990	Requires employer accommodation of individuals with disabilities
Older Workers Benefit Protection Act of 1990	1990	Prohibits age-based discrimination in early retirement and other benefits plans
Civil Rights Act of 1991	1991	Overturns several past Supreme Court decisions and changed damage claims provisions
Congressional Accountability Act	1995	Extends EEO and Civil Rights Act provisions to U.S. Congressional staff

WHO IS COVERED? Title VII, as amended by the Equal Employment Opportunity Act of 1972, covers most employers in the United States. Any organization meeting one of the criteria listed below is subject to rules and regulations that specific government agencies set up to administer the act:

❖ All private employers of 15 or more persons who are employed 20 or more weeks per year

- All educational institutions, public and private
- State and local governments
- Public and private employment agencies
- Labor unions with 15 or more members
- Joint (labor/management) committees for apprenticeships and training[27]

Civil Rights Act of 1991

The major purpose for the passage of the Civil Rights Act of 1991 was to overturn or modify seven U.S. Supreme Court decisions handed down during the 1988–1990 period. Those decisions made it more difficult for individuals filing discrimination charges to win their cases. Also, the 1991 act amended other federal laws, including Title VII of the 1964 Civil Rights Act and Section 1981 of the Civil Rights Act of 1866. The major effects of the 1991 Act are discussed below.

Disparate Impact The Civil Rights Act of 1991 overturned a decision issued in the *Wards Cove Packing v. Atonio* (1989) case.[28] In that case, the Supreme Court's decision made it more difficult for protected-class individuals to use statistics to show that illegal discrimination had occurred. The 1991 act reversed that ruling, relying on earlier reasoning in the *Griggs v. Duke Power* decision.

The Civil Rights Act of 1991 requires that employers show that an employment practice is *job related for the position* and is consistent with *business necessity* if *disparate impact* occurs. The act did clarify that the plaintiffs bringing the discrimination charges must identify the particular employer practice being challenged as causing disparate impact.

According to one study, disparate-impact cases comprised less than 2% of all discrimination suits filed in one two-year period. Most were filed on the basis of discriminatory intent.[29]

Discriminatory Intent The Civil Rights Act of 1991 overturned several court decisions that had made it more difficult for plaintiffs to bring suits based on intentional discrimination. In one of those cases, *Price Waterhouse v. Hopkins* (1989),[30] the U.S. Supreme Court ordered a lower court to rehear Ann Hopkins's charges that the large accounting firm for which she worked had been guilty of sex discrimination. Hopkins charged that she was denied a partnership at Price Waterhouse because of "sexual stereotyping" in which she was viewed as being too macho and aggressive. The Supreme Court ruled that when an employment decision is based on both legitimate and impermissible factors, the employer can avoid liability if the same decision would have been reached without the "impermissible factor" (in this case, gender) being considered, which shifted the burden of proof to the plaintiff.

Under the 1991 act, the plaintiff charging intentional discrimination must show only that protected-class status played *some* factor. For employers, this means that "an individual's race, color, religion, sex, or national origin *must play no factor* in the challenged employment practice."[31] However, the act limits the damages given to a complainant if the employer can demonstrate that the same decision would have been made without the impermissible consideration.

Compensatory and Punitive Damages and Jury Trials The 1991 act allows victims of discrimination on the basis of sex, religion, or disability to receive both compensatory and punitive damages in cases of intentional discrimination. Under the 1991 act, compensatory damages do not include back pay or interest on it, additional pay, or other damages authorized by Title VII of the 1964 Civil

Rights Act. Compensatory damages typically include payments for emotional pain and suffering, loss of enjoyment of life, mental anguish, or inconvenience.[32] However, limits were set on the amount of compensatory and punitive damages, extending from a cap of $50,000 for employers with 100 or fewer employees to a cap of $300,000 for those with over 500 employees.

Additionally, the 1991 act allows jury trials to determine the liability for and the amount of compensatory and punitive damages, subject to the caps just mentioned. Prior to passage of this act, decisions in these cases were made by judges. Generally, this provision is viewed as a victory for those who bring discrimination suits against employers, because juries tend to be more sympathetic to individuals than to employers.

OTHER PROVISIONS OF THE 1991 ACT The Civil Rights Act of 1991 contained a number of sections that addressed a variety of other issues. More detailed discussions of most issues appear later in this chapter or in the next chapter. Briefly, some of the issues and the provisions of the act are as follows:[33]

- *Race Norming.* The act prohibited adjustment of employment test scores or use of alternative scoring mechanisms on the basis of the race or gender of test takers. The concern addressed by this provision is the use of different passing or cut-off scores for protected-class members than for nonprotected-class individuals.
- *International Employees.* The act extended coverage of U.S. EEO laws to U.S. citizens working abroad, except where local laws conflict.
- *Employment Contracts.* The act overturned a Supreme Court decision and made EEO laws apply to employment contracts.[34]
- *"Right to Sue" Notification.* The act amended others dealing with age discrimination to require the EEOC to notify age discrimination complainants when the agency is terminating action of their cases. The individuals then can file civil suits if they wish.
- *Seniority Systems.* The act overturned a Supreme Court decision and allowed protected-class members to challenge the discriminatory operation of seniority systems.[35]
- *Consent Decrees.* The act modified a Supreme Court decision and limited challenges to court-ordered decrees designed to remedy past discriminatory actions. The effect is to restrict nonprotected-class members from challenging the consent decrees.
- *Glass Ceiling Initiative.* Associated with the 1991 act, the Glass Ceiling Act of 1991 established a commission to study and make recommendations on how to eliminate barriers to the advancement of women and other protected-class members to management and executive positions.
- *Government Employee Rights.* Responding to criticism that some government employees were being excluded from EEO law coverage, Congress extended such coverage to employees of the Senate, presidential appointments, and previously excluded state government employees.

EFFECTS OF THE CIVIL RIGHTS ACT OF 1991 By overturning some U.S. Supreme Court decisions, the 1991 act negated many of the more "employer-friendly" decisions made by the Supreme Court from 1988 to 1990. Allowing jury trials and compensatory and punitive damages in cases involving allegations of intentional discrimination means that the costs of being found guilty of illegal discrimination have increased significantly. The number of EEO complaints filed likely will continue to increase because of some of the provisions of the 1991 act.

Consequently, more than ever before, employers must make sure their actions are job related and based on business necessity.

❖ Enforcement Agencies

Government agencies at several levels have powers to investigate illegal discriminatory practices. At the state and local levels, various commissions have enforcement authority. At the federal level, the two most prominent agencies are the Equal Employment Opportunity Commission (EEOC) and the Office of Federal Contract Compliance Programs (OFCCP).

❖ Equal Employment Opportunity Commission (EEOC)

The EEOC, created by the Civil Rights Act of 1964, is responsible for enforcing the employment-related provisions of the act. The agency initiates investigations, responds to complaints, and develops guidelines to enforce various laws. The EEOC has enforcement authority for charges brought under the following federal laws:

- Civil Rights Act of 1964, Title VII
- Civil Rights Act of 1991
- Equal Pay Act
- Pregnancy Discrimination Act
- Age Discrimination in Employment Act
- Americans with Disabilities Act
- Vocational Rehabilitation Act

The EEOC has been given expanded powers several times since 1964 and is the major agency involved with employment discrimination. Over the years, the EEOC has been given the responsibility to investigate equal pay violations, age discrimination, and discrimination based on disability in addition to areas identified by Title VII of the Civil Rights Act of 1964.

An independent regulatory agency, the EEOC is composed of five members appointed by the president and confirmed by the Senate. No more than three members of the commission can be from the same political party. Members serve for seven years. In addition, the EEOC has a staff of lawyers and investigators who do investigative and follow-up work for the commission.

LOGGING ON

LaborBase EEOC Filings Database provides the number of charges filed by year and the new number of findings of probable causes of discrimination. Information is available by state and year for $20.

Http://www.cin.ix.net/anh/eeoc-db.html

❖ Office of Federal Contract Compliance Programs (OFCCP)

While the EEOC is an independent agency, the OFCCP is part of the Department of Labor, established by executive order to ensure that federal contractors and subcontractors have nondiscriminatory practices. A major thrust of OFCCP efforts is to require that federal contractors and subcontractors take affirmative action to overcome the effects of prior discriminatory practices. Affirmative action plans are discussed in detail in the next chapter.

❖ Enforcement Philosophies and Efforts

Since 1964, the various U.S. presidential administrations have viewed EEO and affirmative action enforcement efforts from different philosophical perspectives. Often the thrust and aggressiveness of enforcement efforts have varied depending on whether a Republican or Democratic president and Congress were in office. The purpose of pointing this out is not to suggest who is right or wrong but rather to emphasize that laws are enforced by agencies staffed by presidential appointees. Differing degrees of activism and emphasis result, depending on the philosophical beliefs and priorities held by a particular administration.

❖ State and Local Enforcement Agencies

In addition to federal laws and orders, many states and municipalities have passed their own laws prohibiting discrimination on a variety of bases. Often, these laws are modeled after federal laws; however, state and local laws sometimes provide greater remedies, require different actions, or prohibit discrimination in areas beyond those addressed by federal law. As a result, state and local enforcement bodies have been established to enforce EEO compliance. Fortunately, the three levels of agencies generally coordinate their activities to avoid multiple investigations of the same EEO complaints.

To implement the provisions of the Civil Rights Act of 1964 and the interpretations of it based on court decisions, the EEOC and other federal agencies developed their own compliance guidelines and regulations, each agency having a slightly different set of rules and expectations. Finally, in 1978, the major government agencies involved agreed on a set of uniform guidelines.

❖ Uniform Guidelines on Employee Selection Procedures

The Uniform Guidelines on Employee Selection Procedures apply to the federal EEOC, the U.S. Department of Labor's OFCCP, the U.S. Department of Justice, and the federal Office of Personnel Management. The guidelines provide a framework used to determine if employers are adhering to federal laws on discrimination. These guidelines affect virtually all phases of HR management because they apply to employment procedures, including but not limited to the following:

- Hiring (qualifications required, application blanks, interviews, tests)
- Promotions (qualifications, selection process)
- Recruiting (advertising, availability of announcements)
- Demotion (why made, punishments given)
- Performance appraisals (methods used, links to promotions and pay)
- Training (access to training programs, development efforts)
- Labor union membership requirements (apprenticeship programs, work assignments)
- Licensing and certification requirements (job requirements tied to job qualifications)

The guidelines apply to most employment-related decisions, not just to the initial hiring process. Two major means of compliance are identified by the guidelines: (1) no disparate impact and (2) job-related validation.

❖ No Disparate Impact Approach

Generally, when courts have found discrimination in organizations, the most important issue has concerned the *effect* of employment policies and procedures, regardless of the *intent*. Remember, *disparate impact* occurs whenever there is a substantial underrepresentation of protected-class members in employment decisions. The Uniform Guidelines identify one approach in the following statement: "These guidelines do not require a user to conduct validity studies of selection procedures where no adverse impact results."[36]

***4/5ths Rule**
Rule stating that discrimination generally is considered to occur if the selection rate for a protected group is less than 80% of the group's representation in the relevant labor market or less than 80% of the selection rate for the majority group.

Under the guidelines, disparate impact is determined with the **4/5ths rule.** If the selection rate for any protected group is less than 80% (4/5ths) of the selection rate for the majority group or less than 80% of the group's representation in the relevant labor market, discrimination exists. Thus, the guidelines have attempted to define discrimination in statistical terms. Disparate impact can be checked both internally and externally.

INTERNAL Checking for disparate impact internally requires that employers compare the treatment received by protected-class members with that received by nonprotected-group members. Assume, for example, that Standard Company interviewed both men and women for manufacturing assembly jobs. Of the men who applied, 40% were hired; of the women who applied, 25% were hired. As shown in Figure 5–7, the selection rate for women is less than 80% (4/5ths) of the selection rate for men (40% × 4/5 = 32%). Consequently, Standard Company's employment process does have "disparate impact."

HR activities for which internal disparate impact can be checked internally include:

- Candidates selected for interviews of those recruited
- Performance appraisal ratings as they affect pay increases
- Promotions, demotions, and terminations
- Pass rates for various selection tests

EXTERNAL Employers can check for disparate impact externally by comparing the percentage of employed workers in a protected class in the organization with the percentage of protected-class members in the relevant labor market. The relevant labor market consists of the areas where the firm recruits workers, not just where those employed live. External comparisons can also consider the percentage of protected-class members who are recruited and who apply for jobs to ensure that the employer has drawn a "representative sample" from the relevant

❖ FIGURE 5–7 ❖
INTERNAL DISPARATE IMPACT AT STANDARD COMPANY

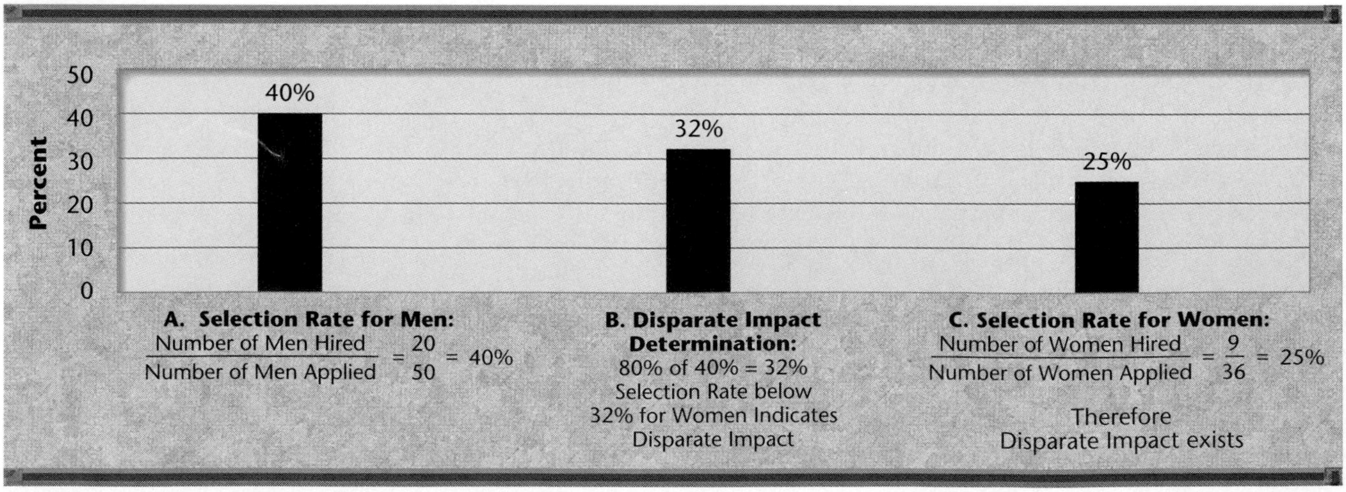

labor market. Although employers are not required to maintain exact proportionate equality, they must be "close." Courts have applied statistical analyses to determine if any disparities that exist are too high.

To illustrate, assume the following situation. In the Valleyville area, Hispanics make up 15% of those in the job market. RJ Company is a firm with 500 employees, 50 of whom are Hispanic. Disparate impact is determined as follows if the 4/5ths rule is applied:

Percent of Hispanics in the labor market	15%
× 4/5	×.8
Disparate-impact level	12%

Comparison:
RJ Co. has 5/500 = 10% Hispanics.
Disparate-impact level = 12% Hispanics.
Therefore, disparate impact exists because fewer than 12% of the firm's employees are Hispanic.

The preceding example illustrates one way external disparate impact can be determined. In reality, statistical comparisons for disparate-impact determination may use more complex methods. Note also that external disparate impact charges make up a very small number of EEOC cases. Instead, most cases deal with the disparate impact of internal employment practices.

Effect of the No Disparate Impact Strategy The 4/5ths rule is a yardstick that employers can use to determine if there is disparate impact on protected-class members. However, to meet the 4/5ths compliance requirement, employers must have no disparate impact at any level or in any job for any protected class. (The next chapter contains more details.) Consequently, using this strategy is not really as easy or risk-free as it may appear. Instead, employers may want to turn to another compliance approach: validating that their employment decisions are based on job-related factors.

❖ Job-Related Validation Approach

Under the job-related validation approach the employment practices that must be valid include such practices and tests as job descriptions, educational requirements, experience requirements, work skills, application forms, interviews, paper-and-pencil tests, and performance appraisals. Virtually every factor used to make employment-related decisions—recruiting, selection, promotion, termination, discipline, and performance appraisal—must be shown to be specifically job related. Hence, the concept of validity affects many of the common tools used to make HR decisions.

Validity is simply the extent to which a test actually measures what it says it measures. The concept relates to inferences made from tests. It may be valid to infer that college admission test scores predict college academic performance. However, it is probably invalid to infer that those same test scores predict athletic performance. As applied to employment settings, a test is any employment procedure used as the basis for making an employment-related decision. For a general intelligence test to be valid, it must actually measure intelligence, not just vocabulary. An employment test that is valid must measure the person's ability to

***Validity**
The extent to which a test actually measures what it says it measures.

perform the job for which he or she is being hired. Validity is discussed in detail in the next section.

The ideal condition for employment-related tests is to be both valid and reliable. **Reliability** refers to the consistency with which a test measures an item. For a test to be reliable, an individual's score should be about the same every time the individual takes that test (allowing for the effects of practice). Unless a test measures a trait consistently (or reliably), it is of little value in predicting job performance.

Reliability
The consistency with which a test measures an item.

Reliability can be measured by several different statistical methodologies. The most frequent ones are test-retest, alternate forms, and internal-consistency estimates. A more detailed methodological discussion is beyond the scope of this text; those interested can consult appropriate statistical references.[37]

❖ Validity and Equal Employment

If a charge of discrimination is brought against an employer on the basis of disparate impact, a *prima facie* case has been established. The employer then must be able to demonstrate that its employment procedures are valid, which means to demonstrate that they relate to the job and the requirements of the job. A key element in establishing job-relatedness is to conduct a *job analysis* to identify the *knowledge, skills,* and *abilities (KSAs)* and other characteristics needed to perform a job satisfactorily. A detailed examination of the job provides the foundation for linking the KSAs to job requirements and job performance. Chapter 7 discusses job analysis in more detail. Both the Civil Rights Act of 1964, as interpreted by the *Griggs v. Duke Power* decision, and the Civil Rights Act of 1991 emphasize the importance of job-relatedness in establishing validity.

The legislation and court decisions mentioned in this chapter are forcing employers to make changes that probably should have been made earlier. Using an invalid instrument to select, place, or promote an employee has never been a good management practice, regardless of its legality. Management also should be concerned with using valid instruments from the standpoint of operational efficiency. Using invalid tests may result in screening out individuals who might have been satisfactory performers and hiring less satisfactory workers instead. Many organizations are increasing their use of instruments that have been demonstrated to be valid. In one sense, then, current requirements have done management a favor by forcing employers to do what they should have been doing previously—using job-related employment procedures.

The 1978 uniform selection guidelines recognize validation strategies measuring three types of validity:

- Content validity
- Criterion-related validity (concurrent and predictive)
- Construct validity

❖ Content Validity

Content Validity
Validity measured by use of a logical, nonstatistical method to identify the KSAs and other characteristics necessary to perform a job.

Content validity is measured when a logical, nonstatistical method is used to identify the KSAs and other characteristics necessary to perform a job. A test is content valid if it reflects an actual sample of the work done on the job in question. For example, an arithmetic test for a retail cashier should contain problems that typically would be faced by cashiers on the job. Content validity is especially useful if the workforce is not large enough to allow other, more statistical approaches.

A content validity study begins with a comprehensive job analysis to identify what is done on a job and what KSAs are used. Then managers, supervisors, and HR specialists must use their judgment to identify the most important KSAs needed for the job. Finally, a test is devised to determine if individuals have the necessary KSAs. The test may be an interview question about previous supervisory experience, or an ability test in which someone types a letter using a word-processing software program, or a knowledge test about consumer credit regulations.

Many practitioners and specialists see content validity as a commonsense way to validate staffing requirements that is more realistic than statistically oriented methods. In the *Washington v. Davis* case, the Supreme Court also appeared to support the content validity approach in that its decision implied approval of a reading comprehension test given to potential police officers that represented actual materials used by police officers in the training academy and on the job.[38] Content validity approaches are growing in use.

❖ Criterion-Related Validity

Employment tests of any kind attempt to predict how well an individual will perform on the job. In measuring **criterion-related validity,** a test is the *predictor* and the desired KSAs and measures of job performance are the *criterion variables.* Job analysis determines as exactly as possible what KSAs and behaviors are needed for each task in the job. Tests (predictors) are then devised and used to measure different dimensions of the criterion-related variables. Examples of tests are: (1) having a college degree, (2) scoring a required number of words per minute on a typing test, and (3) having five years of banking experience. These predictors are then validated against the criteria used to measure job performance, such as performance appraisals, sales records, and absenteeism rates. Some court cases, such as *Albermarle Paper v. Moody,* have pointed out the difficulty in using subjective performance appraisals by supervisors as the criteria against which the tests are validated. However, if the predictors satisfactorily predict job performance behavior, they are legally acceptable and useful.[39]

***Criterion-Related Validity**
Validity measured by means of a procedure that uses a test as the predictor of how well an individual will perform on the job.

A simply analogy is to think of two circles, one labeled *predictor* and the other *criterion variable.* The criterion-related approach to validity attempt to see how well the two circles overlap. The more overlap, the better the performance of the predictor. The degree of overlap is described by a **correlation coefficient,** which is an index number giving the relationship between a predictor and a criterion variable. These coefficients can range from −1.0 to +1.0. A correlation coefficient of +.99 indicates that the test is almost an exact predictor, whereas a +.02 correlation coefficient indicates that the test is a very poor predictor.

***Correlation Coefficient**
An index number giving the relationship between a predictor and a criterion variable.

There are two different approaches to criterion-related validity. *Concurrent validity* represents an "at-the-same-time" approach, while *predictive validity* represents a "before-the-fact" approach.

Concurrent Validity *Concurrent* means "at the same time." As shown in Figure 5–8, when an employer measures **concurrent validity,** a test is given to current employees and the scores are correlated with their performance ratings, determined by such measures as accident rates, absenteeism records, and supervisory performance appraisals. A high correlation suggests that the test can differentiate between the better-performing employees and those with poor performance records.

***Concurrent Validity**
Validity measured when an employer tests current employees and correlates the scores with their performance ratings.

A drawback of the concurrent validity approach is that employees who have not performed satisfactorily are probably no longer with the firm and therefore cannot be tested, while extremely good employees may have been promoted or

❖ FIGURE 5–8 ❖
CONCURRENT VALIDITY

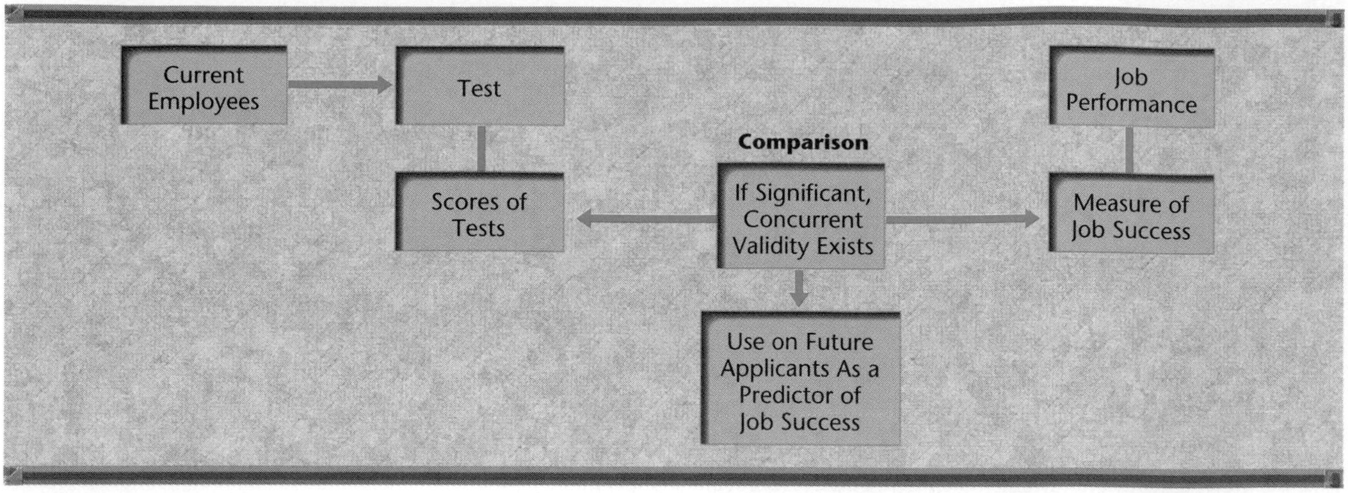

may have left the organization for better jobs. Furthermore, unknown is how people who were not hired would have performed if given opportunities to do so. Thus, the firm does not really have a full range of people to test. Also, the test takers may not be motivated to perform well on the test because they already have jobs. Any learning that has taken place on the job may influence test scores, presenting another problem. Applicants taking the test without the benefit of on-the-job experience might score low on the test but might be able to learn to do the job well. As a result of these problems, a researcher might conclude that a test is valid when it is not or might discard a test because the data indicate that it is invalid when, in fact, it is valid. In either case, the organization has lost because of poor research.

***Predictive Validity**
Validity measured when test results of applicants are compared with subsequent performance.

PREDICTIVE VALIDITY To measure **predictive validity,** test results of applicants are compared with their subsequent job performance. The following example illustrates how a predictive validity study might be designed. A retail chain, Eastern Discount, wants to establish the predictive validity of requiring one year of cashiering experience, a test it plans to use in hiring cashiers. Obviously, the retail outlet wants to use the test that will do the best job of separating those who will do well from those who will not. Eastern Discount first hires 30 people, regardless of cashiering experience or other criteria that might be directly related to experience. Some time later (perhaps after one year), the performance of these same employees is compared. Success on the job is measured by such yardsticks as absenteeism, accidents, errors, and performance appraisals. If those employees who had one year of experience at the time when they were hired demonstrate better performance than those without such experience, as demonstrated by statistical comparisons, then the experience requirement is considered a valid predictor of performance and may be used in hiring future employees. (See Figure 5–9.)

In the past, predictive validity has been preferred by the EEOC because it is presumed to give the strongest tie to job performance. However, predictive validity requires: (1) a fairly large number of people (usually at least 30) and (2) a time gap between the test and the performance (usually one year). As a result, it is not useful in many situations. Because of these and other problems, other types of validity often are used.

❖ FIGURE 5–9 ❖
PREDICTIVE VALIDITY

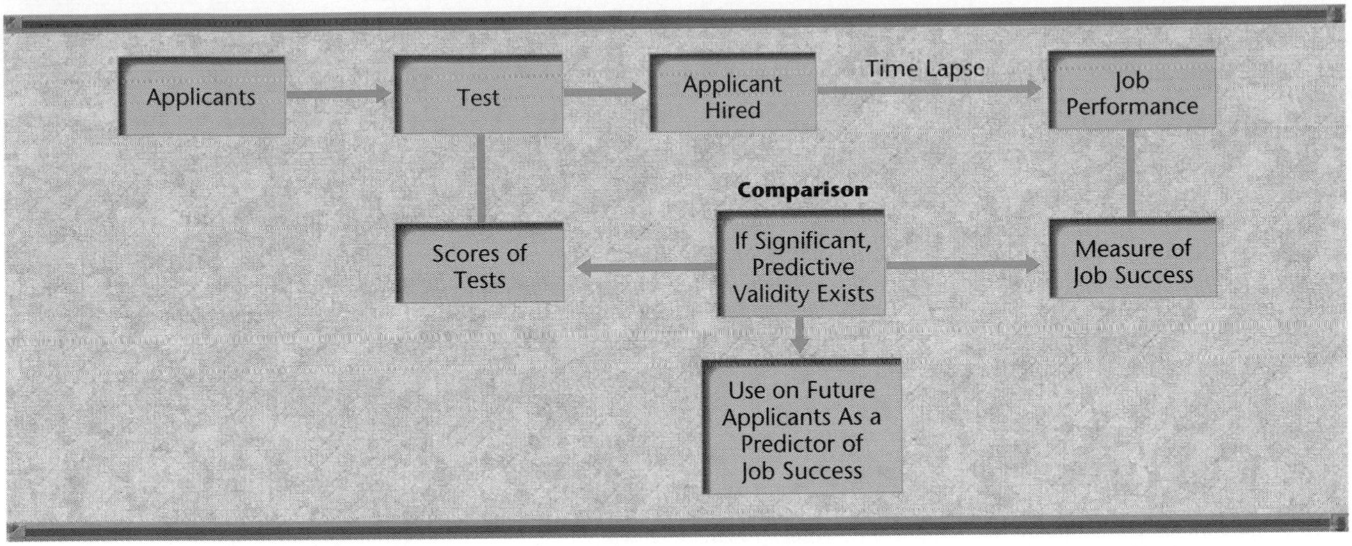

❖ CONSTRUCT VALIDITY

Construct validity shows a relationship between an abstract characteristic inferred from research and job performance. Researchers who study behavior have given various personality characteristics names such as *introversion, aggression,* and *dominance.* These are called *constructs.* Other common constructs for which tests have been devised are creativity, leadership potential, and interpersonal sensitivity. Because a hypothetical construct is used as a predictor in establishing this type of validity, personality tests and tests that measure other such constructs are more likely to be questioned for their legality and usefulness than other measures of validity. Consequently, construct validity is used less frequently in employment selection than the other types of validity.

❖ **Construct Validity**
Validity showing a relationship between an abstract characteristic and job performance.

❖ VALIDITY GENERALIZATION

Validity generalization is the extension of the validity of a test with different groups, similar jobs, or other organizations. Rather than viewing the validity of a test as being limited to a specific situation and usage, one views the test as a valid predictor in other situations as well. Those advocating validity generalization believe that variances in the validity of a test are attributable to the statistical and research methods used; this means that it should not be necessary to perform a separate validation study for every usage of an employment test. Proponents particularly believe validity generalization exists for general ability tests.

Although the approach is controversial, it has been adopted by the U.S. Employment Service, a federal agency, for the General Aptitude Test Battery (GATB). Also, it has been adopted for use throughout the United States in many state and local job service offices. As more and more such job services adopt the approach, more detailed records of results will be available. Anyone interested in learning more about the GATB and validity generalization should contact the job service office in a specific locale to find out how it is used.[40]

❖ **Validity Generalization**
The extension of the validity of a test to different groups, similar jobs, or other organizations.

SUMMARY

❖ Diversity, which recognizes differences among people, is growing as an HR issue.

❖ Organizations have a demographically more diverse workforce than in the past, and continuing changes are expected.

❖ Major demographic shifts include the increasing number and percentage of women working, growth in minority racial/ethnic groups, and the aging of the workforce. Other changes involve the need to provide accommodations for individuals with disabilities and to adapt to workers with differing sexual orientations.

❖ Diversity management is concerned with developing organizational initiatives that value all people equally regardless of their differences.

❖ Effective management of diversity means that firms must go beyond the traditional approaches of affirmative action to develop diversity training and change the culture of organizations.

❖ Equal employment opportunity (EEO) is a broad concept holding that individuals should have equal treatment in all employment-related actions.

❖ Protected classes are composed of individuals identified for protection under equal employment laws and regulations.

❖ Affirmative action requires employers to identify problem areas in the employment of protected-class members and to set goals and take steps to overcome those problems.

❖ The question of whether or not affirmative action leads to reverse discrimination has been intensely litigated, and the debate continues today.

❖ EEO is part of effective management for two reasons: (1) it focuses on using the talents of all human resources; (2) the costs of being found guilty of illegal discrimination can be substantial.

❖ Disparate treatment occurs when protected-class members are treated differently from others, whether or not there is discriminatory intent.

❖ Disparate impact occurs when employment decisions work to the disadvantage of members of protected classes, whether or not there is discriminatory intent.

❖ Employers must be able to defend their management practices based on bona fide occupational qualifications (BFOQ), business necessity, and job-relatedness.

❖ Once a *prima facie* case of illegal discrimination is shown, the burden of proof shifts to the employer to demonstrate that the bases for employment-related decisions were job related.

❖ Retaliation occurs when an employer takes punitive actions against individuals who exercise their legal rights, and it is illegal under various laws.

❖ The 1964 Civil Rights Act, Title VII, was the first significant equal employment law. The Civil Rights Act of 1991 altered or expanded on the 1964 provisions by overturning several U.S. Supreme Court decisions.

❖ The Civil Rights Act of 1991 addressed a variety of issues, such as disparate impact, discriminatory intent, compensatory and punitive damages, jury trials, and EEO rights of international employees.

❖ The Equal Employment Opportunity Commission (EEOC) and the Office of Federal Contract Compliance Programs (OFCCP) are the major federal equal employment enforcement agencies.

❖ The 1978 Uniform Guidelines are used by enforcement agencies to examine recruiting, hiring, promotion, and many other employment practices.

❖ Under the 1978 guidelines, two alternative compliance approaches are identified: (1) no disparate impact and (2) job-related validation.

❖ Disparate impact can be determined through use of the 4/5ths rule.

❖ Job-related validation requires that tests measure what they are supposed to measure (validity) in a consistent manner (reliability).

❖ There are three types of validity: content, criterion-related, and construct.

❖ The content-validity approach is growing in use because it shows the job-relatedness of a measure by using a sample of the actual work to be performed.

❖ The two criterion-related strategies measure concurrent validity and predictive validity. Whereas predictive validity involves a "before-the-fact" measure, concurrent validity involves a comparison of tests and criteria measures available at the same time.

❖ Construct validity involves the relationship between a measure of an abstract characteristic, such as intelligence, and job performance.

Review and Discussion Questions

1. Discuss the following statement: "U.S. organizations must adjust to diversity if they are to manage the workforce of the present and future."
2. Explain why diversity management represents a much broader approach to workforce diversity than providing equal employment opportunity or affirmative action.
3. Regarding the affirmative action debate, why do you support or oppose affirmative action?
4. If you were asked by an employer to review an employment decision to determine if discrimination had occurred, what factors would you consider, and how would you evaluate them?
5. Why is the Civil Rights Act of 1991 such a significant law?
6. Why is the job-related validation approach considered more business-oriented than the no disparate impact approach in complying with the 1978 Uniform Guidelines on Employee Selection Procedures?
7. Explain what validity is and why the content validity approach is growing in use compared with the criterion-related and construct validity approaches.

Terms to Know

4/5ths rule **142**
affirmative action **129**
bona fide occupational qualification (BFOQ) **135**
business necessity **135**
concurrent validity **145**
construct validity **147**
content validity **144**
correlation coefficient **145**
criterion-related validity **145**
disparate impact **135**
disparate treatment **135**
diversity **122**
diversity management **126**
equal employment opportunity (EEO) **128**
predictive validity **145**
protected class **128**
reliability **144**
retaliation **136**
reverse discrimination **129**
validity **143**
validity generalization **147**

Case

The City of San Diego and Diversity

A comprehensive effort in the management of diversity has been developed by the City of San Diego, California. Located in an area in which a widely diverse population must be served, the city has developed a diversity commitment, not a diversity program. It is multifaceted, is wide-ranging in scope, and has received national recognition and numerous awards.

The diversity commitment originated in 1987 when a group of senior managers for the city were reviewing a list of employees for promotion. During their discussion, someone asked how many women and ethnic minorities were on the list. When the response was "relatively few," it caused these managers to ponder the shortcomings of the city in recruiting, hiring, training, and promoting all individuals, not just primarily white males. The City Manager then was charged with addressing the issue of diversity as a human resource concern. To address diversity, the manager of the city's organizational effectiveness program began the efforts that have led the city to reflect its commitment to diversity.

Key to the effort was support from top executives, including public acknowledgment that there were problems and that the city would begin a longer-term effort to remedy them. The top executive in the city throughout most of the efforts has been Jack McGrory, City Manager. McGrory has continued to demonstrate his commitment to diversity in a number of ways, including opening each diversity training program with a presentation on the importance of diversity to the City of San Diego and his support of it. He also has asked that diversity commitment be evaluated during all managerial performance appraisals.

The City of San Diego Commits to Diversity, continued

The continuity of the diversity commitment has been entrusted to the Organizational Effectiveness (OE) Unit. To begin, the OE staff invited about a thousand city employees to group discussions about diversity issues. Participants represented a cross-section of organizational levels, genders, and ethnic groups. Following the focus group discussions, the OE staff developed diversity themes and then held over a hundred feedback sessions to discuss the results. All of this input served to identify the issues of greatest concern and to suggest strategies to address them.

The City Manager then requested funds from the City Council to support the city's diversity commitment. The City Manager pointed out that settling a few lawsuits related to employment discrimination would require an amount equal to or exceeding the amount requested. The funding supplied—$460,000—actually was above the amount originally requested.

To implement the diversity efforts, a steering committee with a diverse membership was established. Then specific activities were identified, including developing diversity training programs. Outside consultants were hired to assist the OE staff. By the mid-1990s, over a thousand city employees, including most supervisors and managers, had participated in the training. The feedback from participants has been very favorable. But just as important, over fifty policy and procedure changes to support the diversity training sessions have been identified through discussions during the diversity training sessions.

Extensive communications and continuing follow-up have all ensured that the City of San Diego maintains its commitment to diversity. All of the original goals of the diversity efforts have been met, and the results have generated a more integrated workforce committed to diversity.[41]

Questions

1. Compare top management's support for diversity at the City of San Diego with that at your current or past place of employment.
2. Why was the use of the focus group initially so important for the diversity efforts of the city?
3. What would you do to keep enthusiasm and commitment to diversity high after diversity training sessions had reached most employees?

Notes

1. Based on Del Jones, "Feds Want Chain to Hire 'Hooters Guys,'" *USA Today*, November 15, 1995; J. Bovard, "The EEOC's War on Hooters," *The Wall Street Journal*, November 17, 1995, A15; and "EEOC Dropping Sex-Bias Inquiry of Hooters Chain," *Albuquerque Journal*, May 2, 1996, A1.
2. M. B. White, "Power Lines: Networks and the Diversity Initiative," *The Diversity Factor*, Winter 1996, 2–7.
3. Throughout the following section, various statistics on workforce composition and trends are taken from U.S. Department of Labor, Bureau of Labor Statistics, and Census Bureau data widely reported in various reference and news media reports. For additional details, pertinent issues of the *Monthly Labor Review* can be consulted.
4. Michael J. Mandel, "How Immigration Caps Choke Off Growth," *Business Week*, October 9, 1995, 44.
5. "Clinton Signs Measure Raising Social Security Earnings Limit," *The Orange County Register*, March 30, 1996, 28.
6. R. Roosevelt Thomas, *Beyond Race and Gender: Unleashing the Power of Your Total Workforce by Managing Diversity* (New York: AMACOM, 1991).
7. "Survey Shows Many Companies Have Diversity Programs, Changes in Affirmative Action Perspectives," *Mosaics*, March 1995, 1.
8. Adapted from "Diversity Management Is a Cultural Change, Not Just Training," 1993 SHRM/CCH Survey, May 26, 1993, *CCH Human Resources Management* (Chicago: Commerce Clearing House, 1993).
9. For additional details on establishing diversity management programs, see Lawrence M. Baytos, *Designing and Implementing Successful Diversity Programs* (Englewood Cliffs, NJ: Prentice Hall, 1995).
10. Barbara Stern, "Holding Executives Accountable: Linking Diversity Performance to Compensation," *The Diversity Factor*, Fall 1995, 11–15.

11. M. L. Williams and Talya N. Bauer, "The Effect of a Managing Diversity Policy on Organizational Attractiveness," *Group and Organization Management* 19 (1994), 295–308.
12. John A. Gray, "Preferential Affirmative Action in Employment," *Labor Law Journal* 43 (1992), 23–30.
13. Charlene M. Solomon, "Are White Males Being Left Out?" *Personnel Journal,* November 1991, 88–94.
14. The authors acknowledge the assistance of Christina Harjehausen in structuring the content of the debate on affirmative action.
15. D. Seligman, "Comes the Revolution," *Fortune,* February 20, 1995, 125.
16. *Adarand Constructors v. Peña* 115 S. Ct. 2097 (1995).
17. *Bakke v. The University of California,* 109 S.Ct. (1978).
18. *Hopwood v. State of Texas,* 78 F.3d 932 (1996).
19. Alison M. Konrad and Frank Linnehan, "Formalized HRM Structures: Coordinating Equal Employment Opportunity or Concealing Organizational Practices?" *Academy of Management Journal* 38 (1995).
20. *Griggs v. Duke Power Co.,* 401 U.S. 424 (1971).
21. Civil Rights Act of 1964, Title VII, Sec. 703e.
22. *McDonnell Douglas v. Green,* 411 U.S. 972 (1973).
23. *Texas Department of Community Affairs v. Burdine,* 25 FEP Cases 113 (1981).
24. EEOC Decision #72-0455, 4 FEP Cases 306.
25. Mark A. Player, *Federal Law of Employment Discrimination* (St. Paul, MN: West Publishing Co., 1992), 166–170.
26. Civil Rights Act of 1964, Title VII, Sec. 103a.
27. U.S. Equal Employment Opportunity Commission, *Affirmative Action and Equal Employment* (Washington, DC: U.S. Government Printing Office, 1974), 12–13.
28. *Wards Cove Packing Co. v. Atonio,* 109 S. Ct. 2115 (1989).
29. John J. Donohue III and Peter Siegleman, "The Changing Nature of Employment Discrimination, *Stanford Law Review* 43 (1991), 983–998.
30. *Price Waterhouse v. Hopkins,* 109 S.Ct. 1775 (1989).
31. Timothy D. Loudon, "The Civil Rights Act of 1991: What Does It Mean and What Is Its Likely Impact?" *Nebraska Law Review* 71 (1992), 304–322.
32. The EEOC enforcement guidelines are identified in Equal Employment Opportunity Commission, "Enforcement Guidance: Compensatory and Punitive Damages Available under Section 102 of the Civil Rights Act of 1991," *Bureau of National Affairs Daily Labor Reporter* 131 (July 8, 1992), E–1.
33. For a discussion of the legal aspects of each of the issues, see Niall A. Paul, "The Civil Rights Act of 1991: What Does It Really Accomplish?" *Employee Relations Law Journal* 17 (1992), 567–591.
34. *Patterson v. McLean Credit Union,* 491 U.S. 164 (1989).
35. *Lorance v. AT&T Technologies, Inc.,* 490 U.S. 900 (1989).
36. "Adoption by Four Agencies of Uniform Guidelines on Employee Selection Procedures (1978)," *Federal Register,* August 15, 1978, Part IV, 38295–38309.
37. For a discussion in the context of employment selection, see Robert D. Gatewood and Hubert S. Feild, *Human Resource Selection,* 2d ed. (Chicago: Dryden Press, 1990), 117–196.
38. *Washington, Mayor of Washington D.C. v. Davis,* 96 S.Ct. 2040 (1976).
39. See *Personnel Psychology* 38 (1985), 697–801, for questions, commentary, and discussion on validity generalization and meta-analysis.
40. The authors express their appreciation to Professor Carl Thornton, BMI Engineering and Management Institute, for his assistance on this section.
41. Based on information in *How to Develop a Diversity Commitment* (Washington, DC: American Association of Retired Persons, 1994). For copies, contact AARP, Workforce Programs Department, 601 E Street N.W., Washington, DC 20049.

CHAPTER 6

IMPLEMENTING EQUAL EMPLOYMENT

After you have read this chapter, you should be able to . . .

- Discuss the two types of sexual harassment and how employers should respond to complaints.
- Give examples of three sex-based discrimination issues besides sexual harassment.
- Identify two age discrimination issues.
- Discuss the major requirements of the Americans with Disabilities Act.
- Describe two bases of EEO discrimination in addition to those listed above.
- Identify typical EEO record-keeping requirements and those records used in the EEO investigative process.
- Discuss the contents of an affirmative action plan (AAP).

HR in Transition

Employer Discrimination is Expensive

Over the 30 years since the passage of the Civil Rights Act of 1964, numerous employers have been found guilty of illegal employment discrimination. Whether based on age, sex, race, disability, or other factors, both large and small employers have paid for their illegal discriminatory actions. But employers continue to engage in discriminatory practices that lead to large fines and settlements. Some examples illustrate that employment discrimination is expensive

Sex Discrimination and Sexual Harassment

- *Del Labs,* based in New York, had to pay $1.185 million to settle a sexual harassment case brought against the firm's CEO by 15 women. That figure did not include the cost of the attorney fees paid by the company in its unsuccessful defense.
- A female *IBM* marketing representative was awarded $65,000 by a California state court. The woman charged that she had been "pressured" by two supervisors to resume a sexual relationship with a senior official in the U.S. Department of Defense. It was hoped that if she did so the firm would be given a multimillion-dollar defense conversion contract. IBM's legal fees were $1.5 million, and the woman's attorneys filed claims against IBM for over $600,000 in attorney fees and costs.
- *AT&T* agreed to a $66 million settlement for 13,000 women who experienced pregnancy discrimination. The settlement covered women who worked for the Western Electric portions of AT&T (prior to the breakup of AT&T into separate companies) between 1965 and 1977). The firm has forced women to take unpaid maternity leaves, had discounted seniority for those on maternity leaves, and had not allowed those returning from maternity leaves to resume their jobs.

The firm had forced women to take unpaid maternity leaves, had discounted seniority for those on maternity leaves, and had not allowed those returning from maternity leaves to resume their jobs.

Racial/Ethnic Discrimination

- *Tempel Steel Co.,* based in Niles, Illinois, settled a race bias case on behalf of African Americans who had applied for or who could show that they would have applied for jobs at the firm. Only 70 of the firm's 1,000 workers were African Americans. The case involved Tempel's recruiting practices, in which job advertisements were placed in Polish- and German-language newspapers where few African Americans would see them. Therefore, the recruiting continued a past pattern of discrimination. In addition to paying $4 million total to the victims of past discrimination, the firm was required to file reports on its hiring practices for four years and pay $500,000 to set up a training program to help African American employees qualify for the higher-skilled, higher-paying jobs in the two factories in the Chicago area.
- An African American lawyer at a national law firm's Washington, D.C., office was awarded $2.5 million for race discrimination. He alleged that even though he was given good performance reviews, he was paid $3,000 less per year than others, was not considered for partnership on the same schedule and was dismissed from the firm due to his race. The firm claimed he was dismissed because the bankruptcy practices in which he worked did not generate sufficient billable hours.

Age Discrimination

- *K-Mart Corporation* was ordered to pay $2.17 million to three pharmacists who had been fired so that younger individuals could be hired as pharmacists, as store managers, and in other jobs. The three pharmacists were aged 63, 65, and 62 when they were fired. Three other older pharmacists did not win their cases.
- *Stites Concrete, Inc.,* in Florida was found to have discriminated against a 75-year-old man who injured himself while working on a company truck. The man was not allowed to return to work following surgery and claimed age discrimination. The man was awarded $38,500 in damages and $28,089 in attorney fees.[1]

> *"Our equality lies in the right for each of us to grow to our full capacity whatever it is."*
> *—Pearl Buck*

As the examples in the opening discussion indicate, the days are past when employers can manage their workforces in any manner they wish. Federal, state, and local laws prohibit unfair discrimination against individuals on a variety of bases.

One of the purposes of this chapter is to discuss the range of issues that have been addressed by EEO laws, regulations, and court decisions. The other purpose is to review what employers should do to comply with the regulations and requirements of various EEO enforcement agencies.

❖ Sex Discrimination

Title VII of the Civil Rights Act of 1964 prohibits discrimination in employment on the basis of sex. Other laws and regulations are aimed at eliminating sex discrimination in specific areas. This section begins with a discussion of sexual harassment and then discusses other forms of sex discrimination.

❖ Sexual Harassment

Sexual Harassment Actions that are sexually directed, are unwanted, and subject the worker to adverse employment conditions or create a hostile work environment.

The EEOC has issued guidelines designed to curtail sexual harassment. A variety of definitions of sexual harassment exist, but generally **sexual harassment** refers to actions that are sexually directed, are unwanted, and subject the worker to adverse employment conditions or create a hostile work environment. Sexual harassment can occur between a boss and a subordinate, among coworkers, and among nonemployees who have business contracts with employees.

There is growing awareness of sexual harassment and less tolerance of it, both among employers and those individuals affected by it.

The victims of sexual harassment are more likely to bring charges and take legal actions against employers and harassing individuals than they were in the past. According to EEOC statistics, well over 90% of the sexual harassment charges filed have involved harassment of women by men. However, some sexual harassment cases have been filed by men against women managers and supervisors. The best-selling book *Disclosure* and the movie based on it illustrated this type of harassment. Also, a few cases have been filed involving a manager and an employee of the same sex.[2] A unique defense was tried in one case involving a Las Vegas hotel and casino. A supervisor at the casino used sexually offensive language to both males and females. The employer claimed that this behavior was not sexual harassment because the supervisor was abusive to all employees, not just women. But a federal court rejected that defense and said that the supervisor's conduct would be offensive to both sexes.[3]

Two types of sexual harassment are defined as follows.

- *Quid pro quo* harassment occurs when an employer or supervisor links specific employment outcomes to the individual's granting sexual favors.
- *Hostile environment* harassment occurs when the harassment has the effect of unreasonably interfering with work performance or psychological well-being or when intimidating or offensive working conditions are created.

Quid pro Quo Linking any condition of employment—including pay raises, promotions, assignments of work and work hours, performance appraisals, meetings, disciplinary actions, and many others—to the granting of sexual favors can be the basis for a charge of *quid pro quo* harassment. Certainly, harassment by supervisors and managers who expect sexual favors as a condition for a raise or promotion is inappropriate behavior in a work environment. This view has been supported in a wide variety of cases.

Hostile Environment The second type of sexual harassment involves the creation of a hostile work environment. One of the most extensive allegations of sexual harassment occurred in 1996 when the EEOC charged Mitsubishi Motor Manufacturing of America with a large number of sexual harassment violations. The EEOC estimated that the company could be required to pay up to $200 million. The company denied that it condoned sexual harassment and pursued its defense in court, where resolution took an extended period of time.

In a landmark case decided by the U.S. Supreme Court, *Meritor Savings Bank v. Vinson,* the Court ruled that creation of a hostile work environment due to sexual harassment is illegal even if the complainant suffered no loss of earnings or job loss. The case was brought by a former female employee who charged that a vice-president of the bank had sexually harassed her.[4]

In *Harris v. Forklift Systems,* the U.S. Supreme Court ruled that in determining if a hostile environment exists the following factors should be considered.[5]

- Whether the conduct was physically threatening or humiliating, rather than just offensive
- Whether the conduct interfered unreasonably with an employee's work performance
- Whether the conduct affected the employee's psychological well-being

Numerous cases in which sexual harassment has been found illustrate that what is harmless joking or teasing in the eyes of one person may be offensive and hostile behavior in the eyes of another. Commenting on dress or appearance, telling jokes that are suggestive or sexual in nature, allowing centerfold posters to be on display, or making continual requests to get together after work can lead to the creation of a hostile work environment.

When determining if sexual harassment occurred, in legal cases there is growing use of the "reasonable woman" standard. In *Ellison v. Brady,* the Court ruled that sexual harassment must be viewed from the perspective of a "reasonable woman," and not just people in general.[6]

Employer Responses to Sexual Harassment Complaints

Employers generally are held responsible for sexual harassment unless they take appropriate action in response to complaints. Employers are also held responsible if they knew (or should have known) of the conduct and failed to stop it. With the passage of the Civil Rights Act of 1991, the costs to employers of being found guilty of sexual harassment likely will increase as a result of jury trials and awards of punitive damages. Therefore, employers must take positive action to eliminate sexual harassment from their workplaces. In the *Ellison v. Brady* case mentioned earlier, the U.S. Supreme Court ruled that employers must take significant action to remedy sexual harassment situations in order to avoid liability. The remedial actions must be forceful, such as separating the two parties involved by job reassignment or discharging the harasser.

In reviewing numerous cases on sexual harassment, one research study found that the complainant won virtually every case if the harassment was severe, if there were witnesses and additional documentation, and if management had been notified of the harassment but had failed to take action. However, if management had taken action, then the employer tended to prevail.

These findings reinforce the fact that employers should have specific sexual harassment complaint procedures and policies that allow a complainant to bypass a supervisor if the supervisor is the harasser. The researchers found that if such a complaint process existed and it was not used by the complainant, the employer was more likely to win the case. Finally, prompt action by the employer to investigate sexual harassment complaints and then to punish the identified harassers aided the employer's defense. In summary, the research revealed that if harassment is taken seriously by employers, the outcomes of cases are more likely to be favorable to them.[7]

Sexual Harassment Policy Every employer should have a policy on sexual harassment. Support for that policy must begin with strong support from top management. The policy should address such issues as the following:[8]

- Instructions on how to report complaints, including how to bypass a supervisor if he or she is involved in the harassment
- Assurances of confidentiality and protection against retaliation by those against whom the complaint is filed
- A guarantee of prompt investigation
- A statement that disciplinary action will be taken against sexual harassers up to and including termination of employment

One case illustrates that by having a policy and enforcing it an employer can avoid liability for the harassment of a female employee by a male supervisor. In this case, the employer investigated the complaint but found insufficient evidence to support the woman's allegations. Nevertheless, the woman was transferred to a job at another facility so that she did not have contact with the supervisor. No disciplinary action was taken against the supervisor. The woman was not satisfied with that solution and filed a discrimination lawsuit against the employer. A federal court ruled that because the employer had adopted appropriate policies and consistently enforced those policies, there was no employer liability in this case.[9]

Communications and Training All employees, especially supervisors and managers, should be informed that sexual harassment will not be tolerated in an organization. To create such awareness, communications to all employees should highlight the employer's policy on sexual harassment and the importance of creating and maintaining a work environment free of sexual harassment. The communications should be ongoing to reinforce to all employees that sexual harassment will not be tolerated and will be dealt with severely.

In addition, training of all employees, especially supervisors and managers, is recommended. The training should identify what constitutes sexual harassment and alert employees to the types of behaviors that create problems.

Investigation and Action Once management has knowledge of sexual harassment, the investigation process should begin. Often, an HR staff member and/or outside legal counsel will spearhead the investigation to provide objectivity. The procedures to be followed should be identified at the time the sexual harassment policy is promulgated, and all steps taken during the investigation should be documented. It is crucial to ensure that the complainant is not subjected to any further harassment or to retaliation for filing the complaint.[10]

Court cases make it clear that employers have a duty to do more than publish a policy.[11] For example, in *Bundy v. Jackson*, a female vocational rehabilitation specialist (Bundy) suffered from sexual propositions and sexual intimidation and was passed over for a promotion. She filed a complaint within the organization, which had a policy against sexual harassment, but no organizational investigation followed. The court decision favored Bundy and found that a violation of Title VII occurred "where an employer created or condoned a substantially discriminatory work environment, regardless of whether the complaining employee lost any tangible job benefits."[12] By failing to investigate this employee's charges, the employer had "condoned" the harassment.

A sidelight to sexual harassment issues involves romances in the workplace. Workplace romances and relationships can create problems for employees and employers alike. The HR Perspective discusses the advisability of limiting workplace romances.

❖ Pregnancy Discrimination

The Pregnancy Discrimination Act (PDA) of 1978 was passed as an amendment to the Civil Rights Act of 1964. Its major provision was that any employer with 15 or more employees had to treat maternity leave the same as other personal or medical leaves. Closely related to the PDA is the Family and Medical Leave Act (FMLA) of 1993, which requires that individuals be given up to 12 weeks of family leave without pay and also requires that those taking family leave be allowed to return to jobs. (See Chapter 15 for details.) The FMLA applies to both men and women.

❖ Compensation Issues and Sex Discrimination

A number of concerns have been raised about employer compensation practices that discriminate on the basis of sex. At issue in several compensation practices is the extent to which men and women are treated differently, with women most frequently receiving less compensation or benefits. Equal pay, pay equity, and benefits coverage are three prominent issues.

HR PERSPECTIVE

Should Workplace Relationships and Romances Be Prohibited?

As more and more men and women work together in teams and on projects, more employers are becoming concerned about personal relationships between employees. Could permitting such relationships lead to liability for sexual harassment claims when relationships end?

The appeal of workplace relationships was succinctly described by a 28-year-old single male information systems specialist: "When you're working 50 to 60 hours per week, the only place to meet women is at work." When work-based friendships lead to romance and off-the-job sexual relationships, managers and employers face a dilemma: Do they monitor for and protect the firm from potential sexual harassment complaints, thereby "meddling" in employees' private, off-the-job lives? Or do they simply ignore such relationships and the potential problems they present?

The greatest concerns are romantic relationships between supervisors and subordinates, because the harassment of subordinates by supervisors is the most frequent type of sexual harassment situation. Though many companies prohibit relatives from having direct reporting relationships, extending this policy to people who are dating raises resistance from those involved, who may believe that what they do after work is none of their employers' concern.

Employment attorneys generally recommend that the HR manager remind both parties in workplace romances of the company policy on sexual harassment and encourage either party to contact the HR department should the relationship cool and become one involving unwanted and unwelcome attentions. Also, the HR manager always should document that such conversations occurred.[13]

EQUAL PAY The Equal Pay Act, enacted in 1963, requires employers to pay similar wage rates for similar work without regard to gender. Tasks performed only intermittently or infrequently do not make jobs different enough to justify significantly different wages. Differences in pay may be allowed because of: (1) differences in seniority, (2) differences in performance, (3) differences in quality and/or quantity of production, and (4) factors other than sex, such as skill, effort, and working conditions.

***Pay Equity**
Similarity in pay for jobs requiring comparable levels of knowledge, skill, and ability, even where actual job duties differ significantly.

PAY EQUITY According to the concept of **pay equity,** the pay for jobs requiring comparable levels of knowledge, skill, and ability should be similar even if actual duties differ significantly. The Equal Pay Act applies to jobs that are substantially the same, whereas pay equity applies to jobs that are *valued* similarly in the organization, whether or not they are the same.

A major reason for the development of the pay equity idea is the continuing gap between the earnings of women and men. As Figure 6–1 shows, that gap has been closing, but it still is sizeable. Men's and women's wage levels are most similar for childless men and women aged 27–33; in this group, women's wages are 98% of those of men. One research study found that the wage gap increases as women and men progress beyond age 35.[14] Another study, by the U.S. Census Bureau, found that the salaries of younger, college-educated women average 92% of those of their male peers. However, the gap widens over time, so that women aged 55–64 are making only 54% of what men that age earn.[15] Industry differences involving occupational choices are significant.[16] The greatest disparity is found when pay for lower-skilled, less-educated women, is compared with pay for lower-skilled, less-educated men. The accompanying cartoon contains more managerial candor than often occurs.

As discussed in more detail in Chapter 13, on compensation, a number of state and local government employers have mandated pay equity for public-sector employees through legislation. Some Canadian provinces have enacted similar laws. But except where state laws have mandated pay equity, U.S. federal

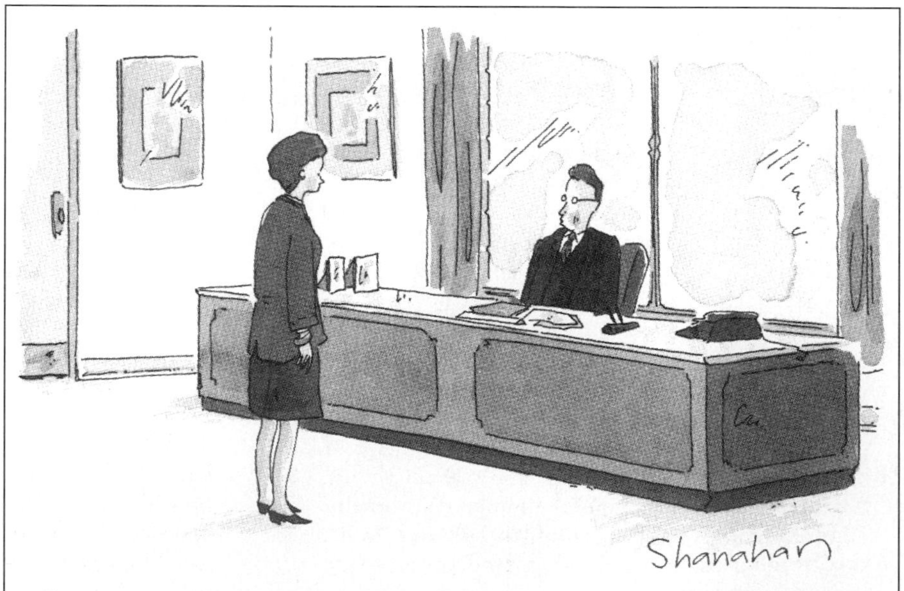

"I've never said this to a woman before, but here goes: We're not paying you enough."

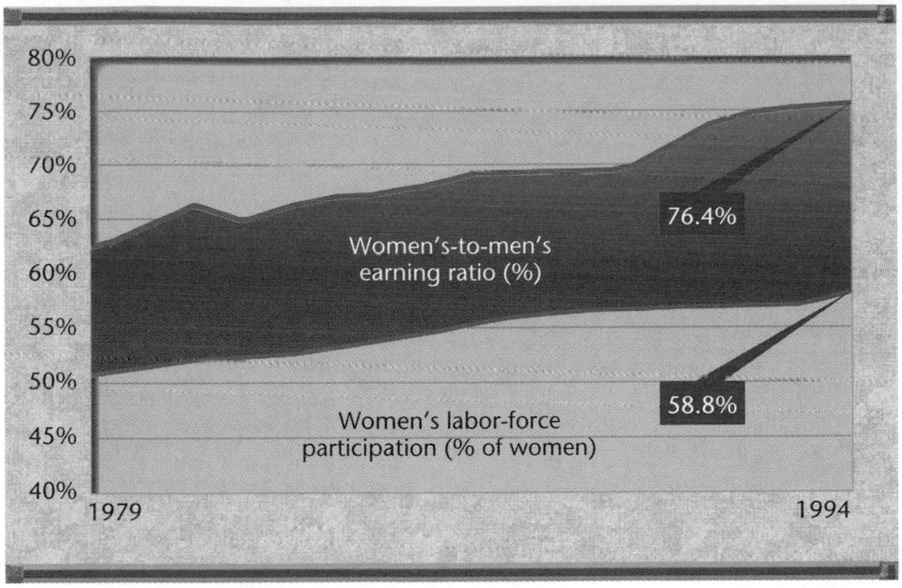

❖ FIGURE 6–1 ❖
COMPARISON OF MEN'S AND WOMEN'S EARNINGS, 1979–1994

SOURCE: Based on information from the U.S. Department of Labor, Bureau of Labor Statistics, presented in *USA Today,* March 14, 1996, 12A.

courts generally have ruled that the existence of pay differences between jobs held by women and jobs held by men is not sufficient to prove that illegal discrimination has occurred.

BENEFITS COVERAGE A final area of sex-based differences in compensation relates to benefits coverage. One concern has been labeled "unisex" pension coverage. The *Arizona Governing Committee v. Norris* decision held that an employer's deferred compensation plan violated Title VII because female employees received lower monthly benefits payments than men received on retirement, despite the fact that women contributed equally to the plan.[17] Regardless of longevity differences, men and women who contribute equally to pension plans must receive equal monthly payments.

❖ SEX DISCRIMINATION IN JOBS AND CAREERS

The selection or promotion criteria that employers use can discriminate against women. Some cases have found that women were not allowed to enter certain jobs or job fields. Particularly problematic is the use of marital or family status as a basis for not selecting women.

NEPOTISM Many employers have policies that restrict or prohibit **nepotism**, the practice of allowing relatives to work for the same employer. Other firms require only that relatives not work directly for or with each other or be placed in a position where potential collusion or conflicts could occur. The policies most frequently cover spouses, brothers, sisters, mothers, fathers, sons, and daughters. Generally, employer anti-nepotism policies have been upheld by courts, in spite of the concern that they discriminate against women more than men (because women tend to be denied employment or leave employers more often as a result of marriage to another employee).

Nepotism
Practice of allowing relatives to work for the same employer.

However, inquiries about previous names (not maiden names) under which an applicant may have worked may be necessary in order to check reference information with former employers, educational institutions, or employers' own files, in the case of former employees. This kind of inquiry is not illegal.

Job Assignments and "Nontraditional Jobs" One result of the increasing number of women in the workforce is the movement of women into jobs traditionally held by men. More women are working as welders, railroad engineers, utility repair specialists, farm equipment sales representatives, sheet metal workers, truck drivers, and carpenters. Many of these jobs typically pay higher wages than the office and clerical jobs often held by women. Nevertheless, women hold fewer than 5% of the blue-collar jobs traditionally held by men, such as welder, carpenter, mechanic, and bricklayer.[18] Thus, it appears there are gender-based groupings of jobs, in which women hold most jobs of certain types and men hold most other types of jobs.[19] Clearly, many kinds of discrimination in the assignment of women to jobs still exist.

The right of employers to reassign women from hazardous jobs to jobs that may be lower paying because of health-related concerns is another issue. Employers' fears about higher health-insurance costs, and even possible lawsuits involving such problems as birth defects caused by damage sustained during pregnancy, have led some employers to institute *reproductive and fetal protection policies.* However, the U.S. Supreme Court has ruled such policies are illegal.[20] Also, having different job conditions for men and women usually is held to be discriminatory.

***Glass Ceiling**
Discriminatory practices that have prevented women and other protected-class members from advancing to executive-level jobs.

The "Glass Ceiling" For years, women's groups have alleged that women encounter a "glass ceiling" in the workplace.The **glass ceiling** refers to discriminatory practices that have prevented women and other protected-class members from advancing to executive-level jobs. The extent of the problem is seen in the fact that white males compose 43% of the workforce but hold 95% of all senior management positions. In the nation's largest corporations, only two women are CEOs, and women compose only 9% of the executive vice-presidents in larger firms.[21] Figure 6–2 shows the percentages of women and minority managers by industry segment. Statistics reveal that women tend to have better opportunities to progress in smaller firms and, of course, when they start their own businesses. Also, in computer-related fields, women are increasing their representation in

❖ Figure 6–2 ❖
Percentages of Women and Minority Managers by Industry Segment

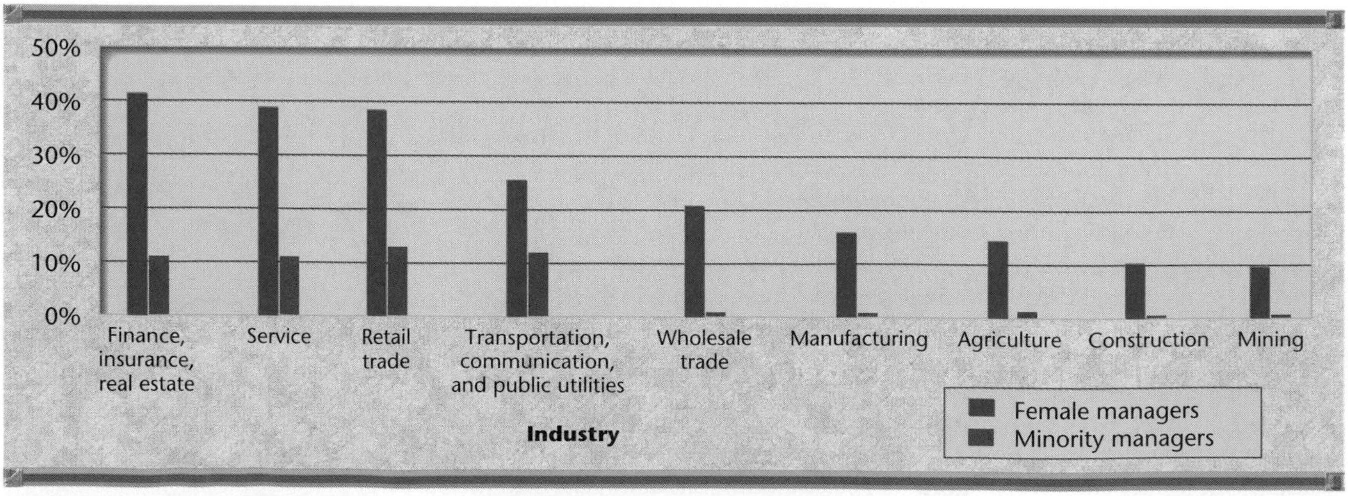

SOURCE: Federal Glass Ceiling Commission Report, 1995.

management, particularly in data processing service and software development firms.[22] One research study found that in the U.S. Government senior executive service, gender was not a major determinant in predicting who progressed to senior-level positions.[23]

The Glass Ceiling Act of 1991 was passed in conjunction with the Civil Rights Act of 1991. A Glass Ceiling Commission was established to conduct a study on how to shatter the glass ceiling encountered by women and other protected-class members. The commission, composed of 21 members, submitted a report in 1995. Key recommendations included the following:[24]

- Employers should include diversity goals in strategic business plans, and managers should be accountable for meeting these goals.
- Affirmative action should be used to encourage firms to recruit more widely and give promotion opportunities to more diverse individuals.
- Women and minorities should be prepared for senior positions by the use of mentoring, training, and other programs.
- Federal government agencies should refine data collection requirements to avoid "double counting" of minority women, so that true statistics and measures of progress can be obtained.
- Increased government enforcement efforts are needed, as well as more funding and staffing of agencies such as the EEOC.

"Glass Walls" and "Glass Elevators" A related problem is that women have tended to advance to senior management in a limited number of functional areas, such as human resources and corporate communications. Because jobs in these "supporting" areas tend to pay less than jobs in sales, marketing, operations, or finance, the overall impact is to reduce women's career progression and income. Limits that keep women from progressing only in certain fields have been referred to as "glass walls" or "glass elevators." Some firms have established formal mentoring programs in order to break down glass walls.[25]

Age Discrimination

For many years, race and sex discrimination cases overshadowed age discrimination cases. Starting with passage of the 1978 amendments to the Age Discrimination in Employment Act (ADEA) of 1967, a dramatic increase in age discrimination suits occurred. However, in recent years, age discrimination still has followed race and sex discrimination as the basis for complaints filed with the EEOC.

Age Discrimination in Employment Act (ADEA)

The Age Discrimination in Employment Act (ADEA) of 1967, amended in 1978 and 1986, makes it illegal for an employer to discriminate in compensation, terms, conditions, or privileges of employment because of an individual's age. The later amendments first raised the minimum mandatory retirement age to 70 and then eliminated it completely. The ADEA applies to all individuals above the age of 40 working for employers having 20 or more workers. However, the act does not apply if age is a job-related occupational qualification.

Prohibitions against age discrimination do not apply when an individual is disciplined or discharged for good cause, such as poor job performance. Older workers who are poor performers can be terminated just as anyone else can be. However, numerous suits under the ADEA have been filed involving workers over 40 who were forced to take "voluntary retirement" when organizational restructuring or workforce reduction programs were implemented.[26]

HR PERSPECTIVE

Forced Retirements and "Overqualified" Older Workers

Many employers have instituted early retirement programs as part of downsizing and restructuring efforts to encourage employees to leave their jobs. While the fact is often unstated, many programs target older individuals, because the eligibility criteria include a combination of age and experience. Older workers tend to have higher salaries because of length of service and job progressions. Thus, by encouraging them to retire, employers may be reducing the most costly portion of their employment budget.

The wave of organizational downsizing has led to a jump in age discrimination claims. Workers filing discrimination charges say that the "voluntary" programs are not truly voluntary. Instead, older workers allege that they are forced to take the retirement buyouts or lose their jobs and get little or no severance payments.

A related problem involves older employees who are not given appropriate consideration for other jobs in an organization when restructuring is done. In one case, an older employee had his position eliminated. He claimed that several open positions for which he was qualified were filled with younger employees. The company did not disagree with the older worker but relied on a defense that the available jobs were not "appropriate" or "suitable" because they were at different pay grades and did not require his advanced technical skills. The issue of "overqualification" also was raised when the employer indicated a concern that the older worker would become frustrated because his knowledge, skills, and abilities would be underutilized.

The court ruled against the employer and said that the employer was relying on assumptions, not facts. Particularly significant was the fact that the older worker had not been asked if he would be willing to take a lower-paying job.

Similar decisions have been reached in other cases. Another court decision summarized the issue as follows:

> Characterizing an applicant in an age discrimination case as overqualified has a connotation that defies common sense: How can a person overqualified by experience and training be turned down for a position given to a younger person deemed better qualified? Denying employment to an older job applicant because he or she has too much experience, training, or education is to employ a euphemism to mask the real reason for refusal, namely, in the eyes of an employer, the applicant is too old.

As a result of such decisions, employers must evaluate older applicants and workers for their knowledge, skills, and abilities, instead of relying on age stereotyping that may be erroneous when applied to a specific older worker.[27]

Age Discrimination and Workforce Reductions In the 1990s, early retirement programs and organizational downsizing have been used by many employers to reduce their employment costs. Illegal age discrimination sometimes occurs in the process when an individual over the age of 40 is forced into retirement or is denied employment or promotion on the basis of age. If disparate impact or treatment for those over 40 exists, age discrimination occurs, as the HR Perspective indicates.

Ensuring that age discrimination—or any kind of illegal discrimination—does not affect employment decisions requires that documentation of performance be completed by supervisors and managers. In the case of older employees, care must be taken that references to age ("good old Fred" or "need younger blood") in conversations are not used with older employees. As mentioned, terminations based on documented performance deficiencies not related to age are perfectly legal.

O'Connor v. Consolidated Coin Caterers A 1996 U.S. Supreme Court decision will affect the way age discrimination cases are viewed in the future. In *O'Connor v. Consolidated Coin Caterers,* a 56-year-old sales manager was fired and replaced by a man aged 40. The employer successfully argued in lower courts that because the replacement also was covered by the ADEA, no age discrimination could exist. However, the Supreme Court unanimously ruled that "The fact that one person in the protected class has lost out to another person in the protected class is irrelevant, so long as he has lost out because of his age." The decision also said that specific evidence of actual age discrimination is needed and that the replacement of an older worker by someone who is insignificantly younger does not necessarily constitute age discrimination. However, the Court did not define what constitutes a significant or an insignificant difference in ages. The actual determination of whether age discrimination had occurred was to be decided by lower courts in this case.[28]

❖ Older Workers Benefit Protection Act (OWBPA)

The Older Workers Benefit Protection Act (OWBPA) of 1990 was passed to amend the ADEA and to overturn a 1989 decision by the U.S. Supreme Court in *Public Employees Retirement System of Ohio v. Betts.*[29] This act requires equal treatment for older workers in early retirement or severance situations. It sets forth some very specific criteria that must be met when older workers sign waivers promising not to sue for age discrimination.

❖ Americans with Disabilities Act (ADA)

The passage of the Americans with Disabilities Act (ADA) in 1990 represented an expansion in the scope and impact of laws and regulations on discrimination against individuals with disabilities. All employers with 15 or more employees are covered by the provisions of the ADA, which are enforced by the EEOC. The ADA was built upon the Vocational Rehabilitation Act of 1973 and the Rehabilitation Act of 1974, both of which applied only to federal contractors.

The ADA affects more than just employment matters, as Figure 6–3 shows, and it applies to private employers, employment agencies, labor unions, and

LOGGING ON

A description of the Americans with Disabilities Act and ways to comply with the law are provided at the following web site.

http://www.igc.apc.org/cwatx/ada.html

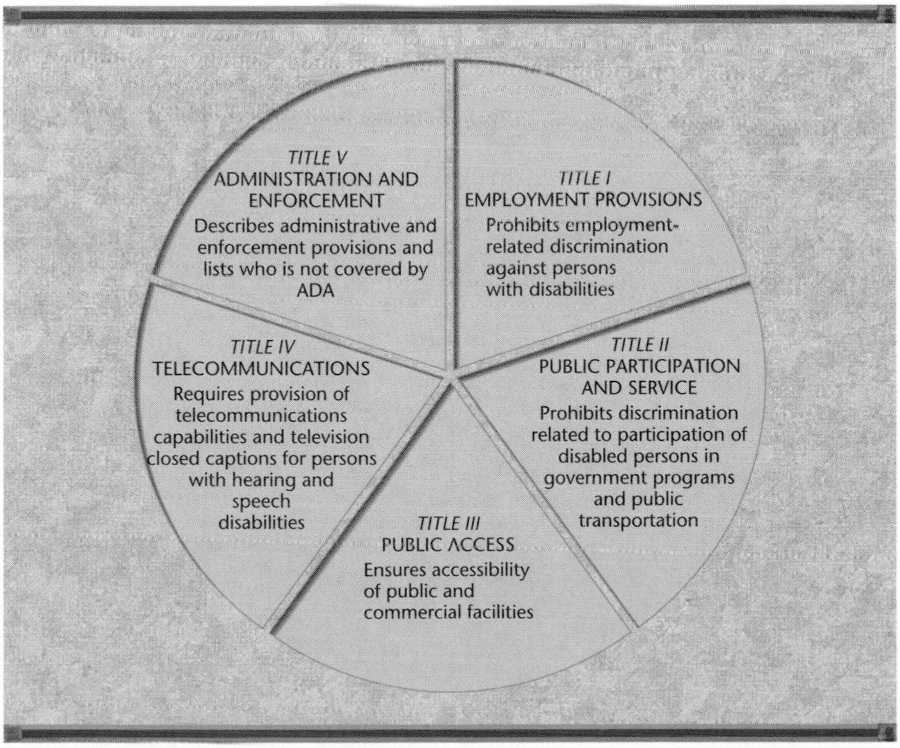

❖ Figure 6–3 ❖
Major Sections of the Americans with Disabilities Act

state and local governments. The ADA contains the following requirements regarding employment:

- Discrimination is prohibited against individuals with disabilities who can perform the *essential job functions,* a standard that is somewhat vague.
- A covered employer must make *reasonable accommodation* for persons with disabilities, so that they can function as employees, unless *undue hardship* would be placed on the employer.
- Preemployment medical examinations are prohibited except after an employment offer is made, conditional upon passing a physical examination.
- Federal contractors and subcontractors with contracts valued at more than $2,500 must take affirmative action to hire qualified disabled individuals.

Discrimination against Individuals with Disabilities

Employers looking for workers with the knowledge, skills, and abilities to perform jobs often have neglected a significant source of good, dedicated people—individuals with physical or mental disabilities. According to U.S. government estimates, there are almost 50 million Americans with some sort of disability. Many of them between the ages of 16 and 64 are unemployed but would like to work if given appropriate opportunities. When individuals with disabilities are hired and placed in jobs that match their capabilities, they often succeed. The accompanying HR Perspective describes a research study on employment discrimination against workers with disabilities.

HR PERSPECTIVE

Research on Employment Discrimination against Workers with Disabilities

Slonaker and Wendt conducted a research study to determine the patterns of employment discrimination against workers with disabilities. The researchers reviewed over 3,500 cases using data from the Ohio Civil Rights Commission. As part of this review, they profiled those who claimed disability discrimination and what types of disabilities they claimed.

As published in *Business Forum,* the results revealed that workers with disabilities composed about 12% of all those filing employment discrimination claims. About two-thirds of those filing disability claims were men, and about 40% of the claimants had manufacturing-related jobs. Interestingly, only 15% claimed that their disabilities were caused on the job. Despite the fact that the rest of the claimants had become disabled due to non-job related injuries, they still filed claims alleging that employers discriminated against them because of their disabilities. Back problems and injuries and impaired movement were the most common disabilities claimed.

Slonaker and Wendt also examined the claims and cases to identify the three most common patterns of employer behaviors that led to disability discrimination complaints. The findings were as follows:

- About 43% of the claims involved employers who were trying to avoid inconveniencing themselves or other workers. Refusal by employers to offer *light-duty work,* whereby individuals do not perform some duties, was a common cause of claims in this area.
- Slightly over 20% of the claimants alleged that their employers did not provide *reasonable accommodation*.
- About 13% of the claimants said employers discharged them because of *absenteeism* caused by disability conditions. In some cases, employers assigned duties that were not recommended by the employees' physicians. Thus, the employees left work, thus creating absenteeism problems.

The results of this study reveal that employers face the greatest likelihood of disability claims under the ADA from existing employees who have or develop disabilities. The study makes clear that employers should not view their employees as "disposable" but should make reasonable accommodations where necessary.[31]

The number of complaints filed under the ADA has skyrocketed in recent years. According to statistics from the EEOC, over 40,000 disability discrimination complaints were filed in the first several years the act was in effect. Over half of those complaints had to do with discharge of employees with disabilities or employees who became disabled. Another 25% dealt with failure to provide reasonable accommodation.[30]

❖ Who Is Disabled?

As defined by the ADA,[32] a **disabled person** is someone who has a physical or mental impairment that substantially limits that person in some major life activities, who has a record of such an impairment, or who is regarded as having such an impairment. Persons who qualify for protection under the act include those who have obvious disabilities such as the absence of a limb, sight or hearing impairments, or other physical disabilities. Individuals with less visible disabilities classified as disabled under the ADA include persons with life-threatening diseases (AIDS, cancer, leukemia), rehabilitated drug users and alcoholics, and persons with major muscular limitations or breathing difficulties. People with various mental disabilities or impairments also qualify under the ADA.[33] Regulations exclude current users of illegal drugs, people with sexual behavior disorders, and compulsive gamblers from being classified as disabled.

❖Disabled Person
Someone who has a physical or mental impairment that substantially limits that person in some major life activities, who has a record of such an impairment, or who is regarded as having such an impairment.

EEOC Guidelines on Disabilities To provide better guidance to those covered by the ADA, the EEOC issued additional clarifications of its guidelines, including the following:[34]

- *Impairment* was defined as a physiological disorder affecting one or more body systems or a mental/psychological disorder. Specifically *excluded* are:
  - Environmental, cultural, and economic disadvantages
  - Homosexuality and bisexuality
  - Normal deviation in height and weight
  - Normal personality traits (rudeness, quick temper, arrogance, and so on)
  - Pregnancy
  - Physical characteristics
- *Thinking, concentrating,* and *interacting with other people* were included as *major life activities.* Individuals impaired in one of these areas are covered by the ADA.
- A *substantial limitation* was clarified to mean a limitation in life activities other than working.

In spite of the EEOC guidelines, there is still some confusion as to who is disabled. For example, some court decisions and laws have protected individuals perceived as impaired to a degree that their employment is affected. Thus, even individuals with facial disfigurements may qualify for protection against employer discrimination. Other court decisions have found individuals who have high blood pressure, epilepsy, allergies, obesity, and color blindness to be disabled.

AIDS and Life-Threatening Illnesses In recent years, the types of disabilities covered by various local, state, and federal acts prohibiting discrimination have been expanded. For example, a U.S. Supreme Court case held that an employer cannot discriminate against an individual whom the employer believes may have a contagious disease. The case involved an individual who had a relapse of tuberculosis and was discharged from her job as a schoolteacher because her employer feared her illness might be contagious.[35]

The most feared contagious disease is acquired immune deficiency syndrome (AIDS). The disease was almost unknown in 1980, but by the mid-1990s, it was estimated that a million people in the United States either had AIDS or were carrying the HIV virus. Over 200,000 people have died from AIDS in the United States.[36]

Unfortunately, employers and employees often react with fear about working with an AIDS victim. Nevertheless, if an employer does have an employee with a life-threatening illness, educating other employees is more appropriate than terminating the victim's employment. A medical leave of absence (without pay if that is the general policy) can be used to assist the AIDS-afflicted employee during medical treatments. Other employees should be told to keep medical records of affected persons confidential. Also, employees who indicate that they will not work with an AIDS victim should be told that their refusal to work is not protected by law and that they could be subject to disciplinary action up to and including discharge.[37]

❖ Essential Job Functions

Essential Job Functions
The fundamental job duties of the employment position that an individual with a disability holds or desires; they do not include marginal functions of the position.

The ADA requires that employers identify for all jobs the **essential job functions**—the fundamental job duties of the employment position that an individual with a disability holds or desires. These functions do not include marginal functions of the position.

The essential functions should be identified in written job descriptions that indicate the amount of time spent performing various functions and their criticality. Most employers have interpreted this provision to mean that they should develop and maintain current and comprehensive job descriptions for all jobs. These job descriptions should list the job functions in the order of "essentiality." Also, the job specification statements that identify the qualifications required of those in the jobs should specify the exact knowledge, skills, abilities, and physical demands involved. For example, hearing, seeing, speaking, climbing, lifting, and stooping should be mentioned when those actions are necessary in performing specific jobs.

❖ Reasonable Accommodation

Reasonable Accommodation
A modification or adjustment to a job or work environment that enables a qualified individual with a disability to enjoy equal employment opportunity.

A **reasonable accommodation** is a modification or adjustment to a job or work environment that enables a qualified individual with a disability to enjoy equal employment opportunity. Employers are required to provide reasonable accommodation for individuals with disabilities to ensure that illegal discrimination does not occur.

There are several areas of reasonable accommodation. First, architectural barriers should not prohibit disabled individuals' *access to work areas or rest rooms.* A second area of reasonable accommodation is the *assignment of work tasks.* Satisfying this requirement may mean modifying jobs, work schedules, equipment, or work area layouts. Some examples include teaching sign language to a supervisor so that a deaf person can be employed, modifying work schedules to assist disabled workers, buying special amplifiers for hearing-impaired employees, and having another worker perform minor duties. There are few specific rules on which an employer can rely in this area, because every situation is considered on its own merits by the courts.

❖ Undue Hardship

Reasonable accommodation is restricted to actions that do not place an "undue hardship" on an employer. An action places **undue hardship** on an employer if it poses significant difficulty or expense. The ADA offers only general guidelines on when an accommodation becomes unreasonable and places undue hardship on an employer.[38] More information on reasonable accommodations is given in Chapter 7, on job analysis and design.

Undue Hardship
Condition created when making a reasonable accommodation for individuals with disabilities would pose significant difficulty or expense for an employer.

Initially, employers were very concerned about facing extensive costs for remodeling facilities or making other accommodations, as some accommodations can be expensive. However, a study done of compliance efforts at Sears, Roebuck, & Company, the large retailer, found that over a five-year period the average cost per accommodation was $121. When some larger projects that cost over $1,000 were removed from the analysis, the average accommodation cost dropped to $36.[39] Examples of accommodations used by other employers and their costs include the following.[40]

- A paper-cup dispenser was placed by a recessed water fountain so that individuals in wheelchairs could get drinks. The cost was $4.95 for each dispenser plus continuing costs of cup refills.
- A one-handed person working in a kitchen could do all jobs except opening food cans. A one-handed electric can opener was purchased for a cost of $35.
- A housekeeper in a motel could not bend to inspect under beds. A mirror was placed on a cleaning wand device for her use. The cost was $11.

❖ Other Bases of Discrimination

The original purpose of the Civil Rights Act of 1964 was to address race discrimination. This area continues to be important today, and employers must be aware of practices that may be discriminatory on the basis of race. Also, the requirements of the EEOC and the affirmative action requirements of the Office of Federal Contract Compliance Programs (OFCCP) specifically designate race as an area for investigation and reporting.

Race is often a factor in discrimination on the basis of national origin. This topic is examined next, followed by discussions of religious discrimination and other types of discrimination.

❖ Discrimination Based on National Origin and Citizenship

What are the rights of people from other countries, especially those illegally in the United States, with regard to employment and equality? Illegal aliens often are called *undocumented workers* because they do not have the appropriate permits and documents from the Immigration and Naturalization Service. The passage of the Immigration Reform and Control Acts (IRCA) in 1986, 1990, and 1996 clarified issues regarding employment of immigrants that had confronted politicians, labor leaders, and employers for many years.

Immigration Reform and Control Acts (IRCA) To deal with problems arising from the continued flow of immigrants to the United States, the Immigration Reform and Control Act (IRCA) was passed in 1986 and revised in 1990. The IRCA makes it illegal for an employer to discriminate in recruiting, hiring, or terminating based on an individual's national origin or citizenship. Many employers were avoiding the recruitment and hiring of individuals who were "foreign looking" or who spoke with an accent, fearing they might be undocumented workers. Hispanic leaders voiced concern about the discriminatory effects of this practice on Hispanics who were U.S. citizens. The 1990 act attempted to address this issue. It also prohibits employers from using disparate treatment, such as requiring more documentation from some prospective employees than from others. In addition, the IRCA requires that employers who knowingly hire illegal aliens be penalized.[41] Later revisions to the IRCA tightened up some of the restrictions on the entry of immigrants to work in U.S. organizations, particularly in "scarce-skill" areas. The number of immigrants allowed legal entry was reduced slightly, and categories for entry visas were revised.

EMPLOYER DOCUMENTATION REQUIREMENTS Under the acts just described, employers are required to examine identification documents for new employees, who also must sign verification forms about their eligibility to work legally in the United States. Employers must ask for proof of identity, such as a driver's license with a picture, Social Security card, birth certificate, immigration permit, or other document. A copy of the I–9 form, which must be completed by all new employees within 72 hours, is included in Chapter 9.

FOREIGN-LANGUAGE AND "ENGLISH-ONLY" REQUIREMENTS Questions about an applicant's language skills should be limited to situations in which workers will have job-related reasons for using a foreign language. The employer is restricted to making such inquiries only in regard to those specific jobs that warrant use of the foreign language. Court decisions in this area generally have rejected attempts by employers to ban employees from speaking foreign languages at all times in work areas.[42] However, some court decisions have supported the idea that some business operations require communication in a single language.

A total of 22 states have passed laws making English the official language of the state. The legal status of those laws is under review by the U.S. Supreme Court, based on appeals from various federal courts.[43] Therefore, employers should monitor developments at both the federal and state levels.

❖ RELIGIOUS DISCRIMINATION

Title VII of the Civil Rights Act identifies discrimination on the basis of religion as illegal. However, religious schools and institutions can use religion as a BFOQ for employment practices on a limited scale.

A major guide in this area was established by the U.S. Supreme Court in *TWA v. Hardison*. In that case, the Supreme Court ruled that an employer is required to make *reasonable accommodation* of an employee's religious beliefs. Because TWA had done so, the ruling denied Hardison's discrimination charges.[44] In summary, employers are advised to offer alternative work schedules, make use of compensatory time off, or otherwise adjust to employees' religious beliefs. Once reasonable accommodation efforts have been made, the employer is considered to have abided by the law.[45]

A major agreement reached with Wal-Mart Stores may set a precedent for other employers. To settle a lawsuit brought by a worker who refused to work on his Sabbath, Wal-Mart agreed to provide guidelines to all managers on how to accommodate workers' religious beliefs and then to conduct training sessions for managers.[46]

Another issue relates to *religious expression*. In the last several years, there have been a number of cases in which employees have sued employers for prohibiting them from expressing their religious beliefs at work. Employers have had to take action because of complaints by other workers. For example, in one case, a devout Catholic woman insisted on wearing an anti-abortion button depicting a fetus. Some coworkers objected, and these employees filed a grievance through their union. The employer offered three options to the woman, but she refused all of them. Following her refusal, the employer terminated her employment, and she sued on the grounds of religious discrimination. A federal court ruled that the employer's efforts had been sufficient, so the employer was not held liable for religious discrimination.[47]

❖ Sexual Orientation and Gay Rights

Recent battles over revising policies for nonheterosexuals in the U.S. military services illustrate the depth of emotions that accompany discussions of "gay rights." Some states and a number of cities have passed laws prohibiting discrimination based on sexual orientation or lifestyle. Even the issue of benefits coverage for "domestic partners," whether heterosexual or homosexual, has been the subject of state and city legislation. That issue is discussed in more detail in Chapter 15. However, at the federal level no laws of a similar nature have been passed. Whether gay men and lesbians have rights under the equal protection amendment to the U.S. Constitution has not been decided by the U.S. Supreme Court.

Regarding transsexuals, who are individuals who have had sex-change surgery, court cases and the EEOC have ruled that sex discrimination under Title VII applies to a person's gender at birth. Thus, it does not apply to the new gender of those who have had gender-altering operations. Transvestites and individuals with other sexual behavior disorders are specifically excluded from being considered disabled under the Americans with Disabilities Act of 1990.

❖ Discrimination and Appearance

Several EEO cases have been filed concerning the physical appearance of employees. Court decisions consistently have allowed employers to have dress codes as long as they are applied uniformly. However, requiring a dress code for women but not for men has been ruled to constitute disparate treatment; therefore, it would be discriminatory. Most of the dress standards contested have required workers to dress in a conservative manner.

Obesity and Facial Hair Individuals have brought cases claiming employment discrimination based on obesity or on unattractive appearance.[48] Employers have lost many of the cases because of their inability to prove any direct job-related value in their requirements. In other cases, some courts have ruled that under the Americans with Disabilities Act (ADA), obese individuals may qualify as having a covered disability when they are perceived and treated as if they have a disability.[49]

Cases also have addressed the issue of beards, mustaches, and hair length and style. Because African American men are more likely than white males to suffer from a skin disease that is worsened by shaving, they have filed suits challenging policies prohibiting beards or long sideburns. Generally, courts have ruled for employers in these cases.

Height/Weight Restrictions Many times, height/weight restrictions have been used to discriminate against women or other protected groups. For example, the state of Alabama violated Title VII in setting height and weight restrictions for correctional counselors. The restrictions (5 feet 2 inches and 120 pounds) would exclude 41.14% of the female population of the country but less than 1% of the men. The Supreme Court found that the state's attempt to justify the requirements as essential for job-related strength failed for lack of evidence. The Court suggested that if strength was the quality sought, the state should have adopted a strength requirement.[50]

❖ Conviction and Arrest Records

Court decisions consistently have ruled that using records of arrests, rather than records of convictions, has a disparate impact on some groups protected by Title VII. An arrest, unlike a conviction, does not imply guilt. Statistics indicate that in some geographic areas, more members of some minority groups are arrested than nonminorities.

Generally, courts have held that conviction records may be used in determining employability if the offense is job related. For example, a bank could use an applicant's conviction for embezzlement as a valid basis for rejection. Some courts have held that only job-related convictions occurring within the most recent five to seven years may be considered. Consequently, employers inquiring about convictions often add a phrase such as "indication of a conviction will not be an absolute bar to employment."

❖ Veterans' Employment Rights

The employment rights of military veterans and reservists have been addressed several times. The two most important laws are highlighted next.

Vietnam-Era Veterans Readjustment Act of 1974 Concern about the readjustment and absorption of Vietnam-era veterans into the workforce led to the passage of the Vietnam-Era Veterans Readjustment Act. The act requires that affirmative action in hiring and advancing Vietnam-era veterans be undertaken by federal contractors and subcontractors having contracts of $10,000 or more.

Uniformed Services Employment and Reemployment Rights Act of 1994 Under the Uniformed Services Employment and Reemployment Rights Act of 1994, employees are required to notify their employers of military service obligations. Employees serving in the military must be provided leaves of absence and have reemployment rights for up to five years. Other provisions protect the right to benefits of employees called to military duty.[51]

❖ Seniority and Discrimination

Conflict between EEO regulations and organizational practices that give preference to employees on the basis of seniority represent another problem area. Employers, especially those with union contracts, frequently make layoff, promotion, and internal transfer decisions by giving employees with longer service first consideration. However, the use of seniority often means that there is disparate impact on protected-class members, who may be the workers most recently hired. The result of this system is that protected-class members who have obtained jobs through an affirmative action program are at a disadvantage because of their low levels of seniority. They may find themselves "last hired, first fired" or "last hired, last promoted." In some cases, the courts have held that a valid seniority system does *not* violate rights based on sex or race. In other cases, gender and racial considerations have been given precedence over seniority.

❖ EEO Compliance

Employers must comply with all EEO regulations and guidelines. To do so, managers should be aware of what specific administrative steps are required and how charges of discrimination are investigated.

❖ EEO Records

All employers with 15 or more employees are required to keep certain records that can be requested by the Equal Employment Opportunity Commission (EEOC). If the organization meets certain criteria, then reports and investigations by the Office of Federal Contract Compliance Programs (OFCCP) also must be addressed. Under various laws, employers also are required to post an "officially approved notice" in a prominent place where employees can see it. This notice states that the employer is an equal opportunity employer and does not discriminate.

EEO Records Retention All employment records must be maintained as required by the EEOC, and employer information reports must be filed with the federal government. Further, any personnel or employment record made or kept by the employer must be maintained for review by the EEOC. Such records include application forms and records concerning hiring, promotion, demotion, transfer, layoff, termination, rates of pay or other terms of compensation, and selection for training and apprenticeship. Even application forms or test papers completed by unsuccessful applicants may be requested. The length of time documents must be kept varies, but generally three years is recommended as a minimum.

Keeping good records, whether required by the government or not, is simply a good HR practice. Complete records are necessary for an employer to respond when a charge of discrimination is made and a compliance investigation begins.

Annual Reporting Form The basic report that must be filed with the EEOC is the annual report form EEO–1 (see Appendix D). The following employers must file this report:

- ❖ All employers with 100 or more employees, except state and local governments
- ❖ Subsidiaries of other companies where total employees equal 100
- ❖ Federal contractors with at least 50 employees and contracts of $50,000 or more
- ❖ Financial institutions in which government funds are held or saving bonds are issued

The annual report must be filed by March 31 for the preceding year. The form requires employment data by job category, classified according to various protected classes.

Applicant Flow Data Under EEO laws and regulations, employers may be required to show that they do not discriminate in the recruiting and selection of members of protected classes. For instance, the number of women who applied and the number hired may be compared with the selection rate for men to determine if adverse impact exists. The fact that protected-class identification is not available in employer records is not considered a valid excuse for failure to provide the data required.

Because collection of racial data on application blanks and other preemployment records is not permitted, the EEOC allows employers to use a "visual" survey or a separate *applicant flow form* that is not used in the selection process. An example of such a form is shown in Figure 6–4. Notice that this form is filled out

❖ FIGURE 6–4 ❖
APPLICANT FLOW DATA FORM

THE C COMPANY

THE FOLOWING STATISTICAL INFORMATION IS REQUIRED FOR COMPLIANCE WITH FEDERAL LAWS ASSURING EQUAL EMPLOYMENT OPPORTUNITY WITHOUT REGARD TO RACE, COLOR, SEX, NATIONAL ORIGIN, RELIGION, AGE OR DISABILITY AS WELL AS THE VIETNAM ERA READJUSTMENT ACT. THE INFORMATION REQUESTED IS VOLUNTARY AND WILL REMAIN SEPARATE FROM YOUR APPLICATION FOR EMPLOYMENT.

A MONTH ☐☐ DAY ☐☐ YEAR ☐☐ APPLICATION DATE

B ☐☐☐ ☐☐ ☐☐☐☐ A APPLICANT SOCIAL SECURITY NUMBER

C ☐ FIRST INITIAL D ☐ MIDDLE INITIAL

D ☐☐☐☐☐☐☐☐☐☐☐☐☐☐☐ LAST NAME

STREET

F ☐☐☐☐☐☐☐☐☐☐☐☐☐☐☐☐☐☐☐☐☐☐☐☐☐☐ ADDRESS

G CITY ☐☐☐☐☐☐☐☐☐☐☐☐☐ STATE (first 2 letters) ☐☐ ZIP ☐☐☐☐☐

H ☐ 1/ EEO CODES

MONTH ☐☐ DAY ☐☐ YEAR ☐☐ BIRTH DATE

EEO CODES 1/

A—White Male
B—White Female
C—Black Male
D—Black Female
E—Hispanic Male (Spanish Origin)
F—Hispanic Female (Spanish Origin)
G—American Indian/Alaskan Native Male
H—American Indian/Alaskan Native Female
I—Asian or Pacific Islander Male
J—Asian or Pacific Islander Female

J ☐ DO YOU HAVE A DISABILITY—Impairment which substantially limits one or more of your life activities?

K ☐ ARE YOU A DISABLED VETERAN— 30% V.A. Compesation or discharged because of disability incurred in line of duty

L ☐ ARE YOU A VIETNAM ERA VETERAN— 180 days Active Duty between Aug. 15, 1964 & May 7, 1975

JOB YOUR HAVE APPLIED FOR ____________________

LOCATION APPLICATION IS MADE FOR ____________________
(City or Town) State

TO BE COMPLETED BY OFFICE ACCEPTING APPLICATION

☐ DIVISION

DEPT. APPLICATION IS MADE FOR

____

HR STAFF USE ONLY

☐☐☐☐☐☐☐☐☐☐

☐☐☐☐ ☐

M ☐ REFERRAL SOURCE

A—Walk in/Write in
B—Ad Response
C—State Employment Agency
D—College Placement Office
E—Minority Referral Agency
F—CETA Referral
G—Private Employment Agency

____
Applicant's Signature

voluntarily by the applicant and that the data must be maintained separately from all selection-related materials. These analyses may be useful in showing that the reason why an employer has underutilized a protected class is because of an inadequate applicant flow of protected-class members, in spite of special efforts to recruit them.[52]

❖ EEO Compliance Investigation

When a discrimination complaint is received by the EEOC or a similar agency, it must be processed. But as Figure 6–5 indicates, the number of complaints has overwhelmed the EEOC's ability to investigate them in a truly timely manner. The backlog has reached over 120,000 complaints at times during the past several years. To address the problem, the EEOC has instituted a system that categorizes complaints into three categories: *priority*, *needing further investigation*, and *immediate dismissal*.[53] If the EEOC decides to pursue a complaint, it uses the process outlined here.

❖ Figure 6–5 ❖
EEOC Complaints Backlog

KINDS OF CASES AWAITING ACTION (some complaints may be filed in multiple categories)	NUMBER OF CASES
Race	34,075
Gender	28,841
Age	20,593
Retaliation	19,680
National origin	8,738
Disability	5,052
Religion	1,801
Equal pay	1,297
Color	742
Other	412

SOURCE: Based on information from EEOC 1995 presented in *USA Today*, March 18, 1996, 13A.

In a typical situation, a complaint goes through several stages before the compliance process is completed.[54] First, the charges are filed by an individual, a group of individuals, or their representative. A charge must be filed within 180 days of when the alleged discriminatory action occurred. Then the EEOC staff reviews the specifics of the charges to determine if it has *jurisdiction*, which means that the agency is authorized to investigate that type of charge. If jurisdiction exists, a notice of the charge must be served on the employer within 10 days after the filing, and the employer is asked to respond. Following the charge notification, the EEOC's major thrust turns to investigating the complaint.

If the charge is found to be valid, the next stage involves mediation efforts by the agency and the employer.[55] If the employer agrees that discrimination has occurred and accepts the proposed settlement, then the employer posts a notice of relief within the company and takes the agreed-on actions. This notice indicates that the employer has reached an agreement on a discrimination charge and reiterates the employer's commitment to avoid future discriminatory actions.

Individual Right to Sue If the employer objects to the charge and rejects conciliation, the EEOC can file suit or issue a **right-to-sue letter** to the complainant. The letter notifies the person that he or she has 90 days in which to file a personal suit in federal court. Thus, if the EEOC decides that it will not bring suit on behalf of the complainant, the individual has the right to bring suit. The suit usually is brought in the U.S. District Court having jurisdiction in the area.

❖**Right-to-Sue Letter**
A letter issued by the EEOC that notifies a complainant that he or she has 90 days in which to file a personal suit in federal court.

Litigation In the court litigation stage, a legal trial takes place in the appropriate state or federal court. At that point, both sides retain lawyers and rely on the court to render a decision. The Civil Rights Act of 1991 provides for jury trials in most EEO cases. If either party disagrees with the court ruling, either can file appeals with a higher court. The U.S. Supreme Court becomes the ultimate adjudication body.

Internal Employer Investigation Many problems and expenses associated with EEO complaints can be controlled by employers who vigorously investigate their employees' discrimination complaints before they are taken to outside agencies. An internal employee complaint system and prompt, thorough responses to problem situations are essential tools in reducing EEO charges and in remedying illegal discriminatory actions.[56] Protecting employee rights is discussed further in Chapter 17.

Tester
A protected-class member who poses as an applicant to determine if employers discriminate in their hiring practices.

Use of "Testers" A controversial policy involves the use of "testers" to see if employers are discriminating illegally or not. A **tester** is a protected-class member who poses as an applicant to determine if employers discriminate in their hiring practices. The purpose of using testers, according to the EEOC, is to identify employers who discriminate illegally. The testers can file charges with the EEOC if they are treated differently from other applicants or believe that they have been discriminated against.

Naturally, employers generally are outraged at this practice. Their argument is that because the testers are not truly applicants, they should not be able to file charges. Also, employers view the use of testers as "entrapment" or "trickery," which is not permitted in criminal law cases.

❖ Preemployment vs. After-Hire Inquiries

Figure 6–6 lists preemployment inquiries and identifies whether they may or may not be discriminatory. All those preemployment inquiries labeled in the figure as "may be discriminatory" have been so designated because of findings in a variety of court cases. Those labeled "may not be discriminatory" are practices that are legal, but only if they reflect a business necessity or are job related for the specific job under review.

Once an employer tells an applicant he or she is hired (the "point of hire"), inquiries that were prohibited earlier may be made. After hiring, medical examination forms, group insurance cards, and other enrollment cards containing inquiries related directly or indirectly to sex, age, or other bases may be requested. Photographs or evidence of race, religion, or national origin also may be requested after hire for legal and necessary purposes, but not before. Such data should be maintained in a separate personnel records system in order to avoid their use in making appraisal, discipline, termination, or promotion decisions.

❖ Affirmative Action Plans (AAPs)

Throughout the last 30 years, employers with federal contracts and other government entities have had to address additional areas of potential discrimination. Several acts and regulations have been issued that apply specifically to government contractors. These acts and regulations specify a minimum number of employees and size of government contracts. The requirements primarily come from Executive Orders 11246, 11375, and 11478.

❖ Executive Orders 11246, 11375, and 11478

Numerous executive orders have been issued that require employers holding federal government contracts not to discriminate on the bases of race, color, reli-

◆ FIGURE 6–6 ◆
GUIDELINES TO LAWFUL AND UNLAWFUL PREEMPLOYMENT INQUIRIES

SUBJECT OF INQUIRY	IT MAY NOT BE DISCRIMINATORY TO INQUIRE ABOUT:	IT MAY BE DISCRIMINATORY TO INQUIRE ABOUT:
1. Name	**a.** Whether applicant has ever worked under a different name	**a.** The original name of an applicant whose name has been legally changed **b.** The ethnic association of applicant's name
2. Age	**a.** If applicant is over the age of 18 **b.** If applicant is under the age of 18 or 21 if job related (i.e., selling liquor in retail store)	**a.** Date of birth **b.** Date of high school graduation
3. Residence	**a.** Applicant's place of residence; length of applicant's residence in state and/or city where employer is located	**a.** Previous addresses **b.** Birthplace of applicant or applicant's parents
4. Race or Color		**a.** Applicant's race or color of applicant's skin
5. National Origin and Ancestry		**a.** Applicant's lineage, ancestry, national origin, parentage, or nationality **b.** Nationality of applicant's parents or spouse
6. Sex and Family Composition		**a.** Sex of applicant **b.** Dependents of applicant **c.** Marital status **d.** Child-care arrangements
7. Creed or Religion		**a.** Applicant's religious affiliation **b.** Church, parish, or holidays observed
8. Citizenship	**a.** Whether the applicant is a citizen of the United States **b.** Whether the applicant is in the country on a visa that permits him or her to work or is a citizen	**a.** Whether applicant is a citizen of a country other than the United States
9. Language	**a.** Language applicant speaks and/or writes fluently, if job related	**a.** Applicant's native tongue; language commonly used at home
10. References	**a.** Names of persons willing to provide professional and/or character references for applicant	**a.** Name of applicant's pastor or religious leader

gion, national origin, or sex. An **executive order** is issued by the president of the United States to provide direction to government departments on a specific issue or area.

During the 1960s, by executive order, the Office of Federal Contract Compliance Programs (OFCCP) in the U.S. Department of Labor was established

***Executive Order**
An order issued by the president of the U.S. to provide direction to government departments on a specific issue or area.

❖ FIGURE 6–6 ❖
GUIDELINES TO LAWFUL AND UNLAWFUL PREEMPLOYMENT INQUIRIES

SUBJECT OF INQUIRY	IT MAY NOT BE DISCRIMINATORY TO INQUIRE ABOUT:	IT MAY BE DISCRIMINATORY TO INQUIRE ABOUT:
11. Relatives	**a.** Names of relatives already employed by the employer	**a.** Name and/or address of any relative of applicant **b.** Whom to contact in case of emergency
12. Organizations	**a.** Applicant's membership in any professional, service, or trade organization	**a.** All clubs or social organizations to which applicant belongs
13. Arrest Record and Convictions	**a.** Convictions, if related to job performance (disclaimer should accompany)	**a.** Number and kinds of arrests **b.** Convictions unless related to job performance
14. Photographs		**a.** Photographs with application, with resume, or before hiring
15. Height and Weight		**a.** Any inquiry into height and weight of applicant except where a BFOQ
16. Physical Limitations	**a.** Whether applicant has the ability to perform job-related functions with or without accommodation	**a.** The nature or severity of an illness or the individual's physical condition **b.** Whether applicant has ever filed workers' compensation claim **c.** Any recent or past operations or surgery and dates
17. Education	**a.** Training applicant has received if related to the job under consideration **b.** Highest level of education attained, if validated that having certain educational background (e.g., high school diploma or college degree) is necessary to perform the specific job	
18. Military	**a.** What branch of the military applicant served in **b.** Type of education or training received in military **c.** Rank at discharge	**a.** Type of military discharge
19. Financial Status		**a.** Applicant's debts or assets **b.** Garnishments

and given responsibility for enforcing nondiscrimination in government contracts. Under Executive Order 11246, issued in 1965, amended by Executive Order 11375 in 1967, and updated by Executive Order 11478 in 1979, the Secretary of Labor was given the power to cancel the contract of a noncomplying contractor or blacklist a noncomplying employer from future government contracts. These orders and additional equal employment acts have required employers to take affirmative action to overcome the effects of past discriminatory practices.

❖ Who Must Have an Affirmative Action Plan?

Even though affirmative action as a concept has been challenged in court, as described in Chapter 5, most federal government contractors still are required to have affirmative action plans (AAPs). Generally, an employer with at least 50 employees and over $50,000 in government contracts must have a formal, written affirmative action plan. A government contractor with fewer than 50 employees and contracts totaling more than $50,000 can be required to have an AAP if it has been found guilty of discrimination by the EEOC or other agencies. The contract size can vary depending on the protected group and the various laws on which the regulations rest.

LOGGING ON

The American Association for Affirmative Action has support materials available at:

http://www.fga.com:80/aaaa

Courts have noted that any employer that is not a government contractor may have a *voluntary* AAP, although the employer *must* have such a plan if it wishes to be a government contractor. Where an employer that is not a government contractor has a required AAP, a court has ordered the employer to have an AAP as a result of past discriminatory practices and violations of laws.

❖ Contents of an Affirmative Action Plan

The contents of an AAP and the policies flowing from it must be available for review by managers and supervisors within the organization. Plans vary in length; some are long and require extensive staff time to prepare. The table of contents of a plan as specified by the OFCCP is shown in Figure 6–7.

Utilization Analysis One of the major sections of an AAP is the **utilization analysis,** which identifies the number of protected-class members employed and the types of jobs they hold. According to Executive Order 11246, employers who are government contractors meeting the required levels for contract size and number of employees must provide data on protected classes in the organization.

❖**Utilization Analysis**
An analysis that identifies the number of protected-class members employed and the types of jobs they hold in an organization.

Availability Analysis As part of the utilization analysis, an **availability analysis** also must be conducted, identifying the number of protected-class members available to work in the appropriate labor market in given jobs. This analysis, which can be developed with data from a state labor department, the U.S. Census Bureau, and other sources, serves as a basis for determining if *underutilization* exists within an organization. The census data also must be matched to job titles and job groups used in the utilization analysis.

❖**Availability Analysis**
An analysis that identifies the number of protected-class members available to work in the appropriate labor market in given jobs.

Underutilization As discussed in Chapter 5, the 4/5ths rule is a guide to calculating the underutilization of protected-class members. Recall that the 4/5ths rule states that discrimination generally is considered to occur if the selection rate for a protected group is less than 80% of the group's representation in the relevant labor market or less than 80% of the selection rate for the majority group. In calculating underutilization, the employer considers the following:

- ❖ Number of protected-class members in the population of the surrounding area
- ❖ Number of protected-class members in the workforce in the surrounding area compared with number in the total workforce in the organization

❖ FIGURE 6–7 ❖
SAMPLE TABLE OF CONTENTS FOR AN AFFIRMATIVE ACTION PLAN

TABLE OF CONTENTS	
	Statement of Confidentiality
I.	Purpose
II.	Policy Statement
III.	Dissemination of Policy
IV.	Responsibility for Implementation
V.	Utilization Analysis
	a) Organization Chart
	b) Workforce Analysis
	c) Job Group
VI.	Availability Analysis
VII.	Goals and Timetables
VIII.	Identification of Problem Areas
IX.	Development, Execution, and Support of Action-Oriented Programs
X.	Internal Audit and Reporting
XI.	Consideration of Minorities and Women Not Currently in the Workforce
XII.	Compliance with Religion and National Origin Guidelines
XIII.	Analysis of Previous Year Goal Accomplishment
XIV.	Lines of Progression
XV.	Compliance with Sex Discrimination Guidelines
XVI.	EEO–1 Reports
XVII.	New Hires and Terminations
XVIII.	Transfers and Promotions
APPENDIX 1	Affirmative Action Program Covering Persons with Disabilities and Vietnam-Era Veterans.

- ❖ Number of unemployed members of protected classes in the surrounding area
- ❖ General availability of protected-class members having requisite skills in the immediate area and in an area in which an employer reasonably could recruit
- ❖ Availability of promotable and transferable protected-class members within the organization
- ❖ Existence of training institutions that can train individuals in the requisite skills
- ❖ Realistic amount of training an employer can do to make all job classes available to protected-class members

Fortunately for many employers, much of the data on the population and workforce in the surrounding area is available in computerized form, so availability analysis and underutilization calculations can be done more easily. However, an employer still must maintain an accurate profile of the internal workforce.

❖ IMPLEMENTATION OF AN AFFIRMATIVE ACTION PLAN (AAP)

The implementation of an AAP must be built on a commitment to affirmative action. The commitment must begin at the top of the organization. A crucial factor is the appointment of an affirmative action officer to monitor the plan.

Once a plan is developed, it should be distributed and explained to all managers and supervisors. It is particularly important that everyone involved in the selection process review the plan and receive training on its content. Also, the AAP plan must be updated and reviewed each year to reflect changes in the utilization and availability of protected-class members. If an audit of an AAP is done by the OFCCP, the employer must be prepared to provide additional details and documentation.[57]

SUMMARY

- ❖ Sexual harassment takes two forms: (a) *quid pro quo* and (b) hostile environment.
- ❖ Employers should have policies on sexual harassment, have identifiable complaint procedures, train all employees on what constitutes sexual harassment, promptly investigate complaints, and take action when sexual harassment is found to have occurred.
- ❖ Sex discrimination can include any of the following: unequal job assignment, sexual harassment, pregnancy discrimination, or unequal compensation for similar jobs.
- ❖ Age discrimination, especially in the form of forced retirements and terminations, is a growing problem.
- ❖ The definition of who is disabled has been expanding in recent years.
- ❖ The Americans with Disabilities Act requires that most employers identify the essential functions of jobs and make reasonable accommodation for individuals with disabilities unless undue hardship results.
- ❖ Discrimination on the basis of national origin still is illegal, but the Immigration Reform and Control Act has affected how employers inquire about and verify citizenship.
- ❖ Reasonable accommodation is a strategy that can be used to deal with religious discrimination situations.
- ❖ Implementation of equal employment opportunity requires appropriate record keeping, such as completing the annual report (EEO–1) and keeping applicant flow data.
- ❖ Many employers are required to develop affirmative action plans (AAPs) that identify problem areas in the employment of protected-class members and initiate goals and steps to overcome those problems.

REVIEW AND DISCUSSION QUESTIONS

1. Give examples that you have experienced or observed of the two types of sexual harassment in employment situations.
2. Based on your past experiences, identify examples of sex discrimination in job conditions, sexual stereotyping, and pregnancy discrimination.
3. Why are age discrimination issues growing in importance?
4. The Americans with Disabilities Act contains several key terms. Define each: (a) *essential job function,* (b) *reasonable accommodation,* and (c) *undue hardship.*
5. Respond to the following comment made by the president of a company: "It's getting so you can't ask anybody anything personal, because there are so many protected classes."
6. Discuss the following question: "How can I report protected-class statistics to the EEOC when I cannot ask about them on my application blank?"
7. Describe how to perform availability analyses and compute underutilization for an affirmative action plan.

Terms to Know

availability analysis 177
disabled person 164
essential job functions 166
executive order 175
glass ceiling 160
nepotism 159
pay equity 158
reasonable accommodation 166
right-to-sue letter 173
sexual harassment 154
tester 174
undue hardship 167
utilization analysis 177

CASE

DENNY'S DEALS WITH DISCRIMINATION

Denny's, a national restaurant chain with over 500 locations, faced a crisis in the 1990s due to discriminatory practices. For a number of years, African Americans and the National Association for the Advancement of Colored People (NAACP) had charged that African American customers were discriminated against in various ways. For instance, in several locations, managers refused to allow African American customers to enter their stores at night. Others required African Americans to pay their bills before they could receive food. According to Denny's critics, a further sign of blatant racism was that only one of the company franchises was minority-owned. Finally, the NAACP and the U.S. Justice Department filed lawsuits against Denny's for illegal discrimination.

Denny's is owned by Flagstar Companies, a conglomerate with a number of subsidiaries. Flagstar signed an agreement with the NAACP to take aggressive action against racism at Denny's. Terms of the agreement included the following:

- A payment of $54 million was made to settle two class-action lawsuits brought under civil rights laws.
- Flagstar promised to increase the number of minority franchisees to 53 by 1997.
- Denny's agreed to purchase over $50 million worth of goods and services from minority-owned firms, representing about 12% of total supply purchases.
- Flagstar agreed to increase the percentage of minorities among employees, managers, and corporate staff. The firm indicated that almost half of its new management positions would be staffed with African Americans by 2000.
- A toll-free number was established at Denny's corporate headquarters to be used by customers to report service problems, including discrimination. The number is displayed in Denny's restaurants. Complaints are investigated by a lawyer independent of the company.

All of the above actions helped Denny's deal with some of its discriminatory practices. But the major change was to replace virtually all of the top management at Denny's. The new management team is headed by James Adamson, Chairman and CEO of Flagstar. The team includes three women and several minorities. Previously, the Denny's executive group had been almost exclusively white males. Adamson, once CEO at Burger King, had a very clear message for employees, managers, and franchisees: "If you discriminate, you're history!"

To change the organizational culture throughout Denny's, a diversity training program was developed, and participation in it is mandatory for managers. Also, a portion of bonus payments to managers is now based on results in reducing customer complaints, including those relating to discrimination. Adamson recognizes that continuing efforts are needed for Denny's to convince customers and employees, both nonminorities and minorities, that it believes in equal opportunity for all.[58]

Questions

1. Discuss why the previous absence of equal employment opportunity at Denny's showed ineffective management of human resources.
2. How likely is it that Denny's treatment of African Americans would have changed without legal intervention? Support your answer.
3. What are the advantages and disadvantages of Denny's approach to taking affirmative action to remedy its past problems with discrimination?

❖ Notes

1. Based on "Women to Receive $1 Million–Plus for Sexual Harassment," *CCH Human Resource Management Ideas & Trends*, August 30, 1995, 1; B. A. Holden, "Former IBM Worker Is Awarded $65,000 in Sexual Harassment Case," *The Wall Street Journal*, July 18, 1995, B14; M. A. Jacobs, "Law Fim Loses Race Discrimination Case," *The Wall Street Journal*, March 25, 1996, B8; "Jury Orders Kmart to Pay $2.17 Million in Miami Age-Bias Case," *The Wall Street Journal*, August 7, 1995, A7; *HR News*, March 1992, A11; *Omaha World-Herald*, January 26, 1993, 3; *Human Resource Executive*, June 1992, 14; *Labor & Employment Update*, November 1992, 1: *Omaha World-Herald*, August 20, 1992, 5; *The Wall Street Journal*, March 27, 1992, B2; *The Wall Street Journal*, November 5, 1991, B1; and *USA Today*, October 7, 1992, B1.

2. Teresa Brady, "Nontraditional Sexual Harassment: What It Is and How Companies Can Avoid It," *Business Forum*, Summer/Fall 1995, 14–16.

3. *Steiner v. Showboat Operating Co.*, CA9, 1994 US App. LEXIS 14197.

4. *Meritor Savings Bank (FBS) v. Vinson*, 106 S.Ct. 57 aff. and remanded 106 S.Ct. 2399 (1986).

5. *Harris v. Forklift Systems, Inc.*, 114 S.Ct. 367 (1993).

6. Howard A. Simon, "*Ellison v. Brady*: A 'Reasonable Woman' Standard for Sexual Harassment," *Employee Relations Law Journal* 17 (1991), 71–80.

7. David E. Terpstra and Douglas D. Baker, "Outcomes of Federal Court Decisions on Sexual Harassment," *Academy of Management Journal* 35 (1992), 164–171.

8. Jonathan A. Segal, "Seven Ways to Reduce Harassment Claims," *HR Magazine*, January 1992, 84–85.

9. *Gary v. Long*, 59 F.3d 1391 (1995).

10. Mark L. Legnick-Hall, "Checking Out Sexual Harassment Claims," *HR Magazine*, March 1992, 77–79.

11. Charles S. Miskind, "Sexual Harassment Hostile Work Environment Class Actions," *Employee Relations Law Journal* 18 (1992), 141–147.

12. *Bundy v. Jackson*, 641 F.2d 934 (D.C.Cir. 1981).

13. Adapted from Anne B. Fisher, "Getting Comfortable with Couples in the Workplace," *Fortune*, October 3, 1994; and "Office Romances Gaining Acceptance," *Omaha World-Herald* February 19, 1995, G1.

14. Phyllis Barnum, Robert C. Liden, and Nancy Ditomaso, "Double Jeopardy for Women and Minorities: Pay Differences with Age," *Academy of Management Journal* 38 (1995), 863–880.

15. U.S. Census Bureau, 1995.

16. Judith Fields and Edward N. Wolff, "Interindustry Wage Differentials and the Gender Wage Gap," *Industrial and Labor Relations Review* 49 (1995), 105–120.

17. *Arizona Governing Committee v. Norris*, 103 S.Ct. 3492 (1983).

18. "Grants to Help Women Gain 'Non-Traditional' Employment," *Omaha World-Herald*, October 22, 1995, G1.

19. For more on gender-based job groupings, see Elissa L. Perry, Allison Davis-Blake, and Carol Tikulik, "Explaining Gender-Based Selection Decisions," *Academy of Management Review* 19 (1994), 786–820.

20. *United Auto Workers v. Johnson Controls*, 111 S.Ct. 1195 (1991).

21. A. Stone and J. Lee, "Glass Ceiling Report Adds Fuel to Debate," *USA Today*, March 17, 1995, 4A; and R. Richards, "More Women Poised for Role as CEO," *USA Today*, March 26, 1996, 2B.

22. Based on data from Equal Employment Opportunity Commission, December 1995.

23. Gary N. Powell and D. Anthony Butterfield, "Investigating the 'Glass Ceiling' Phenomenon: An Empirical Study of Actual Promotions to Top Management," *Academy of Management Journal* 37 (1994), 68–86.

24. Glass Ceiling Commission, *A Solid Investment: Making Use of the Nation's Human Capital* (Washington, DC: U.S. Department of Labor, 1995).

25. Lisa Mainiero, "Getting Anointed for Advancement: The Case of Executive Women," *Academy of Management Executive*, May 1994, 53–67.

26. Cathy Ventrell-Monsees, "The ADEA Backlash," *Textbook Authors Conference Presentation* (Washington, DC: American Association of Retired Persons, 1995), 49–58.

27. Adapted from Cathy Ventrell-Monsees, "Too Much of a Good Thing: Overqualified Older Workers," *Textbook Authors Conference Presentation* (Washington, DC: American Association of Retired Persons, 1992), 34–38.

28. Paul M. Barrett, "Supreme Court Expands Scope of Law on Age Discrimination in Employment," *The Wall Street Journal*, April 2, 1996, B5; and "Age Bias Law Is Strengthened," *Minneapolis Star-Tribune*, April 2, 1996, A1.

29. *Public Employees Retirement System of Ohio v. Betts*, 109 S.Ct. 256 (1989).

30. Equal Employment Opportunity Commission Statistics; Christine Woolsey, "Employers Unsure of Liability Exposure from Bias Allegations by Mentally Disabled," *Business Insurance*, June 27, 1994, 3–6.

31. William M. Slonaker and Ann C. Wendt, "Patterns of Employment Discrimination toward Workers with Disabilities," *Business Forum*, Summer/Fall 1995, 21–25.

32. All of the definitions used in the discussion of the Americans with Disabilities Act are those contained in the act itself or in the *Technical Assistance Manual* issued by the EEOC.

33. Louis Pechnaum, "Mental Disabilities and the ADA," *Benefits & Compensation Solutions*, December 1994, 32–33.

34. "EEOC Issues ADA Guidance," *CCH Human Resource Management Ideas & Trends*, March 29, 1995, 49; and "New EEOC Guidance Defines 'Disability' under the ADA," *Labor & Employment Law Update*, June 1995, 1–2.

35. *School Board of Nassau County, Florida v. Airline*, 107 S.C. 1123 (1987).

36. Romuald A. Stone, "AIDS in the Workplace: An Executive Update," *Academy of Management Executive* August 1994, 52–64.

37. Janice A. Huebner, "What Can You Say About AIDS," *HR Magazine*, December 1994, 86–91; and S. M. Sack, "The HIV-Positive Employees: A New Rulebook," *Benefits & Compensation Solutions*, November 1995, 46–49.

38. John Hollwitz, Deborah F. Goodman, and Dean Bolte, "Complying with the Americans with Disabilities Act: Assessing the Costs of Reasonable Accommodation," *Public Personnel Management* 24 (1995), 149–157.

39. B. P. Noble, "A Level Playing Field for Just $121," *The New York Times*, March 5, 1995, F21.

40. For other examples, see James G. Frierson, *Employer's Guide to the Americans with Disabilities Act* (Washington, DC: Bureau of National Affairs, 1992), 104–105.

41. C. Yang, "Cheese It—the Boss," *Business Week*, November 27, 1995, 128.

(Notes continued on following page)

▼Notes, continued

42. C. Yang, "In Any Language, It's Unfair," *Business Week,* June 21, 1993, 110–111.
43. Tony Mauro, "English-Only to Face Test in High Court," *USA Today,* March 26, 1996, A1.
44. *Trans World Airlines v. Hardison,* 432 U.S. 63 (1977).
45. J. S. Pouliot, "Rising Complaints of Religious Bias," *Nation's Business,* February 1996, 36–37.
46. M. A. Jacobs, "Workers' Religious Beliefs May Get New Attention," *The Wall Street Journal,* August 22, 1995, B1.
47. *Wilson v. U.S. West Communications,* DCNeb, No. CV91–207 (1994).
48. C. J. Martin, "Protecting Overweight Workers against Discrimination," *Employee Relations Law Journal,* 20 (1994), 133–142.
49. R. J. Paul and J. B. Townsend, "Shape Up or Ship Out? Employment Discrimination against the Overweight," *Employee Responsibilities and Rights Journal* 8 (1995), 133–143.
50. *Dothard v. Rawlinson,* 433 U.S. 321 (1977).
51. Public Law 103–353, October 13, 1944.
52. David Ankeny and David Israel, "Preparing for an OFCCP Audit," *HR Magazine,* September 1992, 99–102.
53. "Throw Them Out," *The Wall Street Journal,* December 26, 1995, A1.
54. For more details on the process, see *How to Respond to an EEOC Complaint* (Chicago: Commerce Clearing House, Inc., 1992).
55. Laura M. Litvan, "EEOC Turns to Mediation," *Nation's Business,* June 1995, 38–39.
56. James A. Burns, Jr., "EEO and Employer/Employee Rights," *Employee Relations Law Journal* 17 (1992), 521–529.
57. David C. Anthony and David Israel, "Completing an On-Site OFCCP Audit," *HR Magazine,* March 1993, 89–93.
58. Based on F. Rice, "Denny's Changes Its Spots," *Fortune,* May 13, 1996, 133–142. N. Harris, "A New Denny's—Diner by Diner," *Business Week,* March 25, 1996, 166–168; E. Thomas, "Denny's Shines Its Bad Image with New Deal," *The Wall Street Journal,* November 9, 1994, B1; and Del Jones, "Denny's Strives to Eliminate Racist Elements," *USA Today,* November 2, 1995, 1B.

EXERCISE 3 - Analysis

When SME-TEK or any other company hires new people it is important to have the information necessary to classify them for EEO purposes and to get them paid properly. The chapters in Section 2 talked about questions that could legally be asked and those that could not. However, after a person is hired, any questions (even those illegal before the point of hire) can be asked for EEO classification purposes.

SME-TEK has just hired David Lee as the Marketing Director. Specifics about David are available in the electronic memos on your CD-ROM.

1. Which of the bits of information available on Mr. Lee would have been illegal to ask before hire?
2. Add Mr. Lee to the HRIS database as a "quick hire" and add *employment, personal, compensation and performance*, and *work address* data to his HR record.

SME-TEK

MEMO

TO: HUMAN RESOURCE MANAGEMENT USER

Please join me in welcoming David Lee aboard as our new Marketing Director!

I need you to add David to our database as a quick hire so he can be included in our next payroll cycle.

I will also need you to add the following information to his HR Folder:
employment, personal, compensation and performance, and work address. (Refer to the electronic memos for the details.)

Thanks,

Susan Kyle
Manager, Human Resources

EXERCISE 3 - Procedure

Before completing the memo's request, you need to access the Human Resources module and review the topic "Hiring Process Overview" in the "New Hire" lesson of the Concepts section. The Checkpoint topic in this lesson is optional.

To fulfill the memo's request, access the "New Hire" lesson of the Human Resources Features & Processes section. Then, review the topics "Entering a New Hire," "Accessing the HR Folder," "Entering Employment Information," "Entering Personal Information," "Entering Compensation and Performance Information," sand "Entering a Work Address." Be sure to skip the topic "Entering Compliance Information" for now.

EXERCISE 4 - Analysis

Material in Chapter 4 discusses the ADA essential job functions, and reasonable accommodation. There are few specific rules (as noted) and every situation is considered on its own merit.

David Lee has a hearing impairment that may require some reasonable accommodation and certainly requires note in the HRIS.

1. What reasonable accommodations do you think may be necessary for a marketing director with a hearing problem?
2. Add compliance data for Mr. Lee and in so doing establish a record on his hearing impairment in the ADA window. IRCA information should be properly noted as well in the HRIS.

SME-TEK

MEMO

TO: HUMAN RESOURCE MANAGEMENT USER

We need to add compliance data to David Lee's records. In addition to the standard compliance information, we need to establish a record of his hearing impairment in the ADA window. I've got photocopies of the relevant documents that you can use to enter IRCA information, too.

Please enter this information into his HR folder ASAP.

Thanks,

Susan Kyle
Manager, Human Resources

EXERCISE 4 - Procedure

To fulfill the memo's request, you need to access the "New Hire" lesson of the Human Resources Features

SECTION VIDEO CASES

❖ CASE 1
WILSON BUILDING MAINTENANCE
Keeping Workers and Customers Happy

Anita Oberwortmann meets the challenge of maintaining quality in the building maintenance business by keeping quality people on her payroll. How has she reduced heavy turnover in an industry where it is rampant?

Her Wilson Building Maintenance, which does floor polishing, window cleaning, dusting, etc., for a variety of companies in Wichita, Kansas, has an employee-benefits policy unusual in its industry. It provides health and dental insurance, paying half the premiums; gives holiday and vacation pay; and offers a profit-sharing plan.

A monthly newsletter reporting on such company events as drawings for gift certificates to local merchants—and giving cleaning tips—is distributed to the 170 employees. Since most are Hispanic, there is a Spanish version.

To cut absenteeism, Oberwortmann pays 25-cent-an-hour bonuses for two weeks' perfect attendance. The total last year: more than $50,000.

To deal with problems that might cost customers time and money, Oberwortmann has on-site managers at every job and pagers for direct contact with her front office. There is an after-hours answering service.

Customer retention and growth makes these goodies possible. Wilson Building Maintenance—the name goes back to a former husband, with whom Oberwortmann launched the business in 1978—had more than $2.5 million in sales last year, up 60 percent in three years.

Oberwortmann has come a long way. Divorced not long after the business started, and the sole support of her children, she originally had a lone cleaning contract that brought in $750 a month. She cleaned at night and marketed her services during the day, winning more contracts and taking on help.

Told verbally that she would handle parking-lot sweeping at a major mall, she bought a sweeper. It was priced right, but it was in Atlanta, Georgia. Driving day and night, she brought it back to learn she hadn't gotten the contract.

Increasing her marketing efforts, Oberwortmann landed a contract that would double her company's size. But her bank, fearing she was expanding too fast, would not expand her credit. In fact, it would no longer lend her money short-term to meet payrolls.

Oberwortmann is the daughter of a man who ran janitorial services. Also, she had obtained free counseling on all aspects of her business through SCORE, the Service Corps of Retired Executives.

Working 14 hours a day, she revamped a business plan, got a bank debt consolidation loan guaranteed by the U.S. Small Business Administration, and was able to structure a seven-year expansion program.

Two years ago Oberwortmann, whose present husband works for the company, moved from 4,500 square feet of leased space to a 30,000-square-foot building that the company owns. Today, having survived and expanded in Wichita, she is thinking of expanding to other cities.

1. How does this case illustrate the problems faced by women in the workforce who are single parents and sole providers?
2. How do the obstacles faced by Anita Oberwortmann reflect those often faced by women taking on the management of a small business?

(Excerpts reprinted by permission of The Blue Chip Enterprise Initiative©, *Real-World Lessons for America's Small Businesses* p. 148 copyright 1994 by Connecticut Mutual Life Insurance Company.) ❖

❖ CASE 2
LEWIS SERVICES
Trouble Comes in Threes

Lewis Services, a Lafayette, Louisiana, custodial-janitorial company, would not be in existence today if its owner-general manager had not taken the right steps after three disasters.

- ❖ In 1984 the company lost half of its clientele in a 60-day period.
- ❖ In 1992, through no fault of its own, the business got in big-time trouble with the Internal Revenue Service, was fined heavily, and as a result was unable to borrow funds.
- ❖ Also, because of what owner Lenden Lewis describes as staff incompetence, a client responsible for almost half of the company's revenues left it.

A severe downturn in the oil industry, home of about 80 percent of Lewis Services clients then, caused the 1984 trauma. Owner Lewis, who had started the company three years earlier, reacted with a new marketing strategy. He added services that would appeal to companies outside the oil industry—landscaping, lawn service—and gained new clients. With an increased cash flow, he was able to buy equipment and add food service.

Lewis Services didn't live happily ever after, though. As already indicated, it had a very bad year.

An outside accountant was hired to do payroll, bookkeeping, account payables, and account receivables . At year's end a shocked Lenden Lewis was notified that payroll taxes had not been filed for some of the year.

The accountant was replaced with a new, in-house accountant, and arrangements were made with the IRS to set up a plan for payment of the fines and tax delinquencies. The company obtained new clients, built up receivables, and got by without additional credit. Last year, its tax problem solved, the company became computerized.

Lenden Lewis suffered an injury that disabled him for eight months. Without his supervision, he says, employees were unable to perform competently, resulting in loss of the major client.

To remedy the situation, Lewis hired an operations manager who oversees the 40-odd employees, makes sure jobs are completed on time, and acts as general manager in Lewis' absence. A human relations manager was hired to interview job applicants, check references, and help in employee training and evaluations. Employees who were not performing were terminated. All employees go through a 30-day evaluation period now and must pass any drug tests administered.

The improvement in hiring practices improved the quality of Lewis Services' work and helped it add to its client list, bringing annual sales to an impressive figure. One addition, after 13 months of negotiations, was the major client lost.

1. How has Lewis Services looked to diversity in its staffing?

2. Discuss the importance of "Job related" selection processes to the staffing strategy.

(Excerpts reprinted by permission of The Blue Chip Enterprise Initiative©, *Real-World Lessons for America's Small Businesses* pp. 134, 135; copyright 1994 by Connecticut Mutual Life Insurance Company.) ❖

❖ CASE 3
MICRO OVERFLOW
Removing the "Dis" from Disability

Donald J. Dalton has made a handicap an asset. He runs a company that matches disabled people with computer products that help them overcome their disabilities. Micro Overflow Corp., of Naperville, Illinois, is a success—a fact explainable at least in part by the fact that Dalton is a quadriplegic.

By making himself widely visible, he is a nonwalking advertisement for his company. Potential clients with disabilities that prevent them from speaking, hearing, seeing, talking, or walking figure that if he can function as well as he does, they can do better, too.

Many times, he has left home before sun rise, driven hours to evaluate a client's needs, driven more hours to speak at a dinner where he publicized his company, and gotten back home around midnight. The next day, more of the same.

Dalton, paralyzed in a 1968 diving accident, founded Micro Overflow in 1990. Early on, he and his staff—a total of three then—went to the Illinois capital, Springfield, to talk to the state's Department of Rehabilitation Services about possible sales opportunities. While there, they visited other state agencies. They had no appointments, but in two hours they met six agencies' directors, enabling them to market their services to the agencies from the top down. If you are in a wheelchair, Dalton learned, people don't shut the door in your face; they open it for you.

Agencies or businesses pay for most of Micro Overflow's services, which, though designed to be profitable, sometimes cost less than nonprofit institutions charge.

Micro Overflow keeps costs down. It had no choice at the start. A new enterprise in an unproven industry, it couldn't get financing. That meant it couldn't hire people to take some of the burden off Dalton and the staff. For the first 18 months, there were no salaries, and homemaker wives had to get jobs. All profits were plowed back into the company.

The staff worked out of Dalton's one-car garage. A 12- by 20-foot space held four work stations, two phone lines, a fax machine, a five-computer local area network, a bulletin board, and typically—a half dozen "assistive technology" systems being assembled, tested, and readied for delivery to clients.

What kinds of assistive technology? Dalton himself speaks into a headset to activate a computer keyboard. Another type: a client who was unable to talk can do so now, through a computer and a speech synthesizer. On a recent Mother's Day she used a telephone, for the first time, and called her mother.

When competition developed for Micro Overflow, it kept ahead by being a one-stop shop. It could offer an agency an evaluation of a disabled person, then sell the necessary equipment and train the client in using it. A competitor might offer only equipment—or part of it, leaving the agency to hunt for other components.

Dalton's company today has eight employees and 3,000 square feet of office space. It served more than 320 clients last year, up form 23 its first year and 63 the second. Annual sales are at the $600,000 level.

A mission statement helps the company keep focused. Through "the implementation of modern technologies," it says, "Micro Overflow strives to remove the 'dis' from disability."

1. Discuss how Micro Overflow's products and services allow people with disabilities to have better employment opportunities.

2. How does president Don Dalton's ability to overcome his disabilities illustrate the importance of diversity management efforts?

(Excerpts reprinted by permission of The Blue Chip Enterprise Initiative©, *Real-World Lessons for America's Small Businesses* pp. 201, 202; copyright 1994 by Connecticut Mutual Life Insurance Company.) ❖

SECTION 3

ANALYZING AND STAFFING JOBS

CHAPTER 7

JOB ANALYSIS

After you have read this chapter, you should be able to . . .

- Define *job analysis, job description,* and *job specification.*
- Discuss three behavioral aspects of job analysis.
- Explain how job analysis is used to comply with the Americans with Disabilities Act (ADA) and other legal requirements.
- Identify how job analysis information is used in four other HR activities.
- List and explain four job analysis methods.
- Identify the five steps in conducting a job analysis.
- Write a job description and the job specifications for it.

HR IN TRANSITION

THE GROWTH AND DECLINE OF "JOBS"

Increasingly, commentators and writers are discussing the idea that the nature of jobs and work is changing so much that the concept of a "job" may be obsolete for many people. For other people, the traditional jobs remain but are looking less challenging than previously.

The changing nature of jobs from 1988 to 1993 is seen in a study done by an analyst in the U.S. Department of Labor. That study found that the number of high-paying jobs with pay levels 25% above the median increased 29%, but the number of jobs paying 25% below the median grew almost as fast. What this study suggests is that the U.S. economy increasingly is composed of two tiers of jobs: a higher tier requiring advanced knowledge, skills, and abilities, and a lower tier requiring significantly less education and skill.

In many industries that use lower-skilled workers, traditional jobs continue to exist. For example, jobs in the retail and restaurant industries likely will continue to be staffed by lower-skilled workers. But in many low-paying industries, workers face unpleasant conditions. For instance, workers in the poultry-processing industry work in production environments that are quite difficult. Work-related accidents and repetitive stress injuries occur at twice the normal all-industry rate in many other low paying industries. Nevertheless, for workers who have limited skills or who are located in economically depressed geographic locations, these jobs represent some economic security. Studying these jobs and their work consequences is relatively easy because of the repetitiveness of the work and the limited number of tasks each worker performs.

Employees in these "virtual jobs" must be able to function without job descriptions and without the traditional parameters that are still useful with lower-tier jobs.

In contrast, for many other jobs, even the term *job* may be inappropriate. Instead, in some high-tech industries, employees work in cross-functional project teams and shift from project to project. The focus in these industries is less on performing specific tasks and duties and more on fulfilling responsibilities and attaining results. For instance, a project team of eight employees developing software to allow various credit cards to be used with ATMs worldwide will work on many different tasks, some individually and some with other team members. When that project is finished those employees will move to other projects, possibly with other employers. Such shifts may happen several times per year. Therefore, the basis for selecting and compensating these individuals is their competence and skills, not what they do. Even the "job" of managers changes in such situations, for they must serve their project teams as facilitators, gatherers of resources, and removers of roadblocks.

Clearly, studying the two different types of jobs—the lower-skilled ones and highly technical ones—requires different approaches. Many of the typical processes associated with identifying job descriptions are still relevant with the lower-skilled, task-based jobs. However, for fast-moving organizations in high-tech industries, a job description is becoming an obsolete concept. Employees in these "virtual jobs" must be able to function without job descriptions and without the traditional parameters that are still useful with lower-tier jobs.

HR managers in many organizations therefore must use their knowledge of the traditional structuring of jobs for some parts of organizations, while also reducing jobs in other areas of organizations. The following key questions regarding jobs must be addressed in all organizations:

- Are the right people doing the work of the organization, in terms of competencies?
- Which core tasks central to the organization must be performed inside the organization, and which tasks can be "outsourced" using temporary workers, independent contractors, or vendors?
- Have the people in the various work categories been matched to the realities of the work being performed?
- How should workers be compensated for competencies?
- How has the organization changed to reflect the decline of traditional jobs in some areas and the continuance of task jobs in other areas?

These questions affect both the design of work units in organizations and the methods used in studying work units. They also force HR managers to develop more effective ways to identify worker competencies and then match those competencies to the work to be done.[1]

> "Today's organization is rapidly being transformed from a structure built out of jobs into a field of work ready to be done."
>
> —William Bridges

A primary focus of HR management is on the jobs and work performed by individuals in the organization. The importance of HR actions being job-related has been stressed throughout the previous chapters. But the changing nature of jobs and work, highlighted in the chapter-opening discussion, reveals that the nature of some jobs is shifting to reflect the competitive demands faced by organizations. In addition, individual responses to jobs vary. A job may be fascinating to one person but not to someone else. Depending on how jobs are designed, they may provide more or less opportunity for employees to satisfy their job-related needs. For example, a sales job may furnish a good opportunity to satisfy social needs, whereas a training assignment may satisfy a person's need to be an expert in a certain area. A job that gives little latitude may not satisfy an individual's creative or innovative needs.

Because the nature of jobs is changing, and because jobs must fit so many different situations, managers and employees alike are finding that designing and analyzing jobs require broader perspectives than in the past. Job analysis is the major subject of this chapter.

❖ Nature of Job Analysis

Job Analysis
A systematic way to gather and analyze information about the content and the human requirements of jobs, and the context in which jobs are performed.

Task
A distinct, identifiable work activity composed of motions.

Duty
A larger work segment composed of several tasks that are performed by an individual.

Responsibilities
Obligations to perform certain tasks and duties.

The most basic building block of HR management, **job analysis,** is a systematic way to gather and analyze information about the content and human requirements of jobs, and the context in which jobs are performed. This information is essential to other HR management activities.

Job analysis identifies what the existing tasks, duties, and responsibilities of a job are. A **task** is a distinct, identifiable work activity composed of motions, whereas a **duty** is a larger work segment composed of several tasks that are performed by an individual. Because both tasks and duties describe activities, it is not always easy or necessary to distinguish between the two. For example, if one of the employment supervisor's duties is to "interview applicants," one task associated with that duty would be "asking questions." **Responsibilities** are obligations to perform certain tasks and duties. Because managerial jobs carry greater responsibilities, they are usually more highly paid.

Job analysis usually involves collecting information on the characteristics of a job that differentiate it from other jobs. Information that can be helpful in making the distinction includes the following:

- Work activities and behaviors
- Interactions with others
- Performance standards
- Machines and equipment used
- Working conditions
- Supervision given and received
- Knowledge, skills, and abilities needed

❖ What Is a Job?

Job
A grouping of similar positions having common tasks, duties, and responsibilities.

Position
A job performed by one person.

Although the terms *job* and *position* are often used interchangeably, there is a slight difference in emphasis. A **job** is a grouping of common tasks, duties, and responsibilities. A **position** is a job performed by one person. Thus, if there are two persons operating postage meters in a mail room, there are two positions (one for each person) but just one job (postage meter operator).

A **job family** is a grouping of jobs having similar characteristics. There are a variety of ways of identifying and grouping job families. In all of them, significant emphasis is place on measuring the similarity of jobs.[2] For instance, at one insurance company, the HR director decided that jobs requiring specialized technical knowledge, skills, and abilities related to information systems (IS) should be viewed as a separate job family, regardless of the geographic locations of those jobs. Because of the nature of information systems jobs, attracting and retaining IS professionals was difficult, and special compensation programs were needed to match the compensation packages given by competing employers.

***Job Family**
A grouping of jobs having similar characteristics.

❖ Job Design

Jobs designed to take advantage of important job characteristics are more likely to be received positively by employees. Such characteristics help distinguish between "good" and "bad" jobs.[3] Many of the approaches to enhancing productivity and quality discussed in Chapter 3 reflect efforts to expand some of the job characteristics. Today, more attention is being paid to job design because redesigning jobs can reduce turnover and absenteeism and thus costs.[4]

Job design refers to organizing tasks, duties, and responsibilities into a productive unit of work. It involves determining the content of jobs and the effect of jobs on employees. Identifying the behavioral components of a given job is an integral part of job design. Then redesigning jobs encompasses making jobs "better" from the viewpoint of employees, while also enhancing organizational productivity.

❖ Differentiating Between Job Analysis and Job Design

It is useful to clarify the differences between job design and job analysis. Job design is broader in nature and has as its primary thrust meshing the productivity needs of the organization with the needs of the individuals performing the various jobs. Increasingly, a key aim for job design is to provide individuals meaningful work which fits effectively into the flow of the organization. It is concerned with changing, simplifying, enlarging, enriching, or otherwise making jobs such that the efforts of each worker better fit together with other jobs.

Job analysis has a much narrower focus in that it is a formal system for gathering data about what people are doing in their jobs. The information generated by job analysis may be useful in redesigning jobs, but its primary purpose is to get a clear understanding of what is done on a job and what KSAs are needed to do a job as it has been designed. Documents that capture the elements identified during a job analysis are job descriptions and job specifications.

❖ Job Analysis and Legal HR Practices

Much current interest in job analysis results from the importance assigned to the activity by federal and state courts. The legal defensibility of an employer's recruiting and selection procedures, performance appraisal system, employee disciplinary actions, and pay practices rests in part on the foundation of job analysis. In a number of court cases, employers have lost because their HR processes and practices were not viewed by judges or juries as sufficiently job related. For instance, in *U.S. v. City of Chicago*, the courts found that the performance appraisal system used by the Chicago Police Department discriminated against persons of

Hispanic and African American descent. The court ruled that the performance appraisal system used was not tied directly enough to job-related criteria. Also, the selection and promotion exams for officer and sergeant were found to be discriminatory.[5] Other HR activities also are affected by a wide range of laws and regulations that focus on the jobs performed by employees, which are discussed in more detail later in this chapter.

❖ Components Developed by Job Analysis

Job analysis provides the information necessary to develop job descriptions and specifications. In most cases, the job description and job specifications are combined into one document that contains several different sections.

***Job Description**
Identification of the tasks, duties, and responsibilities of a job.

***Performance Standards**
Indicators of what the job accomplishes and what performance is considered satisfactory in each area of the job description.

Job Descriptions A **job description** indicates the tasks, duties, and responsibilities of a job. It identifies what is done, why it is done, where it is done, and, briefly, how it is done. **Performance standards** should flow directly from a job description, telling what the job accomplishes and what performance is considered satisfactory in each area of the job description. The reason is clear. If employees know what is expected and what constitutes good or poor performance, they have a much better chance of performing satisfactorily. Unfortunately, performance standards often are omitted from job descriptions. Even if performance standards have been identified and matched to job descriptions, they may not be known by employees if the job descriptions are not provided to employees but used only as tools by the HR department and managers. Such an approach limits the value of job descriptions.

***Job Specifications**
List the knowledge, skills, and abilities (KSAs) an individual needs to do the job satisfactorily.

***Knowledge, Skills, and Abilities (KSAs)**
Include education, experience, work skill requirements, personal requirements, mental and physical requirements, and working conditions and hazards.

Job Specifications While the job description describes activities to be done in the job, **job specifications** list the knowledge, skills, and abilities (KSAs) an individual needs to perform the job satisfactorily. **Knowledge, skills,** and **abilities (KSAs)** include education, experience, work skill requirements, personal abilities, and mental and physical requirements. Job specifications for a remote-visual-display-terminal operator might include a required education level, a certain number of months of experience, a typing ability of 60 words per minute, a high degree of visual concentration, and ability to work under time pressure. An example of job specifications for a clerk-typist might be: "Types 50 words per minute with no more than two errors; successful completion of one year of high school English or passing of an English proficiency test." It is important to note that accurate job specifications identify what KSAs a person needs to do the job, not necessarily what qualifications the current employee possesses.

❖ Job Analysis Responsibilities

Most methods of job analysis require that a knowledgeable person describe what goes on in the job or make a series of judgments about specific activities required to do the job. Such information can be provided by the employee doing the job, the supervisor, and/or a trained job analyst. Each source is useful, but each has drawbacks. The supervisor seems to be the best source of information on what *should be* done, but the employee knows most about what actually *is* done. However, both may lack the knowledge needed to complete a job analysis and draw the appropriate conclusions from it. Thus, job analysis requires a high degree of coordination and cooperation between the HR unit and operating managers.

The responsibility for job analysis depends on who can best perform various aspects of the process. Figure 7–1 shows a typical division of responsibilities in organizations that have an HR unit. In small organizations, managers have to perform all the work activities identified in Figure 7–1. In larger companies, the HR unit supervises the process to maintain its integrity and writes the job descriptions and specifications for uniformity. The managers review the efforts of the HR unit to ensure accuracy and completeness. They also may request reanalysis when jobs change significantly.

❖ **FIGURE 7–1** ❖
TYPICAL JOB ANALYSIS RESPONSIBILITIES

HR UNIT	MANAGERS
❖ Prepares and coordinates job analysis procedures ❖ Writes job descriptions and specifications for review by managers ❖ Revises and periodically reviews job descriptions and specifications ❖ Reviews managerial input to ensure accuracy ❖ May seek assistance from outside experts for difficult or unusual analyses	❖ Complete or assist in completing job analysis information ❖ Review and maintain accuracy of job descriptions/job specifications ❖ May request new job analysis as jobs change ❖ Identify performance standards based on job analysis information

❖ JOB ANALYSIS AND THE CHANGING NATURE OF JOBS

As the nature of jobs changes in parts of many organizations, job analysis also must change. For jobs that remain task-based, many of the standard phases of the job analysis process can continue. (These phases are described later in the chapter.) However, for the "virtual jobs" performed by individuals shifting from project to project or working on cross-functional teams that change frequently, the traditional job analysis process must be reshaped.[6] Instead of focusing on tasks, duties, and responsibilities, the analysis must shift to focus on the competencies required and how the KSAs of individuals are assessed and maintained. Job analysts may have to view jobs as broad bands of work flows and task interdependencies.[7] Therefore, identifying the competency groupings, determining when someone has those competencies, and ascertaining how those competencies link to the work done in the organization all must be addressed. It may be that job analysis will shift in order to address the changing nature of broader and looser jobs in some areas, while continuing to be relevant in those areas where jobs remain task-based.

❖ BEHAVIORAL ASPECTS OF JOB ANALYSIS

A detailed examination of jobs, while necessary, can be a demanding and threatening experience for both managers and employees, in part because job analysis can identify the difference between what currently *is* being performed in a job and what *should* be done. Job analysis involves determining what the "core" job is. This determination may require discussion with managers about the design of the job. Often the content of a job may reflect the desires and skills of the incumbent employee. For example, a woman promoted to office manager in one firm continued to spend considerable time opening and sorting the mail because she had done that duty in her old job. Yet she needed to be supervising the work of the eight clerical employees more and should have been delegating the mail duties to one of the clerks. Her manager indicated that opening and sorting mail was not one of the top five tasks of her new job, and the job description was written to reflect this. The manager also met with the employee to discuss what it meant to be a supervisor and what duties should receive more emphasis.

Employees and managers also have some tendency to inflate the importance and significance of their jobs. Because job analysis information is used for compensation purposes, both managers and employees hope that "puffing up" their jobs will result in higher pay levels. Titles of jobs often get inflated also, as the accompanying HR Perspective illustrates.

CURRENT JOB EMPHASIS As suggested earlier, it is important that a job analysis and the resulting job description and job specifications *should not describe just what the person currently doing the job does and what his or her qualifications are.* The person may have unique capabilities and the ability to expand the scope of the job to assume more responsibilities. The company would have difficulty finding someone exactly like that individual if he or she left. Consequently, it is useful to focus on the *core* jobs and *necessary* KSAs by determining what the jobs would be if the current incumbents quit or were no longer available to do the jobs.

EMPLOYEE ANXIETIES One fear that employees may have concerns the *purposes* of a detailed investigation of their job. The attitude behind such a fear might be, "As long as no one knows precisely what I am supposed to be doing, I am safe." Some employees may fear that an analysis of their jobs will put a "straightjacket" on them, limiting their creativity and flexibility by formalizing their duties. However, it does not necessarily follow that analyzing a job will limit job scope or depth. In fact, having a well-written, well-communicated job description can assist employees by clarifying what their roles are and what is expected of them. Management should explain why the job analysis is being done, because some employees may be concerned that someone must feel they have done something wrong if such a searching look is being taken.

HR PERSPECTIVE

JOB TITLE INFLATION

Inflation of job titles has been prevalent for years, but some HR specialists believe that it is becoming worse. Some firms give fancy titles in place of pay raises, while others do it to keep well-paid employees from leaving for "status" reasons. Some industries, such as banking and entertainment, are known for having more title inflation than others. For instance, banking and financial institutions use officer designations to enhance status. In one small midwestern bank, an employee who had three years' experience as a teller was "promoted" with no pay increase to Second Vice-President and Senior Customer Service Coordinator. She basically became the head teller when her supervisor was out of the bank and now could sign a few customer-account forms.

Other examples abound. Some secretarial employees are titled Administrative Assistants or Administrative Office Coordinators. A car salesperson may be called a Vehicle Sales Consultant and a supply clerk an Inventory Technician.

The problems caused by imprecision of job titles led the American Dietetic Association to eliminate job titles as part of a reorganization effort. An executive with the association said, "It sends a message to employees that we're not into status. You don't have to spend time measuring offices." However, the absence of job titles can create other problems. For example, employees cannot identify their job titles on career résumés, they do not have titles on business cards, and they cannot communicate status to others outside of the association.

While the absence of job titles in the American Dietetic Association generally has helped reduce status differences and improve communication across departments, some employees continue to use their old titles unofficially, especially on résumés. Also, some employees have asked how they know if they have received a promotion and how compensation is determined when job titles are not used. In addition, throughout the organization, how to handle National Secretary's Day caused significant discussions, because the job title Secretary does not exist.

Even with the elimination of titles, someone still must be designated as the top official in an organization. The top official at the American Dietetic Association, Beverly Bajus, signs documents and letters as "authorized signature," which could lead to a new title not prevalent in other organizations.[8]

Resistance to Change As jobs change, job descriptions and job specifications should be updated. Because people become used to working within defined boundaries, any attempt to change those "job fences" generates fear, resistance, and insecurity. Suggesting that it is time to revise job descriptions provokes anxiety because the employees' safe and secure job worlds are threatened. They may worry that they may have to take on new and difficult responsibilities. Also, they may fear that change could have a negative impact on their pay. Because resistance to change is a natural reaction, managers should expect it and be prepared to deal with it. Perhaps the most effective way to handle this resistance is to involve employees in the revision process.

Managerial Straitjacket Through the information developed in a job analysis, the job description is supposed to capture the nature of a job. However, if it fails—if some portions of the job are mistakenly left out of the description—some employees may use that to limit managerial flexibility. The resulting attitude, "It's not in my job description," puts a straitjacket on a manager. Such a situation is especially burdensome for management involved in changing jobs in response to changing economic or social conditions. Consequently, some employers refuse to show job descriptions to their employees. The idea is to make it difficult for an employee to say, "I don't have to do that because it is not in my job description." Of course, this idea is incorrect. In some organizations with unionized workforces, very restrictive job descriptions exist.

Because of such difficulties, the final statement in many job descriptions is a *miscellaneous clause,* which consists of a phrase similar to "Performs other duties as needed upon request by immediate supervisor." This statement covers unusual situations that may occur in an employee's job. However, duties covered by this phrase cannot be considered essential functions under the Americans with Disabilities Act (ADA).

❖ Legal Aspects of Job Analysis

Permeating the discussion of equal employment laws, regulations, and court cases in the previous chapters is the concept that legal compliance must focus on the jobs that individuals perform. The 1978 Uniform Selection Guidelines make it clear that HR requirements must be tied to specific job factors if employers are to defend their actions as job related and a business necessity.

❖ Job Analysis and the Americans with Disabilities Act (ADA)

The passage of the Americans with Disabilities Act (ADA) dramatically increased the legal importance of job analysis, job descriptions, and job specifications. HR managers and their organizations must identify job activities and then document the steps taken to create the final job description. One result of the passage of the ADA is increased emphasis by employers on developing and maintaining current and accurate job descriptions. Also, many employers have had to revise their job specifications to reflect the essential prerequisite KSAs, rather than the "puffed up" ones favored by some managers and employees. It is clear that the ADA has had a major impact on job analysis.

Identification of Essential Functions The ADA requires that organizations identify the *essential functions* of jobs. Specifically, the ADA indicates that:

***Essential Functions**
"The fundamental job duties of the employment position that an individual with the disability holds or desires."

essential functions means "the fundamental job duties of the employment position that an individual with the disability holds or desires." The term "essential functions" does not include the marginal functions of the positions.[9]

An important part of job analysis is to obtain information about what duties are being performed and what percentage of time is devoted to each duty. As the ADA suggests, it generally is true that the percentage of time spent on a duty indicates its relative importance.

Another aspect of job analysis is to identify the physical demands and environmental condition of jobs. The accompanying HR Perspective contains a sample page from a job analysis questionnaire for office jobs that requests such information.

Having identified the essential job functions through a job analysis, an employer must be prepared to make reasonable accommodations.[10] Again, the *core* job duties and KSAs must be considered. One manufacturing company with multiple buildings identified that participation in design planning meetings was an essential job function. To accommodate a physically disabled individual, who was otherwise qualified, the firm purchased a motorized cart for the individual and required that all design team meetings be held in first-floor, accessible conference rooms.

Evidence that functions are essential may include, but is not limited to, the following:[11]

- Employer's judgment about which functions are essential
- Job descriptions prepared *before* advertising for or interviewing applicants
- Amount of time on the job spent performing the function
- Consequences of not requiring the employee to perform the function
- Terms of a collective bargaining agreement
- Work experience of past incumbents in the job and/or incumbents in similar jobs

SELECTION AND PERFORMANCE APPRAISAL The ADA makes it even more important that selection criteria and performance appraisal standards be clearly job related. Identifying the essential job functions forms the base for:[12]

- Developing selection interview questions
- Determining what competencies are needed to perform jobs
- Developing any selection tests to determine ability to perform essential functions
- Identifying performance standards for approving employee performance of the essential functions
- Identifying to what extent, if any, job accommodation can be made for a particular individual with a disability
- Evaluating whether making such accommodation would be an unreasonable hardship on the employer

❖ JOB ANALYSIS AND WAGE/HOUR REGULATIONS

Typically, a job analysis identifies the percentage of time spent on each duty in a job. This information helps determine whether someone should be classified as exempt or nonexempt under the wage/hour laws.[13]

As will be noted in Chapter 13, the federal Fair Labor Standards Act (FLSA) and most state wage/hour laws indicate that the percentage of time employees spend on routine, manual, or clerical duties affects whether or not they must be paid overtime for hours over 40 per week. To be exempt from overtime, the

HR PERSPECTIVE

JOB ANALYSIS OBTAINS INFORMATION FOR ADA COMPLIANCE PURPOSES

One result of the Americans with Disabilities Act is that job analysis information on the physical dimensions of jobs must be delineated. With this information, job descriptions and specifications can be written to include the essential functions and knowledge, skills, and abilities (KSAs). By identifying the critical and necessary KSAs, employers will be prepared to deal with current employees with disabilities who apply for job transfers and promotions, as well as external applicants with disabilities.

One mistaken idea that many managers have is that the ADA affects only jobs that are extremely physical, such as those requiring climbing, heavy lifting, or other physical acts. But many office jobs require employees to see well enough to read computer screens, reports, and data printouts. Also, many customer service jobs require hearing capabilities.

The organization can use a job questionnaire to obtain ADA-related information from current employees and their supervisors and managers. Below is a sample page from a job analysis questionnaire that requests such information.

Sample Page from Job Analysis Questionnaire (for office jobs)

PHYSICAL ACTIVITIES AND CHARACTERISTICS:

Please identify the physical requirements associated with this job. For each type of activity, be as specific as possible on how often the activity is performed.

ACTIVITY	% OF TIME	FREQUENCY
a. Seeing and Hearing well enough to:		
b. Standing and Walking well enough to:		
c. Climbing and Balancing well enough to:		
d. Body Movement (kneeling, crawling, stooping, reaching)		
e. Lifting, Pulling, and Pushing (give typical weights/frequency of activity)		
f. Dexterity (fingering, grasping, feeling)		
g. Mobility (moving from one place to another)		

WORKING CONDITIONS:

Please describe the typical work environment in terms of heat, cold, noise, dirt, confined spaces, fumes, or other conditions different from those in a normal office setting.

employees must perform their *primary duties* as executive, administrative, or professional employees. *Primary* has been interpreted to mean occupying at least 50% of the time. Additionally, the exemption regulations state that no more than 20% (40% in retail settings) of the time can be spent on manual, routine, or clerical duties.

Much controversy has revolved around the degree to which jobs traditionally held by men (for example, those that require extensive physical skills) can be compared with those traditionally held by women. The issue is to compare the physical danger of underground coal mining with the mental and emotional demands of nursing or teaching.

Other legal-compliance efforts, such as those involving workplace safety and health, can be aided through the data provided by job analysis, too. In summary, it is extremely difficult for an employer to have a legal staffing system without performing job analysis. Truly, job analysis is the most basic HR activity.

❖ Job Analysis and Other HR Activities

The completion of job descriptions and job specifications, based on a job analysis, is at the heart of many other HR activities, as Figure 7–2 indicates. But even if legal requirements did not force employers to do job analysis, effective HR management would demand it.

❖ HR Planning

HR planning requires auditing of current jobs, as noted in Chapter 2. Current job descriptions provide the basic details necessary for this internal assessment, including such items as what jobs, how many jobs and positions currently exist, and what are the reporting relationships of the jobs.

By identifying what functions are currently being performed and how much time is being spent to perform them, managers and HR specialists can redesign jobs to eliminate unnecessary tasks and combine responsibilities where desirable.

❖ **Figure 7–2** ❖
Job Analysis and Other HR Activities

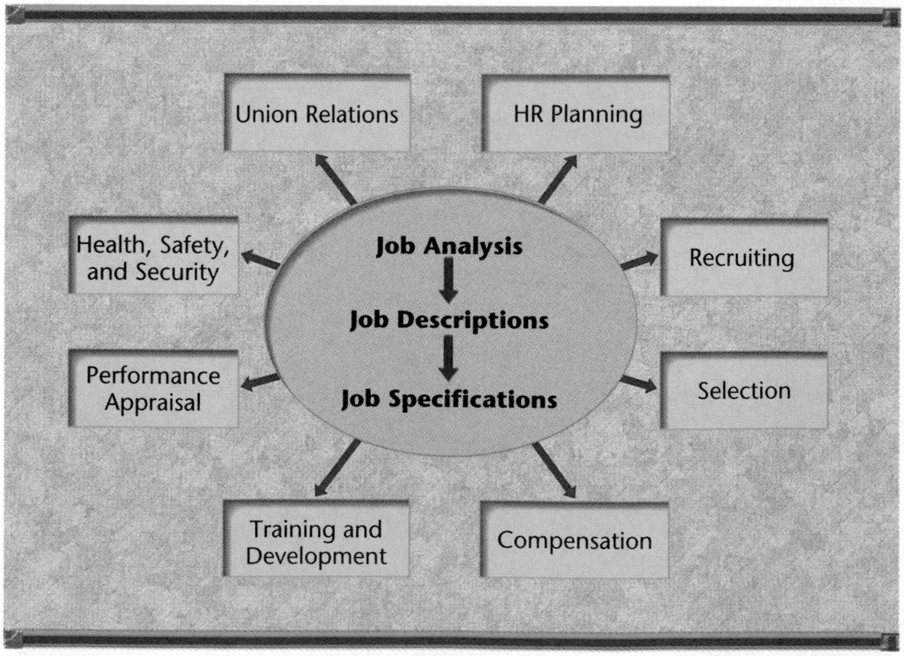

For example, in the sales department of a distribution firm, the sales representatives spent considerable time performing clerical tasks in the office instead of calling on customers. Job analysis helped identify this situation, which the firm remedied by hiring clerical support employees. Consequently, the higher-paid sales representatives were able to spend more time actually selling.

Similarly, managers can analyze a group of jobs to identify how jobs must be adjusted or what jobs can be combined or eliminated.[14] For example, a small communications firm with 28 employees did an analysis of all jobs. When reviewing the information provided by both employees and supervisors, the director of administration and an outside consultant noted that several duties associated with maintaining customer service records were divided among three employees, which often led to delays in recording customer payments and scheduling repair services. Therefore, the various customer service duties were regrouped so that two of the employees performed complete but different functions, and filing activities were concentrated with the third employee, who also served as backup for the other two.

❖ Recruiting and Selection

Equal employment opportunity guidelines clearly require a sound and comprehensive job analysis to validate recruiting and selection criteria.[15] Without a systematic investigation of a job, an employer may be using requirements that are not specifically job related. For example, if a trucking firm requires a high school diploma for a dispatcher's job, the firm must be able to indicate how such an educational requirement matches up to the tasks, duties, and responsibilities of a dispatcher. It must be able to show that the knowledge, skills, and abilities needed by the dispatcher could be obtained only through formal education.

Organizations use job analysis to identify job specifications in order to plan how and where to obtain employees for anticipated job openings, whether recruited internally or externally. For example, a job analysis in a small manufacturer of electric equipment showed that the Accountant II job, which traditionally had required a college-trained person, really could be handled by someone with high school training in bookkeeping and several years of experience. As a result, the company could select from within and promote a current accounting clerk. In addition to saving on recruiting costs, promotion can have a positive impact on employee commitment and career-planning efforts.

❖ Compensation

Job analysis information is very useful in determining compensation. People should be paid more for doing more difficult jobs. Information from job analysis can be used to give more weight, and therefore more pay, to jobs involving more difficult tasks, duties, and responsibilities. Employees' perceptions of fairness and equity are linked to how the extrinsic rewards they receive compare with those given to others, as well as those they expected for themselves.

Job analysis also can aid in the management of various employee benefits programs. For instance, a job analysis can be used to determine what functions can be performed by workers who have been on workers' compensation disability leave.

❖ Training and Development

By defining what activities comprise a job, a job analysis helps the supervisor explain that job to a new employee. In addition, information from job descriptions and job specifications can help in career planning by showing employees what is expected in jobs that they may choose to move to in the future. Job specification information can point out areas in which employees might need to develop in order to further their careers. Employee development efforts by organizations depend on the job descriptions and job specifications generated from job analyses.

❖ Performance Appraisal

By comparing what an employee is supposed to be doing with what the person actually has done, a supervisor can determine the level of the employee's performance. Many organizations publicly embrace the ideal of "pay for performance," meaning that pay should reflect how well a person is performing a job, not just the level of the job. Base comparisons on performance standards that give the employee a clear idea of what is expected in each area of the job. The development of clear and realistic performance standards can reduce communication problems related to performance appraisals.

❖ Safety and Health

Job analysis information is useful in identifying possible job hazards and working conditions associated with jobs. From the information gathered, managers and HR specialists can work together to identify the health and safety equipment needed, specify work methods, and train workers.

❖ Union Relations

Where workers are represented by a labor union, job analysis is used in several ways. First, job analysis information may be needed to determine if the job should be covered by the union agreements. Specifically, management may be able to exclude a supervisory job and its incumbents from the bargaining unit. Second, it is common in unionized environments for job descriptions to be very specific about what tasks are and are not covered in a job. Finally, well-written and specific job descriptions can reduce the number of grievances filed by workers. In one manufacturing plant, a worker refused to sweep up his work area and was disciplined. He filed a grievance and won, because cleaning his work area was not mentioned in the job description.

❖ Job Analysis Methods

Job analysis information can be gathered in a variety of ways. One consideration is who is to conduct the job analysis. Most frequently, a member of the HR staff coordinates this effort. Depending on which of the methods discussed next is used, others who often participate are managers, supervisors, and employees doing the jobs. For more complex analyses, industrial engineers may conduct time and motion studies.

Another consideration is the method to be used. Common methods are observations, interviews, questionnaires, and specialized methods of analysis. Combinations of these approaches frequently are used, depending on the situation and the organization. Each of these methods is discussed in some detail next.

❖ Observation

When the observation method is used, a manager, job analyst, or industrial engineer observes the individual performing the job and takes notes to describe the tasks and duties performed. Observation may be continuous or based on sampling.

Use of the observation method is limited because many jobs do not have complete and easily observed job duties or complete job cycles. Thus, observation may be more useful for repetitive jobs and in conjunction with other methods. Managers or job analysts using other methods may watch parts of a job being performed to gain a general familiarity with the job and the conditions under which it is performed. Multiple observations on several occasions also will help them use some of the other job analysis method more effectively.

Work Sampling As a type of observation, work sampling does not require attention to each detailed action throughout an entire work cycle. Instead, a manager can determine the content and pace of a typical workday through statistical sampling of certain actions rather than through continuous observation and timing of all actions. Work sampling is particularly useful for routine and repetitive jobs.

Employee Diary/Log Another method requires that employees "observe" their own performances by keeping a diary/log of their job duties, noting how frequently they are performed and the time required for each duty. Although this approach sometimes generates useful information, it may be burdensome for employees to compile an accurate log. Also, employees sometimes perceive this approach as creating needless documentation that detracts from the performance of their work.

❖ Interviewing

The interview method of gathering information requires that a manager or HR specialist visit each job site and talk with the employees performing each job. A standardized interview form is used most often to record the information. Frequently, both the employee and the employee's supervisor must be interviewed to obtain a complete understanding of the job. During the job analysis interview, the interviewer must make judgments about the information to be included and its degree of importance.

Group interviews also can be used. Members of the group are usually experienced job incumbents and/or supervisors. This method is expensive because of the number of people involved, and it usually requires the presence of a representative from the HR department as a mediator. However, it does bring together a large body of experience concerning a particular job in one place at one time. For certain difficult-to-define jobs, group interviews are probably most appropriate.

The interview method can be quite time consuming, especially if the interviewer talks with two or three employees doing each job. Professional and managerial jobs often are more complicated to analyze and usually require longer interviews. For these reasons, combining the interview with one of the other methods is suggested. For example, if a job analyst has observed an employee performing a job, a check on observation data can be made by also interviewing the employee. Likewise, the interview frequently is used as a follow-up to the questionnaire method, in which the analyst may ask a supervisor or employee to clarify information on the questionnaire. Also the analyst may be able to get clarification of special terminology used on the questionnaire.

❖ Questionnaires

The questionnaire is a widely used method of gathering data on jobs. A survey instrument is developed and given to employees and managers to complete.

The typical job questionnaire often includes questions in the following areas:

- Duties and percentage of time spent on each
- Special duties performed less frequently
- External and internal contacts
- Work coordination and supervisory responsibilities
- Materials and equipment used
- Decisions made and discretion exercised
- Records and reports prepared
- Knowledge, skills, and abilities used
- Training needed
- Physical activities and characteristics
- Working conditions

Sometimes it is beneficial for the employee and the supervisor to complete the questionnaire independently. At least one employee per job should complete the questionnaire, which is then returned to the supervisor or manager for review before being used in preparing job descriptions.

The major advantage of the questionnaire method is that information on a large number of jobs can be collected inexpensively in a relatively short period of time. However, follow-up observations and discussions often are necessary.

The questionnaire method assumes that employees can accurately analyze and communicate information about their jobs. That may not be a valid assumption in all cases. Research shows that job analysis outcomes are affected by the employees selected to fill out the questionnaire. Different employees produce different job analysis outcomes.[16] Employees may vary in their perceptions of the job, and even in their literacy. The ability to read and write accurately could affect how employees use the questionnaire to describe their jobs. For these reasons, the questionnaire method is usually combined with interviews and observations to clarify and verify the questionnaire information.

One type of questionnaire sometimes used is a *checklist.* Differing from the open-ended questionnaire, the checklist offers a simplified way for employees to give information. Figure 7–3 contains some sample statements from the Organizational Measurement System (OMS) job analysis form.[17] An obvious difficulty with the checklist is constructing it, which can be a complicated and detailed process.

FIGURE 7–3
SAMPLE ORGANIZATIONAL MEASUREMENT SYSTEM (OMS) STATEMENTS

SCOPE

- Do you have access to confidential agreements/contracts?
- What foreign languages do you use (spoken/written) and how much fluency is required?
- What is the total dollar value of customer accounts you represent or handle?
- How much do you travel (%) as part of your job (foreign, domestic)?

TASK STATEMENTS

Include the time you spend *supervising* and *performing* each of the following:

- Analyzing training needs
- Recommending purchase of computer software products
- Entering data into computer system
- Interviewing applicants for clerical openings
- Administering disciplinary procedures
- Developing methods for improving operations

SOURCE: Adapted from Organizational Measurement System, Technical Job Analysis Questionnaire.

SPECIALIZED JOB ANALYSIS METHODS

Several job analysis methods are built on the questionnaire approach. Some of these methods are described next.

POSITION ANALYSIS QUESTIONNAIRE (PAQ) The PAQ is a specialized questionnaire method incorporating checklists. Each job is analyzed on 27 dimensions composed of 187 "elements." The PAQ comprises six divisions, with each division containing numerous job elements. The divisions include:[18]

- *Information input.* Where and how does the worker get information to perform the job?
- *Mental process.* What levels of reasoning are necessary on the job?
- *Work output.* What physical activities are performed?
- *Relationships with others.* What relationships are required to perform the job?
- *Job context.* What working conditions and social contexts are involved?
- *Other.* What else is relevant to the job?

The PAQ focuses on "worker-oriented" elements that describe behaviors necessary to do the job, rather than on "job-oriented" elements that describe the technical aspects of the work. The assumption made in the PAQ is that comparing worker behaviors across jobs is more valid than trying to compare the technological similarities of different jobs in different work fields.

The PAQ can be completed by job analysts who interview workers and observe work as it is being done. It also can be completed by the worker. Although its complexity may deter many potential users, the PAQ is easily quantified and can be used to conduct validity studies on selection tests. It also is useful in helping to ensure internal pay fairness because it considers the varying demands of different jobs.

FUNCTIONAL JOB ANALYSIS (FJA) This method is a comprehensive approach to job analysis. FJA considers: (1) the goals of the organization, (2) what workers do to achieve those goals in their jobs, (3) the level and orientation of what workers do, (4) performance standards, and (5) training content. A functional definition of what is done in a job can be generated by examination of the three components of *data, people,* and *things.*[19] The levels of these components are used to identify and compare important elements of jobs given in the *Dictionary of Occupational Titles (DOT),* a standardized data source provided by the federal government.[20] See Figure 7–4.

FIGURE 7–4
WORK FUNCTIONS FROM *DICTIONARY OF OCCUPATIONAL TITLES*

DATA (4TH DIGIT)	PEOPLE (5TH DIGIT)	THINGS (6TH DIGIT)
0 Synthesizing	0 Mentoring	0 Setting Up
1 Coordinating	1 Negotiating	1 Precision Working
2 Analyzing	2 Instructing	2 Operating-Controlling
3 Compiling	3 Supervising	3 Driving-Operating
4 Computing	4 Diverting	4 Manipulating
5 Copying	5 Persuading	5 Tending
6 Comparing	6 Speaking-Signaling	6 Feeding-Offbearing
	7 Serving	7 Handling
	8 Taking Instructions–Helping	

SOURCE: U.S. Department of Labor, Employment and Training Administration, *Dictionary of Occupational Titles,* 4th ed., revised (Washington, D.C.: Government Printing Office, 1991), xix.

DICTIONARY OF OCCUPATIONAL TITLES (DOT) Functional Job Analysis, as captured in the *DOT,* is a valuable source of job information, regardless of the job analysis method used. The *DOT* describes a wide range of jobs, samples of which are shown in Figure 7–5. A manager or HR specialist confronted with preparing a large number of job descriptions can use the *DOT* as a starting point. The job description from the *DOT* then can be modified to fit the particular organizational situation.

MANAGERIAL JOB ANALYSIS Because managerial jobs are different in character from jobs with clearly observable routines and procedures, some specialized methods have evolved for their analysis. One of the most well known and widely used ones was developed at Control Data Corporation and

❖ FIGURE 7–5 ❖
SAMPLE JOB TITLES FROM THE *DICTIONARY OF OCCUPATIONAL TITLES*

030.162-014 PROGRAMMER-ANALYST (profess. & kin.) alternate titles: applications analyst-programmer
Plans, develops, tests, and documents computer programs, applying knowledge of programming techniques and computer systems: Evaluates user request for new or modified program, such as for financial or human resource management system, clinical research trial results, statistical study of traffic patterns, or analyzing and developing specifications for bridge design, to determine feasibility, cost and time required, compatibility with current system, and computer capabilities. Consults with user to identify current operating procedures and clarify program objectives. Reads manuals, periodicals, and technical reports to learn ways to develop programs that meet user requirements. Formulates plan outlining steps required to develop program, using structured analysis and design. Submits plans to user for approval. Prepares flow charts and diagrams to illustrate sequence of steps program must follow and to describe logical operations involved. Designs computer terminal screen displays to accomplish goals of user request. Converts project specifications, using flowcharts and diagrams, into sequence of detailed instructions and logical steps for coding into language processable by computer, applying knowledge of computer programming techniques and computer languages. Enters program codes into computer system. Enters commands into computer to run and test program. Reads computer printouts or observes display screen to detect syntax or logic errors during program test, or uses diagnostic software to detect errors. Replaces, deletes, or modifies codes to correct errors. Analyzes, reviews, and alters program to increase operating efficiency or adapt to new requirements. Writes documentation to describe program development, logic, coding, and corrections. Writes manual for users to describe installation and operating procedures. Assists users to solve operating problems. Recreates steps taken by user to locate source of problem and rewrites program to correct errors. May use computer-aided software tools, such as flowchart design and code generation, in each stage of system development. May train users to use program. May oversee installation of hardware and software. May provide technical assistance to program users. May install and test program at user site. May monitor performance of program after implementation. May specialize in developing programs for business or technical applications.

166.117-018 MANAGER, PERSONNEL (profess. & kin.) alternate titles: manager, human resources
Plans and carries out policies relating to all phases of personnel activity: Recruits, interviews, and selects employees to fill vacant positions. Plans and conducts new employee orientation to foster positive attitude toward company goals. Keeps record of insurance coverage, pension plan, and personnel transactions, such as hires, promotions, transfers, and terminations. Investigates accidents and prepares reports for insurance carrier. Conducts wage survey within labor market to determine competitive wage rate. Prepares budget of personnel operations. Meets with shop stewards and supervisors to resolve grievances. Writes separation notices for employees separating with cause and conducts exit interviews to determine reasons behind separations. Prepares reports and recommends procedures to reduce absenteeism and turnover. Represents company at personnel-related hearings and investigations. Contracts with outside suppliers to provide employee services, such as canteen, transportation, or relocation service. May prepare budget of personnel operations, using computer terminal. May administer manual and dexterity tests to applicants. May supervise clerical workers. May keep records of hired employee characteristics for governmental reporting purposes. May negotiate collective bargaining agreement with BUSINESS REPRESENTATIVE LABOR UNION (profess. & kin.) 187.167-018

Parts of Occupational Definition

There are seven basic parts to an occupational definition. They present data about a job in a systematic fashion. The parts are listed below in the order in which they appear in every definition:

(1) The Occupational Code Number
(2) The Occupational Title
(3) The Industry Designation
(4) Alternate Titles (if any)
(5) The Body of the Definition
 (a) Lead Statement
 (b) Task Element Statements
 (c) "May" Items
(6) Undefined Related Titles (if any)
(7) Definition Trailer

SOURCE: U.S. Department of Labor, Employment and Training Administration, *Dictionary of Occupational Titles,* 4th ed., revised (Washington, D.C.: Government Printing Office, 1991).

is labeled the *Management Position Description Questionnaire (MPDQ)*. Composed of a listing of over 200 statements, the MPDQ examines a variety of managerial dimensions, including decision making and supervising.[21]

Another approach is the *Executive Checklist (EXCEL)*, which contains approximately 250 statements on planning, decision making, and sales, among others.[22]

❖ Computerized Job Analysis

As computer technology has expanded, researchers have developed computerized job analysis systems. The CMQ System, discussed in the accompanying HR Perspective, illustrates one approach. Others also have been developed, and they all have several common characteristics. First, task statements are used that relate to all jobs. Second, individual employees indicate if and to what degree each task statement is present in their jobs.

A computerized job analysis system often can reduce the time and effort involved in writing job descriptions. These systems have banks of job duty statements that relate to each of the task and scope statements of the questionnaires,

HR Perspective: HRIS and Job Analysis

Just as the computer has changed many other areas of management, so has it enhanced the job analysis process. A variety of software programs now exist to guide the writing of job descriptions.

Blending the administrative convenience of paper and pencil with the power of computerization, one of the new approaches is the Common-Metric Questionnaire: A Job Analysis System (CMQ). The CMQ System consists of a computer-scannable document that is fed into computer-based scoring and reporting services capable of recording, analyzing, and reporting thousands of pieces of information about any job.

The CMQ measures jobs on four major dimensions:

- ❖ Interpersonal
- ❖ Decision making
- ❖ Mechanical and physical activities
- ❖ Work context

For example, the interpersonal dimension examines the human resource responsibility, employee supervision, internal and external contact, and level and impact of interpersonal decisions in each job. A total of 242 core questions make up the CMQ; by pairing these questions with specially designed common-metric rating scales, the CMQ can collect 2,077 different pieces of work activity data.

The CMQ is written at an eighth-grade reading level to ensure its readability by employees with widely varying jobs and skills. Employees and/or their supervisors provide answers to CMQ questions, although some organizations opt to employ trained job analysts to complete the questionnaires on behalf of employees. Typically, it takes less than two hours for a CMQ administration.

An important feature of the CMQ is its behavioral specificity, which allows for the objective verification of job analysis ratings and makes the basis for human resource decisions clear and understandable.

Following collection of the data, the CMQ System performs a variety of statistical analyses and produces a number of different reports. For job descriptions, the CMQ System produces Profile Description Reports, which detail the work activities and environment of each job.

The same data generated and presented in the Profile Description Reports are used to evaluate jobs for compensation purposes, produce performance appraisal forms, and provide criteria for validating employment test results.

For performance appraisal, the CMQ System uses behaviorally-based rating scales to measure performance of relevant work activities for a job. These same performance measures can serve as criteria for selection test validation.

As is evident, the melding of computer technology with psychological methodology allows firms to develop more accurate and comprehensive job descriptions, more equitable compensation programs, and performance-appraisal systems that are more closely job related. In addition, these processes can provide better data for legal defensibility than once was available.[23]

LOGGING ON

Job Analysis
A listing of the completed reports and documents contained in the server that relate to research in job analysis specifically related to the CMQ.

(http://harvey.psyc.vt.edu/ja_reports.htm)

and the job questionnaire data is input into the computer using optical scan forms. Then the data from employees are used to generate behaviorally specific job descriptions. These descriptions categorize and identify the relative importance of various job tasks, duties, and responsibilities.

One advantage of these systems is that the results can be used to develop job evaluation weights and rankings that are tied to pay structures. As each job is scored, it is related to labor market pay data, so that jobs with higher scores are placed in higher pay grades. Also, any mismatches between job scores and pay survey data are highlighted, so that a more intensive job analysis using interviews or other methods can be conducted to resolve the discrepancies.

Another advantage of some computerized systems is that because they are behaviorally based, they can identify the specific skills and abilities required in the job. Thus, job specifications that focus on specific KSAs for each job can be developed, which aids legal-compliance efforts and may improve recruiting, selection, training, and other HR efforts. Some of the skill-based approaches also define the proficiency levels for each job, so that performance appraisals can be made more job specific.[24]

❖ Combination Methods

There are indeed a number of different ways to obtain and analyze information about a job. No specific job analysis method has received the stamp of approval from the various courts in all situations. Therefore, when dealing with issues that may end up in court, care must be taken to document all of the steps taken. Each of the methods has strengths and weaknesses, and a combination of methods generally is preferred over one method alone.

❖ The Job Analysis Process

The process of conducting a job analysis must be done in a logical manner that follows appropriate psychometric practices. Therefore, a multistep process usually is followed, regardless of the job analysis methods used. The steps for a typical job analysis are outlined here. The steps used may vary with the methods used and the number of jobs included. However, the basic process is that shown in Figure 7–6.

❖ A. Identify Jobs and Review Existing Documentation

The first step is to identify the jobs under review. For example, are the jobs to be analyzed hourly jobs, clerical jobs, all jobs in one division, or all jobs in the entire organization? Part of the identification phase is to review existing documentation, such as existing job descriptions, organization charts, previous job analysis information, and other industry-related resources. In this phase, those who will be involved in conducting the job analysis and the methods to be used are identified. Also specified is how current incumbents and managers will participate in the process and how many employees' jobs will be considered.

❖ B. Explain the Process to Managers and Employees

A crucial step is to explain the process to managers, affected employees, and other concerned people, such as union stewards. Explanations should address the natural concerns and anxieties people have when someone puts their jobs under close scrutiny. Items to be covered often include the purpose of the job analysis,

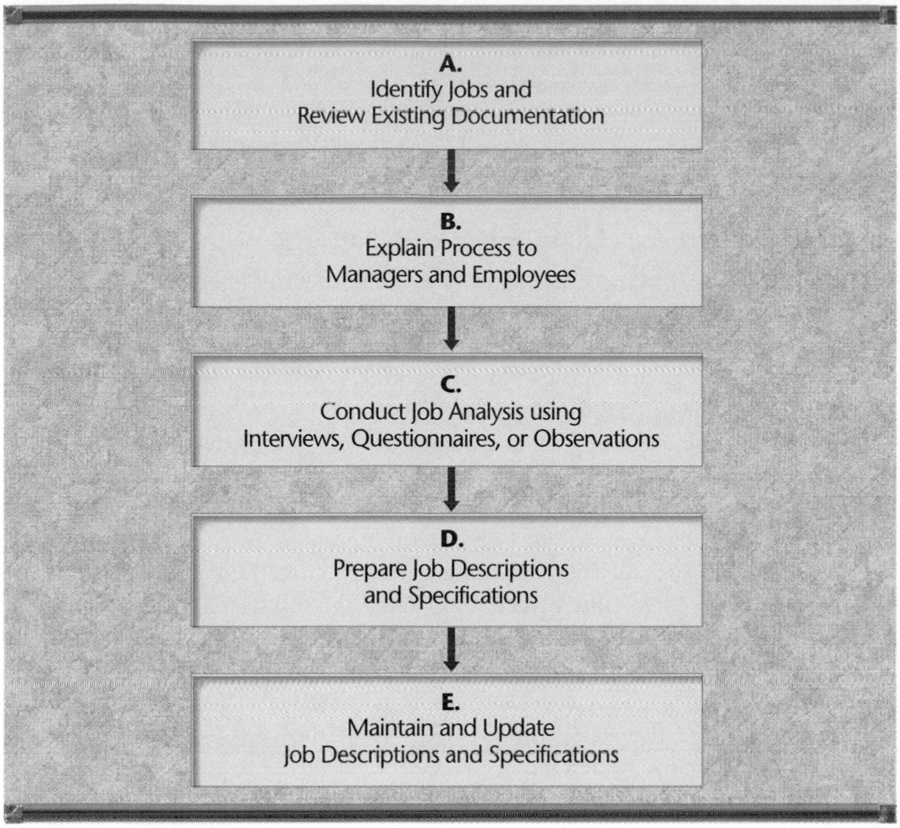

❖ FIGURE 7–6 ❖
TYPICAL JOB ANALYSIS PROCESS

the steps involved, the time schedule, how managers and employees will participate, who is doing the analysis, and whom to contact as questions arise.

❖ C. CONDUCT THE JOB ANALYSIS

The next step is actually gathering the job analysis information. Questionnaires might be distributed, interviews conducted, and/or observations made. Depending on the methods used, this phase often requires follow-up contacts to remind managers and employees to return questionnaires or to schedule interviews. As the job analysis information is received, analysts review it to ensure its completeness. Additional clarifying information can be gathered, usually through interviews.

❖ D. PREPARE JOB DESCRIPTIONS AND SPECIFICATIONS

All job analysis information must be sorted, sifted, and used in drafting the descriptions and specifications for each job. Usually, the drafts are prepared by members of the HR department. Then they are sent to appropriate managers and employees for review. Following the review, all necessary changes are made, and the final job descriptions and specifications are prepared.

Once job descriptions and specifications have been prepared, managers should provide feedback to current job holders, especially those who assisted in the job analysis. One feedback technique is to give employees draft copies of their own job descriptions and specifications for review. Giving current employees the opportunity to make corrections, ask for clarification, and discuss their job duties with the appropriate manager or supervisor enhances manager/employee communications. Questions may arise about how work is done, why it is done that way, and how it can be changed. When employees are represented by a union, it is essential that union representatives be included in reviewing the job descriptions and specifications to lessen the possibility of future conflicts.

❖ E. Maintain and Update Job Descriptions and Specifications

Once job descriptions and specifications have been completed and reviewed by all appropriate individuals, a system must be developed for keeping them current. Otherwise, the entire process, beginning with job analysis, may have to be repeated in several years. Because organizations are dynamic and evolving entities, rarely do all jobs stay the same for years.

Someone in the HR department usually has responsibility for ensuring that job descriptions and specifications stay current. Employees performing the jobs and their managers play a crucial role because, as the ones closest to the jobs, they know when changes occur. One effective way to ensure that appropriate reviews occur is to use job descriptions and job specifications in other HR activities. For example, each time a vacancy occurs, the job description and specifications should be reviewed and revised as appropriate *before* recruiting and selection efforts begin. Similarly, in some organizations, managers review the job description during each performance-appraisal interview. This review enables the job holder and the supervisor to discuss whether the job description still describes the actual job adequately or whether it needs to be revised. In addition, a comprehensive and systematic review may be done during HR planning efforts. For many organizations, a complete review is made once every three years, or as technology shifts occur, and more frequently when major organizational changes are made.

❖ Job Descriptions and Job Specifications

The output from analysis of a job is used to develop a job description and job specifications. Together, they summarize job analysis information in a readable fashion and provide the basis for defensible job-related actions. In addition, they serve the individual employees by providing documentation frorn management that identifies their jobs.

Several events tend to prompt changes in job descriptions and job specifications. One is a change in organization size or structure (growth, restructuring, downsizing). Another is routine periodic review of jobs. The passage and implementation of the Americans with Disabilities Act (ADA) caused many organizations to develop or update job descriptions.

❖ Job Description Components

A typical job description, such as the one in Figure 7–7, contains several major parts. Overviews of the most common ones are presented next.

Identification The first part of the job description is the identification section, in which the job title, reporting relationships, department, location, and date of analysis may be given. Usually, it is advisable to note other information that is useful in tracking jobs and employees through human resource information systems (HRIS).

❖ FIGURE 7–7 ❖
JOB DESCRIPTION AND SPECIFICATIONS

POSITION TITLE:	Human Resources Assistant	JOB NUMBER: ____________	
DEPARTMENT:	Human Resources	GRADE:	OH6
REPORTS TO:	Human Resources Manager	STATUS:	Nonexempt
		CLASS:	Clerical

<u>GENERAL SUMMARY:</u>
Provides support for the Human Resources department by maintaining highly confidential personnel records in physical files, updating Human Resources Database, and preparing reports. Assists in various projects and manages some projects in the absence of the Human Resources manager.

<u>ESSENTIAL JOB FUNCTIONS:</u>
1. Maintains personnel records in files and updates computer records to ensure compliance with regulations. (55%)
2. Retrieves, compiles, and prepares various external and internal reports such as regular and enhanced retiree reports for accounting. (15%)
3. Answers employee questions regarding human resource matters such as benefit inquiries and problems. (10%)
4. Writes, edits, and coordinates printing and layout of company newsletter. (5%)
5. Attends meetings and conducts off-site business on an as-needed basis. (5%)
6. Assists HR Manager with projects as needed. (5%)
7. Performs other related duties as assigned by management. (5%)

<u>KNOWLEDGE, SKILLS, AND ABILITIES:</u>
1. Knowledge of human resource practices and procedures.
2. Knowledge of and skill in using computer software, including WordPerfect or MS Word, and Excel or Lotus.
3. Skill in operating various office equipment, such as personal computer, calculator, facsimile, copy machine, camera, document shredder, typewriter, laminator, and Logitech scanner.
4. Ability to pay close attention to detail and coordinate various activities simultaneously.
5. Ability to communicate with customers, co-workers, and business contacts in a courteous and professional manner.
6. Ability to work with minimal supervision.
7. Ability to maintain confidentiality.

<u>EDUCATION AND EXPERIENCE:</u>
High school graduate or equivalent, plus one to three years specialized secretarial training with emphasis in computers. One year experience in Human Resources or related field. Additional training or education helpful.

<u>PHYSICAL REQUIREMENTS:</u>	0-24%	25-49%	50-74%	75-100%
Seeing: Must be able to read reports and use computer.				X
Hearing: Must be able to hear well enough to communicate with co-workers.				X
Standing/Walking/Mobility: Must be able to stand to open files and operate office machines; mobility between departments and to attend meetings of employees and managers.			X	
Climbing/Stooping/Kneeling:	X			
Lifting/Pulling/Pushing:		X		
Fingering/Grasping/Feeling: Must be able to write, type, and use phone system.				X

<u>PHYSICAL DIMENSIONS:</u>
Medium Work: Exerting up to 50 pounds of force occasionally, and/or up to 20 pounds of force frequently, and/or up to 10 pounds of force constantly to move objects.

Note: The statements herein are intended to describe the general nature and level of work being performed by employees assigned to this classification. They are not intended to be construed as an exhaustive list of all responsibilities, duties, and skills required of personnel so classified.

Commmon items noted in the identifcation section are:

- Job number
- Pay grade
- Fair Labor Standards Act (FLSA) status (exempt/nonexempt)
- EEOC Code (from EEO–1 form)

General Summary The second part, the general summary, is a concise summation of the general responsibilities and components that make the job different form others. One HR specialist has characterized the general summary statement as follows: "In thirty words or less, describe the essence of the job."

Essential Functions and Duties The third part of the typical job description lists the essential functions and duties. It contains clear and precise statements on the major tasks, duties, and responsibilities performed. Writing this section is the most time-consuming aspect of preparing job descriptions.

Job Specifications The next portion of the job description gives the qualifications needed to perform the job satisfactorily. The job specifications typically are stated as: (1) Knowledge, Skills, and Abilities (KSAs), (2) Education and Experience, and (3) Physical Requirements and/or Working Conditions. The components of the job specifications provide information necessary to determine what accommodations might and might not be possible under ADA regulations.

Disclaimer and Approvals The final section on many job descriptions contains approval signatures by appropriate managers and a legal disclaimer. This disclaimer allows employers to change employees' job duties or request employees to perform duties not listed, so that the job description is not viewed as a "contract" between the employer and the employee.

❖ Preparing Job Descriptions

The ADA focused attention on the importance of well-written job descriptions. Legal compliance requires that they accurately represent the actual jobs. Some guidelines to prepare legally satisfactory job descriptions are noted next.

Identifying Titles Job titles should be descriptive of job functions performed. For instance, one firm lumped all clerical jobs into four secretarial categories, even though the actual jobs were for such functions as payroll processor, marketing secretary, and receptionist. When the firm reviewed its descriptions, each job was given a function-related title. However, the jobs were grouped for pay purposes into the same pay grades as before.

Such titles as Senior Worker, Lead Worker, Supervisor, Coordinator, Specialist, Manager, and Director are often misapplied. Titles should reflect the relative responsibilities in the organization and be tied to the pay grade system.

Writing the General Summary and Essential Function Statements Most experienced job analysts have found that it is easier to write the general summary *after* the essential function statements have been completed. Otherwise, there is a tendency for the general summary to be too long.

The general format for an essential function statement is as follows: (1) *action verb,* (2) *to what applied,* (3) *what/how/how often.* There is a real art to writing statements that are sufficiently descriptive without being overly detailed. It is important to use precise action verbs that accurately describe the employee's tasks, duties, and responsibilities.[25] For example, generally it is advisable to avoid the use of vague words such as *maintains, handles,* and *processes.* Compare the statement "Processes expense vouchers" to "Reviews employee expense reports, verifies expense documentation, and submits to accounting for payment." The second statement more clearly describes the scope and nature of the duty performed. However, it is just as important to avoid the trap of writing a motion analysis. The statement "Walks to filing cabinet, opens drawer, pulls folder out, and inserts material in correct folder" is an extreme example of a motion statement. The statement "Files correspondence and memoranda to maintain accurate customer policy records" is sufficiently descriptive without being overly detailed.

The language of the ADA has highlighted the fact that the essential function statements should be organized in the order of importance or "essentiality." If a description has eight statements, it is likely that the last two or three duties described are less essential than the first two or three. Therefore, it is important that job duties be arranged so that the most essential (in terms of criticality and amount of time spent) be listed first and the supportive or marginal ones listed later. Within that framework, specific functional duties should be grouped and arranged in some logical pattern. If a job requires an accounting supervisor to prepare several reports, among other functions, statements relating to the preparation of reports should be grouped together. The *miscellaneous clause* mentioned earlier typically is included to assure some managerial flexibility.

Some job descriptions contain sections about materials or machines used, working conditions, or special tools used. This information is often included in the specific duty statements or in comment sections. Job descriptions of executive and upper-management jobs, because of the wide range of duties and responsibilities, often are written in more general terms than descriptions of jobs at lower levels in the organization.

❖ Writing Job Specifications

Job specifications can be developed from a variety of information sources. Obviously, the job analysis process provides a primary starting point. But any KSA included must be based on what is needed to perform a job duty. Furthermore, the job specifications listed should reflect what is necessary for satisfactory job performance, not what the ideal candidate would have. For example, it is not appropriate for a manager to list as KSAs five years' experience in the specific industry and an MBA when satisfactory performance would require only three years' experience and a bachelor's degree in marketing or advertising.

With this perspective in mind, a job analyst can obtain job specification information by talking with the current holders of the jobs and their supervisors and managers about the qualifications needed to perform the jobs satisfactorily. However, caution is needed here, because the characteristics of the current job occupant should not be the sole basis for the job specification statements. The current incumbent's job qualifications often exceed the minimum KSAs required to perform the job satisfactorily. Checking the job requirements of other organizations with similar jobs is another means of obtaining information for job specifications.

❖ The ADA and Writing KSAs

In writing job specifications, it is important to list specifically those KSAs essential for satisfactory job performance. Only nondiscriminatory, job-related items should be included. For example, a high school diploma should not be required for a job unless the manager can demonstrate that an individual with less education cannot perform the job as well. Because of this concern, some specification statements read, "High school diploma or equivalent acceptable experience."

In light of the ADA, it is crucial that the physical and mental dimensions of each job be clearly identified. If lifting, stooping, standing, walking, climbing, or crawling is required, it should be noted. Also, weights to be lifted should be specified, along with specific visual and hearing requirements of jobs. Refer to Figure 7–7 for examples of KSA statements. Remember, these job specifications are the foundation for evaluating individuals with disabilities for employment.

SUMMARY

- Job analysis is a systematic investigation of the tasks, duties, and responsibilities necessary to do a job.
- The end products of job analysis are: (1) job descriptions, which identify the tasks, duties, and responsibilities in jobs, and (2) job specifications, which list the knowledge, skills, and abilities (KSAs) needed to perform a job satisfactorily.
- A job is a grouping of similar positions.
- Job design is broader than job analysis, with job design concerned with the development and composition of a job and job analysis focusing on obtaining data for jobs that have been designed or that currently exist.
- Job analysis, while seemingly straightforward, has several behavioral implications that managers should consider: employees' fears of the process and resistance to change, management's tendency to overemphasize the current job holder's qualifications, and the danger that job descriptions will limit managerial flexibility.
- Legal compliance in HR must be based on job analysis. The Americans with Disabilities Act (ADA) increased the importance of job analysis and its components.
- Job analysis information is useful in most HR activities: human resource planning, recruiting and selection, compensation, training and development, performance appraisal, safety and health, and union relations.
- Methods of gathering job analysis information include observation, interviews, questionnaires, some specialized methods, and computerized job analysis. In practice, a combination of methods is often used.
- The process of conducting a job analysis is as follows:
  - A. Identify jobs and review existing documentation.
  - B. Explain the process to managers and employees.
  - C. Conduct the job analysis.
  - D. Prepare job descriptions and job specifications.
  - E. Maintain and update job descriptions and job specifications.
- Writing job descriptions and job specifications can be challenging. The essential functions and KSAs should be described clearly.

Review and Discussion Questions

1. Clearly define and differentiate among *job analysis, job description,* and *job specifications.*
2. Job analysis is the most basic HR activity. Discuss why.
3. Discuss why the Americans with Disabilities Act (ADA) has heightened the importance of job analysis activities.
4. How would you deal with employees' behavioral reactions to job analysis?
5. Describe at least three methods of analyzing jobs, devoting two sentences to each method.
6. Explain how you would conduct a job analysis in a company that had never had job descriptions.
7. Discuss how you would train someone to write job descriptions and job specifications for a small bank.

Terms to Know

duty **190**
essential functions **196**
job **190**
job analysis **190**
job description **192**
job family **191**
job specifications **192**
knowledge, skills, and abilities (KSAs) **192**
performance standards **192**
position **190**
responsibilities **190**
task **190**

CASE

JOB ANALYSIS AT BETHPHAGE

Bethphage, Inc., with 2,700 employees, is a not-for-profit organization that provides living and rehabilitative services for individuals with developmental disabilities. The parent corporation has operating entities in 18 states and several foreign countries. Dr. David Jacox, CEO, and the Board of Directors identified the need for a coordinated compensation program because there were inconsistencies between locations and entities in administering wages, and all of the entities administered wages and salaries rather inadequately.

To build a foundation for developing a coordinated compensation program, Raul Saldivar, Senior Vice-President of Human Resources, and a compensation committee of managers and executive directors from the affiliate entities identified the need to take a comprehensive look at all of the jobs in the firm. To begin, a complete job analysis of all jobs was needed. Like many organizations, Bethphage had a small HR staff that was busy with many other HR activities. Consequently, Saldivar gave the responsibility for conducting the job analysis and preparing the job descriptions and specifications to Kelli Jorgensen, Bethphage's Compensation and Benefits Manager.

Jorgensen developed an extensive 12-page job analysis questionnaire tailored to the various job functions common throughout Bethphage. Then questionnaires were distributed to all employees in all locations. In spite of grumbling from some employees about the length of the questionnaire, over 90% of the questionnaires were returned within the allotted period to the appropriate departmental and agency managers for review. They were then sent to Jorgensen and the HR staff. At that point, several HR interns from a local university began the arduous task of writing approximately 300 job descriptions and specifications.

Throughout the drafting of the job descriptions and specifications, questions arose about the content and organization of the jobs. Consequently, follow-up telephone interviews with some employees and managers had to be conducted. In addition, numerous organizational and work-flow issues were identified, and each of them had to be resolved before the job descriptions could be written correctly. Finally, a job titling guide was developed by the compensation committee.

Once draft descriptions were available, Jorgensen coordinated their review by appropriate managers and team leaders. Then the drafts were finalized, reviewed by the compensation committee, and prepared for use in the development of the compensation system. The entire process of conducting the job analysis and developing finalized job descriptions and specifications took four months of intensive effort. The process of developing the compensation and performance appraisal systems took another nine months, and the refinement and implementation of all of the components of the "new and improved" HR activities took over a year. However, it was well worth all of the effort involved, because now Bethphage has a comprehensive and well-designed foundation for managing its HR activities.[26]

Questions

1. Discuss why job analysis was an essential part of Bethphage's change process.
2. Compare the process described in the case with the steps mentioned in the chapter.
3. Discuss how and why managerial and employee behavioral factors were important considerations in the case.

❖ Notes

1. Based on information in "A Trend Toward Quality Jobs?" *Business Week*, October 9, 1995, 30; N. Frederic Crandall and Marc J. Wallace, "The Virtual Workplace," *ACA Journal*, Spring 1995, 6–23; and William Bridges, *Job Shift* (Reading, MA: Addison-Wesley, 1994).

2. Joe Colihan and Gary K. Burger, "Constructing Job Families: An Analysis of Quantitative Techniques Used for Grouping Jobs," *Personnel Psychology*, 48 (1995), 563–586.

3. P. Spector and S. Jex, "Relations of Job Characteristics from Multiple Data Sources with Employee Affect," *Journal of Applied Psychology* 76 (1991), 46–53; and J. Kelley, "Does Job Redesign Theory Explain Job Redesign Outcomes?" *Human Relations* 45 (1992), 753.

4. John Schaubroeck, Daniel C. Ganster, and Barbara E. Kemmerer, "Job Complexity: 'Type A' Behavior and Cardiovascular Disorder," *Academy of Management Journal* 37 (1994), 426–439.

5. *U.S. v. City of Chicago*, 549 FEP F2d 415 (1977). *Cert. denied* 434 US 875 (1977).

6. Juan I. Sanchez, "From Documentation to Innovation: Reshaping Job Analysis to Meet Energizing Business Needs, *Human Resources Management Review* 4 (1994), 51–74.

7. Susan Sonnesyn Brooks, "Managing a Horizontal Revolution," *HR Magazine*, June 1995, 52–58.

8. Adapted from Hal Lancaster, "Life Without Titles," *The Wall Street Journal*, July 16, 1995, B1.

9. "Equal Employment for Individuals with Disabilities," Federal Register 56 (144), 35735.

10. John Hollwitz, Deborah F. Goodman, and Dean Bolte, "Complying with the Americans with Disabilities Act: Assessing the Costs of Reasonable Accommodation," *Public Personnel Management*, 24 (1995), 149–157.

11. "Equal Employment for Individuals with Disabilities."

12. Susana R. Lozada-Larsen, "The Americans with Disabilities Act: Using Job Analysis to Meet New Challenges," paper presented at IPMAAC Conference, Baltimore, MD., June 1992.

13. Robert J. Harvey and Susana R. Lozada-Larsen, "Predicting Pay and Exempt Status Using Higher-Order CMQ Factors," paper presented at the Annual Conference of the Society for Industrial and Organizational Psychology, San Francisco, April 1993.

14. Gopal C. Pati and Elaine K. Bailey, "Empowering People with Disabilities: Strategy and Human Resource Issues in Implementing the ADA," *Organizational Dynamics*, January 1995, 52–59.

15. "How to Hire the Right People," *Supervision*, May 1995, 10.

16. W. Mullins and W. Kimbrough, "Group Composition as a Determinant of Job Analysis Outcomes," *Journal of Applied Psychology* 73 (1988), 657–664.

17. For more details on the Organizational Measurement System, contact Steven Roop, Ph.D., College Station, TX.

18. Ernest J. McCormick et al., *PAQ: Job Analysis Manual* (Logan, Utah: PAQ Services, 1977).

19. For more details, see Sidney A. Fine, *Functional Job Analysis Scales: A Disk Aid* (Milwaukee, WI: Sidney A. Fine, 1992).

20. U. S. Department of Labor, *Dictionary of Occupational Titles*, 4th ed., revised (Washington, D.C.: U.S. Government Printing Office, 1991).

21. W. W. Tornow and P. R. Pinto, "The Development of a Managerial Job Taxonomy: A System for Describing, Classifying, and Evaluating Executive Positions," *Journal of Applied Psychology* 61 (1976), 410–418.

22. Susana R. Lozada-Larsen and Stephen B. Parker, "The Executive Checklist (EXCEL): A Common-Metric Questionnaire for Analyzing Supervisory, Managerial, and Executive Jobs," paper presented at the Sixth Annual Conference of the Society for Industrial and Organizational Psychology, St. Louis, MO, April 1991.

23. Robert J. Harvey, *CMQ: A Job Analysis System* (San Antonio: The Psychological Corp., 1991).

24. Kathleen K. Lundquist and David P. Jones, "Skilled-Based Job Analysis," *Technical & Skills Training*, February–March, 1992, 1–5.

25. Herbert G. Heneman III and Robert L. Heneman, *Staffing Organizations* (Homewood, IL: Mendota Press, 1994), 148–153.

26. Used with permission of Bethphage, Inc.

Chapter 8

Recruiting

After you have read this chapter, you should be able to . . .

- Define *recruiting* and discuss three strategic recruiting issues.
- Discuss why more employers are using flexible staffing.
- Outline a typical recruiting process and identify legal considerations affecting recruiting.
- Compare internal and external sources of candidates.
- Identify three internal sources of candidates.
- List and briefly discuss five external recruiting sources.
- Discuss three factors to consider when evaluating recruiting efforts.

HR in Transition

Recruiting through the Internet

With the explosive growth in popularity and usage of the Internet, more and more employers are using the World Wide Web to recruit employees—primarily professional and technical employees, often in hard-to-fill specialties. Increasingly, employers are identifying potential candidates who would not be reached by traditional means such as newspaper advertisements and professional journals. Also, because it is worldwide, listing employment opportunities on the web gives employers global exposure to potential applicants, which may be advantageous if different language skills or cultural backgrounds are needed as part of job knowledge, skills, and abilities.

Many firms have created their own home pages in order to list job openings. For example, Wells Fargo Bank hired a project manager who had been an independent consultant working on a banking project for another client. The consultant saw Wells Fargo's home page, clicked on the *Employment Opportunities* icon, and saw 60 job openings listed, one of which was for a project manager. The consultant e-mailed his resume in and was hired a month later. Grolier Electronic Publishing has listed openings for editorial directors, and Eli-Lilly Co., a large pharmaceutical company, has recruited chemists and other scientific specialists using its home page. Even newspapers are recognizing the threat that the Internet represents, and six major newspapers have combined to list their help-wanted sections on a common web site called Career Path.com. (http://www.careerpath.com)

As many as 2,000 listings per day flood into the most popular employment news group, (misc.jobs.offered). *Other news groups exist, such as those for different geographical areas or highly specialized fields.*

Employers looking for individuals with information systems and specialized computer skills are finding the Internet to be an especially good recruiting source. Because such individuals already are familiar with using the Internet, they are more likely to be "surfing the net" than individuals with fewer computer capabilities.

Job hunters, especially those familiar with the Internet, frequently view the Internet as the prime source for job leads, rather than checking it after all other sources fail. Individuals who lose jobs because of corporate layoffs or downsizing programs use the Internet to post their resumes electronically to employers located outside their home geographic areas. Also, some employers that cut back their workforces provide employees Internet access to on-line employment services as part of outplacement assistance. The Internet service Usenet has news groups listing jobs throughout the world. As many as 2,000 listings per day flood into the most popular employment news group, *misc.jobs.offered.* Other web sites exist, such as those for different geographical areas or highly specialized fields. Some of the most popular web sites for employment listing, in addition to specific company home pages, are listed below.

- ❖ Jobweb: http://www. jobweb.org
- ❖ Online Career Center: http://www.occ.com/
- ❖ Online Opportunities: http://www.jobnet.com
- ❖ Human Resources Center: http://www.human.resource.center.com
- ❖ Jobcenter: http://www.jobcenter.com/
- ❖ The Monster Board: http://www.monster.com

Regardless of what recruiting processes have been used in the past, it is becoming evident that both employers and applicants increasingly will recruit via the Internet. Those that do not will likely be left behind.[1]

> *"Ability will never catch up with the demand for it."*
> *—Malcolm Forbes*

Recruiting is the process of generating a pool of qualified applicants for organizational jobs. If the number of available candidates only equals the number of people to be hired, there is no selection—the choice has already been made. The organization must either leave some openings unfilled or take all the candidates.

Recruiting
Process of generating a pool of qualified applicants for organizational jobs.

Many employers today are facing shortages of workers with the appropriate knowledge, skills, and abilities. One indication of this problem is revealed by a survey of almost 1,000 small and mid-sized organizations. Finding qualified people was the second greatest concern identified in that survey, surpassed only by dealing with government regulations. About one-fourth of all firms surveyed indicated that they faced significant challenges finding qualified workers. Construction and manufacturing firms faced the greatest difficulties.[2]

❖ Strategic Approach to Recruiting

A strategic approach to recruiting has become more important as competitive pressures have shifted in many industries. As was discussed in Chapter 2, strategic HR planning efforts are made to align HR strategies with organizational strategies. Therefore, it is important that recruiting, as a key HR activity, be viewed strategically. Also, recruiting efforts should reflect the organizational culture.[3] Regardless of organizational size, the following decisions about recruiting must be made:

- How many people does the organization need?
- What labor markets will be tapped?
- Should the organization have its own staff or use other sources such as flexible staffing?
- To what extent should recruiting be focused internally vs. externally?
- What special skills and experience are *really* necessary?
- What legal considerations affect recruiting?
- How can diversity and affirmative action concerns be addressed when recruiting?
- How will the organization spread its message of openings?
- How effective are the recruiting efforts?

❖ HR Planning and Recruiting

An HR plan helps answer the first question by determining the current and projected needs for people in various job categories and any diversity goals the organization may have set. Then the recruiting and selection processes operationalize the HR plan. Thus, recruiting efforts translate human resource plans into action. They also fill openings when unexpected vacancies occur. Even during periods of reduced hiring, implementing long-range plans means keeping in contact with outside recruiting sources to maintain visibility while also maintaining employee recruiting channels in the organization. These activities are essential for management to be able to step up recruiting activity on short notice.

❖ Recruiting and Labor Markets

Labor Markets
The external sources from which organizations attract employees.

Employers compete in a variety of labor markets for employees. **Labor markets** are the external sources from which organizations attract employees. If the organization does not position itself in these markets as a desirable place to work, then its ability to attract and retain employees will be reduced, and its ability to achieve organizational objectives and strategies will be hampered.

There are many ways to identify labor markets, including by geographical area, type of skill, and educational level. Some labor market segments might include managerial, clerical, professional and technical, and blue collar. Classified differently, some markets are local, others regional, others national; and there are international labor markets as well. For instance, an interesting labor market segment opened up with the demise of the Soviet Union. A number of excellent Soviet scientists became available because of the absence of job opportunities in their own countries. Several research organizations, including Sun Microsystems, have recruited them to fill jobs. Many of these recruits have continued to live in their home countries and are linked electronically to their employers in the United States.

Recruiting locally for a job market that is really national will result in disappointing applicant rates. For example, attempting to recruit a senior accounting faculty member in a small town is likely not to be successful. Conversely, it may not be necessary to recruit nationally for workers in unskilled positions on the assembly line. The job qualifications needed and the distribution of the labor supply determine which labor market is relevant.

Changes in a labor market may force changes in recruiting efforts. If a new major employer locates in a regional labor market, then other employers may see a decline in their numbers of applicants. For instance, when three riverboat casinos, employing a total of 3,000 workers, opened in Council Bluffs, Iowa, many employers in the area noticed a dramatic decrease in the number of applicants for job openings outside of the casino industry. Also, some employers, particularly smaller manufacturing firms, had to raise their wages to prevent turnover of existing workers. Similar occurrences have followed the opening of large automobile manufacturing plants in South Carolina, Tennessee, Kentucky, and Alabama.

To understand the components of labor markets in which recruiting takes place, three different categorizations must be considered. Those three groups are *labor force population, applicant population,* and *applicant pool.*

The **labor force population** includes all individuals who are available for selection if all possible recruitment strategies are used. This vast array of possible applicants may be reached in very different ways. Different recruiting methods—for example, newspaper ads versus college recruiting—will reach different segments of the population.

***Labor Force Population**
All individuals who are available for selection if all possible recruitment strategies are used.

The **applicant population** is a subset of the labor force population that is available for selection using a particular recruiting approach. For example, an organization might limit its recruiting for management trainees to MBA graduates from major universities. This recruiting method will result in a very different group of applicants from those who would have applied had the employer chosen to advertise openings for management trainees on a local radio station.

***Applicant Population**
A subset of the labor force population that is available for selection using a particular recruiting approach.

At least four recruiting decisions affect the nature of the applicant population:

1. *Recruiting method* (advertising medium chosen and use of employment agencies)
2. *Recruiting message* (what is said about the job and how it is said)
3. *Applicant qualifications required* (education level and amount of experience necessary)
4. *Administrative procedures* (time of year recruiting is done, follow-ups with applicants, and use of previous applicant files)

***Applicant Pool**
All persons who are actually evaluated for selection.

The **applicant pool** consists of all persons who are actually evaluated for selection. Many factors can affect the size of the applicant pool. For example, the organization mentioned previously is likely to interview only a small percentage of the MBA graduates at major universities because not all graduates will want to be interviewed. The applicant population at this step will depend on the reputation of the organization and industry as a place to work, the screening efforts of the organization, and the information available to the applicant population. Assuming a suitable candidate can be found, the final selection is made from the applicant pool.

❖ Recruiting vs. Flexible Staffing

Increasingly, organizations are examining whether to recruit "employees" or to utilize other staffing arrangements. A growing number of employers have found that the cost of keeping a full-time regular workforce has become excessive and is getting worse because of government-mandated costs. But it is not just the money that is at issue. It is also the number of rules that define the employment relationship, making many employers reluctant to hire new employees even when the economy turns up after a recession. The use of alternative staffing arrangements allows an employer to avoid such issues, as well as the cost of full-time benefits such as vacation pay and pension plans.

As pointed out in Chapter 2, a growing number of employees are "contingent workers" who are employed on a contract, temporary, or part-time basis. Also, outsourcing entire functions or activities of the organization reduces the number of employees needed. Many organizations that traditionally have had to recruit employees are starting to use flexible staffing to accomplish a growing amount of organizational work.[4] The experience of Dannon Yogurt, described in the accompanying HR Perspective, illustrates why.

***Flexible Staffing**
Use of recruiting sources and workers who are not employees.

Flexible staffing makes use of recruiting sources and workers who are not employees. These arrangements use independent contractors, temporary workers, and employee leasing. A look at each of these kinds of workers and some of the important considerations associated with each type follows.

***Independent Contractors**
Workers who perform specific services on a contract basis.

Independent Contractors Some firms employ **independent contractors** to perform specific services on a contract basis. However, those contractors must be independent as determined by a 20-item test identified by the U.S. Internal Revenue Service and the U.S. Department of Labor, which is discussed in greater detail in Chapter 13. Independent contractors are used in a number of areas, including building maintenance, security, and advertising/public relations. Estimates are that employers can save up to 40% by using independent contractors because benefits do not have to be provided.

Temporary Workers Employers who wish to use temporary employees can hire their own temporary staff or use a temporary-worker agency. Such agencies supply workers on a rate-per-day or per-week basis. Originally developed to provide clerical and office workers to employers, agencies now provide workers in many additional areas. Many organizations that use temporary workers do not provide employee benefits thus lowering their overall labor costs. But even if some benefits are provided, there may be advantages for employers to use temporary workers.

The use of temporary workers may make sense for an organization if its work is subject to seasonal or other fluctuations. Hiring regular employees to meet peak employment needs would require that the employer find some tasks to keep employees busy during less active periods or resort to layoffs.

HR PERSPECTIVE

Dannon Yogurt and Flexible Staffing

Today's health-conscious society can't get enough yogurt, especially during New Year's resolution/dieting season and the warm summer months. For 10 years, Manpower International has helped Dannon Yogurt's production and distribution facility in Sidney, Ohio, satisfy consumers' appetite for yogurt by providing temporary workers as needed. Recently, this long-term partnership has grown even closer.

At that time, Dannon created two levels of "flex teams" to support its core workforce of regular employees. The first level, a flex team made up entirely of Manpower employees, is the only point of entry into Dannon's regular workforce. "Dannon accepts no application," says Manpower Manager Pam Heimann. "Anyone who comes to Dannon is given our business card."

When the applicants come to Manpower, the staff evaluates their suitability for Dannon. Heimann says, "Because Dannon is very selective, the temporaries must score well on five separate tests. They must complete the philosophy portion of Manpower's quality training as well as safety training. Then Dannon interviews the candidates. We never compromise Dannon's standards just to fill orders."

Candidates accepted to Manpower's flex team must accept variability in their work schedules. Flex team members may work two days one week and seven the next. "Dannon requires workforce flexibility because it's a just-in-time company," says Heimann. "Turnaround time for customer orders is just two days."

After 90 days on Manpower's flex team, Dannon supervisors evaluate the workers' performances and may move them to the next level of flex teams, which are managed by Dannon. From the Dannon flex team, the workers can move to regular positions with Dannon.

Heimann says that in a tight labor market, Manpower and Dannon must work together to find workers who can handle the schedule flexibility required by the flex team. "It's a very cooperative effort," she says. "In addition to sending all walk-in applicants to Manpower, Dannon lets us use its name in our ads. Dannon has a sterling reputation as an employer, which helps a great deal.

"We make it clear to every applicant that Dannon has no obligation to hire them, but that the opportunity is there," she continues. "We've created a flier that spells out the details of what the flex team is and what Dannon requires of flex team members. We give this flier to applicants before testing, and it does weed out people. For those rejected for Dannon, we direct them to opportunities with other customers."

Since the flex teams were formed, Manpower has supplied more than 140 flex team workers to Dannon, the majority of whom ultimately have been hired for regular positions. "When we helped Dannon start the flex team concept, the hardest sell was Dannon's own supervisors," says Heimann. "They were not sure that Manpower could do a better job of selecting workers than Dannon already did. But the supervisors changed their minds when we administered Ultradex, a specialized skill-based testing system developed by Manpower, to them in order to create a profile of a successful Dannon employee. Going through Ultradex gave the supervisors respect for Manpower's selection system. Also, since Manpower became the point of entry for all Dannon employees, we know that their turnover has decreased."[5]

As suggested, "temp" opportunities are opening up for professional and executive-level jobs, such as chefs, accountants, lawyers, systems analysts, nurses, and managers. Downsizing has taken layers of management out of many firms, and companies may be hesitant to begin adding them back for projects that are temporary. The same downsizing has made available "temporary executives" with experience that would not have been available in years past. Other professionals and executives have taken early retirement but want to continue working on a part-time basis.

Temporary workers can and often do accept regular staff positions. This "try before you buy" approach is potentially beneficial to both employer and employee.[6] However, unlike Manpower, Inc., some temporary service firms bill the client company a placement charge if a temporary worker is hired full time within a certain time period—usually 90 days.

Dilbert® reprinted by permission of United Feature Syndicate, Inc.

Employee Leasing Employee leasing is a concept that has grown rapidly in recent years. The National Association of Professional Employer Organizations estimates that over 1.6 million individuals are employed by more than 2,200 employee leasing firms.[7] The employee leasing process is simple: an employer signs an agreement with an employee leasing company, after which the existing staff is hired by the leasing firm and leased back to the company. For a small fee, a small business owner or operator turns his or her staff over to the leasing company, which then writes the paychecks, pays the taxes, prepares and implements HR policies, and keeps all the required records.

All this service comes at a cost. Leasing companies often charge between 4% and 6% of a monthly salary for their services. Thus, while leasing may save employers money on benefits, it can also increase payroll costs. In addition, employers may encounter some legal problems. Because the leased workers are employees of the leasing company, they may sue the client firm for work-related injuries if there has been negligence by the client because these injuries are not covered by workers compensation.[8] One advantage for employees, if the leasing firm provides benefits, of leasing companies is that they may receive better benefits than they otherwise would have received.

❖ Internal vs. External Recruiting

Both pros and cons are associated with promoting from within (internal source for recruitment) and hiring from outside the organization (external recruitment) to fill openings. Figure 8–1 summarizes some of the most commonly cited advantages and disadvantages of each type of source.

Promotion from within generally is thought to be a positive force in rewarding good work, and some organizations use it well indeed. However, if followed exclusively, it has the major disadvantage of perpetuating old ways of operating. In addition, there are equal employment concerns with using internal recruiting if protected class members are not represented adequately in the organization.

Recruiting externally can infuse the organization with new ideas. Also, it may be cheaper to recruit professionals such as accountants or computer programmers from outside than to train less skilled people promoted from within the organization. But recruiting from outside the organization for any but entry-level positions presents the problem of adjustment time for the new persons. Another serious drawback to external recruiting is the negative impact on current employees that often results from selecting an outsider instead of promoting a current employee.

Most organizations combine the use of internal and external methods. Organizations that operate in a rapidly changing environments and competitive conditions may need to place a heavier emphasis on external sources as well as developing internal sources. However, for those organizations existing in environments that change slowly, promotion from within may be more suitable.[9]

❖ FIGURE 8–1 ❖
ADVANTAGES AND DISADVANTAGES OF INTERNAL AND EXTERNAL SOURCES

ADVANTAGES	DISADVANTAGES
Internal Sources for Recruiting	
❖ Morale of promotee ❖ Better assessment of abilities ❖ Lower cost for some jobs ❖ Motivator for good performance ❖ Causes a succession of promotions ❖ Have to hire only at entry level	❖ Inbreeding ❖ Possible morale problems of those not promoted ❖ "Political" infighting for promotions ❖ Need for management-development program
External Sources for Recruiting	
❖ "New blood" bringing new perspectives ❖ Cheaper and faster than training professionals ❖ No group of political supporters in organization already ❖ May bring industry insights	❖ May not select someone who will "fit" the job or organization ❖ May cause morale problems for internal candidates not selected ❖ Longer "adjustment" or orientation time

❖ THE RECRUITING PROCESS

Based upon an *HR plan*, the organization maintains appropriate *recruiting visibility*. The steps in a typical recruitment process are identified in Figure 8–2. In larger organizations, a manager notifies someone in the HR unit that an opening needs to be filled. Submission of a *requisition* to the HR unit, much as a supply requisition is submitted to the purchasing department, is a common way to trigger recruiting efforts. The HR representative and the manager must *review the job description and job specifications* so that both have clear and up-to-date information on the job duties and the specific qualifications desired of an applicant. For example, whether a job is for a computer programmer or for a systems analyst would significantly affect the screening of applicants and the content of a recruiting advertisement. Familiarity with the job makes it easier to identify the minimum qualifications someone needs to perform the job satisfactorily.

Following this review, the actual recruiting effort begins. *Internal sources* of available recruits through transfers, promotions, and job posting usually are checked first. Then *external sources* are contacted as required, and all applicants are screened through the *selection process*. Finally, *follow-up* is necessary to evaluate the effectiveness of the recruiting efforts and to tie those efforts back into the human resource plan and ongoing recruiting activities.

❖ ORGANIZATIONAL RECRUITING RESPONSIBILITIES

In small organizations, the recruiting process is simplified. For many positions, an advertisement in the local paper may be enough to tap into the local labor market. In very small organizations, the owner/manager often places the ad, determines the recruiting criteria, and makes the decision. However, for some specialist jobs, a regional or national search may be undertaken. Figure 8–3 shows a typical distribution of recruiting responsibilities between the HR department and managers in larger organizations.

❖ FIGURE 8–2 ❖
THE RECRUITING PROCESS

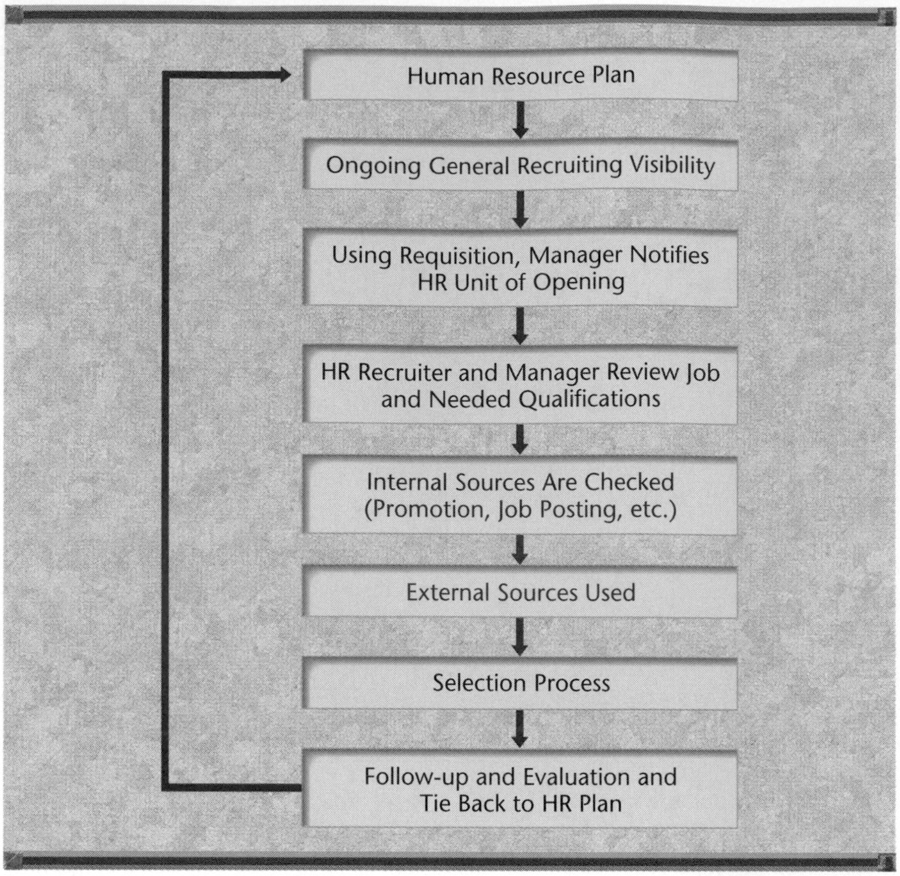

❖ RECRUITING AND LEGAL CONSIDERATIONS

Recruiting as a key employment-related activity is subject to a variety of legal considerations. The wide range of equal employment laws and regulations was discussed in previous chapters, but it is useful to highlight their impact on recruiting activities here.

DISPARATE IMPACT AND AFFIRMATIVE ACTION One facet of legal compliance of the recruiting process is to ensure that external disparate impact is not occurring. Remember that disparate impact occurs when there is underrepresentation of protected class members in relation to the labor markets utilized by the employer.

To determine if disparate impact is occurring, it is necessary for applicant flow information to be maintained in line with the processes discussed in Chapter 6. If disparate impact exists, then the employer may need to make special efforts to persuade protected-class individuals to apply for jobs. For instance, one major midwestern insurance company sends announcements of job openings to over 40 different agencies and organizations that specifically service various protected-class members. For employers with affirmative action plans (AAPs), special ways to reduce disparate impact will be identified as goals listed in those plans.

Some employers that emphasize internal recruiting should take actions to obtain protected-class applicants externally if disparate impact exists in the current workforce. Even using current employees as referral sources can create legal concerns. When the organization has an underrepresentation of a particular protected class, word-of-mouth referral has been considered a violation of Title VII of the Civil Rights Act. An organization composed primarily of nonprotected-class individuals presumably would refer more of the same for consideration as employees.

Employment Advertising Employers covered by equal employment regulations must take care when preparing the wording for employment advertisements. The Equal Employment Opportunity Commission has issued guidelines stating that no direct or indirect references that have gender or age connotations are permitted. Some examples of likely impermissible terminology include the following: *young and enthusiastic, recent college graduate,* and *utility lineman.*[10]

Additionally, employment advertisements should indicate that the employer has a policy of complying with equal employment regulations. Typically, advertisements should contain a general phrase such as *Equal Opportunity Employer* or more specific designations such as *EEO/M-F/AA/ADA.*

❖ **Figure 8–3** ❖
Typical Recruiting Responsibilities

HR UNIT	MANAGERS
❖ Forecasts recruiting needs ❖ Prepares copy for recruiting ads and campaigns ❖ Plans and conducts recruiting efforts ❖ Audits and evaluates recruiting activities	❖ Anticipate needs for employees to fill vacancies ❖ Determine KSAs needed from applicants ❖ Assist in recruiting effort with information about job requirements ❖ Review recruiting efforts

❖ Recruiting Diverse Workers

The growing difficulty that many employers have had in attracting and retaining workers has led them to tap a wide variety of sources. Specifically difficult has been recruiting protected-class individuals under equal employment laws and regulations. If outside agencies are used, equal employment and affirmative action concerns of the actual employers still must be met.[11] What is interesting, though, is that even if the legal stipulations were not present, employers who recruit workers with diverse backgrounds have found these recruits to be valuable employees. Three specific groups that have been attracted into the workforce effectively by some employers are individuals over 55 years of age, persons with disabilities, and persons who are members of racial/ethnic minorities.

Recruiting Older Workers Demographic data reveal that the percentage of the population over the age of 55 continues to increase each year due to increasing life expectancies. When discussing the recruitment of older workers, the first task is to identify what individuals are included in this group. Senior experienced individuals may include the following:

- ❖ Midlife career changers—those who are burned out in their jobs and career fields and leave voluntarily to try new fields
- ❖ Displaced workers under age 62—those who have worked but have been displaced, often involuntarily, through job reductions or plant closings
- ❖ Retirees—those who took early retirement buyouts or retired at age 62 or later

In a research study, the American Association of Retired Persons (AARP) examined recruitment of older workers and found that among the concerns of older workers that must be addressed by potential employers are the following:[12]

- Am I employable if I'm older or lack some education or skills?
- Can I be re-trained and will employers be patient while I learn new knowledge and skills?
- Are working schedules flexible enough given other life demands?
- How will my Social Security benefits be affected if I earn money working full-time or part-time?

Except for the last question, the reality is that most workers of any age would have similar concerns. Therefore, it is important that older workers not be viewed by their age alone. Rather, they should be viewed as experienced workers who may need some training, much as other workers would. In fact, older individuals often already have good skills and work habits. Many employers have found that these workers have lower absenteeism and turnover rates, provide better customer service, have fewer interpersonal conflicts, and serve as mentors for younger workers.[13]

Retirees, in particular, often want part-time work or temporary/seasonal full-time work. Companies such as Grumman Corporation, Traveler's, McDonald's, and Days Inn have found these older workers to be assets. For instance, Days Inn never intended to be an advocate for hiring senior workers, but in the mid-1980s, a labor shortage left the firm trying to grow without the employees it needed. Managers attended a job fair in Atlanta, hired some older people, and were extremely pleased with the results. Years later, 25% of the 600 employees at Days Inn's national reservation centers are seniors.

Employers can set up a "retiree job bank" by first identifying those older employees they would like to reemploy after retirement, perhaps on a temporary basis whenever the work load requires it. Then they must keep track of those employees after they leave. Policy decisions about how long a temporary assignment can last must be made, and pensions must be written so that the retiree is not penalized for returning to work. The question of benefits must be thought through as well. Such efforts seem to be worthwhile in view of the positive reports received thus far on returning retirees to the workplace.

In summary, a growing number of employers are recruiting retirees, both their own and those from other companies. Perhaps what will have to change is the idea that a person is either employed or not employed, retired or not retired. There are clearly points in between.

Recruiting Individuals with Disabilities Another group of individuals providing a potential pool of recruits for jobs are the over 40 million individuals with disabilities covered by the Americans with Disabilities Act (ADA). Many of them are in the workforce, but others have not been able to find employment, particularly those with severe or multiple disabilities.

There are two keys to recruiting individuals with disabilities. First, jobs must be examined to ensure that accommodations could be made so that individuals with certain disabilities can perform the jobs. As mentioned in Chapters 6 and 7, such accommodations may require changes in job duties, work schedules, or work stations and equipment. A study done by an association representing individuals with cerebral palsy found that 76% of businesses employing individuals with disabilities had to make some workplace accommodations.[14]

A second key is to contact associations that specialize in representing individuals with disabilities. By notifying these organizations and discussing the nature of the jobs and the skills needed, employers are able to obtain individuals with disabilities who can perform the essential functions of their jobs. For individuals with disabilities who apply without referrals, those in the employment or

HR office should ensure that appropriate accommodations are discussed. Once hired, as McDonald's Corporation and other employers have found, some additional training time may be necessary, depending on the disabilities of the individuals. But individuals with disabilities generally have been found to be reliable and productive employees.[15]

RECRUITING MEMBERS OF RACIAL/ETHNIC MINORITIES Employers that do business with federal and state governments must have affirmative action plans (AAPs), as discussed in Chapter 6. Consequently, those employers face pressures to increase the number of women employees and employees in racial/ethnic minorities. These pressures often are stronger for managerial, professional, and technical jobs than for unskilled, clerical, and blue-collar jobs.

Employers that are successful in diversifying their workforce use recruiting sources that target the appropriate types of applicants. For example, a firm that needs to ensure hiring of minority engineers may use special minority-oriented publications or recruit at colleges with large numbers of minority students. Media resources that target African Americans include publications such as *Black Careers, Black Enterprise, Black Collegian, Dawn Magazine, National Black Monitor,* and *Dollars and Sense.* Major Hispanic print media are *Hispanic Magazine, Hispanic Business, Hispanic USA Magazine,* and *Vista.*

Other means of recruiting have included participating in job fairs sponsored by certain racial/ethnic organizations, establishing a minority internship program, and using current minority employees to recruit others of similar backgrounds.[16]

❖ MAINTAINING RECRUITING VISIBILITY

Recruiting efforts may be viewed as either continuous or intensive. *Continuous* efforts to recruit have the advantage of keeping the employer in the recruiting market. For example, with college recruiting, it appears to be advantageous for some organizations to have a recruiter on a given campus each year. Those employers that visit a campus only occasionally are less likely to build a following in that school over time.[17]

Intensive recruiting may take the form of a vigorous recruiting campaign aimed a hiring a given number of employees, usually within a short period of time. Such efforts may be the result of failure in the HR planning system to identify needs in advance or to recognize drastic changes in workforce needs due to unexpected work loads.

For many people, the only contact they will have with an organization occurs when they apply for a job there. Of course, the probability is that a given individual will not get the job. If 50 people apply for a job and one is hired, 49 were *not* hired and are potentially unhappy. It is at this point that recruiting can do real damage to the perceptions people have of that organization. In addition to the impressions candidates have of the organization, research shows that recruiter friendliness and other variables affect decisions of job seekers.[18]

❖ INTERNAL RECRUITING SOURCES

Among internal recruiting sources are present employees, friends of present employees, former employees, and previous applicants. Promotions, demotions, and transfers also can provide additional people for an organizational unit, if not for the entire organization.

Among the ways in which internal recruiting sources have an advantage over external sources is that they allow management to observe the candidate for promotion (or transfer) over a period of time and to evaluate that person's potential and specific job performance. Second, an organization that promotes its own employees to fill job openings may give those employees added motivation to do a good job. Employees may see little reason to do more than just what the current job requires if management's policy is usually to hire externally. This concern is indeed the main reason why an organization generally considers internal sources of qualified applicants first.

❖ JOB POSTING AND BIDDING

***Job Posting and Bidding**
A system in which the employer provides notices of job openings within the organization and employees respond by applying for specific openings.

The major means for recruiting employees for other jobs within the organization is *a job posting* system. **Job posting and bidding** is a system in which the employer provides notices of job openings and employees respond by applying for specific openings. The organization can notify employees of all job vacancies by posting notices, circulating publications, or in some other way inviting employees to apply for jobs. In a unionized organization, job posting and bidding can be quite formal; the procedure often is spelled out in the labor agreement. Seniority lists may be used by organizations that make promotions based strictly on seniority, so candidates are considered for promotions in the order of seniority.

Answers to many potential questions must be anticipated: What happens if there are no qualified candidates on the payroll to fill new openings? Is it necessary for employees to inform their supervisors that they are bidding for another job? How much notice should an employee be required to give before transferring to a new department? When should job notices not be posted?

A job posting system gives each employee an opportunity to move to a better job within the organization. Without some sort of job posting and bidding, it is difficult to find out what jobs are open elsewhere in the organization. The most common method employers use to notify current employees of openings is to post notices on bulletin boards in locations such as employee lounges, cafeterias, and near elevators.

Job posting and bidding systems can be ineffective if handled improperly. Jobs generally are posted *before* any external recruiting is done. The organization must allow a reasonable period of time for present employees to check notices of available jobs before it considers external applicants. When employees' bids are turned down, they should have discussions with their supervisors or someone in the HR area regarding the knowledge, skills, and abilities they need in order to improve their opportunities in the future.

❖ PROMOTION AND TRANSFERS

Many organizations choose to fill vacancies through promotions or transfers from within whenever possible. Although most often successful, promotions from within have some drawbacks as well. The person's performance on one job may not be a good predictor of performance on another, because different skills may be required on the new job. For example, not every good worker makes a good supervisor. In most supervisory jobs, an ability to accomplish the work through others requires skills in influencing and dealing with people that may not have been a factor in nonsupervisory jobs.

It is clear that people in organizations with fewer levels may have less frequent chances for promotion. Also, in most organizations, promotions may not be an effective way to speed the movement of protected-class individuals up through the organization if that is an organizational concern.

❖ Current Employee Referrals

A reliable source of people to fill vacancies is composed of friends and/or family members of current employees. Employees can acquaint potential applicants with the advantages of a job with the company, furnish letters of introduction, and encourage them to apply. These are external applicants coming from an internal information source.

Utilizing this source is usually one of the most effective methods of recruiting because many qualified people can be reached at a low cost. In an organization with numerous employees, this approach can develop quite a large pool of potential employees. Some research studies have found that new workers recruited though current employee referral had longer tenure with organizations than those from other recruiting sources.[19]

Some employers pay employees incentives for referring individuals with specialized skills that are difficult to recruit through normal means. One computer firm in the Midwest pays $3,000 to any employee referring a specialized systems analyst after the analyst has worked in the company for six months.

However, as pointed out earlier in the chapter, using only word-of-mouth referrals can violate equal employment regulations if protected-class individuals are underrepresented in the organizational workforce. Therefore, some external recruiting might be necessary to avoid legal problems in this area.

❖ Recruiting Former Employees and Applicants

Former employees and former applicants are also good internal sources for recruitment. In both cases, there is a time-saving advantage, because something is already known about the potential employee.

Former Employees Former employees are considered an internal source in the sense that they have ties to the company. Some retired employees may be willing to come back to work on a part time basis or may recommend someone who would be interested in working for the company. Sometimes people who have left the company to raise a family or complete a college education are willing to come back to work after accomplishing those personal goals. Individuals who left for other jobs might be willing to return for a higher rate of pay. Job sharing and flextime programs may be useful in luring back retirees or others who previously worked for the organization. The main advantage in hiring former employees is that their performance is known.

Some managers are not willing to take back a former employee. However, these managers may change their attitudes toward high-performing former employees as the employment market becomes more competitive. In any case, the decision should depend on the reasons the employee left in the first place. If there were problems with the supervisor or company, it is unlikely that matters have improved in the employee's absence. Concerns that employers have in rehiring former employees include vindictiveness or fear of morale problems among those who stayed.

Former Applicants and Previous "Walk-Ins" Another source of applicants can be found in the organizational files. Although not entirely an internal source, those who have previously applied for jobs can be recontacted by mail, a quick and inexpensive way to fill an unexpected opening.

Applicants who have just "walked in" and applied, may be considered also. These previous "walk-ins" are likely to be more suitable for filling unskilled and semiskilled jobs, but some professional openings can be filled by turning to such applications. One firm that needed two cost accountants immediately contacted qualified previous applicants and was able to hire two individuals who were disenchanted with their current jobs at other companies.

❖ Internal Recruiting Database

Computerized internal talent banks, or applicant tracking systems, are used to furnish a listing of the knowledge, skills, and abilities available for organizations. Employers that must deal with a large number of applicants and job openings have found it beneficial to use such software as part of a human resource information system (HRIS). The accompanying HR Perspective describes how United Parcel Service (UPS) has used one such software package from Resumix.

Software of this type allows employers to enter resumes and then sort the resumes by occupational fields, skills, areas of interests, and previous work histories. For instance, if a firm has an opening for someone with an MBA and marketing experience, the key words *MBA* and *marketing* can be entered, and all resumes containing these two items will be identified.

The advantage of these computerized databases is that they allow recruiters to identify potential candidates more quickly than they could by manually sorting numerous stacks and files of resumes. Employers who have used internal computer databases have found that they reduce recruiting costs associated with advertising expenditures, search-firm fees, and internal processing and record retention expenses.

❖ External Recruiting Sources

If internal sources do not produce an acceptable candidate, many external sources are available. These sources include schools, colleges and universities, employment agencies, temporary-help firms, labor unions, media sources, and trade and competitive sources.

❖ School Recruiting

High schools or vocational/technical schools may be a good source of new employees for many organizations. A successful recruiting program with these institutions is the result of careful analysis and continuous contact with the individual schools. Major considerations for such a recruiting program include the following:

- School counselors and other faculty members concerned with job opportunities and business careers for their students should be contacted regularly.
- Good relations should be maintained with faculty and officials at all times, even when there is little or no need for new employees.
- Recruiting programs can serve these schools in ways other than the placement of students. For instance, the organization might supply educational films, provide speakers, or arrange for demonstrations and exhibits.

Many schools have a centralized guidance or placement office. Contact can be established and maintained with the supervisors of these offices. Promotional brochures that acquaint students with starting jobs and career opportunities can

HR PERSPECTIVE: UPS Airlines Tracks Applicants

How could the HR staff at United Parcel Service (UPS) Airlines process almost 3,000 applications for 145 job openings in a timely and efficient manner? Thanks to Resumix applicant tracking software that can be part of a human resource information system (HRIS), the process, which formerly would have taken several months, became merely a several-day chore in which applicant data were entered into a database so that the HR staff could begin filling positions.

UPS Airlines, headquartered in Louisville, Kentucky, is the largest private employer in that state with more than 11,000 employees. Until 1993, the company had five separate employment functions in Louisville and had job classifications that included administrative, technical, management, and aviation positions. There was no central hiring function, and the manual system for handling the almost 30,000 resumes yearly was cumbersome. The system was overloaded with paper, and it was difficult to track the status of any application. Occasionally recruiters for one division called applicants who already had been hired elsewhere in the company. In addition to problems with outside hiring efforts, current employees were discouraged about possibilities of promotions, concerned that their skills would be overlooked by management.

HR managers realized the need to centralize and automate the hiring process. They examined their current system and documented concerns and recommendations from employees both within the department and companywide, as well as from the community-based labor pool. Using this information, they spent several months identifying requirements for an automated system and chose Resumix.

UPS Airlines has been pleased with the results. Management and administrative staffing hours have been significantly reduced, cost of handling resumes has been lowered, and money has been saved on employment ads. Resumix helps the HR department quickly match each job opening with the best possible candidate. Information on both external and internal candidates is available with Resumix. Normally a hiring manager can receive a list of eligible candidates within a day of identifying the requirements for a new position.

With its policy of "promote from within," UPS Airlines has used Resumix to help employees advance within the company. Patt O'Leary, Project Manager in the UPS HR Department, says, "It's important to us that our employees are confident that they're always being considered for new positions as they develop their skills. Resumix helped us to improve our employees' confidence in the labor environment and in their opportunities here at UPS Air."

The system also is being used to smooth transfers of union members within the company. The old process was a logistical nightmare, with a contract allowing employees up to two transfers per year and a system based wholly on seniority. With Resumix, HR generates lists of union members who bid on each job. Union members can see where they are on the list and bid knowledgeably. Managers can watch the list in order to be ready to replace workers who transfer to other areas.

The HR department continues to search for other ways to use Resumix. Having a separate database to help relatives of transferred employees find jobs in other companies would offset the corporate policy against hiring employees' relatives. The HR department could encourage HR departments in other local companies to consult that database before placing an ad. The company is planning to have a special computer available so that walk-in job applicants can enter data directly into the system. O'Leary says, "Resumix has allowed us to focus on employee relations and the people—not on the procedures and the paper."[20]

be distributed to counselors, librarians, or others. Participating in career days and giving tours of the company to school groups are other ways of maintaining good contact with school sources. Cooperative programs in which students work part time and receive some school credits also may be useful in generating qualified applicants for full-time positions.

❖ College Recruiting

At the college or university level, the recruitment of graduating students is a large-scale operation for many organizations. Most colleges and universities maintain placement offices in which employers and applicants can meet. However, college recruiting presents some interesting and unique problems.

The major determinants that affect the selection of colleges at which an employer conducts interviews are:

- ❖ Current position requirements
- ❖ Past experience with placement offices and previous graduates
- ❖ Organizational budget constraints
- ❖ Cost of available talent (typical salaries)
- ❖ Market competition
- ❖ College reputation

College recruiting can be expensive; therefore, an organization should determine if the positions it is trying to fill really require persons with college degrees. A great many positions do not; yet many employers insist on filling them with college graduates. The result may be employees who must be paid more and who are likely to leave if the jobs are not sufficiently challenging.

To reduce some of the costs associated with college recruiting, some employers and college or university placement services are developing programs using video interviews. More than 70 colleges have purchased the necessary equipment.[21] With these systems, students can be interviewed by interviewers hundreds of miles away. There are advantages for both companies and students. The firms save travel costs and still get the value of seeing and hearing students. For students, the system provides a means of discussing their credentials and job openings without having to miss classes.[22]

There is a great deal of competition for the top students in a college and much less competition for those farther down the ladder. Attributes that recruiters seem to value most highly in college graduates—poise, oral communication skills, personality, appearance, and written communication skills—all typically are mentioned ahead of grade point average (GPA). However, for many, a high GPA *is* a major criterion.

Research has shown that a candidate's impression of an organization often is important because it affects hire rates.[23] The impression of the individual recruiter also is important, as shown in the accompanying HR Perspective. Generally, successful recruiters are those who are enthusiastic and informed, show an interest in the applicant, use interview time well, and avoid overly personal or deliberately stressful questions. Even the gender of recruiters may influence the results. In one study, there was no difference between the way men and women applicants were viewed by male recruiters. But female recruiters viewed male applicants as more qualified than female applicants.[24]

❖ Labor Unions

Labor unions are a source of certain types of workers. In some industries, such as construction, unions have traditionally supplied workers to employers. A labor pool is generally available through a union, and workers can be dispatched to particular jobs to meet the needs of the employers.

In some instances, the union can control or influence recruiting and staffing needs. An organization with a strong union may have less flexibility than a nonunion company in deciding who will be hired and where that person will be placed. Unions also can work to an employer's advantage through cooperative staffing programs, as they do in the building and printing industries.

❖ Media Sources

Media sources such as newspapers, magazines, television, radio, and billboards are widely used.[26] Almost all newspapers carry "Help Wanted" sections, and so

HR PERSPECTIVE

Research on College Recruiting and Job Acceptance

One measure of the effectiveness of college recruiting efforts is the rate at which those recruited accept jobs. The factors that relate to job acceptance were examined in a study by Turban, Campion, and Eyring, and reported in the *Journal of Vocational Behavior.* The study surveyed college recruits of a large Texas petrochemical firm.

The study utilized responses to a survey that were completed by applicants following site visits to the company over a two-year period of time. In the first year, the survey questionnaires were mailed to the applicants after the site visit, while in the second year the applicants were given the survey questions at the end of their site visits. Approximately 70% of all college recruits who made site visits returned questionnaires. Job offers were made to 376 of the 773 applicants that responded, and 135 of them accepted the offers.

The results indicated that overall positive evaluations of the site visit affected job acceptance by the recruits, as would be expected. Additional factors related to job acceptance decisions were applicants' perceptions of the job location and how likeable the company host recruiters were. However, hosts who were viewed as *helpful* versus *likeable* did not influence job acceptance positively, possibly because recruiters who were seen as helpful may have "oversold" the job opportunities.

Another interesting finding concerned how the recruits viewed the location of the jobs offered, most of which were in a smaller community in the southwestern United States. Those recruits that saw the jobs offered as being in a desirable area had higher job acceptance rates. A desirable area seemed to be one offering access to cultural and recreational activities, as well as one providing greater opportunities for social activities. In summary, the location of the job significantly affected job acceptance by the college recruits in the study but the likeableness of the recruiting host also had a positive influence.[25]

do many magazines. For example, *The Wall Street Journal* is a major source used to recruit managerial and professional employees nationally or regionally. Whatever medium is used, it should be tied to the relevant labor market and provide sufficient information on the company and the job.

Newspapers are convenient because there is a short lead time for placing an ad, usually two or three days at most. For positions that must be filled quickly, newspapers may be a good source. However, there can be a great deal of "wasted circulation" with newspaper advertising because most newspapers do not aim to reach any specialized employee markets. Some applicants are only marginally suitable, primarily because employers who compose the ads do not describe the jobs and the necessary qualifications very well. Many employers have found that it is not cost efficient to schedule newspaper ads on days other than Sunday, the only day many job seekers read them.

In addition to newspapers, other media sources include general magazines, television and radio, and billboards. These sources are usually not suitable for frequent use but may be used for one-time campaigns aimed at quickly finding specially skilled workers.

Considerations in Using Media Sources When using recruitment advertisements in the media, employers should ask five key questions:

1. What do we want to accomplish?
2. Who are the people we want to reach?
3. What should the advertising message convey?
4. How should the message be presented?
5. In which medium should it run?

LOGGING ON

Newspaper employment ads from 19 major cities are available here.

http://www.careerpath.com

❖ FIGURE 8–4 ❖
WHAT TO INCLUDE IN AN EFFECTIVE RECRUITING AD

INFORMATION ON THE CANDIDATE

- Years of experience
- Three to five key characteristics of the successful candidate
- Any "preferences" that are not requirements

INFORMATION ON THE JOB AND PROCESS OF APPLICATION

- Job title and responsibilities
- Location of job
- Starting pay range
- Closing date for application
- Whether to submit a resume and cover letter
- Whether calls are invited or not
- Where to mail application or resume

INFORMATION ON THE ORGANIZATION

- That it is an EEO employer
- Its primary business

Figure 8–4 shows the kind of information a good recruiting advertisement should include. Notice that desired qualifications, details on the job and application process, and an overview of the organization are all important.

EVALUATION OF MEDIA RESULTS Recruitment advertising is a form of direct-response marketing. That is, employers are placing ads to generate direct, measurable responses. The more ads they place and track, the better they will become at projecting what responses to expect.

To track responses, an employer first must code the ads. The easiest way to do this is to use different contact names and addresses (for example, specify a department number). Then the employer can note the source of the advertisement each time a response is received. It is best to have one person responsible for opening and coding mailing responses. More people may be needed to respond to call-ins, so they should have some easy and convenient method to record the original source. If one or two people are responsible for screening phone calls, they should ask applicants where they saw the ad. If there are several people regularly taking call-in messages, the organization might consider having a special memo pad just for such inquiries, with a "source" section indicated on the form.

Although the total number of responses should be tracked, judging the success of an ad only by this number is a mistake. For example, it is better to have 10 responses with two qualified applicants than 30 responses with only one qualified applicant.

❖ TRADE AND COMPETITIVE SOURCES

Other sources for recruiting are *professional and trade associations, trade publications,* and *competitors.* Many professional societies and trade associations publish a newsletter or magazine containing job ads. Such publications may be a good source for specialized professionals needed in an industry. Ads in other specialized publications and listings at professional meetings also can be good sources of publicity about professional openings.

An employer may meet possible applicants who are currently employed by a competitor at professional associations and industry meetings. Some employers directly contact individuals working for competitors. Employees recruited from these sources spend less time in training because they already know the industry.[27]

❖ Employment Agencies

Every state in the United States has its own state-sponsored employment agency. These agencies operate branch offices in many cities throughout the state and do not charge fees to applicants or employers.

Private employment agencies also are found in most cities. For a fee collected from either the employee or the employer, usually the employer, these agencies do some preliminary screening for an organization and put the organization in touch with applicants. Private employment agencies differ considerably in terms of the level of service, costs, policies, and types of applicants they provide. Employers can reduce the range of possible problems from these sources by giving them a precise definition of the position to be filled.

❖ Executive Search Firms

Some employment agencies focus their efforts on executive, managerial, and professional positions. These executive search firms are split into two groups: (1) contingency firms that charge a fee only after a candidate has been hired by a client company and (2) retainer firms that charge a client a set fee whether or not the contracted search is successful. Most of the larger firms work on a retainer basis.

The fees charged by executive search firms may be 33% or more of the employee's first-year salary. Most employers pay the fees, but there are some circumstances in which employees pay the fees. For placing someone in a high-level executive job, a search firm may receive $300,000 or more, counting travel expenses, the fee, and other compensation. The size of the fees and the aggressiveness with which some search firms pursue candidates for openings have led to such firms' being called *headhunters*.

Search firms are ethically bound not to approach employees of client companies in their search efforts for another client. As search firms are retained by more corporations, an increasing number of potential candidates become off-limits. At some point, the large search firms feel they may lose their effectiveness, because they will have to shun the best candidates for some jobs because of conflict-of-interest concerns.

❖ External Computerized Databases

In addition to the Internet recruiting sources discussed at the beginning of this chapter, computerized aids for recruiters are growing in usage and complexity. Often, these computerized recruiting aids are used to:

- Compile databases of resumes and application blanks submitted by potential candidates
- Scan the databases to identify potential candidates with specific qualifications and match them to job openings

Typically, an employer pays for tapping into these external databases, either on a per-search basis or on the basis of a monthly or annual fee for a designated number of searches.

❖ Innovative Recruiting Methods

The standard approaches to recruiting just presented are appropriate most of the time. But when it is really difficult to recruit the people needed, some innovative alternatives are available.

Special problems sometimes surface in recruiting efforts. Certain firms, such as those in the fast-food and retailing industries, have had continuing difficulties in recruiting sufficient employees for lower-paying jobs. Also, small employers may have difficulties recruiting against larger ones because smaller organizations often cannot offer extensive training programs or as many benefits. Consequently, creative approaches may be needed.

One small firm in California has successfully recruited salespeople from unusual sources. During earlier years, the firm found that disenchanted schoolteachers were excellent prospects. More recently, newer college graduates working in well-managed restaurants have been a good source. Since they are young, they tend to adapt quickly, and their restaurant experience produces good customer skills.

Recruiting must reach potential applicants such as college students even during spring break, as the HR Perspective describes. Innovative ideas for finding workers include recruiting outside the local area; advertising at cinemas; putting posters

HR PERSPECTIVE

Spring Break Recruiting: Sun, Sand, and Resumes?

One of the more unusual locations for recruiting is the job fair for college students held on Daytona Beach, Florida during the last three weeks of March. Begun in March 1995, by city promoters trying to enhance the out-of-control image of spring break week, the job fair has proved a popular idea, both with recruiters and students. A variety of organizations have been represented, ranging from Walt Disney World Corp. looking for entry-level host jobs to Ernest & Julio Gallo Winery seeking management training prospects. GTE Data Services looked for students to fill internships and training programs, as well as jobs in programming, sales, marketing, and telecommunications. Even the U.S. Secret Service used the opportunity to interview a large number of college students at one time.

Recruiters can find nearly 200,000 students from a myriad of colleges and with diverse backgrounds all in one location during the March period. From such a large pool of potential applicants the recruiters work hard to entice students to think about potential jobs and careers rather than vacations.

Recruiting and interviewing practices are different at this job fair from those at more formal locations. There is definitely a casual atmosphere. Little recruiting occurs in the morning, but afternoons are busier. Application blanks take only five minutes to fill out so students don't miss much sun time. To encourage students to consider employment, some firms have recruiters give out free sunglasses or passes to nightclubs, offer free breakfast buffets, or sponsor beauty contests. Informal dress by applicants is the norm, so recruiters have to become accustomed to evaluating people on qualities other than grooming.

Student responses to the idea of job searching while on spring break vary. Some students reject it altogether, but a number of them accept free offers and talk with recruiters. Some students even bring their resumes with them. Over 600 students interviewed with 28 employers during a recent spring break period. Such an approach indicates how a growing number of employers are using innovative means to recruit employees, especially in technical and professional areas.[28]

in community centers or churches; placing want ads in sections of newspapers other than the help wanted section; and contacting realtors for names of new residents. Other organizations may provide recruiting possibilities. For example, an organization might contact local HR associations for companies with surplus workers or contact persons laid off from their jobs, especially from competing companies. Offering internships to students at educational institutions, contacting vocational rehabilitation centers, and attending job fairs are additional ideas.

Companies that provide desired benefits and advertise those benefits may have more success in finding workers than other organizations. Such benefits can include the following: child care for employees, flexible working hours, tuition reimbursement plans, and discounted housing and meals for hotel workers willing to relocate to resorts during the peak season. Allowing managers flexibility in setting starting wages and offering sign-on bonuses may help in attracting applicants.

❖ Recruiting Evaluation

Evaluating the success of recruiting efforts is important because that is the only way to find out whether the efforts are cost effective in terms of time and money spent. General areas for evaluating recruiting include the following:

- ❖ *Quantity of applicants.* Because the goal of a good recruiting program is to generate a large pool of applicants from which to choose, quantity is a natural place to begin evaluation. Is it sufficient to fill job vacancies?
- ❖ *EEO goals met.* The recruiting program is the key activity used to meet goals for hiring protected-class individuals. This is especially relevant when a company is engaged in affirmative action to meet such goals. Is recruiting providing qualified applicants with an appropriate mix of protected-class individuals?
- ❖ *Quality of applicants.* In addition to quantity, there is the issue of whether the qualifications of the applicant pool are sufficient to fill the job openings. Do the applicants meet job specifications, and can they perform the jobs?
- ❖ *Cost per applicant hired.* Cost varies depending on the position being filled, but knowing how much it costs to fill an empty position puts turnover and salary in perspective. The greatest single expense in recruiting is the cost of having a recruiting staff. Is the cost for recruiting employees from any single source excessive?
- ❖ *Time required to fill openings.* The length of time it takes to fill openings is another means of evaluating recruiting efforts. Are openings filled quickly with qualified candidates, so the work and productivity of the organization are not delayed by vacancies?

❖ Evaluating Recruiting Quantity and Quality

With the broad areas just outlined as a general focus, organizations can compare how their recruiting efforts compare with past patterns and with the performance of other organizations. Brief discussions of some measures follow.

Selection Rates The selection rate is the percentage hired from a given group of applicants. It equals the number hired divided by the number of applicants; for example, a rate of 30% would indicate that 3 out of 10 applicants were hired. The percentage typically goes down as unemployment rates in the job market decrease because fewer qualified candidates typically are available. The selection rate also is affected by the validity of the selection process. A relatively unsophisticated selection program might pick 8 out of 10 applicants for the job. Four of those might turn out to be good employees. A more valid selection process might pick 5 out of 10 applicants and have only one mediocre employee in this group.

BASE RATE In the preceding example, the base rate of good employees in the population is 4 out of 10. That is, if 10 people were hired at random, one would expect 4 of them to be good employees. A good recruiting program should be aimed at attracting the 4 in 10 who are capable of doing well on this particular job. Realistically, no recruiting program will attract *only* the 4 in 10 who will succeed. However, efforts to make the recruiting program attract the largest proportion of those in the base rate group can make recruiting efforts more effective.

Certain long-term measures of recruiting effectiveness are quite useful in indicating whether sufficient numbers of the base rate group are being attracted. Information on job performance, absenteeism, cost of training, and turnover by recruiting source helps to adjust future recruiting. For example, some companies find that recruiting at certain colleges or universities furnishes stable, high performers, whereas other schools provide employees who are more prone to turnover. One survey of employers found that 32.5% of employees recruited from colleges stayed 1 to 3 years, and 23.5% stayed more than 10 years.[29]

***Yield Ratio**
A comparison of the number of applicants at one stage of the recruiting process to the number at the next stage.

YIELD RATIOS Yield ratios can be calculated for each step of the recruiting/selection process. A **yield ratio** is a comparison of the number of applicants at one stage of the recruiting process to the number at the next stage. The result is a tool for approximating the necessary size of the initial applicant pool. Figure 8–5 shows that to end up with 25 hires for the job in question, the company must begin with 300 applicants in the pool, as long as yield ratios remain the same at each step.

❖ FIGURE 8–5 ❖
USING YIELD RATIOS TO DETERMINE NEEDED APPLICANTS

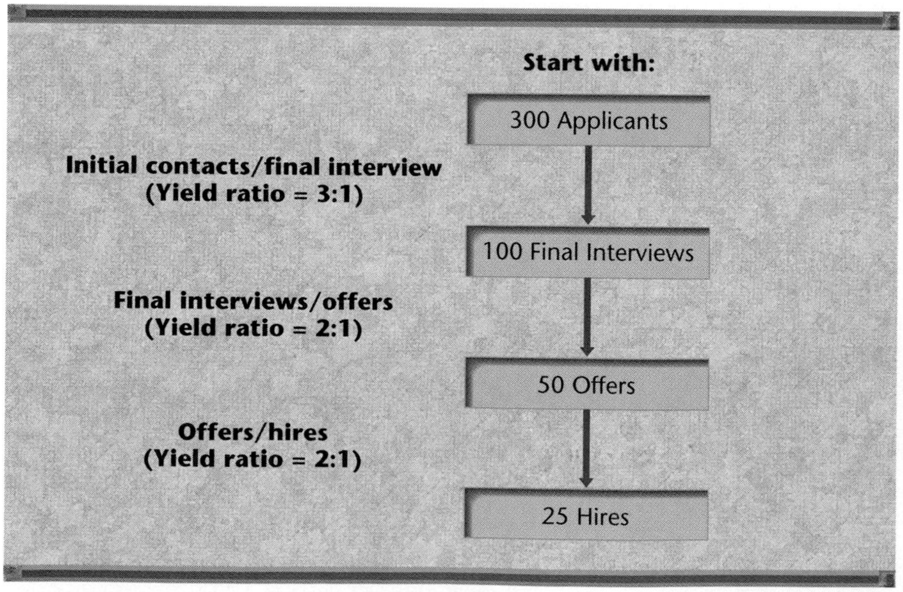

A different approach to evaluating recruiting using ratios suggests that over time organizations can develop ranges for critical ratios. When a given indicator ratio falls outside that range, there may be problems in the recruiting process.[30] For example, in college recruiting the following ratios might be useful.

$$\frac{\text{College seniors given second interview}}{\text{total number of seniors interviewed}} = \text{range of 30–50\%}$$

$$\frac{\text{Number who accept offer}}{\text{number invited to the company for visit}} = \text{range of 50–70\%}$$

$$\frac{\text{Number who were hired}}{\text{number offered a job}} = \text{range of 70–80\%}$$

$$\frac{\text{Number finally hired}}{\text{total number interviewed on campus}} = \text{range of 10–20\%}$$

Timing of Openings If an organization needs a Vice President of Marketing *immediately,* having to wait four months to find the right person presents a problem. Generally speaking, it is useful to calculate the average amount of time it takes from contact to hire for each source of applicants, because some sources may be faster than others for a particular employer.

Figure 8–6 shows some benchmarks from a study done by the Saratoga Institute headed by Jac Fitz-Enz.[31] Two different measures are used:

- *Time to fill openings*—the time from when the requisitions are made to when offers are accepted by candidates for jobs
- *Time to start*—the time from when requisitions are made to when candidates actually start the jobs

Evaluating Recruiting Costs and Benefits

HR managers correctly regard recruiting as an important activity. Inability to generate enough or the appropriate type of applicants for jobs can be costly.

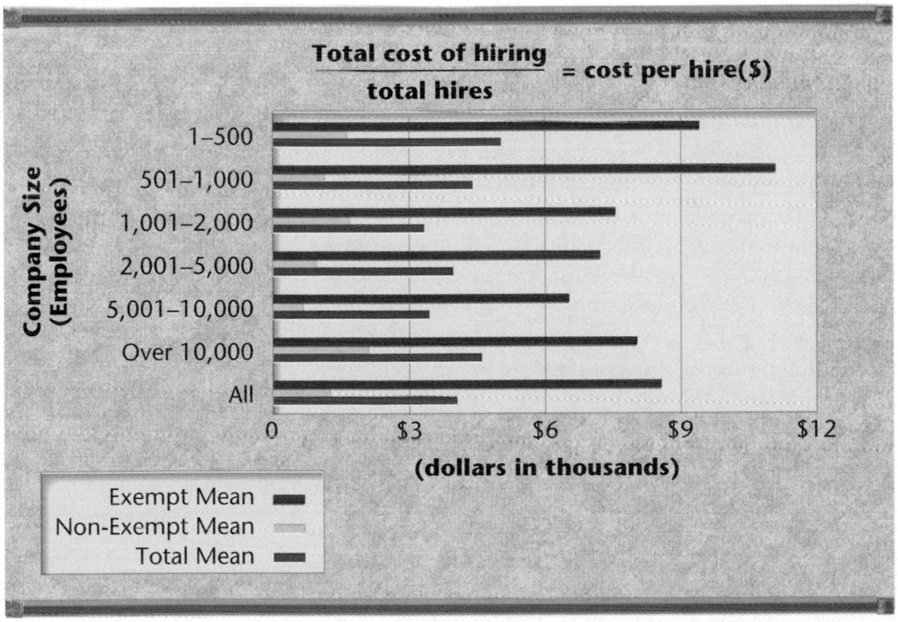

Figure 8–6
Recruiting Costs per Hire

SOURCE: Saratoga Institute, *Human Resource Financial Report,* in *Best Practices in Staffing* (Santa Clara, CA: Resumix, 1995).

When recruiting fails to bring in enough applicants, a common response is to raise starting salaries. This action initially may help recruiting, but often at the expense of others already in the organization. It also may create resentment on the part of employees who started at much lower salaries than the new hires.

In a cost/benefit analysis to evaluate recruiting efforts, costs may include both *direct costs* (advertising, recruiters' salaries, travel, agency fees, telephone) and *indirect costs* (involvement of operating managers, public relations, image). Benefits to consider include the following:

- ❖ Length of time from contact to hire
- ❖ Total size of applicant pool
- ❖ Proportion of acceptances to offers
- ❖ Percentage of qualified applicants in the pool

Cost/benefit information on each recruiting source can be calculated. Comparing the length of time applicants from each source stay in the organization with the cost of hiring from that source offers a useful perspective. Further, yield ratios from each source can help determine which sources generate the most employees.

In summary, the effectiveness of various recruiting sources will vary depending on the nature of the job being filled and the time available to fill it. But unless calculated, the effectiveness may not be entirely obvious.

SUMMARY

❖ Recruiting is the process of generating a pool of qualified applicants for organizational jobs through a series of activities.

❖ Recruiting must be viewed strategically, and discussions should be held about the relevant labor markets in which to recruit.

❖ The applicant population is affected by recruiting method, recruiting message, applicant qualifications required, and administrative procedures.

❖ A growing number of employers are turning to flexible staffing, which makes use of recruiting sources and workers who are not employees. Using temporary employees and employee leasing are two common approaches to flexible staffing.

❖ Two general groups of recruiting sources exist: internal sources and external sources. An organization must decide whether it will look primarily within the organization or outside for new employees, or use some combination of these sources.

❖ The decision to use internal or external sources should be based on the advantages and disadvantages associated with each.

❖ The recruiting process begins with human resource planning and concludes with evaluation of recruiting efforts. Both HR staff and operating managers have responsibilities in the process.

❖ Recruiting is subject to some legal constraints, including avoidance of disparate impact, compliance with EEO requirements and affirmative action plans (AAPs), and use of nondiscriminatory advertising.

❖ Efforts should be made to recruit a diverse workforce, including older workers, individuals with disabilities, and individuals who are racial/ethic minorities.

❖ Current employees, former employees, and previous applicants are the most common internal sources available.

❖ External recruiting sources include schools, colleges and universities, labor unions, media sources, trade and competitive sources, employment agencies, and computerized databases.

❖ Recruiting efforts should be evaluated to assess how effectively they are being performed.

❖ Recruiting evaluation typically includes examining applicant quality and quantity, the time necessary to fill openings, and the costs and benefits of various recruiting sources.

Review and Discussion Questions

1. Discuss what strategic recruiting considerations should be addressed by HR executives at a mid-sized bank with locations in several cities. Give examples, and be specific.
2. What advantages and disadvantages of flexible staffing have you seen in organizations in which you have worked?
3. Design and describe a recruiting process for filling openings for a sales representative's job for a pharmaceutical manufacturer.
4. Discuss the advantages and disadvantages of recruiting internally versus externally.
5. What internal sources for recruiting have you seen work effectively? What internal sources have you seen work ineffectively? Why?
6. Discuss some ways which firms can use to make college recruiting more effective.
7. What should be considered in evaluating the recruiting efforts of a regional discount retailer with 80–100 stores in a geographic area?

Terms to Know

applicant pool **220**
applicant population **219**
flexible staffing **220**
independent contractors **220**
job posting and bidding **228**
labor force population **219**
labor markets **218**
recruiting **218**
yield ratio **238**

Case

Revising the Recruiting Process at Inova Health Systems

Inova Health Systems is a nonprofit health organization based in Falls Church, Virginia. Under the corporate umbrella of Inova are three hospitals, two care centers for longer-term patients, and seven physical therapy centers. Employing over 10,000 people, Inova spends over $500,000 annually on its recruiting efforts. In one year, almost 30,000 applications and resumes were received and processed and over 3,000 interviews held.

But the HR staff and other managers recognized that the recruiting system was not working as smoothly as it should. There was too much overlap of efforts, and some openings were taking too long to fill. In summary, the total recruiting process needed to be reviewed and then revised to become better for applicants, managers, and the HR staff.

Several goals for the "new" recruiting processes were established. One goal was to eliminate redundancies of effort by the various units throughout Inova and to simplify the process and procedures used. Related to this facet was a goal to use computer technology and systems to make information on applicants and openings flow better through all units. Better utilization of staff, space, and facilities was another goal. All of these goals were internal. A major external one was to ensure the satisfaction of applicants and to staff jobs more efficiently and quickly. It was hoped that the revised recruiting system would increase the satisfaction and acceptance rates of both internal and external applicants.

The most significant change made in revising the recruiting process was to establish a centralized employment office. Previously, each of the individual facilities had done its own recruiting. One advantage of centralization was that it allowed Inova to install an HRIS applicant tracking software system. This system allowed HR staff members at Inova to distinguish potential applicants from others in the database. Also, the system provided better handling of records and better compilation of EEO and other government-required compliance reports. Another advantage of centralization was that it allowed for better coordination between entities in the system. With a centralized system, job postings for all locations could be reviewed and employees from all Inova operations could be considered

Revising the Recruiting Process at Inova Health Systems, continued

for transfers and promotions. In addition, employment policies for all of the facilities were reviewed, and common policies developed where possible. Application blanks and other forms were redesigned for common use throughout Inova. In one of the biggest changes, screening of applications and resumes was centralized, so that an individual applicant's credentials could be considered for jobs in all of the Inova facilities, not just in one. Centralization also allowed Inova's HR staff to establish a job vacancy information system. The system now includes a 24-hour job hotline with an 800 number and weekly listings of jobs on the firm's internal e-mail system.

The revised recruiting process has been a success, as judged in several ways. For instance, the numbers of resumes screened and interviews held have been reduced. Also, the number of internal transfers by Inova staff has increased. In summary, the redesign of Inova's recruiting process has provided better coordination, which means that HR staff, managers, employees, and external applicants all get faster and more accurate information on Inova employment opportunities.[32]

❖ *Questions:*

1. Compare the original recruiting process with ones you have observed in organizations where you have worked.
2. Discuss the advantages and disadvantages of centralization of many of the recruiting activities at Inova.
3. What specific measures would be useful to evaluate the effectiveness of the changes in Inova's recruiting process?

❖ *Notes*

1. M. Mannix, "The Home-Page Help Wanteds," *U.S. News & World Report,* October 30, 1995, 86; W. Glaberson, "6 Newspapers Put Job Listings on the Internet," *The Denver Post,* October 22, 1995, 1A; "On-Line Recruiting Offers New Way to Find Computer-Savvy Applicants," *Policies & Practices Update,* August 25, 1995, 1; Samuel Greengard, "Catch the Wave as HR Goes On-Line," *Personnel Journal,* July 1995, 54–68; and Julia King, "Job 'Net' Working," *Computer World,* June 26, 1995, 55.
2. "Scarcity of Workers Worries Small, Mid-Sized Employers," *HR Series, Policies and Practices Update,* August 25, 1995, 4.
3. D. Allen, "Recruitment Management: Finding the Right Fit," *HR Focus,* April 1995, 15.
4. P. Brotherton, "Staff to Suit," *HR Magazine,* December 1995, 50–55.
5. Contributed by Manpower International. Used with permission.
6. Robert Lewis, "Escaping from the Jobless Maze," *AARP Bulletin,* October 1994, 2.
7. "Employee Leasing: A New Dynamic in the Labor Market," *Bankers Trust Research,* January 4, 1995, 1–10.
8. Paul H. Ritter, "Employee Leasing: Risky business or Savvy Management?" *Professional Safety,* November 1994, 36–38.
9. "Jobs Must Be Marketed," *Supplement to Personnel Journal,* January 1996, 1–4.
10. Herbert G. Heneman III and Robert L. Heneman, *Staffing Organizations* (Middleton, WI: Mendota House, 1994), 279.
11. Catherine Rush and Lizabeth Barclay, "Executive Search: Recruiting a Recruiter," *Public Management,* July 1995, 20–23.
12. *How to Recruit Older Workers,* (Washington, DC: American Association of Retired Persons, 1993).
13. *Valuing Older Workers: A Study of Costs and Productivity* (Washington, DC: American Association of Retired Persons, 1995).
14. L. A. Strauss, "Disability Law Adds Smaller Companies," *USA Today,* July 26, 1994, 4B.
15. "Employees with Disabilities Benefit Business," *Supplement to Personnel Journal,* August 1994, 18–19.
16. Laura M. Litvan, "Casting a Wider Employment Net," *Nation's Business,* December 1994, 49–51; and E. Clark, "Job Fairs Help Connect People and Employers," *The Crisis,* August–September, 1995, 34.
17. "Pop Quiz: How Do You Recruit the Best College Grads?" *Supplement to Personnel Journal,* August 1995, 12–18.
18. Sonia M. Goltz and Cristina M. Giannantonio, "Recruiter Friendliness and Attraction to the Job" *Journal of Vocational Behavior* 46 (1995), 109–118.
19. G. Stephen Taylor, "The Relationship between Sources of New Employees and Attitudes toward the Job," *Journal of Social Psychology,* 134 (1994), 99–111.

20. Resumix: Corporate Headquarters, 2953 Bunker Hill Lane, 3rd Floor, Santa Clara, CA 95054. Used with permission.
21. "Video Interview Wave of Future for College Graduates," *Omaha World-Herald*, August 13, 1995, 17G.
22. K. O. Magnusen and K. Galen Kroeck, "Videoconferencing Maximizes Recruiting," *HR Magazine*, August 1995, 70–72.
23. Robert D. Bretz and Timothy A. Judge, "The Role of Human Resource Systems in Job Applicant Decision Processes," *Journal of Management* 20 (1994), 531–552.
24. Laura M. Graves, "The Effect of Sex Similarity on Recruiters' Evaluations of Actual Applicants," *Personnel Psychology* 48 (1995), 85–97.
25. Based on information in Daniel B. Turban, James E. Campion, and Alison R. Eyring, "Factors Related to Job Acceptance Decisions of College Recruits," *Journal of Vocational Behavior* 47 (1995), 193–213.
26. Peter V. Marsden, "The Hiring Process," *American Behavioral Scientist*, June 1994, 979–992.
27. Molly Klimos, "How to Recruit a Smart Team," *Nation's Business*, May 1995, 26.
28. Based on "Job-Hunting College Students May Want to Try the Beach" *Omaha World-Herald*, March 17, 1996, 12A.
29. "A Measure of the HR Recruitment Function," *Journal of Career Planning*, March 1995, 37.
30. Personal communication from Dr. Carl Thornton, GMI Department of Management, Flint, MI.
31. Saratoga Institute, *Human Resource Financial Report*, in *Best Practices in Staffing* (Santa Clara, CA: Resumix, 1995).
32. Based on Phyllis A. Savill, "HR at Inova Reengineers Recruitment Process," *Personnel Journal*, June 1995, 109–114.

CHAPTER 9

SELECTING HUMAN RESOURCES

After you have read this chapter, you should be able to . . .

- Define *selection* and explain several reasons for having a specialized employment unit.
- Diagram a typical selection process in sequential order.
- Discuss the reception and application form phases of the selection process.
- Identify two general and three controversial types of tests.
- Discuss three types of interviews and six key considerations in the selection interview.
- Construct a guide for conducting a selection interview.
- Explain how legal concerns affect background investigations of applicants.
- Discuss why medical examinations, including drug testing, may be useful in selection.

HR IN TRANSITION

SELECTION AND BIZARRE QUESTIONS, ON CAMPUS AND ELSEWHERE

- ❖ If you were at a dinner meeting and the man next to you put his hand on your thigh, what would you do?
- ❖ Is your boyfriend white?
- ❖ Have you ever cheated on your girlfriend?
- ❖ Describe making the perfect banana split.
- ❖ How do you staple a tag to a pig's nose?

These aren't necessarily *illegal* questions, but they are certainly inappropriate ones. They surfaced in college student focus groups discussing the job search. With high-potential candidates, on college campuses or elsewhere, questions like these may defeat the purpose of selection. A candidate may choose not to take the job if it is offered, because he or she was offended. On campus, the word spreads:"The jerk at XYZ company had the nerve to ask me this." Some students report it to their advisors, and companies have been banned from campus as a result.

Getting specific "hard" evidence to see if that person has a particular set of skills is more useful than asking hypothetical questions not job related.

Campus interviews may be conducted by operating managers or executives from outside the HR department. In many cases, these individuals may have had no training in interview techniques or the legalities of interviewing. One consultant, noting that it is cheaper to train an interviewer than hire a lawyer, suggests that untrained interviewers may go on "fishing expeditions" with their questions. These untrained interviewers feel that if they ask predictable questions they will get prepared answers, so they try to use bizarre questions.

Employers sometimes say, "We make efforts to hire minority individuals and we get turned down." A bizarre screening process may provide part of the answer. Candidates receive many subtle signals during the selection process. For example, suppose someone who struggled financially to get through school is asked, "Did you study abroad?" The person may find the question inappropriate. Even if the job is offered, the offer may feel like tokenism, and the person may not accept it.

Arthur Nathan is the Vice President for HR for the Mirage in Las Vegas. In the past five years, the casino/hotel has hired almost 20,000 employees and rejected about 150,000. During that time, the hiring process was challenged only eight times. One challenged decision was an honest mistake; the other seven were appropriate decisions according to Nathan. To keep his interviewers from asking inappropriate questions, Nathan published a list of structured questions to be used in every interview. He trains those who will be interviewing in their use. For each of the 433 distinct jobs at the Mirage, there is a set of questions—non-bizarre ones. Nathan also insists on getting extensive employment history—10 years, in fact. "I look to see if the person stayed a good deal of time," he says.

Maury Hanigan of the Hanigan Consulting Group in New York likes to use behavior-based interviewing that relates behaviors directly to the job—thus keeping the questions relevant and not bizarre. For instance, if conflict resolution is an important skill for a particular job, she might ask the individual being interviewed to describe how he or she has resolved conflict in the past. Getting specific "hard" evidence to see if that person has a particular set of skills is more useful than asking hypothetical questions not job related. "Even if someone tries to answer honestly, the best they can do is guess," she notes. It is better to ask how they *did* respond than to ask hypothetically how they might respond.

Hanigan's advice is do not ask *anything* bizarre. If a candidate with good engineering qualifications is asked, "If you were a box of cereal, what kind of cereal would you be?" the candidate may feel that the hiring decision is arbitrary, because that bizarre question has nothing to do with engineering skills. Imagine yourself in court having to testify why you did not hire someone:"Well, she said she was Rice Krispies and this is a Raisin Bran company." [1]

> "Selecting qualified employees is like putting money in the bank."
> —John Boudreau

Recruiting, as discussed in the previous chapter, provides a group of applicants from which the best potential employees can be chosen. Picking those to be hired is *selection*. For example, deciding which 10 applicants out of 100 who applied are the most likely to be satisfactory employees is the challenge of selection. Selection is an important part of any organizational strategy. Without qualified employees, an organization is not in a position to succeed. A vivid case in point is athletic organizations like the Dallas Cowboys, Atlanta Braves, and Los Angeles Lakers, who fail or succeed on their ability to select the coaches, players, and other employees to win games.

Selection is much more than just picking the "best athlete," however. Selecting the right set of knowledge, skills, and abilities—which come packaged in a human being—is an attempt to get a "fit" between what the applicant can do and wants to do and what the organization needs. That is made more difficult by the fact that one cannot always tell exactly what the applicant really can and wants to do. *Fit* between the applicant and the organization affects not only the employer's willingness to make a job offer but also the applicant's willingness to accept a job.[2]

More than anything else, selection of human resources should be seen as a *matching process*. Gaps between employment skills and requirements of the job are common factors that lead to rejection of applicants. How well an employee is matched to a job affects the amount and quality of the employee's work. This matching also directly affects training and operating costs. Workers who are unable to produce the expected amount and quality of work can cost an organization a great deal of money and time.

Proper matching also is important to the individual applying for a job. The wrong choice of a vocation or improper job placement can result in wasted time for the employee, who could be getting useful experience elsewhere. The mismatched individuals will be unhappy in their jobs and may be dismissed or quit if they prove to be mismatched.

To put selection in perspective, consider that organizations on average reject about five out of six applicants for jobs they need to fill. Figure 9–1 depicts the reasons why employers often reject applicants.[3] Perhaps the best perspective on

❖ FIGURE 9–1 ❖
REASONS APPLICANTS ARE NOT SELECTED

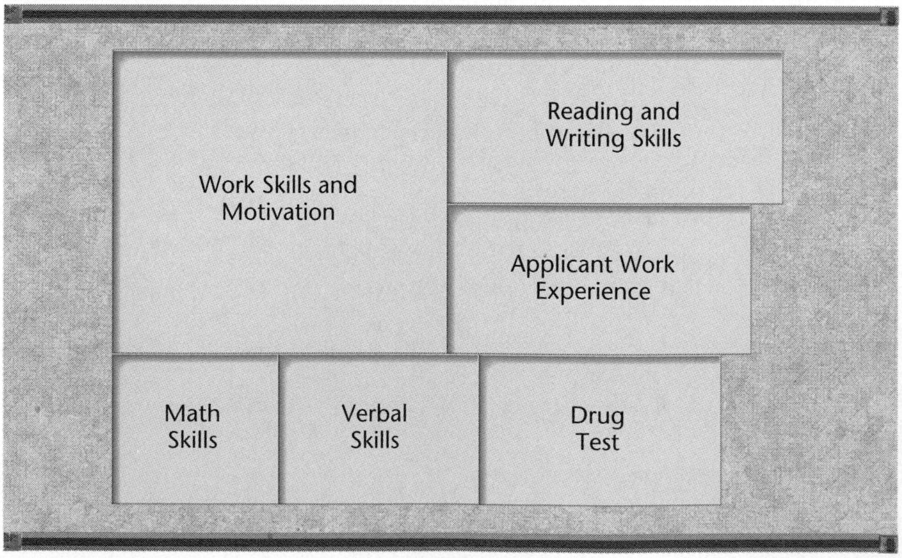

selection comes from two traditional HR "truisms" that clearly identify the importance of effective employment selection.

1. "Good training will not fix bad selection." The implication here is that when the right people are not picked for jobs, it is very difficult to recover later by somehow trying to train those without the proper KSAs to do the jobs well. Further, it has become difficult to dismiss an employee who is marginal without creating the potential for problems.
2. "If you don't hire the right one, your competitor will." There is an opportunity cost in failure to select the right employee, and that cost is that the "right one" went somewhere else. The organization not only *did not* get the "right one" but now may have the "wrong one." Thus, selection is a *very* important HR activity.

❖ Nature of Selection

Selection is the process of choosing individuals who have relevant qualifications to fill jobs in an organization. The selection process begins when a manager or supervisor needs to hire an individual to fill a certain vacancy. In large organizations, a requisition is sent to the in-house employment office or an HR staff member. A *job description,* based on *job analysis,* identifies the vacancy. A *job specifications* statement, which may also accompany the request, describes the knowledge, skills, and abilities a person needs to fill the vacancy. HR specialists use the job description and specifications to begin the recruiting process. From the pool of applicants generated by recruiting activities, one person is selected to fill the job. In small organizations, the manager often handles the whole process.

***Selection**
The process of choosing individuals who have relevant qualifications to fill jobs in an organization.

The process for selecting managers is a bit different. Managers selected from outside the organization often are chosen by upper management on the basis of reference checks, word of mouth, and interviews. The difficulty of specifying *exactly* the behaviors needed to be a successful manager makes management selection more difficult than selection of a good clerk. Middle- and upper-level management selection may be handled outside the customary selection responsibilities detailed in the following discussion.

❖ Selection Responsibilities

Organizations vary in how they allocate selection responsibilities between HR specialists and managers. Until the impact of equal employment opportunity (EEO) regulations became widespread, selection often was carried out in a rather unplanned manner in many organizations. The need to meet EEO requirements has forced them to plan better in this regard. Still, in some organizations, each department screens and hires its own employees. Many managers insist on selecting their own people because they are sure no one else can choose employees for them as well as they can themselves. This practice is particularly prevalent in smaller firms. But the validity and fairness of such an approach may be questionable.

Other organizations maintain the traditional practice of having the HR unit do the initial screening of the candidates, while the appropriate managers or supervisors make the final selection. As a rule, the higher the position within the organization, the greater the likelihood that the ultimate hiring decisions will be made by operating managers rather than HR specialists. Typical selection responsibilities are shown in Figure 9–2 on the next page. These responsibilities are affected by the establishment or existence of a central employment office.

❖ Figure 9–2 ❖
Typical Selection Responsibilities

HR UNIT	MANAGERS
❖ Provides initial employment reception ❖ Conducts initial screening interview ❖ Administers appropriate employment tests ❖ Obtains background and reference information ❖ Refers top candidates to managers for final selection ❖ Arranges for the employment physical examination, if used ❖ Evaluates success of selection process	❖ Requisition employees with specific qualifications to fill jobs ❖ Participate in selection process as appropriate ❖ Interview final candidates ❖ Make final selection decision, subject to advice of HR specialists ❖ Provide follow-up information on the suitability of selected individuals

Centralized Employment Office Selection duties may be centralized into a specialized organizational unit that is part of an HR department. This specialization often depends on the size of the organization. In smaller organizations, especially in those with fewer than 100 employees, a full-time employment specialist or unit may be impractical.

The employment function in any organization may be concerned with some or all of the following operations:(1) receiving applications, (2) interviewing applicants, (3) administering tests to applicants, (4) conducting background investigations, (5) arranging for physical examinations, (6) placing and assigning new employees, (7) coordinating follow-up of these employees, (8) termination interviewing, and (9) maintaining adequate records and reports.

Several reason are generally voiced for conducting employment functions within one unit. One, it is easier for the applicant to have only one place in which to apply for a job. Two, contact with outside applicant sources is easier since issues can be cleared through one central location. Three, centralized employment lets managers concentrate on their operating responsibilities rather than on interviewing. With centralization also comes the expectation that better selection may result because it is handled by a staffing specialist. An applicant advantage is that there may be consideration for a greater variety of jobs. Selection costs may be cut because it avoids duplication of effort. It is also important that people well trained in government regulations handle a major part of the process to prevent future lawsuits and costs associated with them.

Team Staffing The widespread use of teams presents an interesting selection variation. To be successful, teams have to be allowed to control their destiny as much as possible, which means they should be involved in selecting their teammates. When teams hire new members, they have a vested interest in making sure those persons are successful.

However, a good deal of training is required to make sure that teams understand the selection process, testing, interviewing, and legal constraints. Further, a selection procedure in which the team votes for the top choice is inappropriate; the decision should be made by consensus, which may take longer.[4]

❖ Selection Process and Employer Image

In addition to matching qualified people to jobs, the selection process has an important public-relations dimension. Discriminatory hiring practices, impolite interviewers, unnecessarily long waits, inappropriate testing procedures, and lack of follow-up letters can produce unfavorable impressions of an employer. Providing courteous, professional treatment to all candidates during the selection process is important because for most applicants a job contact of any kind is an extremely personal and significant event.

❖ Legal Concerns with Selection

Generally, employers may use a variety of preemployment measures to ensure that applicants will fit available jobs. However, employers may not discriminate or otherwise refuse to hire applicants for any reasons that are against the law. Selection is subject to all the EEO concerns covered in previous chapters. The interview itself is becoming a minefield; one major problem is that there is no standard list of taboo questions but only general areas about which one cannot ask. Small business owners and managers often are the worst offenders, and one of their most common errors is to ask a woman about child-care arrangements, which assumes women are always the ones responsible for child rearing.

As noted in Chapter 6, the EEOC has endorsed the use of employment discrimination **testers**, protected-class members who pose as applicants to determine if employers discriminate in their hiring practices. Testers observe how employer representatives conduct themselves in the selection process, and then file lawsuits if they feel their legal rights as representative job applicants were ignored.[5]

***Testers**
Protected-class members who pose as applicants to determine if employers discriminate in their hiring practices.

It is increasing in importance that companies define more carefully exactly who is an *applicant*, given the legal issues involved. If there is no written policy defining conditions that make a person an applicant, any persons who call or send unsolicited resumes might later claim they were not hired because of illegal discrimination. A policy defining *applicant* might include the conditions shown in Figure 9–3.

It is wise for an organization to retain all applications for three years. Applicant flow data should be calculated if the organization has at least 50 employees.

❖ Figure 9–3 ❖
Employment Application Policies

- Applications are accepted only when there is an opening.
- Only persons filling out application blanks are considered applicants.
- A person's application ceases to be effective after a certain date.
- Only a certain number of applications will be accepted.
- People must apply for a specific job, not "any job"

❖ Selection Criteria and Predictors

Because certain KSAs are so important in being able to perform a given job, they become the standards for selection. **Selection criteria** are those standards that are so important that in order to be hired people *must* meet them. They may be identified through a careful job analysis and job description as critical selection criteria. They are attempts to predict the likelihood of successful job behavior by each applicant. For example, in a bookkeeper, the ability to accurately transcribe numerical amounts from receipts and vouchers to a ledger or database is a selection criterion. The ability of applicants to transcribe accurately can be measured with a test of transcription ability before hiring.

***Selection Criteria**
Standards that become the basis for selection.

The information gathered about an applicant should be a careful attempt to help predict the probability that the applicant can do the job. **Predictors** are information about the likelihood that an applicant will be able to perform the job. They can take many forms, but they should be job-related, valid, and reliable. For instance, a test score can be a predictor of success on the job if it is valid. Previous experience can be a predictor of success if it is related to the necessary performance on the current job. Any selection tool used (for example, application form, test, interview, education requirements, or years of experience required) should *only* be used if it is a valid predictor of job performance. Using

***Predictors**
Information about the likelihood that an applicant will be able to perform the job.

invalid predictors can cause selection of the "wrong" candidate and rejection of the "right" one.

SELECTION PREDICTORS AND ERROR RATES Predictors are used to predict whether someone is likely to meet the job requirements and be a satisfactory employee. Predictors can be any factor that occurs with acceptable work performance. For example, if people who get high scores on a selection test are good performers on the job, the test may be seen as a *valid* predictor of performance. Not all predictors are valid, however. If a manager believes that a firm handshake and good eye contact are good predictors of honesty on the job, she may find that those predictors are *not* valid in many cases. Validity of a predictor refers to whether or not the predictor is accurately related to the performance (or "criterion") desired. However, no single predictor is 100% accurate. If one predictor is accurate 75% of the time and another is accurate 50% of the time, using the two together should increase the probability of selecting a good employee. Adding a third or fourth predictor should further increase the probability. *But* these increases will *only* occur if the predictors are valid. For example, if valid predictors for the job of bank teller are accuracy in keyboard usage and the ability to do arithmetic accurately, a test might be devised to measure these predictors. Any test devised will not always be completely accurate (i.e., someone might have an "off" day with the keyboard and make an unusual number of errors). But, generally, giving keyboarding and arithmetic tests to potential bank tellers should help improve the quality of the work done by the tellers hired.

Figure 9–4 shows how adding additional predictors can affect the applicant pool. When several predictors are used, only in the common area shared by the circles will "qualified" candidates be found. But given that no predictor is 100% accurate, each eliminate good candidates. Having too many predictors—especially

FIGURE 9–4
EFFECT OF ADDING PREDICTORS TO THE SELECTION PROCESS

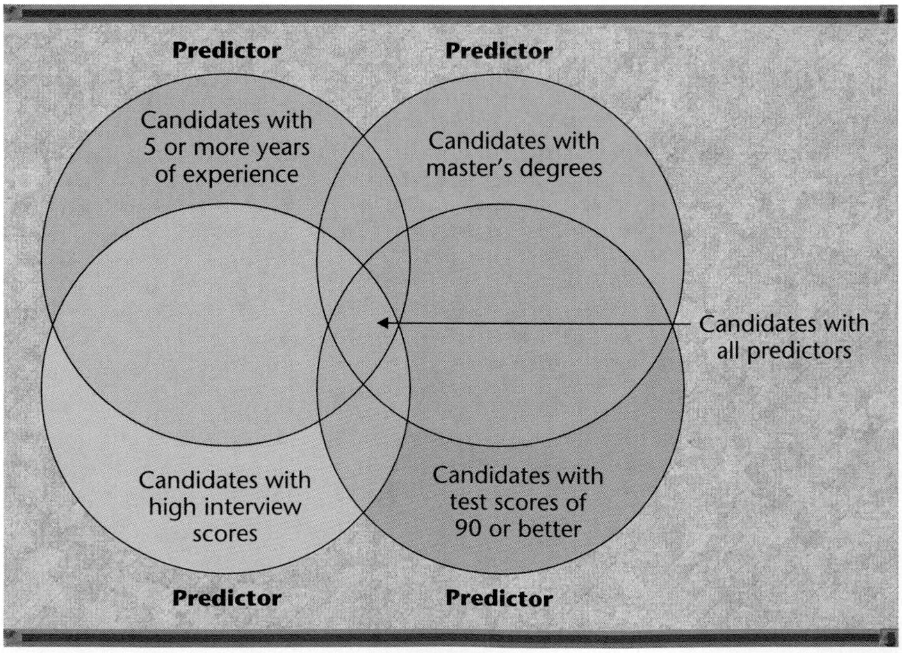

those with lower accuracy rates, may actually harm the quality of selection decisions.

The HR Perspective deals with criteria and predictors for executive career success.

❖ The Selection Process

Most organizations take certain common steps to process applicants for jobs. Variations on this basic process depend on organizational size, nature of jobs to be filled, number of people to be selected, and pressure of outside forces such as EEO considerations. This process can take place in a day or over a much longer period of time. If the applicant is processed in one day, the employer usually

HR PERSPECTIVE

Research on Criteria and Predictors

Timothy Judge and his colleagues examined the extent to which various predictors were related to the criteria associated with executive success. The study was reported in *Personnel Psychology*. They attempted to identify what the predictors of career success are for executives.

If the criteria associated with job success are to be studied, they first must be identified and measured. For this study, the researchers developed an approach that measured both success as identified by others based on relatively objective criteria (*salary* and *number of promotions*) and success as judged by the individuals pursuing careers. The latter measure included feelings of *accomplishment* and *satisfaction with the career.* The sample included 1,388 U.S. executives in a variety of industries.

As the diagram below shows, predictors of promotions and compensation level were age, gender, marital status, and spousal employment. The executives most likely to have high salaries were older, male, and white and had spouses who did not work outside the home. Further, a graduate degree in business or law from an Ivy League school or high-quality university predicted success, as did working in a smaller, successful, publicly traded company; ambition was a good predictor as well.

There was a strong relationship between objective external measures of success and the individual's career satisfaction. An executive with an MBA from a top-rated school and international experience is likely to make $54,000 more per year than an executive without those predictors. Similarly, an executive rated high on accomplishment with 20 years' experience in the job and international experience is likely to earn nearly three more promotions than an executive with average accomplishments, only 10 years' experience, and no international exposure.

Predictors can be used to indicate the likelihood that certain criteria will be achieved. In this case, predictors were used to predict executive success, but the same approach can be used to predict who is most likely to be a satisfactory employee in a given job. First, identify the criteria for a job performance, and then determine which predictors are associated with successful performance and which are linked to unsuccessful performance.[6]

Predictors of Executive Success	Criteria Associated with Successful Executive Performance
Age	Salary
Gender	Promotions
Marital Status	Career Satisfaction
Grad Degree in Business or Law	
Ambition	

checks references after selection. Often, one or more phases of the process are omitted or the order changed, depending on the employer.

The selection process shown in Figure 9–5 is typical of a large organization. Assume a woman applicant, comes to the organization, is directed to the employment office, and is received by a receptionist. Some firms conduct a job preview/interest screen to determine if an applicant is qualified for open jobs before giving out an application form. Next, the receptionist usually gives the individual an application form to complete. The completed application form serves as the basis for an interview or a test. After the interview or test, the applicant may be told that she does not fit any position the company has available. However, if she does appear to have appropriate qualifications, her background and previous employment history may be checked and/or an additional, more in-depth interview may be conducted. If responses are favorable, the applicant may receive a conditional offer of a job, provided she passes a medical and/or drug test.

The remainder of this section describes the first two steps of the selection process: the reception and the job preview/interest screen. The rest of the chapter is devoted to detailed discussions of application forms, selection testing, selection interviewing, and background investigation.

❖ **Figure 9–5** ❖
Selection Process Flowchart

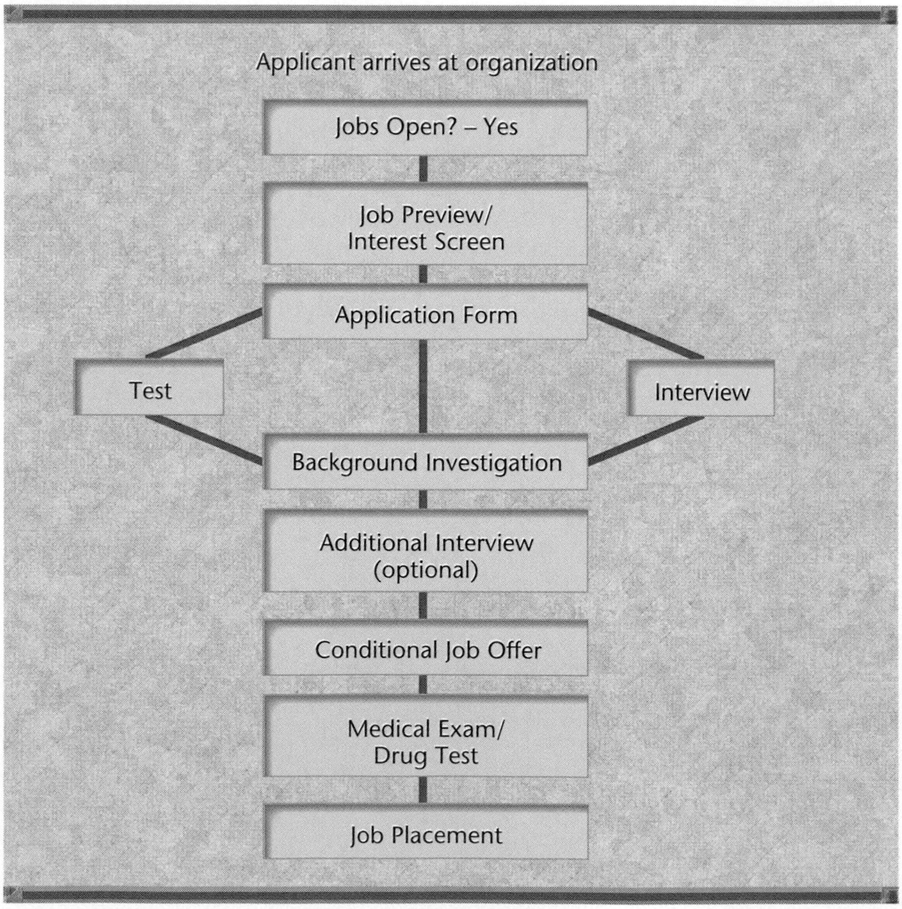

❖ Reception

The job applicant's attitudes about the organization, and even about the products or services it offers, will be influenced by the reception stage of the selection process. Whoever meets the applicant initially should be tactful and able to offer assistance in a courteous, friendly manner. If no jobs are available, applicants can be informed at this point. Any employment possibilities must be presented honestly and clearly.

❖ Job Preview/Interest Screen

In some cases, it is appropriate to have a brief interview, called an *initial screening interview* or a *job preview/interest screen,* to see if the applicant is likely to match any jobs available in the organization before the applicant is allowed to fill out an application form. In most large organizations, this initial screening is done by someone in the employment office or in the HR department. In some situations, the applicant may complete an application form before the short interview.

During the screening interview, the interviewer can determine if the applicant is likely to have the ability to perform available jobs. Typical questions might concern job interests, location desired, pay expectations, and availability for work. One firm that hires security guards and armored-car drivers uses the screening interview to verify whether an applicant meets the minimum qualifications for the job, such as having a valid driver's license, being free of any criminal conviction in the past five years, and having used a pistol. Because these are required minimum standards, it would be a waste of time for any applicant who could not meet them to fill out an application form.

Realistic Job Previews Most job seekers appear to have little information initially about the organizations to which they apply for jobs. The information applicants receive from prospective employers in the recruiting/selection process is apparently given considerable weight in their decisions whether to accept a job and in their performance scores later.[7] Information on pay, nature of the work, geographic location, and opportunity for promotion is important to almost everyone. In addition, information on job security is particularly important to blue-collar applicants.

Some employers oversell their jobs in recruiting advertisements, making them appear better than they really are. The purpose of a **realistic job preview** (RJP) is to inform job candidates of the "organizational realities" of a job so that they can more accurately evaluate their own job expectations. By presenting applicants with a clear picture of the job, the organization hopes to reduce unrealistic expectations and thereby reduce employee disenchantment and ultimately employee dissatisfaction and turnover. A review of research on RJPs found that they do tend to result in applicants having lower job expectations.[8]

***Realistic Job Preview (RJP)**
The process through which an interviewer provides a job applicant with an accurate picture of a job.

A recent court case is of interest here. A federal appeals court heard and upheld an argument that a woman who was fraudulently lured into her job had had her career derailed by the employer. The employee (a lawyer) claimed she left the environmental law department of one law firm to head the start-up environmental law department of another firm, but that department never materialized. This and similar rulings should serve as warnings to employers not to exaggerate opportunities.

Computer and Electronic Interviews A number of firms are using computerized and other electronic interviewing techniques to conduct the initial screen-

❖ FIGURE 9–6 ❖
SAMPLE APPLICATION FORM

Today's Date ____________

APPLICATION FOR EMPLOYMENT
An Equal Opportunity Employer*

Personal Information **Please Print or Type**

Name (Last) (First) (Full Middle Name)				Social Security Number
Current Address	City	State	Zip Code	Phone Number ( )
What position are you applying for?		Date Available for employment?		
Are you willing to relocate ☐ Yes ☐ No	Are you willing to if required? ☐ Yes ☐ No	Any restrictions on hours, weekends, or overtime? If yes, explain.		
Have you ever been employed by this Company or any of its subsidiaries before? ☐ Yes ☐ No	Indicate Locations and Dates			
Can you, after employment, submit verification of your legal right to work in the United States ☐ Yes ☐ No	Have you ever been convicted of a felony? ☐ Yes ☐ No	Convictions will not automatically disqualify job candidates. The seriousness of the crime and date of conviction will be considered.		

Performance of Job Functions

Are you able to perform all the functions of the job for which you are applying with or without accommodation?

☐ Yes, without accommodation ☐ Yes, with accommodation ☐ No

If you indicated you can perform all the functions with an accommodation, please explain how you would perform the tasks and with what accommodation.

Education

School Level	School Name & Address	No. of Years Attended	Did You Graduate?	Course of Study
High School				
Vo-Tech, Business or Trade School				
College				
Graduate School				

Personal Driving Record

This section is to be completed ONLY if the operation of a motor vehicle will be required in the course of the applicant's Employment

How long have you been a licensed driver?	Driver's license number	Expiration date	Issuing state
List any other state(s) in which you have had a driver's license(s) in the past:			
Within the past five years have you had a vehicle accident? ☐ Yes ☐ No	Been convicted of reckless or drunken driving? ☐ Yes ☐ No	If yes, give dates:	Been cited for moving violations? ☐ Yes ☐ No If yes, give dates:
Has your driver's license ever been revoked or suspended? ☐ Yes ☐ No	If yes, explain:	Is your driver's license restricted? ☐ Yes ☐ No	If yes, explain:

*We are an Equal Opportunity Employer. We do not discriminate on the basis of race, religion, color, gender, age, national origin or disability.

ing interview.[9] One example comes from a major hotel chain, where applicants for hotel front-desk jobs view a videotape of certain customer-service situations and then indicate how they believe each situation should be handled. Based on those responses, the applicants are evaluated to determine if they are acceptable candidates for employment.

Great Western Bank in Chatsworth, California, uses a computerized customer-service scenario to test potential tellers. Those who pass the computerized part of the test then go to a manager for an interview. The computer at Great Western can also be used to give a realistic job preview, test applicants on change-making skills, and record applicants' verbal responses to simulated angry customers.

Managers like the approach because it weeds out unqualified people without taking up their time. However, being interviewed by a computer strikes some job hunters as even more depersonalizing than a regular job interview.[10]

❖ Application Forms

Application forms are widely used. Properly prepared, like the one in Figure 9–6, the application form serves four purposes:

- It is a record of the applicant's desire to obtain a position.
- It provides the interviewer with a profile of the applicant that can be used in the interview.
- It is a basic employee record for applicants who are hired.
- It can be used for research on the effectiveness of the selection process.

Many employers use only one application form, but others need several. For example, a hospital might need one form for nurses and medical technicians, another for clerical and office employees, another for managers and supervisors, and another for support persons in housekeeping and food-service areas.

The information received on application forms may not always be completely accurate. This problem is discussed in greater detail later, but an important point must be made here. In an attempt to prevent inaccuracies, many application forms carry a statement that the applicant is required to sign. In effect, the statement reads: "I realize that falsification of this record is grounds for dismissal if I am hired." The statement has been used by employers to terminate people. In fact, in a recent court case, the court held that when a company can show it would not have hired an applicant if it had known the applicant lied on the application form, the employee's claim of discriminatory discharge will not stand.[11]

Application forms traditionally have asked for references and requested that the applicant give permission to contact them. Rather than asking for personal or general references, though, it may be more useful to request the names of previous supervisors on the application form.

❖ EEO Considerations and Application Forms

Although application forms may not usually be thought of as "tests," the Uniform Guidelines of the EEOC and court decisions define them as employment tests. Consequently, the data requested on application forms must be job related. Illegal questions typically found on application forms ask for the following:

- Marital status
- Height/weight
- Number and ages of dependents
- Information on spouse
- Date of high school graduation
- Contact in case of emergency

The reason for concern about such questions is that they can have an adverse impact on some protected groups. For example, the question about dependents can be used to identify women with small children. These women may not be hired because of a manager's perception that they will not be as dependable as those without small children. The high school graduation date gives a close identification of a person's age, which can be used to discriminate against individuals over 40. Or, the question about emergency contact might reveal marital status or other personal information that is inappropriate to ask.

One interesting point to remember is that many employers must collect data on the race and sex of those who apply to fulfill requirements for reporting to the EEOC, but the application blank cannot contain these items. As discussed in Chapter 6, the solution picked by a growing number of employers is to have applicants provide EEOC reporting data on a separate form. It is important that this form be filed separately and not used in any other HR selection activities or the employers may be accused of using the information inappropriately.

❖ Weighted Application Forms

One way employers can make the application form more job related is by developing a weighted form. A job analysis is used to determine the KSAs needed for the job and an application form is developed to include items related to the selection criteria. Then weights, or numeric values, are placed on possible responses to the items based on their predictive value. The responses of applicants can be scored, totaled, and compared.

One interesting example involved a company that had very high turnover among sewing machine operators. It hired a consultant, who took the applications of 100 successful operators who stayed with the company and 100 operators who left or were fired. He identified 10 variables that differentiated the two groups. Some were unusual; one variable identified was that the better performing sewing machine operators weighed more than 300 pounds and did not own a car, among other factors. Based on this analysis, a weighted application form was developed, but its usefulness could be questioned. To develop a weighted application blank, it is necessary to develop questions that differentiate between satisfactory and poor performing employees and that can be asked legally.[12]

There are several problems associated with weighted application forms. One difficulty is the time and effort required to develop such a form. For many small employers and for jobs that do not require numerous employees, the cost of developing the weights can be prohibitive. Also, the form must be updated every few years to ensure that the factors previously identified are still valid predictors of job success. However, on the positive side, using weighted forms enables an employer to evaluate and compare applicants' responses numerically to a valid, job-related set of inquiries.

❖ Resumes

One of the most common methods applicants use to provide background information is the resume. Resumes, also called *vitae* by some, vary in style and length. Technically, a resume used in place of an application form must be treated by an employer as an application form for EEO purposes. Consequently, even if an applicant furnishes some "illegal information" voluntarily on a resume, the employer should not use that information during the selection process. Because resumes contain only information applicants want to present, some employers require that all who submit resumes complete an application form as well, so sim-

❖ FIGURE 9–7 ❖
EMPLOYMENT ELIGIBILITY VERIFICATION FORM I-9

EMPLOYMENT ELIGIBILITY VERIFICATION (Form I-9)

1 EMPLOYEE INFORMATION AND VERIFICATION: (To be completed and signed by employee.)

Name: (Print or Type) Last	First	Middle	Birth Name
Adress: Street Name and Number	City	State	ZIP Code
Date of Birth (Month/Day/Year)		Social Security Number	

I attest, under penalty of perjury, that I am (check a box):

☐ 1. A citizen or national of the United States.
☐ 2. An alien lawfully admitted for permanent residence (Alien Number A ________________).
☐ 3. An alien authorized by the Immigration and Naturalization Service to work in the United States (Alien Number A ________________).
or Admission Number ________________. expiration of employment authorization, if any ________________).

I attest, under penalty of perjury, the documents that I have presented as evidence of identity and employment eligibility are genuine and relate to me. I am aware that federal law provides for imprisonment and/or fine for any false statements or use of false documents in connection with this certificate.

Signature	Date (Month/Day/Year)

PREPARER/TRANSLATOR CERTIFICATION (To be completed if prepared by person other than the employee). I attest, under penalty of prejury, that the above was prepard by me at the request of the named individual and is based on all information of which I have any knowledge.

Signature	Name (Print or Type)		
Address (Street Name and Number)	City	State	Zip Code

2 EMPLOYER REVIEW AND VERIFICATION: (To be completed and signed by employer.)

Instructions:
Examine one document form List A and check the appropriate box, ***OR*** examine one document from List B ***and*** one from List C and check the appropriate boxes.
Provide the ***Document Identification Number*** and ***Expiration Date*** for the document checked.

List A Documents that Establish Identity and Employment Eligibility	List B Documents that Establish Identity	**and**	List C Documents that Establish Employment Eligibility
☐ 1. United States Passport ☐ 2. Certificate of United States Citizenship ☐ 3. Certificate of Naturalization ☐ 4. Unexpired foreign passport with attached Employment Authorization ☐ 5. Alien Registration with photograph	☐ 1. A State-issued driver's license or a State-issued I.D. card with a photograph, or information, including name, sex, date of birth, height, weight, and color of eyes. (Specify State) ________ ☐ 2. U.S. Military Card ☐ 3. Other (Specify document and issuing authority) ________		☐ 1. Original Social Security Number Card (other than a card stating it is not valid for employement) ☐ 2. A birth certificate issued by State, county, or municipal authority bearing a seal or other certification ☐ 3. Unexpired INS Employment Authorization Specify form # ________
Document Identification #________	***Document Identification*** #________		***Document Identification*** #________
Expiration Date (if any) ________	***Expiration Date (if any)*** ________		***Expiration Date (if any)*** ________

CERTIFICATION: I attest, under penalty of perjury, that I have examined the documents presented by the above individual, that they appear to be genuine and to relate to the individual named, and that the individual, to the best of my knowledge, is elibible to work in the United States.

Signature	Name (Print or Type)	Title
Employer Name	Address	Date

Form I-9 (05/07/87)
OMB No. 1115-0136

U.S. Department of Justice
Immigration and Naturalizaion Service

ilar information will be available on all applicants. Individuals who mail in resumes may be sent thank-you letters and application forms to be completed and returned. Appendix C contains some suggestions on resume preparation.

❖ Immigration Requirements

The Immigration Reform and Control Act (IRCA) of 1986, as revised in 1990, requires that within 72 hours of hiring, an employer must determine whether a job applicant is a U.S. citizen, registered alien, or illegal alien. Those not eligible to work in this country must not be hired. Figure 9–7 on the previous page shows the *I-9 form* that employers must use to identify the status of potential employees. Many employers have applicants complete this form during the application process. Others have individuals submit the documents on the first day of employment. Employers do have a responsibility to make sure that documents submitted by new employees, such as U.S. passports, birth certificates, original Social Security cards, and driver's licenses, "reasonably appear on their face to be genuine."

❖ Selection Testing

According to the Uniform Guidelines of the EEOC, any employment requirement is a "test." The focus in this section is on formal tests. As Figure 9–8 shows, a variety of types of tests are used. Notice that most of them focus on specific job-related aptitudes and skills. Some are paper-and-pencil tests (such as a math test), others are motor-skill tests, and still others use machines (polygraphs, for instance). Some employers purchase prepared tests, whereas others develop their own.

Many people claim that formal tests can be of great benefit in the selection process when properly used and administered. Considerable evidence supports this claim. Because of EEO concerns, many employers reduced or eliminated the use of tests beginning in the early 1970s, fearing that they might be judged discriminatory in some way. However, test usage appears to be increasing again.[13]

❖ Test Validity and Test Usage

Any use of a test must be shown to be valid. As described in Chapter 5, *validity* is the extent to which a test actually measures what it says it measures. A high score on a test supposed to measure "ability to learn" should translate to high performance in training if the test is valid. Validity in psychological testing, in particular, should be calculated if the test is to be used for selection.[14]

Validity *coefficients* measure the strength of the relationship between the test and performance. While the coefficient can theoretically range from zero to 1, coefficients of .3 and above are considered good. A coefficient above .5 identifies a highly useful predictor. The results from one study regarding validity coefficients found the following for common predictors.[15]

Method	Validity Coefficient	Method	Validity Coefficient
Ability testing	.53	Experience	.18
Skill testing	.44	Interview	.14
Reference checks	.26	Education	.10
Class rank or grade point average	.21	Interest measures	.10

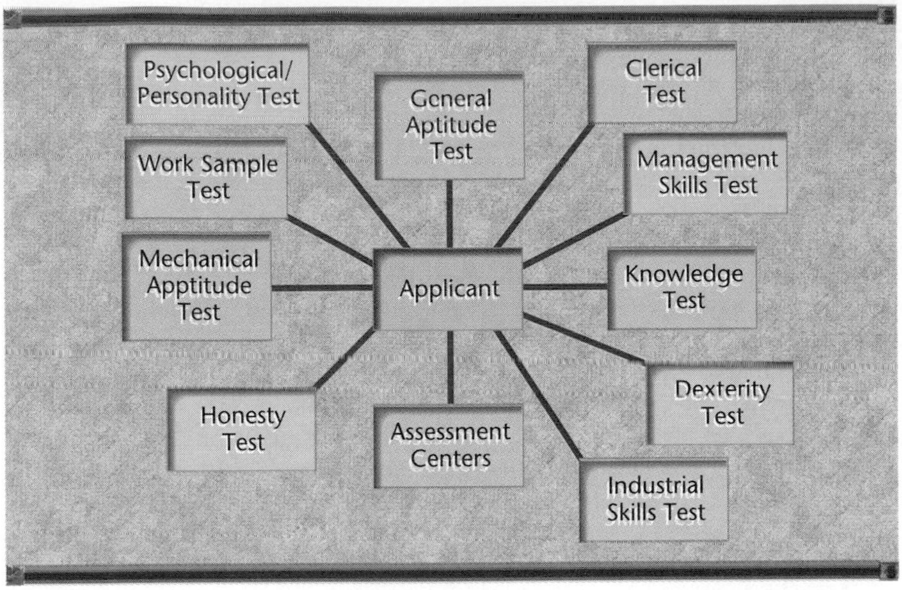

❖ **FIGURE 9–8** ❖
POSSIBLE TESTS USED FOR SELECTION

Interpreting test results is not always straightforward, even if the test is valid. Individuals trained in testing and test interpretation should be involved in establishing and maintaining a testing system. Furthermore, the role of tests in the overall selection process must be kept in perspective: tests represent only one possible data source.[16] Finally, a California court case raises issues relative to testing and privacy that are as yet unresolved. The court found that a psychological test violated the right to privacy afforded all California citizens. Other states with similar guarantees to privacy include Alaska, Arizona, Florida, Hawaii, Illinois, Louisiana, Montana, South Carolina, and Washington.[17]

❖ ABILITY AND APTITUDE TESTS

Ability tests assess the skills that individuals have already learned. **Aptitude tests** measure general ability to learn or acquire a skill. The typing tests given at many firms to secretarial applicants are commonly used ability tests. Other widely used tests measure mechanical ability and manual dexterity.

A type of ability test used at many organizations simulates job tasks. These **work sample tests**, which require an applicant to perform a simulated job task that is part of the job being applied for, are especially useful. Having an applicant for a financial analyst's job prepare a computer spreadsheet is one such test. Requiring a person applying for a truck driver's job to back a truck to a loading dock is another. An "in basket" test is a work sample test in which a job candidate is asked to respond to memos in a hypothetical "in-basket" that are typical of the problems faced by people who hold that job. The key for any work sample test is the behavioral consistency between the criteria in the job and the requirements of the test.

Mental ability tests measure reasoning capabilities. Some of the abilities tested include spatial orientation, comprehension and retention span, and general and conceptual reasoning. The General Aptitude Test Battery (GATB) is a widely used test of this type.

❖ **Ability Tests**
Tests that assess learned skills.

❖ **Aptitude Tests**
Tests that measure general ability to learn or acquire a skill.

❖ **Work Sample Tests**
Tests that require an applicant to perform a simulated job task.

❖ **Mental Ability Tests**
Tests that measure reasoning capabilities.

❖ Assessment Centers

An assessment center is not necessarily a place but is a selection and development device composed of a series of evaluative exercises and tests. The assessment uses multiple exercises and multiple raters. In one assessment center, candidates go through a comprehensive interview, pencil-and paper test, individual and group simulations, and work exercises. The candidates' performances are then evaluated by a panel of trained raters. It is crucial to any assessment center that the tests and exercises reflect the job content and types of problems faced on the jobs for which individuals are being screened.[18]

A number of state and local governments use assessment centers when selecting department or division heads, because they are interested in extensive job-related testing for skills difficult to evaluate from prior work experience. One major city has used the assessment center to select its director of public works, fire chief, city engineer, and employee relations administrator. Assessment centers are especially useful in determining promotable employees and in helping to develop them.

❖ Psychological/Personality Tests

Personality is a unique blend of individual characteristics that affect interaction with the environment and help define a person. Historically, predictive validities have tended to be lower for personality tests used as predictors of performance on the job. However, some studies have shown that carefully chosen personality tests that logically connect to work requirements can help predict the interpersonal aspects of job success. For example, a person's ability to tolerate stress might be a valid concern for a police officer, emotional stability for a nuclear plant operator, and a "people" orientation for a social worker.

Personality profiles must be evaluated by a qualified psychologist. Commonly used profiles are the Thematic Apperception Test and the California Psychological Inventory. Some firms administer standardized psychological profile tests and send them to an industrial psychology company; the company sends back profiles of the strengths and weaknesses of the persons tested.

Such tests are not always valid, because some people who might be poor employees simply take tests well.[19] The Los Angeles police force uses psychological testing to weed out rogue cops, but some argue that this approach does not work and that the Mark Fuhrman and Rodney King situations were examples. One problem is that developing an accurate psychological profile of the "good cop" is difficult because of disagreement as to what makes a "good cop."[20]

❖ Polygraph and Honesty Testing

Several types of tests have been devised to assess honesty. These include polygraph tests and paper-and-pencil honesty tests. Both are controversial.

Polygraphs and the Employee Polygraph Protection Act The polygraph, more generally and incorrectly referred to as the "lie detector," is a mechanical device that measures a person's galvanic skin response, heart rate, and breathing rate. The theory behind the polygraph is that if a person answers incorrectly, the body's physiological responses will "reveal" the falsification through the polygraph's recording mechanisms.

Before 1989, thousands of employers used polygraph results to screen potential employees. The biggest users were in service industries such as retail, fast food, and health care. The purpose of polygraph use was to reduce employee theft. Individuals whose answers revealed a potential pattern of dishonesty were eliminated from employment consideration. However, serious questions were raised about polygraph use in employment settings, especially about its reliability and the invasion of the privacy of those tested.

As a result of those concerns, Congress passed the Employee Polygraph Protection Act of 1988. Effective in 1989, the act bars polygraph use for preemployment screening purposes by most employers. However, federal, state, and local government agencies are exempt from the act. Also exempted are certain private-sector employers such as security companies and pharmaceutical companies. The act does allow employers to continue to use polygraphs as part of internal investigations of theft or losses. But the polygraph test must be administered voluntarily, and the employee can end the test at any time.

HONESTY TESTS The Reid Report and the Stanton Survey are two widely used pencil-and-paper tests that purport to measure employee honesty. Individuals who take honesty tests answer "yes" or "no" to a list of questions. Sample questions include:

- Would you tell your boss if you knew another employee was stealing from the company?
- Is it all right to borrow company equipment to use at home if the property is always returned?
- Have you ever told a lie?
- Have you ever wished you were physically more attractive?

Firms use honesty tests to help reduce losses due to employee theft. With preemployment polygraph testing no longer allowed, a growing number of firms have turned to such tests. These firms believe that giving honesty tests not only helps them to screen out potentially dishonest individuals but also sends a message to applicants and employees alike that dishonesty will not be tolerated.

Concerns about the validity of honesty tests continue to be raised. Many firms using them do not do validation studies on their experiences. Instead, they rely on the general validation results given by the test developers, even though that practice is not consistent with the EEOC's Uniform Guidelines. A review of research on the validity of honesty tests by independent researchers found that honesty tests are valid as broad screening devices for organizations but may not be as good at predicting whether a single individual will steal.[21] Also, the use of these tests can have a negative public-relations impact on applicants. A final concern is that the types of questions asked may constitute invasion of individual privacy.

Using tests that may not measure what they purport to measure raises not only legal questions but ethical ones as well, such as the issue addressed in the HR Perspective on graphology and blood type.

❖ SELECTION INTERVIEWING

A **selection interview** is designed to assess job-related knowledge, skills, and abilities (KSAs) and clarify information from other sources. This in-depth interview is designed to integrate all the information from application forms, tests, and reference checks so that a selection decision can be made. Because of the integration required and the desirability of face-to-face contact, the interview is the most important phase of the selection process in many situations. Conflicting information may have emerged from tests, application forms, and references. As a result, the interviewer must obtain as much pertinent information about the

***Selection Interview**
Interview designed to assess job-related knowledge, skills, and abilities (KSAs) and clarify information from other sources.

HR PERSPECTIVE

Ethical Issues in Using Graphology, Psychics, and Blood Type for Employee Selection

Some *very* questionable tests are used in employee selection. For instance, graphology, psychics, and blood types all have been used by various employers.

Graphology. Graphology is a type of "test" in which an "analysis" is made of an individual's handwriting. Such characteristics as how people dot an "i" or cross a "t", whether they write with a left or right slant, and the size and boldness of the letters they form supposedly tell graphologists about the individuals' personalities and their suitability for employment. The cost of an analysis ranges from $175 to $500 and includes an examination of about 300 personality traits. Formal scientific evaluations of graphology are not easily found and its value as a personality predictor is very questionable. But it is popular in France.

Psychics. Similarly, some firms use psychics to help select managerial talent. The psychics are supposedly able to determine if a person is suited for a job both intellectually and emotionally. However, most businesses would not want anyone to know if they used "psychic advisers."

Blood Type. If using psychics in selection seems outlandish, how about blood type as a predictor of personality? In Japan, many people think blood type is an excellent predictor. Type O blood supposedly indicates a person who is generous and bold; type A, one who is industrious; type B, one who is impulsive and flexible; and Type AB, one who is both rational and creative. A manager at Mitsubishi Electric chose people with type AB to dream up the next generation of fax machines. One nursery school divides children based on their blood types.[22]

Given the lack of formal evidence that handwriting, psychics, or blood type are valid as performance predictors, some have wondered if there is an ethical problem in using them in selection. What do you think?

applicant as possible during the limited interview time, evaluate this information against job standards, and make a decision.

The interview is not an especially valid predictor of job performance, but it has high "face validity"—that is, it *seems* valid to employers. Virtually no employers are likely to hire individuals without interviewing them.

Some interviewers may be better than others at selecting individuals who will perform better. Studies have found that there is very high *intra*rater (the same interviewer) reliability but only moderate-to-low *inter*rater (different interviewers) reliability.[23] Reliability is the ability to pick the same qualities again and again in applicants. Interrater reliability becomes important if there are several interviewers, each of whom is selecting employees from a pool of applicants. If interrater reliability is low, the applicants selected will not be uniformly in possession of the desired characteristics. Many factors affect the accuracy of the interview, from stereotypes carried by interviewers to the order in which interviewees are seen. The accuracy of an interview refers to the extent that an interviewer has drawn the correct conclusions about an applicant's potential from the interview. Whether the interview is a valid selection tool depends on whether the interview results are related to the individual's job performance that follows the selection decision. Obviously, accuracy can affect the validity of the interview as a selection tool. The important point to remember is that the validity of the interview depends on the type of interview used and the capabilities of the individual interviewers.

❖ EEO Considerations and Interviewing

The interview, like a pencil-and-paper test and an application form, is a type of predictor and must meet the standards of job-relatedness and nondiscrimination. Some court decisions and EEOC rulings have attacked the interviewing practices of some organizations as discriminatory.

An interviewer making a hiring recommendation must be able to identify the factors that shaped the decision. If that decision is challenged, the organization must be able to show justification. Everything written or said can be probed for evidence in a lawsuit. Lawyers recommend the following to minimize EEO concerns with interviewing:

- Identify objective criteria related to the job to be looked for in the interview.
- Put criteria in writing.
- Provide multiple levels of review for difficult or controversial decisions.
- Use structured interviews, with the same questions asked of all those interviewed.

Types of Interviews

There are six types of selection interviews: structured, situational, behavioral description, nondirective, stress, and panel interviews. Each type is discussed below.

Structured Interview
Interview that uses a set of standardized questions asked of all job applicants.

Structured Interview The **structured interview** uses a set of standardized questions that are asked of all applicants. Every applicant is asked the same basic questions so comparisons among applicants can more easily be made. This type of interview allows an interviewer to prepare job-related questions in advance and then complete a standardized interviewee evaluation form. Completion of such a form provides documentation if anyone, including an EEO enforcement body, should question why one applicant was selected over another.[24] Sample questions that might be asked of all applicants for a production maintenance management opening are:

- Tell me how you trained workers for their jobs.
- How do you decide the amount of work you and the maintenance crew will have to do during a day?
- How does the production schedule of the plant affect what a mechanic ought to repair first?
- How do you know what the needs of the plant are at any given time and what mechanics ought to be doing?
- How did you or would you go about planning a preventive maintenance program in the plant?

As is evident, the structured interview is almost like an oral questionnaire and offers greater consistency and accuracy than some other kinds of interviews. The structured interview is especially useful in the initial screening because of the large number of applicants in this step of the selection process. Obviously, it is less flexible than more traditional interview formats, and therefore it may be less appropriate for second or later interviews.

Even though a series of patterned questions are asked, the structured interview does not have to be rigid. The predetermined questions should be asked in a logical manner, but the interviewer can avoid reading the questions word for word down the list. The applicant should be allowed adequate opportunity to explain answers clearly. The interviewer should probe until he or she fully understands the applicant's responses.

Research on interviews consistently has found the structured interview to be more reliable and valid than other approaches.[25] The format for the interview ensures that a given interviewer has similar information on each candidate, so there is higher intrarater reliability. Also, the fact that several interviewers ask the same questions of applicants has led to better interrater reliability.

Situational Interview
A structured interview composed of questions about how applicants might handle specific job situations.

SITUATIONAL INTERVIEW The **situational interview** is a structured interview that is composed of questions about how applicants might handle specific job situations. With experienced applicants, the format is essentially one of a job knowledge or work sample test.

Interview questions are based on job analysis and checked by experts in the job so they will be content valid. There are three types of questions:[26]

1. *Hypothetical*—in which an applicant is asked what he or she might do in a certain job situation
2. *Related to knowledge*—which might entail explaining a method or demonstrating a skill
3. *Related to requirements*—in which areas such as willingness to work the hours required and meet travel demands are explored

Job experts also write "good," "average," and "poor" responses to the questions to facilitate rating the answers of the applicant. The interviewer can code the suitability of the answer, assign point values, and add up the total number of points an interviewee received.

Behavioral Description Interview
Interview in which applicants give specific examples of how they have performed or handled a problem in the past.

BEHAVIORAL DESCRIPTION INTERVIEW In a **behavioral description interview,** applicants are required to give specific examples of how they have performed a certain procedure or handled a problem in the past. For example, applicants might be asked the following:

- How did you handle a situation in which there were no rules or guidelines on employee discipline?
- Why did you choose that approach?
- How did your supervisor react?
- How was the issue finally resolved?

Like other structured methods, behavioral descriptions provide better validity than unstructured interviews.

Nondirective Interview
Interview that uses general questions, from which other questions are developed.

NONDIRECTIVE INTERVIEW The **nondirective interview** uses general questions from which other questions are developed. It should be used mainly in psychological counseling, but it is also used in selection. The interviewer asks general questions designed to prompt the applicant to discuss herself or himself. The interviewer then picks up on an idea in the applicant's response to shape the next question. For example, if the applicant says, "One aspect that I enjoyed in my last job was my supervisor," the interviewer might ask, "What type of supervisor do you most enjoy working with?"

Difficulties with a nondirective interview include keeping it job related and obtaining comparable data on various applicants. Many nondirective interviews are only semiorganized; the result is that a combination of general and specific questions is asked in no set order, and different questions are asked of different applicants for the same job.

Stress Interview
Interview designed to create anxiety and put pressure on an applicant to see how the person responds.

STRESS INTERVIEW The **stress interview** is a special type of interview designed to create anxiety and put pressure on the applicant to see how the person responds. In a stress interview, the interviewer assumes an extremely aggressive and insulting posture. Those who use this approach often justify its use with individuals who will encounter high degrees of stress on the job, such as a consumer-complaint clerk in a department store or an air traffic controller.

The stress interview is a high-risk approach for an employer. The typical applicant is already somewhat anxious in any interview, and the stress interview can easily generate a very poor image of the interviewer and the employer. Consequently, an applicant that the organization wishes to hire might turn down the job offer. Even so, one study found that many interviewers deliberately put college seniors under stress.

PANEL INTERVIEWS Usually, applicants are interviewed by one interviewer at a time. But when an interviewee must see several people, many of the interviews are redundant and therefore unnecessarily time consuming. In a **panel interview**, several interviewers interview the candidate at the same time. All the interviewers hear the same responses. On the negative side, applicants are frequently uncomfortable with the group interview format.[27]

Panel Interview
Interview in which several interviewers interview the candidate at the same time.

❖ INTERVIEWING BASICS

Many people think that the ability to interview is an innate talent, but this contention is difficult to support. Just because someone is personable and likes to talk is no guarantee that the person will be a good interviewer. Interviewing skills are developed through training. Some suggestions for good interviewing follow.

PLANNING THE INTERVIEW Effective interviews do not just happen; they are planned. Pre-interview planning is essential to a well-conducted in-depth selection interview. This planning begins with selecting the time and place for the interview. Sufficient time should be allotted so that neither the interviewer nor the interviewee feels rushed. Also, a private location is important so that both parties can concentrate on the interview content. The interviewer should review the application form for completeness and accuracy before beginning the interview and also should make notes to identify specific areas about which to question the applicant during the interview.

CONTROL OF THE INTERVIEW An important aspect of the interview is control. If the interviewer does not control the interview, the applicant usually will. Control includes knowing in advance what information must be collected, systematically collecting it, and stopping when that information has been collected.

Having control of the interview does not mean doing extensive talking. The interviewer should talk no more than about 25% of the time in an in-depth interview. If the interviewer talks more than that, the interviewer is being interviewed.

LOGGING ON

This site describes some software that employers can purchase to prepare job specifications, develop interviews, and evaluate candidate responses to questions.

http://www.cja-careers.com

❖ QUESTIONING TECHNIQUES

The questioning techniques that an interviewer uses can and do significantly affect the type and quality of the information obtained. Some specific suggestions follow.

GOOD QUESTIONS Many questions an interviewer asks assume that the past is the best predictor of the future, and it usually is. An interviewer is less likely to have difficulty when questioning the applicant's demonstrated past performance than when asking vague questions about the future.

Some types of questions provide more meaningful answers than others. Good interviewing technique depends on the use of open-ended questions directed toward a particular goal. An open-ended question is one that cannot be answered "yes" or "no." *Who, what, when, why, tell me, how,* and *which* are all good ways to begin questions that will produce longer and more informative answers. "What was your attendance record on your last job?" is a better question than, "Did you have good attendance on your last job?" because the latter question can be answered simply, "Yes," which elicits less information.

POOR QUESTIONS Certain kinds of questions should be avoided:

1. *Questions that rarely produce a true answer.* An example is, "How did you get along with your coworkers?" This question is almost inevitably going to be answered, "Just fine."
2. *Leading questions.* A leading question is one in which the answer is obvious from the way in which the question is asked. For example, "You do like to talk to people, don't you?" Answer: "Of course."
3. *Illegal questions.* Questions that involve information such as race, age, gender, national origin, marital status, and number of children are illegal. They are just as inappropriate in the interview as they are on the application form.
4. *Obvious questions.* An obvious question is one for which the interviewer already has the answer and the applicant knows it. Questions already answered on the application blank should be probed, not asked again. If an interviewer asks, "What high school did you attend?" the applicant is likely to answer, "As I wrote on my application form, South High School in Caveton." Instead, questions should be asked that probe the information given:"What were your favorite subjects at South High, and why?"
5. *Questions that are not job related.* All questions asked should be directly related to the job for which the interviewee has applied. Some people believe discussions about the weather, sports, or politics help a candidate relax and become at ease. However, those questions consume interview time that could be more appropriately used in other ways. Also, many times, the interviewee does not relax, and the interviewer may not listen to the responses because he or she is using the "chit-chat" time to review the candidate's application form or to otherwise make up for a lack of planning and preparation.

There are certain question areas that an interviewer probably should minimize. These areas can be referred to as "egad" factors and involve the applicant's *expectations, goals, aspirations,* and *desires.* Although the answer to an "egad" question may be meaningful, usually the applicant responds with a prepared "pat" answer. For example, in answer to the question, "What are your aspirations?" the college graduate will often respond that he or she wants to become a company vice-president. The person settles for vice-president instead of president in order not to appear egotistical. Because it is considered culturally desirable in our society to demonstrate a certain amount of ambition, the vice-presidential level appears to be appropriate.

LISTENING RESPONSES The good interviewer avoids *listening responses* such as nodding, pausing, making casual remarks, echoing, and mirroring. A friendly but neutral demeanor is appropriate. Listening responses are an essential part of everyday, normal conversation, but they may unintentionally provide feedback to the applicant. Applicants may try to please the interviewer and look to the interviewer's listening response for cues. Even though the listening responses may be subtle, they do provide information to applicants.

❖ PROBLEMS IN THE INTERVIEW

Operating managers and supervisors most often use poor interviewing techniques because they do not interview often or have not been trained to interview. Some common problems encountered in the interview are highlighted next.

SNAP JUDGMENTS Ideally, the interviewer should collect all the information possible on an applicant before making a judgment. Reserving judgment is much easier to recommend than to do because it is difficult not to form an early impression. Too often, interviewers form an early impression and spend the balance of the interview looking for evidence to support it. This impression may be based on a review of an individual's application blank or on more subjective factors such as dress or appearance. Consequently, many interviewers make a decision on the job suitability of applicants within the first four or five minutes of the interview.

NEGATIVE EMPHASIS As might be expected, unfavorable information about an applicant is the biggest factor considered in interviewers' decisions about overall suitability. Unfavorable information is given roughly twice the weight of favorable information. Often, a single negative characteristic may bar an individual from being accepted, whereas no amount of positive characteristics will guarantee a candidate's acceptance.

HALO EFFECT Interviewers should try to avoid the *halo effect,* which occurs when an interviewer allows a prominent characteristic to overshadow other evidence. The halo effect is present if an interviewer lets a candidate's accomplishments in athletics overshadow other characteristics, which leads the interviewer to hire the applicant because "athletes make good salespeople." *Devil's horns* (a reverse halo effect), such as inappropriate dress or a low grade point average, may affect an interviewer as well.

BIASES Interviewers must be able to recognize their personal biases. For example, studies on the interview process indicate that women are rated lower by both female and male interviewers.[28] Other studies have found that interviewers tend to favor or select people whom they perceive to be similar to themselves. This similarity can be in age, race, sex, previous work experiences, personal background, or other factors. As workforce demographics shift and become more diverse, interviewers will have to be even more aware of this "similarity bias."

The selection of an applicant who falls below standards or the rejection of an applicant who meets standards is an indication that personal bias may have influenced a selection decision. An interviewer should be honest and consider the reasons for selecting a particular applicant. The solution to the problem of bias lies not in claiming that a person has no biases but in demonstrating that they can be controlled.

CULTURAL NOISE The interviewer must learn to recognize and handle *cultural noise*—responses the applicant believes are socially acceptable rather than factual responses. Applicants want jobs; to be hired, they know they must impress the interviewer. They may feel that if they divulge any unacceptable facts about themselves, they will not get the job. Consequently, they may try to give the interviewer responses that are socially acceptable but not very revealing.

An interviewer can handle cultural noise by not encouraging it. If the interviewer supports cultural noise, the applicant will take the cue and continue those kinds of answers. Instead, the applicant can be made aware that the interviewer is not being taken in. An interviewer can say, "The fact that you are the best pitcher on your softball team is interesting, but tell me about your performance on your last job."

❖ WHAT INTERVIEWERS EVALUATE

Overall, interviewers look for evidence that an applicant is well rounded, competent, and successful. The factors most often considered are presented in Figure 9–9.

❖ FIGURE 9–9 ❖
FACTORS INTERVIEWERS CONSIDER IN THE INTERVIEW

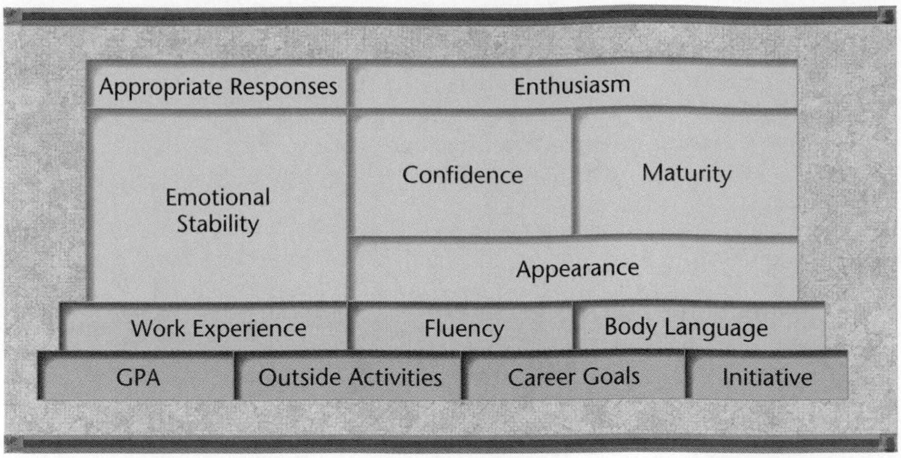

These variables do not include all possible criteria that may be taken into account; a wide variety of other variables may be considered, depending on the job and the interviewer.

❖ BACKGROUND INVESTIGATION

Background investigation may take place either before or after the in-depth interview. It costs the organization some time and money, but it is generally well worth the effort. Unfortunately, applicants frequently misrepresent their qualifications and backgrounds.

Many universities report that inquiries on graduates and former students often reveal that the individuals never graduated. Some did not even attend the university. Another type of credential fraud uses the mail-order "degree mill." To enhance their chances of employment, individuals purchase unaccredited degrees from organizations that grant them for a fee—as one advertisement puts it, "with no exams, no studying, no classes."

It is estimated that many resumes contain at least one lie or "factual misstatement" (see Figure 9–10). The only way for employers to protect themselves from resume fraud and false credentials is to request verification or proof from applicants either before or after hire. If hired, the employee can be terminated for falsifying employment information. It is unwise for employers to assume that "someone else has already checked." Too often, no one took the trouble.

❖ TYPES OF REFERENCES

Background references can be obtained from several sources. Some of the following references may be more useful and relevant than others, depending on the jobs for which applicants are being considered:

- ❖ Academic references
- ❖ Prior work references
- ❖ Financial references
- ❖ Law enforcement records
- ❖ Personal references

Personal references, such as references from relatives, clergy, or family friends, often are of little value; they probably should not even be required. No applicant will ask somebody to write a recommendation who is going to give a negative

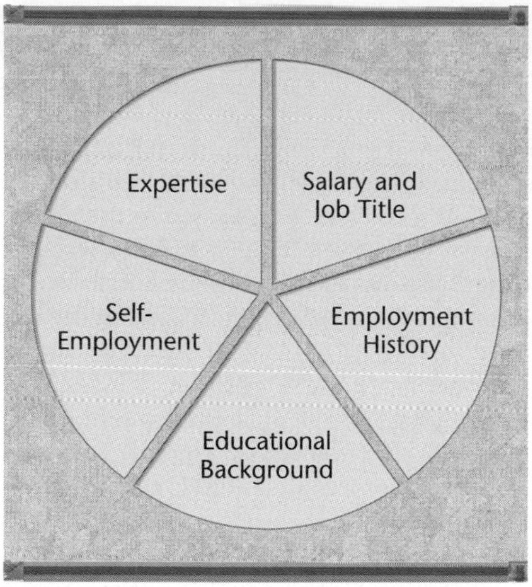

❖ FIGURE 9–10 ❖
COMMON MISREPRESENTATIONS ON RESUMES AND APPLICATIONS

response. Instead, greater reliance should be placed on work-related references from previous employers and supervisors.

❖ LEGAL CONSTRAINTS ON BACKGROUND INVESTIGATIONS

Various federal and state laws have been passed to protect the rights of individuals whose backgrounds may be investigated during preemployment screening. States vary in what they allow employers to investigate. For example, in some states, employers can request information from law enforcement agencies on any applicant. In some states, they are prohibited from getting certain credit information. Several states have passed laws providing legal immunity for employers who provide information on an employee to another employer.[29] Some legal issues are discussed next.

THE PRIVACY ACT OF 1974 Of the laws passed to protect the privacy of personal information, the most important is the Federal Privacy Act of 1974, which applies primarily to government agencies and units. However, bills to extend the provisions of the Privacy Act to private-sector employers have been introduced in Congress at various times. Under the 1974 act, a government entity must have a signed written release from a person before it can give information about that person to someone else.

RISKS OF GIVING REFERENCES ON FORMER EMPLOYEES In a number of court cases, individuals have sued their former employers for slander, libel, or defamation of character as a result of what the employers said to other potential employers that prevented the individuals from obtaining jobs. Two examples illustrate why employers should be careful when giving reference information:

- An executive at one firm remarked that a former employee was a "sociopath." The former employee sued and won $1.9 million in a judgment against the employer and the executive.
- Over $500,000 was paid by both Pan Am World Airways and Equitable Life to settle lawsuits on references given on former employees.

Because of such problems, lawyers advise organizations who are asked about former employees to give out only name, employment date, and title; and many organizations have adopted policies restricting the release of reference information.

LOGGING ON

An example of a firm that conducts background checks for employers can be found at

http://www.emc-corp.com/

Risks of Negligent Hiring The costs of a failure to check references may be high. A number of organizations have found themselves targets of lawsuits that charge them with negligence in hiring workers who committed violent acts on the job. Lawyers say that an employer's liability hinges on how well it investigates an applicant's fitness. Prior convictions and frequent moves or gaps in employment should be cues for further inquiry. Details on the application form provided by the applicant should be investigated to the greatest extent possible, so the employer can show that due diligence was exercised. Also, applicants should be asked to sign releases authorizing the employer to check references, and those releases should contain a statement releasing the reference givers from any future liability actions.

Clearly, employers are in a difficult position. Because of threats of lawsuit, they must obtain information on potential employees but are unwilling to give out information in return. However, many employers hope that changes may eventually result in a reversal of this situation. One attorney speculates that "we are not too far away from the day when the courts will say that Employer A has the duty to divulge negative information to Employer B on the basis of need to know"—the idea of "negligent referral" may be on the horizon.[30]

❖ Reference-Checking Methods

Several methods of obtaining reference information are available to an employer. Telephoning a reference is the most-used method, but many firms prefer written responses.

Telephone Reference Checking Many experts recommend using a structured telephone reference-check form. Typically, such forms focus on factual verification of information given by the applicant, such as employment dates, salary history, type of job responsibilities, and attendance record. Other questions often include reasons for leaving the previous job, the individual's manner of working with supervisors and other employees, and other less factual information. Naturally, many firms will provide only factual information. But the use of the form can provide evidence that a diligent effort was made.

Written Methods of Reference Checking Some organizations send preprinted reference forms to individuals who are giving references for applicants. These forms often contain a release statement signed by the applicant, so that those giving references can see that they have been released from liability on the information they furnish. Specific or general letters of reference also are requested by some employers or provided by applicants.

❖ Medical Examinations

The Americans with Disabilities Act (ADA) prohibits a company from rejecting an individual because of a disability and from asking job applicants any question relative to current or past medical history until a conditional job offer is made. Figure 9–11 shows proper and improper questions about disabilities. It also prohibits the use of preemployment medical exams except for drug tests until a job has been conditionally offered.

Drug Testing Drug testing may be a part of a medical exam, or it may be done separately. Using drug testing as a part of the selection process has increased in the past few years, not without controversy. Employers should remember that such tests are not infallible. The accuracy of drug tests varies according to the type of test used, the item tested, and the quality of the laboratory where the test samples are sent. If an individual tests positive for drug use, then a second, more detailed analysis should be administered by an independent medical laboratory. Because of the potential impact of prescription drugs on test results, applicants should complete a detailed questionnaire on this matter before the testing. Whether urine, blood, or hair samples are used, the process of obtaining, labeling, and transferring the samples to the testing lab should be outlined clearly and definite policies and procedures established.

Drug testing also has legal implications. In a number of cases, courts have ruled that individuals with previous substance-abuse problems who have received rehabilitation are disabled and thus covered by the Americans with Disabilities Act. Also, preemployment drug testing must be administered in a nondiscriminatory manner, not used selectively with certain groups. The results of drug tests also must be used consistently, so that all individuals testing positive are treated uniformly. An applicant for a production-worker position who tests positive should be rejected for employment, just as an applicant to be vice-president of marketing would be.

Challenges to drug testing are less likely to succeed in the private sector than in the government sector. The Fourth Amendment (relating to search and seizure) fails as an argument by employees because the government is not involved.[31]

❖ FIGURE 9–11 ❖
QUESTIONING AN APPLICANT ABOUT DISABILITIES

DO NOT ASK:	DO ASK:
❖ Do you have any physical or other limitations? ❖ Do you have any disabilities? ❖ Have you ever filed for or collected workers' compensation? ❖ How many times were you absent due to illness in the past two years? ❖ Have you been treated for any of the following medical conditions? ❖ Do you have any family members with health problems or history of illness or disabilities? ❖ Why are you using crutches, and how did you become injured?	❖ Have you ever consulted a psychiatrist or psychologist? ❖ Can you perform the essential functions of the job for which you are applying with or without accommodation? Please describe any accommodations needed. ❖ How would you perform the essential tasks of the job for which you have applied? ❖ If hired, how would you perform the tasks outlined in the job description that you have reviewed? ❖ Describe your attendance record on your last job. ❖ Describe any problems you would have reaching the top of a six-foot filing cabinet. Lifting 50-pound boxes up to 25% of the time. Climbing 20-foot ladders up to 50% of the workday. ❖ What did your prior job duties consist of, and which ones were the most challenging?

GENETIC TESTING Another controversial area of medical testing is genetic testing. One survey of large companies revealed that a few firms were using genetic tests and many more were considering their use in the future. However, the general public disapproves strongly of their use.

Employers that use genetic screening tests do so for several reasons. First, the tests may link workplace health hazards and individuals with certain genetic characteristics. Second, genetic testing may be used to make workers aware of genetic problems that could occur in certain work situations. The third use is the most controversial: to exclude individuals from certain jobs if they have genetic conditions that increase their health risks. Because people cannot change their genetic makeup, the potential for discrimination based, for example, on race or sex is very real. For instance, sickle-cell anemia is a condition found primarily in African Americans. If chemicals in a particular work environment can cause health problems for individuals with sickle-cell anemia, African Americans might be screened out on that basis. The question is whether that decision should be made by the individual or the employer.

SUMMARY

❖ Selection is a process that matches individuals and their qualifications to jobs in an organization.

❖ Because of government regulations and the need for better coordination between the HR unit and other mangers, many organizations have established a centralized employment office as part of the HR department.

❖ The selection process—from reception, through initial screening, application, testing, interview, and background investigation, to physical examination—must be handled by trained, knowledgeable individuals.

❖ Application forms must meet EEO guidelines and ask only for job-related information.

❖ All tests used in the selection process must be valid and employers should use valid predictors to identify candidates who can meet important job criteria.

❖ Selection tests include:ability and aptitude tests, assessment centers, and general psychological/personality tests. Also, selection tests should relate directly to the jobs for which individuals apply.

❖ Controversial tests used to select employees include polygraph examinations and honesty tests, among others.

❖ From the standpoints of effectiveness and EEO compliance, the most useful interviews are structured, situational, behavioral description, and panels although nondirective and stress interviews are also used.

❖ Sound interviewing requires planning and control. Applicants should be provided a realistic picture of the jobs for which they are applying. Good questioning techniques can reduce interviewing problems.

❖ Background investigations can be conducted in a variety of areas, but concerns about individual privacy must be addressed.

❖ Care must be taken when either getting or giving reference information to avoid the potential legal problems of defamation, libel, slander, and negligent hiring.

❖ Medical examinations may be an appropriate part of the selection process for some employers, but only after a conditional job offer has been made.

❖ Drug testing has grown in use as a preemployment screening device, in spite of some problems and concerns associated with its accuracy and potential for discrimination on the part of employers.

REVIEW AND DISCUSSION QUESTIONS

1. Why do many employers have a specialized employment office?
2. You are starting a new manufacturing company. What phases will you go through to select your employees?
3. Agree or disagree with the following statement: "A good application form is fundamental to an effective selection process." Explain your conclusion.
4. Discuss the following statement:"We stopped giving tests altogether and rely exclusively on the interview for hiring."
5. Make two lists. On one list, indicate what information you would want to obtain from the screening interview; on the other, indicate what information you would want to obtain from the in-depth interview.
6. Develop a structured interview guide for a 20-minute interview with a retail sales clerk applicant.
7. How would you go about investigating a new college graduate's background? Why would this information be useful in making a selection decision?
8. Discuss how the Americans with Disabilities Act (ADA) has modified the use of medical exams in the selection process.

Terms to Know

ability tests **259**
aptitude tests **259**
behavioral description interview **264**
mental ability tests **259**
nondirective interview **264**
panel interview **265**
predictors **249**
realistic job preview (RJP) **253**
selection **247**
selection criteria **249**
selection interview **261**
situational interview **264**
stress interview **264**
structured interview **263**
testers **249**
work sample tests **259**

CASE

SELECTING MANUFACTURING EMPLOYEES

The manufacturing plant of tomorrow sits on a pot-hole-filled street across from a chicken-processing plant in Arkadelphia, Arkansas. It does not look like a plant—more like an insurance building: sleek, one-story, cleaner than most people's houses. Carrier Corporation makes compressors for air conditioners with its workforce of 150 in the Arkadelphia plant.

What really differentiates this plant from yesterday's plants is its employees. If someone wants a job here, the individual goes through a six-week course before even being considered for employment. The selection process weeds out 15 of every 16 applicants and provides Carrier Corporation with a top-quality workforce. High school graduates take a state test for job applicants first. Only one-third advance to the next step. References are closely checked, and then the applicants are interviewed both by managers *and* by the assembly-line workers with whom they will work. Those who have satisfactory interviews take a six-week course. It meets five nights a week for three hours, with some extra Saturdays. They learn to read blueprints, do math (including metric calculations and statistical process control), use a computer, and engage in problem solving with others. At this point, the applicants have not been hired (or paid) and have no assurance they will be.

Does it work? The compressors produced at the Arkadelphia plant are less expensive and of higher quality than those produced by others in the industry. Carrier executives believe the plant will serve as a model for the future—small, flexible, and staffed with better-educated, better-motivated employees. The president of the compressor division says, "My goal is to sell compressors from Arkansas to Japan."

But this approach does not work everywhere or all the time. Lincoln Electric has had more than 20,000 job applicants in the last 18 months, and most were rejected—yet it has empty positions that it *needs to fill*. A shortage of skilled labor around the country has created a paradox: thousands turned down for factory work by companies who *really need* employees.

Very few of those who applied at Lincoln could do trigonometry (even at the high school level) or read technical drawings. Those skills were needed for even entry-level work. A strong rebound in manufacturing has absorbed the pool of skilled workers. Companies say that those still looking for work are older, high-wage workers who do not have the technological or teamwork skills needed in factories, or who are unwilling to take entry-level jobs.

Some people contend that manufacturers make their labor shortage worse by not paying enough to attract college graduates with technical skills. A bigger problem may be the image of manufacturing. But a college graduate who went to work for Lincoln observed that many of his college classmates were still "working in shoe stores. Everyone thinks and wants to be a manager. But there is no future in that."[32]

❖ *Questions*

1. When using teams to interview applicants, as Carrier Corporation does, what potential problems might exist with the use of invalid predictors and interrater reliability?
2. Explain the selection dilemma at Lincoln Electric using the concepts of criteria and predictors.

❖ Notes

1. Adapted from Stephenie Overman, "Bizarre Questions Aren't the Answer," *HR Magazine,* April 1995, 56.
2. Robert D. Bretz and Timothy A. Judge, "The Role of HR Systems in Job Applicant Decision Processes," *Journal of Management* 20 (1994) 531–551.
3. "How Businesses Search for Qualified Applicants," *Personnel Journal,* Supplement, June 1992,1.
4. Shari Caudron, "Team Staffing Requires New HR Role," *Personnel Journal,* May 1994, 88–94.
5. J. Wymer and Deborah A. Sudbury, "Employment Discrimination 'Testers'—Will Your Hiring Practices 'Pass?'" *Employee Relations Law Journal* 17 (1992), 623.
6. Timothy A. Judge *et al.*, "An Empirical Investigation of the Predictors of Executive Career Success," *Personnel Psychology* 48 (1995), 485–519.
7. R. S. Barrett, "Employee Selection with Performance Priority Survey," *Personnel Psychology* 48 (1995), 653.
8. Cheryl Adkins, "Previous Work Experience and Organizational Socialization," *Academy of Management Journal,* 20 (1995), 842.
9. E. M. Davies, "Wired for Hiring: Microsoft's Slick Recruiting Machine," *Fortune,* February 5, 1996, 123–124.
10. W. M. Bulkeley, "Replaced by Technology: Job Interview," *The Wall Street Journal,* August 22, 1994, B1.
11. R. J. Stevenson, "Application Fraud May Bar Discriminatory Discharge Claim," *Labor and Employment Law Update,* October 1994, 1.
12. S. Oliver, "Slouches Make Better Operators," *Forbes,* August 16, 1993, 104.
13. Charlene M. Solomon, "Testing Is Not at Odds with Diversity Efforts" *Personnel Journal,* March 1993, 100.
14. M. Zeidner and M. Most, eds., *Psychological Testing: An Inside View* (Baltimore: Consulting Psychologists Press, 1992); and T. Maurer *et at.*, "Methodological and Psychometric Issues in Setting Cutoff Scores," *Personnel Psychology* 44 (1991), 235.
15. "Is This Test Valid?" *Personnel Journal,* Supplement, April 1992, 5.
16. K. Murphy and B. Myers, "Modeling the Effects of Bonding in Personnel Selection," *Personnel Psychology* 48 (1995), 61–85.
17. John E. Meyers, "*Soroka v. Dayton Hudson Corp.*—Is the Door Closing on Pre-Employment Testing of Applicants?" *Employee Relations Law Journal* 17 (1992), 645–653.
18. Gary Coulton and Hubert S. Feild, "Using Assessment Centers in Selecting Entry-Level Police Officers," *Public Personnel Management,* June 1995, 223.
19. Julie Bart, "Employee Recruitment Gets Put to the Test," *Denver Post,* January 22, 1996, 1C.
20. Wade Lambert, "Flunking Grade," *The Wall Street Journal,* September 11, 1995, I.
21. H. J. Bernardin and D. K. Cooke, "Validity of an Honest Test in Predicting Theft among Convenience Store Employees," *Academy of Management Journal,* 18 (1993), 1097–1108.
22. C. Deleon, "Firms Look to Psychics When Hiring," *Omaha World Herald,* September 25, 1994, G1; "Handwriting and Business," *Omaha World-Herald,* May 5, 1992, G1; and "Sushi, a Show and a Quick Transfusion," *Business Week,* April 29, 1991, 40.
23. W. S. Dunn *et al.*, "Relative Importance of Personality and General Mental Ability in Manager's Judgments of Applicant's Qualifications," *Journal of Applied Psychology* 80 (1995), 500–509; J. Conway *et al.*, "Meta-Analysis of Interrater and Internal Consistency Reliability of Selection Interviews," *Journal of Applied Psychology* 80(1995), 565–579; M. McDaniel *et al.*, "The Validity of Employment Interviews," *Journal of Applied Psychology* 79 (1994), 599–616.
24. S. Motowidlo and J. Burnett, "Sources of Validity in Structured Employment Interviews," *Organizational Behavior and Human Decision Processes,* March 1995, 239–249.
25. Phillip Lowery, "An Alternative to the Assessment Center?" *Public Personnel Management,* Summer 1994, 201.
26. E. Pulakos and N. Schmitt, "Experience-Based and Situational Interview Questions," *Personnel Psychology* 48 (1995), 289–307.
27. Lisa McDaniel, "Group Assessments Produce Better Hires," *HR Magazine,* May 1995, 72–76.
28. Laura M. Graves and Gary N. Powell, "The Effect of Sex Similarity on Recruiter's Evaluations of Actual Applicants," *Personnel Psychology* 48 (1995), 85–97.
29. Frank Swoboda, "Legislatures Kept Busy Changing Labor Laws in '95," *Denver Post,* March 17, 1996, 3G.
30. P. Perry, "Cut Your Risk When Giving References," *HR Focus,* May 1995, 15–16.
31. M. Harris and L. Heft, "Preemployment Urinalysis Drug Testing," *Human Resource Management Review* 3 (1993), 271–291.
32. Adapted from Raju Narisetti, "Job Paradox," *The Wall Street Journal,* September 8, 1995, 1; and Earle Norton, "Future Factories," *The Wall Street Journal,* January 13, 1993, A1,8.

EXERCISE 5 - Analysis

The material in Section 3 introduces the basic ideas associated with analyzing jobs, defining the duties of those jobs, and picking people to fill them who have the appropriate qualifications.

SME-TEK has hired Mark Tinsley to be an office manager. The job is a combination of two positions (HR manager and recruiter). Mark will spend 80% of his time on the HR manager duties and 20% of his time as a recruiter.

1. Using information from the CD-ROM write a job description for the new office manager's job.
2. In the HRIS, define the new job in the position table window and use the employee positions window to indicate time allocation among duties in the new position.

EXERCISE 5 - Procedure

Before completing the memo's request, you need to access the Position Management module and review the topic "Position Management Overview" in the "What Is Position Management" lesson of the Concepts section. The Checkpoint topic in this lesson is optional.

To fulfill the memo's request, access the "Using Position Managment" lesson of the Position Managment Features & Processes section. Then, review the topics "Defining Positions for a Job" and "Assigning a Position to an Employee."

SME-TEK

MEMO

TO: *HUMAN RESOURCE MANAGEMENT USER*

We've just arranged for Mark Tinsley to take over the new Office Manager job. This job consists of two positions (HR Manager and Recruiter) that need to be defined in the Position Table window.

After creating these two positions in the Position Table window, please use the Employee Positions window to indicate that Mark will spend 80% of his time as an HR manager, and 20% as a recruiter.

Thanks for your help.

Susan Kyle
Manager, Human Resources

EXERCISE 6 - Analysis

The material on recruiting and selection in this section indicated the growing interest in the use of internships. These (typically) summertime experiences have real advantages for both student interns and the companies using them.

SME-TEK has created five intern positions for next summer in sales. The company hopes to find some good candidates for permanent employment when these interns graduate from college.

1. After reviewing the intern position requirements, design a job specification with appropriate KSA's to assist in hiring the right people for the intern jobs.
2. Create a temporary summer intern position in the HRIS in the position table window and budget the five positions into the sales department.

EXERCISE 6 - Procedure

To fulfill the memo's request, access the "Using Position Management" lesson of the Using Position Management Features & Processes section. Then, review the topic "Budgeting for a Temporary Position" The Practice and Checkpoint topics in this lesson are optional.

SME-TEK

MEMO

TO: *HUMAN RESOURCE MANAGEMENT USER*

Our company has five intern positions available for staffing during the summer.

Please create a temporary Summer Intern position in the Position Table window and budget for the five positions in the Sales department.

Thanks,

Susan

SECTION VIDEO CASES

❖ CASE 1
A-1 PIONEER MOVING & STORAGE
Back from Bankruptcy—and Then Some

Douglas Bagley's Salt Lake City, Utah, moving company lost so much ground five years ago that it was forced into bankruptcy. But Bagley reversed its direction quickly. It has been moving forward ever since.

Disagreements with a partner led Bagley, who had founded A-1 Pioneer Moving & Storage decades earlier, to leave it. The two men signed a life-insurance-funded agreement under which Bagley would buy the business in event of the partner's death.

The business piled up debt in following months, and the debt load became heavier when a tractor-trailer carrying $150,000 worth of furniture went up in smoke in the southern California desert. Insurance didn't cover all the loss.

Then the partner died. His widow struggled to run the business until the life insurance proceeds were paid—that took six months—and then Bagley was in the driver's seat.

It was a grim time for him. A family member was in the hospital, and $100,000 of the bills were beyond health plan coverage. And A-1 Pioneer's debt was so heavy that it couldn't meet all its obligations on time.

Bagley took A-1 Pioneer into Chapter 11 bankruptcy protection. The company was out in less than 12 months.

What made that rapid recovery possible? First, Bagley hit the road to assure creditors that they would be paid. Gaining their confidence by outlining plans for his company, he won the freedom to focus on turning it around. Then he hit the road again, to see longtime clients and pledge that A-1 Pioneer would do a good job for them. Although several took their business elsewhere, most did not.

Advertising and hiring salespeople, A-1 Pioneer went after new customers. Government contracts, the business moving and storage market, and long-distance moving were targeted.

Last but not least, Bagley made it a cardinal principle to hire good employees—looking, he says, for people he would be comfortable with in his own home. He set strict standards of service and appearance.

Today he has 37 employees—up from eight in 1989. He also has the revenues to justify the rise in payroll. Sales have increased year by year, from $800,000 in '89 to 1.5 million in '93. They come in equal measure from long-haul moving, local moving, and storage. An 85,000-square-foot company warehouse was filled in August, 1992, for the first time ever, and A-1 Pioneer now has an additional storage site.

1. Describe a program for A-1 to "Find and hire good people."
2. How would you convince the good employees you were trying to recruit to come to work for a company in Chapter 11? Is there an ethical issue here?

(Excerpts reprinted by permission of The Blue Chip Enterprise Initiative©, *Real-World Lessons for America's Small Businesses* pp. 181, 182; copyright 1994 by Connecticut Mutual Life Insurance Company.) ❖

❖ CASE 2
PRESCOTT VALLEY BROADCASTING
Signal Successes

Sanford Cohen and his wife, Terry, has to overcome many challenges in making their dream of owning a radio station come true. Both 28 when they managed to obtain a vacant FM frequency in 1985, the young couple had little capital, no experience in running a business, and only a telephone pole to broadcast from.

The Cohens had settled in the Prescott, Ariz., area, knowing not a soul and building their station, KIHX 106.7 FM Radio, from scratch in Prescott Valley, outside town. They found that no suitable site served by the local power company was available for an antenna tower. And no existing broadcaster would lease them tower space.

As a result, they had a poor signal that limited reception and hurt advertising sales. Working as many as 100 hours a week, the Cohens did some of the announcing and all of the selling, billing, and accounting themselves. But the station lost $2,000 a month. By June, 1986, the Cohens were down to $1,900 out of an original $60,000 in savings. Their Prescott Valley Broadcasting Co., Inc., appeared about to go under.

Instead, it went upward.

The Cohens had leased a site from the state on a 6,160-foot peak that would give a radio signal the range they needed. But running electricity up there would cost more than $100,000, because state law required subterranean wiring. Research led the Cohens to a Scottsdale, Ariz., company that specialized in small, farm-oriented solar power installations. After negotiation, the firm built a photovoltaic power plant on the peak at no initial cost to KIHX and began selling it power.

Not that building the plant was easy. Materials had to be brought up by four-wheel-drive vehicles, and concrete was mixed by hand at the site.

KIHX was now America's only commercial FM station powered by the sun, and it capitalized on that to win the attention of both advertisers and listeners. (It was not the first solar-powered station: The U.S. Energy Department, in an experiment, built a photovoltaic plant in 1980 that a Bryan, Ohio, station has used to power AM operations.)

Things were looking up for the Cohens, and they were able to hire more staff. But life was still hectic. The Cohens were plagued by excessive turnover among advertising salespeople and announcers, colic in a baby daughter, and tough competition.

Then, in January, 1990, they learned that two competing stations had won Federal Communications Commission permission to vastly upgrade the strength of their broadcast signals, to 100,000 watts. KIHX was broadcasting with a weak 3,000 watts, and its solar power system didn't permit a similar upgrade.

The Cohens worked out a deal allowing them to share a local cable company's tower. Without using an attorney, they successfully petitioned the FCC for permission to upgrade to 50,000 watts, and they fought off telephone-company and electric-utility protests that their new operation would interfere with mobile radio systems.

With the upgrade dramatically increasing KIHX's coverage area, there was an equally dramatic increase in ad revenues—most notably, a 22 percent rise in 1992 over '91. And the Cohens can look forward to more of the same. They have bought one of those tough competitors: With a format different than KIHX's, it is on the air under their ownership.

So their dream of owning a radio station has come doubly true.

1. How did the "shoestring" approach to running a radio station affect attracting and retaining employees?

2. How would you structure a recruiting program to hire the right people for the radio stations?

(Excerpts reprinted by permission of The Blue Chip Enterprise Initiative©, *Real-World Lessons for America's Small Businesses* pp. 189, 190; copyright 1994 by Connecticut Mutual Life Insurance Company.) ❖

❖ CASE 3
CAROLINA FINE SNACKS
Finding Help that Wants to Help

"The day David Bruton showed up for work was the day things began to take a dramatic change for the better," says Philip Kosak, a vice president of Carolina Fine Snacks.

Kosak and two fellow Ph.D. food scientists, Craig Bair and Ray Leander, left good jobs at a big company to try entrepreneurship, founding Carolina Fine Snacks in 1982. The Greensboro, N.C., firm, a manufacturer of popcorn, fried cheese curls, fried pork skins, and similar munch food, faced one tough challenge after another. The toughest, Kosak says, was finding reliable workers.

On average, one employee in five would be absent on a given day. Turnover? "With 15 full-time employees, we had over 200 people on the payroll in a little more than a year." Theft was high, productivity low.

Bruton's last job had been with a hotel chain, third shift, cleaning floors. At Carolina Fine Snacks' plant he "immediately began asking what he could do to help, a question we had never heard out of an employee," says Kosak. "He loved the work and was always on time and anxious to start."

His enthusiasm was infectious, and soon there was a new climate in the plant. Other employees worked harder. Some quit.

Invariably, those who quit were replaced by job candidates sent by a local vocational rehabilitation office. Carolina Fine Snacks had hired Bruton there when it took part in an exercise to teach people with disabilities how to handle job interviews. Bruton had a learning disability and was legally blind.

"Within a year over half our staff were persons with disabilities," Kosak says. "The revolving door closed. Turnover and absenteeism dropped to next to nothing. Productivity skyrocketed."

The company raised wages and offered full health benefits and paid vacations to all its employees, who number 20 today.

For three years following its founding, Carolina Fine Snacks had no employees—just Kosak, Bair, and Leander. "We would make a sale and then come back and manufacture the order ourselves," Kosak says.

After volume rose enough to permit hiring, the company ran into a problem comparable in gravity to that of employee quality. Food retailers had begun to charge manufacturers for space on their shelves. In North Carolina the fee was as high as $1,500 per foot. "Even if we had the money, we were unwilling to participate," Kosak says.

Carolina Fine Snacks looked for niche markets. Technology it had developed gave its pork skins a shelf life much longer than competing products'. That provided an edge that landed the firm a government contract. The firm began pursuing international sales, eventually winning approval to sell four products in Japan. It also has two Pacific Rim joint ventures.

When a market developed for nutritionally superior snack foods, the company produced some with lower fat content, higher fiber, less salt, etc. It won contracts with enterprises like Weight Watchers and Amway.

A good reputation won it the opportunity to supply pork skins for George Bush et al. at the 1988 G.O.P. Convention. Subsequent publicity brought the firm to the attention of the vocational rehabilitation office where it found David Bruton.

Today, with annual sales at the $1.2 million level, Carolina Fine Snacks is thriving in an industry where many small firms are collapsing. Says Kosak: "The cream will rise to the top."

1. How did hiring the disabled lead to employees with more motivation and productivity?

2. How does this case illustrate the value of diversity management coupled with Job Descriptions and Specifications?

(Excerpts reprinted by permission of The Blue Chip Enterprise Initiative©, *Real-World Lessons for America's Small Businesses* pp. 24, 25; copyright 1994 by Connecticut Mutual Life Insurance Company.) ❖

SECTION 4

TRAINING AND DEVELOPING HUMAN RESOURCES

CHAPTER 10

ORIENTATION AND TRAINING

After you have read this chapter, you should be able to . . .

- Define *training* and discuss its legal aspects.
- Describe four characteristics of an effective orientation system.
- Discuss the major phases of a training system.
- Identify three ways to determine training needs.
- List and discuss at least four training methods.
- Discuss at least four learning principles that relate to training.
- Give an example for each level of training evaluation.
- Identify three designs used in evaluating training.

HR IN TRANSITION

DEALING WITH DEFICIENCIES

U.S. employers have serious concerns about both job applicants and current employees. Their concerns have less to do with the quantity of applicants available than with their quality: a large and growing segment of the population does not have the basic educational skills to do today's jobs. For example, almost half of the first-year students in the California State University system have to take remedial classes before they can take college courses. The ability to read, write, and do arithmetic are necessary *bona fide* occupational qualifications (BFOQs) in a job market dominated by technology, yet 20 million to 30 million adults in the workforce lack these basic skills. More than half of the Fortune 500 companies report they have to conduct remedial training to bring employees to a minimal level, which costs those firms over $300 million each year. Small and medium-sized companies have the same problem; a survey found one-third of their employees deficient in basic educational skills.

More than half of the Fortune 500 companies report they have to conduct remedial training to bring employees to a minimal level, which costs those firms over $300 million each year.

Over the next decade the mismatch between job skills requirements and the available pool of workers will get worse. Other trends unfavorable for employers were noted earlier in this book, including a decline in population growth, potential reductions in the number of educated immigrants, changing employee values, and the need for greater job flexibility.

Faced with these challenges, U.S. employers have begun to explore three avenues:

1. Forging partnerships with public school districts and community colleges.
2. Establishing advocacy groups to promote better schools and funding.
3. Establishing in-house basic skills training.

Of the jobs available today, 30% require a college degree (or degrees), 36% require training beyond high school but not a college degree, and 34% require less than a high school education.

In-house basic skills training programs are gaining popularity. For example, General Motors (GM) and the United Auto Workers (UAW) union agreed to commit funds and human resources to a formal literacy program. Ford and Chrysler have established similar programs. So far GM operates classrooms in 30 of its facilities and plans to put them in all 150 facilities soon.

An example of how the GM program affects individual people is Ed Castor, age 50, a former GM plant worker with a third-grade reading level. He passed up several promotions because he did not want people to know he could not read well. He had friends fill out his reports when necessary. Finally, his fear of failure and frustration led him to ask for a demotion, but his supervisor found him a tutor instead. Castor received his general equivalency diploma (GED) and now works for GM in the education program.

Smaller companies are getting into the act as well. The Hach Company in Loveland, Colorado, offers its 830 employees basic math and writing education—42 courses in all. Kathryn Hach, Chairman and CEO, notes, "This is the future. If people are educated, it makes running a business that much easier."

Unfortunately, in-house programs do not guarantee student success, and many programs fail. Some students drop out of even successful programs. One study found that 25% of employees drop out of in-house programs. However, this very basic training will have to be done somewhere by someone. Employers cannot have high-tech, complex jobs if their employees cannot read and write adequately which likely will affect productivity.

A recent survey found that employers rated the skills that workers bring to their jobs as follows:

Very good	5%
Good	16%
Adequate	37%
Deficient	42%

Note that 79% of the workers were not perceived as being even good. Would training or education be able to raise the level of employer satisfaction, even if it were forthcoming? The same survey asked employers to rate the most common shortcomings they see in job applicants. The results follow:

Poor attitude and work habits	43%
Oral and written communication deficits	19%
Lack of specific skills	17%
Lack of basic reading and math skills	16%
Lack of work experience	5%

The extent to which some of those shortcomings in the applicant pool can be cured with company-initiated training is an open question.[1]

> "We are forced to rely on people, which is why we put so much emphasis on training them."
> —Henry Block

The strategy an organization chooses to follow has an impact on most of its HR activities—not the least of which is training. If the strategy of the organization is to grow from within, management and technical skills must be developed. If the strategy is to acquire other firms, the training systems of the parent and acquired firms must be integrated and the capacities in both sets of employees assessed and utilized. If the strategy is to divest part of the company, job search skills may be taught, but employees who were leaving would not be taught new job skills.

Training is an *investment* in a person. The employer invests money, and the employee invests time (and sometimes money as well). The lower the likelihood of an employee's leaving the company, the higher the returns an employer receives on that investment. It is clear that certain kinds of investment in human capital are well rewarded by the labor market. For example, compare the current value of a computer science, MBA, or MD degree with that of a high school diploma. At this writing, an experienced machinist familiar with computer-controlled equipment is almost assured of a good job as well.

An organization can use training to try to overcome deficiencies in employees. Often effective training can produce productivity gains that more than offset the cost of the training. Training is especially important in industries with rapidly changing technologies.

Currently U.S. employers spend $55 billion on training, up from $44 billion in 1990.[2] That is about 1.5% of payroll for organizations with more than one hundred employees. Traditionally, about two-thirds of the training expenses have been devoted to developing professional managers and one-third to front-line workers. But that proportion is changing. Organizations are realizing that they need to develop the skills of their front-line workers as much as those of their managers.

Something else is changing as well. An old axiom in HR management was, "When times get tough, training is the first expenditure cut." Accordingly, in the 1982 recession, training was cut disproportionately, because it was little valued by executives. In the most recent recession, though, a survey done by the American Society for Training and Development (ASTD) found that 40% of companies described as "very hard hit" by the recession made no change in their training budgets, 30% increased them, and 30% decreased them. The biggest funding increases went to increase quality management, management development, and computer training. Currently, in-house training is increasing because of a shortage of skilled workers.[3]

❖ The Context of Training

Training
A learning process whereby people acquire skills or knowledge to aid in the achievement of goals.

Training is a learning process whereby people acquire skills or knowledge to aid in the achievement of goals. Because learning processes are tied to a variety of organizational purposes, training can be viewed either narrowly or broadly. In a limited sense, training provides employees with specific, identifiable knowledge and skills for use on their present jobs. Sometimes a distinction is drawn between *training* and *development,* with development being broader in scope and focusing on individuals gaining *new* knowledge and skills useful for both present and future jobs.

❖ Training Responsibilities

A typical division of training responsibilities is shown in Figure 10–1. The HR unit serves as a source of expert training assistance and coordination. The unit often has a more long-range view of employee careers and the development of the entire organization than do individual operating managers. This difference is especially true at lower levels in the organization.

However, managers are likely to be the best source of technical information used in skills training. They also are in a better position to decide when employees need training or retraining. Because of the close and continual interaction they have with their employees, it is appropriate that managers determine and discuss employee career potentials and plans with individual employees.

❖ FIGURE 10–1 ❖
TYPICAL TRAINING RESPONSIBILITIES

HR UNIT	MANAGERS
❖ Prepares skill-training materials ❖ Coordinates training efforts ❖ Conducts or arranges for off-the-job training ❖ Coordinates career plans and employee development efforts ❖ Provides input and expertise for organizational development	❖ Provide technical information ❖ Monitor training needs ❖ Conduct on-the-job training ❖ Continually discuss employees' growth and future potential ❖ Participate in organizational change efforts

❖ LEGAL ASPECTS OF TRAINING

Training is an area targeted by EEO laws and regulations. One area of concern involves the practices used to select individuals for inclusion in training programs. The criteria used must be job related and must not unfairly restrict the participation of protected-class members. Another concern is differences in pay based on training to which protected-class members have not had equal access. A third is the use of training as a criterion for selecting individuals for promotions. In summary, fair employment laws and regulations definitely do apply to training, and employers must be aware of them.

Training is a cost, and some employers have gone to court in an attempt to require individuals who leave their firms after training to repay the cost. For instance, one firm sued a worker who had signed a "promissory note" to repay the firm $9,000 if he left the firm voluntarily or was fired for cause within 24 months of starting a special training program. The employee contested the suit by saying that he did not learn anything he had not already known and thus had received no benefits from the training.

❖ WHERE TRAINING IS CONDUCTED

Good training is tailored specifically to the needs of the trainee and may be conducted inside the organization, outside the organization, or both. Training in on-the-job locations tends to be viewed as being very applicable to the job, it saves the cost of sending employees away for training, and it often avoids the cost of outside trainers. However, trainees who are learning while working can incur costs in the form of lost customers and broken equipment, and they may get frustrated if matters do not go well.

In contrast, the major concerns with off-the-job training are cost and the application of what is learned to the work situation.[4] Figure 10–2 shows the common categories of employees who get training and the sources of their training—in-house or off the job.

Often, technical training is conducted inside organizations. Technical training is usually skills based, for example, training to run precision computer-controlled machinery. Due to rapid changes in technology, the building and updating of technical skills have become crucial training needs. Basic technical skills training is also being mandated by federal regulations in areas where OSHA, the EPA, and other agencies regulate. For example, the HR Perspective explains the importance of technical training for employees who come in contact with hazardous materials.

❖ FIGURE 10–2 ❖
TRAINING IN OR OUT?

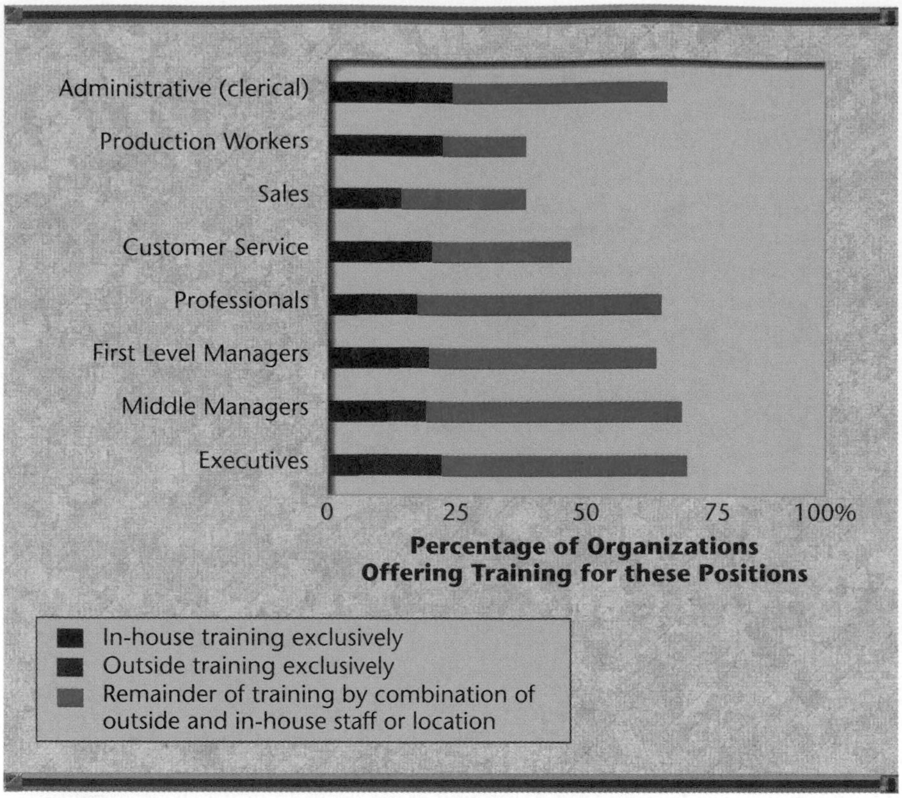

SOURCE: Adapted from "1995 Industry Report–Vital Statistics," *Training,* October 1995, 36, 37. Used with permission.

❖ ORIENTATION: A SPECIAL KIND OF TRAINING

***Orientation**
The planned introduction of new employees to their jobs, coworkers, and the organization.

Orientation is the planned introduction of new employees to their jobs, coworkers, and the organization. However, orientation should not be a mechanical one-way process. Because all employees are different, orientation must incorporate a sensitive awareness to the anxieties, uncertainties, and needs of the individual. Orientation in one form or another is offered by about 90% of all employers.[5]

❖ PURPOSES OF ORIENTATION

The overall goal of orientation is to help new employees learn about their new work environments and get their performances to acceptable levels as soon as possible. The orientation process has several specific purposes: to create an initial favorable impression, to enhance interpersonal acceptance, and to reduce turnover.

TO CREATE AN INITIAL FAVORABLE IMPRESSION A good orientation program creates a favorable impression of the organization and its work. This impression begins even before the new employees report to work. Providing sufficient information about when and where to report the first day, handling all relevant paperwork efficiently, and having personable and efficient people assist the new employee all contribute to creating a favorable impression of the organization.

TO ENHANCE INTERPERSONAL ACCEPTANCE Another purpose of orientation is to ease the employee's entry into the work group.[6] New employees often are concerned about meeting the people in their work units. Furthermore, the expectations of the work group do not always parallel those presented at management's formal orientation. Also, if a well-planned formal orientation is lacking, the new employee may be oriented solely by the group, and thus possibly in ways not beneficial to the organization. For example, at a steel company the work group in the furnace section delighted in telling new employees "the way it really works here." Some of their views were not entirely accurate. Therefore, orientation was essential for management to make certain that new employees knew what their supervisors wanted.[7]

To Reduce Turnover Over half of all new hires may leave their jobs within the first six months in some organizations. But Corning, Inc., found that individuals who had been through more orientation sessions had a lower turnover rate than those who had less orientation (see Figure 10–3). Another firm was able to reduce annual turnover rates 40%, and much of the decline was attributed to more effective orientation of new employees.

Some other benefits of better employee orientation include the following:

- Stronger loyalty to the organization
- Greater commitment to organizational values and goals
- Lower absenteeism
- Higher job satisfaction

HR PERSPECTIVE

Hazmat Technical Training

Almost every recent federal rule requires employers to provide training for employees involved in the areas regulated. This is especially true for organizations regulated by the Occupational Safety and Health Administration (OSHA), the Environmental Protection Agency (EPA), and the Department of Transportation (DOT). Recent regulations for handling hazardous materials (HAZMAT), require industrial training for anyone coming in contact with hazardous substances.

The purpose of this training is twofold: to increase awareness of the dangers of handling HAZMAT and to help prevent HAZMAT incidents mostly caused by human error. The responsibility for doing the training belongs to employers. Furthermore, any new untrained employee must be supervised by a trained employee until the new employee has successfully completed HAZMAT training. Employers are required to have "recurrent" training every two years, records of the training must be maintained for three years, and the trained employees must be tested as part of the process.

The regulations specify four main areas where training must occur:

1. *General awareness.* Training must make the employees aware of the dangers and requirements associated with HAZMAT handling. Some topics include the hazardous material table, United Nations numbering system, 49 CFR HAZMAT regulation, hazard classes and packing groups, etc.
2. *Function specific training.* In this area training for all employees must include how to do their specific jobs safely on a day-to-day basis. Necessary knowledge, skills, and abilities are emphasized.
3. *Safety issues.* Training for all who transport or handle HAZMAT is required to include what to do in the event of a leak or spill. The training covers personal protection to be used, such as clothing, respirators, gloves, and glasses.
4. *Driver training.* Training aimed specifically at over-the-road employees deals with the specifics of transporting HAZMAT over streets and highways. The DOT regulations contain separate rules for handling of radioactive materials and flammable cryogenic liquids.

The federal government has developed modules on each of the basic HAZMAT areas that are available for trainers to use in training new employees. Whatever means and materials are used, employers must comply with the HAZMAT training requirements.[8]

❖ FIGURE 10–3 ❖
ORIENTATION AND TURNOVER AT CORNING, INC.

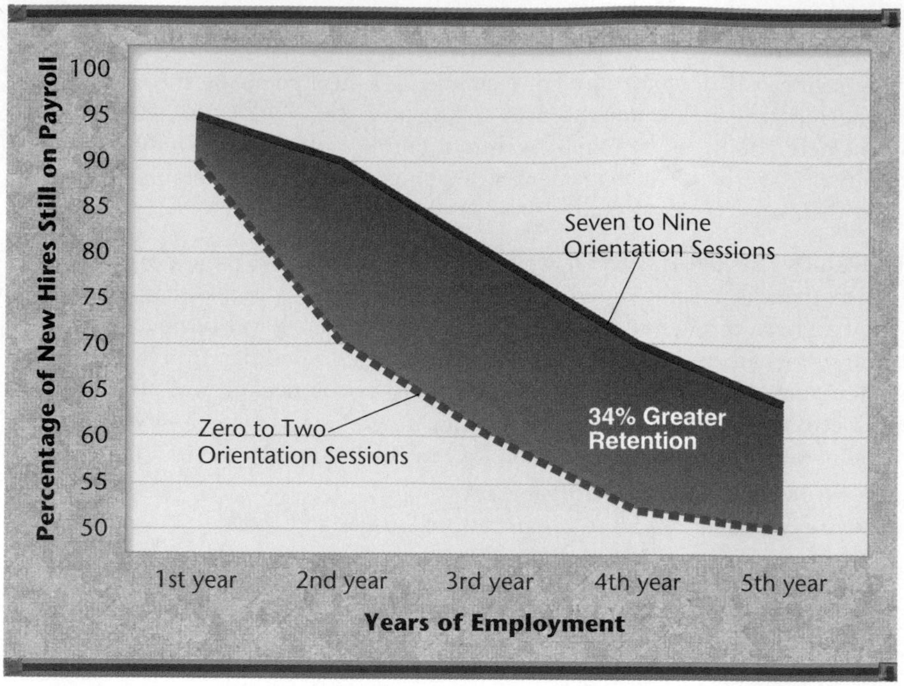

SOURCE: Adapted from Joseph McKenna, "Welcome Aboard," *Industry Week,* November 6, 1992, 34.

❖ ORIENTATION RESPONSIBILITIES

Orientation requires cooperation between individuals in the HR unit and other managers and supervisors. In a small organization without an HR department, such as a machine shop, the new employee's supervisor or manager has the total responsibility for orientation. In large organizations managers and supervisors, as well as the HR department, should work as a team in employee orientation.

Figure 10–4 illustrates a common division of orientation responsibilities in which managers work with HR specialists to orient a new employee. Together they must develop an orientation process that will communicate what the employee needs to learn. Supervisors may not know all the details about health insurance or benefit options, for example, but they usually can best present information on safety rules; the HR department then can explain benefits.

❖ ESTABLISHING AN EFFECTIVE ORIENTATION SYSTEM

A systematic approach to orientation requires attention to attitudes, behaviors, and information that new employees need. Unfortunately, orientation often is conducted rather haphazardly. The general ideas that follow highlight the major components of an effective orientation system: preparing for new employees, providing them with needed information, presenting orientation information effectively, and conducting evaluation and follow-up on the initial orientation.

❖ FIGURE 10–4 ❖
TYPICAL ORIENTATION RESPONSIBILITIES

HR UNIT	MANAGERS
❖ Places employee on payroll ❖ Designs formal orientation program ❖ Explains benefits and company organization ❖ Develops orientation checklist ❖ Evaluates orientation activities	❖ Prepare coworkers for new employee ❖ Introduce new employee to coworkers ❖ Provide overview of job setting and work rules

Preparing for New Employees New employees must feel that they belong and are important to the organization.[9] Both the supervisor and the HR unit should be prepared to give each new employee this perception. For example, an employee would be very uncomfortable arriving at work the first day and hearing a manager say, "Oh, I didn't realize you were coming to work today," or "Who are you?" This type of depersonalization must be avoided.

Further, coworkers as well as the supervisor should be prepared for a new employee's arrival. This preparation is especially important if the new employee will be assuming duties that might be interpreted as threatening a current employee's job status or security. The manager or supervisor should discuss the purpose of hiring the new worker with all current employees before the arrival of the new worker.

Some organizations use coworkers or peers to conduct part of the new employees' orientation. It is particularly useful to involve more experienced and higher-performing individuals who can serve as role models for new employees.

Providing New Employees with Needed Information The guiding question in the establishment of an orientation system is, "What does the new employee need to know *now?*" Often new employees receive a large amount of information they do not immediately need, and they fail to get the information they really need the first day of a new job.

Some organizations systematize this process by developing an orientation checklist. Figure 10–5 indicates the items to be covered by the HR department representative, the new employee's supervisor, or both. A checklist can ensure that all necessary items have been covered at some point, perhaps during the first week. Many employers have employees sign the checklist to verify that they have been told of pertinent rules and procedures.

Often, employees are asked to sign a form indicating that they have received the handbook and have read it. This requirement gives legal protection to employers who may have to enforce policies and rules later. Employees who have signed forms cannot deny later that they were informed about policies and rules.

Several types of information usually are included in the orientation process. The information ranges from the nature of the organization and its culture to the routines of a normal workday. A general organizational overview might include a brief review of the organization; the history, structure, key executives, purpose, products, and services of the organization; how the employee's job fits into the big picture; and other general information. If the employer prepares an annual report, a copy may be given to a new employee. Also, some organizations give new employees a list of terms that are used in the industry to help them learn regularly used vocabulary.

To help them understand the organization fully, new employees also should be oriented to the culture of the organization. Giving informal information on such factors as typical dress habits, lunch practices, and what executives are called will help new employees to adjust.

Another important type of initial information to give employees is information on the policies, work rules, and benefits of the company. Policies about sick leave, tardiness, absenteeism, vacations, benefits, hospitalization, parking, and safety rules must be made known to every new employee immediately. Also, the employee's supervisor or manager should describe the routine of a normal workday for the employee the first morning.

❖ FIGURE 10–5 ❖
ORIENTATION CHECKLIST

Name of Employee ______________
Starting Date ______________
Department ______________

HR DEPARTMENT

Prior to Orientation

__ Complete Form A and give or mail to new employee
__ Complete Form B
__ Attach Form B to "Orientation Checklist—Supervisor" and give to supervisor

Prior to Orientation

Organization and Employee Policies and Procedures

__ History of XYZ Inc.
__ Organization Chart
__ Purpose of company
__ Employee classifications

Insurance Benefits

__ Group health plan
__ Disability insurance
__ Life insurance
__ Worker compensation

Other Benefits

__ Holidays
__ Vacation
__ Jury and election duty
__ Funeral leave
__ Health services
__ Professional discounts
__ Child care

End of Orientation—First Day

__ Make appointment for second day
__ Introduce supervisor

Other Items

__ Job posting
__ Bulletin board—location/use
__ Safety
__ Alcohol/drug use
__ Where to get supplies
__ Employee's records—updating

____
Employee Signature

____
Date

Name of Employee ______________
Starting Date ______________
Department ______________
Position ______________

SUPERVISOR

Employee's First Day

__ Introduction to coworkers
__ Tour of department
__ Tour of company

Location of

__ Coat closet
__ Restroom
__ Telephone for personal use and rules concerning it

Working Hours

__ Starting and leaving
__ Lunch
__ Breaks
__ Overtime
__ Early departures
__ Time clock

Pay Policy

__ Pay Period
__ Deposit system

Other Items

__ Parking
__ Dress

Employee's Second Day

__ Pension retirement plan
__ Sick leave
__ Personal leave
__ Job posting
__ Confidentiality
__ Complaints and concerns
__ Termination
__ Equal Employment Opportunity

During Employee's First Two Weeks

Emergencies

__ Medical
__ Power Failure
__ Fire

At the end of the employee's first two weeks, the supervisor will ask if the employee has any questions concerning any items. After all questions have been discussed, both the employee and the supervisor will sign and date this form and return it to the HR Department.

____
Orientation Conducted By

Presenting Orientation Information Effectively Managers and HR representatives should determine the most appropriate ways to present orientation information. One common failing of many orientation programs is *information overload*. New workers presented with too many facts may ignore important details or inaccurately recall much of the information. For example, rather than telling an employee about company sick leave and vacation policies, an employee handbook that includes this information might be presented on the first day. The manager or HR representative then can review this information a few days later to answer any of the employee's questions, and the employee can review it as needed. Some companies present certain information on videotapes or computer.[10]

Indeed, employees will retain more of the orientation information if it is presented in a manner that encourages them to learn. In addition to the videotapes and computers already mentioned, some organizations have successfully used filmstrips, movies, slides, and charts. However, the emphasis should be on presenting information, not on entertaining the new employee. Materials such as handbooks and information leaflets should be reviewed periodically for updates and corrections.

Logging On

An example of an organization that can develop interactive employee orientation materials is available at

http://www.intechnic.com/

Evaluation and Follow-up A systematic orientation program should have an evaluation and/or reorientation phase at some point after the initial orientation. An HR representative or manager can evaluate the effectiveness of the orientation by conducting follow-up interviews with new employees a few weeks or months after the orientation. Employee questionnaires also can be used. Some organizations even give new employees a written test on the company handbook two weeks after orientation.

Too often, typical orientation efforts assume that once oriented, employees are familiar with everything they need to know about the organization forever. Instead, orientation should be viewed as a never-ending process of introducing both old and new employees to the current state of the organization. To be assets to their organizations, employees must know current organizational policies and procedures, and these may be altered from time to time.

❖ Systems Approach to Training

The success of orientation or any other type of training can be gauged by the amount of learning that occurs and is transferred to the job. Too often, unplanned, uncoordinated, and haphazard training efforts significantly reduce the learning that could have occurred.[11] Training and learning will take place, especially through informal work groups, whether an organization has a coordinated training effort or not. Employees learn from other employees.[12] But without a well-designed, systematic approach to training, what is learned may not be what is best for the organization. Figure 10–6 shows the relevant components of the three major phases in a training system: (1) the assessment phase, (2) the implementation phase, and (3) the evaluation phase.[13]

In the *assessment* phase, planners determine the need for training and specify the objectives of the training effort. Looking at the performance of clerks in a billing department, a manager might find that their data-entry and keyboard abilities are weak and that they would profit by having instruction in these areas. An objective of increasing the clerks' keyboard entry speed to 60 words per minute without errors might be established. The number of words per minute without errors is the criterion against which training success can be measured,

❖ FIGURE 10–6 ❖
MODEL OF A TRAINING SYSTEM

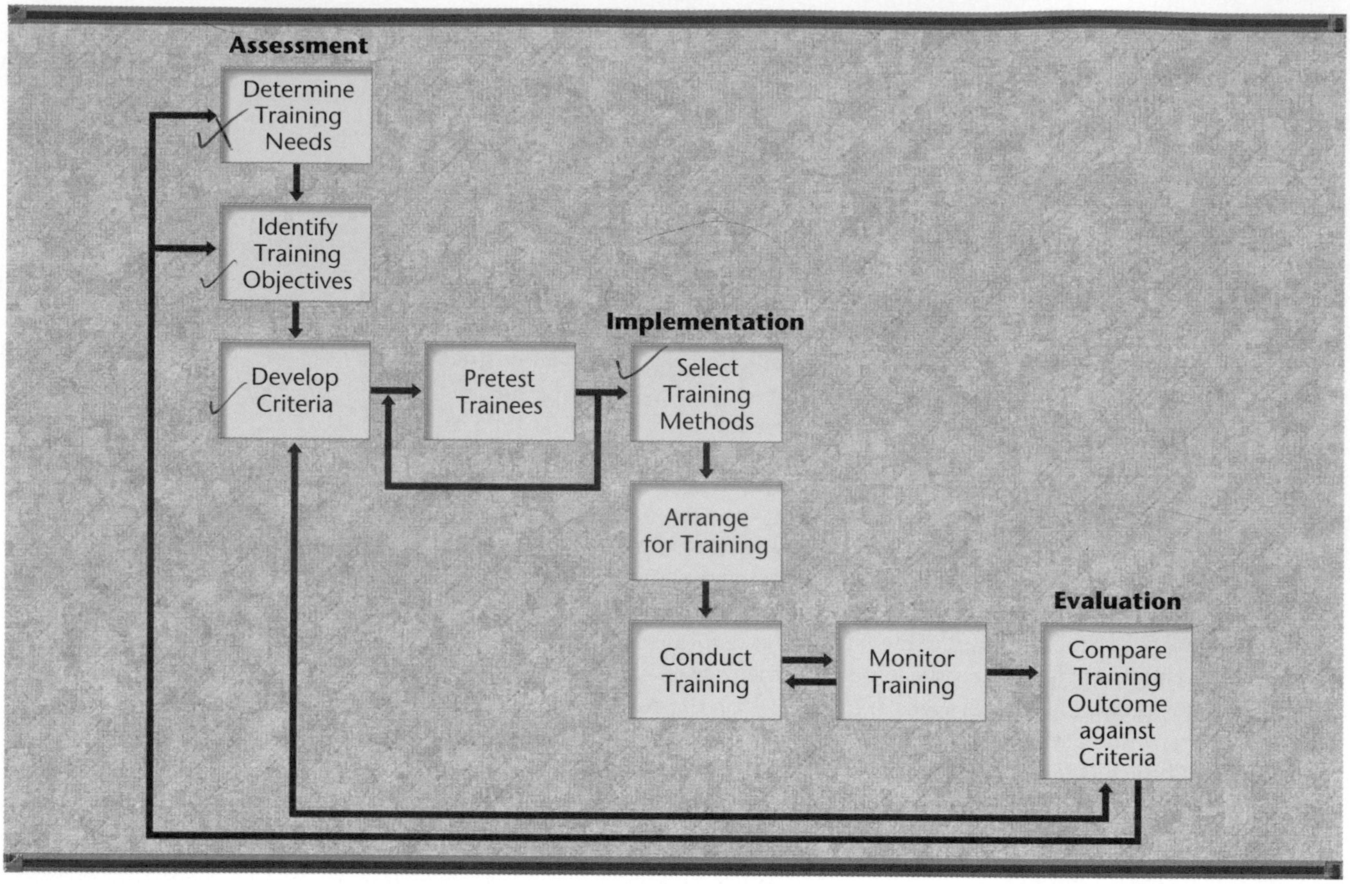

and it represents the way in which the objective is made specific. To make the bridge between assessment and implementation, the clerks would be given a keyboard data-entry test.

Using the results of this test, *implementation* can begin. For instance, the billing supervisor and an HR training specialist could work together to determine how to train the clerks to increase their speeds. Arrangements for instructors, classrooms, materials, and so on would be made at this point. A programmed instruction manual might be used in conjunction with a special data-entry class set up at the company. Then training is actually conducted.

The *evaluation* phase is crucial. It focuses on measuring how well the training accomplished what its originators expected. Monitoring the training serves as a bridge between the implementation and evaluation phases.

❖ TRAINING NEEDS ASSESSMENT

Training is designed to help the organization accomplish its objectives. Determining organizational training needs is the diagnostic phase of setting training objectives. Just as a patient must be examined before a physician can prescribe medication to deal with an ailment, an organization or an individual employee must be studied before a course of action can be planned to make the "patient" function better. As Figure 10–7 indicates, managers can identify training needs through three types of analyses:

- ❖ Organizational analyses
- ❖ Task analyses
- ❖ Individual analyses

❖ ORGANIZATIONAL ANALYSES

The first way to diagnose training needs is through organizational analysis, which considers the organization as a system. An important part of the company's strategic human resource planning is the identification of the knowledge, skills, and abilities that will be needed by employees in the future as both jobs and the organization change. Both internal and external forces that will influence the training of workers must be considered. The problems posed by the technical obsolescence of current employees and an insufficiently educated labor pool from which to draw new workers should be confronted before those training needs become critical.

For example, assume that in its five-year business plan, a manufacturer of mechanical equipment identifies the need to shift production to computer-based electronic equipment. As the organization implements its plans, current employees will need to be re-trained so that they can do electronic instead of mechanical assembly work.

Organizational analyses also can be done using various operational measures of organizational performance. On a continuing basis, detailed analyses of HR data can show training weaknesses. Departments or areas with high turnover, high absenteeism, low performance, or other deficiencies can be pinpointed. After such problems are analyzed, training objectives can be developed. Specific

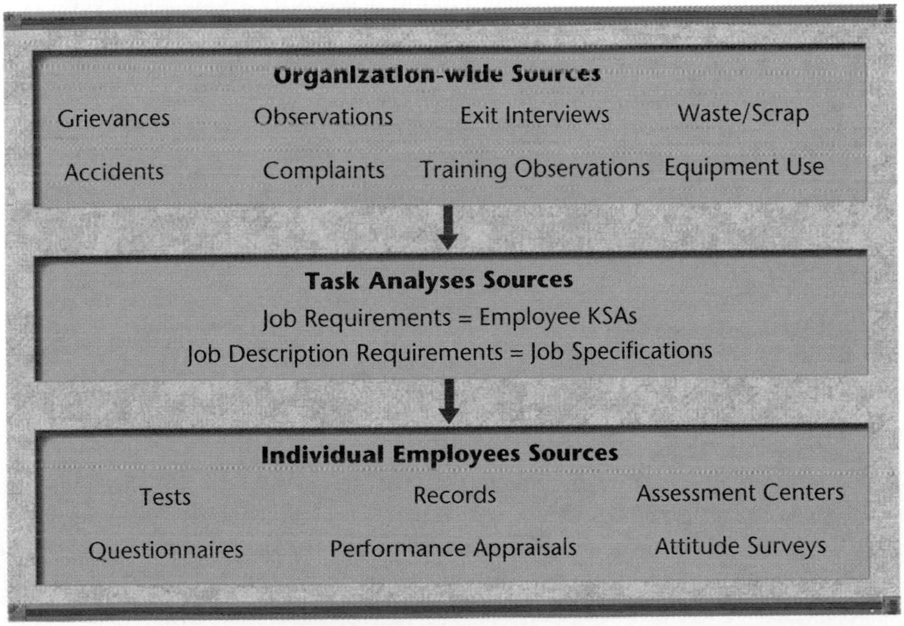

❖ FIGURE 10–7 ❖
LEVELS OF TRAINING NEEDS ASSESSMENT

sources of information and operational measures for an organizational-level needs analysis may include the following:

- Grievances
- Accident records
- Observations
- Exit interviews
- Complaints from customers
- Equipment utilization figures
- Training committee observations
- Waste/scrap/quality control data

❖ Task Analyses

The second way to diagnose training needs is through analyses of the tasks performed in the organization. To do these analyses, it is necessary to know the job requirements of the organization. Job descriptions and job specifications provide information on the performances expected and skills necessary for employees to accomplish the required work. By comparing the requirements of jobs with the knowledge, skills, and abilities of employees, training needs can be identified.

One firm used task analyses to identify the tasks to be performed by engineers who were to be trained as instructors to train other employees. By listing the tasks required of a technical instructor, management established a program to teach specific skills needed by the engineers to become successful instructors.

❖ Individual Analyses

The third means of diagnosing training needs focuses on individuals and how they perform their jobs. The use of performance appraisal data in making these individual analyses is the most common approach. In some instances a good HR information system can be used to help identify individuals who require training in specific areas.[14] To assess training needs through the performance appraisal process, an employee's performance inadequacies first must be determined in a formal review. Then some type of training must be designed to help the employee overcome the weaknesses. Figure 10–8 shows how analyses of the job and the person mesh to identify training needs.

Another way to assess individual training needs is by asking employees. Both managerial and nonmanagerial employees can be surveyed, interviewed, and tested. The results can inform managers about what employees believe their problems are and what actions they recommend.

A survey can take the form of questionnaires or interviews with supervisors and employees on an individual or group basis. The purpose is to gather information on problems perceived by the individuals involved. The following are among the sources of information for surveys:

- Questionnaires
- Job knowledge tools
- Skill tests
- Attitude surveys
- Records of critical incidents
- Data from assessment centers
- Role-playing results

❖ Determining Training Priorities

Because training seldom is an unlimited budget item and there are multiple training needs in an organization, it is necessary to prioritize needs. Ideally, training needs are ranked in importance on the basis of organizational objectives. The training most needed to improve the health of the organization is done first in order to produce visible results more quickly.

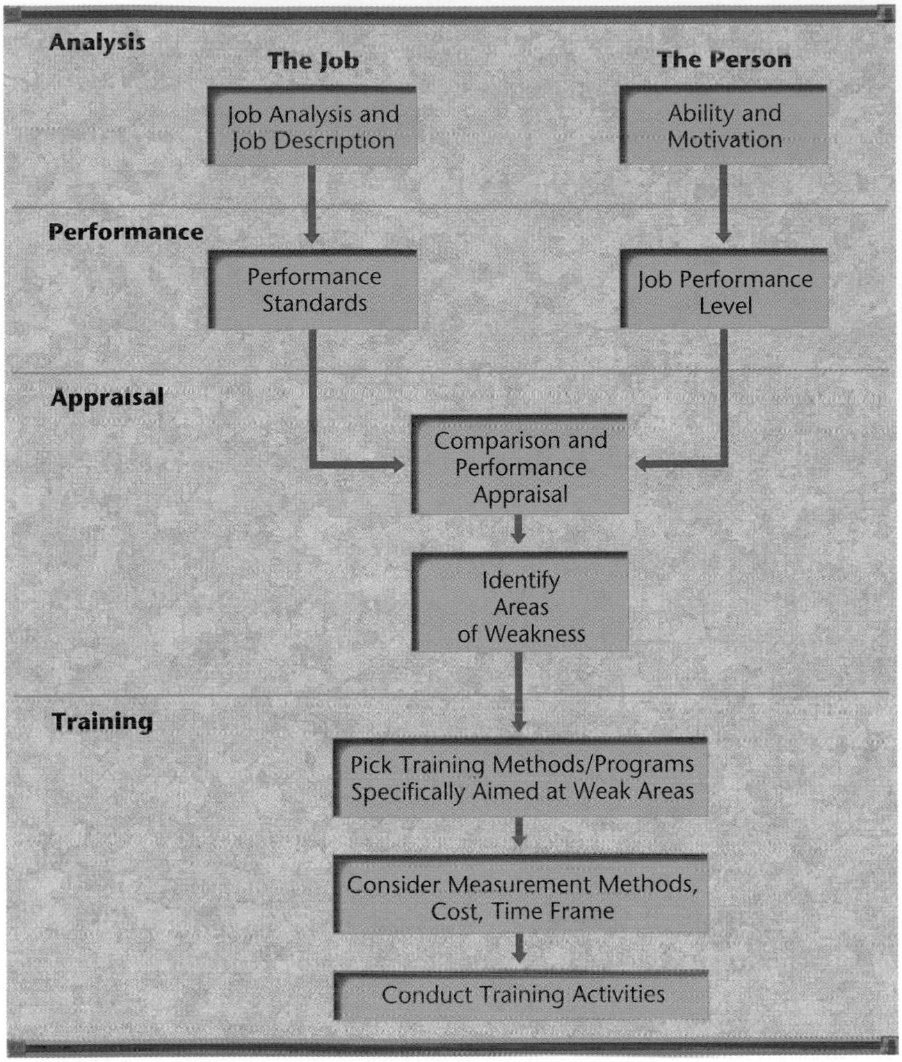

❖ FIGURE 10–8 ❖
USING JOB PERFORMANCE TO ANALYZE TRAINING NEEDS

However, other considerations may enter into the decision-making process:

- ❖ Upper management choices
- ❖ Time
- ❖ Trainers' abilities and motivations
- ❖ Money
- ❖ Likelihood of tangible results

❖ SETTING TRAINING OBJECTIVES

Objectives for training should relate to the training needs identified in the needs analysis. The success of the training should be measured in terms of the objectives set. Good objectives are measurable. For example, an objective for a new salesclerk might be to "demonstrate the ability to explain the function of each product in the department within two weeks." This objective serves as a check on internalization, or whether the person really learned.

Objectives for training can be set in any area by using one of the following four dimensions:

- ❖ *Quantity of work* resulting from training (for example, number of words per minute typed or number of applications processed per day)

- *Quality of work* after training (for example, dollar cost of rework, scrap loss, or errors)
- *Timeliness of work* after training (for example, schedules met or budget reports turned in on time)
- *Cost savings* as a result of training (for example, deviation from budget, sales expense, or cost of downtime)

❖ Training Approaches

Objectives have been determined, and now actual training can begin. Regardless of whether the training is job specific or broader in nature, the appropriate training approach must be chosen. The following overview of common training approaches and techniques classifies them into several major groups. Other methods that are used more frequently for management development are discussed in the next chapter, although there can be overlap in the use of some of the methods.

❖ On-the-Job Training

The most common type of training at all levels in an organization is *on-the-job training (OJT)*. Whether or not the training is planned, people do learn from their job experiences, particularly if these experiences change over time. On-the-job training usually is done by the manager, other employees, or both. A manager or supervisor who trains an employee must be able to teach, as well as to show, the employee what to do.

A special, guided form of OJT is *job instruction training (JIT)*. Developed during World War II, JIT was used to prepare civilians with little experience for jobs in the industrial sector producing military equipment. Because of its success, JIT is still used. In fact, its logical progression of steps is an excellent way to teach trainers to train. Figure 10–9 shows the steps in the JIT process.

On-the-job training is by far the most commonly used form of training, because it is flexible and relevant to what the employee is doing. However, OJT has some problems as well. A common problem is that OJT often is haphazardly

For Better or For Worse, copyright 1994 Lynn Johnston Prod., Inc. Reprinted with permission of Universal Press Syndicate. All rights reserved.

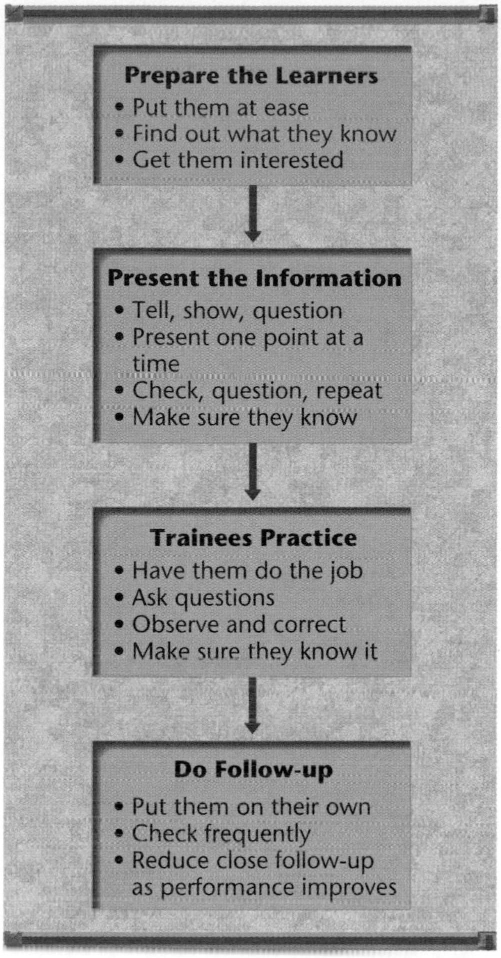

❖ FIGURE 10–9 ❖
JOB INSTRUCTION TRAINING (JIT) PROCESS

done. Trainers may have no experience in training, no time to do it, and no desire to participate. Under such conditions, learners essentially are on their own, and training likely will not be effective. Another problem is that OJT can disrupt regular work. Unfortunately, OJT can amount to no training at all in some circumstances, especially if the trainee simply is abandoned by an ineffective trainer to learn the job alone. However, well-planned and well-executed OJT can be very effective. For instance, the Dodson Group has begun using senior sales representatives as instructors in training sessions. The training gets them involved and helps customize training for the company. The training is viewed by the trainees as being relevant. Rather than listen to an outsider, the trainees get advice, lessons, and tips from those who have experience in the job. The trainees also are more likely to pay attention because they know the training is relevant to their job.[15]

❖ SIMULATION

Simulation is a training approach that uses a training site set up to be identical to the work site. In this setting, trainees can learn under realistic conditions but be away from the pressures of the production schedule. For example, having an employee practice on a PBX console in a simulated setting before taking over as a telephone receptionist allows the person to learn the job more easily and without stress. Consequently, there may be fewer mistakes in handling actual incoming calls. Airlines use simulators to train pilots and cabin attendants, astronauts train in mock-up space capsules, and nuclear power plant operators use model operations control rooms and consoles.[16]

Simulated training must be realistic to be effective. The equipment should be similar to the type the trainee actually will use so that transfer of learning can be made easily. Behavioral simulations and computer-generated virtual reality hold promise for training simulation in the future.[17] Virtual reality uses three-dimensional environments to replicate a job. Computers, audio equipment, and video equipment may be part of a virtual reality training approach. It is very useful where danger to the learner or to expensive equipment is involved, such as teaching pilots to fly a 757 aircraft or teaching police officers when to use their weapons and when to hold their fire in situations where their lives may be in danger.

❖ Cooperative Training

There are two widely used cooperative training methods: internships and apprenticeships. Both mix classroom training and on-the-job experiences.

Internships An internship is a form of on-the-job training that usually combines job training with classroom instruction in trade schools, high schools, colleges, or universities. According to one study, over 200,000 college students per year worked full or part time in cooperative programs and internships. Many fields were represented, including accounting, engineering, newspaper reporting, and HR management.[18]

Internships are advantageous to both employers and interns. Interns get "real-world" exposure, a line on the *vita* (resume), and a chance to examine a possible employer closely.[19] Employers who hire from campuses get a cost-effective selection tool that includes a chance to see an intern at work before a final hiring decision is made.[20]

Apprenticeships Another form of cooperative training that is used by employers, trade unions, and government agencies is apprentice training. An apprenticeship program provides an employee with on-the-job experience under the guidance of a skilled and certified worker. Certain requirements for training, equipment, time length, and proficiency levels may be monitored by a unit of the U.S. Department of Labor. According to government sources, in one recent year approximately 280,000 apprentices were in training, and there were about 44,000 apprentice programs in operation. Apprentice training is used most often to train people for jobs in skilled crafts, such as carpentry, plumbing, photoengraving, typesetting, and welding.[21] Apprenticeships usually last two to five years, depending on the occupation. During this time the apprentice receives lower wages than the certified individual.

Apprentice programs seem to be experiencing a revival for people who are not planning to go to college. They are much more widely used in Europe, especially in Germany.[22] In the United States about 1% of the workforce learns the job through apprenticeships. In Germany about 60% of the high school graduates who do not go to college enroll in apprenticeship programs, and many combine college and apprenticeship to increase their employability.[23]

❖ Behaviorally Experienced Training

Some training efforts focus on emotional and behavioral learning. **Behaviorally experienced training** focuses less on physical skills than on attitudes, perceptions, and interpersonal issues. As Figure 10–10 shows, there are a number of different types of behaviorally experienced training. Employees can learn about behavior by *role playing,* in which individuals assume identities in a certain situation and act it out. *Business games, case studies,* other cases called *incidents,* and short work assignments called *in-baskets* are other behaviorally experienced learning methods. *Sensitivity training,* or *laboratory training,* is an example of a method used for emotional learning. *Diversity training* seeks to shape attitudes about a work environment with differing kinds of employees. Figure 10–10 compares some of the commonly used forms of behaviorally experienced training.

❖Behaviorally Experienced Training Training methods that deal less with physical skills than with attitudes, perceptions, and interpersonal issues.

The critical issue in any of these methods is the purpose of the exercise. Employees may perceive role playing as fun or annoying, but they should understand clearly what the exercise is attempting to teach. Also, they must be able to transfer the learning back to their jobs. In addition, some behavioral methods are controversial and raise ethical issues.

One of the more controversial training methods that some firms have used is New Age (NA) training. This training was developed by Werner Erhard, also known for founding the *est* human potential movement. During NA sessions, trainees are required to reveal intimate and personal episodes in their lives. The training uses meditation, yoga, self-hypnosis, and other behavioral techniques to change employee attitudes, values, and beliefs. NA training raises ethical issues about the rights of employees and employers when individuals are requested to participate in training by their employers, particularly when the training focuses on changing the employees' values, beliefs, and behaviors.

❖ Figure 10–10 ❖
Common Forms of Behaviorally Experienced Training

Role Playing	Participants acting out roles in work-related situations. Works to improve interpersonal skills, but many see it as a game.
Business Games	Computer simulations where the trainee makes management decisions and gets feedback on success. Trains people to make business decisions without actually affecting the business. May be expensive and time-consuming.
Sensitivity Training	Unstructured attempt to show how others see you. Can provide insight into how you come across to others. May not relate to the job.
Diversity Training	Classroom lecture approach to easing racial or gender tensions at work. Often found enlightening, but not all attendees feel comfortable with the topic.
In-Basket	A series of memos or letters that must be dealt with, usually in a rapid fashion. Can be made relevant to real job decisions. Takes much time and effort to build an in-basket for a specific company.
Case Studies/Incidents	Descriptions of real companies or situations that require dealing with lots of facts and making decisions. Can provide a great deal of exposure to many different companies and problems. Some participants complain they do not have enough information.

❖ Classroom and Conference Training

Training seminars, courses, and presentations can be used in both job related and developmental training. Lectures and discussions are a major part of this training. The numerous management development courses offered by trade associations and educational institutions are examples of conference training.

Company-conducted short courses, lectures, and meetings usually consist of classroom training, whereas company sales meetings are a common type of conference training. Both classroom and conference training frequently make use of training techniques such as case discussions, films and tapes to enhance the learning experience.[24]

LOGGING ON

The Training Registry contains a directory of training courses and vendors listed by category and topic. It can be found at

http:/www.tregistry.com/ttr/home.htm

Training methods of this kind are familiar to trainees because they have experienced them in school. However, they are essentially one-way communications. Although they may be good for knowledge enhancement, they probably are not appropriate for motor skills acquisition unless some practice also is included.

❖ TRAINING MEDIA

Several aids are available to trainers presenting information. Some aids can be used in many settings and with a variety of training methods. The most common ones are computer-assisted instruction and audiovisual aids. Another is distance training and learning using interactive two-way television or computer technology.

❖ COMPUTER-ASSISTED INSTRUCTION

Computer-assisted instruction (CAI) allows trainees to learn by interacting with a computer. Application of CAI technology is driven by the need to improve the efficiency or effectiveness of a training situation and to enhance the transfer of learning to improve job performance. Computers lend themselves well to instruction, testing, drill and practice, and application through simulation.

Training programs in the United States are becoming increasingly high-tech. Interactive media such as computers can take the place of more expensive instructor-led classroom training. However, two issues are sometimes a problem with computer-assisted instruction:

- Will employees being trained on technological changes resist those changes?
- How computer literate is the training target audience?[25]

A major advantage of CAI is that it allows self-directed instruction, which many users prefer. Computers used as a training tool allow self-paced approaches and often can be used at the usual place of business. In contrast, instructor-based teaching in a campus-based setting requires employees to spend considerable time away from their jobs.

One firm is experimenting with interactive technology that can be combined with CD-ROM-based courses already available.[26] By combining text, graphics, sound, animation, and video, an entertaining program for learning can be put together in CD-ROM format.[27]

❖ AUDIOVISUAL AIDS

Other technical training aids are audio and visual in nature, including audiotapes and videotapes, films, closed-circuit television, and interactive video teleconferencing. All but interactive video are one-way communications. They may allow the presentation of information that cannot be presented in a classroom. Demonstrations of machines, experiments, and examinations of behavior are examples. Interactive video capability adds audio and video capabilities to CAI, but it uses touch-screen input instead of a keyboard. Audio and visual aids also can be tied into satellite communications systems to convey the same information, such as new product details, to sales personnel in several states.

❖ DISTANCE TRAINING/LEARNING

Many colleges and universities are using interactive two-way television to present classes. The medium allows an instructor in one place to see and respond to a "class" in any number of other towns. If a system is fully configured, employees can take courses from anywhere in the world—at their job or home.[28] Colleges are designing courses and even degrees for companies who pay for delivery to their employees. Both a satellite-based training business and a "World Community College" based on the Internet are operational, if somewhat new.

Trainers must avoid becoming dazzled with the machines and remember that the real emphasis is on learning and training. The effectiveness of the technologies and media needs to be examined in the evaluation. Whatever technology or approach to training is taken will have to fit the way people learn. The discipline of psychology has studied learning for a very long time. Some basic learning principles must be considered in the design of any training program.

❖ Learning Principles: The Psychology of Learning

Working in organizations is a continual learning process, and learning is at the heart of all training activities. Different learning approaches are possible, some apparently more effective than others.[29] Learning is a complex psychological process that is not fully understood by practitioners or research psychologists.

Often, trainers or supervisors present information and assume that merely by presenting it they have ensured that it will be learned. But learning takes place only when information is received, understood, and internalized in such a way that some change or conscious effort has been made to use the information. Managers can use the research on learning to make their training efforts more effective. Some of the major learning principles that guide training efforts are presented next.

❖ Intention to Learn

People learn at different rates and are able to apply what they learn differently. *Ability* to learn must be accompanied by motivation, or *intention,* to learn. Motivation to learn is determined by answers to questions like the following: "How important is my job to me?" "How important is it that I learn that information?" "Will learning this help me in any way?" and "What's in it for me?"

People vary in their beliefs about their ability to learn things through training. These perceptions may have nothing to do with their actual ability to learn but rather reflect the way they see themselves. People with low *self-efficacy* (low level of belief that they can learn something) benefit from one-on-one training. People with high self-efficacy seem to do better with conventional training. Because self-efficacy involves a motivational component, it affects a person's intention to learn.[30]

People are more willing to learn when the material is important to them. Some of the following goals may affect intention to learn in certain people:

- Achievement
- Advancement
- Authority
- Comprehension
- Coworkers' influence
- Creativity
- Curiosity
- Fear of failure
- Recognition
- Responsibility
- Status
- Variety

❖ Whole Learning

It is usually better to give trainees an overall view of what they will be doing than to deal immediately with the specifics. This concept is referred to as *whole learn-*

HR PERSPECTIVE

Seeing the "Big Picture" *First* Helps Learning

Read this passage, and be prepared to recall the details when you have finished. Is it easy to understand and learn?

The procedure is actually quite simple. First you arrange items into different groups. Of course one pile may be sufficient, depending on how much there is to do. If you have to go somewhere else due to a lack of facilities, then that is the next step; otherwise, you are pretty well set. It is important not to overdo things. That is, it is better to do too few things at once than too many. In the short run this may not seem important but complications can easily arise. A mistake can be expensive as well.

At first, the whole procedure will seem complicated. Soon, however, it will become just another facet of life. It is difficult to foresee any end to the necessity for this task in the immediate future, but then, one never can tell. After the procedure is completed, one arranges the materials into different groups again. Then they can be put into their appropriate places. Eventually they will be used once more; then the whole cycle will have to be repeated. However, that is part of life.[31]

Now read the upside-down sentences below.

The preceding passage is written about washing clothes. Reread it with that in mind. Does it make more sense when you have that "big picture"?

ing or *Gestalt learning*. As applied to job training, this means that instructions should be divided into small elements *after* employees have had an opportunity to see how all the elements fit together. For example, in a plastics manufacturing operation, it would be desirable to explain to trainees how the raw chemical material comes to the plant and what is done with the plastic moldings after they are used in the manufacturing process before explaining the trainees' specific jobs. The information should be presented as an entire, logical process so that trainees can see how the various actions fit together into the big picture.[32] Then the supervisor can break the information into the specifics with which the trainees must deal. See the accompanying HR Perspective feature for a good illustration.

❖ Reinforcement

Reinforcement
A concept based on the law of effect, which states that people tend to repeat responses that give them some type of positive reward and avoid actions that are associated with negative consequences.

The concept of **reinforcement** is based on the *law of effect*, which states that people tend to repeat responses that give them some type of positive reward and avoid actions associated with negative consequences. (This subject will be explored in more depth later in this chapter in connection with behavior modification.) The rewards (reinforcements) an individual receives can be either external or internal. For example, a registered nurse receives an external reward for learning how to use a new electrocardiograph machine by receiving a certificate of completion. The internal reward may be a feeling of pride in having learned something new. Consider also a machinist who learns to use a new lathe in the machine shop. At first he makes many mistakes. With time and practice he begins to do better and better. One day he knows he has mastered the lathe. His feeling of accomplishment is a type of internal reward.

Many training situations provide both internal and external rewards.[33] A new salesclerk who answers a supervisor's question correctly and is complimented for doing so may receive both an external reward (the compliment) and an internal reward (a feeling of pride). A person who is positively reinforced for learning will continue to learn.

❖ IMMEDIATE CONFIRMATION

Another learning concept is **immediate confirmation**: people learn best if reinforcement is given as soon as possible after training. Feedback on whether a learner's response was right or wrong should be given as soon as possible after the response.[34] To illustrate, suppose a corporate purchasing department has developed a new system for reporting inventory information. The new system is much more complex than the old one and requires the use of a new form that is longer and more difficult to complete. However, it gives computerized information much more quickly and helps eliminate errors in the recording process that delay the total inventory report. The purchasing manager who trains inventory processors may not have the trainees fill out the entire inventory form when teaching them the new procedure. Instead, the manager may explain the total process and then break it into smaller segments and have each trainee complete the form a section at a time. By checking each individual's form for errors immediately after each section is complete, the purchasing manager can give immediate feedback, or confirmation, before the trainees fill out the next section. This immediate confirmation corrects errors that, if made throughout the whole form, might establish a pattern that would need to be unlearned.

❖Immediate Confirmation
The concept that people learn best if reinforcement is given as soon as possible after training.

❖ PRACTICE

Learning new skills requires practice. Research and experience show that the following considerations must be addressed when designing training practice applications: active practice and spaced versus massed practice.

ACTIVE PRACTICE **Active practice** occurs when trainees perform job-related tasks and duties during training. It is more effective than simply reading or passively listening. Once some basic instructions have been given, active practice should be built into every learning situation. It is one of the advantages of good on-the-job training. Assume a person is being trained as a customer service representative. After being given some basic selling instructions and product details, the trainee should be allowed to call on a customer to use the knowledge received.

❖Active Practice
The performance of job-related tasks and duties by trainees during training.

SPACED VS. MASSED PRACTICE Active practice can be structured in two ways. The first, **spaced practice,** occurs when several practice sessions are spaced over a period of hours or days. The other, **massed practice,** occurs when a person does all of the practice at once. Spaced practice works better for some kinds of learning, whereas massed practice is better for others. If the trainee is learning physical skills (like learning to ski), several practice sessions spaced over a period of hours or days result in greater learning than the same amount of practice in one long period. Training cashiers to operate a new machine could be alternated with having the individuals do tasks they already know how to do. Thus, the training is distributed instead of being concentrated into one period. To take advantage of spaced practice, some organizations spread their orientation of new employees over an entire week by devoting an hour or two daily to orientation, instead of covering it all in one day. This incremental approach to skills acquisition minimizes the physical fatigue that deters learning.

❖Spaced Practice
Several practice sessions spaced over a period of hours or days.

❖Massed Practice
The performance of all of the practice at once.

For other kinds of tasks, such as memorizing tasks, massed practice is usually more effective. Can you imagine trying to memorize the list of model options for a dishwasher one model per day for 20 days as an appliance distribution salesperson? By the time you learned the last option you would have forgotten the first one.

❖ FIGURE 10–11❖
COMMON LEARNING CURVES

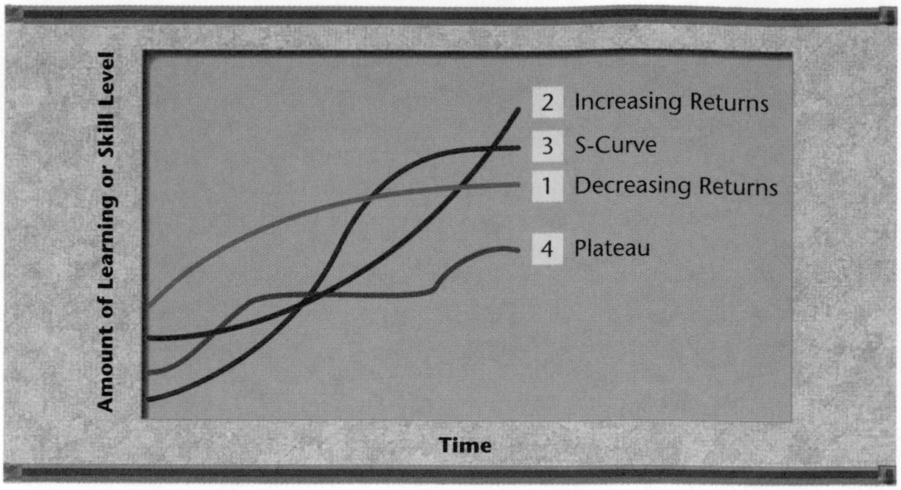

❖ LEARNING CURVES

People learn in different patterns in different training situations. These patterns are called *learning curves.* The kind of learning curve typical of a given task has implications for the way the training program is designed. Figure 10–11 shows the learning curves mentioned in this discussion. In the *decreasing returns* (Curve 1) pattern, the amount of learning and/or the skill level increases rapidly at first; then the rate of improvement slows. For example, when an employee first learns to operate a stamping machine, the rate of production increases rapidly at first and then slows as the normal rate is approached. Learning to perform most routine jobs follows such a curve.

The *increasing returns* (Curve 2) pattern is much less common. It occurs most often when a person is learning a completely unfamiliar task. Starting a completely new job with little formal orientation or training might require a slow beginning while the important vocabulary and relationships are learned. Then the learner begins to pick up expertise quickly.

A third pattern, the *S-shaped curve* (Curve 3), is a combination of the decreasing returns and increasing returns curves. S-curves usually result when a person tries to learn an unfamiliar, difficult task that also requires insight into the basics of the job. In this pattern, learning occurs slowly at first, then increases rapidly for a while, and then flattens out. Learning to debug computer systems is one example, especially if the learner has little previous contact with computers.

The *plateau* (Curve 4) in a learning curve indicates that as knowledge, skill, or speed is being acquired, the learner often reaches a point where there is no apparent progress. At this point, trainees should be encouraged and advised that these plateaus are expected, common, understandable, and usually followed by new surges in learning.

❖ TRANSFER OF TRAINING

The training from a class must be transferred to the job.[35] For effective *transfer of training* to occur, two conditions must be met:

1. The trainees must be able to take the material learned in training and apply it to the job context in which they work.
2. Use of the learned material must be maintained over time on the job.

To aid transfer of training to job situations, the training should be as much like the jobs as possible. In the training situation, trainees should be able to experience the types of situations they can expect on the job. For example, training managers to be better interviewers should include role playing with "applicants" who respond in the same way that real applicants would.

❖ Two Processes Underlying Learning

Behavior modification and behavior modeling are two ways people learn, both on and off the job. These processes are based on the learning principles just described and can be incorporated into the design of training programs.

Behavior Modification A comprehensive approach to training has been developed based on the concept of reinforcement. This popular approach, *behavior modification,* use the theories of psychologist B. F. Skinner who stated that "learning is not doing; it is changing what we do."

Behavior modification makes use of four means of changing behavior, labeled *intervention strategies.* The four strategies are positive reinforcement, negative reinforcement, punishment, and extinction.

A person who receives a desired reward receives **positive reinforcement.** If an employee is on time every day during a week and, as a result, receives extra pay equivalent to one hour of normal work, the employee has received positive reinforcement of his or her good attendance by receiving a desired reward.

***Positive Reinforcement**
A person receives a desired reward.

Negative reinforcement occurs when an individual works to avoid an undesirable consequence. An employee who arrives at work on time every day may do so to avoid a supervisor's criticism. Thus, the potential for criticism leads to the employee's taking the desired action.

***Negative Reinforcement**
An individual works to avoid an undesirable consequence.

Action taken to repel a person from undesirable action is **punishment.** A grocery manager may punish a stock clerk for leaving the stockroom dirty by forcing her to stay after work and clean it up.

***Punishment**
Action taken to repel a person from an undesired action.

Behavior can also be modified through a technique known as **extinction,** which is the absence of an expected response to a situation. Assume that an employee dresses in a new style to attract the attention of his superior. The supervisor just ignores the new type of dress. There is no reinforcement, positive or negative, and no punishment is given. With no reinforcement of any kind, it is likely that the employee will quit dressing in that fashion. The hope is that unreinforced behavior will not be repeated.

***Extinction**
The absence of an expected response to a situation.

All four strategies can work to change behavior, and combinations may be called for in certain situations. But research suggests that for most training situations, positive reinforcement of the desired behavior is most effective.

Behavior Modeling The most elementary way in which people learn—and one of the best—is **behavior modeling,** or copying someone else's behavior. A variation of modeling occurs when people avoid making mistakes they see others make. The use of behavior modeling is particularly appropriate for skill training in which the trainees must use both knowledge and practice. But modeling also can be used to affect ethical values, as the accompanying HR Perspective feature illustrates.

***Behavior Modeling**
Copying someone else's behavior.

In training situations that use behavior modeling, individuals must learn specific information and then apply it. For example, a workshop that trains managers to conduct job interviews might include a presentation of information on equal employment regulations and the types of questions to ask and not to ask. Next, the trainees can be shown a videotape of an interview in which the inter-

HR PERSPECTIVE

Ethical Issues with Allstate and Scientology

Allstate, the large insurance corporation, acknowledged that it hired a consultant to teach training classes who taught "unacceptable" Church of Scientology principles as a part of the courses. Scientology is a religious-scientific movement founded by the late L. Ron Hubbard. Critics call it a cult. More than 3,500 Allstate workers participated in approximately 200 seminars that "taught them to disregard ethics" in the quest for greater productivity.

The seminars focused mostly on "management by statistics," a concept that charted income and production on weekly graphs. An employee who produced "up" statistics was never to be questioned for unethical behavior. A worker with "down" statistics had no protection and "tends to be hounded," the materials used in training said. The "Fair Game Law" written by Hubbard says any enemy of scientology is "Fair Game" and can be deprived of property or injured by any means by any Scientologist without any church discipline. These enemies may be "tricked, sued, or lied to or destroyed."

Allstate agents contend that the "Fair Game" approach allowed management by intimidation, that it was vindictive, and that it was a way to remove people. David Richardson, a former Allstate manager, claims that colleagues developed a system under which the worst-performing agent and manager would be required to reach a series of daily, weekly, and monthly goals that were frequently unreachable. He says that "we would harass agents" by calling them and visiting them frequently.

Although Allstate has repudiated the courses, their impact is still being felt because more than 3,500 supervisors and agents had participated in 200 seminars based on Scientology. For instance, Allstate agents in Florida have tried to unionize their workforce, and they use the "scientology training" as a reason for attacking management. The program also led to employment lawsuits on religious grounds and wrongful discharge suits. Complaints of harassment and intimidation also persisted.[36]

viewers use the information previously presented. Then the trainees can apply their knowledge to conducting interviews in role-playing situations. By videotaping the role-playing interviews, the managers can receive feedback and reinforce their performances.

Most training programs are not structured to take adequate advantage of modeling. Passive classroom training in which individuals listen to lectures allows little modeling, while training that uses videotapes of people showing the desired behavior allows much more. When modeling is used, it is important to select a model who exhibits the desired behaviors. An informal group leader who shares management's values often is a good choice. Likewise, a longer-service employee can become a newer one's mentor by using modeling and other psychological processes.

❖ Evaluation of Training

Evaluation of training compares the post-training results to the objectives expected by managers, trainers, and trainees. Too often, training is done without any thought of measuring and evaluating it later to see how well it worked. Because training is both time-consuming and costly, evaluation should be an integral part of the program. Research examining the success of training programs has produced mixed results. People usually like the training and learn the material taught, but behavior and performance do not always reflect the extent of training delivered and supposedly learned.[37]

The management axiom that "nothing will improve until it is measured" may apply to training assessment. In fact, at some firms, what employees learn is directly related to what they earn, which puts this principle of measurement into direct practice. Knowledge is measured every six months and compared against performance measures.

One way to evaluate training is to examine the costs associated with the training and the benefits received through **cost/benefit analysis**. Comparing costs and benefits is easy until one has to assign an actual dollar value to some of the benefits. The best way is to measure the value of the output before and after training. Any increase represents the benefit resulting from training. However, careful measurement of both the costs and the benefits may be difficult in some cases. Figure 10–12 shows some costs and benefits that may result from training. Furthermore, some benefits (such as attitude changes) are hard to quantify. However, a cost/benefit comparison remains the best way to determine if training is cost effective.[38] For example, one firm evaluated a traditional safety training program and found the program did not lead to a reduction in accidents. Therefore, the program was redesigned so that better safety practices resulted.

***Cost/Benefit Analysis**
Compares costs of training with the benefits received.

❖ FIGURE 10–12 ❖
COSTS AND BENEFITS IN TRAINING EVALUATION

COSTS	BENEFITS
❖ Trainer's salary	❖ Increase in production
❖ Materials for training	❖ Reduction in errors
❖ Living expenses for trainer and trainees	❖ Reduction in turnover
❖ Cost of facilities	❖ Less supervision necessary
❖ Equipment	❖ Ability to advance
❖ Transportation	❖ New skills that lead to ability to do more jobs
❖ Trainee's salary	❖ Attitude changes
❖ Lost production (opportunity cost)	
❖ Preparation time	

❖ LEVELS OF EVALUATION

It is best to consider how training is to be evaluated *before* it begins. Donald L. Kirkpatrick identified four levels at which training can be evaluated.[39] According to him, evaluation of training becomes more rigorous and specific as the levels advance. Later research has examined this schematic and raised questions about how independent each level is from the others, but the four levels are used to focus on the importance of evaluating training.

REACTION Organizations evaluate the reaction level of trainees by conducting interviews or by administering questionnaires to the trainees. However, the immediate reaction may measure only how much the people liked the training rather than how it benefited them.

LEARNING Organizations evaluate learning levels by measuring how well trainees have learned facts, ideas, concepts, theories, and attitudes. Tests on the training material are commonly used for evaluating learning and can be given both before and after training to compare scores. To evaluate training courses at some firms, test results are used to determine how well the courses have provided employees with the desired content. If test scores indicate learning problems, instructors get feedback, and the courses are redesigned so that the content can be delivered more effectively. Of course, learning enough to pass a test does not guarantee that the trainee can *do* anything with what was learned.

BEHAVIOR Evaluating training at the behavioral level involves measuring the effect of training on job performance through interviews of trainees and their coworkers and observations of job performance. But behavior is more difficult to measure than reaction and learning. Even if behaviors do change, the results that management desires may not be obtained.

RESULTS Employers evaluate results by measuring the effect of training on the achievement of organizational objectives. Because results such as productivity, turnover, quality, time, sales, and costs are relatively concrete, this type of evaluation can be done by comparing records before and after training.

The difficulty with measuring results is pinpointing whether it actually was training that caused the changes in results. Other factors may have had a major impact as well. For example, a department manager who has completed a supervisory training program on controlling turnover can be measured on turnover before and after the training. But turnover is also dependent on the current economic situation, the demand for product, and the quality of employees being hired. Therefore, when evaluating results, managers should be aware of all issues involved in determining the exact effect of the training.

❖ Evaluation Designs

There are many ways to design the evaluation of training programs to determine their effects.[40] The three most common designs are shown in Figure 10–13. The rigor of the designs increases with each level.

❖ **Figure 10–13** ❖
Training Evaluation Designs

10–13a

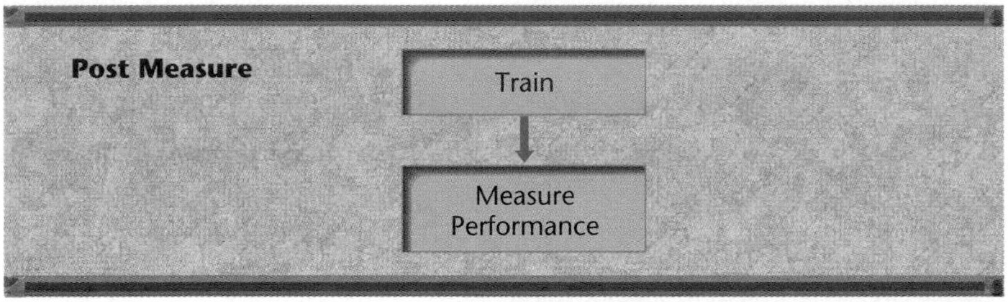

Post-Measure The most obvious way to evaluate training effectiveness is to determine after the training whether the individuals can perform the way management wants them to perform. Assume that a manager has 20 typists who need to improve their typing speeds. They are given a one-day training session and then given a typing test to measure their speeds. If the typists can all type the required speed after training, was the training beneficial? It is difficult to say; perhaps they could have done as well before training. It is difficult to know whether the typing speed is a result of the training or could have been achieved without training.

10–13b

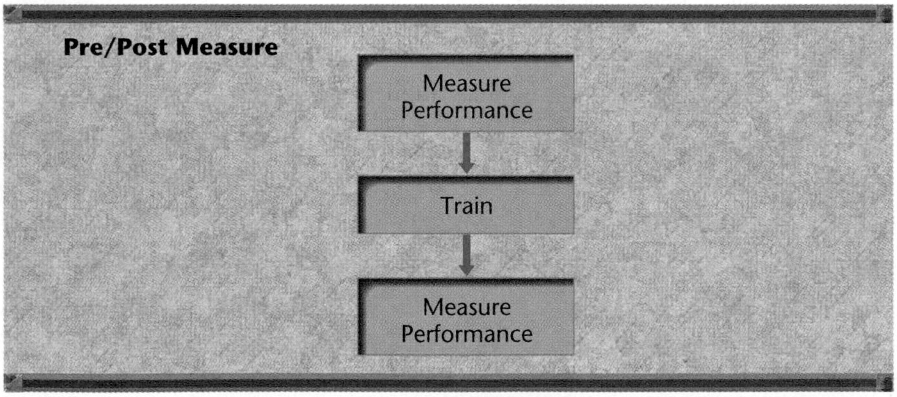

Pre-/Post-Measure By designing the typing speed evaluation differently, the issue of pretest skill levels could have been considered. If the manager had measured the typing speed before and after training, we could have known whether the training made any difference. However, a question remains. If there was a change in typing speed, was the training responsible for the change, or did these people simply type faster because they knew they were being tested? People often perform better when they know they are being tested on the results.

Pre-/Post-Measure with Control Group Another evaluation design can address this problem. In addition to the 20 typists who will be trained, a manager can test another group of typists who will not be trained to see if they do as well as those who are to be trained. This second group is called a *control group*. If, after training, the trained typists can type significantly faster than those who were not trained, the manager can be reasonably sure that the training was effective. The final portion of Figure 10–13 shows the pre-/post-measure design with a control group.

Other designs also can be used, but these three are the most common ones.[41] When possible, the pre-/post-measure or pre-/post-measure with control group design should be used, because each provides a much stronger measurement than the post-measure design alone.

Figure 10–13c

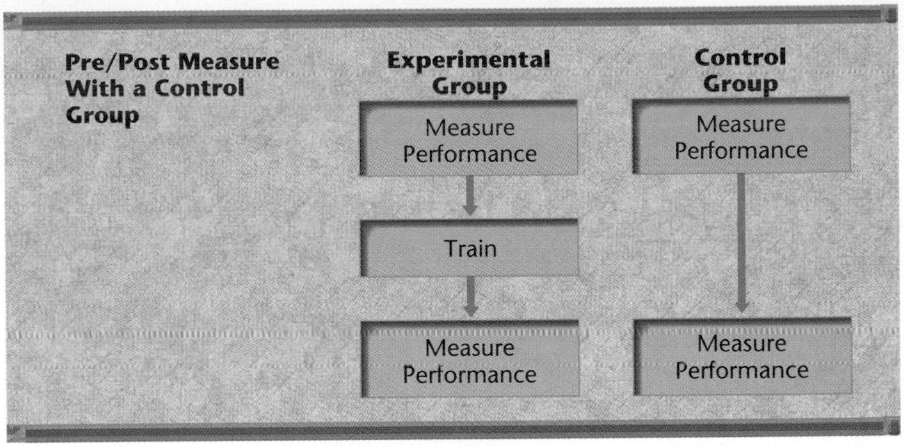

SUMMARY

❖ Remedial training and retraining of existing workers are two of the major challenges facing employers in many industries.

❖ Training is a learning process whereby people acquire skills or knowledge to aid in the achievement of goals.

❖ Training has legal implications, such as who is selected for training, the criteria used for the selection, pay differences based on training, and use of training when making promotion decisions.

❖ Orientation is a special kind of training designed to help new employees learn about their jobs, coworkers, and the organization.

❖ Components of an effective orientation system include preparing for new employees; determining what information is needed and when it is needed by the employees; presenting information about the workday, organization, policies, rules, and benefits; and doing evaluation and follow-up.

❖ A training system includes assessment, implementation, and evaluation.

❖ Of the many training methods, on-the-job training (OJT) is the most often used (and abused) method.

❖ Two widely used cooperative training methods are internships and apprenticeships.

❖ Training media such as computer-assisted instruction and audio and visual aids each have advantages and disadvantages. They should be matched with training situations where they best apply, because they will not all work in all situations.

❖ Basic learning principles that guide training efforts include intention to learn, whole learning, reinforcement, immediate confirmation, practice, learning curves, transfer of training, behavior modification, and behavior modeling.

❖ Evaluation of training success is important, because if the training does not return as much in benefits as it costs, there is no reason to train. Training can be evaluated at four levels: reaction, learning, behavior, and results.

❖ A pre-/post-measure with control group design is the most rigorous training evaluation design, but others can be used as well.

Review and Discussion Questions

1. Why must employers be concerned about complying with equal employment requirements when selecting people for training?
2. Discuss the importance of orientation, and tell how you would orient a new management trainee.
3. What are the three major phases in a training system? Identify the processes within each phase.
4. Assume that you want to identify training needs for a group of sales employees in a luxury-oriented jewelry store. What would you do?
5. You are training someone to use a word-processing computer software program. What training methods would you use?
6. Describe how you would use some of the learning concepts discussed in the chapter to train someone to operate a fax machine.
7. You want to evaluate the training received by some data-input operators.
   (a) Give examples of how to evaluate the training at four different levels.
   (b) What type of training design would you use, and why?

Terms to Know

active practice **301**
behavior modeling **303**
behaviorally experienced training **297**
cost/benefit analysis **305**
extinction **303**
immediate confirmation **301**
massed practice **301**
negative reinforcement **303**
orientation **284**
positive reinforcement **303**
punishment **303**
reinforcement **300**
spaced practice **301**
training **282**

Case

Omaha Property and Casualty Insurance Company

Omaha Property and Casualty Insurance Company (OPAC) expanded its Customer Service Operations (CSO) Department to include responsibilities of making telephone responses to various customers; processing policy changes on-line; and processing new business applications, renewals, and various other policy changes. These functions are performed by customer service representatives (CSRs). By merging these functions, the department has the flexibility to respond quickly to fluctuating volumes of inbound telephone calls.

CSO established knowledge and skill criteria for the CSR position. Among other requirements, individuals in these positions must obtain a property and casualty agent's license before they can become CSRs.

To accomplish this goal as quickly as possible, the HR Department worked closely with CSO management to develop a training program. Objectives of the program included meeting current, as well as future, needs.

The needs assessment phase of this project determined that all new entrants into CSO needed basic insurance knowledge, product knowledge, coverage knowledge, an understanding of underwriting guidelines, enhanced customer service skills, and enhanced telephone skills. The HR Department assisted CSO by conducting courses on insurance, product, and coverage knowledge, as well as a telephone skills workshop.

The training program consisted of two purchased courses, short quizzes, and a comprehensive examination for each course. These courses covered basic insurance, product, and coverage information. The HR Training Coordinator conducted these classes and incorporated OPAC-specific products into these courses. In addition, experts from the underwriting and claims departments were invited to assist in clarifying complex issues. A minimum examination score of 70% was established to mirror the criteria for obtaining the agent's license. A desired examination score of 90% was set for the insurance examination. Individuals in the training program who scored less than 90% were encouraged to retake the examination. The HR Training Coordinator also developed and conducted a telephone skills workshop.

During the examination phase of this project it became clear that a number of individuals in the program were apprehensive over taking the actual agent's examination. Thus, practice license tests were given, along with helpful hints on how to take examinations. One-on-one training was also available.

The HR Department continues to conduct this training for new CSR trainees. In addition to the above program, new entrants in the department are given basic data-entry training for processing new business by the HR Training Coordinator. The HR Department developed a visual timetable to assist trainees with program expectations. The Training Coordinator evaluates class participants to determine further individual training needs. The assistance of the HR Department with training gives CSO management time to focus on other issues.

An evaluation of the training program indicates the program is a success. One hundred percent of the program participants have received their agent's license, with 80% of this group passing the test on the first attempt. All program participants have met the knowledge and skill criteria within the designated time frame to qualify for promotion to customer service representative.

The most challenging aspect for HR has been keeping abreast of product revisions and insurance regulations that affect the licensing process. Communication with various OPAC departments is the key to keeping the training program current.[42]

Questions

1. Fit each part of OPAC's training approach to the systems model in Figure 10–6.
2. What other criteria might OPAC use to evaluate the success of its program in addition to the percentage of participants receiving licenses?

Notes

1. Based on information from "Reader's Views on Job Training," *Nation's Business*, October 1995, 93; "The 'Basics' of In-House Skills Training," *HR Magazine*, February 1991, 74–78; E. Jeanings, "Helping to Educate Small Firms' Workers," *The Wall Street Journal*, June 26, 1992, B1; L. Armstrong and G. Smith, "Productivity Assured or We'll Fix Them Free," *Business Week*, November 25, 1991, 34; K. Miller, "A + GM, The Three R's Are the Big Three," *The Wall Street Journal*, July 3, 1992, B1; D. Machan, "Eager Pupils," *Forbes*, September 16, 1991, 188; Joe Marquette, "Working at Education," *USA Today*, March 29, 1995, A1; and "Half of CSU Freshman Need Help," *Sacramento Bee*, January 6, 1995, B5.
2. William Tracey, "How to Weigh the Costs and Benefits of Training," *Benefits & Compensation Solutions*, December 1995, 52.
3. "In-House Training Increases," *The Wall Street Journal*, January 30, 1996, 1.
4. F. Maidment, "Send Managers Back to School at the Local University," *Human Resource Professional*, July/August 1995, 29–30.
5. "Training and Continuous Learning," SHRM Survey Report Executive Summary, Alexandria, VA: Society for Human Resource Management, 1994), 2.
6. W. Hopkins et al., "Training Priorities for a Diverse Work Force," *Public Personnel Management*, Fall 1994, 429–435.
7. J. C. Meister, "Training Workers in the 3 C's," *Nation's Business*, September 1994, 51.
8. B. Cropp and C. McMillan, "Performance-Oriented Training," *Occupational Health and Safety*, February 1995, 50–57.
9. K. Smith-Jentsch et al., "Can Pretraining Experiences Explain Individual Differences in Learning?" *Journal of Applied Psychology* 8 (1996), 110–116.
10. Bob Kronemeyer, "Basic Training," *Business News*, Fall 1995, 41–43.
11. "Company Illustrates Power of Investing in Human Beings," *Omaha World-Herald*, January 3, 1993, 12G.
12. Sandra Phillips, "Team Training Puts Fizz in Coke Plant's Future," *Personnel Journal*, January 1996, 87–92.
13. Adapted from I. L. Goldstein, *Training in Organizations* (Monterey CA: Brooks-Cole, 1986).
14. William Matlack, "Automated Job Placement," *Benefits & Compensation Solutions*, June 1995, 24.
15. Bill Kelley, "Selling Employees on Training," *Human Resource Executive*, June 20, 1994, 41.
16. D. Leeds, "Show-Stopping Training," *Training and Development*, March 1995, 34–36.
17. G. Mitchell, *The Trainer's Handbook* (New York: AMACOM, 1993).
18. A. Horarhoff, "Working for Nothing Pays Off," *Career Woman*, Fall 1993, 18–21.

(Notes continued on following page)

Notes, continued

19. B. Kroneyer, "Trying Out a Career: Internships and Shadowing," *Career World*, May 1993, 27–30.

20. David Sommers, "Critical Thinking, Experimental Learning and Internships," *Journal of Management Education*, May 1993, 260–262.

21. T. Nhan, "Company Aims to Fill Worker Void with Apprentices," *World Herald*, December 3, 1995, 15G.

22. J. R. Veum, "Sources of Training and Their Impact on Wages," *Industrial and Labor Relations Review*, 48 (1995) 812–825.

23. "Apprenticeship Training and College Combine for Success in Germany," *Manpower Argus*, March 1996, 8.

24. T. A. Stewart, "How a Little Company Won Big by Betting on Brainpower," *Fortune*, September 4, 1995, 121–122.

25. C. Katz and P. Katz, "Ask the Right Questions to Ease Computer Learning," *HR Magazine*, February 1996, 67–70.

26. U. Gupta, "TV Seminars and CD-ROM Train Workers," *The Wall Street Journal*, January 3, 1996, B1.

27. Judy Lanier, "Computer-Based Training Gains Favor," *TeleProfessional*, November/December 1995, 18–19.

28. P. Theibert, "Train and Degree Them—Anywhere," *Personnel Journal*, February 1996, 28–37.

29. M. J. Ree, et. al., "Role of Ability and Prior Job Knowledge in Complex Training Performance," *Journal of Applied Psychology*, 80 (1995), 721–730.

30. Alan M. Saks, "Longitudinal Field Investigation of the Moderating and Mediating Effects of Self-Efficacy on the Relationship between Training and Adjustment," *Journal of Applied Psychology* 80 (1995), 211–225.

31. D. Lavitt, "Framework for Learning," *Training and Development Journal*, June 1992, 17.

32. H. Lancaster, "Company Puts 'Big Picture' on Game Board," *Omaha World-Herald*, February 12, 1995, 11G.

33. M. A. Quinones, "Pretraining Context Effects: Training Assignments as Feedback," *Journal of Applied Psychology* 80 (1995), 226–238.

34. J. Martorchio and J. Dulebohn, "Performance Feedback Effects in Training: The Role of Perceived Controllability," *Personnel Psychology* 47 (1994), 357–373.

35. J. B. Tracey et al., "Applying Trained Skills to the Job," *Journal of Applied Psychology* 80 (1995), 239–252.

36. Adapted from "Allstate Admits Unacceptable Training," *Denver Post*, March 23, 1995, A5; and Rochelle Sharpe, "In Whose Hands," *The Wall Street Journal*, March 22, 1995, 1.

37. James Georges, "The Myth of Soft Skills Training," *Training*, January 1996, 48–54.

38. William Tracey, "How to Weigh the Costs and Benefits of Training," *Benefits and Compensation Solutions*, December 1995, 52–56.

39. Donald L. Kirkpatrick, "Four Steps to Measuring Training Effectiveness," *Personnel Administrator*, November 1983, 19–25.

40. Jack Phillips, "Was It the Training?" *Training and Development*, March 1996, 28–32.

41. Robert Haccoun and T. Hamtiaux, "Optimizing Knowledge Tests for Inferring Learning Acquisition Levels in Single Group Training Evaluation Designs," *Personnel Psychology* 47 (1994), 573–605.

42. Written by Marlene Heider, PHR, and used with permission.

CHAPTER 11

HUMAN RESOURCE DEVELOPMENT AND CAREERS

After you have read this chapter, you should be able to . . .

- Define *human resource development,* and explain how it differs from training.
- Describe the development process.
- List and describe at least four on-the-job and four off-the-job development methods.
- Discuss specific advantages and problems associated with assessment centers.
- Differentiate between organization-centered and individual-centered career planning.
- Explain how dual career ladders for engineers and scientists function.
- Identify how dual-career marriages affect career paths and strategies of individuals and organizations.

HR in Transition

Development and Careers in a World without Managers

When organizational strategies seem to be endless reorganization and downsizing, it is difficult to know what a career is, much less how to develop one. Further, why worry about "development" for managers when it looks like there will be no managers left in the future?

These views are extreme, but three factors do indeed appear to have changed:

- The middle management ladder upward in organizations is much altered—to some extent replaced by computers.
- Many firms have a tightened focus on their core competencies and outsourced much of the rest.
- Project-based work is growing, making careers a series of projects, not steps upward in a given organization.

These changes in human resources have led to booming outplacement offices, more temporary staffers, and a restructured concept of middle management. But make no mistake—middle management is reduced, but it is *not* gone. There are now 11.17 managers per 100 employees, compared with 11.83 per 100 in 1990.

But make no mistake—middle management is reduced, but it is not gone.

The "massive delayering" portrayed in the popular press is creating some opportunities for managers where they did not exist before, albeit often in other firms. For example, technologies that replace workers need managers to oversee them. Outsourcing creates jobs for companies that need managers. More complex white-collar work may actually require *more* managers in some cases. The need for managers to deal more with customers rather than just supervise employees makes management both more similar to marketing and more necessary. Finally, with responsibility being moved lower in the organization, more people at lower levels are getting management responsibility.

Middle-level management hiring has doubled in some fields: information technology, systems planning, technical services, and emerging technologies. Further, the wireless communication industry is exploding, and currently there is a limited amount of management talent in that field.

Nevertheless, career changes are wrenching for people involved in them, and they are continuing. One industry, banking, provides a good illustration of where careers have been and where they are going. Few industries have experienced as much consolidation and restructuring as banking has in the last 10 years. Competition from mutual funds, brokerage firms, and other financial service companies has been intense. Total industry employment declined from 2.3 million to 2.1 million in one five-year period. The number of U.S. banks has dropped from 14,000 to 10,000. There is speculation that only about 5,000 will be left after the turn of the century.

Where are all the bankers going? Estimates are that now roughly half find jobs somewhere in the financial service industry. But as the industry continues to shrink, the chances of finding similar employment in the financial industry will decrease. Other former banking employees have gone into consulting, insurance, and information services. Regardless of which industry they end up in, they stay at roughly the same organizational level but receive an average pay cut of 8%. One knowledgeable observer of the banking situation says, "Everyone in this industry ought to be planning for career changes." Those who remain will find a different climate that places more emphasis on sales and customer service and less on check-clearing, loan-processing, and back-office operations. Development thus will continue to be necessary for those who remain to follow careers in banking.[1]

> "Information is pretty thin stuff, unless mixed with experience."
> —Clarence Day

Development is different from training in that it is often the result of experience and the maturity that comes with it. It is possible to train most people to run a postage meter, drive a truck, operate a computer, or assemble a radio. However, development in such areas as judgment, responsibility, decision making, and communications is much more difficult, because such factors may or may not develop over time with the experiences of life or as part of a planned program. Managers, particularly, need a variety of experiences to enhance their development; but a planned system of development experiences for all employees can help expand the overall level of abilities in an organization and increase its productivity, quality, and flexibility. Figure 11–1 contrasts development and training.

❖ Human Resource Development

Development
Efforts to improve employees' ability to handle a variety of assignments.

Development can be thought of as bringing about capacities that go beyond those required by the current job; it represents efforts to improve an employee's ability to handle a variety of assignments. As such, it can benefit both the organization and the individual's career. Employees and managers with appropriate experiences and abilities enhance the ability of an organization to compete and adapt to a changing competitive environment. In the development process, the individual's career also gains focus and evolves.

Specific development needs, especially for the organizations of the future, can be identified by HR planning. Currently, more jobs are taking on the characteristics of *knowledge work,* meaning that people in these jobs must combine mastery of technical expertise with the ability to work in teams with other employees, form relationships with customers, and analyze their own practices in order to improve. The practice of management increasingly involves guiding and integrating autonomous, highly skilled people. Figure 11–2 shows an estimate from the Bureau of Labor Statistics on how development dollars are spent. Managers and professionals account for almost half of the expenditures.

❖ **Figure 11–1** ❖
Development versus Training

	Training	Development
Focus:	Learn specific behaviors and actions; Demonstrate techniques and processes	Understand information concepts, context; Develop judgment; Expand capacities for assignments
Time Frame:	Shorter-term	Longer-term
Effectiveness Measures:	Performance appraisals, cost/benefit analysis, passing tests or certification	Qualified people available when needed; promotion from within possible; HR-based competitive advantage

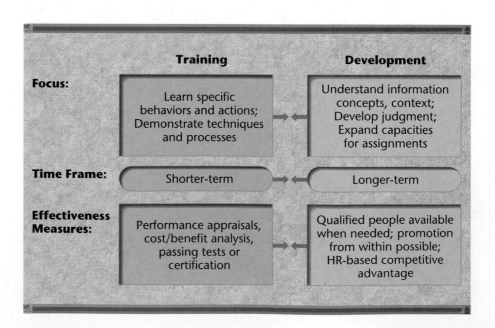

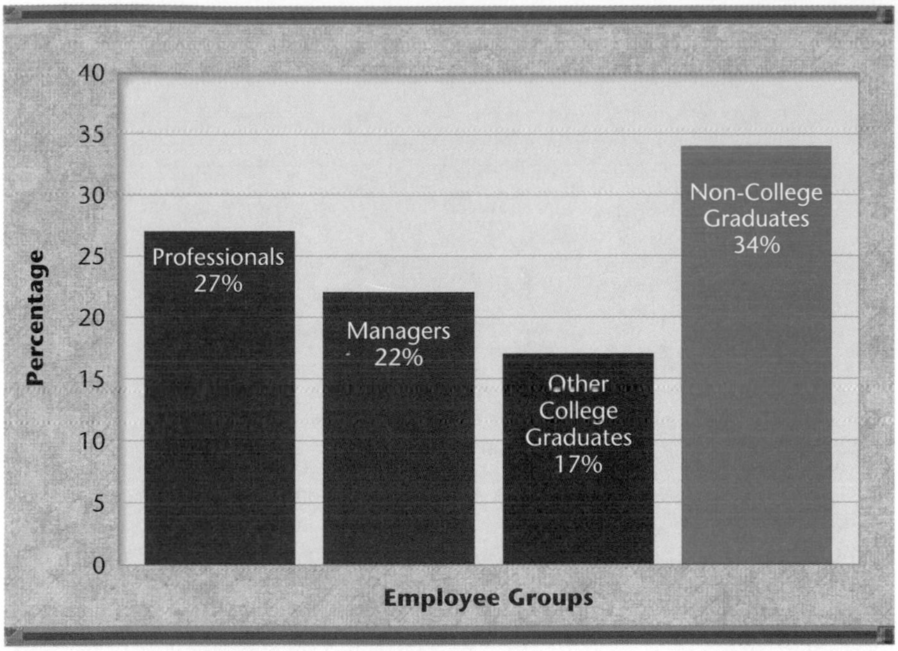

❖ FIGURE 11–2 ❖
HOW COMPANIES SPEND DEVELOPMENT DOLLARS

SOURCE: U.S. Bureau of Labor Statistics as reported in *USA Today,* March 26, 1995, p. A1.

Developing human resources in an organization can help provide a *sustained competitive advantage* as long as three basic requirements are met:

1. The workforce adds positive economic benefits to the production of goods and services.
2. The abilities of the workforce provide an advantage over competitors.
3. Those abilities are not easily duplicated by a competitor.[2]

Employers to some extent face a "make or buy" choice: develop competitive human resources or "buy" them already developed from someone else. Current trends indicate that technical and professional people are hired according to the amount of skill development they have already achieved rather than their ability to learn or their behavioral traits.[3] There is an apparent preference to "buy" rather than "make" scarce employees in today's labor market. However, buying rather than developing human resource capacities does not contribute to the requirements for sustained competitive advantage through human resources noted above.

❖ THE DEVELOPMENT PROCESS

Development should begin with the HR plans of the firm. Such plans deal with analyzing, forecasting, and identifying the organizational HR needs. Development allows anticipation of the movement of people through the organization due to retirement, promotion, and transfers. It helps identify the kinds of abilities that will be needed and the development necessary to have people with those abilities on hand when needed.

Figure 11–3 diagrams the HR development process. As the figure shows, HR plans first identify necessary abilities and capacities. Such capacities can influence planning in return. The specific abilities needed also influence decisions as to who will be promoted and what the succession of leaders will be in the organization. Those decisions both influence and are influenced by an assessment of

❖ FIGURE 11–3 ❖
THE HR DEVELOPMENT PROCESS

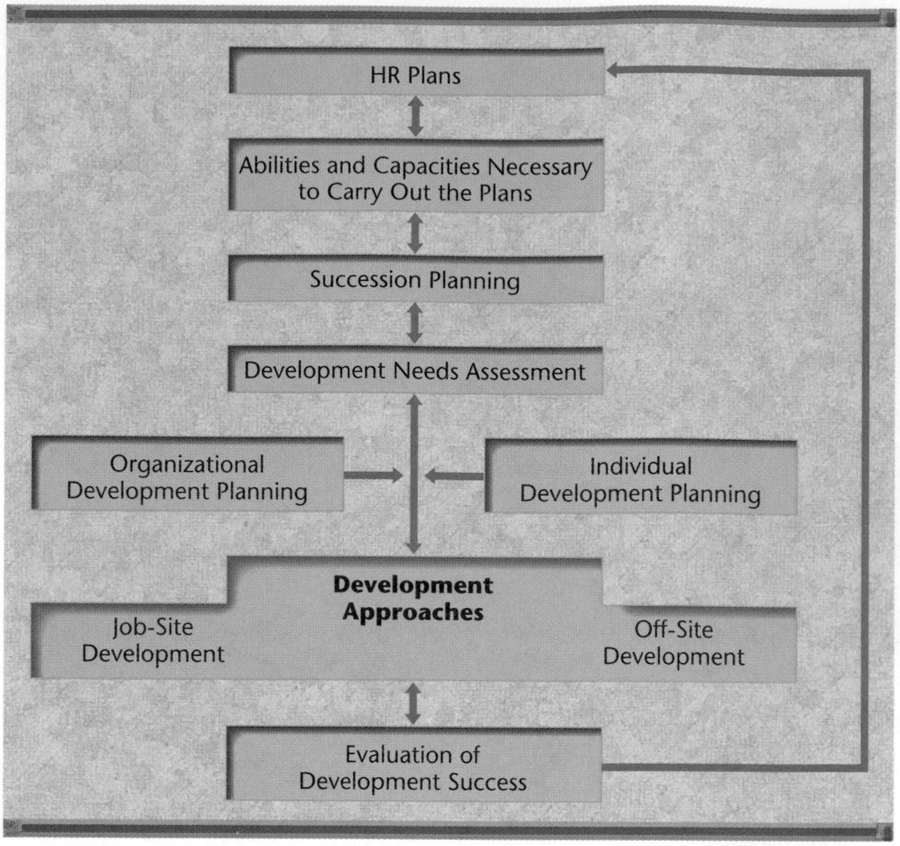

development needs in the organization. Various approaches to development follow from this needs assessment. Finally, the process must be evaluated and changes made as necessary over time.

HR planning for necessary abilities has already been described in Chapter 2. Succession planning to identify replacements and provide management continuity will be described next, as the model in Figure 11–3 guides the discussion that follows.

❖ SUCCESSION PLANNING

Succession planning can be an important part of development. For example, combined with skills training, management development, and promotion from within, it has been linked to "turning around" a plant acquired by another company. The general result for the plant was a large increase in capacity over four years with virtually no infusion of new managers or employees. Existing talent was developed instead.

SUCCESSION PLANNING IN SMALL-, MEDIUM-SIZED, AND CLOSELY HELD FIRMS Succession planning can be especially important in small- and medium-sized firms, but studies show that these firms have done the least in this area. Only 22% of small- and medium-sized firms have formal succession plans.[4]

In closely held firms (those that are not publicly traded on the stock exchanges), most CEOs plan to pass the business on to a family member. Planning in advance for the orderly succession and development needs of the successor is important to avoid a host of potential problems.[5]

Replacement Charts Traditional career paths in a company include a range of possible moves: lateral moves across departments, vertical moves within departments, and others. Each possible path represents actual positions, the experience needed to fill the positions, and the relationships of positions to each other. Replacement charts (similar to depth charts used by football teams to show the backup players at each position) give a simple model of the process. The purpose of replacement charts is to ensure that the right individual is available at the right time and has had sufficient experience to handle the job.

Replacement charts can be part of the development planning process. Such a chart can specify the kind of development each individual needs for promotion. This information can be used to identify development needs and "promotion ladders" for people.

❖ Development Needs Analysis

Either the company or the individual can analyze what a given person needs by way of development. The goal, of course, is to identify strengths and weaknesses. Methods used by organizations to assess development needs include assessment centers, psychological testing, and performance appraisals.

***Assessment Center**
A collection of instruments and exercises designed to diagnose a person's development needs.

Assessment Centers **Assessment centers** are not places as much as they are collections of instruments and exercises designed to diagnose a person's development needs. They are used both for developing and for selecting managers. Police departments as well as many other types of large organizations use assessment centers.

Typically, in an assessment-center experience, a potential manager spends two or three days away from the job performing many activities. These activities may include role playing, pencil-and-paper tests, cases, leaderless group discussions, management games, peer evaluations, and in-basket exercises, in which the trainee handles typical problems coming across a manager's desk. For the most part, the exercises are samples of managerial situations that require the use of managerial skills and behaviors. During the exercises, participants are observed by several specially trained judges.

Assessment centers are seen as an excellent means for determining management potential.[6] These centers are praised because they are thought to overcome the biases inherent in interview situations, supervisor ratings, and written tests.[7] Experience has shown that such key variables as leadership, initiative, and supervisory skills are almost impossible to measure with paper-and-pencil tests alone. Another advantage of assessment centers is that they help identify employees with potential in large organizations. Supervisors may nominate people for the assessment center, or employees may volunteer. The opportunity to volunteer especially is valuable for talented people who may not be recognized as such by their supervisors.

Assessment centers also can raise problems. Some managers may use the assessment center as a way to avoid difficult promotion decisions. Suppose a plant supervisor has personally decided that an employee is not a qualified candidate for promotion. Rather than stick by the decision and tell the employee, the supervisor may send the employee to the assessment center, hoping that the report will show that the employee is not qualified for promotion. Problems between the employee and the supervisor will be worse if the employee earns a positive report. If the report is negative, the supervisor's views are validated, but using the assessment center in this way is not recommended because it does not aid the development of the employee.

Two further difficulties often encountered with assessment centers are making sure the exercises in the assessment center are valid predictors of management performance and properly selecting and training the assessors.

Yet another concern is that assessment centers are expensive. The actual cost for each candidate who goes through a center varies from organization to organization but ranges from $600 to $6,000. Of course, the cost of making a mistake in management selection is great, too. According to some estimates, the cost of terminating a department head far exceeds $20,000 in legal, salary, and benefit payments. Many major firms that have created assessment centers, including General Electric, Union Carbide, AT&T, and IBM, have decided they are worth the cost.

Psychological Testing Psychological pencil-and-paper tests have been used for several years to determine employees' developmental potential and needs. Intelligence tests, verbal and mathematical reasoning tests, and personality tests are often used. Such testing can furnish useful information to employers about such factors as motivation, reasoning abilities, leadership styles, interpersonal response traits, and job preferences.

The biggest problem with psychological testing lies in interpretation, because untrained managers, supervisors, and workers usually cannot accurately interpret test results. After a professional reports a test taker's scores to someone in the organization, the interpretation often is left to untrained managers who may attach their own meanings to the results. It also should be recognized that some psychological tests are of limited validity, and test takers can easily fake desirable responses. Thus, psychological testing is appropriate only when the testing and feedback process is closely supervised by a qualified professional throughout.

Performance Appraisals Well-done performance appraisals can be a source of development information. Performance data on productivity, employee relations, job knowledge, and other relevant dimensions can be measured this way. As noted in Chapter 12, appraisals that are designed for development purposes may be more useful than appraisals designed strictly for administrative purposes.

❖ Individual and Organizational Development Planning

In deciding which approaches to development hold most promise in a particular case, both an organizational plan for a person and the person's plans must receive consideration. Individuals may do some *self-assessment* as part of the process. Many tests, workshops, and books are available to assist in self-assessment. Software, such as *Career Architect,* is available is well.[8] A person's interests and long-range plans must be consistent with what the organization has in mind for development if development is to be successful. Cultural differences such as those described in the HR Perspective can play a role.

The actual development approaches available are described next under two major headings: job-site development and off-site development. Both are appropriate in developing managers and other employees.

❖ Development Approaches: Job-Site Methods

A number of job-site development methods are available. A major difficulty with development that takes place on the job site is that too often unplanned activi-

HR PERSPECTIVE

Global Management Development Issues in Japanese and American Cultures

As business contact between Japan and the United States has increased, a better understanding of the basic differences between the values of the two cultures has grown. For those who must manage organizations and employees in the other culture, development is crucial.

The extensive diversity of the United States has been produced by waves of immigrants from many different countries. Immigrants have found a country defined by Judeo-Christian thinking that emphasizes individual choice and separates spiritual and business life. Rebellion against authority is often esteemed. Individual effort is seen as leading to accomplishment.

In contrast, Japanese society evolved from a homogeneous population shaped by religions that teach a love of natural form, social order, and self-denial. Strict codes of social conduct and a strict social hierarchy maintain order.

A Japanese who comes to America to manage, or an American who goes to Japan, is likely to meet with unpleasant surprises because of practices counter to familiar values. Four areas stand out in this regard:

1. In *community life,* the Japanese manager confronts unfamiliar social diversity, violence and crime, poverty, and ignorance of foreign ways. The American does not understand long-standing Japanese customs and sees an aloof, clannish community.
2. In *business practices,* the Japanese manager encounters a legal minefield, a short time horizon, hasty deals, and less emphasis on service. The American is frustrated in Japan by what is seen as vagueness and delay, ethical violations, overworked employees, and influence peddling.
3. In *organizational dynamics,* the Japanese manager sees narrow careerism, political confrontation, employee disloyalty, and a lack of spiritual quality in the organization. The American manager in Japan sees lack of managerial accountability, a closed inner circle, stifled employees, and discriminatory practices.
4. In *interpersonal dealings,* the Japanese manager encounters unaccustomed assertiveness, frankness, egoism, and impulsiveness. The American finds distrust and secrecy, arrogance, caution, and excessive sensitivity.

To the Japanese manager, American society seems chaotic and dangerous and American businesses too quick to act and change. Organizations appear to be filled with dissention, and people seem offensively blunt, aggressive, and disrespectful of authority.

The American manager sees Japanese society as closed to outsiders, businesses as slow moving, organizations as abusive and obsessed with saving face. The people seem timid, risk-averse, and too easily embarrassed.

Despite this gloomy picture, managers of both nations *do* develop in the other culture and grow to appreciate its strengths. However, the initial culture shock, brought on by impressions based on very different values, presents a formidable hurdle.[9]

ties are regarded as development. It is imperative that managers plan and coordinate development efforts so that the desired development actually occurs.

Coaching
Daily training and feedback given to employees by immediate supervisors.

COACHING The oldest on-the-job development technique is **coaching,** which is the daily training and feedback given to employees by immediate supervisors. Coaching involves a continual process of learning by doing. For effective coaching, a healthy and open relationship must exist between employees and their supervisors or managers. Many firms conduct formal training courses to improve the coaching skills of their managers.

Unfortunately, like other on-the-job methods, coaching can be temptingly easy to implement without any planning at all. Even if someone has been good at a job or a particular part of a job, there is no guarantee that he or she will be able to coach someone else to do it well—but that is often the assumption made. It is easy for the "coach" to fall short in guiding the learner systematically, even if he or she knows which systematic experiences are best. Sometimes, too, doing a full day's work gets priority over learning and coaching. Also, many skills have an intellectual component that might be better learned from a book or lecture before coaching occurs.

COMMITTEE ASSIGNMENTS Assigning promising employees to important committees can give these employees a broadening experience and can help them to understand the personalities, issues, and processes governing the organization. For instance, assigning employees to a safety committee may give them the safety background they need to become supervisors. Also, they may experience the problems involved in maintaining employee safety awareness. But managers should be aware that it is possible for committee assignments to become time-wasting activities, too.

❖Job Rotation
The process of shifting an employee from job to job.

JOB ROTATION **Job rotation** is the process of shifting an employee from job to job. In some organizations, job rotation is unplanned, whereas other organizations have elaborate charts and schedules precisely planning the program for each employee.

Job rotation is widely used as a development technique. For example, a promising young manager may spend three months in the plant, three months in corporate planning, and three months in purchasing. When properly handled, such job rotation fosters a greater understanding of the organization. At one large firm, job rotation is used during a 15-month sales training program. Trainees work in at least three areas, such as industrial sales, retail sales, and product training.

Especially when opportunities for promotion are scarce, job rotation through lateral transfers may be beneficial in rekindling enthusiasm and developing new talents. The best lateral moves do one or more of the following:

- ❖ Move the person into the core business
- ❖ Provide closer contact with the customer
- ❖ Teach new skills or perspectives

In spite of its benefits, managers should recognize that job rotation can be expensive. Furthermore, a substantial amount of managerial time is lost when trainees change positions because they must become acquainted with different people and techniques in each new unit.

"ASSISTANT-TO" POSITIONS An "assistant-to" position is a staff position immediately under a manager. Through such jobs, trainees can work with outstanding managers they might not otherwise have met. Some organizations have "junior boards of directors" or "management cabinets" to which trainees may be appointed. Assignments such as these are useful if trainees have the opportunity to deal with challenging or interesting assignments.

❖ DEVELOPMENT APPROACHES: OFF-SITE METHODS

Off-the-job-site development techniques can be effective because they give the individual an opportunity to get away from the job and concentrate solely on what is to be learned. Moreover, meeting with other people who are concerned with somewhat different problems and come from different organizations may provide an employee with new perspectives on old problems. Various off-site methods are used.

CLASSROOM COURSES AND DEGREES Many off-the-job development programs include some classroom instruction. The advantage of classroom training is that it is widely accepted because most people are familiar with it. But a disadvantage of classroom instruction is the lecture system, which encourages passive listening and reduced learner participation. Sometimes trainees have little opportunity to question, clarify, and discuss the lecture material. The effectiveness of classroom instruction depends on the size of the group, the ability of the instructor, and the subject matter.

Organizations often send employees to externally sponsored seminars or professional courses. These programs are offered by many colleges and universities and by professional associations such as the American Management Association. Some larger organizations have established training centers exclusively for their own employees.

Many organizations encourage continuing education by paying for employees to take college courses. A very high proportion of organizations reimburses employees for school tuition. Some employers encourage employees to study for advanced degrees such as MBAs in this manner. Employees often earn these degrees at night after their regular workdays end.[10]

LOGGING ON

Information on management development sources available through the American Management Association can be found at

http://www.tregistry.com/ttr/ama.htm

Human Relations Training Human relations training originated with the well-known Hawthorne studies. Initially, the purpose of the training was to prepare supervisors for "people problems" brought to them by their employees. This type of training focuses on the development of the human relations skills a person needs to work well with others. Many human relations training programs are aimed at new or relatively inexperienced first-line supervisors and middle managers. Human relations programs typically have sessions on motivation, leadership, employee communication, and humanizing the workplace.

The problem with such programs is the difficulty in measuring their effectiveness. The development of human relations skills is a long-range goal; tangible results are hard to identify over the span of several years. Consequently, such programs often are measured only by participants' reactions to them. As mentioned in the previous chapter, reaction-level measurement is the weakest form of evaluating the effectiveness of training.

Case Studies The case study is a classroom-oriented development technique that has been widely used. Cases provide a medium through which trainees can study the application of management or behavioral concepts. The emphasis is on application and analysis, not mere memorization of concepts.

One common complaint is that cases sometimes are not sufficiently realistic to be useful. Also, cases may contain information inappropriate to the kinds of decisions that trainees would make in a real situation. This also can be one of the values of case studies, though, if the focus is to test whether or not students can select appropriate information.

Role Playing **Role playing** is a development technique requiring the trainee to assume a role in a given situation and act out behaviors associated with that role. Participants gain an appreciation of the many behavioral factors influencing on-the-job situations. For instance, a labor relations director may be asked to play the role of a union vice-president in a negotiating situation in order to give the director insight into the constraints and problems facing union bargaining representatives. Role playing is a useful tool in some situations, but a word of caution applies: Trainees are often uncomfortable in role-playing situations, and trainers must introduce the situations well so that learning can occur.

Role Playing
A development technique requiring the trainee to assume a role in a given situation and act out behaviors associated with that role.

Simulations (Business Games) Several business games, or simulations, are available commercially. A **simulation** requires the participant to analyze a situation and decide the best course of action based on the data given. Some are computer-interactive games in which individuals or teams draw up a set of mar-

Simulation
A development technique that requires the participant to analyze a situation and decide the best course of action based on the data given.

keting plans for an organization to determine such factors as the amount of resources to allocate for advertising, product design, selling, and sales effort.[11] The participants make a variety of decisions, and then the computer tells them how well they did in relation to competing individuals or teams. Simulations have been used to diagnose organizational problems as well.

When properly done, a simulation can be a useful management development tool. However, simulation receives the same criticism as role playing: Realism is sometimes lacking, so the learning experience is diminished. Learning must be the focus, not just "playing the game."

***Sabbatical Leave**
Paid time off the job to develop and rejuvenate oneself.

Sabbaticals and Leaves of Absence A **sabbatical leave** is paid time off the job to develop and rejuvenate oneself. Popular for many years in the academic world, where professors take a leave to sharpen their skills and advance their education or conduct research, sabbaticals have been adopted in the business community as well. More than 10% of U.S. corporations offer sabbaticals.[12] For example, Xerox Corporation gives some of its employees six months or more off with pay to work on "socially desirable" projects. Projects include training people in urban ghettos and providing technical assistance to overseas countries. Sabbaticals are often spent in some form of corporate volunteer program.[13] Sabbaticals are most commonly given to executives in high-tech businesses with around-the-clock projects. They are becoming popular in other countries, including the United Kingdom, as well.

Companies offering sabbaticals speak well of the results. They say sabbaticals help prevent burnout, offer advantages in recruiting and retention, boost morale, and enable people to carry heavier workloads upon their return.

One of the disadvantages of paid sabbaticals is the cost. Also, the nature of the learning experience is not within the control of the organization and is left somewhat to chance.

Outdoor Training Many organizations send executives off to ordeals in the wilderness, called outdoor training, as a development tool. General Foods, Xerox, GE, Honeywell, Burger King, AMEX, Sears, and other organizations have sent executives and managers to the outdoors for stays of several days or even weeks. The rationale for these wilderness excursions is as follows: For individuals, such experiences can increase self-confidence and help them reevaluate personal goals and efforts. For work units, a shared risk outside the office environment can create a sense of teamwork. The challenges may include rock climbing in the California desert, whitewater rafting on the Rogue River, backpacking in the Rocky Mountains, or handling a longboat off the coast of Maine.

The survival-type management development course may have more impact than many other management seminars. There are perils, however, and some participants have not been able to handle the physical and emotional challenges associated with rappeling down a cliff or climbing a 40-foot tower. The decision whether to sponsor such programs should depend on the personalities of the employees who will be involved.

Figure 11–4 summarizes the major advantages and disadvantages of the various on-site and off-site approaches to development. Some recent research suggests that the method chosen affects the compensation received later in a person's career. Company-sponsored development and seminars outside the workplace were positively related to wage-level increases when compared with correspondence courses, vocational courses, and apprenticeships.[14]

❖ FIGURE 11–4 ❖
ADVANTAGES AND DISADVANTAGES OF MAJOR DEVELOPMENT APPROACHES

Job-Site Methods	Advantage	Disadvantage
Coaching	Natural and job-related	Difficulty in finding good coaches
Committee Assignments	Participants are involved in critical processes	Can be time waster
Job Rotation	Gives excellent overview of the organization	Long start-up time
"Assistant to" Positions	Provides exposure to an excellent manager	Possible shortage of good assignments

Off-Site Methods	Advantage	Disadvantage
Classroom Courses and Degrees	Familiar, accepted, status	Does not always improve performance
Human Relations Training	Deals with important management skills	Difficult to measure effectiveness
Case Studies	Practical; those involved can learn from real management	Information may be inadequate for some decision makers
Role Playing	May lead to attitude change in difficult interpersonal situations	Trainees may be uncomfortable
Simulations	Realism and integration	Inappropriate "game playing"
Sabbaticals	Rejuvenating as well as developmental	Expensive and employees may lose contact with job
Outdoor Training	Physical challenges can increase self-confidence and teamwork	Not appropriate for all because of physical nature; dangerous

❖ MANAGEMENT DEVELOPMENT

Development is important for all employees but especially so for managers. Unless managers are appropriately developed, resources (including employees) throughout the organization may not be managed well. Management development should be seen as a way of imparting the knowledge and judgment needed by managers to meet the strategic objectives of the organization. Among these skills are leading, dealing with change, helping (coaching and advising) subordinates, controlling when necessary, and providing feedback.

Experience is an important part of management development. Indeed, experience often contributes more to the development of senior managers than classroom training does, but much of that experience occurs informally on the job over time. Development on the job is related to the extent to which the job pre-

❖ Figure 11–5 ❖
Opportunities to Learn Managerial Lessons through Experience on the Job

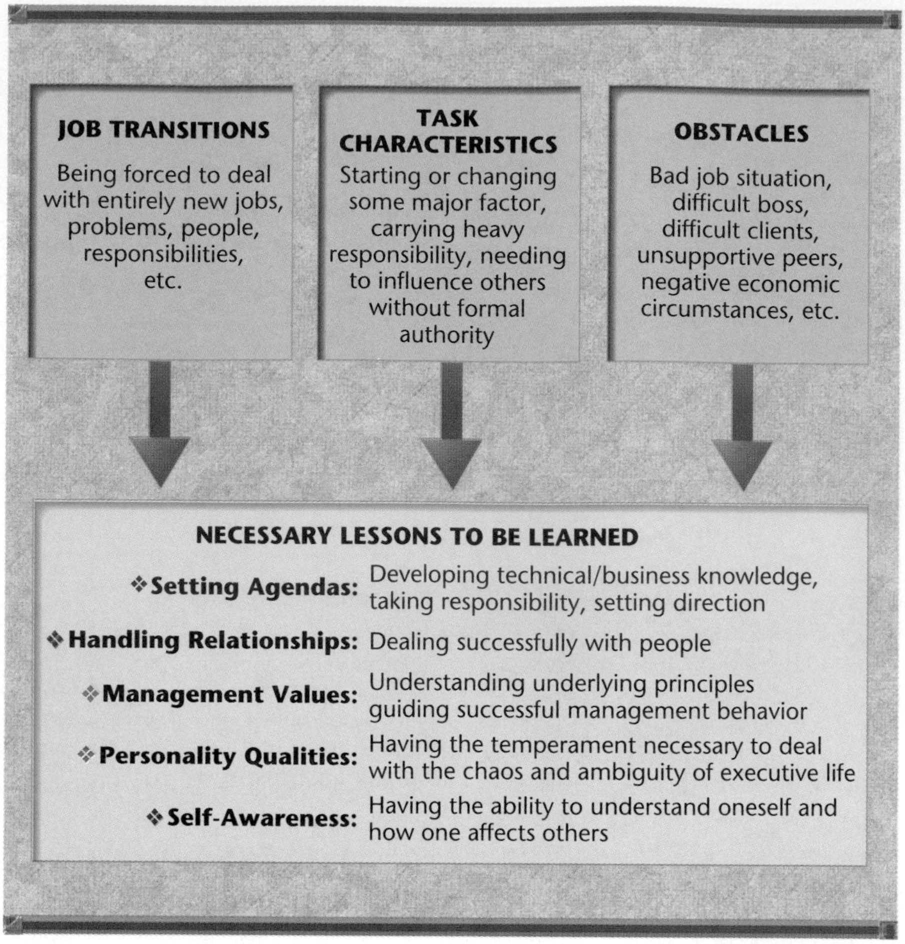

sents a challenge and offers development opportunities. Figure 11–5 shows some of the lessons and features of the job that are important for effective management development.[15] Next some specific management development methods are examined.

❖ Managerial Modeling

❖Behavior Modeling
Copying someone else's behavior.

A common adage in management development says managers tend to manage as they were managed. Another way of saying this is that managers learn by **behavior modeling**, or copying someone else's behavior. This is not surprising because a great deal of human behavior is learned by modeling. Children learn by modeling the behaviors of parents and older children, which means they are familiar with the process by the time they grow up. Management development efforts can take advantage of natural human behavior by matching young or developing managers with appropriate models and then reinforcing the desirable behaviors exhibited.

It is important to note that modeling is not a straightforward imitation, or copying, process; it is considerably more complex. For example, one can learn what *not* to do by observing a model. Thus, exposure to both positive and negative models can be beneficial to a new manager.

❖ Management Coaching

Coaching combines observations with suggestions. Like modeling, it is a very natural way for humans to learn. In the context of management development, coaching is best accomplished when it involves a relationship between two managers for a brief period of time as they perform their jobs. Coaching has many applications. It has found some success in solving behavioral problems that threaten to derail managers; abrasive or inflexible managers may benefit from coaching by the right executive.[16] Coaching does not have to be oriented toward aberrant behavior, however; just sharing with another manager how a problem might be approached is coaching, too.

❖ Mentoring

Mentoring is a relationship in which managers at the midpoints in their careers aid individuals in the first stages of their careers. Technical, interpersonal, and political skills can be conveyed in such a relationship from the older to the younger person. Not only does the younger one benefit, but the older one may enjoy the challenge of sharing his or her wisdom. The four stages in most successful mentor/learner relationships are shown in Figure 11–6.[17]

***Mentoring**
A relationship in which managers at midpoints in careers aid individuals in the first stages of careers.

Mentoring has been studied enough to allow some conclusions to be drawn. First, it apparently works. Women with mentors were found to move up faster than those without mentors, for example. As they moved to the top, they in turn became mentors.[18] Mentoring may be a useful way to attack the "glass ceiling" phenomenon, discussed next.

The term *glass ceiling* describes the situation in which women fail to progress to top management positions. Little real research has been done on the glass ceiling phenomenon; much of the literature is based on narratives from individuals.[19] However, in all countries, the proportion of women holding managerial jobs is less than the proportion of men holding such jobs. Situations are changing in both the private and federal sector, but not with great speed.[20] Successful women executives suggest that breaking the glass ceiling requires developing political sophistication, building credibility, refining a management style, and shouldering responsibilities.[21]

❖ Figure 11–6 ❖
Stages in Mentor/Learner Relationships

STAGE	LENGTH OF TIME	YOUNGER MANAGER	OLDER MANAGER
Initiation	6–12 months	Admires the senior manager's competence; recognizes him or her as source of support and guidance	Realizes younger manager is someone with potential and "is coachable"
Cultivation	2–5 years	Gains self-confidence, new attitudes, values, and styles of operation	Provides challenging work, coaching, visibility, protection, and sponsorship
Separation	6–12 months	Experiences independence and autonomy; has feelings of turmoil, anxiety, and loss at times	Demonstrates his or her success at developing management talent as they move apart
Redefinition	Ongoing	Responds with gratitude for the early years but is not dependent; relationship becomes a friendship	Continues to be a supporter; takes pride in the younger manager's accomplishments; relationship becomes a friendship

Mentoring is not without its problems. Young minority managers report difficulty finding white mentors. Men are less willing than women to be mentors. Further, mentors who are dissatisfied with their jobs and those who teach a narrow or distorted view of events may not help a young manager's development. However, most managers have a series of advisors/mentors during their careers, and they may find advantages in learning

HR PERSPECTIVE

Sink or Swim—Management Development at Retail

Michael Quinn is an African American, a college dropout, 25 years old, and the manager of his own Wal-Mart store. The promising young store manager is an example of the fast-track approach to management taken by retail stores. Michael says, "It amazes me that I'm in charge of a business that has sales of $22 million a year and more than 200 associates." Including bonuses, his annual earnings will be about $75,000.

Rapid growth by numerous retailers has left the industry short of what is generally cited as the *key ingredient* in a successful store—good management. Over the past few years and continuing into the future thousands of managers must be hired to run new Wal-Mart, Home Depot, Target, Circuit City, and Computer City stores. These store manager jobs can pay well into six figures and offer rapid advancement.

Typically, 22-year-old college graduates receive a few weeks of training and then get a department in a store. A few weeks out of school and the novice managers may find themselves with 20 employees and an $8-million-a-year department. However, the opportunity comes with a cost. Work weeks average 60 hours and often demand something nearer 80. Relocation is frequent—Quinn has moved seven times with Wal-Mart.

But advancement can be rapid. Target's management trainees can become managers of small stores in as little as three years, making $50,000 plus bonuses. After that, district manager and regional vice-president positions can follow. Advancement is not limited to one company. Discounter retailers often raid the competition for good store managers with increasing frequency.

Of course, not everyone succeeds. The inability to deal with employee turnover, theft, and the unrelenting pressure for sales and profit takes its toll. For example, Quinn's promotion came at the expense of an older manager who was "busted down." "The bottom line," Quinn says, "is, if you don't keep performing you don't last." Sink or swim. Only the strong survive which is managerial Darwinism, represented by on-the-job development![22]

from many perspectives. For example, the experience of having many mentors may help them to identify key behaviors in management success and failure. Further, they may find that their previous mentors provide useful sources for networking.[23]

❖ Problems with HR Development Efforts

Development efforts are subject to certain common mistakes and problems. The HR Perspective illustrates one type of management development that may work for some retailers, but it may not be as appropriate in other industries. Most of the problems result from inadequate planning and a lack of coordination of HR development efforts. Common problems include the following:

- ❖ Inadequate needs analysis
- ❖ Trying out fad programs or training methods
- ❖ Abdicating responsibility for development to staff
- ❖ Trying to substitute training for selection
- ❖ Lack of training among those who lead the development activities
- ❖ Using only "courses" as the road to development
- ❖ Encapsulated development

❖Encapsulated Development
Situation in which an individual learns new methods and ideas in a development course and returns to a work unit that is still bound by old attitudes and methods.

The last item on the list may require some additional explanation. **Encapsulated development** occurs when an individual learns new methods and ideas in a development course and returns to a work unit that is still bound by old attitudes and methods. The reward system and the working conditions have not changed. Although the trainee has learned new ways to handle certain situations, these methods cannot be applied because of resistance from those having an investment in the status quo. The new knowledge remains encapsulated in the classroom setting. Encapsulated development is an obvious waste of time and money. For example, in some organizations, diversity training efforts have been wasted because follow-up and reinforcement were not done.

❖ CAREERS

A **career** is the sequence of work-related positions a person occupies throughout life. While it is still possible to build a long career with a single organization, that certainly is not the norm today. People pursue careers to satisfy deeply individual needs. At one time, identity with one employer seemed to fulfill many of those needs.[24] But now, the distinction between an individual's career as the organization sees it and the career as the individual sees it is important.

❖Career
The sequence of work-related positions a person occupies throughout life.

❖ ORGANIZATION-CENTERED VERSUS INDIVIDUAL-CENTERED CAREER PLANNING

The nature of career planning can be somewhat confusing because different perspectives exist. Career planning can be organization centered, individual centered, or both.

Organization-centered career planning focuses on jobs and on constructing career paths that provide for the logical progression of people between jobs in an organization. These paths represent ladders that individuals can climb to advance in certain organizational units. For example, a person might enter the sales department as a sales counselor, then be promoted to account director, to sales manager, and finally to vice-president of sales.

❖Organization-Centered Career Planning
Career planning that focuses on jobs and on constructing career paths that provide for the logical progression of people between jobs in an organization.

Some argue that there are ethical questions connected with organizational involvement in individuals' career planning and advising. For example, organizational commitment to "lifetime employment" is obviously fading fast in the United States because of competition and cost cutting. For organizations where lifetime employment is unlikely, career planning for employees may risk creating unrealistic expectations about the employees' future. Even more serious is the dilemma that may arise if the best career move an employee could make would be to leave the organization: Would an HR staff member or manager say so, if the person was a valuable contributor?

Individual-centered career planning focuses on individuals' careers rather than organizational needs. As done by employees themselves, individual goals and skills are the focus of the analysis. Such analyses might consider situations both within and outside the organization that could expand a person's career. The points of focus for organization- and individual-oriented career planning are compared in Figure 11–7.

❖Individual-Centered Career Planning
Career planning that focuses on individuals' careers rather than on organizational needs.

Retrenchment and downsizing have changed career plans for many people. In particular, middle-aged managers and nonmanagerial employees have found themselves in "career transition"—in other words, in need of finding another job. As mentioned, employers can no longer be counted on for lifetime employment. In the last 10 years, the number of people changing occupations has almost doubled, from 6.6 million to 10 million a year.[25] Small businesses, some started by early retirees from big companies, provide many of the new career opportunities.

❖ HOW DO PEOPLE CHOOSE CAREERS?

Four general individual characteristics affect how people make career choices.

1. *Interests.* People tend to pursue careers that they believe match their interests.

❖ **Figure 11–7** ❖
Organizational and Individual Career-Planning Perspectives

ORGANIZATIONAL CAREER PERSPECTIVE	INDIVIDUAL CAREER PERSPECTIVE
❖ Identify future organizational staffing needs ❖ Plan career ladders ❖ Assess individual potential and training needs ❖ Match organizational needs with individual abilities ❖ Audit and develop a career system for the organization	❖ Identify personal abilities and interests ❖ Plan life and work goals ❖ Assess alternative paths inside and outside the organization ❖ Note changes in interests and goals as career and life stage change

2. *Self-image.* A career is an extension of a person's self-image, as well as a molder of it.[26]
3. *Personality.* This factor includes an employee's personal orientation (for example, whether the employee is realistic, enterprising, artistic) and personal needs (including affiliation, power, and achievement needs).
4. *Social backgrounds.* Socioeconomic status and the education and occupation level of a person's parents are a few factors included in this category.

Less is known about how and why people choose specific organizations than about why they choose specific careers.[27] One obvious factor is the availability of a job when the person is looking for work. The amount of information available about alternatives is an important factor as well. Beyond these issues, people seem to pick an organization on the basis of a "fit" between the climate of the organization as they perceive it and their own personal characteristics.[28] The HR Perspective discusses research on existing jobs and careers.

❖ General Career Progression

The typical career today probably will include many different positions, transitions, and organizations—more so than in the past, when employees were less

HR PERSPECTIVE

Research on Existing Jobs and Individuals' Interests

Meredith Downes and K. Galen Kroeck researched an interesting question on careers. As discussed in the *Journal of Vocational Behavior,* they noted that even during periods of high unemployment, there are jobs for which few employees can be found. There are many reasons for this phenomenon, but could one reason be that the interests of the labor force are different from the needs of employers?

The researchers attempted to answer this question by identifying the career interest areas in which demand for employees will be the greatest and the areas in which jobs will not be very plentiful despite strong interest among potential employees. The study used a sample of 819 high school students and 656 working adults. The researchers collected interest data on these subjects using the Holland occupational interest measure.

Data on existing positions were collected from *Monthly Labor Review* (MLR), a Bureau of Labor Statistics publication. The MLR lists the total numbers employed in the U.S. in each of the 292 jobs it recognizes and the outlook for employment in each. Comparing the two sets of data indeed did show that certain job categories were likely to be undersubscribed because of lack of interest, while others would be oversubscribed because too many people were interested.

Job categories with too little interest included many managerial occupations—airport, hotel, motel, and financial institution managers, for example. Among high school students, practical jobs involving work with tools or machines were not sufficiently interesting, but these jobs were interesting to working adults. High school students were highly interested in jobs in the artistic, investigative, and social interest areas. However, the greatest needs for employees will not be in these areas but will be in the areas of math, computer science, personal services, and protective services.

The researchers note that the differences found between students and adults is evidence that interests can change during a person's lifetime. It is good that interests can and do change, since it appears that high school interests are not especially well aligned with career needs.[29]

❖ FIGURE 11–8 ❖
GENERAL PERIODS IN CAREERS

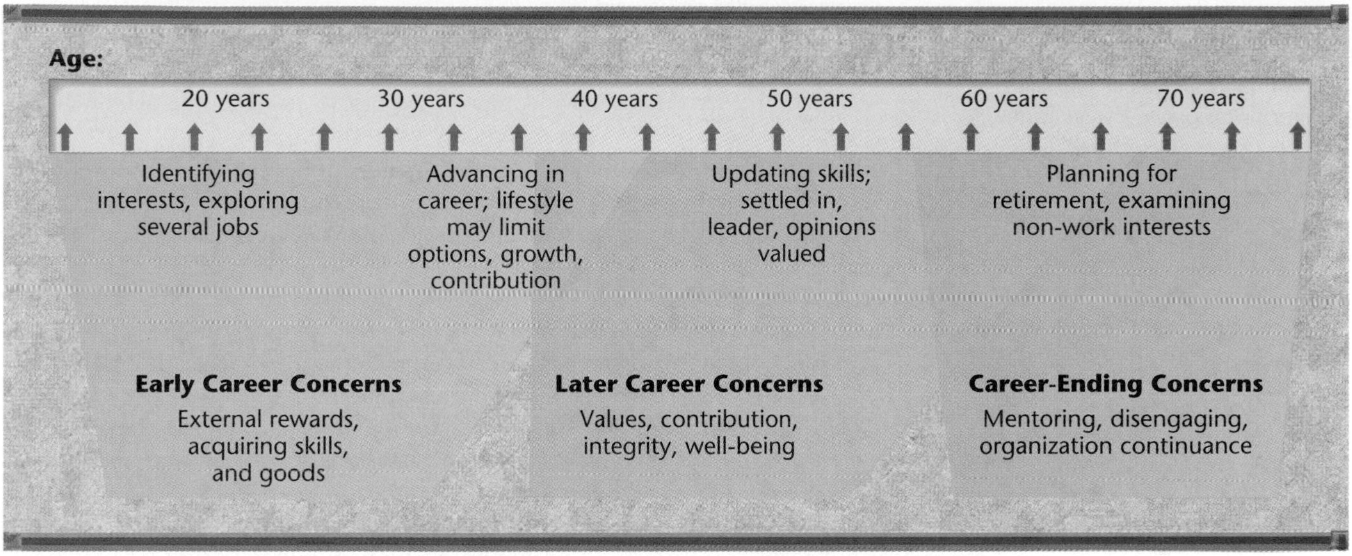

mobile and organizations more stable as long-term employers. In this context, it is useful to think about general patterns in people's careers and in their lives.

Many theorists in adult development describe the first half of life as the young adult's quest for competence and a way to make a mark in the world. According to this view, happiness during this time is sought primarily through external achievement and the acquisition of skills and goods. The second half of life is different. Once an adult starts to measure time from the expected end of his or her life rather than from the beginning, the need for competence and acquisition changes to the need for integrity, values, and well-being. Internal values take precedence over external scorecards for many. In addition, mature adults already have certain skills, so their focus may shift to other interests. Career-ending concerns reflect additional shifts also. Figure 11–8 shows a model identifying general periods in a career and a lifetime.

Contained within this view is the idea that careers and lives are not predictably linear but cyclical. Periods of high stability are followed by transition, by less stability, and by inevitable discoveries, disappointments, and triumphs. Therefore, lives and careers must be viewed as cycles of structure and transition. This view may be a useful perspective for those suffering the negative results of downsizing and early career plateaus in large organizations. Such a perspective argues for the importance of flexibility in an individual's career and may encourage a willingness to acquire diverse skills.

❖ RETIREMENT

Whether retirement comes at age 50 or 70, it can require a major adjustment for many people. Some common emotional adjustments faced by retirees include:

- *Self-management.* The person must adjust to being totally self-directed after retirement. There is no longer any supervisor or work agenda dictating what to do.
- *Need to belong.* When a person retires, he or she is no longer a member of the work group that took up so much time and formed an important social structure for so many years. What takes its place?

LOGGING ON

An example of a career planning system for employees working in the State of Washington is found at

http://www.wagov/esd/lstop/

- *Pride in achievement.* Achievement reinforces self-esteem and is often centered around work. In retirement, past achievements quickly wear thin as a source of self-esteem.
- *Territoriality.* Personal "turf," in the form of office, company, and title, is lost in retirement. Other ways to satisfy territorial needs must be found.
- *Goals.* Organizations provide many of a person's goals. Some people may be unprepared to set their own goals when they retire.

Of course, from the standpoint of the organization, retirement is an orderly way to move people out at the ends of their careers. Mindful of the problems that retirement poses for some individuals, however, some organizations are experimenting with *phased retirement* through gradually reduced workweeks and increased vacation time. These and other preretirement and postretirement programs aimed at helping employees deal with problems aid in transition to a useful retirement.

The phenomenon of "forced" early retirement that began in the 1980s has required thousands of managers and professionals to determine what is important to them while they are still young and healthy and to plan accordingly. Because of economic factors, many organizations have used early retirement to reduce their workforces. Some of these young retirees "go fishing," but many begin second careers. Tom Peterson, Jr., of Dallas retired early and discovered he was not ready to retire. Within six months, he had found another job. He now collects a pension from the first career and is working at the second. Tom is not unusual; 73% of male retirees aged 50 to 54 have jobs. Among those aged 55 to 61, about half are working.[30] In Tom's case, it was not the need for money that caused him to return to work (although that *is* the case most often). He simply needed to have the responsibility of a job. Another major reason retirees have gone back to work is to afford health insurance, as many companies have eliminated retiree health benefits.

❖ Career Planning: Individual Issues

Effective career planning at the individual level first requires self-knowledge. A person must face a number of issues: How hard am I really willing to work? What is most important in life to me? What trade-off between work and family or leisure am I willing to make? These questions and others must be confronted honestly before personal goals and objectives can be realistically set in a career plan. Professional counseling may be helpful.

As suggested earlier, changing jobs and careers has become an accepted practice in recent years, and it can be financially rewarding. However, "job-hopping" (changing jobs very frequently) can cause problems with retirement, vacation, seniority, and other benefits. Perhaps more important is the perception that job-hopping is a sign of instability, especially in more mature managers.

❖ Career Plateaus

Those who do not job-hop may face another problem: career plateaus. As the baby boom generation reaches midlife, and as large employers cut back on their workforces, increasing numbers of managers will find themselves at a career plateau. Plateauing may seem a sign of failure to many people, and plateaued employees can cause problems for employers when frustration affects performance.[31]

Perhaps, in part, because of plateauing, surveys show that middle managers' optimism about opportunity for advancement has declined. Indeed, large industrial organizations have dealt with the problem of overstaffing by laying off many middle managers. As pointed out earlier, though, middle managers are not a disappearing breed. In small- and middle-sized organizations across the country, the ranks of middle managers actually are growing. The result for these firms is a bonanza of talent and experience.[32] (But one consultant, in a bit of an overstatement, says of large companies that "Their only career program is outplacement."[33]) Meanwhile, for the middle managers left behind in large companies, the world has changed. They have additional responsibility and more influence in the decision-making process, making for a leaner, more competitive organization.

Figure 11–9 shows how a new "portable" career path may be evolving in keeping with the apparent movement away from an orderly series of cyclic alterations at prescribed chronological ages.[34] This evolution means that careers are less predictable than in previous decades.

❖ FIGURE 11–9 ❖
THE NEW "PORTABLE" CAREER PATH

The "New Portable" Career Path

Beginning
Spend several years at large company to learn skills and build network

Expanding
Begin moonlighting to develop broader skills and make contacts; establish good reputation

Changing
Start a company; go to work for smaller companies; change industries

Mid-Career
Refresh skills; take a sabbatical; go back to school for new credentials; gain experiences in a nonprofit organization

Toward End of Career
Move to appealing projects as a temporary employee or subcontractor

❖ DUAL CAREER PATHS FOR TECHNICAL AND PROFESSIONAL WORKERS

Technical and professional workers, such as engineers and scientists, present a special challenge for organizations. Many of them want to stay in their labs or at their drawing boards rather than move into management; yet advancement frequently *requires* a move into management. Most of these people like the idea of the responsibility and opportunity associated with advancement, but they do not want to leave the technical puzzles and problems at which they excel.

The *dual career ladder* is an attempt to solve this problem. As shown in Figure 11–10, a person can advance up either the management ladder or a corresponding ladder on the technical/professional side. Dual career paths have been used at IBM, Union Carbide, and AT&T/Bell Labs for years. They are most common in technology-driven industries such as pharmaceuticals, chemicals, computers, and electronics. Pacific Bell has created a dual career ladder in its data-processing department to reward talented technical people who do not want to move into management. Different tracks, each with attractive job titles and pay opportunities, are provided.

Unfortunately, the technical/professional ladder sometimes is viewed as leading to "second-class citizenship" within the organization. For a second or third career track to be taken seriously, management must apply standards as rigorous as those applied to management promotions. Studies have shown that dual career paths are ineffective when organizations fail to document and define performance qualifications and standards.[35]

❖ DUAL-CAREER COUPLES

The increasing number of women in the workforce, particularly in professional careers, has greatly increased the number of dual-career couples, as noted in Chapter 2. The U.S. Bureau of Labor Statistics estimates that 81% of all couples are dual-career couples.[36] Marriages in which both mates are managers, professionals, or technicians have doubled since 1970. Leading areas of growth in the number of dual-career couples are the West Coast, Denver, Chicago, New York, and the Washington, D.C.–Baltimore area. Problem areas involving dual-career couples include recruitment, transfer, and family issues.

It is important that the career-development problems of dual career couples be recognized as early as possible, especially if they involve transfer, so that realistic alternatives can be explored. Early planning by employees and their supervisors can prevent crisis. Whenever possible, having both partners involved, even when one is not employed by the company, has been found to enhance the success of such efforts.

❖ FIGURE 11–10 ❖
DUAL CAREER PATH FOR ENGINEERS

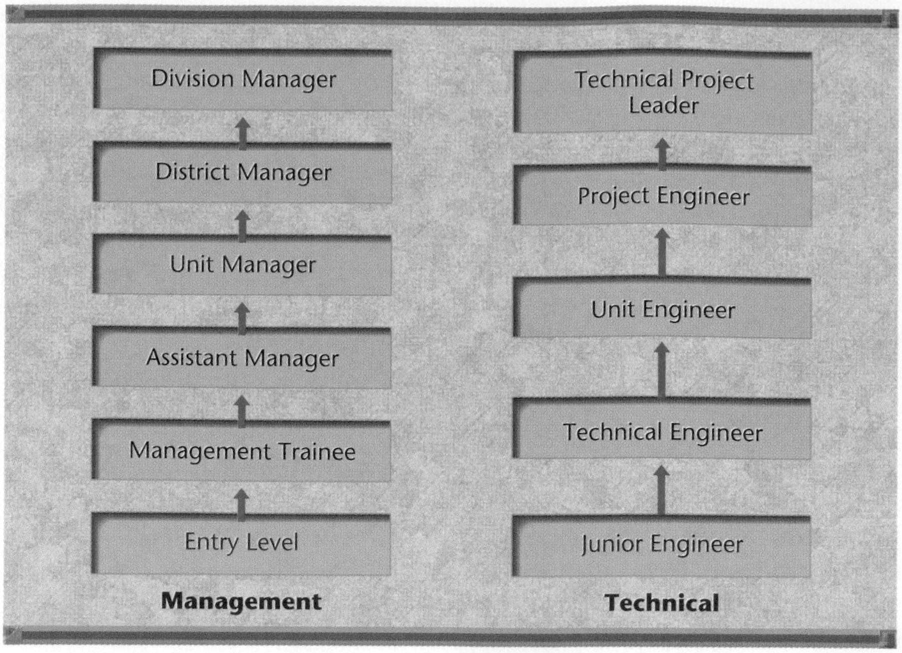

For dual-career couples with children, family issues may conflict with career progression. Thus, in job transfer situations, one partner may be more willing to be flexible in the type of job taken for the sake of the family. Part-time work, flex-time, and work-at-home arrangements may be options considered especially for parents with younger children.

RECRUITMENT PROBLEMS WITH DUAL-CAREER COUPLES Recruiting a member of a dual-career couple increasingly means making an equally attractive job available for the candidate's partner at the new location. Dual-career couples have more to lose when relocating and, as a result, often exhibit higher expectations and request more help and money in such situations.

RELOCATION OF DUAL-CAREER COUPLES Traditionally, transfers are part of the path upward in organizations. However, the dual-career couple is much less mobile because one partner's transfer interferes with the other's career.[37] Dual-career couples, besides having invested in two careers, have established support networks of friends and neighbors to cope with their transportation and dependent-care needs. These needs, in a single-career couple, would normally be met by the other partner. Relocating one partner in a dual-career couple means upsetting this carefully constructed network or creating a "commuting" relationship.

If a company has no partner-assistance program, an employee may be hesitant to request such services and may turn down the relocation. The dual-career family has not been the norm for very long, and traditional role expectations remain.[38] A male employee may still fear he will appear "unmanly" should his partner refuse to defer in support of his career, while a female employee may feel guilty about violating the traditional concept of male career dominance.

When relocation is the only way to handle a staffing situation, employers increasingly provide support services to help the couple adapt to the new location. Some companies go so far as to hire the spouse at the new location or find the partner a job with another company.[39] At times, companies have agreed to pay part of the salary or benefits when another company hires the partner and to reciprocate at some future time. When such arrangements cannot be made, professional job search counseling can be obtained for the partner. It makes sense to take into account the dual-career social trend when revising HR policies on employee relocation assistance. Some approaches that could be considered are:

- Paying employment agency fees for the relocating partner
- Paying for a designated number of trips for the partner to look for a job in the proposed new location
- Helping the partner find a job within the same company or in another division or subsidiary of the company.
- Developing computerized job banks to share with other companies in the area that list partners who are available for job openings

CAREERS, WORK, AND FAMILY ISSUES The pressures exerted by work and family issues affect individual careers, but they affect employers' strategic choices as well. Those strategic choices result in changes in the way employers are dealing with family/work issues.[40] Employers are concerned about balancing the needs of families and employee development because high-performing managers are difficult to recruit and to keep. Further, there is evidence that many job candidates are giving higher priority to the quality of family and personal life when choosing employers.

The conflict between family and work is not new, but it has greatly intensified with the trend toward families' having two working parents. In view of the predicted shortage of certain high-demand workers, employers may find the interplay of careers and family responsibilities one of the most pressing issues of the next decade.[41]

MOONLIGHTING AS A CAREER STRATEGY

Moonlighting traditionally has been defined as work outside a person's regular employment that takes 12 or more additional hours per week. More recently, the concept of moonlighting has been expanded to include such activities as self-employment, investments, hobbies, and other interests for which additional remuneration is received. The perception that moonlighting is a fixed outside commitment is no longer sufficiently broad, since the forms that it may take are varied and sometimes difficult to identify.

*Moonlighting
Work outside a person's regular employment that takes 12 or more additional hours per week.

Moonlighting is no longer just a second job for the underpaid blue-collar worker but also a career development strategy for some professionals. A growing number of managers are dividing their work efforts by moonlighting as consultants or self-employed entrepreneurs. Consulting not only increases their income but also provides new experiences and diversity to their lives. Many individuals also view such activities as providing extra security, especially in these times of layoffs among middle managers.

Most moonlighting managers cannot afford to walk away from their corporate salaries, but they are looking elsewhere for fulfillment. An HR manager at a TV network moonlights by working for a training firm that she and a friend set up. An advertising executive at a cosmetics company accepts freelance assignments from his employer's clients. A computer software expert secretly develops a home computer program to market on his own.

If someone is working for a company and freelancing in the same field, questions about whose ideas and time are involved are bound to arise. Some organizations threaten to fire employees who are caught moonlighting, mainly to keep them from becoming competitors. But that does not seem to stop the activities. Other organizations permit freelance work so long as it is not directly competitive. Many believe their staff members should be free to develop their own special interests.

There is evidence that some people who hold multiple jobs work a second job in preparation for a career change. Whether or not a career change is sought, the concept of "job insurance" plays a role, as mentioned earlier. Moonlighting can be viewed in the same context as auto, car, home, or life insurance. The second job can serve as a backup in the event the primary job is lost.

Moonlighting is not without its problems. The main argument against moonlighting has been that energy is being used on a second job that should be used on the primary job. This division of effort may lead to poor performance, absenteeism, and reduced job commitment. However, these arguments are less valid with ever-shorter average workweeks.

Key for employers in dealing with moonlighting employees is to devise and communicate a policy on the subject. Such a policy should focus on defining those areas in which the employer limits employee activities because of business reasons.

SUMMARY

- ❖ Development is different from training because it focuses on less tangible aspects of performance, such as attitudes and values.
- ❖ Successful development requires top management support and an understanding of the relationship of development to other HR activities.
- ❖ Replacement charts are like football depth charts. From them, decisions can be made about whether to develop people internally or go outside for new talent.
- ❖ Assessment centers provide valid methods of assessing management talent and development needs.
- ❖ On-the-job development methods include coaching, committee assignments, job rotation, and "assistant to" positions.
- ❖ Off-the-job development methods include classroom courses, human relations training, case studies, role playing, simulations, sabbatical leaves, and outdoor training.
- ❖ Mentoring and modeling are two ways for younger managers to acquire the skills and know-how necessary to be successful. Mentoring follows a four-stage progression in most cases.
- ❖ Career planning may focus on organizational needs, individual needs, or both.
- ❖ A person chooses a career based on interests, self-image, personality, social background, and other factors.
- ❖ A person's life is cyclical, as is his or her career. Putting the two together offers a useful perspective.
- ❖ Retirement often requires serious emotional adjustments.
- ❖ Dual-career ladders are used with scientific and technical employees.
- ❖ Dual-career marriages increasingly require relocation assistance for the partners of transferring employees.
- ❖ Moonlighting is growing in usage by managers and others.

Review and Discussion Questions

1. What is HR development, and why is top management support so important?
2. You are the head of a government agency. What two methods of on-the-job development would you use with a promising supervisor? What two off-the-job methods would you use? Why?
3. Why have many large organizations started assessment centers?

to analyze the development needs of ee's
" select those ee's who would make the best mgr
non-bias → conducted by group of judges
while an expensive process, the costs associated w/ term a mgr. are much greater

Terms to Know

assessment center 317
behavior modeling 324
career 327
coaching 319
development 314

4. Discuss whether you would prefer organization-centered or individual centered career planning.
5. List reasons why dual-career paths for professional and technical workers may grow in importance in the future.
6. Assume you must develop a company policy to address concerns about dual-career couples. What would you propose for such a policy?

adress transfers - spousal support / assistance w/ job hunt at new location
" involvement in move process
family issues - flex-time, tele-commuting / work at home
recruitment -

CASE

DEVELOPMENT CHANGES AT CHEVRON

San Francisco–based Chevron Corporation had just revised its career development program when brutal economic realities forced downsizing and layoff of 8,000 employees. Even the name of the previous program, "employee career development," sounded inappropriate after the layoffs. The company knew it could not promise career development because development implied that upward movement would be possible—and it would *not* be possible. Remaining employees were concerned about job security, and the company was operating in a slow-to-no-growth environment.

To address the problem, the company changed to a "career enrichment" program designed to help employees find meaning in their current work. The process is designed to help employees enhance their effectiveness and satisfaction, develop new skills, and become better prepared to meet future needs of the company. Participation is voluntary, and there is no guarantee of higher salaries or promotions, but the program enables employees to take more responsibility for their own career development.

The key components of the plan are as follows:

- *Preparation.* This phase includes self-assessment, organizational assessment, and goal-setting sessions.
- *Joint planning.* The employee and the employee's manager review assessment results and agree on an "enrichment plan" for the next year.
- *Plan review.* The plan is presented by the manager to a group of managers who form a plan review committee. The committee provides the employee with feedback on lateral moves, options, and opportunities that might be available.
- *Implementation.* The employee is responsible for implementing the plan, but managers are available for help if needed.
- *End-of-cycle review.* Results are reviewed, and the cycle for the next year is begun.

There was once an understanding that if employees were loyal, they would be assured a job, one manager noted. That is not the case any longer. Employees must understand the business and its needs as well as their own values and skills in order to align their personal goals with the goals of the organization.[42]

Questions

1. What are the advantages and disadvantages of Chevron's new system?
2. What modifications, if any, would you make in the plan? Why?

❖ Notes

1. Based on Thomas Steward, "Planning a Career in a World without Managers," *Fortune,* March 20, 1995, 72–80; Joann S. Lublin, "AT&T Outplacement Manager's Phone Rings Nonstop," *The Wall Street Journal,* January 25, 1996, B1; Alex Markels, "Restructuring Alters Middle-Management Role but Leaves It Robust," *The Wall Street Journal,* September 25, 1995, 1, 10; James Alley, "Where the Laid-Off Workers Go," *Fortune,* October 30, 1995, 45–48; and "Multiple Mergers Leave Banker's Career Derailed," *Omaha World-Herald,* January 21, 1996, 17G.
2. Wayne Cascio, "Whither Industrial and Organizational Psychology in a Changing World of Work?" *American Psychologist,* November 1995, 931.
3. P. Osterman, "Skill, Training and Work Organization in American Establishments," *Industrial Relations,* 34 (1995), 125–145.
4. Blackman and Associates, "Succession Planning Is Crucial to a Firm's Future," *Law Firm Management,* Winter 1995, 3.
5. Blackman and Associates, "Planning a Successful Succession," *Viewpoint on Value,* March/April 1995, p. 5.
6. L. W. Joyce, P. W. Thayer, and S. B. Pond, "Managerial Functions: An Alternative to Traditional Assessment Center Dimensions?" *Personnel Psychology* 47 (1994), 109–120.
7. J. Schneider and N. Schmitt, "An Exercise Design Approach to Understanding Assessment Center Dimension and Exercise Constructs," *Journal of Applied Psychology* 77 (1992), 32–41.
8. H. Lancaster, "Managing Your Career," *The Wall Street Journal,* August 29, 1995, B1.
9. R. Linowes, "The Japanese Manager's Traumatic Entry into the U.S.," *Academy of Management Executive,* November 1993, 21–40.
10. J. O. Sample, "Fast Track MBA Programs Boom," *Denver Post,* May 8, 1995, E1.
11. W. M. Bulkeley, "Business War Games Attract Big Warriors," *The Wall Street Journal,* December 22, 1994, B1.
12. Rochelle Sharpe, "Corporate Sabbaticals," *The Wall Street Journal,* August 8, 1995, 1.
13. Shari Caudron, "Volunteerism and the Bottom Line," *Industry Week* 243 (1994), 13–18; C. Ramono, "Pressed to Service: Corporate Volunteer Programs," *Management Review* 83 (1994) 37–40.
14. J. R. Veum, "Sources of Training and Their Impact on Wages," *Industrial and Labor Relations Review,* 49 (1995), 812.
15. Figure 11–5 is based on research noted in C. D. McCauley *et al.,* "Assessing the Developmental Components of Managerial Jobs," *Journal of Applied Psychology* 79 (1994), 544–560.
16. Richard Koonce, "One on One," *Training and Development,* February 1994, 34–40; Wayne Cascio, "Whither I/O Psychology in a Changing World of Work?" *American Psychologist,* November 1995, 930.
17. Adapted from information in K. E. Kram, "Phases of the Mentor Relationship," *Academy of Management Journal* 26 (1983), 608–625.
18. Carol Hymowitz, "How a Dedicated Mentor Gave Momentum to a Woman's Career," *The Wall Street Journal,* April 24, 1995, B1.
19. Gary N. Powell and D. Anthony Butterfield, "Investigating the Glass Ceiling," *Academy of Management Journal* 37 (1994), 69.
20. A. Carol Rusaw, "Mobility for Federal Women Managers: Is Training Enough?" *Public Personnel Management,* Summer 1994, 257–262.
21. Lisa Mainiero, "On Breaking the Glass Ceiling," *Organizational Dynamics,* Winter 1996, 5–20.
22. Adapted from K. Helliker, "Sold on the Job," *The Wall Street Journal,* August 25, 1995, A1.
23. Luann Gaskill, "A Conceptual Framework for the Development of Formal Mentoring Programs," *Journal of Career Development,* Winter 1993, 147–160.
24. B. Dumaine, "Why Do We Work?" *Fortune,* December 26, 1994, 196–204.
25. P. Mergenbagen, "Doing the Career Shuffle," *American Demographics,* November 1991, 42.
26. T. Parham and H. Austin, "Career Development and African Americans," *Journal of Vocational Behavior* 44 (1994) 139–154.
27. N. Betz, "Self-Concept Theory in Career Development," *The Career Development Quarterly,* September 1994, 32.
28. M. Duarte, "Career Concerns, Values and Role Salience in Employed Men," *Career Development Quarterly,* June 1995, 339–349.
29. M. Downes and K. G. Kroeck, "Discrepancies between Existing Jobs and Individual Interests: An Empirical Application of Holland's Model," *Journal of Vocational Behavior* 48 (1996), 107–117.
30. Robert Lewis, "More Midlife Men Combine Pensions with New Careers," *AARP Bulletin,* July/August 1995, 1.
31. Julie Connelly, "Have You Gone As Far As You Can Go?" *Fortune,* December 26, 1994, 231.
32. "Career Opportunities," *The Economist,* July 8, 1995, 59.
33. L. S. Richman, "How to Get Ahead in America," *Fortune,* May 16, 1994, 50.
34. R. Smart and C. Peterson, "Stability vs. Tradition in Woman's Career Development," *Journal of Vocational Behavior* 45 (1994), 241–260.
35. A. Penzias, "New Paths to Success," *Fortune,* July 12, 1995, 90.
36. "The Career Couple Challenge," *Personnel Journal* (Supplement), September 1995, 1.
37. P. Capell, "The Right Move?" *The Wall Street Journal,* February 26, 1996, R7.
38. Robin Martin, "The Effects of Prior Moves on Job Relocation Stress," *Journal of Occupational and Organizational Psychology* 68 (1995), 49–56.
39. "Statistics on Relocation," *Solutions,* June 1995, 59.
40. J. Goodstein, "Institutional Pressures and Strategic Responsiveness: Employer Involvement in Work-Family Issues," *Academy of Management Journal* 37 (1994), 350–382.
41. Keith H. Hammonds, "Balancing Work and Family," *Business Week,* September 16, 1996, 74–80.
42. Adapted from Shari Caudron, "Chevron Changes Focus from Career Development to Career Enrichment," *Personnel Journal* (Special Report), April 1994, 64.

CHAPTER 12

PERFORMANCE MANAGEMENT AND APPRAISAL

After you have read this chapter, you should be able to:

- Distinguish between job criteria and performance standards and discuss criterion contamination and deficiency.
- Identify the two major uses of performance appraisal.
- Explain several rater errors by giving examples of them.
- Describe both the advantages and disadvantages of multi-source (360°) appraisal.
- Identify the nature of behavioral approaches to performance appraisal and management by objectives (MBO).
- Discuss several concerns about appraisal feedback interviews.
- Identify the characteristics of a legal and effective performance appraisal system.

HR IN TRANSITION

360° PERFORMANCE APPRAISAL

You have been x-rayed, CAT scanned, poked, prodded and palpated in all the most embarrassing places. . . . Only it's not your lower intestine that's about to be discussed, but something even more personal: *you*. Your personality. The way you deal with people. Your talents, your values, your ethics, your leadership. And the folks who did the poking and temperature taking weren't anonymous technicians but a half dozen or more of your closest colleagues at work.[1]

The latest attempt to improve performance—multisource assessment, or 360° performance appraisal (PA)—increasingly has found favor with a growing number of organizations. Unlike traditional performance appraisals, which typically come from superiors to subordinates, 360° appraisal uses feedback from "all around" the appraisee. Superiors, subordinates, peers, customers—and perhaps a self-appraisal as well—provide input for the performance appraisal process. Such feedback obviously can be used for the *development* of managers, leaders, and others. Indeed, it is most often intended to serve a developmental role. But in some organizations, it is being used as input for evaluating performance in order to determine compensation adjustments and other more traditional *administrative* performance purposes.

Should managers do the performance appraisals, should team leaders do them, or should team members evaluate each other?

Driving factors in 360° PA include the growing use of teams and an emphasis on customer satisfaction that comes from quality enhancement operations. Use of 360° PA with teams presents a problem, however. Should managers do even performance appraisals, should team leaders do them, or should team members evaluate each other? Further, after downsizing, many managers have seen their roles change, with more people reporting to them directly and a shift in accountability lower in the organization. Shouldn't these people have something to say about how well the manager has done?

As mentioned, most 360° programs emphasize employee development. For example, at Mobil Oil, the process attempts to identify areas where a manager can be more successful. Feedback is aimed toward a "development plan." Certainly, the more sources of feedback, the more likely that a complete view of performance will be available. However, 360° assessment has several potential problems that may restrict its applicability to development uses:

- ❖ The process generates a great deal of paper, with evaluations from many people. It may require collecting ratings on computers.
    - ❖ Confidentiality is an issue. If people do not believe their comments will be anonymous, they will not be as honest as they otherwise would be.
    - ❖ Raters will require training so they understand the system and the position of the person they are rating.
- ❖ Determining who will be selected for assessment teams is important. Friends, enemies, or both?
- ❖ The organization must address how it will handle very high or very low ratings by one person who is apparently out of step with everyone else.[1]

Much is left to learn about 360° performance feedback, but the potential to provide *better* feedback where appropriate is great with this human resource approach.

> *"How would you like a job where, if you made a mistake, a big red light goes on and 18,000 people boo?"*
>
> *—Former hockey goalie, Jaques Plante*

Human resource performance is an important issue in the strategy most organizations must follow to achieve their goals. Whether that strategy is to offer the lowest-priced goods, the highest-quality goods, or constant innovation in design, performance by employees will be a key factor in the success or failure of the strategy. This chapter discusses performance measurement, appraisal, and reporting, or feedback, as well as performance improvement.

Performance Management Systems
Attempts to monitor, measure, report, improve, and reward employee performance.

Performance management systems are attempts to monitor, measure, report, improve, and reward employee performance. Performance management also should include some development planning designed to improve or expand employees' core capabilities. Performance management is the link between strategy and organizational results, as shown in Figure 12–1.

Monitoring and Measuring Performance

Employee performance is not controlled by management but ultimately by the employees themselves. A manager's job is to assist employees by making sure they understand how to do their jobs, what constitutes good performance, how they are doing, and how to improve if necessary. Understanding how to do the job and if employee performance is at an acceptable level requires identifying critical job dimensions and performance standards.

Critical Job Dimensions and Performance Standards

Critical Job Dimensions
Elements of a job on which performance is measured.

Job analysis helps identify the most important duties and tasks of jobs, as pointed out in Chapter 7. From the job analysis, it is important to develop **critical job dimensions**, which are elements of a job on which performance is measured. For example, one dimension for a word processor's job might be speed; another might be accuracy. If jobs have been properly designed, critical job dimensions will reflect what needs to be done to advance the strategy of the organization.

Performance Standard
The expected level of performance.

Each critical job dimension should be associated with a **performance standard**, which is the expected level of performance. For the word processing job, the standard might be 50 words per minute with no more than two errors.

This example illustrates that performance is almost never one-dimensional. In baseball, job performance might include home runs, batting average, fielding

Figure 12–1
The Linkage between Strategy, Outcomes, and Organizational Results

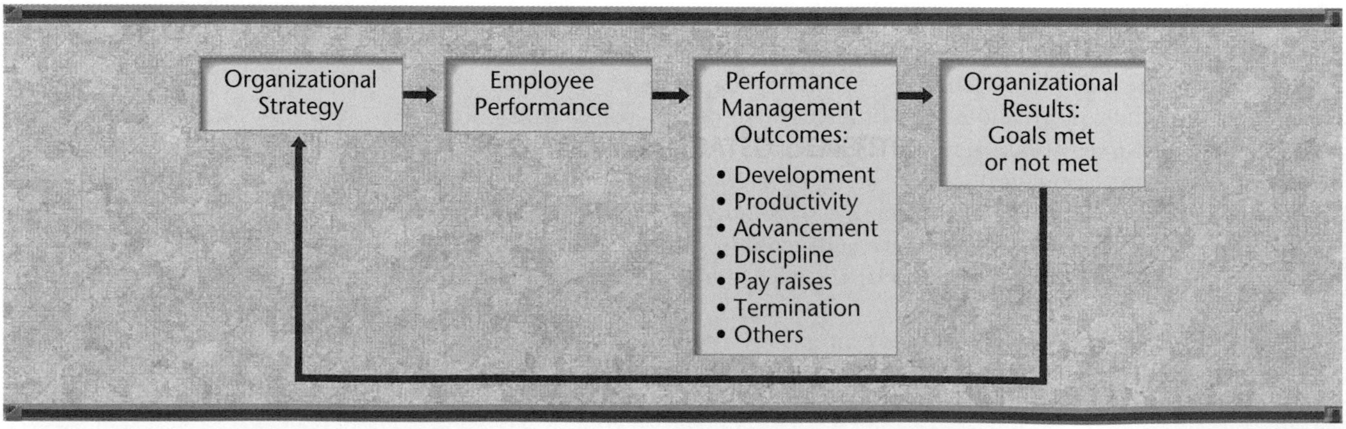

percentage, and on-base performance, to name a few dimensions. The leading home-run hitter may not be the best fielder and may not even hit for the highest average. Both in sports and many other jobs, multiple job dimensions are the rule rather than the exception for all but the simplest jobs.

The various dimensions for a given job also might be *weighted* to reflect the relative importance of the criteria. For example, in the word processing job, speed might be twice as important as accuracy, and accuracy might be equally important as getting to work on time and being there every day. Thus, the weighting might be:

Critical Job Dimensions	Weight
Input speed	2
Accuracy	1
Attendance	1
Tardiness	1

❖ Types of Performance Criteria

Performance criteria are standards commonly used for testing or measuring performances. Criteria for evaluating job performance can be classified as trait-based, behavior-based, or results-based. A *trait-based* criterion identifies a subjective character trait such as "pleasant personality," "initiative," or "creativity" and has little to do with the specific job. Such traits tend to be ambiguous, and courts have held that evaluations based on traits such as "adaptability" and "general demeanor" are too vague to use as the basis for performance-based HR decisions.

Performance Criteria
Standards commonly used for testing or measuring performances.

Behavior-based criteria focus on specific behaviors that lead to job success. For example, a salesperson who can exhibit appropriately the behavior of "verbal persuasion" has satisfied a behavior-based criterion. Behavioral criteria are more difficult to develop but have the advantage of clearly specifying the behaviors management wants to see. A potential problem is that there may be several behaviors, all of which can be successful in a given situation.

Results-based criteria look at what the employee has done or accomplished. For some jobs where measurement is easy and appropriate, a results-based approach works very well. However, that which is measured tends to be emphasized, and equally important but nonmeasurable parts of the job may be left out. For example, a car salesman who gets paid only for sales may be unwilling to do any paperwork not directly necessary to sell cars. Further, when only results are emphasized and not *how the results were achieved,* ethical or even legal issues may arise.

❖ Criterion Relevance

When measuring performance, it is important that relevant criteria be used. Generally, criteria are relevant when they measure employees on the most important aspects of their jobs. For example, measuring a customer service representative in an insurance claims center on "appearance" may be less relevant than measuring the number of calls handled properly. The HR Perspective discusses issues associated with using performance appraisals in public school systems.

❖ Criteria Problems

Jobs usually include many duties and tasks, and so measuring performance usually requires more than one dimension. If the performance criteria leave out some important job duties, they are *deficient.* If some irrelevant criteria are

HR PERSPECTIVE

Performance Appraisal in Public School Systems

Determining how well an employee is doing his or her job and communicating that information is common in American business. Even in the public sector, performance appraisal is common—but it has not been as common for teachers in public schools until recently.

Teaching presents some special problems for performance appraisal. The key question is what performance standards should be set? How well the teacher gets along with the students and how neat the room appears seem beside the point. Standards based on changes in pupils' abilities or teachers' behaviors that can be clearly linked by research to learning seem more appropriate. But the idea that there is a single best method of teaching may prevent an unbiased evaluation of just how good a teacher is performing. In summary, there are no agreed-upon, measurable standards of what is most important in good teaching.

When (or if) proper criteria for appraising the performance of teachers are identified and used, like any other organization, both public and private school systems will have another hurdle to overcome—acceptance of the performance appraisal process. This concern is magnified because performance appraisal can be used to remove teachers who are not rated as satisfactory or better. For example, in one school district, the teachers themselves helped to draw up the performance appraisal system. But they began to fear that the system would be misused by new administrators. The teachers felt that if an administrator wanted to remove a teacher, the administrator would only have to rig the performance appraisal system to rank the teacher low, and that teacher would be gone.

Clearly, teacher evaluation at any level is difficult and controversial. Even appraising the performance of the top administrators in school systems—the superintendents—also is controversial. Roger L. Barnes, superintendent of a rural Ohio district, promised to quit if ninth graders did not improve on a state proficiency test by 10%. He did quit, after scores went up only 3%. Such arrangements are becoming more common elsewhere. In Houston, Texas, the district's 12 superintendents—in exchange for 15% salary increases—have two years to improve test scores.

Skeptics argue that it is not fair to tie administrators' and teachers' pay to the performance of students, because a great many factors are beyond the control of teachers and administrators. Poverty, funding, and violence are among those commonly cited. Some experts warn that too much concern with measuring performance also could lead to cheating on test scores.[3] In summary, the ultimate outcomes associated with these experiments in performance management systems are still to be determined.

included, the criteria are said to be *contaminated.* Managers use deficient or contaminated criteria for measuring performance much more than they should.[4]

Performance measures can be thought of as *objective* or *subjective* as well. Objective measures are directly counted amounts—for example, the number of cars sold or the number of invoices processed. One example of a subjective measure is a supervisor's ratings of an employee's performance.[5] Objective measures tend to be narrowly focused and perhaps subject to deficiency for that reason. However, subjective measures may be prone to contamination or random errors. Neither is a panacea, and both should be used carefully.

The level of achievement of standards often is expressed in numbers or adjectives—for example "outstanding" or "unsatisfactory." It may be difficult to reach agreement on exactly what the level of performance has been relative to the standard. Figure 12–2 shows terms used in evaluating employee performance on standards at one company. Notice that each level is defined in terms of performance standards.

❖ Establishing Useful Performance Standards

Realistic, measurable, clearly understood performance standards benefit both the organization and the employees. In a sense, standards show the "right way" to do the job. It is important to establish standards *before* the work is performed so that all involved will understand the level of accomplishment expected.

Standards often are established for the following:

- Quantity of output
- Quality of output
- Timeliness of results
- Manner of performance
- Effectiveness in use of resources

Supervisory ratings of *quantity* of work produced have been found to be accurate, but measuring *quality* against standards is less precise, possibly because quality is more subjective in some cases.[6] Sales quotas and production output standards are familiar quantity performance standards. Another standard of performance is that a cashier must balance the cash drawer at the end of each day.

Standards are often set by someone external to the job, but they can be written effectively by employees as well. Experienced employees know what constitutes satisfactory performance of tasks on their job descriptions. Their supervisors do as well. Therefore, these individuals often can collaborate with good effect. For example, two performance standards for difficult duties that were derived jointly are as follows:

FIGURE 12–2
TERMS USED TO DEFINE STANDARDS AT ONE COMPANY

Outstanding. The person is so successful at this job criterion that special note should be made. Compared with the usual standards and the rest of the department, this performance ranks in the top 10%.
Very Good. Performance at this level is one of better than average performances in the unit, given the common standards and unit results.
Satisfactory. Performance is at or above the minimum standards. This level of performance is what one would expect from most experienced, competent employees.
Marginal. Performance is somewhat below the minimum-level standard on this job dimension. However, there appears to be potential to improve the rating within a reasonable time frame.
Unsatisfactory. Performance on this item in the job is well below standard, and there is serious question as to whether the person can improve to meet minimum standards.

Duty: Keep current on supplier technology.
Performance Standards:
1. Every six months, invite suppliers to make presentation of newest technology.
2. Visit supplier plants once per year.
3. Attend trade shows.

Duty: Do price or cost analysis as appropriate.
Performance Standard: Performance will be acceptable when all requirements of the procedure "Price and Cost Analysis" are followed.[7]

PERFORMANCE APPRAISAL

Performance Appraisal (PA) The process of determining how well employees do their jobs compared with a set of standards and communicating that information to those employees.

Performance appraisal (PA) is the process of evaluating how well employees do their jobs compared with a set of standards and communicating that information to those employees. It also has been called *employee rating, employee evaluation, performance review, performance evaluation,* and *results appraisal.*

Performance appraisal sounds simple enough; and research shows that it is widely used for wage/salary administration, performance feedback, and identification of individual employee strengths and weaknesses. Well over 80% of U.S. companies have PA systems for office, professional, technical, supervisory, middle management, and nonunion production workers.[8]

In situations in which an employer must deal with a strong union, performance appraisals may be conducted only on salaried, nonunion employees. Generally, unions emphasize seniority over merit, which precludes the use of performance appraisal. Unions view all members as equal in ability; therefore, the worker with the most experience is considered to be the most qualified; thus, a performance appraisal is unnecessary.

Performance appraisal often is management's least favored activity. There may be good reasons for that feeling. Not all performance appraisals are positive, and for that reason, discussing ratings with the employee may not be pleasant. It may be difficult to differentiate among employees if good performance data are not available. Further, some supervisors are uncomfortable with "playing God" with employees' raises and careers, which they may feel results from conducting performance appraisals.

In general terms, performance appraisal has two roles in organizations, and these roles often are seen as potentially conflicting. One role is to measure performance for the purpose of rewarding or otherwise making *administrative* decisions about employees. Promotions or layoffs might hinge on these ratings, making them difficult at times. Another role is *development* of individual potential. In this case, the manager is featured more as a counselor than as a judge, and the atmosphere is often different. Emphasis is on identifying potential and planning growth. Figure 12–3 shows the two potentially conflicting roles for performance appraisal.

❖ Administrative Uses

A performance appraisal system is often the link between the reward employees hope to receive and their productivity. The linkage can be thought of as follows:

productivity → performance appraisal → rewards

This approach to compensation is at the heart of the idea that raises should be given for merit rather than for seniority. Under merit systems, employees receive raises based on performance. The manager's role historically has been as evaluator of a subordinate's performance, and the focus is usually on comparison of performance levels among individuals. If any part of the process fails, the most productive employees will not receive the larger rewards, resulting in all the problems that come from perceived inequity in compensation.

Most American workers perceive little connection between the levels of their efforts and the sizes of their paychecks. According to one survey of 5,000 American employees, only 28% saw a link. Further, only about one-third of the sample rated their supervisors as good at giving performance feedback.[9] Most research indicates that the use of performance appraisal to determine pay is very common. Consequently, research indicating that it is not perceived as equitable warrants close attention.

❖ FIGURE 12–3 ❖
CONFLICTING ROLES FOR PERFORMANCE APPRAISAL?

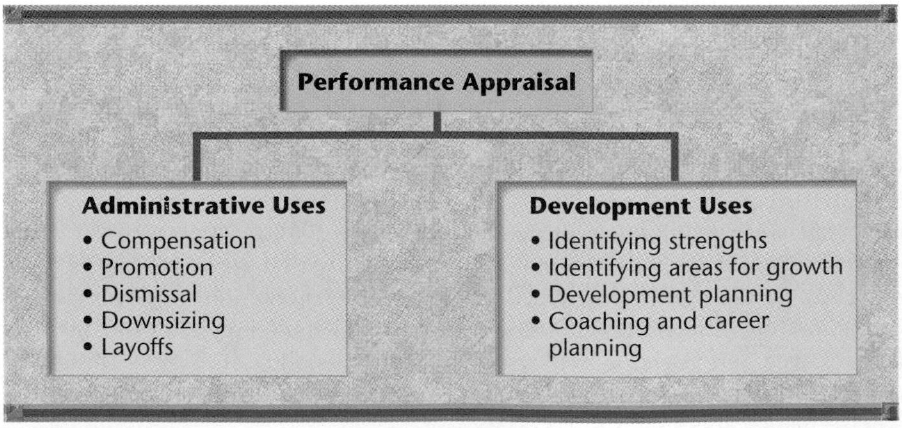

Administrative uses of performance appraisal, such as decisions on promotion, termination, layoff, and transfer assignments, are very important to employees. For example, the order of layoffs can be justified by performance appraisals. For this reason, if an employer claims that the decision was performance-based, the performance appraisals must document clearly the differences in employee performance. Similarly, promotion or demotion based on performance must be documented with performance appraisals.

Performance appraisals are necessary when organizations terminate, promote, or pay people differently, as they are a crucial defense if employees sue over such decisions.[10] Thus, necessity likely accounts for the widespread administrative use of performance appraisals. But certain problems, including leniency, are common when ratings are to be used for administrative purposes.[11]

❖ Development Uses

Performance appraisal can be a primary source of information and feedback for employees, which is key for their future development. When supervisors identify the weaknesses, potentials, and training needs of employees through PA feedback, they can inform employees about their progress, discuss what skills they need to develop, and work out development plans.

The manager's role in such a situation is like that of a coach. The coach's job is to reward good performance with recognition, explain what improvement is necessary, and show employees *how* to improve. After all, people do not always know where they could improve, and managers really cannot expect improvement if they are unwilling to explain where and how improvement can occur.

The purpose of developmental feedback is to change or reinforce individual behavior, rather than to compare individuals as in the case of administrative uses of performance appraisal. Positive reinforcement for the behaviors the organization wants is an important part of development. Research suggests that developmental performance appraisal increases feedback and development planning, as well as satisfaction with the feedback, and improvements in performance may result.[12]

The development function of performance appraisal also can identify areas in which the employee might wish to grow. For example, in a performance appraisal interview that was targeted exclusively to development, an employee found out that the only factor keeping her from being considered for a management job in her firm was a working knowledge of cost accounting. Her supervisor suggested that she consider taking such a course at night at the local college.

The use of teams provides a different set of circumstances for developmental appraisal. The manager may not see all of the employee's work, but team members do. Teams *can* provide developmental feedback, as we saw earlier in the feature on 360° appraisal. However, it is still an open question whether teams can handle administrative appraisal. When teams are allowed to design appraisal systems, they prefer to "get rid of judgment," and they apparently have a very hard time dealing with differential rewards.[13] Perhaps, then, group appraisal is best used for development purposes.

❖ Informal Vs. Systematic Appraisal

Performance appraisal can occur in two ways, informally or systematically. An *informal appraisal* is conducted whenever the supervisor feels it is necessary. The day-to-day working relationship between a manager and an employee offers an opportunity for the employee's performance to be judged. This judgment is communicated through conversation on the job or over coffee or by on-the-spot examination of a particular piece of work. Informal appraisal is especially appropriate when time is an issue. The longer feedback is delayed, the less likely it is to motivate behavior change. Frequent informal feedback to employees can also avoid surprises (and therefore problems) later when the formal evaluation is communicated. However, informal appraisal can become *too* informal, as the following observation from *The Wall Street Journal* suggests:[14]

> A senior executive at a big auto maker so dreaded face-to-face evaluations that he recently delivered one manager's review while both sat in adjoining stalls in the men's room. The boss told the startled subordinate: "I haven't had a chance to give you a performance appraisal this year. Your bonus is going to be 20%. I am really happy with your performance."

A *systematic appraisal* is used when the contact between manager and employee is formalized and a system is established to report managerial impressions and observations on employee performance. Although informal appraisal is useful, it should not take the place of formal appraisal. When a formalized or systematic appraisal is used, the interface between the HR unit and the appraising manager becomes more important.

❖ Appraisal Responsibilities

The appraisal process can be quite beneficial to the organization and to the individuals involved if done properly. It also can be the source of a great deal of discontent.

Figure 12–4 shows that the HR unit typically designs a systematic appraisal system. The manager does the actual appraising of the employee, using the procedures developed by the HR unit. As the formal system is being developed, the manager usually offers input on how the final system will work. Only rarely does an HR specialist actually rate a manager's employees.

❖ Figure 12–4 ❖
Typical Appraisal Responsibilities

HR UNIT	MANAGERS
❖ Designs and maintains formal system ❖ Establishes formal report system ❖ Makes sure reports are on time ❖ Trains raters	❖ Typically rate performance of employees ❖ Make formal reports ❖ Review appraisals with employees

Timing of Appraisals The timing of appraisals is important. Systematic appraisals typically are conducted once or twice a year. Appraisals most often are conducted once a year, usually near the employee's anniversary date. For new employees, an appraisal 90 days after employment, again at six months, and annually thereafter is common timing.

This regular time interval is a feature of formal appraisals and distinguishes them from informal appraisals. Both employees and managers are aware that performance will be reviewed on a regular basis, and they can plan for performance discussions. In addition, informal appraisals should be conducted whenever a manager feels they are desirable.

Appraisals and Pay Discussions The timing of performance appraisals and pay discussions should be different, some argue, for the following reasons:

- ❖ Pay decisions may include factors other than performance. For example, a good performer may get the same raise as a poor employee because raises are granted "across the board" that year.

- Performance appraisal can be reinforcing by itself, especially if there are not raises in a given year. The reinforcement value may be lost if pay is discussed at that point.
- People may focus more on the pay amount than on what they have done well or need to improve.
- Sometimes managers may manipulate performance appraisal ratings to justify the desired pay treatment for a given individual.

Not everyone agrees that performance appraisal and pay are best discussed separately. In fact, research provides conflicting evidence. One study found that discussing pay during the performance review did not affect future behavior, and another found mixed results.[15]

Who Conducts Appraisals?

Performance appraisal can be done by anyone familiar with the performance of individual employees. Possibilities include the following:

- Supervisors who rate their employees
- Employees who rate their superiors
- Team members who rate each other
- Outside sources
- Employee self-appraisal
- Multisource (360°) appraisal

The first method is the most common. The immediate superior has the sole responsibility for appraisal in most organizations, although it is common practice to have the appraisal reviewed and approved by the supervisor's boss. Any system should include a face-to-face discussion between rater and ratee.

Because of the growing use of teams and a concern with customer input, two fast-growing sources of appraisal information are team members and sources outside the organization. Also, as the chapter opening discussion highlighted, multisource appraisal (or 360° appraisal) is a combination of all the methods and has grown in usage recently.

Supervisory Rating of Subordinates

Traditional rating of employees by supervisors is based on the assumption that the immediate supervisor is the person most qualified to evaluate the employee's performance realistically, objectively, and fairly. The *unity of command* notion—the idea that every subordinate should have only one boss—underlies this approach.

As with any rating system, the supervisor's judgment should be objective and based on actual performance. Toward this end, some supervisors keep performance logs noting what their employees have done. These logs provide specific examples when rating time arrives. They also serve to jog the memory, because supervisors cannot be expected to remember every detail of performance over a six-month or one-year period. A supervisor's appraisal typically is reviewed by the manager's boss to make sure that a proper job of appraisal has been done. Figure 12–5 shows the traditional review process in which supervisors conduct performance appraisals on employees.

Managers and employees evaluate performance appraisal systems on different bases. Managers tend to evaluate the systems on how well they aid in communicating with employees about their performance levels and if they aid in enhancing better performance.

❖ FIGURE 12–5 ❖
TRADITIONAL APPRAISAL PROCESS

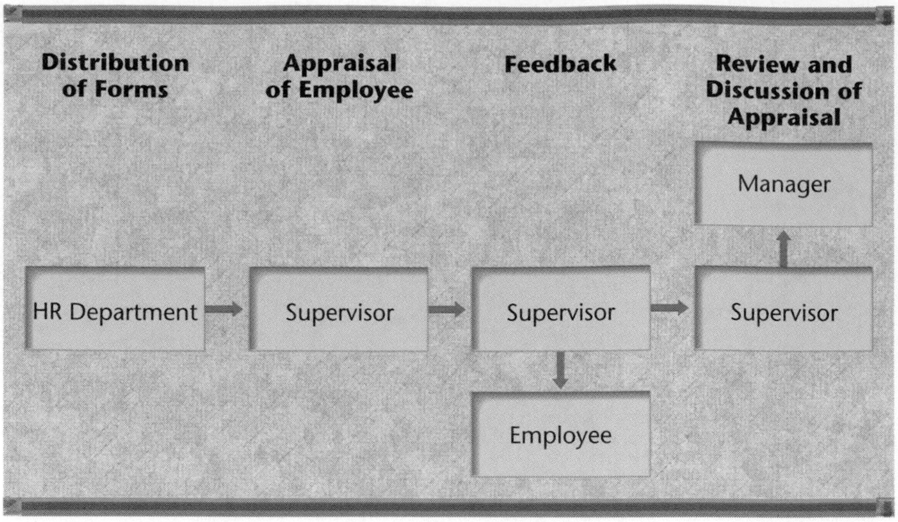

Employees rate the fairness of a performance appraisal higher if the following characteristics exist:

- Ratings are based on actual performance.
- Standards are consistently applied.
- Two-way communication is allowed during the interview.

❖ EMPLOYEE RATING OF MANAGERS

The concept of having supervisors and managers rated by employees or group members is being used in a number of organizations today. A prime example of this type of rating takes place in colleges and universities where students evaluate the performance of professors in the classroom. Industry also uses employee ratings for developmental purposes.

ADVANTAGES There are three primary advantages of having employees rate managers. First, in situations where manager/employee relationships are critical, employee ratings can be quite useful in identifying competent managers. The rating of leaders by combat soldiers is an example. Second, this type of rating program can help make the manager more responsive to employees, though this advantage can quickly become a disadvantage if it leads the manager to try to be "nice" rather than to try to manage. Nice people without other qualifications may not be good managers in many situations. Finally, it can be the basis for coaching as part of a career development effort for the managers. The hope is that the feedback will assist their managerial development.

DISADVANTAGES A major disadvantage is the negative reaction many superiors have to being evaluated by employees.[16] The "proper" nature of manager/employee relations may be violated by having workers rate managers. Also, the fear of reprisal may be too great for employees to give realistic ratings. In addition, employees may resist rating their bosses because they do not perceive it as part of their jobs. If this situation exists, workers may rate the manager only on the way the manager treats them and not on critical job requirements.

The problems associated with having employees rate managers seem to limit the usefulness of this appraisal approach to certain situations, except for managerial development uses. The traditional nature of most organizations appears to restrict the applicability of employee rating except for self-improvement purposes.

Should employees rating a boss be held accountable for their comments, or should the comments be anonymous? The effects of both these options are discussed in the accompanying HR Perspective on feedback accountability.

❖ Team/Peer Ratings

The use of peer groups as raters is another type of appraisal with potential both to help and to hurt. For example, if a group of salespersons meets as a committee to talk about one another's ratings, then they may share ideas that could be used to improve the performances of lower-rated individuals. Alternatively, the criticisms could lead to future work relationships being affected negatively.

Peer ratings are especially useful when supervisors do not have the opportunity to observe each employee's performance but other work group members do. As mentioned earlier, it may be that team/peer evaluations are best used for development purposes rather than for administrative purposes. However, some contend that *any* performance appraisal, including team/peer ratings, can affect teamwork and participative management efforts negatively.

Team Appraisal and TQM Total quality management (TQM) and other participative management approaches emphasize teamwork and team performance rather than individual performance. Effectiveness is viewed as the result of systematic factors rather than the product of individual efforts. Individual accomplishment occurs only through working with others. In this view, individual performance appraisal is seen as producing fear and hindering the development of teamwork. If management does not appraise team members in high involvement/high commitment groups, some contend that it is more likely that other team members will focus informally on helping those whose performance is deficient. But even if formal appraisals seem inappropriate, informal appraisals by peers or team leaders still may be necessary at times.

HR PERSPECTIVE

Research on "Feedback Accountability" in Upward Appraisal Rating

Upward appraisals allow subordinates to evaluate the performance of managers. Previous research has found that managers did develop into better managers as a result of anonymous upward appraisals. However, the purpose and structure of the appraisal may affect the ratings that are given. Other research has suggested that some employees rated their bosses differently if the ratings were to be used in the manager's personal administrative PA. Furthermore, raters in general dislike giving poor ratings, and when the ratees will know who gave the ratings, the raters are especially adverse to giving low appraisals.

As reported in *Personnel Psychology,* Antonioni studied 38 managers with positions ranging from supervisors to vice-presidents in a large midwestern insurance company. Another 183 people (the managers' subordinates) participated in the study as well.

Managers viewed feedback more positively if it came from individuals whose identities were known than if it came from anonymous individuals. But subordinates were more comfortable giving anonymous responses than subordinates whose identities were not protected. Further, subordinates whose identities were known rated their managers significantly higher than subordinates protected by the cloak of anonymity. Antonioni concluded that upward appraisal processes where the raters' identities are known may produce inflated ratings of managerial performance.

The author suggested that organizations that use upward appraisals keep those appraisals anonymous, because managers have more power in the working relationship and reprisals could occur. Ratings that are not anonymous may be of little use for development or administration. He noted that it is understandable that managers want their subordinates to be held accountable, because anonymous appraisals could result in unfair evaluations.[17]

The noted management consultant W. Edwards Deming saw performance appraisal as one of the "seven deadly diseases" afflicting American management practice. He argued that such appraisals (even peer appraisals) inappropriately attribute negative variation in performance to individuals rather than to problems in the system. Deming contended that variation in individual performance is generally due to factors outside of individual control.[18]

TEAM RATING DIFFICULTIES Although team members have good information on one another's performance, they may not choose to share it. They may unfairly attack or "go easy" to spare feelings. For example, at Baxter International, Inc., an employee task force agreed that peer appraisals would be used to determine pay raises and that appraisals would *not* be anonymous. The result was that no one said anything bad about anyone. The HR Director indicated that feedback became rather distorted. She noted that the following year the decision was made to separate pay and appraisals so that the appraisal feedback became a self-development tool.[19]

Some organizations attempt to overcome such problems by using anonymous appraisals and/or having a consultant or manager interpret peer ratings. However, there is some evidence that using outsiders to facilitate the rating process does not necessarily result in the system being seen as more fair by those being rated.[20] Whatever the solution, team/peer performance ratings are important and probably inevitable, especially where work teams are used extensively.[21]

❖ SELF-RATINGS

Self-appraisal works in certain situations. Essentially, it is a self-development tool that forces employees to think about their strengths and weaknesses and set goals for improvement. If an employee is working in isolation or possesses a unique skill, the employee may be the only one qualified to rate his or her own behavior. However, employees may not rate themselves as supervisors would rate them; they may use quite different standards. Some research shows that people tend to be more lenient when rating themselves, whereas other research does not.[22] Despite the difficulty in evaluating self-ratings, employee self-ratings can be a valuable and credible source of performance information.

❖ OUTSIDE RATERS

Rating also may be done by outsiders. Outside experts may be called in to review the work of a college president, for example; or a panel of division managers might evaluate a person's potential for advancement in an organization. Outsiders may furnish managers with professional assistance in making appraisals, but there are obvious disadvantages. The outsider may not know all the important contingencies within the organization. In addition, outsider appraisals are time consuming and expensive.

The customers or clients of an organization are obvious sources for outside appraisals. For salespeople and other service jobs, customers may provide the only really clear view of certain behaviors. One corporation uses measures of customer satisfaction with service as a way of helping to determine bonuses for top marketing executives.

❖ MULTISOURCE RATING

As noted in the chapter opening discussion multisource, or 360°, rating is growing in popularity.[23] Figure 12–6 shows graphically some of the parties who may

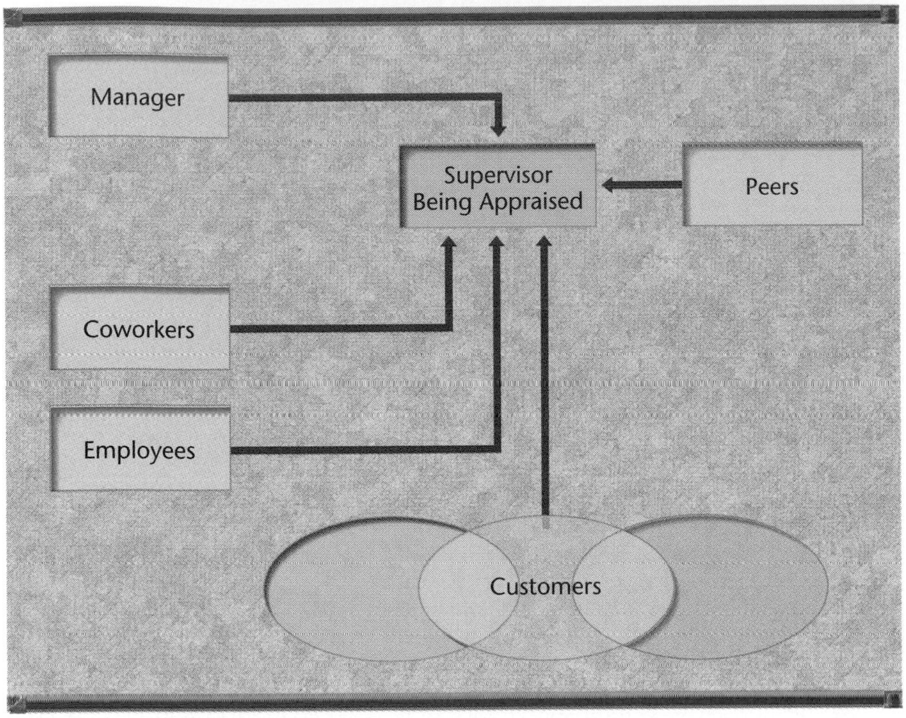

❖ FIGURE 12–6 ❖
MULTISOURCE APPRAISAL

be involved in 360° rating. In this figure the supervisor is the focus of the multisource appraisal. Multisource feedback recognizes that the manager is no longer the sole source of performance appraisal information. Instead, feedback from various colleagues and constituencies is obtained and given to the manager, thus allowing the manager to help shape the feedback from all sources. The manager remains a focal point both to receive the feedback initially and to engage in appropriate follow-up, even in a 360° system. Thus, the manager's perception of an employee's performance is still an important part of the process.

The research on 360° feedback is relatively new and not large in volume. A review of the research suggests there is typically limited agreement among rating sources.[24] However, it should be remembered that the purpose of 360° feedback is *not* to increase reliability by soliciting like-minded views. Rather, the intent is to capture all of the differing evaluations that bear on the individual employee's different roles.

Multisource feedback has been seen by participants as useful, but follow-up on the development activities identified as a result of the feedback has been found to be the most critical factor in the future development of a manager's skills.[25] Appraisees are generally supportive of subordinate appraisal when they receive feedback from *both* their managers and their subordinates.[26] However, supervisors' enthusiasm for subordinates' ratings dims considerably when such ratings are used to help determine pay.[27]

Some potential problems clearly are present when 360° feedback is used for administrative purposes. Differences among raters can present a challenge, especially in the use of 360° ratings for discipline or pay decisions. Bias can just as easily be rooted in customers, subordinates, and peers as in a boss, and their lack of accountability can affect the ratings.[28] Multisource approaches to performance appraisal are possible solutions to the well-documented dissatisfaction with today's legally necessary administrative performance appraisal. But a num-

LOGGING ON

Advance/360 describes a 360° feedback system in a Windows environment which is flexible and can be customized.

http://www.west.net/~teamware/adv360.html

❖ FIGURE 12–7 ❖
PERFORMANCE APPRAISAL METHODS

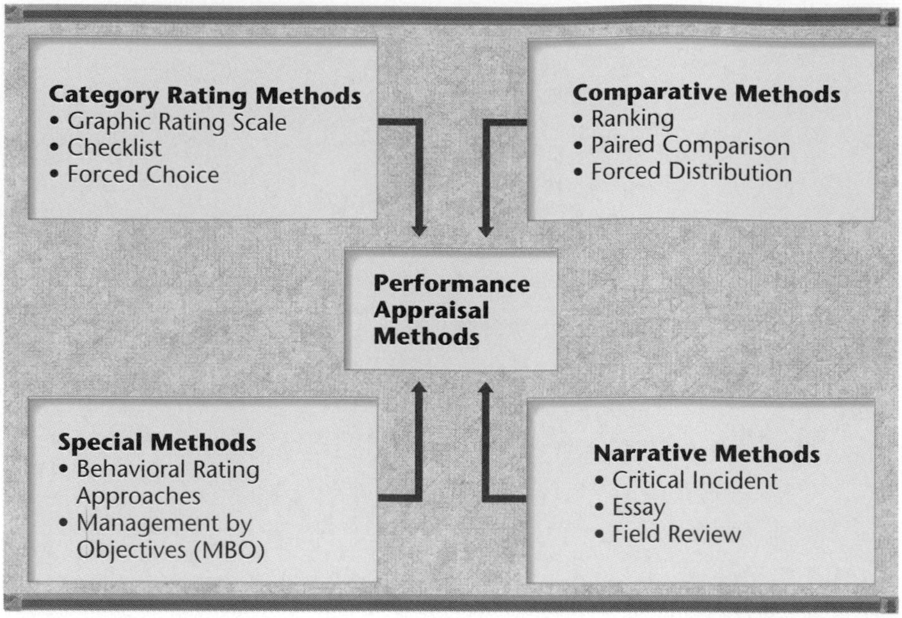

ber of questions arise as multisource appraisals become more common. One concern is whether 360° appraisals improve the process or simply multiply the number of problems by the total number of raters. Also, some wonder if multisource appraisals really will create better decisions than conventional methods, given the additional time investment. Another concern is by blurring accountability, multisource appraisals may generate disruptive conflicts among individuals or groups. Additionally, there is a question about raters being both *willing* and *able* to participate in a meaningful sense in the rating process. Finally, the culture/climate of the organization may not be conducive to using multisources for performance appraisal ratings.

It seems reasonable to assume that these issues are less a concern when the 360° feedback is used *only for development* because the process is usually less threatening. But those concerns may negate multisource appraisals as an administrative tool in many situations.

❖ METHODS FOR APPRAISING PERFORMANCE

Performance can be appraised by a number of methods. In Figure 12–7, various methods are categorized into four major groups.

❖ CATEGORY RATING METHODS

The simplest methods for appraising performance are category rating methods, which require a manager to mark an employee's level of performance on a specific form. The graphic rating scale and checklist are common category rating methods. Another is the forced choice method.

❖Graphic Rating Scale
A scale that allows the rater to mark an employee's performance on a continuum.

GRAPHIC RATING SCALE The **graphic rating scale** allows the rater to mark an employee's performance on a continuum. Because of its simplicity, this method is the one most frequently used. Figure 12–8 shows a graphic rating scale form used by managers to rate office employees. The rater checks the appropriate

❖ FIGURE 12–8 ❖
SAMPLE PERFORMANCE APPRAISAL FORM (SIMPLIFIED)

APPRAISAL FORM

Date sent 4-7-97 Return by 4-21-97
Name Alicia Williamson Job Title Shipping and Receiving Clerk
Department Shipping and Receiving Supervisor Robert Martinez
Full-time ☐ Part-time ☐ Date of Hire 4/93
Appraisal Period: From 4/96 To 4/97
Reason for appraisal (check one): Regular interval ☐ Probationary ☐ Counseling only ☐ Discharge ☐

Major job duties

Job duty 1: Receive and check in inventory, noting quantity errors

Lowest — Satisfactory — Highest
1 — 2 — 3 — 4 — 5

Explanation for rating ______

Job duty 2: Identify damaged goods and complete credit request forms

Lowest — Satisfactory — Highest
1 — 2 — 3 — 4 — 5

Explanation for rating: ______

Job duty 3: Wrap and seal packages for shipment

Lowest — Satisfactory — Highest
1 — 2 — 3 — 4 — 5

Explanation for rating ______

Overall Rating: Consider a general view of the employee's job performance during the rating period.

______

place on the scale for each duty listed. More detail can be added in the space for comments following each factor rated.

There are some obvious drawbacks to the graphic rating scale. Often, separate traits or factors are grouped together, and the rater is given only one box to check. Another drawback is that the descriptive words sometimes used in such scales may have different meanings to different raters. Terms such as *initiative* and *cooperation* are subject to many interpretations, especially in conjunction with words such as *outstanding, average,* and *poor.* Graphic rating scales in many forms are used widely because they are easy to develop; but for the same reason, they encourage errors on the part of the raters, who may depend too heavily on them.

***Checklist**
Performance appraisal tool that uses a list of statements or words that are checked by raters.

CHECKLIST The **checklist** is composed of a list of statements or words. Raters check statements most representative of the characteristics and performance of employees. The following are typical checklist statements:

_______ can be expected to finish work on time
_______ seldom agrees to work overtime
_______ is cooperative and helpful
_______ accepts criticism
_______ strives for self-improvement

The checklist can be modified so that varying weights are assigned to the statements or words. The results can then be quantified. Usually, the weights are not known by the rating supervisor and are tabulated by someone else, such as a member of the HR unit.

There are several difficulties with the checklist: (1) as with the graphic rating scale, the words or statements may have different meanings to different raters; (2) raters cannot readily discern the rating results if a weighted checklist is used; and (3) raters do not assign the weights to the factors. These difficulties limit the use of the information when a rater discusses the checklist with the employee, creating a barrier to effective developmental counseling.

***Forced Choice**
Appraisal approach in which raters choose between two statements to describe employee performance.

FORCED CHOICE A **forced choice** format is an attempt to improve rater objectivity by disguising the "best" of two responses. Both items may be positive. For example:

Choose the statement that best describes this employee:
_______ (1) Listens objectively to criticism or
_______ (2) Asks for input on difficult projects

One of the two is more important for the job in question, but raters cannot necessarily tell which it is. The intention is to reduce the opportunity for deliberate inflation of ratings. One of the choices would be scored one point and the other zero. Clearly, one problem with the forced choice format is developing statements so that the intent is not entirely obvious.

❖ COMPARATIVE METHODS

Comparative methods require that managers directly compare the performances of their employees against one another. For example, a data-entry operator's performance would be compared with that of other data-entry operators by the computing supervisor. Comparative techniques include ranking, paired comparison, and forced distribution.

***Ranking**
Listing of all employees from highest to lowest in performance.

RANKING The **ranking** method consists of listing all employees from highest to lowest in performance. The primary drawback of the ranking method is that the size of the differences among individuals is not well defined. For example, there may be little difference in performance between individuals ranked second and third but a big difference in performance between those ranked third and fourth. This drawback can be overcome to some extent by assigning points to indicate the size of the gaps. Ranking also means that someone must be last. It is possible that the last-ranked individual in one group would be the top employee in a different group. Further, ranking becomes very unwieldy if the group to be ranked is very large.

Paired Comparisons The rater using the **paired comparison** method formally compares each employee with every other employee in the rating group one at a time. The number of comparisons can be calculated using the following formula:

$$\frac{n(n-1)}{2} \qquad [n = \text{number of people rated}]$$

For example, a manager with 15 employees would compare each employee's performance with that of each of the other 14 employees. The manager would have to make 105 different comparisons on each rating factor.

The paired comparison method gives more information about individual employees than the straight ranking method does. Obviously, the large number of comparisons that must be made is the major drawback of this method.

Paired Comparison
Formal comparison of each employee with every other employee in the rating group one at a time.

Forced Distribution With the **forced distribution** method, the ratings of employees' performances are distributed along a bell-shaped curve. Using the forced distribution method, for example, a head nurse would rank nursing personnel along a scale, placing a certain percentage of employees at each performance level. Figure 12–9 shows a scale used with a forced distribution. This method assumes that the widely known bell-shaped curve of performance exists in a given group. Forced distribution is a comparative technique but without the drawback of the large number of comparisons required by the paired-comparison method.

Forced Distribution
Performance appraisal method in which ratings of employees' performance are distributed along a bell-shaped curve.

There are several drawbacks to the forced distribution method. One problem is that a supervisor may resist placing any individual in the lowest (or the highest) group. Difficulties may arise when the rater must explain to the employee why he or she was placed in one grouping and others were placed in higher groupings. Further, with small groups, there may be no reason to assume that a bell-shaped distribution of performance really exists. Finally, in some cases the manager may feel forced to make distinctions among employees that may not exist.

In fact, generally, the distribution of performance appraisal ratings does not approximate the normal distribution of the bell-shaped curve. It is common for 60% to 70% of the workforce of an organization to be rated in the top two performance levels. This pattern could reflect outstanding performance by many employees, or it could reflect *leniency bias*, discussed later in this chapter.

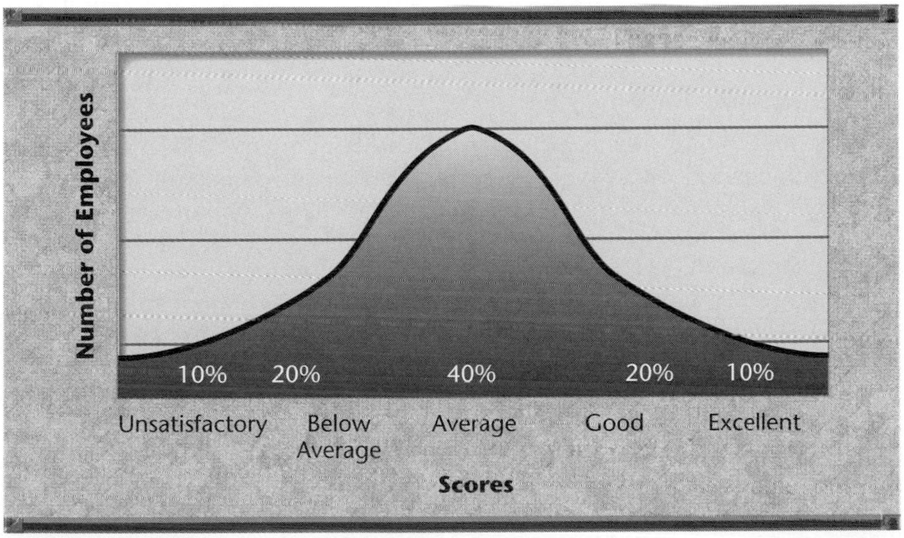

❖ Figure 12–9 ❖
Forced Distribution on a Bell-Shaped Curve

❖ Narrative Methods

Some managers and HR specialists are required to provide written appraisal information. Documentation and description are the essence of the critical incident, the essay, and the field review methods. These records describe an employee's actions rather than indicating an actual rating.

Critical Incident In the critical incident method, the manager keeps a written record of both highly favorable and unfavorable actions in an employee's performance. When a "critical incident" involving an employee occurs, the manager writes it down. A list of critical incidents is kept during the entire rating period for each employee. The critical incident method can be used with other methods to document the reasons why an employee was rated in a certain way.

The critical incident method also has its unfavorable aspects. First, what constitutes a critical incident is not defined in the same way by all supervisors. Next, producing daily or weekly written remarks about each employee's performance can take considerable time. Further, employees may become overly concerned about what the superior writes and begin to fear the manager's "black book."

Essay The essay, or "free-form," appraisal method requires the manager to write a short essay describing each employee's performance during the rating period. The rater usually is given a few general headings under which to categorize comments. The intent is to allow the rater more flexibility than other methods do. As a result, the essay is often combined with other methods.

Field Review In the field review, the HR unit becomes an active partner in the rating process. A member of the unit interviews the manager about each employee's performance. The HR representative then compiles the notes from each interview into a rating for each employee. Then the rating is reviewed by the supervisor for needed changes. This method assumes that the representative of the HR unit knows enough about the job setting to help supervisors give more accurate and thorough appraisals.

The major limitation of the field review is that the HR representative has a great deal of control over the rating. Although this control may be desirable from one viewpoint, supervisors may see it as a challenge to their managerial authority. In addition, the field review can be time-consuming, particularly if a supervisor has to rate a large number of employees.

❖ Behavioral Rating

One attempt to overcome some of the difficulties of the methods just described are several different behavioral approaches. Behavioral approaches hold promise for some situations in overcoming some of the problems with other methods.

❖**Behavioral Rating Approach**
Assesses an employee's behaviors instead of other characteristics.

Behavioral Rating Approaches **Behavioral rating approaches** attempt to assess an employee's *behaviors* instead of other characteristics. Some of the different behavioral approaches are: *Behaviorally anchored rating scales* (BARS), *behavioral observation scales* (BOS), and *behavioral expectation scales* (BES). BARS match descriptions of possible behaviors with what the employee most commonly exhibits. BOS are used to count the number of times certain behaviors are exhibited. BES order behaviors on a continuum to define outstanding, average, and unacceptable performance.[29] BARS were developed first and are used here as an example of behavioral rating approaches.

❖ FIGURE 12–10 ❖
CUSTOMER SERVICE SKILLS

Example behaviors of a telephone customer service representative taking orders for a national catalog retailer.

The customer service representative:

Excellent	5	← Used positive phrases to explain product features.
	4	← Offered additional pertinent information when asked questions by customer.
Satisfactory	3	← Referred customer to another product when requested item was not available.
	2	← Discouraged customer from waiting for an out-of-stock item.
Unsatisfactory	1	← Argued with customer about suitability of requested product.

Behavioral rating approaches describe examples of employee job behaviors. These examples are "anchored," or measured, against a scale of performance levels. Figure 12–10 shows a behavioral observation rating scale that rates customer service skills. What constitutes various levels of performance is clearly defined in the figure. Spelling out the behavior associated with each level of performance helps minimize some of the problems noted earlier for other approaches.

❖ FIGURE 12–11 ❖
DEVELOPMENT PROCESS FOR BEHAVIORAL ANCHORS

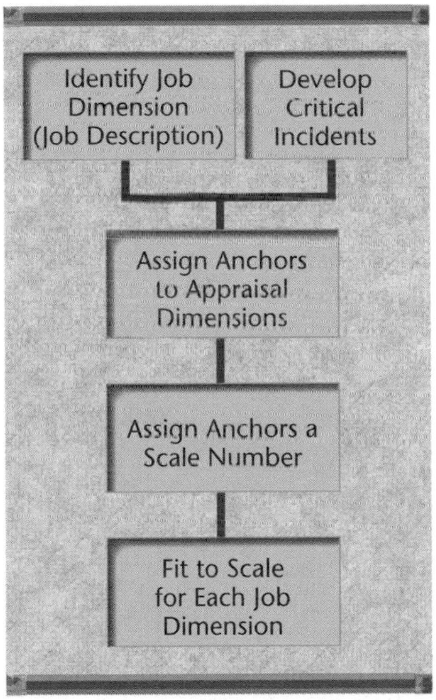

CONSTRUCTING BEHAVIORAL SCALES Construction of a behavioral scale begins with identification of important *job dimensions*. These dimensions are the most important performance factors in an employee's job description. For example, for a college professor, the major job dimensions associated with teaching might be: a) Course organization, b) Attitude toward students, c) Fair treatment, d) Competence in subject area.

Short statements, similar to critical incidents, are developed that describe both desirable and undesirable behaviors (anchors). Then they are "retranslated," or assigned to one of the job dimensions. This task is usually a group project, and assignment to a dimension usually requires the agreement of 60% to 70% of the group. The group, consisting of people familiar with the job, then assigns each "anchor" a number, which represents how good or bad the behavior is. When numbered, these anchors are fitted to a scale. Figure 12–11 shows a flow diagram for developing behavioral anchors.

There are several problems associated with the behavioral approaches that must be considered. First, developing and maintaining behaviorally anchored rating scales require extensive time and effort. In addition, several appraisal forms are needed to accommodate different types of jobs in an organization. In a hospital, nurses, dietitians, and admission clerks all have different jobs; separate BARS forms would need to be developed for each distinct job.

❖ MANAGEMENT BY OBJECTIVES (MBO)

Management By Objectives (MBO) specifies the performance goals that an individual hopes to attain within an appropriate length of time. The objectives that each manager sets are derived from the overall goals and objectives of the

Management by Objectives (MBO)
Specifies the performance goal that an individual hopes to attain within an appropriate length of time.

❖ FIGURE 12–12 ❖
MBO PROCESS

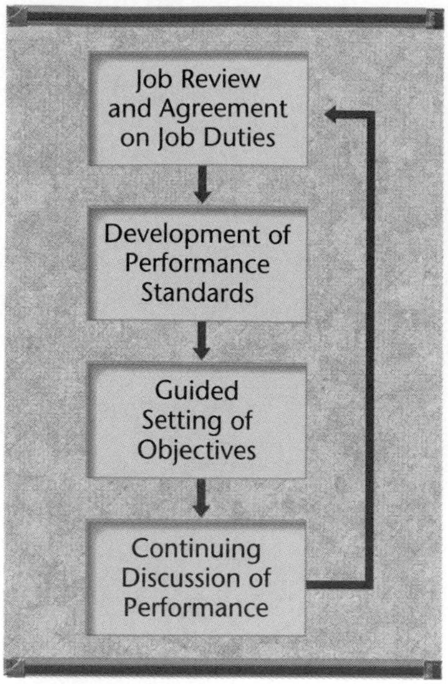

organization, although MBO should not be a disguised means for a superior to dictate the objectives of individual managers or employees. Although not limited to the appraisal of managers, MBO is most often used for this purpose. Other names for MBO include *appraisal by results, targeting-coaching, work planning and review, performance objectives,* and *mutual goal setting.*

KEY MBO IDEAS Three key assumptions underlie an MBO appraisal system. First, if an employee is involved in planning and setting the objectives and determining the measure, a higher level of commitment and performance may result.

Second, if the objectives are identified clearly and precisely, the employee will do a better job of achieving the desired results. Ambiguity and confusion—and therefore less effective performance—may result when a superior determines the objectives for an individual. By having the employee set objectives, the individual gains an accurate understanding of what is expected.

Third, performance objectives should be measurable and should define results. Vague generalities, such as "initiative" and "cooperation," which are common in many superior-based appraisals, should be avoided. Objectives are composed of specific actions to be taken or work to be accomplished. Sample objectives might include:

- Submit regional sales report by the fifth of every month
- Obtain orders from at least five new customers per month
- Maintain payroll costs at 10% of sales volume
- Have scrap loss less than 5%
- Fill all organizational vacancies within 30 days after openings occur

THE MBO PROCESS Implementing a guided self-appraisal system using MBO is a four-stage process. These phases are shown in Figure 12–12 and discussed next.

1. *Job review and agreement.* The employee and the superior review the job description and the key activities that comprise the employee's job. The idea is to agree on the exact makeup of the job.
2. *Development of performance standards.* Specific standards of performance must be mutually developed. In this phase a satisfactory level of performance that is specific and measurable is determined. For example, a quota of selling five cars per month may be an appropriate performance standard for a salesperson.
3. *Guided objective setting.* Objectives are established by the employee in conjunction with, and guided by, the superior. For the automobile salesperson, an objective might be to improve performance; the salesperson might set a new objective of selling six cars per month. Notice that the objective set may be different from the performance standard. Objectives should be realistically attainable.
4. *Continuing performance discussions.* The employee and the superior use the objectives as bases for continuing discussions about the employee's performance. Although a formal review session may be scheduled, the employee and the manager do not necessarily wait until the appointed time to discuss performance. Objectives are modified mutually, and progress is discussed during the period.

MBO CRITIQUE No management tool is perfect, and certainly MBO is not appropriate for all employees or all organizations. Jobs with little or no flexibility are not compatible with MBO. For example, an assembly-line worker usually has so little job flexibility that performance standards and objectives are already determined. The MBO process seems to be most useful with managerial personnel and employees who have a fairly wide range of flexibility and control over their jobs. When imposed on a rigid and autocratic management system, MBO may fail. Extreme emphasis on penalties for not meeting objectives defeats the development and participative nature of MBO.

❖ Rater Errors

There are many possible sources of error in the performance appraisal process. One of the major sources is mistakes made by the rater. There is no simple way to eliminate these errors, but making raters aware of them is helpful. A variety of rater errors are discussed next.

❖ Problems of Varying Standards

When appraising employees, a manager should avoid using different standards and expectations for employees performing similar jobs, which is certain to incur the anger of employees. Such problems are likely to exist when ambiguous criteria and subjective weightings by supervisors are used.

Even if an employee actually has been appraised on the same basis as others, his or her perception is critical. If a student felt a professor had graded his exam harder than another student's exam, he might ask the professor for an explanation. The student's opinion might not be changed by the professor's claim that she had "graded fairly." So it is with performance appraisals in a work situation. If performance appraisal information is to be helpful, the rater must use the same standards and weights for every employee and be able to defend the appraisal. The HR Perspective describes some computer software that can be useful when preparing appraisals.

HR PERSPECTIVE

HRIS Technology and Performance Appraisal

When managers need to write memos, they can use their computers and software such as WordPerfect or Microsoft Word. If a sales analyst needs to crunch sales numbers, the analyst can use Lotus 1-2-3 or Microsoft Excel and move the numbers around until the analysis is completed. Fortunately, managers and supervisors can now use HRIS software to complete performance appraisals using various programs. Clearly, using a "software assist" will not absolve the manager of responsibility for rating performance. But the software may be useful in some situations. A brief description of three of these programs follows:[30]

Performance Now! Users are asked to rate employees on a scale of one to five on various skills. The program then generates descriptive text that supports the rating. The user adds specific examples.

Review Writer Users choose from a list of predefined templates for different jobs. Goals are entered, and categories for performance are selected. Statements on performance appear, and users rate employees by agreeing or disagreeing with the statements.

Employee Appraiser This program provides sample text that can be used as part of a narrative appraisal. It also includes extensive coaching for managers on how to give feedback and how to improve employee performance.

❖ Recency Effect

***Recency Effect**
An error whereby the rater gives greater weight to recent occurrences when appraising an individual's performance.

The **recency effect** is present when a rater gives greater weight to recent occurrences when appraising an individual's performance. Giving a student a course grade based only on his performance in the last week of class or giving a drill press operator a high rating even though she made the quota only in the last two weeks of the rating period are examples.

The recency effect is an understandable rater error. It may be difficult for a rater to remember performance that took place seven or eight months ago. Employees also become more concerned about performance as formal appraisal time approaches. Some employees may attempt to take advantage of the recency factor by currying favor with their supervisors shortly before their appraisals are conducted. The problem can be minimized by using some method of documenting both positive and negative performance.[31]

❖ Rating Patterns

***Central Tendency Error**
Rating all employees in a narrow band in the middle of the rating scale.

Students are well aware that some professors tend to grade easier or harder than others. Likewise, a manager may develop a *rating pattern.* Appraisers who rate all employees within a narrow range (usually the middle or average) commit a **central tendency error.** For example, Dolores Bressler, office manager, tends to rate all her employees as average. Even the poor performers receive an average rating from Dolores. Jane Carr, the billing supervisor, believes that if employees are poor performers, they should be rated below average. An employee of Jane's who is rated average may well be a better performer than one rated average by Dolores.

Similarly, rating patterns may exhibit leniency or strictness. The *leniency error* occurs when ratings of all employees are at the high end of the scale.[32] The *strictness error* occurs when a manager uses only the lower part of the scale to rate employees.

❖ Rater Bias

***Rater Bias**
Error that occurs when a rater's values or prejudices distort the rating.

Rater bias occurs when a rater's values or prejudices distort the rating. Rater bias may be unconscious or quite intentional. If a manager has a strong dislike of certain ethnic groups, this bias is likely to result in distorted appraisal information for some people. Age, religion, seniority, sex, appearance, or other arbitrary classifications may be reflected in appraisals if the appraisal process is not properly designed. Examination of ratings by higher-level managers may help correct this problem.

One reason that positive rater bias or leniency may exist is that supervisors are concerned about damaging a good working relationship by giving an unfavorable rating. Or they may wish to avoid giving negative feedback, which is often unpleasant, so they inflate the ratings. Reasons for a rating biased on the low side might include sending the employee a "message" or documenting a case leading to dismissal.[33] Rater bias is difficult to overcome, especially if a manager is not aware of the bias or will not admit to it.

❖ Halo Effect

***Halo Effect**
Rating a person high or low on all items because of one characteristic.

The **halo effect** occurs when a manager rates an employee high or low on all items because of one characteristic. For example, if a worker has few absences, her supervisor might give her a high rating in all other areas of work, including quantity and quality of output, because of her dependability. The manager may not really think about the employee's other characteristics separately.

An appraisal that shows the same rating on all characteristics may be evidence of the halo effect. Clearly specifying the categories to be rated, rating all employees on one characteristic at a time, and training raters to recognize the problem are some means of reducing the halo effect.

❖ Contrast Error

Rating should be done on the basis of established standards. The **contrast error** is the tendency to rate people relative to other people rather than to performance standards. For example, if everyone else in a group is doing a mediocre job, a person performing somewhat better may be rated as excellent because of the contrast effect.[34] But in a group performing well, the same person might have received a poor rating. Although it may be appropriate to compare people at times, the rating should reflect performance against job requirements, not against other people.

❖Contrast Error
Tendency to rate people relative to other people rather than to performance standards.

❖ The Appraisal Feedback Interview

Once appraisals have been made, it is important to communicate them so that employees have a clear understanding of how they stand in the eyes of their immediate superiors and the organization. It is fairly common for organizations to require that managers discuss appraisals with employees. The appraisal feedback interview can clear up misunderstandings on both sides. In this interview, the manager should emphasize counseling and development, not just tell the employee, "Here is how you rate and why." Focusing on development gives both parties an opportunity to consider the employee's performance and its potential for improvement.

The appraisal interview presents both an opportunity and a danger. It is an emotional experience for the manager and the employee because the manager must communicate both praise and constructive criticism. A major concern for managers is how to emphasize the positive aspects of the employee's performance while still discussing ways to make needed improvements. If the interview is handled poorly, the employee may feel resentment, and conflict may result, which could be reflected in future work. Figure 12–13 summarizes hints for an effective appraisal interview for supervisors and managers.

Employees usually approach an appraisal interview with some concern. They often feel that discussions about performance are very personal and important to their continued job success. At the same time, they want to know how the manager feels they have been doing.

❖ Figure 12–13 ❖
Hints for Managers in the Appraisal Interview

DO	DON'T
❖ Prepare in advance ❖ Focus on performance and development ❖ Be specific about reasons for ratings ❖ Decide on specific steps to be taken for improvement ❖ Consider the supervisor's role in the subordinate's performance ❖ Reinforce desired behaviors ❖ Focus on future performance	❖ Lecture the employee ❖ Mix performance appraisal and salary or promotion issues ❖ Concentrate only on the negative ❖ Do all the talking ❖ Be overly critical or "harp on" a failing ❖ Feel it is necessary that both parties agree in all areas ❖ Compare the employee with others

❖ Reactions of Managers

Managers and supervisors who must complete appraisals of their employees often resist the appraisal process. As mentioned earlier, managers may feel they

are put in the position of "playing God." A major part of the manager's role is to assist, encourage, coach, and counsel employees to improve their performance. However, being a judge on the one hand and a coach and counselor on the other may cause internal conflict and confusion for the manager.

The fact that appraisals may affect an employee's future career may cause raters to alter or bias their rating. This bias is even more likely when managers know that they will have to communicate and defend their ratings to the employees, their bosses, or HR specialists. From the manager's viewpoint, providing negative feedback to an employee in an appraisal interview can be easily avoided by making the employee's ratings positive. Reactions such as these are attempts to avoid unpleasantness in an interpersonal situation. Avoidance helps no one. A manager *owes* an employee a well-considered appraisal.

❖ Reactions of Appraised Employees

Many employees view appraising as a zero-sum game—that is, one in which there must be a winner and a loser. Employees may well see the appraisal process as a threat and feel that the only way to get a higher rating is for someone else to receive a low rating. This win/lose perception is encouraged by comparative methods of rating.[35] However, appraisals can also be non-zero-sum in nature—that is, both parties can win and no one must lose. Emphasis on the self-improvement and developmental aspects of appraisal appears to be the most effective means to reduce zero-sum reactions from those participating in the appraisal process.[36]

Another common employee reaction is similar to students' reactions to tests. A professor may prepare a test he or she feels is fair, but it does not necessarily follow that students will feel the test is fair. They simply may see it differently. Likewise, employees being appraised may not necessarily agree with the manager doing the appraising. In most cases, however, employees will view appraisals done well as what they are meant to be—constructive feedback.

❖ Effective and Legal Performance Appraisals

A growing number of court decisions have focused on performance appraisals, particularly in relation to equal employment opportunity (EEO) concerns. In addition, legal consequences are associated with certain ethical issues, as the

HR PERSPECTIVE

ETHICS OF DISMISSING A "SATISFACTORY" EMPLOYEE

"We should never have kept him in that job so long. It was a mistake and now we have to bite the bullet." "We were wrong. Fred should have been told years ago that his performance was marginal." "We should have fired Fred 10 years ago."

So went the comments just before the decision was made to dismiss Fred Johnson, a supervisor and 20-year employee of a large firm in the telecommunications industry. But his performance had consistently been rated satisfactory—3 on a 5-point scale. No one had ever said anything to him that would cause him to be concerned about his future. There were certainly no rave reviews, but there were no condemning comments either, and he had received "merit" pay increases over his 20 years with the company. But the ground rules had changed, and suddenly he was out.

If management wants to make employment changes, it clearly has the right to do so. However, is it ethically proper to disregard years of performance that is satisfactory by management's own rating? Or should Fred's boss identify the specific goals to be met and set a timetable for meeting them, knowing full well that Fred is likely to fail? Is there an age discrimination issue here as well?

Dentists allegedly extract their mistakes; physicians are said to bury theirs. What is the ethical course of action a company should take when changes must be made but when years of past performance appraisals do not indicate that anything is wrong with an individual's performance?

acompanying HR Perspective indicates. The Uniform Guidelines issued by the Equal Employment Opportunity Commission (EEOC) and other federal enforcement agencies make it clear that performance appraisals must be job related and nondiscriminatory.

❖ PERFORMANCE APPRAISALS AND THE LAW

It may seem unnecessary to emphasize that performance appraisals must be job related, because appraisals are supposed to measure how well employees are doing their jobs. Yet in numerous cases, courts have ruled that performance appraisals were discriminatory and not job related.[37]

One court case provides an important illustration. Fort Worth Bank and Trust was a relatively small bank with 80 employees. It hired Clara Watson as a proof operator. Two years later, she was promoted to teller. Eight years after going to work for the bank, she was promoted to commercial teller. Over the next year and a half, she applied for four different promotions. In each case, a white employee was selected over Watson, who was a member of a racial minority group. The bank admitted it had no precise formal criteria to evaluate good performance for the positions for which Watson had applied. It relied instead on the subjective judgment of supervisors. Watson resigned, sued, and won. In *Watson v. Fort Worth Bank and Trust,* the U.S. Supreme Court ruled that a violation of Title VII of the Civil Rights Act could occur when an employer's *subjective* promotion criteria resulted in disproportionately fewer minority employees receiving promotions. The Court noted that an "undisciplined system of subjective decision making" could have the same negative consequences as a process that was intended to discriminate. Performance appraisal systems without formal criteria and standards appear to qualify as subjective.[38]

ELEMENTS OF A LEGAL PERFORMANCE APPRAISAL SYSTEM The elements of a performance appraisal system that can survive court tests can be determined from existing case law. Various cases have provided guidance. The elements of a legally-defensible performance appraisal are as follows:

- ❖ Performance appraisal criteria based on job analysis
- ❖ Absence of disparate impact and evidence of validity
- ❖ Formal evaluation criteria that limit managerial discretion
- ❖ Formal rating instrument
- ❖ Personal knowledge of and contact with appraised individual
- ❖ Training of supervisors in conducting appraisals
- ❖ Review process that prevents one manager acting alone from controlling an employee's career
- ❖ Counseling to help poor performers improve

It is clear that the courts are interested in fair and nondiscriminatory performance appraisals. Employers must decide how to design their appraisal systems to satisfy the courts, enforcement agencies, and their employees.

❖ Effective Performance Appraisals

Regardless of which method is used, an understanding of what an appraisal is supposed to do is critical. When performance appraisal is used to develop employees as resources, it usually works. When management uses appraisal as a punishment or when raters fail to understand its limitations, it fails. The key is not which form or which method of performance appraisal is used but whether managers and employees understand its purposes. In its simplest form, performance appraisal is a manager's statement: "Here are your strengths and weaknesses, and here is a way to shore up the weak areas." It can lead to higher employee motivation and satisfaction if done right.

❖ Figure 12–14 ❖
Positives and Negatives of Performance Appraisal Systems

POSITIVES OF EFFECTIVE APPRAISAL SYSTEMS	NEGATIVES OF MANY APPRAISAL SYSTEMS
❖ Establish a process and criteria for evaluating performance ❖ Provide documentation in the event of legal action ❖ Can clarify goals and development needs ❖ Can use feedback as a reward	❖ Time consuming ❖ Individual focus may cause problems for team approaches ❖ Emotionally unpleasant at times ❖ May decrease morale in some cases ❖ Sometimes seen as unfair

The "perfect" PA system does not exist because all PA systems have positives and negatives. Figure 12–14 shows the positives and negatives most often mentioned. Unfortunately, many performance appraisal systems have not met their potential. Although most organizations (at least larger ones) have them, appraisal systems often are poorly designed and frequently fail to tie pay to performance or help improve employee motivation.[39] However, PA systems usually do let employees know where they stand, provide input about their jobs, and help establish and clarify goals.

An effective performance appraisal system will be:

- ❖ Consistent with the strategic mission of the organization
- ❖ Useful as a development tool
- ❖ Useful as an administrative tool
- ❖ Legal
- ❖ Viewed as generally fair by employees
- ❖ Documentation of employee performance

Most appraisal systems can be improved by training of the appraising supervisors. Training should focus on minimizing rater errors and providing a common frame of reference on how raters observe and recall information. Feedback on how well a supervisor has rated employees is an excellent method of improving rating effectiveness. In many organizations, managers and supervisors have had little appraisal training. Training appraisers gives them confidence in their ability to make appraisals and handle appraisal interviews. Familiarity with common rating errors and training on how to avoid them can improve rater performance as well.

Organizationally, there is a tendency to distill performance appraisals into a single number that can be used to support pay raises. Systems based on this concept reduce the complexity of each individual's contribution in order to satisfy compensation-system requirements. Such systems are too simplistic to give employees feedback or help managers pinpoint training and development needs. In fact, use of a single rating often is a barrier to performance discussions, because what is emphasized is attaching a label to a person's performance and defending or attacking that label. Effective performance appraisal systems evolve from a recognition that human behaviors and capabilities collapsed into a single score have limited use in developing human resources.

SUMMARY

- ❖ Performance management systems attempt to monitor, measure, report, improve, and reward employee performance.
- ❖ Performance is the link between an organization's strategy and results.
- ❖ Job criteria are job dimensions, such as accuracy and speed, that are being measured.
- ❖ Relevance, contamination, and deficiency of criteria affect performance measurement.
- ❖ Appraising employee performance is useful for development and administrative purposes.
- ❖ Performance appraisal can be done either informally or systematically. Systematic appraisals usually are done annually.
- ❖ Appraisals can be done by superiors, employees, teams, outsiders, or a combination of raters. Employees also can conduct self-appraisals.
- ❖ Superiors' ratings of employees are most frequently used.
- ❖ Four types of appraisal methods are available: category rating methods, comparative methods, narrative methods, and special methods.
- ❖ Category rating methods, especially graphic rating scales and checklists, are widely used.
- ❖ Ranking, paired comparison, and forced distribution are comparative methods.
- ❖ Narrative methods include the critical incident technique, the essay approach, and the field review.
- ❖ Two special methods of appraisal include behavioral rating approaches and management by objectives (MBO).
- ❖ Construction of a behaviorally-oriented rating scale requires a detailed job analysis so that the rating criteria and anchors are job specific.
- ❖ Management by objectives (MBO) is an approach that requires joint goal setting by a superior and an employee.
- ❖ A major source of performance appraisal problems is rater error. Rater errors include varying standards, recency effect, rater bias (such as leniency bias), rating patterns (such as central tendency error), halo effect, and contrast error.
- ❖ The appraisal feedback interview is a vital part of any appraisal system.
- ❖ Both managers and employees may resist performance appraisals, and perfect systems do not exist.
- ❖ Federal employment guidelines and numerous court decisions have scrutinized performance appraisals. The absence of specific job-relatedness can create legal problems, as can subjectivity.
- ❖ Training appraisers and guarding against the tendency to reduce an appraisal to a single number are important for an effective appraisal system.

Review and Discussion Questions

1. What is the difference between performance standards and job criteria, and why do the criteria problems of contamination and deficiency exist?
2. How can the developmental and administrative uses of performance appraisals conflict?
3. Suppose you are a supervisor. What errors might you make when preparing a performance appraisal on a clerical employee?
4. What sources are typically included in 360° performance appraisal?
5. Explain the similarities and differences between the behavioral approaches to performance appraisal and Management By Objectives (MBO).
6. Construct a plan for a post-appraisal interview with an employee who has performed poorly.
7. Discuss the following statement: "Most performance appraisal systems in use today would not pass legal scrutiny."
8. Why is the training of appraisers so vital to an effective performance appraisal system?

Terms to Know

behavioral rating approach **356**
central tendency error **360**
checklist **354**
contrast error **361**
critical job dimensions **340**
forced choice **354**
forced distribution **355**
graphic rating scale **352**
halo effect **360**
management by objectives (MBO) **357**
paired comparison **355**
performance appraisal (PA) **343**
performance criteria **341**
performance management systems **340**
performance standard **340**
ranking **354**
rater bias **360**
recency effect **360**

Case

Revising the Performance Appraisal System at St. Luke's Hospital

Recently St. Luke's Hospital in Jacksonville, Florida, a thoroughly modern hospital, had a thoroughly modern problem. Its performance appraisal system was rapidly becoming an insurmountable pile of papers; and with 1325 employees, the HR staff recognized that changes were needed.

Performance appraisal forms can range from a simple single sheet of paper to very lengthy and complex packets. St. Luke's performance appraisal system had evolved over the years into a form with about 20 pages per employee. Although some of the length was due to concerns about meeting numerous federal, state, and health-care industry requirements, other facets of the system had been developed for administrative reasons.

The existing performance appraisal system was based on a combination of job descriptions and a performance appraisal. In addition, health care accreditation requirements necessitated using a competency management program focusing on employee development and education. As a result, St. Luke's had combined the competency profiles with the job descriptions and performance appraisal forms. To complete an appraisal on employees, supervisors and managers scored employee performance on formal weighted criteria and then summarized the information by compensation and benefits class. Those summaries were reviewed by upper management for consistency, as one would expect. The overall performance appraisal process was paper-intensive, slow, and frustrating because it required a total of 36 different steps.

A steering committee was formed to oversee the process of changing to a better performance appraisal system. The committee established that it was crucial for the new system to better fit the needs of those using it. Also, the committee wanted the system to use more technology and less paper. Based on these general objectives, brainstorming was conducted to find bottlenecks and identify what the ideal automated process would look like. At this point the committee understood the current systems and what key users wanted. After reviewing literature on performance appraisal systems, surveying other hospitals, and looking at software packages, the committee decided it would have to design its own system.

The option chosen consisted of moving the numerical criteria scores from the individual pages of the job description to a summary sheet that provided for scoring up to 6 employees on one form. Then total scores were calculated by the computer. Also, written comments were moved to a summary sheet dealing only with exceptions to standards.

The most difficult part proved to be the design of the database. It had to be designed from scratch and had to interface with the existing HR systems already in place. A software program was written to do the calculations using data already in place and another program was written to do the calculations. The new process reduced the paperwork from 20 to 7 pages per employee. Supervisors and managers were given the option of using computerized comment sheets. Another time saver was the ability to use the system to record and document noteworthy employee performance incidents, both positive and negative in nature, as they occurred throughout the year. This documentation feature eliminated the need for a separate note-keeping system that many managers had been using.

To implement the new performance appraisal system, training for supervisors and managers was crucial. When the training program was developed for the new system, all 97 supervisors and managers were required to attend. During the training, attendees were given a sample package with appraisal forms, a checkoff timeline, a resource text, and directions for using the on-line performance appraisal forms.

To determine if the original goals had been met, the committee developed an evaluation form. After the new appraisal system had been in use, an evaluation revealed that 90% of the supervisors and managers felt that the process had indeed been streamlined. The new process was viewed as easier to understand, a significant reduction in paper had occurred, arithmetic errors were prevented, and the appraisal information was clearer and more concise.

The next year the committee reconvened to examine the first year operation and identify areas for improvement. Since then minor revisions have been made in the performance appraisal system, updates on computer hardware and software were undertaken and data screens have been simplified for management users. Also, efforts have begun to fully automate the performance appraisal system. In summary, the revision of the performance appraisal system met its objectives.[40]

❖ *Questions:*

1. Explain why the new performance appraisal system at St. Luke's Hospital is more likely to result in more accurate performance appraisals.
2. Describe some of the advantages and disadvantages of combining job descriptions, performance appraisals, and competency profiles for development as St. Luke's did.

Notes

1. Brian O'Reilly, "360° Feedback Can Change Your Life," *Fortune,* October 17, 1994, 93.
2. Based upon information in M. London and J. W. Smithers, "Can Multi-Source Feedback Change Perceptions . . . ? Theory-Based Applications and Directions for Research," *Personnel Psychology* (1995), 803–839; R. Hoffman, "Ten Reasons You Should Be Using 360 Degree Feedback," *HR Magazine,* April 1995, 84; and Michael Bennett, "360 Ratings," *ACA News,* April 1995, 12–15.
3. Based on S. Lubman, "Schools Tie Salaries to Pupil Performance," *The Wall Street Journal,* March 10, 1995, B1.
4. R. S. Barrett, "Employee Selection with the Performance Priority Survey," *Personnel Psychology* 48 (1995), 653–663.
5. William Bommer et al., "On the Interchangeability of Objective and Subjective Measures of Employee Performance: A Meta-Analysis," *Personnel Psychology* 48 (1995), 587–605.
6. P. Bobko and A. Colella, "Employee Reactions to Performance Standards: A Review and Research Proposition," *Personnel Psychology* 47 (1994), 1–29.
7. Carolyn Pye, "Setting Employee Standards," *NAPM Insights,* May 1995, 18–21.
8. S. L. Thomas and Robert D. Bretz, "Research and Practice in Performance Appraisal: Evaluating Employee Performance in America's Largest Companies," *S.A.M. Advanced Management Journal,* Spring 1994, 28–34.
9. D. Daley, "Pay for Performance, Performance Appraisal, and TQM," *Public Productivity and Management Review,* Fall 1992, 39–50.
10. Joann S. Lublin, "It's Shape-up Time for Performance Reviews," *The Wall Street Journal,* October 3, 1994, B1.
11. Michael M. Harris, D. E. Smith, and D. Champagne, "A Field Study of Performance Appraisal Purpose: Research versus Administrative Based Ratings," *Personnel Psychology* 48 (1995), 151.
12. Phyllis Tharenov, "The Impact of a Developmental Performance Appraisal Program on Employee Perceptions in an Australian Federal Agency," *Group and Organization Management,* September 1995, 245.
13. M. Moravec, R. Juliff, and K. Hesler, "Partnerships Help a Company Manage Performance," *Personnel Journal,* January 1995, 105–108, and T. Labriola, "Quality System Tracks Work," *HR Magazine,* February 1994, 67–72.
14. Lublin, "Performance Reviews," B1.
15. Robert D. Bretz, G. Milkovich, and W. Read, "The Current Stage of Performance Appraisal Research: Concerns, Directions, and Implications," *Journal of Management* 18 (1992), 321–352.
16. Joann S. Lublin, "Turning the Tables: Underlings Evaluate Bosses," *The Wall Street Journal,* October 4, 1994, B1.
17. Based on David Antonioni, "The Effects of Feedback Accountability on Upward Appraisal Ratings," *Personnel Psychology* 47 (1994), 349–356.
18. K. Carson et al., "Performance Appraisal As Effective Management or Deadly Management Disease," *Group and Organizational Studies* 16 (1991), 145–146.
19. S. Shellenbarger, "Reviews from Peers Instruct and Sting," *The Wall Street Journal,* October 4, 1994, B1.
20. J. H. Barclay and L. K. Harland, "Peer Performance Appraisals," *Group and Organization Management,* March 1995, 39–60.
21. R. J. Trent and R. M. Monczka, "Guidelines for Developing Team Performance Appraisal Systems," *NAPM Insights,* July 1994, 30–32.
22. M. London and J. W. Smithers, "Can Multi-Source Feedback Change Perceptions of Goal Accomplishment, Self Evaluations and Performance Related Outcomes?" *Personnel Psychology* 48 (1995), 803–839.
23. M. Edwards and A. Ewen, "Moving Multi-Source Assessment Beyond Development," *ACA Journal,* Winter 1995, 82–93.
24. Robert L. Cardy and Gregory H. Dobbins, *Performance Appraisal: Alternative Perspectives* (Cincinnati: South-Western Publishing, 1994).
25. M. London and R. Beatty, "360 Degree Feedback as Competitive Advantage," *Human Resource Management* 32 (1993), 353–373.
26. M. London, *Self and Interpersonal Insight: How People Learn About Themselves and Others in Organizations* (New York: Oxford Press, 1995).
27. W. W. Tornow, "Editor's Note," *Human Resource Management* 32 (1993), 211–219.
28. N. Merz and S. Motowidlo, "Effects of Rater Accountability on the Accuracy and Favorability of Performance Ratings," *Journal of Applied Psychology* 80 (1995), 517–524.
29. U. J. Wiersma, P. T. Van Den Berg, and G. P. Latham, "Dutch Reactions to Behavioral Observation, Behavioral Expectation, and Trait Scales," *Group and Organization Management,* September 1995, 297–309.
30. A. L. Sprout, "Surprise! Software to Help You Manage," *Fortune,* April 17, 1995, 197–200, and E. C. Baig, "So You Hate Rating Your Workers?" *Business Week,* August 22, 1994, 14.
31. A. J. Kinicki et al., "Effects of Category Prototypes on Performance-Rating Accuracy," *Journal of Applied Psychology* (1995), 354–370.
32. Yitzhak Fried and Robert Tiegs, "Supervisor's Role Conflict . . . ," *Journal of Applied Psychology* (1995), 282–291.
33. Michael M. Harris, "Rater Motivation in the Performance Appraisal Context: A Theoretical Framework," *Journal of Management* (1994), 737–756.
34. Yozv Ganzach, "Negativity and Positivity in Performance Evaluation: Three Field Studies," *Journal of Applied Psychology* (1995) 491–499.
35. J. W. Smithers, A. J. Wohlers, and M. London, "A Field Study of Reactions to Normative vs. Individualized Upward Feedback," *Group and Organization Management,* March 1995, 61–89.
36. M. Korsgaard and L. Roberson, "Procedural Justice in Performance Evaluation," *Journal of Management* 21 (1995) 657–669.
37. G. Jonathan Meng, "The Legal Side of Performance Appraisals," *PAYTECH,* July/August 1994, 22–25.
38. G. Mertens, "*Watson v. Fort Worth Bank and Trust:* Unanswered Questions," *Employee Relations Law Journal* 14 (1988), 163–173.
39. David Antonioni, "Improve the Performance Management Process before Discontinuing Performance Appraisals," *Compensation and Benefits Review,* May/June 1994, 29–37.
40. Based upon: L. Aderhold, N. O'Keefe, and D. Burke, "Critical Care for Review Process," *Personnel Journal,* April 1996, 115–120.

EXERCISE 7 - Analysis

Throughout this section the importance of providing training internally has been emphasized. Larger organizations often have a number of training and development courses accessible for which employees can enroll.

SME-TEK has several courses that employees may take to enhance their overall skills. One of the classes is Presentation Skills (PUBS0001, class 001). An employee, Henry Aston, has called to enroll in that course.

1. Given the content that typically might be covered in a course on Presentation Skills, how could the effectiveness of that course be evaluated?
2. Please register Mr. Aston in that class and then use the class table to find out if there are fewer than five participants enrolled. If that is true, then the class may have to be combined with section 002.

> SME-TEK
>
> MEMO
>
> TO: *HUMAN RESOURCE MANAGEMENT USER*
>
> Henry Aston called to enroll in the upcoming Presentation Skills training. Please register him in the system for the course PUBS0001, class number 001.
>
> When done, please use the Class Table to find out how many employees have registered for the 1st (001) Presentation Skills class. If fewer than five participants are enrolled, we may have to combine this class with the second one (002).
>
> Thanks,
>
> Ann Smith

EXERCISE 7 - Procedure

Before completing the memo's request, you need to access the Basic Training module and review the topics "What is Basic Training?" in the "Overview" lesson of the Concepts section. The Checkpoint topic in this lesson is optional.

To fulfill the memo's request, access the "Course Enrollment" lesson of the Basic Training Features & Processes section. Then, review the topics "Enrolling an Employee in a Class" and "Viewing Class Enrollments."

EXERCISE 8 - Analysis

One common type of training offered in many organizations is to provide safety-related classes. Partly due to Occupational Safety and Health Administration (OSHA) requirements, a certain number of individuals must be trained in first-aid, including cardiopulmonary resuscitation (CPR).

SME-TEK offers a CPR class (SAFE 101, class 001) to its employees. Two employees have called to enroll in the CPR class, and a different employee has called to cancel attendance at the CPR class.

1. Why would the CPR training be seen as beneficial to employees beyond aiding SME-TEK in complying with OSHA regulations?
2. Enroll Alice Tudwell and Cathy Salmons in the CPR class and cancel the enrollment for Craig Kimball. Also, update the class record so that another employee can be admitted if necessary.

> SME-TEK
>
> MEMO
>
> TO: *HUMAN RESOURCE MANAGEMENT USER*
>
> Two more employees have decided to enroll in the CPR course we are offering next month (course SAFE101, class number 001). One is Alice Tudwell, the other Cathy Salmons. Since Alice notified me first, give her priority if the class is nearing full capacity.
>
> Also, Craig Kimball called to cancel his enrollment in the CPR class. Please update the class record ASAP so you can admit a new employee if necessary.
>
> Thanks,
>
> Ann

EXERCISE 8 - Procedure

To fulfill the memo's request, access the "Course Enrollment" lesson of the Basic Training Features & Processes section. Then, review the topics "Enrolling an Employee in a Full Class" and "Canceling an Employee's Enrollment." The Practice and Checkpoint topics in this lesson are optional.

EXERCISE 9 - Analysis

Many employers offer tuition assistance so that employees can take courses and obtain college degrees. SME-TEK provides tuition aid to employees and reimburses employees for most of the costs. One of the SME-TEK employees, Scott Carson, completed a course (BA 821 - Accounting II) at the University of Texas, and appropriate notation and credit need to be made so that he can be reimbursed.

1. How does having a tuition assistance plan contribute to the longer-term development of organizational human resources?
2. Enter the information on Mr. Carson's accounting class in which he received an A, so that his reimbursement check can be processed.

EXERCISE 9 - Procedure

To fulfill the memo's request, access the "Tuition Reimbursement" lesson of the Basic Training Features & Processes section. Then, review the topic "Adding Tuition Reimbursement Data." The Practice and Checkpoint topics in this lesson are optional.

SME-TEK

MEMO

TO: *HUMAN RESOURCES MANAGEMENT USER*

Scott Carson completed a course in accounting at the University of Texas. He is eligible for an 80% reimbursement of his tuition expenses, which totaled $400.00. The course he took is BA821—Accounting II. He began this course last quarter and received an A as his final grade. Please enter the information necessary to record his reimbursement so we can get a check to him as quickly as possible.

Thanks,

Jon Hanson

SECTION VIDEO CASES

❖ CASE 1
ROBOTRON
Qualifying for Global Competition

Robotron Corp., a Southfield, Michigan, manufacturer, used to think the equipment it produced for the auto industry was above average in quality, says CEO Leonard Brzozowski. That, he adds, "was largely because none of our customers ever complained about it."

Then General Motors gave Robotron an order for induction bonding machines to cure adhesive in auto door joints. The machines went to a Michigan plant of Sanyo Manufacturing Co., which GM was trying out as a door builder.

The Japanese firm was unhappy with the equipment. Brzozowski went to its plant and "learned that they had a completely different expectation of quality than our usual American customers." Inspection was more demanding. Tolerances allowed were much smaller.

"For the first time," Brzozowski says, "we realized that the philosophy, engineering, management, and shop practices of our company did not qualify us for global competition." He and other managers "resolved to launch a revolution" at Robotron.

A group of hourly employees were immediately driven to the Sanyo plant. "Their opportunity to actually see the customer's disappointment, hear his complaints, and compare our equipment with that manufactured by Sanyo," Brzozowski says, accomplished more than scores of meetings or managers' could have. The ride home was filled with discussions about things to do to improve quality.

Soon Robotron had established new inspection procedures, bought more accurate inspection tools, changed internal control procedures, and developed yardsticks against which to measure progress.

It began sending out teams to check on cusotmer satisfaction within six months after equipment deliveries. A hot line that any customer could call was set up, and customers were given home numbers of Brzozowski and his staff.

To give all the company's 115 employees a stake in its success, Robotron substituted a bonus program for merit reviews of pay. Now 21 percent of pretax profit goes into the program for distribution to everyone, from Brzozowski to the newest shop trainee.

Robotron's revolution appears to have paid off in customer satisfaction. Claims under warranty dropped 40 percent in three years—a period in which orders rose at a compound annual rate of 13.5 percent.

1. Evaluate the idea of "people learning from customers" as a training technique.
2. Creativity and innovation are *developed* not trained. Discuss Robotron's approach as a way to develop creativity in your Human Resources.

(Excerpts reprinted by permission of The Blue Chip Enterprise Initiative©, *Real-World Lessons for America's Small Businesses* pp. 70, 71; copyright 1994 by Connecticut Mutual Life Insurance Company.) ❖

❖ CASE 2
LANDMARK TITLE
Recession as Opportunity

Landmark Title, Inc., had to retrench when a recession struck, but it fought back with a "customer first—everyone in the trenches" strategy.

Another label that the title search, title insurance, and closing firm devised also describes its attitude: "recession as opportunity." Those words are prominent in a "recession charter" conceived at a planning meeting of key staff members. Meetings involving the whole staff followed, and everyone became "totally customer-driven," says Landmark President Michael Massey.

Landmark, based in Manchester, N.H., was seriously threatened when the real estate market slumped severely and its bank failed. Its revenues dropped 26 percent, and it was shut off from capital.

It had recently lost two key employees, but now it had to lose more. The staff was cut to 25, from 35. Everyone went on a four-day week.

There was no cutback, however, in employee training or in marketing. In reorganizing the work force and focusing on the customer, says Massey, "it became painfully obvious that we were spending a great deal of time correcting documentation errors and title issues after the transaction closed." Monitoring such post-closing errors, Landmark retrained employees as needed. A pre-closing review process was established to catch errors earlier.

The company checks with customers after each closing and now reports a 98 percent "excellent" quality rating.

To get more business, Landmark diversified, but without straying far from what it knew. For example, the company had software that automated reporting to the Internal Revenue Service on proceeds from real estate sales. So it offered law firms a service: It would provide reports their clients had to make to the IRS on such sales. Also, an increase in real estate tax liens had placed pressure on municipal tax collectors. Landmark developed a software program to calculate required notice fees, generate the notices, and print mailing labels.

Despite cost-containment and marketing efforts, there were periods of critical cash shortfall. To meet payroll, Massey obtained a home equity loan. A friend made him a short-term loan at another critical point.

The building where Landmark is headquartered was bought at a foreclosure sale in 1991. Landmark negotiated an agreement to manage the building for a fee, and, at its most critical cash-flow point, won permission to hold off on rent payments, pledging its management fee against them.

Today Landmark has a new banking relationship, which should make such measures unnecessary in the future. Growing revenues—jumps of 60 percent in 1992 and 40 percent in '93—should also make them unnecessary. The company now has 44 employees, and it sees new opportunities ahead in the post-recession period.

1. Explain how retrenching can generate the need for retraining.

2. Discuss advantages of cross training for this Company in the future.

(Excerpts reprinted by permission of The Blue Chip Enterprise Initiative©, *Real-World Lessons for America's Small Businesses* pp. 20, 21; copyright 1994 by Connecticut Mutual Life Insurance Company.) ❖

❖ CASE 3
TRAU & LOEVNER
Changing with the Times

Mark H. Loevner's company is a lot different from what it was when his grandfather founded it in 1897—or what it was when he took it over in the 1980s. If he hadn't met the challenge of changing it, it might well not be around today.

When Loevner joined Trau & Loevner, Inc., in 1956 after service in the Air Force, the Pittsburgh, Pa., firm was wholesaling men's and boys' furnishings to mom and pop stores and junior department stores, as it had since his grandfather's day.

But retailing began to change, Loevner points out—"Kresge became Kmart, Woolworth stores became Woolco stores, the Wal-Mart type of store was born.... Manufacturers began bypassing the wholesaler and selling direct to the retailer."

Under an older cousin, Trau & Loevner added three divisions that handled separate lines of apparel. Each was a money-loser. Loevner and his cousin disagreed on strategy, and ultimately, in the early 1980s, Loevner bought the cousin out.

He closed the three divisions, and sales dropped to $2.6 million from $7 million. The original wholesale business was still above break-even, although Loevner didn't know for how long.

There wasn't enough work for all 17 of the company's remaining employees, but if Loevner was to save the business, he needed a work-force nucleus. "I paid all these people a week's wages but dismissed most of them before lunch each day," he recalls. He cut his own pay by two thirds.

Then he made a fateful switch: He decided that the company's future lay in sportswear custom-imprinted under license. Ending wholesaling, he hooked up with a friend who had a New York sales office and a following among mass merchandisers and department stores. He also hooked up, thanks to past contacts, with U.S. textile mills and sewing plants to make clothing that Trau & Loevner would imprint.

Loevner recognized that manufacturing was changing, just as merchandising had. He couldn't skimp on technology: The plant foreman was sent to trade shows to buy state-of-the-art silk screening equipment. Production employees were sent to seminars to improve techniques. Computer equipment with customized software was procured for design artwork, which had been done by hand. Artwork that used to take four hours to produce was now done, geometrically perfect, in five minutes.

Trau & Loevner is now the country's fifth largest manufacturer of licensed college apparel—and the four ahead of it are subsidiaries of public companies. Sales last year topped $30 million, and there are 104 employees.

Loevner's son, Howard, and nephew, Steve, joined the company in the 1980s and today are co-presidents, with Howard heading up sales and Steve in charge of operations.

An executive noted for philanthropy, Mark Loevner, who is chairman, has charged the younger generation of Loevners to be philanthropic, too, and to continue the company's growth. That might well entail more change.

1. Discuss the need to develop and train employees as part of the business changes at Trau and Loevner.

2. What training needs had to be addressed for Trau and Loevner to successfully transition to its new market?

(Excerpts reprinted by permission of The Blue Chip Enterprise Initiative©, *Real-World Lessons for America's Small Businesses* pp. 33, 34; copyright 1994 by Connecticut Mutual Life Insurance Company.) ❖

Section 5

Compensating Human Resources

CHAPTER 13

COMPENSATION

After you have read this chapter, you should be able to . . .

- Identify the three types of compensation and discuss two compensation philosophies.
- Discuss different bases for compensation.
- Describe three equity considerations and how organizational justice is related to compensation.
- Identify the basic provisions of the Fair Labor Standards Act.
- Define *job evaluation* and discuss four methods of performing it.
- Outline the process of building a wage and salary administration system.
- Discuss how a pay-for-performance system is established.

HR IN TRANSITION

BROADBANDING COMPENSATION

As work has become broader and more cross-functional, organizations have had to make their compensation programs more flexible. One means of doing so is *broadbanding*, which uses fewer pay grades having broader ranges than traditional compensation systems. Interest in broadbanding has been growing, as evidenced by a survey of 2,300 companies that found that 10% of the firms surveyed were considering broadbanding, even though only 7% actually had implemented the approach.

There are several reasons why it is beneficial to reduce the number of pay grades and broaden pay ranges. First and foremost, broadbanding is more consistent with the flattening of organizational levels and the growing use of jobs that are multi-dimensional in nature. For example, at General Electric, four bands that are 130% wide (that is, that cover a range of 130% from minimum to maximum) are used for all salaried employees below the executive level. Previously, there were fourteen grades that had 50% ranges from minimum to maximum. With fewer bands and broader ranges, employees can shift responsibilities as market conditions and organizational needs change. Traditional questions from employees about when a promotion to a new grade occurs and what pay adjustments will be made for temporarily performing some new job responsibilities are unnecessary.

With fewer bands and broader ranges, employees can shift responsibilities as market conditions and organizational needs change.

A closely related second reason for broadbanding is to reduce the administrative demands associated with traditional compensation programs. Many HR professionals spend a large number of hours managing the "bureaucratic" policies and rules that have developed with traditional compensation programs. But with broadbanding, operating managers have more responsibility and flexibility within broad parameters. Therefore, HR managers function more in advising operating managers than in interpreting policies and rules and approving or disapproving what managers do. With many traditional compensation plans, employees and managers spend significant time trying to justify changing the grades and ranges for jobs in order to reflect small changes in responsibilities. With broadbanding, many of the control mechanisms traditionally enforced by HR departments are removed, and authority for more compensation decisions is decentralized down to operating managers.

A third advantage of broadbanding is that employee career development can be enhanced when the artificial barriers of numerous pay grades are removed. By allowing employees to move into other job areas and broaden their knowledge, skills, and abilities without having to deal with a large number of contracts imposed by a compensation program, the organization encourages employees to move between departments, divisions, and locations. Compensation is adjusted based on the needs and budgeting constraints of the operating entities. At Eli Lilly, employees are encouraged to move across business units and apply for openings in areas of the company other than where they have been working. This cross-functional development is beneficial to Lilly because it creates more employees who have greater flexibility and broader sets of capabilities.

However, broadbanding is not appropriate for every organization. Philip Morris appointed a task force to evaluate broadbanding, and the decision was to stay with the traditional Hay compensation system established several years before. One factor in that decision was that broadbanding did not appear to be compatible with the organizational culture at Philip Morris. Many organizations still operate in a relatively structured manner, and the flexibility associated with broadbanding is not consistent with the traditional hierarchical way in which executives and managers have been operating.

Another disadvantage of broadbanding is that the decentralization of decision making authority to operating managers requires considerable training Without the traditional limitations or adequate training of decision makers, questions about favoritism, inconsistency across departments, and other concerns can arise.

Another problem with broadbanding is that many employees have become "conditioned" to the idea that a promotion is accompanied by a pay raise and movement to a new pay grade. As a result of removing this grade progression, the organization may be seen as having fewer upward promotion opportunities. Furthermore, a number of individuals do not want to move across the organization into other areas. One insurance firm found that when broadbanding was adopted, resistance to broadening job titles was greater than expected, especially among employees who used titles outside the firm on business cards.

Despite these and other problems, it is likely that broadbanding will continue to grow in usage. As more and more organizations face changes due to competition and other strategic factors, the flexibility of broadbanding may be needed.[1]

> "What is needed in many situations is a new approach to management that includes new pay-system assumptions and practices."
>
> —E. E. Lawler

Compensation is fundamentally about balancing human resource costs with the ability to attract and keep employees. By providing compensation, most employers attempt to provide fair remuneration for the knowledge, skills, and abilities of their employees. In addition, the compensation system should support organizational objectives and strategies, as the discussion of broadbanding indicates.

❖ Basic Compensation Considerations

Compensation serves the function of allocating people among employers based on the attractiveness of jobs and compensation packages. Employers must be reasonably competitive with several types of compensation in order to hire and keep the people they need.

❖ Types of Compensation

Compensation can be both tangible and intangible. Regarding tangible (financial) compensation, there are two general types: direct and indirect. With the direct type of compensation, the actual tangible benefits are provided by the employer. The most common forms of direct compensation are *pay* and *incentives*.

Pay is the basic compensation an employee receives, usually as a wage or salary. An **incentive** is compensation that rewards an employee for efforts beyond normal performance expectations. Examples of incentives include bonuses, commissions, and profit-sharing plans.

With indirect compensation, employees receive the tangible value of the rewards without receiving the actual cash. A **benefit** is an indirect reward, such as health insurance, vacation pay, or retirement pensions, given to an employee or group of employees as a part of organizational membership.

As mentioned, rewards also may be intangible. The praise given to an employee for completing a special project is one example. The psychological and social effects of compensation are discussed later.

Pay
The basic compensation an employee receives, usually as a wage or salary.

Incentive
Compensation that rewards an employee for efforts beyond normal performance expectations.

Benefit
An indirect reward given to an employee or group of employees as a part of organizational membership.

❖ Compensation Responsibilities

Compensation costs are significant expenditures in most organizations. At one large hotel, employee payroll and benefits expenditures comprise about 50% of all business costs. Although compensation costs are relatively easy to calculate, the value derived by employers and employees is much more difficult to identify. To administer these expenditures wisely, HR specialists and other managers must work together.

A typical division of compensation responsibilities is illustrated in Figure 13–1. HR specialists usually guide the overall development and administration of an organizational compensation system by conducting job evaluations and wage surveys. Also, because of the technical complexity involved, HR specialists typically are the ones who develop wage and salary structures and policies. Operating managers try to match employees'

❖ FIGURE 13–1 ❖
TYPICAL COMPENSATION RESPONSIBILITIES

HR UNIT	MANAGERS
❖ Develops and administers compensation system ❖ Conducts job evaluation and wage surveys ❖ Develops wage/salary structures and policies	❖ Attempt to match performance and rewards ❖ Recommend pay rates and pay increases based on guidelines from HR unit ❖ Monitor attendance and productivity for compensation purposes

efforts with rewards by using guidelines provided by the HR unit when recommending pay rates and pay increases. Much managerial activity goes into monitoring employee attendance and productivity. Because time and productivity are the bases for compensation, this monitoring is a vital part of any manager's job.

❖ Strategic Compensation

Because compensation is such a key activity, compensation philosophies and objectives must reflect the overall culture, philosophies, and strategic plans of the organization. The compensation practices that typically exist in a new organization may be different from those in a mature, bureaucratic organization. For example, if a firm wishes to create an innovative, entrepreneurial culture, it may offer stock equity programs so that employees can participate in the growth and success of the company but pay can be kept at modest levels. However, for a large, stable organization, highly structured pay and benefit programs may be more appropriate.

❖ Compensation and Organizational Culture

It is critical that organizations align their compensation practices with their organizational cultures, especially if efforts are made to change the cultures because of competitive pressures. For instance, a telecommunications firm faced major changes in the industry after government restrictions on pricing were removed and cable television firms were allowed to provide telephone service. The firm could not continue to offer the wages it had paid when government agencies allowed the pricing of services to cover full cost recovery and a set level of profits. When changing organizational culture, organizations must change their compensation systems if they are to avoid sending mixed signals to employees.[2] The opening discussion about broadbanding illustrates the importance of matching compensation practices to the organizational culture.

❖ Compensation Philosophies

Compensation first must be seen strategically. Because so many organizational funds are spent on compensation-related activities, it is critical for top management and HR executives to view the "strategic" fit of compensation with the objectives of the organization as they identify the compensation philosophy to guide compensation planning.[3]

There are two basic compensation philosophies, which should be seen as opposite ends of a continuum. At one end of the continuum is the *entitlement* philosophy; at the other end, the *performance-oriented* philosophy.

Entitlement Orientation The entitlement philosophy can be seen in many organizations that traditionally have given automatic increases to their employees every year. Most of those employees receive the same or nearly the same percentage increase each year as well. Employees and managers who subscribe to the entitlement philosophy believe that individuals who have worked another year are *entitled* to a raise in base pay and that all incentives and benefit programs should continue unchanged, regardless of changing industry or economic conditions. Commonly, in organizations following an entitlement philosophy, pay increases are referred to as *cost-of-living* raises, whether or not they are tied specifically to economic indicators. Following an entitlement philosophy ultimately means that as employees continue their employment lives, employer costs increase, regardless of employee performance or other organizational competitive pressures.

Performance Orientation Where a *performance-oriented* philosophy is followed, no one is guaranteed compensation just for adding another year to organizational service. Instead, pay and incentives are based on performance differences among employees. Employees who perform well get larger compensation increases, and those who do not perform satisfactorily receive little or no increase in compensation.[4] Thus, employees who perform satisfactorily should keep up or advance in relation to the labor market for their jobs, whereas poor or marginal performers should fall behind. Few organizations are totally performance-oriented in all facets of their compensation practices, but breaking the entitlement mode increasingly is occurring in the organizational restructurings common throughout many industries.

❖ Compensation Bases

Another strategic issue is how compensation philosophies and objectives are reflected in the design of compensation systems, particularly base pay programs. There are several bases that can be used, and different bases may be used in different parts of the organization.

Time vs. Productivity Employees of organizations can be paid for the amount of time spent on the job or on the amount of work produced. Many organizations use two pay categories, *hourly* and *salaried,* which are identified according to the way pay is distributed and the nature of the jobs. Hourly pay is the most common means of payment based on time; employees who are paid hourly are said to receive **wages**, which are payments directly calculated on the amount of time worked. In contrast, people who are paid a **salary** receive payment that is consistent from period to period despite the number of hours worked. Being salaried typically has carried higher status for employees than being paid wages. Some organizations have switched to an all-salaried approach with their manufacturing and clerical employees in order to create a greater sense of loyalty and organizational commitment. The complexities of a time-based system and the value of a computerized HR information system are shown in the HR Perspective "The Computerized Time Clock and HRIS."

***Wages**
Payments directly calculated on the amount of time worked.

***Salary**
Payment that is consistent from period to period despite the number of hours worked.

Another general basis for compensation is performance or productivity. A direct productivity-based system, called a **piece-rate system,** is one in which an employee is paid for each unit of production. For example, an employee who works in a telemarketing firm may be paid an amount for every sale made.

***Piece-Rate System**
A productivity-based compensation system in which an employee is paid for each unit of production.

Merit or *pay-for-performance* systems, discussed later in the chapter, also attempt to link employee performance to pay-increase decisions. Two other main issues must be decided by management when pay-for-performance systems are used.

- ❖ Should performance be measured and rewarded based on individual, group, or organizational performance?
- ❖ Should the length of time for measuring performance be short term (less than one year) or long term (more than one year)? The latter issue is particularly important for executive and managerial jobs.[5]

Task- vs. Knowledge- and Skill-Based Pay Most base compensation programs are designed to reward employees for the tasks, duties, and responsibilities performed. It is the jobs done that determine, to a large extent, which employees have higher base rates than others. Employees are paid more for doing jobs that

HR PERSPECTIVE

The Computerized Time Clock and HRIS

As more hourly employees have begun to work flexible schedules and/or take advantage of various incentive programs, manual timekeeping systems have been overwhelmed by the complexity of all the calculations. Computerization and technological advances have made the recording of employees' work time more automated and the calculation of employees' paychecks less prone to error. The experience at a Calgon Carbon plant in Cattlettsburg, Kentucky, illustrates the advantages of melding the traditional time clock with a human resource information system.

A "crisis" at the Calgon plant was triggered by the retirement of the employee who had handled payroll data entry. That person had become the "indispensable" expert on the complexities of paying Calgon's 300 employees, who worked a variety of rotating shifts. Under the old manual system, the payroll person took the time card data, which often included penciled-in changes by workers and supervisors, and entered it into a payroll program. Typically, the process took three days each week. But with the retirement of the payroll processor, Calgon's management decided that the timing was appropriate to convert to an automated system.

Ultimately, Calgon management decided it needed a system that could track all the variations of individual schedules. Also, a system was needed that could be changed as new provisions were implemented under Calgon's contract with the labor union representing many employees. To ensure its support, Calgon management involved the union in selecting an integrated payroll and timekeeping software system.

In the new system, employees have been trained to enter their work time on computer terminals. That information then is captured and immediately used to determine payroll data. As a result, the time required for entry of payroll data has decreased dramatically, and the amount of time for processing the data to issue payroll checks has been reduced to one day. A side benefit has been that all workers must use computers, and those anxious about computers now see the advantages of computerization. As a result, Calgon management believes it can begin distributing job-related information such as operating manuals electronically to computer terminals accessible by most workers throughout the plant.[6]

require more variety of tasks, more knowledge and skills, greater physical effort, or more demanding working conditions.

A growing number of organizations are paying employees, particularly hourly ones, for the skills or competencies they have rather than for the specific tasks being performed. Paying for skills rewards employees who are more versatile and have continued to develop their skills.[7] In these *knowledge-based pay* (KBP) or *skill-based pay* (SBP) systems, employees start at a base level of pay and receive increases as they learn to do other jobs or gain other skills and therefore become more valuable to the employer. For example, a printing firm has two-color, four-color, and six-color presses. The more colors, the more skill required of the press operators. Under a KBP or SBP system, press operators increase their pay as they learn how to operate the more complex presses, even though sometimes they may be running only two-color jobs.

A survey sponsored by the American Compensation Association (ACA) found that the success of KBP and SBP plans requires managerial commitment to a philosophy different from the one that has existed traditionally in organizations.[8] This approach places far more emphasis on training employees and supervisors. Also, work flow must be adapted to allow workers to move from job to job as needed.

According to the ACA survey, knowledge- and skill-based pay systems produce significant positive outcomes at both the organizational level and the employee level, as shown in Figure 13–2 on the next page.

❖ FIGURE 13–2 ❖
POSITIVE OUTCOMES OF KNOWLEDGE- OR SKILL-BASED PAY SYSTEMS

ORGANIZATION-RELATED OUTCOMES	EMPLOYEE-RELATED OUTCOMES
❖ Greater workforce flexibility ❖ Increased effectiveness of work teams ❖ Fewer bottlenecks in work flow ❖ Increased worker output per hour	❖ Enhanced employee understanding of organizational "big picture" ❖ Greater employee self-management capabilities ❖ Improved employee satisfaction ❖ Greater employee commitment

When an organization moves to an SBP or KBP system, considerable time must be spent identifying what the required knowledge or skills are for various jobs.[9] Then each *block* of skills and knowledge must be priced using market data. Progression of employees must be possible, and they must be paid appropriately for all of their knowledge and skills. Any limitations on the numbers of people who can acquire the top knowledge and skill levels should be identified clearly. Training in the appropriate knowledge and skills is critical. Important also to SBP and KBP systems is a system for *certification* of employees who have acquired certain knowledge and skills. Further, a process must exist for verifying that employees maintain their competency.[10]

Because these plans focus on having knowledgeable and skilled employees, those employees who continue to develop their capabilities and competencies to receive pay raises are the real winners. As more organizations recognize their employees as valuable human resources, it is likely that SBP and KBP systems will spread.

❖ COMPENSATION STRATEGIES AND OBJECTIVES

The changes in many industries and organizations have led to forecasts that traditional compensation practices followed in the past are currently evolving and will be significantly different in the future. Figure 13–3 compares compensation strategies of yesterday, today, and tomorrow. Notice that the shifts from yesterday to tomorrow parallel shifts from entitlement-oriented philosophies to more performance-oriented thrusts.

In virtually every organization, a compensation program should address three objectives:

- ❖ Legal compliance with all appropriate laws and regulations
- ❖ Cost effectiveness for the organization
- ❖ Internal, external, and individual equity for employees

A look at each of these objectives follows next.

❖ LEGAL COMPLIANCE

First, the compensation program must comply with all *legal* constraints and regulations in all compensation areas in which the organization operates. Numerous laws and regulations affect pay, incentives, and benefits. The design and implementation of compensation programs must be built with the various legal restrictions in mind. The most important legal concerns are addressed later in the chapter.

❖ COST EFFECTIVENESS

Second, compensation must be *cost-effective* and affordable for the organization, given the competitive pressures it faces. A firm that provides compensation that is too high may have difficulty competing with lower-paying, more efficient com-

YESTERDAY	TODAY	TOMORROW
❖ Fixed salary	❖ Variable pay as add-on to salary	❖ Low fixed salary, more variable pay
❖ Bonuses/perks for executives only	❖ Variable pay emerging throughout organization	❖ Variable pay common throughout the organization
❖ Fixed benefits, reward long tenure	❖ Flexible benefits	❖ Portable benefits
❖ Company based career, "moving up"	❖ Industry-based career, "moving around"	❖ Skill-based career, interim employment
❖ Hierarchical organizations	❖ Flatter, team-based organizations	❖ Networked "virtual" organizations
❖ "Cookie cutter" pay plans	❖ Total compensation (Look at benefits, too)	❖ Customized, integrated pay systems; pay, benefits, intangibles

❖ FIGURE 13–3 ❖
CHANGING COMPENSATION STRATEGIES

SOURCE: Reprinted from September 1996 *ACA News,* with permission from the American Compensation Association (ACA), 14040 N. Northsight Blvd., Scottsdale, Arizona 85260; telephone 602/951-9191; fax 602/483-8352. ©ACA.

petitors. As the earlier discussion on changing corporate strategies illustrates, more and more organizations are adapting variable pay programs tied to organizational and individual performance in order to have greater cost flexibility.

❖ EQUITY

People want to be treated fairly in all facets of compensation, including base pay, incentives, and benefits. This is the concept of **equity**, which is the perceived fairness of the relation between what a person does (inputs) and what the person receives (outcomes). *Inputs* are what a person brings to the organization and include educational level, age, experience, productivity, and other skills or efforts. The items received by a person, or the *outcomes,* are the rewards obtained

***Equity**
The perceived fairness of the relation between what a person does (inputs) and what the person receives (outcomes).

©1995 Creators Syndicate, Inc.

in exchange for inputs. Outcomes include pay, benefits, recognition, achievement, prestige, and any other rewards received. Note that an outcome can be either tangible (extrinsic rewards such as pay and economic benefits) or intangible (internal rewards such as recognition and achievement).

Equity within the Organization Internally, equity means that employees receive compensation in relation to the knowledge, skills, and abilities they use in their jobs and their responsibilities and accomplishments. To monitor internal equity, organizations use job evaluation systems to evaluate the relative difficulty of jobs across departments and organizational levels. Various job evaluation methods are discussed later in this chapter.

Equity with Other Organizations Externally, the organization must provide compensation that is seen as equitable in relation to the compensation provided employees performing similar jobs in other organizations. If an employer does not provide compensation that is viewed as fair by its employees, that organization may have higher turnover of employees, may have more difficulty recruiting qualified and scarce-skill employees, and may attract and retain individuals with less knowledge, skills, and abilities, resulting in lower overall organizational productivity. Organizations track external equity by using pay surveys, which are discussed later in the chapter.

Individual Equity Additionally, individuals judge equity in compensation by comparing the effort and performance they give with the effort and performance of others.[11] Assume you are a laboratory technician in a hospital. You exchange talents and efforts for the tangible and intangible rewards the hospital gives. Then you compare your inputs (what you did) and your outcomes (what you received) with those of others to determine the equity of your compensation, as Figure 13–4 shows. You will compare your inputs and outcomes with those of lab technicians both inside your hospital and at other hospitals. You also will compare your talents, skills, and efforts with those of other hospital employees. Your perception—correct or incorrect—significantly affects your valuation of your inputs and outcomes. A sense of inequity occurs when the comparison process results in an imbalance between inputs and outcomes.

Pay and other types of compensation offer a symbolic means of "keeping score" and a sense of achievement. If a cost accountant receives a raise, he may see his change in compensation as recognition of his efforts, and he may derive

❖ FIGURE 13–4 ❖
EQUITY EVALUATIONS

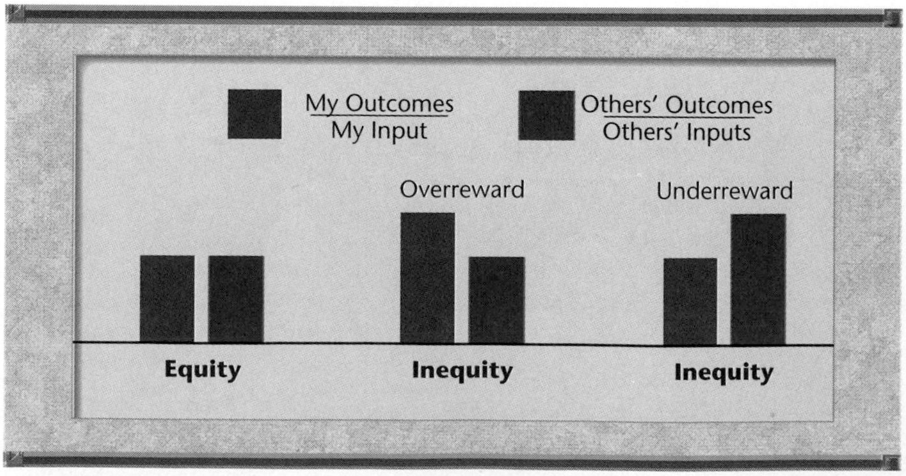

a sense of achievement from his work. This internal satisfaction may mean more to him than what he can buy with the additional money. Conversely, the absence of adequate compensation may cause him to become discouraged or dissatisfied.

Perceptions of status also are based on pay and the perceived *equity* of pay. For example, a division manager might compare her pay, and therefore her *status* in the organization, with that of other division managers. She may be satisfied with her pay, or she may become dissatisfied because other division managers have higher pay and higher status. Because compensation can symbolize status, it often remains important even after the basic material needs of an employee are satisfied. Consider the case of the professional baseball player whose status needs are unfulfilled by a multimillion-dollar paycheck when another player had a higher paycheck.

❖ Procedural and Distributive Justice in Compensation

A growing equity issue in organizational research is organizational justice. Two major sub-areas are *procedural justice* and *distributive justice*. **Procedural justice** is the perceived fairness of the process and procedures used to make decisions about employees, including their pay. The process of determining the base pay for jobs, the allocation of pay increases, and the measurement of performance must be perceived as fair.[12] Two critical issues are how appropriate and fair the process is that is used to assign jobs to pay grades and how the pay ranges for those jobs are established. If employees believe that managers play favorites, then the credibility of the entire pay system will be in question.[13]

❖Procedural Justice
The perceived fairness of the process and procedures used to make decisions about employees, including their pay.

Distributive justice, which refers to the perceived fairness of the amounts given for performance, must be considered also. For example, one study of U.S. government workers revealed that managers who had received performance bonuses had a much more positive view of a new pay system. Also, those who viewed the system more favorably were more likely to view their pay as market competitive.[14]

❖Distributive Justice
The perceived fairness of the amounts given for performance.

To address concerns about justice, some organizations establish *appeals procedures*. In public-sector organizations, appeals procedures usually are identified formally, whereas in private-sector firms they are usually more informal. Typically, employees can contact the HR department after they have discussed their concerns with their immediate supervisors and managers.

❖ Secret vs. Open Pay Systems

Another equity issue concerns the degree of openness or secrecy that organizations allow regarding their pay systems. Pay information kept secret in "closed" systems includes how much others make, what raises others have received, and even what pay grades and ranges exist in the organization.

Policies that prohibit discussion of individual pay are likely to be violated. Coworkers do share pay information, and explaining the pay system may prevent the spreading of misinformation through the grapevine. Because comparison is such a critical part of how employees view compensation, some theorists advocate the need for *open pay systems,* in which employees are informed about the pay of coworkers. By having pay openness, organizations that truly base pay on performance can emphasize the importance of performance to higher pay. This approach is particularly useful when objective measures of individual performance exist, such as in some sales jobs.

A growing number of organizations are opening up their pay systems to some degree by informing employees of compensation policies, providing a general description of the basis for the compensation system, and indicating where an individual's pay is within a pay grade. Such information allows employees to make more accurate equity comparisons. It is crucial in an open pay system that managers be able to explain satisfactorily any pay differences that exist.

❖ Legal Constraints on Pay Systems

Compensation systems must comply with a myriad of government constraints. Minimum wage standards and hours of work are two important areas that are addressed by the laws. The following discussion examines the laws and regulations affecting base compensation, while laws and regulations affecting incentives and benefits are examined in later chapters.

❖ Fair Labor Standards Act (FLSA)

The major law affecting compensation is the Fair Labor Standards Act (FLSA). The act has three major objectives:(1) to establish a minimum wage floor, (2) to encourage limits on the number of weekly hours employees work through overtime provisions, and (3) to discourage oppressive use of child labor. The first two objectives are the most relevant in this chapter. Passed in 1938, the FLSA has been amended several times to raise minimum wage rates and expand employers covered.

Employers Covered Unless otherwise noted in the discussion that follows, both private- and public-sector employers are affected by the act. Generally, private-sector employers engaged in interstate commerce and retail service firms with two or more employees and gross sales of at least $500,000 per year are covered by the act. Very small, family-owned and -operated entities and family farms generally are excluded from coverage. Most federal, state, and local government employers are also subject to the provisions of the act, except for military personnel, volunteer workers, and a few other limited groups. Covered employers must keep accurate time records on all employees subject to the act, and the government can request access to those records.[15]

Enforcement Compliance with the provisions of the FLSA is enforced by the Wage and Hour Division of the U.S. Department of Labor. To meet its requirements, employers must keep accurate time records and maintain these records for three years. Inspectors from the Wage and Hour Division investigate complaints filed by individuals who believe they have not received the overtime payments due them. Also, certain industries that historically have had a large number of wage and hour violations can be targeted, and firms in those industries can be investigated. Penalties for wage and hour violations often include awards of back pay for affected current and former employees for up to two years.

Exempt and Nonexempt Status Under the FLSA, employees are classified as exempt or nonexempt. **Exempt employees** are those who hold positions classified as *executive, administrative, professional,* or *outside sales,* to whom employers are not required to pay overtime. **Nonexempt employees** are those who must be paid overtime under the Fair Labor Standards Act.

❖Exempt Employees
Employees classified as executive, administrative, professional, or outside sales, to whom employers are not required to pay overtime under the Fair Labor Standards Act.

❖Nonexempt Employees
Employees who must be paid overtime under the Fair Labor Standards Act.

Three major factors are considered in determining whether an individual holds an exempt position:

- Discretionary authority for independent action
- Percentage of time spent performing routine, manual, or clerical work
- Earnings level

Under provisions of the FLSA, jobs can be categorized in three groupings:

- Hourly
- Salaried-nonexempt
- Salaried-exempt

Hourly jobs require employers to pay overtime and comply with the FLSA. Each salaried position must be identified as *salaried-exempt* or *salaried-nonexempt.* Employees in positions classified as salaried-nonexempt are covered by the overtime provisions of the FLSA and therefore must be paid overtime. Salaried-nonexempt positions sometimes include secretarial, clerical, and salaried blue-collar positions. Figure 13–5 shows the impact of these factors on each type of exemption.

Minimum Wage The FLSA sets a minimum wage to be paid to the broad spectrum of covered employees. The actual minimum wage can be changed only by congressional action. A lower minimum-wage level is set for "tipped" employees who work in such firms as restaurants, but their payment must at least equal the

Figure 13–5
Wage/Hour Status under Fair Labor Standards Act

EXEMPTION CATEGORY	A DISCRETIONARY AUTHORITY	B PERCENT OF TIME	C EARNINGS LEVELS
Executive	1. Primary duty is managing 2. Regularly directs work of at least two others 3. Authority to hire/fire or recommend these	1. Must spend 20% or less time doing clerical, manual, routine work (less than 40% in retail or service establishments)	1. Paid salary at $155/wk or $250/wk if meets A1–A2
Administrative	1. Responsible for nonmanual or office work related to management policies 2. Regularly exercises discretion and independent judgment and makes important decisions 3. Regularly assists executives and works under general supervision	1. Must spend 20% or less time doing clerical, manual, routine work (less than 40% in retail or service establishments)	1. Paid salary at $155/wk or $250/wk if meets A1–A2
Professional	1. Performs work requiring knowledge of an advanced field *or* creative and original artistic work *or* works as teacher in educational system 2. Must do work that is predominantly intellectual and varied	1. Must spend 20% or less time doing nonprofessional work	1. Paid salary at least $170/wk or $250/wk if meets A1
Outside Sales	1. Customarily works away from employer site *and* 2. Sells tangible or intangible items *or* 3. Obtains orders or contracts for services	1. Must spend 20% or less time doing work other than outside selling	1. No salary test

NOTE: For more details, see *Executive, Administrative, Professional, and Outside Sales Exemptions under the Fair Labor Standards Act,* WH Publication no. 1363 (Washington, DC: U.S. Department of Labor, Employment Standards Administration, Wage and Hour Division).

minimum wage when *average* tips are included. Although recent efforts resulted in raising the minimum wage, concerns continue to exist that increasing the minimum wage will reduce the number of jobs for lower-skilled individuals.[16]

OVERTIME PROVISIONS The FLSA establishes overtime pay requirements. Its provisions set overtime pay at one and one-half times the regular pay rate for all hours in excess of 40 per week, except for employees who are not covered by the law. Overtime provisions do not apply to farm workers, who also have a lower minimum wage schedule.

The work week is defined as a consecutive period of 168 hours (24 hours × 7 days) and does not have to be a calendar week. Hospitals are allowed to use a 14-day period instead of a 7-day week as long as overtime is paid for hours worked beyond 8 in a day or 80 in a 14-day period. No daily number of hours requiring overtime is set, except for special provisions relating to hospitals and other specially designated organizations. Thus, if a manufacturing firm has a 4-day/10-hour schedule, no overtime pay is required by the act.

❖Compensatory Time Off
Time off given in lieu of payment for extra time worked.

COMPENSATORY TIME OFF Often called *comp-time,* **compensatory time off** is given in lieu of payment for extra time worked. However, unless it is given at the rate of one and one-half times the hours worked over a 40-hour week, comp-time is illegal in the private sector. Also, comp-time cannot be carried over from one pay period to another.

The only major exception to those provisions are for public-sector employees, such as fire and police employees, and a limited number of other workers. Because they often are on 24-hour duty, these individuals may receive compensatory time off. Police and fire officers can accumulate up to 480 hours; all other covered public-sector employees can accumulate up to 240 hours. When those hours are used, the employees must be paid their normal rates of pay, and the comp-time hours used *do not* count as hours worked in the paid week.

CHILD-LABOR PROVISIONS The child-labor provisions of the FLSA set the minimum age for employment with unlimited hours at 16 years. For hazardous occupations (see Chapter 16), the minimum is 18 years of age. Those aged 14 to 15 years old may work outside school hours with the following limitations:

1. No more than 3 hours on a school day, 18 hours in a school week, 8 hours on a nonschool day, or 40 hours in a nonschool week.
2. Work may not begin before 7 A.M. nor end after 7 P.M., except between June 1 and Labor Day, when 9 P.M. is the ending time.

Many employers require age certificates for employees because the FLSA places the responsibility on the employer to determine an individual's age.[17] The certificates may be issued by a representative of a state labor department, a state education department, or a local school district.

❖ INDEPENDENT CONTRACTOR REGULATIONS

The growing use of contingent workers by many organizations has called attention to another group of legal regulations—those that identify the criteria that independent contractors must meet. Classifying someone as an independent contractor rather than an employee offers two primary advantages. First, the employer does not have to pay Social Security, unemployment, or benefits. These additional payroll levies could add 10% or more to the costs of hiring the individual as an employee. Second, if the person is classified as an employee and is doing a job considered nonexempt under the federal Fair Labor Standards Act, then the employer may be responsible for overtime pay at the rate of time-and-a-half for any week in which the person works more than 40 hours.

The criteria for deciding independent contractor status have been identified by the Internal Revenue Service (IRS), and most other federal and state entities rely on those criteria. The IRS has identified 20 factors that must be considered in making such a determination. Of those 20, the following are the primary factors that indicate independent contractor status:

- *Investment.* Has the individual invested in and does he or she own the facilities and equipment used in the performance of the work for the employer?
- *Profit or loss.* Can the individual incur a profit or a loss, so that some economic risk is involved, other than the risk of not getting paid by the employer?
- *Availability of services.* Does the individual offer the same or similar services to the general public and other firms on a regular basis?
- *Multiple clients.* Does the individual perform work, particularly the same type of work, for more than one employer at a time?

The remaining criteria relate to matters such as control over hours, place, and time of work and reporting relationships. The HR Perspective gives examples of independent contractor status.

HR PERSPECTIVE

EMPLOYEE OR CONTRACTOR?

One of the major HR planning problems facing many small businesses involves whether a person who is hired to perform certain services is an *employee* (for whom the firm must pay Social Security taxes) or an *independent contractor* (for whom no taxes need be paid).

PISA Brothers Travel Service, a New York travel agency, has agreements with independent contractors working as travel agents. The contractors pay the agency a share of their sales and pay rent. In exchange, they get space, computers, and other services. Unlike the company's 20 full-time employees, they pay their own income and Social Security taxes.

The IRS audited PISA Brothers and assessed the company $274,000 in income and Social Security taxes—an amount it claimed the company should have paid over three years for its contractors. The President of PISA noted that the assessment exceeded the company's annual net profit.

The test that the IRS uses to distinguish an employee from an independent contractor is complicated and subjective. Under the current system, a contractor may be considered an employee if only one criterion is unmet. A large group of small-business people recently voted this the most vexing problem that small business has with government. Certainly it makes planning for personnel needs more difficult.[18]

Here is the current IRS test:

AN EMPLOYEE

- Must comply with instructions about when, where, and how to work
- Renders services personally
- Has a continuing relationship with an employer
- Usually works on the premises of the employer
- Normally is furnished significant tools, materials, and other equipment by the employer
- Can be fired by an employer
- Can quit at any time without incurring liability

AN INDEPENDENT CONTRACTOR

- Can hire, supervise, and pay assistants
- Generally can set his or her own hours
- Usually is paid by the job or on straight commission
- Has a significant investment in facilities
- Can make a profit or suffer a loss
- Generally is free to provide services to two or more unrelated persons or firms at the same time
- Makes his or her services available to the public

SOURCE: Internal Revenue Service.

❖ Equal Pay Act of 1963

The Equal Pay Act was passed as a major amendment to the FLSA in 1963. The original act and subsequent amendments focus on wage discrimination on the basis of sex. The act applies to both men and women and prohibits paying different wage scales to men and women performing substantially the same jobs. Except for differences justifiable on the basis of merit (better performance), seniority (longer service), quantity or quality of work, or any factor other than sex, similar pay must be given for jobs requiring equal skills, equal effort, or equal responsibility or jobs done under similar working conditions.

Most of the equal-pay cases decided in court have involved situations in which women were paid less than men for doing similar work, though under different job titles. For example, equal-pay violations have been found in health-care institutions in which male "physician assistants" were paid significantly more than females with equal experience and qualifications who were called "nurse practitioners" but performed the same job duties. Note that pay equity, as discussed in Chapter 6 and later in this chapter, is an issue different from the issue of equal pay for equal worth, in that pay equity relates to comparable skills in different jobs.

❖ Walsh-Healey and Service Contracts Acts

The Walsh-Healey Public Contracts Act and Service Contracts Act require companies with *federal supply or service contracts* exceeding $10,000 to pay a prevailing wage. Both acts apply only to those who are working directly on the contract or who substantially affect its performance. The *prevailing wage* is determined by a formula that considers the rate paid for a job by a majority of the employers in the appropriate geographic area.

❖ Davis-Bacon Act of 1931

Still in force with many of the original dollar levels intact, the Davis-Bacon Act of 1931 affects compensation paid by firms engaged in federal construction projects valued in excess of $2,000. It deals only with federal construction projects and requires that the "prevailing wage" rate be paid on all federal construction projects. A growing number of critics believe that the Davis-Bacon Act should be repealed because it inflates the costs of federal construction projects. But construction unions have defended the law as still being necessary to prevent nonunion contractors from lowering wages paid to construction workers.[19] States have had their own versions of the Davis-Bacon provisions, but many of them are being dropped.

❖ State Laws

Modified versions of federal compensation laws have been enacted by many state and municipal government bodies. These laws tend to cover workers included in intrastate commerce not covered by federal law. If a state has a higher minimum wage than that set under the Fair Labor Standards Act, the higher figure becomes the required minimum wage.

Many states once had laws that limited the number of hours women could work. However, these laws generally have been held to be discriminatory in a variety of court cases. Consequently, most states have dropped such laws.

❖ Garnishment
A court action in which a portion of an employee's wages is set aside to pay a debt owed a creditor.

❖ Garnishment Laws

Garnishment of an employee's wage occurs when a creditor obtains a court order that directs an employer to submit a part of the employee's pay to the creditor for debts owed by the employee. Regulations passed as a part of the Consumer Credit Protection Act established limitations on the amount of wages that can be garnished and restricted the right of employers to discharge employees whose pay is subject to a single garnishment order. All 50 states have laws that apply to wage garnishments.

❖ Wage and Salary Administration

The development, implementation, and ongoing maintenance of a base pay system usually is described as **wage and salary administration**. The purpose of wage and salary administration is to provide pay that is both competitive and equitable. Underlying the administered activities are pay policies that set the overall direction of pay within the organization.

***Wage and Salary Administration**
The activity involved in the development, implementation, and maintenance of a base pay system.

❖ Pay Policies

Organizations must develop policies as general guidelines to govern pay systems. Uniform policies are needed for coordination, consistency, and fairness in compensating employees. One specific organizational policy decision defines the relationship between pay expenditures and such factors as productivity, sales, or number of customers. In the retail industry, it is common to have a policy of maintaining payroll expenditures at about 10% of gross sales volume. Such policies reflect a major consideration in management decision making:how much an organization can afford to pay employees.

Market Competitiveness A major policy decision must be made about the comparative level of pay the organization wants to maintain. Specifically, an employer must identify how competitive it wishes to be in the market for employees. Organizations usually want to "pay market"—that is, to *match* the "going rates" paid to employees by competitive organizations in order to ensure external equity.

Some organizations choose to *lead* the market by paying above market rates. This policy aids in attracting and retaining employees. One transportation firm that pays about 10% to 15% above local market medians for clerical employees consistently has a waiting list for qualified word-processing and other office workers. By paying above market, the firm feels that it deters efforts of its office workers to unionize.

Firms that have monopolies in their markets or that operate in regulated "cost-plus" markets also may have higher-than-market wages. For instance, the electric utility industry generally pays rates higher than local averages to clerical employees. These higher wage rates are included in the cost structure for setting consumer electric rates.

In contrast, some employers may deliberately choose to *lag* the market by paying below market. If there is an excess of qualified workers in an area, an adequate number of people are willing to work for lower pay. Also, organizations in declining industries and some small businesses may not be able to afford to pay going rates because of financial pressures. However, paying rates below market can result in higher turnover or in having to hire less qualified employees.

Market Pricing Some employers do not establish a formal wage and salary system. Smaller employers particularly may assume that the pay set by other employers is an accurate reflection of a job's worth, so they set their pay rates at **market price**, the prevailing wage paid for a job in the immediate job market.

***Market Price**
The prevailing wage rate paid for a job in the immediate job market.

One difficulty with this approach is the assumption that jobs are the same from organization to organization, which is not necessarily the case. Also, obtaining market information often means calling one or two other firms, which may not give an accurate picture of the market. Further, direct market pricing does not adequately consider the impact of economic conditions, employer size, and other variables. Consequently, more complex methods have been developed.

❖ Unions and Compensation

A major variable affecting an employer's pay policies is whether any employees are represented by a labor union. In nonunion organizations, employers have significantly more flexibility in determining pay levels and policies. Unionized employees usually have their pay set according to the terms of a collective bargaining contract between their employer and the union that represents them. Because pay is a visible issue, it is natural for unions to emphasize pay levels.

According to U.S. Bureau of Labor Statistics data, employers having unionized employees generally have higher wage levels than nonunion employers. The strength and extent of unionization in an industry and in an organization affect wage levels. The levels generally are higher in firms in heavily unionized industries with highly unionized workforces. As union strength in heavily unionized industries have declined, pay increases for nonunion employees have diminished somewhat in recent years.

❖ Development of a Base Pay System

Once pay policies have been determined, the actual development of a base pay system begins. Because most organizations use task-based systems that focus on individuals in specific jobs, that is the focus of this discussion. If skill-based or team pay systems are used, then many of the activities discussed here must be modified.

As Figure 13–6 shows, the development of a wage and salary system assumes that accurate job descriptions and job specifications are available. The job descriptions then are used in two activities: *job evaluation* and *pay surveys*. These activities are designed to ensure that the pay system is both internally equitable and externally competitive. The data compiled in these two activities are used to design *pay structures*, including *pay grades* and minimum-to-maximum *pay ranges*. After the pay structures have been developed, individual jobs must be placed in the appropriate pay grades and employees' pay adjusted based on length of service and performance. Finally, the pay system must be monitored and updated.

❖ Job Evaluation

❖Job Evaluation
The systematic determination of the relative worth of jobs within an organization.

Job evaluation provides a systematic basis for determining the relative worth of jobs within an organization. It flows from the job analysis process and is based on job descriptions and job specifications. In a job evaluation, every job in an organization is examined and ultimately priced according to the following features:

- ❖ The relative importance of the job
- ❖ The skills needed to perform the job compared with other jobs
- ❖ The difficulty of the job compared with other jobs

It is important that employees perceive their pay as appropriate in relation to pay for jobs performed by others. Because jobs may vary widely in an organization,

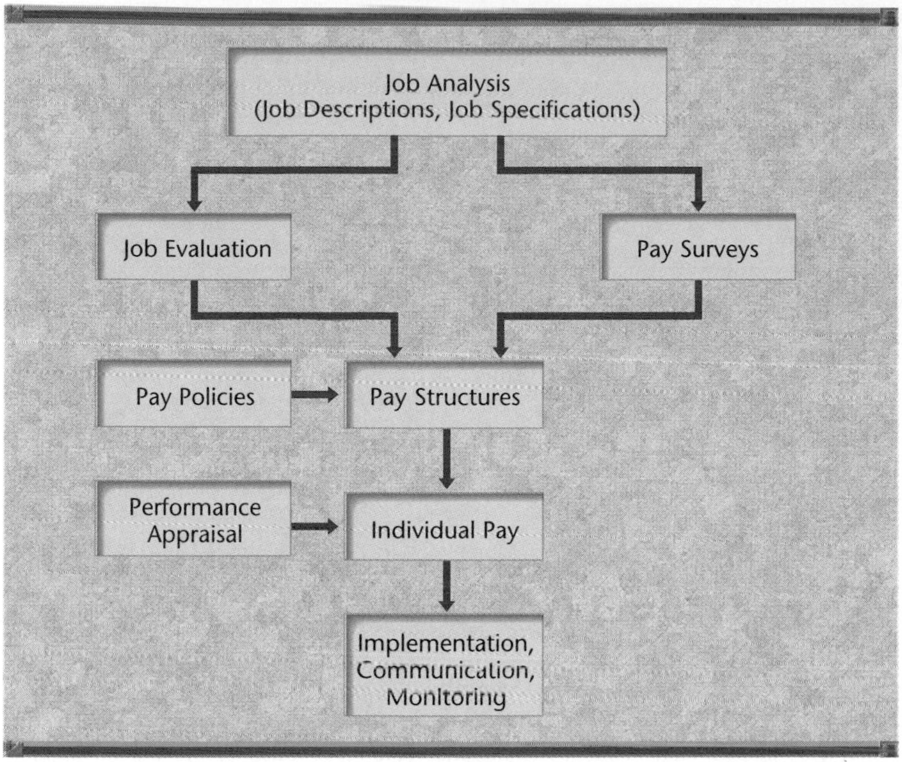

❖ FIGURE 13–6 ❖
COMPENSATION ADMINISTRATION PROCESS

it is particularly important to identify **benchmark jobs**— jobs that are found in many other organizations and are performed by several individuals who have similar duties that are relatively stable and that require similar KSAs. For example, benchmark jobs commonly used in clerical/office situations are accounts payable processor, word-processing operator, and PBX receptionist. Benchmark jobs are used with all of the job evaluation methods discussed here because they provide "anchors" against which unique jobs can be evaluated.

Benchmark Job
Job found in many organizations and performed by several individuals who have similar duties that are relatively stable and that require similar KSAs.

Systematic evaluation of jobs is a way to reduce favoritism. However, subjective judgments cannot be avoided entirely, so managers and HR specialists should not overemphasize the objectivity of a job evaluation system.[20] Using a job evaluation committee in which several evaluators rate jobs can help improve the reliability of the evaluation. However, unions generally distrust job evaluations and view them as being manipulated for the benefit of management. For this reason, among others, firms often bring in outside consultants to perform the job evaluation.

Several methods are used to determine internal job worth through job evaluation. All methods have the same general objective, but they differ in complexity and means of measurement. Regardless of the method used, the intent is to develop a usable, measurable, and realistic system to determine compensation in an organization.

RANKING METHOD The ranking method is one of the simplest methods of job evaluation. It places jobs in order, ranging from highest to lowest in value to the organization. The entire job is considered rather than the individual components. Several different methods of ranking are available, but all present problems.

Ranking methods are extremely subjective, and managers may have difficulty explaining why one job is ranked higher than another to employees whose pay is affected by these rankings. When there are a large number of jobs, the ranking method also can be awkward and unwieldy. Therefore, the ranking method is more appropriate in a small organization having relatively few jobs.

CLASSIFICATION METHOD The classification method of job evaluation was developed under the old U.S. Civil Service system and was widely copied by state and local government entities. A number of classes, or *GS grades,* are defined. The various jobs in the organization are put into grades according to common factors such as degree of responsibility, abilities or skills, knowledge, duties, volume of work, and experience needed. The grades are then ranked into an overall system.

The major difficulty with the classification method is that subjective judgments are needed to develop the grade descriptions and to place jobs accurately in them. With a wide variety of jobs and generally written grade descriptions, some jobs may appear to fall into two or three different grades.

Another problem with the classification method is that it relies heavily on job titles and duties and assumes that they are similar from one organization to another. For these reasons, many federal, state, and local government entities have shifted to point systems.

POINT METHOD The point method, the most widely used job evaluation method, is more sophisticated than the ranking and classification methods. It breaks down jobs into various compensable factors and places weights, or *points,* on them. A **compensable factor** is one used to identify a job value that is commonly present throughout a group of jobs. The factors are determined from the job analysis. For example, for jobs in warehouse and manufacturing settings, *physical demands, hazards encountered,* and *working environment* may be identified as factors and weighted heavily. However, in most office and clerical jobs, those factors are of little importance. Consequently, the compensable factors used and the weights assigned must reflect the nature of the job under study.

Compensable Factor
Factor used to identify a job value that is commonly present throughout a group of jobs.

Figure 13–7 helps to illustrate how the system is used. The individual using the point chart in the figure looks at a job description and identifies the degree to which each element is necessary to perform the job satisfactorily. For example, the points assigned for a payroll clerk for education might be 42 points, third degree. To reduce subjectivity, such determinations often are made by a group of people familiar with the jobs. Once points have been identified for all factors, the total points for the payroll clerk job are computed. After point totals have been determined for all jobs, the jobs are grouped together into pay grades.

A special type of point method used by a consulting firm, Hay and Associates, has received widespread application, although it is most often used with exempt employees. The *Hay system* uses three factors and numerically measures the degree to which each of these factors is required in each job. The three factors and their sub-factors are as follows:[21]

Know-How	Problem Solving	Accountability
❖ Functional expertise	❖ Environment	❖ Freedom to act
❖ Managerial skills	❖ Challenge	❖ Impact of end results
❖ Human relations		❖ Magnitude

The point method has grown in popularity for several reasons. It is a relatively simple system to use. It considers the components of a job rather than the total job and is much more comprehensive than either the ranking or classification method. Once points have been determined and a job evaluation point manual has been developed, the method can be used easily by people who are not spe-

❖ FIGURE 13–7 ❖
JOB EVALUATION POINT CHART

CLERICAL GROUP

FACTOR	1ST DEGREE POINTS	2ND DEGREE POINTS	3RD DEGREE POINTS	4TH DEGREE POINTS
1. Education[a]	14	28	42	56
2. Experience	22	44	66	88
3. Initiative and ingenuity	14	28	42	56
4. Contacts with others	14	28	42	56
Responsibility				
5. Supervision received	10	20	35	50
6. Latitude and depth	20	40	70	100
7. Work of others	5	10	15	20
6. Trust imposed	10	20	35	50
9. Performance	7	14	21	28
Other				
10. Work environment	10	25	45	
11. Mental or visual demand	10	20	35	
12. Physical effort	28			

[a]The specific degrees and points for education are as follows:

Education is the basic prerequisite knowledge essential to satisfactorily perform the job. This knowledge may have been acquired through formal schooling such as grammar school, high school, college, night school, correspondence courses, company education programs or through equivalent experience in allied fields. Analyze the minimum requirements of the job and not the formal education of individuals performing it.

1st Degree—Requires knowledge usually equivalent to a two-year high school education. Requires ability to read, write, and follow simple written or oral instructions and to use simple arithmetic processes involving counting, adding, subtracting, dividing, and multiplying whole numbers. May require basic typing ability.

2nd Degree—Requires knowledge equivalent to a four-year high school education. Requires ability to perform advanced arithmetic processes involving adding, subtracting, dividing, and multiplying or decimals and fractions and ability to maintain or prepare routine correspondence, records, and reports. May require knowledge of advanced typing and/or basic knowledge of shorthand, bookkeeping, drafting, etc.

3rd Degree—Requires knowledge equivalent to a four-year high school education plus some specialized knowledge/training in a particular field such as advanced stenographic, secretarial, or business fields; elementary accounting; or general blueprint reading or engineering practices.

4th Degree—Requires knowledge equivalent to two years of college education. Requires ability to understand and perform work involving general engineering or accounting theory. Requires ability to originate and compile statistics and interpretive reports and prepare correspondence of a difficult or technical nature.

cialists. The system can be understood by managers and employees, which gives it a definite advantage.

Another reason for the widespread use of the point method is that it evaluates the components of a job and determines total points before the current pay structure is considered. In this way, an employer can assess relative worth instead of relying on past patterns of worth.

One major drawback to the point method is the time needed to develop a system. For this reason, manuals and systems developed by management consultants or other organizations often are used by employers. Also, point systems have been criticized for reinforcing traditional organizational structures and job rigidity. Although not perfect, the point method of job evaluation generally is better than the classification and ranking methods because it quantifies job elements.

FACTOR COMPARISON The factor-comparison method is a quantitative and complex combination of the ranking and point methods. It involves first determining the benchmark jobs in an organization, selecting compensable factors, and ranking all benchmark jobs factor by factor. Next, the jobs are compared with market rates for benchmark jobs, and monetary values are assigned to each factor. The final step is to evaluate all other jobs in the organization by comparing them with the benchmark jobs.

One of the major advantages of the factor-comparison method is that it is tied specifically to one organization. Each organization must develop its own key jobs and its own factors. For this reason, buying a packaged system may not be appropriate. Further, factor comparison not only tells which jobs are worth more but also indicates how much more, so factor values can be more easily converted to monetary wages.

The major disadvantages of the factor-comparison method are its difficulty and complexity. It is not an easy system to explain to employees, and it is time consuming to establish and develop. Also, a factor-comparison system may not be appropriate for an organization with many similar types of jobs. Managers attempting to use the method should consult a specialist or one of the more detailed compensation books or manuals that discuss the method.

COMPUTERIZED JOB EVALUATION The advent of computerized job analysis programs has led to computerized job evaluation programs. Generally, the computerized processes still must identify the prevalence of compensable factors in jobs. Some computerized programs integrate market pricing into the job evaluation ratings as well. Some experts question whether computer-assisted job evaluation is a separate method; it may simply be an application of computer techniques and analyses to the point or factor-comparison method.

❖ LEGAL ISSUES AND JOB EVALUATION

Employees usually view evaluating jobs to determine rates of pay as a separate issue from selecting individuals for those jobs or taking disciplinary action against individuals. But because job evaluation affects the employment relationship, specifically the pay of individuals, it involves legal issues that must be addressed.

JOB EVALUATION AND THE AMERICANS WITH DISABILITIES ACT (ADA) As emphasized in Chapter 7, the Americans with Disabilities Act (ADA) requires employers to identify the essential functions of a job. However, all facets of jobs are examined when a job evaluation is done. The central issue is whether this total examination is appropriate or whether the job evaluation should consider only the essential functions. For instance, assume a production job requires a punch press operator to drill holes in parts and place them in a bin of finished products. Every three hours, the operator must push that bin, which may weigh two hundred pounds or more, to the packaging area. The movement of the bin probably is not an essential function. But if job evaluation considers the physical demands associated with pushing the bin, then the points assigned may be different from the points that would be assigned if only the essential functions were considered. Thus, based on the ADA, it generally would seem more appropriate that those determining the worth of jobs through job evaluation should focus on essential functions and limit consideration of marginal functions.[22]

JOB EVALUATION AND PAY EQUITY Many employers base their pay rates heavily on external equity comparisons in the labor market, which is their major defense for adopting the pay systems they use. Undoubtedly, with additional court decisions, government actions, and research, job evaluation activities will face more pressures to address pay equity.

As noted previously in Chapter 6, **pay equity** is the concept that the pay for all jobs requiring comparable knowledge, skills, and abilities should be similar even if actual duties and market rates differ significantly. Growing concerns about comparable worth have been translated into laws designed to address *pay equity*. These laws focus on public-sector jobs, especially those in state governments. States with comparable-worth policies include Hawaii, Iowa, Maine, Michigan, Minnesota, Montana, Ohio, Oregon, Washington, and Wisconsin.

***Pay Equity**
The concept that the pay for jobs requiring comparable knowledge, skills, and abilities should be similar even if actual duties and market rates differ significantly.

Pay equity advocates have attacked typical job evaluations as gender biased. Many jobs traditionally held by women are clerical and service jobs, whereas many jobs dominated by men are craft and manual jobs. Critics have charged that traditional job evaluation programs place less weight on knowledge, skills, and working conditions for many female-dominated jobs than on the same factors for male-dominated jobs. Also, jobs typically are compared only with others in the same job "family."

In spite of these criticisms, studies of job evaluations of female- and male-dominated jobs usually show that the jobs are compensated appropriately when compared with market rates.[23] Except where state (in the United States) or provincial (in Canada) laws have required pay equity, simply showing that there are pay differences for jobs that are different has not been sufficient to prove discrimination in court.[24]

❖ Pay Surveys

Another part of building a pay system is surveying the pay that other organizations provide for similar jobs. A **pay survey** is a collection of data on compensation rates for workers performing similar jobs in other organizations. An employer may use surveys conducted by other organizations or may decide to conduct its own survey.

***Pay Survey**
A collection of data on existing compensation rates for workers performing similar jobs in other organizations.

Using Prepared Pay Surveys Many different surveys are available from a variety of sources. National surveys on many jobs and industries are available through the U.S. Department of Labor, Bureau of Labor Statistics, and through national trade associations. In many communities, employers participate in a wage survey sponsored by the Chamber of Commerce to provide information to new employers interested in locating in the community.

When using surveys from other sources, it is important to use them properly.[25] Some questions that should be addressed before using a survey are:

1. Is the survey a realistic sample of those employers with whom the organization competes for employees?
2. Is the survey balanced so that organizations of varying sizes, industries, and locales are included?
3. How current are the data (determined by when the survey was conducted)?
4. How established is the survey, and how qualified are those who conducted it?
5. Does it contain job summaries so that appropriate matchups to organizational job descriptions can be made?

LOGGING ON

For pay survey and other data from the U.S. Bureau of Labor Statistics, see

http://www.stats.bls.gov

Developing a Pay Survey If needed pay information is not already available, the employer can undertake its own pay survey. Employers with comparable positions should be selected. Also, employers considered to be "representative" should be surveyed. Even if the employer conducting the survey is not unionized, the pay survey probably should examine unionized as well as nonunionized organizations. Developing pay competitive with union wages may deter employees from joining a union.

The positions to be surveyed also must be decided. Not all jobs in all organizations can be surveyed, and not all jobs with the same titles in all organizations are the same. For example, an accounting clerk in a city government office and an accounting clerk in a credit billing firm might perform different jobs. Therefore, managers should select jobs that can be easily compared, have common job elements, and represent a broad range of jobs. Key or benchmark jobs are especially important ones to include. Also, it is advisable to provide brief job descriptions for jobs surveyed in order to ensure more accurate matches. For executive-level jobs, data on total compensation (base pay and bonuses) often are gathered as well.

In the next phase of the pay survey, managers decide what compensation information is needed for various jobs. Information such as starting pay, base pay, overtime rate, vacation and holiday pay and policies, and bonuses all can be included in a survey. However, requesting too much information may discourage survey returns.

The results of the pay survey usually are made available to those participating in the survey in order to gain their cooperation. Most surveys specify confidentiality, and data are summarized to assure anonymity. Different job levels often are included, and the pay rates are presented both in overall terms and on a city-by-city basis to reflect regional differences in pay.

Legal Issues and Pay Surveys One reason for employers to use outside consultants to conduct pay surveys is to avoid charges that the employers are attempting to "price-fix" wages. The federal government has filed suit in the past alleging that by sharing wage data, employers may be attempting to hold wages down artificially in violation of the Sherman Anti-Trust Act.

A key case involved the Utah Society for Healthcare Human Resource Administration and nine hospitals in the Salt Lake City area. The consent decree that resulted prohibits all health-care facilities in Utah from designing, developing, or conducting a wage survey. The hospitals can participate in surveys conducted by independent third-party firms only if some specific privacy safeguards are met. Specifically, only aggregate data that are summarized may be provided, and no data from an individual firm may be identified.[26] As a result, it is likely that fewer firms will conduct their own surveys, and more will contract with outside consultants instead.

❖ Pay Structure

Once survey data have been gathered, the pay structure for the organization can be developed by the process depicted in Figure 13–8. As indicated in that figure, one means of tying pay survey information to job evaluation data is to plot a *wage curve,* or *scattergram.* This plotting involves first making a graph that charts job evaluation points and pay survey rates for all surveyed jobs. In this way, the distribution of pay for surveyed jobs can be shown, and a linear trend line can be developed by use of the *least-squares regression method.* Also, a curvilinear line can be developed by use of multiple regression and other statistical techniques. The end result is the development of a *market line.* This line shows the relationship between job value as determined by job evaluation points, and wage/salary survey rates,

❖ FIGURE 13–8 ❖
ESTABLISHING A PAY STRUCTURE

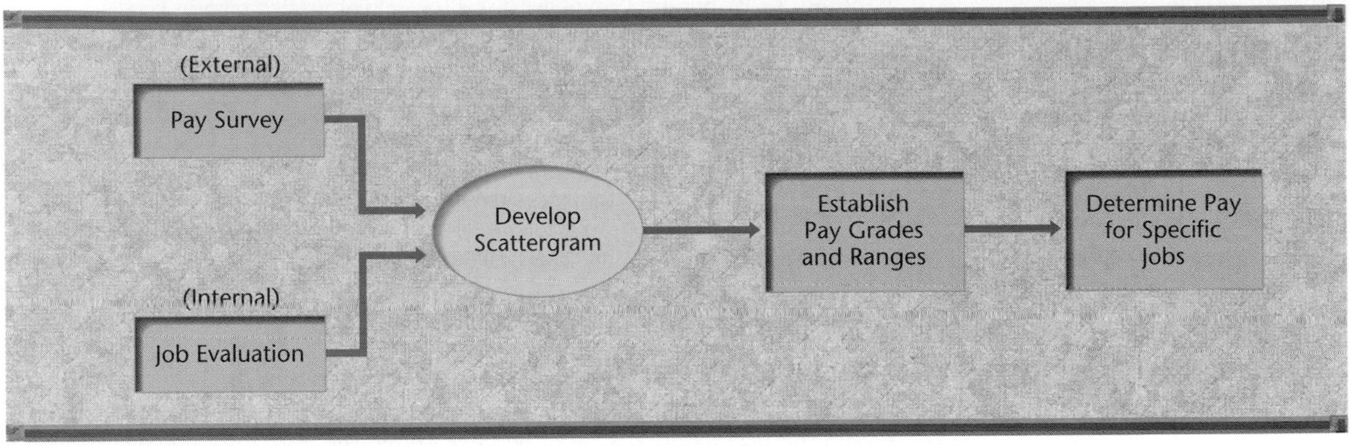

as shown in Figure 13.9. (Details on these methods can be found in any basic statistics text.)

Use of pay survey data links the internal rating jobs through job evaluation to external market considerations. This linkage ensures that the internal view of jobs can be checked against the external "realities." One study of approximately 400 corporate compensation managers found that when differences between job evaluation and pay survey data existed, these managers gave more emphasis to the market data.[27] Such a market emphasis is even more likely for scarce-skill occupational groups.

ESTABLISHING PAY GRADES In the process of establishing a pay structure, organizations use **pay grades** to group together individual jobs having approximately the same job worth. While there are no set rules to be used in establishing pay grades, some overall suggestions have been made. Generally, 11 to 17 grades are

***Pay Grade**
A grouping of individual jobs having approximately the same job worth.

❖ FIGURE 13–9 ❖
PAY SCATTERGRAM

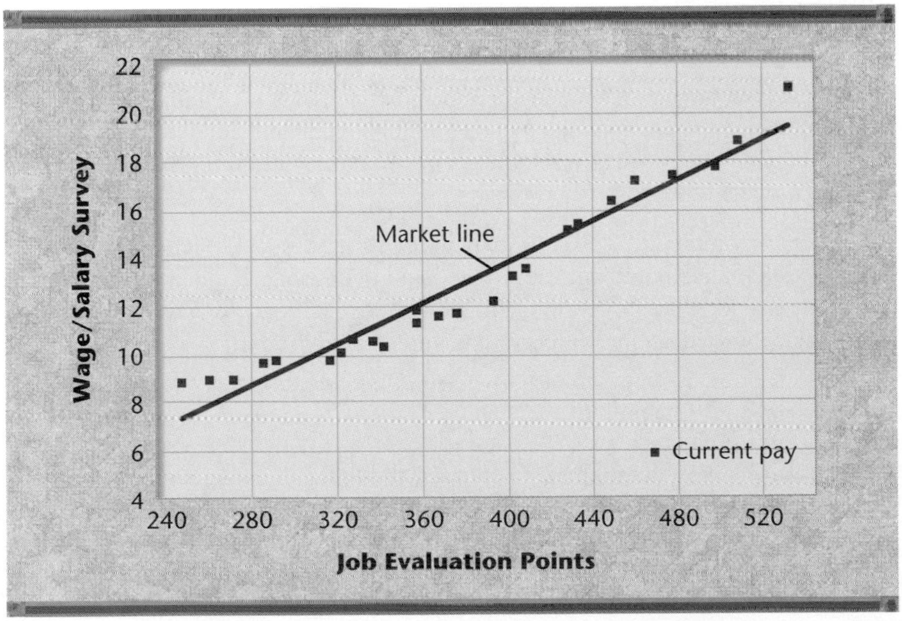

used in small companies. However, as the chapter opening discussion indicates, a growing number of employees are reducing the number of grades by broadbanding. **Broadbanding** involves using fewer pay grades having broader ranges then traditional compensation systems.

***Broadbanding**
Practice of using fewer pay grades having broader ranges than traditional compensation systems.

By using pay grades, management can develop a coordinated pay system without having to determine a separate pay rate for each job in the organization. All the jobs within a grade have the same range of pay regardless of points. As discussed previously, the factor-comparison method of job evaluation uses monetary values, so an employer using that method can easily establish and price pay grades. A vital part of the classification method is developing grades. Organizations that use the ranking method can group several ranks together to create pay grades.

PAY RANGES The pay range for each pay grade also must be established. Using the market line as a starting point (see Figure 13–8), the employer can determine maximum and minimum pay levels for each pay grade by making the market line the midpoint line of the new pay structure. For example, in a particular pay grade, the maximum value may be 20% above the midpoint and the minimum value 20% below it.

A smaller minimum-to-maximum range should be used for lower-level jobs than for higher-level jobs, primarily because employees in lower-level jobs tend to stay in them for shorter periods of time and have greater promotion possibilities. For example, a clerk-typist might advance to the position of secretary or word-processing operator. However, a design engineer likely would have fewer possibilities for upward movement in an organization. At the lower end of a pay structure, the pay range may be 20% (minimum to maximum), whereas upper-level ranges may be as high as 100% (minimum to maximum). This approach recognizes that individual performance can vary more greatly among people in upper-level jobs than in lower-level jobs. However, using the same percentage range at all levels can make administration of a pay system easier in small firms. If broadbanding is used, then much wider ranges, often exceeding 100%, may be used.

❖ FIGURE 13–10 ❖
EXAMPLE OF PAY GRADES AND RANGES

GRADE	POINT RANGE	MINIMUM PAY	MIDPOINT PAY	MAXIMUM PAY
1	240–269	$ 5.92	$ 7.26	$ 8.59
2	270–299	6.94	8.50	10.06
3	300–329	7.96	9.75	11.54
4	330–359	8.98	11.00	13.02
5	360–389	10.00	12.25	14.50
6	390–419	11.01	13.49	15.97
7	420–449	11.79	14.74	17.69
8	450–479	12.79	15.99	19.18
9	480+	14.51	18.14	21.77

Experts recommend having overlap between grades, such as those in Figure 13–10, so that an experienced employee in a lower grade can be paid more than a less experienced employee in a job in the next pay grade. Overlap between three adjacent grades, but no more than three, is advised.

❖ INDIVIDUAL PAY

Once managers have determined pay ranges, they can set the specific pay for individuals. Each of the dots in Figure 13–11 represents an individual employee's current pay in relation to the pay ranges that have been developed. Setting a range for each pay grade gives flexibility by allowing individuals to progress within a grade instead of having to be moved to a new grade each time they receive a raise.

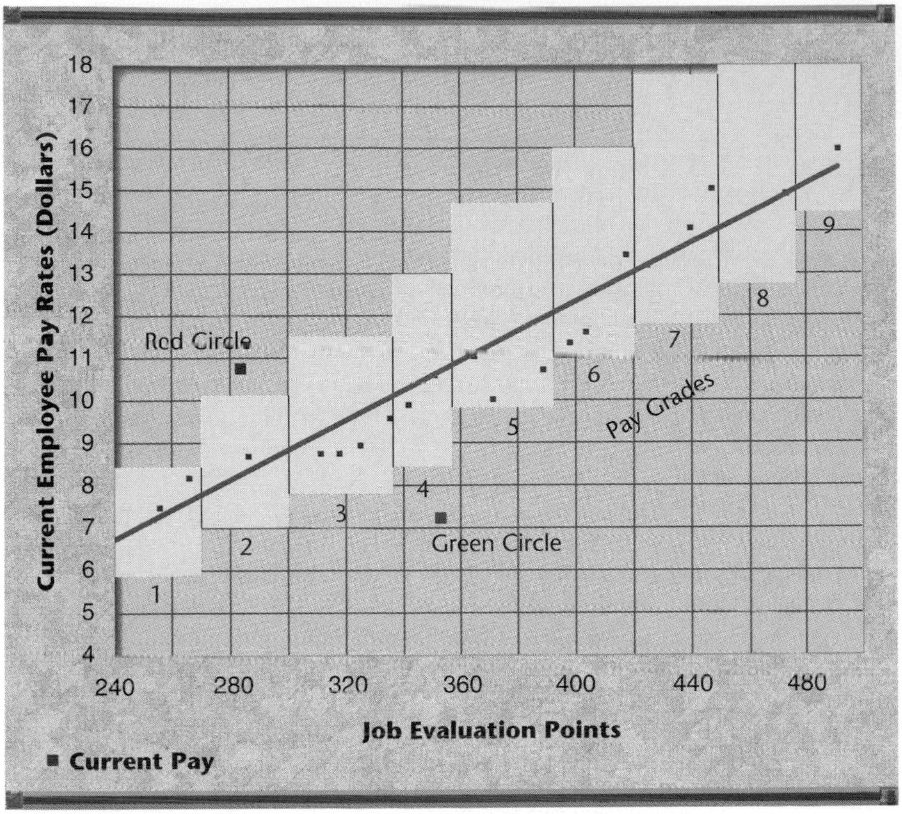

❖ FIGURE 13–11 ❖
PAY STRUCTURE DEPICTED GRAPHICALLY

Also, a pay range allows managers to reward the better-performing employees while maintaining the integrity of the pay system.

❖ RATES OUT OF RANGE

Regardless of how well constructed a pay structure is, there usually are a few individuals whose pay is lower than the minimum or higher than the maximum. These situations occur most frequently when firms that have had an informal pay system develop a new, more formalized one.

RED-CIRCLED EMPLOYEES A red-circled job is shown on the graph in Figure 13–10. A **red-circled employee** is an incumbent who is paid above the range set for the job. For example, assume that an employee's current pay is $10.92 per hour but that the pay range for that grade is between $6.94 and $10.06. The person would be red circled, and attempts would be made over a period of time to bring the employee's rate into grade. Typically, the red-circled job is filled by a longer-service employee who has declined promotions or has been viewed as unpromotable. For instance, consider a long-service employee who started as a forklift driver right out of high school, eventually became a warehouse manager, and has held that job for some time. The employee probably does not have the formal educational background needed to become Purchasing/Inventory Manager. Yet the individual may have continued to receive large pay increases.

***Red-Circled Employee**
An incumbent who is paid above the range set for the job.

Several approaches can be used to bring a red-circled person's pay into line. Although the fastest way would be to cut the employee's pay, that approach is not recommended and is seldom used. Instead, the employee's pay may be frozen until the pay range can be adjusted upward to get the employee's pay rate back into the grade. The employee also can be transferred to a job with a higher grade or can be given more responsibilities, which will result in greater job evaluation worth, thus justifying the job's being upgraded. Another approach is to give the employee a small lump-sum payment but not adjust the pay rate when others are given raises.

***Green-Circled Employee**
An incumbent who is paid below the range set for the job.

GREEN-CIRCLED EMPLOYEES An individual whose pay is below the range is a **green-circled employee.** Promotion is a major cause of this situation. Assume someone receives a promotion that significantly increases his or her responsibilities and pay grade. Typical promotion adjustments are 8% to 15%, but such an adjustment may leave the individual still below the minimum of the new pay range. Because the promotion represents such a significant increase in responsibilities, the employer may not work to increase the person's pay to the minimum until all facets of the new job are being performed fully. Generally, it is recommended that the green-circled individual receive pay increases to get to the pay grade minimum fairly rapidly. More frequent increases can be given if the increase to minimum would be large.

❖ PAY COMPRESSION

***Pay Compression**
Situation in which pay differences among individuals with different levels of experience and performance in the organization become small.

One major problem many employers face is **pay compression,** which occurs when the range of pay differences among individuals with different levels of experience and performance becomes small. Pay compression occurs for a number of reasons, but the major one involves the situation in which labor market pay levels increase more rapidly than an employer's pay adjustments.

Occasionally, in response to competitive market shortages of particular job skills, managers may have to deviate from the priced grades to hire people with scarce skills. For example, suppose the worth of a welder's job is evaluated at $8 to $12 an hour in a company but welders are in short supply and other employers are paying $14 an hour. The firm must pay the higher rate. But suppose several welders who have been with the firm for several years started at $8 an hour and have received 4% increases each year (these have been typical amounts in recent years). These welders may still be making less than the $14 an hour paid to new welders with lesser experience. One solution to pay compression is to have employees follow a step progression based on length of service, assuming performance is satisfactory or better.

Compression between first-line supervisors and those they supervise is a common problem, especially when few first-line supervisors receive overtime pay and their employees do. One strategy is to have a policy of maintaining a percentage differential between supervisors' pay and the pay of those supervised—for example, 15% to 20%—when compression occurs.

❖ PAY INCREASES

Once pay ranges have been developed and individuals' placements within the ranges identified, managers must look at adjustment to individual pay. Decisions about pay increases often are critical ones in the relationships among employees, their managers, and the organization. Individuals have expectations about their pay and about how much increase is "fair," especially in comparison with the increases received by other employees. There are several ways to determine pay increases.

PAY-FOR-PERFORMANCE SYSTEMS Many employers profess to have a pay system based on performance. But relying on performance-appraisal information for making pay adjustments assumes that the appraisals are done well; and this is not always the case, especially for employees whose work cannot be measured easily. Consequently, some system for integrating appraisals and pay changes must be developed and applied equally. Often, this integration is done through the use of a *pay adjustment matrix,* or *salary guide chart* (see Figure 13–12).

Pay adjustment matrices base adjustments in part on a person's **compa-ratio,** which is the pay level divided by the midpoint of the pay range. To illustrate from Figure 13–12, the compa-ratio for two employees would be:

***Compa-Ratio**
Pay level divided by the midpoint of the pay range.

$$\text{Employee R} = \frac{\$13.90 \text{ (current pay)}}{12.25 \text{ (midpoint)}} \times 100 \rightarrow \text{Compa-ratio} = 113$$

$$\text{Employee J} = \frac{\$11.00 \text{ (current pay)}}{12.25 \text{ (midpoint)}} \times 100 \rightarrow \text{Compa-ratio} = 89$$

Such charts reflect a person's upward movement in an organization. Upward movement depends on the person's performance, as rated in an appraisal, and on the person's position in the pay range, which has some relation to experience as well. A person's placement on the chart determines what pay raise the person should receive. For example, if employee J is rated as exceeding expectations (3) with a compa-ratio of 89, that person is eligible for a raise of 7% to 9% according to the chart in Figure 13–12.

Notice that as employees move up the pay range, they must exhibit higher performance to obtain the same percentage raise as those lower in the range performing at the "meets performance expectations" (2) level. This approach is taken because the firm is paying above the market midpoint but receiving only

❖ **FIGURE 13–12** ❖
PAY ADJUSTMENT MATRIX

Compa-ratio (Percent of Midpoint)	Does Not Meet Performance Expectations 1	Meets Performance Expections 2	Exceeds Performance Expectations 3	Significantly Exceeds Performance Expectations 4	Grade 5 (Hourly rates)
Maximum 120% – 112%	A1 0%	A2 0%	A3 0 - 3%	A4 3 - 5%	Maximum = $14.50
112% – 104%	B1 0%	B2 0 - 3%	B3 3 - 5%	B4 5 - 7%	Employee R $13.90
104% – 96% (100% of Midpoint)	C1 0 - 3%	C2 3 - 5%	C3 5 - 7%	C4 7 - 9%	Midpoint = $12.25
96% – 88%	D1 0 - 3%	D2 5 - 7%	D3 7 - 9%	D4 9 - 11%	Employee J = $11.00
88% – Minimum 80%	E1 0 - 3%	E2 7 - 9%	E3 9 - 11%	E4 11 - 13%	Minimum = $10.00

Performance Appraisal

satisfactory performance rather than "above-market" performance. Charts can be constructed to reflect the specific pay-for-performance policy and philosophy in an organization.

In many organizations, pay-for-performance systems are becoming a very popular way to change the way pay increases are distributed. In a truly performance-oriented system, no pay raises are given except for increases in performance. Giving pay increases to people because they have 10 to 15 years' experience, even though they are mediocre employees, defeats the approach. Further, unless the performance-based portion of a pay increase is fairly significant, employees may feel it is not worth the extra effort.[28] Giving an outstanding industrial designer making $40,000 a year the "standard raise" of 4% plus 1% for merit means only $400 for merit versus $1,600 for "hanging around another year."

COST-OF-LIVING ADJUSTMENTS (COLA) A common pay-raise practice is the use of a *standard raise* or *cost-of-living adjustment* (COLA). Giving all employees a standard percentage increase enables them to maintain the same real wages in a period of economic inflation. Often, these adjustments are tied to changes in the Consumer Price Index (CPI) or some other general economic measure. (Critics increasingly have charged that the CPI overstates the actual cost of living, however.[29]) Unfortunately, some employers give across-the-board raises and call them *merit raises,* which they are not. If all employees get a pay increase, it is legitimately viewed as a cost-of-living adjustment having little to do with merit or good performance. For this reason, employers should reserve the term *merit* for any amount above the standard raise, and they should state clearly which amount is for performance and which is the "automatic" COLA adjustment.

SENIORITY Seniority, or time spent in the organization or on a particular job, also can be used as the basis for pay increases. Many employers have policies requiring that persons be employed for a certain length of time before they are eligible for pay increases. Pay adjustments based on seniority often are set as automatic steps once a person has been employed the required length of time, although performance must be at least satisfactory in many nonunion systems.

***Maturity Curve**
Curve that depicts the relationship between experience and pay rates.

A closely related approach uses a **maturity curve,** which depicts the relationship between experience and pay rates. Pay rises as an employee's experience increases, which is especially useful for professionals and skilled craft employees. Unlike a true seniority system, in which a pay raise occurs automatically once someone has put in the required time, a system using maturity curves is built on the assumption that as experience increases, proficiency and performance also increase, so pay raises are appropriate. If proficiency does not increase, theoretically pay adjustments are reduced, although that seldom happens in practice. Once a person plateaus in proficiency, then the pay progression is limited to following the overall movement of the pay structure.

LUMP-SUM PAY INCREASES (LSI) Most employees who receive pay increases, either for merit or seniority, fist have their base pay adjusted and then receive an increase in the amount of their regular monthly or weekly paycheck. For example, an employee who makes $1,200 per month and then receives a 6% increase will get gross pay of $1,272 per month.

***Lump-Sum Increase (LSI)**
A one-time payment of all or part of a yearly pay increase.

In contrast, a **lump-sum increase** (LSI), sometimes called a *performance bonus,* is a one-time payment of all or part of a yearly pay increase. For example, an employee in an LSI plan would receive a check for $864 (before taxes are deducted) instead of getting $72 per month for 12 months. Some organizations place a limit on how much of a merit increase can be taken as a lump-sum payment. Other organizations split the lump sum into two checks, each representing one-half the year's pay raise.

Organizations that use an LSI plan often limit eligibility for the plan to employees with longer service who are not in high-turnover groups. Some employers treat the lump-sum payment as an advance, which must be repaid if the employee leaves the firm before the year is finished.

As with any plan, there are advantages and disadvantages. The major advantage of an LSI plan is that it heightens employees' awareness of what their performance "merited." A lump-sum check also gives employees some flexibility in their spending patterns so that they can buy big-ticket items without having to take out a loan. In addition, the firm can slow down the increase of base pay, so that the compounding effect of succeeding raises is reduced.[30] Unionized employers, such as Boeing and Ford, have negotiated LSI plans as a way to hold down base wages, which also holds down the rates paid for overtime work. Pension costs and some other benefits, often tied to base wages, can be reduced as well.

One disadvantage of LSI plans is administrative tracking, including a system to handle income tax and Social Security deductions from the lump-sum check. Also, workers who take a lump-sum payment may become discouraged because their base pay has not changed. Unions generally resist LSI programs because of this and because of the impact on pensions and benefits. To some extent, this problem can be reduced if the merit increase is split to include some in the base pay and the rest in the lump-sum payment.

SUMMARY

- Compensation provided by an organization can come through pay (base wages and salaries), incentives (performance-based rewards), and benefits (indirect compensation).
- Compensation responsibilities of both HR specialists and managers must be performed well. Compensation practices are closely related to organizational culture, philosophies, strategies, and objectives.
- A continuum of compensation philosophies exists, ranging from an entitlement-oriented philosophy to a pay-for-performance philosophy.
- Bases for determining compensation include time, productivity, tasks, knowledge and skills, and a combination of these.
- Compensation strategies are shifting to reflect competitive and organizational pressures that differ from those faced in the past.
- The objectives of a compensation program are to comply with legal requirements, to be cost-effective, and to provide equity internally, externally, and individually.
- Organizational justice, both procedural and distributive, affects the way that employees view compensation.
- The Fair Labor Standards Act (FLSA), as amended, is the major federal law that affects pay systems. It requires most organizations to pay a minimum wage and to meet certain overtime provisions, including appropriately classifying employees as exempt or nonexempt and as independent contractors or employees.
- Other laws place restrictions on employers who have federal supply contracts or federal construction contracts or who garnish employees' pay.
- Administration of a wage and salary system requires the development of pay policies that incorporate internal and external equity considerations.
- Job evaluation determines the relative worth of jobs. Several different evaluation methods exist, with the point method being the most widely used.
- Once the job evaluation process has been completed, pay survey data must be collected and a pay structure developed. An effective pay system requires that changes continue to be made as needed.
- Developing a pay structure includes grouping jobs into pay grades and establishing a pay range for each grade. Broadbanding, which uses fewer pay grades with broader ranges, is growing in popularity.
- Individual pay must take into account employees' placement within pay grades. Problems involving rates above or below range and pay compression must be addressed.
- Individual pay increases can be based on performance, cost-of-living adjustments, seniority, or a combination of approaches.

Review and Discussion Questions

1. Discuss what compensation philosophies seemed to be used at several organizations where you have worked.
2. Identify some jobs that you believe could be compensated using a skill-based approach instead of a task-based approach. mfg., production, IS ?
3. Discuss the following statement: "If employees believe that subjectivity and favoritism shape the pay system in an organization, then it does not matter that the system was properly designed and implemented."
4. What factors should be considered to determine if an employee who works over 40 hours in a week is due overtime under the FLSA?
5. Considering all methods, why is the point method the most widely used for job evaluation?
6. You have been named compensation manager for a hospital. How would you establish a pay system?
7. Why are pay-for-performance systems growing in importance?

Terms to Know

benchmark job 391
benefit 376
broadbanding 398
compa-ratio 401
compensable factor 392
compensatory time off 386
distributive justice 383
equity 381
exempt employees 384
garnishment 388
green-circled employee 400
incentive 376
job evaluation 390
lump-sum increase (LSI) 402
market price 389
maturity curve 402
nonexempt employees 384
pay 376
pay compression 400
pay equity 395
pay grade 397
pay survey 395
piece-rate system 378
procedural justice 383
red-circled employee 399
salary 378
wage and salary administration 389
wages 378

Case

Skill-Based Pay at the City of Englewood

Changing compensation programs from an entitlement-oriented, time-based framework to a skill-based plan has benefited the city of Englewood, New Jersey. The changes in the compensation plan were connected with efforts made by the city to alter its mission and organizational culture.

The traditional plan used until the early 1990s was based on the Hay system and benchmark jobs. Pay ranges were developed, and employees received increases each six months, supposedly based on performance appraisals. However, in reality, performance truly was not considered significant, and employees received automatic step increases each six months until they reached the top of their ranges after 18 months on the job. At that point, increases were limited to cost-of-living adjustments made when the ranges were moved each year. There was no differentiation for individual or group performance, so high performers left for other organizations.

To address these concerns, the Employee Services Division of the city began to develop a skill-based compensation system that tied into career development plans. At the heart of the new system was the development or revision of job descriptions to identify skills. After the skills had been identified, they were classified into two groups: (1) essential skills and (2) skills of excellence. The essential skills were those necessary to perform each core job, while the skills of excellence incorporated additional duties performed and licensing or certification requirements. Next, monetary amounts were linked to all facets of the jobs. Finally, pay survey data on individual jobs were gathered and used to develop broader pay ranges.

As a result of the changes, employees can now advance and receive pay increases by gaining additional skills and/or performing better. For example, an employee who obtains and masters a skill that is worth 5% of the midpoint pay for the job can receive an appropriate increase at the next performance review, assuming performance was satisfactory or better. Conversely, employees who do not maintain their skills or who perform poorly are subject to having their pay decrease somewhat.

Performance reviews are conducted periodically, with departmental managers having the option of conducting reviews quarterly, semiannually, or annually. As part of the performance appraisal discussion, employees set goals, and progress against those goals is considered in subsequent reviews.

One advantage of the new system is that it links employees to a career development planning process. By focusing on skills, Englewood has been able to compile an inventory of employee skills, which aids in future job placement. Also, employees know that if they develop additional skills, they will be rewarded for them and will have greater career development opportunities.

After several years, approximately half of the city's employees are participating in the plan, while others remain on the traditional plan. According to Monica Lopez, the city's Human Resource Administrator, the program has been a success. Employees appear to view the program positively and to view their performance appraisals as important. Better communication between employees and managers also has been noticed. Finally, the new plan has paid for itself through direct and indirect cost savings, including retaining employees who might otherwise have left. As a result of the success of the Englewood program, a number of other cities and private-sector employers have contacted Englewood to obtain details for revising their own compensation programs.[31]

Questions

1. Discuss how shifting the emphasis of the compensation system affected the organizational culture at the city of Englewood.
2. Compare the traditional and new compensation programs at Englewood to a program used by an organization where you have worked.

Notes

1. P. V. LeBlanc and C. M. Ellis, "The Many Faces of Banding," *ACA Journal,* Winter 1995, 52–62; J. Kanin-Lovers and M. Cameron, "Broadbanding—a Step Forward of a Step Backward?" *Journal of Compensation and Benefits,* March–April 1994, 39–42; K. S. Abosch, D. Gilbert, and S. M. Dempsey, "Broadbanding: Approaches of Two Organizations," *ACA Journal,* Spring 1994, 46–53; and K. S. Abosch and J. S. Hard, "Characteristics and Practices of Organizations with Broadbanding," *ACA Journal,* Autumn 1994, 6–17.
2. Elizabeth J. Hawk, "Cultural Rewards: A Balancing Act," *Personnel Journal,* April 1995, 30–37.
3. E. E. Lawler, III, *Strategic Pay: Aligning Organizational Strategies and Pay Systems* (Northbrook, IL: Brace-Park Press, 1995).
4. G. Bassett, "Merit Pay Increases Are a Mistake," *Compensation and Benefits Review,* March–April 1994, 20–22.
5. Luis R. Gomez-Mejia and David B. Balkin, *Compensation, Organizational Strategy, and Firm Performance* (Cincinnati: South-Western Publishing, 1992), 39–49.
6. Adapted from Kimberly Charlet, "Give the Boot to Punching a Clock," *Benefits & Compensation Solutions,* September 1995, 36–37.
7. S. A. Snell and J. W. Dean, Jr., "Strategic Compensation for Integrated Manufacturing: The Moderating Effect of Jobs and Organizational Inertia," *Academy of Management Journal* 37 (1994), 1109–1140.

(Notes continued on following page)

▼Notes, continued

8. G. D. Jenkins, G. E. Ledford, N. Gupta, and D. H. Doty, *Skill-Based Pay* (Scottsdale, AZ: American Compensation Association, 1992).

9. Reginald Shareef, "Skill-Based Pay in the Public," *Review of Pubic Personnel Administration,* Summer 1994, 60–74.

10. Edward G. Vogeley and Louise J. Schaeffer, "Link Employee Pay to Competencies and Objectives," *HR Magazine,* October 1995, 75–81.

11. Gary Blau, "The Effect of Level and Importance of Pay Reflects on Pay Level Satisfaction," *Human Relations* 47 (1994), 1251–1268.

12. Blair H. Sheppard, Ray J. Lewichi, and John W. Minton, *Organizational Justice* (New York: Lexington Books, 1992), 122–129.

13. Martin M. Greller and Charles K. Parsons, "Contingent Pay Systems and Job Performance Feedback," *Group & Organization Management* 20 (1995), 90–108.

14. Marcia P. Miceli, I. Jung, Janet P. Near, and D. B. Greenberger, "Predictors and Outcomes of Reactions to Pay-for-Performance Plans," *Journal of Applied Psychology* 76 (1991), 508–521.

15. For more specifics, see *Handy Reference Guide to the Fair Labor Standards Act,* WH Publication no. 1282 (Washington, DC: U.S. Department of Labor, Employment Standards Administration, Wage and Hour Division).

16. Mike McNamee, "A Minimum-Wage Hike Spells Maximum Damage," *Business Week,* January 30, 1995, 36; and "The Minimum-Wage Debate," *The Economist,* September 10, 1994, 84.

17. For more details, see J. E. Kalet, *Primer on FLSA and Other Wage & Hour Laws,* 3rd ed. (Washington DC: Bureau of National Affairs, 1994).

18. M. Seiz and S. Mehta, "Small Businesses Get Big Bills as IRS Targets Free-Lancers," *The Wall Street Journal,* August 24, 1995, B1.

19. Dorothy J. Gailer, "The Davis-Bacon Act Comes Under Attack by an Odd Alliance," *The Wall Street Journal,* May 3, 1995, A1; and George F. Will, "Dumbest Law? Davis-Bacon Act," *Washington Post,* February 6, 1995, B7.

20. Donald V. Brookes, "Reality-Based Job Evaluation," *Benefits & Compensation Solutions,* April 1995, 54–55; and Gundars E. Kaupins, "Lies, Damn Lies, and Job Evaluation," *Personnel,* November 1989, 62–65.

21. For a detailed discussion of the Hay system, see Richard I. Henderson, *Compensation Management,* 6th ed. (Englewood Cliffs, NJ: Prentice-Hall, 1994), 288–305.

22. M. F. Karsten, M. K. Schroeder, and M. A. Surrette, "Impact of the Americans with Disabilities Act on Job Evaluation," *Labor Law Journal* 46 (1995), 436–439.

23. M. Gray, "Pay Equity through Job Evaluation," *Compensation and Benefits Review,* July 1992, 46–58.

24. George T. Milkovich and Jerry M. Newman, *Compensation,* 5th ed. (Chicago: Irwin, 1995), 531–543.

25. Suggestions for pay survey usage are in L. Kate Beatty, *The Use and Abuse of Salary Surveys* (Deerfield, IL: William M. Mercer, 1993).

26. *District of Utah, U.S. District Court v. Utah Society for Healthcare Human Resources Administration, et al. Federal Register,* March , 1994, 14203.

27. Caroline L. Weber and Sara L. Rynes, "Effects of Compensation Strategy on Job Pay Decisions," *Academy of Management Journal* 34 (1991), 86–109.

28. A. Mitra, N. Gupta, and G. D. Jenkins, "How People See Their Pay Raises," *Compensation and Benefits Review,* May–June 1995, 71–76.

29. Brian S. Klaas and Joseph C. Ullman, "Sticky Wages Revisited: Organizational Responses to a Declining Market-Clearing Wage," *Academy of Management Journal* 20 (1995), 281–310.

30. H. Stein, "The Consumer Price Index: Servant or Master?" *The Wall Street Journal,* November 1, 1995, A10.

31. Based on Bill Leonard, "Creating Opportunities to Excel," *HR Magazine,* February 1995, 47–51; and Monica Z. Lopez, "Creating Opportunities to Excel," *Benefits & Compensation Solutions,* September 1994, 10–11.

Chapter 14

Incentives and Executive Compensation

After you have read this chapter, you should be able to . . .

- Define *incentive* and give examples of three categories of incentives.
- Identify four guidelines for successful incentive programs.
- Discuss three types of individual incentives.
- Define *gainsharing* and explain several types of gainsharing plans.
- Explain why profit-sharing and employee stock ownership plans (ESOPs) are important as organizational incentive plans.
- Identify the components of executive compensation.
- Discuss several criticisms of board compensation committees and long-term incentives for executives.

HR in Transition

Stock Incentives for Employees
What Happens at Wal-Mart When Stock Prices Fall?

Incentives can take many forms, from commissions on sales to bonuses for a good year. Incentives are designed to encourage productivity and to tie employees more closely to the company. Retail discounter Wal-Mart has traditionally used incentives in the form of stock purchases (at a discount, of course) to motivate its employees.

Retail employees are often not especially well paid, and the opportunity to participate in a stock purchase plan promising appreciation on the investment can be attractive. For example, someone who paid $1,650 for 100 shares of Wal-Mart stock in 1970 would have had shares worth $3.5 million after the recent stock split.

Wal-Mart "associates" buy shares of the company's stock through a payroll deduction plan at a 15% discount. The firm feels it is very important to have employee shareholders, as do other firms who use shares of stock as incentives. Federal Express, MCI, Home Depot, and Southwest Airlines have similar stock incentive plans.

The impact of offering an incentive that has become uncertain at best is quite apparent. Some say morale is down at Wal-Mart. There are increasing attempts to unionize, and employees are demanding better benefits and wages in some places.

Wal-Mart's plan has been well subscribed. Less than 50% of the company's employees have worked there more than three years, but more than 55% join in the payroll deduction stock purchase plan. The theory behind investing is quite compelling: effective work leads to rising sales and profits, which will contribute to rising stock prices. Also, Wal-Mart's sales and profits *have* continued to rise. The company expects to add about $17 billion in sales for the year in which this is being written. Wall Street analysts see the company's earnings growing 19% per year over the next five years. That is excellent performance for a *very* large company.

But Wal-Mart's stock price is *down*. Since the stock split, the value of a share has fallen roughly 40%. Executives try to reassure employees that if sales continue to go up and profits go up, the stock prices will eventually go up as well. Investors, however, are not convinced that the company has the same competitive advantage it had in the 1980s. Apparently, investors' dollars have gone to stocks with higher performance potential, reducing the price of Wal-Mart stock.

The impact of offering an incentive that has become uncertain at best is quite apparent. Some say morale is down at Wal-Mart. There are increasing attempts to unionize, and employees are demanding better benefits and wages in some places. Wal-Mart employees have been long praised for their loyalty to the company and the stores' friendly, family-like atmosphere. But one former company director is disturbed to see restrooms not kept clean, spilled merchandise unshelved, and the famous smiling greeting from employees missing. One married pair of employees now in their 70s had planned to retire, but the value of Wal-Mart stock in their profit sharing account had dropped so much they no longer felt they could do so.

The use of stock purchases to give employees a sense of ownership and loyalty seems sensible. However, the incentive value clearly is reduced when the stock's worth falls, perhaps even below what it cost. Organizations using such incentives may discover, as Wal-Mart has, that when prices are going up rapidly, stock incentives motivate. But stock prices do not always go up![1]

"Incentives merely—and temporarily—change what we do."
—A. Kohn

***Performance Incentives**
Compensation that attempts to link pay with performance.

Some employees have long been accustomed to **performance incentive** plans which provide compensation that attempts to link pay with performance. For example, executives' compensation has traditionally been linked to the performances of the organizations they manage by short-term incentives such as bonuses or long-term incentives such as stock option plans. Recently, interest in linking pay and performance more closely has been high, as in the Wal-Mart example just discussed. This opportunity to align employee interests with the interests of the organization promises both better performance and greater reward for employees.

The need for new ways of paying people to increase their productivity has resulted in many different approaches, plans, and ideas. Generally, performance incentive systems are based on some simple assumptions:

- Some jobs contribute more to organizational success than others.
- Some people do better work than others.
- Employees who do more should receive more.

Contrast these assumptions with a pay system based on seniority only:

- Time spent each day is the primary measure of short-term contribution.
- In the long term, length of service with the organization is the primary differentiating factor among people.
- Everyone is equal in his or her contribution to the unit, and units are equal in organizational contribution.

A study of 629 organizations found that their top compensation goals were, in order: (1) linking pay to performance, (2) controlling costs, (3) linking pay to quality, and (4) encouraging teamwork. The study also found that one-third of the organizations had increased the incentive portion as a percent of compensation in the previous two years. Also, incentives are not just being used for top executives. About 33% of the respondents said that incentives have spread to lower-level managers, 26% to professional and technical staff members, and 22% to all administrative, clerical, and hourly employees.[2]

But experts say that about half of the performance incentive plans they see *don't work*! Poor design and poor administration are the culprits. Indeed, linking pay to performance may not always be appropriate. For example, if the output cannot be objectively measured, management may not be able to reward the higher performers with more pay. Managers may not even be able to identify accurately the higher performers. Requirements for successful incentive plans and executive compensation programs are discussed in this chapter.

❖ INCENTIVES

***Incentive**
Compensation that rewards an employee for efforts beyond normal performance expectations.

Incentives are attempts to tie employee reward to output. **Incentives** are compensation that rewards an employee for performance beyond normal expectations.

❖ THREE FOCUS POINTS FOR INCENTIVES

As Figure 14–1 shows, incentives can be focused on individual performance, team or group performance, or organization-wide performance. The three focuses have different impacts on cooperation among people.

Individual incentives neither require nor foster much cooperation among individuals. In pursuit of individual rewards, an employee may withhold information from others, sabotage efforts of a competing employee, focus *only* on what is rewarded, or refuse to do anything that is not tied directly to the incentive

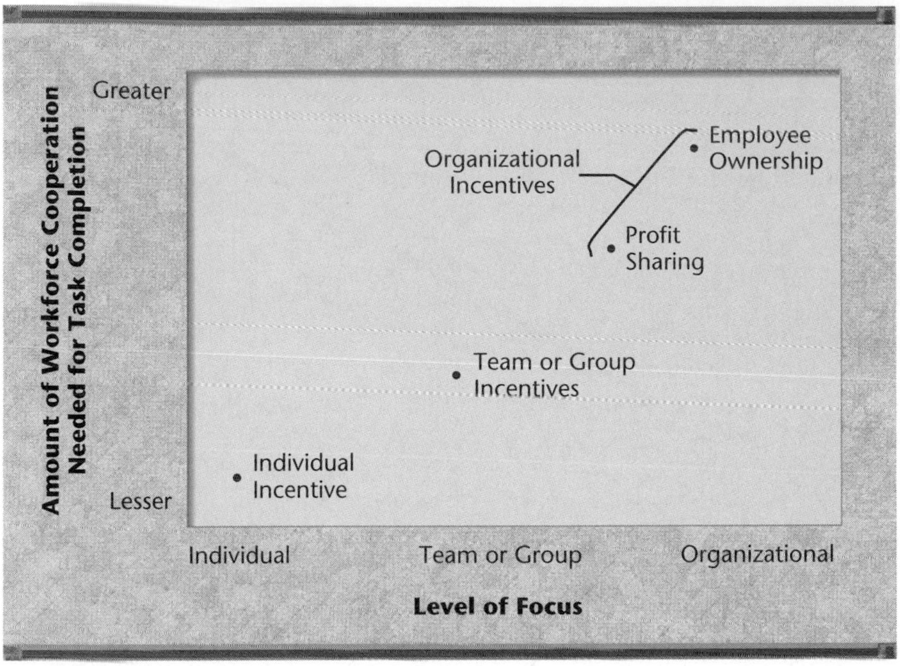

❖ FIGURE 14–1 ❖
INCENTIVE PLANS: FOCUS AND COOPERATION REQUIREMENTS

reward. Despite such undesirable behaviors, individual incentives may be very successful if doing the job does not require a great deal of cooperation among employees.

When an entire work group or *team* is rewarded for its performance, more cooperation among the members is required and usually forthcoming. However, competition among different teams for rewards can lead to decline in overall performance under certain circumstances.

Organizational incentives reward people for the performance of the entire organization. This approach reduces individual and team competition and assumes that all employees working together can generate financial gain, which is then shared.

❖ GUIDELINES FOR INCENTIVE SYSTEMS

Incentive systems can be complex and can take many forms. However, certain general guidelines are useful in establishing and maintaining incentive systems.

RECOGNIZE ORGANIZATIONAL CULTURE AND RESOURCES An important factor in the success of any incentive program is that it be consistent with both the culture and the financial resources of the organization. For example, if an organization is autocratic and adheres to traditional rules and procedures, an incentive system that rewards flexibility and teamwork is likely to fail. The incentive plan is being "planted" in the wrong growing environment.

Any incentive system requires an organizational climate of trust and cooperation between employees and managers. As the amount of trust between employees and managers increases, and the objectivity of the criteria used for determining rewards becomes greater, the likelihood of a successful incentive program increases. If workers have a high level of trust and good working relationships with their superiors, they may accept more subjective performance measures. But low trust of management leads to a low probability of success for

❖ FIGURE 14–2 ❖
RELATIONSHIP BETWEEN TRUST AND OBJECTIVITY IN INCENTIVE SYSTEM SUCCESS

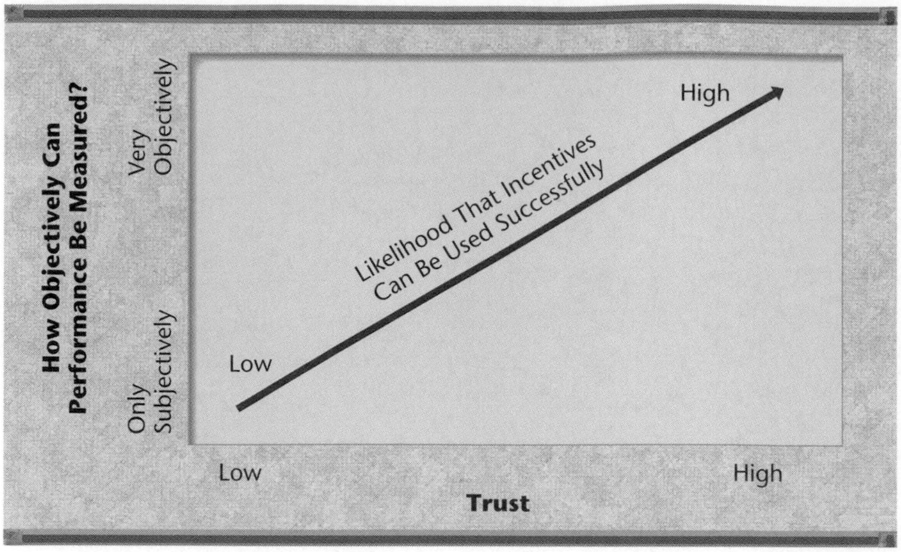

an incentive program.[3] Employees will see rewards as being associated with friendship or other factors rather than performance and will not work hard to get a reward they are convinced will not be forthcoming. Figure 14–2 illustrates how the factors of trust and objectivity are related.

TIE INCENTIVES TO DESIRED PERFORMANCE Incentive systems should be tied as much as possible to desired performance. Employees must see a direct relationship between their efforts and their rewards. Further, both employees and managers must see the rewards as equitable and desirable. Expectancy theory indicates that incentives are most effective when employees can see clearly that their extra efforts lead to increased performance and desirable rewards. Otherwise, stress can be created.

Because people tend to produce what is measured and rewarded, it is important to make sure that what is being rewarded is *really* what is needed and that nothing important is being left out. For example, assume a hotel reservation center sets incentives for its employees to increase productivity by lowering their time spent per call. That reduction may occur, but customer service and the number of reservations made might drop as employees rush callers to reduce talk time.

Additionally, employee competition for incentives may produce undesirable results. Paying salesclerks in a retail store a commission may encourage "fighting" over customers. Some salesclerks may be reluctant to work in departments that sell low-cost items if their commissions are figured on the basis of total sales. For example, clerks in a department store may concentrate on selling major appliances without giving adequate attention to small household appliances.

KEEP INCENTIVE PLANS CURRENT An incentive system should consistently reflect current technological and organizational conditions. Offering an incentive for salesclerks to sell outdated merchandise in order to clear it out of stock might be appropriate until that merchandise is gone, but no incentive may be needed to sell high-demand fashion items.

Incentive systems should be reviewed continually to determine whether they are operating as designed. Follow-up, through an attitude survey or other means, will determine if the incentive system is actually encouraging employees to perform better. If it is not, then managers should consider changing the system.[4]

Recognize Individual Differences Incentive plans should provide for individual differences. People are complex, and a variety of incentive systems may have to be developed to appeal to various organizational groups and individuals. Not everybody will want the same type of incentive rewards. For this and other reasons, individual incentive systems must be designed carefully.

As illogical as it may seem, informal group pressure and sanctions commonly are used to restrict the amount that individuals produce, even if individual pay is reduced as a result. Those who seek to maximize their earnings by exceeding group-imposed limits are labeled "rate busters" or something even more graphic. Rate restrictors often feel they are being made to suffer by comparison with the higher producers.

Separate Plan Payments from Base Pay Successful incentive plans separate the incentive payment from base salary. That separation makes a clear connection between performance and pay. It also reinforces the notion that one part of the employee's pay must be "re-earned" in the next performance period. Many employees prefer the security of automatic increases in pay based on length of service in the organization to having incentives paid based on performance as judged by their immediate supervisors.[5]

❖ Individual Incentives

Individual incentive systems attempt to relate individual effort to pay. Conditions that favor the use of individual incentive plans are as follows:[6]

- Individual performance must be capable of being identified and isolated by the nature of the job performed.
- A substantial amount of independent work must be performed, allowing individual contributions to be identified.
- The individuals must not be too interdependent with other workers; or if they are, competition among employees must be desirable.
- The organizational culture must emphasize individual achievements and rewards.

❖ Piece-Rate Systems

The most individual incentive system is the piece-rate system, whether of the straight or differential type. Under the **straight piece-rate system,** wages are determined by multiplying the number of units produced (such as garments sewn or customers contacted) by the piece rate for one unit. The rate per piece does not change regardless of the number of pieces produced. Because the cost is the same for each unit, the wage for each employee is easy to figure, and labor costs can be accurately predicted.

❖Straight Piece-Rate System
A pay system in which wages are determined by multiplying the number of units produced by the piece rate for one unit.

A **differential piece-rate system** pays employees one piece-rate wage for units produced up to a standard output and a higher piece-rate wage for units produced over the standard. Developed by Frederick W. Taylor in the late 1800s, this system is designed to stimulate employees to achieve or exceed established standards of production.

❖Differential Piece-Rate System
Pays employees one piece-rate wage for units produced up to a standard output and a higher piece-rate wage for units produced over the standard.

Managers often determine the standards, or quotas, by using time and motion studies. For example, assume that the standard quota for a worker is set at 300 units per day and the standard rate is 14¢ per unit. For all units over the standard, however, the employee receives 20¢ per unit. Under this system, the worker who produces 400 units in one day will get $62 in wages (300 × 14¢) + (100 × 20¢). There are many possible combinations of straight and differential piece-rate systems. The specific system used by a firm depends on many situational factors.

Despite their incentive value, piece-rate systems are difficult to use because standards for many types of jobs are difficult and costly to determine.[7] In some instances, the cost of determining and maintaining the standards may be greater than the benefits derived. Jobs in which individuals have limited control over output or in which high standards of quality are necessary also may be unsuited to piecework. Though the system still is widely used in certain industries, such as the garment industry, it seldom is used in white-collar, office, and clerical jobs, in which an individual employee's performance often is affected by factors beyond the employee's control.

❖ COMMISSIONS

***Commission**
Compensation computed as a percentage of sales in units or dollars.

An individual incentive system widely used in sales jobs is the **commission,** which is compensation computed as a percentage of sales in units or dollars. Commissions are integrated into the pay given to sales workers in three common ways: straight commission, salary plus commission, and bonuses.

STRAIGHT COMMISSION In the straight commission system, a sales representative receives a percentage of the value of the sales made. Consider a sales representative working for a consumer products company. She receives no compensation if no sales are made, but for all sales made in her territory, she receives a percentage of the total amount. The advantage of this system is that the sales representative must sell to earn. The disadvantage is that it offers no security for the sales staff. This disadvantage can be especially pronounced when the product or service sold is one that requires a long lead time before purchasing decisions are made. One sales representative with a telecommunications firm spent five months working with a large corporation to sell a $1 million phone and communication system, for which the representative received a sizable commission. But during the five months, he received no income; he was paid only when the sale was closed and the equipment installed.

***Draw**
An amount advanced from and repaid to future commissions earned by the employee.

For that reason, some employers use a **draw** system, in which the sales representative can draw advance payments against future commissions. The amount drawn then is deducted from future commission checks. From the employer's side, one of the risks in a draw system is that future commissions may not be large enough to repay the draw, especially for a new or marginally successful salesperson. In addition, arrangements must be made for repayment of drawn amounts if an individual leaves the organization before earning the draw in commission.

SALARY PLUS COMMISSION The most frequently used form of sales compensation is the *salary plus commission,* which combines the stability of a salary with the performance aspect of a commission. A common split is 80% salary to 20% commission, although the split varies by industry and with other factors.

Consultants criticize many sales commission plans as being too complex to motivate sales representatives. Others are too simple, focusing only on the salesperson's pay, not on organizational objectives. Although a majority of companies use overall sales growth as the only performance measure, performance would be much better if these organizations used a variety of criteria, including obtaining new accounts and selling high-value versus low-value items that reflect marketing plans.[8]

❖ Bonuses

As mentioned, sales workers may receive commissions in the form of lump-sum payments, or **bonuses.** Other employees may receive bonuses as well. Bonuses are less costly than general wage increases, since they do not become part of employees' base wages, upon which future percentage increases are figured. One method of determining an employee's annual bonus is to compute it as a percentage of the individual's base salary. Often, such programs pay bonuses only if specific individual and organizational objectives have been achieved. Though technically this type of bonus is individual, it comes close to being a group or organizational incentive system. Because it is based on the profits of the division, management must consider the total performance of the division and its employees.

***Bonus**
A payment made on a one-time basis which does not become part of the employee's base pay.

Bonuses have gained in popularity recently. Individual incentive compensation in the form of bonuses often is used at the executive or upper-management levels of an organization, and it is increasingly used at lower levels, too. The HR Perspective describes how a bonus program was used at Taco Bell.

A bonus recognizes performance by both the employee and the company. When both types of performance are good, bonuses go up. When both are bad, bonuses go down. When an employee has done poorly in a year that was good for the company, most employers base the employee's bonus on individual performance. It is not always as clear what to do when an employee does well but the company does not. However, a growing number of companies are asking employees to put a portion of their pay "on the line." While offering big incen-

HR PERSPECTIVE

Managerial Incentives at Taco Bell

In order to keep pace with the growth in new restaurants, Taco Bell Corporation had to revise its managerial incentive program. During a recent two-year period, Taco Bell added more than 350 new restaurants. As a result, the company implemented a new field organization structure. Because of concerns that Taco Bell would not be able to recruit and retain a sufficient number of managers to have one manager in each restaurant, the firm decided to make existing restaurant managers responsible for two locations, not just one.

In compensating these managers for the additional responsibilities and demands placed on them, Taco Bell had two choices. The first, which was rejected, was to increase the base salaries for the managers. Instead, a decision was made to institute a new managerial incentive program. Under the previous bonus program, most managers (whose base salaries averaged about $30,000) received $1,000 bonuses every quarter. However, under the new managerial incentive program, managers whose performance is outstanding can earn up to $5,000 twice a year, more than twice the amount possible under the old program. In this way, managers with responsibilities for two restaurants receive more than twice as much additional compensation.

The new program, instituted for over 1,600 restaurant managers, uses three measures of performance: (1) targeted profit, (2) customer service, and (3) store sales. Using the performance objectives set under the new program, 60% to 70% of the managers typically meet their objectives for each six-month period, compared with 85% who met the easier goals set under the old program. Those who do not measure up lose out on up to $10,000 per year, not $4,000, which provides stronger incentives for managers to meet their objectives.

In addition to rewarding performance more, Taco Bell has seen better results in other areas throughout the chain. In the first months after implementation of the new managerial incentive program, profit records were broken, customer service scores were higher than ever before, and food costs as a percentage of store sales decreased. These results indicate that the revised managerial incentive program has had the positive impact desired.[9]

tive bonuses for high performance, they are withholding them when performance is poor and insisting that employees share *both* the risks and rewards of business.[10]

Bonuses also can be used to reward new ideas and development of skills. Typically, managers or teams identify skills the organization needs. When the skills are acquired by an employee, a pay increase or a one-time bonus may follow. Tests usually are used to confirm that skills have indeed been acquired. Also, skill training itself can be used as a reward. Dow Corning–Australia rewards individuals in TQM programs with outside skill-training opportunities.[11]

❖ Special Incentive Programs

Although special incentive programs can be developed for groups and for entire organizations, they focus on rewarding only high-performing individuals. Giving the salesperson who sells the most new cars a trip to Las Vegas is one example of a special incentive program. Sales contests, productivity competitions, and other incentive schemes can be established so that individual employees receive extra compensation.

Special incentive programs are used widely in sales-related jobs. Cash, merchandise, travel, and combinations of those are the most frequently used rewards. The main reasons for using awards are to achieve immediate sales gains and to focus attention on selling specific products or obtaining new accounts.

One type of incentive program is becoming less popular. Firms like IBM, Scott Paper, Merck, and American Express recently have eliminated rewards for longevity with the company. Giving the traditional "gold watch" for long service and other service awards may be awkward in a time of many layoffs. For example, Bank of America announced layoffs right after mailing out invitations to its 25-year-service awards dinner—an interesting mixed message.[12]

❖ Team-Based Incentives

Today, about two-thirds of U.S. companies assign some work to self-managed teams—up from 28% in 1987.[13] For many of these companies, individual-centered incentives no longer make sense. Figure 14–3 shows some reasons that companies

❖ Figure 14–3 ❖
Why Organizations Establish Team Incentives

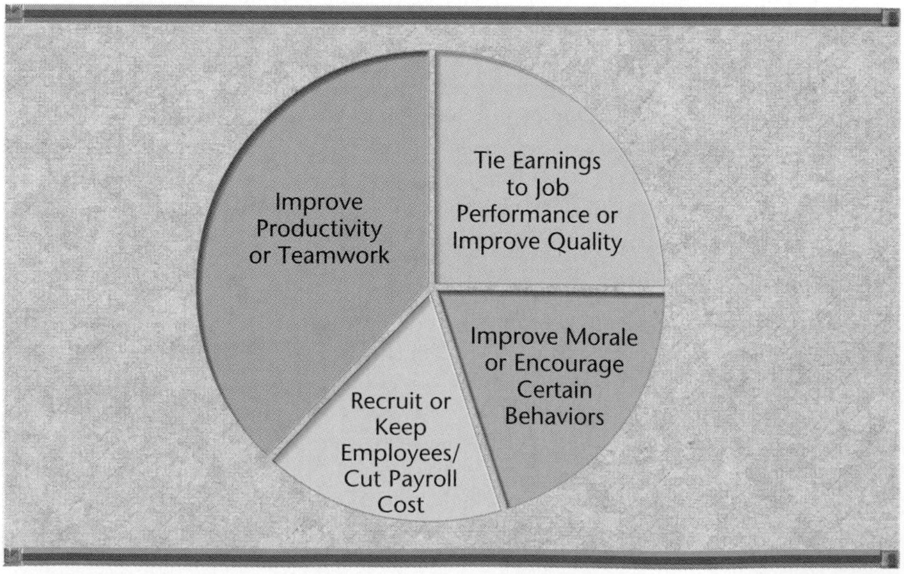

establish group incentive programs. One company is with over 700 employees operating in teams split up incentive payments based on how well members have achieved goals.

Although some teams actually make decisions on bonuses for their members, this practice seems to be the exception rather than the rule. Many companies find teams unwilling to handle pay decisions for co-workers. Team-based bonus plans present other problems as well. Should a member be rewarded for trying hard but not quite succeeding? What happens when extra money for a "superstar" has to come from other group members' foregoing their own bonuses to some extent? Team-based incentives present both opportunities and challenges when they are developed and implemented.

❖ Successful Team-Based Incentives

The size of the group is critical to the success of team-based incentives. If it becomes too large, employees may feel their individual efforts will have little or no effect on the total performance of the group and the resulting rewards. Incentive plans for small groups are a direct result of the growing number of complex jobs requiring interdependent effort. Team-based incentive plans may encourage teamwork in small groups where interdependence is high. Such plans have been used in many service-oriented industries where a high degree of contact with customers requires teamwork.

Group incentives seem to work best when certain criteria are present:

- Significant interdependence exists among the work of several individuals, and teamwork and cooperation are essential.
- Difficulties exist in identifying exactly who is responsible for differing levels of performance.
- Management wants to create or reinforce teamwork and cooperation among employees.

If these conditions cannot be met, then either individual or organizational incentives may be more appropriate.

❖ Problems with Team-Based Incentives

Team-based incentive plans can pose problems for the design and difficulties in the administration of team-based incentives. Furthermore, groups, like individuals, may restrict output, resist revision of standards, and seek to gain at the expense of other groups. Compensating different employee teams with different incentives may cause them to overemphasize certain efforts to the detriment of the overall organizational good. For example, conflict often arises between the marketing and production functions of organizations because marketing's incentive compensation often is based on what is sold, while production's incentive compensation may be based on having unit production costs as low as possible. Marketing representatives may want to tailor products to customers' needs to increase their sales, but production managers emphasize production of identical items to lower costs. The overall company performance and profitability therefore may be sidetracked.

Another problem with team-based incentives occurs when a poorly performing individual influences the group results negatively.[14] For instance, suppose holding data-entry errors to below 2% is an objective that triggers payment of a group incentive. The presence of one or two poor performers who make numerous errors can result in the group being denied an incentive payment for a month. Unfortunately, even if management retrains or removes the poor performers, some incentive amounts already have been lost.

❖ Organizational Incentives

An organizational incentive system compensates all employees in the organization based on how well the organization as a whole performs during the year. The basic concept behind organizational incentive plans is that overall efficiency depends on organizational or plantwide cooperation. The purpose of these plans is to produce teamwork. For example, conflict between marketing and production can be overcome if management uses an incentive that emphasizes organizational profit and productivity. To be effective, an organizational incentive program should include everyone from nonexempt employees to managers and executives. Common organizational incentive systems include gainsharing, profit sharing, and employee stock ownership plans (ESOPs).

❖ Gainsharing

❖Gainsharing
The sharing with employees of greater-than-expected gains in profits and/or productivity.

Gainsharing is the sharing with employees of greater-than-expected gains in profits and/or productivity. Gainsharing attempts to increase "discretionary efforts"—that is, the difference between the maximum amount of effort a person can exert and the minimum amount of effort necessary to keep from being fired. It can be argued that workers currently are not paid for discretionary effort in most organizations. They are paid to meet the minimum acceptable level of effort required. However, when workers do exercise discretionary efforts, the organization can afford to pay them more than the going rate, because the extra efforts produce financial gains over and above the returns of minimal efforts.

A study of gainsharing-type plans found that the surveyed firms used financial measures, productivity measures, and quality measures to determine when to pay some of the gains generated to employees. This study also revealed that employees received about 35% of the gains generated, while organizations retained about 65% of the gains.[15]

Determining Payment and Performance Measures To begin a gainsharing program, management must identify the ways in which increased productivity, quality, and financial performance can occur and decide that some of the gains should be shared with employees. The most critical step is to involve employees at all levels in the gainsharing process, often by establishing a gainsharing taskforce composed of managers and nonmanagers alike. Once the taskforce meets, there are two crucial decisions to be made: (1) How much gain is to be shared with employees? (2) What are the performance measures to be used?

Payouts of the gains can be made monthly, quarterly, semiannually, or annually, depending on management philosophy and the performance measures used. The more frequent the payouts, the greater the visibility of the rewards to employees. Therefore, given a choice, most firms with gainsharing plans have chosen to make the payouts more frequently than annually. The rewards can be distributed in four ways:

- A flat amount for all employees
- Same percentage of base salary for all employees
- Percentage of the gains by category of employees
- Amount or percentage based on individual performance against measures

The first two methods generally are preferred because they promote and reward teamwork and cooperation more than the other two methods.

Where performance measures are used, only those measures that employees actually can affect should be considered. Often, measures such as labor costs, overtime hours, and quality benchmarks are used. Both organizational measures and departmental measures may be used, with the gainsharing weighting being split between the two categories. Naturally, an individual's performance must be satisfactory in order for that individual to receive the gainsharing payments. Figure 14–4 shows that bonuses of all kinds as a proportion of payroll have been increasing throughout the decade.

SUCCESS IN GAINSHARING The success or failure of incentive programs begins with the culture of the organization. Putting a gainsharing program in autocratically or in desperation to save a badly managed firm virtually guarantees failure. Inadequate financial information systems, severe external competitive conditions, and government constraints also inhibit the success of gainsharing programs. Simply offering gainsharing payouts may not be enough to generate much participation in the plan. Negative attitudes toward the gainsharing plan and management can lead to nonparticipation by the employees.

However, gainsharing certainly *can* work to improve performance. At Panhandle Eastern Corporation of Houston (a natural gas firm), employees have turned into cost-cutting vigilantes as a result of their gainsharing program. Like most natural gas firms, Panhandle had no incentives to keep costs low when its rates were set by government regulations; but after deregulation and the institution of a gainsharing plan, cost control has become the rule. If Panhandle earns \$2.00 per share, each employee receives a bonus of 2% of his or her salary. If earnings are \$2.10 a share or more, the bonus is 3%. The first year of the program produced a 24% increase in earnings over the previous year. Upper management attributes that increase to aggressive cost-cutting efforts by employees.[16]

IMPROSHARE A number of gainsharing-type plans have been devised. One is Improshare, which stands for Improved Productivity through Sharing. Improshare was created by Mitchell Fein, an industrial engineer. It is similar to a piece-rate plan except that it rewards all workers in the organization. Input is measured in

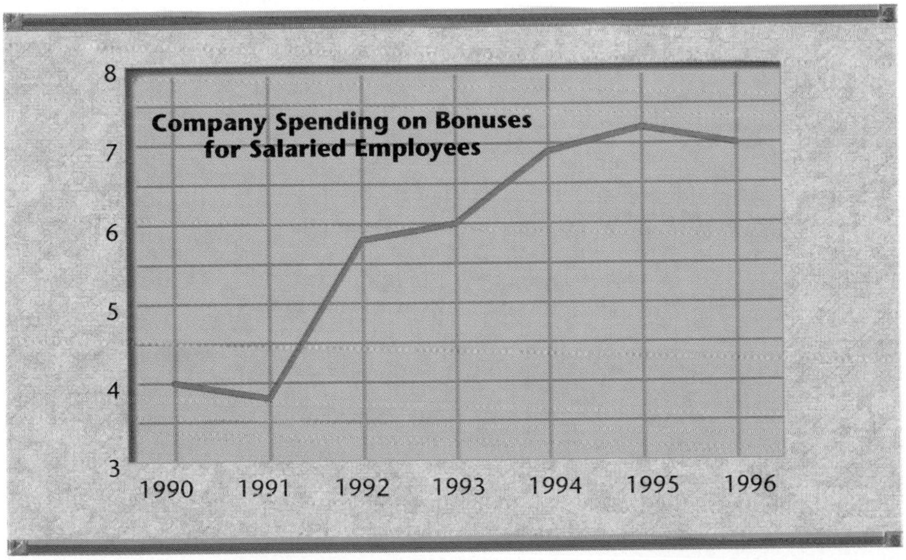

❖ FIGURE 14–4 ❖
INCREASE IN BONUS PAYMENTS IN THE 1990S AS A PERCENTAGE OF PAYROLL

SOURCE: Adapted from Hewitt Associates, *On Compensation,* September/October, 1995, 1.

hours and output in physical units. A standard is calculated and weekly bonuses are paid based on the extent to which the standard is exceeded. The impact of Improshare programs was identified in a survey of 112 firms using these programs. The firms had a median productivity increase of 8% during the first year and productivity gains of 17.5% by the third year.[17]

Scanlon Plan Since its development in 1927, the Scanlon plan has been implemented in many organizations, especially in smaller unionized industrial firms. The basic concept underlying the Scanlon plan is that efficiency depends on teamwork and plantwide cooperation. The plan has two main features: (1) a system of departmental committees and a plant screening committee to evaluate all cost-saving suggestions and (2) direct incentive rewards to all employees to improve efficiency.

The system is activated through departmental employee committees that receive and review cost-saving ideas submitted by employees. Suggestions beyond the scope of the departmental committees are passed to the plant screening committee for review. Savings that result from suggestions are passed on to all members of the organization.

Incentive rewards are paid to employees on the basis of improvements in preestablished ratios. Ratios of labor costs to total sales value or total production or total hours to total production are most commonly used. Savings due to differences between actual and expected ratios are placed in a bonus fund. A predetermined percentage of this fund is then split between employees and the organization.

The Scanlon plan is not a true profit-sharing plan, because employees receive incentive compensation for reducing labor costs, regardless of whether the organization ultimately makes a profit. Organizations that have implemented the Scanlon plan have experienced an increase in productivity and a decrease in labor costs. Also, employee attitudes have become more favorable, and cooperation between management and workers has increased.

Rucker Plan The Rucker plan, almost as old as the Scanlon plan, was developed in the 1930s by the economist Allan W. Rucker. The Scanlon formula measures performance against a standard of labor costs in relation to the dollar value of production, whereas the Rucker formula introduces a third variable: the dollar value of all materials, supplies, and services that the organization uses to make its product. The Rucker formula is:

$$\frac{\$\text{ Value of Labor Costs}}{\$\text{ Value of Production} - \$\text{ Value of Materials, Supplies, Services}}$$

The result is what economists call the "value added" to a product by the organization. The use of value added rather than the dollar value of production builds in an incentive to save on other inputs.

❖ Profit Sharing

Profit Sharing
A system to distribute a portion of the profits of the organization to employees.

As the name implies, **profit sharing** distributes a portion of organizational profits to employees. Typically, the percentage of the profits distributed to employees is agreed on by the end of the year before distribution. In some profit-sharing plans, employees receive portions of the profits at the end of the year; in others, the profits are deferred, placed in a fund, and made available to employees on retirement or on their leaving the organization. Figure 14–5 shows how profit-sharing plans can be set up.

Unions used to be skeptical of profit-sharing plans, because the system only works when there are profits to be shared. Often, the level of profits is influenced by factors not under the employees' control, such as marketing efforts, competition, and elements of executive compensation. However, in recent years, organized labor has supported profit-sharing plans in which employees' pay increases are tied to improved company performance.

❖ FIGURE 14–5 ❖
PROFIT-SHARING PLAN OPTIONS

HOW THE EMPLOYER MIGHT DETERMINE CONTRIBUTIONS TO PROFIT SHARING:
❖ Fixed Percentage of Profit ❖ Sliding Percentage Based on Sales or Return on Assets ❖ Unit Profits ❖ Some Other Formula
HOW PROFITS MIGHT BE ALLOCATED TO INDIVIDUAL EMPLOYEES:
❖ Equally to All Employees ❖ Based on Employee Earnings ❖ Based on Earnings and Years of Service ❖ Based on Contribution

OBJECTIVES AND DRAWBACKS OF PROFIT-SHARING PLANS The primary objectives of profit-sharing plans are to:

- ❖ Improve productivity
- ❖ Recruit or retain employees
- ❖ Improve product/service quality
- ❖ Improve employee morale

When used throughout an organization, including lower-echelon workers, profit-sharing plans can have some drawbacks. First, management must be willing to disclose financial and profit information to employees. As many people know, both the definition and level of profit can depend on the accounting system used and decisions made. Therefore, to be credible, management must be willing to disclose sufficient financial and profit information to alleviate the skepticism of employees, particularly if profit-sharing levels are reduced from previous years. Second, profits may vary a great deal from year to year—resulting in windfalls and losses beyond the employees' control. Third, the payoff may be seen as too far removed from employees' efforts to serve as a strong link between better performance and higher rewards. However, there is evidence that even when effective programs have been stopped, there may be positive long-term improvement in performance that continues.[18]

❖ EMPLOYEE STOCK OWNERSHIP PLANS (ESOPS)

A common type of profit sharing is the **employee stock ownership plan (ESOP)**. An ESOP is designed to give employees stock ownership of the organization for which they work, thereby increasing their commitment, loyalty, and effort. During one recent 17-year period, more than 9,000 ESOP plans were established, with some being used by employees to buy out firms that might otherwise have been closed.[19]

❖Employee Stock Ownership Plan (ESOP)
A plan whereby employees gain stock ownership in the organization for which they work.

ESTABLISHING AN ESOP An organization establishes an ESOP by using its stock as collateral to borrow capital from a financial institution. Once the loan repayment begins through the use of company profits, a certain amount of stock is released and allocated to an employee stock ownership trust (ESOT). Employees are assigned shares of company stock, kept in the trust, based on length of service and pay level. On retirement, death, or separation from the organization, employees or their beneficiaries can sell the stock back to the trust or on the open market, if the stock is publicly traded.[20]

Employee stock ownership plans are subject to certain tax laws. Generally, the employers who have treated all employees alike are most advantaged. Those that provide different levels of benefits for different groups of employees are penalized in the tax laws.

Advantages and Disadvantages of ESOPs Establishing an ESOP creates several advantages. The major one is that the firm can receive favorable tax treatment of the earnings earmarked for use in the ESOP. Second, an ESOP gives employees a "piece of the action" so that they can share in the growth and profitability of their firm. Employee ownership may be effective in motivating employees to work harder.[21]

Almost everyone loves the concept of employee ownership as a kind of "people's capitalism." However, the sharing also can be a disadvantage because employees may feel "forced" to join, thus placing their financial future at greater risk. Both their wages or salaries and their retirement benefits depend on the performance of the organization. This concentration is even riskier for retirees because the value of pension fund assets also depends on how well the company does.

Another drawback is that ESOPs have been used as a management tool to fend off unfriendly takeover attempts. Holders of employee-owned stock often align with management to turn down bids that would benefit outside stockholders but would replace management and restructure operations. Surely, ESOPs were not created to entrench inefficient management. Despite these disadvantages, ESOPs have grown in popularity.[22]

FASB Rules on ESOPs Perhaps in part because of the increase in popularity of ESOPs, companies have been required to disclose how much they would have earned if the stock options they gave employees had been charged against company income. The Financial Accounting Standards Board (FASB) has been concerned that stock options were treated as a "gift from the gods," entailing no cost. Employees got richer, but the company did not record an expense and was apparently none the poorer. The FASB will now require companies to report the value of the stock options they give employees—but there is some real controversy over how to value the options. The net effect may be to chill company enthusiasm for ESOPs.[23]

❖ Do Incentive Plans Work?

Incentive plans are not new, but recent concern with linking performance and pay have brought about a renewed interest in incentives. From individual bonuses to employee ownership of the company, a variety of incentives are being used to improve productivity. The HR Perspective "Research on Cross-Cultural Reward Preferences" shows that the American culture and the Chinese culture may be undergoing changes in the assumptions they make about incentives at work.

There are, of course, successes and failures. In general, though, neither of the polar extremes—the view that incentives do not work versus the view that incentives are a panacea—appears to be the case. The key to success seems to be to combine incentives with employee participation in the process. In addition, it is clear that worker participation programs are "fragile and difficult to sustain."[24] Incentives do work under the proper conditions mentioned earlier, but administering the system of incentives is a challenge.

❖ Executive Compensation

Many organizations, especially large ones, administer executive compensation somewhat differently than compensation for lower-level employees. An executive typically is someone in the top two levels of an organization, such as Presi-

HR PERSPECTIVE

Research on Cross-Cultural Reward Preference

Chao Chen recently studied the current reward allocation preferences of employees in two U.S. companies and three Chinese companies as reported in the *Academy of Management Journal*. The two nations are known to have different traditions of individualism and collectivism. Previous research has shown that these factors are tied to the way employees feel rewards should be given. Cross-cultural studies have shown that Chinese workers have preferred allocations that use equal treatment as the norm. Americans however, generally prefer different levels of reward based on contribution to the organization (i.e., the best producer gets the most reward).

But reward systems are changing in both countries. In many cases U.S. companies are changing their individual-based reward systems to reflect a team-based approach in an effort to foster cooperation. Chinese companies have been changing reward systems that treat everyone the same in an effort to establish individual responsibility and competition. This reflects a change in China from enterprises that were essentially political and welfare institutions before 1978 to businesses that emphasize economic goals—even profit. Reduced protection by the state and competitive open markets in many industries have created economic gains, and labor productivity has in many cases achieved priority over social and ideological considerations.

The three Chinese companies in Chao Chen's study (a steel manufacturer, an oil company, and a transportation company) had been undergoing change since 1980. Employees in these companies and in the two U.S. companies were asked to play the role of the company president and make some decisions about how rewards should be allocated. The rewards were material (pay/bonus) and socioemotional (managerial friendliness or an invitation to a party).

The Chinese people emphasized the economic goals of the organization and favored giving out both the material and socioemotional rewards differentially on the basis of contribution to the company. The Americans agreed that performance should be the basis for allocating material rewards but preferred that everyone be treated the same in allocating the socioemotional rewards.[25] These results might not have been predicted 10 years ago.

dent or Senior Vice-President. Executive compensation programs often include incentives, as well as other forms of compensation. Two objectives influence executive compensation: (1) tying the overall performance of the organization over a period of time to the compensation paid executives, and (2) ensuring that the total compensation packages for executives are competitive with the compensation packages in other firms that might employ them.

❖ Board Members' Compensation

Although they are not executives of the firm, outside members of the board of directors receive compensation as well. A recent commission report on pay for members of Boards of Directors recommended linking board pay more closely to shareholder interest. It was recommended that directors be paid primarily in stock.[26] That recommendation seems to give support to a trend that has apparently begun already, as the proportion of companies providing equity-based pay for directors has jumped from 63% to 78% of the companies paying directors.[27]

❖ The Compensation Committee

A **compensation committee** usually is a subgroup of the board of directors composed of directors who are not officers of the firm. Compensation committees generally make recommendations to the board of directors on overall pay policies, salaries for top officers, supplemental compensation such as stock options and bonuses, and additional perquisites ("perks") for executives. As the HR Perspective on the next page indicates, the "independence" of board compensation committees increasingly has been criticized.

Compensation Committee
Usually a subgroup of the board of directors composed of directors who are not officers of the firm.

HR PERSPECTIVE

Ethical Issues Regarding the Independence of Board Compensation Committees

Critics point out that many U.S. corporate CEOs make 95 to 150 times more than average workers in their firms make, whereas in Japan the ratio is 15 to 1 and in Europe 20 to 1. Also, Japanese CEOs are paid about one-third of what U.S. CEOs of comparable-sized firms are paid. Stock options are seldom used in Japan and many other countries, and base salaries and bonuses often are significantly lower as well.

A major cause for the high total compensation for CEOs in the United States is the use of executive stock options, which give executives the right to purchase shares of corporate stock at a specific price. For example, suppose a CEO has an option granted in 1992 to purchase 10,000 shares for $10 per share in the future. If the price of the stock rises to $50 per share by 1997, then the executive can exercise the option and make $40 per share, or $400,000. Supporters of stock options point out that the company shareholders also benefit by a $40 per share gain. However, critics say that giving one person that much credit for improving the performance in a corporation employing 20,000 people is not reasonable.

One major concern voiced by many critics is that the base pay and bonuses of CEOs often are set by board compensation committee members, many of whom are CEOs of other companies with similar compensation packages. Also, the compensation advisors and consultants to the CEOs often collect large fees, and critics charge that those fees distort the objectivity of the advice given. For example, one of the directors on the compensation committee of Coca-Cola heads a firm that received $24 million in investment fees in six years from Coke. Similarly, the law firm of a director at Philip Morris received about $25 million in fees over a three-year period. Situations such as these give the impression of self-serving conflicts of interest.

A related problem exists when the board compensation committee in one firm is composed solely of executives of other companies, each of whose compensation often is compared against the compensation of the others. A director obviously may have self-serving reasons for supporting higher compensation for executives, so that the director will benefit when the compensation committee in his own firm looks at his compensation package. Also, if an executive from Firm A sits on the board compensation committee of Company X, and the CEO of Company X sits on the compensation committee of Firm A, how "independent" is each of them likely to be?

To counter criticism, some corporations are changing the composition of the compensation committee and giving it more independence. Some of the changes include prohibiting "insider" company officers and board members from serving on compensation committees and empowering the compensation committee to hire pay and compensation consultants without executive management involvement.[28] Further, the SEC is toughening its proxy-disclosure requirements about director pay.

❖ Elements of Executive Compensation

At the heart of most executive compensation plans is the idea that executives should be rewarded if the organization grows in profitability and value over a period of years. Because many executives are in high tax brackets, their compensation often is provided in ways that offer significant tax savings. Therefore, their total compensation packages are more significant than their base pay. Especially when the base salary is $1 million or more, the executive often is interested in the mix of items in the total package, including current and deferred compensation. Figure 14–6 shows the components of executive compensation, which are *salaries,* annual *bonuses, long-term incentives, benefits,* and *perquisites.*

❖ Executive Salaries

A provision of the 1993 tax act prohibits a publicly traded company from deducting pay of more than $1 million for each of its top five officers unless that pay is based on performance criteria approved by outside directors and shareholders. A recent study shows that about 75% of such companies had obtained shareholder approval for their executive pay plans.[29]

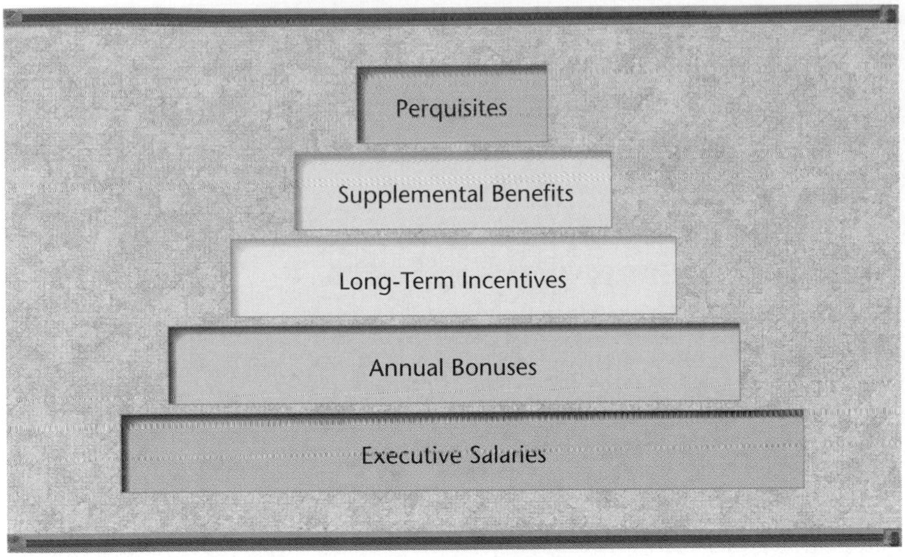

❖ FIGURE 14–6 ❖
EXECUTIVE COMPENSATION COMPONENTS

Salaries of executives vary by type of job, size of organization, region of the country, and industry. On average, salaries make up about one-third of the typical top executive's annual compensation total.

❖ EXECUTIVE BONUS PLANS

Because executive performance may be difficult to determine, bonus compensation must reflect some kind of performance measure if it is to be meaningful. As an example, a retail chain with over 250 stores ties annual bonuses for managers to store profitability. The bonuses have amounted to as much as 35% of a store manager's base salary.

Bonuses for executives can be determined in several ways. A discretionary system whereby bonuses are awarded based on the judgments of the chief executive officer and the board of directors is one way. However, the absence of formal, measurable targets is a major drawback of this approach. Also, as noted, bonuses can be tied to specific measures, such as return on investment, earnings per share, or net profits before taxes. More complex systems create bonus pools and thresholds above which bonuses are computed. Whatever method is used, it is important to describe it so that executives trying to earn bonuses understand the plan; otherwise, the incentive effect will be diminished. Figure 14–7 shows the proportion of compensation given as salary and other compensation in the United States and selected other countries during the early 1990s.

❖ PERFORMANCE INCENTIVES—LONG TERM VERSUS SHORT TERM

Performance-based incentives, often in the form of stock options, attempt to tie executive compensation to the long-term growth and success of the organization. However, whether the emphasis is really on the long term or merely represents a series of short-term rewards is controversial. Short-term rewards based on quarterly or annual performance may not result in the kind of long-run-oriented decisions necessary for the company to continue to do well.

A **stock option** gives an individual the right to buy stock in a company, usually at an advantageous price. Different types of stock options have been used depending on the tax laws in effect. Stock options have increased in use as a

❖**Stock Option**
A plan that gives an individual the right to buy stock in a company, usually at a fixed price for a period of time.

❖ FIGURE 14–7 ❖
PROPORTION OF EXECUTIVE COMPENSATION GIVEN AS SALARY

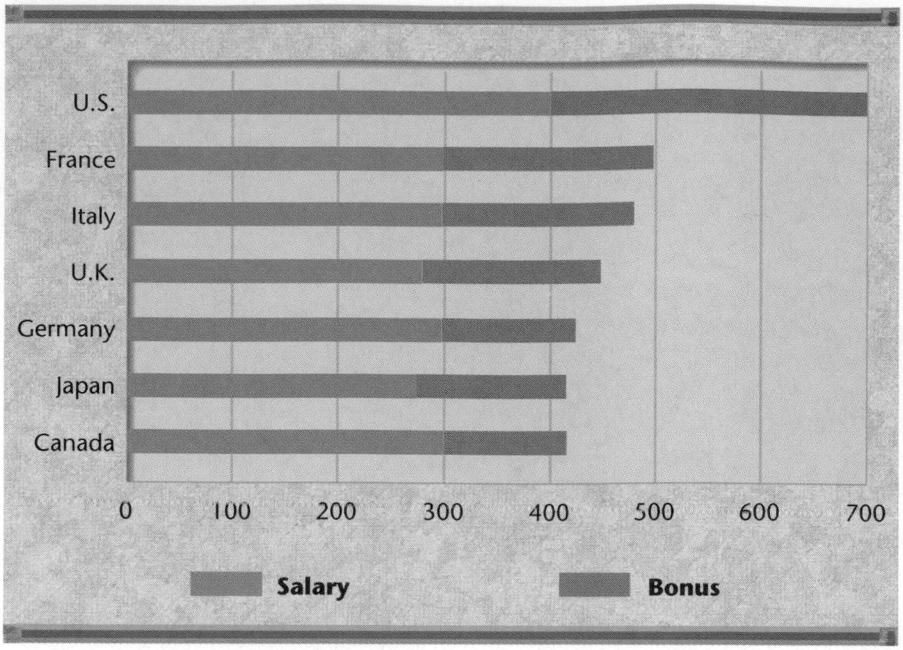

SOURCE: Adapted from J. Abowd and M. Bognano, "Nice Work," *The Economist,* December 10, 1994, 67.

component of executive compensation during the past 10 years, and employers may use a variety of very specialized and technical approaches to them, which are beyond the scope of this discussion. However, the overall trend is toward using stock options as performance-based long-term incentives.

Most privately held companies also try to base long-term incentive programs on ownership. One study found that, among the surveyed firms, where CEOs had greater levels of ownership, the firms performed better.[30] Where stock is closely held, firms may grant "stock equivalencies" in the form of *phantom stock* or *appreciation rights.* These plans pay recipients the cash value of increased value of the stock in the future, determined by a base valuation made at the time the phantom stock or share appreciation rights are given.

❖ EXECUTIVE BENEFITS

As with non-executive employees, benefits for executives may take several forms including traditional retirement, health insurance, vacations, and so on. However, executive benefits may include some things that other employee benefits do not. For example, executive health plans with no co-payments, deductibles, or limits on physician choice are popular among small and middle-sized businesses. Corporate-owned life insurance on the life of the executive is popular and pays *both* the executive's estate *and* the company in the event of death. Trusts of various kinds may be designed by the company to help the executive deal with estate issues. Deferred compensation is another possible means used to help executives with tax liabilities caused by incentive compensation plans.

❖ EXECUTIVE PERQUISITES

***Perquisites (Perks)** Special benefits—usually noncash items—for executives.

In addition to the regular benefits received by all employees, executives often receive benefits called perquisites. **Perquisites (perks)** are special executive benefits—usually noncash items. Perks are useful in tying executives to organizations and in demonstrating their importance to the companies. It is the status enhancement value of perks that is important to many executives. Visible symbols of status allow executives to be seen as "very important people (VIPs)" both inside and outside their organizations. In addition, perks can offer substantial tax savings because many perks are not taxed as income. Figure 14–8 lists some perks that are commonly available.

A special perk available to some executives, a **golden parachute,** provides protection and security to executives in the event that they lose their jobs or their firms are acquired by other firms. Typically, employment contracts are written to give special compensation to executives if they are negatively affected in an acquisition or merger.

Golden parachutes often are criticized for giving executives protection, while lower and middle-level managers and other employees are left vulnerable when mergers or acquisitions occur. As a result, some firms have established **silver parachutes,** severance and benefit plans to protect nonexecutives if their firms are acquired by other firms. For example, Herman Miller, a Zeeland, Michigan, manufacturer of office furniture, has designed a generous severance pay and benefits plan that goes into effect if a hostile takeover threatens any of the 3,500 employees' jobs. Whether golden or silver, the parachute phenomenon is a clear response to the takeover strategy that many organizations have faced.[31]

❖ FIGURE 14–8 ❖
COMMON EXECUTIVE PERKS

Physical Exams
Company Car
Financial Counseling
Company Plane
First-Class Air Travel
Income Tax Preparation
Club Memberships
Personal Liability Insurance
Estate Planning
Travel for Spouse
Chauffeur Service

Golden Parachute
A severance benefit that provides protection and security to executives in the event that they lose their jobs or their firms are acquired by other firms and they are negatively affected.

Silver Parachute
A severance and benefit plan to protect nonexecutives if their firms are acquired by other firms.

❖ THE REASONABLENESS OF EXECUTIVE COMPENSATION

A number of criticisms have been directed at executive compensation. One is that it does not offer really long-term rewards. Instead, performance in a given year may lead to large rewards even though corporate performance over time may be mediocre. This difference is especially apparent if the yearly measures are carefully chosen. Executives can even manipulate earnings per share by selling assets, liquidating inventories, or reducing research and development expenditures. All these actions may make organizational performance look better, but they may impair the long-term growth of the organization.[32]

Another potential problem is that, although supplements such as bonuses and stock options are supposed to be tied to the performance of the organization, research results conflict as to whether or not this linkage exists.

For critics, the existence of perks highlights problems with the overall compensation of executives, particularly if the executives continue to receive the perks even when their organizations are performing poorly. In the future, it is likely that more restrictions will be placed on the tax-deductibility of some perks, just as excessive executive compensation has been attacked. However, the spread of performance-oriented incentives throughout the organization at all levels may help to mute some of the criticism.

Overall, the reasonableness of executive compensation is often calculated through market salary surveys, but these usually provide a range of salaries that requires interpretation. A recent tax court case suggested some interesting criteria to determine if executive pay was "reasonable" in a specific instance:

- Would another company hire this person as CEO?
- Is the company so tenuous that a premium must be paid?
- How does this compensation compare with that in similar companies?
- Is the CEO's pay consistent with pay for the other employees?
- What would an investor pay for this CEO's level of performance?[33]

SUMMARY

❖ An incentive is compensation received for efforts beyond normal performance expectations.

❖ Three types of incentive systems are individual, group, and organizational.

❖ An effective incentive program should recognize organizational culture and resources, tie incentives to performance, be kept current, recognize individual differences, and separate plan payments from base pay.

❖ Individual incentives include piece-rate systems, commissions, bonuses, and special incentive programs.

❖ To overcome some problems associated with individual incentives, team-based incentive systems encourage and reward teamwork and group effort.

❖ One organizational incentive system is gainsharing, which provides rewards based on greater-than-expected gains in profits and/or productivity.

❖ Types of gainsharing plans include Improshare, Scanlon, and Rucker plans.

❖ Profit-sharing plans set aside a portion of the profits earned by organizations for distribution to employees.

❖ An employee stock ownership plan (ESOP) enables employees to gain ownership in the firm for which they work.

❖ Executive compensation must be viewed as a total package composed of salaries, bonuses, long-term performance-based incentives, benefits, and perquisites (perks).

❖ A compensation committee, which is a subgroup of the board of directors, has authority over executive compensation plans.

❖ Performance-based incentives often represent a significant portion of an executive's compensation package. Stock options, phantom stock, and stock appreciation rights are widely used.

❖ Perks provide additional noncash compensation to executives.

Review and Discussion Questions

√ 1. Identify what an incentive is and discuss why team-based and organizational incentives are growing in usage.
√ 2. Give several examples of individual incentives that you have received or that have been used in an organization by which you were employed. What problems did you observe with them?
3. What are the advantages and disadvantages of using a piece-rate incentive plan?
√ 4. Why do you think that increased emphasis on productivity in the United States has led to greater interest in gainsharing?
5. Why would an employee stock ownership plan (ESOP) be seen by employees both as an attraction and as a risk?
6. Locate a corporate annual report and review it to identify the components of executive compensation discussed in it.
7. What is your view of criticisms of board compensation committees? What changes would you recommend?

Terms to Know

bonus **415**
commission **414**
compensation committee **423**
differential piece-rate system **413**
draw **414**
employee stock ownership plan (ESOP) **421**
gainsharing **418**
golden parachute **427**
incentive **410**
performance incentives **410**
perquisites (perks) **426**
profit sharing **420**
silver parachute **427**
stock option **425**
straight piece-rate system **413**

CASE

INCENTIVES PAY OFF FOR VIKING FREIGHT SYSTEMS

The success of an incentive plan can be measured by a number of different methods. By virtually all measures, the incentive pay program at Viking Freight System has been very successful. Viking Freight is a trucking and shipping carrier based in San Jose, California, with 4,500 employees.

The deregulation of the trucking industry changed the business environment for most trucking firms, including Viking. To respond to those changes, Terry Stambaugh (Vice-President of Human Resources), Ron Pelzel (Executive Vice-President), and Phil Smith (Vice-President of Corporate Planning) reviewed the incentive compensation programs at Viking. Their review clarified that employee productivity and performance were critical to success in a deregulated industry. To reward employees for superior performance and productivity, they developed the Viking Performance Earnings Plan (VPEP).

In VPEP, all Viking employees except corporate officers receive monthly rewards for achievement of objectives. Once employees complete a 90-day probation program, they are eligible for VPEP. The officers have a separate Management Incentive Compensation Plan (MICP).

Under VPEP, each employee group has its own set of objectives appropriate for its operating area. For instance, each freight terminal has its own objectives, and appropriate objectives are set for maintenance, sales, claims, and other departments. Performance is measured every four weeks, and payments are made on the accomplishment of objectives for that four-week period. The performance measures and standards are established by Viking's performance engineers and executive committee. For support staff in clerical and other areas where it is difficult to identify specific work standards, the payouts are based on the operating ratio of the firm. This ratio is as follows:

$$\frac{\text{Operating Expenses}}{\text{Revenues before Interest and Taxes}}$$

The ratio is applicable for other areas as well, because the operating ratio for a four-week period must be below 95% (including the cost of VPEP payouts) for there to be any payouts, regardless of group or individual performance. Also, any employee who has an avoidable accident forfeits the VPEP payout for the four-week period.

Incentive payouts are computed as a percentage of the employee's four-week gross pay as follows:

Hourly employees	7.5%
Salaried supervisors	11.25
Salespeople	12.25
Department managers	15.0
Terminal managers	20.0

The criteria for freight terminal performance (with weights) are:

Revenue attainment	30%
Labor performance	30
On-time service	30
Claims ratio	10

This system is communicated clearly to all terminal employees, and they know how important performance in each area is.

Incentives Pay Off for Viking Freight Systems, continued

When the plan was implemented, the VPEP payouts averaged less than $50. Three years later, the average payout check had increased to over $125 per period, which represents about 5.5% of the average gross pay. More importantly, corporate performance rose and remains at a high level. For example, for a recent year, Viking had an on-time ratio of 98.1% and a claims ratio of .9%, both much better than is typical in the trucking industry.[34]

❖ *Questions*

1. What is the importance of having separate incentive programs for corporate officers and for all other employees?
2. What is the significance of saying that the level for the operating ratio must be below 95% or no payouts occur, regardless of group or individual performance?
3. Discuss why you believe VPEP had a key role in generating Viking's superior corporate performance.

❖ *Notes*

1. Adapted from Bob Ortega, "Life without Sam," *The Wall Street Journal,* January 4, 1995, 1.
2. "Performance-Based Incentives Spreading through the Ranks," *Employee Benefit News,* February 1993, 45.
3. R. C. Mayer, et al., "An Integrative Model of Organizational Trust," *Academy of Management Review,* July 1995, 709–734.
4. Susan Sonnesyn Brooks, "Incentives Research," *HR Magazine,* April 1994, 41.
5. H. Glaeser and J. Miller, "Recognition Awards and Incentives," *Human Resource Executive,* November 15, 1993, 93.
6. Luis R. Gomez-Mejia and David B. Balkin, *Compensation, Organizational Strategy, and Firm Performance* (Cincinnati: South-Western Publishing Co., 1992), 260–261.
7. Thomas B. Wilson, "Is It Time to Eliminate the Piece-Rate Incentive System?" *Compensation and Benefits Review,* March–April 1992, 43–49.
8. T. M. Welbourne and D. M. Cable, "Group Incentives and Pay Satisfaction: Understanding the Relationship through an Identity Theory Perspective," *Human Relations* 48 (1995), 711–725.
9. Adapted from Shari Caudron, "Variable-Pay Program Increases Taco Bell's Profits," *Personnel Journal,* June 1993, 641.
10. H. Gleckman, et al., "Bonus Pay: Buzzword or Bonanza?" *Business Week,* November 14, 1995, 62.
11. S. B. Knouse, "Variations on Skill Based Pay for Total Quality Management," *Advanced Management Journal* 60 (1995), 34–37.
12. Alex Markels and Joann S. Lublin, "Longevity-Reward Programs Get Short Shrift," *The Wall Street Journal,* April 27, 1995, B1.
13. Joann S. Lublin, "My Colleague, My Boss," *Wall Street Journal,* April 12, 1995, R4.
14. John A. Wagner III, "Studies of Individualism-Collectivism: Effects on Cooperation in Groups," *Academy of Management Journal* 38 (1995), 152–172.
15. Jerry L. McAdams and Elizabeth J. Hawk, "Capitalizing on Human Assets through Performance-Based Rewards," *ACA Journal,* Autumn 1992, 60–72.
16. E. Nelson, "Gas Company's Gain Sharing Plan," *The Wall Street Journal,* September 29, 1995, B1.
17. R. T. Kaufman, "The Effects of Improshare on Productivity," *Industrial and Labor Relations Review* 45 (1992), 311–322.
18. T. R. Stenhouse, "The Long and Short of Gainsharing," *Academy of Management Executive,* February 1995, 77.
19. *Employee Benefits News,* June 1993, 3.
20. Blackman and Associates P.C., "Viewpoint on Value," November/December 1995, 1–3.
21. J. S. Hirsch, "Avis Employees Find Stock Ownership Is a Mixed Blessing," *The Wall Street Journal,* May 2, 1995, B1.
22. J. C. Szabo, "Giving Workers a Company Stake," *Nation's Business,* June 1994, 54–55.
23. R. Lowenstein, "The Cost of Employee Stock Options, Now Hidden, Might Earn a Footnote," *The Wall Street Journal,* July 6, 1995, C1.
24. "A Firm of Their Own," *The Economist,* June 11, 1994, 59.
25. Chao C. Chen, "New Trends in Reward Allocation Preferences: A Sino–U.S. Comparison," *Academy of Management Journal* 38 (1995), 408–428.
26. Joann S. Lublin, "Give the Board Fewer Perks, a Panel Urges," *The Wall Street Journal,* June 19, 1995, B1.
27. "Directors Take Stock," *Business Week,* July 17, 1995, 10.
28. Lawrence M. Baytos, "Board Compensation Committees: Collaboration or Confrontation?" *Compensation and Benefits Review,* May–June 1991, 33–38.
29. "Executive Pay Plans," *The Wall Street Journal,* June 7, 1995, A1.
30. Gene Koretz, "When the Boss Has a Big Stake," *Business Week,* February 13, 1995, 28.
31. M. Dunlop, "Tax-Effective Executive Benefits," *Employee Benefits Journal,* June 1994, 29–35.
32. J. Welsh, "Think Short," *The Wall Street Journal,* April 12, 1995, R6.
33. Ira Weinberg and John Heller, "How to Determine the Reasonableness of Executive Pay," *Journal of Compensation and Benefits,* May–June 1994, 39–44.
34. Adapted from Terry Stambaugh, "An Incentive Pay Success Story," *Personnel Journal,* April 1992, 48–54.

CHAPTER 15

EMPLOYEE BENEFITS

After you have read this chapter, you should be able to . . .

- Define *benefit* and identify approximate average benefit costs.
- Identify strategic reasons an employer might choose to offer benefits.
- Distinguish between mandated and voluntary benefits and list three of each.
- Describe two security benefits.
- Explain why health-care cost management has become important and list some methods of achieving it.
- List and define at least six pension-related terms.
- Discuss several types of financial and related benefits.
- Identify typical time-off benefits.
- Discuss benefits communication and flexible benefits as considerations in benefits administration.

HR in Transition

Employee Benefits After Merger, Acquisition, or Spin-Off

Mergers and acquisitions have been numerous for the last decade, and the trend shows little evidence of ceasing in the 1990s. Such combinations often are driven by the attraction of economies of scale and increased market share. The jointed companies usually want to combine their benefit plans to reduce administrative costs and to provide the same benefits for all employees. But often unnoticed in the atmosphere surrounding the merger or take-over are the difficulty and potential costs of merging benefits programs.

The "buzzword" in the benefits industry to describe an ideal merger of benefits is "seamless." An uneventful transition is less disruptive for employees, who will not be caught in the "seam" between plans. But seamless benefits combinations are difficult, because dealing with benefits plans is probably one of the most complicated areas of a merger.

But seamless benefits combinations are difficult, because dealing with benefits plans is probably one of the most complicated areas of a merger.

Hidden liabilities make costing the plans difficult initially, and similarities and differences in coverage for both active and retired employees require attention. For example, unfunded retiree medical obligations can be a substantial cost and are difficult to value. Health insurance consolidation regarding deductibles, preexisting conditions, claims in progress, and compatible coverage can be very difficult and expensive to resolve in a seamless fashion.

Pension plans can be just as complex. Will credit toward retirement be given for service with the prior employer? Are there termination liabilities in an acquired company's pension plan? Is an existing plan appropriate for the combined company's future operations?

These and other complexities have caused some companies to rethink benefits altogether when organizational changes occur. For example, Capitol One Financial Corporation was formed after a spin-off from Signet Bank/Virginia. The new company felt it was constrained by Signet Bank's HR management practices. The practices were appropriate for a retail bank but did not fit for an information-based firm that developed new customized financial products, needed a high level of innovation and flexibility, and hired very analytical, well-educated, quantitatively oriented employees. Within a year after the spin-off, Capitol One had changed its approach to compensation by reducing or eliminating "entitlement" benefits such as life insurance and supplemental retirement. Changes were made (with input from employees) in paid time-off, medical programs, and others. Costs were offset by reductions in some plans and administrative savings. The philosophy of the benefits program shifted from being based on years of service to offering stock-based plans tied to increases in the shareholder value of the company.

Mergers, acquisitions, and spin-offs present difficulties in merging or redoing benefits plans. But they also present opportunities to rethink what the employers want to get for their benefits dollars and why the benefits are offered.[1]

> "We used to call them "fringe benefits," but we quit using the word "fringe" when we saw the magnitude of that figure."
>
> —*James Morris*

Employee benefits are a smorgasbord of indirect compensations, such as pensions, health insurance, time-off with pay, and others. A **benefit** is a form of indirect compensation. Unlike employers in many other countries, in the United States employers have become a major provider of benefits for citizens. In many other nations, citizens and employers are taxed to pay for the government's provision of such benefits as health care and retirement. Although U.S. employers are required to provide some benefits, they voluntarily provide others.

Benefit
Indirect compensation given to employees for organizational membership.

❖ Benefits in Perspective

Why do employers provide benefits? Individuals could purchase their own health insurance and save for their own retirement. Certainly the money that employers spend on benefits could be given instead to employees in cash, and they could spend that cash for any benefits they might want. That amount is not insignificant. It is most recently estimated at $14,678 per full-time employee. Total benefits payments as a percentage of payroll average 40.7%[2] Figure 15–1 shows how the average benefit dollar is spent.

Benefits must be viewed as part of total compensation, and total compensation is one of the key strategic decision areas in human resources. **Total compensation** includes money paid directly (such as wages and salaries), money paid indirectly (such as benefits), and nonmonetary rewards (such as praise, job satisfaction, and recognition). Too often, both managers and employees think of only wages and salaries as total compensation and fail to consider the additional 40% contributed by benefits.

Total Compensation
The sum of money paid directly, money paid indirectly, and nonmonetary rewards.

❖ Figure 15–1 ❖
How the Benefit Dollar Is Spent

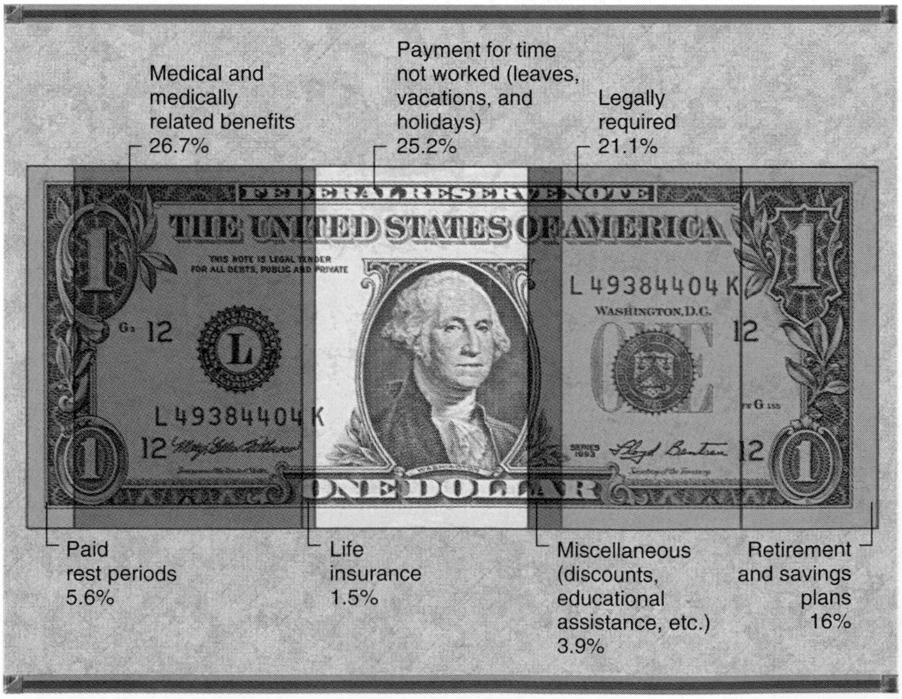

SOURCE: *Employee Benefits, 1994 Edition,* (Washington, D.C.: U.S. Chamber of Commerce, 1994). Used with permission.

❖ Strategy and Total Compensation

Total labor compensation amounts to 60% of total costs in many manufacturing operations and even more in some service operations. For example, around 80% of the U.S. Post Office budget is labor compensation. Because total compensation is such a significant part of organizational costs, and because benefits are a significant part of total compensation, several strategic concerns about benefits should be addressed:

- What is expected from benefits?
- What is an appropriate mix of benefits?
- How much total compensation, including benefits, should be provided?
- What part should benefits comprise of the total compensation of individuals?
- What expense levels are acceptable for each benefit offered?
- Why is each type of benefit offered?
- Which employees should be given or offered which benefits?
- What is being received in return for each benefit?
- How does having a comprehensive benefits package aid in minimizing turnover or maximizing recruiting and retention of employees?
- How flexible should the package of benefits be?

❖ Strategic Reasons for Offering Benefits

Major benefits attempt to protect employees and their dependents from financial risk associated with illness, disability, unemployment, and old age. From management's perspective, benefits are thought to contribute to several strategic goals:

- *Help attract employees.* An employer with a more attractive benefits package may have a differential advantage over other employers in hiring qualified employees *if* the prospective employees know about the advantage.
- *Help retain employees.* An employee who receives benefits such as profit sharing, stock ownership, and elder care may have difficulty finding a job with the same total compensation elsewhere. In fact, such benefits may create "golden handcuffs."
- *Elevate the image of the organization with employees and other organizations.* Image may contribute to the competitive edge in HR matters, or it may not, but some employers value being able to cultivate an image of generosity and demonstrating care for their employees. Concern with image drives benefits programs more than do rational economic concerns in some organizations.
- *Increase job satisfaction.* Benefits can contribute to employees' overall good feelings toward the employer *if* the employees are aware of the benefits they receive. However, research suggests that many employees do not know exactly what benefits they receive or their value, leading to the description of benefits as a "hidden paycheck."[3]

❖ Historical Reasons for Offering Benefits

Historically, benefits were not employers' primary compensation components. In 1929, wages and salaries accounted for 99% of the total compensation in the private sector. It was not until the period of the 1930s through the 1950s that benefits really became widely established. Several developments occurred during that period to encourage employers to include benefits as part of the compensathat period to encourage employers to include benefits as part of the compensation package.

Wage Controls During both World War II and the Korean War, wage and price controls constrained employers' ability to give pay raises. A pension plan, more vacation time, or sick leave might be used to keep or attract good employees who otherwise would leave because their wages could not be raised.

Unions During this period, unions gained steadily in power. Both to avoid further unionization and as a result of bargaining with union representatives, employers added benefits. Management found that benefits were highly desired by employees.

❖ Taxation As a Reason to Offer Benefits

Benefits generally are not taxed as income to employees. For this reason, they represent a somewhat more valuable reward to employees than an equivalent cash payment. For example, assume that employee Henry Schmidt is in a 25% tax bracket. If Henry earns an extra $400, he must pay $100 in taxes on this amount (disregarding exemptions). But if his employer provides prescription drug coverage in a benefit plan, and he receives the $400 as payments for prescription drugs, he is not taxed on the amount; he receives the value of the entire $400. This feature makes benefits a desirable form of compensation to employees, and more benefits are more desirable.

❖ Competition

Some employers have chosen to recruit in difficult labor markets on the basis of their excellent benefits plans. Wellness programs, child care, flexible benefits, and profit sharing are viewed positively by certain segments of the potential pool of employees. Employers that offer these benefits may be more attractive if base pay is similar with competing firms.

❖ Federal Social Legislation and Benefits

A variety of laws, from the Social Security Act, to the Family/Medical Leave Act have required that certain employers provide benefits to certain employees. These laws are covered in this chapter. The number and total cost of mandated benefits has increased over the years, causing the total cost of keeping employees on the job to increase as well, even for employers who offer no voluntary benefits. As a result, a growing number of employers have begun to have existing employees work overtime rather than hiring new employees in an attempt to save on such benefit costs.[4]

❖ Legally Mandated Benefits

Mandated Benefits
Those benefits which employers in the United States must provide to employees by law.

Mandated benefits are those benefits which employers in the United States must provide to employees by law. Social Security and unemployment insurance are funded through a tax paid by the employer based on the employee's compensation. Worker's compensation laws exist in all states. In addition, employers must offer unpaid leave to employees during certain medical or family difficulties. Other mandated benefits are available through Medicare, which provides health care for those 65 and over. It is funded in part through an employer tax through Social Security. The Consolidated Omnibus Budget Reconciliation Act

(COBRA) mandates that an employer extend health-care coverage to employees after they leave the organization. The following sections explain many of these requirements in detail.

Mandated benefits have been *proposed* for many other areas, but as yet none of the proposals has been adopted. Areas in which coverage has been proposed include:

- Universal health-care benefits for all workers
- Child-care assistance
- Pension plan coverage that can be transferred by workers who change jobs
- Core benefits for part-time employees working at least 500 hours per year

A major reason for these proposals is that federal and state governments want to shift many of the social costs for health care and other expenditures to employers. This shift would relieve some of the budgetary pressures facing governments to raise taxes and cut spending.

❖ COBRA Provisions

Legal requirements in the Consolidated Omnibus Budget Reconciliation Act (COBRA) require that most employers (except churches and the federal government) with 20 or more employees offer *extended health-care coverage* to the following groups:

- Employees who voluntarily or involuntarily quit, except those terminated for "gross misconduct."
- Widowed or divorced spouses and dependent children of former or current employees.
- Retirees and their spouses whose health-care coverage ends.

Employers must notify eligible employees and/or their spouses and qualified dependents within 60 days after the employees quit, die, get divorced, or otherwise change their status. The coverage must be offered for 18 to 36 months, depending on the qualifying circumstances. The individual no longer employed by the organization must pay the premiums, but the employer may charge this individual no more than 102% of the premium costs to insure a similarly covered employee.

For most employers, the COBRA requirements mean additional paperwork and related costs. For example, firms must not only track the former employees but also notify their qualified dependents. The 2% premium addition generally does not cover all relevant costs; the costs often run several percentage points more. Consequently, management efforts to reduce overall health benefits costs have become even more of a concern to employers.

❖ Social Security

The Social Security Act of 1935, with its later amendments, established a system providing *old age, survivor's, disability,* and *retirement benefits.* Administered by the federal government through the Social Security Administration, this program provides benefits to previously employed individuals. Employees and employers share in the cost of Social Security through a tax on employees' wages or salaries.

Social Security Changes Since the system's inception, Social Security payroll taxes have risen from 2% to 12.4%. In addition, Medicare taxes have more than doubled, to 2.9%. But benefits also became increasingly generous during the 1960s and 1970s. When generous benefits collided with a steep drop in labor-force growth, which slowed the growth of the amount being paid in to the system, problems emerged.[5] Several other factors have created additional pressures: Social Security payments were tied to the cost of living (through the Consumer Price Index) which brought about automatic increases in payments. Increasing numbers of persons are covered by the Social Security system. Further, the aging of the U.S. population may place severe strains on the system in the future as more and more people become eligible for payments. All these problems have raised concerns about the availability of future funds from which to pay benefits. Figure 15–2 shows projections for Social Security's future.

Because the Social Security system affects a large number of individuals and is government operated, it is a politically sensitive program. Congress has in part been responding to popular pressure when it has raised payments *and* introduced cost-of-living adjustments. At the same time, Congress must respond to criticism that the system is in trouble. Yet critics believe that further changes will be needed to ensure the viability of the Social Security system after 2000.[6] The United States is not the only country facing difficulties with national health and pension programs. See the accompanying HR Perspective on the next page for a look at similar programs in Eastern Europe.

❖ Workers' Compensation

Workers' Compensation
Provides benefits to persons injured on the job.

Workers' compensation, which provides benefits to persons injured on the job, started with the Federal Employees' Compensation Act of 1908. Laws were enacted by California, New Jersey, Washington, and Wisconsin in 1911. Workers' compensation laws to aid injured employees have spread to all the remaining states. Federal employees are covered under the Federal Employees' Liability Act, administered by the U.S. Department of Labor.

❖ Figure 15–2 ❖
Social Security Projections

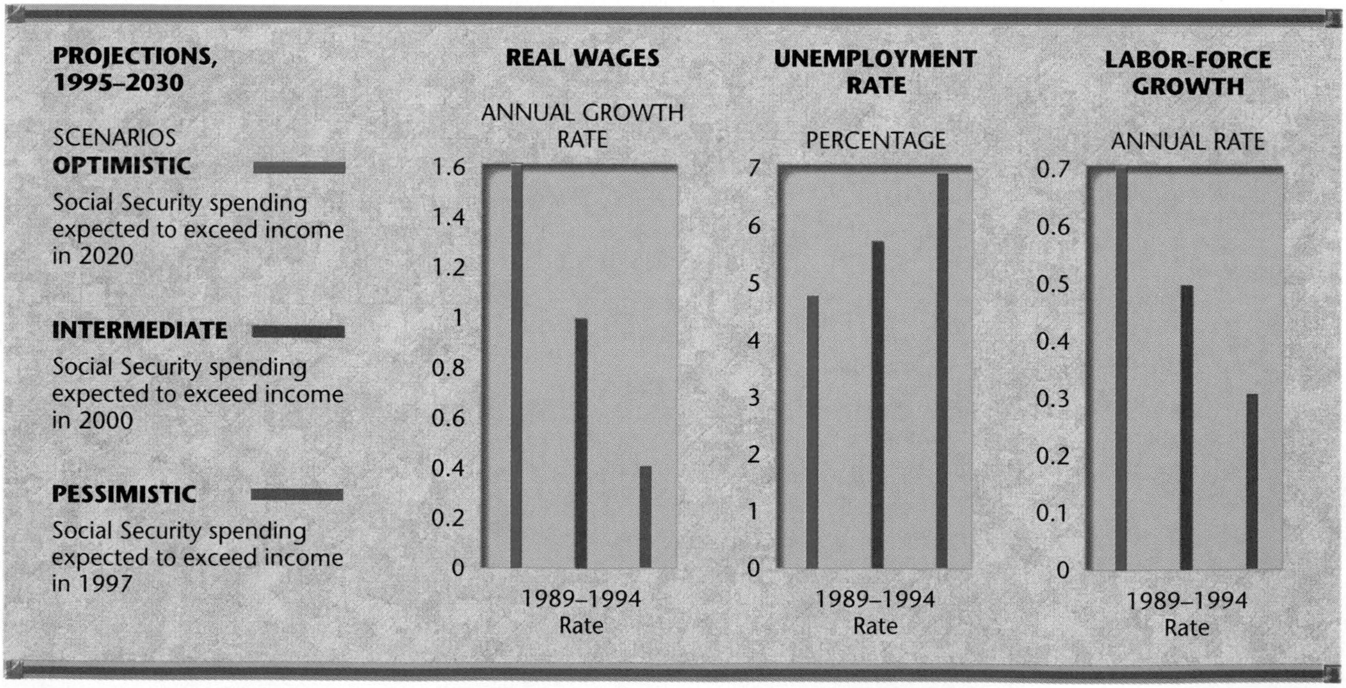

SOURCE: U.S. Government, Social Security Administration.

HR PERSPECTIVE

Benefits on the International Scene

Political changes in Eastern Europe and Russia are bringing about changes in government-provided benefits. For example, Hungary's social programs are being privatized. Poland, on the other hand, still provides extensive benefits for citizens through the government but is introducing tax incentives for private industry to supplement those public plans. Russia introduced a national health-insurance reform that changed the government health-care system to a private one with both mandatory and voluntary coverage. Private pension funds are allowed, but private benefits are still rare because the government-provided benefits are so comprehensive.

Examples of current benefits in the medical and pension areas are as follows:

COUNTRY	MEDICAL	PENSION
Hungary	Free for most workers and dependents who contribute to the program	53% of average monthly earnings after 20 years
Poland	Free for all employees, dependents, and retirees	Minimum retirement age 65/men, 60/women; 24% of average national wage
Russia	Mandatory and voluntary coverage for all citizens; state pays coverage for many	Minimum retirement age 60/men, 55/women; 55% of highest 5-year average earnings; 25 years of service

According to Foster-Higgins, an international benefits consulting firm, growing foreign investment in these areas means employers will need to establish benefit programs to attract scarce skilled labor.

In summary, in these and other formerly communist countries, major changes have had to be made. Voluntary employer-provided benefits may include pensions, annuities, ESOPs, and life, health, and disability insurance.[7]

Workers' compensation systems require employers to give cash benefits, medical care, and rehabilitation services to employees for injuries or illnesses occurring within the scope of their employment. Employees are entitled to quick and certain payment from the workers' compensation system without proving that the employer is at fault. In exchange, employees give up the right of legal actions and awards, so employers enjoy limited liability for occupational illnesses and injury.

Employers provide workers' compensation coverage by purchasing insurance from a private carrier or state insurance fund or by providing self-insurance. Employers that self-insure are required to post a bond or deposit securities with the state industrial commission. State laws usually require that employers have a minimum number of employees before they are permitted to self-insure. Group self-insurance is permitted in some states and is useful for groups of small businesses.

Workers' compensation has been faced with rapidly escalating costs. A related problem is bogus workplace injuries, which are apparently a growing trend. For example, David Vaughn, working the night shift at Kinko's Copies in Rockford, Illinois, had a friend shoot him in the shoulder in a fake robbery attempt. He hoped to get workers' compensation and an insurance settlement—but he got caught instead.[8] Recommendations by experts for reducing workers' compensation claims include conducting pre-injury training, auditing claims, instituting return-to-work programs, and other approaches.[9] Workers' compensation will be covered in more detail in Chapter 16.

❖ Unemployment Compensation

Another benefit required by law is unemployment compensation, established as part of the Social Security Act of 1935. Each state operates its own unemployment compensation system, and provisions differ significantly from state to state.

Employers finance this benefit by paying a tax on the first $7,000 (or more, in 37 states) of annual earnings of each employee. The tax is paid to state and federal unemployment compensation funds. The percentage paid by individual employers is based on "experience rates," which reflect the number of claims filed by workers who leave. An employee who is out of work and is actively looking for employment normally receives up to 26 weeks of pay, at the rate of 50% to 80% of normal pay. Most employees are eligible. However, workers fired for misconduct or those not actively seeking employment generally are ineligible.

Criticism of Unemployment Insurance Changes in unemployment insurance laws have been proposed in bills at both state and federal levels for two reasons: (1) Abuses are estimated to cost billions each year, and (2) many state unemployment funds are exhausted during economic slowdowns. Some states allow union workers who are on strike to collect unemployment benefits, a provision bitterly opposed by many employers.

Supplemental Unemployment Benefits (SUB) Supplemental unemployment benefits (SUB) are closely related to unemployment compensation, but they are *not required by law.* First obtained by the United Steelworkers in 1955, a SUB program is a benefit provision negotiated by a union with an employer as part of a collective bargaining agreement. The provision requires organizations to contribute to a fund that supplements the unemployment compensation available to employees from federal and/or state sources.

❖ Family Leave

In 1993, President Clinton signed into law the Family and Medical Leave Act (FMLA), which covers all employers with 50 or more employees who live within 75 miles of the workplace and includes federal, state, and private employers. Only employees who have worked at least 12 months and 1,250 hours in the previous year are eligible for leaves under FMLA. The law requires that employers allow eligible employees to take a total of 12 weeks' leave during any 12-month period for one or more of the following situations:

- Birth, adoption, or foster-care placement of a child
- Caring for a spouse, child, or parent with a serious health condition
- Serious health condition of the employee

❖Serious Health Condition
A health condition requiring inpatient, hospital, hospice, or residential medical care or continuing physician care.

A **serious health condition** is one requiring inpatient, hospital, hospice, or residential medical care or continuing physician care. An employer may require an employee to provide a certificate from a doctor verifying such an illness.

Regarding taking leaves, FMLA provides for the following:

- Employees taking family and medical leave must be able to return to the same job or a job of equivalent status or pay.
- Health benefits must be continued during the leave at the same level and conditions. If, for a reason other than serious health problems, the

employee does not return to work, the employer may collect the employer-paid portion of the premiums from the nonreturning employee.
- The leave taken may be intermittent rather than in one block, subject to employee and employer agreements, when birth, adoption, or foster-child care is the cause. For serious health conditions, employer approval is not necessary.
- Employees can be required to use all paid-up vacation and personal leave before taking unpaid leave.
- Employees are required to give 30-day notice, where practical.

Since passage of the act, several factors have become apparent. First, many employers have not paid enough attention to the law. One study found that some employers are not guaranteeing that workers will get their jobs back. Others are not continuing health benefits. More than half of the employers surveyed said they would not develop an appeal procedure as suggested.[10] At the same time, some employees are invoking the law for ailments like anxiety attacks, hemorrhoids, and vasectomies. "The FMLA has become the most powerful tool for the problem employee to avoid discharge for excessive absenteeism," an expert on the FMLA contends. For perspective, 26% of the employers in one survey found the act had negative or highly negative impact on productivity, and 65% found it had *no* impact.[11]

A Classification of Benefits

Benefits continue to evolve as an HR issue. A primary driver of benefits in the past was the federal tax code. The U.S. Congress from time to time has shifted the tax code to influence employers' conduct regarding benefits, giving tax breaks for certain types of programs such as employee stock ownership plans (ESOPs) and health care. But in the past decade, the government has cut back on these tax adjustments (for example, completely eliminating tax credit for ESOPs). Decreases in tax advantages, along with the uncertainty created by constant legislative tinkering, have caused many employers to redesign benefits packages based on an employee-needs approach.[12] Using focus groups and surveys, employers are basing benefits on employee input.

A classification of typical benefits is presented in Figure 15–3. Voluntary and mandated benefits are distinguished in the figure. The following sections describe the benefit classes in detail. Note that because of the changing focus just discussed, the benefits included look somewhat different from those available five years ago, and the benefits available in the future will probably look different still.

Security Benefits

Mandatory security benefits such as workers' compensation, Social Security, and unemployment compensation were discussed earlier in this chapter. Benefits related to severance pay, legal insurance, and family issues are explained here.

Severance Pay

Severance pay is a security benefit voluntarily offered by employers to employees who lose their jobs. Severed employees may receive lump-sum severance payments if their employment is terminated by the employer. For example, if a facility closes

***Severance Pay**
A security benefit voluntarily offered by employers to employees who lose their jobs.

❖ FIGURE 15–3 ❖
BENEFITS CLASSIFIED BY TYPE

Government Mandated | Employer Voluntary

SECURITY
- Workers' compensation
- Unemployment compensation
- Social Security (retirement, old age, survivor's, and disability insurance)
- Severance pay
- Supplemental unemployment insurance
- Family Issues: child care, elder care

FINANCIAL, INSURANCE, AND RELATED
- Life insurance
- Legal insurance
- Disability insurance
- Stock plans
- Financial counseling
- Credit unions
- Company-provided car and expense account
- Educational assistance
- Relocation and moving assistance

HEALTH CARE
- COBRA provisions
- Medical
- Dental
- Vision care
- Prescription drugs
- Psychiatric counseling
- Wellness programs
- HMO or PPO health-care plans

SOCIAL AND RECREATIONAL
- Tennis courts
- Bowling leagues
- Service awards
- Sponsored events (athletic and social)
- Cafeteria
- Recreation programs

RETIREMENT
- Social Security
- Early retirement
- Preretirement counseling
- Disability retirement benefits
- Health care for retirees
- Pension plans
- IRA, 401(k), Keogh plans

TIME OFF
- Family and medical leaves
- Military reserve time off
- Election and jury leaves
- Lunch and rest breaks
- Holidays and vacations
- Funeral and bereavement leaves

because it is outmoded and no longer economically profitable to operate, the employees who lose their jobs may receive lump-sum payments based on their years of service. Severance pay provisions often appear in union/management agreements and usually provide larger payments for employees with longer service.[13] Many firms also provide *outplacement* assistance in the form of resume-writing instruction, interviewing skills workshops, and career counseling.

The Worker Adjustment and Retraining Notification Act (WARN) of 1988 requires that many employers give 60 days' notice if a mass layoff or facility closing is to occur. The act does not require employers to give severance pay.

❖ Family Security Issues

Family-related security issues include child care and elder care. Different lifestyles in the United States give rise to other issues as well.

Child Care Balancing work and family responsibilities is a major challenge for many workers. Whether single parents or dual-career couples, these employees often experience difficulty in obtaining high-quality, affordable child care.

Employers are addressing the child-care issue in several ways. Some organizations provide on-site day-care facilities. Relatively few such facilities have been established, primarily because of costs and concerns about liability and attracting sufficient employee use. However, at least one study found that on-site child care had a positive impact on employees who used the service. The study found that the greater the use of the care service, the more favorable employees' attitudes toward management and their employer.[14]

Other options for child-care assistance include:

- ❖ Providing referral services to aid parents in locating child-care providers
- ❖ Establishing discounts at day-care centers, which may be subsidized by the employer
- ❖ Arranging with hospitals to offer sick-child programs partially paid for by the employer
- ❖ Developing after-school programs for older school-age children, often in conjunction with local public and private school systems

Elder Care Another family-related issue of growing importance is caring for elderly relatives. Various organizations have surveyed their employees and found that as many as 30% of them have had to miss work to care for an aging relative. Elder-care assistance provided by caregivers includes transportation and assistance with shopping, meals, laundry, housecleaning, feeding, bathing, dressing, medication, and financial affairs.[15] The responsibilities associates with caring for elderly family members have resulted in reduced work performance, increased absenteeism, and more personal stress for the affected employees. Many more employers will have to respond to this issue as the U.S. population continues to age.[16]

Benefits for Domestic Partners and Spousal Equivalents As lifestyles have changed in the United States, employers are being confronted with requests for benefits by employees who are not married but have close personal relationships with others. The employees who are submitting these requests are:

- ❖ Gay and lesbian employees requesting benefits for their partners
- ❖ Unmarried employees who have living arrangements with individuals of the opposite sex.

The terminology most often used to refer to individuals with such living arrangements are *domestic partners* and *spousal equivalents*.

The argument made by these employees is that if an employer provides benefits for the spouses of married employees, then benefits should be provided for employees with alternative lifestyles and relationships as well. This view is reinforced by: (1) the fact that more gays and lesbians are being open about their lifestyles; and (2) data showing that a significant percentage of heterosexual couples live together before formally marrying.

Some employers have offered benefits to eligible domestic partners voluntarily. These firms include Lotus Development Corporation, Walt Disney, Levi Strauss & Company, and Ben & Jerry's Homemade, Inc. At Lotus, both the employee and the "eligible partner" must sign an "Affidavit of Spousal Equivalence." In this affidavit, the employee and the partner are asked to affirm that:

- Each is the other's only spousal equivalent.
- They are of the same sex and/or not blood relatives.
- They are living together and jointly share responsibility for their common welfare and financial obligations.

Disney's decision to extend benefits to partners of gay and lesbian employees came under attack from Florida lawmakers. Currently, about 150 employers nationwide offer benefits to partners of gay and lesbian employees; however, only 2% to 3% of all employees use the benefits for partners.[17]

❖ Health-Care Benefits

Employers provide a variety of health-care and medical benefits, usually through insurance coverage. The most common ones cover medical, dental, prescription-drug, and vision-care expenses for employees and their dependents. Basic health-care insurance to cover both normal and major medical expenses is highly desired by employees. Dental insurance is also important to many employees. Many dental plans include orthodontic coverage, which is usually very costly. Some employer medical insurance plans also cover psychiatric counseling.

The *Health Portability and Accountability Act* allows employees who switch from one company's health insurance plan to another's to get the new health coverage regardless of pre-existing conditions. The legislation also prohibits group insurance plans from dropping coverage from a sick employee, and requires them to make individual coverage available to people who leave group plans.

Experimental *Medical Savings Accounts* are included for small businesses, self-employed, and uninsured people. These are seen by some as a way to help control medical expenses. Their success will be evaluated in the year 2000 and they will be continued or discontinued depending on effectiveness.

❖ Health-Care Costs

The costs of health-care insurance escalated at a rate well in excess of inflation for three decades. In 1960, about $26 billion was spent on health care, representing 5.4% of the nation's gross domestic product (GDP). By the mid-1990s, health-care costs had risen to $1 trillion, about 16% of the GDP. Employers have felt the impact of the increase in insurance premium costs. However, because of concerted efforts by employers to control costs, medical premium increases have finally fallen below the rate of inflation. Figure 15–4 shows the trend.

❖ Health-Care Cost Management Strategies

Employers are using a variety of strategies to contain health-care costs. Instead of offering health insurance to employees and paying all or most of the premiums, they are establishing managed care plans and using other cost-control means.

Managed Care Preferred provider organizations (PPOs) and health maintenance organizations (HMOs) are often called **managed care** plans. Such approaches are designed to monitor and reduce medical costs using good management practices and the market system. Managed care plans have become an important health-care option, as Figure 15–5 shows. These plans emphasize primary and preventative care, the use of specific providers who will charge lower prices, restrictions on certain kinds of treatment, and prices negotiated with hos-

❖Managed Care
Approaches designed to monitor and reduce medical costs using good management practices and the market system.

❖ Figure 15–4 ❖
Medical Insurance Costs and Inflation

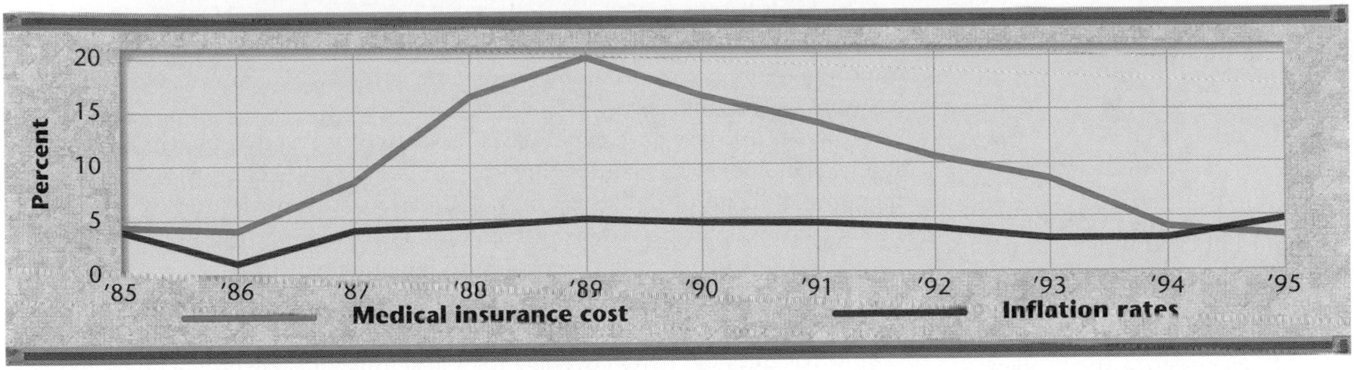

SOURCE: Data from U.S. Department of Labor, Bureau of Labor Statistics, 1996.

pitals and physicians. Managed care programs are saving companies billions of dollars by reducing claims.[18] Such efforts to reduce costs lead to higher costs for employees and a shift in satisfaction with company-provided health plans.[19]

Preferred Provider Organizations (PPOs) One type of managed care plan is the **preferred provider organization** (PPO), a health-care provider that contracts with an employer or an employer group to provide health-care services to employees at a competitive rate. Employees have the freedom to go to other providers if they want to pay the difference in costs. *Point of service* plans are somewhat similar; and offer financial incentives to encourage employees to use designated medical providers.

***Preferred Provider Organization (PPO)**
A health-care provider that contracts with an employer or an employer group to provide health-care services to employees at a competitive rate.

Health Maintenance Organizations (HMOs) A **health maintenance organization** (HMO) provides services for a fixed period on a prepaid basis. The HMO emphasizes prevention as well as correction. An employer contracts with an HMO, which has doctors and medical personnel on its staff, to furnish complete medical care, except for hospitalization. The employer pays a flat rate per enrolled employee or per family. The covered individuals may then go to the

***Health Maintenance Organization (HMO)**
Managed care plan that provides services for a fixed period on a prepaid basis.

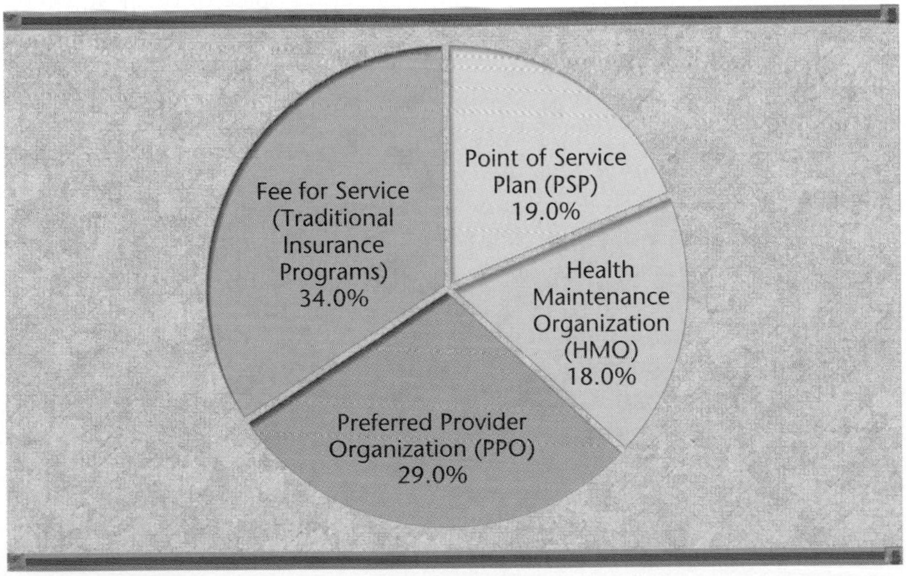

❖ Figure 15–5 ❖
Health-Care Cost Containment Approaches by Employers

SOURCE: Data from L. Dainis, "Health Care Costs Finally Stabilize," Reprinted with permission from *Benefits & Compensation Solutions*, January 1996, 28.

HMO for health care as often as they need to. Supplemental policies for hospitalization also are provided.

The HMO Act of 1973 requires that if employers with 25 or more employees provide other health-care coverage, then they also must offer an HMO as an option to their employees if one is available in the local area. As a result, HMOs have grown in popularity.

However, HMOs have experienced a flurry of mergers, alliances, and acquisitions. Employers are contending that in some cases, competing HMOs are spending millions of dollars on business matters such as destructive price wars and acquiring other businesses instead of focusing on innovation in health care. Employers in some areas are choosing to negotiate with smaller groups of doctors and hospitals, provide employees with information and vouchers, and let them shop among competing medical groups.[20]

IBM has offered HMO coverage for a long time but recently decided to evaluate its offerings to the more than 50,000 employees and retirees in the HMOs. The company collected data in four areas: quality of clinical care, administrative effectiveness, flexibility of plan design, and organizational stability. Then each HMO was assessed for cost effectiveness and the company encourages enrollment in these "best practice" plans.[21]

LOGGING ON

The Massachusetts Association of HMOs provides information about HMOs for both HMO members and HMO professionals at

http://www.mahmo.org/

OTHER COST MANAGEMENT TOOLS Other means used to contain health-care costs include co-payment, utilization reviews, and wellness/communication programs.

Co-payment In the past, many employers offered *first-dollar coverage.* With this type of coverage, all expenses, from the first dollar of health-care costs, were paid by the employee's insurance. Previously, a very small deductible amount was paid by the employee; but many basic coverage plans did not require an employee-paid deductible. Experts say that when first-dollar coverage is included in the basic plan, many employees see a doctor for every slight illness, which results in an escalation of the costs of the benefits.

As health insurance costs rose, employers shifted some of those costs to employees. The **co-payment** strategy requires employees to pay a portion of the cost of both insurance premiums and medical care. Many employers have raised the deductible per person from $50 to $250 or more.

***Co-payment**
Employee's payment of a portion of the cost of both insurance premiums and medical care.

Utilization Review Many employers have found that some of the health care provided by doctors and hospitals is unnecessary, incorrectly billed, or deliberately overcharged. Consequently, both employers and insurance firms are requiring that medical work and charges be audited and reviewed through a **utilization review.** This process may require a second opinion, review of procedures used, and review of charges for procedures done.

***Utilization Review**
An audit and review of the services and costs billed by health-care providers.

Wellness/Communication Programs Wellness programs try to encourage employees to have more healthy lifestyles. Included in wellness programs are activities such as smoking cessation classes, diet and nutrition counseling, exercise and physical fitness centers and programs, and health education. Wellness programs are discussed in more detail in Chapter 16.

Employers also are educating employees about health-care costs and how to reduce them. Newsletters, formal classes, and many other approaches are used, all designed to make employees more aware of why health-care costs are increasing and what employees can do to control them.

Finally, some employers are offering financial incentives for improving health habits. These programs reward employees who stop smoking, lose weight, wear seat belts, and participate in exercise programs.[22]

❖ Retirement Benefits

Few people have financial reserves to use when they retire, so retirement benefits attempt to provide income for employees on retirement. Ninety-one percent of employers with 200 or more workers offer some kind of retirement plan.[23] However, financial resources and pension plans are only part of the broader issues in national retirement policies.

❖ National Retirement Policies and Trends

Private pensions serve several purposes for employees: they increase annual income and, among union members, they improve the distribution of earned income.[24] Generally, private pensions are a critical part of providing income for people after retirement. With the baby boomer generation closing in on retirement, pressures on private pensions, as well as Social Security, are likely to arise. Figure 15–6 shows the numbers in various age groups currently.

As a result of a 1986 amendment to the Age Discrimination in Employment Act, most employees cannot be forced to retire at any age. Previously, age 65 for men and age 62 often were considered to be normal retirement age. As a result employers have had to develop different policies to comply with these regulations. In many employer pension plans "normal retirement" is the age at which employees can retire and collect full pension benefits. Employers must decide whether individuals who continue to work past age 65 should receive the full benefits package, especially pension credits. As possible changes in Social Security increase the age for full benefits past 65, these policies likely will be modified.

❖ Figure 15–6 ❖
Baby Boomers and Retirement

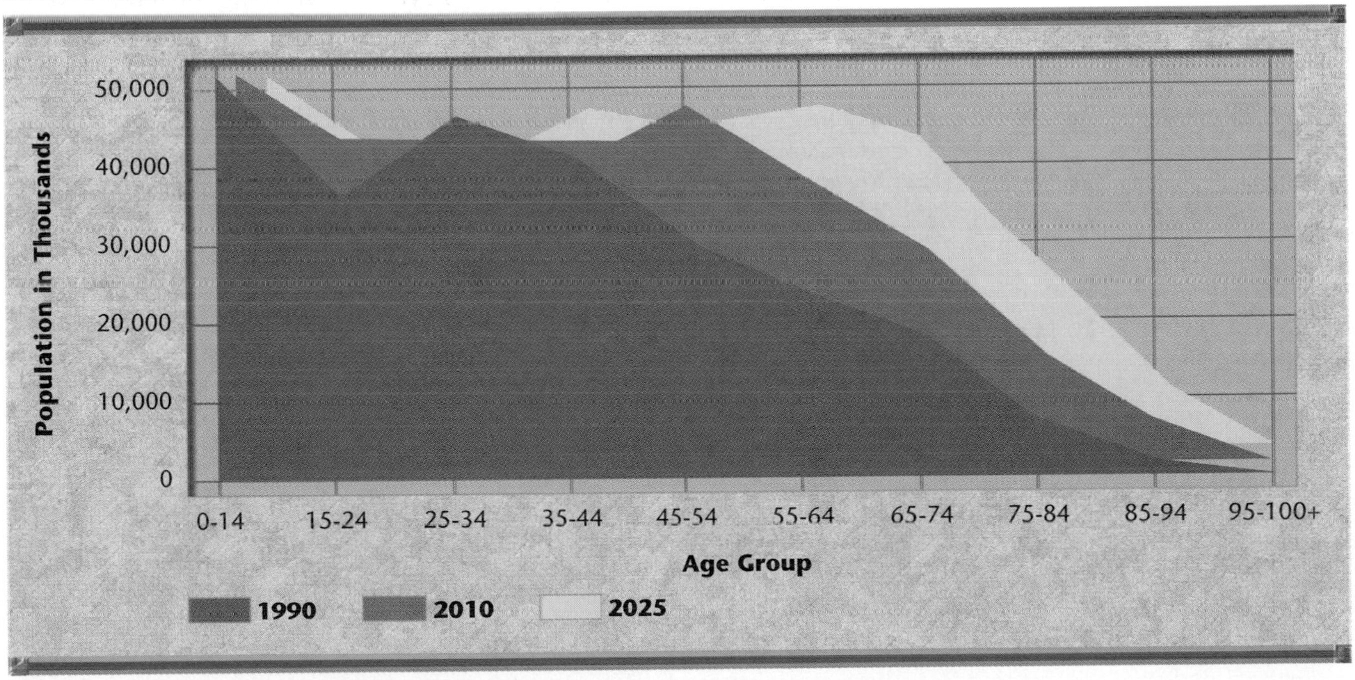

SOURCE: Data from U.S. Bureau of the Census.

Despite the removal of mandatory retirement provisions, the age at which individuals retire has continued to decline in the United States. In 1990, the average retirement age was 62, and the U.S. Bureau of Labor Statistics has predicted that the age will decline slightly by the year 2000.

❖ Early Retirement and Preretirement Counseling

Provisions for early retirement currently are included in many pension plans. Early retirement gives people an opportunity to get away from a long-term job; individuals who have spent 25 to 30 years working for the same employer may wish to use their talents in other areas. Phased-in and part-time retirements also are used by some individuals and firms.

Some employers use early retirement buyout programs to cut back their workforces and reduce costs. Care must be taken to make these early retirement programs truly voluntary. Forcing workers to take advantage of an early retirement buyout program has led to age discrimination suits.

Preretirement counseling is aimed at easing employees' anxieties and preparing them for retirement and the benefits associated with it. The biological changes of aging may be a concern, but suddenly having no job can cause even more anxiety and stress. Preretirement counseling should not begin just before retirement; it should be a systematic process of gradual preparation. Topics most frequently covered are health, housing, Social Security, legal and financial considerations, and use of leisure time.

Companies sometimes use preretirement counseling to provide information to employees considering early retirement. However, preretirement counseling often raises emotional issues for many people, and research suggests that attempts to use it as a strategy to encourage employees to retire may backfire and discourage retirement instead.[25]

❖ Retirees and Health Care-Benefits

Some employers choose to offer health-care benefits to their retirees, paid by the retirees, the company, or both. These benefits are usually available until the retiree is eligible for Medicare.

The costs of such coverage have risen dramatically, and to ensure that firms adequately reflect the liabilities for retiree health benefits, the Financial Accounting Standards Board (FASB) in 1992 issued a Rule 106 requiring that firms establish accounting reserves for funding retiree health-care benefits. Prior to 1992, most firms had not set aside funds for these benefits, paying instead out of current yearly income. FASB Rule 106 affected many firms, which now must reflect the liability on financial statements and reduce their current earnings each year to fund retiree health-care benefits. Huge write-offs against earnings have been taken by many firms in order to comply with FASB 106. For instance, AT&T took a one-time charge of $7.5 billion, and General Motors charged $23 billion against earnings.

❖ Pension Plans

❖Pension Plans
Retirement benefits established and funded by employers and employees.

Pension plans are retirement benefits established and funded by employers and employees. Organizations are not required to offer pension plans to employees, and only 40% to 50% of U.S. workers are covered by them. Smaller firms offer them less often than large ones. Many employers do not offer pension plans primarily because of the costs and administrative burdens imposed by government legislation.

Employee Retirement Income Security Act (ERISA) It was widespread criticism of many pension plans that led to the passage of the Employee Retirement Income Security Act (ERISA) in 1974. The purpose of this law is to regulate private pension plans in order to assure that employees who put money into them or depend on a pension for retirement funds actually will receive the money when they retire.[26]

ERISA essentially requires many companies to offer retirement plans to all employees if they are offered to any employees. Accrued benefits must be given to employees when they retire or leave. The act also sets minimum funding requirements. Plans that do not meet these requirements are subject to IRS financial penalties. Employers are required to pay plan termination insurance to ensure that employee pensions will be there even if the company goes out of business.

Pension Contributions Pension plans can be either contributory or noncontributory. In a **contributory plan,** money for pension benefits is paid in by both the employee and the employer. In a **noncontributory plan,** the employer provides all the funds. As would be expected, the noncontributory plan is preferred by employees and labor unions.

***Contributory Plan**
Pension plan in which the money for pension benefits is paid in by both employees and employers.

***Noncontributory Plan**
Pension plan in which all the funds for pension benefits are provided by the employer.

Pension Benefits Payment of benefits can follow one of two plans. In a **defined-contribution plan,** the employer makes an annual payment to an employee's pension account. The key to this plan is the *contribution rate;* employee retirement benefits depend on fixed contributions and employee earnings levels. Profit-sharing plans, employee stock ownership plans (ESOPs), and thrift plans often are defined-contribution plans. Because these plans hinge on the investment returns on the previous contributions, which can vary according to profitability or other factors, employees' retirement benefits are less secure and predictable. But because of their structure, these plans are preferred by younger, shorter-service employees.

***Defined-Contribution Plan**
Pension plan in which the employer makes an annual payment to an employee's pension account.

In a **defined-benefit plan,** an employee is promised a pension amount based on age and service. The employer's contributions are based on actuarial calculations that focus on the *benefits* to be received by employees after retirement and the *methods* used to determine such benefits. The amount of an individual employee's benefits is determined by the person's length of service with the organization and the person's average earnings over a five-year or longer period. A defined-benefit plan gives the employee greater assurance of benefits and greater predictability in the amount of benefits that will be available at retirement. Therefore, it generally is preferred by older workers.

***Defined-Benefit Plan**
Pension plan in which an employee is promised a pension amount based on age and service.

If the funding in a defined-benefit plan is insufficient, the employers may have to make up the shortfall. Therefore, a growing number of employers are dropping defined-benefit plans in favor of defined-contribution plans so that their contribution liabilities are known.[27]

Portability Another feature of some employee pensions is **portability.** In a portable plan, employees can move their pension benefits from one employer to another. A commonly used portable pension system in colleges and universities is the Teacher Insurance Annuity Association (TIAA) system. Under this system, any faculty or staff member who accumulates pension benefits at one university can transfer these benefits to another university within the TIAA system. If they leave before retirement, individuals who are not in a portable system must take a *lump-sum settlement* made up of the money that they contributed to the plan plus accumulated interest on their contribution.

***Portability**
A pension plan feature that allows employees to move their pension benefits from one employer to another.

Vesting
The right of employees to receive benefits from their pension plans.

VESTING RIGHTS Certain rights are attached to employee pension plans. The right of employees to receive benefits from their pension plans is called **vesting.** Typically, vesting assures employees of a certain pension, provided they have worked a minimum number of years. If employees resign or are terminated before they are vested (that is, before they have been employed for the required time), no pension rights accrue to them except the funds that they have contributed. If employees stay the allotted time, they retain their pension rights and receive benefits from the funds contributed by both the employer and themselves.

DISCRIMINATION IN PENSION PLANS The pension area is like many others in HR management—it is constantly changing. Some relatively recent changes are concerned with making pension plans nondiscriminatory. Here, the term *nondiscriminatory* refers to discrimination against women.

Statistics have shown that women generally live longer than men. As a result, before 1983, women received lower benefits than men for the same contributions. However, this kind of discrimination was declared illegal by a U.S. Supreme Court decision. The *Arizona Governing Committee v. Norris* ruling forced pension plan administrators to use "unisex" mortality tables that do not reflect the gender differential in mortality.[28] To bring legislation in line with this decision, the Retirement Equity Act was passed in 1984 as an amendment to ERISA and the Internal Revenue Code. It liberalized pension regulations that affect women, guaranteed access to benefits, prohibited pension-related penalties owing to absences from work such as maternity leave, and lowered the vesting age.

INDIVIDUAL RETIREMENT BENEFIT OPTIONS

The availability of several retirement benefit options makes the pension area more complex. Three such options are individual retirement accounts (IRAs), 401(k) plans, and Keogh plans. These may be available *in addition* to a pension plan.

Individual Retirement Account (IRA)
A special account in which an employee can set aside funds on which taxes are deferred until the employee retires.

INDIVIDUAL RETIREMENT ACCOUNTS (IRAS) An **individual retirement account (IRA)** is a special account in which an employee can set aside funds that will not be taxed until the employee retires. The major advantages of an IRA are the ability to accumulate extra retirement funds and the shifting of taxable income to later years, when total income, and therefore taxable income, is likely to be lower. Until 1987, many workers took advantage of IRAs offered by financial institutions, insurance companies, and brokerage firms. However, with the passage of the Tax Reform Act of 1986, IRA use became more limited.

401(k) Plan
An agreement in which a percentage of an employee's pay is withheld and invested in a tax-deferred account.

401(K) PLANS The **401(k) plan** gets its name from Section 401(k) of the federal tax code and is an agreement in which a percentage of an employee's pay is withheld and invested in a tax-deferred account. It allows employees to choose whether to receive cash or have employer contributions from profit-sharing and stock-bonus plans placed into tax-deferred accounts. Employees can elect to have their current pay reduced by a certain percentage and that amount paid into a 401(k) plan.

The use of 401(k) plans and the assets in them have grown significantly in the past few years, as shown in Figure 15–7. The advantage to employees is that they can save up to approximately $8,500 per year (as a ceiling) of pre-tax income toward their retirement. Typically, employers match employee contributions at a 50% rate up to a certain percentage of employee pay, and often employees can contribute additional funds of their own up to the ceiling set by the Internal Rev-

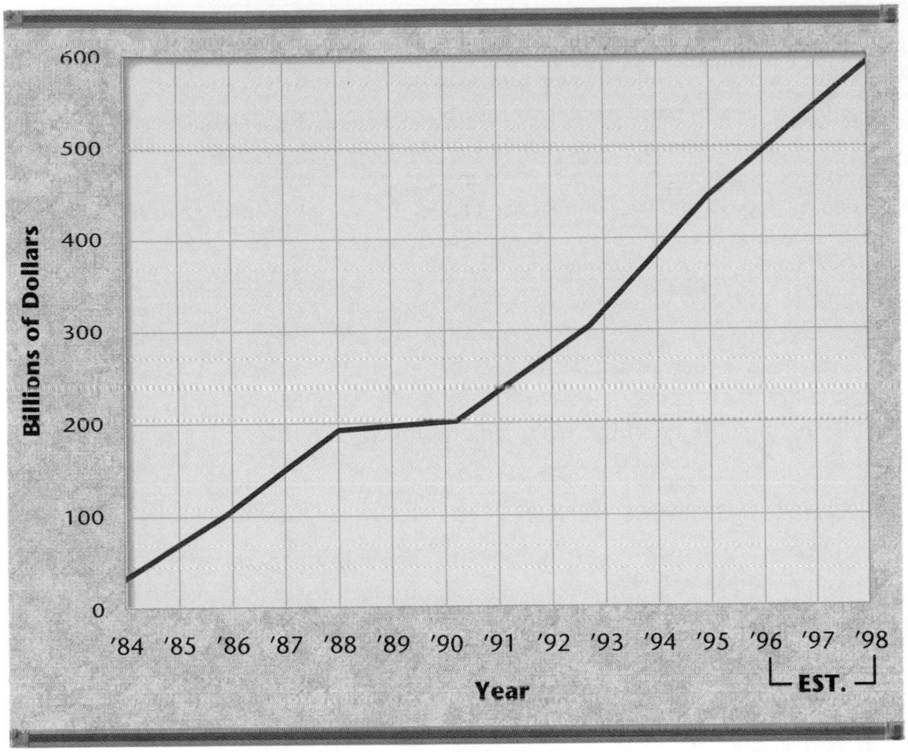

❖ FIGURE 15–7 ❖
GROWTH OF 401(K) PLANS

SOURCE: Data from U.S. Department of Labor, Bureau of Labor Statistics.

enue Service. When employers match employee contributions, substantial increases in employee participation occur; but at higher rates of matching, employee contributions fall.[29]

KEOGH PLANS A **Keogh plan** is a special type of individualized pension plan for self-employed persons. These individuals can set aside a percentage of their incomes in pension accounts. Keogh plans can either be defined-contribution or defined-benefit plans. Because of the complexity of Keogh plans and the special regulations covering them, many self-employed individuals seek advice from tax specialists before establishing one.

***Keogh Plan**
A type of individualized pension plan for self-employed individuals.

❖ FINANCIAL AND OTHER BENEFITS

Employers may offer workers a wide range of special benefits—financial benefits, insurance benefits (in addition to health-related insurance), educational benefits, social benefits, and recreational benefits. From the point of view of the employer, such benefits can be useful in attracting and retaining employees. Workers like receiving special benefits which often are not taxed as income.

❖ FINANCIAL BENEFITS

Financial benefits include a wide variety of items. A *credit union* provides saving and lending services for employees. *Purchase discounts* allow employees to buy goods or services from their employers at reduced rates. For example, a furniture manufacturer may allow employees to buy furniture at wholesale cost plus 10%; a bank may offer the use of a safety deposit box and free checking to its employees.

Employee *thrift, saving,* or *stock-investment plans* may be made available. Some employers match a portion of the employee's contribution. These plans are especially attractive to executive and managerial personnel. To illustrate, in a stock-purchase plan, the corporation provides matching funds equal to the amount invested by the employee to purchase stock in the company. In this way, employees can benefit from the future growth of the corporation. Also, it is hoped that employees will develop a greater loyalty and interest in the organization and its success.

Financial planning and counseling are especially valuable to executives, who may need information on investments, tax shelters, and comprehensive financial counseling because of their higher levels of compensation. These financial planning benefits likely will grow as a greater percentage of workers approach retirement age.

Numerous other financial-related benefits may be offered as well. These include the use of a company car and company expense accounts and assistance in buying or selling a house when an employee is transferred.

❖ Other Insurance Benefits

In addition to health-related insurance, some employers provide other types of insurance. These benefits offer major advantages for employees because many employers pay some or all of the costs. Even when employers do not pay any of the costs, employees still benefit because of the lower rates available through group programs.

Life Insurance It is common for employers to provide *life insurance* for employees. Life insurance is bought as a group policy, and the employer pays all or some of the premiums, but the level of coverage is usually low and is tied to the employee's base pay. A typical level of coverage is one-and-a-half or two times an employee's annual salary. Some executives may get higher coverage as part of executive compensation packages.

Disability Insurance Other insurance benefits frequently tied to employee pay levels are *short-term* and *long-term disability insurance.* This type of insurance provides continuing income protection for employees who become disabled and unable to work. Long-term disability insurance is much more common because many employers cover short-term disability situations by allowing employees to accrue the sick leave granted annually.[30]

Legal Insurance Legal insurance is offered as a benefit through some employers, often as part of cafeteria benefit plans, which let workers choose from many different benefits. Legal insurance plans operate in much the same way health maintenance organizations do. Employees (or employers) pay a flat fee of a set amount each month. In return, they have the right to use the service of a network of lawyers to handle their legal problems.

❖ Educational Benefits

Another benefit used by employees comes in the form of *educational assistance* to pay for some or all costs associated with formal education courses and degree programs, including the costs of books and laboratory materials. Some employers pay for schooling on a proportional schedule, depending on the grades received; others simply require a passing grade of C or above.

Unless the education paid for by the employer meets certain conditions, the cost of educational aid must be counted as taxable income by employees. To qualify as nontaxable income under Section 127 of the Internal Revenue Code, the education must be:[31]

- *Job-related,* in that it is used to maintain or improve a person's skills for the current job
- *Expressly required,* either to meet specific current job requirements or to maintain required professional standing, such as licenses or continuing education
- *Above minimum standards,* meaning that it is not education necessary for the person to qualify for a job initially

Because of U.S. federal budget deficits, repeated attempts have been made to include all educational benefits as taxable income to employees, thereby raising the taxes to be paid by employees using those benefits. Some proposals have attempted to narrow the criteria for deciding if education is job related and expressly required. As of the writing of this text, those efforts have been unsuccessful, and many employer-provided educational benefits remain nontaxable to employees.

Social and Recreational Benefits

Some benefits and services are social and recreational in nature, such as bowling leagues, picnics, parties, employer-sponsored athletic teams, organizationally owned recreational lodges, and other sponsored activities and interest groups. As interest in employee wellness has increased, more firms have begun to provide recreational facilities and activities. But employers should retain control of all events associated with their organizations because of possible legal responsibility.

The idea behind social and recreation programs is to promote employee happiness and team spirit. Employees *may* appreciate this type of benefit, but managers should not necessarily expect increased job productivity or job satisfaction as a result. Other benefits too numerous to detail here are made available by various employers as well. The HR Perspective on the next page describes some of them.

Time-Off Benefits

Employers give employees paid time off in a variety of circumstances. Paid lunch breaks and rest periods, holidays, and vacations are the most well known. But leaves are given for a number of other purposes as well. Time-off benefits are estimated to represent from about 5% to 13% of total compensation. Some of the more common time-off benefits include holiday pay, vacation pay, and leaves of absence.

Holiday Pay

Most, if not all, employers provide pay for a variety of holidays, as Figure 15–8 shows. Other holidays are offered to some employees through laws or union contracts. As an abuse-control measure, employers commonly require employees to work the last scheduled day before a holiday and the first scheduled workday after a holiday to be eligible for holiday pay. Some employers pay time-and-a-half to hourly employees who must work holidays.

Figure 15–8
Most Common Paid Holidays in the United States

1. Christmas
2. New Year's Day
3. Thanksgiving
4. Independence Day
5. Labor Day
6. Memorial Day
7. Day after Thanksgiving
8. Presidents' Day
9. Good Friday
10. Christmas Eve
11. New Year's Eve
12. Veterans Day
13. Columbus Day
14. Martin Luther King, Jr., Day
15. Employee's Birthday

HR PERSPECTIVE

Unusual Benefits

Many employers offer their employees a wide range of benefits other than those considered standard. Food services, counseling services, paid professional memberships, uniforms, and employee discounts are common ones. Other firms offer more unusual benefits, as the following examples illustrate:

- Employees at Ben and Jerry's, the New England–based ice cream firm, are allowed to have up to three pints of ice cream per day free.
- Most airlines allow employees to fly free on a stand-by basis, and immediate family members of airline employees can fly stand-by at significantly reduced rates.
- A Livermore, California, employer, Lawrence Livermore National Laboratory, sponsors over 100 clubs for employees, including karate, chess, and computer clubs. The clubs meet after work hours.
- Numerous firms have "dress-down" or "jeans" days, often on Fridays. Microsoft, the large software firm, has no dress code anytime.
- Free breakfast every day is given to employees at Computer Associates International, based in Islandia, N.Y.
- The manufacturer of Budweiser and Michelob beer, Anheuser-Busch, allows employees to take home two cases of beer per month at no cost.
- Because of unhappiness with the local school system in Moorpark, California, the owner of a 25-employee plumbing company established a school for employee's children in a company warehouse. In operation for more than six years, the school serves 15 to 20 students each year.
- Apple Computer gives each new employee a free personal computer.
- On his or her birthday each employee at Mary Kay Cosmetics in Dallas, Texas, receives a birthday card and a coupon for free lunch or movie tickets for two. After five years with the company, employees receive a $100 U.S. Savings Bond.
- Johnson and Johnson provides eight weeks paid *paternity* leave.
- IBM set up a $50 million fund designated for child and elder care.

The reason organizations offer such benefits is to reward employees in ways not readily available elsewhere. These organizations hope to create greater employee loyalty, which will enhance employee retention. They also hope that offering unusual benefits will help differentiate them when recruiting workers, particularly scarce-skill professionals and managers.[32]

Vacation Pay

Paid vacations are a common benefit. Employers often use graduated vacation-time scales based on employees' length of service. Some organizations allow employees to accumulate unused vacation. As with holidays, employees often are required to work the day before and the day after a vacation to prevent abuse. Figure 15–9 shows the average number of vacation days earned in the United States.

Leaves of Absence

Leaves of absence, taken as time off with or without pay, are given for a variety of reasons. All of the leaves discussed here add to employer costs even when they are unpaid, because usually the missing employee's work must be covered, either by other employees working overtime or by temporary employees working under contract.

Family Leave As mentioned earlier in the chapter, the passage of the Family and Medical Leave Act helped clarify the rights of employees and the responsibilities of most employers. Even though *paternity leave* for male workers is avail-

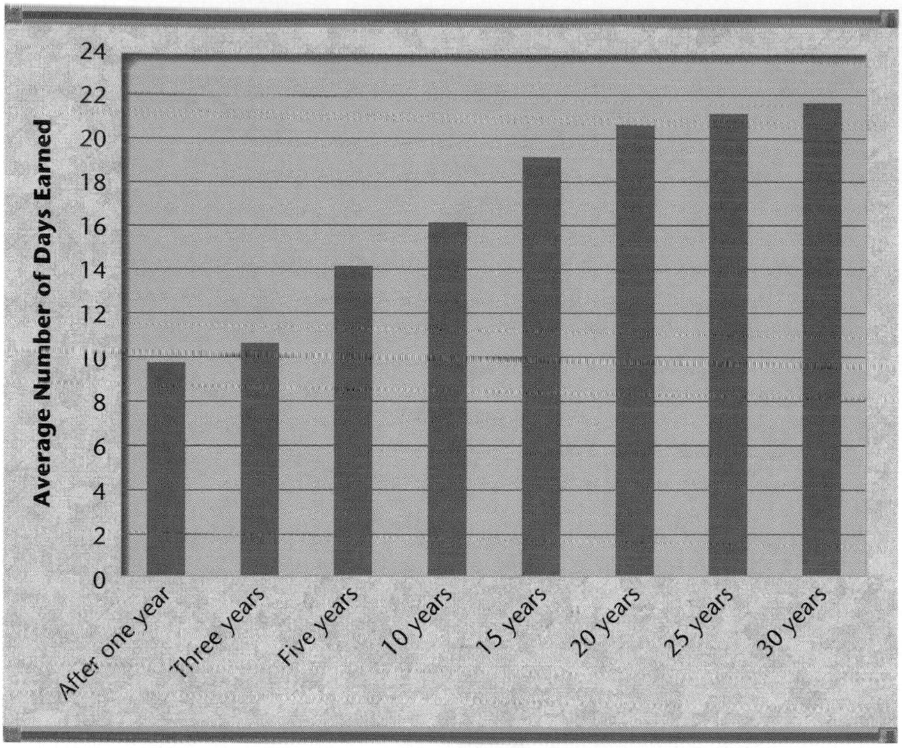

❖ **FIGURE 15–9** ❖
AVERAGE PAID VACATION DAYS EARNED IN THE UNITED STATES

SOURCE: Data from U.S. Department of Labor, U.S. Bureau of Labor Statistics.

able under FMLA, a relatively low percentage of men take it. The primary reason for the low usage is a perception that it is not as socially acceptable for men to stay home for child-related reasons. That view likely will change as a result of the increase in dual-career couples in the workforce.[33]

MEDICAL AND SICK LEAVE Medical and sick leave are closely related. Many employers allow their employees to miss a limited number of days because of illness without losing pay. Some employers allow employees to accumulate unused sick leave, which may be used in case of catastrophic illnesses. Others pay employees for unused sick leave.

Some organizations have shifted emphasis to reward people who do not use sick leave by giving them **well-pay**—extra pay for not taking sick leave. Other employers have made use of the **earned-time plan,** which combines sick leave, vacations, and holidays into a total number of hours or days that employees can take off with pay. One organization found that when it stopped designating a specific number of sick-leave days and an earned-time plan was implemented, absenteeism dropped, time off was scheduled better, and employee acceptance of the leave policy improved.

❖**Well-Pay**
Extra pay for not taking sick leave.

❖**Earned-Time Plan**
Plan that combines all time-off benefits into a total number of hours or days that employees can take off with pay.

PAID TIME-OFF (PTO) PLANS Still other firms are using *time-off-banks,* which lump the various time-off-with-pay days together in one package to be used at the employee's discretion. The new programs provide more flexibility in using time off, and some say they add dignity to the process of taking time off. Employers note that they save administrative costs as well.[34] However, such plans prohibit workers from carrying over unused vacation time to the next year because of IRS code restrictions on deferred benefits.[35]

Other Leaves Other types of leaves are given for a variety of purposes. Some, such as *military leave, election leave,* and *jury leave,* are required by various state and federal laws. Employers commonly pay the difference between the employee's regular pay and the military, election, or jury pay. Some firms grant employees military time off and give them regular pay while the employees also receive military pay. Federal law prohibits taking discriminatory action against military pay. Federal law prohibits taking discriminatory action against military reservists by requiring them to take vacation time to attend summer camp or other training sessions. However, the leave request must be reasonable and truly required by the military.

Funeral or *bereavement leave* is another common leave offered. Leave of up to three days for immediate family members is usually given, as specified in many employers' policy manuals and employee handbooks. Some policies also give unpaid time off for the death of more distant relatives or friends.

❖ Benefits Administration

With the myriad of benefits and regulations, it is easy to see why many organizations must make coordinated efforts to administer benefits programs. Figure 15–10 shows how benefits administration responsibilities can be split between HR specialists and other managers. The greatest role is played by HR specialists, but managers are responsible for the communication aspects of benefits administration. One of the greatest advances in administering benefits has been the development of computer software to help employers track benefits ranging from workers' compensation to retirement.[36]

❖ Figure 15–10 ❖
Typical Benefits Administration Responsibilities

HR UNIT	MANAGERS
❖ Develops and administers benefit systems ❖ Answers employees' technical questions on benefits ❖ Assists employees in filing benefit claims ❖ Coordinates special preretirement programs	❖ Answer simple questions on benefits ❖ Maintain liaison with HR specialists on benefits ❖ Maintain good communications with employees near retirement

❖ Benefits Communication

Employees generally do not know much about the values and costs associated with the benefits they receive from employers. Yet benefits communication and benefits satisfaction are linked. Many employers have instituted special benefits communication systems to inform employees about the value of the benefits provided. Explaining benefits during new employee orientation programs, holding periodic meetings, preparing special literature, and using in-house employee publications to heighten awareness of benefits are among the methods used.

Many employers also give employees annual "personal statements of benefits" that translates benefits into dollar amounts. Federal regulations under ERISA require that employees receive an annual pension-reporting statement, which also can be included in the personal statements. By having a personalized statement, each employee can see how much his or her own benefits are worth. Employers hope that by educating employees on benefits costs, they can manage expenditures better and can give employees a better appreciation for the employers' payments.[37]

❖Flexible Benefits Plan
Benefits plan that allows employees to select the benefits they prefer from groups of benefits established by the employer.

❖ Flexible Benefits

A **flexible benefits plan,** sometimes called a *flex* or *cafeteria* plan, allows employees to select the benefits they prefer from groups of benefits established by the employer. By making a variety of "dishes," or benefits, available, the organization allows each employee to select an individual combination of benefits within some overall limits. As a result of the changing composition of the workforce, flexible benefits plans have grown in popularity. These systems recognize that individual employee situations differ because of age, family status, and lifestyles. For instance, individuals in dual-career couples may not want the same benefits from two different employers. Under a flex plan, one of them can forgo some benefits available in the partner's plan and take other benefits instead.

FLEXIBLE SPENDING ACCOUNTS Under current tax laws (Section 125 of the Tax Code administered by the Internal Revenue Service), employees can divert some income before taxes into accounts to fund certain benefits. These **flexible spending accounts** allow employees to contribute pretax dollars to buy additional benefits. An example illustrates the advantage of these accounts to employees. Assume an employee earns $3,000 per month and has $100 per month deducted to put into a flexible spending account. That $100 does not count as gross income for tax purposes, so her taxable income is reduced. The employee uses the money in the account to purchase additional benefits.

***Flexible Spending Account**
Account that allows employees to contribute pre-tax dollars to buy additional benefits.

Under tax law at the time of this writing, the funds in the account can be used only to purchase the following: (1) *additional health care* (including offsetting deductibles), (2) *life insurance,* (3) *disability insurance,* and (4) *dependent-care benefits.* Furthermore, tax regulations require that if employees do not spend all of the money in their accounts by the end of the year, they forfeit it. Therefore, it is important that employees estimate very closely the additional benefits they will use.[38]

Flexible spending accounts have grown in popularity as more flexible benefits plans have been adopted by more employers. Of course, such plans and their tax advantages can be changed as Congress passes future health-care and tax-related legislation.

ADVANTAGES OF FLEXIBLE BENEFITS PLANS The flexible benefits approach has several advantages. First, this scheme takes into consideration the complexity of people and situations. Because employees in an organization have different desires and needs, they can *tailor benefit packages* to fit their individual life situations within the limits of legal restrictions.

The second advantage, and certainly an important one to most employers, is that flex plans can aid in *benefits cost-control efforts.* The impact of flex plans is seen in a study done over several years that compared flex plans with more fixed plans. The study found that for employers without flex plans, medical care costs rose 41.1%, while employers with flex plans experienced an increase of only 22.7%.[39] Although employers without flex plans can take cost-containment steps, the decision by employers to reduce benefits or increase co-payments is made easier and is more palatable to employees when these measures are integrated into flex plans.

Another advantage of the flexible benefits approach is heightened *employee awareness* of the cost and the value of the benefits. Because they must determine what benefits they will receive, employees know what the trade-offs are.

The fourth advantage is that employers with flexible benefits plans can recruit, hire, and retain employees more easily because of the *attractiveness* of flexible plans. If they can tailor benefits to their needs, employees may not be as interested in shifting to other employers with fixed benefits plans.

DISADVANTAGES OF FLEXIBLE BENEFITS PLANS The flexible approach to benefits is not without some drawbacks. The major problem is the *complexity* of keeping track of what each individual chooses, especially if there are a large number of employees. Sophisticated computer software is now available to manage these complexities. Also, the *increase in benefits communications costs* is a concern. As more benefits are made available, employees may be less able to understand the options because the benefits structure and its provisions may become quite complicated.

A third problem is that an *inappropriate benefits package* may be chosen by an employee. A young construction worker might not choose disability benefits; however, if he or she is injured, the family may suffer financial hardship. Part of this problem can be overcome by requiring employees to select a core set of benefits (life, health, and disability insurance) and then offering options on other benefits.

Adverse Selection
Situation in which only higher-risk employees select and use certain benefits.

A final problem can be **adverse selection,** whereby only higher-risk employees select and use certain benefits. Because many insurance plans are based on a group rate, the employer may face higher rates if insufficient numbers of employees select an insurance option.

Despite these disadvantages, it is likely that flex plans will continue to grow in popularity. The ability to match benefits to differing employee needs, while also controlling some costs, is so attractive that employers will try to find ways to overcome the disadvantages while attuning their benefits plans to the 21st century.

One such "tuning" attempt is underway at Owens-Corning Fiberglass for current employees. The company is replacing its fixed-benefits structure with "credits" workers can use to buy items like disability insurance, health insurance, and even extra vacation days. Alternatively, they can keep the cash. However, for employees hired in the future new plans are intended to keep costs down in bad times and reward more during good times. Benefits credits will be variable. This approach to benefits is already attracting interest from other companies.[40]

SUMMARY

- ❖ Benefits provide additional compensation to employees as a reward for organizational membership.
- ❖ Because benefits generally are not taxed, they are highly desired by employees. The average employee now receives an amount equal to about 40% of his or her pay in benefit compensation.
- ❖ What part of total compensation benefit expenses will comprise is a major HR strategic decision.
- ❖ Strategic reasons for offering benefits include attracting and retaining employees, improving the company's image, and enhancing job satisfaction.
- ❖ Historically, benefits have been offered because of wage controls, unions, favorable tax treatment, competition, and federal legislation.
- ❖ An important distinction is made between mandated and voluntary benefits. Mandatory benefits are required by law.
- ❖ Social Security, workers' compensation, and unemployment compensation are three prominent mandated benefits.
- ❖ The general types of benefits include security benefits, retirement benefits, health-care benefits, financial benefits, social and recreational benefits, and time-off benefits.
- ❖ Security concerns include family-related issues such as complying with the Family and Medical Leave Act of 1993 and offering both child-care and elder-care assistance.
- ❖ Health-care benefits are the most costly insurance-related benefits. Employers have become more aggressive in managing their health-care costs.
- ❖ Organizations that provide retirement-related benefits should develop policies on early retirement, offer preretirement counseling, and plan how to integrate Social Security benefits into employees' benefit plans.
- ❖ Retiree health-care costs represents an area of increasing concern for employers.
- ❖ The pension area is a complex are governed by the Employee Retirement Income Security Act (ERISA).
- ❖ Individual retirement accounts, 401(k) plans, and Keogh plans are important individual options available for supplementing retirement benefits.

❖ Various types of insurance, financial planning assistance, tuition aid, and other benefits that employer may offer enhance the appeal of benefits to employees.

❖ Holiday pay, vacation pay, and various leaves of absence are means of providing time-off benefits to employees.

❖ Because of the variety of benefit options available and the costs involved, employers need to develop systems to communicate these options and costs to their employees.

❖ Flexible benefits systems, which can be tailored to individual needs and situations, have grown in popularity.

Review and Discussion Questions

1. Why have benefits grown in strategic importance to employers?
2. Discuss the following statement:"Employers should expect that more benefits will become mandatory just as those mandated by the Family and Medical Leave Act did."
3. Why are workers' compensation, unemployment compensation, and Social Security appropriately classified as security-oriented benefits?
4. Define the following terms:(a) *contributory plan,* (b) *defined-benefit plan,* (c) *portability,* and (d) *vesting.*
5. Discuss the following statement: "Health-care costs are out of control in the United States, and it is up to employers to put pressure on the medical system to reduce costs."
6. What types of financial and other benefits would you most prefer? Why?
7. Some experts have forecast that time-off benefits will expand in the future. Why?
8. Why are benefits communications and flexible benefits systems so intertwined?

Terms to Know

401(k) plan **450**
adverse selection **458**
benefit **434**
co-payment **446**
contributory plan **449**
defined-benefit plan **449**
defined-contribution plan **449**
earned-time plan **455**
flexible benefits plan **456**
flexible spending account **457**
health maintenance organization (HMO) **445**
individual retirement account (IRA) **450**
Keogh plan **451**
managed care **444**
mandated benefits **436**
noncontributory plan **449**
pension plans **448**
portability **449**
preferred provider organization (PPO) **445**
serious health condition **440**
severance pay **441**
total compensation **434**
utilization review **446**
vesting **450**
well-pay **455**
workers' compensation **438**

Case

Concord Management and Health Care Costs

Concord Management is a real-estate management firm in Grand Rapids, Michigan that employs nine people and uses a health plan that rewards people for pinching pennies. The firm dropped its expensive Blue Cross and Blue Shield plan to avoid further premium increases.

Instead Concord purchased a less expensive "catastrophic" policy that covers only major expenses above $1,500 per person and $2,000 per family annually. The company used the savings to set up medical savings accounts (MSAs) for employees to cover expenses before the insurance begins. Any unused amount at the end of the year goes to employees to keep.

Concord Management and Health Care Costs, continued

The effect has been to make the employees cost-conscious shoppers. Employees often don't know or care what a physician charges because insurance pays the cost. But Richard Norton, who suffers from asthma, is a good example of how the new plan works. He began asking questions of his physician and pharmacist about the price of his medication when the new plan began. "I wanted to find out if there were treatments that cost less," he said. They were—his new prescription costs 1/4 of what the old one did. He got a check for $750, the unspent balance of his $1,500 medical savings account at the end of the year.

For the employer, total health care costs have slowed since the new plan. Management notes that employees are making fewer claims and the cost increases in medical insurance premiums have declined dramatically.

This approach is getting attention in Congress. The combination of MSAs and catastrophic health insurance is being touted by some as a nonbureaucratic approach to health care reform and cost containment. Advocates want to allow employers and employees to contribute to MSAs like 401(k) plans with pre-tax dollars, and then allow employees to have the portability to move those accounts from job to job.

❖ *Questions*

Encourage EE's to shop around for providers

1. Explain the mechanism whereby medical savings accounts (MSAs) could actually reduce the rate of increase in medical costs to employers.
2. Why would MSA's be politically controversial in comparison to the employer-provided medical insurance many employees receive.

❖ *Notes*

1. M. A. Hart, "Benefits Design and Delivery for Mergers and Acquisitions," *ACA Journal,* Winter 1995, 39–40; Blackman and Associates, "Employee Benefit Plans after the Merger," *Viewpoint on Value,* May/June 1995, 1–4; D. H. Liberson, "How Capitol One Recreated Its Human Resources Strategy Following a Spin-Off," *ACA Journal,* Winter 1995, 32–35; and Hewitt Associates, "A Perspective on Outsourcing and Benefit Service Delivery," *On Employee Benefits,* November/December 1995, 1.
2. Roger Thompson, "Benefit Costs Shift into Reverse," *Nation's Business,* February 1996, 50.
3. G. Noceti, "Hidden Paycheck," *Solutions,* October 1994, 42.
4. Roger Thompson, "Benefit Costs Shift into Reverse," *Nation's Business,* February 1996, 50.
5. Paul Magnusson, "Social Security:Apocalypse Soon—or Sooner," *Business Week,* May 1, 1995, 138.
6. "Anti-Social Security," *The Economist,* January 21, 1995, 30.
7. "Benefits Arise in Eastern Europe and Russia's New Free Markets," *World Link,* February–March 1995, 1–2.
8. "Cashing In: Bogus Workplace Injuries Become Growing Scam," *The Wall Street Journal,* October 17, 1995.
9. M. J. Killian, "Reducing Workers' Compensation Costs," *Journal of Health Care Benefits,* May/June 1994, 26–31; N. C. Tompkins, "The New Round of Workers' Compensation Controls," *Compensation and Benefits Review,* May/June 1995, 45–50; and C. L. Lorenz, "Nine Practical Suggestions for Streamlining Workers' Compensation Costs," *Compensation and Benefits Review,* May/June 1995, 40–44.
10. S. Shellenbarger, "Work and Family," *The Wall Street Journal,* March 16, 1994, B1.
11. Joann S. Lublin, "Family-Leave Law Can Be Excuse for a Day Off," *The Wall Street Journal,* July 7, 1995, B1.
12. A. T. Steinberg, "Beyond the Tax Code: How Employee Needs Are Driving Benefits Design," *Compensation and Benefits Review,* January/February 1995, 29–32.
13. Gillian Flynn, "Does Your Severance Plan Make the Cut?" *Personnel Journal,* August, 1995, 32–40.
14. E. E. Kosseh and V. Nichol, "The Effects of On-Site Child Care on Employee Attitudes and Performance," *Personnel Psychology* 45 (1992), 485–507.
15. Laura Beller, "Elder Care's Growing Presence Is an HR Matter," *Benefits & Compensation Solutions,* October 1995, 21.
16. S. Shellenbarger, "Work and Family," *The Wall Street Journal,* August 2, 1995, B1.
17. Del Jones and A. Willette, "Critics Claim Disney's Gay Policies Are Anti-Family," *USA Today,* October 19, 1995, B1.
18. Ellen Schultz, "Advantages of Employer Health Plans Are Disappearing," *The Wall Street Journal,* June 17, 1994, C1.
19. Melissa Barringer and Olivia Mitchell, "Workers' Preferences among Company-Provided Health Insurance Plans," *Industrial and Labor Relations Review,* 47 (1994), 141.

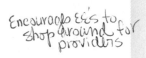

20. Ron Winslow, "Employer Group Rethinks Commitment to Big HMOs," *The Wall Street Journal*, July 21, 1995, B1.
21. "IBM Adopts Strategic Framework to Evaluate HMOs," in *On Health Care* (Lincolnshire, IL: Hewitt Associates, 1995), 4.
22. D. Shanks, "Improve Communication about Health Care," *Benefits & Compensation Solutions*, December 1995, 48–49; Olga Padilla, "Empowering Employees through Health Care Education: Changing Attitudes and Behavior," *Employee Benefits Journal*, June 1994, 13–14; and Camille Haltom, "Shifting the Health Care Focus from Sickness to Wellness," *Compensation and Benefits Review*, January–February 1995, 47–53.
23. "The Sky Isn't Falling," *The Wall Street Journal*, June 13, 1995, A1.
24. Mary Ellen Benedict and Kathryn Shaw, "The Impact of Pension Benefits on the Distribution of Earned Income," *Industrial and Labor Relations Review*, July 1995, 240–256.
25. Jim Sullivan, "Retirement Planning," *Benefits & Compensation Solutions*, March 1994, 18; Sidney Siegel, "A Comparative Study of Preretirement Programs in the Public Sector," *Public Personnel Management*, Winter 1994, 631–647; and D. Veeneman, "How Employees' Investment Decisions Are Linked to Your Bottom Line," *Compensation and Benefits Review*, January/February 1995, 38–40.
26. R. Allen (ed.), "ERISA:The Twentieth Anniversary," *Working Age*, 10 (September/October 1994).
27. "A Balancing Act," *The Economist*, November 26, 1994, 91.
28. *Arizona Governing Committee v. Norris*, 103 S.Ct. 3492, 32FEP Cases 233 (1983).
29. L. E. Papke, "Participation in and Contributions to 401(k) Pension Plans," *The Journal of Human Resources*, Spring 1995, 311–323.
30. J. F. Marlowe and W. P. Jones, "Managed Disability Savings Opportunities," *Journal of Compensation and Benefits*, May/June 1994, 18–25; and D. Coleman, "Disability Insurance," *Lifelines*, Fall 1995, 3–6.
31. T. S. Davidson, "Educational Assistance Programs," *Basics*, Second quarter 1994.
32. L. Dianis, "The Dream Team of Corporate Benefits," *Benefits & Compensation Solutions*, January 1996, 20–21; Julia Lawlor, "Offbeat Perks Can Perk Up Workers," *USA Today*, July 20, 1993, B2; and "Perks Can Make the Difference," *Omaha World-Herald*, April 11, 1993, 1G.
33. "Survey: Few Workers Use 'Emergency' Unpaid Leave," *Omaha World Herald*, October 29, 1995, C1.
34. Ellen Schultz, "Time-Off Bank Lets Employees Choose," *The Wall Street Journal*, September 27, 1994, C1.
35. Alex Markels, "Use It or Lose It: Vacation Time Expires Now," *The Wall Street Journal*, December 28, 1995, B1.
36. "Supplier Solutions," *Benefits & Compensation Solutions*, October 1995, 61.
37. M. L. Williams, "Antecedents of Employee Benefit Level Satisfaction: A Test of a Model," *Journal of Management* 21 (1995), 1097–1128.
38. J. F. Levy and A. Z. Krebs, "Flexible Spending Accounts: Medreal IRA's and Partner's Reimbursement Accounts," *Paytech*, July/August 1994, 38–42.
39. "Tough Choices: Extra Vacation or a Free Trip to the Dentist," *Finance Executive*, May 1989, 6–7.
40. "What Benefits," *The Wall Street Journal*, November 14, 1995, 1.
41. Based on Laura M. Litvan, "Building Nest Eggs for Medical Bills," *Nation's Business*, July 1995, 31–32.

EXERCISE 10 - Analysis

Employee benefits plans vary in scope and complexity from employer to employer. As the opening vignette in Chapter 15 discusses, one of the greatest challenges when firms merge or acquire other firms is combining benefits plans.

SME-TEK now faces this challenge, as the benefits offered by XYZ Communications contain vision insurance. However, SME-TEK currently does not offer vision insurance, which must be added to the HRIS database listing of benefits.

1. What are the advantages and disadvantages of allowing employees in an acquired firm to maintain their benefits unchanged for a period of time?
2. In the HRIS, establish vision insurance as a category and enroll Susan Mackey, hired from XYZ Communications, in the vision insurance program.

SME-TEK

MEMO

TO: *HUMAN RESOURCE MANAGEMENT USER*

SME-TEK has just acquired XYZ Communications. The former XYZ employees are being permitted to retain their benefits for the remainder of the current plan year. However, their plan contains vision insurance which SME-TEK does not offer, so we need to add this benefit to our benefit plan tables.

When you've set up the plan, please enroll Susan Mackey, whom we have just hired from XYZ Communications, in the Vision plan.

Thanks,

Mary Steedman
Employee Benefits Coordinator

EXERCISE 10 - Procedure

Before completing the memo's request, you need to access the Human Resources module and review the topic "Employee Benefits Tables" in the "Employee Benefits" lesson of the Concepts section. The Checkpoint topic in this lesson is optional.

To fulfill the memo's request, access the "Employee Benefits" lesson of the Human Resources Features & Processes section. Then, review the topics "Setting Up Benefit Plans" and "Managing Employee Benefits."

EXERCISE 11 - Analysis

Family and dependent benefits are of major value to many employees. Often, access to health benefits and the extent of coverage may affect whether individuals choose one employer over other possibilities. But for new employees, as well as existing ones, it is crucial to have accurate information so that employee claims get paid promptly and accurately. If the organization offers family benefits, then information on family status changes must be tracked also.

Carmen Jiminez, a SME-TEK employee, had her first baby last week, so her records need to be updated.

1. Discuss benefits issues associated with the birth of a child by an employee, including the requirements under the Family/Medical Leave Act.
2. Enter the information on Carmen Jimenez's new child into the HRIS, based upon the data contained in the CD-ROM.

SME-TEK

MEMO

TO: *HUMAN RESOURCE MANAGEMENT USER*

Carmen Jimenez had her first baby last week. Please enter Carmen's new child into her records as a dependent, then add this new dependent to her medical plan.

Thanks!

Susan Kyle
Manager, Human Resources

EXERCISE 11 - Procedure

To fulfill the memo's request, access the "Employee Benefits" lesson of the Human Resources Features & Processes section. Then, review the topic "Changing Plans and Covering Dependents." The Practice and Checkpoint topics in this lesson are optional.

EXERCISE 12 - Analysis

One of the greatest uses of an HRIS is to comply with the requirements of the provisions of COBRA, the general provisions of which are highlighted in Chapter 15. There are a number of qualifying events that trigger COBRA notification requirements.

In this exercise you can review some of the details of COBRA and then take action to provide COBRA notification to David Cadiz, who has been terminated from employment at SME TEK. But, COBRA continuation coverage generally is not available for dependents age 18 and above.

1. Give some examples of situations that would be "qualifying events" for COBRA, and then discuss why COBRA is beneficial to employees, but an administration burden on employers.
2. Remove David Cadiz (Employee No. 1080) from employment and send him a COBRA election letter. Also, in his records remove his son Jeffrey, who turned 18 yesterday, and add a daughter Cherise Cadiz born a few days ago.

EXERCISE 12 - Procedure

Before completing the memo's request, you need to access the COBRA module and review the topics "Qualifying Events and Coverage" and "COBRA Administration Folder" in the "COBRA Overview" lesson of the Concepts section.

To fulfill the memo's request, access the "Getting Started" lesson of the COBRA Initial Steps section and review the topic "Terminating and Moving an Employee to COBRA." When done, access the "COBRA Administration" lesson of the COBRA Features & Processes section. Then, review the topics "Viewing and Entering Qualifier Information," "Tracking COBRA Election Correspondence," "Adding and Updating Benefit Coverage," and "Adding and Updating Dependent Data." The Practice and Checkpoint topics in this lesson are optional.

MEMO:

TO: *HUMAN RESOURCE MANAGEMENT USER*

Please terminate David Cadiz (Employee No. 1080) and move his records to COBRA. We will need to send him a COBRA election letter and change any of his benefits during this Open Enrollment period, if desired.

His son Jeffrey just turned 18 yesterday, triggering a second COBRA qualifying event that you also need to enter into the system. Update David's COBRA record to add his daughter Cherise Cadiz (born 4 days ago) and remove Jeffrey Cadiz, who turned 18 yesterday.

Thanks,

Susan Kyle

SECTION VIDEO CASES

❖ CASE 1
ACE
Fun and Profit Centers

When a California defense contractor, no loner in the Pentagon's good graces, abruptly had to stop buying machine gun and tank parts it had contracted for from Ace Co., Inc., a dozen years ago, the small Boise, Idaho, manufacturer and machine shop was shellshocked.

The California firm, whose troubles were unrelated to Ace, had become Ace's largest customer. Ace had invested heavily in the defense job, hiring and training people and buying equipment.

Now it had to decide whether to liquidate and pay off its creditors or borrow more money to continue. It stayed in business, knowing that the going would be rough. Henceforth it could borrow no more and must survive on cash flow alone. There were job cuts, and salaries of those who remained were frozen. President Raliegh Jensen took a pay cut.

He also took a hard look at company operations. A way of doing things eventually evolved, he says, that—relying on employees' help—narrowed down to honest commitment, on-time delivery, and quality parts.

Most job shop operators tell customers, "We will do the best we can," but in doing so are not making honest commitments, Jensen says. At Ace the customer is told the truth about a delivery date, even if that means losing an order. The commitment comes from the people who actually make the parts, through their supervisors, who deal directly with the customer.

Since they are thus associated with the customer, Jensen says, they have a heightened interest in the parts' quality. "Quality awareness is a characteristic that selected individuals instill in the rest of the group," he says, adding that a no-compromise attitude on quality has taken years to develop at his company and has required management dedication.

Ace has been split into groups, none containing more than 20 of its 90 employees, and each is a profit center with its own quarterly profit and loss statement. Groups share tools and machinery and form purchasing and marketing alliances. But they don't necessarily go to one another for work they don't do themselves. They are free to get it done on the outside.

Profit center managers are independent chief operating officers. Jensen and two other corporate officers keep an eye on them and offer advice, while maintaining control of the company's basic direction and finances.

Employees, who are polled on their group managers' effectiveness, get bonuses on the basis of how well their groups do and for good individual attendance. As many as 13 employees have missed no time for any reason in a whole year.

Jensen says Ace's structure "would probably not work for large corporations," but "we do not plan on being a large corporation." It has worked for Ace.

Sales, $5 million in 1993, have risen an average of 15.6 percent a year for a decade. The company has no complaints about profits.

Says Jensen: "Business is fun when you are successful and in a financial comfort zone. It looks like we are about to have a lot more fun."

1. Discuss the use of Profit Sharing and a 401K plan given ACE's Commitment to Customer Service and Quality.

2. Explain the interaction between a team approach and the incentive systems ACE has designed.

(Excerpts reprinted by permission of The Blue Chip Enterprise Initiative©, *Real-World Lessons for America's Small Businesses* pp. 53, 54; copyright 1994 by Connecticut Mutual Life Insurance Company.) ❖

❖ CASE 2
GALE & WENTWORTH
While the Herd Ran the Other Way

Within two years of its founding in 1988, Gale & Wentworth, a New Jersey property developer, faced an unfortunate market development: one of the century's most serious downturns in real estate.

America was in recession—New Jersey's economy was especially hard-hit—and office vacancy rates more than doubled peak rates of the early '80s recession. As landlords vied for tenants, lowering rents, some building values toppled to a quarter of they had been a few years before. Construction loans were hard to get, and new construction came to a virtual standstill.

Partners Stanley C. Gale and Finn Wentworth faced this challenging environment by adopting a contrarian strategy. They moved forward aggressively, diversifying vigorously.

Their firm, headquartered in the town of Florham Park but also operating at five other locations, had been a developer of upscale commercial properties. By expanding its in-house services and putting them to work for others, Gale & Wentworth became much more than that. Now it also manages office buildings and retail outlets, develops and manages residential properties, represents financial institutions in real estate negotiations, and is a major property investor. Having the foresight and resources to capitalize on a buyer's market, it has bought undervalued, top-of-the-line properties while the herd ran the other way.

Stan Gale and Finn Wentworth knew their strategy was risky, but they could see an immediate payoff on the services side and a future payoff when the market came back.

Employee incentives were a key element of the strategy. The company was split into four operating divisions—commercial, residential, asset management, construction—each with a manager given responsibility for the group. The division heads share in company profits and, in turn, distribute profits among their employees. When the company does well, everyone does.

In choosing division heads, the partners looked for people who could generate new business as well as handle what was in hand.

To fill the commercial construction void, the construction division sought out third-party business and completed $15 million worth of projects in a year. The residential division, targeting young families priced out of detached housing, created affordable single-family homes in prime locations. The division has built its reputation on offering quality construction and service.

Today Gale & Wentworth can look back on a rise in annual revenues to $20 million from $6.5 million in 1988 and an increase in employees to 185 from 35. The company has branched out to Long Island in New York and plans to open offices in Philadelphia, Westchester County, N.Y., and Fairfield, Conn. Eventually, its owners hope, it will go national. They are still moving forward aggressively.

1. Explain how employee incentives were a critical part of Gale & Wentworth's recovery.

2. What is unique about this business (industry) that lends itself to the use of incentives for employees?

(Excerpts reprinted by permission of The Blue Chip Enterprise Initiative©, *Real-World Lessons for America's Small Businesses* pp. 18, 19; copyright 1994 by Connecticut Mutual Life Insurance Company.) ❖

SECTION 6

EMPLOYEE AND LABOR RELATIONS

CHAPTER 16

HEALTH, SAFETY, AND SECURITY

After you have read this chapter, you should be able to . . .

- Define *health*, *safety*, and *security* and explain their importance in organizations.
- Explain how workers' compensation and child labor laws are related to health and safety.
- Identify the basic provisions of the Occupational Health and Safety Act of 1970.
- Describe the Occupational Safety and Health Administration (OSHA) inspection and record-keeping requirements.
- Identify and briefly discuss three different approaches to safety that comprise effective safety management.
- Discuss three different health problems and how employers are responding to them.
- Discuss workplace violence as a security issue and some components of an effective security program.

HR in Transition

Workplace Violence: Murder at Work

Traditionally, when employers have addressed worker health, safety, and security, they have been concerned about reducing workplace accidents, improving workers' safety practices, and reducing health hazards at work. A shocking statistic is that *homicide* (meaning murder) is the second leading cause of workplace fatalities, following only transportation-related deaths.

During the last few years, workplace homicide has been the number one cause of job deaths in several states. In one year, approximately one thousand individuals were killed at work, and an additional two million people were attacked at work. About 70% of the workplace fatalities involved armed robberies.

Workers such as police officers, taxi drivers, and convenience store clerks are more likely to be murdered on the job than employees in many other occupations. Often, these deaths occur during armed robbery attempts. But what has shocked many employers in a variety of industries has been the number of disgruntled employees or former employees who have resorted to homicide in the workplace to deal with their anger and grievances. Some examples include the following:

But what has shocked many employers in a variety of industries has been the number of disgruntled employees or former employees who have resorted to homicide in the workplace to deal with their anger and grievances.

- Clifton McCree worked for the city of Ft. Lauderdale, Florida, for 18 years cleaning beaches. Then he was fired for being rude to citizens, threatening coworkers, and failing a drug test. Two years later, he returned to the office where his work crew met and killed five parks workers and critically wounded a sixth worker.
- A younger worker at Wendy's Restaurant in Tulsa shot and wounded three employees and three customers. He was upset because he had not received a raise. Also, he had been turned down for a date by a coworker.
- A Los Angeles city electrician, Willie Woods, was angered by a poor rating on a performance review. Believing that his supervisors picked on him, he returned to work and shot and killed the four supervisors.
- Postal workers in several cities have been killed by coworkers or ex-employees. Workplace killings of this type have occurred in recent years in Dana Point, California; Edmund, Oklahoma; and Dearborn, Michigan, among other sites.
- A 22-year-old female employee at a Houston, Texas, insurance company was killed at work by a former boyfriend. At a retail store in another state, a disgruntled husband shot and killed his wife, who was working as a cashier.

The violence committed at work against employees by co-workers and former co-workers is a growing concern for employers. Also, employers have faced legal action by employees or their survivors for failure to protect workers from violence at work caused by disgruntled spouses or boyfriends/girlfriends.

These concerns have led a number of employers to conduct training for supervisors and managers on how to recognize the signs of a potentially violent employee and what steps should be taken. During the training at many firms, supervisors learn the typical profile of potentially violent employees. They are trained to notify the HR department and to refer employees to outside counseling professions, whose services are covered by employee assistance programs offered by the employers. The Liz Claiborne firm has held seminars on domestic violence issues. Polaroid Company works with women who have been threatened to tap their phones, provide escorts to and from parking lots, and assist them in filing for legal restraining orders against abusers.

All of the above examples illustrate that employers must provide for the health, safety, and security of employees at work in ways beyond just preventing workplace accidents and complying with federal and state safety requirements. At many workplaces, the HR staff has been thrust into a broadened role affecting employee selection, development of policies, and training of supervisors and managers.[1]

> "If only it weren't for the people always getting tangled up with the machinery. . . Earth would be an engineer's paradise."
>
> —Kurt Vonnegut

Employers are obligated to provide employees with safe, healthy, and secure work environments. But as the opening discussion on workplace violence indicates, meeting that general goal is not easy, nor can all situations affecting employee health, safety, and security always be anticipated. Nevertheless, both managers and HR specialists have responsibilities for health, safety, and security in organizations. Requiring employees to work with unsafe equipment or in areas where hazards are not controlled is a highly questionable practice that has led to the passage of workplace safety and health laws. Managers also must ensure that employees are safety conscious and are encouraged to maintain good health.

❖ Health, Safety, and Security

❖Health
A general state of physical, mental, and emotional well-being.

❖Safety
Condition in which the physical well-being of people is protected.

❖Security
Protection of employer facilities and equipment from unauthorized access and protection of employees while on work premises or work assignments.

The terms *health, safety,* and *security* are closely related. The broader and somewhat more nebulous term is **health**, which refers to a general state of physical, mental, and emotional well-being. A healthy person is one who is free of illness, injury, or mental and emotional problems that impair normal human activity. However, the question of exactly what is healthy or normal behavior is open to interpretation. Health management practices in organizations strive to maintain the overall well-being of individuals.

Typically, **safety** refers to protection of the physical well-being of people. The main purpose of effective safety programs in organizations is to prevent work-related injuries and accidents.

The purpose of **security** is to protect employer facilities and equipment from unauthorized access and to protect employees while they are on work premises or work assignments. Certainly, preventing unauthorized persons from having access to organizational premises and internal systems such as computer systems is part of protecting employees. Also, security may include providing emergency assistance programs to employees who encounter health problems while traveling on business internationally. With the growth of workplace violence, security at work has become an even greater concern for employers and employees alike.

❖ Health, Safety, and Security Responsibilities

As Figure 16–1 indicates, the primary health, safety, and security responsibilities in an organization usually fall on supervisors and managers. An HR manager or safety specialist can help coordinate health and safety programs, investigate accidents, produce safety program materials, and conduct formal safety training. However, department supervisors and managers play key roles in maintaining safe working conditions and a healthy workforce. For example, a supervisor in a ball-bearing plant has several health and safety responsibilities: reminding employees to wear safety glasses; checking on the clean-

❖ Figure 16–1 ❖
Typical Health, Safety, and Security Responsibilities

HR UNIT	MANAGERS
❖ Coordinates health and safety programs ❖ Develops safety reporting system ❖ Provides accident investigation expertise ❖ Provides technical expertise on accident prevention ❖ Develops restricted-access procedures and employee identification systems ❖ Trains managers to recognize and handle difficult employee situations	❖ Monitor health and safety of employees daily ❖ Coach employees to be safety conscious ❖ Investigate accidents ❖ Observe health and safety behavior of employees ❖ Monitor workplace for security problems ❖ Communicate with employees to identify potentially difficult employees ❖ Follow security procedures and recommend changes as needed

liness of the work area; observing employees for any alcohol, drug, or emotional problems that may affect their work behavior; and recommending equipment changes (such as screens, railings, or other safety devices) to specialists in the organization.

Regarding security, HR managers and specialists must coordinate their efforts with those in other operating areas to develop access restriction and employee identification procedures, contract or manage organizational security services such as guards, and train all managers and supervisors to handle potentially explosive situations. Managers and supervisors must observe work premises to identify potential security problems and communicate with employees exhibiting signs of stress that could lead to workplace violence.

❖ Legal Requirements for Safety and Health

Complying with a variety of federal and state laws is fundamental for employers developing a healthy, safe, and secure workforce and working environment. A look at a few major legal areas follows next.

❖ Evolution of Workplace Health, Safety, and Security Concerns

Before the passage of workers' compensation laws, an employee might not recover damages for an injury, even if it happened because of hazards inherent in the job or because of the negligence of a fellow worker. Workers who died or became disabled as a result of occupational injury or disease received no financial guarantees for their families. Employers (and society) assumed that safety was the employee's responsibility. With changing attitudes in society came the passage of the first workers' compensation law in 1911 in Wisconsin. Similar laws were later passed in all states, and the Occupational Safety and Health Act was passed at the national level in 1970.

Employers once thought that accidents and occupational diseases were unavoidable by-products of work. This idea was replaced with the concept of using prevention and control to minimize or eliminate health and safety risks in the workplace. Recently, increased occurrences of workplace violence and unauthorized access to computer systems have led to growing concern about workplace security.

❖ Workers' Compensation

Workers' compensation coverage is provided by employers to protect employees who suffer job-related injuries and illnesses, as discussed in Chapter 15. Workers' compensation costs are borne by employers. The types of injuries covered include more than on-the-job physical injuries: Coverage has been expanded in many areas to include emotional impairment that may have resulted from physical injury, as well as job-related strain, stress, anxiety, and pressure. Some cases of suicide also have been ruled to be job-related, with payments due under workers' compensation.

Workers' Compensation and the ADA The passage of the Americans with Disabilities Act (ADA) of 1990 created new problems for employers. Employers sometimes try to return injured workers to "light-duty" work in order to reduce workers' compensation costs. However, under the ADA, in making accommodations for injured employees through light-duty work, employers may be undercutting what really are *essential job functions*. By making such accommodations for injured employees for extended periods of time, an employer may have to make accommodation for applicants with disabilities.

Controlling Workers' Compensation Costs Workers' compensation costs have increased dramatically in the past and have become a major issue in many states. These costs comprise from 2% to 10% of payroll for most employers. During a 10-year period, the costs of workers' compensation claims increased 300%, so that the average claim costs $19,444.[2] Major contributors to the increases have been higher litigation expenses and medical costs. Another reason for increases is an increase in accident rates.

Industrial accidents cost billions of dollars each year in direct and indirect costs to employers. Calculating the cost of accidents is useful, because top management can review such data, and expenditures for improving worker health and safety are justified more easily.

Employers continually must monitor their workers' compensation expenditures. To reduce accidents and workers' compensation costs, an employer should have a well-managed safety program, which typically results in: (1) reduction in insurance premiums, (2) savings of litigation costs, (3) fewer wages paid for lost time, (4) less expense in training new workers, (5) less overtime, and (6) greater productivity. Efforts to reduce workplace injuries and illnesses can reduce workers' compensation premiums and claims costs. Many of the safety and health management suggestions discussed later in this chapter can be used to reduce workers' compensation costs.

❖ Child Labor Laws

Another area of safety concern is reflected in restrictions affecting younger workers, especially those under the age of 18. Child-labor laws, found in Section XII of the Fair Labor Standards Act (FLSA), set the minimum age for most employment at 16 years. For "hazardous" occupations, 18 years is the minimum. Figure 16–2 lists 17 occupations considered by the government to be hazardous for children who work while attending school.

In addition to complying with workers' compensation and child labor laws, most employers must comply with the Occupational Health and Safety Act of 1970. This act has had a tremendous impact on the workplace; therefore, any person interested in HR management must develop a knowledge of the provisions and implications of the act, which is administered by the Occupational Safety and Health Administration (OSHA).

❖ Occupational Safety and Health Act

The Occupational Safety and Health Act of 1970 was passed "to assure so far as possible every working man or woman in the Nation safe and healthful working conditions and to preserve our human resources." Every employer engaged in commerce who has one or more employees is covered by the act. Farmers having fewer than 10 employees are exempt. Covered under other health and safety acts are employers in specific industries such as coal mining. Federal, state, and local government employees are covered by separate provisions or statutes. The importance of the act is seen in Figure 16–3, which shows the types of illnesses and injuries that occurred in a recent year, when 2.3 million occupational illnesses and injuries were reported.

❖ Basic Provisions

The act established the Occupational Safety and Health Administration, known as OSHA to administer its provisions. The act also established the National Institute of Occupational Safety and Health (NIOSH) as a supporting body to do research and develop standards. In addition, the Occupational Safety and Health Revision Commission (OSHRC) has been established to review OSHA enforcement actions and disputes between OSHA and employers cited by OSHA inspectors.

"General Duty" Clause Section 5a(1) of the act is known as the "general duty" clause. This section requires that in areas in which no standards have been adopted, the employer has a *general duty* to provide safe and healthy working conditions. Employers who know of, or who should reasonably know of, unsafe or unhealthy conditions can be cited for violating this clause. The existence of standard practices or of a trade association code

❖ Figure 16–2 ❖
Child Labor and Hazardous Occupations (18 Is Minimum Age in These Occupations)

1. Manufacturing or storing explosives
2. Driving a motor vehicle and being an outside helper
3. Coal mining
4. Logging and sawmilling
5. Using power-driven woodworking machines*
6. Exposure to radioactive substances and to ionizing radiations
7. Operating power-driven hoisting apparatus
8. Operating power-driven, metal-forming, punching, and shearing machines*
9. Mining, other than coal mining
10. Slaughtering, or meat packing, processing, or rendering*
11. Using power-driven bakery machines
12. Operating power-driven paper-products machines*
13. Manufacturing brick, tile, and related products
14. Using power-driven circular saws, band saws, and guillotine shears*
15. Wrecking, demolition, and shipbreaking operations
16. Roofing operations*
17. Excavation operations*

*In certain cases, the law provides exemptions for apprentices and student learners in these occupations.

SOURCE: Employment Standards Administration, Wage and Hour Division, U.S. Department of Labor, *Child Labor Requirements in Nonagricultural Occupations,* WH Publication no. 1330 (Washington DC: U.S. Government Printing Office).

❖ Figure 16–3 ❖
Occupational Illnesses and Injuries

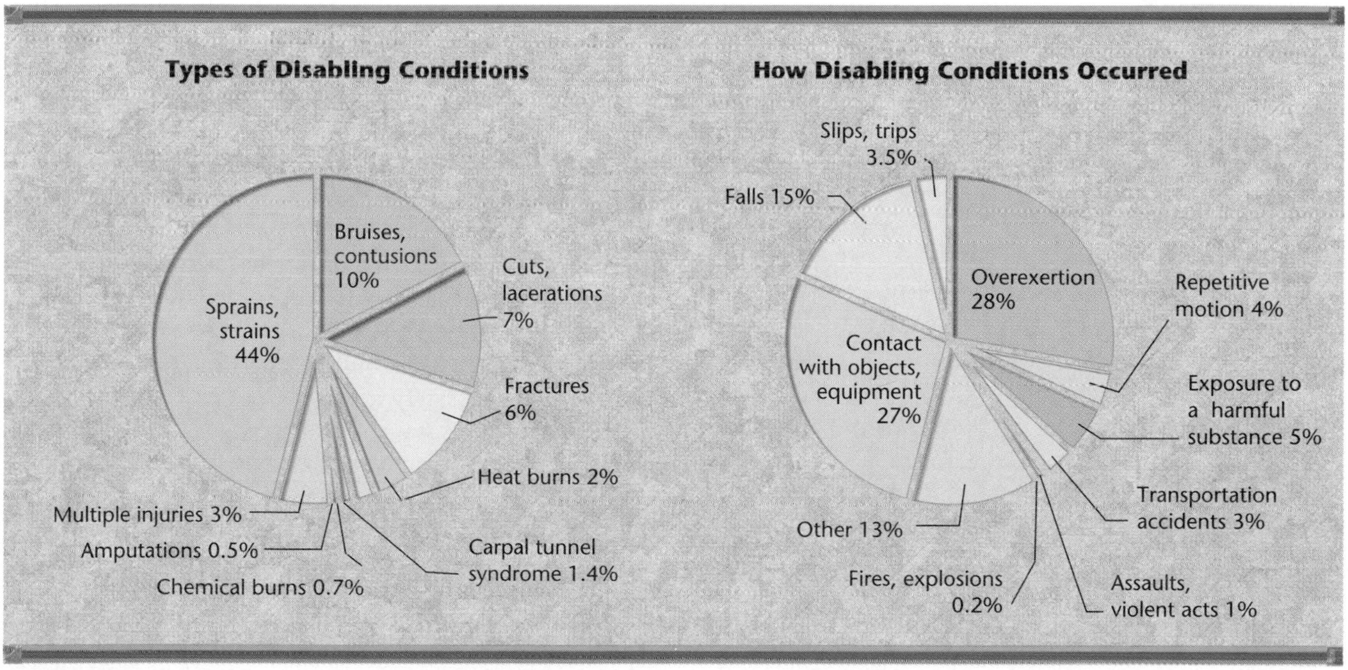

SOURCE: *HR Magazine,* October 1994, 58. Used with permission.

not included in OSHA standards often is used as the basis for citations under the general duty clause. Employers are responsible for knowing about and informing their employees of safety and health standards established by OSHA and for displaying OSHA posters in prominent places. In addition, they are required to enforce the use of personal protective equipment and to provide communications to make employees aware of safety considerations. The act also states that employees who report safety violations to OSHA cannot be punished or discharged by their employers.

Refusing Unsafe Work Both union and nonunion workers have refused to work when they considered the work unsafe. Although such actions may appear to be insubordination, in many cases they are not. Two important Supreme Court cases have shed light on this issue. In *Whirlpool v. Marshall* (1980), employees and unions won a major victory. The U.S. Supreme Court unanimously ruled that workers have the right to walk off a job without fear of reprisal from the employer if they believe it is hazardous. The Court ruled that "employees have the right not to perform an assigned task because of a reasonable apprehension of health or serious injury coupled with a reasonable belief that no less drastic alternative is available.[3] *Gateway Coal v. the United Mine Workers* clarified the necessary requirements by which employees can refuse unsafe work.[4] Current legal conditions for refusing work because of safety concerns are:

- The employee's fear is objectively reasonable.
- The employee has tried to get the dangerous condition corrected.
- Using normal procedures to solve the problem has not worked.

Work Assignments and Reproductive Health Related to unsafe work is the issue of assigning employees to work in areas where their ability to have children may be affected by exposure to chemical hazards. Women who are able to bear children or who are pregnant have presented the primary concerns, but in some situations, the possibility that men might become sterile also has been a concern.

In a court case involving reproductive health, the Supreme Court held that Johnson Controls' policy of keeping women of childbearing capacity out of jobs that might lead to lead exposure violated the Civil Rights Act and the Pregnancy Discrimination Act. To protect unborn children from the toxic effects of lead, Johnson Controls (which made lead batteries) barred women from jobs working around the lead. The Court said, "Decisions about the welfare of future children must be left to the parents who conceive, bear, support, and raise them rather than to the employers who hire those parents."[5]

There is very little research on reproductive health hazards. Yet employers need to protect themselves from liability for the effects of workers' exposure to threats to reproductive health. One attorney suggests the following:[6]

- Maintain a safe workplace for all by seeking the safest methods.
- Comply with all state and federal safety laws.
- Inform employees of any known risks.
- Document employee acceptance of any risks.

However, it should be noted that there is no *absolute* protection from liability for employers.

LOGGING ON

OSHA standards and related documents are available from OSHA at

http://www.osha-slc.gov/OshStd_toc

Enforcement Standards To implement OSHA, specific standards were established regulating equipment and working environments. National standards developed by engineering and quality control groups are often used. Figure 16–4 shows the OSHA standard for personal protective equipment (PPE) as an illustration of the form and terminology used. OSHA rules and standards often are very complicated and technical. Small business owners and managers who do not have specialists on their staffs may find the standards difficult to read and understand. In addition, the presence of many minor standards has hurt OSHA's credibility. To counter criticism in this area, OSHA has revoked about 900 minor or confusing standards. As an example, in 1995, OSHA decided to stop citing employers for failure to post the OSHA general information poster. Instead, an OSHA compliance officer will supply a poster and put it on a bulletin board in the work area.[7]

❖ FIGURE 16–4 ❖
SAMPLE OSHA STANDARD

OSHA standard 1910.132, General Requirements for Personal Protective Equipment for General Industry, requires employers to

- Perform a hazard assessment and equipment selection.
- Inform all affected employees of the hazards and the type of equipment that will be used to protect them.
- Ensure that each employee is properly fitted.
- Verify that the required workplace hazard assessment has been performed through a written certification that identifies the workplace and the person certifying that the evaluation has been performed.
- Mandate that defective or damaged PPE shall not be used and determine the extent of applicable "defect or damage."
- Train each employee to know, at a minimum, the following: when PPE is necessary; what PPE is necessary; how to properly don, doff, adjust, and wear PPE; PPE's limitations; and proper care, maintenance , life, and disposal of PPE.
- Test employees or otherwise ensure that employees can demonstrate understanding of the training covered and the ability to use the PPE properly before being allowed to perform work requiring the use of PPE. The employer must first define the learning objectives of the training required.
- Retrain an employee when there is reason to believe that an affected employee who has undergone training does not have the understanding and skill required.
- Verify that each affected employee has received and understands the required training through a written certification bearing the name of each employee trained and the subjects of certification.

SOURCE: General Industry Standards. USDOL Pamphlet OSHA No. 2206, OSHA Safety & Health STDS (29 CFR1910).

HAZARD COMMUNICATION OSHA also has enforcement responsibilities for the federal Hazard Communication Standard, which requires manufacturers, importers, distributors, and users of hazardous chemicals to evaluate, classify, and label these substances. Employers also must make available to employees, their representatives, and health professionals information about hazardous substances. This information is contained in *Material Safety Data Sheets* (MSDSs), which must be kept readily accessible to those who work with chemicals and other substances. The MSDSs also indicate antidotes or actions to be taken should someone contact the substances.

PERSONAL PROTECTIVE EQUIPMENT (PPE) One thrust of OSHA has been to develop standards for personal protective equipment (PPE). (Refer again to Figure 16–4.) These standards require that employers conduct analyses of job hazards, provide adequate PPE to employees in those jobs, and train employees in the use of PPE.[8] An example of a job hazard analysis is shown in Figure 16–5.

BLOODBORNE PATHOGENS OSHA issued a standard in 1992 "to eliminate or minimize occupational exposure to Hepatitis B Virus (HBV), Human Immunodeficiency Virus (HIV), and other bloodborne pathogens."[9] This regulation was developed to protect employees who regularly are exposed to blood and other such substances. Obviously, health-care laboratory workers, nurses, and medical technicians are at greatest risk. However, all employers covered by OSHA regulations must be prepared in workplaces where cuts and abrasions are common. Employers with the most pronounced risks are required to have written control and response plans and to train workers to follow the proper procedures.

EMERGING AREAS FOR STANDARDS With the shift of jobs from manufacturing to service industries, OSHA has begun to examine additional areas for setting stan-

❖ FIGURE 16–5❖
JOB HAZARD ANALYSIS

Date 2/3/96
Performed by John Berns
Verified by D. Kneipp
Title of employee doing job Automotive Mechanic
Job or operation title P.M. service on car or light truck
Department/division PU/Municipal Garage
Job location All locations
Special or primary hazard Dirt in eyes; foreign objects in eyes
Personal protective equipment required or recommended Safety glasses, safety shoes, dust mask

Basic Job Steps	**Existing or Potential Hazards**	**Recommended Corrective Measures**
1. Pull vehicle into shop and onto lift.	Hitting other parked vehicles in parking area. Hitting fixed object or vehicle in shop.	Do a circle of safety before moving vehicle. Check for clearances.
2. Jack up or raise vehicle on lift.	Vehicle falling off jack stand or lift.	Make sure jack stand or lift is properly set.
3. Drain oil, remove oil filters, check fluids under vehicle, and lube chassis.	Dropping parts or tools on feet. Debris in eye.	Wear safety shoes. Clean excessive dirt and debris from work area. Wear proper safety glasses.
4. Inspect and evaluate tires and wheels.	Back strain.	Use proper lifting technique.
5. Inspect and evaluate brake shoes and related parts.	Inhaling brake dust. Dropping tools or parts on feet.	Wear dust mask. Wear safety shoes.
6. Put oil in engine and add other fluids.	Liquid splashing in eye.	Wear proper safety glasses.
7. Close hood.	Closing hood on hand.	Make sure hand and other body parts are clear.
8. Inspect and evaluate light bulbs.	Glass bulb breaking, cutting hand, or glass in eye.	Wear work gloves. Wear safety glasses.

SOURCE: Michael B. Gunn, "Implementing the PPE Standard," *Occupational Health & Safety,* September, 1995, 63. Used with permission.

dards. Two of the most prominent areas in which OSHA has proposed standards are cumulative trauma disorders (CTD) and second-hand smoke. Because of resistance from a majority of members of the U.S. Congress, the proposed standards have not been implemented. But despite Congressional resistance, there are growing problems in these two areas, and they are discussed later in the chapter.

❖ INSPECTION REQUIREMENTS

The act provides for on-the-spot inspection by OSHA representatives called *compliance officers* or *inspectors.* Under the original act, an employer could not refuse entry to an OSHA inspector. Further, the original act prohibited a compliance officer from notifying an organization before an inspection. Instead of allowing an employer to "tidy up," this *no-knock provision* permits inspection of normal operations. The provision was challenged in numerous court suits. Finally, in 1978, the U.S. Supreme Court ruled on the issue in the case of *Marshall v. Barlow's, Inc.* In that case, an Idaho plumbing and air conditioning firm, Barlow's, refused entry to an OSHA inspector. The employer argued that the no-knock provision violated the Fourth Amendment of the U.S. Constitution, which deals with "unreasonable search and seizure." The government argued that the no-knock provision was necessary for enforcement of the act and that the Fourth Amendment did not apply to a business situation in which employees and customers have access to the firm.

The Supreme Court rejected the government's arguments and held that safety inspectors must produce a search warrant if an employer refuses to allow an inspector into the plant voluntarily. However, the Court ruled that an inspector does not have to prove probable cause to obtain a search warrant. A warrant can be obtained if a search is part of a general enforcement plan.[10]

TARGETED INSPECTIONS Beginning in 1995, OSHA adopted a targeted inspection process aimed at employers with the worst health and safety records, as evidenced by OSHA reporting forms and workers' compensation claims. The targeted program was developed to respond to employer and Congressional concerns about OSHA and to use OSHA budget resources more effectively, given funding cuts made by the U.S. Congress. OSHA also will continue to investigate workplaces based on employee complaints.

CONDUCT OF INSPECTIONS When an OSHA compliance officer arrives, managers should request to see the inspector's credentials. Next, the HR representative for the employer should insist on an opening conference with the compliance officer.[11] The compliance officer may request that a union representative, an employee, and a company representative be present as the inspection is conducted. In the inspection, the officer checks organizational records to see if they are being maintained and to determine the number of accidents that have occurred. Following this review of the safety records, the officer conducts an on-the-spot inspection and may use a wide variety of equipment to test compliance with standards. After the inspection, the compliance officer can issue citations for violations of standards and provisions of the act.

VOLUNTARY INSPECTIONS AND SAFETY CONSULTATION In conjunction with state and local governments, OSHA has established a safety consultation service. An employer can contact the state agency and have an authorized safety consultant conduct an advisory inspection. The consultant cannot issue citations or penalties and generally is prohibited from providing OSHA with any information obtained during the consultation visit. Such a visit provides an employer with safety information to help prevent future difficulties when OSHA does conduct an inspection.[12] The program has become so popular that OSHA has not been able to keep up with the demand for the consultation service.[13]

❖ CITATIONS AND VIOLATIONS

As noted, OSHA inspectors can issue citations for violations of the provisions of the act. Whether a citation is issued depends on the severity and extent of the problems and on the employer's knowledge of them. In addition, depending on the nature and number of violations, penalties can be assessed against employers. The nature and extent of the penalties depends upon the type and severity of the violations as determined by OSHA officials.

❖ FIGURE 16–6 ❖
MOST FREQUENTLY CITED OSHA VIOLATIONS

CITATION	FREQUENCY	EXPLANATION
1. 1910.1200 E1	4,728	Hazcom: Written hazard communication program
2. 1904.002 A	3,944	Recordkeeping: OSHA log and summary
3. 1910.1200 H	3,833	Hazcom: Employee information and training
4. 1926.059 E1	3,463	(Construction) Hazcom: Written program
5. 1926.059 H	2,277	(Construction) Hazcom: Employee information and training
6. 1910.147 C1	1,958	Lockout/tagout/program (temporary *off* for machines/electricity)
7. 1910.212 A1	1,887	Machine guarding
8. 1910.215 B9	1,737	Machine guarding: Abrasive wheel
9. 1910.1200 F5	1,729	Hazcom: Labeling of containers
10. 1910.1200 G1	1,627	Absence of Material Safety Data Sheets

SOURCE: Adapted from information reported by U.S. Department of Labor, Occupational Safety and Health Administration, Office of Compliance.

The most common violations and citations are shown in Figure 16–6. There are basically five types of violations, ranging from severe to minimal and including a special category for repeated violations:

- Imminent danger
- Serious
- Other than serious
- *De minimis*
- Willful and repeated

IMMINENT DANGER When there is reasonable certainty that the condition will cause death or serious physical harm if it is not corrected immediately, an imminent-danger citation is issued and a notice posted by an inspector. Imminent danger situations are handled on the highest priority basis. They are reviewed by a regional OSHA director and must be corrected immediately. If the condition is serious enough and the employer does not cooperate, a representative of OSHA may go to a federal judge and obtain an injunction to close the company until the condition is corrected. The absence of guard railings to prevent employees from falling into heavy machinery is one example.

SERIOUS When a condition could probably cause death or serious physical harm, and the employer should know of the condition, a serious-violation citation is issued. Examples are the absence of a protective screen on a lathe or the lack of a blade guard on an electric saw.

OTHER THAN SERIOUS Other-than-serious violations could have an impact on employees' health or safety but probably would not cause death or serious harm. Having loose ropes in a work area might be classified as an other-than-serious violation.

DE MINIMIS A *de minimis* condition is one that is not directly and immediately related to employees' safety or health. No citation is issued, but the condition is mentioned to the employer. Lack of doors on toilet stalls is a common example of a *de minimis* violation.

WILLFUL AND REPEATED Citations for willful and repeated violations are issued to employers who have been previously cited for violations. If an employer knows about a safety violation or has been warned of a violation and does not correct the problem, a second citation is issued. The penalty for a willful and repeated violation can be very high. If death results from an accident that involves a safety violation, a jail term of six months can be imposed on responsible executives or managers.

❖ RECORD-KEEPING REQUIREMENTS

OSHA has established a standard national system for recording occupational injuries, accidents, and fatalities. Employers are generally required to maintain a detailed annual record of the various types of accidents for inspection by OSHA representatives and for submission to the agency. Employers that have had good safety records in previous years and that have fewer than 10 employees are not required to keep detailed records. However, many organizations must complete OSHA form 200 shown in Figure 16–7.

❖ FIGURE 16–7 ❖

OSHA FORM 200

U.S. Department of Labor

For Calendar Year 19__ Page ___ of ___

Company Name

Establishment Name

Establishment Address

Form Approved
O.M.B. No. 1220-0029

Extent of and Outcome of INJURY						Type, Extent of, and Outcome of ILLNESS												
Fatalities	Nonfatal Injuries					Type of Illness							Fatalities	Nonfatal Illnesses				
Injury Related	Injuries With Lost Workdays				Injuries Without Lost Workdays	CHECK Only one Column for Each Illness *(See other side of form for terminations or permanent transfers.)*							Illness Related	Illnesses With Lost Workdays				Illness Without Lost Workdays
Enter DATE of death Mo./day/yr.	Enter a CHECK if injury involves days away from work, or days of restricted work activity, or both.	Enter a CHECK if injury involves days away from work.	Enter number of DAYS *away from work.*	Enter number of DAYS of *restricted work activity.*	Enter a CHECK if no entry was made in columns 1 or 2 but the injury is recordable as defined above.	Occupational skin diseases or disorders	Dust diseases of the lungs	Respiratory conditions due to toxic agents	Poisoning (systemic effects of toxic materials)	Disorders due to physical agents	Disorders associated with repeated trauma	All other occupational illnesses	Enter DATE of death Mo./day/yr.	Enter a CHECK if illness involves days away from work, or days of restricted work activity, or both.	Enter a CHECK if illness involves days away from work.	Enter number of DAYS *away from work.*	Enter number of DAYS of *resticted work activity.*	Enter a CHECK if no entry was made in columns 8 or 9.
(1)	(2)	(3)	(4)	(5)	(6)	(7)							(8)	(9)	(10)	(11)	(12)	(13)
						(a)	(b)	(c)	(d)	(e)	(f)	(g)						

Those organizations requried to complete OSHA 200 reports are:

- Firms having frequent hospitalizations, injuries, or illnesses
- Firms having work-related deaths
- Firms included in OSHA's annual labor statistics survey

No one knows how many industrial accidents go unreported. It may be many more than anyone suspects, despite the fact that OSHA has increased its surveillance of accident-reporting records. OSHA guidelines state that facilities whose accident record is below the national average rarely need inspecting.

Accident Frequency Rate Accident frequency and severity rates must be calculated. Regulations from OSHA require organizations to calculate injury frequency rates per 100 full-time employees on an annual basis. Employers compute accident severity rates by figuring the number of lost-time cases, the number of lost workdays, and the number of deaths. These figures are then related to total work hours per 100 full-time employees and compared with industrywide rates and other employers' rates.

Reporting Injuries and Illnesses Four types of injuries or illnesses are defined by the act:

1. *Injury- or illness-related deaths.*
2. *Lost-time or disability injuries.* These include job-related injuries or disabling occurrences that cause an employee to miss his or her regularly scheduled work on the day following the accident.
3. *Medical care injuries.* These injuries require treatment by a physician but do not cause an employee to miss a regularly scheduled work turn.
4. *Minor injuries.* These injuries require first-aid treatment and do not cause an employee to miss the next regularly scheduled work turn.

The record-keeping requirements for these injuries and illnesses are summarized in Figure 16–8. Notice that only minor injuries do not have to be recorded for OSHA. Managers may attempt to avoid reporting lost-time or medical care injuries. For example, if several managers are trained in first aid, some minor injuries can be treated at the worksite.

❖ Evaluating Effects of OSHA

By making employers and employees more aware of safety and health considerations, OSHA has had a significant impact on organizations. But how effective the act has been is not clear. It does appear that OSHA regulations have been able to reduce the number of accidents and injuries in some cases. But while some studies have shown that OSHA has had a positive impact, others have shown that OSHA has had no impact. Work-related injuries and illnesses per 100 workers had declined from 11 per 100 in 1973 to 8.5 per 100 workers by 1996. However, in the past few years, workplace fatalities have exceeded six thousand per year.

OSHA has been criticized on several fronts. Because the agency has so many worksites to inspect, many employers have only a relatively small chance of being inspected. Some suggest that many employers pay little attention to OSHA enforcement efforts for this reason. Labor unions and others have criticized OSHA and Congress for not providing enough inspectors. For instance, one review found that 75% of the worksites at which workers suffered severe injuries or deaths had not been inspected in the previous five years.[14]

❖ FIGURE 16–8 ❖
GUIDE TO RECORDABILITY OF CASES UNDER THE OCCUPATIONAL SAFETY AND HEALTH ACT

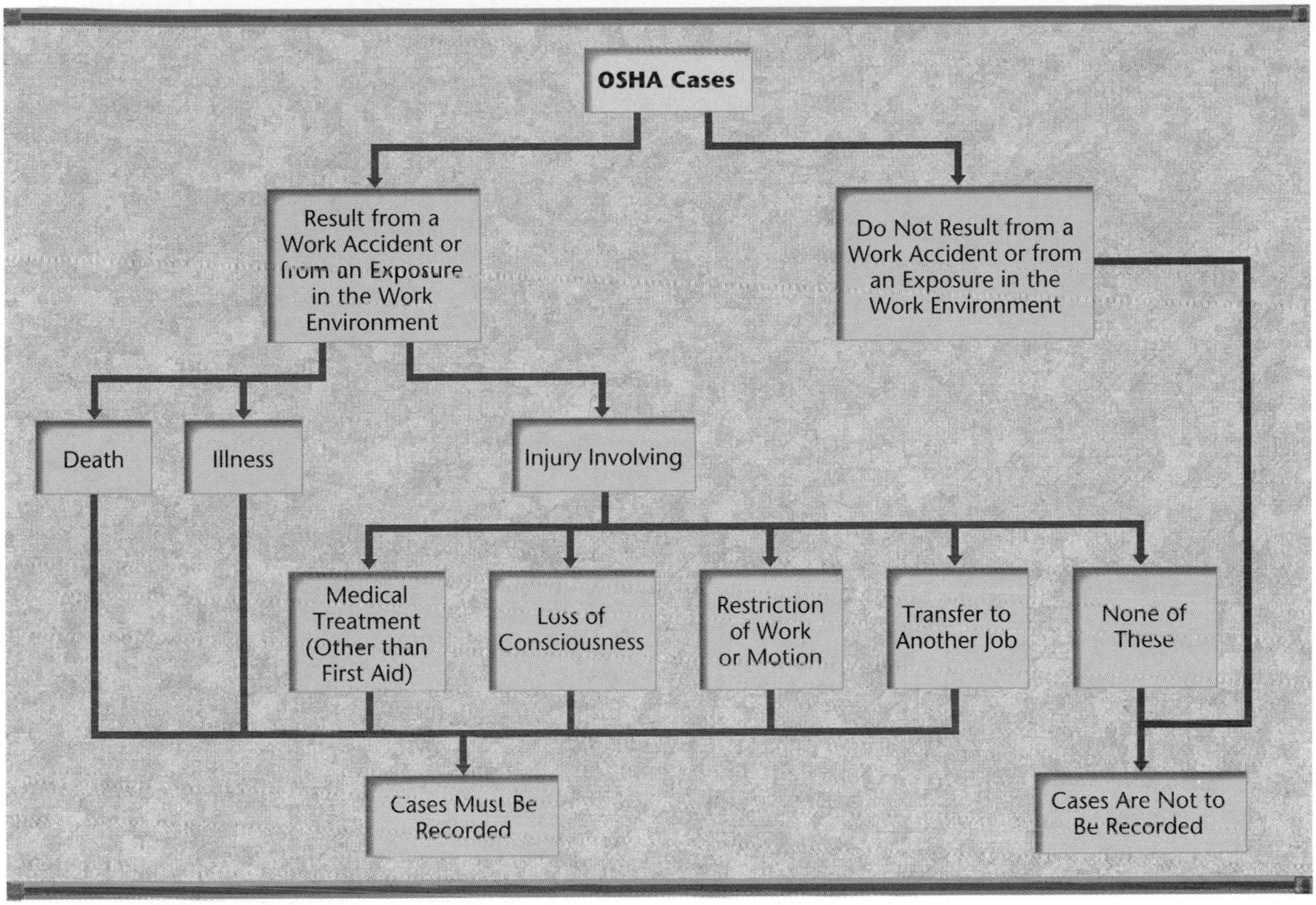

SOURCE: U.S. Department of Labor Statistics, *What Every Employee Needs to Know About OSHA Record Keeping* (Washington DC: U.S. Government Printing Office).

Employers, especially smaller ones, continue to complain about the complexity of complying with OSHA standards and the costs associated with penalties and with making changes required to remedy problem areas. Small employers point out that according to statistics from OSHA, small businesses already have significantly lower work-related injury and illness rates than larger ones.[15] For larger firms, the costs of penalties and required changes may be larger, but incurring such costs does not appear to affect significantly the way the firms are viewed by outsiders. One study over a 10-year period found that announcement of OSHA penalties had little or no effect on the stock prices of the violators during a period shortly after the announcements.[16]

❖ SAFETY MANAGEMENT

Effective safety management begins with organizational commitment to a comprehensive safety effort. This effort should be coordinated from the top level of management to include all members of the organization. It also should be reflected in managerial actions. If the president of a small electrical manufacturing firm does not wear a hard hat in the manufacturing shop, he can hardly expect to enforce a requirement that all employees wear hard hats in the shop. Unfortunately, sincere support by top management often is missing from safety programs. The importance of a commitment to safety is seen in the fact that both public and private organizations are rejecting contract bids from firms with poor safety records.[17]

Today, many firms are integrating an organizational commitment to safety with efforts to obtain ISO certification (see Chapter 3) and to implement total quality management (TQM). It is interesting that the processes used to reduce workplace hazards are very compatible with those advocated by Deming, Crosby, and other quality gurus. When a broader commitment is made, then firms attempting to obtain ISO 9000 certification must commit to safety.[18]

Once the organization has made a commitment to safety, three different approaches can be used, as Figure 16–9 illustrates. With all facets of safety addressed, then safety management becomes integrated with effective HR management throughout the organization.

❖ Organizational Safety Management

Once a commitment is made to safety, planning efforts must be coordinated, with duties assigned to supervisors, managers, safety specialists, and HR specialists. Naturally, duties vary according to the size of the organization and the industry. For this reason, it is impossible to suggest a single proper mixture of responsibilities. The focus of any systematic approach to safety is the continued diligence of workers, managers, and other personnel. Employees who are not reminded of safety violations, who are not encouraged to be safety conscious, or who violate company safety rules and policies are not likely to be safe.

Safety Policies and Discipline Enforcing safety policies and rules and disciplining violators are important components of safety efforts. Frequent reinforcement of the need for safe behavior and feedback on positive safety practices are extremely effective in improving worker safety.

❖ Figure 16–9 ❖
Approaches to Effective Safety Management

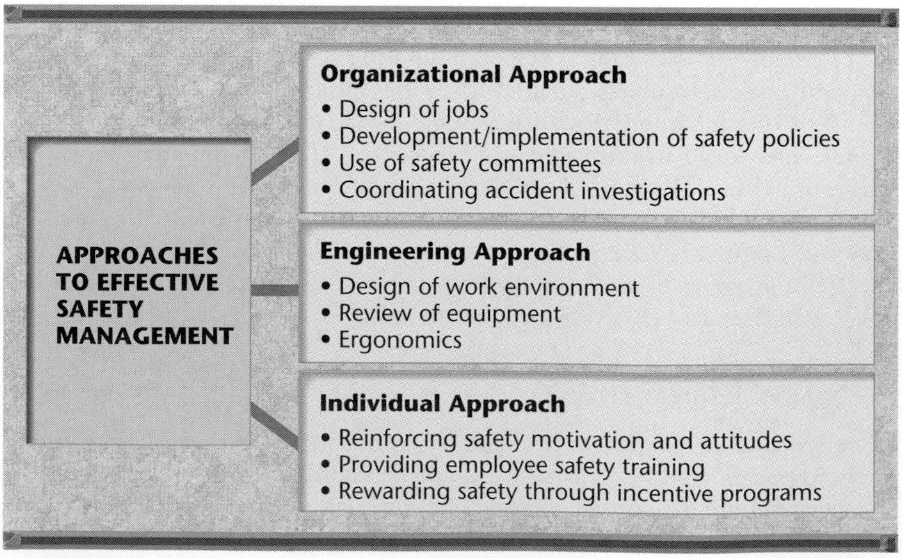

Consistent enforcement has been used by employers as a defense against OSHA citations. In one situation, a utility foreman was electrocuted while operating an overhead crane. However, the company was exonerated because it had consistently enforced safety rules and penalized violators. The employee who was killed had violated a safety rule for grounding equipment even though the company had given him regular safety training, had posted signs prominently, and had warned all employees about grounding equipment. The OSHA district director ruled that the employee's action was an isolated incident and management was not to blame.

SAFETY TRAINING AND COMMUNICATIONS One way to encourage employee safety is to involve all employees at various times in safety training sessions and committee meetings and to have these meetings frequently. In addition to safety training, continuous communication to develop safety consciousness is necessary. Merely sending safety memos is not enough. Posting safety policies and rules is part of this effort. Contests, incentives, and posters are all ways to heighten safety awareness. Changing safety posters, continually updating bulletin boards, and posting safety information in visible areas also are recommended. Safety films and videotapes are additional ways to communicate safety ideas.[19]

SAFETY COMMITTEES Workers frequently are involved in safety planning through safety committees, often composed of workers from a variety of levels and departments. A safety committee generally has regularly scheduled meetings, has specific responsibilities for conducting safety reviews, and makes recommendations for changes necessary to avoid future accidents. Usually, at least one member of the committee is from the HR unit.[20]

Care must be taken that managers do not compose a majority on a safety committee. Otherwise, the employer may be in violation of some provisions of the National Labor Relations Act. That act, as explained in detail in Chapter 18, prohibits employers from dominating a *labor organization*. Some safety committees have been ruled to be labor organizations because they deal with working conditions.[21]

In approximately 32 states, all but the smallest employers may be required to establish safety committees. From time to time, legislation has been introduced at the federal level to require joint management/employee safety committees. But as yet, no federal provisions have been enacted.[22]

SAFETY INSPECTION AND ACCIDENT INVESTIGATION It is not necessary to wait for an OSHA inspector to inspect the work area for safety hazards. Such inspections may be done by a safety committee or by the safety coordinator. They should be done on a regular basis because OSHA may inspect organizations with above-average lost workday rates more frequently.

In addition, when accidents occur, they should be investigated. In investigating the *scene* of an accident, it is important to determine the physical and environmental conditions that contributed to the accident. Poor lighting, poor ventilation, and wet floors are all possible contributors. Investigation at the scene should be done as soon as possible after the accident to ensure that the conditions under which the accident occurred have not changed significantly. One way to obtain an accurate view of the accident scene is with photographs or videotapes.

The second phase of the investigation is the *interview* of the injured employee, his or her supervisor, and witnesses to the accident. The interviewer attempts to determine what happened and how the accident was caused. These interviews may also generate some suggestions on how to prevent similar accidents in the future. In the third phase, based on observations of the scene and interviews, investigators complete an *accident investigation report.* This report form provides the data required by OSHA.

Finally, *recommendations* should be made on how the accident could have been prevented and what changes are needed to avoid similar accidents. Identifying why an accident occurred is useful, but taking steps to prevent similar accidents from occurring is important also.

ACCIDENT RESEARCH Closely related to accident investigation is research to determine ways to prevent accidents. Employing safety engineers or having outside experts evaluate the safety of working conditions is useful. If many similar accidents seem to occur in an organizational unit, a safety education training program may be necessary to emphasize safe working practices. As an example, a publishing company reported a greater-than-average number of back injuries by employees who lifted heavy boxes. Safety training on the proper way to lift heavy objects was initiated to prevent back injuries.

EVALUATION OF SAFETY EFFORTS Organizations need to monitor their safety efforts. Just as organizational accounting records are audited, a firm's safety efforts should be periodically audited as well. Accident and injury statistics should be compared with previous accident patterns to determine if any significant changes have occurred. This analysis should be designed to measure progress in safety management. A manager at a hospital might measure its safety efforts by comparing the hospital's accident rate with hospital industry figures and with rates at other hospitals of the same size in the area. The HR Perspective describes a successful safety effort at Horizon Steel.

Another part of safety evaluation is updating safety materials and safety training aids. The accident investigation procedures and accident-reporting methods also should be evaluated continually to make sure they are actually generating ideas useful in reducing accidents. Safety policies and regulations should be reviewed and made to comply with all standards set by OSHA, state agencies, and professional agencies.

❖ ENGINEERING APPROACH TO SAFETY AND HEALTH

Logic and reason suggest that both work design and human work behaviors contribute to safety. Yet some approaches to reducing accidents focus on one or the other exclusively. Both approaches are valuable, so they tend to be most effective when considered together. The engineering approach to safety and health is examined first.

PHYSICAL SETTING OF WORK Designing jobs properly requires consideration of the physical setting of a job. The way the work space surrounding a job is utilized can influence the worker's performance of the job itself. Several job-setting factors have been identified, including: size of work area, kinds of materials used, sensory conditions, distance between work areas, and interference from noise and traffic flow. Temperature, noise, and light levels are sensory conditions that affect job performance.[23] For example, noise decreases performance on complex mental tasks, tasks requiring speed, and tasks requiring high levels of perceptual capacity. "Personal space" is another factor to be considered. Some people need more space than others, and space needs vary from culture to culture. Violation

HR PERSPECTIVE

Catching Safety at Horizon Steel Erectors

Dramatic stories of several workers *not* being injured in falls from 60 to 100 feet have resulted from a cooperative effort in Atlanta, Georgia, among Horizon Steel Erectors Company, its insurance carrier, Argonaut Insurance Company, and OSHA's Atlanta East office. All workers were wearing full body harnesses and shock-absorbing lanyards and were tied off, so none was injured.

The three entities began working together through the initiative of OSHA as part of a pilot project in the Atlanta East office to change the way OSHA operates and interacts with employers. In the project, OSHA works with employers to establish comprehensive safety and health programs, not just enforce regulations. Argonaut Insurance Company, which specializes in underwriting workers' compensation, was chosen by OSHA because it was already working with clients to implement health and safety programs. Horizon Steel agreed to participate in the program to reduce injuries and costs of accidents. The following goals were set at Horizon Steel for the project: (1) reduce total claim costs per work hour, (2) reduce maximum claim costs, and (3) reduce potential OSHA penalties through risk assessment.

Risk assessment was conducted by the OSHA state consultation program; during assessment, citations and fines were suspended. Argonaut Insurance helped Horizon develop a supervisor accountability program in which safety was tied to the performance appraisal system. Bonuses for the supervisors were based on the safety record. Argonaut focused on supervisors because they are the long-term employees at any construction site, so they have a key role in creating a safety culture.

The current OSHA fall protection standard for steel erection is 25 feet for exterior construction. Typically, employees working more than 25 feet off the ground had to wear full body harnesses and shock-absorbing lanyards. However, Horizon Steel decided to require complete fall protection for all workers above *six feet* and to provide 100% fall protection. The equipment used by Horizon for this protection was more expensive than that required by OSHA, but by using it the company avoided costs of back injuries from falls. Even though Horizon had been in compliance with OSHA regulations, in the pilot project Horizon Steel went beyond the regulations and used more stringent requirements.

Results from the program exceeded goals. Claim cost per work hour was reduced by 96%. Maximum claim costs were reduced to $13,200, well below the target goal of $25,000. Managers at Horizon Steel believe that the success of their new program is the result of cooperation with OSHA and their insurance company. Best of all, the program helped to reduce injuries in the workplace.[24]

of space requirements makes people feel either isolated or crowded. Both reactions may cause stress and related safety and health problems.

Sick Building Syndrome The Environmental Protection Agency (EPA) defines *sick building syndrome* as a situation in which occupants experience acute health problems and discomfort that appear to be linked to time spent in a building. As an example, judges, lawyers, jurors, and employees who stayed in the Suffolk County Courthouse in Boston for any length of time complained of headaches, dizziness, sore throats, and other illnesses. After extensive study, the problems were traced to a waterproof coating used when the building was renovated in the early 1990s. The problems were so severe that approximately 200 workers had to be relocated for several years while various solutions were tried.[25] Unfortunately, this building is not the only example of this problem.

One cause of sick buildings is poor air quality, which arises in "sealed" buildings where windows cannot be opened. Inadequate ventilation, as well as airborne contamination from carpets, molds, copy machines, adhesives, and fungi, can cause sick buildings. Also, problems may result when the air flow and circulation controls are too sophisticated for the people who maintain them or when operators try to cut corners to save energy. OSHA officials estimate that over 20 million workers have health problems caused by sick buildings and bad air quality.[26] Air quality and the effects of secondhand smoke have become issues in the efforts to ban smoking at work.

Clearly, employers must examine the engineering design and the operations of air and ventilation equipment. Regular monitoring of air quality by building engineers is essential. When employees start complaining of becoming sick in certain parts of a building, HR professionals and managers should conduct investigations and develop remedies, just as they do when an industrial accident occurs.[27]

ENGINEERING WORK EQUIPMENT AND MATERIALS If accidents are caused by *dangerous work,* one obvious solution is to reengineer that work and the workplace to eliminate the accidents. This solution suggests an approach to the problem of accidents that is different from an approach based on the belief that *people* and their carelessness, reduced awareness, or limited capacities are the causes of accidents.

Employers can prevent some accidents by designing machines, equipment, and work areas so that workers who daydream periodically or who perform potentially dangerous jobs cannot injure themselves or others. Providing safety equipment and guards on machinery and installing emergency switches often forestall accidents. To prevent a punch-press operator from mashing her finger, a safety guard is attached to a machine so her hand cannot accidentally slip into the machine. Actions such as installing safety rails, keeping aisles clear, and installing adequate ventilation, lighting, and heating and air conditioning can all help make work environments safer.

***Ergonomics**
The proper design of the work environment to address the physical demands experienced by people.

ERGONOMIC APPROACH TO SAFETY **Ergonomics** is the proper design of the work environment to address the physical demands experienced by people. The term comes from the Greek *ergon,* meaning "work," and the suffix *-omics,* meaning "management of." An ergonomist studies physiological, psychological, and engineering design aspects of a job, including such factors as fatigue, lighting, tools, equipment layout, and placement of controls. Human factors engineering is a related field.

Most recently, attention has focused on the application of ergonomic principles to the design of workstations where computer operators work with personal computers and video display terminals (VDTs) for long periods of time. Workstations, tools, and jobs must "fit" a person just as a pair of shoes must "fit," or injuries can occur. Many eyestrain problems are related to glare and poor lighting or poor screen resolution. Ergonomically correct workstations focus on chair adjustment and support, VDT area and quality, station height, lighting, glare, noise levels, document placement, and screen flicker; rest breaks and employee training are also emphasized.[28] Figure 16–10 shows an ergonomically correct PC/VDT workstation. Notice that the level of the table, vision line of the screen, and chair height are all designed ergonomically.

***Cumulative Trauma Disorders (CTDs)**
Muscle and skeletal injuries that occur when workers repetitively use the same muscles to perform tasks.

CUMULATIVE TRAUMA AND REPETITIVE STRESS Repetitive stress injuries, repetitive motion injuries, cumulative trauma disorders, carpal tunnel syndrome, ergonomic hazards—this listing of serious-sounding problems applies to many workplaces. **Cumulative trauma disorders (CTDs)** occur when workers repetitively use the same muscles to perform tasks, resulting in muscle and skeletal injuries. These problems are occurring in a variety of work settings. The meatpacking industry has the highest level of CTDs.[29] But office workers increasingly are experiencing CTDs, primarily from extensive typing and data entry on computers and computer-related equipment. Grocery cashiers also have experienced CTDs from repetitively twisting their wrists when they scan bar codes on canned goods.

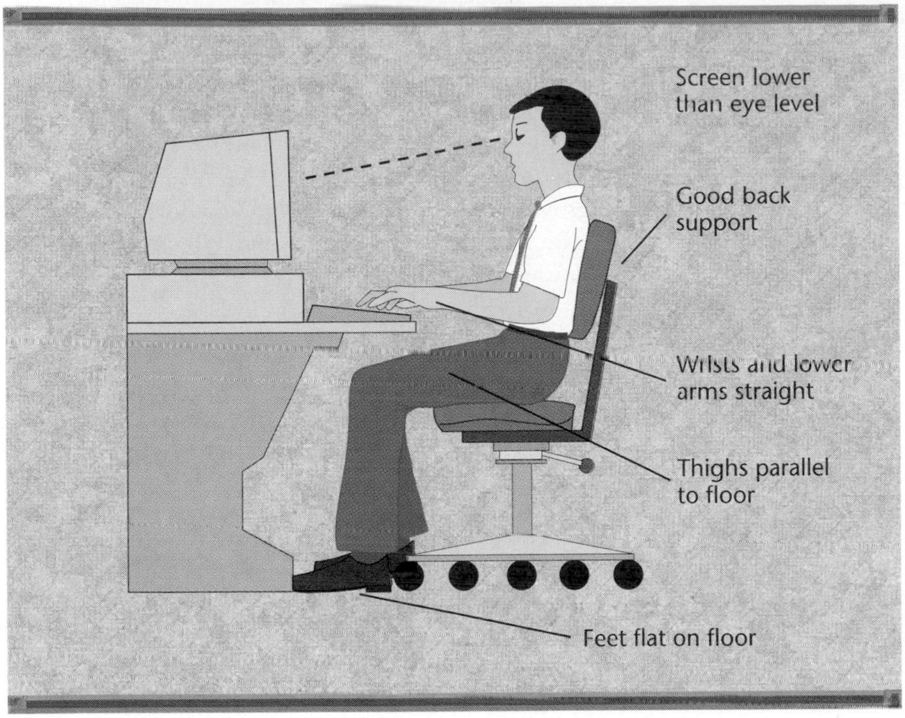

❖ FIGURE 16–10 ❖
AN ERGONOMICALLY CORRECT WORKSTATION

Carpal tunnel syndrome, one of the most common cumulative trauma disorders, has existed for years, but its incidence appears to be increasing. It is an injury common to people who put their hands through repetitive motions such as typing, playing certain musical instruments, cutting, or sewing. The motion irritates the tendons in the "carpal tunnel" area of the wrist. As the tendons swell, they squeeze the median nerve. The result is pain and numbness in the thumb, index finger, and middle finger. The hands of victims become clumsy and weak. Pain at night increases, and at advanced stages not even surgery can cure the problem. Victims eventually lose feeling in their hands if they do not receive timely treatment.

As a result of the growth in CTDs seen in many industries, OSHA proposed some standards that focus on the 2.6 million workers most affected by CTDs. However, the proposal met resistance from Congress and employer groups. Consequently, OSHA did not issue its regulation and is working to reduce the scope and effects of its proposal.

But employers should not wait for OSHA or state authorities to address cumulative trauma disorders. The costs of these injuries affect workers' compensation rates and reduce worker productivity. To address CTDs, it is recommended that three approaches be used.[30]

- *Assessment.* The worksites, jobs, and activities of workers in jobs most subject to CTDs should be studied and a detailed assessment made of typical injuries and what is needed to reduce them.
- *Ergonomic job design.* Work equipment should be modified if it is contributing to CTDs. For instance, ergonomically designed computer keyboards can be purchased. Also, rotating tasks so that employees vary their motions and activities every two hours is a typical approach. For example, a grocery chain has checkers restock shelves every two hours, providing them with a break from twisting their wrists as they use price scanners.

- *Training.* Both managers and employees should receive training to identify ways to reduce CTDs. Managers should be trained to use rotation of tasks as part of developing work schedules. Employees should be trained in how to work in ways that reduce CTDs and how to use equipment properly.

Undoubtedly, cumulative trauma disorder will continue to grow as an occupational problem with the growth in use of computers and automation of equipment.[31] Therefore, it will be critical for managers and HR professionals to identify potential CTD situations and address them.

LOGGING ON

For more information on human factors engineering see details on the Human Factors & Ergonomics Society at

http://www.hfes.vt.edu/HFES.

❖ Individual Factors and Safety Management

Engineers approach safety from the perspective of redesigning the machinery or the work area. Industrial psychologists see safety differently. They are concerned with the proper match of people to jobs and emphasize employee training in safety methods, fatigue reduction, and health awareness.

Behavioral Approach to Safety Industrial psychologists have conducted numerous field studies with thousands of employees looking at the "human factors" in accidents. The results show a definite relationship between emotional factors, such as stress, and accidents. Other studies point to the importance of individual differences, motivation, attitudes, and learning as key factors in controlling the human element in safety. The accompanying HR Perspective discusses a study that used behavioral feedback to reduce accident rates in a manufacturing plant.

HR PERSPECTIVE

Research Using Goal Setting and Feedback to Reduce Accidents

Four British researchers conducted a study to determine if goal setting and feedback techniques would be useful in reducing accidents at a plant manufacturing cellophane film. The plant was a three-shift operation with over 500 workers.

To begin, the researchers gathered accident data from the previous two years and classified it by department and type of accident. They also identified the degree to which the behaviors of individual workers had contributed to causing the accidents. Then those behaviors were verified in interviews with some of the workers.

Next, the researchers conducted briefings with managers on goal setting and feedback. Safety observers were recruited from senior production managers, and these observers were trained to observe workers' behaviors and then give feedback to them. Next, and crucial to the process, departmental meetings were held with all workers. In these meetings, checklists were distributed, and workers in groups and departments were asked to set goals for reducing accidents over the following 16 weeks. Workers were assured that the weekly results would be posted and meetings held to discuss the results.

The results generally were positive. Safe behavior rose from an average of 52.5% of goals initially to 75.6% of goals 12 weeks later. However, during the final four-week period, safe behavior dropped to 70% of goals as a result of accidents in one department in which maintenance was done haphazardly. Nine of the 14 departments showed significant improvements in safety, while two departments that already had 100% safety records showed no decline during the study. The other three departments did not do as well. The accident rate for the entire year showed a 21% decline compared with the rate for the previous year, and lost-time accidents declined by 82%.

Overall, then, the study appears to show that having workers set goals and giving them regular feedback on safety performance can improve safety management. A key element of the success appeared to be the participation and continuing involvement of all workers in departmental teams and groups.[32]

ACCIDENT RATES AND INDIVIDUALS Attitudinal variables are among the individual factors that affect accident rates. Attitudes toward working conditions, accidents, and safe work practices are very important because more problems are caused by careless employees than by machines or employer negligence. At one time, workers who were dissatisfied with their jobs were thought to have higher accident rates. However, this assumption has been questioned in recent years. One study found that individual workers who are constantly exposed to safety and health risks experience lower job satisfaction and greater job stress.[33] Thus, although employees' personalities, attitudes, and individual characteristics apparently have some influence on accidents, exact cause-and-effect relationships are difficult to establish.

ACCIDENT RATES AND WORK SCHEDULES Work schedules can be another cause for accidents. The logic to explain the relationship between work schedules and accidents is as follows: Fatigue based on physical factors rarely exists in today's industrial workplace. But fatigue defined as boredom, which occurs when a person is required to do the same tasks for a long period of time, is rather common. As fatigue of this kind increases, motivation is reduced; along with decreased motivation, workers' attention wanders, and the likelihood of accidents increases.

A particular area of concern in work scheduling is overtime. One study found that overtime work was related to accident incidence. Further, the more overtime worked, the more severe the accident appeared to be.[34]

Another area of concern is the relationship of accident rates to different shifts, particularly late night shifts. Many late-night shiftworkers experience sleeplessness during the day, so that they arrive back at work tired and not as alert. Also, because the number of supervisors and managers tends to be fewer in the "graveyard" shifts, workers tend to receive less training and supervision. Both of these factors lead to higher accident rates.

EMPLOYEE SAFETY MOTIVATION Convincing employees to keep safety standards continuously in mind while performing their jobs is difficult. Often, employees think that safety measures are bothersome and unnecessary until an injury occurs. For example, it may be necessary for employees to wear safety glasses in a laboratory most of the time. But if the glasses are awkward, employees may resist using them, even when they know they should have protection. Some employees may have worked for years without wearing the glasses and may think this requirement is a nuisance. Because of such problems, all safety training and communication efforts must address safety issues so that employees view safety as important and are motivated to follow safe work practices.[35]

SAFETY INCENTIVES To encourage employees to work safely, many organizations have used safety contests and have given incentives to employees for safe work behavior. Jewelry, clocks, watches, and even vacation trips have been given as rewards for good safety records. For example, safe driving awards for drivers in trucking firms have been quite successful in generating safety consciousness. Belt buckles and lapel pins are especially popular with the drivers. The effect of a safety incentive program is seen in the experience of the city of Port Lavaca, Texas, in which incentives reduced lost-time incidents dramatically. As a result, the city's workers' compensation premiums declined $150,000.[36]

❖ HEALTH

Employee health problems are varied—and somewhat inevitable. They can range from minor illnesses such as colds to serious illnesses related to the jobs performed. Some employees have emotional problems; other have alcohol or drug problems. Some problems are chronic; others are transitory. But all may affect organizational operations and individual employee productivity. A look at some common health problems follows next.

❖ AIDS and Other Life-Threatening Illnesses

Employers are increasingly confronted by the problems associated with employees who have AIDS or other life-threatening illnesses such as cancer. First, there is eventual decline in productivity and attendance brought on by progressive deterioration. Then, with AIDS specifically, there are the problems associated with anxiety in the workplace born of misunderstanding and misinformation.

Some firms have policies to deal with AIDS and other life-threatening illnesses. Firms that have lost an employee to one of these diseases are more likely to have a policy than those that have not. But estimates are that only 25% of the larger employers in the United States have a policy on life-threatening illness.[37]

It appears that many companies feel that it is unnecessary to adopt specific policies that deal solely with AIDS and other life-threatening illnesses because they do not want to draw attention to the problem and unnecessarily alarm employees. No matter what information experts might offer to assuage fear, an employee with AIDS, whether on the shop floor or in the executive offices, creates feelings of anxiety and unease among other employees, suppliers, and customers. To meet this problem and yet address the needs of afflicted employees, some companies are electing to continue to pay the employees full salary, medical, and retirement benefits on the stipulation they not return to work. However, more progressive employers have instituted education and training programs to educate employees about AIDS and other life-threatening illnesses.[38] Also, employers must ensure that they are complying with the bloodborne pathogens standards issued by OSHA.

❖ Smoking at Work

Arguments and rebuttals characterize the smoking-at-work controversy, and statistics are rampant. A multitude of state and local laws have been passed that deal with smoking in the workplace and public places. Passage of these laws has been viewed by many employers positively, as they relieve employers of the responsibility for making decisions on smoking issues. But the courts have been hesitant to address the smoking-at-work issue. They clearly prefer to let employers and employees resolve their differences rather than prohibiting or supporting the right to smoke.

Workplace Smoking Bans As a result of health studies, complaints by nonsmokers, and state laws, many employers have established no-smoking policies throughout their workplaces. Although smoking employees tend to complain initially when a smoking ban is instituted, they seem to have little difficulty adjusting within a few weeks, and many quit smoking or reduce the number of cigarettes they use each workday. One study tracked smokers in a hospital that instituted a ban on smoking. Those who were smokers reduced their cigarette consumption by a pack a week after the ban.[39] At Merck Corporation, there was a 25% decrease in the number of employees who smoked after a companywide ban on smoking was established.[40] Employers have also offered smoking cessation workshops and even cash incentives to employees who quit smoking, and these measures seem to reduce smoking by employees.

Environmental Tobacco Smoke at Work A growing area of concern is the effects on nonsmokers of others' cigarette smoke, which is referred to as *second-hand smoke* or *environmental tobacco smoke (ETS)*. The reasons for the concern are seen in a study done by a group of medical researchers who studied 25 different workplaces and collected air quality samples. In organizations where smoking was allowed, a majority of air samples at nonsmokers' desks exceeded levels classified as posing *significant risk*.[41]

Concerns about ETS have led OSHA to conduct research on ETS and to draft regulations requiring employers to take action to reduce the exposure of nonsmoking employees to workplace smoke. Some health agencies have urged OSHA to issue a total ban on workplace smoking. But because of pressure from the tobacco industry and many employers concerned about how to comply with the proposed restrictions, OSHA tabled the regulations. Nevertheless, action has been taken by courts at the state level. For instance, a New York Court of appeals ruled that employees who become ill from ETS at work can collect workers' compensation benefits.[42] It is likely that further court cases and regulatory action will develop to reduce ETS in workplaces.

❖ Substance Abuse

Substance abuse is defined as the use of illicit substances or the misuse of controlled substances, alcohol, or other drugs. There are millions of substance abusers in the workforce, and they cost the United States billions of dollars annually. The incidence of substance abuse is greatest among white men aged 19 to 23. At work it is higher among men than women and higher among whites than minority-group members. Blue-collar workers are more likely to abuse substances than white-collar workers.[43]

***Substance Abuse**
The use of illicit substances or the misuse of controlled substances, alcohol, or other drugs.

Employers are concerned about substance abuse because it alters work behaviors. The effects may be subtle, such as tardiness, increased absenteeism, slower work pace, higher rate of mistakes, and less time spent at the workstation. Research has shown that substance abuse also has altered behaviors at work so that more withdrawal (physical and psychological) and antagonistic behaviors were present.[44]

Substance Abuse and the ADA The Americans with Disabilities Act (ADA) determines how management can handle substance-abuse cases. The practicing illegal drug abuser specifically is excluded from the definition of *disabled* under the act. However, addiction to legal substances (alcohol, for example) is *not* excluded. Previous legislation and various government agencies have defined *disabled* differently, but the medical community seems to be in accord that both alcohol and drug abuse are mental disorders. Therefore, addiction is generally regarded as a disease, similar to mental disorders. Further, the regulations developed to administer ADA define both alcoholism and drug addiction that have been treated as disabilities.[45] Therefore, the prudent employer would probably be wise to consider recovering substance abusers as disabled under the ADA and proceed accordingly in considering them for employment and making accommodations for them to receive treatment.

Drug Free Workplace Act The Drug Free Workplace Act of 1988 states that any employer who has contracts with the U.S. government must maintain a drug-free environment for its workers. Failure to do so can lead to contract termination. Tobacco and alcohol are not considered controlled substances under the act, and off-the-job drug use is not included.

To be in conformance with the Drug Free Workplace Act, employers must do the following:

- Inform employees of drug-free workplace requirements
- Outline actions to be taken for violations
- Establish awareness programs and supervisory training

Substance Abuse and Managerial Responsibility To encourage employees to seek help for their substance-abuse problems, a *firm-choice* option is usually recommended and has been endorsed legally. In this procedure, the employee is privately confronted by a supervisor or manager about unsatisfactory work-related behaviors. Then, in keeping with the disciplinary system, he or she is offered a choice between help, possibly through an employee assistance program (discussed later in the chapter), and discipline. Treatment options and consequences of further unsatisfactory performance are *clearly* discussed. What the company will do is made clear. Confidentiality and follow-up are critical when the firm-choice option is used by employers.

Stress

The pressures of modern life, coupled with the demands of a job, can lead to emotional imbalances that are collectively labeled *stress.* Not all stress is unpleasant. To be alive means to respond to the stimulation of achievement and the excitement of a challenge. In fact, there is evidence that people *need* a certain amount of stimulation and that monotony can bring on some of the same problems as overwork. What is usually meant by the term *stress* is excessive stress.

Evidence of stress can be seen everywhere, from the 35-year-old executive who dies suddenly of a heart attack to the dependable older worker who unexpectedly commits suicide. Some studies indicate that some people who abuse alcohol and/or drugs do so to help reduce stress.[46]

When an emotional problem (stress-related or otherwise) becomes so severe that it disrupts an employee's ability to function normally, the employee should be directed to appropriate professionals for help. Because emotional problems are difficult to diagnose, supervisors and managers should not become deeply involved. If a worker is emotionally upset because of marital difficulties, for example, a supervisor should not give advice but should refer the employee to a program staffed by professionals.

Employer Responses to Health Issues

Employers who are concerned about maintaining a healthy workforce must move beyond simply providing safe working conditions and must address employee health and wellness in other ways. Next, some of the major ways employers address employee health issues are discussed.

Wellness Programs Employers' desires to improve productivity, decrease absenteeism, and control health-care costs have come together in the "wellness" movement. **Wellness programs** are designed to maintain or improve employee health before problems arise. Wellness programs encourage self-directed lifestyle changes. Early wellness programs were aimed primarily at reducing the risk of disease. Newer programs have emphasized healthy lifestyles and environment. Typical programs may include the following:

Wellness Programs
Programs designed to maintain or improve employee health before problems arise.

- Screenings (risk factors, blood pressures, cardiovascular disease, etc.)
- Exercise programs (endurance, aerobics, strength, etc.)

Peanuts reprinted by permission of United Feature Syndicate, Inc.

- ❖ Education/awareness programs (stress reduction, weight control, prevention of back pain, etc.)
- ❖ Skills programs (CPR, first aid, etc.)

Organizations have entered the "wellness business" not just because they have suddenly developed a higher social conscience, but because in each year employers spend billions of dollars on group life and health insurance premiums. Much of that money goes to finance care after emergencies (such as heart attacks) that are, at least to some degree, preventable.

There are a number of ways of assessing the effectiveness of wellness programs. Participation rates by employees vary by type of activity, but generally 20 to 40% of employees participate in several different activities over a longer period of time. While clearly more participation would be beneficial, the programs have resulted in healthier lifestyles for more employees. Cost/benefit analyses tend to support the continuation of wellness programs. Generally, at least two dollars in benefits are obtained for every dollar the programs cost.[47]

Employee Assistance Programs (EAPs) One method that organizations are using to respond broadly to employee health issues is the **employee assistance program** (EAP), which provides counseling and other help to employees having emotional, physical, or other personal problems. In such a program, an employer establishes a liaison relationship with a social service counseling agency. Employees who have problems may then contact the agency, either voluntarily or by employer referral, for assistance with a broad range of problems. Counseling costs are paid for by the employer in total or up to a preestablished limit.

***Employee Assistance Program (EAP)**
Program that provides counseling and other help to employees having emotional, physical, or other personal problems.

EAPs are attempts to help employees with a variety of problems. Some HR managers feel that EAPs make their other HR programs more effective. For example, in one large company, the Vice-President of Human Resources found that much of his department's time was being consumed by such problems as employee anxiety reactions, suicide attempts, alcohol- and drug-related absences, and family disturbances. Further, the medical department was not able to provide accurate information on whether affected employees could successfully return to work. The Vice President decided an EAP might save a great deal of time and money and was able to convince the President of the firm to fund the costs of the EAP.

Currently, many employers have EAPs. One survey found that 64% of all employers and more than 80% of larger employers have such programs.[48] Typically, about 10% of eligible employees use EAPs. A study of relatively new EAPs offered to over 2,000 employees found that about 80% knew about the program

❖ FIGURE 16–11 ❖
TYPICAL AREAS ADDRESSED BY EMPLOYEE ASSISTANCE PROGRAMS (EAPS)

- Career Counseling
- 24-Hour Crisis Hot Line
- AIDS Education/Support Groups
- Health Risk Screening
- Financial Counseling
- Retirement Counseling
- Legal Counseling
- Alcohol/Drug Abuse Programs
- Counseling for Marital/Family Problems
- Counseling for Mental Disorders/Emotional Stress
- Health Education (Smoking, Weight)
- Termination/Outplacement Assistance

and 6% actually had used the EAP. Usage by men and women did not differ significantly.[49] It is especially important to have such programs available when dealing with a potentially violent employee or one involved with substance abuse. Also, those with life-threatening illnesses or suffering from extreme stress can be referred to EAPs. (See Figure 16–11).

Unfortunately, it is hard to find an objective assessment of how effective EAPs have been. On the one hand, the Employee Assistance Professionals Association contends that for every dollar employers invest in EAPs, they recover an estimated three to five dollars in reduction of other costs or increased productivity.[50] On the other side of the issue are those who contend that EAPs cause health-care costs to go up, not down, because of difficulty in measuring effectiveness.[51] Further, there are many areas of potential liability arising out of EAPs for employers that must be considered before establishing EAPs.

❖ SECURITY

Security activities provide protection to employees and organizational premises, equipment, and systems. Many examples can be cited of security concerns at work. Security in workplaces is incresing as an HR issue. Vandalism against organizational property, theft of company equipment and employees' personal property, and unauthorized "hacking" on organizational computers are all examples of major security concerns today. Another growing concern is workplace violence, which may be seen in attacks by outsiders or coworkers on employees.

❖ WORKPLACE VIOLENCE

As the chapter-opening discussion indicated, workplace violence is a growing concern. The following occupations have the highest homicide rates at work:

- Taxi drivers and chauffeurs
- Police officers
- Hotel clerks
- Gas station workers
- Security guards
- Sales clerks
- Store owners
- Bartenders

People in these and some other occupations traditionally have faced a higher risk of violence from criminals. But the violent actions of employees and ex-employees also cause concern for HR professionals.

It is crucial that HR professionals and other supervisors and managers be trained to identify potentially violent employees. Research on the individuals who have committed the most violent acts indicates that a relatively common profile emerges, as Figure 16–12 indicates. One common sign is seen in employees who become very emotional over minor "injustices" that they have suffered or that

❖ FIGURE 16–12 ❖
WHO'S MURDERED ON THE JOB?

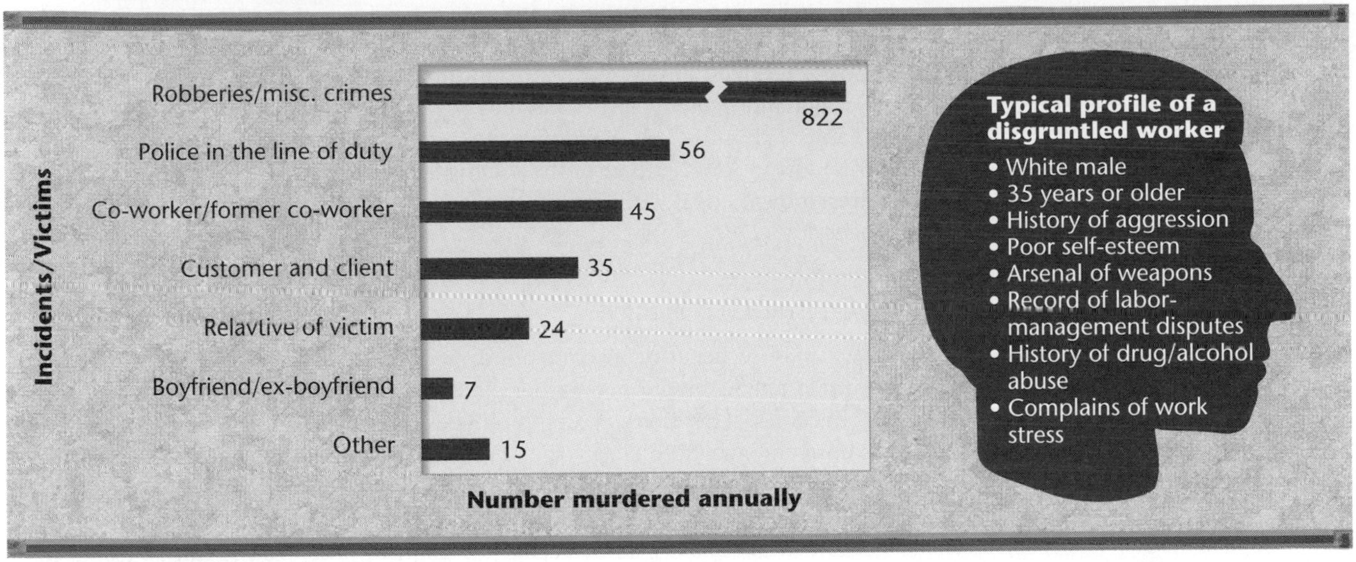

SOURCE: Monty Baumann, *USA TODAY,* April 5, 1994, 11a. Used with permission.

they perceive to have occurred. Another common sign is the voicing of threats to supervisors or other employees.

Some experts recommend that supervisors talk with employees who voice threats in order to allow the employees to vent some of their hostility and anger. Also, supervisors should try to get HR professionals involved. Often, an HR staff member can arrange for the upset employee to talk with trained professionals available through employee assistance programs. Another approach is to establish a violence response team composed of employees trained to handle violent individuals. Members of this team can discuss and/or deal with potentially violent employees and customers.[52]

However, employers must be careful, because they may face legal action for discrimination if they discharge employees for behaviors that often precede violent acts. For example, in several cases, employees who were terminated or suspended for making threats or even engaging in physical actions against coworkers have sued their employees, claiming they had mental disabilities under the Americans with Disabilities Act (ADA). In one case, the court ruled that a postal worker had a stress disorder; he therefore was able to collect $75,000 for actual distress and several thousand dollars in back pay.[53]

Workplace violence is only one workplace security issue. Actions that may be taken to address broader security concerns are discussed next.

❖ SECURITY AUDIT/VULNERABILITY ANALYSIS

Conducting a comprehensive analysis of the vulnerability of the security of an organization is the purpose of a **security audit**. Oftentimes, such an audit uses both managers inside the organization, such as the HR manager and facilities manager, and outsiders, such as security consultants, police officers, fire officials,

***Security Audit**
A comprehensive analysis of the vulnerability of the security of an organization.

manager, and outsiders, such as security consultants, police officers, fire officials, and computer security experts.[54]

Typically, a security audit begins with a survey of the area around the facility. Such factors as lighting in parking lots, traffic flow, location of emergency response services, crime in the surrounding neighborhood, and the layout of the buildings and grounds are evaluated. Also included is an audit of the security available within the firm, including the capabilities of guards and others involved with security. Another part of the security audit is a review of *disaster plans*, which address how to deal with natural disasters such as floods, fires, and civil disturbances.[55]

❖ Controlled Access

A key part of security is controlling access to the physical facilities of the organization. As mentioned earlier, 70% of all workplace homicides occur during robberies. Therefore, those employees most vulnerable, such as taxi drivers and convenience store clerks, must be provided secure areas to which access is limited. For instance, providing plexiglass partitions and requiring use of cash trays have reduced deaths in some convenience store/gasoline station locations.

Many organizations limit access to facilities and work areas by using electronic access or keycard systems. While not foolproof, these systems can make it more difficult for an unauthorized person, such as an estranged husband or a disgruntled ex-employee, to enter the premises. Access controls also can be used in elevators and stairwells to prevent unauthorized persons from entering certain areas within a facility.

Yet another part of security is controlling access to computer systems. With so many transactions and records being handled by computers, it is crucial that adequate security provisions be in place to prevent unauthorized access to computer systems, including human resource information systems (HRIS). The security of human resource information systems is discussed in the last chapter.

❖ Employee Screening and Selection

A key facet of providing security is to screen applicants for jobs. As discussed in Chapter 9, there are limits on what can be done, particularly regarding the use of psychological tests and checking of references. However, firms that do not screen employees adequately may be subject to liability if an employee commits crimes later. For instance, an individual with a criminal record for assault was hired by a Florida firm to perform interior maintenance of sound equipment. The employee used a passkey to enter a home and assault the owner, and the employer was ruled liable.[56] Of course, employers must be careful when selecting employees to use only valid, job-related screening means and to avoid violating federal EEO laws and the Americans with Disabilities Act.

❖ Security Personnel

Having sufficient security personnel who are adequately trained is a critical part of security management. Many employers contract this service out to firms specializing in security. If employees are to be used, they must be selected and trained to handle a variety of workplace security problems, ranging from dealing with violent behavior by an employee to taking charge in natural disasters.

SUMMARY

❖ Health is a general state of physical, mental, and emotional well-being.

❖ Safety involves protection of the physical well-being of people.

❖ Security involves protection of employer facilities and equipment from unauthorized access and protection of employees while on work premises or work assignments.

❖ Workers' compensation coverage is provided by employers to protect employees who suffer job-related injuries and illnesses. The costs are paid by employers, who must make efforts to control them.

❖ The Fair Labor Standards Act (FLSA) limits the types of work that employees under the age of 18 can perform.

❖ The Occupational Safety and Health Act states that employers have a general duty to provide safe and healthy working conditions, and enforcement standards have been established to aid in that process.

❖ The Occupational Safety and Health Administration (OSHA) conducts inspections of workplaces and can issue citations for several different levels of violations. Also, OSHA requires employers to keep records on occupational illnesses and injuries.

❖ Effective safety management requires integrating three different approaches: organizational, engineering, and individual.

❖ Among the organizational approaches to safety management, key elements include organizational commitment, safety policies and discipline, safety training and communications, safety committees, safety inspections and accident investigations, accident research, and evaluation of safety efforts.

❖ Accident prevention should be approached from both engineering and individual perspectives.

❖ Some work environments pose health problems, such as sick building syndrome. Fetal protection concerns may also arise in some environments.

❖ The engineering approach to safety and health considers the physical setting of work, work equipment and materials, and ergonomics to address problems such as cumulative trauma disorder (CTD).

❖ Accidents and industrial health concerns are major problems, both from cost and personal standpoints. Worker attitudes play a major role in accidents and accident prevention.

❖ Various health issues have grown in importance for organizations and employees. AIDS, smoking at work, substance abuse, and job stress are among the most prevalent.

❖ Employers have responded to health problems by establishing and supporting wellness programs and employee assistance programs (EAPs).

❖ Security of workplaces has grown in importance, particularly in light of the increasing frequency in which workplace violence occurs.

❖ Employers can enhance security by conducting a security audit, controlling access to workplaces and computer systems, screening employees adequately, and providing security personnel.

REVIEW AND DISCUSSION QUESTIONS

1. Identify the purpose of health, safety, and security as HR activities and discuss how they are interrelated.
2. Discuss how controlling workers' compensation costs is related to effective health, safety, and security practices.
3. Describe the Occupational Safety and Health Act and some of its key provisions, including current issues and standards.
4. What should an employer do when faced with an OSHA inspection, and what records should be available?
5. Why must safety management address organizational, engineering, and individual perspectives to be effective?
6. Discuss the following statement by a supervisor: "I feel it is my duty to get involved with my employees and their personal problems to show that I truly care about them."
7. Consider an organization where you have worked and describe some of the security issues discussed in the chapter as they might be identified in a security audit.

Terms to Know

cumulative trauma disorders (CTDs) **484**
employee assistance program (EAP) **491**
ergonomics **484**
health **468**
safety **468**
security **468**
security audit **493**
substance abuse **489**
wellness programs **490**

CASE

IMPROVING SAFETY AND HEALTH AT ONEIDA SILVERSMITHS

Oneida Silversmiths is a manufacturer of silver flatware and utensils located in Oneida, New York. In the early 1990s, Oneida was experiencing 137 lost-time incidents per year; these were cases in which a work-related injury or illness caused an Oneida worker to miss at least one scheduled workday. Also, Oneida was experiencing 7.3 lost-time accidents per 100 full-time workers. While both of these statistics were below national averages, they were still too high for Oneida. The firm's management knew that occupational injuries and illnesses affected productivity and insurance costs. But being concerned about their employees, Oneida's management also recognized that having workers miss work disrupted work-team activities and results and caused problems for employees and their families.

Oneida's management decided a multifaceted effort was needed to reduce occupational illnesses and injuries. A key manager in this effort was Dr. Scott Treatman, Oneida's medical director. Oneida's approach used both reactive and proactive efforts.

Reactive efforts included actions taken after injuries and illnesses had occurred to: (1) prevent them from occurring again and (2) reduce the associated costs. A more thorough injury investigation process was instituted, with the manager of the department where the injured employee worked playing a key role. Part of this process involved identifying how and understanding why the accident occurred and what changes were needed to prevent future accidents. Because back injuries were common at Oneida (and throughout the flatware industry), particular attention was given to reducing the number and severity of back injuries. Now, in addition to having medical assessments of their back disabilities, employees who lose work time due to a back injury must attend "back school training" before returning to their jobs. The focus of this training is to teach workers how to lift objects and move correctly in order to prevent back injuries. Additionally, the firm began monitoring its workers' compensation costs and claims more closely.

Proactively, Oneida began an ergonomics review of jobs in the firm, particularly those in which the greatest number of occupational illnesses and injuries occurred. Under the direction of a coordinator, departmental ergonomics teams now assess ergonomic hazards, identify potential solutions, and monitor changes after they are made. Regular team meetings are held, and the coordinator reviews the team's activities with senior managers every six months.

An on-site exercise program was started as well. Employees are shown stretching exercises and other movements that will help reduce fatigue and muscle tension. A wellness program builds on this program and focuses on employee health more broadly.

As a result of all of these efforts, over a four-year period, the number of lost-time incidents decreased to fewer than 50, and the number of accidents per 100 full-time workers declined from 7.3 to 1.0. In summary, safety management clearly paid off for Oneida and its workers.[57]

Questions

1. Discuss how the facets of the organizational approach to safety management contributed to the changes at Oneida.
2. Oneida integrated the engineering and individual approaches to safety management. Identify some examples, and discuss why you believe they were successful.

Notes

1. Donna Rosaton, "On-the-Job Deaths: Homicide No. 2 Cause," *USA Today*, August 4, 1995, A1; "Fired City Worker Kills Five Former Colleagues," *Wichita Eagle-Beacon*, February 10, 1996, 10A; Michael R. Mantell, "Let's Put a Stop to Workplace Violence," *USA Today*, April 5, 1994, 11A; Eric Malnic, Jeff Leeds, and Bettina Boxall, "City Worker Held after Four Supervisors Are Slain," *Los Angeles Times*, July 20, 1995, A1, A18; Shankar Vedantam, "Signs of Workplace Violence Often Ignored," *Omaha World Herald*, September 24, 1995, G1, G5; Joseph Pereira, "Employers Confront Domestic Abuse," *The Wall Street Journal*, March 2, 1995; and "Death on the Job," *The Economist*, December 3, 1994, 39.

2. Kevin Powers and Caren Arnstein, "Getting Them Back to Work Safely," *Occupational Health & Safety*, February 1995, 42–68.

3. *Whirlpool v. Marhsall*, 445 U.S. 1 (1980).

4. *Gateway Coal Co. v. the United Mine Workers of America*, 94, S.Ct. 641 (1981).

5. *United Autoworkers v. Johnson Controls, Inc.* 111 S.Ct. 1196 (1991).

6. Howard A. Simon, "Mixed Signals: The Supreme Court's Title VII Decisions," *Employee Relations Law Journal* 7 (1991), 214.

7. R. Blake Smith, "Where Is OSHA Going?" *Occupational Health & Safety*, October 1995, 41–46.

8. C. R. Diaz, "The ABCs of Emergency Response," *Occupational Health & Safety*, February 1996, 39–40.

9. "Occupational Exposure to Bloodborne Pathogens," *Federal Register* 56 (March 6, 1992).

10. *Marshall v. Barlow's Inc.*, 98 S.Ct. 1816 (1978).

11. For specific suggestions on handling an OSHA inspection, see William J. Goldsmith, "Preparing for and Managing an OSHA Inspection," *SHRM Legal Report*, Summer 1994, 1–4.

12. Laura M. Litvan, "A Low-Stress OSHA Review" *Nation's Business*, January 1995, 37.

13. Barbara Marsh, "Small-Business Owners Get Clean-Up Tips from OSHA," *The Wall Street Journal*, July 12, 1994, B1.

14. Earle Eldridge, "Study Links Job Deaths to OSHA Failure," *USA Today*, September 6, 1995, B1.

15. U. S. Department of Labor, Bureau of Labor Statistics, 1995.

16. W. N. Davidson, III, D. Worrell, and L. T. W. Cheng, "The Effectiveness of OSHA Penalties: A Stock-Market Test," *Industrial Relations* 33 (1994), 283–296.

17. D. Stripp, "Officials Reject Contract Bids on Proof of Poor Safety Records," *The Wall Street Journal*, February 6, 1995, B1.

18. R. Blake Smith, "Safety, Health, and ISO 9000," *Occupational Health & Safety*, October 1995, 119–121.

19. Janine S. Pouliot, "A Visual Approach to Employee Safety," *Nation's Business*, February 1995, 225–226.

20. N. C. Tompkins, "Getting the Best Help from Your Safety Committee," *HR Magazine*, April 1995, 76–80.

21. Henry J. Zaccardi and Scott D. MacDonald, "Worker Safety Committees and the Law," *Occupational Health & Safety*, November 1995, 48–57.

22. J. W. Vigen and Timothy S. Brady, "Safety and Health Teams," *NBDC Report*, March 1995, 1–4.

23. Karen Crawford, "Environmental Design in the Call Center," *TeleProfessional*, November/December 1995, 38–40.

24. Based on Ellen S. Carnevale, "Reinventing an OSHA Relationship," *Occupational Health & Safety*, October 1995, 57–64.

25. Barbara Carton, "Odor in the Court!" *The Wall Street Journal*, July 27, 1995, A1.

26. "Bad Air a Hazard at Work," *Omaha World-Herald*, May 7, 1995, G1.

27. J. N. Janczewski and S. J. Caldeira, "Improving Air Quality," *Occupational Health & Safety*, October 1995, 31–37.

28. Linda Thornburg, "Workplace Ergonomics Makes Sense," *HR Magazine*, October 1994, 58–60.

29. Laura M. Litvan, "Controlling Wrist and Back Injuries," *Nation's Business*, August 1994, 44–46.

30. Elizabeth Sheley, "Preventing Repetitive Motion Injuries," *HR Magazine*, October 1995, 57–60.

31. J. R. Davis, "Automation and Other Strategies for Compliance with OSHA," *Industrial Engineering*, February 1995, 48–52.

32. M. D. Cooper, R. A. Phillips, V. J. Sutherland, and P. J. Makin, "Reducing Accidents Using Goal-Setting and Feedback," *Journal of Occupational and Organizational Psychology* 67 (1994), 219–240.

33. David L. McLain, "Responses to Health and Safety Risk in the Work Environment," *Academy of Management Journal* 38 (1995), 1726–1743.

34. Michael Schuster and Susan Rhodes, "The Impact of Overtime Work on Industrial Accident Rates," *Industrial Relations* 26 (1985), 234–246.

35. E. Lightfoot and J. Bennett, "Train Me . . . If You Can," *Occupational Health & Safety*, February 1996, 47–49.

36. Jerry Laws, "The Power of Incentives," *Occupational Health & Safety*, January 1996, 25–26.

37. Romuald A. Stone, "AIDS in the Workplace: An Executive Update," *Academy of Management Executive*, August 1994, 52–61.

38. Nancy L. Breur, "Emerging Trends for Managing AIDS in the Workplace," *Personnel Journal*, June 1995, 125–134.

39. J. Brigham, J. Gross, M. L. Stitzer, and L. J. Felch, "Effects of a Restricted Work-Site Smoking Policy on Employees Who Smoke," *American Journal of Public Health*, May 1994, 773–779.

40. "Company Smoking Bans," *The Wall Street Journal*, April 12, 1994, A1.

41. S. Katharine Hammond, Glorian Sorenson, Richard Youngstrom, and Judith K. Ockene, "Occupational Exposure to Environmental Tobacco Smoke," *Journal of the American Medical Association*, September 27, 1995, 956–961.

42. Christine Woolsey, "N.Y. Court Awards Work Comp Benefits for Illness Tied to Second-Hand Smoke," *Business Insurance*, June 27, 1994, 1.

43. P. Gleason *et al.*, "Drug and Alcohol Use at Work: A Survey of Young Workers," *Monthly Labor Review*, August 1991, 3–7.

44. W. Lehman and D. Simpson, "Employee Substance Use and On-the-Job Behaviors," *Journal of Applied Psychology* 77 (1992), 309.

45. 45 CFR 84–3 (J)(2)(i).

46. M. R. Frone, Marcia Russell, and M. Lynne Cooper, "Job Stressors: Job Involvement and Employee Health," *Journal of Occupational and Organizational Psychology* 68 (1995), 1–11.

47. Richard A. Wolfe and Donald F. Parker, "Employee Health Management: Challenges

(Notes continued on following page)

▼ Notes, continued

and Opportunities," *Academy of Management Executive*, May 1994, 22–31.
48. A. G. King, "Employee Assistance Programs on the Rise," *USA Today*, May 1, 1995, 2B.
49. Ronald J. Burke, "Utilization of Employees' Assistance Program in a Public Accounting Firm," *Psychological Report*, August 1994, 264–267.
50. D. Kirrane, "EAPs: Dawning of a New Age," *HR Magazine*, January 1990, 34.
51. See the following for discussions on evaluating EAPs and some of their problems: W. Afield, "Running Amok," *Business Insurance*, May 1989; E. Settineri, "Effectively Measuring Costs of EAPs," *HR Magazine*, April 1991, 53; and R. Stolz (ed.), "A Closer Look at EAPs," *Employee Benefit News*, March 1992, 4–15.
52. Charles E. Labig, *Preventing Violence in the Workplace* (New York: AMACOM, 1995).
53. E. Felsenthal, "Potentially Violent Employees Present Bosses with a Catch-22," *The Wall Street Journal*, April 1995, B1.
54. W. L. Gregory, "Halt? Is Your Security System Secure?" *HR Focus*, February 1994, 9–11.
55. M. Kutler, "Coping with Crisis," *Occupational Health & Safety*, February 1996, 22–24.
56. *Williams v. Feather Sound*, 386 So.2d 1238 (Fla.App 1980).
57. Based on information in Scott L. Treatman, "The Shotgun Approach," *Occupational Health & Safety*, August 1995, 65–70.

CHAPTER 17

EMPLOYEE RIGHTS AND DISCIPLINE

After you have read this chapter, you should be able to . . .

- Explain how employee rights and HR policies are interrelated.
- Identify three exceptions to employment-at-will used by the courts.
- List elements to consider when developing an employee handbook.
- Explain the concept of just cause and how it is determined.
- Discuss the issues and problems associated with drug tests.
- Identify the major concerns about polygraph and honesty testing.
- Outline a progressive discipline sequence.
- Explain three alternative dispute resolution methods.

HR in Transition

Trying to Settle Employment Arguments out of Court

Employers and employees do not always agree. These days, disagreements often mean lawsuits and big legal bills to determine settlements. An alternative is arbitration, which uses a neutral third party to decide without going to court.

Legal precedent holds that when two parties agree to have disputes settled in such a way, the decision is "insulated" from review by the courts. That means that the arbitrator can make a binding final decision on the problem, and neither one of the parties then can sue to try (once again) to win their case. Generally speaking, the arbitration process has worked very well.

Arbitration often has been a feature in union contracts. Recently, the U.S. Supreme Court cleared the way for the use of *predispute arbitration agreements* in nonunion settings. In the precedent-setting case, a New York stockbroker and his company had both signed a form stating that "any dispute, claim, or controversy . . . arising out of the employment or termination of employment . . . is required to be arbitrated." The Supreme Court held that the stockbroker's later claim of dismissal because of age discrimination therefore belonged before an arbitrator, not in federal court. A week later, the Court in a similar case extended the ruling to most race, sex, and age discrimination claims under Title VII of the Civil Rights Act.

The simple answer is that lawsuits over employment-related matters have exploded and many courts are bogged down in employment litigation. Especially in the states where employers have been hardest hit (California, Michigan, and Illinois), the arbitration approach seems to make sense.

At almost the same time, the National Conference of Commissioners on Uniform State Laws suggested that the states adopt a uniform employment statute at state level that would let most fired employees take their cases to a neutral arbitrator instead of resorting to the court system. The commission says its plan would cover 60 million workers and estimates that 10% of the 2 million workers who are fired each year would have valid claims.

Why all the interest in arbitration? The simple answer is that lawsuits over employment-related matters have exploded and many courts are bogged down in employment litigation. Especially in the states where employers have been hardest hit (California, Michigan, and Illinois), the arbitration approach seems to make sense. In California, employees win 70% of the jury trials and collect awards averaging $300,000 to $500,000 before legal costs. Employers' legal fees on such cases average $75,000; workers', $40,000. In contrast, arbitration costs a total of about $15,000 per case. Also, arbitration is much quicker. Only one of several "alternative dispute resolution" methods employers are beginning to consider, arbitration holds obvious promise.

But there can be a problem with arbitration. As the use of arbitration has grown, many employers have adopted stiff, self-serving arbitration rules that prohibit punitive damages or put severe restrictions on the process for employees. Of course, employees had to sign an agreement on the arbitration process to get or keep their jobs.

U.S. District Judge Norman Black shook up the firms that saw binding arbitration as a way around employee rights law. He held that a Houston firm can no longer use the company's arbitration agreement because it violates employees' civil rights. The judge was especially angry that employees had been expected to sign an agreement but had never been given a chance to read the policy. He did not say that arbitration policies are illegal but said that employers who use such policies need to make sure such agreements are fair to employees.

While the judge's orders do not constitute legal precedent, it is clear that one-sided agreements are going to be a problem for employers. The American Arbitration Association can provide guidance to fair and equitable arbitration processes. Perhaps the promise of dispute arbitration can be realized, but it will require an even-handed approach.[1]

> "The right to be left alone—the most comprehensive of rights and the most valued by civilized men."
>
> —Louis Brandeis

This chapter considers three related and important issues in the management of human resources: employee rights, HR policies and rules, and discipline. At first, these may seem separate issues, but in truth they are not. The policies and rules that an organization enacts define employee rights to a certain extent and also constrain those rights (sometimes inappropriately or illegally). Similarly, discipline of those who fail to follow policies and rules often is seen as a fundamental right of employers.

The three concepts are not only interconnected but also constantly changing as laws and societal values change. Although the U.S. Constitution grants citizens rights to freedom and due process, not all such rights are necessarily present in the workplace. Indeed, the right of management to run organizations as it chooses was at one time so strong that employee rights were practically nonexistent. Federal, state, and local laws and labor/management contracts have been necessary to grant employees certain rights at work. Laws in such areas as equal employment opportunity, collective bargaining, and safety have changed traditional management prerogatives. These laws and their recent interpretations have been the subjects of considerable dispute.

❖ Employee Rights and Responsibilities

Right
That which belongs to a person by law, nature, or tradition.

Responsibility
A duty or obligation to be accountable for an action.

Generally, rights do not exist in the abstract. They exist only when someone is successful in demanding their practical applications. A **right** belongs to a person by law, nature, or tradition. Of course, there is considerable potential for disagreement as to what really is a right. Pressures placed by employers on employees with "different" lifestyles illustrate one area in which conflicts can occur. Moreover, *legal* rights may or may not correspond to certain *moral* rights, and the reverse is true as well.

Rights are offset by **responsibilities,** which are duties or obligations to be accountable for actions. Jeremy Bentham, the European reformer, observed that when one party is given a "right," another party is obligated to maintain a certain behavior for the exercise of that right by the first party. Put another way, when a person has a "moral right" to do or have something, then some other person has a corresponding obligation.[2] For example, if an employee has the right to a safe working environment, the employer has an obligation to provide a safe workplace. Because rights and responsibilities are reciprocal, the employer also has a right to expect uninterrupted, high-quality work from the employee, meaning that the worker has the responsibility to be on the job and do the job carefully. Thus, employment is a reciprocal relationship (both sides have obligations), and employee rights arise in exchange for reciprocal employee responsibilities such as loyalty and service.

The reciprocal nature of rights and responsibilities suggests that each party to an employment relationship should regard the other as having equal rights and should treat the other accordingly, with respect.[3] Demanding rights without an awareness of corresponding responsibilities shows knowledge of only part of the issue. The HR Perspective discusses one view of employees' rights.

❖ Rights As a Citizen vs. Rights As an Employee

Some rights have applications both on and off the job. Health and safety rights, the right to free speech, and the right to due process are three examples. Other rights might apply in the workplace but not the home, and vice versa. For exam-

HR PERSPECTIVE

Ethics in an Employee Bill of Rights?

Thomas Michaud, an ethics professor, has suggested the following "employee bill of rights," which would apply to employees' relations and communications with other employees at work.[4] It illustrates that rights and responsibilities go together.

Employee Bill of Rights

You have the right to . . .	and the obligation to . . .
❖ Refuse requests without feeling guilty	❖ Help if you reasonably can
❖ Change your mind	❖ Have good reasons for your decision
❖ Be forgiven for honest mistakes	❖ Forgive the honest mistakes of others
❖ Accept gifts of nominal value	❖ Refuse gifts that may be too valuable
❖ Stand up for your own interests	❖ Remember others may also have needs
❖ Express views, positive or negative	❖ State them so they don't injure others
❖ Criticize	❖ Communicate criticisms constructively
❖ Make requests in the workplace	❖ Request help from one capable of helping
❖ Start and build relationships	❖ Stop attempts at friendship if the other party is unwilling

ple, an employer may have restrictions on employees' right to smoke at work but not on their right to smoke at home off the job. Sometimes, management and employees do not have a clear agreement as to which rights exist in the workplace. Unions have tried over the years to define workplace rights, often through confrontation. Although unionism has declined, increased legal restrictions on employers' HR practices through state legislation and court decisions have increased employee rights.

❖ Statutory Rights and Contractual Rights

Employees' **statutory rights** are the result of specific laws passed by federal, state, or local governments. The legal right to form or join unions is one such right.

Statutory Rights
Rights based on laws.

An employee's **contractual rights** are based on an agreement or contract with an employer, such as the arbitration agreements mentioned in the opening of this chapter. Unions and management may agree on contracts that specify certain rights. Those contracts are legally enforceable in court. **Employment contracts** spell out details of an employment agreement. These contracts are usually written and very detailed. However, courts are enforcing "unwritten" promises and finding such items as an employee handbook to be part of an employment contract.[5]

Contractual Rights
Rights based on a specific contractual agreement between employer and employee.

Employment Contracts
Agreements that spell out the details of employment.

The proliferation of court-backed employee rights mirrors a change in society's attitude toward work. To live within the new employee rights environment, employers must ensure that HR procedures are fair and are not applied arbitrarily or capriciously. Rights and responsibilities of the employee to the employer may be spelled out in a job description, in an employment contract, or in HR policies, buy many are not. They may exist only as unwritten employer expectations about what is acceptable behavior or performance on the part of the employee. Figure 17–1 shows a possible division of responsibilities between the

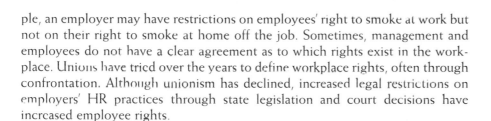

HR unit and operating managers with regard to employee rights and discipline issues.

❖ Rights and Employee/Employer Relations

❖ Figure 17–1 ❖
Typical Division of Responsibilities for Employee Rights and Discipline

HR UNIT	MANAGERS
❖ Designs HR procedures that incorporate employees' legal and moral rights ❖ Designs progressive discipline process if nonunion ❖ Trains managers on the protection and limits of employees' rights and on the discipline process	❖ Keep informed of concerns related to employees' rights ❖ Operate under the discipline system—make disciplinary decisions and dismiss employees who violate policies and rules ❖ Provide feedback to HR on situations not covered by the disciplinary process

Workplace litigation has reached epidemic proportions as employees who feel their rights have been violated sue their employers. Advocates for expanding employee rights warn that management policies abridging free speech, privacy, or due process will lead to national legislation to regulate the relationship. At the same time, management is under pressure to maintain a lean, efficient, flexible, drug-free workforce. HR professionals argue that they must protect management's traditional employment-at-will prerogatives (discussed later in this chapter) to hire and fire and promote and demote employees as they see fit. If efficiency and quality are to be maintained, poor performers cannot be tolerated.

As employees increasingly regard themselves as free agents in the workplace—and as the power of unions declines—the struggle between employee and employer "rights" is heightening. Employers frequently do not fare very well in court. Further, it is not only the employer that is liable in many cases. Individual managers and supervisors have been found liable when hiring or promotion decisions have been based on discriminatory factors or when they have had knowledge of such conduct and have not taken steps to stop it.

Some feel that a new workplace relationship between employer and employee is evolving in the United States. In its most basic form, it seems to be stated by employers as: You will be employed here as long as you add value to the organization. There will not be job security. You are responsible for finding ways to add value. In return, you have the right to interesting work, freedom to do that work, pay that reflects your contribution, and the experience and training necessary to be employed here or elsewhere.[6] This relationship is an outgrowth of the changing nature of the psychological contract between employers and employees that was highlighted in Chapter 3. Whether such an arrangement is indeed evolving can only be determined at a future time. But at present, the relationship is certainly in a state of flux.

Current employee rights, as widely defined under various laws, are divided here into three major categories:

1. Rights affecting the employment agreement, involving:
   - ❖ Employment-at-will
   - ❖ Implied employment contracts (employee handbooks)
   - ❖ Due process
   - ❖ Dismissal for just cause.
2. Employee privacy rights, involving:
   - ❖ Employee review of records
   - ❖ Substance abuse and drug testing
   - ❖ Polygraph and honesty testing

3. Other employee rights, involving:
   - Workplace investigation
   - Potential hazards and unsafe working conditions
   - Free speech and whistle-blowing
   - Notification of plant closings
   - Security at work

❖ Rights Affecting the Employment Agreement

Although it can be argued that all employee-rights issues affect the employment relationship, four basic issues predominate: employment-at-will, implied contracts, due process, and dismissal for just cause.

❖ Employment-at-Will (EAW)

Employment-at-will (EAW) is a common-law doctrine stating that employers have the right to hire, fire, demote, or promote whomever they choose, unless there is a law or contract to the contrary. Employers often defend EAW based on one or more of the following reasons:

1. The right of private ownership of a business guarantees EAW.
2. EAW defends employees' right to change jobs, as well as employers' right to hire and fire.
3. Interfering with EAW reduces productivity in the economy.

Employment-at-Will (EAW)
A common-law doctrine stating that employers have the right to hire, fire, demote, or promote whomever they choose, unless there is a law or contract to the contrary.

History of EAW EAW is a by-product of the 19th-century industrial revolution. Laissez-faire social thought encouraged rapid economic expansion and granted business complete flexibility in the way employees were handled. Very little changed until the 20th century, when unionized labor gained protection from arbitrary and capricious discharge through grievance arbitration procedures in most union contracts. In disputed cases, a neutral arbitrator ruled on whether there were adequate grounds for dismissal. Over time, both management and unions generally became familiar with restraints placed on employers who discharged employees. Many public-sector employees were granted due process protection under civil service regulations, whether or not they were represented by a union. Nonunion employees remained under the EAW doctrine. In the 1960s, however, an increasing number of state courts began to create exceptions to EAW ideas even for nonunion employees. Courts questioned the *fairness* of an employer's decision to fire an employee without just cause and due process. The suits implied that employees have job rights that must be balanced against EAW.

EAW and the Courts Nearly all states have adopted one or more statutes that limit an employer's right to discharge. The universal restrictions include race, age, sex, national origin, religion, and handicap. Restrictions on other areas vary from state to state. Employers who discharge employees in violation of these statutes are guilty of wrongful discharge.

In addition, states may choose to recognize certain nonstatutory grounds for wrongful-discharge suits. Courts in California and New York have taken two very different approaches in this regard. These positions represent the extreme ends of a continuum of approaches being taken nationwide. In New York, courts have refused to take EAW cases, saying that EAW is a legislative concern, not one for the courts to decide. On the other hand, in California, courts will take EAW cases almost without exception.

In general, courts have recognized three different rationales for hearing EAW cases.[7]

1. *Public policy exception.* This exception to EAW holds that an employee can sue if he or she was fired for a reason that violates public policy. For example, if an employee refused to commit perjury and was fired, he could sue.
2. *Implied employment contract.* This approach holds that the employee will not be fired as long as he or she does the job. Long service, promises of continued employment, and lack of criticism of job performance imply continuing employment.
3. *Good faith and fair dealing.* This approach suggests that a covenant of good faith and fair dealing exists between the employer and at-will employees. If the employer has broken this covenant by unreasonable behavior, the employee has legal recourse.

A landmark court case in this area is *Fortune v. National Cash Register Company.* The case involved the firing of a salesman (Fortune) who had been with National Cash Register (NCR) for 25 years.[8] Fortune was fired shortly after winning a large order that would have earned him a big commission. From the evidence, the court concluded that he was fired because NCR wanted to avoid paying him the commission, which violated the covenant of good faith. The courts generally have held that unionized workers cannot pursue EAW actions as at-will employees because they are covered by an alternative remedy: the grievance-arbitration process.

The lesson of wrongful-discharge suits is that employers should take care to see that dismissals are handled properly, that all HR management systems are in order, and that due process and fair play are observed. Suggestions for preparing for the defense of any such lawsuits are shown in Figure 17–2.

Wrongful-discharge lawsuits have become a major concern for many firms.[9] Such lawsuits (according to one study) cost an average of $80,000 to defend. Further, a Rand Corporation study found that "firms can avoid the legal threat

❖ **Figure 17–2**
Keys for Defense in Wrongful Discharge: The "Paper Trail"

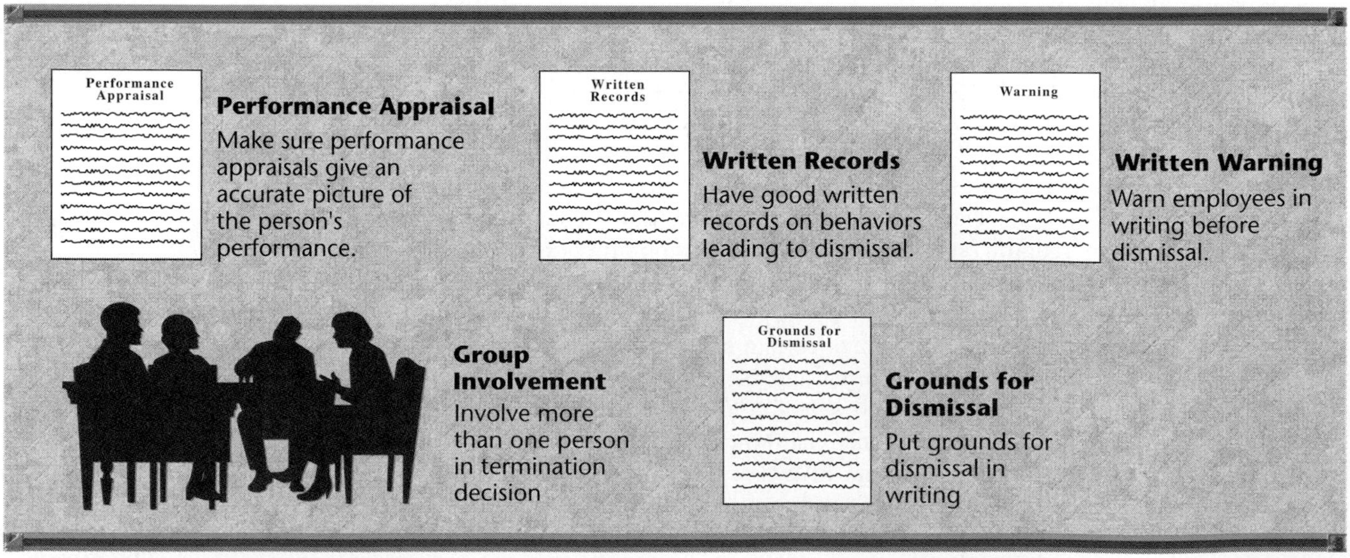

Performance Appraisal
Performance Appraisal
Make sure performance appraisals give an accurate picture of the person's performance.
Written Records
Written Records
Have good written records on behaviors leading to dismissal.
Warning
Written Warning
Warn employees in writing before dismissal.
Group Involvement
Involve more than one person in termination decision
Grounds for Dismissal
Grounds for Dismissal
Put grounds for dismissal in writing

[only] by not firing workers even when justified by economic conditions or poor job performance . . . trading off production efficiency for diminished exposure to legal liability."[10] In addition, companies are hiring fewer full-time employees and using more temporary workers and overtime to reduce the threat of wrongful-discharge lawsuits.[11]

Indeed, wrongful discharge has become a dilemma even for well-intentioned firms, as the following example illustrates. Federal law requires employers to maintain a workplace free of sexual harassment. But some states allow workers to sue if they are discharged without good reason. The fired sexual harasser frequently sues the company, contesting the "good reason." When the court hears the case, the legal question becomes whether EEOC guidelines requiring "immediate and appropriate corrective action" when an employee complains of sexual harassment take precedence over state law and employment agreements that say the employer must have "just cause" before firing.

❖ Rights in the Employment Contract (Employee Handbooks)

The idea that a contract (even an implied, unwritten one) exists between workers and their employers affects the employment relationship. Several courts have held that if an employer hires someone for an indefinite period and promises job security or gives specific procedures for discharge, the employer has lost the right to terminate at will. These actions establish employee expectations. When the employer fails to follow up on them, the employee has recourse in court. In essence, the courts have held that such promises, especially when contained in an employee handbook, constitute a contract between an employer and its employees, even though there is no signed document. A landmark case is *Pine River State Bank v. Mettile,* but many other cases have led to similar conclusions: that handbooks are implied contracts. The legal remedy for a broken contract requires the party breaking the contract to perform and keep its contracted obligation. However, courts have also imposed compensatory and punitive damages for breaking such implied contracts.[12]

❖ Due Process

***Due Process**
The opportunity to defend oneself against charges.

Due process is the opportunity to defend oneself against charges. For unionized employees, due process usually refers to the right to use the grievance procedure specified in the union contract. Due process may include specific steps in the grievance process, time limits, arbitration procedures, and providing knowledge of disciplinary penalties.

Compared with due process procedures specified in union contracts, procedures for at-will employees are more varied and may address a broader range of issues. Attempts by at-will employees to use their rights of due process often run into difficulties for several reasons. Figure 17–3 shows some questions to ask about situations in which employees argue they were not granted "due process." These questions usually must be addressed by HR managers and their employers if due process procedures

❖ Figure 17–3 ❖
Due Process (Fair Treatment)

QUESTIONS TO DETERMINE WHETHER DUE PROCESS EXISTS:

- ❖ Does the organization have a precedent or process spelled out for handling similar situations?
- ❖ Is the process reasonable?
- ❖ Was the process followed?
- ❖ Did the employee have an opportunity to use a grievance procedure?
- ❖ Did the employee have help in preparing his/her defense?
- ❖ Is there protection for employees who use a grievance procedure against retaliatory actions by management ?
- ❖ Was the final decision independent of the original management decision maker?
- ❖ Would a reasonable person find the ultimate action and process "fair"?

are to be perceived as fair by the courts. Employees certainly must be given the opportunity to present their sides of the stories during the disciplinary process.

Nonunion organizations are well advised to have a grievance procedure providing due process for their employees. Just the presence of procedural fairness can be a positive indication that an employee has been given due process. Further, if the due process procedure is seen as fair, discharged employees are less likely to sue.

NOTIFICATION OF PLANT CLOSINGS When an employer chooses to close a facility, the employees may experience severe economic and psychological problems.[13] A federal law requires employers to give a 60-day notice before a "massive layoff" or "plant closing" involving more than 50 people. The Worker Adjustment and Retraining Notification (WARN) Act imposes stiff fines on employers who do not follow the required process and give notice.

DISTRIBUTIVE JUSTICE AND PROCEDURAL JUSTICE Employees' perceptions of fairness or justice in their treatment reflect at least two factors. First, people prefer favorable *outcomes* for themselves. They decide how favorable their outcomes are by comparing them with those of others, given their relative situations. This decision involves the concept of **distributive justice**, which deals with the question: Is the way the outcomes were distributed fair?

❖Distributive Justice
Perceived fairness in the distribution of outcomes.

❖Procedural Justice
Perceived fairness of the process used to make a decision.

Procedural justice also is involved in whether an action will be viewed as fair by an employee. It focuses on whether the *procedures* that led to an action were appropriate, were clear, and gave appropriate opportunity for input. Procedural justice deals with the question: Was the process used to make the decision fair?

ORGANIZATIONAL OMBUDSMAN One means some organizations use to ensure process fairness is through an **ombudsman**, who is a person outside the normal chain of command who acts as a problem solver for management and employees. For example, one firm uses an ombudsman to resolve complaints from employees that cannot be settled through the employee's supervisor or the HR department. The ombudsman first reviews the employee's information and complaint. After the problems have been discussed with other individuals, such as the employee's supervisor or a representative of the HR department, the ombudsman recommends a solution to the problem. Making such an individual available gives employees the opportunity to talk freely about complaints and frustrations that may not otherwise surface until they become serious problems. Using an ombudsman also can be a way to make sure that employees are given fair hearings and due process in attempting to address their problems.

❖Ombudsman
Person outside the normal chain of command who acts as a problem solver for management and employees.

❖ DISMISSAL FOR JUST CAUSE

As with due process, what constitutes **just cause** as sufficient justification such as dismissal usually is spelled out in union contracts but often is not as clear in at-will situations. While the definition of *just cause* varies, the criteria used by courts have become well-defined. They appear in Figure 17–4.

❖Just Cause
Sufficient justification for actions.

Related to just cause is the concept of **constructive discharge**, which occurs when an employer deliberately makes conditions intolerable in an attempt to get an employee to quit. Under normal circumstances, an employee who resigns rather than being dismissed cannot later collect damages for violation of legal rights. An exception to this rule occurs when the courts find that the working conditions are so intolerable as to *force* a reasonable employee to resign. Then, the resignation is considered a discharge. For example, an employee had been told he should resign

❖Constructive Discharge
Occurs when an employer deliberately makes conditions intolerable in an attempt to get an employee to quit.

but refused. He was then given lesser assignments, publicly ridiculed by his supervisor, and threatened each day with dismissal. He finally resigned and sued his employer, and the judge held that he had been "constructively discharged." His employer had to pay damages because it had forced him to resign.

❖ FIGURE 17–4 ❖
CRITERIA FOR DETERMINATION OF JUST CAUSE FOR DISCIPLINARY ACTION

- ❖ Was the employee warned of the consequences of his or her conduct?
- ❖ Was the company's rule reasonable?
- ❖ Did management investigate before disciplining?
- ❖ Was the investigation fair and impartial?
- ❖ Was there evidence of guilt?
- ❖ Were the rules and penalties applied in an evenhanded fashion?
- ❖ Was the penalty reasonable, given the offense?

BEHAVIOR OFF THE JOB Discharge for "just cause" is especially difficult to establish when the case involves an employee's off-the-job behavior. The basic premise is that an employer should not control the lives of its employees off the job. There are exceptions, however. In one case, a company fired an employee because he lied about his arrest for possession of marijuana. The arbitrator upheld the dismissal because the company's need for accurate information from the employee was important in his job.

However, in general, disciplinary action for off-the-job behavior of employees is unsettling to both employers and employees. Further, the general public is leery of employers' investigating the off-the-job behavior of their workers. For example, one poll found that the vast majority of people believe the boss has no right to ask about employees' private lives, lifestyles, and off-work activities. Nearly 80% of those surveyed said that recreational activities, political activities, and factors such as smoking should not be considered in employment decisions. However, about the same proportion said it was all right to differentiate in employee health-care premiums for off-the-job smokers.[14] Other polls have shown that a similar number believe that employers do not have the right to monitor personal telephone conversations, forbid an employee to date an employee of a rival firm, or require an employee to diet.[15] Twenty-three states have laws that prohibit firing workers for privately using legal products (like tobacco and alcohol) or engaging in legal activities when away from the job.[16]

UNETHICAL EMPLOYEE BEHAVIOR Whether at work or off the job, unethical employee behavior is becoming an increasingly serious problem for organizations.[17] On the job, unethical behavior includes theft, illegal drug and excessive alcohol use, falsification of documents, and misuse of company funds, among others. The management of such behaviors has become more important as employers have become more responsible for the behaviors of employees.

❖ FREE SPEECH (WHISTLE-BLOWING)

A person who reports a real or perceived wrong committed by his or her employer is called a **whistle-blower**. Two key questions in regard to whistle-blowing are: (1) When do employees have the right to speak out with protection from retribution? (2) When do employees violate the confidentiality of their jobs by speaking out? Often, the answers are difficult to determine. Whistle-blowing is an important right, but it is a right that can be abused.

Whistle-Blower
Person who reports a real or perceived wrong committed by his or her employer.

A widely publicized whistle-blowing case involved an employee in the U.S. Defense Department who revealed that significant cost overruns on an airplane contract were being concealed from the U.S. Congress. Attempts were made by his superiors to transfer him, demote him, or fire him. The whistle-blower ultimately left the Defense Department, but not before Congress held a series of public hearings and investigations.

Whistle-blowers are less likely to lose their jobs in public employment than in private employment because most civil service systems have rules protecting whistle-blowers. However, there is no comprehensive whistle-blowing law that protects the right to free speech of both public and private employees. If an individual is fired or made miserable for reporting a perceived wrongdoing, that person may not receive proper redress.[18] Research on retaliation against whistle blowers suggests that it is more likely to occur when the whistle-blower tried to stay anonymous, when the wrongdoing harmed the public, or when the wrongdoing harmed the organization.[19]

❖ Employee Privacy Rights

Three categories of employee privacy rights are considered here: (1) employee rights to review records, (2) rights involving substance abuse and drug testing, and (3) rights involving polygraph and honesty testing.

❖ Employee Right to Review Records

As a result of concerns about the protection of individuals' privacy rights, the Privacy Act of 1974 was passed. It includes provisions affecting HR record systems. This law applies *only* to federal agencies and organizations supplying services to the federal government; but similar state laws, somewhat broader in scope, also have been passed. Regulation of private employers on this issue for the most part is a matter of state rather than federal law. Public-sector employees have greater access to their files in most states than do private-sector employees.

The following legal issues are involved in employee rights to privacy and HR records:

- Right to access personal information
- Opportunity to respond to unfavorable information
- Right to correct erroneous information
- Right to be notified when information is given to a third party
- Right to know how information is being used internally
- Right to reasonable precautions, assuring the individual that the information will not be misused

An employer probably may run afoul of laws on employee records when another employer asks for information about a former employee. Many lawyers recommend that only the most basic employment history, such as job title, dates of employment, and ending salary, be given. Although that information may be safe, it probably is not especially helpful to the employer seeking the reference, because it does not answer questions a potential employer may have about an employee's suitability. Recently, several states have passed laws that protect employers who provide employment information from being sued.[20]

Some employees are quite concerned about what is in their records at work—perhaps for good reason. For instance, employee assistance programs (EAPs) are designed to help employees with drug or alcohol problems, emotional difficulties, or family concerns. Counselors who help these employees sometimes may provide information to the employer. The result is that workers who sue employers for discrimination, wrongful termination, or the like may find their EAP records used against them in court.[21]

Access to HR records is discussed further in Chapter 20. Figure 17–5 shows some guidelines for maintaining privacy in employee records.

❖ FIGURE 17–5 ❖
GUIDELINES FOR PRIVACY IN EMPLOYEE RECORDS

- ❖ Disclose to employees the records kept on them and the company's policy on records.
- ❖ Have a policy that limits record use and allows employees to see their files.
- ❖ Review contents regularly and destroy outdated items as appropriate.
- ❖ Designate a file custodian.
- ❖ Restrict the establishment of separate files by supervisors and managers.
- ❖ Train managers on documentation of employee actions.

❖ SUBSTANCE ABUSE AND DRUG TESTING

The issue of substance abuse and drug testing at work has received a great deal of attention. The importance of the problem to HR management is clear. At best, workers on drugs operate at about 75% of their capacity.[22] In addition, the accident rate, illness rate, workers' compensation rate, absenteeism rate, and voluntary turnover rate range from 3 to 16 times higher for drug users. It is easy to see why management is in favor of drug testing. However, the trade-off between employers' need to test for drugs and employees' right to privacy involves difficult issues.

On the one hand, testing can help ensure a safe workplace. Safety concerns are especially important in some areas. For example, the U.S. Department of Transportation has very comprehensive rules about both drug and alcohol use by workers employed in transportation, for the protection of the general public. Because of these and other concerns, most employers are testing for drugs, especially in major companies.[23]

On the other hand, there are several arguments against drug testing: (1) It violates employees' rights. (2) Drugs may not affect job performance in every case. (3) Employers may abuse the results of tests. (4) Often, drug tests are inaccurate, or the results are misinterpreted.

EMPLOYEE ATTITUDES TOWARD DRUG TESTING Surveys show that employee attitudes toward drug testing have changed. Apparently, experience with workplace drug problems has made managers and employees less tolerant of drug users.[24] Drug testing appears to be most acceptable to employees when they see the procedures being used as fair and when characteristics of the job (such as danger to other people) require that the employee be alert and fully functioning. *Procedural justice* appears to be an important issue in perceptions of fairness of drug testing, but drug testing raises less concern about employee rights than it once did.

DRUG TESTING AND THE LAW Two misconceptions about privacy in the workplace should be clarified. First, federal constitutional rights, such as the right to protection from unreasonable search and seizure, protect an individual only against the activities of the government. Thus, employees can be searched at work by representatives of the employer. This principle was reaffirmed by a U.S. Supreme Court decision that held that even employers in government workplaces may search desks and files without search warrants if they believe that a work rule was violated.

Second, termination of an employee because of substance-abuse problems must be in keeping only with the due process described in an employer's policy. Unless state or local law prohibits testing, employers have a right to require employees to submit to a blood test or urinalysis. But court decisions generally have indicated that random drug testing may be unconstitutional and that public agencies must have "probable cause" to test.

Drug testing can be done before and/or after hiring. If done afterwards, three different methods may be used: (1) random testing of everyone at periodic inter-

LOGGING ON

Information from the Institute for a Drug-Free Workplace can be found at

http://www.drugfreeworkplace.org/

vals; (2) testing only when there is probable cause; or (3) after accidents. Each method raises its own set of problems. From a policy standpoint, it is most appropriate to test for drugs when the following conditions exist:

- Job consequences of abuse are so severe they outweigh privacy concerns.
- Accurate test procedures are available.
- Consent of the employee in writing is obtained.
- Results are treated confidentially, as with any medical record.
- Employers have a complete drug program including counseling assistance for drug users.

The U.S. Supreme Court has ruled that certain drug-test plans do not violate the Constitution. But private employer programs are governed mainly by state laws, which currently are a confusing hodgepodge. Passage of the Drug-Free Workplace Act in 1988 required government contractors to take steps to eliminate employee drug usage. The U.S. Transportation Department is testing truck and bus drivers, train crews, mass-transit employees, airline pilots and mechanics, pipeline workers, and licensed seamen.

TYPES OF TESTS FOR DRUGS The most common tests for drug use are urinalysis, radioimmunoassay of hair, and fitness testing. Urinanalysis is the test most frequently used. It requires a urine sample that must be tested at a lab. There is concern about sample switching, and the test detects drug use only over the past few days. But urinalysis is accurate and well accepted.

Hair radioimmunoassay requires a strand of an employee's hair, which is analyzed for traces of illegal substances. A 1.5-inch sample provides a 90-day

HR PERSPECTIVE

FITNESS-FOR-DUTY TESTS

A smiling sailor pops onto the computer screen. He has a row of diamonds in one hand and hearts in the other. Do the hearts (or diamonds) at his feet match those in is hands? It gets tougher when the sailor is turned upside down or backwards, especially for someone who is impaired by substance abuse or fatigue. When a crew of delivery-truck drivers come to work, they "play" a similar video game—with serious consequences. Unless the machine presents a receipt saying they "passed" the test, they are not allowed to drive their trucks that day.

Known as *fitness-for-duty tests,* these video games measure whether employees have the hand/eye coordination to perform their jobs on a given day. The computer has already established a baseline for each employee. Subsequent testing measures the employees against these baselines. Interestingly, most failures are *not* drug- or alcohol-related. Initial results suggest that fatigue, illness, and personal problems render a person unfit to perform a sensitive job more frequently. Whatever the reason for poor performance, for one company, accidents fell 67%, errors declined 92%, and workers' compensation claims fell 64% after one year of using the fitness-for-duty tests.

At Domino's Pizza Distribution, truck drivers, warehouse workers, and dough makers are tested. Plant workers need to be alert when using machinery, or they can get caught in it. If some workers flunk the test, they spend the day doing paperwork or painting—jobs in which they cannot hurt themselves or others.

Not everyone likes fitness-for-duty testing. One federal drug official questions the reliability of such tests in detecting impairment. And a union official opposes the tests on the principle that management could come in and establish a company baseline to get rid of older members. But another union president notes, "It's a hell of a lot better than asking our people to urinate in a jar." And indeed, it may be—a common saying is that in some dangerous jobs the urinalysis results always arrive just in time for the funeral.[26]

profile. Sample swapping is more difficult, and the longer time period covered is advantageous. However, this test is somewhat controversial.[25]

Both NASA and the U.S. Air Force have used a test of tracking ability to detect impairment due to drug use. The test is easier and quicker than urinalysis. It can be used to assess a worker's fitness on the spot before he or she goes to work. The test operates much like a video game. It measures fine hand/eye coordination and reaction time and takes less than a minute to administer. The accompanying HR Perspective details fitness-for-duty tests, which are growing in use.

❖ Workplace Investigations

Another area of concern regarding employee rights involves workplace investigations. Public-sector employees are protected by the Constitution in the areas of due process, search and seizure, and privacy. But employees in the private sector are not protected.

Employee theft is the number-one cause of retail inventory loss, costing U.S. retailers an estimated $25 billion per year. A study done at the University of Florida estimates that 43% of the merchandise that disappears is stolen by employees and 32% by shoplifters.[27]

As a result of these problems, employers have increased their attempts to investigate employee theft and substance abuse in their organizations. For example, General Motors operated a "sting" operation to identify drug users in some of its plants. As a result, some 200 persons were arrested. Drug abuse, dishonesty, and unethical behavior are the focus of such investigations. Figure 17–6 shows methods most commonly used to conduct workplace investigations.

Polygraph and Honesty Testing The theory behind a polygraph is that the act of lying produces stress, which in turn causes observable physical changes. An examiner can thus interpret the physical responses to specific questions and make a judgment as to whether the person being tested is practicing deception. However, the Polygraph Protection Act prohibits the use of polygraphs for most preemployment screening and for judging a person's honesty while employed.

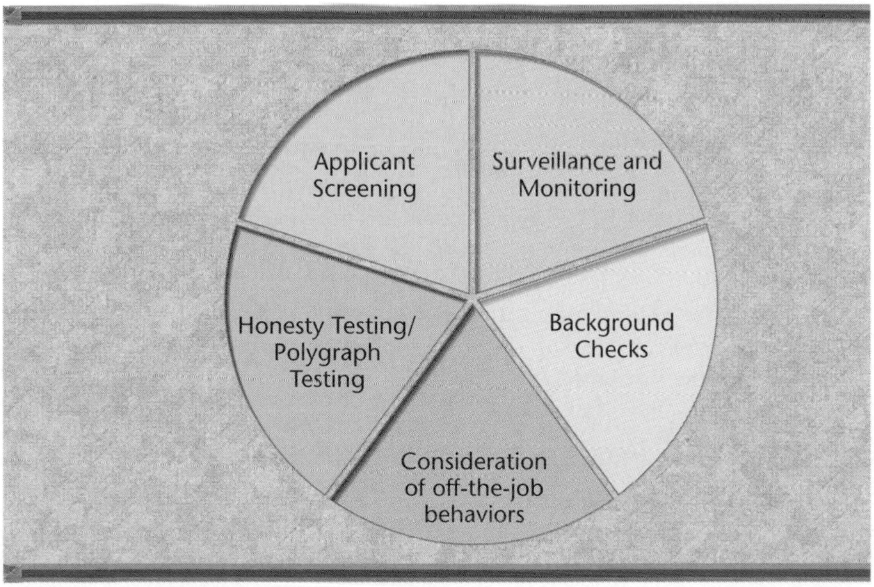

❖ Figure 17–6 ❖
Methods of Workplace Investigations

"Pencil-and-paper" honesty tests have gained popularity recently. They are not restricted by the Polygraph Protection Act nor by the laws of most states. Many organizations are using this alternative to polygraph testing, and over two dozen variations of such tests are being sold.

Honesty tests were developed from test items that differentiated between people known to be honest and those known to be dishonest. (This is similar to the way personality tests are developed.) It is not always easy to determine who is honest for the purpose of validating the tests, but the tests have generally been shown to be valid.[28] In the private sector, honesty tests do not violate any legal rights of employees if employers adhere to state laws. The Fifth Amendment (which protects persons from compulsory self-incrimination) may be a basis for prohibiting such tests in public-sector employment.

Employee Monitoring Employee monitoring may be done to measure performance (amount produced, for example), to check for theft, or to enforce company rules or laws.[29] The common concern in a monitored workplace is usually not whether monitoring should be used but how it should be conducted, how the information should be used, and how information should be communicated to employees.

As employers take advantage of increasingly sophisticated technology, electronic monitoring—or "spying," as some call it—is on the increase.[30] The following employee responses have been associated with electronic monitoring or surveillance: increases in performance on simple tasks, increased effort and stress, and decreases in job satisfaction.[31] Two-way communication and employee involvement in the design of the system reduces stress and increases perceptions of fairness. Procedural justice seems to moderate the negative effects of monitoring.

Monitoring of Electronic Communications Voice mail and e-mail systems increasingly are seen by employers as areas where employers have a right to monitor what is said and transmitted. A key question is are these communications subject to the privacy rights of employees, or subject to employer surveillance? For instance, when a male worker began having an affair with a coworker and exchanging steamy messages via voice mail, he found his messages had been retrieved and played for his wife and his boss. About 22% of managers in one survey admitted to monitoring voice mail, e-mail, or computer files. Many did so without workers' knowledge.[32]

To minimize ethical concerns, an employer should consider establishing the following policies:

- Voice mail, e-mail, and computer files are provided by the employer and are for business use only.
- Use of these media for personal reasons is prohibited.
- All computer pass codes must be available to the employer.
- The employer reserves the right to monitor or search any of the above without notice for business purposes.[33]

HR Policies, Procedures, and Rules

It is useful at this point to consider some guidelines for HR policies, procedures, and rules. They greatly affect employee rights (just discussed) and discipline (discussed next). Where there is a choice among actions, **policies** act as general guidelines that regulate organizational actions. Policies are general in nature,

Policies
General guidelines that regulate organizational actions.

while procedures and rules are specific to the situation. The important role of policies in guiding organizational decision making requires that they be reviewed regularly, because obsolete policies can result in poor decisions and poor coordination. Policy proliferation also must be carefully monitored. Failure to review, add to, or delete policies as situations change may lead to problems.

Procedures are customary methods of handling activities and are more specific than policies. For example, a policy may state that employees will be given vacations. Procedures will establish a specific method for authorizing vacation time without disrupting work.

***Procedures**
Customary methods of handling activities.

Rules are specific guidelines that regulate and restrict the behavior of individuals. They are similar to procedures in that they guide action and typically allow no discretion in their application. Rules reflect a management decision that action be taken—or not taken—in a given situation and provide more specific behavioral guidelines than policies. For example, one welding company has a policy stating that management intends to provide the highest-quality welding service in the area. The rule that a welder with fewer than five years of welding experience will not be hired promotes this policy. This rule constrains HR selection decisions.

***Rules**
Specific guidelines that regulate and restrict the behavior of individuals.

❖ Responsibilities for HR Policy Coordination

For policies, procedures, and rules to be effective, coordination between the HR unit and other managers is vital. As Figure 17–7 shows, managers are the main users and enforcers of rules, procedures, and policies and should receive some training and explanation in how to carry them out. The HR unit supports managers, reviews disciplinary rules, and trains managers to use them. It is critical that any conflict between the two entities be resolved so that employees receive fair and coordinated treatment.

FIGURE 17–7 ❖
TYPICAL RESPONSIBILITIES FOR HR POLICIES AND RULES

HR UNIT	MANAGERS
❖ Designs formal mechanisms for coordinating HR policies ❖ Provides advice in development of organizationwide HR policies, procedures, and rules ❖ Provides information on application of HR policies, procedures, and rules ❖ Explains HR rules to managers ❖ Trains managers to administer policies, procedures, and rules	❖ Help in developing HR policies and rules ❖ Review policies and rules with employees ❖ Apply HR policies, procedures, and rules ❖ Explain rules and policies to employees

❖ Guidelines for HR Policies and Rules

Well-designed HR policies and rules should be consistent, necessary, applicable, understandable, reasonable, and distributed and communicated. A discussion of each characteristic follows.

CONSISTENT Rules should be consistent with organizational policies, and policies should be consistent with organizational goals. The principal intent of policies is to provide written guidelines and to specify actions. If some policies and rules are enforced and others are not, then all tend to lose their effectiveness.

NECESSARY HR policies and rules should reflect current organizational philosophy and directions. To this end, managers should confirm the intent and necessity of proposed rules and eliminate obsolete ones. Policies and rules should be reviewed whenever there is a major organizational change. Unfortunately, this review is not always done, and outdated rules are still on the books in many organizations.

Applicable Because HR policies are general guidelines for action, they should be applicable to a large group of employees. For policies that are not general, the appropriate areas or people must be identified. For instance, if a sick-leave policy is applicable only to nonexempt employees, that should be specified in the company handbook. Policies and rules that apply only to one unit or type of job should be developed as part of specific guidelines for that unit or job.

Understandable HR policies and rules should be written so employees can clearly understand them. One way to determine if policies and rules are understandable is to ask a cross-section of employees with various positions, education levels, and job responsibilities to explain the intent and meaning of a rule. If the answers are extremely varied, the rule should be rewritten.

Reasonable Ideally, employees should see policies as fair and reasonable. Policies and rules that are perceived as being inflexible or as penalizing individuals unfairly should be reevaluated. For example, a rule forbidding workers to use the company telephone for personal calls may be unreasonable if emergency phone calls are occasionally necessary. Limiting the amount of time the telephone can be used for personal business and the number of calls might be more reasonable.

Some of the most ticklish policies and rules involve employee behavior. Dress codes are frequently controversial, and organizations that have them should be able to justify them to the satisfaction of both employees and outside sources who might question them.

Distributed and Communicated In order to be effective, HR policies must be distributed and communicated to employees. Employee handbooks can be creatively designed to explain detailed policies and rules so that people can refer to them at times when no one is available to answer a question. Supervisors and managers can maintain discipline by reminding their employees about policies and rules. Because employee handbooks are used so widely, guidelines for their preparation are discussed next.

❖ Guidelines for an Employee Handbook

An employee handbook gives employees a reference source for company policies and rules and can be a positive tool for effective management of human resources. Even smaller organizations can prepare handbooks relatively easily using computer software such as *Personnel Policies Expert* or others. However, management should consider several factors when preparing handbooks.[34]

Readability The specialists who prepare employee handbooks may not write at the appropriate level. One review of the reading level of some company handbooks revealed that on average they were written at the third-year college level, which is much higher than the typical reading level of employees in most organizations. One solution is to test the readability of the handbook on a sample of employees before it is published.

Use Another important factor to be considered in preparing an employee handbook is its method of use. Simply giving an employee a handbook and saying, "Here's all the information you need to know," is not sufficient. Employee handbooks often are ranked third behind supervisors and "the grapevine" as sources of information about the organization.

Some organizations distribute handbooks as part of the orientation process. One company periodically gives all employees a written test on the company handbook. In this company, the HR managers use questions that are consistently missed to focus their communication efforts. These tests also are used in updating the handbook.

LEGAL REVIEW OF LANGUAGE As mentioned, there is a current legal trend to use employee handbooks against employers in lawsuits charging a broken "implied" contract. But that is no reason to abandon employee handbooks as a way to communicate policies to employees. *Not* having an employee handbook with HR policies spelled out can also leave an organization open to costly litigation and out-of-court settlements.

A more sensible approach is first to develop sound HR policies and employee handbooks to communicate them and then have legal counsel review the language contained in them. Recommendations include the following:

- *Eliminate controversial phrases.* For example, the phrase "permanent employee" often is used to describe those people who have passed a probationary period. This wording can lead to disagreement over what the parties meant by "permanent." A more appropriate phrase is "regular employee."
- *Use disclaimers.* Contract disclaimers have been upheld in court. However, there is a trade-off between disclaimers and the image presented by the handbook, so disclaimers should not be overused. A disclaimer also should appear on application forms. A disclaimer in the handbook can read as follows.

  > This employee handbook is not intended to be a contract or part of a contractual agreement between the employer and the employee. The employer reserves the right to modify, delete, or add to any policies set forth herein without notice and reserves the right to terminate an employee at any time with or without cause.

- *Keep the handbook current.* Many employers simply add new material to handbooks rather than deleting old, inapplicable rules. Those old rules can become the bases for new lawsuits. Consequently, handbooks and HR policies should be reviewed periodically and revised every few years.

EMPLOYEE DISCIPLINE

Employee rights have been an appropriate introduction to employee discipline because employee rights are often an issue in disciplinary cases. **Discipline** is a form of training that enforces organizational rules. The goal of preventive discipline is to heighten employee awareness of organizational policies and rules. Knowledge of disciplinary actions may prevent violations. The emphasis on preventive discipline is similar to the emphasis on preventing accidents. Counseling by a supervisor in the work unit can have positive effects. Many times people simply need to be made aware of rules.

Discipline
A form of training that enforces organizational rules.

The disciplinary system (see Figure 17–8) also can be viewed as an application of behavior modification for marginal or unproductive employees. The best discipline is clearly self-discipline; when most people understand what is required at work, they can usually be counted on to do their jobs effectively. Yet some find that the prospect of external discipline helps their self-discipline.

Even though an employer's description of discipline is purposely upbeat and nonnegative in tone, there are times when discipline involves the use of punishment. Under such circumstances, managers must see to it that punishment is *corrective* in nature and not purely punitive.

❖ FIGURE 17–8 ❖
THE DISCIPLINARY SYSTEM

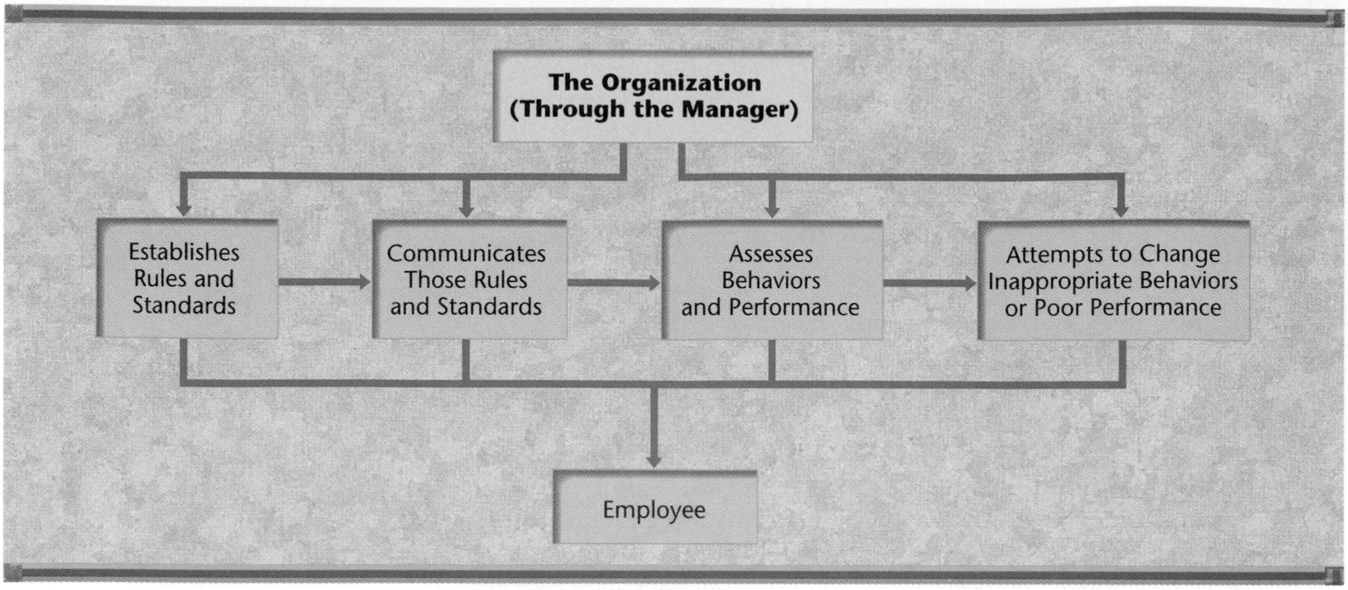

❖ DIFFICULT OR PROBLEM EMPLOYEES

Fortunately, problem employees comprise a small number of employees, but they often are the ones who cause the most problems. If employers fail to deal with problem employees, negative effects on other employees and work groups often result. Common disciplinary problems caused by problem employees include absenteeism, tardiness, productivity deficiencies, alcoholism, and insubordination.

❖ PROGRESSIVE DISCIPLINE

Progressive discipline incorporates a sequence of steps into the shaping of employee behaviors. Figure 17–9 shows a typical progressive discipline system. Like the procedures in the figure, most progressive discipline procedures use verbal and written reprimands and suspension before resorting to dismissal. Thus, progressive discipline suggests that actions to modify behavior become progressively more severe as the employee continues to show improper behavior. For example, at one manufacturing firm, failure to call in when an employee is to be absent from work may lead to a suspension after the third offense in a year.

An employee is given every opportunity, as well as help, if appropriate, to correct deficiencies before being dismissed. Following the progressive sequence ensures that both the nature and the seriousness of the problem have been clearly communicated to the employee. Not all steps in the progressive discipline procedure have to be followed in every case. The idea is to impress on the offender the seriousness of the problem and the manager's determination to see that the behavior is changed.

❖ COUNSELING AND DISCIPLINE

Counseling can be an important part of the discipline process. The focus should be on fact-finding and guidance to encourage desirable behavior, instead of on using penalties to discourage undesirable behavior. The philosophy is that violations are actions that usually can be constructively corrected without penalty.

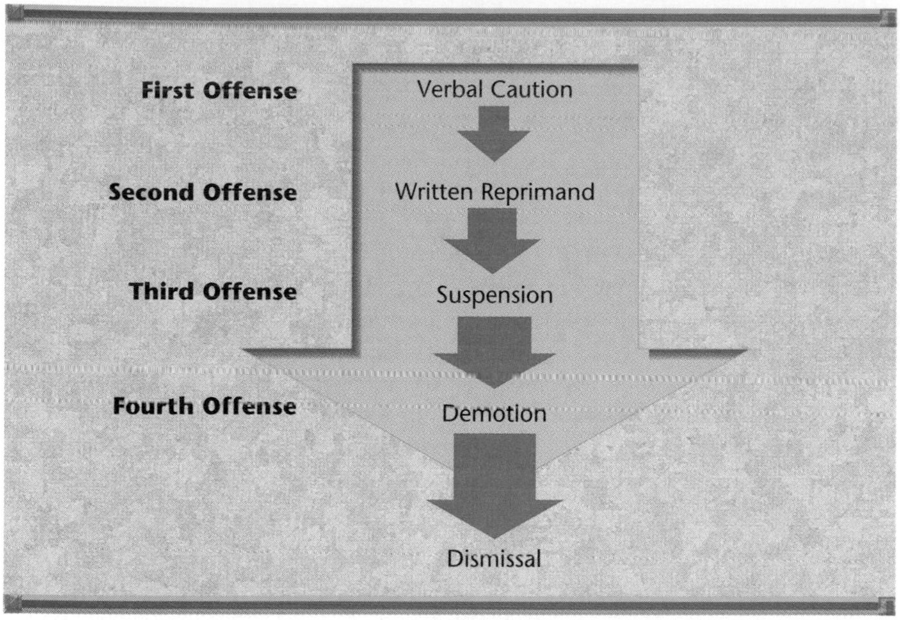

❖ FIGURE 17–9 ❖
PROGRESSIVE DISCIPLINE PROCEDURES

As can be seen in Figure 17–10, typically, there is a sequence of events in counseling and discipline. Often, an employee's first violation results in a meeting with the immediate supervisor. A second violation brings another discussion with the supervisor on how this kind of behavior can be avoided in the future. The next violation leads to counseling with the same manager and that manager's immediate superior. A fourth infraction results in "final counseling" with top management. The offender is typically sent home for the rest of the day without pay and told that any further violation will result in termination. If the employee has no further violations for a year, his or her personnel file is wiped clean. Any new violations start the process all over again. Certain serious offenses are exempted from the procedure and may result in immediate termination.

❖ FIGURE 17–10 ❖
COMMON IMMEDIATE TERMINATION OFFENSES

PROBLEM
Intoxication at work Fighting Possession of weapons Theft Drug use at work Falsifying employment application Outside criminal activities

❖ REASONS WHY DISCIPLINE MIGHT NOT BE USED

Sometimes managers are reluctant to use discipline. There are a number of reasons why discipline may not be used:

1. *Lack of support.* Many managers do not want to use discipline because they fear that their decisions will not be supported by higher management.
2. *Guilt.* Some managers feel that before they became managers, they committed the same violations as their employees, and they cannot discipline others for doing something they used to do.
3. *Loss of friendship.* Managers who allow themselves to become too friendly with employees may fear losing those friendships if discipline is used.
4. *Time loss.* Discipline, when applied properly, requires considerable time and effort. Sometimes it is easier for managers to avoid taking the time disciplining, especially if their actions may be overturned by higher management.
5. *Fear of lawsuits.* Managers are increasingly concerned about being sued for disciplining someone, particularly for taking the ultimate disciplinary step of dismissal.

A study of federal government supervisors found that 78% had encountered at least one employee with a performance problem, but only 23% had taken steps to solve the problem. The managers agreed it is difficult, if not impossible, to fire a federal employee.[35]

❖ Effective Discipline

Because of legal aspects, managers must understand discipline and know how to administer it properly. Effective discipline should be aimed at the behavior, not at the employee personally because the reason for discipline is to improve performance.

The manager administering discipline must consider the effect of actions taken by other managers and of other actions taken in the past. *Consistent* discipline helps to set limits and informs people about what they can and cannot do. Inconsistent discipline leads to confusion and uncertainty.

Effective discipline requires *accurate written record keeping* and written notification to the employee. In many cases, the lack of written notification has been evidence for an employee's argument that he or she "did not know." Also, effective discipline requires that *people know the rules.* When people perceive discipline as unfair, it is often on the basis that they did not realize they had broken a rule.

Additionally, effective discipline is *immediate.* The longer the time that transpires between the offense and the disciplinary action, the less effective the discipline will be. Finally, effective discipline is handled *impersonally.* Managers cannot make discipline an enjoyable experience, but they can minimize the unpleasant effects somewhat by presenting it impersonally and by focusing on behaviors, not on the person.

That discipline can be positively related to performance surprises those who feel that discipline can only harm behavior. However, although employees may resist unjustified discipline from a manager, actions taken to maintain legitimate standards actually may reinforce productive group norms and result in increased performance and feelings of fairness. A work group may perceive that an inequity has taken place when one individual violates standards. An individual who violates standards may also be violating group norms, so lack of discipline can cause problems for the group as well as for the manager. Distributive and procedural justice suggest that if a manager tolerates this unacceptable behavior, the group may feel it is not fair.

❖ Discharge: The Final Alternative

The final stage in the discipline process is termination. A manager may feel guilty when dismissing an employee, and sometimes guilt is justified. If an employee fails, it may be because the manager was not able to create an appropriate working environment. Perhaps the employee was not adequately trained, or perhaps management failed to establish effective policies. Managers are responsible for their employees, and to an extent, they share the blame for failures.

An interesting approach to dismissal is used by some employers that have adopted systems that require employees who have been warned about deficiencies to create their own improvement plans. Terminating workers because they do not keep their own promises is more likely to appear equitable and defensible to a jury. Also, such a system seems to reduce the emotional reactions that lead fired workers to sue in the first place.

❖ Alternative Dispute Resolution

Alternatives to lawsuits in cases involving employee rights are being used with increasing frequency.[36] The most common of these alternative dispute resolution (ADR) methods are arbitration, peer review panels, and mediation.

ARBITRATION Arbitration was the subject of the chapter-opening feature. The Supreme Court has sanctioned the use of mandatory arbitration for employment claims. But as the chapter opener points out, some companies have tried to limit employees' rights too much with arbitration agreements. The method can work, but reasonable design of the process is important.

PEER REVIEW PANELS Some employers allow employees to appeal discharge to a committee or panel of their peers. Such peer review panels are really the last part of a formal grievance procedure for nonunion employees. They have worked well to settle contested dismissals and to keep the process out of court. In general, these methods reverse management's decisions much less frequently than one might think, reduce lawsuits, and provide a good defense in cases that do go to court.

MEDIATION Mediation is different from arbitration in that a mediator tries to get two parties to agree on a mutual position to resolve a dispute. In arbitration, the arbitrator makes the decision. Mediation appears to be more limited for employment disputes.

LOGGING ON

Subscribing to a mailing list on alternative dispute resolution is available at

http://www.law.emory.edu/FOCAL/adjoin.html

"Hank, when you're finished firing this gentleman I have some rather unfortunate news for you as well."

SUMMARY

❖ Ideas about employee rights, HR policies and rules, and discipline have continued to change and evolve.

❖ The employment relationship is viewed as a reciprocal one in which the employee, in return for loyalty and service, has moral rights.

❖ Employee rights affecting the employment agreement include employment at will, implied employment contracts, due process, and dismissal for just cause.

❖ Employment-at-will relationships are changing in the courts, which have found public policy exceptions, implied contract exceptions, and good faith/fair dealing exceptions.

❖ Although due process is not guaranteed for at-will employees, the courts expect to see evidence of due process in employee discipline cases. Furthermore, following due process is good management.

❖ Employee rights to review records vary considerably from state to state. Government employees have consistent rights and guarantees in this regard.

❖ Drug testing generally is legal and is widely used as employers try to deal with increasing drug problems at work.

❖ Polygraph testing appears to be relatively inaccurate, and its use has declined. Pencil-and-paper honesty tests are being used in its place.

❖ Miscellaneous employee rights include rights involving workplace investigations, workplace hazards, whistle-blowing, notification of plant closings, and security at work.

❖ In order to be effective, HR policies and rules should be consistent, necessary, applicable, understandable, reasonable, and distributed and communicated.

❖ Employee handbooks have been viewed as contracts by the courts. This presents no problem as long as the handbook conforms to certain standards. HR policies that are expressed verbally also have been viewed as unwritten contracts, so it is best to have all policies clearly written in a handbook.

❖ Facts to be considered in preparing an employee handbook include readability, use, and legal review of language.

❖ Discipline is best thought of as a form of training. Although self-discipline is the goal, sometimes counseling or progressive discipline is necessary to encourage self-discipline.

❖ Managers may fail to discipline when they should for a variety of reasons.

❖ Effective discipline can have positive effects on the productivity of employees.

❖ Alternative dispute resolution methods include arbitration, peer review, and mediation.

REVIEW AND DISCUSSION QUESTIONS

1. Where do employee rights originate?
2. Explain the public policy exception to employment-at-will.
3. Discuss the differences and similarities between the issues of due process and just cause.
4. What would be the pros and cons of giving a prospective employer honest information about a former employee of yours who stole from the company?
5. Design a checklist of items to remember in investigating an employee suspected of drug use in your company.
6. What does it mean for discipline to be viewed as a progressive process?

Terms to Know

constructive discharge 508
contractual rights 503
discipline 517
distributive justice 508
due process 507
employment-at-will (EAW) 505
employment contracts 503
just cause 508
ombudsman 508
policies 514
procedural justice 508
procedures 515
responsibility 502
right 502
rules 515
statutory rights 503
whistle-blower 509

CASE

YOU CAN'T FIRE ME!

Paul Zimmerman went to work for H. E. Butt Grocery, a Texas grocery chain, and was a fine employee. In fact, the company President told him, "You've done a really good job; you've earned your way, and you have a contract for life." Zimmerman was sacked six years later for stealing inventory and trying to hide it.

He sued for breach of contract. Contract employees *can* be fired, of course, but the employer must prove that there was just cause. Zimmerman argued that he had not stolen and had not falsified records and had therefore been fired without cause. The company countered that Zimmerman did not have a contract but was an "at-will" employee.

Zimmerman was awarded $391,000 in damages at trial. The judge found that he did have a contract because he had signed an employee handbook that his boss had told him was a contract. Further, the company had treated the handbook as a contract.

But later, a three-judge panel of the Fifth Circuit Court reversed every aspect of the judge's finding. They held that there was no language in the handbook that said employees could be fired only for cause. They also held that lifetime contracts must be in writing to be enforceable. The moral of the story: Employers, watch what you say. Employees, get it in writing.[37]

Questions

1. Under what circumstances is it realistic to think of "employment for life" in any business?
2. Explain "just cause" and "at-will employee" in the context of this case.

Notes

1. C. M. Sixel, "Employer Passion for Arbitration Cooling," *Omaha World-Herald*, February 2, 1996, G1; and Wade Lambert, "Employee Pacts to Arbitrate Sought by Firms," *The Wall Street Journal*, October 22, 1993, B1.

2. Yg Chimezie and A. B. Osigweh, "Elements of an Employee Responsibilities and Rights Paradigm," *Journal of Management* 16 (1990), 835–850.

3. Ibid., 839.

4. Thomas Michaud, quoted in Vikki Kratz, "Proactive Employee Relations," *Business Ethics*, September/October, 1995, 16. Used with permission.

5. "Attorney Suggests Employment Contracts for Workers at All Levels," *BNAC Communicator*, Fall 1994, 19.

6. Brian O'Reilly, "The New Deal," *Fortune*, June 13, 1994, 44.

7. Adapted from Mark A. Player, *Federal Law of Employment Discrimination* (St. Paul: West Publishing, 1991).

8. *Fortune v. National Cash Register Co.*, 373 Mass. 96, 36 NE 2d 1251, 1977.

9. J. D. Thorne, "How to Head Off Termination Suits," *Nation's Business*, May 1995, 28.

10. D. Frum, "The Right to Fire," *Forbes*, October 26, 1992, 76–77.

11. Milo Geyelin, "Rulings on Wrongful Firing Curb Hiring," *The Wall Street Journal*, April 7, 1992, B3.

12. J. R. Derr, "Employee Handbook—Friend or Foe?" *Nebraska Employment Law Letter*, December 1995, 2–3.

13. M. Barrier, "Easing the Pain of Layoffs," *Nation's Business*, January 1996, 17–18.

14. Michael R. Losey, "Workplace Privacy," *Modern Office Technology*, May 1993, 56–58.

15. B. Tarrant, "Alaskans Believe Off-Duty Time Is Off-Limits to Bosses," *Anchorage Times*, January 17, 1992, C1.

16. M. Schaefer, "Two States Pass Privacy Rights Laws," *Human Resource Executive*, June 1992, 14.

17. B. R. Crossen, "Managing Employee Unethical Behavior without Invading Individual Privacy," *Journal of Business and Psychology*, Winter 1993, 227.

18. "The Uncommon Good," *The Economist*, August 19, 1995, 55–56.

19. Marcia Miceli and Janet Near, "Relationships among Value Congruence, Perceived Victimization, and Retaliation against Whistleblowers," *Journal of Management*, 20 (1994), 773–794.

20. F. Swoboda, "Legislatures Kept Busy Changing Labor Laws in '95," *Denver Post*, March 17, 1996, G3.

21. Ellen Schutz, "If You Use Firm's Counselors, Remember Your Secrets Could Be Used Against You," *The Wall Street Journal*, May 26, 1994, C1.

22. Z. Kahn, *et al.*, "Ethics of Drug Testing: What Are Worker's Attitudes?" *Business Forum*, Summer/Fall 1995, 17.

(Notes continued on following page)

▼Notes, continued

23. Todd Allen, "DOT Drug-Testing Rules Require Detailed Plans," *HR News,* March 1996, 3.

24. Michael A. Verespej, "Drug Users—Not Testing—Anger Workers," *Industry Week,* February 17, 1992, 33; and Z. Kahn et al.,"Ethics of Drug Testing: What Are Workers' Attitudes?" *Business Forum,* Summer/Fall 1995, 17–20.

25. Margaret Kirk, "Hair Target of Newest Drug Tests," *Omaha World-Herald,* January 28, 1996, G1.

26. J. Hamilton, "A Video Game That Tells If Employees Are Fit for Work," *Business Week,* June 3, 1991, 36; and L. McGinley, "Fitness Exams Help to Measure Worker Activity," *The Wall Street Journal,* April 21, 1992, B1.

27. Randy Tucker, "Retailer Survey: Employee Theft Top Cause of Inventory Loss," *Omaha World-Herald,* April 30, 1995, M1.

28. H. J. Bernardin and D. K. Cooke, "Validity of an Honesty Test in Predicting Theft among Convenience Store Employees," *Academy of Management Journal* 36 (1993) 1097–1108.

29. S. R. Hawk, "Effects of Computerized Performance Monitoring: An Ethical Perspective," *Journal of Business Ethics,* December 1994, 949–957.

30. Julie Lopez, "Privacy Eroding in Workplace, Labor Specialists Say," *Omaha World-Herald,* November 26, 1995, G1; Ken Western, "Ethical Spying," *Business Ethics,* September/October 1995, 22; and K. Eike-Peat, "Electronic Eavesdropping," *HRM Highlights,* August 1995, 4.

31. R. Kidwell and N. Bennett, "Employee Reactions to Electronic Control Systems," *Group and Organization Management,* June 1994, 203–208; S. R. Hawk, "Effects of Computerized Performance Monitoring: An Ethical Perspective," *Journal of Business Ethics,* December 1994, 949–957; and M. Picard, "Working Under an Electronic Thumb," *Training,* February 1994, 47–51.

32. F. McMorris, "Is Office Voice Mail Private?" *The Wall Street Journal,* February 28, 1995, B1.

33. K. Eike-Peat, "Electronic Eavesdropping," *HRM Highlights,* August 1995, 4.

34. J. Luna, "Case Studies," *CCH Ideas and Trends,* August 30, 1995, 149.

35. S. Barr, "Discipline Is Lax among Federal Managers, Survey Finds," *Washington Post,* October 27, 1995, A23.

36. "Alternative Dispute Resolution Gaining in Popularity," *CCH Ideas and Trends,* March 29, 1995, 1.

37. Based on J. Lyons, "You Can't Fire Me," *Forbes,* September 16, 1991, 164.

Chapter 18

Union/Management Relations

After you have read this chapter, you should be able to . . .

- Describe what a union is and discuss why employees join unions.
- Explain reasons for the decline in the percentage of U.S. workers represented by unions.
- Explain the acts that compose the National Labor Code.
- Identify and discuss the stages in the unionization process.
- Define *decertification* and explain how it occurs.

HR in Transition

Resurgence in Unions?

Many articles have been written in recent years that chronicle the decline of unions. Numerous statistics are cited—for example, that union membership has declined from 22 million in 1975 to 16 million in 1995 and that the percentage of the U.S. private-sector workforce that is unionized has declined from 24% to 16% during that same time period. There are many reasons for the decline, some of which are discussed later in the chapter. But there are also reasons why unions may be ready for a resurgence in membership and prominence. Those reasons are aggressive union leadership, increased emphasis on diverse employees, workers' fears of job insecurity, and growth in unions representing public-sector employees.

Aggressive Leadership

Several factors contribute to optimism among union supporters. First, a transition in the leadership of the major union federation, the AFL-CIO, in 1995 brought a new breed of union leaders to the forefront. Prior to 1995, the AFL-CIO and many unions had been headed by older leaders who had been in leadership positions for many years.

A major reason for renewed interest in unions on the part of many workers is the job insecurity caused by seemingly endless mergers, downsizings, and workforce consolidations.

The new president is John Sweeney, who had headed the Service Employees International Union (SEIU). Although over 60, Sweeney was different from previous AFL-CIO leaders in orientation. He and his union had emphasized organizing lower-paid workers in various service industries. The most widely publicized campaign the SEIU had conducted was "Justice for Janitors," which added 35,000 members over a 10-year period. That campaign was marked by street demonstrations, protests, blockages of sidewalks in major cities, and other aggressive tactics. For instance, a major New York City bank was targeted because the bank used a non-union contractor to clean its buildings. The SEIU and its supporters put advertising on buses and in subway stations telling people to withdraw their money and close their accounts at the bank. The SEIU also asked union workers in other firms, such as trucking and delivery firms, to refuse to cross its picket lines in order to disrupt the internal operations of the bank. Similar tactics have been used in other industries as well. Naturally, business owners and managers object to the new tactics, calling them "smear tactics" and "economic terrorism." But with Sweeney now heading a more active union movement, more employers are likely to face similar campaigns.

Emphasis on Diverse Employees

Many employees holding lower-paying jobs are non-white. Because such diverse groups make up an increasing portion of the workforce, the unions are targeting these workers. The AFL-CIO has established the Organizing Institute, sponsored by 14 different unions, to train union organizers. The institute has recruited trainees from college campuses by focusing on students from poor or working-class backgrounds whose parent are union members. Each summer, 200 participants are trained in Washington, D.C. Seventy percent of those trained have been female and/or people of color and with diverse backgrounds. Regional organizing institutes have trained hundreds of other organizers.

Worker Fear and Job Insecurity

A major reason for renewed interest in unions on the part of many workers is the job insecurity caused by seemingly endless mergers, downsizings, and workforce consolidations. Those employees who still have jobs see all of the turmoil and recognize that *job security* has become an oxymoron, because they could be the next ones "right-sized" out of jobs. As a result, unions have been stressing job security and recruiting members with promises to negotiate job security provisions. For those unions with contracts with major employers, wage and benefit increases have become lower, but the unions have insisted on job security provisions.

Public-Sector Growth

While union membership overall has been declining, workers in public-sector organizations increasingly have been joining unions. By the late 1990s, it is estimated that 38–40% of public-sector workers will be unionized and that they will comprise about 45% of all union members. The growth in public-sector unions has been occurring at a time when federal government employment has been declining, so most of the growth has involved state and local government employees.

All of the above factors indicate that unions are far from dead. With their new aggressiveness, unions may be able to begin adding total members and stabilizing the percentage of the workforce that they represent. Much of the success or failure of these efforts will be determined by employers and how they respond to employee issues and concerns, not just to union organizing efforts.[1]

> "If employees have problems that you aren't addressing, unions will."
> —Michael Severns, Mountain States Employers' Council

A **union** is a formal association of workers that promotes the interests of its members through collective action. The status of unions varies among countries depending on the culture and the laws that define union/management relationships. This chapter takes a broad look at union/management relations and explains how unions become employee representatives.

Union
A formal association of workers that promotes the interests of its members through collective action.

❖ Nature of Union/Management Relations

When employees choose a union to represent them, management and union representatives enter into formal collective bargaining over certain issues such as pay scales, benefits, and working conditions. Once these issues have been resolved in a labor contract, management and union representatives must work together to manage the contract and deal with grievances which are formal complaints filed by workers with management. Collective bargaining and grievance procedures, then, are two important interfaces between management and labor unions, and both areas are examined in Chapter 19.

❖ HR Responsibilities with Unions

Figure 18–1 shows a typical division of responsibilities between the HR unit and operating managers in dealing with unions. This pattern may vary among organizations. In some organizations, HR is not involved with labor relations because operating management handles them. In other organizations, the HR unit is almost completely in charge of labor relations. The typical division of responsibilities shown in Figure 18–1 is a midpoint between these extremes.

❖ Figure 18–1 ❖
Typical Labor Relations Responsibilities

HR UNIT	MANAGERS
❖ Deals with union organizing attempts at the company level ❖ Monitors "climate" for unionization and union relationships ❖ Helps negotiate labor agreements ❖ Provides detailed knowledge of labor legislation as needed	❖ Promote conditions conducive for positive relationships with employees ❖ Avoid unfair labor practices during organizing efforts ❖ Administer the labor agreement on a daily basis ❖ Resolve grievances and problems between management and employees

❖ Why Employees Unionize

Whether a union targets a group of employees or the employees themselves request union assistance, the union still must win sufficient support from the employees if it is to become their legal representative. Research consistently reveals that employees join unions for one primary reason: They are dissatisfied with their employers and how they are treated by their employers and feel the union can improve the situation. If the employees do not get organizational justice from their employers, they turn to the unions to assist them in getting what they believe is equitable. Important factors seem to be wages and benefits, job security, and supervisory treatment.

The primary determinant of whether employees unionize is management. If management treats employees like valuable human resources, then employees generally feel no need for outside representation. That is why providing good working conditions, fair treatment by supervisors, responsiveness to worker complaints and concerns, and reasonably competitive wages and benefits are antidotes to unionization efforts. In addition, many workers want more cooperative dealings with management, rather than being autocratically managed.[2] As would be expected, individuals who tend to be more independent or who gen-

would be expected, individuals who tend to be more independent or who generally view unions negatively are the most likely to oppose unionization efforts.

A variety of studies have attempted to determine why employees become interested in unions and ultimately join them. One study found that the pressures and views of coworkers, family members, and others in their job categories influence individuals' intention to vote for or against union representation. Another study found that cultural background may make a difference in enthusiasm for joining a union. African Americans were found to have the most favorable attitude toward joining a union; Hispanics, the least.[3]

A study on union loyalty looked at 71 apprentices in a union/management training program. Each apprentice was assigned to a journeyman who was also a union member. The variables that most influenced apprentices' loyalty to the union were the attitudes they brought with them about unions and their satisfaction with the training.[4]

Clearly more research on the topic is necessary if we are to understand why some people are loyal and committed to the union and others are not. But the research done to date suggests that how well the union is succeeding in providing services to members may be the most important factor in fostering union commitment today.

❖ Unions in the United States

Unionism in the United States has followed a pattern somewhat different from that in other countries. In such countries as Italy, England, and Japan, the union movement has been at the forefront of nationwide political trends. For the most part, this politicalization has not occurred in the United States. Perhaps workers here tend to identify with the American free enterprise system. Further, class consciousness and conflict between the working class and the management class is less in the United States than in many other countries.

Over the past several decades, the statistics on union membership have told a disheartening story for organized labor in the United States. As shown in Figure 18–2, unions represented over 30% of the workforce from 1945 through 1960. But by the mid-1990s, unions represented less than 16% of all private-sector workers. Also, as mentioned in the chapter-opening discussion, the number of union members has declined significantly even though the workforce has expanded in the past decade. From 1975 to 1995, union membership declined from 22 million to 16.7 million. Also, 1994 was the only year between 1985 and 1994 in which union membership actually increased at all.[5] But as the HR Perspective indicates, unions in other countries are facing declining membership, just as in the United States. Some of the reasons for the shifts in union membership are addressed next.

❖ Unions and Job-Related Legislation

Economists speculate that several issues have sparked union decline: deregulation, foreign competition, a larger number of people looking for jobs, and a general perception by firms that dealing with unions is expensive compared with the nonunion alternative. Also, management has taken a much more activist stance against unions than during the previous years of union growth.

The primary role of unionism in the United States has been collective pursuit of "bread-and-butter" economic gains. Unions have emphasized helping workers

❖ FIGURE 18–2 ❖
UNION MEMBERSHIP AS A PERCENTAGE OF U.S. WORKFORCE

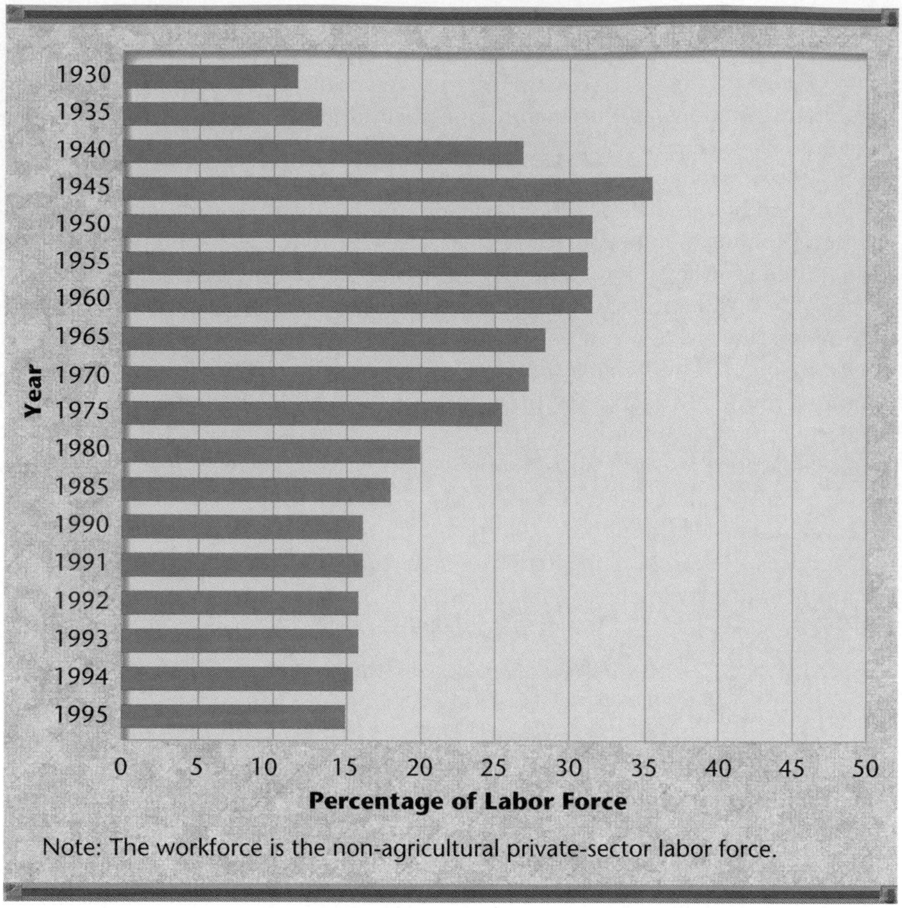

Data from Bureau of Labor Statistics, U.S. Department of Labor.

obtain higher wages, shorter working hours, job security, and safe working conditions from their employers. Ironically, some believe that one cause for the decline of unions has been their success in getting their important worker issues passed into laws.

Achieving their goals through passage of laws has meant that unions have had to be politically active. The result has been federal and state laws oriented toward specific workplace issues such as health and safety, minimum wage increases, and pension protection. Increasingly, unions also have taken positions on broad social and economic issues. For example, unions have been in the forefront of those pushing for mandatory parental leave, universal health insurance for most workers, and child-care tax credits for working parents.

As a result of union activism in the political arena, most workers now have laws guaranteeing them protection and benefits that previously were available only to members of unions who negotiated for these items with employers. Therefore, unions are not as necessary for many employees, even though they enjoy the results of past union efforts to influence legislation.

❖ WORKFORCE CHANGES AND UNIONS

Many of the workforce changes discussed earlier have contributed to the decline in union representation of the labor force. The primary growth in jobs in the United States has been in service industries having large numbers of white-collar

HR PERSPECTIVE

Global Decline of Unions

COUNTRY	% UNION MEMBERSHIP
France	9
Spain	15
United States	16
Netherlands	22
Japan	24
Sweden	84
Finland	75
Denmark	58
Norway	56
United Kingdom	33

Like U.S. unions, the unions in other countries are facing pressures affecting their membership. As the chart shows, the percentage of union membership in the workforce varies by country. However, it is important to emphasize that in many of the Northern European countries, workers must join unions to be eligible to receive some social welfare benefits or to get jobs in certain industries. Also, union membership is much higher in public-sector jobs than in private firms.

The greatest difficulties for unions are in the Western European countries. In the past, there have been strong national unions in these countries linked closely to political parties, such as the Labour Party in England. But because of the economic pressures highlighted in Chapter 3, the unemployment, productivity, and wage rates in many European countries are much less favorable than those in the United States. As a result, membership in European unions has declined. Another cause in the decline of European unions is that European manufacturers have been reducing operations in Europe and moving jobs to the United States, as well as to low-wage countries such as China, Thailand, and the Philippines. Further, the need to reduce expenditures for social benefits, such as welfare and pensions, have forced European countries to reduce jobs in their public sectors, which traditionally have been highly unionized. Compounding the problems, many large employers in Western European countries are wholly or partially owned by the national government. For instance, Air France and Alitalia, large international airlines, have significant government ownership. When efforts have been made to cut workers and reduce costs to more competitive levels, massive resistance has occurred. France has seen the most turmoil. Air France employees have blockaded French airports to protest job cuts and wage reductions proposed by the French government. A 21-day strike by French public-sector workers paralyzed the train system when freezes in pension expenditures and job reductions were proposed. The French government ultimately backed down on most of the reforms, which still left it facing large public budget deficits.

In Great Britain, unions have been facing a continuing drop in membership. For instance, the Transport and General Workers union had over two million members in 1980, but it had fewer than 800,000 members by the mid-1990s. Also, much as in the United States, there were leadership battles between old-line labor leaders and a new generation of leaders who wanted the labor union movement to become more aggressive and modernize its appeal to Britain's workers.

The global competitiveness of economies and firms will continue to put pressures on unions throughout the world. Over the next decade, it will be interesting to observe whether the decline in other countries will be as large as that in the United States.[6]

jobs. Also, the influx of women into the workforce and the growth in part-time workers indicate the changing mix of jobs. But unions traditionally have had the greatest difficulty convincing white-collar workers and women to join.

White-Collar Unionism White-collar workers include clerical workers, insurance claims representatives, data input processors, nurses, teachers, mental health aides, computer technicians, loan officers, auditors, and salespeople. Efforts to organize white-collar workers have been increasing because advances in technology have boosted their numbers in the workforce.

However, one major difficulty that unions face in organizing these workers is that many of them see unions as resistant to change and not in touch with the concerns of the more educated workers in technical and professional jobs. In addition, many white-collar workers exhibit a mentality and a set of preferences quite different from those held by blue-collar union members. Professionals define fairness in pay differently than do blue-collar workers. They prefer pay based on individual performance, while blue-collar workers always have preferred pay based on equality of job title and seniority, two basic tenets of traditional unionism.

Unions and Women Workers As mentioned, unions generally have not been as successful in organizing women workers as they have in organizing men. Figure 18–3 shows that the percentage of women who are union members is lower than that for men workers. There are some indications that unions are trying to focus on recruiting women members. Unions have been in the forefront in the push for legislation on such family-related goals as child care, maternity and paternity leave, pay equity, and flexible work arrangements. Unions in the garment and service industries, which have high concentrations of female workers, generally emphasize the conflicting demands of work and family and the inequality of women's wages compared with men's. One study found that the styles union organizers were using to try to get lower-paid women to consider unionizing differ from the styles used with other groups. A particular concern is that these women tend to take longer to be convinced to consider being unionized because they have higher levels of fear of retaliation by their employers.[7]

❖ Geographic Changes and Unions

Over the past decade, job growth in the United States has been the greatest in states located in the South, Southwest, and Rocky Mountains. Most of these states have relatively small percentages of unionized workers, partly because of

❖ **Figure 18–3** ❖
Union Membership by Industry

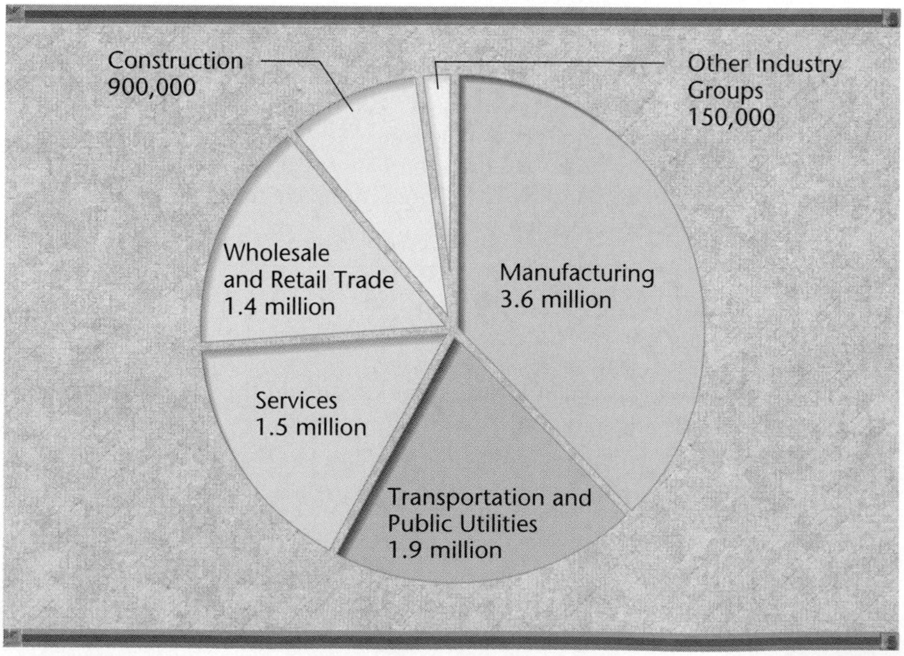

SOURCE: Data from Bureau of Labor Statistics, U.S. Department of Labor.

"employer-friendly" laws passed to attract new plants and those relocated from Northern states, where unions traditionally have been stronger. One study of 100 North Carolina counties found that foreign competition, automation, and the lack of organizational facilities were the main barriers to unionizing efforts in the South.[8]

Another geographic movement involves movement of many lower-skill jobs outside the United States. Primarily because of cheaper labor, many manufacturers have moved a significant number of low-skill jobs to Mexico, the Philippines, China, Thailand, and other lower-wage countries. Even some white-collar processing jobs are being moved out of the country. For instance, a major airline has data entry of airline tickets being done by workers on two different Caribbean islands.

A major impetus for moving low-skill, low-wage jobs to Mexico was the passage of the North American Free Trade Agreement (NAFTA). It removed tariffs and restrictions affecting the flow of goods and services among the United States, Canada, and Mexico. Because wage rates are significantly lower in Mexico, a number of jobs that would be susceptible to unionization are now being moved there. Supporters of NAFTA make the case that jobs are created in the United States as well, but many of those jobs are at higher levels and in areas less likely to be unionized. The overall result, then, is that jobs that otherwise could lead to unionization and the growth of unions have been moving out of the reach of U.S. unions.

❖ Public-Sector Unionism

An area where unions have had some measure of success is with public-sector employees. Particularly with state and local government workers have unions been successful.

State and Local Government Unionism Unionization of state and local government employees presents some unique problems and challenges. First, many unionized local government employees are in exclusive and critical service areas. Allowing police officers, firefighters, and sanitation workers to strike endangers public health and safety. Consequently, over 30 states have laws prohibiting public employee work stoppages. These laws also identify a variety of ways to resolve negotiation impasses, including arbitration. But unions still give employees in these areas greater security and better ability to influence legislators for wages and benefits.

Second, state and local government unions operate under laws and hiring policies that vary widely from city to city and state to state. Civil service and so-called merit systems make the public sector vastly different from the private sector. State and local laws, not federal labor laws, take precedence, so unique legal situations often occur. Additionally, local and state officials who lack experience with unions and collective bargaining processes may hamper union/management relations. Consider a farmer and a dentist serving on a county board; their limited knowledge of union-related activities and processes might easily stand in the way of effective union/management decisions. Finally, public employee wage increases are another concern, because the taxpaying general public is increasingly critical of state and local government expenditures. Thus, wage demands by public employees often become political issues.

Unionism and the Federal Government Although unions in the federal government hold the same basic philosophy as unions in the private sector, they do differ somewhat. Through past executive orders and laws, methods of labor/management relations that consider the special circumstances present in the federal government have been established. For example, because of limitations on collective bargaining, federal government unions cannot bargain over wages. The Office of Personnel Management has considerable control over HR policies and regulations.

❖ Union Structure

Craft Union
A union whose members do one type of work, often using specialized skills and training.

Industrial Union
A union that includes many persons working in the same industry or company, regardless of jobs held.

American labor is represented by many different kinds of unions. But regardless of size and geographic scope, there are two basic types of unions that have developed over time. A **craft union** is one whose members do one type of work, often using specialized skills and training. Examples include the International Association of Bridge, Structural, and Ornamental Iron Workers and the American Federation of Television and Radio Artists. An **industrial union** is one that includes many persons working in the same industry or company, regardless of jobs held. Examples are the United Food and Commercial Workers, the United Auto Workers, and the American Federation of State, County, and Municipal Employees.

Federation
A group of autonomous national and international unions.

Labor organizations have developed complex organizational structures with multiple levels. The broadest level is a **federation,** which is a group of autonomous national and international unions. The federation allows individual unions to work together and present a more unified front to the public, legislators, and members. The most prominent federation in the United States is the AFL-CIO, which is a confederation of national and international unions.

LOGGING ON

The AFL-CIO has a home page describing union news and Organizing Institute information.

http://www.afl-cio.org

❖ National Unions

National or international unions are not governed by the federation even if they are affiliated with it. They collect dues and have their own boards, specialized publications, and separate constitutions and bylaws. Such national–international unions as the United Steel Workers and the American Federation of State, County, and Municipal Employees determine broad union policy and offer services to local union units. They also help maintain financial records, and provide a base from which additional organization drives may take place.

❖ Local Unions

Local unions may be centered around a particular employer organization or around a particular geographic location. Officers in local unions are elected by the membership and are subject to removal if they do not perform satisfactorily. For this reason, local union officers tend to be concerned with the effect of their actions on the perceptions of the membership. They tend to react to situations as politicians do because they, too, are concerned about obtaining votes. One study found that women generally did not hold local union offices except when there was a large percentage of women members in the union local.[9]

Business Agent
A full-time union official employed by the union to operate the union office and assist union members.

Union Steward
An employee of a firm or organization who is elected to serve as the first-line representative of unionized workers.

Local unions typically have business agents and union stewards. A **business agent** is a full-time union official employed by the union to operate the union office and assist union members. The agent runs the local headquarters, helps negotiate contracts with management, and becomes involved in attempts to unionize employees in other organizations. A **union steward** is an employee of a firm or organization who is elected to serve as the first-line representative of unionized workers. Stewards negotiate grievances with supervisors and generally represent employees at the worksite.

❖ Evolution of U.S. Unions

The evolution of the union movement began with early collective efforts by employees to address job concerns and counteract management power. As early as 1794, shoemakers organized a union, picketed, and conducted strikes. However, in those days, unions in the United States received very little support from the courts. In 1806, when the shoemaker's union struck for higher wages, a Philadelphia court found union members guilty of engaging in a "criminal conspiracy" to raise wages.

In 1842, the Massachusetts Supreme Court handed down a decision in the case of *Commonwealth v. Hunt* that became an important legal landmark. The court ruled, "For a union to be guilty of conspiracy, either its objective or the means used to reach it must be criminal or unlawful."[10] As a result of this decision, unions were no longer seen as illegal conspiracies in the eyes of the courts, the conspiracy idea lost favor, and employees were no longer legally precluded from forming unions.

❖ Labor Organizations

The end of the Civil War in 1865 was followed by rapid industrial expansion and a growth of giant business trusts. The 1870s were characterized by industrial unrest, low wages, long hours, and considerable unemployment. In 1877, great railroad strikes spread through the major U.S. railroad companies as union members protested against the practices of railroad management. Eight years later, a group of workers formed the Knights of Labor. The leaders of the Knights of Labor believed that a large, national union was necessary to counter-balance the huge business trusts of that time. They emphasized political reform and establishment of work cooperatives. But after their peak in 1885, the Knights soon faded from the labor scene.

American Federation of Labor (AFL) In 1886, the American Federation of Labor (AFL) was formed as a federation of independent national unions. Its aims were to organize skilled craft workers, like carpenters and plumbers, and to emphasize such bread-and-butter issues as wages and working conditions. Samuel Gompers was the AFL's chief spokesman and served as president until his death in 1924. At first the AFL grew slowly. Six years after its formation, its total membership amounted to only 250,000. However, it managed to survive in the face of adversity while other labor groups withered and died.

Congress of Industrial Organizations (CIO) The Civil War gave factories a big boost, because factory mass-production methods using semiskilled or unskilled workers were necessary to supply the armies; and as mentioned, further industrial expansion followed the Civil War. Though factories provided a potential area of expansion for unions, they were hard to organize. Unions found that they could not control the semiskilled workers entering factory jobs because these workers had no tradition of unionism. It was not until 1938, when the Congress of Industrial Organizations (CIO) was founded, that a labor union organization focused on semiskilled and unskilled workers. Years later, the AFL and the CIO merged to form one coordinating federation, the AFL-CIO.

❖ Early Labor Legislation

The right to organize workers and engage in collective bargaining is of little value if workers are not free to exercise it. Historical evidence shows that management developed practices calculated to prevent workers from using this right. The federal government has taken action to both hamper unions and protect them.

SHERMAN AND CLAYTON ACTS The passage of the Sherman Antitrust Act in 1890 forbade monopolies and certain efforts to restrain trade. Later, as a result of a 1908 Supreme Court case *(Loewe v. Lawlor)*, union boycott efforts were classed as attempts to restrain trade.

In 1914, the Clayton Act, which limited management's use of legal injunctions to stop labor disputes, was passed. But it had little effect because of the way it was interpreted by the Supreme Court. As a result, union strength declined throughout the 1920s.

RAILWAY LABOR ACT The Railway Labor Act (1926) represented a shift in government regulation of unions. As a result of a joint effort between railroad management and unions to reduce transportation strikes, this act gave railroad employees "the right to organize and bargain collectively through representatives of their own choosing." In 1936, airlines and their employees were added to those covered by the act. Both these industries are still covered by this act instead of by others passed later.

NORRIS-LAGUARDIA ACT The crash of the stock market and the onset of the "Great Depression" in 1929, led to massive cutbacks by employers. In some industries, resistance by employees led to strikes and violence. Under the laws at that time, employers could go to court to get a federal judge to issue injunctions that ordered workers to return to work. In 1932, Congress passed the Norris-LaGuardia Act, which guaranteed workers some rights to organize and restricted the issuance of court injunctions in labor disputes. The Norris-LaGuardia Act substantially freed union activity from court interference and made the infamous *"yellow dog" contract* illegal. Under this type of contract, signed by the worker as a condition of employment, the employee agreed not to join a union on penalty of discharge. It was called a yellow dog contract because, according to union sympathizers, only a "yellow dog" would take a job under such conditions.

In 1933, the National Industry Recovery Act (NIRA) was passed. It contained, among other clauses, provisions extending the policies of the Railway Labor Act for railroad employees into interstate commerce. Also, the act set up election machinery permitting employees to choose collective bargaining representatives. However, the NIRA was declared unconstitutional in 1935 and was replaced by the National Labor Relations Act (Wagner Act).

❖ THE "NATIONAL LABOR CODE"

The economic crises of the early 1930s and the restrictions on workers' ability to organize into unions led to the passage of landmark labor legislation. Later acts reflected other pressures and issues that had to be addressed legislatively. Together, three acts passed over a period of almost 25 years comprise what has been labeled the "National Labor Code": (1) the Wagner Act, (2) the Taft-Hartley Act, and (3) the Landrum-Griffin Act. Each of the acts was passed to focus on some facet of the relationships between unions and management. Figure 18–4 shows each segment of the code and describes the primary focus of each act.

❖ WAGNER ACT (NATIONAL LABOR RELATIONS ACT)

The *National Labor Relations Act,* more commonly referred to as the Wagner Act, has been called the Magna Carta of labor and is, by anyone's standards, *pro-union*.

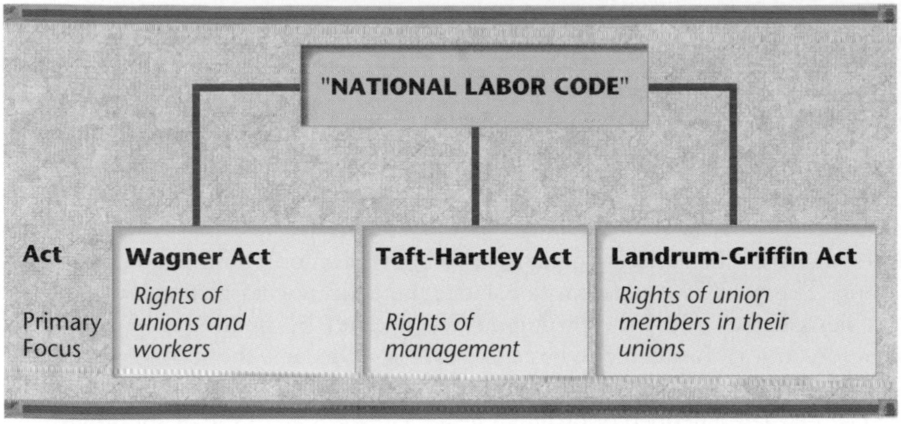

❖ FIGURE 18–4 ❖
THE NATIONAL LABOR CODE

Passed in 1935, the Wagner Act was an outgrowth of the Great Depression. With employers having to close or cut back their operations, workers were left with little job security. Unions stepped in to provide a feeling of solidarity and strength for many workers.

The Wagner Act declared, in effect, that the official policy of the U.S. government was to encourage collective bargaining. It helped union growth in three ways:

1. It established workers' right to organize, unhampered by management interference.
2. It defined unfair labor practices on the part of management.
3. It established the National Labor Relations Board (NLRB) as an independent entity to enforce the provisions of the Wagner Act.

The Wagner Act established the principle that employees would be protected in their right to form a union and to bargain collectively. To protect union rights, the act prohibited employers from undertaking the following five unfair labor practices:[11]

1. Interfering with, restraining, or coercing employees in the exercise of their right to organize, bargain collectively, and engage in other concerted activities for their mutual aid or protection. (Examples would be threatening or spying on employees.)
2. Dominating or interfering with the formation or administration of any labor organization or contributing financial or other support to it. (An example would be encouraging employees to select one union over another.)
3. Encouraging or discouraging membership in any labor organization by discriminating with regard to hiring or tenure or conditions of employment, subject to an exception for a valid union security agreement. (An example would be firing someone for being pro-union.)
4. Discharging or otherwise discriminating against an employee because he or she filed charges or gave testimony under the act. (Examples would be discharging or denying promotion to someone who filed a complaint with the NLRB.)
5. Refusing to bargain collectively with representatives of the employees. (Examples would be refusing to meet with the union representative or not bargaining in "good faith.")

The NLRB administers all of the provisions of the Wagner and subsequent labor relations acts. Although it was set up as an impartial umpire of the organizing process, the NLRB has changed its emphasis depending on which political party is in power to appoint members.

❖ Taft-Hartley Act (Labor-Management Relations Act)

When World War II ended, pent-up demand for consumer goods was frustrated by numerous strikes—about three times as many as before the war. The passage of the *Labor-Management Relations Act,* better known as the Taft-Hartley Act, in 1947 answered the concerns of many who felt that union power had become too strong. This act was an attempt to balance the collective bargaining equation. It was designed to offset the pro-union Wagner Act by limiting union actions; therefore, it was considered to be *pro-management.* It became the second part of the "National Labor Code."

The new law amended or qualified in some respect all of the major provisions of the Wagner Act and established an entirely new code of conduct for unions. The Taft-Hartley Act forbade a series of unfair labor practices by unions:[12]

1. Restraining or coercing employees in the exercise of their rights under the act; restraining or coercing any employer in the selection of a bargaining or grievance representative
2. Causing or attempting to cause an employer to discriminate against an employee on account of membership or nonmembership in a labor organization, subject to an exception for a valid union security agreement
3. Refusing to bargain collectively in good faith with an employer if the union has been designated as bargaining agent by a majority of the employees
4. Inducing or encouraging employees to stop work to force anyone to join a union or to force an employer or other person to stop doing business with any other persons (*boycott provisions*)
5. Inducing or encouraging employees to stop work with the object of forcing an employer to assign particular work to members of a union instead of to members of another union (*jurisdictional strike*)
6. Charging an excessive or discriminatory fee as a condition of becoming a member of the union
7. Causing or attempting to cause an employer to pay for services that are not performed or not to be performed (*featherbedding*)

National Emergency Strikes The Taft-Hartley Act also allows the president of the United States to declare that a strike presents a national emergency. A **national emergency strike** is one that would affect an industry or a major part of it such that the national health or safety would be impeded. Under the Taft-Hartley Act, the president can delay such strikes up to 80 days, called a *cooling-off period.* The national emergency provisions of the act require: (1) the appointment of a fact-finding board, (2) resumption of bargaining by the parties, (3) obtaining an injunction against the strike from federal courts, and (4) a report to Congress. These provisions were upheld following a challenge by the United Steel Workers in 1959.[13]

***National Emergency Strike**
A strike that would affect an industry or a major part of it such that the national health or safety would be impeded.

The Right to Work One specific provision of the Taft-Hartley Act, Section 14(b), deserves special explanation. This so-called right-to-work provision affects the **closed shop**, which requires individuals to join a union before they can be hired. Because of concerns that a closed shop allows a union to "control" who may be considered for employment and who must be hired by an employer,

***Closed Shop**
A firm that requires individuals to join a union before they can be hired.

Section 14(b) prohibits the closed shop except in construction-related occupations. The act does allow the **union shop,** which requires that an employee join the union, usually 30 to 60 days after being hired. The act also allows the **agency shop,** which requires employees who refuse to join the union to pay amounts equal to union dues and fees in return for the union's representative services.

The Taft-Hartly Act allows states to pass laws that restrict compulsory union membership. Accordingly, some states have passed **right-to-work laws,** which prohibit both the closed shop and the union shop. The laws were so named because they allow a person the "right to work" without having to join a union. The states that have enacted these laws are shown in Figure 18–5.

***Union Shop**
A firm that requires that an employee join a union, usually 30 to 60 days after being hired.

***Agency Shop**
A firm that requires employees who refuse to join the union to pay equivalent amounts equal to union dues and fees for the union's representative services.

***Right-to-Work Laws**
State laws that prohibit both the closed shop and the union shop.

❖ Landrum-Griffin Act (Labor-Management Reporting and Disclosure Act)

In 1959, the third segment of the "National Labor Code," the *Landrum-Griffin Act,* was passed. A congressional committee investigating the Teamsters Union, headed by Dave Beck and James Hoffa, had found corruption in the union. The law was aimed at protecting the rights of individual union members against such practices.

❖ **Figure 18–5** ❖
Right-to-Work States

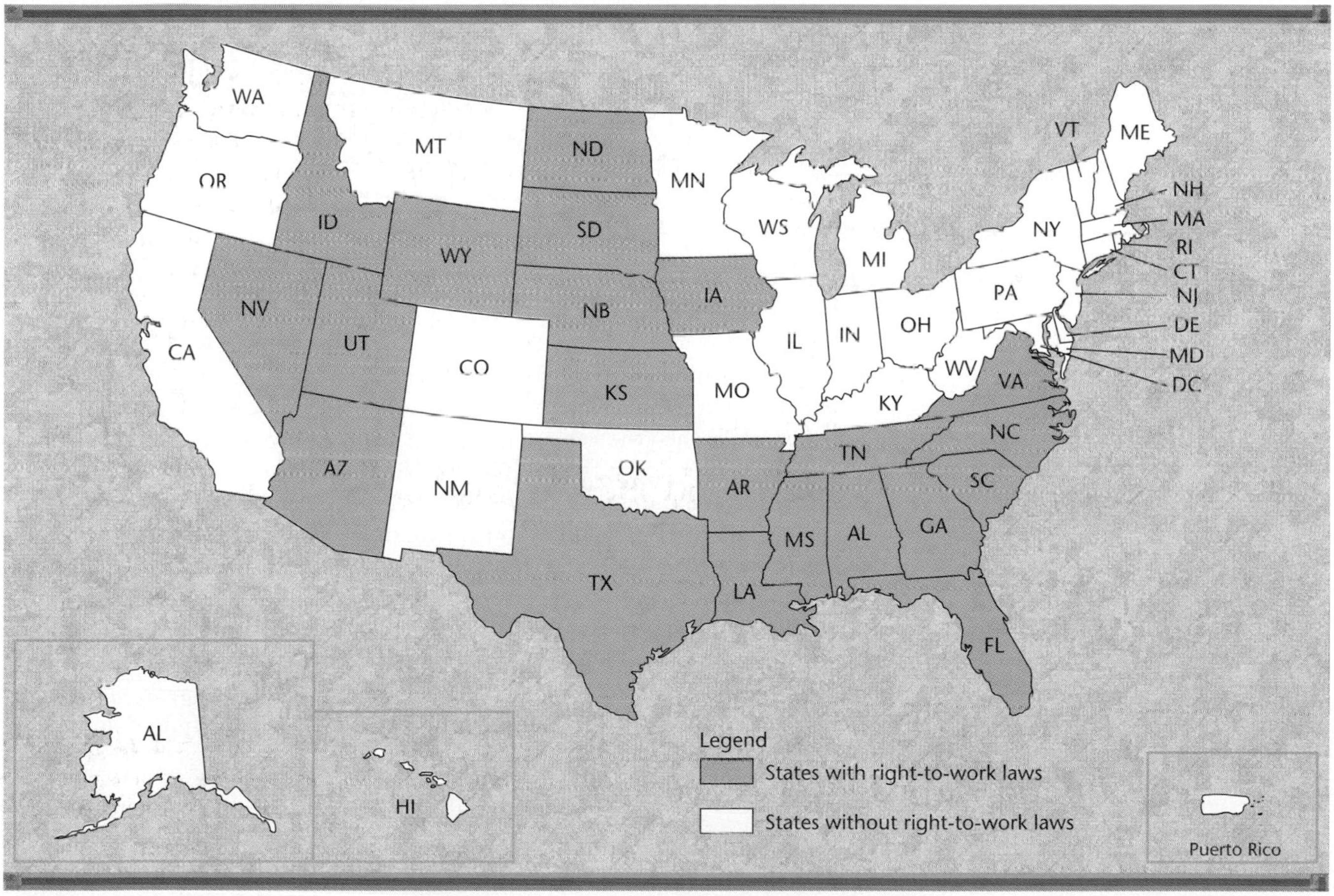

Among the provisions of the Landrum-Griffin Act are the following:[14]

1. Every labor organization must have a constitution and bylaws containing certain minimum standards and safeguards.
2. Reports on the union's policies and procedures, as well as an annual financial report, must be filed with the Secretary of Labor and must be disclosed to the union's members.
3. Union members must have a bill of rights to protect their rights.
4. Standards are established for union trusteeship and union elections.
5. Reports on trusteeships must be made to the Secretary of Labor.
6. A fiduciary relationship is imposed on union officers.
7. Union leaders are required to file reports with the Secretary of Labor on conflict-of-interest transactions.
8. The Secretary of Labor is to act as a watchdog of union conduct and a custodian of reports from unions and their officers and has the power to investigate and prosecute violations of many of the provisions of the act.

UNION MEMBERS' RIGHTS A union is a democratic institution in which union members vote on and elect officers and approve labor contracts. The Landrum-Griffin Act was passed in part to ensure that the federal government protects those democratic rights. Some important rights guaranteed to individual union members are as follows:

- Right to nominate and vote on officers
- Right to attend and participate in union meetings
- Right to have pension funds properly managed

In a few instances, union officers have attempted to maintain their jobs by physically harassing or attacking individuals who try to oust them from office. In other cases, union officials have "milked" pension fund monies for their own use. Such instances are not typical of most unions but illustrate the need for legislative oversight to protect individual union members.

❖ CIVIL SERVICE REFORM ACT OF 1978

Passed as Title VII of the Civil Service Reform Act of 1978, the Federal Service Labor-Management Relations statute made major changes in how the federal government deals with unions. The act also identified areas that are and are not subject to bargaining. For example, as a result of the law, wages and benefits are not subject to bargaining. Instead, they are set by Congressional actions.

The act established the Federal Labor Relations Authority (FLRA) as an independent agency similar to the NLRB. The FLRA was given authority to oversee and administer union/management relations in the federal government and to investigate unfair practices in union organizing efforts. The FLRA is a three-member body appointed on a bipartisan basis, and each member is appointed for five years. In addition, the act gave the Federal Service Impasse Panel (FSIP) the authority to investigate situations in which union/management negotiations reach an impasse. The FSIP also was empowered to resolve impasses in new contract negotiations. Because unions in the federal sector are prohibited from going on strike, the FSIP becomes a means of resolving bargaining conflicts.

❖ THE UNIONIZATION PROCESS

The process of unionization may begin in one of two primary ways: (1) union targeting of an industry or company or (2) employee requests. In the former case, the local or national union identifies a firm or industry in which it believes unionization can succeed. Usually, the industry has a significant number of employees who may be amenable to organizing. For example, the insurance industry in several midwestern cities was targeted because many of its workers were women in lower-paying clerical jobs, almost none of them represented by a union. The logic for targeting is that if the union is successful in one firm or a portion of the industry, then many other workers in the industry will be more willing to consider unionizing. The accompanying HR Perspective discusses aggressive union organizing effectiveness.

The second type of impetus for union organizing occurs when individual workers in an organization contact a union and express a desire to unionize. The employees themselves or the union then may begin a campaign to win support among the other employees. Whether a union pursues the unionization effort is determined by such factors as how large the potential employee unit is, how expensive it will be to campaign for support, and whether the requesting employees' complaints are an accurate gauge of employee feelings.

Once the unionization efforts begin, all activities must conform to the requirements established by labor laws and the National Labor Relations Board for private-sector employees or the appropriate federal or state governmental agency for public-sector employees. Both management and the unions must adhere to those requirements, or the results of the effort can be appealed to the NLRB and overturned. With those requirements in mind, the union can embark on the typical union organizing process, shown in Figure 18–6.

❖ Organizing Campaign

Like other entities seeking members, a union usually mounts an organized campaign to persuade individuals to support its efforts. This persuasion takes many forms, including personally contacting employees outside of work, mailing materials to employees' homes, inviting employees to attend special meetings away from the company, and publicizing the advantages of union membership. The accompanying HR Perspective discusses the ethics of some organizing efforts.

Handbilling
Practice in which unions give written publicity to employees to convince the employees to sign authorization cards.

Handbilling **Handbilling** is a practice in which unions give written publicity to employees to convince them to sign authorization cards. Brochures, leaflets,

❖ Figure 18–6 ❖
Typical Unionization Process

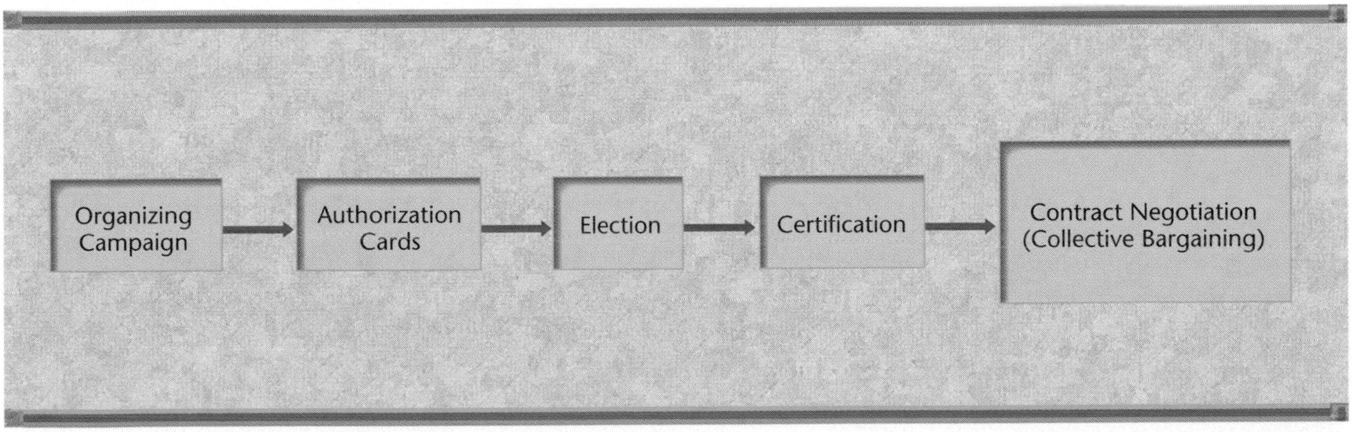

HR PERSPECTIVE

Ethics of Aggressive Union Organizing Efforts

The new aggressiveness of organized labor raises questions about how fair and ethical some of the tactics are, just as questions about the tactics used by employers have been raised in the past. As mentioned in the chapter opener, the use of aggressive tactics has been expanded under John Sweeney, new head of the Service Employees International Union. Some tactics used by this union, as well as some tactics used by another union, are described here.

United Food and Commercial Workers (UFCW)
To overcome resistance to a union organizing effort by Food Lion, a supermarket chain on the East Coast, the United Food and Commercial Workers Union (UFCW) persuaded ABC News to broadcast a story that claimed Food Lion regularly sold rotten fish and meat. The union even gave "pre-hire training" and a false letter of reference so the reporter could be employed at Food Lion. The veracity of the claim has been disputed by Food Lion, which sued ABC.

Through a separate consumer organization it co-sponsors, the UFCW also issued a press release claiming that Food Lion frequently sold past-dated infant formula. The consumer organization did not study any other supermarkets. The concerns of Food Lion customers reached such proportions that the federal Food and Drug Administration had to issue a press release that stated that outdated infant formula does not pose health hazards.

As a result of these union organizing tactics, Food Lion's earnings declined $174 million in one year. Food Lion ended up closing almost 100 stores and laying off over 3,000 employees. Not all of the decline was due to the UFCW efforts, but they certainly contributed to Food Lion's problems.

Service Employees International Union (SEIU)
The SEIU has used very aggressive tactics to try to organize workers at the Hillhaven Corporation, a nursing-home chain. In addition to the typical use of pickets, the SEIU filed a lawsuit challenging a merger between Hillhaven and another nursing-home chain. The union also posted information to Hillhaven shareholders on the Internet asking them to oppose the merger. A major HMO in California stopped sending patients to Hillhaven after the SEIU picketed the HMO.

Given the consequences to employers at targeted firms, some have questioned whether the unions really were concerned about the employees or were just trying to get members at any cost. Also, questions have been raised about the ethics of some union organizing efforts that are very aggressive.[15]

and circulars are all handbills. These items can be passed out to employees as they leave work, mailed to their homes, or even attached to their vehicles, as long as they comply with the rules established by laws and the NLRB.

Employers have fought handbilling efforts by going to court. In one U.S. Supreme Court decision, the Court held that an employer may prohibit nonemployee union organizers from engaging in unionization efforts on company-owned or company-controlled property.[16] A subsequent decision ruled that an employer can prohibit nonemployees from giving out handbills claiming that the employer is paying inadequate wages.[17]

"SALTING" A 1995 U.S. Supreme Court decision affects the ability of employers to discriminate against organizers paid by unions to infiltrate a targeted employer for the purpose of trying to organize other workers. The practice, known as **salting**, involves unions' hiring and paying people to apply for jobs at certain companies; when the people are hired, they begin union organizing efforts. The Supreme Court ruled that refusing to hire otherwise qualified applicants, even if they also are paid by a union, violates the Wagner Act.[18] The unions saw this decision as a major victory. The specific focus of the case was "salting" construction companies in order to gain union representation. One for-

Salting
Practice in which unions hire and pay people to apply for jobs at certain companies; when the people are hired, they begin union organizing efforts.

mer "salt" said he was hired and then reported back unfair treatment by supervisors. The union would use those examples when approaching workers to try to get them to sign authorization cards.[19]

❖ Authorization

A **union authorization card** is signed by an employee to designate a union as his or her collective bargaining agent. At least 30% of the employees in the targeted group must sign authorization cards before an election can be called. If at least 50% of the targeted employees sign authorization cards, the union can request that the employer recognize the union as the official bargaining agent for all of the employees, meaning that no election need be held. However, as would be expected, most employers refuse this request. Consequently, the union must petition the NLRB to hold a representation election.

Union Authorization Card
Card signed by an employee to designate a union as his or her collective bargaining agent.

In reality, the fact that an employee signs an authorization card does not mean that the employee is in favor of a union; it means only that he or she would like the opportunity to vote on having one. Employees who do not want a union still might sign authorization cards to attract management's attention to the fact that employees are disgruntled.

❖ Representation Election

An election to determine if a union will represent the employees is supervised by the NLRB for private-sector organizations and by other legal bodies for public-sector organizations. If two unions are attempting to represent employees, the employees will have three choices: union A, union B, or no union.

Bargaining Unit Before the election is held, the appropriate bargaining unit must be determined. A **bargaining unit** is composed of all employees eligible to select a single union to represent and bargain collectively for them. If management and the union do not agree on who is and who is not included in the unit, the regional office of the NLRB must make a determination. Ultimately, disputes about the bargaining unit can be appealed to the NLRB at the national level.

Bargaining Unit
All employees eligible to select a single union to represent and bargain collectively for them.

One of the major criteria used in deciding the composition of a bargaining unit is what the NLRB has called a "community of interest." This concept means that the employees have mutual interests in the following areas:

- Wages, hours, and working conditions
- Traditional industry groupings for bargaining purposes
- Physical location of employees and the amount of interaction and working relationships among employee groups
- Supervision by similar levels of management

Another consideration involves employees who regularly work with confidential data, such as a human resource assistant who prepares data for union negotiations. These employees can be excluded from the bargaining unit. Also, since the passage of the Taft-Hartley Act, first-line supervisors can be excluded from the bargaining unit. For instance, the U.S. Supreme Court ruled that certain licensed practical nurses could qualify as supervisors under the Wagner Act and therefore could be excluded from the bargaining unit.[20]

The NLRB issued some proposed new parameters for determining bargaining units in 1996. Those regulations would make it easier for unions to organize two separate locations that are near each other, such as two fast-food restaurants two miles apart. Previously, each restaurant was considered a separate bargaining unit.[21] But employers have gone to court to block the NLRB from using this new rule.

❖ **FIGURE 18–7** ❖
LEGAL DO'S AND DON'TS FOR MANAGERS DURING THE UNIONIZATION PROCESS

DO (LEGAL)	DON'T (ILLEGAL)
❖ Tell employees about current wages and benefits and how they compare with those in other firms ❖ Tell employees that the employer opposes unionization ❖ Tell employees the disadvantages of having a union (especially cost of dues, assessments, and requirements of membership) ❖ Show employees articles about unions and relate negative experiences others have had elsewhere ❖ Explain the unionization process to employees accurately ❖ Forbid distribution of union literature during work hours in work areas ❖ Enforce disciplinary policies and rules in a consistent and fair manner	❖ Promise employees pay increases or promotions if they vote against the union ❖ Threaten employees with termination or discriminate when disciplining employees ❖ Threaten to close down or move the company if a union is voted in ❖ Spy on or have someone spy on union meetings ❖ Make a speech to employees or groups at work within 24 hours of the election (before that, it is allowed) ❖ Ask employees how they plan to vote or if they have signed authorization cards ❖ Urge employees to persuade others to vote against the union (such a vote must be initiated solely by the employee)

UNFAIR LABOR PRACTICES Employers and unions engage in a number of activities as authorization cards are being solicited and after an election has been requested. Both the Wagner Act and the Taft-Hartley Act place restrictions on these activities.

A number of tactics may be used by management representatives to try to defeat a unionization effort. Such tactics often begin when handbills appear or when authorization cards are being distributed. Some employers hire experts who specialize in combatting unionization efforts. The use of these "union busters," as they are called by unions, appears to enhance employers' chances of winning the representation election.[22] Figure 18–7 lists some common tactics that management legally can use and some tactics it cannot use.

Unions have constraints on their activities as well. For example, the Supreme Court has held that union organizers who were not company employees did not have to be allowed into the parking lot to distribute handbills. This ruling addressed the balance between employer property rights and employee rights to organize.[23]

ELECTION PROCESS Assuming an election is held, the union need receive only the votes of a *majority of those voting* in the election. For example, if a group of 200 employees is the identified unit, and only 50 people vote, only 50% of the employees voting plus one (26) would need to vote "yes" in order for the union to be named as the representative of all 200.

If either side believes that unfair labor practices have been used by the other side, the election results can be appealed to the NLRB. If the NLRB finds that unfair practices were used, it can order a new election. Assuming that no unfair practices have been used and the union obtains a majority in the election, the union then petitions the NLRB for certification.

Over the years, unions have won representation elections about 45% to 50% of the time. Statistics from the NLRB consistently indicate that the smaller the number of employees in the bargaining unit, the higher the percentage of elections won by unions.[24] In one recent period, unions won 40% of elections in the manufacturing sector but only 32% of elections in mining. Studies have found that various factors affect the "win rate" of unions.[25] An AFL-CIO study found that win rates were higher when the campaign focused on working conditions, grievance procedures, and dignity on the job. When unions focused only on wages, they won about half as frequently.[26] The HR Perspective presents research done on union organizing effectiveness.

❖ Certification and Decertification

Official certification of a union as the legal representative for employees is given by the NLRB (or by the relevant body for public-sector organizations). Once certified, the union attempts to negotiate a contract with the employer. The employer *must* bargain, as it is an unfair labor practice to refuse to bargain with a certified union. Negotiation of a labor contract is one of the most important methods that unions use to obtain their major goals. A general discussion of collective bargaining is contained in Chapter 19.

Employees who have a union and no longer wish to be represented by it can use the election process called **decertification.** The decertification process is similar to the unionization process. Employees attempting to oust a union must obtain decertification authorization cards signed by at least 30% of the employees in the bargaining unit before an election may be called. If a majority of those voting in the election want to remove the union, the decertification effort succeeds. One caution: Management may not assist the decertification effort in any way by providing assistance or funding.

Decertification
A process whereby a union is removed as the representative of a group of employees.

Decertification elections often result in the union losing. According to data from the NLRB, unions have lost about 30% of all decertification elections in

HR PERSPECTIVE

Research on Union Organizing Effectiveness

The effectiveness of a national union in attracting and retaining members was the focus of a research study done by Fiorito, Jarley, and Delaney. The researchers had determined through reviews of other studies that environmental and organizational factors affected union organizing effectiveness. Environmental factors included demand for union services, employer opposition, and employment growth. Organizational influences with regard to the union included its resources, bureaucracy, and others.

To determine effectiveness, the researchers conducted structured telephone interviews with top-level union officials in 111 national unions; 275 interviews in all were conducted. (The interviews covered unions representing about 95% of all unionized employees in the United States.) The researchers also reviewed the constitutions of all 111 unions and used a coding procedure to classify the union structure and governance processes.

Measurement of union organizing effectiveness was based on data from the NLRB on certification elections won and lost, vote shares in those elections, and organizing activities. Decertification election data of a similar nature also was obtained. Finally, the researchers obtained data on members gained from other unions and membership growth.

Some of the findings of the study included the following:

- ❖ Union officials considered effectiveness to be actually getting union members, not just making efforts to sign up members.
- ❖ Winning elections by significant margins of votes—not just winning—was important to the union officials.
- ❖ Two broad organizing strategies were identified. (1) Relatively few specific organizations and situations can be targeted. (2) Wider organizing efforts in more organizations and settings can be undertaken, which results in a lower success rate.
- ❖ Unions that avoid decertification bids are more effective in getting workers to unionize in other elections.

Overall, these findings provide insights into unions' efforts to reduce declines in membership. Each union must develop its own strategies.[27]

recent years. One study found that labor market conditions affected the likelihood that decertification would be successful.[28] Some other reasons that employees decide to vote out a union include the following:[29]

- Better treatment by employers, so employees no longer feel they need a union to protect their interests.
- Efforts by employers to discredit the union, resulting in employees' initiating decertification.
- The inability of some unions to address the changing needs of a firm's workforce.
- Declining image of unions, coupled with lack of confidence in aging labor leaders on the part of younger, more educated workers.

SUMMARY

- A union is a formal association of workers that promotes the interests of its members through collective action.
- Workers join unions primarily because of management's failure to address major job-related concerns.
- Union membership as a percentage of the workforce is down from over 30% in 1960 to below 16% currently.
- Unions are attempting to reverse this decline in membership, in part, by organizing more white-collar workers, women, and government workers.
- The structural levels of unions include federations, national or international unions, and local unions. Business agents and union stewards work at the local level.
- Unions in the United States have survived many ups and downs but experienced their greatest growth in earlier days and have suffered declining numbers lately.
- The "National Labor Code" is composed of three laws that provide the legal basis for labor relations today. The three laws are the Wagner Act, the Taft-Hartley Act, and the Landrum-Griffin Act.
- The Wagner Act was designed to protect unions and workers. The Taft-Hartley Act restored some powers to management, and the Landrum-Griffin Act was meant to protect individual union members.
- The Civil Service Reform Act of 1978 made major revisions in the union/management relations process in the federal government.
- The process of organizing includes an organizing campaign, authorization, a representation election, NLRB certification, and collective bargaining.
- The process can be reversed through decertification.

REVIEW AND DISCUSSION QUESTIONS

1. Describe why you would or would not consider joining a union in your current job or in a former hourly job.
2. Discuss the following statement: "I think anybody who anticipates that unions will reverse their decline in membership during the next 10 years is dreaming."
3. Identify the three parts of the "National Labor Code" and the key elements of each.
4. A coworker has just brought you a union leaflet that urges each employee to sign an authorization card. What events would you expect to occur from this point on?

Terms to Know

agency shop **539**
bargaining unit **543**
business agent **534**
closed shop **538**
craft union **534**
decertification **545**
federation **534**
handbilling **541**
industrial union **534**
national emergency strike **538**
right-to-work laws **539**
salting **541**
union **528**
union authorization card **543**
union shop **539**
union steward **534**

CASE

Unionization Efforts at Whole Foods

It is well known that unions target employers whose management practices are deficient. But what about trying to organize workers at a company that has been recognized for having a variety of "employee-friendly" policies and practices? The battle between the United Food and Commercial Workers (UFCW) and Whole Foods Market, Inc., reveals some aspects of situations faced by unions today.

Whole Foods opened its first store in 1980 in Austin, Texas. By the mid-1990s, Whole Foods had 35 stores in eight states, some under other names, and an annual sales volume of over $400 million per year. In a number of locations, Whole Foods has been targeted by the UFCW because Whole Foods employees are paid less than standard UFCW wages at other supermarkets. For instance, at the Whole Foods store in St. Paul, Minnesota, employees earned $5.50 per hour, while UFCW wages were $6 per hour. In California, the UFCW had contracts with some competitive supermarket chains whereby, though beginning workers earned only $4.90 to $5.30 per hour, full-time employees earned as much as $16 per hour plus benefits. At all Whole Foods stores, employees start at $5.50 per hour, but raises beyond that level are based on store profit percentages and team performance. The CEO of Whole Foods claims that the firm's benefits package is equal to that of the UFCW and that after stores have been open for several years, employees at Whole Foods stores that meet performance and profit goals will be making wages close to those paid at UFCW-represented companies.

The UFCW has had difficulties organizing Whole Foods workers. One reason has been the employee-friendly policies and practices used throughout the firm. For instance, most of the managers in Whole Foods stores started as hourly employees. One store manager started as a stocker and two years later was promoted to assistant store manager with an attendant pay raise. Whole Foods workers also can transfer to other stores in other areas. In addition, Whole Foods employees get a 20% discount on all purchases at their stores, and the firm gives bonuses to workers who get more training. For the longer term, Whole Foods has established an employee stock ownership plan.

Nevertheless, the UFCW has persisted in its organizing efforts, conducting unionization campaigns at Whole Foods Stores in several states. Its major goal is to raise the wages of Whole Foods workers to a level equal to that at competing supermarkets where UFCW members work. Otherwise, Whole Foods will continue to have a major labor cost advantage. Also, the president of a UFCW local addresses a broader concern when he says, "Our society can't survive on $6 to $7 an hour jobs." So the union plans to continue picketing Whole Foods and running advertisements urging consumers to shop elsewhere until Whole Foods employees select the UFCW to represent them.[30]

Questions

1. Discuss how management at Whole Foods illustrates why union membership has declined.
2. What are the reasons supporting and negating the need for the UFCW's activities to organize workers at Whole Foods stores?

Notes

1. J. Worsham, "Labor Comes Alive," *Nation's Business*, February 18, 1996, 24–26; R. L. Rose, "John Sweeney Plots a Revolution at AFL-CIO," *The Wall Street Journal*, June 14, 1995, B1; S. Caudron, "The Changing Union Agenda," *Personnel Journal*, March 1995, 42–49; J. B. Judis, "Can Labor Come Back? Why the Answer May Be Yes," *The New Republic*, May 23, 1994, 25–29; and R. L. Rose, "Love of Labor: Training the Newest Generation of AFL-CIO Organizations," *The Wall Street Journal*, October 26, 1995, B1.

2. Joel Rogers, "Talking Union," *The Nation*, December 26, 1994, 784–786.

3. R. S. Iverblatt and R. J. Amann, "Race, Ethnicity, Union Attitudes, and Voting Predictions," *Industrial Relations* 30 (1991), 271–285.

4. C. Fullagar et al., "The Socialization of Union Loyalty," *Journal of Organizational Behavior* 13 (1992), 13–26; also see a related study, J. Barling et al., "Pre-employment Predictors of Union Attitudes: The Role of Family Socialization and Work Beliefs," *Journal of Applied Psychology* 76 (1991), 725–731.

5. Diane Crispell, "Have Unions Stopped Shrinking?" *American Demographics*, June 1994, 14.

6. P. Bassett, "Union Elections Highlight the Struggle for Influence," *The Times*, May 31, 1995, 23; J. Warner, "Clinging to the Safety Net," *Business Week*, March 11, 1996, 62; and "France Trails Europe in Union Membership," *Manpower Argus*, February 1996, 11.

7. Marion Crain, "Gender and Union Organizing," *Industrial and Labor Relations Review*, 47 (1994), 227–248.

8. Vincent J. Roscigno and M. Keith Kimble, "Elite Power, Race, and the Persistence of Low Unionization in the South," *Work and Occupations* 22 (1995), 271–301.

9. Steven Mellor, "Gender Composition and Gender Representation on Local Unions," *Journal of Applied Psychology* 80 (1995), 706–721.

10. *Commonwealth of Massachusetts v. Hunt*, Massachusetts, 4 Metcalf 3 (1842).

11. "National Labor Relations Act," *United States Statutes at Large* 49, 449.

12. "Labor-Management Relations Act, 1947" (PL 101, 23 June 1947), *United States Statutes at Large* 61, 136–162.

13. *United Steel Workers v. United States*, 45 LRRM 2066 (1959).

14. "Labor-Management Reporting and Disclosure Act of 1959" (PL 86–257, 14 September 1959), *United States Statutes at Large* 73, 519–546.

15. Adapted from S. Baker, "The Yelping over Labor's New Tactics," *Business Week*, October 23, 1995, 75; T. J. DiLorenzo, "Fishy Campaign Targets Nonunion Grocer," *The Wall Street Journal*, November 16, 1995, 18; and W. Zellner, "Tactics That Joe Hill Never Dreamed Of," *Business Week*, October 30, 1995, 120.

16. *Lechmere, Inc. v. NLRB*, 112 S.Ct. 841 (1992).

17. Clifford R. Oviatt, "Employer Property Rights Upheld in Handbilling Case," *HR News*, December 1995, 20.

18. *NLRB v. Town & Country Electric, Inc. and Ameristaff Contractors, Ltd.*, 115 S.Ct. 450 (1995).

19. R. J. Grossman, "Employers Brace for 'Salting' after High Court Ruling," *HR News*, January 1996, 1.

20. *NLRB v. Health Care & Retirement Corporation of America*, 114 S.Ct. 1778 (1994).

21. Clifford R. Oviatt, "Bargaining-Unit Proposal Has Far-Reaching Impact," *HR News*, November 1995, 11.

22. Bruce E. Kaufman and Paula E. Stephan, "The Role of Management Attorneys in Union Organizing Campaigns," *Journal of Labor Research* 16 (1995), 439–455.

23. Paul Barrett, "Employers Win Supreme Court Ruling," *The Wall Street Journal*, January 28, 1992, A4.

24. "Union Win Rate," *Bulletin to Management*, June 16, 1994, 188–190.

25. C. Scott, J. Simpson, and S. Oswald, "An Empirical Analysis of Union Election Outcomes in the Electrical Utility Industry," *Journal of Labor Research* 14 (1993), 355–366.

26. Stephanie Overman, "The Union Pitch Has Changed," *HR Magazine*, December 1991, 46.

27. Adapted from Jack Fiorito, Paul Jarley, and John Thomas Delaney, "National Union Effectiveness in Organizing: Measures and Influences," *Industrial and Labor Relations Review*, 48 (1995), 613–635.

28. David Meyer and Trevor Bain, "Union Decertification Election Outcomes," *Journal of Labor Research* 15 (1994), 117–137.

29. Marvin J. Levine, "Double-Digit Decertification Activity: Union Organizational Weakness in the 1980s," *Labor Law Journal* 40 (1989), 311–315.

30. Based on Beth Mattson, "New Age Hooey?" *Business Ethics*, October 1995, 20–21.

Chapter 19

Collective Bargaining and Grievance Management

After you have read this chapter, you should be able to . . .

- Define *collective bargaining* and identify at least four bargaining relationships.
- Explain the three categories of collective bargaining issues.
- Identify and describe a typical collective bargaining process.
- Discuss how union/management cooperation has been affected by NLRB rulings.
- Define *grievance* and describe the importance and extent of grievance procedures.
- Explain the basic steps in a grievance procedure.

HR IN TRANSITION

STRIKE AT GM OVER JOB SECURITY AND OUTSOURCING

The competitive forces faced by both companies and unions are illustrated by union/management conflicts between General Motors (GM) and the United Auto Workers (UAW). A 17-day strike at a GM plant in Dayton, Ohio, points up several fundamental issues.

PRODUCTION AND WORKING DEMANDS

First, GM had instituted a "just-in-time" production strategy at many of its parts plants. As a result, many other GM assembly plants depended on having a steady flow of parts such as brake components from the Dayton plant. Because of a shortage of brake components, the UAW members at the Dayton plant had been working significant amounts of overtime. The company had refused to hire more workers, assuming the shortage of workers might turn to a surplus if demand for GM vehicles softened.

COST PRESSURES AND OUTSOURCING

From GM's viewpoint, it faced major cost problems with the UAW members. For instance, the average GM worker received wages and benefits averaging $43 per hour, including $16 per hour worth of benefits. By comparison, non-union workers at a non-GM brake plant in South Carolina received wages and benefits valued at $23 per hour, including $5 per hour worth of benefits.

In summary, the UAW members and GM had priced their labor too high, and GM took a stand starting in Dayton to begin cost reductions.

Under the union contract, GM was allowed to outsource some parts production—that is, purchase some parts from outside suppliers—and production costs for the outsourced parts were lower. By using the South Carolina producer of brake parts, GM saved considerable money but shifted the equivalent of 88 jobs out of the Dayton plant.

One major trigger for the Dayton strike was a demand by GM to increase outsourcing in order to be competitive with Ford Motor Company and Chrysler Corporation. Whereas GM used outsourcing for 30% of its components, Chrysler used outsourcing for 70% of its parts. The cost differential was so large that Chrysler could sell its cars and trucks slightly cheaper and still make significantly higher profits per vehicle. In summary, the UAW members and GM had priced their labor too high, and GM took a stand starting in Dayton to begin cost reductions.

JOB SECURITY

Another major concern of the UAW members was job security. As outsourcing at GM increased, more jobs were being "transferred out" to non-union subcontractors. With those jobs gone, the UAW lost membership, and the slow decline in the number of jobs could put the long-term viability of the Dayton plant in question.

BROADER CONTRACT POSITIONING

Another factor contributing to the strike was that both sides were using the Dayton situation to position themselves for broader negotiations, to begin in September 1996 when the UAW contract with GM expired. From the union perspective, taking a tough stand on job security and outsourcing at the Dayton plant established that those issues would be major ones in the upcoming negotiations. For GM, it was important to take a firm stand on its right to outsource and its intent to increase the percentage of components produced by outside suppliers.

RESOLVING THE STRIKE

The strike ended after 17 days. During that period, over 175,000 UAW members at the Dayton plant and other GM locations lost wages. Without a continuous flow of parts from the Dayton plant, assembly lines in 24 of GM's 29 car and truck assembly plants had been forced to close, causing 125,000 workers to be laid off. But the costs were high to GM also. Total production lost was about 250,000 cars and trucks, and company earnings were reduced by $400 million. Other suppliers to GM also had to lay off workers and lost earnings. One economist estimated that in total the strike cost the U.S. economy $5.4 billion, which represented about 1% of the gross domestic product.

Under the terms of the settlement, GM retained its right to continue and increase outsourcing. Specifically, GM could buy brake systems for several new models from the South Carolina firm, which ultimately will cost the Dayton plant 120 jobs.

The UAW retained the right to authorize strikes at other local plants, which GM had wanted to eliminate until the national contract negotiations began. Also, GM promised to add new jobs at the plant, based on new business needs.

So who won? It depends on which of the various factors are deemed to be the most important. Observers generally believed that if there was a winner, it was GM.

But what the Dayton strike indicates is that for unions today, job security and outsourcing are more important concerns than wage and benefit increases. It is likely that these concerns will be evident in numerous other industries as workers fight for job security and employers strive to lower their labor costs.[1]

> *"There are only two forces that unite men—fear and interest."*
> *Napoleon Bonaparte*

Collective bargaining takes center stage in an organization following a successful unionization attempt. This final stage of the unionization process involves the negotiation and signing of a contractual agreement between a union and an employer. In this chapter, the process of contract negotiation through collective bargaining is discussed. Also, day-to-day union/management relations that occur as part of through grievance management are examined.

❖ NATURE OF COLLECTIVE BARGAINING

❖Collective Bargaining
The process whereby representatives of management and workers negotiate over wages, hours, and other terms and conditions of employment.

Collective bargaining is the process whereby representatives of management and workers negotiate over wages, hours, and other terms and conditions of employment. It is a give-and-take process between representatives of two organizations for the benefit of both. It is also a power relationship. The power relationship in collective bargaining involves conflict, and the threat of conflict seems necessary to maintain the relationship. But perhaps the most significant aspect of collective bargaining is that it is a continuing relationship that does not end immediately after agreement is reached. Instead, it continues over the life of the labor agreement and beyond.

❖ TYPES OF BARGAINING RELATIONSHIPS

The attitude of management toward unions is one major factor in determining the collective bargaining relationship. This attitude plays a crucial role in management's strategic approach to collective bargaining. For instance, especially after a bitter organizing campaign, a union may take months to win an initial contract. Some employers continue the fight in courts, charging unfair practices, and the resulting delays can run several years.[2] Some unions never reach contract agreements and voluntarily relinquish their certification.

Management/union relationships in collective bargaining can follow one of several patterns. Figure 19–1 shows the relationship as a continuum, ranging from conflict to collusion. On the left side of the continuum, management and union see each other as enemies. On the right side, the two entities join together illegally. In smaller firms traditional collective bargaining occurs through such approaches as armed truce, power bargaining, and accommodation. However, more contentious, conflict-oriented situations had grown in fre-

❖ FIGURE 19–1 ❖
COLLECTIVE BARGAINING RELATIONSHIP CONTINUUM

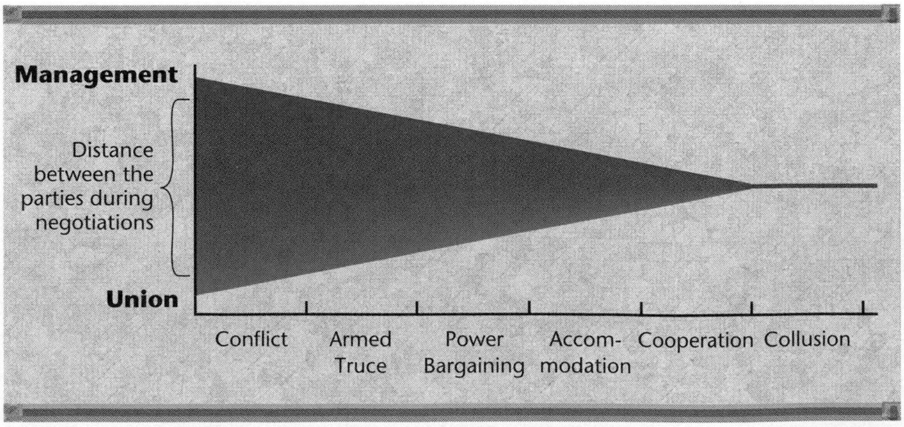

quency.[3] There are a number of positions in between and a discussion of the six strategies follows.[4]

Conflict In the conflict strategy, management takes a totally uncompromising view, which leads to an uncompromising approach by the union, or vice versa. A desire to "bust the union" may underlie the use of the conflict strategy. To paraphrase a saying from old western movies, management's attitude is that "the only good union is a dead union!"

Armed Truce Management representatives who practice the armed-truce strategy take the position that they are well aware of the vital interests of the organization, while the union is poles away and always will be. However, management realizes that forcing conflict is not in the best interests of either party and that the union is not likely to disappear. Consequently, management is willing to negotiate a basic agreement. Many union/management relationships, especially in smaller businesses, have not progressed beyond this armed-truce stage.

Power Bargaining Managers engaged in a power bargaining relationship can accept the union; many even pride themselves on the sense of "realism" that forces them to acknowledge the union's power. Managerial philosophy here assumes that management's task is to increase its power, then use it whenever possible to offset the power of the union. The union engages in power bargaining by using tactics that have an impact on the employer's pocketbook such as lawsuits, public hearings, demonstrations, and appeals to legislators.

Accommodation In accommodation, management and the union learn to tolerate each other and attempt to minimize conflict and to conciliate whenever necessary. The accommodation strategy in no way suggests that management goes out of its way to help organized labor, but merely that it recognizes the need to reduce confrontation in dealing with common problems often caused by external forces, such as imports and government regulations.

Cooperation The cooperation strategy involves full acceptance of the union as an active partner in a formal plan. In this strategy, management supports both the right and the desire of unions to participate in certain areas of decision making. The two parties jointly resolve human resource and production problems as they occur. Labor/management committees and quality-improvement groups are examples of cooperation.

Collusion Collusion, relatively rare in American labor history, is illegal. In the collusion strategy, union and management may engage in labor price fixing designed to inflate wages and profits at the expense of the general public. Or they may institute "sweetheart" deals that benefit management and union officials at the expense of the employees.

❖ Bargaining Structures

Collective bargaining can be structured in several different ways. Here, the structures are classified according to whether they involve one employer or multiple employers.

One Employer The *one-employer, one-union* structure is the simplest and most common. Here, an employer has just one unionized operating facility and negotiates with just one union. If an employer has several facilities and the same union represents employees at all the facilities, then the collective bargaining structure is *one employer, multiplant.* For example, if a printing company has three facilities, each located in a different state, then a collective bargaining contract can be negotiated for all plants at the same time. Then the provisions of the contract will apply to all company locations.

The *one-employer, multiunion* structure may be used when a large employer has employees represented by different unions, and contracts with all the unions are negotiated at the same time. This model is common in the construction industry, where one employer may face several different building trade unions representing a number of different crafts.

MULTIEMPLOYER Another structure, *multiemployer, one union,* was developed in the coal-mining industry. This structure also has been used extensively in the steel industry in the form of a *master contract* that applies to all companies. This master agreement then is supplemented by a *local contract* dealing with individual company and/or plant issues.

The final bargaining structure is the *multiemployer, multiunion* structure. It has been used in the construction industry. Here, a group of unions negotiates with a contractors' association representing all of the unionized construction companies in a geographic area.

CHOICE OF A BARGAINING STRUCTURE The choice of a bargaining structure is made for a variety of reasons, many of which reflect the bargaining power and pressures that each party believes it can exert. The structure may change over time as both parties attempt to stay up to date with industry changes.

Employers prefer different bargaining structures for different reasons. For example, an employer that must bargain with multiple unions may spend less time and get more consistent contracts by negotiating with all unions at once. Or an employer may prefer a one-employer, multiplant structure to get similar contracts at widely diverse plants, which also may put pressure on individual locals to agree to similar concessions.

Unions also take various approaches. Some unions favor negotiating with one company and then using the contract gained as a model for other firms in the same industry. This approach has been labeled *pattern bargaining.* It has been used by the United Auto Workers with General Motors, Ford, and Chrysler. One study found that the degree of centralization of bargaining by national unions varies depending on the size of local affiliates and the percentage of unionization in the industry, as well as other factors.[5]

❖ ISSUES FOR BARGAINING

The Wagner Act clearly expects management and the union to bargain over "wages, hours, and other terms and conditions of employment." What specifically is included in those categories has been defined over the years by the National Labor Relations Board (NLRB) and Supreme Court rulings. They have defined bargaining issues as falling into three groupings: mandatory, permissive, and illegal issues.

❖Mandatory Issues
Those issues that are identified specifically by labor laws or court decisions as being subject to bargaining.

MANDATORY ISSUES Those issues that are identified specifically by labor laws or court decisions as being subject to bargaining are **mandatory issues.** If either party demands that issues in this category be bargained over, then bargaining must occur. Generally, mandatory issues relate to wages, benefits, nature of jobs, and other work-related subjects.

The following issues have been ruled to be mandatory subjects for bargaining:[6]

- Discharge of employees
- Job security
- Grievances
- Work schedules
- Union security and dues checkoff
- Retirement and pension coverage
- Vacations
- Christmas bonuses
- Rest- and lunch-break rules
- Safety rules
- Profit-sharing plans
- Required physical exams

PERMISSIVE ISSUES Those issues that are not mandatory but relate to jobs are **permissive issues.** Some examples that can be bargained over if both parties agree are:

- Benefits for retired employees
- Product prices
- Performance bonds

Permissive Issues Those issues that are not mandatory but relate to jobs.

Illegal Issues Those issues that would require either party to take illegal action.

ILLEGAL ISSUES A final category is **illegal issues,** those that would require either party to take illegal action, such as giving preference to individuals who have been union members when hiring employees. If one side wants to bargain over an illegal issue, the other can refuse.

TYPICAL CONTRACT ITEMS Typical items in a formal labor contract are shown in Figure 19–2. Aside from the issues just discussed, two areas of common concern in contract bargaining are management rights and union security agreements.

FIGURE 19–2
TYPICAL ITEMS IN A LABOR CONTRACT

1. Purpose of agreement	11. Separation allowance
2. Nondiscrimination clause	12. Seniority
3. Management rights	13. Bulletin boards
4. Recognition of the union	14. Pension and insurance
5. Wages	15. Safety
6. Incentives	16. Grievance procedure
7. Hours of work	17. No-strike or lockout clause
8. Vacations	18. Definitions
9. Sick leave and leaves of absence	19. Terms of the contract (dates)
10. Discipline	20. Appendices

Management Rights Virtually all labor contracts include **management rights,** which are those rights reserved to the employer to manage, direct, and control its business. Such a provision often reads as follows:

> The employer retains all rights to manage, direct, and control its business in all particulars, except as such rights are expressly and specifically modified by the terms of this or any subsequent agreement.[7]

Management Rights Those rights reserved to the employer to manage, direct, and control its business.

By including such a provision, management is attempting to preserve its unilateral right to decide or make changes in any areas not identified in a labor contract. Some labor contracts spell out in more detail the issues that fall under management rights, while others use the general language just quoted. As would be expected, management representatives want to have as many issues defined as "management rights" as they can.

Union Security A major concern of union representatives when bargaining is to negotiate **union security provisions** to aid the union in obtaining and retaining members. One union security provision is the **dues checkoff,** which provides that union dues will be deducted automatically from the payroll checks of members. This provision makes it much easier for the union to collect its funds, which otherwise it must collect by billing each individual member.

Union Security Provisions Contract provisions to aid the union in obtaining and retaining members.

Dues Checkoff Provision that union dues will be deducted automatically from payroll checks of union members.

Another form of union security involves *requiring union membership* of all employees, subject to state right-to-work laws. As mentioned in Chapter 18, the closed shop

❖ FIGURE 19–3 ❖
TYPICAL COLLECTIVE BARGAINING PROCESS

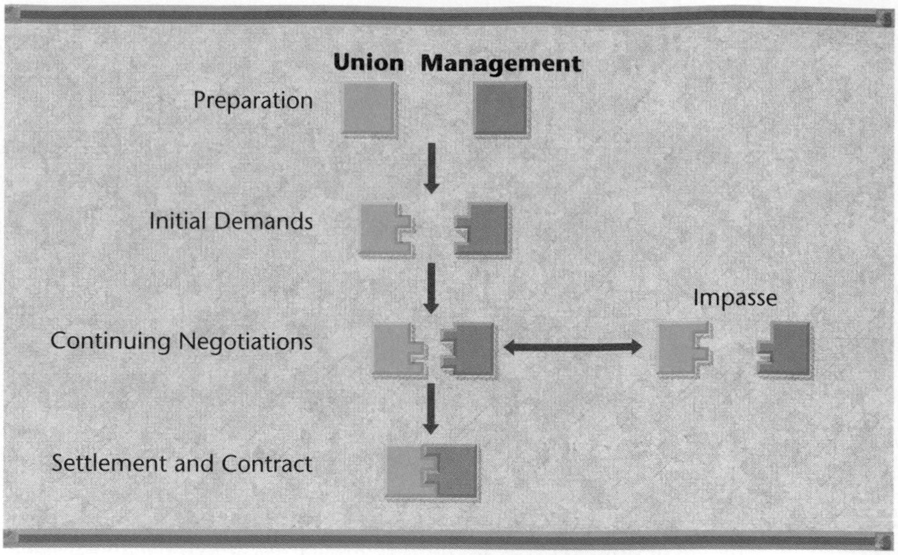

is illegal except in limited construction-industry situations. But other types of arrangements can be developed, including *union shops, maintenance-of-membership,* and *agency shops.*

A growing facet of union security in labor contracts is the *no-layoff* policy, or *job security* guarantee. The job security concerns at General Motors' Dayton plant, described in the opening discussion, illustrate how important such provisions are becoming to many union workers. This is especially true in light of all of the mergers, downsizings, and job reductions in many industries.

❖ PROCESS OF COLLECTIVE BARGAINING

The collective bargaining process is made up of a number of stages. Over time, each situation develops slight modifications, which are necessary for effective bargaining. The process shown in Figure 19–3 is typical.

❖ PREPARATION

Both labor and management representatives spend much time preparing for negotiations. If a previous contract is expiring, the grievances filed under the old contract will be reviewed to identify contract language changes to be negotiated. Employer and industry data concerning wages, benefits, working conditions, management and union rights, productivity, and absenteeism are gathered. Once the data are analyzed, each side identifies what its priorities are and what strategies and tactics it will use to obtain what it wants. Each tries to allow itself some flexibility in order to trade off less important demands for more critical ones.

The courts have stated that unions cannot represent workers in a competent manner if they do not have necessary company information. Therefore, management must provide the necessary data. If the organization argues that it cannot afford to pay what the union is asking, the employer's financial situation and accompanying data are all the more relevant. However, the union must request such information before the employer is obligated to provide it.[8]

❖ Initial Demands

Typical bargaining includes initial proposals of expectations by both sides. The amount of rancor or calmness exhibited sets the tone for future negotiations between the parties. Union and management representatives who have been part of previous negotiations may adopt a pattern that has evolved over time. In negotiations for the first contract between an employer and a union, the process can be much more difficult. Management representatives must adjust to dealing with a union, and employees who are leaders in the union must adapt to their new roles.

❖ Continuing Negotiations

After opening positions have been taken, each side attempts to determine what the other values highly so the best bargain can be struck. For example, the union may be asking the employer to pay for dental benefits as part of a package that also includes wage demands and retirement benefits. However, the union may be most interested in the wages and retirement benefits and may be willing to trade the dental payments for more wages. Management has to determine which the union wants more and decide exactly what to give up.

During negotiations, both management and union must evaluate cost proposals concerning changes in wages, benefits, and other economic items quickly and accurately. A mathematical modeling system tied to a computer spreadsheet will perform the calculations and produce a total cost figure almost immediately. Such issues as an extra day off or a 10-cent-an-hour pay raise can be converted easily to annual cost figures for comparison.

Good Faith Provisions in federal labor law require that both employer and employee bargaining representatives negotiate in *good faith*. In good faith negotiations, the parties agree to send negotiators who can bargain and make decisions, rather than people who do not have the authority to commit either group to a decision. Meetings between the parties cannot be scheduled at absurdly inconvenient hours. Some give-and-take discussions also must occur. After decisions are made in good faith, neither party can renege on the agreement. Blatant anti-union or anti-management propaganda cannot be used during the bargaining process. The specifics of the good faith relationship for collective bargaining are defined by a series of NLRB and court rulings.[9]

Bargaining Power The factors affecting the outcomes of collective bargaining are shown in Figure 19–4. As that model shows, four sets of factors determine the bargaining power of management and the union, all of which must be considered by the negotiators in their give-and-take discussions.

Obviously, *economic factors* are vital. What a firm can afford without jeopardizing its economic health is important to both management and the union. The various *organizational factors* reflect the relative strengths or weaknesses of the union. *Sociodemographic factors* affect the types of proposals made by management and union. For example, if the workers represented by the union are older and predominately male, then certain benefits, such as maternity coverage and child-care assistance, may not be desired as much as additional pension contributions. Both parties must comply with all *legal restraints and regulations* on bargaining procedure and outcomes. Depending on the analyses of those factors, the parties use their bargaining power to obtain concessions from the other party. Ultimately, the outcomes are represented as provisions in the labor contract.

❖ FIGURE 19–4 ❖
DETERMINANTS OF COLLECTIVE BARGAINING ACTIONS

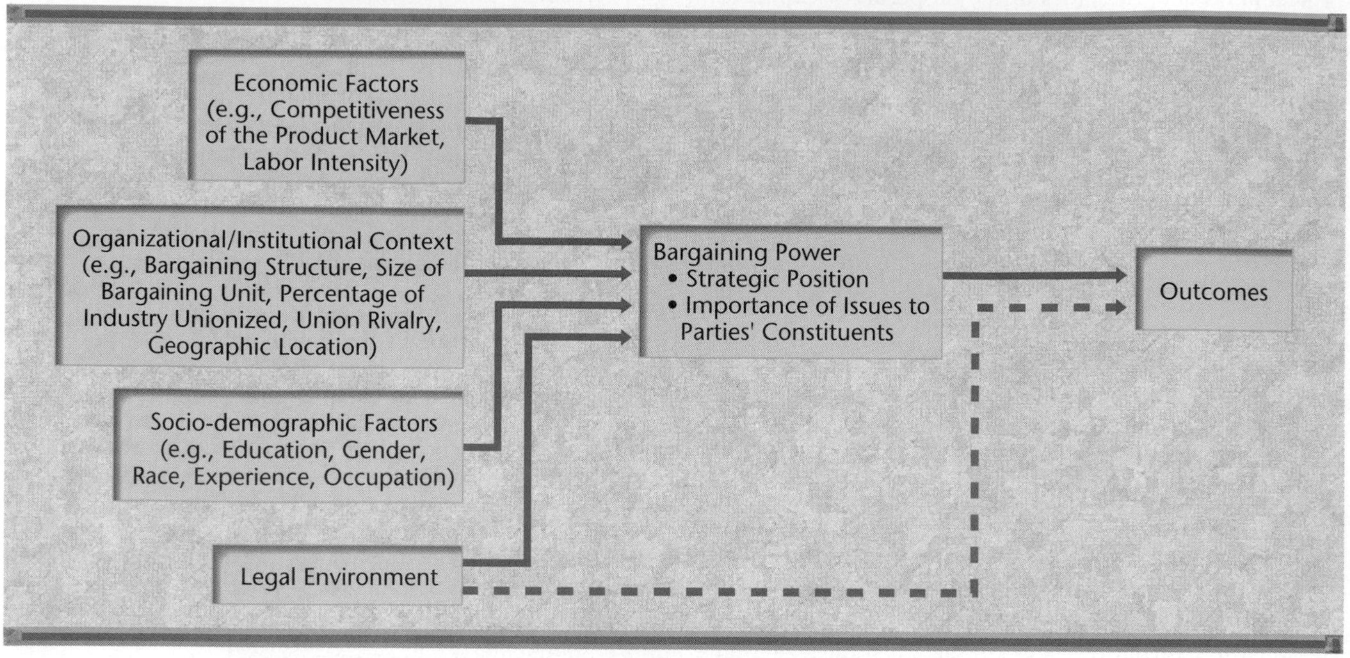

SOURCE: John Thomas Delaney and Donna Sochell, "The Mandatory-Permissive Distinction and Collective Bargaining Outcomes," *Industrial and Labor Relations Review* 42 (1989), 571. © 1989 Cornell University. Used with permission.

BARGAINING BEHAVIOR Collective bargaining is not always a strictly logical, rational process. The behavior of the negotiators is critical. Representatives may exhibit any of four behavior subprocesses in collective bargaining.[10]

1. *Distributive bargaining* occurs when one party must win and the other must lose over a particular issue. If a union wants a dues checkoff, and the employer does not want a checkoff, only one side can win. Either there will or will not be a checkoff.
2. *Integrative bargaining* occurs when both management and union face a common problem and must work together for a solution. For example, the two parties might negotiate a joint program for handling alcoholism, both agreeing to provide some funds to pay for alcohol treatment activities, because there are joint gains to be had from such a program in terms of reduced absenteeism and discipline problems.
3. *Attitudinal structuring* occurs when each side attempts to affect the tone, or "climate," of the negotiations. The result will determine which of the six bargaining strategies identified earlier is adopted during negotiations.
4. *Intraorganizational bargaining* occurs when disagreements exist *within* labor or management. Union negotiators may not be addressing the concerns of all union members in some areas. For instance, some union members may feel that dental insurance should be included in a union proposal, while other union members feel that higher retirement benefits are more important. Some consensus will have to be reached before the negotiators go to the bargaining table. Sometimes union negotiators have members rank their preferences for specific benefits.

❖ Settlement and Contract Agreement

After an initial agreement has been made, the two sides usually return to their respective constituencies to determine if what they have informally agreed on is acceptable. A particularly crucial stage is **ratification** of the labor agreement, which occurs when union members vote to accept the terms of a negotiated agreement. Prior to the ratification vote, the union negotiating team explains the agreement to the union members and presents it for a vote. If approval is voted, the agreement is then formalized into a contract. The agreement also contains language on the duration of the contract.[11] The HR Perspective discusses research on factors affecting ratification.

***Ratification**
Process by which union members vote to accept the terms of a negotiated labor agreement.

Concessionary Bargaining In a variety of industries, unions have engaged in **concessionary bargaining**, which occurs when the union agrees to reduce wages, benefits, or other factors during collective bargaining. Unions have agreed to concessions in such industries as auto, airline, rubber, meat processing, steel, and trucking. When the unions have refused to grant concessions, companies have simply shut down or hired replacement non-union workers at lower wage and benefit levels.

***Concessionary Bargaining**
Collective bargaining through which a union agrees to reduce wages, benefits, or other factors.

HR Perspective: Research on Union Contract Ratification

At the conclusion of the collective bargaining process, when management and union representatives have reached agreement on a contract, that contract usually must be ratified by a vote of the union members. Research by Martin and Berthiaume provides some insights on factors affecting union members and their decision to vote for or against contract ratification.

The researchers gathered data from union members covered by a labor contract involving 40 retail stores in the Midwest. When the old agreement expired, a new agreement was negotiated by union/management representatives but rejected by the union members, with 62% voting to reject the contract. Following that rejection, the negotiators developed a new contract, which was ratified by 69% of the voting members.

Prior to the expiration of the initial contract, the researchers sent surveys to over 18,000 individuals in the bargaining unit. That questionnaire gathered information on union members' attitudes and preferences for various contract provisions. The researchers also obtained demographic data on the members of the union, based on union records. Finally, using vote tallies by store, the researchers compared the questionnaire data with the voting patterns by demographic group and store grouping.

Union officers had indicated that they thought the two most important bargaining issues to their members were dependent medical insurance coverage for part-time employees and wage increases. Given that over 80% of the employees worked part time, those issues would be expected to be important. In the contract that was rejected, subsidized dependent health insurance was available to all employees, and pay in some lower-tier jobs was increased, but employees in high-tier jobs received only lump-sum payments. After that contract was rejected, the new contract provided more to workers in higher-tier jobs.

The researchers used statistical analyses to compare the voting on the second contract with their earlier survey data. As would be expected, the results revealed that how well the union is perceived as representing members' interests affects the voting to accept or reject a contract. Also, the material facets of the contract, such as wages and insurance benefits, significantly influence union members' votes. Another interesting result was that union members consider their security and employment options when voting to accept or reject a contract or to go on strike. Those who perceived they had fewer employment options were more likely to vote to ratify a contract than those who felt they had more options.

In summary, this research provides insights for both union representatives and management negotiators on factors to consider when constructing a labor contract. If a contract does not match the perceptions and interests of those it covers, then the likelihood of ratification decreases.[12]

Two-Tier Wage Structure
Wage structure in which new union members receive lower wages and fewer benefits than existing members performing similar jobs.

Two-Tier Wage Structure Another approach taken to reduce labor costs yet provide job security for union members is a **two-tier wage structure,** in which new union members receive lower wages and fewer benefits than existing members performing similar jobs. As unionized firms negotiated two-tier contracts, they brushed aside predictions that such plans would inevitably cause friction on the job. But the plans are not popular with the new employees, and the longer-service workers fear that their high wages give management an incentive to get rid of them. In summary, two-tier wage schemes, which may have been a triumph of collective bargaining when they were negotiated, now seem to have lost some of their appeal.[13]

❖ Bargaining Impasse

Regardless of the structure of the bargaining process, labor and management do not always reach agreement on the issues. If impasse occurs, then the disputes can be taken to conciliation, mediation, or arbitration.

Conciliation
Process by which a third party attempts to keep union and management negotiators talking so that they can reach a voluntary settlement.

Mediation
Process by which a third party assists negotiators in their discussions and also suggests settlement proposals.

Conciliation and Mediation In conciliation or mediation, an outside party attempts to help two deadlocked parties continue negotiations and arrive at a solution. In **conciliation,** the third party attempts to keep union and management negotiators talking so that they can reach a voluntary settlement but makes no proposals for solutions. In **mediation,** the third party assists the negotiators in their discussions and also suggests settlement proposals. In neither conciliation nor mediation does the third party attempt to impose a solution.

Conciliators and mediators usually are experienced neutrals who act as counselors to reopen communication, clarify problems, and try to find areas in which the two parties can agree. The success of mediators often is linked to their having significant previous experience, being flexible, and taking an active role in keeping the parties negotiating.[14]

Often, mediators and conciliators are provided by the Federal Mediation and Conciliation Service (FMCS). This agency assists in union and management negotiations when impasses arise. The FMCS has offices in most major cities and employs several hundred trained labor experts. Employees of the FMCS sit down with the negotiators from both union and management and attempt to forestall strikes or lockouts.

LOGGING ON

U.S. Collective Bargaining Law and Arbitration. This site contains information on U.S. collective bargaining law and arbitration relating to negotiations between employers and unions.

http://www.law.cornel.edu/topics/collective_bargaining.html

Arbitration
Process by which negotiating parties submit their dispute to a third party to make a decision.

Arbitration The process of **arbitration** is a means of deciding a dispute in which negotiating parties submit the dispute to a third party to make a decision. It can be conducted by either an individual or a panel of individuals. Arbitration is used to solve bargaining impasses primarily in the public sector. This "interest" arbitration is not frequently used in the private sector because companies generally do not want an outside party making decisions about their rights, wages, benefits, and other issues. However, grievance, or "rights," arbitration is used extensively in the private sector. Arbitration will be discussed in more detail when the grievance process is presented later in this chapter.

Strike
Work stoppage in which union members refuse to work in order to put pressure on an employer.

❖ Strikes and Lockouts

If deadlocks cannot be resolved, then an employer may revert to a lockout or a union may revert to a strike. During a **strike,** union members refuse to work in order to put pressure on an employer. Often, the striking union members picket or demonstrate against the employer outside the place of business by carrying placards and signs. In a **lockout,** management shuts down company operations to prevent union members from working. This action may avert possible damage or sabotage to company facilities or injury to employees who continue to work. It also provides leverage to managers.

Both strikes and lockouts place pressure on the other party. By striking, the union attempts to pressure management into making some concessions and signing a contract. However, management may respond by hiring replacement workers or may operate the company by using supervisors and managers to fill in for striking workers.[15] By locking out workers, an employer puts economic pressure on union members in the hope that they will make concessions and support a contract agreement.

***Lockout**
Shutdown of company operations undertaken by management to prevent union members from working.

TYPES OF STRIKES The following types of strikes can occur:

- *Economic strikes* occur when the parties fail to reach agreement during collective bargaining.
- *Unfair labor practice strikes* occur when union members walk away from their jobs over what they feel are illegal employer actions, such as refusal to bargain.
- *Wildcat strikes* occur during the life of the collective bargaining agreement without approval of union leadership and violate a no-strike clause in a labor contract. Strikers can be discharged or disciplined.
- *Jurisdictional strikes* occur when one union's members walk out to force an employer to assign work to them instead of to another union.
- *Sympathy strikes* express one union's support for another involved in a dispute, even though the first union has no disagreement with the employer.

Workers' rights vary depending on the type of strike that occurs. For example, in an economic strike, an employer is free to replace the striking workers. But with an unfair labor practice strike, workers who want their jobs back at the end of the strike must be reinstated.

Work stoppages due to strikes and lockouts are relatively rare. Overall, as has been discussed previously, there has been a decline in union power, paralleling the decline of heavy industry in the United States and decreased public support of unions. Thus, many unions are reluctant to go on strike because of the financial losses their members would incur or the fear that the strike would cause the employer to go bankrupt. One study found that the economic environment of the time affects both whether strikes will occur and how long they will last.[16] Certainly, the GM strike described in the chapter opener illustrates this finding. In addition, management has shown its willingness to hire replacements, and some strikes have ended with union workers losing their jobs.

REPLACEMENT OF STRIKERS Management has always had the ability to simply replace workers who struck, but the option was not widely used. A strike by the United Auto Workers (UAW) against Caterpillar in 1992 changed that, as the HR Perspective on the next page describes.

A growing number of employers appear to be willing to hire replacement workers, and of course, the threat of being replaced reduces the attractiveness of striking to the unionized workers.[17] In response, organized labor proposed legislation prohibiting employers from hiring permanent replacement workers. The union movement argued that such legislation was necessary to restore balance to the collective bargaining process. However, others contended that such legislation would do just the opposite by tilting the balance too far in favor of striking employees. As a result, legislation to ban the use of striker replacements did not pass the U.S. Congress.

HR PERSPECTIVE

Caterpillar Beats the UAW Using Replacement Workers

One of the most bitter and prolonged strikes in recent times occurred at Caterpillar, Inc. A strike called by the United Auto Workers (UAW) against Caterpillar began in 1991 and finally ended in 1995. The clear winner was Caterpillar, which used replacement of striking workers as a key part of its management strategy to counterattack the efforts of the UAW.

The chronology of the strike reveals how a determined employer willing to use replacement workers can outlast a large union with an $800 million strike fund. In late 1991, the UAW began a partial strike when the previous UAW contract expired. Caterpillar responded by locking out UAW members at some Caterpillar plants for several months. Then the UAW began a companywide strike.

At that point, in April 1992, Caterpillar threatened to replace strikers permanently by hiring new non-union workers. The UAW responded by calling off its strike but began "in-plant" tactics to pressure Caterpillar to reach a new contract. For instance, the UAW initiated a campaign to increase dramatically the number of grievances that were filed. The UAW members also initiated a number of wildcat strikes over unresolved grievances.

Finally, in mid-1994, the UAW called a national strike. In response, Caterpillar kept production flowing and plants open by moving salaried office workers, supervisors, and managers into production jobs. Also, Caterpillar hired over 5,000 replacement workers from a huge pool of applicants who wanted the high-paying jobs at the company. In addition, over 4,000 temporary employees were hired. By the end of 1994, Caterpillar had met most of its production goals, and the company reported record profits. Interestingly, many of the workers who were hired as replacements or who crossed the UAW picket line indicated that working relations and productivity were much better with the UAW strikers out of the plant.

By 1995, the leadership of the UAW recognized that the union had lost the fight and resumed negotiations to settle the strike. But Caterpillar insisted that many of the replacement members had been hired as permanent replacements and UAW members would be called back to work only as jobs were available. Finally, in December 1995, the UAW rejected the company's proposal for a contract but ended the strike anyway.

When the UAW workers returned to work, they were confronted with a detailed, structured list of expectations and rules. The 8,700 strikers and all other workers in the plant were given "standards of conduct." Prohibited were buttons, caps, and T-shirts with slogans favoring either the union or the company. However, logos for either the UAW or Caterpillar were allowed as long as they were generic and noncontroversial. Use of derogatory terms, such as *scab,* in conversation also was prohibited. In response, the UAW filed unfair labor practice charges with the NLRB against Caterpillar. But the company indicated that if the NLRB ruled in favor of the union, then Caterpillar would file court appeals so that the standards could continue to be used. In summary, Caterpillar continued to be aggressive in its relations with the UAW.[18]

Executive Order 12954 Despite Congress's rejection of striker-replacement legislation, in 1995 President Bill Clinton signed Executive Order 12954, which prohibits firms that hire permanent replacement workers for striking union workers from receiving U.S. government contracts valued at $100,000 or more.[19] However, the legality of the executive order has been challenged in court by various employer groups. In a lower federal court hearing, the court ruled that President Clinton had exceeded his authority and that the executive order was unenforceable. However, the Clinton administration directed that an appeal be filed with a higher court. Therefore, whether the executive order remains in force will be the subject of future court actions.

❖ Union/Management Cooperation

The adversarial relationship that naturally exists between unions and management may lead to the impasses and conflicts discussed previously. But there is also a growing recognition by many union leaders and employer representatives that cooperation between management and labor unions is essential if organizations are going to compete in a global economy.

Many leaders in both unions and management realize that without changes, there will be fewer companies and fewer jobs. Union/management cooperation has taken many forms, as the following examples illustrate:[20]

- National Steel Corporation began a union/management cooperation program in 1986. Data on company performance and profits are shared with union officers, and the company adopted a no-layoff policy for the 9,500 union members. As a result of cooperation, the number of hours needed to make a ton of steel at the company's main plant in Michigan has declined 33%, to be among the best in the entire steel industry.
- Scott Paper Company established a committee of top managers and union officials to discuss company issues. As a result of its success in reducing costs and boosting quality, Scott has become a model that is being emulated by other paper companies.
- Saturn, a division of General Motors, has used union/management cooperation at its Spring Hill plant. The "co-managed" facility has produced cars known for their quality, and employees take pride in the Saturn reputation for customer service and quality. The teamwork seen at Saturn sharply contrasts with the situation at GM's Dayton brake plant, discussed earlier.

There are many more examples, of course, one of which is discussed in the HR Perspective on Xerox. Some hail these successes as a new era in bargaining in which labor and management have begun to focus on the *process* of change, not just the results. Others suggest that the process of change is far from complete and note that the commitment to joint programs is quite varied. Some in the labor movement fear that such programs may lead to an undermining of union support by creating a closer identification with the company's concerns and goals. In fact, for a while it was unclear whether the NLRB would continue to allow union/management cooperation or outlaw it, as discussed next.

Employee Involvement and the NLRB

Suggesting that union/management cooperation or involving employees in making suggestions and decisions could be bad seems a little like arguing against

HR PERSPECTIVE

Union/Management Cooperation at Xerox

Xerox Corporation, the large manufacturer of office equipment, developed a cooperative relationship with the Amalgamated Clothing and Textile Workers Union (ACTWU). Among the employee involvement programs developed by the company and the union were *focus factories*. The focus factories were redesigned to include self-managing production cells and to enhance productivity, flexibility, quality, and employee teamwork. The union agreed to work with the company, modifying the union contract where necessary.

The focus factories met their major goals. Several years after their inception, product development costs had decreased 30%, quality had doubled, and return on investment had increased 75% at the factories. Also, the number of supervisors needed had declined, because the work teams have coaches, who are workers on the teams, to provide guidelines and training to other team members. In addition, the teams do their own scheduling, including balancing of overtime needs, and determine parts needed.

As a result of the success of the focus factories, in 1994 the company and the union signed a seven-year labor contract. A key provision in that contract was that Xerox guaranteed jobs to unionized workers in the focus factories, relieving the anxiety caused by layoffs and restructuring occurring throughout the industry. A Xerox executive said, "This relationship has developed successfully because we don't view each other as adversaries or enemies."[21]

motherhood, the flag, and apple pie. Yet some decisions by the National Labor Relations Board appear to have done just that. Some historical perspective is required to understand the issues that surrounded the decisions.

In the 1930s, when the Wagner Act was written, certain employers would form sham "company unions" and coerce workers into joining them in order to keep legitimate unions from attempting to organize the employees. As a result, the Wagner Act contained prohibitions against employer-dominated labor organizations. These prohibitions were enforced, and company unions disappeared.

Electromation Decision Because of the Wagner Act, some or all of the 30,000 employee involvement programs set up in recent years may be illegal, according to an NLRB decision dealing with Electromation, an Elkhart, Indiana, firm. Electromation used teams of employees to solicit other employees' views about such issues as wages and working conditions. The NLRB labeled them "labor organizations" as defined by the Wagner Act in 1935. It further found that they were "dominated" by management, which had formed them, set their goals, and decided how they would operate.[22]

DuPont Decision In a subsequent decision, the DuPont Corporation was ordered by the NLRB to dissolve six safety committees. The NLRB ruled that because the safety committees dealt with working conditions and had been established by the employer, they were "labor organizations" and thus were covered by the Wagner Act. A major concern of the NLRB was that the committees were created by the company and that the membership included managers as well as employees. Because of the structure and operations of the safety committees, the NLRB ruled that management dominated the committees, which made them illegal.[23]

❖ Future of Employee Involvement Efforts

As a result of these decisions, many employers have had to rethink and restructure their employee involvement efforts. While the NLRB rulings will not put an end to union/management efforts to cooperate, it is likely that these efforts will become more formalized and feature less involvement by managers.[24] Also, in unionized organizations, the various committees will have to be established with union participation, not just as a part of management practices.[25]

LOGGING ON

Developed by advocates for the Team Act, this web site contains information on the Act.

http://www.teamwork.org/

TEAM Act Employer responses to the NLRB decisions have led to the drafting of a new act, the Teamwork for Employees and Managers Act. Called the TEAM Act, it passed the U.S. House of Representatives, with most Republicans voting for it and most Democrats voting against it. The act amends the Wagner Act to allow non-union employees in team-based situations to work with management concerning working conditions and workplace situations.[26] However, it is unlikely that the bill will ever become law. Because of strong union opposition, President Clinton vetoed the bill. Nevertheless, the act showed that there was considerable support for overturning the NLRB decisions. Interestingly, a number of provisions of the TEAM Act are similar to recommendations from the Dunlop Commission, appointed by President Clinton.

Dunlop Commission Following the Electromation and DuPont decisions, President Clinton appointed Professor John Dunlop, a former Secretary of Labor, to head a commission on the future of worker/management relations. The commission was charged with developing recommendations on what was needed to modernize U.S. labor laws and policies in order to foster better union/management relations in future years.

The commission, composed of union leaders, business executives, academicians, and government experts, submitted its report. Some of the recommendations of the commission were as follows:[27]

- Encourage more union/management cooperation efforts.
- Focus cooperation efforts more narrowly on specific HR practices, rather than dealing with productivity generally.
- Recognize that the responsibilities of employees and supervisors are becoming intermingled as work is redesigned. Therefore, the definition of who is a supervisor needs to be narrowed.
- Make greater use of mediation and alternative dispute resolution procedures to resolve union/management conflicts.
- Require the NLRB to hold union elections within two weeks after an election petition has been filed.

Unions generally applauded the recommendations, while employer groups rejected the commission's report as being biased in favor of unions and against employers. It is uncertain which, if any, of the commission's recommendations ultimately will be translated into action.

❖ Union Ownership

Unions have become active participants in the restructuring of American industry by encouraging workers to become partial or complete owners of the companies that employ them. These efforts were spurred by concerns that firms were preparing to shut down or to be merged or bought out by financial investors who the unions feared would cut union jobs.

Unions have been active in assisting members in putting together employee stock ownership plans (ESOPs) to purchase all or part of some firms, as highlighted in Chapter 14. Unions also have made offers to purchase firms to head off financially leveraged takeovers by other investors. One of the best known purchases is the employee buyout of United Airlines. The unions representing United Airlines employees made a counteroffer after a takeover bid. In conjunction with the top management group at United Airlines, the pilots' union persuaded the unions representing machinists and other employees, excluding the flight attendants, to back the buyout offer.[28]

Some firms also have union representatives on their boards of directors. The best known example is Chrysler Corporation, in which a representative of the United Auto Workers was given a seat on the board in exchange for assistance in getting federal government financial help in the late 1970s. This practice is very common in European countries, where it is called *co-determination,* as discussed in Chapter 4.

❖ Grievance Management

Alert management knows that employee dissatisfaction is a potential source of trouble whether or not it is expressed. Hidden dissatisfaction grows and creates reactions that may be completely out of proportion to the original concerns. Therefore, it is important that dissatisfaction be given an outlet. A **complaint,** which is merely an indication of employee dissatisfaction that has not been submitted to a formal settlement process, is one outlet. For instance, if an employee

❖Complaint
An indication of employee dissatisfaction that has not been submitted to a formal settlement process.

says, "My supervisor does not like me," that is a complaint—a reflection of the employee's dissatisfaction. However, if the employee is represented by a union, and the employee says, "I should have received the job transfer because I have more seniority, which is what the union contract states," then that complaint may become a grievance. A **grievance** is an alleged misinterpretation, misapplication, or violation of a provision in a union/management agreement. Management should be concerned with both complaints and grievances, because complaints are good indicators of potential problems within the workforce. Also, unresolved complaints may turn into grievances in a union environment.

Grievance
An alleged misinterpretation, misapplication, or violation of a provision in a union/management agreement.

❖ Union Vs. Non-Union Grievance Management

Union and non-union firms handle grievances differently. In an organization with a union, grievances might occur over interpretation of the contract, disputes not covered in the contract, and problems of individual employees. In non-union organizations, complaints cover a variety of concerns that for a unionized organization would be covered in the contract: wages, benefits, working conditions, and equity. Grievance procedures almost always are specified in labor/management contracts. Relatively few non-union firms have grievance procedures, although more and more are beginning to have them, as discussed in Chapter 17.

The reason that virtually all labor contracts specify grievance procedures is that such procedures are extremely important for effective employee/employer relations in unionized firms. From the standpoint of the union, grievance systems allow employees a way to dispute management's implementation of the collective bargaining agreement. Management benefits from a grievance system, too. Without a grievance procedure, management may be unable to respond to employee concerns because managers are unaware of them. Such information does not always come to the attention of top management automatically. A great deal of discontent is dismissed at lower levels and never rises to the managers who have the authority to make decisions to solve the problems. For these reasons, a formal grievance procedure is a valuable communication tool for the organization.

A crucial measure of the performance of a grievance system is the rate of grievance resolution. Grievances that have been resolved become feedback to help resolve future grievances at an earlier stage. One study found that as management and union representatives work together to resolve grievances, the process of handling grievances becomes more efficient and effective.[29]

❖ FIGURE 19–5 ❖
TYPICAL GRIEVANCE RESPONSIBILITIES

HR UNIT	MANAGERS
❖ Assists in designing the grievance procedure ❖ Monitors trends in grievance rates for the organization ❖ May assist in preparation of grievance cases for arbitration ❖ May have responsibility for settling grievances	❖ Operate within the grievance procedure ❖ Attempt to resolve grievances where possible as "person closest to the problem" ❖ Document grievance cases for the grievance procedure ❖ Have responsibility for grievance prevention

❖ Grievance Responsibilities

The typical division of responsibilities between the HR unit and line managers for handling grievances is shown in Figure 19–5. These responsibilities vary considerably from one organization to another, even between unionized firms. But the HR unit usually has a more general responsibility. Managers must accept the grievance procedure as a possible constraint on some of their decisions.

❖ Approaches to Grievances

A formal grievance procedure sometimes leads management to conclude that the proper way to handle grievances is to abide by the "letter of the law." Therefore, management does no more nor less than what is called for in the contract. Such an approach can be labeled the *legalistic approach* to the resolution of grievances. A much more realistic approach, the *behavioral approach*, recognizes that a grievance may be a symptom of an underlying problem that management should investigate and rectify.

It is important to consider the behavioral aspects of grievances in order to understand why grievances are filed and how employees perceive them. Regarding why grievances have been filed, research has found that union stewards rather than employees tend to initiate grievances over job descriptions. Also, grievances over work rules are the least likely ones to be settled informally without resort to the use of grievance procedures.[30]

Management should recognize that a grievance is a behavioral expression of some underlying problem. This statement does not mean that every grievance is symptomatic of something radically wrong. Employees do file grievances over petty matters as well as over important concerns, and management must be able to differentiate between the two. However, to ignore a repeated problem by taking a legalistic approach to grievance resolution is to miss much of what the grievance procedure can do for management.

❖ Fact Finding and Mediation

Labor and management sometimes tend to ignore potential problem areas in a relationship until it is too late. The result can be an explosive dispute that does a great degree of harm. Fact finding and grievance mediation can minimize this sort of difficulty. It is the duty of a mediator to meet periodically with union and management representatives to discuss areas of potential trouble between the parties. Although the use of a mediator is not a panacea for resolving difficulties in labor/management relations, it can be a useful tool. One plan calls for continuing discussions with the assistance of a mediator during a 60-day period, during which time hopefully the problem can be solved in a calm and considered manner.

❖ Grievance Procedure

Grievance procedures are formal communications channels designed to settle a grievance as soon as possible after the problem arises. First-line supervisors are usually closest to a problem; however, the supervisor is concerned with many other matters besides one employee's grievance and may even be the subject of an employee's grievance.

❖Grievance Procedure
A formal channel of communications used to resolve grievances.

Supervisory involvement presents some problems in solving a grievance at this level. For example, William Dunn, a 27-year-old lathe operator at a machine shop, is approached by his supervisor, Joe Bass, one Monday morning and told that his production is lower than his quota. Bass advises him to catch up. Dunn reports that a part on his lathe needs repair. Bass suggests that Dunn should repair it himself to maintain his production because the mechanics are busy. Dunn refuses, and a heated argument ensues; as a result, Bass orders Dunn home for the day.

The illustration shows how easily an encounter between an employee and a supervisor can lead to a breakdown in the relationship. This breakdown, or failure to communicate effectively, could be costly to Dunn if he loses his job, a day's wages, or his pride. It also could be costly to Bass, who represents management, and to the owner of the machine shop if production is delayed or halted. Grievance procedures can resolve such conflicts.

In this particular case, the machine shop has a contract with the International Brotherhood of Lathe Operators, of which Dunn is a member. The contract specifically states that company plant mechanics are to repair all manufacturing equipment. Therefore, Bass appears to have violated the union contract. What is Dunn's next step? He may use the grievance procedure provided for him in the contract. The actual grievance procedure is different in each organization. It depends on what the employer and the union have agreed on and what is written in the labor contract.

❖ Individual Rights in a Grievance

A unionized employee generally has a right to union representation if he or she is being questioned by management and if discipline may result. If these so-called *Weingarten rights* (named after the court case that established them) are violated and the employee is dismissed, he or she usually will be reinstated with back pay.

However, individual union members do not always feel that their best interests are properly served by the union. Workers and unions may not agree on the interpretation of a contract clause. For example, a worker suspended for drinking may feel strongly that her interests are not sufficiently represented by the union because the shop steward (her union representative) is a teetotaler.

If an individual does not feel the union has properly and vigorously pursued the grievance, he or she may have recourse to the federal court system. Such cases attempt to pinpoint individual rights inside the bargaining unit and determine what those rights are for a person who has been denied due process through the grievance procedure. In fact, an individual can pursue a grievance against an employer on his or her own if a union does not back the claim.

❖ Steps in a Grievance Procedure

Grievance procedures can vary in the number of steps they include. Figure 19–6 shows a typical one, which includes the following steps:

1. The employee discusses the grievance with the immediate supervisor.
2. The employee then discusses the grievance with the union steward (the union's representative on the job) and the supervisor.
3. The union steward discusses the grievance with the supervisor's manager.
4. The union grievance committee discusses the grievance with the unit plant manager or the employer's HR department.
5. The representative of the national union discusses the grievance with the company general manager.
6. The final step may be use of an impartial umpire or arbitrator for ultimate disposition of the grievance.

The grievance can be settled at any stage. The following discussion illustrates the steps with reference to the example involving William Dunn.

Employee and Supervisor Dunn has already discussed his grievance with the supervisor. Although not the case with Dunn's grievance, this first step should eliminate the majority of gripes and complaints that employees may view as legitimate grievances.

Supervisors are generally responsible for understanding the contract so that they can administer it fairly on a day-to-day basis. They must be accessible to

❖ FIGURE 19–6 ❖
STEPS IN A GRIEVANCE PROCEDURE

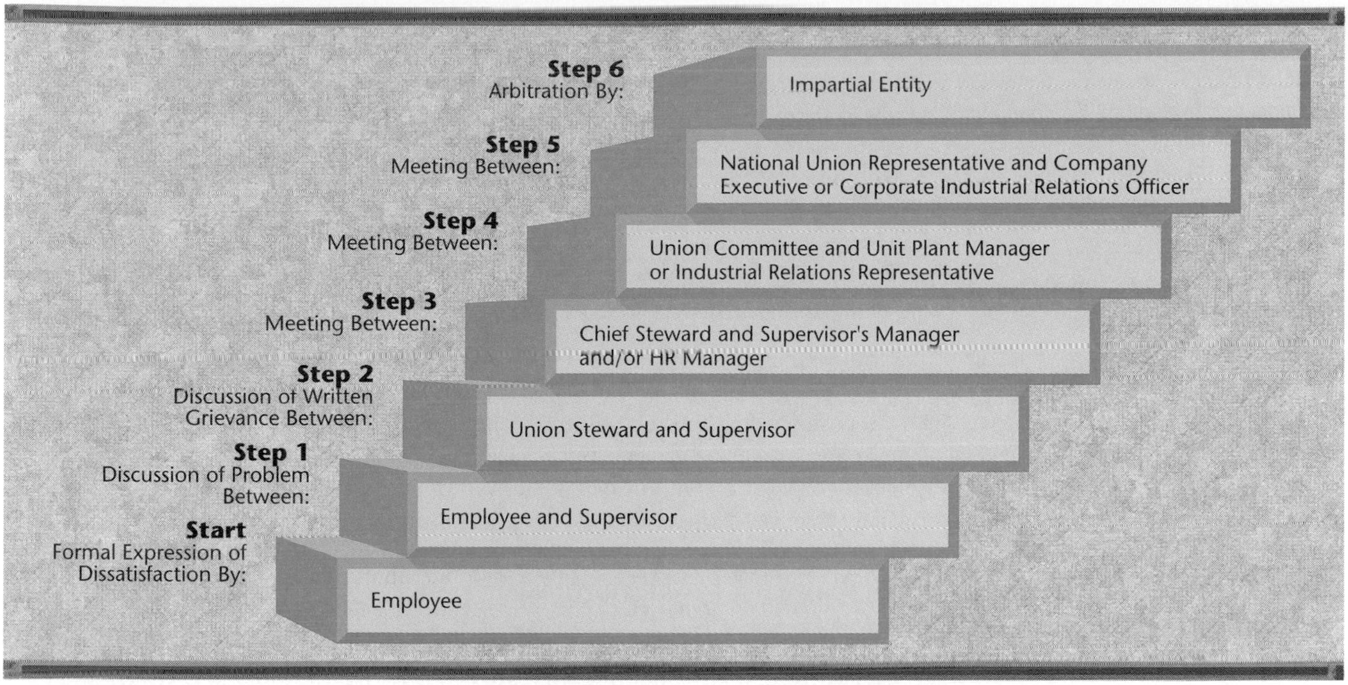

employees for grievance investigation and must gather all the pertinent facts and carefully investigate the causes, symptoms, and results. But the filing of grievances does create some risks for employees. The reactions of supervisors to employees who file grievances may affect the employees' performance ratings, especially when the supervisor is the target of the grievance. Such factors are reasons why seniority is preferred by unions as a basis for promotions and pay changes.

UNION STEWARD AND SUPERVISOR The second step involves the union steward, whose main task is to present the grievance of a union member to management. Because of their union status, union stewards can challenge managerial and supervisory decisions without being insubordinate, as long as they do so in a manner consistent with the labor agreement. Research indicates that union stewards have to balance a dual commitment, one to their employers for their jobs and one to their unions to represent employees with grievances.[31]

Assume that Dunn's grievance remains unsettled after the second step. The steward contacts Bass's boss and/or the unit's HR manager. In most grievance procedures, the grievance is documented and, until it is settled, much of the communication between management and the union is in writing. This written communication is important because it provides a record of each step in the procedure and constitutes a history for review at each subsequent step.

One study found that an employee's previous work history with an organization influences managerial decisions on grievances at the second and third stages. An employee whose work history shows that he or she has been disciplined less, has more tenure on the job, and has compiled a better performance record is more likely to have a grievance upheld by management. This study underscores the impact of behavioral factors on the grievance process.[32]

Union Grievance Committee and Unit Manager Pressure tends to build with each successive step, because grievances that are not precedent setting or difficult are screened out earlier in the process. If the department manager (who is supervisor Bass's boss) backs Bass against the chief steward at the third step, the grievance goes to the next step. The fourth step brings in the local union grievance committee. In our case, the grievance committee of the union convinces the plant manager that Bass violated the contract and Dunn should be brought back to work and paid for the time he missed. The plant manager gives in, partly because she thinks the company has a weak case and partly because, if the grievance continues past her, it will probably go to arbitration, and she does not feel the issue is worth the cost. Although in Dunn's case, a grievance committee was used, not all grievance procedures use committees.

National Representatives and Arbitrators If the grievance had remained unsettled, representatives for both sides would have continued to meet to resolve the conflict. On rare occasions, a representative from the national union might join the process. Or a corporate executive from headquarters (if the firm is a large corporation) might be called in to help resolve the grievance. If not solved at this stage, the grievance goes to arbitration.

❖ Grievance Arbitration

Arbitration is flexible and can be applied to almost any kind of controversy except those involving criminal matters. Advisory, or voluntary, arbitration may be used in the negotiation of agreements or in the interpretation of clauses in existing agreements. Because labor and management generally agree that disputes over the negotiation of a new contract should not be arbitrated in the private sector, the most important role played by arbitration in labor relations is as the final step in the grievance procedure.

❖Grievance Arbitration
A means by which disputes arising from different interpretations of a labor contract are settled by a third party.

Grievance arbitration is a means by which disputes arising from different interpretations of a labor contract are settled by a third party. This should not be confused with contract arbitration, discussed earlier, which is arbitration to determine how a contract will be written. Grievance arbitration is a deeply ingrained part of the collective bargaining system, although it was not always so. In earlier times, arbitration was not considered useful in settling labor disputes.

However, in 1957, a court decision that established the right of unions to sue for specific performance arbitration awards gave arbitration new strength.[33] Later court cases added more powers to the arbitration process. The legal standing of grievance arbitration was clarified in a series of cases involving the United Steelworkers union, called the "Steelworkers trilogy."[34] To summarize the results of these three cases, it was ruled that a company had to arbitrate all issues not specifically excluded in the contract. Courts were directed not to rule on the appropriateness of an arbitration award unless misinformation, fraud, or negligence was involved.

❖ Grievance Arbitration Process

The wording and meaning of a contract clause is a common arbitration issue. It is important to spell out the types of disputes that may be taken to arbitration. Most collective bargaining contracts suggest that either party may start arbitration proceedings. Others state that only the union can initiate arbitration proceedings. Still others permit arbitration only when both parties agree.

Assuming that a grievance has not been resolved and the labor contract calls for arbitration, the arbitration process begins with the selection of a single arbitrator or a panel of arbitrators, usually three in number. Before it is necessary to select an arbitrator, the important selection factors should be identified.[35] Typically, the past record of the arbitrator is checked by both sides. The manner of selecting arbitrators varies, but usually each party eliminates names from a list of potential arbitrator candidates until only one name remains. If a panel is used, then the union selects one name, management selects one name, and the "neutral" is selected in the manner just noted. Most contracts call for union and management to share equally in the cost of arbitration.

Some parties may have a permanent arbitrator, but more typically the arbitrator is selected from a list supplied by either the Federal Mediation and Conciliation Service or the American Arbitration Association.

❖ Arbitration Hearing

There is no single way to conduct an arbitration hearing. The purpose is to gather the information necessary for the arbitrator to make a decision. A formal hearing may resemble a courtroom trial. A less formal hearing has little of the courtroom atmosphere—witnesses make presentations and are questioned by the opposition. The style depends on the arbitrator, but most hearings have the following parts:

- Opening the hearing
- Defining the issue
- Making opening statements
- Swearing in witnesses
- Presenting the case
- Making closing arguments

Following the hearing, each side may be asked to submit a post-hearing brief. The arbitrator then reviews all the evidence, including the applicable section of the labor contract, and makes a decision. This decision also is called an *award* and is enforceable in federal court if the labor contract indicates that arbitration decisions are binding on both parties.

Grievance arbitration presents several problems. It has been criticized as being too costly, too legalistic, and too time-consuming. Also, one study found that arbitrators generally treated women more leniently than men in disciplinary grievance situations.[36] In addition, many feel that there are too few qualified and experienced arbitrators. Nevertheless, arbitration has been successful and is currently seen as a potentially superior solution to traditional approaches to resolving union/management problems.

SUMMARY

❖ Collective bargaining occurs when management negotiates with representatives of workers over wages, hours, and working conditions.

❖ Different collective bargaining relationships exist. Conflict, armed truce, power bargaining, accommodation, cooperation, and collusion are recognized as types of relationships.

❖ Various collective bargaining structures are used, ranging from one employer bargaining with one union to multiple employers bargaining with multiple unions.

❖ The issues subject to collective bargaining fall into three categories: mandatory, permissive, and illegal.

❖ Provisions on management rights and union security typically appear in labor contracts.

❖ The collective bargaining process includes preparation, initial demands, negotiations, and settlement.

❖ Once an agreement (contract) is signed between labor and management, it becomes the document governing what each party can and cannot do.

❖ The bargaining power of both management and union is determined by economic, organizational, sociodemographic, and legal factors.

❖ During bargaining, different types of behavior may be exhibited, including distributive bargaining, integrative bargaining, attitudinal structuring, and intraorganizational bargaining.

❖ Efforts to resolve impasses include conciliation, mediation, and arbitration.

❖ When impasse occurs, work stoppages through strikes or lockouts can be used to pressure the other party.

❖ One major trend in collective bargaining has been union/management cooperation.

❖ Grievances express worker dissatisfaction or differences in contract interpretations. Grievances follow a formal path to resolution.

❖ A formal grievance procedure is usually specified in a union contract, but it should exist in any organization to provide a system for handling problems.

❖ Grievances can be approached by management from either a behavioral or a legalistic viewpoint; however, the behavioral approach is recommended.

❖ A grievance procedure begins with the first-level supervisor—and ends (if it is not resolved along the way) with arbitration.

❖ Arbitration has worked well in settling union/management grievances.

Review and Discussion Questions

1. Why do collective bargaining relationships differ?
2. Give several examples of mandatory, permissive, and illegal bargaining issues.
3. What are the stages in a typical collective bargaining process?
4. Assume that a bargaining impasse has occurred. What would be the differences between using mediation and arbitration to resolve the impasse?
5. Discuss how union/management cooperation has been affected by NLRB rulings.
6. Give an example of a grievance and how both unionized and non-union firms might handle it.
7. What steps are followed in a typical grievance process? Why is arbitration, as the final step of a grievance process, important and useful?

Terms to Know

arbitration **560**
collective bargaining **552**
complaint **565**
concessionary bargaining **559**
conciliation **560**
dues checkoff **555**
grievance **566**
grievance arbitration **570**
grievance procedure **567**
illegal issues **555**
lockout **561**
management rights **555**
mandatory issues **554**
mediation **560**
permissive issues **555**
ratification **559**
strike **560**
two-tier wage structure **560**
union security provisions **555**

CASE

THE "STOLEN" ORANGE JUICE

Grievances can be filed over large or small matters. The following case represents a grievance that was decided by an arbitrator hired by Greyhound Food Management (Warren, Michigan) and the United Catering Restaurant, Bar, & Hotel Workers, Local 1064.[37]

The grievance was filed by the union on behalf of Tom, a union member working as a fast-food attendant at a Greyhound-operated cafeteria. The Greyhound Food Service provided food-service management on a contract basis for many firms, including Hydra Matic, a manufacturing company located in Warren, Michigan.

Tom had been working for Greyhound for almost a year and was working the 1 P.M.–8:30 P.M. shift making $5.25 an hour at the time of his discharge from the company. The company justified Tom's employment termination by asserting that he had attempted to steal a six-once container of orange juice, which normally sold for 58 cents.

Tom's supervisor testified that from his office he had observed Tom attempting to leave the premises with the container of orange juice hidden under his jacket. After stopping Tom, the supervisor had accused him of attempting to steal the orange juice. Then the supervisor had telephoned the assistant manager for instructions. The assistant manager had told the supervisor to document the incident and had stated that he (the assistant manager) would take care of the matter the next morning. The supervisor's written report stated that he had heard the refrigerator door slam, then had heard Tom walking toward the door. The supervisor had asked Tom twice what Tom had in his coat, after which Tom had pulled the juice out of his coat, dropping and spilling it over the floor.

The following morning, the assistant manager called Tom and the union steward into his office and confronted them with the supervisor's written description of the incident. Tom denied that he had attempted to steal the orange juice, saying that the supervisor had just seen some orange juice on the floor. At a meeting later that morning, the assistant manager terminated Tom's employment. Tom filed a grievance, which was immediately denied. Tom and the union then requested arbitration, as was allowed under the company/union labor contract.

The arbitrator reviewed several documents, including statements from the supervisor, the assistant manager, a former employee, and the union steward. Also, he reviewed the relevant sections of the labor contract on management rights, seniority, and the grievance procedure. Finally, the arbitrator reviewed the list of company rules and regulations posted by the time clock, one of which said that disciplinary action ranging from reprimand to immediate discharge could result from rule violation. The first rule prohibited "stealing private, company, or client's property."

Company Position

The company's position was that Tom had knowledge of the posted work rules, the first of which clearly prohibited theft. The company also had a policy that no company property was to leave the restaurant. The testimony of the supervisor established that Tom had attempted to steal and remove company property. It was not relevant that Tom's impermissible act had not succeeded. The detection by management of the theft before Tom left the premises did not excuse the act. Also, the company said that the size or dollar amount of the theft was immaterial. Therefore, because the company followed the terms of the union contract that provided for dismissal of employees for "just cause," and because Tom knew, or

The "Stolen" Orange Juice, continued

should have known, of the rule against stealing, the arbitrator should rule for the company.

Union Position

The union's position was that the act of attempting to steal a container of orange juice valued at 58 cents involved moral turpitude and therefore required the application of a "high degree of proof." The employer carried the burden of convincing the arbitrator beyond a reasonable doubt through the witnesses that Tom had attempted to steal the orange juice. The union contended that even though Tom had been subject to some other minor disciplinary actions in the past, termination was too harsh a penalty and therefore the arbitrator should rule for Tom and the union.

Questions

1. How important is the value of the item in comparison with the alleged act of stealing?
2. Because Tom never left the company premises with the juice, did he actually steal it?
3. How would you rule in this case? (Your instructor can give you the actual decision of the arbitrator.)

Notes

1. Earle Eldridge, "Dayton Strikers' Key Demand: Respect," *USA Today,* March 18, 1996, 3B; Rebecca Blumstein and Nicole Christian, "GM, UAW Tentatively Settle Walkout," *The Wall Street Journal,* March 22, 1996, A3; Michael Clements and Micheline Maynard, "GM, Local 969 Strike Deal," *USA Today,* March 22, 1996, 1A; Nichole Christian and Anita Sharpe, "Rich Benefits Plan Gives GM Competitors Cost Edge," *The Wall Street Journal,* March 21, 1996, B1; and Bill Vlasic, "Bracing for the Big One," *Business Week,* March 25, 1996, 34–35.
2. G. P. Zachary, "Long Litigation Often Holds Up Union Victories," *The Wall Street Journal,* November 15, 1995, B1.
3. J. Cutcher-Gershenfeld, P. McHugh, and D. Power, "Collective Bargaining in Small Firms: Preliminary Evidence of Fundamental Change," *Industrial and Labor Relations Review* 49 (1996), 195–212.
4. The six strategies are adapted from R. E. Allen and T. B. Keavany, *Contemporary Labor Relations* (Reading, MA: Addison-Wesley, 1988), 126.
5. Wallace E. Hendricks, Cynthia L. Gramm, and Jack Fiorito, "Centralization of Bargaining Decisions in American Unions," *Industrial Relations* 32 (1993), 367–390.
6. John J. Kenney, *Primer of Labor Relations,* 23rd ed. (Washington, DC: Bureau of National Affairs, 1986), 46–47.
7. Adapted from William H. Holley and Kenneth M. Jennings, *The Labor Relations Process,* 3rd ed. (Chicago, Dryden Press, 1988), 395.
8. C. J. Martin, "Current Developments in Labor-Management Relations," *Employee Relations Law Journal* 17 (1991), 139–144.
9. D. Cantrell, "Spontaneous Strike Notice: Who Is Responsible?" *Personnel Journal,* July 1990, 38–39.
10. Richard E. Walton and Robert B. McKersie, *A Behavioral Theory of Labor Negotiations* (New York: McGraw-Hill, 1965).
11. K. Murphy, "Determinants of Contract Duration in Collective Bargaining Agreements," *Industrial and Labor Relations Review* 45 (1992), 352.
12. James E. Martin and Ruth D. Berthiaume, "Predicting the Outcome of a Contract Ratification Vote," *Academy of Management Journal,* 38 (1995), 916–928.
13. S. Thomas and M. Kleiner, "The Effect of Two-Tier Collective Bargaining Agreements on Shareholder Equity," *Industrial and Labor Relations Review* 45 (1992), 339–351; and D. McFarland and M. Frone, "A Two-Tiered Wage Structure in a Non-Union Firm," *Industrial Relations* 29 (1990), 145.
14. M. E. McLaughlin and P. Carnevale, "Professional Mediators' Judgements of Mediation Tactics," *Journal of Applied Psychology* 76 (1991), 465; and J. Wall and D. Rude, "The Judge As Mediator," *Journal of Applied Psychology* 76 (1991), 54.
15. B. P. Sunoo, "Managing Strikes, Minimizing Loss," *Personnel Journal,* January 1995, 50–60.
16. J. I. Ondrich and J. F. Schnell, "Strike Duration and the Degree of Disagreement," *Industrial Relations* 32 (1993), 412–431.
17. Peter C. Cramton and Joseph S. Tracy, "The Determinants of U.S. Labor Disputes," *Journal of Labor Economics* 12 (1994), 180–209.
18. P. T. Kilborn, "Union Capitulation Shows Strike Is Now Dull Sword," *The New York Times,* December 5, 1995, A 16; R. L. Rose, "Caterpillar Continues to Stand Tough As Strikers Return," *The Wall Street Journal,* December 8, 1995, B1; and R. L. Rose, "Caterpillar Prepares Rules for Conduct," *The Wall Street Journal,* December 5, 1995, A4.
19. "Clinton Signs Striker Replacement Ban," *Facts on File,* March 30, 1995, 226; and J. P. Krupin, "Sidestepping Congress," *The National Law Journal,* May 15, 1995, A21.

20. "Why America Needs Unions but Not the Kind It Has Now," *Business Week*, May 23, 1994, 70–82.

21. Based on Dawn Anfuso, "Xerox Partners with the Union to Regain Market Share," *Personnel Journal*, August 1994, 46–53.

22. *Electromation*, 142LRRM1001 (1992).

23. 311 NLRB No. 88 (1993).

24. Randall Hanson, Rebecca I. Porterfield, and Kathleen Ames, "Employee Empowerment at Risk: Effects of NLRB Rulings," *Academy of Management Executive*, May 1995, 45–56.

25. Audrey Anne Smith, "The Future of Labor Management Cooperation Following Electromation and E. I. DuPont," *Santa Clara Law Review* 35 (1995), 225.

26. "TEAM Act Passes House," *HR News*, November 1995, 5.

27. For more details, see M. H. Cimini and C. J. Muhl, "Dunlop Commission Issues Report," *Compensation and Working Conditions*, April 1995, 40; and M. H. Yarborough, "Reactions Differ Over Commission Recommendations," *HR Focus*, May 1995, 9–10.

28. Susan Chandler, "United We Own," *Business Week*, March 18, 1996, 96–100.

29. David Meyer, "The Political Effects of Grievance Handling by Stewards in a Local Union," *Journal of Labor Research* 15 (1994), 33–52.

30. Brian Bemmels, "The Determinants of Grievance Initiation," *Industrial and labor Relations Review* 47 (1994), 285–301.

31. Brian Bemmels, "Dual Commitment: Unique Construct or Epiphenomenon?" *Journal of Labor Research* 16 (1995), 401–423.

32. Brian S. Klaas, "Managerial Decision Making about Employee Grievances: The Impact of the Grievant's Work History," *Personnel Psychology* 42 (1989), 53–68.

33. *Textile Workers Union of America v. Lincoln Mills of Alabama* 353 U.S. 448 (1957).

34. The cases involved are *United Steelworkers of America v. American Manufacturing Co.*, 363 US 564 (1960); *United Steelworkers of America v. Warrior and Gulf Navigation Co.*, 363 US 574 (1960); and *United Steelworkers of America v. Enterprise Wheel and Car Corp.*, 363 US 593 (1960).

35. C. A. Goldberger and P. W. Gurahian, "Six Steps to Succeeding in Arbitration," *Trial*, June 1995, 36–42.

36. Brian Bemmels, "Gender Effects in Grievance Arbitration," *Industrial Relations* 30 (1991), 150.

37. 89 LA 1138 (1987)

Chapter 20

Assessing Human Resource Effectiveness

After you have read this chapter, you should be able to . . .

- Identify three general areas in which HR departments should set goals.
- Discuss three major reasons why HR records are necessary.
- Identify several uses of a human resource information system (HRIS).
- Differentiate between primary and secondary research, and identify four methods for researching HR problems.
- Discuss why assessing HR effectiveness is important, and identify two approaches for doing so.
- Identify an HR audit and describe how one is conducted.

HR in Transition

Benchmarking HR at Goodyear

Goodyear Tire and Rubber Company, like most businesses, has seen massive change and has tried to focus on finding new and better ways to get work done. As part of that search, the company has used benchmarking to help identify the "best practices" for all facets of its operations, including human resources. By measuring itself and comparing the measurements against those of other companies, Goodyear has managed to find more efficient ways to get work done.

The idea behind benchmarking is that it is possible to examine the best practices of other organizations and make changes in operations based on what is learned. More than 70% of the Fortune 500 companies use benchmarking regularly. A benefit of benchmarking is that it forces companies to focus on the specific factors that lead to success or failure.

When Goodyear begins a benchmarking project, it spends up to three months planning. There are major discussions about what the company hopes to accomplish. Those who are participants receive training in the process. From the highly focused questions that are developed by the benchmark team come answers about specific practices and results. Developing these questions and answers may require conducting interviews in person or over the phone, bringing in an academic to design a scientific study to examine a problem, or using outside consultants to gather information. But obtaining information about Goodyear's practices and those of the other company (or companies) is the key thrust. Communicating information so that comparisons can be made and new ideas generated is the basis for benchmarking.

The idea behind benchmarking is that it is possible to examine the best practices of other organizations and make changes in operations based on what is learned.

Recently, when the company, as part of the broader benchmarking process, examined compensation strategies, it put together an internal team with individuals from many departments. The team developed questions and studied topics such as variable pay, pay for top performers, and the role of education and training in compensation. Team members first determined what the company needed to learn and then created an agenda to gather the information. After conducting interviews and gathering data from many other sources, the team compared notes on the practices of various successful companies. Then it made its recommendations for changes at Goodyear.

When HR began to benchmark its own practices, it examined a wide range of issues. Leadership development, succession planning, benefits, safety, and compensation were all benchmarked. The company wanted to tie employee compensation to individual performance and the firm's goals of improving customer service and shareholder satisfaction.

After about six months of examining several Fortune 100 companies, Goodyear's HR staff made several changes, including altering the way the company approached its compensation program. It concluded that to remain competitive and provide better customer service, it needed to better define the employee performance appraisal process and tie that activity to Goodyear's business objectives. That link meant clearly communicating what each position was expected to contribute and what its responsibilities were. As a result, even part of the Chairman's compensation is now "at risk," depending on the company's financial performance.

The HR Director has summarized Goodyear's use of benchmarking as a way to evaluate the success of company practices and to assess effectiveness. He says, "If your goal is continuous improvement, your company will always want to learn what other companies are doing. And it is important for HR to be aligned with the corporate strategy and be recognized as a valuable resource for change."[1]

"Direction and control are impossible without data."

—Jac Fitz-Enz

There is a myth of long standing that one cannot measure what the human resources function does. That myth has hurt HR departments in some cases because it suggests that any value added by HR is somehow mystical or magical. None of that is true, and HR—like marketing, legal, or finance—must be evaluated based on the value it adds to the organization. Defining and measuring HR effectiveness is not as straightforward as it might be in some more easily quantifiable areas, but it can be done. Assessing the contribution made by HR management activities and processes is the subject of this chapter.

Effectiveness
The extent to which goals have been met.

Efficiency
The degree to which operations are done in an economical manner.

Effectiveness for organizations is often defined as the extent to which goals have been met. **Efficiency** is the degree to which operations are done in an economical manner. Efficiency can also be thought of as cost per unit of output. Organizations must be able to achieve their goals within the constraints of limited resources. For example, providing on-site child care for all employees might help an employer to achieve the goal of reducing turnover, but it could be too expensive for that employer to implement.

Problems can arise in determining whether an organization (or its HR department) is effective, because people in management may have multiple or conflicting goals. Furthermore, agreement on the appropriate goals for the organization may be subject to the varying viewpoints of society, employees, and/or shareholders. This *multiple constituency* view allows for multiple evaluations of effectiveness from different groups, somewhat like 360° performance appraisal. However, where the HR function in an organization is concerned, identifying the relevant constituency is somewhat easier. The other departments, managers, and employees are the main "customers" for HR services. If those services are lacking, too expensive, or of poor quality, then consideration may have to be given to outsourcing some HR activities.

Like other organizations and entities, HR departments must set goals and measure effectiveness. The following general concerns are common to all:

- Acquiring resources
- Producing proper outputs
- Conforming to codes of behavior
- Performing administrative tasks
- Using resources efficiently
- Investing in the organization
- Satisfying varying interests

The HR department is an organization within an organization. What it does (or does not do) affects the whole system. To function effectively, HR needs a vision as to what it does and whom it serves. That perspective should unify the HR staff and provide a basis for making decisions. HR can position itself as a partner in an organization, but only by demonstrating to the rest of the organization that there are real links between what it does and organizational results.

To demonstrate to its customer—the rest of the organization—that it is a partner with a positive influence on the bottom line of the business, HR must be prepared to collect measurement data on what it does. Then it must communicate that information to the rest of the organization. Next, this chapter considers sources of information for measuring effectiveness: *HR records, human resource information systems (HRIS), research data,* and *benchmarking.*

Human Resource Records

Many organizations, regardless of size, are addressing the need for more detailed and timely data and information on which to base HR decisions and measure effectiveness. The terms *information* and *data* are often used as if they are the same. But to

HR professionals their meanings differ. **Data** are raw facts that have yet to be processed or organized for meaningful use, such as a listing of all employees who have quit a firm in the previous twelve months. **Information** is processed and organized data. When the percentage of employees who quit is identified by department, for example, the data becomes information. When the frequency with which employees with certain skills quit is compared to the frequency for other groups and departments, the information becomes even more useful. Gathering and maintaining records on a variety of HR activities are necessary for three reasons:

- Compliance with government regulations
- Documentation
- Assessment of HR effectiveness

***Data**
Facts that have yet to be processed or organized for meaningful use.

***Information**
Processed and organized data.

❖ Government Requirements and HR Records

Federal, state, and local laws require that organizations keep numerous records on employees. Figure 20–1 shows some HR records and data sources that can be maintained in an HR department. The requirements are so varied that it is difficult to identify exactly what should be kept and for how long. Each specific case must be dealt with separately.[2] Generally, records relating to employment, work schedules, wages, performance appraisals, merit and seniority systems, and affirmative action programs should be kept by all employers who are subject to provisions of the Fair Labor Standards Act. Other records may be required on issues related to EEO, OSHA, or the Age Discrimination Act. The most commonly required retention time for such records is three years.

❖ Figure 20–1 ❖
Examples of HR Records and Data Sources

❖ Accidents	❖ Terminations
❖ Employment requisitions	❖ Job specifications
❖ Promotion inventories	❖ Job descriptions
❖ Applicant tracking	❖ Salary increases
❖ Interview results	❖ Training programs
❖ Turnover	❖ Personal histories
❖ Job transfers	❖ Affirmative action records
❖ Payroll	❖ Medical records
❖ Work schedules	❖ Insurance usage
❖ Test scores	❖ Employee benefit choices
❖ Performance appraisals	❖ Committee meetings
❖ Grievances	❖ Recruiting expenses
❖ Occupational health records	❖ Attitude/morale survey results
❖ Job bidding	❖ Open jobs
❖ Exit interviews	❖ Labor market data

Americans with Disabilities Act (ADA) and Medical Records Record-keeping and retention practices have been affected by the following provision in the Americans with Disabilities Act (ADA):

> Information from all medical examinations and inquiries must be kept apart from general personnel files as a separate confidential medical record available only under limited conditions specified in the ADA.[3]

As interpreted by attorneys and HR practitioners, this provision requires that all medical-related information be maintained separately from all other confidential files. Also, specific access restrictions and security procedures must be adopted for medical records of all types, including employee medical benefit claims and treatment records.[4]

Establishment of Several Employee Files The result of all the legal restrictions is that many employers are establishing several separate files on each employee. The following files may be established:

1. Current file containing only the last few years of employee-related information
2. Confidential file containing such items as reference letters and promotability assessments

HR PERSPECTIVE

Legal and Ethical Issues Regarding Employee Records

One ethical issue that HR professionals must address regularly is the right of an employee to inspect the information kept by the employer in the employee's HR file. Related concerns are the types of information kept in those files and the methods used to acquire that information.

In other business-related areas, federal laws have been passed that allow individuals access to their own files, such as credit records and medical records. But only in some states have laws been passed to require employers to give employees access to their HR records, or parts of them. Many of these state laws allow employers to exclude certain types of information from inspection, such as reference letters written by former employers. Some employers in states without access laws nevertheless allow employees access to certain records.

The most common records kept include performance appraisals, salary history, and disciplinary actions. However, maintenance of individual medical records and background investigation reports in separate confidential files is common.

Most employers require that an HR staff member be present while employees view their files. Some firms allow access but limit or restrict the photocopying of certain items. It is recommended that firms allow employees to provide additional statements or dispute the accuracy of details in their files.

It appears that maintaining records on individuals to which access is limited is crucial. Enabling individuals to comment on or correct details in their files ensures that HR records are accurate.[5]

3. Confidential medical file as required by the ADA
4. Individual personnel file containing older information and nonconfidential, nonmedical benefits documents

Employee Access to HR Records One concern that has been addressed in various court decisions and laws is the right of employees to have access to their own files. As mentioned in Chapter 17, many employees have little knowledge of what information is contained in their own HR files. The accompanying HR Perspective discusses the legal and ethical issues involved.

❖ Assessing HR Effectiveness Using Records

With the proliferation of government regulations, the number of required records has expanded; of course, the records are only useful if they are kept current and properly organized. Managers who must cope with the paperwork have not always accepted such record-keeping requirements easily.[6] Also, many managers feel that HR records can be a source of trouble because they can be used to question past managerial actions.

Another view of HR record-keeping activities is that HR records serve as important documentation should legal challenges occur. Disciplinary actions, past performance appraisals, and other documents may provide the necessary "proof" that employers need to defend their actions as job related and nondiscriminatory. Records and data can also provide a crucial source of information to audit or assess the effectiveness of any unit, and they provide the basis for research into possible causes of HR problems.

Jac Fitz-Enz, who studies HR effectiveness, has suggested some measures to check the effectiveness of the HR function. The measures are shown in Figure 20–2. Note how each requires accurate records and a complete human resource information system.

A problem organizations often face with HR record keeping is the inability to retrieve needed information without major difficulties. Better HR decisions can be made if managers have good information on such matters as the causes and severity of accidents, the reasons for absenteeism, and the distribution of performance appraisals. But in many organizations, such information is not readily available. A solution is a well-designed human resource information system (HRIS).

❖ **FIGURE 20–2** ❖
POSSIBLE MEASURES OF HR EFFECTIVENESS FROM HR RECORDS

❖ Revenue per employee	❖ Retiree benefit cost per retiree
❖ Expense per employee	❖ Cost of hires
❖ Compensation as a percentage of revenue	❖ Time to fill jobs
❖ Compensation as a percentage of expenses	❖ Worker's compensation cost per employee
❖ HR Department expense as a percentage of company expenses	❖ Absence rate
❖ HR Department expense per company employee	❖ Turnover rate
❖ Benefits cost as a percentage of compensation	❖ Ratio of job offers to acceptances
	❖ "Customer" satisfaction with HR

SOURCE: Adapted from Jac Fitz-Enz, *How to Measure Human Resources Management* (New York: McGraw Hill, 1995), 33.

❖ HUMAN RESOURCE INFORMATION SYSTEM (HRIS)

Computers have simplified the task of analyzing vast amounts of data, and they can be invaluable aids in HR management, from payroll processing to record retention. With computer hardware, software, and databases, organizations can keep records and information better, as well as retrieve them with greater ease. A **human resource information system** (HRIS) is an integrated system designed to provide information used in HR decision making. Although an HRIS does not have to be computerized, most are.

❖**Human Resource Information System (HRIS)**
An integrated system designed to provide information used in HR decision making.

❖ PURPOSES OF HRIS

An HRIS serves two major purposes in organizations. One relates to efficiency, the other to effectiveness. The first purpose of an HRIS is to improve the efficiency with which data on employees and HR activities is compiled. Many HR activities can be performed more efficiently and with less paperwork if automated. When on-line data input is used, fewer forms must be stored, and less manual record keeping is necessary.[7] Much of the reengineering of HR activities has focused on identifying the flow of HR data and how the data can be retrieved more efficiently for authorized users. Workflow, automation of some HR activities, and automation of HR record keeping are key to improving HR operations by making workflow more efficient.[8]

The second purpose of an HRIS is to provide HR information more rapidly and more easily for use by management in making decisions.[9] For example,

Dilbert® reprinted by permission of United Feature Syndicate, Inc.

instead of manually doing a turnover analysis by department, length of service, and educational background, a specialist can compile such a report quickly by using an HRIS and various sorting and analysis functions. HR management has grown in strategic value in many organizations; accordingly, there has been an increased emphasis on obtaining and using HRIS data for strategic planning and human resource forecasting, which focus on broader HR effectiveness over time.

❖ Uses of HRIS

There are many uses for an HRIS in an organization. The most basic use is the automation of payroll and benefits activities. With an HRIS, employees' time records are entered into the system, and the appropriate deductions and other individual adjustments are reflected in the final paychecks. As a result of HRIS development and implementation in many organizations, a number of payroll functions are being transferred from accounting departments to HR departments. Another common use of HRIS is EEO/affirmative action tracking. Beyond these basic activities, many other HR activities can be affected by the use of an HRIS, as Figure 20–3 notes.

❖ Figure 20–3 ❖
Uses of HRIS

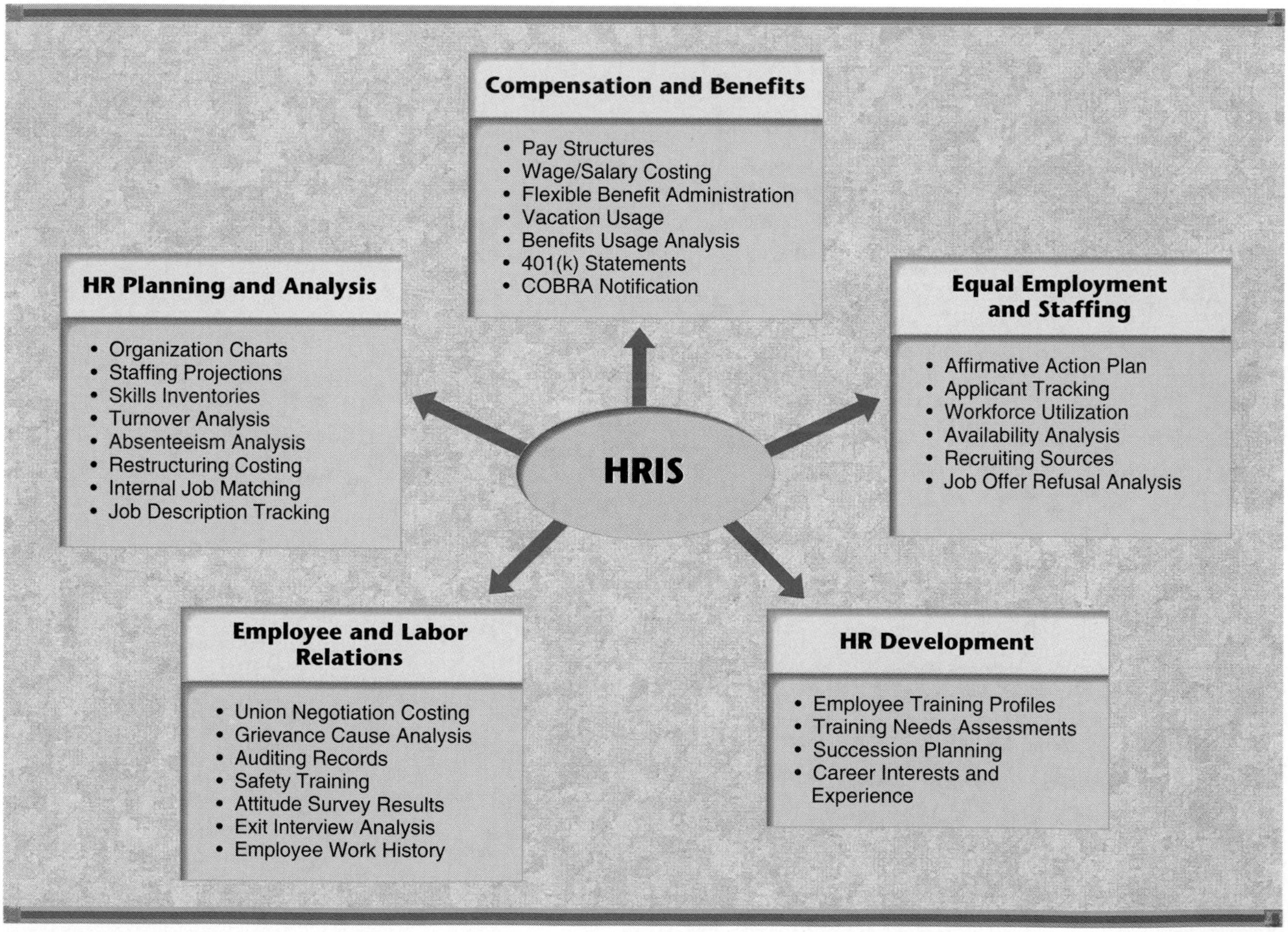

Throughout the text, the use of HRIS for specific HR activities, as highlighted in HR Perspectives, has indicated the breadth of benefits available from having an HRIS. Also, the Ceridian CD-ROM that accompanies the book has given readers opportunities to use HRIS applications.

❖ Establishing an HRIS

Design, implementation, and training are all important elements of establishing an HRIS. Security and privacy are also important issues.

Design and Implementation To design an effective HRIS, experts advise starting with questions about the data to be included:

- What information is available, and what information will be needed about people in the organization?
- To what uses will the information be put?
- In what format should the output be presented to fit with other company records?
- Who needs the information?
- When and how often is it needed?

Answers to these questions help pinpoint the necessary hardware and software. Experts recommend that a *project team* be established and extensive planning be done.[10] This team often includes representatives from several departments in the organization, including the HR and management information/data-processing areas. The team serves as a steering committee to review user needs, identify desired capabilities of the system, solicit and examine bids from software and hardware vendors, and identify the implementation process required to install the system. By involving a cross-section of managers and others, the organization attempts to ensure that the HRIS fulfills its potential, is accepted by users, and is

HR PERSPECTIVE

Installing HRIS at Green Tree Financial

Green Tree Financial Corporation, based in St. Paul, Minnesota, provides financial and mortgage services to a growing number of customers. To handle the business growth, Green Tree has increased its workforce from 1,700 employees several years ago to over 3,500 currently in 160 offices across the United States. The addition of more employees meant that improvements were essential in the payroll and HR information systems at the firm. As a result, Green Tree established a new HRIS with assistance from Ceridian Corporation.

The reasons that Green Tree decided to establish the new system were summarized by Jean Kensy, Green Tree's Manager of Payroll and HRIS. "We wanted our payroll and HR information in one database to simplify running reports," Kensy said. "Before, it took a lot of time to pull information from one system and use it in the other. The new system changed all that." She cited the salary increases report as an example: "This report contains such information as the salary increase percentages for each department and average merit increase. Before, I had to do the report manually, and it took 16 hours of weekend work. Now it's done in two hours."

The new system also provides much greater control for Kensy and her staff. "The payroll portion is much more user-friendly and flexible than the previous system used," she said. "We can change things ourselves. For example, the status codes in the system allow us to control when a deduction is taken, and we can see immediately how it affects taxability."

Kensy and her six-person staff are now tracking more information than ever before and doing it more efficiently. Just as important, Kensy and the other HR professionals at Green Tree are able to be more responsive to senior managers and others who request information on HR activities.[11]

implemented in an organized manner. The successful implementation of a new HRIS at Green Tree Financial is detailed in the HR Perspective.

Training Training those who will be using the system is critical to the successful implementation of an HRIS. This training takes place at several levels. First, everyone in the organization concerned with data on employees has to be trained to use new recording forms compatible with the input requirements of the system. In addition, in the HR department, staff members, including the executive in that area, must be trained on the system. For some HR professionals, this training may be their first detailed exposure to computers. Support and instruction from hardware and software vendors also are important in order for the organization to realize the full benefits of the system.

Security and Privacy Two other issues of concern are *security* and *privacy*. Controls must be built into the system to restrict indiscriminate access to HRIS data on employees. For instance, health insurance claims might identify someone who has undergone psychiatric counseling or treatment for alcoholism, and access to such information must be limited. Likewise, performance appraisal ratings on employees must be guarded. Often, data disks are kept in specially locked cabinets. In addition, restricted passwords are used to access different parts of the HRIS database.

❖ Using HR Research for Assessment

HR Research
The analysis of data from HR records to determine the effectiveness of past and present HR practices.

HR research is the analysis of data from HR records to determine the effectiveness of past and present HR practices. HR research data can be used in the following ways:

- ❖ Monitoring current HR activities
- ❖ Identifying HR problem areas and possible solutions to these problems
- ❖ Forecasting trends and their impact on HR management
- ❖ Evaluating the costs and benefits of HR activities.

Conducting research is often crucial to solving HR problems because it is difficult to make good decisions without appropriate information. Just as a physician must make a diagnosis before treating an illness, HR professionals must research and analyze current HR practices to ensure that future HR programs and activities are more effective. Many managers are intimidated by the word *research* and its academic connotations. But research can be quite simple and straightforward, as when an employer uses a questionnaire to ask employees about work scheduling options. For example, employees in a state education agency did a simple survey of work schedule preferences. This survey pointed out problem areas that would otherwise not have been discovered. As a result, the revised work schedules offered were more compatible with the desires of employees.

❖ Types of Research

Primary Research
Research method in which data are gathered firsthand for the specific project being conducted.

Secondary Research
Research method using data already gathered by others and reported in books, articles in professional journals, or other sources.

Research in general can be categorized as *primary* or *secondary*. In **primary research**, data are gathered firsthand for the specific project being conducted. Attitude surveys, questionnaires, interviews, and experiments are all primary research methods. **Secondary research** makes use of research already done by others and reported in books, articles in professional journals, or other sources.

Individuals who plan to do primary research should decide first what they wish to study. Examples of primary research topics are causes of nursing employee turnover, employee attitudes about flextime, and the relationship of preemployment physical exams to workers' compensation claims.

HR practitioners do *primary research* when they conduct a pay survey on computer system jobs in other companies in their geographic area or a study of turnover costs and reasons that employees in technical jobs leave more frequently during the first 24 to 30 months of employment. Thus, primary research has very specific applications to resolving actual HR problems in particular organizations. Examples of primary research can be found in the *Academy of Management Journal, Personnel Psychology,* and the other research-oriented journals listed in Appendix B. The research studies described in these journals can offer HR professionals guidance on factors affecting HR problems and the impact of management approaches to HR issues.[12]

As noted, *secondary research* uses the primary research done by others. Several computerized literature databases are available to HR researchers. Pay and benefits surveys prepared by government agencies or management consulting firms illustrate another common source of secondary research data on HR activities. Other secondary research might give investigators insight into how to use statistical methods or how well evaluation techniques are being applied.[13]

The following sections describe some primary methods often used in HR research: experiments and pilot projects, employee and attitude surveys, and exit interviews.

❖ Experiments and Pilot Projects

Experiments and pilot projects can provide useful HR insights. An **experiment** involves studying how factors respond when changes are made in one or more variables, or conditions. For instance, to test the impact of flextime scheduling on employee turnover, a firm might allow flexible scheduling in one department on a pilot basis. If the turnover rate of the employees in that department drops in comparison with the turnover in other departments still working set schedules, then the experimental pilot project may indicate that flexible scheduling can reduce turnover. Next, the firm might extend the use of flexible scheduling to other departments.

***Experiment**
Research to determine how factors respond when changes are made in one or more variables, or conditions.

The biggest problem with experiments and pilot projects in HR research is that HR management is practiced in the "real world." Unlike chemistry and other pure sciences, HR management is an applied science, and in real organizations it may be very difficult to control outside factors. For example, in the flexible scheduling situation, other factors may be influencing turnover in the pilot department. The investigators can address this problem by using another department as a *control group*; this control group has a population similar to that of the experimental group, but no changes are introduced. After the scheduling is changed in the pilot department, turnover in the department can be compared with that in the control department. A logical assumption may be that any differences are the result of the experimental group variable (flextime).

❖ Employee and Attitude Surveys

One type of research uses questionnaires to give employees opportunities to voice their opinions about specific HR activities. Employee opinion surveys can be used to diagnose specific problem areas, identify employee needs or preferences, and reveal areas in which HR activities are well received or are viewed negatively. For example, questionnaires may be sent to employees to collect ideas for revising a performance appraisal system. Or employees may be asked to evaluate specific organizational communication methods, such as the employee handbook or the company suggestion system. One common use of a questionnaire is to determine if employees are satisfied with their benefits programs. In addition, some organizations survey employees before granting new benefits to see if they are desired.

Questionnaires can be distributed and collected by supervisors, given out with employee paychecks, or mailed to employees' homes. More accurate information usually is obtained if employees can return information anonymously. New ways to obtain employee survey information include electronic mail (e-mail) surveys and interactive telephone surveys using touch-tone responses.

Attitude survey
A special type of survey that focuses on employees' feelings and beliefs about their jobs and the organization.

A special type of research is the **attitude survey,** which focuses on employees' feelings and beliefs about their jobs and the organization. By serving as a sounding board to allow employees to air their feelings about their jobs, their supervisors, their coworkers, and organizational policies and practices, these surveys can be starting points for improving productivity. Some employers conduct attitude surveys on a regularly scheduled basis (such as every year), while others do it intermittently. As the use of e-mail has spread, more organizations have begun conducting employee surveys electronically.[14] The accompanying HR Perspective describes how one firm used electronic mail inappropriately to conduct an employee survey.

Attitude surveys can be custom-designed to address specific issues and concerns in an organization. But only surveys that are valid and reliable can measure attitudes accurately. Often a "research" survey developed in-house is poorly structured, asks questions in a confusing manner, or leads employees to respond in a way that will give the desired results. For these reasons, consultants often are hired to develop and conduct customized attitude surveys. Prepared attitude surveys also are available from a wide variety of vendors. One drawback to the use

HR PERSPECTIVE

E-Mail Research

With the evolution of new technologies have come additional ways of conducting HR research. Electronic mail (e-mail) systems allow anyone with a computer account to compose and send memos, leave messages, and otherwise communicate with others in the organization. Large- and medium-sized organizations increasingly are using e-mail. One of the most intriguing uses is to obtain survey information from employees.

Electronic mail is a feasible way to conduct employee surveys because a researcher can electronically transmit a questionnaire to all or selected e-mail addresses. The respondents then provide their answers and send them back to the researcher. If desired, the responses can be anonymous.

However, this method is not without its problems. For example, the CEO of a manufacturing firm convened an electronic "town hall." All questions from employees were welcome, and comments could be anonymous. The results were disastrous. Inquiries about budget cuts were so explicit that upper management declined to answer. Unpopular managers were viciously attacked. Furious executives criticized "flame throwers" for hiding behind anonymity. Equally furious employees responded that the organization punished honesty instead of rewarding it. At the end of the second day, the CEO discontinued the input process.[15]

Technology-generated opportunities to communicate are transforming the information that companies can gather about themselves. However, some cautions still must be observed about how to do it properly.

of standardized surveys is that they may not cover special concerns. If HR managers choose a standardized survey, they should check published reliability and validity statistics before using it. Figure 20–4 shows sample questions from an attitude survey.

❖ FIGURE 20–4 ❖
SAMPLE QUESTIONS FROM AN ATTITUDE SURVEY

Questions in an attitude survey conducted for an insurance company asked employees to identify how much they agreed or disagreed with the following statements (among others):

- My immediate supervisor seeks out the thoughts and feelings of others.
- I find real enjoyment in my job.
- I would not consider taking another job with another firm.
- In this firm, high standards for performance are set.
- If you do good work, you will receive rewards and recognition.
- Unnecessary requirements and rules are kept to a minimum.
- I am rewarded fairly for the experience I have.
- I have little control over how I carry out my daily tasks.
- I think top management makes an effort to get opinions from the employees.
- Staying with this organization is a matter of necessity as much as desire.

When undertaking an attitude survey, HR management must get the support of top management. In addition, the specific purposes and objectives of an attitude survey should be identified before the survey is conducted. By asking employees to respond candidly to an attitude survey, management is building up employees' expectations that action will be taken on the concerns identified. Therefore, a crucial part of conducting an attitude survey is to provide feedback to those who participated in it. It is especially important that negative survey results be communicated to avoid fostering the appearance of hiding the results or placing blame. Generally, it is recommended that employee feedback be done through meetings with managers, supervisors, and employees, often in small groups to encourage interaction and discussion. That approach is consistent with the most common reason for conducting an attitude survey—to diagnose strengths and weaknesses so that actions can be taken to improve the HR activities in an organization.

❖ EXIT INTERVIEWS

A research interview is an alternative to a survey and may focus on a variety of problems. One widely used type of interview is the **exit interview**, in which those who are leaving the organization are asked to identify the reasons for their departure. This information can be used to correct problems so that others will not leave. HR specialists rather than supervisors usually conduct exit interviews, and a skillful interviewer can gain useful information. A wide range of issues can be examined in exit interviews, including reasons for leaving, supervision, pay, training, and the best-liked and least-liked aspects of the job. Exit interviews are usually voluntary for employees who are leaving. Most employers who do exit interviews use standard questions so the information is in a format that allows summarizing and reporting to management for assessment.

***Exit Interview**
An interview in which those leaving the organization are asked to identify the reasons for their departure.

Departing employees may be reluctant to divulge their real reasons for leaving because they may wish to return to their jobs some day. They may also fear that candid responses will hinder their chances of receiving favorable references. One major reason an employee commonly gives for leaving a job is an offer for more pay elsewhere. Although this reason is acceptable, the pay increase may not be the only factor. To uncover other reasons, it may be more useful to contact the departing employee a week or so after departure. Former employees may be more willing to provide information on questionnaires mailed to their homes or in telephone conversations conducted some time after they have left the organization.

❖ IMPORTANCE OF HR RESEARCH

HR decisions can be improved through research because better information leads to better solutions. Effective management comes through analyzing problems and applying experience and knowledge to particular situations. A manager who just "supposes" that a certain result may occur is not likely to be effective. In increasing numbers of organizations, systematic programs of HR research are used to assess the overall effectiveness of HR activities.

❖ Benchmarking for Assessment

Benchmarking
Comparing specific measures of performance against data on those measures in "best practices" organizations.

One approach to assessing HR effectiveness is **benchmarking**, which compares specific measures of performance against data on those measures in "best practices" organizations.

Those attempting to benchmark try to locate organizations that do some activities very well to become the "benchmarks." They then develop a relationship with those organizations in order to share data for the purpose of mutual learning. A successful benchmarking project will leave the benchmarker with a mass of potentially useful information regarding specific functions, processes, and practices. Benchmarking is *not* an exercise in imitation. It yields data, not solutions.[16]

❖ Nature of Benchmarking HR Activities

As applied to HR activities, benchmarking comparisons let the HR staff know how their activities and accomplishments compare with those in other organizations. HR benchmarking can lead to:

- Identifying areas where performance can be improved
- Evaluating HR policies and practices
- Comparing practices to "best practices and results"
- Setting performance goals to narrow the gap between current practices and best practices.

To do benchmarking, planning is required, evaluation methods must be established, best practices must be identified, and changes must be implemented based on the gaps that are identified.

HR data most frequently used as indicators of HR performance include the items highlighted in Figure 20–5. Compensation is one of the HR areas that is most frequently benchmarked.

❖ Figure 20–5 ❖
Sample Indicators of HR Performance

- Total compensation as a percentage of income (net income of the organization before taxes)
- Percentage of workforce unionized
- Number or percentage of management positions filled internally
- Dollar sales per employee
- Benefits as a percentage of payroll costs

Investigators can develop benchmark data by contacting organizations identified by the HR staff as "best practices" organizations. For example, benchmarking data can be collected through telephone calls. The calls may be followed up with questionnaires and site visits to benchmarking partners. Other, more general data are available as well. For instance, the Society for Human Resource Management (SHRM) and the Saratoga Institute have developed benchmarks based on data from over 500 companies, presented by industry and by organizational size.

Benchmarking looks at the "best practices" in other companies (or other divisions in a really big company) and asks "What can we adapt from that to our situation?" The HR Perspective "Research on Sharing 'Best Practices'" demonstrates how some companies are using computer systems in this process.

HR PERSPECTIVE

Research on Sharing "Best Practices"

Several large firms are exchanging "best practices" through computer systems that link geographically disparate units. Xerox, Motorola, and Anderson Consulting are among these "benchmarkers."

In the United States, companies maintain almost 30 million electronic mailboxes, and sales of connection software (or "groupware") that allows users to share databases have soared. Many companies believe that networked personal computers running powerful connection software allow their organizations to share data in a beneficial way. These data can be used to provide information on best practices and how well they work for the company using them.

For example, Tandem Computer has 11,000 employees worldwide involved in manufacturing and selling its products. The company's e-mail system is organized into three classes, with one reserved for information requests. Any employee can e-mail requests for help to all other employees around the world. Any employee can respond with ideas or solutions to the problem. Those responses are stored in a public file. In addition, subsequent solutions or modifications can be added to the file.

The sharing of best practices within a company—or "internal benchmarking"—is a useful but sometimes problematic tool. Researchers asked a group of managers, salespeople, and service technicians about best practices they had encountered. Of 78 people, 69 had adapted a best practice, but not all were actually implemented. That is, in some cases, all the information was collected, but because of other job demands the method was never put to use.

The impact of those "best practices" that were used was mixed. Fifteen of the best practices solved a technical problem with a specific machine. Twenty-two created better attitudes or work behaviors. Only two directly affected business results. The links between best practices and improved results are not strong or clear. They appeared in this study to result in small incremental improvements, not "home runs." Perhaps service technicians will be able to solve problems on a piece of equipment faster, or a better inventory control method will be implemented. However, a single adapted practice may not lead to major shifts in organizational indicators.[17]

❖ Professional Organizations As Information Sources for Benchmarking

HR specialists can gain information and insights from managers and specialists in other organizations by participating in professional groups. The most prominent professional organizations are the Society for Human Resource Management (SHRM) and the International Personnel Management Association (IPMA). These organizations publish professional journals and newsletters, conduct annual meetings and conferences, and offer many other services, often through local chapters. SHRM is composed primarily of private-sector HR professionals, whereas members of IPMA are HR managers from local, state, and federal government agencies.

Professional HR journals and publications of professional organizations are a useful communication link among managers, HR specialists, researchers, and other practitioners. Appendix A contains a list of journals that often publish HR management information.

Surveys done by various professional organizations can also provide useful perspectives. Some organizations, such as the Bureau of National Affairs and the Conference Board, sponsor surveys on HR practices in various communities, states, and regions. The results are distributed to participating organizations.

Finally, private management consulting firms and local colleges and universities can assist in HR research. These outside researchers may be more knowledgeable and unbiased than people inside the organization. Consultants skilled in questionnaire design and data analysis can give expert advice on HR research.

LOGGING ON

The website of the Association for Human Resource Management (AHRM) has links to the websites of 16 different HR associations at

http://www.ahrm.org

Appendix B contains a list of organizations and agencies having information useful to HR specialists and other managers.

❖ Communication and HR Information Transfer

It has been observed that "best practices" companies communicate much more, in greater detail, to more levels than other organizations, and use more technology in doing so. For example, HR at Mellon Bank uses an employee service center staffed by six customer service representatives who answer routine questions about the company's 56 HR services and products. Each representative uses a computer that allows him or her to see the employee's personal profile while the employee is on the phone. In addition, the company uses an employee newsletter, brochures, and other innovations to improve communications with employees.[18]

Communication not only deals with data for assessment and new ideas for making the organization more effective, it also provides the *context* in which work is performed. It enables management to convey objectives, values, and strategies to those who will implement them.[19]

At the heart of organizational communication is *information transfer:* providing information to those who need it in a format that is useful to them. HRIS may be a part of information transfer. But communication of reasons, goals and purpose is as important as merely transmitting data. Communication affects the management of people as much as, or more than, any other process over which management has influence. Many people think of communication primarily as interpersonal in nature. However, communication throughout organizations is just as important. There is no attempt here to cover all organizational communication, just that with special relevance for HR.

❖ Communication Throughout Organizations

HR communication focuses on the receipt and dissemination of HR data and information throughout the organization. *Downward communication* flows from top management to the rest of the organization and is essential so that employees know what is and will be happening in the organization and what top management expectations and goals are. *Upward communication* also is important so that managers know what the ideas, concerns, and information needs of employees are. Both formal means to encourage upward communication, such as suggestion systems and grievance procedures, and informal means, such as the grapevine, are used.

Informal Communication: The Grapevine As anyone who has ever worked in any organization knows, an important part of organizational communication is carried out through informal information channels, referred to as the *grapevine.* Just as jungle drums in old Tarzan movies indicated trouble, activity along the grapevine may reflect employee concerns and organizational problems. If there is a relatively trusting climate in an organization, then managers may be able to tap into current grapevine messages and listen for major distortions. However, without a favorable organizational climate, managers are more likely to be seen as "spies" and be cut out of the grapevine network. Activity in the grapevine depends on how important a topic is and on the presence (or absence) of official communication about it.

It is not possible to eliminate the grapevine. Absence of an observable grapevine in an organization might indicate either that employees are too scared to talk or that they care so little about the organization that they do not want to talk about it. Because the grapevine is a fact of organizational life, it is important that managers share information and communicate details to reduce the need for inaccurate rumors and gossip.

FORMAL DOWNWARD COMMUNICATION: PUBLICATIONS AND MEDIA Organizations communicate with employees through internal publications and media, including newspapers, company magazines, organizational newsletters, videotapes, and computer technology. Whatever the formal means used, managers should make an honest attempt to communicate information employees need to know. Communication should not be solely a public relations tool to build the image of the organization. Bad news, as well as good news, should be reported objectively in readable style. For example, an airline publication has a question-and-answer section in which employees anonymously can submit tough questions to management. Management's answers are printed with the questions in every issue. Because every effort is made to give completely honest answers, this section has been very useful. The same idea fizzled in another large company because the questions were answered with "the company line" and employees soon lost interest in the less-than-candid replies.

Some employers produce *audiotapes* or *videotapes* explaining benefit programs, corporate reorganizations, and revised HR policies and programs, which are shipped to each organizational branch. At those locations, the tapes are presented to employees in groups, then questions are addressed by a manager or someone from headquarters.

FORMAL UPWARD COMMUNICATION: SUGGESTION SYSTEMS A **suggestion system** is a formal method of obtaining employee input and upward communication. Such programs are becoming even more important as they are integrated with gainsharing or total quality management (TQM) efforts. Giving employees the opportunity to suggest changes or ways in which operations could be improved can encourage loyalty and commitment to the organization.[20] Often, an employee in the work unit knows more about how waste can be eliminated, how hazards can be controlled, or how improvements can be made than do managers, who are not as close to the actual tasks performed. Many suggestion systems give financial rewards to employees for cost-saving suggestions, and often payments to employees are tied to a percentage of savings, up to some maximum level.[21] Often committees of employees and managers are used to review and evaluate suggestions.[22]

Suggestion System
A formal method of obtaining employee input and upward communication.

❖ ELECTRONIC COMMUNICATION: E-MAIL AND TELECONFERENCING

As electronic and telecommunications technology has developed, many employers have added more technologically based methods of communicating with employees. The growth of information systems in organizations has led to the widespread use of electronic mail. With the advent of e-mail systems, communication throughout organizations can be almost immediate. E-mail systems can operate worldwide through networks. Replies can be returned at once rather than in a week or more. One feature of e-mail systems is that they often result in the bypassing of formal organizational structure and channels.

Some organizations also communicate through *teleconferencing*, in which satellite technology links facilities and groups in various locations. In this way, the same message can be delivered simultaneously to various audiences. For example, Domino's Pizza uses a satellite network to communicate information on new products, store operations, ideas, and other information. Others using satellites are J. C. Penney, Texas Instruments, and Federal Express.

❖ Approaches for Assessing HR Effectiveness

This chapter has discussed many sources of information about HR effectiveness. The final section describes some specific approaches to measuring effectiveness. A study of 968 large and medium-sized firms in 35 U.S. industries looked at accounting profits, productivity, employee turnover, and human resource practices. A solid relationship was found between the best HR practices and reduced turnover and increased employee productivity. Further, those practices enhanced profitability and market value of the firms studied. A high-quality, highly motivated workforce is hard for competition to replicate. It is an advantage that improves organizational performance, and it comes from effective HR management.[23] Specific approaches and ideas about measuring effectiveness follow.

❖ HR Audit

❖HR Audit
A formal research effort that evaluates the current state of HR management in an organization.

One general means for assessing HR effectiveness is through an HR audit, similar to a financial audit. An **HR audit** is a formal research effort that evaluates the current status of HR management in an organization. Through the development and use of statistical reports and research data, HR audits attempt to evaluate how well HR activities have been performed, so that management can identify what needs to be improved.[24]

An HR audit begins with a determination by management of the objectives it wants to achieve in the HR area. The audit compares the actual state of HR activities with these objectives, as the sample audit in Figure 20–6 does. A variety of research sources may be used to assess HR effectiveness during the audit. Review of all relevant HR documents is helpful. Common documents to be reviewed include employee handbooks, organization charts, job descriptions, and many of the forms used, such as performance appraisals, benefit statements, and labor union contracts. Also, interviews are conducted with a cross-section of executives, managers, supervisors, and HR staff members to obtain information about HR practices and problems. In some organizations, the HR staff members conduct the HR audit. However, a more objective assessment may be achieved if the organization uses external consultants for this task. Regardless of who conducts the HR audit, it is important to prepare a written report. This report should identify the methods used, specific observations on the state of HR activities, and recommendations for improvements. The report should go to top management, as well as HR staff members, to obtain greater commitment to implementing the recommendations. As part of an audit a checklist that consists of specific questions based on the objectives set during the HR planning process can be developed. These questions expand on the various areas of HR activities.

❖ Ratio Analyses

A useful way to evaluate HR involves calculating ratios. The ratios can be calculated and compared from year to year, providing information about changes in HR operations. For example, one suggested series of ratios and measures to consider is shown in Figure 20–7.[25]

Effectiveness is best determined by comparing ratio measures with national statistics using benchmarking. The comparisons should be tracked internally

❖ FIGURE 20–6 ❖
SAMPLE HR AUDIT CHECKLIST

HR Audit

This HR management audit allows you to rate the extent to which an organization has basic HR activities in place and how well they are being performed. In deciding upon your rating, consider also how other managers and employees would rate the activities. The total score provides a guide for actions that will improve HR activities in your organization.

Instructions: For each of the items listed below, rate your organization using the following scale:

VERY GOOD (complete, current, and done well)	3 points
ADEQUATE (needs only some updating)	2 points
WEAK (needs major improvements/changes)	1 point
BASICALLY NONEXISTENT	0 points

I. LEGAL COMPLIANCE

_____ **1.** Equal employment opportunity (EEO) requirements
_____ **2.** Immigration reform
_____ **3.** Health and safety (OSHA)
_____ **4.** Wage and hour laws (FLSA)
_____ **5.** Employment-at-will statements
_____ **6.** Privacy protection
_____ **7.** ERISA reporting/compliance
_____ **8.** Family/medical leave (FMLA)

II. OBTAINING HUMAN RESOURCES

_____ **9.** Current job descriptions and specifications
_____ **10.** HR supply-and-demand estimates (for 3 years)
_____ **11.** Recruiting process and procedures
_____ **12.** Job-related selection interviews
_____ **13.** Physical exam procedures

III. MAINTAINING HUMAN RESOURCES

_____ **14.** Formal wage/salary system
_____ **15.** Current benefits programs/options
_____ **16.** Employee recognition programs
_____ **17.** Employee handbook/personnel policy manual
_____ **18.** Absenteeism and turnover control
_____ **19.** Grievance resolution process
_____ **20.** HR record-keeping/information systems

IV. DEVELOPING HUMAN RESOURCES

_____ **21.** New employee orientation program
_____ **22.** Job skills training programs
_____ **23.** Employee development programs
_____ **24.** Job-related performance appraisal
_____ **25.** Appraisal feedback training of managers

_______ **TOTAL POINTS**

HR Audit Scoring

Evaluate the score on the HR audit as follows:

60–75	HR activities are complete, effective, and meeting legal compliance requirements.
45–59	HR activities are being performed adequately, but they are not as complete or effective as they should be. Also, it is likely that some potential legal risks exist.
30–44	Major HR problems exist, and significant attention needs to be devoted to adding to and changing the HR activities in the organization.
Below 30	Serious potential legal liabilities exist, and it is likely that significant HR problems are not being addressed.

SOURCE: Developed by Robert L. Mathis. May not be reproduced without permission.

over time. Saratoga Institute in Santa Clara, California, surveys employers annually and compiles information that allows individual employers to compare HR costs against national figures, such as those in Figure 20–8.

❖ RETURN ON INVESTMENT (ROI) AND ECONOMIC VALUE ADDED (EVA)

Return on investment (ROI) and economic value added (EVA) are two related approaches to measuring the contribution and cost of HR. Both calculations are a bit complex, so they are just highlighted here.

❖ FIGURE 20–7 ❖
HR RATIOS AND MEASURES

HR FUNCTION	USEFUL RATIOS	
• Selection	Long-term vacancies / Total jobs	Vacancies filled internally / Total vacancies
	Time to fill vacancy / Total vacancies	
• Training	Number of days training / Number of employees	Total training budget / Total employees
• Compensation	Total compensation costs / Total revenue	Basic salary cost / Total compensation cost
• Employee relations	Resignations / Total employees per year	Length of service / Total employees
	Absences / Days worked per months	Total managers / Total employees
• Overall HR	Part-time employees / Total employees	HR professionals / Total employees

Return On Investment (ROI) Calculation showing the value of expenditures for HR activities; it also can be used to show how long it will take for the activities to pay for themselves.

Return on investment (ROI) can show the value of expenditures for HR activities and can also be used to show how long it will take for the activities to pay for themselves. The following formula can be used to calculate return on investment (ROI) for a new HR activity: $(A - B) - C + D = ROI$

where:

A = current operating costs for the time period
B = operating costs for a new or enhanced system for the time period
C = one-time cost of acquisition and implementation
D = value of gains from productivity improvements for the time period

Economic Value Added (EVA) A firm's net operating profit after the cost of capital is deducted.

Economic value added (EVA) is a firm's net operating profit after the cost of capital is deducted. Cost of capital is the minimum rate of return demanded by shareholders. When a company is making more than the cost of capital, it is creating wealth for shareholders. An EVA approach requires that all policies, procedures, measures, and methods use cost of capital as a benchmark against which their return is judged. Human resources decisions can be subjected to the same analysis. Both of these methods are useful, and specific information on them is available from other sources.[26]

❖ UTILITY OR COST/BENEFIT ANALYSES

Utility Analysis Analysis in which economic or other statistical models are built to identify the costs and benefits associated with specific HR activities.

In **utility analysis,** economic or other statistical models are built to identify the costs and benefits associated with specific HR activities. These models generally contain equations that identify the relevant factors influencing the HR activity under study. According to Jac Fitz-Enz—a pioneer in measuring HR effectiveness—formulas and measures should be derived from a listing of activities and the variables associated with those activities. Figure 20–9 contains an example that quantifies selection interviewing costs.

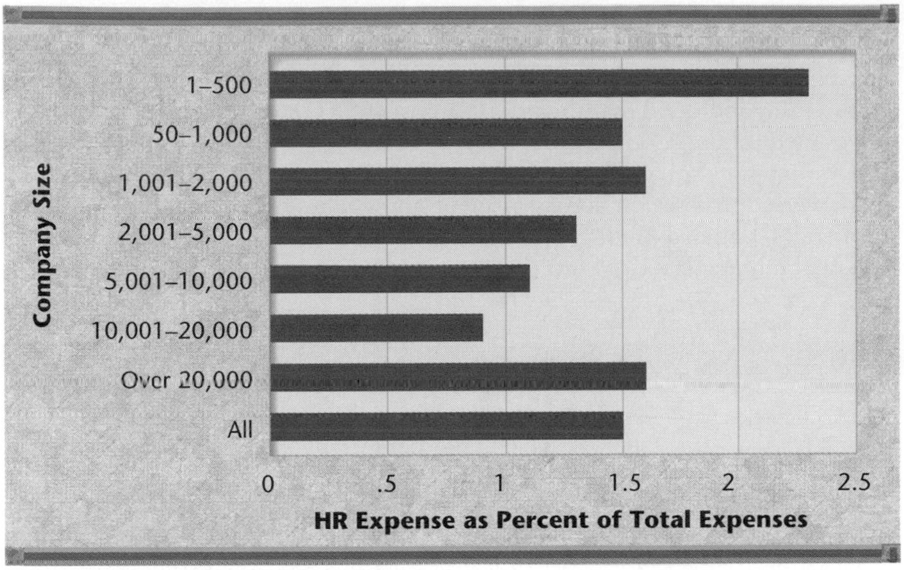

❖ **FIGURE 20–8** ❖
HR EXPENSE BY COMPANY SIZE

SOURCE: Saratoga Institute, Santa Clara, CA. *Human Resource Financial Report.* Used with permission.

Two examples illustrate how cost/benefit analyses have been beneficial, one at Union Bank in Los Angeles and one at AT&T.[27] At Union Bank in Los Angeles, a child-care facility was established at the operations center. By use of a cost/benefit analysis, it was estimated that during the first year the day-care center saved the bank approximately $200,000, compared with costs of about $105,000. The costs identified were the subsidies paid by the bank to cover expenditures that exceeded the fees paid by parents. Most of the savings were attributed to a reduction in employee turnover and absenteeism. The data collected indicated that turnover among employees who had used the child-care center was 2.2%, whereas turnover among employees using other day-care options was 9.5% and total bank turnover was 18%. When the costs of turnover were included, savings as high as $157,000 were identified. Regarding absenteeism, employees using the bank's day-care facility were absent about two days less per year and had maternity leaves one week shorter than those not using the facility. The savings attributed to the lower absenteeism were calculated to be about $35,000. In addition, the bank received significant publicity, news stories, and other media exposure that would have cost an estimated $40,000 to purchase.

The second example involves AT&T's assessment measures for identifying the costs and benefits associ-

❖ **FIGURE 20–9** ❖
SELECTION INTERVIEWING COSTS

SOURCE: Adapted from Jac Fitz-Enz, *How to Measure Human Resource Management,* (New York: McGraw-Hill, 1984), 64–65.

Here Is an example of how HR costing models can be developed. The following equations show how to compute interviewing costs.

$$C/I = \frac{ST + MT}{I}$$

where:

C/I = *cost of interviewing*
ST = total *staff time* spent interviewing (interviewer's hourly rate × hours)
MT = *management time* spent interviewing (manager's hourly rate × hours)
I = number of applicants interviewed

An example helps to illustrate use of the formula. Assume that an employment interview specialist is paid $12 an hour and interviews eight applicants for a job for an hour each. Following the personal interview, the applicants are interviewed by a department manager paid $20 an hour for 30 minutes each. The interview costs would be:

$$\frac{\overset{ST}{(\$12 \times 8 \text{ hours})} + \overset{MT}{(\$20 \times 4 \text{ hours})}}{8 \text{ interviews}} = \frac{\$96 + \$80}{8} = \frac{\$176}{8} = \$22 \text{ per applicant}$$

What this equation might indicate is the benefit of reducing the number of applicants interviewed by using better employment screening devices. Obviously, the costs of those screening items, such as a paper-and-pencil test, must be included when total selection costs are calculated.

ated with an employee wellness program. For the four-year program, in which over 75,000 employees participated, the firm compared the medical claims of participants and nonparticipants on various demographic characteristics. Results of the study indicated that the program costs of $175 per person were offset by lower medical benefits costs for AT&T.

Continuing efforts to cost-justify expenditures will require HR professionals to be versed in research and assessment approaches and methods. To face the challenges outlined throughout this text, effective HR management will be essential in organizations both in the United States and globally.

SUMMARY

- HR departments must set goals and measure effectiveness.
- HR records provide a basis for government compliance, documentation, and research on the effectiveness of HR actions.
- An HRIS is an integrated system designed to improve the efficiency with which HR data is compiled and to make HR records more useful to management as a source of information.
- An HRIS offers a wide range of HR uses, with payroll, benefits administration, and EEO/affirmative action tracking being the most prevalent.
- Establishment of an HRIS generally is done by a project team. Once the key components are identified, training must be done and security and privacy issues must be addressed.
- Research on HR activities answers questions with facts, not guesswork.
- Primary researchers gather data directly on issues, whereas secondary researchers use research done by others and reported elsewhere.
- Research information can be gathered from several sources, including experiments, pilot projects, various types of surveys, and exit interviews.
- Systematic programs of HR research are used to assess the overall effectiveness of HR activities.
- Benchmarking allows an organization to compare its practices against "best practices" in other organizations.
- Professional organizations provide sources of information on HR activities.
- A variety of employee publications and audiovisual media can be used to enhance formal HR communication efforts.
- Suggestion systems can be a good source of new ideas if employee suggestions are handled properly.
- HR audits can be used to gather comprehensive information on how well HR activities in an organization are being performed.

REVIEW AND DISCUSSION QUESTIONS

1. Discuss the following statement: "Recordkeeping is a necessary but mundane part of HR management."
2. If you had to establish an HRIS for a firm with 500 employees, how would you proceed?
3. Give some examples of how you would communicate with and receive communication from employees about implementing a flextime scheduling system in a firm with 200 employees.
4. How would you conduct HR research on turnover and absenteeism problems in a bank?
5. Using the HR audit checklist in Figure 20–6, rate an organization where you have worked.
6. Why is assessing and measuring the effectiveness and efficiency of HR programs so important?

Terms to Know

attitude survey **586**
benchmarking **588**
data **579**
economic value added (EVA) **594**
effectiveness **578**
efficiency **578**
exit interview **587**
experiment **585**
HR audit **592**
HR research **584**
human resource information system (HRIS) **581**
information **579**
primary research **584**
return on investment (ROI) **594**
secondary research **584**
suggestion system **591**
utility analysis **594**

Case

Prognosis: Healthy HRIS at HealthVISION

HealthVISION, Inc., develops and markets computerized health-care information systems for hospitals, doctor's groups, and HMOs. The company's headquarters are in Santa Rosa, California, and it has offices in 14 states, Canada, Australia, and the United Kingdom. Like many companies "on the grow," HealthVISION found its HR/payroll system inadequate for its expanding requirements.

"Actually, we had no computerized HR system at all," said Katherine Ketzer, HealthVISION's Human Resource Manager. "And the payroll system, which was outsourced to a major vendor, was inadequate for our needs. At the rate Health VISION was expanding, we needed a system that would grow with us, offering diversity, with a comprehensive data source."

The solution was an integrated HR/payroll system developed by Ceridian Corporation. In one stroke, HealthVISION moved into the 1990s with a system that allows integrated information exchange between HR and payroll.

Installed in October 1995, the new system has more than lived up to expectations, Ketzer said. "Efficiency and accuracy are much improved. All input and processing is done at our in-house convenience. Reports are generated for employee benefit programs, such as cafeteria and 401(k) plans, as well as accounting reporting. Manual checks are always precise, with up-to-date system payroll data." Ketzer noted that compatibility with Microsoft Windows NT is a plus, as is the ability to work with other Windows programs such as Excel and Word.

Ketzer said that HealthVISION has just begun to tap the potential of the new system, especially with regard to HR applications. She plans to take advantage of the system's ability to track and report employee information to meet government requirements. The custom benefits administration application will also be expanded to include all employee health benefits, savings plans, and leave reporting, as well as salary and performance reports.[28]

Questions

1. Discuss why payroll and HR information applications must be closely linked.
2. How will the efficiency of the new system aid HR in maintaining its growth?

Notes

1. Adapted from Samuel Greengard, "Discover Best Practices," *Personnel Journal,* November 1995, 62–73.
2. Barry A. Harstein, "Rules of the Road in Dealing with Personnel Records," *Employee Relations Law Journal* 17 (1992), 673–692.
3. Equal Opportunity Commission, *Technical Assistance Manual of the Employment Provisions (Title I) of the Americans with Disabilities Act,* as presented in *HR News, ADA Special Supplement,* April 1992, C32.
4. William Tracey, "Auditing ADA Compliance," *HR Magazine,* October 1994, 88–90.
5. "Personnel Records Are an Open Book at Some Big Companies," *The Wall Street Journal,* May 7, 1996, 1; and Harold P. Coxson, "The Double-Edged Sword of Personnel Files and Employee Records," *SHRM Legal Report,* Fall 1992, 1–5.
6. "Have You Looked at Your Personnel Files Lately?" *The Personnel News,* August 1993, 24.
7. Samuel Greengard, "Client Server: HR's Helping Hand?" *Personnel Journal,* May 1996, 90–98.
8. Michael LaBrie and Mary Myhre, "Harnessing Workflow Automation in Human Resources," *The Review,* April/May 1996, 36–48.
9. A. M. Townsend and A. R. Henrickson, "Recasting HRIS as an Information Resource," *HR Magazine,* February 1996, 91–94.
10. K. Barardi, "How to Select an HRIS System," *Benefits & Compensation Solutions,* March 1996, 32–34.
11. Based on information provided by Green Tree Financial Corporation and Ceridian Employer Services, Ceridian Corporation. Used with permission.
12. A. A. Lado and M. C. Wilson, "Human Resource Systems and Sustained Competitive Advantage: A Competency Based Perspective," *Academy of Management Review,* October 1994, 699–727.

(Notes continued on following page)

Notes, continued

13. G. J. Medsker, *et al.*, "A Review of Current Practices for Evaluating Causal Models in Organizational Behavior and Human Resources Management Research," *Journal of Management* 20 (1994), 439.

14. Thomas M. Hastings, "Fast-Tracking the Survey Process," *HR Magazine*, December 1995, 71–73.

15. M. Schrage, "Manager's Journal," *The Wall Street Journal*, November 7, 1994, A18.

16. Paul Goodman and Eric Darr, "Exchanging Best Practices through Computer-Aided Systems," *Academy of Management Executive*, May 1996, 7–19.

17. Jac Fitz-Enz, *Benchmarking Staff Performance* (San Francisco: Josey-Bass), 1993, 34.

18. Jac Fitz-Enz, *Best in America Guidebook* (Santa Clara, CA: Saratoga Institute, 1994), 1X.

19. Joel Head, *et al.*, "The New Realism; Maximizing Employee Value through HR Alignment," *Employment Relations Today*, Autumn 1995, 3.

20. M. Barrier, "Beyond the Suggestion Box," *Nation's Business*, July 1995, 34.

21. R. Schmidt, "Building a Better Suggestion Box," *The Rotarian*, October 1994, 18.

22. "Business Bulletin: The Suggestion Box Thrives in Updated Format for Brainstorming," *The Wall Street Journal*, March 23, 1995, 1.

23. M. Zigarelli, "Human Resources and the Bottom Line," *Academy of Management Executive*, May 1996, 63.

24. K. Dawson and S. Dawson, "How to Select the Best Service," *HR Magazine*, January 1996, 75–83.

25. Adapted from J. Hiltrop and C. Despres, "Benchmarking the Performance of HR Management," *Long Range Planning*, December 1994, 53.

26. G. B. Stewart III, "EVA Works—but Not If You Make These Common Mistakes," *Fortune*, May 1, 1995, 117; "Can EVA Deliver Profits in the Post Office?" *Fortune*, July 10, 1995, 29; and S. E. O'Connell, "Calculate the Return on Your Investment for Better Budgeting," *HR Magazine*, October 1995, 39.

27. Adapted from Julie Soloman, "Companies Try Measuring Cost Savings from New Types of Corporate Benefits," *The Wall Street Journal*, December 29, 1988, B1.

28. Based on information provided by HealthVISION Corporation and Ceridian Employer Services, Ceridian Corporation. Used with permission.

EXERCISE 13 - Analysis

The recordkeeping requirements of OSHA are detailed in Chapter 16. As accidents occur, they must be tracked, both for compliance purposes and for safety management follow-up. Because of the wide number of types of accidents and injuries that can occur in work settings, it is important to have accurate classification information.

At SME-TEK two health and safety incidents have to be tracked. One involves an employee who cut his finger at work, and the other involves a chronic respiratory situation.

1. How could data on the different types of injuries and illnesses be used as part of safety management efforts?
2. Identify two new codes on the OSHA Incident Table for CUT AND RESP to reflect the two recent safety and health situations. Also record that Vincent Johnson seriously cut his finger and lost 1-1/2 days of work, which makes the incident reportable to OSHA.

> SME-TEK
>
> MEMO
>
> TO: *Human Resource Management User*
>
> Recently, an employee seriously cut his finger while at work, warranting an OSHA incident report. Today another employee was notified that he is suffering from a chronic respiratory illness. Before these incidents can be recorded, I need you to enter two new codes (CUT and RESP) in the OSHA incident table.
>
> When done, please record the OSHA incident involving Vincent Johnson, the employee who cut his finger. He lost a day and a half of work. This incident is reportable to OSHA.
>
> Thanks,
>
> Sam Jacobs

EXERCISE 13 - Procedure

Before completing the memo's request, you need to access the Employee Profile module and review the topic "Employee Profile Overview" in the "Overview" lesson of the Concepts section. The Checkpoint topic in this lesson is optional.

To fulfill the memo's request, access the "OSHA" lesson of the Employee Profile Features & Processes section. Then, review the topics "Updating the Incident Table" and "Recording an OSHA Incident." The Practice and Checkpoint topics in this lesson are optional.

EXERCISE 14 - Analysis

Disciplinary incidents must be documented which provides better legal protection for an employer. One of the most common disciplinary problems is chronic absenteeism, even after individuals have had such problems pointed out by their supervisors. To begin the formal progressive discipline process common in many companies, including SME-TEK, a formal verbal warning may be given, and the fact that such a warning occurred should be documented by a supervisor. At SME-TEK, Sheila Wilson, a supervisor, has given a verbal warning to Lorie Evans for chronic absenteeism.

1. Even though they are called verbal warnings, why must documentation occur? How might that documentation be valuable later if disciplinary problems with an employee continue?
2. Record a verbal warning issued by Sheila Wilson to Lorie Evans for chronic absenteeism. Also, compile a listing of disciplinary actions against Ms. Evans over the past six months, as her performance appraisal is due soon.

> SME-TEK
>
> MEMO
>
> TO: *Human Resource Management User*
>
> On the first of this month, I had to issue a verbal warning to Lorie Evans because she has been chronically late for work. Please make note of this incident in her records, so that we can reference it should further action need to be taken.
>
> Since it's performance appraisal time again, I'll also need you to notify me if any other disciplinary actions have been taken against her, specifically in the last six months. I need this information by the end of the week.
>
> Thanks,
>
> Sheila Wilson
> Supervisor

EXERCISE 14 - Procedure

To fulfill the memo's request, access the "Disciplinary Action" lesson of the Employee Profile Features & Processes section. Then, review the topics "Recording a Disciplinary Action" and "Selection Criteria." The Practive and Checkpoint topics in this lesson are optional.

EXERCISE 15 - Analysis

In most unionized situations, employees can file grievances if they believe that some provisions of a labor agreement have been violated. Sometimes grievances are triggered by perceived unfair or inconsistent treatment of one employee when compared to another employee. Even in non-union situations, formal grievance procedures may exist as well. At SME-TEK an employee, Kaye Santos, filed a grievance regarding a travel reimbursement claim.

1. Why is it beneficial to record and analyze grievances by type and frequency?
2. Add a code for Expense Reimbursement (ER) to the Grievance Table in the Ceridian® CD-ROM, and enter the grievance filed by Kaye Santos to the appropriate records.

Exercise 15 - Procedure

To fulfill the memo's request, access the "Employee Grievances" lesson of the Employee Profile Features & Processes section. Then, review the topics "Updating the Grievance Table" and "Recording an Employee Grievance." The Practice and Checkpoint topics in this lesson are optional.

SME-TEK

MEMO

TO: *HUMAN RESOURCE MANAGEMENT USER*

Two days ago Kaye Santos filed a grievance in which she claims she was not fully reimbursed for expenses on her trip to headquarters in Boulder, even though a coworker submitted the same expenses and received full reimbursement.

I need you to add the code (ER—Expense Reimbursement) to the Grievance Table, then enter a record of this incident using the CII Grievance window.

Thanks,

Karen Jones

SECTION VIDEO CASES

❖ CASE 1
BRADBURY & STAMM CONSTRUCTION
An Old Firm's New Tack

The healthy growth and profits it had enjoyed for 63 years were rudely interrupted at Bradbury & Stamm Construction Co., Inc., one of New Mexico's largest private contractors.

A disastrous energy market in neighboring Texas, traditional source of most capital for New Mexican development, and passage of the Tax Reform Act, which removed significant investment incentives, sent New Mexico's building industry into a tailspin. Hundreds of companies declared bankruptcy.

Under Jim King, a 14-year employee who became BSC's third president that year, succeeding Robert Stamm, the Albuquerque firm acted to ensure that it wouldn't have to follow suit.

BSC had primarily relied on negotiated contracts with private developers, seldom bidding on public agencies' projects. That had to change, now that so many developers were going belly up.

The company went head to head with contractors accustomed to bid work and found to its surprise that it had an edge. Dealing with developers driven by the profit motive, BSC had developed strict-to-the-penny cost estimating tools. Because its new competitors' cost forecasting was not as precise, it was successful on bid after bid.

Seeking other markets new to it, BSC also ventured outside New Mexico, soliciting work in surrounding states. It developed a separate company in El Paso, Tex., Bradbury & Stamm of Texas.

Meanwhile, to cut costs, BSC had to downsize—and to end the union shop called for in its union contract, which was up for renewal. The company had built vast reserves of goodwill in dealings with unions and individual employees. Explaining its uncertainty about its future to union representatives, it was able to go to a merit shop and pare its payroll without a damaging strike.

Next, responsibility was spread across a wider spectrum of the company. A vertical organization chart was deactivated, and four self-sufficient teams were created to handle large projects, renovation and smaller projects, multifamily residential work, and high tech and correctional facilities projects. Each team had its own manager.

Three women were promoted to team technician slots and eventually became project managers—first of their sex in so high a position among New Mexican contractors.

Another aspect of BSC's operations also needed attention: safety. High workers' compensation insurance costs affected the company's bids. A one-on-one safety-first campaign began, and all employees pledged to follow through. There was a dramatic drop in accidents and in the insurance rate.

One cost was never cut, though. BSC maintained a policy of donating 5 percent of profits to charities. It has twice been named "most admired company" by New Mexico's top 100 private businesses.

Today BSC, which has 198 employees—30 more than three years ago, but half the number it had—is doing well. Annual sales are at the $65 million to $70 million level.

"We're a whole lot leaner, smarter, and more customer-oriented than just a few years ago," says Jim King. "We've learned to respond positively to obstacles, and we've thrown away the panic button."

1. Explain the potential problems in getting union workers in a union shop to buy into a team format.

2. How could BSC cut the cost of accidents further through the use of a systems approach to safety?

(Excerpts reprinted by permission of The Blue Chip Enterprise Initiative©, *Real-World Lessons for America's Small Businesses* pp. 5, 6; copyright 1994 by Connecticut Mutual Life Insurance Company.) ❖

❖ CASE 2
WILHEIT PACKAGING MATERIALS
Pulling Together after a Fire

When Gainesville, Ga., firefighters responded to an alarm at the headquarters of Wilheit Packaging Materials Co., Inc., they didn't realize the magnitude of the blaze.

A group went into the building and were caught in a backdraft. Flames were all around them. Fortunately, other firefighters were able to work their way in and rescue them. But no one could save the building; all the company's offices and 50,000 square feet of warehouse were destroyed.

Philip A. Wilheit, the firm's president, learned of the fire while at a son's basketball game. "When I got to the building it was burning badly," he says, "but I ran in with one of the firemen and, between us, we were able to salvage the main computer brain, accounts receivable, inventory books, and other miscellaneous items." It was too dangerous to save more, he adds. "The firemen ordered me out."

The blaze, which cost his business $2.1 million, could have been costly to other businesses, too. Wilheit's company distributes packaging materials on a just-in-time basis, and, he says, "If our supply was destroyed and not replaced immediately, half of the city of Gainesville's production lines would be affected."

But, Wilheit says, quick and cooperative action "helped us to recoup almost immediately." Employees pitched in to help. So did suppliers. Customers were supportive. Competitors didn't take advantage of the situation.

The company had a 110,000-square-foot warehouse a few blocks away, and what had been salvaged from the fire was moved there.

"As my employees started to arrive," says Wilheit, "we began using all cars that had mobile phones to call our major suppliers and customers. Our suppliers—some got out of bed for us—began replacing inventory, and within a 12-hour period we began receiving new supplies. Our customers were assured that it would be business as usual."

The company proved it could live up to a promise under adverse conditions. Not a delivery was missed. Customers stayed with Wilheit Packaging, and it had its largest billing month ever.

Wilheit Packaging, which has 46 employees, has now built more warehouse space than it lost. Its annual sales, currently at the $31 million level, have been rising, and it is well on the way to making up for the money that the fire cost.

"Here is proof," says Philip Wilheit, "that when people pull together and support each other, what almost seems impossible can be accomplished."

1. Why does this case illustrate the importance of safeguarding organizational records including those on employees?

2. Given the growth of the business after the fire, how would you go about measuring HR effectiveness?

(Excerpts reprinted by permission of The Blue Chip Enterprise Initiative©, *Real-World Lessons for America's Small Businesses* p. 214; copyright 1994 by Connecticut Mutual Life Insurance Company.) ❖

❖ CASE 3
VIRGINIA SEMICONDUCTOR
A New Beginning

Fredericksburg, Va., home of Virginia Semiconductor, Inc., has a fascinating past—it is rich in Civil War and Colonial history—but VSI is focused on up-to-the-minute technology and the future.

It is a successful small business: Only once in the past eight years has it failed to record annual sales growth of at least 20 percent. However, if President Thomas C. Digges, Jr., hadn't chosen the right course in 1985, the company might not be around today.

Digges and his brother Robert H. Digges founded VSI in 1978, establishing a niche as a manufacturer of small-diameter, single-crystal silicon wafers used for a number of microelectronic products. Volume made up for low profit margins per wafer.

Without notice, two major customers that represented 65 percent of VSI's business stopped buying. Digges desperately needed new customers.

He decided to go after markets where the volume of products his company made would be comparatively unimportant, but profit margins could be high because of the value of engineering research and expertise involved. That proved to be an ideal environment for a small, versatile enterprise.

The first opportunity was to make a silicon wafer that was two inches in diameter, 75 microns thick (a micron is one millionth of a meter), and polished on both sides. Such wafers, needed by several customers, had never been offered before. VSI delivered 25 in a few months. They sold for more than 10 times the price of conventional silicon wafers.

Soon VSI was offering wafers two to four microns thick, wafers with textured surfaces for infrared applications, wafers with micromachined holes or shapes... all in highly specialized markets. The company nimbly delivered custom orders in three or four weeks—faster than competitors were delivering standard silicon products.

VSI had made a new beginning. To get there, it had made sacrifices, but it hadn't sacrificed any of its 25 skilled employees. There were no layoffs. Digges took an 80 percent pay reduction for a time, and the workweek dropped to 32 hours, but everyone worked. Inventory was tightly controlled, extended-payment terms were negotiated with suppliers, and expenses were cut to the bone.

The company had never had long-term debt and, remarkably, it managed to get through its transition period without taking on any. VSI benefits from that today. The absence of large monthly debt payments enables it to respond quickly to new production needs.

Cross training has improved production quality, and marketing strategy has successfully been reinforced by N. Perry Cook, VSI's marketing manager since 1986. The company has participated in State of Virginia economic-development efforts that have brought it markets in Europe, Japan, Korea, and Israel. Exports now represent 40 percent of VSI's businesses, compared to 1 percent in 1985.

As VSI continues to come up with new products—one, an ultramachining wafer, has become a key component in auto air bags—it comes up with new customers. It has more than 300 active ones today, as against fewer than 50 in 1985. The company hardly misses the two big ones it lost that year.

1. How does the case illustrate viewing people as Human Resources when business becomes difficult?

2. The effectiveness appears to have increased at the company. How would you document that growth?

(Excerpts reprinted by permission of The Blue Chip Enterprise Initiative©, *Real-World Lessons for America's Small Businesses* p. 80, 81; copyright 1994 by Connecticut Mutual Life Insurance Company.) ❖

Appendix A - Current Literature in HR Management

Students are expected to be familiar with the professional literature in their fields of study. The professional journals are the most immediate and direct communication link between the researcher and the practicing manager. Two groups of publications are listed below:

A. Research Oriented Journals. These journals contain articles that report on original research. Normally these journals contain either sophisticated writing and quantitative verifications of the author's findings or conceptual models and literature reviews of previous research.

Academy of Management Journal
Academy of Management Review
Administrative Science Quarterly
American Journal of Psychology
American Behavioral Scientist
American Journal of Sociology
American Psychologist
American Sociological Review
Annual Review of Psychology
Applied Psychology: An International Review
Behavioral Science
Behavioral Science Research
British Journal of Industrial Relations
Cognitive Studies
Decision Sciences
Group and Organization Studies
Human Organization
Human Relations
Industrial & Labor Relations Review
Industrial Relations
Interfaces
Journal of Abnormal Psychology
Journal of Applied Behavioral Science
Journal of Applied Business Research
Journal of Applied Psychology
Journal of Business
Journal of Business and Industrial Marketing
Journal of Business and Psychology
Journal of Business Communications
Journal of Business Research
Journal of Communications
Journal of Counseling Psychology
Journal of Experimental Social Psychology
Journal of Human Resources
Journal of Industrial Relations
Journal of International Business Studies
Journal of Labor Economics
Journal of Management
Journal of Management Studies
Journal of Occupational and Organizational Psychology
Journal of Organizational Behavior
Journal of Personality and Social Psychology
Journal of Social Policy
Journal of Social Psychology
Journal of Vocational Behavior
Labor History
Labor Relations Yearbook
Management Science
Occupational Psychology
Organizational Behavior and Human Decision Processes
Personnel Psychology
Psychological Monographs
Psychological Review
Social Forces
Social Science Research
Sociology Perspective
Sociometry
Work and Occupations

B. Management-Oriented Journals. These journals generally cover a wide range of subjects. Articles in these publications normally are aimed at the practitioner and are written to interpret, summarize, or discuss past, present, and future research and administrative applications. Not all the articles in these publications are management-oriented.

ACA Journal
Academy of Management Executive
Administrative Management
Arbitration Journal
Australian Journal of Management
Benefits and Compensation Solution
Business
Business Horizons
Business Management
Business Monthly

Business Quarterly
Business and Social Review
California Management Review
Canadian Manager
Columbia Journal of World Business
Compensation and Benefits Review
Directors and Boards
Employee Benefits News
Employee Relations Law Journal
Employment Decisions Practices
Employment Relations
Employment Relations Today
Entrepreneurship Theory and Practice
Forbes
Fortune
Harvard Business Review
Hospital and Health Services Administration
HR Magazine
Human Resource Executive
Human Resource Management
Human Resource Planning
Human Behavior
INC.
Incentive
Industrial Management
Industry Week
International Management
Journal of Business Strategy
Journal of Pension Planning
Journal of Systems Management
Labor Law Journal
Long-Range Planning
Manage
Management Consulting
Management Planning
Management Review
Management Solutions
Management Today
Management World
Managers Magazine
Michigan State University Business Topics
Monthly Labor Review
Nation's Business
Organizational Dynamics
Pension World
Personnel Journal
Personnel Management
Psychology Today
Public Administration Review
Public Opinion Quarterly
Public Personnel Management
Recruiting Today
Research Management
SAM Advanced Management Journal
Security Management
Sloan Management Review
Supervision
Supervisory Management
Training
Training and Development Journal
Working Woman

C. Abstracts & Indices. For assistance in locating articles, students should check some of the following indices and abstracts that often contain subjects of interest.

ABI Inform
Applied Science and Technology Index
Business Periodicals Index
Dissertation Abstracts
Employee Relations Index
Human Resources Abstracts
Index to Legal Periodicals
Index to Social Sciences and Humanities
Management Abstracts
Management Contents
Management Research Abstracts
Personnel Management Abstracts
Psychological Abstracts
PsychLit
Reader's Guide to Periodical Literature
Sociological Abstracts
Work-Related Abstracts

Appendix B - Important Organizations in HR Management

Academy of Management
Pace University
235 Elm Road
Briarcliff Manor, NY 10510-8020
(914) 923-2607

Administrative Management Society
4622 Street Road
Trevose, PA 19047
(215) 953-1040

AFL-CIO
815 – 16th Street, N.W.
Washington, DC 20006
(202) 637-5000

American Arbitration Association
140 W. 51st Street
New York, NY 10020
(212) 484-4800

American Compensation Association
14040 N. Northsight Blvd.
Scottsdale, AZ 85260
(602) 951-9191

American Management Association
135 W. 50th
New York, NY 10020-1201
(212) 586-8100

American Society for Healthcare Human Resources Administration
840 N. Lakeshore Drive
Chicago, IL 60611
(312) 280-6111

American Society for Industrial Security
1655 N. Fort Meyer Drive
Arlington, VA 22209-3108
(703) 522-5800

American Society for Public Administration
1120 G Street, NW, Suite 500
Washington, DC 20005
(205) 393-7878

American Society for Training and Development
1630 Duke Street
Alexandria, VA 22312
(703) 683-8100

American Society of Pension Actuaries
1700 K Street, NW, Suite 404
Washington, DC 20006
(202) 659-3620

American Society of Safety Engineers
1800 East Oakton
Des Plaines, IL 60018
(312) 692-4121

Association of Executive Search Consultants, Inc.
151 Railroad Avenue
Greenwich, CT 06830
(203) 661-6606

Association for Health and Fitness
965 Hope Street
Stamford, CT 06902
(203) 359-2188

Association of Human Resource Systems Professionals
P.O. Box 801646
Dallas, TX 75380
(214) 661-3727

Bureau of Industrial Relations
University of Michigan
Ann Arbor, MI 48104

Bureau of Labor Statistics (BLS)
U.S. Department of Labor
3rd Street & Constitution Avenue., NW
Washington, DC 20210

Canadian Public Personnel Management Association
220 Laurier Avenue, West, Suite 720
Ottawa, Ontario K1P 5Z9
Canada
(613) 233-1742

Employee Benefit Research Institute
2121 K Street, NW, Suite 860
Washington, DC 20037
(202) 659-0670

Employee Relocation Council
1720 N. Street, NW
Washington, DC 20036-2097
(202) 857-0857

Employee Management Association
5 West Hargett, Suite 1100
Raleigh, NC 27601
(919) 828-6614

Equal Employment Opportunity Commission (EEOC)
2401 E Street, NW
Washington, DC 20506

Human Resource Certification Institute (HRCI)
606 N. Washington
Alexandria, VA 22314

Human Resource Planning Society
317 Madison Avenue, Suite 1509
New York, NY 10017
(212) 837-0632

Industrial Relations Research Association
7726 Social Science Blvd.
Madison, WI 53706
(608) 262-2762

Institute of Personnel Management
IPM House
Camp Road, Wimbleton
London SW19 4UX
England

Internal Revenue Service (IRS)
1111 Constitution Avenue, NW
Washington, DC 20224
(202) 566-3171

International Association for Human Resource Management
14643 Dallas Parkway, Suite 525
Dallas, TX 75240
(214) 661-3727

International Association for Personnel Women
194-A Harvard Street
Medford, MA 02155
(617) 391-7436

International Foundation of Employee Benefit Plans
18700 Blue Mound Road
Brookfield, WI 53008
(414) 786-6700

International Personnel Management Association
1617 Duke Street
Alexandria, VA 22314
(703) 549-7100

International Society of Pre-Retirement Planners
2400 South Downing Street
Westchester, IL 60153
(617) 495-4895

Labor Management Mediation Service
1620 I Street, NW, Suite 616
Washington, DC 20006

National Association for the Advancement of Colored People (NAACP)
4805 Mt. Hope Drive
Baltimore, MD 21215
(212) 481-4800

National Association of Manufacturers (NAM)
1331 Pennsylvania Avenue, NW, Suite 1500N
Washington, DC 20004
(202) 637-3000

National Association of Personnel Consultants
3133 Mt. Vernon Avenue
Alexandria, VA 22305-2640
(703) 684-0180

National Association of Temporary Services
119 South St. Asaph
Alexandria, VA 22314
(703) 549-6287

National Employee Services & Recreation Association
2400 S. Downing Avenue
Westchester, IL 60153
(312) 562-8130

National Labor Relations Board
1717 Pennsylvania Avenue, NW
Washington, DC 20570
(202) 632-4950

National Public Employer
Labor Relations Association
1620 I Street, NW, 4th Floor
Washington, DC 20006
(202) 296-2230

Occupational Safety and
Health Association (OSHA)
200 Constitution Ave., NW
Washington, DC 20210
(202) 523-8045

Office of Federal Contract
Compliance Programs (OFCCP)
200 Constitution Ave., NW
Washington, DC 20210

Pension Benefit Guaranty Corporation
P.O. Box 7119
Washington, DC 20044

Profit Sharing Council of America
200 N. Wacker Drive, Suite 1722
Chicago, IL 60606
(312) 372-3411

Society for Human Resource
Management (SHRM)
606 N. Washington
Alexandria, VA 22314
(703) 548-3440

U.S. Chamber of Commerce
1615 H Street, NW
Washington, DC 20062

U.S. Department of Labor
200 Constitution Ave., NW
Washington, DC 20210

Appendix C - Starting a Career

Starting Your Career

As students reach their Junior and Senior years of college, getting a job after graduation often becomes their number one priority. Many students feel lost or uncertain about how to approach this process. This appendix provides an outline of the steps to follow, and helpful tips to increase your chance of success in the job market. There are many other resources available to you and you are encouraged make use of as many of these as possible.

Beginning the Job Search

You are looking for the best opportunity and setting in which to begin your career. In order to identify such an opportunity and setting, you must begin by knowing who you are. The first step is to sit down and determine your abilities, skills, work values, interests, strengths and weaknesses. Next go back through your list and determine which of these you would most like to use in your first job. For example, if you are good at understanding and explaining how systems or processes work and like solving problems, you may want to consider employers that value these skills. What you are willing and able to do will begin to shape your job search. You will use this information in determining types of positions that are of interest, employers that you want to contact, in the construction of your resume and cover letters, and in preparing for your interviews. You must be honest with yourself and know your strengths and weaknesses. Only then will you head down the right path to landing a job that fits you as a person.

Next, you need to investigate the job market. Newspapers and business magazines often carry headlines regarding employment trends and company layoffs. This is just one source of information. Check with the Career Center at your school for information particular to the degrees being granted. Campus career fairs featuring employers hiring for different areas provide a wonderful opportunity to collect information on available jobs and preferred skills. Most states publish employment information through their Department of Labor or Commerce. The federal government annually publishes the *Occupational Outlook Handbook*. These are all sources of supply and demand information. Professional associations for your field can often offer information on careers and job outlook. It is also important to know which employers are hiring and what skills they are seeking. Employers look for the following things regardless of a student's major: academic preparation, willingness to start at the bottom, good work ethic, communication skills, willingness to learn, global focus, some knowledge of technology, willingness to work the job not the hours, and a "can do" attitude. Also, if at all possible, you need to be geographically flexible. A major complaint from employers is that students are not willing to relocate.

The authors are thankful to Jo Chytka, the Director of the Career Services Center at the University of Wyoming for providing the excellent advice contained in this Appendix.

Once you have determined who you are, and what the job market looks like in your field, you can begin to determine which employers you will pursue. The principles you learned in your marketing classes will come into play here. You must have an organized plan for contacting employers. The first part of the plan is to identify those companies in which you are interested. Start with a small list of 10 to 20 and then build on this if needed. This allows you to focus on a small number and not feel overwhelmed. This list may include companies that interview on your campus as well as those that don't. The accessibility of the employer will determine how you approach them. For example, if they interview on your campus, your approach will be to sign up for that interview, thoroughly research the company, and use your resume and interviewing skills to pursue getting the job. If they do not interview on your campus, you will use your resume and cover letter to secure an interview on site.

There are many resources available to determine employers in your field. Your college or university career center is a good starting point as they will have information on employers specifically looking for new college graduates. Membership directories for professional associations can provide member information by field and geographic location. The school or public library may also have company directories and annual reports. The Internet and World Wide Web contain many company home pages that provide information on employment opportunities, as well as several sites available for conducting a job search. Be aware that some of these sites require the user to pay a subscription fee. Campus or regional career fairs provide opportunities to visit in person with employees regarding careers and/or job openings. Many business schools offer free lectures from visiting executives. Attend and take advantage of the information presented in these lectures. Your faculty may also have contacts in various organizations—let them know of your interests.

Once you have determined your list of potential employers, you need to put together your package—your resume, cover letter, interview preparation and follow up plans. You also need to purchase a personal day planner and/or large calendar with which to track your job search progress. You may also need to purchase an answering machine. Most employers call you to set up and follow up with interviews. By having an answering machine you can increase the chance of their reaching you. Make sure you check your initial recording on the machine. It should at minimum identify the number they have called, sound professional, and be easy to understand.

Your Resume

Many students put off constructing a resume for fear that they don't have enough information to put on the page or because of a lack of personal focus. If you have completed the first step of the job search process, knowing who you are, it will be easier to construct your resume. The resume is a very important document. It is the first impression the employer will have of you as a candidate. IT MUST BE PERFECT!! This is the means by which you promote yourself and present your skills. Unfortunately, the employers initially may spend only 20 seconds looking at this document; therefore, you must make it as easy as possible for them to find what they are looking for.

There are some hard and fast rules for resume construction:

Rule #1 Keep it to one page. Again employers may only look at it initially for 20 seconds. Keep it to the point and on one page.

Rule #2 No mistakes!! This is your presentation of your skills; your lack of attention to the details of your resume will speak a thousand words to the employer. Have three knowledgeable people proofread it, then correct any mistakes in spelling, punctuation and grammar.

Rule #3 No personal information. The employer can't legally ask about your marital status, weight, health, height, or age, and the resume is not the place to provide this information.

Rule #4 Make sure to include your name, address, phone number, and if you wish, your e-mail address at the top. Use your school address. (You may want to include a permanent address if you are nearing the end of the term or graduation.)

Rule #5 Keep your resume uncluttered. Many computer programs allow you to dress up your resume with graphics, but do not distract from your text. There are some fields where the use of graphics is more appropriate than others—check with your career center. Many employers receive resumes by fax. Make sure yours will be easy to read.

Rule #6 Place your most important information near the top—your name, address, phone, number, objective, education, skills, and related work experience. Make it easy for the employer to find the things they need.

Rule #7 Use action verbs and avoid using "I." Your resume will include incomplete sentences. It is assumed that you have done the things indicated, therefore you do not need to use "I" in your text.

Rule #8 Do not put your references on the resume. You may, however, attach a list of references.

Figure C-1 shows an example of a suggested format for a chronological resume for a new graduate. There are other formats such as targeted, functional, and the resume letter. For most new graduates the chronological format is preferred by employers. There are exceptions, for example, if you are changing fields after returning to school. If you have an accumulation of skills that you want to highlight, the functional format may be more appropriate.

Rule #9 Use a good quality printer and a good quality bond paper. The additional expense of bond paper is a good investment. The color paper should be conservative and give a professional look. Never print on the back of your resume.

Many companies scan resumes electronically. If you know that your resume will be scanned you will need to use a certain text and font size. You will also need a keyword section that is made up of nouns not verbs. Figure C-2 shows an example of an electronic resume. These same requirements can also apply when you send your resume electronically over the Internet or World Wide Web. There are many publications available that discuss electronic resumes.

❖ FIGURE C–1 ❖

Chronological Resume

Sam Jones
e-mail jonesa@uwyo.edu

School Address	Permanent Address
2777 East 6th Street, #77	1717 Concord Dr.
Laramie, WY 82070	Austin, TX 98997
(307) 989-7675	(405) 995-8723

OBJECTIVE: Management trainee position in a retail or services environment. Willing to relocate and travel.

EDUCATION: **Bachelor of Science, Management**, University of Wyoming, Laramie, WY. Expected date of graduation, May, 1997.
GPA 3.4 (A=4.00) Dean's List 6 semesters.
Coursework has included:

Retail Management	Service Marketing
Organizational Behavior	Human Resources Management

INTERNSHIP EXPERIENCE:

Summer 1996 Intern, Management Development Program, Federal Reserve Bank of Kansas City, Denver Branch. Interned in the Business Development area, wrote publications, assisted in developing public programs and seminars.

Summer 1995 Intern, Target Stores, Minneapolis. Interned in the corporate headquarters on projects involved with new business development. Worked with site development, writing proposals and conducting research. Recognized as **Intern of the Month** for July.

Summer 1994 Intern, City of Austin, Parks and Recreation Department. Worked with department managers to promote park and recreation programs city wide. Wrote public service announcements, flyers, and contributed to monthly newsletters.

ACTIVITIES:
Vice President, Alpha Kappa Psi 1995-96
Peer Assistant, College of Business, University of Wyoming 1996
Chair, Public Relations Committee, Associated Students University of Wyoming Spring, 1995
Volunteer, Big Brothers, Big Sisters Fun Night, 1994, 1995, 1996
Phon-a-thon, University of Wyoming Development for College of Business 1995, 1996, **highest return on pledges, 1996.**

COMPUTER SKILLS:
Excel   Harvard Graphics   PageMaker   Word Perfect 6.1

INTERESTS: Intramural sports, skiing, fly fishing, golf, reading business publications.

❖ FIGURE C–2 ❖

Electronic Resume

Jane C. Smith
1717 8th Street
Laramie, WY 82070
(307)742-5757 (work)
(307)745-7654 (home)

e-mail jcsmth@uwyo.edu

KEYWORDS

Year End Statements. Tax Returns. Accounts Payable. Accounting Systems. Payroll. Financial Reports. Inventory. Lotus 1-2-3. Microsoft Office. Excel. DacEasy Instant Accounting. Word. Harvard Graphics. Quattro Pro. Cost Accounting Systems. Sales Tax Forms. Tax Code.

Education: Bachelor of Science, Accounting, University of Wyoming, May **1996 GPA 3.40 (A=4.0)**

CPA Exam, May 1996.

Coursework included:
Cost Accounting
Income Tax
Automated Accounting Systems
Accounting for Non-For-Profit Organizations
Auditing Principles
Auditing Electronic Computer Systems
Accounting Information Systems

Employment:

School Years
1994.95.96

Bookkeeper, Holiday Inns of Wyoming. Laramie WY
Handled accounts payable, payroll and preliminary preparation of financial statements, and year end reports. Handled restaurant inventory. Worked full time summers, 15-20 hours per week during school year.

Tax Season
1994.95.96

Income Tax Preparation, Laramie WY
Assisted with tax preparation for individuals through Beta Alpha Psi

Activities:

Beta Alpha Psi, Accounting Honorary , 1994.95.96
Kappa Kappa Gamma Sorority, 1994.95.96 **President**
Big Brothers Big Sisters 1995. **Volunteer**
College of Business Phon-a-thon 1995 **Committee Chair**

Cover Letters

The cover letter is the most difficult component to write. The purpose of the letter is to tell the employer why you are writing, and to persuade them to consider you for an interview if an opening exists, or to consider you for future openings. Never send a resume without an accompanying cover letter. The letter must be specific to the company and demonstrate that you know what they do and how you might fit into that organization. It should be directed to a specific person, or to a title, if a person's name is not available. It is best to send this to the division or area you are interested in working for rather than the HR department unless otherwise instructed. The HR department may receive hundreds of such letters each week. It is more likely that your resume/cover letter will receive the attention you want from the actual department in which you are interested.

The same rules that apply to your resume also apply to your cover letter. It must be error free, one page in length, printed on a good quality bond paper plus be specific to the company and to the position of interest. There are two types of cover letters—the letter of inquiry and the letter of application. You use the letter of inquiry to make initial contact with an employer for the sake of inquiring what position(s) may be coming open. You may also use it when you have been referred by someone else. For example, a professor suggests you contact a certain person in XYZ corporation that he/she knows. The letter of application indicates that you are writing to apply for a specific position.

In each case, the letter is typically three to four paragraphs in length. The first paragraph details why you are writing (to inquire to apply or at the suggestion of so-and-so). In the second paragraph you use the information you have gained from prior research of the employer to draw parallels between your qualifications. Do not lie or exaggerate. If you do not possess a certain skill, leave it alone. In the third paragraph you refer to your enclosed resume and ask for an interview. You should indicate if you are going to be in the area during a certain time period. Many companies will be happy to visit with you if you are already there. School breaks are a great time to schedule such interviews. You should give them a time frame for responding to your letter and indicate, you will be back in touch by a certain date. This is where your calendar or daily planner is helpful. Mark the date you are to contact them again. Many employers wait to see if you will follow through and make that second contact. The letter ends with a closing such as 'Sincerely' and your signature followed by your typed name. This should then be sent with your resume. Proofread carefully and make sure you sign it before you put it in the mail.

Applications

Some employers will ask you to complete an application prior to being considered for employment. Make sure you are thorough and complete all sections to the best of your ability. On occasion you may run into what may be illegal questions on the application form. Questions can only be asked if they can be shown to concern Bona Fide Occupational Qualifications (BFOQ). Therefore questions pertaining to age, gender, marital status, race, national origin, religion, and mental and physical limitations are usually not allowed. It is best if you, as the applicant, leave these questions blank or put a dash (-) in the blank. Employers asking questions for the purpose of EEO compliance should provide these questions on a separate form after you have been hired. If possible, type your application and again, make sure it is free from error.

Getting the Interview

The purpose of the cover letter and resume is to generate an interview. Once you know you have an interview you must begin to prepare for it. Many students have no idea of what to expect in an employment interview. The interview is a conversation with a purpose—finding the best candidate for the job. You can assist the interviewer in this pursuit by being prepared and professional. The key to a successful interview is to know yourself, to know the employer and the position for which you are being interviewed, and to be professional and enthusiastic in your approach.

You should already have done some self-inquiry during the first step of your job search process. The key now is to take those results and apply them to this employer. To do that you need to know what the employer does, where they are located, and the requirements and description of the position(s) for which they are hiring. It is highly appropriate to ask the employer for an annual report, job description, or other company information. You career center may also have this information. Read these—but go beyond that by going to your library and searching for recent information in the news. Ninety percent of the candidates will not do this. After reviewing the company information, match your skills and experiences to their profile. This will allow you to give specific examples in the interview and show that you have done your homework. Prepare a list of questions to ask them. Remember this is a two way street and you will also be making a decision on where the best place is to start your career. It is not appropriate during a screening interview to ask about benefits or salary. Also, read your resume and cover letter again to refresh your memory.

Being Prepared for the Interview

It is strongly suggested that you participate in a practice interview prior to the real thing. Many career centers offer videotaped practice interviews. By doing this you will increase your confidence and comfort level. Also, take a look at potential interview questions and think of how you would answer each one.

You need to make sure that you present a professional appearance. A suit and tie for men and a skirted suit for women are the most appropriate attire. You should be conservative with accessories, jewelry, make-up, and cologne or perfume. Your hair should be clean and off the face. This is your first step into the professional world and you need to look the part. Take the time to make sure everything is clean and pressed because first impressions last the longest. Also make sure your attitude is in order. Are you excited and willing to go to work? Are you enthusiastic about your future? Appearance and attitude are important to a potential employer.

During the Interview

On the day of the interview plan to arrive 10 to 15 minutes early. This will give you time to compose yourself and relax. If you are headed to an unfamiliar site, map your route ahead of time and plan for the unexpected. While being lost and flat tires make funny stories later, your potential employer will not be impressed. Do not smoke before you walk into the door and remember to get rid of your gum. It is acceptable to carry a leather portfolio with extra resumes and simple notes into the interview.

You may initially be greeted by a receptionist or secretary. Be polite and follow their instructions. When the person with whom you will be interviewing comes to get you, stand, smile, and extend your hand. The person is already forming an impression of you based on this initial interaction.

During the interview sit straight but be comfortable and maintain an acceptable amount of eye contact with the employer. It is important that you listen to each question in its entirety as it may contain more than one part. Answer the questions to the best of your ability and when appropriate use an example to personalize your answer. This also allows you to demonstrate your knowledge of the company. It is appropriate to ask for clarification if you do not understand a question but don't do that with each question! As previously mentioned, you should be given the opportunity to ask your questions. At the end of the interview, the interviewer should indicate the next step in the selection process and when that will occur. If they do not provide this information it is acceptable to ask.

The employer may invite you back for a second extensive interview. This second interview may include managers, coworkers, and human resource professionals. It may also include having a meal with the employer. Many students do not think about the meal until it is about to occur. Proper etiquette is very important especially if you will be placed in situations where you will be dining with clients or customers. Brush up on your dining etiquette prior to the interview. For example, do not order foods that are difficult to eat, do not order an alcoholic drink even if the employer does, and learn which utensils are appropriate for each course.

Follow Up

At the conclusion of the interview, shake the interviewer's hand, thank them for the interview, and it if has not already been provided ask them for their business card. When you get home, take a moment to jot down your impression of the interview, what you could have done differently, and your impression of the company. This will help you later in preparing for additional interviews and in making your employment decision. Also make sure you take time to send a thank you note. If you interviewed with several people in the company, send a thank you note to the hiring manager and your host. In the note thank them for their time and re-express your interest in the position. If you are no longer interested in the position, send a thank you note and indicate this.

Accepting a Position

This is the step you hope to get to quickly! Prior to accepting a position make sure you have in writing the starting salary and start date, the benefit package, and the location. Once you have accepted a position you should cease your job search. It is unethical to continue to interview once you have accepted a position and it could have long term ramifications for your career.

Concluding Thoughts

You have worked long and hard to get to this point. With preparation, determination, and persistence you will be able to reach your goal. The main points are to know yourself and what you are looking for, to know the employer and what they are looking for, and to be able to communicate these things in writing and in person. The easier you can make it for the employer to see that the qualifications you offer fit what they need, the more successful you will be. Good Luck!

Appendix D - Annual Report Form EEO-1

Standard Form 100
(Rev. 12-76)
Approved GAO B-180541 (R0077)
Expires 12-31-78

EQUAL EMPLOYMENT OPPORTUNITY
EMPLOYER INFORMATION REPORT EEO-1

Joint Reporting Committee

- Equal Employment Opportunity Commission
- Office of Federal Contract Compliance Programs

Section A — TYPE OF REPORT
Refer to instructions for number and types of reports to be filed

1. Indicate by marking in the appropriate box the type of reporting for which this copy of the form is submitted (MARK ONLY ONE BOX).

(1) ☐ Single-establishment Employer Report

Multi-establishment Employer:
(2) ☐ Consolidated Report
(3) ☐ Headquarters Unit Report
(4) ☐ Individual Establishment Report (submit one for each establishment with 25 or more employees)
(5) ☐ Special Report

2. Total number of reports being filed by this Company (Answer on Consolidated Report only) ______

Section B — COMPANY IDENTIFICATION *(To be answered by all employers)*

OFFICE USE ONLY

1. Parent Company
   a. Name of parent company (owns or controls establishment in item 2) omit if same as label — a.

Name of receiving office				Address (Number and street)	b.
City or town	County	State	ZIP code	b. Employer Identification No.	

2. Establishment for which this report is filed. (Omit if same as label)
   a. Name of establishment — c.

Address (Number and street)	City or town	County	State	ZIP code	d.

b. Employer identification No. | | | | | | | | | (If same as label, skip)

3. Parent company affiliation (Multi-establishment Employers: Answer on Consolidated Report)
   a. Name of parent—affiliated company b. Employer Identification No.

Address (Number and street)	City or town	County	State	ZIP code

Section C — EMPLOYERS WHO ARE REQUIRED TO FILE *(To be answered by all employers)*

☐ Yes ☐ No 1. Does the entire company have at least 100 employees in the payroll period for which you are reporting?

☐ Yes ☐ No 2. Is your company affiliated through common ownership and/or centralized management with other entities in an enterprise with a total employment of 100 or more?

☐ Yes ☐ No 3. Does the company or any of its establishments (a) have 50 or more employees AND (b) is not exempt as provided by 41 CFR 60-1.5. AND either (1) is a prime government contractor or first-tier subcontractor, and has a contract, subcontract, or purchase order amounting to $50,000 or more, or (2) serves as a depository of Government funds in any amount or is a financial institution which is an issuing and paying agent for U.S. Saving Bonds and Saving Notes?

NOTE: if the answer is yes to ANY of these questions, complete the entire form; otherwise skip to Section G.

Section D — EMPLOYMENT DATA

Employment at this establishment--Report all permanent, temporary, or part-time employees including apprentices and on-the-job trainees unless specifically excluded as set forth in the instructions. Enter the appropriate figures on all lines and in all columns. Blank spaces will be considered as zeros.

JOB CATEGORIES	NUMBER OF EMPLOYEES										
		MALE					FEMALE				
	OVERALL TOTALS (SUM OF COL B THRU K) A	WHITE (NOT OF HISPANIC ORIGIN) B	BLACK (NOT OF HISPANIC ORIGIN) C	HISPANIC D	ASIAN OR PACIFIC ISLANDER E	AMERICAN INDIAN OR ALASKAN NATIVE F	WHITE (NOT OF HISPANIC ORIGIN) G	BLACK (NOT OF HISPANIC ORIGIN) H	HISPANIC I	ASIAN OR PACIFIC ISLANDER J	AMERICAN INDIAN OR ALASKAN NATIVE K
Officials and Managers											
Professionals											
Technicians											
Sales Workers											
Office and Clerical											
Craft Workers (Skilled)											
Operatives (Semi-Skilled)											
Laborers (Unskilled)											
Craft Workers (Skilled)											
TOTAL											
Total employment reported in previous EEO-I report											

(The trainees below should also be included in the figures for the appropriate occupational categories above)

Formal On-the-job trainees	White collar										
	Production										

1. NOTE: On consolidated report, skip questions 2-5 and Section E.
2. How was information as to race or ethnic group in Section D obtained?
   1. ☐ Visual Survey
   2. ☐ Employment Record
   3. ☐ Other — Specify ____________
3. Dates of payroll period used –
4. Pay period of last report submitted for this establishment ____________
5. Does this establishment employ apprentices?
   This year? 1. ☐ Yes 2. ☐ No
   Last year? 1. ☐ Yes 2. ☐ No

Section E — ESTABLISHMENT INFORMATION

1. Is the location of the establishment the same as that reported last year?
   1. ☐ Yes 2. ☐ No 3. ☐ Did not report last year 1. ☐ Reported on combined basis
2. Is the major business activity at this establishment the same as that reported last year?
   1. ☐ Yes 2. ☐ No 3. ☐ No report last year 4. ☐ Reported on combined basis
3. What is the major activity of this establishment? (Be specific, i.e., manufacturing steel castings, retail grocer, wholesale plumbing supplies, title insurance, etc. Include the specific type of product or type of service provided, as well as the principal business or industrial activity.

OFFICE USE ONLY

e.

Section F — REMARKS

Use this item to give any identification data appearing on last report which differs from that given above. Explain major changes in composition or reporting units, and other pertinent information.

Section G — CERTIFICATION (See instructions G)

Check one
1. ☐ All reports are accurate and were prepared in accordance with the instructions (check on consolidated only).
2. ☐ This report is accurate and was prepared in accordance with the instructions.

Name of Certifying Official	Title.	Signature			Date
Name of person to contact regarding this report (Type or print)	Address (number and street)				
Title	City and State	ZIP code	Telephone Area Code	Number	Extension

All reports and information obtained from individual reports will be kept confidential as required by Section 709 (e) of Title VII.

Appendix E - HRCI Content Outline of the HR Body of Knowledge

Following each of the major functional sub-areas are the weightings for that sub-area. The first number in the parentheses is the PHR percentage weighting and the second number is the SPHR percentage weighting. These weightings should help you allocate your time in preparing for each respective examination.

I. Management Practices (22%, 29%)

A. Role of HR in Organizations (3.1%, 4.0%)

1. HR Roles: Advisory Role, Service Role, Control Role
2. Change agent role
3. HR's Role in Strategic Planning
4. HR Generalist and HR Specialist Roles
5. Effects of Different Organizational Contexts and Industries on HR Functions
6. HR. Policies and Procedures
7. Integration and Coordination of HR Functions

B. Human Resource Planning (3.0%, 4.0%)

1. Environmental Scanning
2. Forecast of International HR Supply and Demand
3. Inventory of Human Resources
4. Human Resource Information Systems
5. Action Plans and Programs
6. Evaluation of Human Resource Planning

C. Organizational Design and Development (2.1%, 3.2%)

1. Organizational Structures
2. Organizational Development

D. Budgeting, Controlling and Measurement (1.3%, 1.8%)

1. HR Budgeting Process
2. HR Control Process
3. Evaluating HR Effectiveness

E. Motivation (1.7%, 2.1%)

1. Motivation Theories
2. Applying Motivation Theory in Management

F. Leadership (1.8%, 2.3%)

1. Leadership Theories
2. Effect of Leadership In Organizations
3. Leadership Training
4. Roles in Leadership: Leader's Role, Follower's Role

G. Quality and Performance Management/TQM (2.2%, 2.8%)

1. Performance Planning: Identifying Goals/Desired Behaviors
2. Setting and Communicating Performance Standards
3. Measuring Results and Providing Feedback
4. Implementing Performance Improvement Strategies
5. Evaluating Results

H. Employee Involvement Strategies (2.4%, 2.8%)

1. Work Teams
2. Job Design and Redesign
3. Employee Ownership/ESOPs
4. Employee Suggestions System
5. Participative Management
6. Alternative Work Schedules
7. Role of HR in Employee Involvement Programs

I. HR Research (1.2%, 1.7%)

1. Research Design and Methodology
2. Quantitative Analysis
3. Qualitative Research

J. International HR Management (1.4%, 2.2%)

1. Cultural Differences
2. Legal Aspects of International HR
3. Expatriation and Repatriation
4. Issues of Multinational Corporations
5. Compensation and Benefits for Foreign Nationals and Expatriates
6. The Role of HR in International Business

K. Ethics (1.8%, 2.1%)

1. Ethical Issues
2. Establishing Ethical Behavior in the Organization

II. Selection and Placement (20%, 15%)

A. Legal and Regulatory Factors Affecting Selection and Placement: Definitions, Requirements, Proscribed Practices, Exemptions, Enforcement, Remedies, and Case Histories (6.1%, 4.4%)

1. Title VII of the Civil Rights Act (1964) as amended (1972, 1991)
2. Executive Order 11246 (1965) as amended by 11375 (1967), Executive Order 11478 (1969)
3. Age Discrimination in Employment Act (1967) as amended
4. Consumer Credit Protection Act: Fair Credit Reporting (1970)
5. Vocational Rehabilitation Act (1973) as amended
6. Vietnam Era Veterans Readjustment Act (1974)
7. Pregnancy Discrimination in Employment Act (1978)
8. Immigration Reform and Control Act (1986)
9. Employee Polygraph Protection Act (1988)
10. Uniform Guidelines on Employee Selection Procedures
11. Worker Adjustment and Retraining Notification Act (1988)
12. Americans with Disabilities Act (1990)
13. Common Law Tort Theories

B. Equal Employment Opportunity/Affirmative Action (2.6%, 2.1%)

1. Legal Endorsement of EEO: Supreme Court Decisions
2. Equal Employment Opportunity Programs
3. Affirmative Action Plans
4. Special Programs to Eliminate Discrimination

5. Fairness Issues: Reverse Discrimination, Quota Hiring vs. Merit Hiring

C. Recruitment (3.1%, 2.3%)

1. Determining Recruitment Needs and Objectives
2. Identifying Selection Criteria
3. Internal Sourcing
4. External Sourcing
5. Evaluating Recruiting Effectiveness

D. Selection (6.5%, 4.7%)

1. Application Process
2. Interviewing
3. Pre-employment Testing
4. Background Investigation
5. Medical Examination
6. Hiring Applicants with Disabilities
7. Illegal Use of Drugs and Alcohol
8. Validation and Evaluation of Selection Process Components

E. Career Planning and Development (1.7%, 1.5%)

1. Accommodating Organizational and Individual Needs
2. Mobility Within the Organization
3. Managing Transitions

III. Training and Development (12%, 12%)

A. Legal and Regulatory Factors Affecting Training: Definitions, Requirements, Proscribed Practices, Exemptions, Enforcement, Remedies, and Case Histories (2%, 1.9%)

1. Title VII of the Civil Rights Act (1964, 1991), Americans with Disabilities Act (1990), and other applicable employment discrimination statutes
2. National Lab or Relations Act (1935), Labor-Management Relations Act (1947), and other applicable labor relations statutes
3. Copyright Statutes
4. OSHA Mandated Training

B. HR Training and the Organization (1.7%, 2.0%)

1. Linking Training to Organizational Goals, Objectives, and Strategies
2. Funding the Training Function
3. Cost/Benefit Analysis of Training

C. Training Needs Analysis (1.0%, 1.0%)

1. Training Needs Analysis Process
2. Methods of Assessing Training Needs

D. Training and Development Programs (5.1%, 4.9%)

1. Trainer Selection
2. Design Considerations and Learning Principles
3. Types of Training Programs
4. Instructional Methods and Processes
5. Training Facilities Planning
6. Training Materials

E. Evaluation of Training Effectiveness (2.2%, 2.2%)

1. Sources for Evaluation
2. Research Methods for Evaluation
3. Criteria for Evaluating Training

IV. Compensation and Benefits (2.1%, 18%)

A. Legal and Regulatory Factors Affecting Compensation and Benefits: Definitions, Requirements, Proscribed Practices, Exemptions, Enforcement, Remedies, and Case Histories (4.1%, 3.0%)

1. Early Compensation Laws: Davis-Bacon Act (1931); Anti-kickback (Copland) Act (1934); Public Contracts (Walsh-Healy) Act (1936)
2. Fair Labor Standards Act (1938) as amended
3. Equal Pay Act (1963)
4. Title VII of the Civil Rights Act (1964) as amended (1972, 1991)
5. Age Discrimination in Employment Act (1967) as amended
6. Consumer Credit Protection Act: Wage Garnishment (1968), Fair Credit Reporting (1970)
7. HMO (Health Maintenance Organization Act) (1973)
8. ERISA (Employee Retirement Income Security Act) (1974)
9. Pregnancy Discrimination in Employment Act (1978)
10. COBRA (Consolidated Omnibus Budget Reconciliation Act) (1990)
11. Workers' Compensation and Unemployment Compensation Laws/Regulations
12. Social Security Laws/Regulations

B. Tax and Accounting Treatment of Compensation and Benefit Programs (0.5%, 0.5%)

1. FASB Regulations
2. IRS Regulations

C. Economic Factors Affecting Compensation (1.0%, 1.0%)

1. Inflation
2. Interest Rates
3. Foreign Competition
4. Economic Growth

D. Total Compensation Philosophy, Strategy, and Policy (1.6%, 1.5%)

1. Fitting Strategy and Policy to the External Environment and to the Organization's Culture, Structure, and Objectives
2. Training and Communication Compensation Programs
3. Making Compensation Programs Achieve Organizational Objectives
4. Establishing Administrative Controls

E. Compensation Programs: Types, Characteristics, and Advantages/Disadvantages (2.0%, 1.7%)

1. Base Pay
2. Differential Pay
3. Incentive Pay
4. Pay Programs for Selected Employees

F. Job Analysis, Job Description, and Job Specification (1.6%, 1.1%)

1. Methods of Job Analysis
2. Types of Data Gathered in a Job Analysis
3. Uses of Job Analysis

4. Job Descriptions
5. Job Specifications
6. Validity and Reliability of Job Analysis, Job Description, and Job Specification

G Job Evaluation Methods (1.8%, 1.5%)

1. Compensable Factors
2. Ranking Method
3. Classification/Grading Method
4. Factor Comparison Method
5. Point Method
6. Guide Chart-Profile Method (Hay method)

H. Job Pricing, Pay Structures, and Pay Rate Administration (1.7%, 1.3%)

1. Job Pricing and Pay Structures
2. Individual Pay Rate Determination
3. Utilizing Performance Appraisal in Pay Administration
4. Reflecting Geographic Influences in Pay Structures
5. Wage Surveys

I. Employee Benefit Programs: Types, Objectives, Characteristics, and Advantages/Disadvantages (2.6%, 1.9%)

1. Legally Required Programs/Payments
2. Income Replacement
3. Insurance and Income Protection
4. Deferred Pay
5. Pay for Time Not Worked
6. Unpaid Leave
7. Flexible Benefit Plans, Cafeteria Plans
8. Recognition and Achievement Awards

J. Managing Employee Benefit Programs (2.9%, 3.1%)

1. Employee Benefits Philosophy, Planning, and Strategy
2. Employee Need/Preference Assessment: Surveys
3. Administrative Systems
4. Funding/Investment Responsibilities
5. Coordination with Plan Trustees, Insurers, Health Service Providers and Third-Party Administrators
6. Utilization Review
7. Cost-Benefit Analysis and Cost Management
8. Communicating Benefit Programs

K. Evaluating the Effectiveness of Total Compensation Strategy and Programs (1.2%, 1.4%)

1. Budgeting
2. Cost Management
3. Assessment of Methods and Processes

V. Employee and Labor Relations (18%, 19%)

A. Legal and Regulatory Factors Affecting Employee and Labor Relations: Definitions, Requirements, Proscribed Practices, Exemptions, Enforcement, Remedies, and Case Histories (2.6%, 2.5%)

1. Federal Anti-Injunction (Norris-LaGuardia) Act (1932)
2. National Labor Relations (Wagner) Act (1935)
3. Labor Management Relations (Taft-Hartley) Act (1947)
4. Labor Management Reporting and Disclosure (Landrum-Griffin) Act (1959)
5. Title VII of the Civil Rights Act (1964) as amended (1991) and other applicable employment discrimination statutes
6. Age Discrimination in Employment Act (1967) as amended
7. Employee Polygraph Protection Act (1988)
8. Worker Adjustment and Retraining Notification (Plant Closing) Act (1988)
9. Americans with Disabilities Act (1990)

B. Union Representation of Employees (1.4%, 1.6%)

1. Scope of the Labor Management Relations (Taft-Hartley) Act (1947)
2. Achieving Representative Status
3. Petitioning for an NLRB Election
4. Election Campaign
5. Union Security

C. Employer Unfair Labor Practices (1.5%, 1.6%)

1. Procedures for Processing Unfair Labor Practice
2. Interference, Restraint, and Coercion
3. Domination and Unlawful Support of Labor Organizations
4. Employee Discrimination to Discourage Union Membership
5. Retaliation
6. Remedies

D. Union Unfair Labor Practices, Strikes, and Boycotts (1.4%, 1.6%)

1. Responsibility for Acts of Union Agents
2. Union Restraint or Coercion
3. Duty of Fair Representation
4. Inducing Unlawful Discrimination by Employer
5. Excessive or Discriminatory Membership Fees
6. Strikes and Secondary Boycotts
7. Strike Preparation

E. Collective Bargaining (2.3%, 2.9%)

1. Bargaining Issues and Concepts
2. Negotiation Strategies
3. Good Faith Requirements
4. Notice Requirements
5. Unilateral Changes in Terms of Employment
6. Duty to Successor Employers or Unions: Buyouts, Mergers, or Bankruptcy
7. Enforcement Provisions
8. Injunctions
9. Mediation and Conciliation
10. National Emergency Strikes

F. Managing Organization-Union Relations (1.0%, 1.0%)

1. Building and Maintaining Union-Organization Relationships: Cooperative Programs
2. Grievance Processes and Procedures
3. Arbitration Process
4. Maintaining Nonunion Status

G. Public Sector Labor Relations (1.0%, 1.0%)

1. Right to Organize
2. Federal Labor Relations Council

3. Limitations on Strikes
4. Mediation and Conciliation

H. *Employment Policies and Practices (1.6%, 1.4%)*
1. Discipline
2. Absenteeism and Tardiness
3. Sexual Harassment
4. Terminations

I. *Individual Employment Rights (1.0%, 1.1%)*
1. Common Law Tort Theories
2. Job-As-Property Doctrine
3. Employment-At-Will Doctrine
4. Exceptions to Employment-At-Will

J. *Performance Appraisals (3.1%, 3.1%)*
1. Performance Measurement - The Criterion
2. Criterion Problems
3. Documenting Employee Performance
4. Category Rating Appraisal Methods
6. Narrative Appraisal Methods
7. Special Appraisal Methods: MBO, BARS, BOS
8. Types of Appraisals
9. Rating Errors
10. Appraisal Interview
11. Linking Appraisals to Selection, Compensation, and Training and Development
12. Legal Constraints on Performance Appraisal

K. *Employee Attitudes, Opinions, and Satisfaction (1.1%, 1.1%)*
1. Measurement
2. Feedback
3. Intervention
4. Confidentiality and Anonymity of Surveys

VI. **Health, Safety, and Security (7.0%, 7.0%)**

A. *Legal and Regulatory Factors Affecting Health, Safety and Security: Definitions, Requirements, Proscribed Practices, Exemptions, Enforcement, Remedies, and Case Histories (1.4%, 1.3%)*
1. Occupational Safety and Health Act (1971)
2. Vocational Rehabilitation Act (1973) as amended
3. Drug-Free Workplace Act (1988)
4. Hazard Communication Standards (1986)
5. Americans with Disabilities Act (1990)

B. *Health (2.7%, 2.6%)*
1. Analysis of Environmental factors: Epidemiology, Environmental Toxicology
2. Employee Assistance Programs
3. Employee Wellness Programs
4. Fetal Protection Policies
5. Chemical Dependency
6. Communicable Diseases in the Workplace
7. Employer Liabilities
8. Stress Management
9. Smoking Policies
10. Recordkeeping and Reporting

C. *Safety (1.8%, 1.7%)*
1. Organization of Safety Program
2. Safety Promotion
3. Accident Investigation
4. Safety Inspections
5. Human Factors Engineering (ergonomics)
6. Special Safety Considerations
7. Sources of Assistance

D. *Security (1.1%, 1.4%)*
1. Organization of Security
2. Control Systems
3. Protection of Proprietary Information
4. Crisis Management and Contingency Planning
5. Theft and Fraud
6. Investigations and Preventive Corrections

Glossary

4/5ths Rule Rule stating that discrimination generally is considered to occur if the selection rate for a protected group is less than 80% of the group's representation in the relevant labor market or less than 80% of the selection rate for the majority group.
401(k) Plan An agreement in which a percentage of an employee's pay is withheld and invested in a tax-deferred account.
Ability Tests Tests that assess learned skills.
Active Practice The performance of job-related tasks and duties by trainees during training.
Adverse Selection Situation in which only higher-risk employees select and use certain benefits.
Affirmative Action A process in which employers identify problem areas, set goals, and take positive steps to guarantee equal employment opportunities for people in a protected class.
Agency Shop A firm that requires employees who refuse to join the union to pay equivalent amounts equal to union dues and fees for the union's representative services.
Applicant Pool All persons who are actually evaluated for selection.
Applicant Population A subset of the labor force population that is available for selection using a particular recruiting approach.
Aptitude Tests Tests that measure general ability to learn or acquire a skill.
Arbitration Process by which negotiatingparties submit their dispute to a third party to make a decision.
Assessment Center A collection of instruments and exercises designed to diagnose a person's development needs.
Attitude survey A special type of survey that focuses on employees' feelings and beliefs about their jobs and the organization.
Autonomy The extent of individual freedom and discretion in the work and its scheduling.
Availability Analysis An analysis that identifies the number of protected-class members available to work in the appropriate labor market in given jobs.

Balance-Sheet Approach An approach to international compensation that provides international employees with a compensation package that equalizes cost differences between the international assignment and the same assignment in the home country of the individual or the corporation.
Bargaining Unit All employees eligible to select a single union to represent and bargain collectively for them.
Behavior Modeling Copying someone else's behavior.
Behavioral Description Interview Interview in which applicants give specific examples of how they have performed or handled a problem in the past.
Behavioral Rating Approach Assesses an employee's behaviors instead of other characteristics.
Behaviorally Experienced Training Training methods that deal less with physical skills than with attitudes, perceptions, and interpersonal issues.
Benchmark Job Job found in many organizations and performed by several individuals who have similar duties that are relatively stable and that require similar KSAs.
Benchmarking Comparing specific measures of performance against data on those measures in "best practices" organizations.
Benefit Indirect compensation given to employees for organizational membership.
Bona Fide OccupationalQualification (BFOQ) A characteristic providing a legitimate reason why an employer can exclude persons on otherwise illegal bases of consideration.
Bonus A payment made on a one-time basis which does not become part of the employee's base pay.
Broadbanding Practice of using fewer pay grades having broader ranges than traditional compensation systems.
Business Agent A full-time union official employed by the union to operate the union office and assist union members.
Business Necessity A practice necessary for safe and efficient organizational operations.
Business Process Reengineering The fundamental rethinking and redesign of work to improve cost, service, and speed.

Career The sequence of work-related positions a person occupies throughout life.
Central Tendency Error Rating all employees in a narrow band in the middle of the rating scale.
Checklist Performance appraisal tool that uses a list of statements or words that are checked by raters.
Closed Shop A firm that requires individuals to join a union before they can be hired.
Co-Determination A practice whereby union or worker representatives are given positions on a company's board of directors.
Co-payment Employee's payment of a portion of the cost of both insurance premiums and medical care.
Coaching Daily training and feedback given to employees by immediate supervisors.
Collective Bargaining The process whereby representatives of management and workers negotiate over wages, hours, and other terms and conditions of employment.
Commission Compensation computed as a percentage of sales in units or dollars.
Compa-Ratio Pay level divided by the midpoint of the pay range.
Compensable Factor Factor used to identify a job value that is commonly present throughout a group of jobs.
Compensation Committee Usually a subgroup of the board of directors composed of directors who are not officers of the firm.
Compensatory Time Off Time off given in lieu of payment for extra time worked.
Complaint An indication of employee dissatisfaction that has not been submitted to a formal settlement process.
Compressed Workweek Workweek in which a full week's work is accomplished in fewer than five days.

Concessionary Bargaining Collective bargaining through which a union agrees to reduce wages, benefits, or other factors.
Conciliation Process by which a third party attempts to keep union andmanagement negotiators talking so that they can reach a voluntarysettlement.
Concurrent Validity Validity measured when an employer tests current employees and correlates the scores with their performance ratings.
Construct Validity Validity showing a relationship between an abstract characteristic and job performance.
Constructive Discharge Occurs when an employer deliberately makes conditions intolerable in an attempt to get an employee to quit.
Content Validity Validity measured by use of a logical, nonstatistical method to identify the KSAs and other characteristics necessary to perform a job.
Contractual Rights Rights based on a specific contractual agreement between employer and employee.
Contrast Error Tendency to rate people relative to other people rather than to performance standards.
Contributory Plan Pension plan in which the money for pension benefits is paid in by both employees and employers.
Correlation Coefficient An index number giving the relationship between a predictor and a criterion variable.
Cost/Benefit Analysis Compares costs of training with the benefits received.
Craft Union A union whose members do one type of work, often using specialized skills and training.
Criterion-Related Validity Validity measured by means of a procedure that uses a test as the predictor of how well an individual will perform on the job.
Critical Job Dimensions Elements of a job on which performance is measured.
Culture The societal forces affecting the values, beliefs, and actions of a distinct group of people.
Cumulative Trauma Disorders (CTDs) Muscle and skeletal injuries that occur when workers repetitively use the same muscles to perform tasks.

Data Facts that have yet to be processed or organized for meaningful use.
Decertification A process whereby a union is removed as the representative of a group of employees.
Defined-Benefit Plan Pension plan in which an employee is promised a pension amount based on age and service.
Defined-Contribution Plan Pension plan in which the employer makes an annual payment to an employee's pension account.
Development Efforts to improve employees' ability to handle a variety of assignments.
Differential Piece-Rate System Pays employees one piece-rate wage for units produced up to a standard output and a higher piece-rate wage for units produced over the standard.
Disabled Person Someone who has a physical or mental impairment that substantially limits that person in some major life activities, who has a record of such an impairment, or who is regarded as having such an impairment.
Discipline A form of training that enforces organizational rules.
Disparate Impact Situation that exists when there is a substantial underrepresentation of protected-class members as a result of employment decisions that work to their disadvantage.
Disparate Treatment Situation that exists when protected-class members are treated differently from others.
Distributive Justice Perceived fairness in the distribution of outcomes.
Diversity Differences among people.
Diversity Management Efforts concerned with developing organizational initiatives that value all people equally, regardless of their differences.
Downsizing Reducing the size of an organizational workforce.
Draw An amount advanced from and repaid to future commissions earned by the employee.
Due Process The opportunity to defend oneself against charges.
Dues Checkoff Provision that union dues will be deducted automatically from payroll checks of union members.
Duty A larger work segment composed of several tasks that are performed by an individual.

Earned-Time Plan Plan that combines all time-off benefits into a total number of hours or days that employees can take off with pay.
Economic Value Added (EVA) A firm's net operating profit after the cost of capital is deducted.
Effectiveness The extent to which goals have been met.
Efficiency The degree to which operations are done in an economical manner.
Employee Assistance Program (EAP) Program that provides counseling and other help to employees having emotional, physical, or other personal problems.
Employee Stock Ownership Plan (ESOP) A plan whereby employees gain stock ownership in the organization for which they work.
Employment Contracts Agreements that spell out the details of employment.
Employment-at-Will (EAW) A common-law doctrine stating that employers have the right to hire, fire, demote, or promote whomever they choose, unless there is a law or contract to the contrary.
Encapsulated Development Situation in which an individual learns new methods and ideas in a development course and returns to a work unit that is still bound by old attitudes and methods.
Environmental Scanning The process of studying the environment of the organization to pinpoint opportunities and threats.
Equal Employment Opportunity (EEO) The concept that individuals should have equal treatment in all employment-related actions.
Equity The perceived fairness of the relation between what a person does (inputs) and what the person receives (outcomes).
Ergonomics The proper design of the work environment to address the physical demands experienced by people.
Essential Functions "The fundamental job duties of the employment position that an individual with the disability holds or desires."
Essential Job Functions The fundamental job duties of the employment position that an individual with a disability holds or desires; they do not include marginalfunctions of the position.

Exempt Employees Employees classified as executive, administrative, professional, or outside sales, to whom employers are not required to pay overtime under the Fair Labor Standards Act.
Exit Interview An interview in which those leaving the organization are asked to identify the reasons for their departure.
Expatriate An employee working in a unit or plant who is not a citizen of the country in which the unit or plant is located but is a citizen of the country in which the organization is headquartered.
Expectancy The probability that if the employee puts forth more effort, it will lead to performance.
Experiment Research to determine how factors respond when changes are made in one or more variables, or conditions.
Extinction The absence of an expected response to a situation.

Federation A group of autonomous national and international unions.
Feedback The amount of information received about how well or how poorly one has performed.
Flexible Benefits Plan Benefits plan that allows employees to select the benefits they prefer from groups of benefits established by the employer.
Flexible Spending Account Account that allows employees to contribute pre-tax dollars to buy additional benefits.
Flexible Staffing Use of recruiting sources and workers who are not employees.
Flextime A scheduling arrangement in which employees work a set number of hours per day but vary starting and ending times.
Forced Choice Appraisal approach in which raters choose between two statements to describe employee performance.
Forced Distribution Performance appraisal method in which ratings of employees' performance are distributed along a bell-shaped curve.
Forecasting Identifying expected future conditions based on information from the past and present.

Gainsharing The sharing with employees of greater-than-expected gains in profits and/or productivity.
Garnishment A court action in which a portion of an employee's wages is set aside to pay a debt owed a creditor.
Glass Ceiling Discriminatory practices that have prevented women and otherprotected-class members from advancing to executive-level jobs.
Global Organization An organization that has corporate units in a number of countries that are integrated to operate as one organization worldwide.
Golden Parachute A severance benefit that provides protection and security to executives in the event that they lose their jobs or their firms are acquired by other firms and they are negatively affected.
Graphic Rating Scale A scale that allows the rater to mark an employee's performance on a continuum.
Green-Circled Employee An incumbent who is paid below the range set for the job.
Grievance An alleged misinterpretation, misapplication, or violation of a provision in a union/management agreement.
Grievance Arbitration A means by which disputes arising from different interpretations of a labor contract are settled by athird party.
Grievance Procedure A formal channel of communications used to resolve grievances.

Halo Effect Rating a person high or low on all items because of one characteristic.
Handbilling Practice in which unions give written publicity to employees to convince the employees to sign authorization cards.
Health A general state of physical, mental, and emotional well-being.
Health Maintenance Organization (HMO) Managed care plan that provides services for a fixed period on a prepaid basis.
Host-Country National An employee working in a unit or plant who is a citizen of the country in which the unit or plant is located, but where the unit or plant is operated by an organization headquartered in another country.
HR Audit A formal research effort that evaluates the current state of HR management in an organization.
HR Generalist A person with responsibility for performing a variety of HR activities.
HR Research The analysis of data from HR records to determine the effectiveness of past and present HR practices.
HR Specialist A person with in-depth knowledge and expertise in a limited area of HR.
Human Capital The total value of organizational human resources.
Human Resource (HR) Planning The process of analyzing and identifying the need for and availability of human resources so that the organization can meet its objectives.
Human Resource Information System (HRIS) An integrated system designed to provide information used in HR decision making.
Human Resource (HR) Management The design of formal systems in an organization to ensure the effective and efficient use of human talent to accomplish organizational goals.

Illegal Issues Those issues that would require either party to take illegal action.
Immediate Confirmation The concept that people learn best if reinforcement is given as soon as possible after training.
Importing and Exporting The phase of international interaction in which an organization begins selling and buying goods and services with organizations in other countries.
Incentive Compensation that rewards an employee for efforts beyond normal performance expectations.
Incentive Compensation that rewards an employee for efforts beyond normal performance expectations.
Independent Contractors Workers who perform specific services on a contract basis.
Individual Retirement Account (IRA) A special account in which an employee can set aside funds on which taxes are deferred until the employee retires.
Individual-Centered Career Planning Career planning that focuses on individuals' careers rather than on organizational needs.
Individualism Dimension of culture referring to the extent to which people in a country prefer to act as individuals

Industrial Union A union that includes many persons working in the same industry or company, regardless of jobs held.
Information Processed and organized data.
Instrumentality The probability that performance will lead to the desired rewards.
Interfaces Areas of contact between the HR unit and managers within the organization.

Job A grouping of similar positions having common tasks, duties, and responsibilities.
Job Analysis A systematic way to gather and analyze information about the content and the human requirements of jobs, and the context in which jobs are performed.
Job Description Identification of the tasks, duties, and responsibilities of a job.
Job Design Organizing tasks, duties, and responsibilities into a productive unit of work.
Job Enlargement Broadening the scope of a job by expanding the number of different tasks to be performed.
Job Enrichment Increasing the depth of a job by adding employee responsibility for planning, organizing, controlling, and evaluating the job.
Job Evaluation The systematic determination of the relative worth of jobs within an organization.
Job Family A grouping of jobs having similar characteristics.
Job Posting and Bidding A system in which the employer provides notices of job openings within the organization and employees respond by applying for specific openings.
Job Rotation The process of shifting a person from job to job.
Job Rotation The process of shifting an employee from job to job.
Job Specifications List the knowledge, skills, and abilities (KSAs) an individual needs to do the job satisfactorily.
Just Cause Sufficient justification for actions.

Keogh Plan A type of individualized pension plan for self-employed individuals.
Knowledge, Skills, and Abilities(KSAs) Include education, experience, work skill requirements, personal requirements, mental and physical requirements, and working conditions and hazards.
Labor Force Population All individuals who are available for selection if all possible recruitment strategies are used.
Labor Markets The external sources from which organizations attract employees.
Lockout Shutdown of company operations undertaken by management to prevent union members from working.
Long-Term Orientation Dimension of culture referring to values people hold that emphasize the future, as opposed to short-term values, which focus on the present and the past.
Lump-Sum Increase (LSI) A one-time payment of all or part of a yearly pay increase.

Managed Care Approaches designed to monitor and reduce medical costs using good management practices and the market system.
Management by Objectives (MBO) Specifies the performance goal that an individual hopes to attain within an appropriate length of time.
Management Rights Those rights reserved to the employer to manage, direct, and control its business.
Mandated Benefits Those benefits which employers in the United States must provide to employees by law.
Mandatory Issues Those issues that are identified specifically by labor laws or court decisions as being subject tobargaining.
Market Price The prevailing wage rate paid for a job in the immediate job market.
Masculinity/Femininity Dimension of culture referring to the degree to which "masculine" values prevail over "feminine"values.
Massed Practice The performance of all of the practice at once.
Maturity Curve Curve that depicts the relationship between experience and pay rates.
Mediation Process by which a third party assists negotiators in their discussions and also suggests settlement proposals.
Mental Ability Tests Tests that measure reasoning capabilities.
Mentoring A relationship in which managers at midpoints in careers aid individuals in the first stages of careers.
Moonlighting Work outside a person's regular employment that takes 12 or more additional hours per week.
Motivation The desire within a person causing that person to act.
Multinational Enterprise (MNE) An organization with units located in foreign countries.

National Emergency Strike A strike that would affect an industry or a major part of it such that the national health or safety would be impeded.
Negative Reinforcement An individual works to avoid an undesirable consequence.
Nepotism Practice of allowing relatives to work for the same employer.
Noncontributory Plan Pension plan in which all the funds for pension benefits are provided by the employer.
Nondirective Interview Interview that uses general questions, from which other questions are developed.
Nonexempt Employees Employees who must be paid overtime under the Fair Labor Standards Act.
Ombudsman Person outside the normal chain of command who acts as a problem solver for management and employees.
Organization-Centered Career Planning Career planning that focuses on jobs and on constructing career paths that provide for the logical progression of people between jobs in an organization.
Organizational Commitment The degree to which employees believe in and accept organizational goals and desire to remain with the organization.
Organizational Culture A pattern of shared values and beliefs giving members of an organization meaning and providing them with rules for behavior.
Orientation The planned introduction of new employees to their jobs, coworkers, and the organization.
Outplacement A group of services provided to displaced employees to give them support and assistance.
Outsourcing Contracting with another organization to provide operations that were previously handled internally.

Paired Comparison Formal comparison of each employee with every other employee in the rating group one at a time.
Panel Interview Interview in which several interviewers interview the candidate at the same time.
Pay The basic compensation an employee receives, usually as a wage or salary.
Pay Compression Situation in which pay differences among individuals with different levels of experience and performance in the organization become small.
Pay Equity The concept that the pay for jobs requiring comparable knowledge, skills, and abilities should be similar even if actual duties and market rates differ significantly.
Pay Grade A grouping of individual jobs having approximately the same job worth.
Pay Survey A collection of data on existing compensation rates for workers performing similar jobs in other organizations.
Pension Plans Retirement benefits established and funded by employers and employees.
Performance Appraisal (PA) The process of determining how well employees do their jobs compared with a set of standards and communicating that information to those employees.
Performance Criteria Standards commonly used for testing or measuring performances.
Performance Incentives Compensation that attempts to link pay with performance.
Performance Management Systems Attempts to monitor, measure, report, improve, and reward employee performance.
Performance Standard The expected level of performance.
Permissive Issues Those issues that are not mandatory but relate to jobs.
Perquisites (Perks) Special benefits—usually noncash items—for executives.
Piece-Rate System A productivity-based compensation system in which an employee is paid for each unit of production.
Policies General guidelines that regulate organizational actions.
Portability A pension plan feature that allows employees to move their pension benefits from one employer to another.
Position A job performed by one person.
Positive Reinforcement A person receives a desired reward.
Power Distance Dimension of culture referring to the inequality among the people of a nation.
Predictive Validity Validity measured when test results of applicants are compared with subsequent performance.
Predictors Information about the likelihood that an applicant will be able to perform the job.
Preferred Provider Organization (PPO) A health-care provider that contracts with an employer or an employer group to provide health-care services to employees at a competitive rate.
Primary Research Research method in which data are gathered firsthand for the specific project being conducted.
Procedural Justice Perceived fairness of the process used to make a decision.
Procedural Justice The perceived fairness of the process and procedures used to make decisions about employees, including their pay.
Procedures Customary methods of handling activities.
Production Cells Groupings of workers who produce entire products or components of products.
Productivity A measure of the quantity and quality of work done, considering the cost of the resources it took to do the work.
Profit Sharing A system to distribute a portion of the profits of the organization to employees.
Protected Class Those individuals who fall within a group identified for protection under equal employment laws and regulations.
Psychological Contract The unwritten expectations that employees and employers have about the nature of their workrelationships.
Punishment Action taken to repel a person from an undesired action.

Quality Circle A small group of employees who monitor productivity and quality and suggest solutions to problems.

Ranking Listing of all employees from highest to lowest in performance.
Rater Bias Error that occurs when a rater's values or prejudices distort the rating.
Ratification Process by which union members vote to accept the terms of anegotiated labor agreement.
Realistic Job Preview (RJP) The process through which an interviewer provides a job applicant with an accurate picture of a job.
Reasonable Accommodation A modification or adjustment to a job or work environment that enables a qualified individual with a disability to enjoy equal employment opportunity.
Recency Effect An error whereby the rater gives greater weight to recent occurrences when appraising an individual's performance.
Recruiting Process of generating a pool of qualified applicants for organizational jobs.
Red-Circled Employee An incumbent who is paid above the range set for the job.
Reengineering Rethinking and redesigning work to improve cost, service, and speed.
Reinforcement A concept based on the law of effect, which states that people tend to repeat responses that give them some type of positive reward and avoid actions that are associated with negative consequences.
Reliability The consistency with which a test measures an item.
Repatriation The process of bringing expatriates home.
Responsibilities Obligations to perform certain tasks and duties.
Responsibility A duty or obligation to be accountable for an action.
Retaliation Punitive actions taken by employers against individuals who exercise their legal rights.
Return On Investment (ROI) Calculation showing the value of expenditures for HR activities; it also can be used to show how long it will take for the activities to pay for themselves.
Reverse Discrimination A condition that may exist when a person is denied an opportunity because of preferences given to protected-class individuals who may be less qualified.
Right That which belongs to a person by law, nature, or tradition.

Right-to-Sue Letter A letter issued by the EEOC that notifies a complainant that he or she has 90 days in which to file a personal suit in federal court.
Right-to-Work Laws State laws that prohibit both the closed shop and the union shop.
Role Playing A development technique requiring the trainee to assume a role in a given situation and act out behaviors associated with that role.
Rules Specific guidelines that regulate and restrict the behavior of individuals.

Sabbatical Leave Paid time off the job to develop and rejuvenate oneself.
Safety Condition in which the physical well-being of people is protected.
Salary Payment that is consistent from period to period despite the number of hours worked.
Salting Practice in which unions hire and pay people to apply for jobs at certain companies; when the people are hired, they begin union organizing efforts.
Secondary Research Research method using data already gathered by others and reported in books, articles in professional journals, or other sources.
Security Audit A comprehensive analysis of the vulnerability of the security of an organization.
Security Protection of employer facilities and equipment from unauthorized access and protection of employees while on work premises or work assignments.
Selection Criteria Standards that become the basis for selection.
Selection Interview Interview designed to assess job-related knowledge, skills, and abilities (KSAs)and clarify information from other sources.
Selection The process of choosing individuals who have relevant qualifications to fill jobs in an organization.
Self-Directed Work Team An organizational team composed of individuals who are assigned a cluster of tasks, duties, and responsibilities to be accomplished.
Serious Health Condition A health condition requiring inpatient, hospital, hospice, or residential medical care or continuing physician care.
Severance Pay A security benefit voluntarily offered by employers to employees who lose their jobs.
Sexual Harassment Actions that are sexually directed, are unwanted, and subject the worker to adverse employment-conditions or create a hostile work environment.
Shamrock Team An organizational team composed of a core of members, resource experts who join the team as appropriate, and part-time/temporary members as needed.
Silver Parachute A severance and benefit plan to protect nonexecutives if their firms are acquired by other firms.
Simulation A development technique that requires the participant to analyze a situation and decide the best course of action based on the data given.
Situational Interview A structured interview composed of questions about how applicants might handle specific job situations.
Skill Variety The extent to which the work requires several different activities for successful completion.
Skills Inventories Listings of the skills of all employees in an organization.
Spaced Practice Several practice sessions spaced over a period of hours or days.
Special-Purpose Team An organizational team that is formed to address specific problems and may continue to work together to improve work processes or the quality of products and services.
Statutory Rights Rights based on laws.
Stock Option A plan that gives an individual the right to buy stock in a company, usually at a fixed price for a period of time.
Straight Piece-Rate System A pay system in which wages are determined by multiplying the number of units produced by the piece rate for one unit.
Stress Interview Interview designed to create anxiety and put pressure on an applicant to see how the person responds.
Strike Work stoppage in which union members refuse to work in order to put pressure on an employer.
Structured Interview Interview that uses a set of standardized questions asked of all job applicants.
Substance Abuse The use of illicit substances or the misuse of controlled substances, alcohol, or other drugs.
Suggestion System A formal method of obtaining employee input and upward communication.

Task A distinct, identifiable work activity composed of motions.
Task Identity The extent to which the job includes a "whole" identifiable unit of work that is carried out from start to finish and that results in a visible outcome.
Task Significance The amount of impact the job has on other people.
Tax Equalization Plan Compensation plan used to protect expatriates from negative tax consequences.
Telecommuting The process of going to work via electronic computing and telecommunications equipment.
Tester A protected-class member who poses as an applicant to determine if employers discriminate in their hiring practices.
Testers Protected-class members who pose as applicants to determine if employers discriminate in their hiring practices.
Third-Country National An employee who is a citizen of one country, working in a second country, and employed by an organization headquartered in a third country.
Total Compensation The sum of money paid directly, money paid indirectly, and nonmonetary rewards.
Total Quality Management (TQM) A comprehensive management process focusing on the continuous improvement of organizational activities to enhance the quality of the goods and services supplied.
Training A learning process whereby people acquire skills or knowledge to aid in the achievement of goals.
Turnover Process in which employees leave the organization and have to be replaced.
Two-Tier Wage Structure Wage structure in which new union members receive lower wages and fewer benefits than existing members performing similar jobs.

Uncertainty Avoidance Dimension of culture referring to the preference of people in a country for structured situations instead of unstructured situations.

Undue Hardship Condition created when making a reasonable accommodation for individuals with disabilities would pose significant difficulty or expense for an employer.
Union A formal association of workers that promotes the interests of its members through collective action.
Union Authorization Card Card signed by an employee to designate a union as his or her collective bargaining agent.
Union Security Provisions Contract provisions to aid the union in obtaining and retaining members.
Union Shop A firm that requires that an employee join a union, usually 30 to 60 days after being hired.
Union Steward An employee of a firm or organization who is elected to serve as the first-line representative of unionized workers.
Unit Labor Cost The total labor cost per unit of output, which is the average wages of workers divided by their levels of productivity.
Utility Analysis Analysis in which economic or other statistical models are built to identify the costs and benefits associated with specific HR activities.
Utilization Analysis An analysis that identifies the number of protected-class members employed and the types of jobs they hold in an organization.
Utilization Review An audit and review of the services and costs billed by health-care providers.

Valence The strength of the individual's valuation of the reward.
Validity Generalization The extension of the validity of a test to different groups, similar jobs, or other organizations.
Validity The extent to which a test actually measures what it says it measures.
Vesting The right of employees to receive benefits from their pension plans.

Wage and Salary Administration The activity involved in the development, implementation, and maintenance of a base pay system.
Wages Payments directly calculated on the amount of time worked.
Well-Pay Extra pay for not taking sick leave.
Wellness Programs Programs designed to maintain or improve employee health before problems arise.
Whistle-Blower Person who reports a real or perceived wrong committed by his or her employer.
Work Sample Tests Tests that require an applicant to perform a simulated job task.
Workers' Compensation Provides benefits to persons injured on the job.

Yield Ratio A comparison of the number of applicants at one stage of the recruiting process to the number at the next stage.

Name Index

Subject Index

System Requirements for Ceridian's® Integrated HR/Payroll System II on CD-ROM

- Microsoft MS-DOS® 3.3 or higher
- Microsoft Windows 3.1 or higher
- a Windows-compatible computer with a 66MHz 80486 processor and CD-ROM drive
- A Windows-compatible mouse or other pointing device
- a hard disk with 5MB of free disk space for CD-Installation, or 95MB for hard-drive installation
- at least 8MB of RAM; 12 MB or more is recommended
- a graphics adapter card (VGA, Super VGA, or other Windows-compatible card)
- a VGA monitor that can display 640 x 480 resolution in 256 color

CD-ROM Installation Instructions

Before Installing the CD-ROM, you need to consider whether you will run the program from the CD or from your hard drive. If you will not be using your own PC to view the CD materials, or if your PC does not meet the system requirements, you will need to run the program directly from the CD. Instructions follow for each type of installation

Running the Exercises Directly from the CD

Windows 3.x

1. From Program Manager or File Manager choose File from the menu bar, then Run.
2. In the Run dialog box, type the command line of the module you would like to run (shown in the table below)
3. Click OK.
4. When the splash panel displays, click the Menu button to access the Section Menu.

Windows 95

1. Click the Start button on the taskbar, then click Run.
2. In the Run dialog box, type the command line of the module you would like to run (shown in the table below).
3. Click OK.
4. When the splash panel displays, click the Menu button to access the Section Menu.

Command lines for running the exercises from CD:

Module Name	Command Line
Basic Training	d:*\p2krun.exe bt**
COBRA	d:\p2krun.exe co
Employee Profile	d:\p2krun.exe ep
Human Resources	d:\p2krun.exe hr
Position Management	d:\p2krun.exe mp

* Where d is the letter of your CD-ROM drive
** Note that there is a space between the executable name and the 2-letter code.

Running the Exercises from Your Hard Drive

Windows 3.x

1. In File Manager, click c:\ at the top of your hard drive's directory tree.
2. Choose File from the menu bar, then Create Directory.
3. Enter Ceridian as the name of the new directory, then click OK.
4. Copy all of the files from the CD-ROM into the new directory.
5. Exit File Manager and return to Program Manager.
6. From Program Manager choose File on the menu bar, then New.
7. Select the Program Group option, then click OK.
8. In the Program Group Properties dialog box, enter Ceridian CBT as the name of the group, then click OK.
9. From Program Manager, click in the Ceridian CBT group to activate it.
10. Choose File on the menu bar, then New.
11. Select the Program Item option, then click OK.
12. In the Program Item Properties dialog box, enter the name of the first module you'd like to set up as the Description.
13. In Command Line, enter the corresponding command line from the table below.
14. In Working Directory, enter c:\ceridian.
15. Click OK.
16. Repeat steps 10-15 for the remaining 4 modules.
17. To run a module, double click its program icon in the Ceridian CBT group.
18. When the splash panel displays, click the Menu button to access the Section Menu.

CD-ROM Installation Instructions, *continued*

Windows 95

1. Double-click My Computer.
2. Double-click the icon of your computer's hard drive.
3. On the File menu, point to New, and then click Folder.
4. Type Ceridian as the name of the new folder, then press ENTER.
5. Copy all of the files from the CD into the new folder.
6. On the Desktop, click the right mouse button and point to New, then click Folder.
7. Type Ceridian CBT as the name of the new folder, then press ENTER.
8. Double-click the new folder to open it.
9. On the File menu, point to New, and then click Shortcut.
10. Enter the command line of the first module you would like to add to the new folder (refer to the table below), then click Next>.
11. Enter the module name as the name of the shortcut, then click Finish.
12. Repeat steps 9-11 to add shortcuts for the remaining four modules.
13. To run a module, double-click its shortcut icon in the Ceridian CBT folder.
14. When the splash panel displays, click the Menu button to access the Section Menu.

Command lines for running the exercises from the hard drive:

Module Name	Command Line
Basic Training	c:\ceridian\p2krun.exe bt*
COBRA	c:\ceridian\p2krun.exe co
Employee Profile	c:\ceridian\p2krun.exe ep
Human Resources	c:\ceridian\p2krun.exe hr
Position Management	c:\ceridian\p2krun.exe mp

* Note that there is a space between the executable name and the 2-letter code.

Getting Started with the Exercises

Before performing any of the exercises in the Sections that follow, you should familiarize yourself with the naming and navigational conventions used in Ceridian's computer-based training (CBT). The easiest way to do this is to take the lesson "How to Use Ceridian's CBT" contained in the materials on your CD-ROM. To access this lesson, start the Human Resources module. In the Section Menu, click the Introduction button. From the Lesson Menu, click the button to the left of the item "How to Use This CBT." In the Topic Menu, click "How to Use Ceridian's CBT." After completing this lesson, you'll feel comfortable using the rest of the CBT topics that are a required part of this course.

Keep in mind that certain features that you learn about in the topic "How to Use Ceridian's CBT" will be slightly different in the student version of the training. On the navigational panel, there is no Help button, nor is there an Index button. In addition, when you choose to exit the CBT, you will be given the option of saving your progress report.

Caution: Do not choose to save your progress data unless you are using the CD materials on your own PC. When you save your progress data, the information is stored on the hard drive of the computer you are using to access the materials. Therefore, you must always use the same computer to preserve the integrity of your scores.

If you're new to the Windows operating system, it is a good idea to take the lesson on Windows Skills. To access this lesson, start the Human Resources module. In the Section Menu, click the Introduction button. From the Lesson Menu, click the button to the left of the item "Introduction to Windows." In the Topic Menu, click "CII Windows Skills." After completing this lesson ,you will be up to speed on the skills you'll need to use Ceridian's CBT.

Materials to be Appended to the What is an HRIS? Section

To get a feel for Ceridian's HRIS, you need to look at some of the introductory materials on the CD-ROM. In the Human Resources module, click the Introduction button in the Section Menu. From the Lesson Menu, click the button to the left of the item "Introduction to CII." Look at all of the topics in this lesson and then proceed to the following lesson, "Introduction to PIT," to learn more about the features of Ceridian's Integrated HR/Payroll System II (CII).

After completing this topic, you will possess the necessary background information to be able to assist SME-TEK in some of its routine HR transactions using CII's CBT.

Troubleshooting Tips

If you have trouble initializing the CBT, check to see that you've followed the instructions exactly as they appear above. If you are following the instructions exactly and are still having problems, search for the file ciicbt.ini in the root directory of your computer's hard drive. Delete this file and try again to start the CBT. This should take care of the problem.